THE VICTORIA HISTORY
OF THE
COUNTIES OF ENGLAND

A HISTORY OF
MIDDLESEX

VOLUME IV

THE VICTORIA HISTORY
OF THE
COUNTIES OF ENGLAND

EDITED BY R. B. PUGH

DIEU ET MON DROIT

THE UNIVERSITY OF LONDON
INSTITUTE OF
HISTORICAL RESEARCH

Oxford University Press, Ely House, 37 Dover Street, London, W1X 4AH

GLASGOW   NEW YORK   TORONTO   MELBOURNE   WELLINGTON
CAPE TOWN   SALISBURY   IBADAN   NAIROBI   DAR ES SALAAM   LUSAKA   ADDIS ABABA
BOMBAY   CALCUTTA   MADRAS   KARACHI   LAHORE   DACCA
KUALA LUMPUR   SINGAPORE   HONG KONG   TOKYO

SBN 19 722727 9

PRINTED IN GREAT BRITAIN
AT THE UNIVERSITY PRESS, OXFORD
BY VIVIAN RIDLER
PRINTER TO THE UNIVERSITY

INSCRIBED TO THE

MEMORY OF HER LATE MAJESTY

QUEEN VICTORIA

WHO GRACIOUSLY GAVE THE TITLE TO

AND ACCEPTED THE DEDICATION

OF THIS HISTORY

THE GRAND JUNCTION CANAL AT SOUTHALL MILL, c. 1806

A HISTORY OF THE
COUNTY OF
MIDDLESEX

EDITED BY J. S. COCKBURN

AND T. F. T. BAKER

VOLUME IV

PUBLISHED FOR

THE INSTITUTE OF HISTORICAL RESEARCH

BY

OXFORD UNIVERSITY PRESS

1971

LIST OF ILLUSTRATIONS

Thanks are offered to the following for permission to reproduce material in their possession and for the loan of prints: All Souls College, Oxford; City of London, Guildhall Library; the Greater London Record Office (Middlesex Records); King's College, Cambridge; London Borough of Ealing, Central Library; London Borough of Ealing, Southall Library; London Borough of Hillingdon, Uxbridge Library; the National Monuments Record (indicated below by the initials N.M.R.); the Trustees, Norwood (Middlesex) Charities; the Society of Friends. Coats of arms were drawn by C. W. Scott-Giles.

LIST OF ILLUSTRATIONS

LIST OF MAPS AND PLANS

All the maps except those of Edgware village and Ruislip village were drawn by K. J. Wass of the Department of Geography, University College, London. The hundred maps are based upon C. G. Greenwood's Map of Middlesex (1819), information for the map of Harrow and Pinner parishes has been taken from estate maps in the Greater London Record Office (Middlesex Records), and the other parish maps are based on the inclosure maps. The map of Harrow's development and the plans of Uxbridge and Harrow-on-the-Hill are based upon the Ordnance Survey, with the sanction of the Controller of H.M. Stationery Office, Crown Copyright reserved. For details of the Edgware and Ruislip village maps see List of Illustrations.

EDITORIAL NOTE

THE revival of the *Victoria History of Middlesex* in 1955 is described in the Editorial Note to Volume III, and later modifications in the arrangements in that to Volume I. The University of London again records its true appreciation of the generous grants made by the Local Authorities. The membership of the Middlesex *Victoria County History* Council in 1970 is set out below. Mr. G. R. Thomas, appointed Assistant County Editor (formerly known as Assistant Local Editor) in 1968, resigned in 1969 and was succeeded by Mr. G. C. Tyack.

The present volume is the fourth to be published in the Middlesex set, and broadly follows the usual scheme of 'topographical' volumes of the *Victoria History*. It was begun under the editorship of Mr. H. P. F. King, shortly before his resignation in 1963. The structure and aims of the *Victoria History* series as a whole are outlined in the *General Introduction* to the *History* (1970).

Many people have helped in the compilation of the volume by providing information or by reading and commenting on parts of the text before it was printed. The co-operation of the town clerks, education officers, and librarians of the various Local Authorities, both before and after the administrative changes of 1965 following from the London Government Act, 1963, is gratefully acknowledged, together with that of the members of their respective staffs. Among so many, special mention is to be made of the following: Miss E. J. Humphreys, formerly Branch Librarian, Middlesex County Libraries, at Uxbridge; Mr. J. D. Lee, Reference Librarian of the London Borough of Hillingdon; Miss E. D. Mercer, Archivist to the Greater London Council and formerly Middlesex County Archivist; Miss A. M. Pollard, Reference Librarian at the Central Reference Library, Harrow; and Mr. E. R. West, formerly Town Clerk of Uxbridge. Help of a similar nature has been given by Mr. M. Bawtree, of West Drayton, Mr. C. H. Keene, of Northolt, Mr. L. E. Morris, of Ruislip, Mr. A. H. Murgatroyd, Archivist of the Wembley History Society, Mr. K. R. Pearce, of Uxbridge, and Miss Susan Reynolds, formerly editor of the *Victoria History of Middlesex*. To them, and to the many people named in footnotes as supplying information or allowing access to documents, thanks are gratefully rendered.

MIDDLESEX
VICTORIA COUNTY HISTORY
COUNCIL

As at 1 July 1970

Chairman
R. M. ROBBINS, ESQ.†

Representatives of the following Local Authorities
The Greater London Council

London Boroughs

Barnet	Enfield	Hillingdon
Brent	Haringey	Hounslow
Ealing	Harrow	Richmond-upon-Thames

Urban Districts

Potters Bar	Staines	Sunbury-on-Thames

Representatives of
The London and Middlesex Archaeological Society
The Institute of Historical Research

Co-opted Members
DR. IRENE J. MARSINGALL-THOMAS†
MISS SUSAN REYNOLDS†
Hon. Secretary: A. H. HALL, ESQ.†
Hon. Treasurer: E. B. EAGLES, ESQ.†
General Editor: PROFESSOR R. B. PUGH†

Executive Committee

MISS F. M. GREEN	G. M. NOBLE, ESQ.
MISS E. D. MERCER	DR. F. H. W. SHEPPARD
SIR CHRISTOPHER COWAN	

together with the persons marked with a dagger

LIST OF CLASSES OF DOCUMENTS
IN THE PUBLIC RECORD OFFICE
USED IN THIS VOLUME
WITH THEIR CLASS NUMBERS

Chancery

	Proceedings
C 1	Early
C 2	Series I
C 3	Series II
C 47	Miscellanea[1]
C 54	Close Rolls
C 66	Patent Rolls
C 78	Decree Rolls
C 93	Proceedings of Commissioners of Charitable Uses, Inquisitions, and Decrees
C 131	Extents for Debts
	Inquisitions post mortem
C 134	Series I, Edw. II
C 135	Edw. III
C 136	Ric. II
C 139	Hen. VI
C 140	Edw. IV
C 142	Series II
C 145	Miscellaneous Inquisitions
	Ancient Deeds
C 147	Series CC

Court of Common Pleas

	Feet of Fines
C.P. 25(1)	Series I
C.P. 25(2)	Series II
C.P. 43	Recovery Rolls

Exchequer, King's Remembrancer

E 106	Extents of Alien Priories
E 112	Bills, Answers, etc.
E 142	Ancient Extents
	Inquisitions post mortem
E 150	Series II
E 178	Special Commissions of Inquiry
E 179	Subsidy Rolls etc.
	Ancient Deeds
E 210	Series D
E 212	Series DS

Exchequer, Augmentation Office

E 301	Certificates of Colleges and Chantries
E 305	Deeds of Purchase and Exchange
E 310	Particulars for Leases
E 315	Miscellaneous Books

E 318	Particulars for Grants of Crown Lands
	Ancient Deeds
E 326	Series B
E 329	Series BS

Ministry of Education

Ed. 7	Public Elementary Schools, Preliminary Statements

Home Office

H.O. 67	Acreage Returns
	Various, Census
H.O. 107	Population Returns
H.O. 129	Ecclesiastical Returns

Justices Itinerant, Assize and Gaol Delivery Justices, etc.

J.I. 1	Eyre Rolls, Assize Rolls, etc.

Ministry of Agriculture, Fisheries, and Food

M.A.F. 68	Agricultural Returns: Parish Summaries

Maps and Plans

M.R. (documents with the call-mark M.R. belong to various classes).

Court of Requests

Req. 2	Proceedings

Special Collections

S.C. 2	Court Rolls
S.C. 6	Ministers' Accounts
	Rentals and Surveys
S.C. 11	Rolls
S.C. 12	Portfolios

State Paper Office

	State Papers Domestic
S.P. 17	Chas. I

Court of Star Chamber

	Proceedings
Sta. Cha. 2	Hen. VIII
Sta. Cha. 4	Mary
Sta. Cha. 8	Jas. I

---

[1] In 1970, when the volume was in the press, part of the class Chancery, Miscellanea, was subject to rearrangement. The former references ceased to apply but new references were not then available.

SELECT LIST OF CLASSES OF DOCUMENTS IN THE
GREATER LONDON RECORD OFFICE
(MIDDLESEX RECORDS)
USED IN THIS VOLUME
WITH THEIR CLASS NUMBERS

Deposited Records

Acc. 76	Northwick Collection
Acc. 180	Hayes Collection
Acc. 249	Hawtrey-Deane
Acc. 401	Lord Hillingdon
Acc. 405	Earl of Jersey
Acc. 435	Earl of Jersey
Acc. 436	Earl of Jersey
Acc. 446	Marquess of Anglesey
Acc. 538	Manor and Borough of Uxbridge etc.
Acc. 590	Harrow Local Archives Committee
Acc. 643	Northwick Collection
Acc. 794	Northwick Collection
Acc. 974	Northwick Collection
Cal. Mdx. Recs.	Calendar of Sessions Records, 1607–12
Cal. Mdx. Sess. Bks.	Calendar of Sessions Books, 1638–1752
D.R.O. 3	Diocesan Records, Harrow-on-the-Hill Parish Records
D.R.O. 8	Diocesan Records, Pinner Parish Records
E.M.C.	Extra-Mural Collections
F	Facsimile
H.T.	Hearth Tax Assessment
L.A. HW.	Harrow Local Government Records
L.T.A. Mdx.	Land Tax Assessment
MJ/OC.	Middlesex Justices, Orders of Court
L.V.	Licensed Victuallers' Lists
P.S.	Petty Sessional Records
S.R.	Sessions Roll

NOTE ON ABBREVIATIONS

Among the abbreviations and short titles used the following may require elucidation:

Brewer, *Beauties of Eng. and Wales*, x(5)
J. N. Brewer, vol. x (1816) of *The Beauties of England and Wales* (1810–16), ed. E. W. Brayley and J. Britton. The part of the work cited is alternatively known either as the fifth part, or as the second part of vol. iv, of *London and Middlesex*, which is itself vol. x of *The Beauties*

Ft. of F. Lond. & Mdx.
Calendar to the Feet of Fines for London and Middlesex, ed. W. J. Hardy and W. Page (2 vols. 1892–3)

Foot, *Agric. of Mdx.*
P. Foot, *General View of the Agriculture of the County of Middlesex* (1794)

Gen. Reg. Off.
The General Register Office, Somerset House, London

Guildhall MSS.
City of London, Guildhall Library. The collection includes bishops' registers (MS. 9531), diocesan administrative records (MSS. 9532–60), and records of bishops' estates (MSS. 10234–51)

Hennessy, *Novum Repertorium*
G. Hennessy, *Novum Repertorium Ecclesiasticum Parochiale Londinense* (1898)

Hist. Mon. Com. *Mdx.*
Royal Commission on Historical Monuments, *An Inventory of the Historical Monuments in Middlesex* (H.M.S.O. 1937)

Kelly's Dir. Mdx.
The Post Office Directories. The directories for Middlesex between 1845 and 1863 are published as part of the *Home Counties Directory*

Lond. Dioc. Bk.
Yearbook of the diocese of London (1940 to date)

Lysons, *Environs of Lond.*
D. Lysons, *The Environs of London* (1792–6), vols. ii and iii (1795)

Lysons, *Mdx. Pars.*
D. Lysons, *An Historical Account of those parishes in the County of Middlesex which are not described in the Environs of London* (1800)

M.L.R.
Middlesex Land Registry. The enrolments are at the Greater London Record Office (Middlesex Records), the volumes and indexes throughout are at the Greater London Record Office

M.R.O.
Middlesex Record Office. On the incorporation of Middlesex within Greater London on 1 April 1965 the office became known as the Greater London Record Office (Middlesex Records)

Mdx. Cnty. Recs.
Middlesex County Records [1550–1688], ed. J. C. Jeaffreson (4 vols. 1886–92)

Mdx. Cnty. Recs. Sess. Bks. 1689–1709
Middlesex County Records, Calendar of the Sessions Books 1689 to 1709, ed. W. J. Hardy (1905)

Mdx. Sess. Recs.
Calendar to the Sessions Records [1612–18], ed. W. le Hardy (4 vols. 1935–41)

Middleton, *View*
J. Middleton, *View of the Agriculture of Middlesex* (1798)

Newcourt, *Repertorium*
R. Newcourt, *Repertorium Ecclesiasticum Parochiale Londinense* (2 vols. 1708–10)

P.N. Mdx. (E.P.N.S.)
The Place-Names of Middlesex (English Place-Name Society, vol. xviii, 1942)

Pevsner, *Mdx.*
N. Pevsner, *The Buildings of England, Middlesex* (1951)

Robbins, *Middlesex*
M. Robbins, *Middlesex* (1953)

Thorne, *Environs*
J. Thorne, *Handbook to the Environs of London* [alphabetically arranged in two parts] (1876)

T.L.M.A.S.
Transactions of the London and Middlesex Archaeological Society (1856 to date). Consecutive numbers are used for the whole series, although vols. vii–xvii (1905–54) appeared as N.S. i–xi

W.A.M.
Westminster Abbey Muniments

THE HUNDRED OF ELTHORNE

(continued)

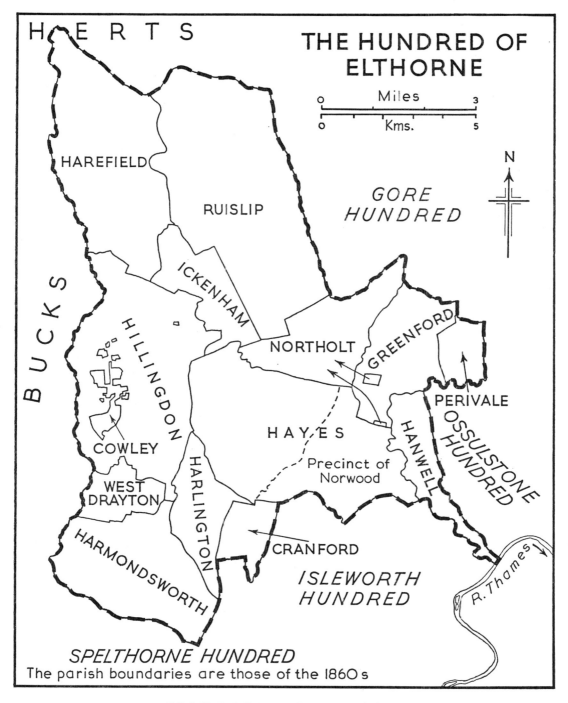

THE HUNDRED OF ELTHORNE

Miles

Kms.

N

HERTS

BUCKS

HAREFIELD

RUISLIP

GORE HUNDRED

ICKENHAM

HILLINGDON

NORTHOLT

GREENFORD

PERIVALE

COWLEY

HAYES

HANWELL

OSSULSTONE HUNDRED

WEST DRAYTON

HARLINGTON

Precinct of Norwood

HARMONDSWORTH

CRANFORD

ISLEWORTH HUNDRED

R. Thames

SPELTHORNE HUNDRED
The parish boundaries are those of the 1860 s

HARMONDSWORTH

THE ANCIENT parish of Harmondsworth lay on the western boundary of Middlesex, adjoining Coln- brook (Bucks.) and between West Drayton to the north and Stanwell and Bedfont on the south. More than half of its area is covered by London Airport (Heathrow), on which work started in 1944.[1] Previously the parish had included Harmondsworth village, three other villages, Heathrow, Longford, and Sipson, and a farm with a few scattered cottages called Perry Oaks. In the Middle Ages there was also a hamlet called Southcote.[2] Covering in 1951 some 3,308 a., the parish was almost 2½ miles from west to east, and, except where a narrow leg extended northward between West Drayton and Harlington to the boundary with Hillingdon parish, under 2 miles from north to south. To the west the parish and county boundary was formed by the Bigley Ditch and the Wyrardisbury River, both branches of the River Colne, and most of the southern boundary was marked by the Duke of Northumberland's River. In the 1940s the Duke's River was diverted and thereafter ran across the southern portion of the airport. The eastern and northern boundaries ran across fields shared with Bedfont, Harlington, and West Drayton. In 1949 the civil parish of Harmondsworth was merged in that of Yiewsley and West Drayton, which now forms part of the London Borough of Hillingdon.[3]

Harmondsworth parish is almost entirely flat and lies just over 75 ft. above sea level.[4] The soil along the rivers and in the west is alluvium; Taplow Gravel covers the area south of the Bath Road, and continues northward in a very narrow strip alongside the alluvium; the remainder is brickearth.[5] The parish is extensively watered on the western side by the Colne and its branches. The Colne itself and four tributary streams, two of which are artificial, runs from north to south across the parish west of Longford. In the north-west runs the Bigley Ditch, which leaves the Colne at West Drayton.[6] West of Harmondsworth village the ditch joins the Wyrardisbury River, formerly also known as Hawthorn's River,[7] and the Pyle or Poyle Mill Stream, which also left the Colne at West Drayton. In 1586 land on either side of the river was charged with the upkeep of Mad Bridge,[8] which carried the Bath Road across the river.[9] During the 18th and early 19th centuries this bridge was maintained by the Colnbrook turnpike trustees, who presumably erected in 1834[10] the bridge with cast-iron parapets which was still standing in 1968.[11] Slightly to the east of the Wyrardisbury River runs the Colne itself, having divided into two streams on the north boundary of the parish. The main stream follows the western branch, formerly called the Middle River or the Drayton and Staines Mill Stream, while the eastern branch runs southward into the Duke of Northumberland's River. This eastern branch, in the early 19th century

called the Old River, formerly rejoined the main stream at its confluence with the Longford River,[12] but by 1826 seems to have been diverted to run straight into the Duke's River.[13] The Duke of Northumberland's River and the Longford River are both artificial, and run east and west respectively of Longford village. The Duke's River (formerly the Isleworth Mill River) was constructed to increase the water driving Isleworth mill in or about 1543,[14] although work seems to have begun as early as 1530.[15] It seems possible, however, that the cut was made along the course of a much earlier stream.[16] The Longford River, constructed by Charles I to improve the water supply at Hampton Court,[17] did not receive its present name until the 20th century, having been called variously the New River, the King's River, the Queen's River, the Cardinal's River, the Hampton Court Cut, and the Hampton Court Canal. The river was stopped up in 1648 or 1649 without authority and petitions were lodged in 1653 against its re-opening because of flood damage to crops and livestock.[18] In the late 1940s, to help the building of Heathrow Airport, both the Duke's River and the Longford River were diverted southward into a single channel.[19]

The Colne, the Longford River, and the Duke's River are all bridged by the Bath Road. The Colne is crossed by Moor or High Bridge, which existed in the 15th century,[20] when there was also an unidentified bridge called Middle Bridge.[21] In 1627 the maintenance of High Bridge was charged on a Sipson farm.[22] The bridge was rebuilt or repaired in 1652 when it was called Middle Bridge.[23] A new bridge was erected in 1809, and in 1826 was still maintained out of the Sipson property. The Longford River was presumably bridged when the river was constructed. This bridge was demolished in 1648,[24] but had been replaced by 1675.[25] In the 19th century, when it was called Stone Bridge, the Crown was responsible for its upkeep.[26] In 1960 it was called King's Bridge. The Bath Road crosses the Duke of Northumberland's River by Longford Bridge at the east end of Longford village. A bridge called Longford Bridge was probably first erected in the 14th century, but, as the two rivers that flow through Longford are both artificial, it is possible that Longford Bridge itself stood in the place of either Mad or High Bridge. This conjecture is supported by the fact that in the 14th century neighbouring parishes had helped to repair it.[27] On the other hand, as the Duke's River may have been cut along an older watercourse it seems more likely that the long ford and the later bridge have been in substantially their present position since the 14th century. In the late

[1] See below and plate facing p. 6. This article was written in 1960. Any references to later years are dated.
[2] See below.
[3] See p. 17.
[4] O.S. Maps 1/2,500, Mdx. xiv. 16; xix. 3, 4, 7, 8, 12; xx. 5, 9 (1932–5 edn.).
[5] Geol. Survey Map, sheet 269 (drift).
[6] Harmondsworth Incl. Map *penes* Yiewsley and West Drayton U.D.C.; *Rep. Cttee. of Magistrates on Public Bridges in Mdx.* (1826), 250–2.
[7] Harmondsworth Incl. Map.
[8] C 66/1284/13.
[9] *Rep. on Bridges in Mdx.* 250–2.
[10] Date on bridge.
[11] Pevsner, *Mdx.* 124.
[12] Harmondsworth Incl. Map.
[13] *Rep. on Bridges in Mdx.* 250–2.
[14] *L. & P. Hen. VIII*, Addenda (ii), p. 545; see also *V.C.H. Mdx.* iii. 86.
[15] *L. & P. Hen. VIII*, Addenda (i), p. 239. This is identified by the editor, almost certainly wrongly, as the Longford River.
[16] *V.C.H. Mdx.* iii. 188.
[17] Hist. MSS. Com. *7th Rep.* 77–78.
[18] Ibid.
[19] Ex inf. Air Ministry.
[20] M.R.O., Acc. 446/L 1/15; S.C. 2/1196/7.
[21] S.C. 2/1196/7.
[22] M.R.O., Acc. 498/1.
[23] M.R.O., *Cal. Mdx. Sess. Bks.* ii. 23.
[24] Hist. MSS. Com. *7th Rep.* 78.
[25] J. Ogilby, *Britannia* (1675), 20.
[26] *Rep. on Bridges in Mdx.* 250–2.
[27] *Public Works in Medieval Law*, ii (Selden Soc. xl), 25.

14th and early 15th centuries the maintenance of the bridge was the responsibility of the lord of the manor.[28]

Evidence of early settlement north-east of Heathrow has been discovered. About twelve hut sites were found within an earthwork, which also contained the remains of a temple. The huts produced evidence of a domestic occupation approximately dating to the early Iron Age from c. 500 B.C. onwards.[29] Before the excavation of the site in 1944 the earthwork, ploughed flat about 1906, had been thought to contain a Roman camp.[30] In the 8th century A.D., probably in 780, land amounting to 20 *mansiones* in the place called Hermonds in the Middle Saxon province, was granted by Offa, King of Mercia, to his servant Ældred.[31]

Early settlement in the area appears to have been dominated by the Bath Road which bisects the parish from east to west. Of the five settlements only one grew up on the road. The village of Harmondsworth, which was probably in existence before 1086,[32] lies in the north-west of the parish, about ½ mile north of the Bath Road, and less than ¼ mile inside the northern parish boundary. Sipson, first mentioned in 1214,[33] lies on the same latitude as Harmondsworth, but nearly a mile to the east. Longford, the only medieval settlement to grow up along the Bath Road, was in existence by 1337.[34] Longford was presumably situated on a river, which has not been clearly identified, although it seems likely to have been along the course of the later Duke's River. The position of Southcote hamlet, which was in existence by 1265,[35] is not accurately known. In the 13th and 14th centuries a Southcote family lived in the parish but their earliest holding seems to have been in Sipson. The family does not appear to have acquired land in Southcote itself until 1310.[36] The earliest indication of the situation of Southcote is in a rental of 1337 where the holding at Perry of John, son of Robert de Perry, is listed under the hamlet of Southcote.[37] In 1349 Southcote was described as 'juxta Colnbrook',[38] and in the early 15th century a meadow was described as lying near High Bridge between Colney stream and Southcotes.[39] All available evidence places the hamlet in the south-west of the parish. In the 15th century Southcote became known as 'Southcoterow', and, in 1450, 'Southcoterow' included the Perry lands and land called Padburys.[40] In 1583 both Perry and Padburys lay in Heathrow.[41]

Heathrow itself, the last definite area of settlement in the parish, began to appear in the early 15th century at about the same time as Southcote became known as 'Southcoterow'. A man said in 1403 to be of 'Southcoterow'[42] was described in 1416 as of Heathrow.[43] Records throughout the century are confused: in 1450 'Southcoterow' but not Heathrow was listed in a manorial rental,[44] and in 1453 tallage collectors were appointed for Heathrow and the other hamlets but not for 'Southcoterow'.[45] Both settlements appear in a rental of 1493–4,[46] but thereafter Heathrow almost always appears alone. It seems most likely that Southcote itself lay nearer to Perry Oaks, a later settlement about 1¼ mile south of Harmondsworth, than to Heathrow. Perry itself was called a hamlet in 1354,[47] and as it is not so mentioned again until the 16th century the reference may be to Southcote. In the 14th century the name Southcote was also associated with a manor which lay partly in Harmondsworth and partly in Ruislip parish.[48]

By 1337 the settlement areas, almost all situated in the west of the parish, were clearly defined. There were 48 houses on Moor and Sheep lanes in Harmondsworth, 30 in Longford, and 17 in Southcote, but only 14 houses at Sipson in the north-east. These areas were surrounded by cultivated land.[49] The absence of settlement in the south-east is explained by the intrusion of Hounslow Heath, which covered this area until the 19th century. Apart from encroachments on the heath this pattern of settlement appears to have remained virtually unchanged until the 20th century. In the early 15th century there were houses on four roads in Harmondsworth, Moor Lane, Sherlane, Ash Lane, and Sipson Way, and also on the square called the Place.[50] Heathrow in 1583 contained 14 houses,[51] but until the mid-18th century little further is known. Harmondsworth and Sipson were mentioned by Norden,[52] and Longford is recorded by Ogilby.[53]

The first definite picture of the parish is supplied by Rocque's map of 1754, where the settlement pattern is clearly shown. At Longford, Harmondsworth, and Sipson there were small, compact groups of houses. At Longford they lined both sides of the Bath Road from the east bank of the Longford River up to and across the Duke of Northumberland's River. Harmondsworth was mainly grouped south and west of the church and along the south side of Moor Lane. Hatch Lane led south to the Bath Road, and continued south to Perry Oaks as Long Lane; Holloway Lane led north to West Drayton; while Harmondsworth Lane, running east to Sipson, and continuing to Harlington as Sipson Lane, was only a track across the open fields. The main settlement at Sipson lay south of Harmondsworth Lane, and was grouped on both sides of Sipson Road; a few houses were situated at Sipson Green where the road joined the Bath Road. From the Bath Road at King's Arbour to its southernmost point dwellings,

[28] B.M. Lansdowne MS. 328, ff. 14, 17.
[29] Ex inf. Prof. W. F. Grimes who, as Director of the London Mus., was in charge of the excavation in 1944. See also *V.C.H. Mdx.* i. 51.
[30] *V.C.H. Mdx.* ii. 3–4. There is no evidence to support this view.
[31] S.C. 11/444. This document, dated *temp.* Ric. II, consists of copies of earlier documents. The grant by Offa is the earliest, and has been much rubbed, making it almost illegible.
[32] *V.C.H. Mdx.* i. 123–4.
[33] *Cur. Reg. R.* vii. 165.
[34] S.C. 11/443.
[35] *Cal. Inq. Misc.* i, p. 246.
[36] See p. 136.   [37] S.C. 11/443.
[38] E 326/B 4526.

[39] M.R.O., Acc. 446/L 1/15.
[40] S.C. 11/446.
[41] M.R.O., Acc. 446/EM. 37.
[42] S.C. 2/191/17.
[43] M.R.O., Acc. 446/M 98/5. See also S.C. 2/191/20.
[44] S.C. 11/446.
[45] S.C. 2/191/24.
[46] E 315/409.
[47] *Public Works in Medieval Law*, ii (Selden Soc. xl), 25.
[48] For this see p. 136.
[49] S.C. 11/443.
[50] M.R.O., Acc. 446/EM. 1.   [51] Ibid. 37.
[52] J. Norden, *Speculum Britanniae*, pt. 1 (1593), pp. 25, 40.
[53] Ogilby, *Britannia*, 20.

collectively known as Heathrow, lined the side of Heathrow Road. At the south end two tracks left the road and ran over the heath, one southward to Bedfont and the other east to Hatton. Another track to Hatton ran south-east from King's Arbour. Perry Oaks consisted of one house. From it the later Oaks Road led south to Stanwell and another road south-west to Stanwell Moor. Heathrow Road itself turned north to the Bath Road again as Tithe Barn Lane.

In 1754 the greater part of the parish was open. Around all the settlements were inclosed lands, but there appears to have been none elsewhere. The uncultivated area west of the rivers was known as Harmondsworth moors, although south of the Bath Road the area between the Colne and the Longford rivers was meadowland, and between the Longford and the Duke's rivers arable. Arable covered the rest of the parish to the eastern boundary north of the Bath Road and to Heathrow Road in the south. Harmondsworth Field lay north of the Bath Road and south of Harmondsworth Lane, while Sipson Field covered the area north of Harmondsworth and Sipson lanes. Heathrow Field lay south of the main road and behind Heathrow. Hounslow Heath covered the area south and west of Heathrow. In 1754, therefore, both ends of the parish consisted of uncultivated moor or heath, while the central portion, ringed with settlements and a belt of inclosed land, formed the cultivated area.[54]

Between 1754 and the Parliamentary inclosure of 1819 inclosure increased, mainly in the north- and south-west, and settlement spread between Heathrow and Perry Oaks, although still on the northern side of the road.[55] At inclosure few of the roads were altered. Harmondsworth and Sipson lanes were both made along the old tracks. Long Lane, then called Lord Lane, was made a private road, and other private roads continued from Moor Lane in Harmondsworth over the moors. Cain's Lane was laid out over the heath but ran south-east to Bedfont, and not east as it had previously done. High Tree Lane was made approximately along the old track to Bedfont, but the track from King's Arbour over the heath disappeared. At this date most of the fields can be identified,[56] although the Perry fields, which existed both in the 17th century[57] and in 1839,[58] were not mentioned. Apart from Harmondsworth, Sipson, and Heathrow fields, the older fields and meadows appear to be Little Field,[59] Wide Mead,[60] and Bury Mead.[61] A Southcote Field is mentioned in 1431,[62] and an Oldfield in Heathrow in 1597,[63] but these cannot now be identified.

By 1839 the cultivated area of the parish had been considerably extended. Over 770 a. of former heath and moorland had been brought under cultivation, although the extreme western end of the parish was still rough pasture. There were also almost 30 small orchards scattered across the parish. In Harmondsworth village, cottages had extended over the Colne, and there were also a few houses

near Mad Bridge. Sipson Green, lying on both sides of the Bath Road, was almost as large as Sipson itself, but both Sipson Green and Sipson were smaller than Harmondsworth (the largest village), Longford, and Heathrow. There were village shops at Harmondsworth, Longford, and Sipson, but Heathrow had only a public house.[64]

During the 19th and early 20th centuries the parish was comparatively little built upon. By 1900 houses in Harmondsworth extended down Hatch Lane on both sides of the road and buildings behind Moor Lane had been erected. In Sipson houses had been built along Sipson Lane, Sipson Road, and Harmondsworth Lane, while a few dwellings were erected at Sipson Green. A few houses were built along Heathrow Road and Cain's Lane but this area remained largely rural until the Second World War. After 1850, however, arable land in the parish diminished and extensive orchards were planted. These lay mainly on the periphery of the parish, on the moors, surrounding Sipson and Sipson Green, in Cain's Lane, and surrounding Perry Oaks. The centre remained arable. There were also several glasshouses at Sipson.[65]

The character of the parish started to change gradually in 1929 with the opening of the Colnbrook by-pass, which left the Bath Road at the junction with Hatch Lane and by-passed Longford to the north. Industrial development began in 1930 with the opening of the Road Research Laboratory on the Colnbrook by-pass. In the same year the Fairey Aviation Co. opened an airfield, the Great West Aerodrome, south-west of Heathrow. This formed the nucleus of the later airport,[66] and the Fairey hangar was eventually incorporated into Heathrow Airport as a fire station. By the late 1930s some residential building had taken place, although almost entirely in the northern half of the parish. Small estates were built off Hatch Lane around Candover Close and Zealand Avenue and further building took place along Sipson Road, around Blunts Avenue, and along the north side of the Bath Road at Sipson Green. Longford remained virtually untouched. A brick-works was established by the corner of Cain's Lane and Heathrow Road and the area of former heathland was extensively worked for gravel, sand, and grit. The county council also opened a large sewage pumping station to the west of Perry Oaks. The Great South West Road from Brentford to Staines also crossed the south-east corner of the parish but played no part in its development. Although many of the orchards survived, their numbers had been greatly reduced and it seems probable that much of the former fruit-growing area was being used for market gardening.[67] In 1944 Harmondsworth and Sipson retained their agricultural character despite some suburban housing. It was then suggested that further expansion in the Yiewsley and West Drayton area should be curtailed, as the land was primarily in demand for agriculture;[68] this proposal has largely been followed.

[54] J. Rocque, *Map of Mdx.* (1754).
[55] Harmondsworth Incl. Map; Harmondsworth Incl. Award *penes* Yiewsley and West Drayton U.D.C. TS. copy in M.R.O.
[56] Harmondsworth Incl. Map.
[57] S.P. 17/H 18. vi, f. 611.
[58] Par. survey (1839) *penes* Yiewsley and West Drayton U.D.C.   [59] E 315/463 (dated 1540).
[60] S.C. 6/1126/7 (dated 1433–4).

[61] S.C. 12/11/20 (dated *temp.* Ric. II).
[62] S.C. 2/191/21.
[63] M.R.O., Acc. 446/EM. 6.   [64] Par. survey (1839).
[65] O.S. Maps 1/2,500, Mdx. xiv. 16; xix. 3, 4, 7, 8, 12; xx. 5, 9 (1867 and later edns.).
[66] Ex inf. Road Research Laboratory and Air Ministry.
[67] O.S. Maps 1/2,500, Mdx. xiv. 16; xix. 3, 4, 7, 8, 12; xx. 5, 9 (1932–5 edn.).
[68] P. Abercrombie, *Greater Lond. Plan* (1944), 151.

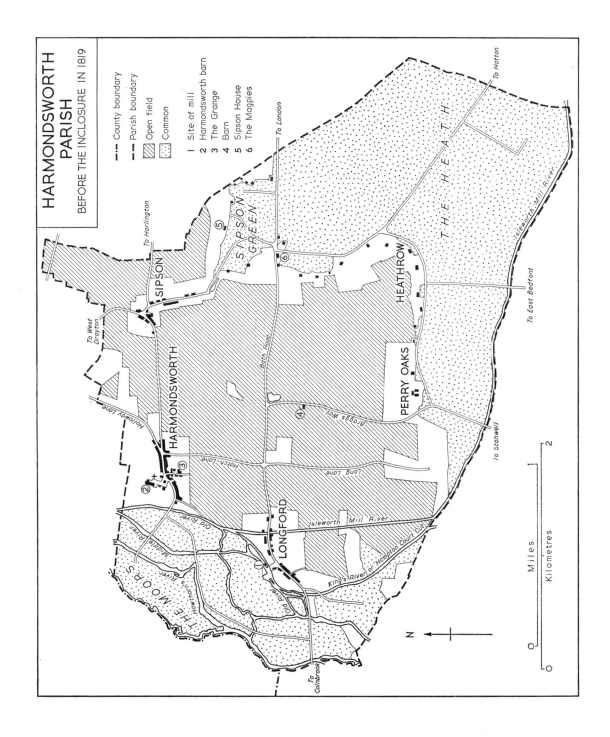

HARMONDSWORTH
PARISH

BEFORE THE INCLOSURE IN 1819

— ·· — County boundary
— — — Parish boundary
[hatched] Open field
[dotted] Common

1 Site of mill
2 Harmondsworth barn
3 The Grange
4 Barn
5 Sipson House
6 The Magpies

SIPSON

SIPSON GREEN

HARMONDSWORTH

HEATHROW

THE HEATH

PERRY OAKS

LONGFORD

THE MOORS

To Harlington

To West Drayton

To London

To Hatton

To East Bedfont

To Stanwell

To Colnbrook

Holloway Lane

Bath Road

Hatch Lane

Long Lane

Braggs Way

Isleworth Mill River

Isleworth Mill River

King's River or Hampton Court Cut

Old River

Middle River

Hawthorn's River

Old River

Miles

Kilometres

N

5

In 1944, however, the modern pattern of Harmondsworth began to emerge with the transfer of the Fairey airfield to the Royal Air Force and its subsequent development by the Air Ministry as Heathrow R.A.F. station. This entailed the complete demolition of Heathrow and Perry Oaks hamlets, and widespread draining of the old flooded gravel pits. Many of the small buildings along the south side of the Bath Road that were still standing in 1960 were erected by the R.A.F. Although R.A.F. personnel were using the airfield in 1944–5, the construction of the base's three runways had not been completed by 1945.[69] The end of the Second World War left the R.A.F. with no need of a long-haul transport airfield,[70] and it was proposed that the station should be converted into an international civil airport. In 1946 Heathrow Airport came officially into being and was transferred to the Ministry of Civil Aviation; regular services started in January 1946,[71] and civil flights from Northolt were transferred to Heathrow after 1952.[72] A plan to extend the airport by building three runways on the north side of the Bath Road, in addition to the six under construction in the main part of the airport[73] was, however, abandoned. The expansion of the airport during the late 1940s entailed road and river diversions. Heathrow Road, Cain's Lane, High Tree Road, and Oaks Road were all destroyed. Long Lane was diverted slightly but in 1960 still existed as a private road for airport use and as an approach to the sewage works. In place of these roads the ministry constructed Stanwell New Road between 1947 and 1949. This runs south to Stanwell and Staines from the Bath Road between Moor and King's bridges. During construction of the runway the sewage works were moved north, and both the Duke of Northumberland's and the Longford rivers diverted to run southward in one channel. In 1960 most of the airport's 2,850 a. lay in Harmondsworth. The area in the parish included runways 1 to 7 laid out in the form of a star of David, the central terminal buildings designed by Frederick Gibberd, the north terminal buildings, the southern air-traffic control centre, and the large maintenance base of British European Airways.[74] The M 4 motorway from London to the west, opened in 1964, cuts through the northernmost tip of Harmondsworth parish before entering West Drayton. A branch road to the south, passing east of Sipson and beneath Sipson Lane, Sipson Road and the Bath Road, links the motorway with the airport. North of the airport and the Bath Road the appearance of the parish has otherwise changed little. Flat and hedgeless, its fields lay open, and in the west by the rivers it remained rough pasture.

Apart from the church[75] and the barn,[76] the two most notable buildings in Harmondsworth village are in Summerhouse Lane. The Grange is a two-story brick house, with a hipped, tiled roof, and windows mostly two-light and transomed. It was built in 1675 and in the south wall there is a painted sundial dated 1695. Harmondsworth Hall, opposite the Grange, was reconstructed in the 18th century but incorporates a 17th-century chimney.[77] At the west end of the village street, where the road widens to form a small green, the Sun House, a timber-framed range probably dating from the 16th century, was remodelled in the 18th century.[78] The Lodge, an imposing early 19th-century residence at the far end of the street, stood derelict in 1968, by which time the 16th-century Centre House in Holloway Lane had already been demolished.

At the west end of Longford, Weekly House, on the south side of the Bath Road, dates from c. 1700, and Longford Close, opposite, from the late 18th century. In the middle of the village a restored timber-framed house with cross-wings, dating from the 16th century, faces the White Horse Inn, and in a lane leading to the river a range of 1739 had recently been renovated as two houses in 1968. Further east a group of timber-framed buildings includes Longford Cottage and the house now called the Stables, both much restored. Sipson House, dating from the late 18th century, stands near the south end of Sipson Lane opposite the main entrance to London Airport.[79]

Nothing is known of the inns of the parish before the mid 18th century. In 1748 there were nine inns[80] of which the 'Magpies', the 'King's Head', and the 'White Horse' became the best known. The 'Magpies', later called the 'Old Magpies', stood at the corner of Heathrow Road and the Bath Road. The house, built in the 16th century and later much altered,[81] was demolished in the 1950s. A few yards up the road was another inn called the 'Three Magpies', which may be that known in 1765 as the 'Three Pigeons' and later as the 'Magpie and Pigeon'.[82] This 18th-century house was still standing in 1960. In Harmondsworth village the Five Bells, 17th-century but refaced with brick, looks eastward down the main street from the green. At Longford the 'White Horse', dating from the 17th century, is much restored. The 'King's Head' at Longford originally stood just east of the Duke's River on the north side of the Bath Road. It acquired its later name of the 'Peggy Bedford' from the family of licensees who are first found at the 'King's Head' in 1775,[83] and were still there in 1824.[84] It is said that Peggy Bedford herself died in 1859 and that the inn was burned down later in the century.[85] It was rebuilt on its present corner site on the Colnbrook by-pass and the Bath Road in the 1930s.

The Domesday Survey mentions 44 people on the monastic estate in Harmondsworth, and two villeins on a further hide, which belonged to Colham manor.[86] In the mid 12th century there were said to be 86 people in the parish,[87] and in the 1330s 43 men were listed on a muster roll.[88] By 1337 the manor of Harmondsworth had 16 tenants in

[69] Ex inf. Air Ministry.
[70] *Jnl. Transport Hist.* iii(1), 21.
[71] Ex inf. Air Ministry.
[72] See p. 132.
[73] *London Airport* (H.M.S.O. 1948), 6–10.
[74] Ex inf. Air Ministry; Pevsner, *Mdx.* 124.
[75] See p. 19.
[76] See p. 8.
[77] Hist. Mon. Com. *Mdx.* 62.
[78] Ibid. 63. See below, p. 18.
[79] Hist. Mon. Com. *Mdx.* 62–64; Pevsner, *Mdx.* 95–96.

[80] M.R.O., L.V. 6/84.
[81] Hist. Mon. Com. *Mdx.* 63.
[82] M.R.O., L.V. 8/39, 86, 9/91.
[83] M.R.O., L.V. 9/2.
[84] M.R.O., L.V. 24/1789–92.
[85] S. A. J. MacVeigh, *West Drayton Past and Present*, 62. Stories of Peggy Bedford can be found in *Lond. and Mdx. Note Bk.* (1892), 34.
[86] *V.C.H. Mdx.* i. 123–4; see below, p. 70.
[87] S.C. 12/11/20.
[88] M.R.O., F 37/4.

HARMONDSWORTH: LONDON AIRPORT FROM THE NORTH-WEST IN 1954

The terminal buildings are under construction, the Bath Road runs across the centre of the picture, and Harmondsworth village is in the right foreground

Southall: King Street, *c.* 1900

Harmondsworth: the medieval Barn at Manor Farm

Ruislip.[89] In 1530 there was an increase, probably temporary, of 42 labourers who were working on the new river cut from Longford,[90] and in 1547 there were 245 communicants in the parish.[91] In 1642 143 adult males took or failed to take the protestation oath,[92] and 107 people were assessed to the hearth tax in 1664.[93] Twelve years later there were said to be 200 conformists and 48 nonconformists in the parish.[94] In 1801 the population was 879. From that date it has risen fairly steadily; the numbers appear stationary between 1841 and 1861, and the increase is again slow between 1881 and 1901. The largest single increase came during the decade from 1921 to 1931 when the population rose from 2,288 to 3,084. There were 3,365 people resident in the parish in 1951 and 3,321 in 1961.[95]

Few famous people have been associated with the parish. General Sir John Byng, who fought throughout the Peninsular War and at Waterloo, was in 1835 created Baron Strafford of Harmondsworth and later Earl of Strafford. William Heather, a late-16th-century musician, founder of the professorship of music in the University of Oxford, was born at Harmondsworth about 1563.[96]

MANORS AND OTHER ESTATES. Before 1066 the manor of *HARMONDSWORTH* was owned by Earl Harold, and at the Conquest it passed to William I.[97] In 1069 it was granted by the king to the Benedictine Abbey of Holy Trinity, Rouen, afterwards known as St. Catherine's,[98] which held it in 1086.[99] Some time later a small cell was founded at Harmondsworth, although a prior is not mentioned until 1211.[1] Thereafter the prior seems in effect to have become lord of the manor, and indeed sometimes appeared in law-suits as the lord rather than as the representative of his abbot.[2] Richard de Cruce, who claimed to hold the manor at farm, quitclaimed his interest to the abbey in 1209.[3] In the late 12th or early 13th century the abbey exchanged some land in Southcote[4] for 33 a. in Harmondsworth.[5] Apart from this transaction it does not appear that the abbey acquired much land in addition to the original grant. The priory and manor were taken into the king's hands after a murder in 1279.[6] In spite of the confiscations suffered by alien priories in the 14th century,[7] the priors of Harmondsworth seem to have retained the custody of the manor and priory, paying

the king £80 for the farm from 1338 to 1369.[8] The manor and advowson, together with those of Tingewick (Bucks.), were acquired from the abbey and prior in 1391 by William of Wykeham, Bishop of Winchester, and formed part of the endowment of Winchester College. This grant did not include the knights' fees held in the king's hands nor the property farmed out by the priory,[9] which possibly consisted of the several manor farms described below. Winchester College retained the manor until 1543 when it was surrendered to Henry VIII[10] in exchange for property elsewhere.[11] It has been suggested that by means of the surrendered lands the king wished to enlarge Hampton Court chase,[12] but there is no indication that this extension ever stretched as far north as Harmondsworth, which lay on the far side of Hounslow Heath. Four years later, in 1547, the lordship and manor were granted to William, later Lord, Paget (d. 1563),[13] who had obtained the neighbouring manor of West Drayton in 1546.[14] Paget's second son, Thomas, Lord Paget (d. 1590), was attainted in 1587.[15] The queen then leased the manor of Harmondsworth to Sir Christopher Hatton,[16] who died in 1591. Thomas's son, William Paget, was granted Harmondsworth and West Drayton in fee in 1597,[17] and was finally restored in blood in 1604.[18] Thereafter the manor remained in the hands of the Pagets, later earls of Uxbridge and marquesses of Anglesey,[19] until the mid 19th century when it was sold by Henry, Marquess of Anglesey (d. 1869).[20]

When the manor passed to Winchester College in 1391 it seems to have been farmed out in various lots,[21] the college appointing a bailiff responsible for the whole.[22] Leases of the whole manor, however, became common in the mid and late 16th century, the first one, for 10 years, appearing to have been made in 1540 to William Noke.[23] A lease in reversion was granted by the king in 1544,[24] Noke sub-let in 1549,[25] and other leases were granted by the Crown during the sequestration from the Pagets.[26] In 1589 the Crown retained 49 a. in demesne,[27] and at one time in the 18th century the Pagets themselves held 389 a. in the manor.[28] The location of most of the manor lands is uncertain. Holdings were scattered among the hamlets; in the early 15th century there were about 408 a. in Southcote hamlet, 366 a. at Harmondsworth, 351 a. at Sipson, and 212 a. at Longford.[29] In 1450 the amount of land held in

[89] S.C. 11/443.
[90] *L. & P. Hen. VIII*, Addenda (i), p. 239. For the river, see p. 2.
[91] E 301/34/147.
[92] Hse. of Lords, Mdx. Protestation Rets.
[93] M.R.O., H.T. 6.
[94] William Salt Libr., Stafford, Salt MS. 33, p. 40.
[95] *Census*, 1801–1961.
[96] *D.N.B.*
[97] *V.C.H. Mdx.* i. 123–4.
[98] *Regesta Regum Anglo-Normannorum*, i, ed. H. W. C. Davis, no. 29. See also *Eng. Hist. Docs.* ii. 918.
[99] *V.C.H. Mdx.* i. 123–4.
[1] *Pipe R. 1211* (P.R.S. n.s. xxviii), 136. A history of the priory appears in *V.C.H. Mdx.* i. 200–202.
[2] *Cal. Close, 1279–88*, 70; *Feudal Aids*, iii. 373.
[3] *Pipe R. 1209* (P.R.S. n.s. xxiv), 37.
[4] For a discussion of the location of Southcote see p. 3.
[5] M.R.O., Acc. 446/ED. 106.
[6] *Cal. Pat. 1272–81*, 166.
[7] e.g. E 142/82(2); C 145/139/19; Winchester Coll. Mun., 10744, 11436.
[8] *Cal. Pat. 1338–40*, 56; 1343–5, 547; *Cal. Fine R. 1369–77*, 22.

[9] *Cal. Pat. 1388–92*, 378, 434; E 212/D.S. 98; M.R.O., Acc. 446/ED. 108.
[10] *L. & P. Hen. VIII*, xviii (2), p. 124.
[11] C 66/729/6.
[12] MacVeigh, *West Drayton*, 39.
[13] *Cal. Pat. 1547–8*, 45.
[14] *L. & P. Hen. VIII*, xxi, p. 351; *V.C.H. Mdx.* iii. 192.
[15] *Complete Peerage*, x. 282–3.
[16] M.R.O., Acc. 446/EM. 42.
[17] *Cal. S.P. Dom. 1595–7*, 468.
[18] *Complete Peerage*, x. 282–3.
[19] For the genealogy of the Pagets see *Complete Peerage*, i. 138 sqq.; x. 276 sqq.
[20] Thorne, *Environs of Lond.* 320.
[21] See below.
[22] S.C. 6/1126/6; 1126/7; Winchester Coll. Mun., 11501–4.
[23] E 315/463, ff. 8–11.
[24] *L. & P. Hen. VIII*, xix, p. 648.
[25] M.R.O., Acc. 446/EM. 37.
[26] Ibid./EM. 42; C 66/1404/21.
[27] E 178/1430.
[28] M.R.O., Acc. 446/45.
[29] Ibid.,/EM. 1.

Harmondsworth itself was the smallest, at 321 a., of any in the four hamlets,[30] but had risen to by far the largest in 1494.[31] The demesne lands were probably situated in the north of the parish, as in 1530 they lay principally in Harmondsworth, with a small amount of land in Sipson.[32] Both in the 1380s and in 1591 two acres of common meadow in Colnbrook (Bucks.) lay in the demesne of Harmondsworth manor,[33] and the manor also owned land in Ruislip.[34] There were 2½ a. of meadow in Stanwell that were owned by Godfrey atte Perry in 1411.[35] This estate subsequently became part of Harmondsworth manor, and was sold by William, Lord Paget (d. 1678), in 1672.[36]

A 'court' on the manor is mentioned in 1293–4,[37] and a capital messuage, a garden, and two pigeon-houses are recorded in 1324–5.[38] A manor-house, with 23 a. around it, is mentioned in 1583,[39] and fifty years later a large house called Court Lodge, with 216 a. of land, was leased by Lettice, Lady Paget. It seems likely that this was the old manor-house and demesne land, as the lease included the gate-house, pigeon-house, court barns, and the customary works of the tenants.[40] This building, leased out by the Paget family until at least 1698,[41] may have been the manor-house, a 'rich and quaint pile' with many ornamented gables, which is said to have been pulled down in 1774.[42] In 1794 a timber-framed, double-fronted house under two plain gables, perhaps a farm-house, was called the manor-house,[43] although the present Manor Farm House near the barn dates from the early 19th century.

In 1484–5 Winchester College spent over £40 on new buildings.[44] The college was almost certainly responsible for building the tithe barn west of the church. In 1426–7 a new barn at Harmondsworth was being made and roofed[45] under the charge of William Kypping, a carpenter employed by the college,[46] and in 1434–5 another new barn was being built on the manor by an Uxbridge carpenter.[47] Two bays of the 'great barn' were included in a lease of the Court Lodge property in 1688,[48] and in 1698 another lease included a 'tithe barn' on part of the property and one other barn called the 'great barn'.[49] A 'tithe barn' standing in 1819 on Braggs Way, the lane leading from the Bath Road to Perry Oaks, still existed in 1934, when the lane was known as Tithe

Barn Lane;[50] the airport now covers this site. Rocque shows the present barn at Harmondsworth as L-shaped[51] but there is nothing else to support the tradition that a wing of this building was removed to Heathrow and re-erected.[52] At Heathrow itself three barns of 16th- or 17th-century date were demolished, with the farm-house, during the building of the airport.[53] The barn at Harmondsworth, one of the most notable surviving medieval barns in the country, stands about 70 yds. west of the church and is an aisled building of twelve bays, 190 ft. long. It is of timber construction on a stone base and is weather-boarded externally.[54] The roof, continuous over 'nave' and aisles, has kingpost trusses with curved braces below the tie beams; there are also curved braces longitudinally between the principal posts and the ties which span the aisles have curved braces below and curved struts above.[55] West of the barn, traces of a moat survived in 1968.

The manor or manor farm of *PERRY* or *PERRY OAKS* evolved from the holdings in the parish of the Perry family.[56] There was a Robert de Perry on Harmondsworth manor in the 12th century,[57] and in 1308 Robert atte Perry acquired 13 a. of heath from Roger atte Crouch of Sipson. John, son of Robert de Perry,[58] held a tenement at Perry in 1337.[59] Henry atte Perry held land in 1405,[60] but the main holding was that of Godfrey atte Perry and his wife Mirabel, who were in the parish at least from 1375 to 1411.[61] In 1411 Godfrey sold the reversion on his property after the death of his wife to Nicholas Walpole of Suffolk.[62] The reversionary interest passed through a number of hands between 1419 and 1430,[63] when it was held by Robert Long to whom Mirabel, Godfrey's widow, and her second husband, Richard Edward, quitclaimed their rights.[64] It was sold again in 1431 to Thomas Hering,[65] from whom it passed before 1443 to Sir Thomas Lewkenore and Henry Sever.[66] Sever sold his interest in 1444[67] and by 1486 the property had passed to four men who in that year sold it to Robert Frost or Frosten.[68] His son, another Robert, still held Perry in 1511,[69] when he mortgaged it to Nicholas Tichebourn and two priests, John Rede and John Webb.[70] In 1523, however, William Frost and Robert Wallop quitclaimed the property to Winchester College,[71] and in 1542 the house, Perry Place, and its land were leased by

[30] S.C. 11/446. The figures were: Sipson 430 a., South-coterow 427 a., Longford 341 a., Harmondsworth 321 a.
[31] E 315/409. The figures were: Harmondsworth 800 a., Longford 193 a., Southcoterow 192 a., Sipson 191 a., Heathrow 15 a.
[32] S.C. 11/450.
[33] S.C. 12/11/20; E 310/19/94/24.
[34] B.M. Add. MS. 9368; see p. 135.
[35] E 210/D 4229.
[36] M.R.O., Acc. 446/ED. 121. For this property see below *sub* Perry.
[37] B.M. Add. MS. 6164, p. 98.
[38] E 142/83(2).
[39] M.R.O., Acc. 446/EM. 37.
[40] Ibid./ED. 151.
[41] Ibid./ED. 151–9, 162, 164.
[42] Thorne, *Environs of Lond.* 320.
[43] Illustrated copy of Lysons, *Mdx. Pars.* in Guildhall Libr.
[44] Winchester Coll. Mun., 22151.
[45] Ibid. 22104.
[46] J. H. Harvey, *Eng. Medieval Architects*, 156.
[47] Winchester Coll. Mun., 22111.
[48] M.R.O., Acc. 446/ED. 162.
[49] Ibid./ED. 164.
[50] Harmondsworth Incl. Map *penes* Yiewsley and West

Drayton U.D.C; O.S. Maps 1/2,500, Mdx. xix. 8 (1867 and 1934 edns.).
[51] Rocque, *Map of Mdx.* (1754).
[52] Thorne, *Environs of Lond.* 319.
[53] Hist. Mon. Com. *Mdx.* 63.
[54] See plate facing p. 7.
[55] Hist. Mon. Com. *Mdx.* 61–62.
[56] The alternative spellings Pyrie, Pirye, Pyrye, Pyro, Purye, and Pury have been standardized as Perry.
[57] S.C. 12/11/20.
[58] S.C. 12/11/28. Roger atte Crouch is probably identifiable with Roger de Cruce of Sipson, see p. 136 *sub* Southcote manor.
[59] S.C. 11/443.
[60] S.C. 2/191/17.
[61] E 210/D 8217, 4229.
[62] E 329/B.S. 282.
[63] Ibid.; C.P. 25(1)/152/87/32; E 210/D 5878.
[64] C.P. 25(1)/152/89/42.
[65] C.P. 25(1)/152/89/46; S.C. 2/191/21.
[66] E 210/D 2342.
[67] E 210/D 6065.
[68] Cal. Inq. p.m. Hen. VII, i, p. 27.
[69] E 210/D 4834.
[70] C.P. 25(2)/27/178/9.
[71] E 210/D 9865.

the college to George Brighouse.[72] Thereafter the property followed the descent of Harmondsworth manor.[73] Perry was leased by Elizabeth I[74] and by the Pagets,[75] and in 1672 William, Lord Paget, sold the house and estate to Thomas Wood of Littleton,[76] to whose descendants, Edward and William Wood, it belonged in 1708.[77] Thomas Wood the elder sold the manor in 1776 to Edward Baron and Robert Hudson, when it was linked to a Yorkshire estate.[78]

It is almost certain that the Perry property was never independent of Harmondsworth manor: John de Perry held his land in 1337 from that manor;[79] Godfrey atte Perry owed services to the manor;[80] Henry atte Perry appeared in the court rolls as a tenant;[81] and in 1431 Nicholas Carewe and Thomas Hering were entered in the rolls as the tenants of Perry Place and its land.[82] It may, however, have formed part of the property which was farmed out in 1391 and therefore exempted from the grant to Winchester College. It was first styled a manor in 1424–5[83] but was not so described again until 1542, when it belonged to the college.[84] Perry Place was called a farm in 1580,[85] and in 1587 formed part of the demesne of Harmondsworth manor.[86]

There are no known valuations of Perry manor. In 1542[87] and 1587[88] a rent of £8 was paid to Harmondsworth manor. In 1662 there was a reserved rent on Perry Place of £5 6s., and rents from 9 men on Perry manor were estimated to amount to £84 15s.[89] In 1430 the manor consisted of 4 houses and 260 a. of land,[90] which in 1424–5 included 143 a. of heath, 100 a. of which was called Perry Heath.[91] In the 15th century there were at least 200 a. in the manor,[92] and by 1580 this had risen to 240 a.[93] In 1640 the manor comprised 278 a., 2½ a. of which lay in Stanwell,[94] and had been owned by Perry at least since 1411.[95] During the 17th century the manor was partially split up in leases,[96] but in 1672, when the whole property was sold, it amounted to 261 a.[97]

There were four houses on the manor in 1419.[98] One of these was presumably the manor-house, as in 1424–5 the gate of the manor is mentioned.[99] In the mid 15th century there was a manor-house with a gate-house, two gardens, and a dovecote,[1] and in 1511 one of the four houses on the manor was expressly called Perry Place.[2] In the mid 17th cen-

tury the house was described as a spacious mansion, with two great gate-houses, three gardens, and two pigeon-houses.[3] Nothing is known of the house after this date; the gate-houses do not appear to have survived and in the 19th and 20th centuries the only buildings at Perry Oaks were a late-16th-century farm-house, a dovecote, and barns.[4] These were demolished during the construction of Heathrow Airport.[5]

The manor farm of *PADBURY* has no known connexion with the John de Padbury who held land in the parish in 1349.[6] In the late 14th century property called 'Padburylands' was held by John Ley or Lye of London and John Dodd of Staines. Some time before 1400 they conveyed it to Peter Lodington or Luddington, who in turn conveyed it to five people, among whom were Godfrey atte Perry and Alan Wombe, Vicar of Harmondsworth. In 1400 'Padburylands' was conveyed by these five to John Hore or Okebourne.[7] It was acquired from Okebourne in 1401 by John Kundell and others,[8] but in 1402 Okebourne still appeared to have rights in the property.[9] Padbury was probably included in the lands of Robert Okebourne which were sold to Rose, widow of Robert Tentirden, in 1428,[10] and by her to Winchester College in 1430.[11] The property is mentioned as a tenement in Harmondsworth manor in 1450[12] and was being administered by Winchester College after 1475, together with the two other manor farms, Luddingtons and Barnards.[13] The first known lease was made by the college in 1541 to Nicholas Parker.[14] A lease was granted by Elizabeth I in 1592,[15] and during the 17th and early 18th centuries the Pagets leased it to Matthew East and his son John.[16] The later descent of the property is unknown.

The property, said in 1450 to be in Southcote-row,[17] was described in 1542 as being in Heathrow. It then consisted of a house and 109 a., rented at £5, and formed part of the manor of Harmondsworth.[18] In 1541 Padbury had comprised only 100 a., of which the greatest portion, 93 a., lay in Heathrow Field.[19] In 1583 the manor-house of Padbury was surrounded by 6 a. of inclosed land.[20] The house was still standing in 1749.[21] In 1450 Padbury appears in a rental of Harmondsworth manor, and in 1587 it

[72] E 315/463, pp. 4–6.
[73] See above.
[74] E 310/19/96/26; S.P. 17/H/18. vi.
[75] M.R.O., Acc. 446/ED. 175–7; B.M. Add. Ch. 56058, 56058*, 56062.
[76] M.R.O., Acc. 446/ED. 121; B.M. Add. Ch. 56059.
[77] B.M. Add. Ch. 56064.
[78] M.R.O., Acc. 423/1–2.
[79] S.C. 11/443.
[80] Winchester Coll. Mun., 11503.
[81] S.C. 2/191/17.
[82] S.C. 2/191/21, 22.
[83] S.C. 12/11/28.
[84] E 318/1233.
[85] Req. 2/163/128.
[86] E 310/19/96, m. 26; E 178/1430.
[87] E 315/463, p. 16.
[88] E 178/1430.
[89] M.R.O., Acc. 446/EM. 15.
[90] Cal. Close, 1429–35, 34.
[91] S.C. 12/11/28.
[92] M.R.O., Acc. 446/L 1/15. This document is an undated survey of Perry manor. It has here been ascribed to the 15th cent., although it possibly dates from the late 14th cent.
[93] Req. 2/163/128.
[94] S.P. 17/H/18. vi, ff. 611–12.
[95] E 329/B.S. 282.

[96] M.R.O., Acc. 446/ED. 176–7; B.M. Add. Chs. 56058, 56058*, 56062.
[97] B.M. Add. Ch. 56059. The other surviving copy of this sale, M.R.O., Acc. 446/ED. 121, lists only 249 a. This omits 3 closes and cuts 1 a. off a fourth close.
[98] C.P. 25(1)/152/87/32.
[99] S.C. 12/11/28.
[1] M.R.O., Acc. 446/L 1/15.
[2] E 210/D 4834.
[3] S.P. 17/H/18. vi, ff. 611–12.
[4] Kelly's Dir. Mdx. (1886); Hist. Mon. Com. Mdx. 63.
[5] Ex inf. Air Ministry.
[6] E 326/B 4526, and see p. 136 sub Southcote manor.
[7] E 210/D 1302.   [8] E 315/48/299.
[9] Cal. Close, 1399–1402, 557.
[10] E 210/D 4430.
[11] Cal. Close, 1429–35, 49–50.
[12] S.C. 11/446.
[13] Winchester Coll. Mun., 11473–91. The bailiffs' accounts in the three manors extend from 1475 to 1521.
[14] E 315/463, ff. 11–13.
[15] M.R.O., Acc. 446/ED. 142.
[16] Ibid./ED. 144, 146, 148, 150; /EM. 35.
[17] S.C. 11/446.
[18] E 315/463, ff. 16–19.
[19] Ibid. ff. 11–13.
[20] M.R.O., Acc. 446/EM. 37.
[21] Ibid./EM. 35.

was said to be part of the Harmondsworth demesne;[22] in 1662, however, it was described as a farm, with an annual rent of £22 10s.[23] It is doubtful whether it ever had an independent existence, at any rate after the beginning of the 15th century.

The manor farm of *LUDDINGTONS* followed a descent similar to that of Padbury. A Robert de Luddington held land at Sipson in 1337,[24] but in the late 14th century the land that became the manor farm had belonged to William atte Aronle, and later to John Ley and John Dodd. This property, comprising a house, garden, and ½ acre in Sipson, came into the possession of Peter and Maud Luddington in 1393.[25] In the same year Luddington acquired other land in Harmondsworth parish, formerly held by Alexander Tresom, from John Mann, Vicar of Harlington, and Alan Wombe, Vicar of Harmondsworth.[26] Luddington's lands, after the death of his mother Maud, reverted to Thomas Aunger of London, but in 1402 Aunger quitclaimed his rights to John Hore or Okebourne.[27] After a dispute in 1425 the property passed to Robert Okebourne.[28] Three years later he sold his land in Harmondsworth, Sipson, Southcoterow, and Longford to Rose, widow of Robert Tentirden,[29] who herself sold the estate to Winchester College in 1430.[30] Thereafter the property presumably became part of Harmondsworth manor, and after 1475 was administered by Winchester with Padbury and Barnards.[31] In 1542 Luddingtons was leased by the college at an annual rent of £2 13s.[32] In a rental of 1549, and in later years, the property was styled a manor, and consisted of a house, 64 a. in Sipson, and 4 a. of meadow in Wide Mead south of Longford.[33] It was let at £20 in 1662[34] and leased until the early 18th century.[35]

The origin of the manor farm of *BARNARDS* is not known. The property, first mentioned in 1450 as a tenement on Harmondsworth manor,[36] was administered by Winchester after 1475,[37] and was leased in 1521 as the manor of Barnards to Roger and Thomas Watts. It consisted of the manor and 54 a., held at a yearly rent of £3 4s.,[38] and was situated at Sipson.[39] In 1549 Thomas Watts, the assignee of James Annesley, held the manor and 55 a.[40] Other leases from the Paget family were granted during the 16th and 17th centuries,[41] the manor being joined in 1621 with Longford mills[42] and another tenement called Malinhawe with 9 a. of land and 2 a. of meadow in Colnbrook.[43] In 1542 Malinhawe and its

land had been an independent holding in the manor.[44] Like the other manor farms, it is improbable that Barnards ever had a separate manorial existence.

Part of the manor of *SOUTHCOTE* lay in Harmondsworth parish until at least the 14th century. Although the extent of the manor and its relationship to the parishes of Harmondsworth and Ruislip is obscure, it seems unlikely that there were two manors of Southcote, as Lysons suggests.[45] Since the bulk of the estate appears to have lain in Ruislip from the late 14th century onwards, a full discussion is reserved for that article.[46]

ECONOMIC AND SOCIAL HISTORY. The manor of Harmondsworth, which had been worth £25 before the Conquest, was worth only £12 when the abbey received it, but in 1086 it was valued at £20.[47] The value increased to £61 in 1293–4,[48] only to fall to below £30 during the sequestrations of the 14th century.[49] After the manor had passed to Winchester College the value rose again,[50] and in the early 16th century the property was thought to be worth £108.[51] A rental of 1662 shows that over £630 was received from the manor in rent and tithe.[52]

In 1086 the manor was assessed at 30 hides,[53] and in the late 14th[54] and early 15th[55] centuries it was reckoned to consist of about 1,321 a. By 1450 the area seems to have been at least 1,620 a.,[56] but it fell again in 1494 to about 1,392 a.[57] The demesne lands, which were assessed at 8 hides in 1086,[58] were estimated at over 230 a. in 1294,[59] and at over 290 a. in 1325.[60] By 1340 the demesne had fallen to 165 a.,[61] but in the late 14th century it rose to over 300 a.[62]

The Domesday population of the monastic estates at Harmondsworth and Colham comprised an unidentified knight, an uncertain number of Frenchmen, 26 villeins, 7 cottars, 6 bordars, and 6 serfs.[63] In the 12th century there were said to be 39 virgaters and 47 cottars.[64] In 1324 the manorial servants, who were paid in kind, included a keeper, a reeve, a hayward, 2 ploughmen, 2 drovers, a carter, a swineherd, and a cowman; there was also a smith, who received 12d. in money.[65] By 1337 there were a cobbler and a tailor in Harmondsworth, and a smith and at least one fisherman in Longford.[66] By the 1430s there were 6 ploughmen employed on the

22 E 310/19/96/26.
23 M.R.O., Acc. 446/EM. 15.
24 S.C. 11/443.
25 E 210/D 661.
26 E 210/D 2492.
27 *Cal. Close*, 1399–1402, 562; E 326/B 9174.
28 *Cal. Close*, 1422–9, 208, 209, 210.
29 E 210/D 4430.
30 *Cal. Close*, 1429–35, 49–50, 52. This sale excluded a house and 7 a. in Sipson held from Dawley manor, in Harlington, and 2 a. of meadow in Stanwell.
31 Winchester Coll. Mun., 11473–91.
32 E 315/463, ff. 16–19.
33 M.R.O., Acc. 446/EM. 37.
34 Ibid./EM. 15.
35 Ibid./ED. 119, 178–81; E 310/19/94/21.
36 S.C. 11/446.
37 Winchester Coll. Mun., 11473–91.
38 Ibid. 11418.
39 E 315/463, ff. 16–19; E 318/1233.
40 M.R.O., Acc. 446/EM. 37.
41 Ibid./ED. 120, 135, 138–41.
42 See p. 14.
43 M.R.O., Acc. 446/ED. 136.
44 E 315/463, ff. 16–19.
45 Lysons, *Mdx. Pars.* 140, 209.
46 See pp. 136–7.
47 *V.C.H. Mdx.* i. 124.
48 B.M. Add. MS. 6164, p. 98.
49 E 142/83(2); C 145/139/19.
50 S.C. 12/11/20. This is an undated valor of Harmondsworth manor *temp.* Ric. II.
51 S.C. 11/450.
52 M.R.O., Acc. 446/EM. 15.
53 *V.C.H. Mdx.* i. 123.
54 S.C. 12/11/20.
55 M.R.O., Acc. 446/EM. 1.
56 S.C. 11/446.
57 E 315/409.
58 *V.C.H. Mdx.* i. 123.
59 B.M. Add. MS. 6164, pp. 96, 98.
60 E 142/83(2).
61 C 145/139/19.
62 S.C. 12/11/20.
63 *V.C.H. Mdx.* i. 123–4.
64 S.C. 12/11/20.
65 S.C. 6/1126/5.
66 S.C. 11/443.

manor, and also a cook, baker, and dairyman, all paid in money.[67]

During the Middle Ages arable farming predominated in the manor, with some dairy and pig farming.[68] There was land for 20 ploughs in 1086, when the Frenchmen and villeins had 10 ploughs, and the lord 3 ploughs on his 8 demesne hides.[69] The amount of arable, exclusive of the demesne, remained fairly constant at about 230 a. from the late 13th to the mid 15th century. The maximum amount cultivated during this period was 269 a. in 1397–8, and the minimum appears to have been the 140 a. under cultivation in May 1340.[70] The latter figure may, however, refer to the demesne. The area cultivated in demesne in 1293–4 was 240 a. in addition to 233 a. on the manor. Farming during the late 13th and early 14th century appears to have been mixed. In 1294 wheat and oats were being grown in almost equal proportions of 56 and 50 a. respectively. Rye and barley accounted for 40 and 39 a. respectively, and peas for 24 a. A further 24 a. were fallow. By 1337 wheat, grown on 72 a., was by far the largest crop, while the area in oats had fallen to a mere 16 a. Mixed wheat and rye were grown on 59 a., barley on 52 a., and peas and rye were also grown. The amount of land in wheat continued to increase during the later 14th century, and by 1397–8 it was grown on 110 a. By this date the second main crop was barley, grown on 82 a. The only other crops grown were pulse (haras') and oats, the latter used almost exclusively for fodder. Until the mid 15th century, when the manorial accounts cease, the proportions of wheat, barley, and pulse remained virtually unchanged, although even fewer oats were grown.

By the end of the 14th century about a third of the wheat yield was used for seed, and about a third sold, this amount in 1397–8 being over 1,198 bu. Of the remaining third, the bulk was used for domestic purposes. In the 15th century much less wheat was sold. In 1406–7 only 482 bu. were sold, and 955 bu. in 1450–1. In 1433–4 wheat was used for payments in kind to the manorial servants, and the increased amount of wheat sold in 1450–1 may mark the beginning of money stipends to the servants. Of the barley yield well over half was sold in 1397–8, and during the 15th century sales of barley rose as those of wheat declined: 1,362 bu. were sold in 1406–7 and 1,032 bu. in 1450–1. Some barley was also retained as seed, and throughout the Middle Ages it was used for malt.[71] Lesser quantities of pulse and oats were also sold.

The rotation of the crops is uncertain, but in 1324, 50 a. of winter corn and 46 a. of winter maslin were sown. Winter crops seem to have remained the custom in Harmondsworth, as a lease of October 1540 specifies that the lessee was to return the manor in ten years with 74 a. fallowed, well manured, and ready to be sown with wheat. At the same time it is noticeable that there was to be more barley in the granary than wheat or oats.[72]

There were 20 carucates of meadowland in 1086 and pasture sufficient for the beasts of the vill.[73] There appears to have been little meadow or pasture on the manor later in the Middle Ages. In 1293–4 there were 24 a. of meadow in the demesne, and a separate pasture is also mentioned. This demesne land had fallen by 1340 to 17 a. of meadow and 8 a. of pasture,[74] and at about the same date there were said to be 100 a. of meadow in the parish.[75] The amount of demesne meadow and pasture remained unaltered in 1379,[76] and at about the same time the manor owned 44 a. of meadow, 40 a. of which were in Burymead.[77] This was unchanged by the mid 15th century,[78] when the meadows were usually reckoned to produce 20 loads of hay, used for winter fodder.

Cattle and pig farming was also carried on in the manor during the Middle Ages. The manor's herd of 20 cows in 1293–4 had dwindled by the early 14th century to only eight or nine, but by the end of the 14th and during the early 15th century it had risen again to about 25. A few hens, geese, and swans were also kept, five or six of the geese producing a flock of 28 or 29 a year.[79] The woodland supported 500 pigs in 1086,[80] and the manor itself seems to have kept a herd of 100 to 140 pigs.[81] Pannage was paid on 350 pigs in 1394,[82] and references to pigs and amounts paid in pannage occur frequently in the court rolls. The scarcity of sheep on the manor is remarkable especially as Harmondsworth lay on the north side of Hounslow Heath. 'Sheeplane', however, existed in Harmondsworth village in 1337.[83] In 1397 there were 200 sheep on the manor and 178 in 1398.[84] These are the sole references to sheep belonging to the manor, except for four lambs which were included in a list of manorial stock in 1540.[85] The unfree tenants of the manor seem to have kept some sheep, and in 1411 and 1416 bondage tenants were presented for grazing 140 sheep on the lord's land.[86] Tithes in the hands of Winchester College about 1400 included 12 lambs and wool worth 8s.[87] At the end of the 15th and in the early 16th century sheep were also kept on the manor farms of Padbury, Barnards, and Luddingtons. Between 1475 and 1521 these farms were administered by the college as one estate, and, apart from 30 to 35 a. of wheat with some barley and pulse, their main farming consisted of a constant flock of 120 sheep. There were also 40 lambs each year.[88] Little is known of the grazing or stinting regulations enforced on the manors except that by the end of the 15th century pigs were not allowed on the common land between March and September.[89]

Much is known about relations between the lord

[67] S.C. 6/1126/7.
[68] Except where specified this and the following paragraphs are based on bailiffs' accounts and extents of the manor dating from 1294 to 1451: B.M. Add. MS. 6164, pp. 98–99 (for 1294); S.C. 6/1126/5 (for 1324); /6 (for 1388–9); /7 (for 1433–4); C 47/18/1/12 (for 1337); Winchester Coll. Mun., 11501 (for 1386–7), 11502 (for 1397–8), 11503 (for 1406–7), and 11504 (for 1450–1).
[69] V.C.H. Mdx. i. 123.
[70] C 145/139/19.
[72] E 315/463, ff. 8–11.
[73] V.C.H. Mdx. i. 124.
[74] Winchester Coll. Mun., 11338.
[75] Inq. Non. (Rec. Com.), 198.
[71] See p. 14

[76] Winchester Coll. Mun., 10744.
[77] S.C. 12/11/20.
[78] S.C. 11/445.
[79] See above, note 68.
[80] V.C.H. Mdx. i. 124.
[81] See above, note 68.
[82] S.C. 2/191/16.
[83] S.C. 11/443.
[84] Winchester Coll. Mun., 11502.
[85] E 315/463.
[86] S.C. 2/191/19; M.R.O., Acc. 446/M 98/5.
[87] Guildhall MS. 9531/3, ff. 206–7.
[88] Winchester Coll. Mun., 11473–91.
[89] S.C. 2/191/28.

of Harmondsworth and his tenants, and there appears to have been considerable unrest, during the ownership of both Rouen and Winchester College. Disturbances, occurring at regular intervals from the 1220s to the 1450s, were too widespread to be the work of one man or one family, and it seems equally improbable that discontent stemmed from a succession of over-harsh lords. The earliest known lawsuit between the Abbot of Holy Trinity and his Harmondsworth tenants occurred in 1227,[90] but no details have survived. In 1233 thirty tenants protested in court that the abbot should not demand customs from them.[91] This plea was rejected,[92] but in 1275 it was repeated with the additional claim that Harmondsworth formed part of the ancient demesne of the Crown. This was again rejected[93] and during the next four years there appears to have been open warfare between lord and tenants. The tenants carried off the lord's muniments,[94] felled his trees, killed his men, and burned his houses. The king ordered the Sheriff of Middlesex and the Constable of Windsor to go to Harmondsworth and assist the abbot and his prior to distrain the men.[95] The tenants complained against tallage in 1278, repeated that they held in ancient demesne, and refused to return the stolen muniments.[96] In 1279 the king himself threatened them with 'castigation' if they remained recalcitrant and denied service and tallage to the abbot.[97] Twelve Harmondsworth people were in gaol in 1281 for burning the priory buildings,[98] and there were further disputes over services in 1289.[99] Four years later the prior was appealed of having caused a murder in the village by the widow of the victim,[1] who had herself been in gaol in 1281.[2] Apart from a charge of extortion against the prior in 1354,[3] the parish seems to have remained peaceful until in 1358 the houses and goods of the priory were said to have been burned.[4] In 1391 the escheator was sent to investigate reports of 'unlawful assemblies' in Harmondsworth and of great hosts of armed men disturbing and terrorizing the people.[5] Between 1420 and 1436 there were constant petty disputes between Winchester College and the tenants over timber and fishing rights. These included armed raids on college woods and heath,[6] although disturbances do not appear to have reached the proportions of earlier quarrels. A Chancery petition lodged in the early 1450s against payment of customary services and works to the college[7] only resulted in an order to the tenants to pay their services and keep the peace towards the college servants.[8] This appears to mark the end of two centuries of discord.

The manor court rolls reveal much unrest in the years after the Black Death and immediately preceding the Peasants' Revolt.[9] The customary services which were so much in dispute are first detailed in a late-14th-century document, said to be a copy of a 12th-century custumal.[10] Another 14th-century copy, however, assigns the custumal to 1226-7.[11] Little is known about commutation of services in Harmondsworth, but temporary sales of works are recorded as early as 1397-8, when 18 manual works were sold at 1½d. each and Godfrey atte Perry sold all his services for 3s. 4d.[12] In 1450-1 there were sales of the customary works of ploughing, harrowing, mowing hay, and of carting, tossing, and stacking wheat and hay;[13] this was by then presumably the accepted custom. Increasing commutation may also explain the absence of further bitter disputes between lord and tenant.

Very little is known of the economy of the parish after the Pagets assumed possession. Although the sale of works had apparently been the custom earlier, in 1587 ploughing, harrowing, and carrying works were still being exacted; timber on the manorial estate was carefully reckoned, and there was still a notable absence of sheep on the capital manor.[14] By about 1640, however, Perry manor was keeping 400 to 500 sheep, and shearing them on the premises.[15] These were presumably grazed on the heath, 143 a. of which had been included in Perry manor as early as 1424-5.[16] In the 1640s Perry was predominantly arable and the 82-acre Great Perry Field was sown with barley, peas, vetches, and oats. Some wheat was also grown in other fields.[17] This suggests that the 15th-century pattern of arable farming had not yet changed.

In the early 18th century the timber on Perry manor, of which in the 1640s there had been more than 24 a., was in dispute between the parish and the owners of Perry manor who finally allowed the parish surveyors two pollard oaks a year.[18] In the early 17th century malting and brewing were still carried on in an oast house in Sipson belonging to the Tillyer family. This family also grew wheat and rye, and kept at least 20 sheep.[19] In the late 18th century there are a few scattered references to sheep being kept on the manor,[20] and prohibitions against cross-cropping the arable had been written into earlier leases granted by the Pagets.[21] In the late 18th century the rotation of crops in the Harmondsworth area was: clover; peas, beans, or tares; wheat with turnips on the stubble; barley; and oats.[22] In 1801 there were 1,350 a. in Harmondsworth under arable cultivation, slightly over a third of the parish. Wheat (500 a.) and barley (450 a.) were the main crops.

90 *Rot. Litt. Claus.* (Rec. Com.), 211b.
91 *Close R.* 1231–4, 294.
92 S.C. 11/444.
93 Ibid.; *Cal. Close*, 1272–9, 247; *Plac. Abbrev.* (Rec. Com.), 188.
94 *Cal. Pat.* 1272–81, 236.
95 S.C. 11/444.
96 *Cal. Pat.* 1272–81, 290, 292.
97 S.C. 11/444.
98 *Cal. Pat.* 1272–81, 467.
99 S.C. 11/444.
1 J.I. 1/544, m. 50d.
2 *Cal. Pat.* 1272–81, 467.
3 S.C. 11/444.
4 *Cal. Close*, 1354–60, 472.
5 Ibid. 1389–92, 391.
6 M.R.O., Acc. 446/L 1/1–18.
7 Ibid./M 98/1. This is undated and addressed to the Cardinal Archbishop of York, Chancellor of England. The only man who fulfils all three conditions in the 15th cent. is Cardinal Kemp, Chancellor 1426–32, 1450–4.
8 *Cal. Close*, 1447–54, 334–5.
9 *V.C.H. Mdx.* ii. 80–83. In this article extracts from the court rolls are also given.
10 S.C. 12/11/20; *V.C.H. Mdx.* ii. 66–69.
11 S.C. 11/444.
12 Winchester Coll. Mun., 11502.
13 Ibid. 11504.
14 E 178/1430.
15 S.P. 17/H/18. vi, f. 611.
16 S.C. 12/11/28.
17 S.P. 17/H/18. vi.
18 B.M. Add. Ch. 56064.
19 M.R.O., Acc. 498/1.
20 M.R.O., Acc. 446/EF. 46/17, 1/22.
21 Ibid./EM. 35.
22 Foot, *Agric. of Mdx.* 20.

Peas and beans each occupied 150 a., and some oats, turnips, rape, potatoes, and rye were also grown. The vicar, who made the return, commented that most of the waste land could be sown with corn to much greater advantage.[23]

At Domesday Harmondsworth had been one of the few Middlesex manors cultivating vines, of which there was one arpent.[24] There is no further reference to viticulture, but by the 18th century the parish seems to have become a fruit-growing area, which developed considerably in the 19th century. In the mid 18th century there were at least three 'fruiterer' families in the parish,[25] and in the early 19th century there were extensive orchards, said to be of 'ancient standing',[26] at Longford.

Before the early 19th century comparatively little inclosure had taken place. In 1583 Perry Place with 138 a. had the largest amount of inclosed land; there were 26 inclosed a. at Longford and 6 a. surrounding the manor-house of Padbury.[27] By 1754 inclosure had taken place only around the settlement areas at Harmondsworth, Sipson, and Longford, and the long straggle of scattered houses from Sipson Green southward to Heathrow and Perry Oaks.[28] In 1801 there were said to be no fewer than 1,300 a. of waste in the parish and inclosure was being considered.[29] The Inclosure Act was passed in 1805[30] but no award was made, and an amending Act was passed in 1816.[31] Finally in 1819 1,170 a. of waste and 1,100 a. in fields and meadows were inclosed.[32]

Inclosure had little immediate effect on agrarian practice. In the 1830s the price of peas, which had hitherto been supplied to the London market, was too low to encourage their cultivation; oats and barley were still grown, but the latter was often of inferior quality and so could not be used for malting. White wheat was grown principally for bread, but was also used as fodder. Straw was sent to London[33] or used in Hounslow barracks. In exchange dung was obtained from the barracks, without which the heavy cropping rotation of ⅓ green crop, ⅓ wheat, and ⅓ barley and oats would have been impossible.[34] In the 1830s wheat was grown on the former open-field land, while on the old open common land oats were grown and sheep for the London butchers were kept.[35] A survey of the parish in 1839 shows that the centuries-old pattern was gradually changing and that the district was developing like many Middlesex parishes that were influenced by the London markets. The amount of arable had nearly doubled since 1800 with the cultivation of former heath and commons. There were also over 100 a. of orchards and three market gardens.[36] Arable land had increased little by the 1860s but orchards covered over 240 a. These were almost all small-holdings but some of the arable fields extended over large areas of 70, 90, and 100 a.[37] In the 1840s a Harmondsworth farmer had ploughed, sown with wheat, harrowed, and rolled 100 a. in one day for a wager.[38] During the later 19th century, however, arable farming slowly declined and was replaced by fruit growing and market gardening. From the 1880s until the First World War orchards occupied nearly 1,000 a. in the parish,[39] and the number of market gardeners rose from 3 in 1870 to 25 in 1917, one of their principal crops being strawberries for London.[40] By the 1930s both orchard and market-garden land had decreased, but there were still seven farms in the parish.[41] There was little industry or building, and by the end of the Second World War the West Drayton area had been reserved for agriculture,[42] although the growth of Heathrow Airport in the post-war years swallowed up over half the available agricultural land. In 1960 most of the parish untouched by the airport remained open under cultivation, mainly in market gardens supplying potatoes and other vegetables for the London market. A little wheat and barley were still grown, and some orchards remained, although the trees were exhausted and decaying.[43] Nursery gardening was carried on south of Longford under the threat of airport extension.[44] Pig farming was also carried on in the north of the parish.

In 1086 there were three mills, worth in all 60s., on Harmondsworth manor.[45] By 1293–4 there were only two water-mills.[46] One of these was most probably a corn mill, and the other may have been a malt mill.[47] In 1324 there was definitely a corn mill on the manor,[48] and in 1325 there were both corn and malt water-mills.[49] These two mills operated throughout the 14th century,[50] both corn malt and barley malt being produced.[51] The mills were repaired in the late 14th century[52] and were let at £6 13s. a year.[53] By 1406 the rent, which had increased to £8, included a fishery in the river.[54] In 1433–4 only one mill, the corn mill at Longford, was being farmed, but the malt mill was almost certainly still working since barley malt was being produced and there was at this time a thatched malt-house on the manor.[55] The miller of Harmondsworth mill at Longford is mentioned in 1449,[56] and two years later the mill was farmed at £10,[57] although a second mill is not mentioned. One water-mill only

[23] H.O. 67/16.
[24] V.C.H. Mdx. i. 124.
[25] Par. Recs., Reg. 1670–1802.
[26] Brewer, Beauties of Eng. and Wales, x(5), 623.
[27] M.R.O., Acc. 446/EM. 37.
[28] Rocque, Map of Mdx. Settlement and its areas are more fully described on pp. 3–4.
[29] H.O. 67/16.
[30] L.J. xlv. 413a.
[31] Ibid. i. 743a.
[32] Harmondsworth Incl. Award.
[33] Rep. Cttee. on Agric. Distress, H.C. 79, pp. 194–8 (1836), viii (1).
[34] Ibid. 188–94; Mins. before Sel. Cttee. on Agric., H.C. 464, pp. 293–5 (1837), v.
[35] Mins. before Sel. Cttee. on Agric. (1837), 293–5.
[36] Survey (1839) penes Yiewsley and West Drayton U.D.C.
[37] O.S. Area Bk.
[38] Home Cnties. Dir. (1845).
[39] O.S. Maps 1/2,500, Mdx. xiv. 16; xix. 3, 4, 7, 8, 12;

xx. 5, 9 (1895–6 and 1913–14 edns.).
[40] Kelly's Dirs. Mdx. (1870–1917).
[41] Ibid. (1922–37); O.S. Maps 1/2,500, Mdx. xiv. 16; xix. 3, 4, 7, 8, 12; xx. 5, 9 (1932–5 edn.).
[42] Abercrombie, Greater Lond. Plan (1944), 151.
[43] Ex inf. Mr. H. E. Purser, Manor Farm.
[44] Ex inf. Mr. J. F. W. Philp, Fairview Farm.
[45] V.C.H. Mdx. i. 123.
[46] B.M. Add. MS. 6164, p. 98.
[47] Ibid. pp. 96, 98.
[48] S.C. 6/1126/5.
[49] E. 142/83(2).
[50] C 145/139/19; Winchester Coll. Mun., 10744.
[51] S.C. 6/1126/6.
[52] S.C. 12/11/20.
[53] Ibid.; Winchester Coll. Mun., 11502.
[54] Winchester Coll. Mun., 11503.
[55] S.C. 6/1126/7.
[56] S.C. 2/191/23.
[57] Winchester Coll. Mun., 11504.

at Longford was rented in 1493–4,[58] but in 1501 Harmondsworth mills, comprising a wheat mill and a malt mill in two houses at Longford, and the fishery of the mill stream, were leased by Winchester College to John Smallbroke of Longford, who received a livery of clothing from the college.[59] When the manor was exchanged with the king in 1543 there appears to have been only one mill,[60] and a single mill was specified in the grant to William Paget in 1547,[61] although in the preceding year the king had leased Longford mills for 60 years to Sir Philip Hoby.[62] Hoby sold his interest in 1548 to Sir Thomas Paston and in 1560 Edward Fitzgarret, who had married Paston's widow, sold the lease to Thomas Warde of Longford. It was acquired in 1565 by Edmund Downing and in 1566 by John Tamworth, who in turn sold it to Arnold Lumley in 1568.[63] Longford mills are mentioned in 1583[64] and 1587,[65] but Edward Fitzgarret was returned in a rental of 1587 as holding the only mill.[66] A lease of 1615 to Thomas, Lord Knyvett, and William Steere of Loughborough (Leics.), mentions the mills,[67] and in 1621 a lease of Barnards manor farm included two corn water-mills in one house at Longford.[68] In 1622 one of these wheat mills was said to have been formerly a fulling mill.[69] The situation of two mills under one roof at Longford probably explains why they are sometimes referred to in the singular and sometimes in the plural. In 1627 Longford mill is again mentioned.[70] By 1647 the house described as formerly a fulling mill had been converted into a malt mill, with fishing rights along the Middle River as far as Blackengrove, which lay on the boundary with Stanwell. The wheat mill, 'furnished with French stones', stood on Colney stream, and was called Longford mills.[71] The malt and corn mills are again mentioned in 1648,[72] but are not afterwards expressly named. Later references to mills at Longford probably refer to the paper mills.

It is not known when paper mills were first started in Longford, but in 1636 Longford mill was among the Middlesex paper mills closed because of the plague.[73] This mill must have been rebuilt, for in 1647 there were three newly built mills adjoining the wheat mill in Longford, one driving 24 hammers and the others 15 hammers each. There were also two drying houses.[74] In 1656 Thomas Holland, the miller and papermaker, agreed with Lord Paget to carry out repairs and enlarge the mills.[75] In 1662 Longford mills, probably the paper mills, were let at

£33 10s.;[76] in 1694 the paper mills were valued at £90;[77] and in 1695–6 one year's rent of the mill was £100.[78] The paper mills were repaired in 1697 and new machinery to make 'fine white writing paper' was installed.[79] In 1697 and 1701 the two writing-paper mills were let to Nicholas Faulcon of St. Giles, Cripplegate, at £65 a year. Apart from the two mill houses, the property comprised two vat rooms, two drying lofts, a sizeing room, a water house, and a drywork house. The mills stood on opposite sides of the river, one being 'next to Longford town'.[80] Further repairs were carried out in 1704, and between January 1705 and May 1707 the mills sold slightly over 8,576 reams of paper.[81] There was a dwelling-house with 2 a. of land attached to the paper mills in 1715.[82] Paper-makers worked in the parish at least until 1762,[83] but after this date there are no references to any mills until the mid 19th century, when a map of the Colne and its tributaries showed the site of former calico mills at Longford.[84] The existence of a calico mill in Longford is supported by the mention in 1829 of Matthew Ferris of Longford, a calico printer.[85]

Notwithstanding these mills there was little industry in Harmondsworth before the 20th century, and even by 1960 there had been, in comparison with nearby parishes, little industrial development. In 1739 a bell-founder, Thomas Swain, moved his foundry from Holborn to Longford, but nothing more is known of the works, although some of Swain's bells hang in churches in Surrey and Sussex.[86] In the 18th century there was said to be a trade in lampreys which were sold both to home consumers and to the Dutch as fish bait.[87] In the 1820s there was a printing works in Longford,[88] but this was disused by 1834.[89] A jam factory[90] was established at Sipson in the late 1890s in an old farm, and some additional buildings were erected. Production seems to have ceased after the First World War, and the buildings were taken over by Sims & Brooks, furniture makers, in 1935. In 1947 manufacture changed from furniture to caravans, and in 1960 the firm, Sipson Caravans, employed about 20 people.[91]

All other industry in the parish was established in the 20th century. In the early 1930s there was a brick-works on the road to Heathrow,[92] and in 1937 there were in the parish five firms dealing in sand and gravel, and one brick-making firm, the West London Brick Co. Ltd.[93] There is no previous record

[58] E 315/409.
[59] Winchester Coll. Mun., 11402.
[60] E 315/463; E 318/1233.
[61] *Cal. Pat.* 1547–8, 45.
[62] *L. & P. Hen. VIII*, xxi(2), p. 435.
[63] B.M. Harl. Ch. 80, F. 36.
[64] M.R.O., Acc. 446/EM. 37.
[65] Ibid./EM. 40.
[66] E 178/1430.
[67] M.R.O., Acc. 446/ED. 167.
[68] Ibid./ED. 136.
[69] Ibid./ED. 165.
[70] C 142/448/113.
[71] M.R.O., Acc. 446/ED. 168.
[72] Ibid./ED. 169.
[73] M.R.O., Acc. 249/822.
[74] M.R.O., Acc. 446/ED. 168.
[75] Ibid./ED. 170. Holland is here called a miller, but in 1657 he is described as a paper-maker: B.M. Add. Ch. 56058.
[76] M.R.O., Acc. 446/EM. 15.
[77] M.R.O., F 34/114. This is a schedule of par. assessments at 4s. in the £ for the war with France; Mr. Briscoe paid £18 for Lord Paget's paper mills.
[78] M.R.O., Acc. 446/EF. 28/2.
[79] Ibid./EF. 28/3.
[80] Ibid./ED. 171.
[81] Ibid./EF. 29.
[82] Ibid./ED. 122.
[83] Par. Recs., Register 1670–1802. Paper-makers 1699–1761 are listed in A. H. Shorter, *Paper Mills and Paper Makers in Eng. 1495–1800*, 214.
[84] M.R.O., F 32.
[85] M.R.O., Acc. 601/12.
[86] *V.C.H. Mdx.* ii. 167.
[87] MacVeigh, *West Drayton*, 62.
[88] *Pigot's Lond. Dir.* (1826–7).
[89] *Rep. Poor Law Com. App. B(2)*, H.C. 44, p. 100g (1834), xxxv–vi.
[90] *Kelly's Dir. Mdx.* (1898).
[91] Ex inf. Sipson Caravans.
[92] Maxwell, *Highwayman's Heath*, 292. This is shown on Ministry of Defence maps.
[93] *Kelly's Dir. Mdx.* (1937).

of brick-making in the parish, although there were brick-fields in West Drayton and Hillingdon,[94] and, during the Middle Ages, on Harmondsworth manor's estate at Ruislip.[95]

The opening of the Colnbrook by-pass in 1929 was followed quickly by ribbon industrial development along the Bath Road. In 1930 the Ministry of Transport opened a road-testing laboratory, which in 1933 was taken over by the Department of Scientific and Industrial Research and formed the nucleus of the Road Research Laboratory. In 1960 the laboratory occupied a site of 22 a. and employed approximately 420 people. Only about 10 of these, however, were resident in the parish. The Harmondsworth buildings housed the main offices for the Road Research department, and also the materials and construction division.[96] Technicolor Ltd. opened a factory at Harmondsworth in 1936 with 200 employees. Occupying an 11-acre site on the Bath Road, the works in 1960 processed films in colour, about 60 per cent. being for the export market, and employed approximately 1,100 people, of whom about 200 were local residents.[97] West's Piling & Construction Co. Ltd. was also established in the early 1930s on the Bath Road, and, among many other projects, was responsible for the ocean terminal at Southampton.[98] In 1938, three years after their first publication, Penguin Books opened their present headquarters in the Bath Road,[99] although they later acquired premises for storage in West Drayton.[1] The last major firm to settle in the parish, Black & Decker Ltd., occupied a site on the Bath Road in 1940 with about 250 employees. In 1960 a large proportion of the firm's output of electric tools was exported and their employees numbered over 1,100.[2]

There were also in 1960 a number of small industries, mainly established after 1945 and each employing fewer than a dozen people. They included a granite works whose stock of stone was drawn from old Waterloo Bridge, a non-ferrous iron foundry in the former smithy in Harmondsworth village, and a precision engineering firm at Longford in a former wheelwright's shed.[3]

The largest single industrial unit in the parish is Heathrow Airport. In 1946 the airport had a staff of approximately 200 people. Since 1946 the premises have been repeatedly enlarged and by the late 1950s Heathrow had become the major airport for London. By 1960 it employed about 27,000 people.[4] Few of these, however, were drawn from Harmondsworth.

Few details of social life in the parish have survived. There was a friendly society in the village by 1813 and this had 97 members by 1815;[5] in 1845 it

met at the 'White Horse' in Longford.[6] The average wage of agricultural labourers in the 1830s was 12s. a week,[7] and there were reports of discontent in the district.[8] Even by 1900 the average wage of a 'cottager' had not risen above 17s. The vicarage hall was erected in 1885 by the vicar and in the 1920s was used as a club and by the Women's Institute.[9] Nothing further is known of a fair at Harmondsworth mentioned in 1879.[10] The British Legion bought land on the Bath Road in 1933, but lacked the money to build. In 1939 they exchanged their site for one in Sipson Road and a building was finally erected in 1959. The Harmondsworth Community Association was formed about 1947.[11]

LOCAL GOVERNMENT. A manor court is first mentioned in Harmondsworth in 1222.[12] Consecutive court rolls exist from 1377 to 1530;[13] these, to some extent, have already been examined in an earlier volume.[14]

In 1274 the vill of Harmondsworth was said not to owe suit to the hundred.[15] This statement and the holding at Harmondsworth in 1500 of a view of frankpledge for Harmondsworth, Longford, and Southcote,[16] are the only indications that Harmondsworth manor ever exercised an independent jurisdiction. In the 12th century there was a court every winter at Martinmas,[17] but by the late 14th century no clearly defined sequence is apparent, although courts were rarely held at less than quarterly intervals. During the later 15th century the business of the court slackened, and meetings were normally held twice a year;[18] although the October or November court was the larger, little business was transacted either in the spring or in the autumn. The courts were usually reserved to the lord in leases of the manor, and during the sequestration in the late 16th century the Crown followed the same practice.[19] By this time courts were held at Easter and Michaelmas, the perquisites going to the lord.[20] Courts continued to meet at least until 1772,[21] but there is little indication of their frequency.

During the Middle Ages the manor court dealt with all aspects of local life and agricultural organization. As well as fines and surrenders of land, the court regulated pannage and tallage.[22] Courts before 1391 were presumably held by the Prior of Harmondsworth, or his deputy, and at least once after that date the Warden of Winchester College himself held the court.[23] Officials of the manor were occasionally elected there, as were a beadle and keeper of the heath in 1377, and a reeve in 1378,[24] but these appointments seem to have been exceptional. The

[94] V.C.H. Mdx. iii. 199; see below.
[95] See p. 139.
[96] Ex inf. Road Research Laboratory.
[97] Ex inf. Technicolor Ltd.
[98] Yiewsley and West Drayton Official Guide.
[99] E. W. Williams, The Penguin Story, 10, 30–33; R. M. Robbins, Middlesex, 278.
[1] V.C.H. Mdx. iii. 196.
[2] Ex inf. Black & Decker Ltd.
[3] Ex inf. Morgan & Son Ltd.; A. Bennett, Non-Ferrous Iron Foundry; N. G. Loges & Co. Ltd.
[4] Ex inf. Min. of Aviation; see also p. 6.
[5] Rets. on Expense and Maintenance of Poor, H.C. 82, pp. 262–3 (1818), xix.
[6] M.R.O., C.P. Reg. of Socs., ii, p. 19.
[7] Rep. Cttee. on Agric. Distress, H.C. 79, pp. 194–8 (1836), viii(1).
[8] Rep. Poor Law Com. App. B(2), H.C. 44, p. 100f

(1834), xxxv–vi.
[9] Char. Com. files.
[10] MacVeigh, West Drayton, 60.
[11] Char. Com. files.
[12] W. H. Hale, Domesday of St. Paul's (Camd. Soc. lxix), 101.
[13] S.C. 2/191/14–31.
[14] V.C.H. Mdx. ii. 73–75.
[15] J.I. 1/540, m. 13d.
[16] S.C. 2/191/13.
[17] S.C. 12/11/20.
[18] S.C. 2/191/14–31.
[19] E 310/19/96/39.
[20] E 178/1430.
[21] M.R.O., Acc. 446/EF. 8.
[22] S.C. 2/191/14–31.
[23] Winchester Coll. Mun., 11502.
[24] S.C. 2/191/14.

beadle, who received an allowance of grain from the manor in 1388,[25] was evidently a form of constable, and after 1394 the rolls frequently contain details of his attachments.[26] He seems to have been chiefly concerned with grazing offences, poaching, unauthorized wood-cutting, and the like. He was still receiving an allowance of grain in 1398[27] but is not often mentioned in the 15th century. There was, however, a constable of Harmondsworth village in 1405[28] and this officer might be identifiable with the earlier beadle, although the beadle reappears in the 1450s.[29] By the late 1430s there were two sub-constables for the parish.[30] The bailiff was a servant of the lord of the manor rather than an official of the manor court. He was receiving a salary of 40s. in 1434, when the steward, mentioned for the first time, was paid only 16s. 8d.[31] The bailiff's salary was unchanged in 1451,[32] and he was probably responsible for much of the work on the manor, the steward occupying a higher and perhaps more honorary post. In the mid 16th century the bailiff was appointed for life by letters patent at a salary of £4 a year, and at the same time a chief steward was appointed by the Crown.[33] The reeve seems to have been the chief officer of the manor in the 12th century[34] but is rarely mentioned later. In the 14th century tenants on the Harmondsworth land at Ruislip were under the authority of a woodward who was responsible for making presentments and attachments.[35] The tenants at Ruislip were also bound to render suit of court at Harmondsworth.[36]

There were probably court buildings on the manor by 1293–4 when the site of the 'court' is mentioned.[37] In 1337 the door or gate of the court is recorded,[38] and references to a house standing by the door of the court are frequently repeated.[39] In 1688 the lease of the Court Lodge property included the court house;[40] later leases, however, do not mention it, nor is it known where the building stood. In the late 18th century court dinners were held by the Pagets, the last known dinner being in 1800.[41] These may have taken place in the court house, if it was still standing at that date.

Little is known of the growth of the parish administration which succeeded the manorial organization. In 1642 there were 2 constables, 2 churchwardens, and an overseer.[42] Subsequently parish business was presumably transacted by the vestry, which became select after 1819. By 1834 the vestries were said to be rarely fully attended, and parish business was conducted by the churchwardens, overseers, and 2 or 3 inhabitants.[43] The vestry

was responsible for the workhouse which was in existence at least as early as 1776 when it had 40 inmates.[44] During the first two decades of the 19th century the numbers fell to between 20 and 30.[45] In 1834 the workhouse contained 21 people classed as 'idle and illiterate', who were alleged to make the other poor dissatisfied. Workhouse poor were farmed at 3s. 6d. per head and their labour.[46] The workhouse, which stood at Sipson Green, was still standing in 1839[47] but had been demolished by the 1860s.[48] The vestry remained in sole charge of affairs in the civil parish until 1895, and its only salaried officer appears to have been the assistant overseer. He was first appointed in 1833,[49] and in 1893 was receiving a salary of £40 a year.[50]

A parish council was formed in 1895. It met four times a year and had a membership of nine. The council appointed one man as assistant overseer and clerk in 1896, and a clerk to the surveyors of the highways was appointed in 1897.[51] Before the First World War, however, a great deal of local administration was still undertaken by the vestry.[52] This may have been because at first the parish council was extremely unpopular. The vicar was bitterly hostile, and in 1899 all but two of the members were ousted after a vote.[53] By 1914 the vestry was still conducting charity business, the piping of gas and water, and the clearing of all ditches, and it was the body which negotiated with the police for a speed limit on the Bath Road at Longford. The parish council, on the other hand, was mainly concerned with sanitary conditions, the fire engine, and the provision of allotments. In many cases, however, membership of both bodies was the same. After 1919 the vestry usually met only once a year. The parish council took over practically all local administration during the war, and, among other functions, elected the burial board and school managers. No permanent council offices were built. In about 1918 meetings moved from the Sipson and Heathrow school on the Bath Road to the parish room, on the same road,

LONDON BOROUGH OF HILLINGDON. *Per pale gules and vert, an eagle displayed per pale or and argent, in the dexter claw a fleur-de-lis or and in the sinister a cog-wheel argent; on a chief or four civic crowns vert*
[Granted 1965]

and this was subsequently termed the Council Offices.

[25] S.C. 6/1126/6d.
[26] S.C. 2/191/16 contains the first list in 1394.
[27] Winchester Coll. Mun., 11502.
[28] Cal. Pat. 1405–8, 57.
[29] S.C. 2/191/24.
[30] M.R.O., F.37/4.
[31] S.C. 6/1126/7.
[32] Winchester Coll. Mun., 11504.
[33] L. & P. Hen. VIII, xxi(1), pp. 770, 776; M.R.O., Acc. 446/EM. 37.
[34] S.C. 12/11/20.
[35] Ibid.; see also p. 141.
[36] S.C. 11/444.
[37] B.M. Add. MS. 6164, p. 98.
[38] S.C. 11/443.
[39] e.g. ibid./446, /449; E 315/416.
[40] M.R.O., Acc. 446/ED. 162.
[41] Ibid./EF. 46/1, 17, 73.
[42] Hse. of Lords, Mdx. Protestation Rets.
[43] Rep. Poor Law Com. App. B(2), H.C. 44, p. 100 f

(1834), xxxv–vi.
[44] Rep. Sel. Cttee. on Rets. by Overseers, 1776, Ser. 1, ix, p. 396.
[45] Rets. on Expense and Maintenance of Poor, H.C. 175, p. 294 (1803–4), xiii; H.C. 82, pp. 262–3 (1818), xix.
[46] Rep. Poor Law Com. App. B(2), H.C. 44, p. 100 f (1834), xxxv–vi.
[47] Par. Survey (1839) penes Yiewsley and West Drayton U.D.C.
[48] The building is not marked on the first edition of the Ordnance Survey.
[49] Rep. Poor Law Com. App. B(2), H.C. 44, p. 100 f (1834), xxxv–vi.
[50] Vestry Min. Bk. 1888–1929 penes Yiewsley and West Drayton U.D.C.
[51] Par. Council Min. Bk. 1895–1913 penes Yiewsley and West Drayton U.D.C.
[52] Ibid.; Vestry Min. Bk. 1888–1929.
[53] Char. Com. files.

The exact location of the room is not definitely known, but it was possibly attached to the mission church of St. Saviour. It may, however, merely have been a room in the school.[54]

In 1930 the parish council was dissolved on the transference of Harmondsworth civil parish from Staines R.D. to Yiewsley and West Drayton U.D., which took over all the independent parish administration. The civil parish of Harmondsworth itself was absorbed in 1949 into the civil parish of Yiewsley and West Drayton.[55] After this date, therefore, Harmondsworth existed only as an ecclesiastical area. Since 1965 Yiewsley and West Drayton have formed part of the London Borough of Hillingdon.[56]

CHURCH. In 1069 the parish church was granted, with the manor, to the Abbey of Holy Trinity, Rouen.[57] The rectory thereafter followed the descent of the manor until the late 18th century, its appropriation to Holy Trinity being rescinded in 1391, when it was appropriated to Winchester College.[58] The rectory was sold in 1772 by Henry, Lord Paget, later Earl of Uxbridge, to Sir William Heathcote, who in turn sold it in 1789 to George Byng, who represented Middlesex in Parliament.[59] The Byngs still owned the rectory in 1835,[60] but its later history is obscure.

During the ownership of Winchester College the rectory is known to have been farmed out at least twice. It was farmed in 1415,[61] and this was probably the usual custom. The first surviving lease of the rectory is to William Noke in 1540, in which the patronage was reserved to the college.[62] Later an under-lease was granted, and also a lease in reversion.[63] The rectory formed part of the dower of Anne, Lady Paget, in 1564,[64] and in 1587, on Lord Paget's attainder, it was included in the lease of the manor from Queen Elizabeth I to Sir Christopher Hatton.[65] It was leased again by the queen in 1593 to Thomas and William Duck,[66] after Hatton's death. During the 17th and 18th centuries, after it had been restored to the Pagets,[67] the rectory was usually leased out together with the tithes and tithe barn.[68]

About 1247 the church was valued at 25 marks.[69] By 1291 the sum had increased to £20[70] and in 1293–4 the church was worth £17 6s. 8d.[71] By 1324 the figure had fallen to £10,[72] and although in 1340 it was again reckoned to be £20, the actual value to the rector was only £13 6s. 8d., the rest being assigned to the vicar.[73] The sum of £20 remained

a standard figure quoted in the late 14th and early 15th centuries.[74] In the 16th century and thereafter the rectory was almost always leased together with the tithes, and so no independent figures can be obtained. The farm of the rectory and tithes rose progressively from £25 in 1530 to £270 in 1738.[75]

The Abbey of Holy Trinity, as the impropriate rector, collected the great tithes,[76] and in the early 15th century the great tithe of flax and hemp was paid on all lands and gardens cultivated with a plough.[77] At about the same time the rectorial tithes of grain and hay were valued at 40 marks or more.[78] When the rectory was owned by Winchester College the great tithes formed part of the income of the college and manor. In 1433, for instance, part of the tithe money was raised by the sale of lime, chalk, and the previous year's hay crop.[79] In the mid 17th century the tithes, leased at £210 a year, constituted part of the Pagets' income from the manor;[80] a century later they were leased at £250.[81] The rectorial tithes were extinguished at Michaelmas 1806, after the first Inclosure Act, and 369 a. in lieu of tithes were awarded to George Byng, the impropriate rector, in 1819 under the second Inclosure Act.[82] No glebe land appears to have been attached to the rectory at any time.

The precise date of the ordination of the vicarage is not known, but it probably occurred at the same time as or shortly after the appropriation to Holy Trinity Abbey; there was certainly a vicarage by about 1247.[83] In 1321 and doubtless long before the patronage of the vicarage was exercised by the abbey.[84] While the rectory remained the property of the lord of the manor the advowson of the vicarage also remained in the lord's hand, being expressly reserved to him in leases of the rectory and tithes. In 1755, some years before the sale of the rectory, the vicarage was consolidated with that of West Drayton, the Pagets owning both.[85] In the same year Henry Paget, Earl of Uxbridge, sold the advowson to the Revd. George Booth. It passed to Thomas Ives in 1756, to the Revd. William Harvest in 1760, and to Culling Smith of Hadley in 1776. Smith sold the advowson in 1785 to a Mr. Burt, from whom it was acquired in 1786 by John Hubbard.[86] By 1808 it was in the possession of James Godfrey de Burgh of West Drayton.[87] The Dean and Chapter of St. Paul's, however, who had an alternate right of presentation to the church of West Drayton,[88] also claimed in 1808 the right of alternate presentation to the vicarage of Harmondsworth.[89] Hubert de Burgh

[54] Vestry Min. Bk. 1888–1929; Par. Council Min. Bks. 1895–1913, 1914–30.
[55] Census, 1931, 1951.
[56] London Govt. Act, 1963, c. 33.
[57] Regesta Regum Anglo-Normannorum, i, ed. Davis, no. 29.
[58] Cal. Papal Letters, iv. 441.
[59] Hennessy, Novum Repertorium, 200–1.
[60] Rep. Com. Eccl. Rev. [67], p. 650, H.C. (1835), xxii.
[61] Winchester Coll. Mun., 11416.
[62] E 315/463, ff. 8–11.
[63] M.R.O., Acc. 446/EM. 37; L. & P. Hen. VIII, xix(1), p. 648.
[64] M.R.O., Acc. 446/ED. 125.   [65] Ibid./EM. 42.
[66] C 66/1404; E 310/19/96/40.
[67] M.R.O., Acc. 446/ED. 104; Cal. S.P. Dom. 1603–10, 391; see p. 7.
[68] Home Cnties. Mag. ii. 282–3; M.R.O., Acc. 446/ED. 127–33.
[69] St. Paul's MS. W.D.9, f. 84v.
[70] Tax. Eccl. (Rec. Com.), 17.
[71] B.M. Add. MS. 6164, p. 98.
[72] E 142/83(2).
[73] Cal. Inq. Misc. ii, p. 418; C 145/139/19.
[74] Winchester Coll. Mun., 11436; Feudal Aids, iii. 378.
[75] S.C. 11/450; E 315/463, ff. 8–11; M.R.O., Acc. 446/EF. 15/2, /EM. 40, /ED. 133; Home Cnties. Mag. ii. 282–3.
[76] Winchester Coll. Mun., 11338.
[77] S.C. 2/191/18.
[78] Guildhall MS. 9531/3, f. 207. See below note 1.
[79] S.C. 6/1126/7.
[80] M.R.O., Acc. 446/EM. 15.   [81] Ibid./EM. 35.
[82] Harmondsworth Incl. Award.
[83] St. Paul's MS. W.D.9, f. 84v.
[84] Reg. Baldock, Segrave, Newport, and Gravesend (Cant. & York Soc. vii), 268.
[85] V.C.H. Mdx. iii. 203.
[86] For the descent of the advowson, see Lysons, Mdx. Pars. 39; Hennessy, Novum Repertorium, 201.
[87] Guildhall MS. 9557.
[88] V.C.H. Mdx. iii. 202.
[89] Guildhall MS. 9558.

held the patronage in 1835,[90] and it seems to have remained in the de Burgh family until 1866, when Harmondsworth was separated from West Drayton, and sold to a Miss Rainsford. In 1875 it was bought by the Revd. Henry Worsley, who sold it in 1879 to Nicholas Richard Sykes. Sykes sold it in 1883 to John Charles Taylor[91] who in 1886 was also lord of the manor.[92] In 1894 the patronage was exercised by Taylor's trustees, who still owned it in 1937.[93] In 1965 the patron was the Revd. H. M. S. Taylor.[94]

The vicarage was valued at 3 marks c. 1247[95] and at £2 in 1291.[96] In 1340 ten marks were being assigned out of the income of the rectory for the maintenance of the vicar.[97] In the mid 14th century the rectory and vicarage were valued together at £45 6s. 8d.,[98] the vicarage being valued alone in 1347 at 40s.[99] In the late 14th or early 15th centuries the vicarage seems to have been worth about 75s.,[1] and in the earlier 16th century to have had a net annual value of £12.[2] Worth £40 a year in 1656,[3] and £60 in the early 18th century,[4] its value had risen to £180 in 1780 and to £250 by 1813.[5] In 1835 the gross and net income of the consolidated benefices of Harmondsworth and West Drayton was £530.[6]

About 1340 some of the tax on the church was remitted, because the small tithes, which belonged to the vicarage, had been greatly reduced owing to the dry summers which had burned up the land.[7] In 1407 the small tithes of flax and hemp were given to the vicar from garden and other ground dug with a spade.[8] A late-14th or early-15th century inquisition shows that the small tithes, worth 60s. 8d., were also in the possession of Winchester College. Nearly half of this money came from gifts, and most of the remainder from pigs, geese, lambs, and wool. Small tithes were also levied on apples, honey, wax, milk, cheese, hemp, and flax. The college was presumably taking the tithes during a vacancy of the vicarage.[9]

In the early 15th century the vicar provided a lamp in Harmondsworth church at his own expense.[10] This was probably the same lamp that he maintained before the statue of the Virgin at about the same date, and which was supported from an acre of manorial land given to the church by Roger Mortimer.[11] This acre, called 'lamp land', was granted, together with other property, to John Walton and John Cressett by the Crown in 1586. It had been given for the maintenance of obits, lights, and lamps in Harmondsworth church, and had been held by the churchwardens.[12] In 1510 the Vicar of Harmondsworth, John Horne, bequeathed 4d. for every

light burning before the statue of every saint in the church, and requested that his executors should ordain a priest for three years to read, sing, and pray in the church for the dead.[13] In 1547 there were said to be no chantries, obits, or lights,[14] but in 1562 land granted by the Crown to Cecily Pickerell included property in Harmondsworth that had been given for an obit in the church.[15] In 1586, together with the acre of 'lamp land', the Crown granted to Walton and Cressett a house lying immediately west of the churchyard that had been given for the maintenance of obits, lights, and lamps, and 2 a. of pasture in Harmondsworth held by William Geffrey, the income of which had been used partly for prayers for the dead, and partly to help the maintenance of Mad Bridge. Land in Stanwell was granted for the same purpose.[16]

In 1745 William Wild gave to trustees the land which had been granted out by the Crown in 1586. The rents were to be applied to the repair of the parish church, and in 1823 the property consisted of the Sun Inn and 2 a. awarded at inclosure. Later assertions that the charity had been created by the grant of 1586 are therefore inaccurate. In the mid 19th century the property included a butcher's shop, and a large part of the income had been used to build a vestry onto the church in 1858–9. The charity was regulated by a Charity Commission Scheme in 1862. The 'Sun' was closed by the licensing authorities in 1913, compensation being granted, and was converted into a private house. The 2 a. owned by the charity lay in Heathrow, and were sold to the Air Ministry in 1947. In 1958 the income of the Church Estate was about £62.[17]

By about 1400 there was a vicarage house.[18] Throughout the 15th and early 16th centuries manorial rentals record payments by the churchwardens of Harmondsworth for the house next to the court,[19] and there is one payment for the house next to the churchyard gate.[20] Glebe land, of which there were 12 a., is first mentioned in a late-14th or early-15th-century inquisition.[21] In 1587 the vicar was holding 20 a. from the manor,[22] and in 1656 there were 20 a. of glebe, a house, and an orchard, worth in all £40, but the salary of the resident minister was above £40.[23] At inclosure in 1819 the vicar was allotted 193 a. in lieu of tithes and glebe.[24] The vicarage was rebuilt in 1845 on a site east of the churchyard.[25] It is a plain building of brown brick with a central porch and a later 19th-century addition incorporating a tower at its east end.

90 *Rep. Com. Eccl. Rev.* [67], p. 650, H.C. (1835), xxii.
91 Hennessy, *Novum Repertorium*, 201.
92 *Kelly's Dir. Mdx.* (1886).
93 Ibid. (1894, 1937).
94 *Lond. Dioc. Bk.* (1965).
95 St. Paul's MS. W.D.9, f. 84v.
96 *Tax. Eccl.* (Rec. Com.), 20.
97 *Cal. Inq. Misc.* ii, p. 418; C 145/139/19.
98 *Inq. Non.* (Rec. Com.), 198.
99 *Cal. Papal Letters*, iii. 239.
1 Guildhall MS. 9531/3, ff. 206–7. This inquisition from Braybroke's register is dated 1438. The dating and its apparent insertion in an earlier register are unexplained, and the hand is contemporary with the rest of the register. It can safely be dated after 1391, and seems likely to have been an inquisition taken shortly after the acquisition of the manor and church by William of Wykeham.
2 *Valor Eccl.* (Rec. Com.), i. 434; E 301/34/147.
3 *Home Cnties. Mag.* ii. 282–3.
4 Guildhall MS. 9550.
5 Ibid. 9557.

6 *Rep. Com. Eccl. Rev.* [67], p. 650, H.C. (1835), xxii.
7 *Inq. Non.* (Rec. Com.), 198.
8 S.C. 2/191/18.
9 Guildhall MS. 9531/3, ff. 206–7; see above note 1.
10 Guildhall MS. 9531/3, f. 207.
11 M.R.O., Acc. 446/EM. 1.
12 C. 66/1284/14.
13 P.C.C. 35 Bennett.
14 E 301/34/147.
15 *Cal. Pat.* 1560–3, 258.
16 C 66/1284/13, /14.
17 Char. Com. files.
18 Guildhall MS. 9531/3, ff. 206–7.
19 S.C. 11/443, 449; E 315/409, 416; M.R.O., Acc. 446/EM. 1.
20 S.C. 11/446.
21 Guildhall MS. 9531/3.
22 E 178/1430.
23 *Home Cnties. Mag.* ii. 282–3.
24 Harmondsworth Incl. Award.
25 Date on building.

Even before the formal union of Harmondsworth vicarage with that of West Drayton in 1755 one minister had often served both cures. Thomas Tyson, Vicar of Harmondsworth 1713–27, seems to have been the last vicar resident at Harmondsworth, although he too held West Drayton. His successor, John Lidgould, lived at West Drayton and employed a curate for Harmondsworth.[26] In the early 19th century the curates lived at the vicarage.[27] After the separation of the benefices, however, curates do not seem to have been appointed.

Almost nothing is known of the religious life of the parish. In the 15th century Richard Wiche, Vicar of Harmondsworth, was burned for heresy.[28] At Harmondsworth in the late 18th and early 19th centuries, when the vicarage was consolidated with West Drayton, there was one service only in the morning.[29]

The church of *ST. MARY* stands to the north of the green at the west end of Harmondsworth village and consists of chancel, nave, north and south aisles, north chapel, south-west tower, south porch, and north vestry. The exterior is mainly of flint rubble with stone dressings but the upper stages of the tower are of red brick. The oldest work in the church is in the south aisle which has a re-set south doorway of the mid 12th century, one of the two finest in Middlesex.[30] It consists of a semi-circular arch of three orders, the inner order decorated with carved rosettes and similar designs, the middle with beak-heads, and the outer with chevron ornament; the middle order rests on enriched shafts with scalloped capitals, much worn. The south aisle itself, together with the piece of the south arcade, are probably of the later 12th century, although the arcade arches are pointed and may thus represent an alteration of after 1200. It has been suggested that there is also 12th-century work in the north wall of the present tower which perhaps formed part of the Norman nave.[31] The church was largely remodelled in the early 13th century when the nave and north aisle were built or rebuilt and the north arcade constructed. The plain octagonal font of Purbeck marble dates from *c.* 1200. The north chapel is apparently a 14th-century addition and the present chancel, incorporating sedilia and a piscina in its south wall, is largely of the 15th century. The north side of the chancel and the north chapel were altered *c.* 1500 when the arcade between them was given four-centred arches and extended into the east bay of the nave; the hammer-beam roof of the chapel and its piscina are of this date. The south-west tower is also of the late 15th or early 16th century, much restored.[32] Its upper stages are of brick and it is surmounted by a domed cupola and an embattled parapet with angle pinnacles. The north vestry and timber south porch are 19th-century additions.

The chancel was described as ruinous in 1673,

when the ceiling, floor, and windows all required repairs.[33] The church was extensively restored in 1862–3. The walls, arcades, and roofs, which had been plastered, were stripped and the 15th-century nave roof of crown-post construction was revealed.[34] The commandment boards and the royal arms were removed,[35] but the early 16th-century oak pews, described as 'irregular and uncomfortable',[36] were retained and pine pews of similar design were added. The exterior, having been rough-cast over the stone and brick, was also stripped in 1862–3.

Some brasses were stolen from the church during the restoration, and also the communion plate, which was replaced in 1887 by a flagon, two cups, and a paten made by Garrards.[37] There are no outstanding monuments. Wall tablets in the chancel commemorate John Bush (d. 1713) and Anna and Richard Bankes (d. 1735 and 1750). Those in the north chapel commemorate Thomas Willing (d. 1773), Sir Walter Erskine (d. 1786), and Susannah, Lady Stirling (d. 1806), a paternal descendant of William of Wykeham. In the north aisle are wall monuments to past vicars and there are three of the late 17th and 18th centuries with achievements of arms. In the churchyard, north-east of the church, is the tomb of Richard Cox (d. 1845), a brewer who perfected the first Cox's Orange Pippin at Colnbrook End, in the adjoining parish of Stanwell.[38] The registers, which are complete, record baptisms and burials from 1670 and marriages from 1671. There are 6 bells, of which four are dated 1658 and are by Brian Eldridge; the other two are modern.

A mission chapel dedicated to *ST. SAVIOUR* was erected at Heathrow in 1880 by Claude Brown a former curate.[39] The church seems to have been sited on the Bath Road at or near where its successor stood in 1960.[40] This rectangular brick building, called the Church Hall of St. Saviour, was intended to serve the western side of the parish and to become a parish church if residential building was extended. As this did not occur, the hall remained a mission church.[41]

ROMAN CATHOLICISM. In 1640 there were two known recusants, both women, and a family suspected of recusancy had recently left the village.[42] In 1642 the two women were still in the parish,[43] but by 1706 there were said to be no Roman Catholics in Harmondsworth.[44] In 1960 Roman Catholics in the parish were served by the West Drayton church of St. Catherine the Martyr.[45]

PROTESTANT NONCONFORMITY. By 1669 the Society of Friends held meetings in a private room at Longford. In 1673 the meeting bought

[26] Guildhall MS., 9550.
[27] Ibid. 9560.
[28] R. Fabyan, *Chronicles of Eng. and France* (1811), 613; J. Foxe, *Actes and Monuments* (1837), iii. 702; *Cal. Pat. 1436–41*, 426.
[29] Guildhall MS. 9558.
[30] Hist. Mon. Com. *Mdx.* 60–61, pl. 135; Pevsner, *Mdx.* 95. See plate facing p. 36. The other and more elaborate doorway is at Harlington.
[31] D. M. Rust, *St. Mary's Parish Ch., Harmondsworth* (1966).
[32] Hist. Mon. Com. *Mdx.* 61, pl. 136.
[33] Guildhall MS. 9537/20.
[34] Char. Com. files.

[35] A. H. Cox, *Harmondsworth Heritage*, 6.
[36] Char. Com. files.
[37] E. Freshfield, *Communion Plate of Mdx.* 28.
[38] A. Simmonds, *A Horticultural Who was Who* (Royal Horticultural Soc. 1940), 14–16; *V.C.H. Mdx.* iii. 36.
[39] *Kelly's Dir. Mdx.* (1882).
[40] O.S. Map 1/2,500, Mdx. xix. 4 (1896 and later edns.).
[41] Ex inf. the vicar.
[42] B.M. Add. MS. 38856, f. 52. See also Hse. of Lords, Mdx. Protestation Rets. for 3 people who failed to take the protestation oath in 1642.
[43] Guildhall MS. 9582.
[44] Ibid. 9800.
[45] *Catholic Dir.* (1959); *V.C.H. Mdx.* iii. 204.

a plot of land, and a meeting-house was built in 1676.[46] In that year there were said to be 48 nonconformists in Harmondsworth parish, although the sect or sects to which they belonged are not stated.[47] The earlier 18th century saw a decline in the Quaker congregation, but during the later half of the century numbers increased as Quaker families settled in Uxbridge and Staines. The 19th century, however, saw a steady decline, and the Longford meeting was amalgamated with Westminster in 1864. In its early days the meeting appointed its own overseers of the poor, but between 1690 and 1717 a few Quakers were supported by the parish.[48] In 1778 there were said to be Anabaptists in the parish, with a meeting-house at Longford,[49] but these may have been Quakers. The meeting-house is mentioned in 1792 and 1793,[50] and in 1839 the meeting owned a cottage and garden in Longford.[51]

In 1810 there were about 98 dissenters in Harmondsworth parish, the majority described as Anabaptists and the rest as Independents. Their numbers were said to be decreasing steadily.[52] In 1820 a house in Longford was registered for worship by the Independents,[53] but in 1835 there were said to be no chapels of any sort in the parish.[54] The Baptists built the Zoar Baptist Chapel in Longford in 1859.[55] It consisted of a small annexe to a private house, the name of the chapel being later altered to Zion Chapel.[56] The chapel fell into disuse in the late 19th and early 20th centuries[57] and, although the building was still standing in 1960, it was not used for religious purposes.

There were Baptists in Harmondsworth village itself in 1833, by which time they had established a Sunday school attended by 54 boys.[58] By 1846 Harlington Baptist Chapel had a branch at Harmondsworth, which probably consisted of a Sunday school, and before 1855 there was a chapel in the village under the control of the Harlington chapel. The Harmondsworth chapel had belonged to John Hunt, who sold it to Harlington in 1855 on leaving for Australia.[59] This chapel, probably in a private house, evidently declined, and in 1880 a mission room was built[60] and registered for non-denominational worship.[61] The building was enlarged in 1884,[62] still as an unsectarian mission room. Its registration was cancelled in 1891.[63] The Harmondsworth Baptist Chapel was formed in 1896;[64] at first it may have occupied the mission building, before a new site was

found on the corner of Moor Lane and Hatch Lane.[65] In 1936 the Baptists registered an old chapel at the back of Blacksmith's Row,[66] but in 1959 the chapel on the corner of Moor Lane and Hatch Lane was the only Baptist meeting-house in Harmondsworth.[67]

There are traces of nonconformity in Sipson by 1708, when dissenters met in William Wild's house.[68] In 1886 the Y.M.C.A. registered a mission room in Sipson,[69] and in 1887 a packing shed belonging to Thomas Wild was registered for the use both of the Y.M.C.A. and the Salvation Army.[70] Both registrations were cancelled in 1896. A Salvation Army hall, registered from 1891 to 1901,[71] stood at the corner of Sipson Lane and Sipson Road.[72] The building, of yellow and red brick, was erected in 1891 and enlarged in 1900.[73] In 1907 Sipson Baptist Chapel was formed;[74] this most probably occupied the same corner site as the Salvation Army hall.[75]

In Heathrow nonconformity appeared with the Primitive Methodists in 1870, and by July 1871 a chapel had been built and registered.[76] Its site is not certain, as in 1888 it was said to be some distance away from Heathrow, where the Methodists had erected a new chapel which was more convenient.[77] Late-19th-century maps show a disused Methodist chapel in Cain's Lane.[78] The only registration of a Primitive Methodist chapel in Heathrow was in 1890, and this registration was cancelled six years later.[79] A Salvation Army barracks at Heathrow was registered between 1899 and 1903,[80] and in the early 20th century there was a mission room, also in Cain's Lane opposite the old Methodist chapel.[81] This was said to have been erected for the Sipson Baptists in 1901.[82] All of these buildings were destroyed during the construction of Heathrow Airport.

EDUCATION. The earliest reference to education in Harmondsworth parish dates from 1694, when Edward Griffin was encouraged by the Quakers to open a school at the Longford meeting-house. This scheme, however, did not succeed.[83] In the late 18th century there were schoolmasters in Harmondsworth[84] and presumably there was a school of some kind in the village. In 1819, however, there was said to be no school in the parish.[85]

By 1833 there were three day schools in the parish, in which 28 boys and 38 girls were educated at their

[46] W. Beck and T. F. Ball, *London Friends' Meetings* (1869), 283–93.
[47] William Salt Libr., Stafford, Salt MS. 33, p. 40.
[48] Beck and Ball, *London Meetings*, 283–93.
[49] Guildhall MS. 9558.
[50] M.R.O., Acc. 446/EF. 32.
[51] Par. Survey (1839) *penes* Yiewsley and West Drayton U.D.C.
[52] Guildhall MS. 9558. The assessment may be subjective.
[53] Guildhall MS. 9580/5.
[54] *Rep. Com. Eccl. Rev.* [67], p. 650, H.C. (1835), xxii.
[55] Date on building.
[56] Inscription on building, where ZION has been cut over ZOAR.
[57] *Kelly's Dirs. Mdx.* (1886–1910).
[58] *Educ. Enq. Abstract*, H.C. 62, p. 564 (1835), xlii.
[59] Ex inf. deacon of Harlington Baptist chapel.
[60] *Kelly's Dir. Mdx.* (1882).
[61] Gen. Reg. Off., Wship. Reg. 24959.
[62] *Kelly's Dir. Mdx.* (1886).
[63] Gen. Reg. Off., Wship. Reg. 28590.
[64] Ibid. 36026.
[65] *Kelly's Dir. Mdx.* (1898). The description of the Bap-

tist chapel is identical with the earlier one of the mission room. On the other hand, the map shows the mission room on Hatch Lane, and the later Baptist church on the corner: O.S. Map 1/2,500, Mdx. xix. 3 (1895–6 and 1932–5 edns.).
[66] Gen. Reg. Off., Wship. Reg. 56584.
[67] *Baptist Handbk.* (1959).
[68] *Mdx. Cnty. Recs. Sess. Bks. 1689–1709*, 328.
[69] Gen. Reg. Off., Wship. Reg. 29333.
[70] Ibid. 30074.   [71] Ibid. 32947.
[72] O.S. Map 1/2,500, Mdx. xix. 4 (1896 edn.).
[73] Dates on building.
[74] Gen. Reg. Off., Wship. Reg. 42574.
[75] Ibid. 38154.
[76] Char. Com. files. No registration has, however, been found in the Worship Reg.
[77] Char. Com. files.
[78] O.S. Map 1/2,500, Mdx. xix. 8 (1895 edn.).
[79] Gen. Reg. Off., Wship. Reg. 32092.
[80] Ibid. 37012.
[81] O.S. Map 1/2,500, Mdx. xix. 8 (1914 edn.).
[82] *Kelly's Dirs. Mdx.* (1910, 1914).
[83] Beck and Ball, *London Meetings*, 292.
[84] Par. Recs., Reg., 1670–1802.
[85] *Digest of Parochial Rets.* H.C. 244, p. 588 (1819), ix (1).

parents' expense. There were also Anglican and Baptist Sunday schools.[86] Harmondsworth National School was built in 1846 and in 1857 was attended by 40 boys and 31 girls. There was no endowment and fees were only 1d. or 2d. The children were taught by a master and mistress, neither of whom was trained or certificated, and although new teachers were appointed in 1857 and their salary raised, they too were untrained.[87] The school, which was said to have been erected by public subscription,[88] stood slightly south of Moor Lane.[89] A school board of five members was formed in 1874,[90] and by the end of the 19th century this school was known as the Harmondsworth Board School. It had accommodation for 208 boys and girls and in 1899 had an average attendance of 141.[91] New buildings were erected in 1906–7 by the local authority, when it was called a mixed county primary school. It was also designed to take older children and infants from the Sipson and Heathrow school, also then called the National School, until repairs to that school were carried out.[92] In 1960 it was attended by 77 children.[93]

In 1863 the Sipson Infants School was established under the National Society, and managed by Mrs. R. L. de Burgh, wife of the incumbent of West Drayton. The building was privately owned and the 26 children occupied one room with the mistress, who was certificated. The fees were 4d. for boys and 3d. for girls.[94] The Sipson and Heathrow Council School was established in 1875 with 107 children. The buildings were borrowed, the boys' room consisting of a converted cart-shed about 30 yards from the girls' and infants' rooms which were in a private house. The staff comprised a master, mistress, and infant teacher.[95] Permanent buildings were erected in 1877 on land lying on the north side of the Bath Road nearly opposite the 'Magpies'[96] and given to the school board by Lord Strafford.[97] The school was enlarged in 1891, and by the end of the century the attendance had risen to 194.[98] In 1960 it was attended by 112 children.[99]

CHARITIES FOR THE POOR.[100] The earliest known charity was the Stock Money Land, founded in 1678 when the parish paid £90 to Miles Pool and his wife Elizabeth for 6 a. scattered in the Sipson fields. The purchase money was said to have belonged already to the poor, but its origin is not known. The rent of the land was to be paid to the churchwardens who were to distribute it to the poor. On inclosure 9 a. were allotted to the trustees, which brought in about £9 10s. a year. This was distributed when needed in sums varying from 5s. to 10s. to poor families not receiving parish relief. By 1862 the money was paid in sums of 10s. to poor women on their confinement or sickness. The gift of William Culley or Cullee of 10s. a year charged on an acre lying near the Bath Road was made by deed in 1680.

Payments fell into arrears before 1820, but had been made up before 1823 and the charity was thereafter distributed by the churchwardens in bread. Dowsett and Hickman's charity was founded by two Cranford men, John Dowsett, whose will was dated 1722, and William Hickman, whose will was dated 1729, each of whom left 10s. to the poor of Harmondsworth. In 1823 both charities were distributed as quartern loaves, although Hickman's bequest had specified a money distribution. By 1862 Hickman's 10s. was given in money, and Dowsett's had been joined with Tillyer's charity[101] which was distributed in 4-lb. loaves of bread. In 1747 Elizabeth, Dowager Countess of Uxbridge, gave £100 stock to the parish to be distributed to ten poor families who did not receive parish relief, no one family receiving more than 10s. a year. The trustees were allowed to purchase land or to leave the money in the funds. There was also an allowance of 5s. to whomsoever collected the money in London and paid it to the churchwardens. In 1823 this charity was regarded as irregular. John Tillyer founded by will a charity of 20s. a year which was charged on an acre of land. The date of Tillyer's foundation is not known but was probably in the late 18th century. In the 19th century it was joined with Dowsett's charity. Allotments to the poor in lieu of fuel and common rights were made at inclosure when just over 75 a. were settled in trust in two parcels.[102] It is not certain how much of this actually came into the hands of the trustees, as in 1823 the poor allotment was said to amount to just over 51 a. This in 1808 brought in over £91 a year which was normally used for buying coal, which was then sold to the poor at a price ranging from 6d. to 1s. a bushel. In 1823 there was a substantial balance in hand which was kept against a fall in rents. By 1862 the rent from nearly 52 a. brought in £151 which was distributed as coal at Christmas.

After an inquiry in 1862 these six charities were combined by the Charity Commissioners in 1863. The proceeds were usually distributed in coal. In 1906 seventy-six coal tickets for amounts varying from 2s. 6d. to 7s. 6d. were issued, but in 1908 there were about 800 tickets issued, it being observed that in such a large agricultural district almost everyone wanted coal. At this date the land that maintained the coal charities amounted to just over 42 a. A new Scheme was made for the six charities in 1909 when they were called the United Charities. This provided for pensions varying from 5s. to 10s. for a term of 3 years, which could be prolonged for one further term. It was also to be used for supplying medical and nursing attention, clothes, bedding, and fuel up to a limit of £20 a year. No pensions were ever paid and in 1958 a request to the commissioners to raise the limit of £20 to £50 because of the rise in the price of coal was refused. Dowsett and Hickman's charity was redeemed for £40 in 1932 and

[86] *Educ. Enq. Abstract*, H.C. 62, p. 564 (1835), xlii.
[87] Ed. 7/86.
[88] *Kelly's Dir. Mdx.* (1855).
[89] O.S. Map 1/2,500, Mdx. xix. 3 (1867 and later edns.).
[90] *Kelly's Dir. Mdx.* (1886).
[91] *Ret. of Schools, 1899* [Cd. 315], H.C. p. 580 (1900), lxv(2).
[92] Ed. 7/86.
[93] Ex inf. Yiewsley and West Drayton U.D.C.
[94] Ed. 7/86.
[95] Ibid.
[96] O.S. Map 1/2,500, Mdx. xix. 4 (1896 edn.).

[97] Inscription on building.
[98] *Ret. of Schools, 1899* [Cd. 315], H.C. p. 580 (1900), lxv(2).
[99] Ex inf. Yiewsley and West Drayton U.D.C.
[100] Except where otherwise stated this section is based on Char. Com. files and *9th Rep. Com. Char.* H.C. 258, pp. 226–9 (1823), ix.
[101] See below.
[102] Harmondsworth Incl. Award. It seems, however, that poor land was in existence earlier than 1819, and some inclosure may have taken place after the first Act in 1805.

Tillyer's charity was redeemed for the same amount in 1939; 18 a. of the stock money land were sold in 1947 and the Ministry of Aviation redeemed a £10 rentcharge on Fairview Farm, the property of the Air Ministry, in 1959. The United Charities accounted for over £390 in 1956, of which more than £267 were disbursed.

The Blanket Charity was created by the will of Henry Smith of Harmondsworth Hall in 1875. He bequeathed £300 to be given to the poor in blankets.[103] Some of the stock was transferred in 1878 to the use of the National School. In 1958 the charity income amounted to over £7, from which six blankets were purchased.

HAYES

THE ANCIENT parish of Hayes, which in 1961 formed part of the urban district of Hayes and Harlington[1] and now forms part of the London Borough of Hillingdon,[2] lay between Hanwell and Hillingdon on the south-east and north-west, Greenford and Northolt to the north-east, and Heston and Harlington on the south-west. Although it was not until 1859 that two civil parishes of Hayes and Norwood with Southall were formed out of this area, ecclesiastically it had been divided since the Middle Ages. The boundary between Hayes and its dependent chapelry of Norwood ran through the open fields and continued in a more or less straight line down the Yeading Brook. After 1801 the Paddington Canal replaced the undefined open-field line as the northern part of this boundary. Since the history of Norwood with Southall is treated in a separate account,[3] all references in this article to Hayes and its parish apply to that part of Hayes which lies to the west and north-west of the Yeading Brook and the Paddington Canal. This area covers approximately 3¼ miles from north-west to south-east, and about 2¾ miles from north-east to south-west. In 1754 the boundary of Hayes ran south and south-east along a road from Ickenham to Bulls Bridge, where it turned sharply north-east up the Yeading Brook, and continued in the same direction through the open fields towards Northolt and Greenford. Turning north-west it continued across the open fields until it turned north and finally due west again just north of Charville Lane.[4] By 1814 there was no road along the west until the boundary, running through the open fields, met and followed Dawley Lane.[5] In 1863 Hayes parish contained 3,311 a.[6] and since that date its boundaries have not altered. The parish is predominantly flat, lying at about 50 feet, and nowhere exceeding 100 feet. The soil, described in 1876 as 'clay, loam, and gravel',[7] consists of brickearth to the south and east of Hayes village, of London Clay to the north, along the Yeading Brook, and of Boyn Hill Gravel along the road to Hillingdon and Uxbridge.[8] The parish is watered by a single stream, the Yeading Brook, which forms part of the eastern boundary and also runs through the north-eastern part of the parish.

Early settlement in the Hayes area is suggested by palaeolithic implements found at Botwell[9] in the southern part of the parish. In 757 an area called 'Geddinges', usually identified as Yeading in the north of the parish, was given by Æthelbald, King of Mercia, to Withred and his wife,[10] and in 793 Offa, King of Mercia, gave 60 *tributarii* to Archbishop Æthelheard in 'Linga Haese' and 'Geddingas'.[11] In 831 Archbishop Wulfred received a further grant of 5 *cassatae* of land in 'Botewaelle' (Botwell) from the Mercian king, Wiglaf. This grant again mentions Hayes.[12] Anglo-Saxon settlement in Hayes, Yeading, and Botwell, three of the five later hamlets of the parish, therefore seems probable. Hayes church is situated nearly in the centre of the parish, a quarter of a mile south of the medieval highway known as Uxbridge Road, but there is no evidence to show that settlement first grew up around it. Botwell lay almost a mile to the south, and Yeading about a mile to the north-east. The other two hamlets in the parish, Hayes End and Wood End, although not mentioned until the early 16th century,[13] were probably settled earlier. Hayes End lay on Uxbridge Road about 1¼ mile west and slightly north of the church, while Wood End lay between Hayes and Hayes End, and about half a mile from the former. Thus only one of the five hamlets actually lay on the main road. The village of Hayes itself was at this date called Cotman's Town, and this name survived as late as the early 20th century. Cotman's Town is almost certainly identifiable with Hayes village itself, or that part of Hayes grouped round the church. The other hamlets can all be identified and there is no evidence to suggest early settlement elsewhere in the parish. The vill of Hayes was called Cotman's Town in 1598,[14] and Cotman's Town appears regularly in the land tax assessments.[15] It is mentioned in 1814,[16] although Hayes Town occurs three years later.[17] In 1874 Cotman's Town was said to be the group of dwellings to the east of the church.[18] In 1929 there is a reference in a court book to Hayes Town formerly called Cotman's Town.[19]

During the Middle Ages manor and parish seem to have been conterminous, but with the appearance in the 15th century of the sub-manor of Yeading, the boundaries of Hayes manor probably retreated from the north-eastern part of the parish. By the early 19th century the manorial property was confined to the north-westerly end of the parish. Many

---

[103] J. Webb, *Hist. of Charities and Fishing Rights in Harmondsworth* (1880), 13–14.

[1] This article was written in 1961. Any references to a later time are dated.
[2] See p. 33.
[3] See p. 40.
[4] J. Rocque, *Map of Mdx.* (1754).
[5] M.R.O., Hayes Incl. Map.
[6] O.S. Area Bk.; *Census*, 1931.
[7] Thorne, *Environs of Lond.* 335.
[8] Geol. Survey Map, sheet 255 (drift).

[9] C. E. Vulliamy, *Archaeology of Mdx. and Lond.* 56.
[10] *Cart. Sax.*, ed. Birch, i. 259–60.
[11] Ibid. 369.
[12] Ibid. 556–7.
[13] Sta. Cha. 2/8/92.
[14] B.M. Add. MS. 24812.
[15] e.g. M.R.O., L.T.A. 649, 671.
[16] M.R.O., Acc. 180/82.
[17] Ibid. /83.
[18] T. Mills, *Hist. of Hayes Par.* (1874), 46.
[19] M.R.O., Acc. 180/12, p. 343.

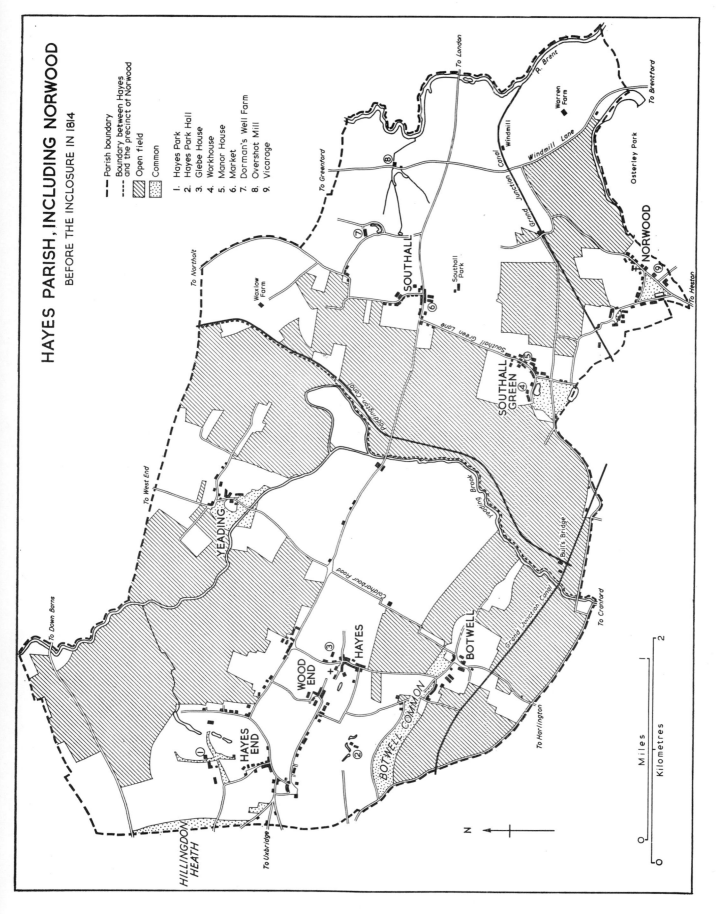

HAYES PARISH, INCLUDING NORWOOD

BEFORE THE INCLOSURE IN 1814

Parish boundary
Boundary between Hayes
and the precinct of Norwood
Open field
Common

1. Hayes Park
2. Hayes Park Hall
3. Glebe House
4. Workhouse
5. Manor House
6. Market
7. Dorman's Well Farm
8. Overshot Mill
9. Vicarage

To London

R. Brent

To Brentford

Warren Farm

Windmill

Grand Junction Canal

Windmill Lane

Osterley Park

To Greenford

NORWOOD

To Heston

SOUTHALL

Southall Park

To Northolt

Woxlow Farm

Southall Green Lane

SOUTHALL GREEN

Yeading Brook

To West End

YEADING

Yeading Brook

Bull's Bridge

To Down Barns

Coldharbour Road

BOTWELL

Grand Junction Canal

To Cranford

WOOD END

HAYES

BOTWELL COMMON

To Harlington

HAYES END

HILLINGDON HEATH

To Uxbridge

N

Miles
Kilometres

23

field names survive from the late 14th century,[20] and in 1573 Bag Lane (widened in the 20th century and called Park Lane) and Heath Lane are mentioned.[21] The first detailed description of Hayes is contained in an incomplete survey of 1596–8 made for Roger, Lord North.[22] At this date the largest hamlet was Wood End which consisted of 25 dwellings, 16 of them cottages. All were surrounded by inclosed land, amounting in all to nearly 129 a. Hayes End, with 22 dwellings of which only 7 were cottages, was surrounded by more than 203 a. of inclosed land. Cotman's Town had 12 dwellings and 23 inclosed a., while there was only a tenement, a cottage, and 7 a. of inclosed land at Botwell. Yeading was not mentioned. Three of the large open fields, Broadmead Field (270 a.), Greathedge Field (226 a.), and Crouch Field (224 a.), lay around Hayes End, Wood End, and Cotman's Town, presumably to the north-east where they were at inclosure. There were three other small fields amounting in all to approximately 45 a. Botwell had further inclosures of 33 a. and 3 large open fields: South Field (199 a.), West Field (161 a.), and North or East Field (119 a.). The exact location of these fields is not known although their names are partly explanatory.[23] The demesne was wholly inclosed. The main area of inclosure probably lay north-west of Botwell and to the south-west of Hayes End. Few roads or lanes are mentioned: Smetlane and Fotes Lane in Cotman's Town; Foot Lane in Wood End; Bag Lane in Hayes End. London Way, presumably identifiable with Uxbridge Road, the Shireway, and Batford Bridge are also mentioned. About a century later the largest hamlet was still apparently Wood End with 29 householders, followed closely by Hayes with 27. Hayes Town had 18 householders, Botwell and the Town both had 17, and Yeading was the smallest with only 13.[24] The precise areas of settlement denoted by Hayes, Hayes Town, and the Town are uncertain.

The first detailed map showing the parish is that made by Rocque in 1754. Settlement at that date was almost entirely confined to the south-western side of the main road to Uxbridge which, running north-east in an almost straight line, divided the parish in half. Hayes End, Wood End, and Hayes itself formed a continuous area of houses. Hayes End was built on Park Lane (formerly Bag Lane) and Hayes End Road; Wood End ran round Angel and Morgan's Lanes, down Wood End Green Road, and along Church Walk and Grange Road. Hayes itself was said to be a small area of houses down Botwell Lane, but was separated from Botwell by the Heath. From Wood End, Hemmen Lane and Hesa Road led to Coldharbour Lane, which itself led to Botwell. Although Hayes End lay north-east of the main road, practically all the eastern half of the parish was covered by open fields, those named being Greathedge, Broadmead, Barnhill, Crouch, Rolls Ditch,

and Dunstable fields. A small group of houses was clustered on the main road, where a lane leading to Yeading left it opposite Church Road, which then curved east through the open fields to Yeading. The only open fields shown south-west of the main road were Botwell Heath and Dawley Field.[25] In 1796 the Grand Junction Canal was cut through the south-western corner of the parish to the south of Botwell and in 1814 open fields of over 1,000 a. were inclosed. These lay on the northern and southern edges of the parish, the central area surrounding the main road and the lanes of Hayes End and Wood End being practically all inclosed previously. All the open fields had been reduced in area since 1754 and the course of some of the roads had been altered. Botwell Lane (then Wood End Green and Botwell Road) and Church Road (then Hayes and Botwell Road) both led to Botwell, while Yeading Lane, or Highway, led straight to Uxbridge Road and continued south to Botwell and over the canal. Pump Lane in Botwell and Barnhill Lane in Yeading were both field lanes, while West End Lane led to Northolt, and Dawley Lane and the later-named Station Road led to Harlington. There were 12 farms at this date, also mainly in the eastern half of the parish.[26] By 1827 brick-fields, cottages, and docks on the canal had been laid out near Botwell, and brickfields and brick-makers' cottages had also appeared at Yeading,[27] although in 1834 the parish was described as being purely agricultural. At that time there were about 200 houses or cottages, owned mainly by tradesmen.[28] In 1838 the G.W.R. line was driven across the southern edge of the parish, and, although Hayes station at Botwell was not opened until 1864,[29] the G.W.R. Co. owned warehouses and shops in Botwell by 1842.[30]

Although the number of commercial premises increased during the later 19th century,[31] the appearance of the parish altered little before 1900. A few factories in Dawley Road and a small terrace of houses along North Hyde Road were built.[32] After 1850 an increasing number of private estates was advertised and sold for building purposes.[33] By 1874 there were 597 houses in the parish, and a large proportion of the population lived in Hayes End, Wood End, Botwell, and Yeading rather than in Hayes, which was described as an 'irregular, commonplace collection of houses'. There were 'many farms, few good residences, fewer resident gentry', and while a few years previously it had been observed that at Yeading 'dirt, ignorance, and darkness reign supreme', in 1874 the inhabitants of Yeading were 'always found civil'.[34] Following representations by the parish council in 1902 about the unsatisfactory and infrequent train services,[35] the G.W.R. services were improved,[36] and between 1901 and 1903 the London United Tramways Co. extended its line from Southall to Uxbridge along the main road.[37]

[20] M.R.O., Acc. 401/1–8.   [21] S.C. 2/191/32.
[22] B.M. Add. MS. 24812.
[23] Some of them are mentioned by name as early as the 13th cent.: Lambeth Palace, Estate MS. 2068.
[24] M.R.O., H.T. 55.
[25] Rocque, Map of Mdx.
[26] M.R.O., Hayes Incl. Award and Map. No precise figures for the Hayes inclosure can be given as Norwood is included in the award and on the map.
[27] Hayes and Harlington U.D.C., Hayes Valuation (1827).
[28] Rep. Poor Law Com. App. B(2), H.C. 44, pp. 101 f–k (1834), xxxv–vi.

[29] T. B. Peacock, G. W. Suburban Services, 45.
[30] Hayes and Harlington U.D.C., Hayes Valuation (1842).
[31] Kelly's Dirs. Mdx. (1866 and later edns.).
[32] O.S. Maps 1/2,500, Mdx. xiv. 8, 12; xv. 1, 5, 6, 9, 13 (1865 and 1895–6 edns.).
[33] e.g. M.R.O., Acc. 180/501, 505, 512.
[34] Thorne, Environs of Lond. 334–6.
[35] Hayes and Harlington U.D.C., Par. Meeting Min. Bk. 1864–1904.
[36] Peacock, G. W. Suburban Services, 4.
[37] Hayes and Harlington U.D.C., Par. Coun. Min. Bk 1899–1904, p. 73.

Some building occurred before the First World War. In Wood End the north ends of Tudor, Cromwell, and North roads were built up; some houses were erected around Hemmen Lane and Church Road, and in Botwell a line of factories appeared between the canal and the railway, with housing along Printing House Lane (then Workhouse Lane).[38]

In the years between the wars the bulk of house and factory building took place, a large part of the former being a result of the industrial development. By 1924 Botwell was described as the modern shopping and residential area of Hayes, and between 1919 and 1924 the council erected 766 'working-class houses' at Botwell.[39] By 1938 the number had risen to 1,213 dwellings around Botwell, with 116 on the Park Farm estate between Cromwell Road and York Avenue, and 20 houses in Yeading.[40] Other large private estates laid out before 1935 were the Townfield estate built around Central Avenue on the west side of Coldharbour Lane; the Minet estate erected between Birchway and Mount Road on the west side of Coldharbour Lane; and a large estate that extended north-east from Uxbridge Road up Lansbury Drive, Woodrow Avenue, and Fairholme Crescent. The area between Carlyon Road and Uxbridge Road was also built up, as was the land between Brookside Road and the Yeading Brook.[41] The cottage hospital in Grange Road, opened in 1898, was enlarged in 1932.[42] The railway bridge at Botwell was rebuilt and enlarged in 1937[43] and a bus service to Ruislip was instituted in 1938.[44] Building continued on a large scale between 1935 and 1940, and the area between Woodrow Avenue, Kingshill Avenue, and Charville Lane was built up. Balmoral Drive was extended; Warley Road and the Shakespeare Avenue area were built up; and there was further development in and around Yeading. There was also some further building south-west of Judge Heath Lane and north of Botwell.[45] By 1944 Hayes was described as an area consisting entirely of working-class housing and mainly serving the industrial area of Botwell. Industry was increasing and housing was in short supply. The layout of the area was 'crude and monotonous' and the parish was considered deficient in open spaces.[46] Post-war housing development was mainly limited to the area north and east of Yeading where the land between Green Way and Attlee and Owen roads was built over. By May 1961 the council had erected 2,426 houses and flats in Hayes.[47]

The area lying between Wood End and the parish church at Hayes, however, remained in the 1960s almost unaffected by the spread of building elsewhere. The extensive graveyard and, adjacent to it, the grounds of former private houses with established trees gave the church a surprisingly peaceful setting. South-west of the church is Hayes Court, a farm-house owned by the Minet family from 1766 until 1967[48]; an octagonal 18th-century dovecote stands near the main residence, which was rebuilt c. 1800. The house stood derelict in 1968, when there were plans to build on the site.[49] A small green south-east of the church is faced by a range of four yellow brick cottages dated 1867. Until after 1914 these cottages overlooked a pond, as did others, demolished by 1935, which stood next to the lychgate.[50] Church Road contains the former Rectory, now called Manor House,[51] and several 19th-century buildings, including the refaced Wistowe House, and there are some weather-boarded cottages in Freeman's Lane. Angel Lane, Morgan's Lane and other roads off both sides of Woodend Green Road contain many brown brick houses and cottages of the early 19th century and later. In contrast to Hayes village, now served mainly by shops in Uxbridge Road, Botwell has developed as a shopping and industrial centre. Botwell House, Whitehall, and Bell House,[52] early 19th-century residences in their own grounds survive in Botwell Lane.

Although a victualler, Mary Hill, is mentioned c. 1636,[53] the earliest recorded inn was the 'Adam and Eve' in 1665.[54] In 1748, as well as the 'Adam and Eve', there were four further inns in Hayes: the 'White Hart', the 'Angel', the 'Turnpike', and the 'Queen's Head'.[55] In 1751 there was at least one unlicensed alehouse at the 'Cock'.[56] In the early 19th century only four inns are found at Hayes, the 'Queen's Head' and the 'Turnpike' disappearing and being replaced by the 'Waggon and Horses'.[57] The 'Adam and Eve' included a brewery in 1827,[58] and a new inn at Yeading, the 'Union', was opened in the same year.[59] Thereafter public houses proliferated and by 1864 there were at least eighteen.[60]

At Domesday 108 people were recorded on the manor of Hayes. Of these one was a priest, 3 were knights, and 74 were villeins; there were also 16 bordars, 12 cottars, and 2 serfs.[61] These figures, however, presumably include the precinct of Norwood. In 1547 there were 270 communicants in the parish of Hayes.[62] In 1642 in Hayes parish 178 adult males took the protestation oath.[63] Hearth tax was assessed on 76 houses in 1664 and a further 45 were exempt.[64] The same number, 121 houses, occurs later in the century.[65] In 1801 the population was 1,026. This figure had increased to 2,076 by 1851. A large increase in 1861 is accounted for by the opening of the St. Marylebone parochial schools and by the erection of large numbers of cottages for

[38] O.S. Maps 1/2,500, Mdx. xiv. 8, 12; xv. 1, 5, 9, 13 (1914 edn.).

[39] *Southall-Norwood and Hayes Official Guide* (1924), 33.

[40] *Hayes and Harlington Official Guide* (1938), 14.

[41] O.S. Maps 1/2,500, Mdx. xiv. 8, 12; xv. 1, 5, 9, 13 (1935 edn.).

[42] *Hayes, Harlington and Cranford Official Guide* (1932), 20–21.

[43] Ibid. (1938), 21–22.

[44] M.R.O., Hist. Notes, 29/11/50.

[45] O.S. Map 1/2,500, Mdx. xv. 5, 6, 9, 10 (1940 edn.).

[46] Abercrombie, *Greater Lond. Plan* (1944), 148–9.

[47] Ex inf. Engineer and Surveyor's Dept., Hayes and Harlington U.D.C.

[48] Ex inf. Messrs. Collissons, Barnard and Douglas-Mann.

[49] Ex inf. the Town Clerk, London Bor. of Hillingdon.

[50] O.S. Maps 1/2,500, Mdx. xv. 9 (1865 and later edns.).

[51] See p. 35.

[52] See p. 37.

[53] *Mdx. and Herts. N. & Q.* iv. 79.

[54] M.R.O., Acc. 180/2, f. 150.

[55] M.R.O., L.V. 84.

[56] Par. Recs., Register 1707–84, *sub* burials 1751.

[57] M.R.O., L.V. 10/93; 17/7; 21/6.

[58] M.R.O., Acc. 180/497.

[59] Hayes and Harlington U.D.C., Hayes Valuation (1827).

[60] Ibid. (1864).

[61] *V.C.H. Mdx.* i. 119.

[62] E 301/34/165.

[63] Hse. of Lords, Mdx. Protestation Rets.

[64] M.R.O., H.T. 6.

[65] Ibid. 55.

brick-workers. A slow increase until 1881 was followed by a slight decline, so that in 1901 there were only 2,594 people in the parish. The population had nearly doubled by 1911 and ten years later numbered over 6,303 people. Since that date the population has risen steeply to over 19,000 in 1931 and to 49,650 in 1951. The total population of Hayes and Harlington was 67,915 in 1961.[66] This large increase, unlike that in many Middlesex parishes, can be related more to the opening of communications and the coming of large industry than to the expansion of a mainly dormitory population.

Few well-known people have resided in the parish, but a number of the rectors have been distinguished men.[67] In the early 16th century Thomas Howard, Duke of Norfolk (d. 1554), lived at Hayes, but he had left the parish by 1531.[68] John Heath, a judge of the Common Pleas from 1780 to 1816, had a house in Hayes, of which a view survives.[69] He is commemorated in the parish by Judge Heath Lane.

MANORS AND OTHER ESTATES. Land in Yeading is mentioned as early as 757 and land in Botwell and Hayes was included in a grant dated 831.[70] In the following year Werhard, a Canterbury priest, devised 32 hides in Hayes to Christ Church, Canterbury.[71] This formed the bulk of the holding later known as *HAYES* manor which remained in the possession of the see of Canterbury until 1545. From that date until 1613 its descent followed that of Harrow manor.[72] In the early 16th century successive archbishops leased out the manorial demesne for 15-year terms at an annual farm of £16.[73] The estate was leased out to the Milletts of Hayes as early as 1526, and they continued to farm the property after its transfer to the king in 1545 and its sale to the North family in 1546. In 1613 Dudley, Lord North, sold Hayes to John and Richard Page, who later in the same year resold it to John Millett of Hayes, presumably the son of a former lessee, Richard Millett.[74] John Millett died in 1629, and was succeeded by his son John,[75] who in 1641 sold Hayes to Sir John Franklin. Richard Franklin sold the manor to Roger Jenyns in 1677 and it remained in the Jenyns family until 1729, when James Jenyns conveyed the property to Sir George Cooke of Harefield.[76] Cooke died about 1770 when the manor was put up for sale.[77] It apparently was not sold until 1777 when Cooke's son, George John Cooke, disposed of the estate to Francis Ascough of Southall.[78] Francis was succeeded by his son, George Merrick Ascough, whose trustees sold Hayes manor in 1800 to the executors of Robert Child in trust for the children of Sarah Fane, Countess of Westmorland,

Child's daughter.[79] By the marriage of George Villiers (later Child-Villiers), Earl of Jersey (d. 1859), with Sarah Sophia Fane, the grand-daughter of Robert Child, Hayes manor passed to the Jersey family.[80] In 1829, however, the Earl and Countess of Jersey sold the property to Robert Willis Blencowe, an already extensive landholder in Hayes,[81] who had held a mortgage on the estate since 1813. He was succeeded by his son, also called Robert Willis Blencowe, who sold the manor in 1858 to Charles Mills, the banker, who lived at Hillingdon.[82] Mills was created a baronet in 1868, and was succeeded in 1872 by his son, Sir Charles Henry Mills who, in 1886, was created Lord Hillingdon.[83] He retained Hayes until his death in 1898 when the estate was broken up.

In 1086 Hayes manor was assessed at 59 hides, with 12 hides in demesne.[84] The manor was then presumably conterminous with the ancient parish, and probably included the area which later formed the precinct of Norwood. Very little is known of the extent of the non-demesne land of the manor after this date, but during the Middle Ages the area of Hayes manor was reduced by the formation of small sub-manors and the larger sub-manors of Norwood and Southall.[85] These two eventually covered almost the whole of the area of Norwood precinct. In 1553 and 1598, however, Hayes manor still had extensive holdings in both Southall and Northcott,[86] and as Norwood and Southall manors were always considered to be held of Hayes manor, it is doubtful whether the lands of Hayes manor were finally confined to Hayes parish, excluding the precinct of Norwood, until the 18th or 19th centuries. As late as 1800 the 'mansion-house' of the Hayes manor estate was Southall Park in Southall.[87]

In the 13th century[88] the Hayes demesne comprised woodland and 595 a. in North Field, Middle Field, South Field, Bromcroft, and Chalcroft. About 1598 the demesne covered just over 663 a.[89] An estate of 658 a. divided into halves is described in 1677; that half which centred on the manor-house and consisted of 327 a. probably formed the demesne. The other 331 a. were farmed out in seven parts.[90] In 1800 the manorial property, including three farms of which one was at Dorman's Well in Norwood, covered 632 a.[91] This had increased by 1858 to nearly 726 a. and at this date, when Charles Mills acquired not only Hayes but also Norwood and Southall manors, the property covered all the northern part of Hayes parish, between the Yeading Brook and Hillingdon on the east and west and Uxbridge Road to the south. No land at all appeared to lie in Norwood precinct or parish.[92]

There was almost certainly a manor-house in Hayes from an early date, as in 1095 Archbishop

[66] *Census*, 1801–1961.
[67] See p. 35.
[68] Sta. Cha. 2/25/145; *Complete Peerage*.
[69] Mills, *Hist. of Hayes*, 9; prints in Guildhall Libr.
[70] *Cart. Sax.*, ed. Birch, i. 259–60, 556–7; see above, p. 22.
[71] *Cart. Sax.*, ed. Birch, i. 558–9.
[72] See p. 203.
[73] Lambeth Palace, Estate MSS. 1213–21; F. R. H. Du Boulay, 'Calendar of Archbishopric Demesne leases, 1503–32', *Kent Recs.* xviii. 270 sqq.; C 78/104; Canterbury Cathedral Libr., Regs. T1, T2, *passim*.
[74] C 66/2009/74, /100.
[75] C 142/450/93; B.M. Harl. MS. 756, f. 257.
[76] Lysons, *Environs of Lond.* ii. 590, quoting the title deeds.
[77] M.R.O., Acc. 264/123.
[78] M.L.R., 1777/3/116.
[79] M.R.O., Acc. 397/19; Acc. 400/16.
[80] *Complete Peerage*, vii. 91–92.
[81] M.L.R., 1829/7/553.
[82] M.R.O., Acc. 401/349. See also E. G. B., *Hist. of the House of Glyn, Mills & Co.* (c. 1933), *passim*.
[83] *Complete Peerage*, vi. 523.
[84] *V.C.H. Mdx.* i. 119.
[85] See below, pp. 43–44.
[86] M.R.O., Acc. 76/222a; B.M. Add. MS. 24812.
[87] M.R.O., Acc. 436/16.
[88] Lambeth Palace, Estate MS. 2068.
[89] B.M. Add. MS. 24812.
[90] M.R.O., Acc. 262 (St. 35).
[91] M.R.O., Acc. 436/16.
[92] M.R.O., Acc. 401/349.

Anselm was ordered by the king to move to Hayes so as to be nearer Windsor.[93] A hall, two granges, and a cattle shed are mentioned in 1398,[94] and numerous minor repairs to the hall and other manorial buildings are recorded in the later 15th century.[95] The site of the manor, presumably the house and garden, was occupied by the farmer, Richard Millett, in 1594,[96] and in 1598 the dwelling and outhouses stood in 6 a. of land.[97] During the early 17th century the house, called Hayes Court, continued to be occupied by the Milletts,[98] and in 1677 Hayes Court was the residence of William Wayland and the centre of a 327-acre estate which was probably the manorial demesne.[99] In 1770 the manor-house was described as very large, but since the sale of property included both Norwood and Southall manors as well as Hayes,[1] this house could have been Southall manor-house, and not that of Hayes. This seems likely since in 1800 the 'mansion-house' of the manor of Hayes was the house called Southall Park.[2] The present 'Manor House' stands opposite the junction of the modern Church Road and Church Walk. In the 1860s, however, this house was merely called the Rectory, and another building on the north side of Freeman's Lane, at the Church Road end, was called the Manor House.[3] Whether either of these houses was correctly styled is open to question, as it seems most doubtful whether any specific manor-house existed after the Middle Ages. Many of the owners of the manor are known to have had their own houses either in the parish or in the neighbourhood.[4]

A park at Hayes is mentioned in 1274,[5] and both a pleasure park and a deer park are recorded in 1398.[6] Part of the park probably formed the nucleus of an estate held in the 15th century by the Green family, lords of Cowley Peachey manor,[7] which later became known as the sub-manor of *HAYES PARK HALL*. In 1481 Cecily Green, widow of Sir Robert Green, was said to be seised of an estate called the manor of Hayes, which she held in fee of the Archbishop of Canterbury.[8] This was almost certainly the holding later known as Hayes Park Hall, since twelve years later a jury reaffirmed the rights of the archbishop to the capital manor of Hayes.[9] The lesser estate with which the capital manor had apparently been confused probably descended to Thomas Burbage, son of another Cecily Green who had married William Burbage.[10] Hayes Park Hall was first mentioned by name in 1560 when it was included, together with Cowley Peachey manor, in a settlement made by Robert Burbage, Thomas's son, and his wife Mary.[11] The property was the subject of a family dispute between the Burbages and their son-in-law,

William Goring, in the 1570s,[12] and was included in a survey of Hayes manor about 1598.[13] The estate then included a moated house, called Hayes Park Hall in 1577,[14] and approximately 160 a. The manor was said to have belonged to Lady Dacre, widow of Gregory Fiennes, Lord Dacre, the owner of Dorman's Well in Norwood, to whom it had probably been transferred in 1582.[15] In 1598 Sir Edward Fenner claimed to hold Hayes Park Hall by gift from Lady Dacre. A few months before his death in 1612 Fenner appears to have sold the manor to Vincent Barry and Michael Shorediche.[16] In 1640 Roland Reynolds died holding both the manor of Hayes Park Hall and the house of the same name. Both were then held of Edward Millett who was presumably a relative of John Millett, the lord of Hayes manor at this time.[17] Reynolds left two daughters as coheirs, but the property seems to have been divided into at least three parts. By 1658 one part, together with property in Hillingdon and Uxbridge, had been acquired by the Purefoy family and a second by William Roberts.[18] In 1662 Roberts sold Hayes Park Hall to Robert Child,[19] who died in possession in 1675. The estate was then sold by trustees,[20] to be held in trust for William Vannam. In 1678 Nathaniel Bennet held the manor in trust for a widow, Elizabeth Vannam. By 1703 it was again divided into two moieties, one of which passed to John Vannam, son of William, and the other to Robert and his wife Elizabeth, who was the daughter of the late George Vannam, another of William's sons.[21] By 1741 the estate was apparently again consolidated in the hands of the Dodd family of Swallowfield (Berks.), lords of Colham manor.[22] Hayes Park Hall passed in the Dodd family until the late 18th century when John Dodd sold it to the father of Joseph Fraine who held the property in 1795.[23] At that date Hayes Park Hall adjoined a moated site south of Uxbridge Road; the house was occupied by John Heath, the judge, who lived there until his death in 1816.[24] A quit-rent to Hayes manor for what was styled the 'Park' was paid in 1806 by a Mr. Fortescue, presumably the John Faithful Fortescue who at inclosure in 1814 held 174 a. in the parish.[25] In 1816 it was paid by 'Admiral' Fortescue. After this date the descent of the manor of Hayes Park Hall is obscure. The manor-house had been demolished by 1865, when its site was occupied by Park Farm, which itself disappeared between 1914 and 1935.[26] By 1937 the moat had been almost entirely filled in,[27] and after the Second World War the site was covered by houses.

North of Uxbridge Road a mansion belonging to

[93] Eadmer, *Hist. Novorum* (Rolls Ser.), 70–71.
[94] C 145/263/22.
[95] Lambeth Palace, Estate MSS. 1214–20.
[96] C 78/104.
[97] B.M. Add. MS. 24812.
[98] *Mdx. Pedigrees* (Harl. Soc. lxv), 138; C 142/450/93.
[99] M.R.O., Acc. 262 (St. 35).
[1] M.R.O., Acc. 264/123.
[2] M.R.O., Acc. 436/16.
[3] See p.   .
[4] e.g. the Cookes at Harefield; the Childs at Osterley.
[5] J.I. 1/540, m. 12d.
[6] C 145/263/22.
[7] See *V.C.H. Mdx.* iii, 173.
[8] C 140/76/54/5.
[9] *Cal. Inq. p.m. Hen. VIII*, iii, p. 493.
[10] *V.C.H. Mdx.* iii. 173.
[11] C.P. 25(2)/171/2 & 3 Eliz. Mich.
[12] Req. 2/174/69; /178/112; /58/43.

[13] B.M. Add. MS. 24812.
[14] Req. 2/178/112. It seems likely that there had been a house called Hayes Park since the 15th cent.: *V.C.H. Mdx.* iii. 173.
[15] *V.C.H. Mdx.* iii. 173.
[16] C.P. 25(2)/324/10 Jas. I, Trin.
[17] B.M. Harl. MS. 411, p. 114.
[18] C.P. 25(2)/1657, Mich.; 1658, Mich.
[19] C.P. 25(2)/13–14 Chas. II, Hil.
[20] Hist. MSS. Com. *Hse. of Lords Calendar*, ix(2), 119a; *L.J.* xiii. 254; *C.J.* ix. 508.
[21] C 78/1904/6.
[22] See p. 71.
[23] Lysons, *Environs of Lond.* ii. 591.
[24] M.R.O., Acc. 264/106, 116; see above, p. 26.
[25] M.R.O., Acc. 264/106, 116; Hayes Incl. Award and Map.
[26] O.S. Maps 1/2,500, Mdx. xv. 9 (1865 and later edns.).
[27] Hist. Mon. Com. *Mdx.* 70.

Robert Willis Blencowe was substantially rebuilt about 1820 as a two-story dwelling with a central, porticoed doorway.[28] After Blencowe had purchased the manor of Hayes in 1829 this house, Hayes Park, seems to have descended with the capital manor.[29] From about 1850, however, the house was used as a private mental home.[30] It served this purpose until the break-up of the manorial estate after the death of Charles, Lord Hillingdon, in 1898 when the house and 60 a. were sold for use as a nursing home.[31] The remaining 100 a. of the estate were sold separately to Dalton's Dairies Ltd.[32] In 1959 H. J. Heinz Ltd. purchased Hayes Park and the two parcels of land, amounting in all to 160 a., for use as a research centre and offices. Three years later the house was demolished and new offices built on the site.

An estate at *YEADING* owned by William de Pilardington was styled a manor in 1337.[33] Hugh, son of Stephen de Pilardington, had acquired a carucate in Yeading as early as 1243,[34] and in 1279 John de Pilardington did homage for half a knight's fee in Hayes.[35] By 1383 this estate was clearly a sub-manor of Hayes, as the lord of Yeading was paying for suit of court at Hayes.[36] During the earlier 14th century members of a Yeading (*Yedding*) family are mentioned,[37] but they do not appear to have been the owners of the manor until 1387 when John Yeading, who held a grant of the manor for life, was granted the reversion to it.[38] The property then included a house and 60 a. in Yeading. A William Yeading was a Middlesex coroner in the early 15th century and an Adam Yeading was committed for debt in 1413,[39] but it is not known whether they were also owners of the manor. Nothing further is known of the estate until 1539 when Thomas Bullock sold the reversion on Yeading manor to John Roys, a London mercer, the manor then belonging to Thomas's father Richard Bullock.[40] In 1540 Richard and Thomas Bullock and John Roys disposed of their interests in the manor to John Hughes. At this date it was said to comprise 10 houses, 490 a., and 100s. rents in Yeading and Hayes.[41] The manor was subject to settlements in 1582 and 1585,[42] and in 1586 Robert, son of Thomas Hughes, sold it to William Hewitt. The property was then said to be held of the lord of Hayes manor at an annual rent of 6d.[43] Robert King held the estate in 1596,[44] but whether as a tenant or owner is not known. Henry Arundell was apparently the owner in 1653.[45] Throughout the

18th century quit-rents for Yeading were paid to Hayes manor; by Lady Wiseman in 1702, by the heirs of Mr. Lambert in 1735, and by Benjamin Lethieullier in 1770.[46] The Revd. Lascelles Iremonger owned the manor by 1807;[47] at inclosure in 1814 Iremonger owned 180 a. in the parish.[48] He was still in possession in 1816,[49] but the later history of the holding is unknown.

There is no record that courts were held by the owners of Yeading, and business was probably always transacted through the Hayes manor court. A manor-house with a hall, chambers, kitchen, parlour, and gatehouse was contracted to be built in 1653.[50] In the 18th century the manor certainly owned both copyhold land and quit-rents,[51] but the extent of its property is unknown.

Hugh, son of Hugh de Northburgh and a relative of Roger Northburgh, Bishop of Coventry and Lichfield, acquired a house and 92 a. in Hayes and Yeading in 1337.[52] This estate seems to have originated in a conveyance of 1325 from William de Pilardeston, who is probably identifiable with the Pilardington who owned Yeading manor at this date.[53] In 1347 Henry Frowyk owned 2 houses and 180 a. in Yeading which he had acquired from John Dalling, a London mercer.[54] In 1430 an estate, possibly identifiable with the earlier Frowyk property, consisting of part of a house and 186 a. in Yeading, was sold by Henry and Joan Southwell to John Holme.[55] By 1479 this property had passed to William Chadborne, a London baker, and his son Thomas, who disposed of it in 1479 to John Shodewell, a clerk.[56] Other land in Yeading was bought in 1419 by Richard King from Thomas Bullock.[57] Two smaller estates, of 61 and 40 a. respectively, lay in both Hayes and Norwood.[58] Ankerwyke Priory (Bucks.) held some woodland in Hayes in the 16th century, if not earlier,[59] and this was granted in 1537 by the king to Bisham Abbey (Berks.).[60]

Little else is known of freehold property in Hayes before the 19th century. Elisha Biscoe held approximately 170 a. in Hayes, which passed on his death to Sir Joseph Banks.[61] At inclosure in 1814 502 a. in Hayes were in the possession of Hughes Minet,[62] whose relative, William Minet, is said to have acquired the estate in 1767.[63] By 1827 John Lewis Minet had increased his estate to 585 a. Another large landowner was John Hambrough, with 479 a., and there were at least two others, Louis Hayes Pettit and A. A. Powell, who owned about 180 a.

[28] M.R.O., Hayes Incl. Award and Map; Guildhall Libr. prints; ex inf. H. J. Heinz Ltd.
[29] Hayes and Harlington U.D.C., Hayes Valuation (1864).
[30] Ex inf. Heinz Ltd.; *Census*, 1861–1921.
[31] Ex inf. Miss Helen Lloyd.
[32] Ex inf. Heinz Ltd.
[33] *Cal. Close*, 1337–9, 115.
[34] C.P. 25(1)/147/13/224.
[35] *Reg. Pecham*, pt. i. (Cant. & York Soc. pt. xiv), 16.
[36] M.R.O., Acc. 401/1, m. 5.
[37] e.g. *Cal. Close*, 1337–9, 115; C 47/1/12/16; *Cal. Fine R.* 1347–56, 119.
[38] C.P. 25(1)/151/78/86.
[39] *Close R.* 1405–9, 495; *Cal. Fine R.* 1405–13, 260.
[40] C 54/421/60.
[41] C.P. 25(2)/27/183.
[42] C.P. 25(2)/172/24 Eliz. Trin.; /27 Eliz. Trin.
[43] M.R.O., Acc. 401/7, mm. 21, 24.
[44] Ibid. m. 36.
[45] M.R.O., Acc. 249/1298.
[46] M.R.O., Acc. 180/21, 25, 55.

[47] M.R.O., Acc. 264/106.
[48] M.R.O., Hayes Incl. Award and Map.
[49] M.R.O., Acc. 264/116.
[50] M.R.O., Acc. 249/1298.
[51] M.R.O., Acc. 210/17; 264/123.
[52] C.P. 25(1)/150/57/111.
[53] C.P. 25(1)/149/52/333.
[54] C.P. 25(1)/150/62/227.
[55] C.P. 25(1)/152/89/50.
[56] *Cal. Close*, 1476–85, 150.
[57] C.P. 25(1)/152/87/26.
[58] C.P. 25(2)/27/179 15 Hen. VIII East.; /171 3 Eliz. East. For other medieval freeholds see C.P. 25(1)/149/50/274;/150/57/105; /152/93/135; /152/93/139; /152/101 19 Hen. VII Hil.; C.P. 25(2)/27/181 22 Hen. VIII Mich.; /74/630 4 & 5 Phil. and Mary Mich.
[59] S.C. 6/Hen. VIII, 234; S.C. 6/Hen. VIII, 109, m. 75d.
[60] C 66/2009/28.
[61] M.R.O., Acc. 398/13.
[62] M.R.O., Hayes Incl. Award and Map.
[63] *Hayes, Harlington and Cranford Official Guide* (1932), 33.

each.[64] In 1866 Oscar Holden Hambrough sold a house and 379 a. to Charles Mills, the owner of the manor.[65] William Minet still owned property in the parish in 1932, and the Minet housing estate built round Central Avenue and Longmead Road is the only example in Hayes of a housing development carried out by a landed proprietor.[66]

ECONOMIC AND SOCIAL HISTORY. Before the Conquest the manor of Hayes had been worth £40, although this had dropped to £30 by 1086.[67] In 1291 the lands, rents, and customs were valued at almost £50.[68] More than £55 was rendered to the archbishop's receiver-general in 1425;[69] although the farm in 1459 was only rated at £41,[70] it had been raised to £61 by 1467, at which sum it remained for the rest of the 15th century.[71] In 1566 the manor was valued at £7 10s.,[72] although it had been leased in 1539 and 1555 at nearly £16.[73] The fines and quit-rents of the manor were valued in 1770 at only £60,[74] but in 1800 the rights and profits had an estimated value of £3,000.[75]

Until the mid 19th century the economy of the parish was almost exclusively agrarian. There was a mill, worth 4s., on Hayes manor in 1086, although whether it lay within Hayes parish is doubtful.[76] At this date the archbishop's manor was assessed at 59 hides, 12 of which were in demesne. The 3 knights shared 6½ hides, and the priest and two villeins each held one hide. Of the other villeins, 12 had ½ hide each, 20 had one virgate, and the other 40 held ½ virgate each. The bordars shared 2 hides. The land was capable of supporting 40 ploughs, but the free-men and villeins had only 26; there were also two on the demesne. In addition there was a carucate of meadow, pasture sufficient for the animals, and woods to support 400 pigs.[77] Early 13th-century evidence suggests that Hayes and Harrow manors formed a single agricultural unit to supply other archiepiscopal manors. For instance in 1233 the two manors produced 48 cartloads of charcoal, of which 40 were sent to London, 6 were kept for Harrow, and 2 for Hayes.[78] At about the same date wheat and maslin from Hayes were being sent to Harrow, Lambeth, and Mortlake, rye and oats to Mortlake, and barley to Mortlake, Lambeth, and Wimbledon. Some wheat was also used for domestic consumption and seed, while 8 loads were sold. Rye was sold, though most of the crop was used to seed 99 a., while barley was used for payments in kind to the manorial servants.[79] The manor was farmed for the profit of the king during vacancies, and in 1270–1 he

took the profits from the sale of wheat and rye, receiving the barley in kind. Oats and maslin were bought for the manor in large quantities.[80] In the 14th century the amount of grain sold apparently increased. Wheat, oats, hay, rye, and peas were all sold in varying quantities. Rye, oats, and hay were also used for cattle fodder.[81] Cattle and pigs were kept by 1270–1,[82] and sheep are mentioned in 1348, although none was included in the list of stock for that year.[83] By 1383 there was at least one ram on the manor, and pannage was paid on 210 pigs.[84] There-after the court rolls provide many examples of pre-sentments for letting sheep on to the corn.[85] At the end of the 14th century pasture on the demesne consisted of 180 a. Arable amounted to only 120 a., and there were 18 a. of meadow.[86] This seems to mark a change from the earlier 13th century when agriculture was principally arable.

In the 13th century the tenants owed haymaking, harvesting, sheep-shearing, and carrying services, as well as the obligation to provide haywards within the manor.[87] Commutation seems to have begun about 1270 when over £4 was raised from the sale of works.[88] In 1348 741 autumn works and 249 winter works were sold. By this date 16 hides owed 10 works each during the harvest at two a day; 7 *cot-manni* owed 35 works and 3 freemen owed 15 works. Customary tenants rendered heavier services; some owed winter ploughing, harrowing, and sowing obligations.[89] In the 1230s money stipends were paid to 4 full-time ploughmen and 2 others, and to a treasurer, a bailiff, and a collector. Stipends in kind were paid to 4 harrowers, 2 oxherds, a carter, cowman, gardener, beadle, and reeve.[90] In 1242 there were only 2 bailiffs for Hayes, Harrow, Lambeth, Croydon, and Wimbledon, and one serjeant for Hayes and Harrow.[91] A swineherd received a stipend in 1270–1,[92] but no shepherds are mentioned.

During the 16th century there is some evidence of sheep farming in the parish. About 1530 150 lambs were sold[93] and in 1584 sheep were stinted on the common fields at two an acre.[94] Arable farming, however, almost certainly still predominated, and in 1531 there were 9 wheat fields, 9 bean fields, and others with different crops.[95] By the mid 16th cen-tury the virgate in Hayes was apparently reckoned at 48 a., and in a rental of 1553 it was still a common unit of area measurement.[96] The first extant survey of the parish was made for Roger, Lord North, between 1596 and 1598. At this date there were over 1,304 a. in 11 open fields. Three of these, Broad-mead Field, Greathedge Field, and Crouch Field

[64] Hayes and Harlington U.D.C., Hayes Valuation List (1827).
[65] M.R.O., Acc. 401/351a.
[66] *Hayes, Harlington and Cranford Official Guide* (1932), 33.
[67] *V.C.H. Mdx.* i. 120.
[68] *Tax. Eccl.* (Rec. Com.), 14b.
[69] Lambeth Palace, MS. C.R. 1343.
[70] Ibid. 1213.
[71] Ibid. 1214–8, 1220.
[72] B.M. Add. MS. 39401.
[73] C 78/104.
[74] M.R.O., Acc. 264/123.
[75] M.R.O., Acc. 436/16.
[76] See p. 46.
[77] *V.C.H. Mdx.* i. 119–20.
[78] *Cal. Lib.* 1226–40, 200. For the economic history of Harrow see below, pp. 218–34.
[79] Lambeth Palace, MS. C.R. 1193.

[80] S.C. 6/1128/1: 29 qr. maslin and 102 qr. oats were bought in 1270–1.
[81] S.C. 6/1128/2; /9.
[82] S.C. 6/1128/1.   [83] S.C. 6/1128/12.
[84] M.R.O., Acc. 401/1, mm. 2d–3.
[85] e.g. ibid. m. 13.
[86] C 145/263/22.
[87] Lambeth Palace, Estate MS. 2068; Canterbury Cathedral Libr., Lit. E 24, f. 148; see below, p. 220.
[88] S.C. 6/1128/1.
[89] Ibid./12.
[90] Lambeth Palace, MS. C.R. 1193; *Cal. Lib.* 1226–40, 237; see also B.M. Add. MS. 29794.
[91] *Cal. Lib.* 1240–5, 131–2.
[92] S.C. 6/1128/1.
[93] Sta. Cha. 2/25/69.
[94] M.R.O., Acc. 401/7, m. 19.
[95] Sta. Cha. 2/8/89–90.
[96] M.R.O., Acc. 76/222a, m. 20d.

were well over 200 a. each, and three more, Botwell West, Botwell South, and Botwell North or East fields were all over 100 a.[97] Almost all the land was apparently arable, and only 48 a. were definitely meadow. The various hamlets were surrounded by over 395 a. in house land and inclosures.[98] Lammas lands within the manor were opened for common use each year,[99] and many of the manor-court regulations dealt with hedging, ditching, cleaning, and making water courses, repairing gates and stiles, and similar measures.[1] Cattle and horses were grazed in the open fields after the harvest, and were stinted at one animal for every three acres, and one cow and one bullock for every cottage.[2] The appearance of other field names in the late 16th and 17th centuries —Dawley Field, Yeading Green, Yeading Bean Field, Rolls Ditch Field—suggests that the large open fields of 1598[3] were gradually being broken down into smaller units. In the 1650s the stinting regulations in the three largest fields were altered to 2 beasts for each cottager, and the fields were to be closed on 1 November. All common land was to be opened either on 1 August or when the crop was off.[4] By the end of the 18th century the crop rotation practised in the Hayes area was a three-year one of fallow, wheat, and barley or oats with clover.[5] In 1805, shortly before inclosure, wheat, oats, peas, beans, tares, and clover, were all grown in the parish.[6]

Inclosures are first mentioned in 1348 when 6 a. in folds or inclosures were fallow.[7] In 1424 a man was presented at the manor court for inclosing Whiting Field,[8] a field name that was subsequently lost. Sherfield, another lost name, which was part of the glebe about 1530, was said always to have been inclosed, and its cultivation to alternate between wheat and pasture.[9] By the end of the 16th century all the manorial demesne, amounting to approximately 663 a., was inclosed, and another 395 a. of inclosures and gardens surrounded the hamlets of the parish.[10] By 1600, therefore, about a third of Hayes parish had been inclosed. In the early 17th century there are a few presentments for unlicensed inclosing,[11] a process which presumably continued. In 1809 the Hayes Inclosure and Tithe Extinguishment Act was passed[12] but no award was made until 1814 when over 1,000 a. were inclosed. The former open-field land was contained in 12 fields and some smaller common closes. The fields around Botwell had changed their names since 1598 and then comprised Townfield, Orange Field, and Bulls Bridge Field, as well as Dawley Field and Botwell Common. Nearly half the land in the parish was concentrated in three large estates.[13]

Unlike other places in this area of Middlesex arable farming continued to predominate after inclosure. The main crops on the Blencowe estate were wheat and beans, the rotation being either fallow, wheat, and beans, or fallow, wheat, clover, wheat, and beans. The grassland produced hay for the London markets but by 1830 the land was said to be exhausted from over-cropping.[14] Four years later the situation had not improved; hedging and drainage had been ignored, and young plantations had been wilfully cropped down.[15] The parish was then described as purely agricultural and, because of the concentration of two or more farms in a single person's hand, unemployment was rising. At this date the average wage of an agricultural labourer was 8s. a week or £20 a year.[16] Although arable land was valued in 1838 at 20s.–30s. an acre, and pasture at 25s.–40s. an acre,[17] in the 1860s the parish contained over 1,600 a. of arable to 1,260 a. of pasture.[18] Towards the end of the 19th century the main crops were wheat, oats, hay, and fruit,[19] and the jam factories that were a feature of Hayes in the early 20th century were based on the local fruit-growing industry.[20] There were at least 11 farms in the parish in 1890, but by 1922 there were only two. Two market-gardens and one nursery-garden survived, however, until at least 1937.[21]

Brick-making was the first industry to appear in Hayes, and its development probably resulted from the opening of the Grand Junction Canal in 1796, and the Paddington Canal, which branches from the earlier waterway at Bulls Bridge, in 1801. There is no evidence to support the assertion that brick-making began in the late 15th century.[22] In 1805 and 1806 land in the south of the parish around Botwell and the canal was advertised as containing 'exceeding good brickearth',[23] and in 1806–7 a quit-rent for his brick-field was paid to Hayes manor by Joseph Stroud.[24] By 1824 there was a brick-field at Yeading, situated about a quarter of a mile from the canal and surrounded by fields of exploitable brickearth.[25] By 1827 there were 5 brickfields, amounting to over 45 a., situated either in Yeading or by the canal at Botwell. Edward Shackle owned three of these, and brick-workers' cottages were attached to the sites.[26] There were only two brick-fields in 1842, one still owned by the Shackles, but the acreage being worked remained the same.[27] In 1847 Edward Shackle was discovered to be taking brickearth from copyhold land and was compelled under threat of legal action to seek a licence for so doing from the lord of the manor. These licences set a royalty of 2d. on every thousand bricks.[28] By 1864 many of the old brick-fields had been worked out, but the Yeading

97 B.M. Add. MS. 24812. The figures are: Broadmead (279 a.), Greathedge (226 a.), Crouch (224 a.), Botwell South (199 a.), Botwell West (160 a.), Botwell North or East (118 a.).
98 B.M. Add. MS. 24812.
99 M.R.O., Acc. 401/7, m. 14d.
1 e.g. S.C. 2/191/32.
2 M.R.O., Acc. 401/7, m. 47d.
3 Ibid. /8, m. 20; S.C. 2/191/32.
4 M.R.O., Acc. 180/1, 2.
5 Foot, Agric, of Mdx. 21.
6 M.R.O., Acc. 264/124.
7 S.C. 6/1128/12.
8 M.R.O., Acc. 401/3, m. 4d.
9 Sta. Cha. 2/25/69.
10 B.M. Add. MS. 24812.
11 e.g. M.R.O., Acc. 401/8, m. 25.
12 L.J. xlvii. 342a.

13 M.R.O., Hayes Incl. Award; see above, p. 28.
14 M.R.O., Acc. 180/176.
15 Ibid. /203.
16 Rep. Poor Law Com. App. B(2), H.C. 44, pp. 101 f-k (1834), xxxv-vi.
17 M.R.O., Acc 180/211.
18 O.S. Area Bk.
19 Kelly's Dir. Mdx. (1890).
20 M.R.O., County Development Plan (1951), p. 45.
21 Kelly's Dirs. Mdx. (1890–1937).
22 Mills, Hist. of Hayes. 42.
23 M.R.O., Acc. 264/123–30.
24 Ibid. /106.
25 B.M. Add. MS. 12543, m. 2.
26 Hayes and Harlington U.D.C., Hayes Valuation (1827).
27 Ibid. (1842).
28 M.R.O., Acc. 180/181–3.

brick-field contained at least 20 stools.[29] In 1876 brick-making was still largely carried on at Yeading,[30] but by 1890 the brickearth had nearly all been worked out. Two brick-makers survived at Dawley, however,[31] and in 1951 the East Acton Brick Works & Estates Co. Ltd. worked a 22-acre site at Yeading. Production then was only 25 per cent. of the pre-war figure, but it was reckoned that manufacture could continue for at least 30 years.[32]

During the 19th century industry in Hayes was virtually confined to brick-making. In the 1830s some gravel was dug, and on the manorial estate gravel, which cost 6d. to raise, could be sold at 2s. 6d. a load.[33] The poor were also employed by the overseers on gravel-digging.[34] There was a brewery between the church and Freeman's Lane in Hayes in the 1860s, but this was disused by 1895.[35] Earlier, in 1827, the 'Adam and Eve' had a brewery attached to it.[36] The opening of Hayes station in 1864[37] appears to have had little effect on the industrialization of the parish, for large-scale industry did not arrive until the early 20th century. The first large factory established was that of the British Electric Transformer Co. which moved to Hayes in 1901.[38] By 1908 this had been joined by brewing, sugar, tube, turpentine, and two floor manufacturers,[39] and in 1907 by the Gramophone Co. that became, in 1931, Electric & Musical Instruments Ltd.[40] By 1913 there was an increasing demand for cottages and houses, as several large factories had recently been built.[41] During the 1920s and 1930s the industrial concentration round Botwell greatly expanded with the appearance of such firms as Nestlé's, Kraft, and Smith's Potato Crisps.[42] By 1944 Hayes was considered to be over-industrialized, and the labour saturation point had been passed. Labour demands were increasing and the shortage of housing was acute. Industry was organized in large units[43] and in 1951 was said to be divided between engineering and electrical goods, vehicle manufacture, and the production of food, drink, and tobacco. Over 60 per cent. of the insured population were employed by four firms,[44] one of which, Fairey Aviation and Westland Helicopters, was sited just within Harlington parish, although the firm was normally considered as an important and integral part of the Hayes industrial complex. In 1951 the Minet industrial estate was the only area considered available for industrial expansion,[45] and new industries were not encouraged. In 1961 the largest single employer of labour in Hayes was E.M.I. Ltd., who owned factories covering 150 a. in and around Blyth Road. The firm's labour force has grown from approximately 3,000 in 1920 to 7,000 in 1929, and to 14,000 by 1961. They produced a wide variety of electrical, radio, and electronic equipment.[46] In 1950 a factory in Hayes was acquired by the Public Record Office as an intermediate depository, where departmental records could be sorted before destruction or transfer for preservation in the Public Record Office itself.[47]

The *Hayes, Harlington and District Chronicle* was first published in 1933, its name being changed to the *Hayes Chronicle* ten years later. The *Hayes News* was first published in 1939, and the *Middlesex Advertiser* produced a Hayes edition between 1939 and 1945; this was continued after 1945 as the *Hayes Gazette*. The *Hayes Post* was first published in 1954.[48]

Little is known of the social life of the parish. In the 1530s sports such as dice, cards, tennis, bowls, and football were popular,[49] and in the 18th century cockfights were held in the churchyard.[50] There were four friendly societies in 1803–4 with over 230 members,[51] and the Hayes United Friendly Society ranked the lord of the manor among its members in 1820.[52] The Working Mens' Institute and tennis, football, and cricket clubs were all in existence by 1895.[53] The present Hayes Football Club was founded in 1909 as the Botwell Mission F.C., only changing its name in 1930.[54] By 1932 organizations in the parish included the silver prize band, two rate-payers' associations, and the chamber of commerce.[55] A cinema was opened at Botwell in 1926 and two others were being built in Uxbridge Road in 1938.[56]

LOCAL GOVERNMENT. Hayes belonged to the Archbishop of Canterbury's bailiwick or liberty of Harrow.[57] A court was held at Hayes, as well as at Harrow, in 1242,[58] and in 1270 the pleas and perquisites were worth 102s.[59] Under the North family there were a reeve and a beadle, who rendered separate accounts[60] and who were elected in the Hayes manor court.[61] The court rolls exist from 1381 to 1778 and the court books from 1728 to 1930.[62]

The manor court normally held a view of frank-pledge every Easter, and 3 or 4 courts baron in between; the bailiff usually held the court on behalf of the archbishop.[63] In 1383 the lord of Yeading manor commuted his suit of court at Hayes,[64] and in 1386 ale-tasters for both Hayes and Southall are

[29] Hayes and Harlington U.D.C., Hayes Valuation (1864).
[30] Thorne, *Environs of Lond.* 335–6.
[31] *Kelly's Dir. Mdx.* (1890).
[32] M.R.O., County Development Plan (1951), p. 137.
[33] M.R.O., Acc. 180/203.
[34] *Rep. Poor Law Com. App. B(2)*, H.C. 44, pp. 101 *f-k* (1834), xxxv–vi.
[35] O.S. Map 1/2,500, Mdx. xv. 9 (1865 and 1895 edns.).
[36] M.R.O., Acc. 180/497.
[37] Peacock, *G. W. Suburban Services*, 45.
[38] Ex inf. British Electric Transformer Co. Ltd.
[39] *Kelly's Dir. Mdx.* (1908).
[40] Ex inf. E.M.I. Ltd.
[41] Char. Com. file.
[42] *Southall-Norwood Official Guide* (1924), 33; *Hayes, Harlington and Cranford Official Guide* (1934), 14.
[43] Abercrombie, *Greater Lond. Plan* (1944), 148–9.
[44] M.R.O., County Development Plan (1951), pp. 51, 57.
[45] Ibid. 65.
[46] Ex inf. E.M.I. Ltd.; *Daily Sketch*, 12 Feb. 1929.
[47] *111th Dep. Kpr's. Rep.* 6.

[48] B.M. Newspaper Catalogue.
[49] Sta. Cha. 2/25/69; 2/8/85–86; *L. & P. Hen. VIII*, vii, pp. 208–9.
[50] Par. Recs., Register 1707–84, *sub* Burials, 1754.
[51] *Rets. on Expense and Maintenance of Poor*, H.C. 175, p. 294–5 (1803–4), xiii (demi-folio).
[52] M.R.O., Acc. 180/238.
[53] *Kelly's Dir. Mdx.* (1895).
[54] Ex inf. Hayes F.C.
[55] *Hayes, Harlington and Cranford Official Guide* (1932), 29.
[56] *Southall-Norwood and Hayes Official Guide* (1926), 39; *Hayes and Harlington Official Guide* (1938), 15.
[57] See p. 238.
[58] *Cal. Lib. R.* 1240–5, 131.
[59] S.C. 6/1128/1.
[60] M.R.O., Acc. 76/220, 221, 222a.
[61] M.R.O., Acc. 401/7, m. 19; /8, m. 19.
[62] M.R.O., Acc. 401/1–16 are court rolls; Acc. 180/6–12 are court books.
[63] M.R.O., Acc. 401/1–16.
[64] Ibid. /1, m. 5.

mentioned.[65] In 1402 the court elected four constables, one of whom was for Southall, and beadles for Hayes, Botwell, and Southall.[66] By the 16th century the number of officials elected by the court was apparently increasing, and in 1572 two constables and two headboroughs were elected for Hayes, and one of each for Norwood.[67] According to Lysons Norwood manor held courts certainly from 1481,[68] but the appointment of the Norwood officials by the Hayes court indicates the subservience of Norwood manor to that of Hayes. By 1610 two constables and two ale-tasters were elected for Hayes, together with an under-constable or headborough for each of the 5 hamlets of Yeading, Hayes End, Wood End, Botwell, and Cotman's Town; Norwood and Southall had a constable and aletaster each, and shared 3 under-constables.[69] Throughout its existence the court was primarily concerned with making economic regulations. There was perhaps a court house as early as 1270, when the doors of the court are mentioned,[70] but there is no further evidence of such a building until c. 1640, when a building called the Court House was in private occupation.[71] By the 19th century one court baron was held in the spring every year, the last being in 1864,[72] and court dinners were held at the 'Adam and Eve'.[73] After 1864 only purely formal business was transacted.

The vestry is not mentioned until the early 19th century, although it was presumably in existence long before this. In 1531 the parish clerk was dismissable by the churchwardens, who were themselves probably answerable to the vestry, and in the same year a man gave 10s. towards repairing the highways.[74] During the 17th century Norwood probably developed an independent jurisdiction.[75] In the early 19th century the vestry met occasionally in the church and then in the workhouse, usually about 4 times a year, with an average attendance of 5–8 people. The meetings were almost solely for administering the poor law, electing overseers, and occasionally for levying a church rate. Under the Sturges Bourne Act the vestry was converted into a select vestry of 20 members including the vicar and 4 officials. The average attendance rose during the 1830s and 1840s to between 15 and 18. During 1839 meetings were held at the 'Adam and Eve', but in 1841 were moved to the National School. In 1839 the vestry elected 8 officers, consisting of 2 each of guardians of the poor, overseers of the poor, highway surveyors, and assessors and collectors of taxes. In 1839, on the vicar's refusal to do so, they also appointed a vicar's warden and a year later they refused for a time to appoint a churchwarden at all,

because a warden might be imprisoned for not going to church.[76]

During the early 19th century the principal occupation of the vestry was the administration of the poor laws. Between 1783 and 1785 the average amount spent annually on the poor was over £298, the rates being over £300,[77] and by 1803 they had doubled to £661.[78] In the early part of the century the poor were said to be farmed out, but this practice was later discontinued.[79] By 1803 the parish had acquired a workhouse, and in 1814 this and its garden, together occupying over 2 a., stood on the south side of Botwell Lane,[80] near Printinghouse Lane (earlier Workhouse Lane).[81] The workhouse usually had about 24 inmates, the old men working in the garden and women in the house.[82] The vestry owned a room in the poorhouse and bought an oak chest in which to keep their documents there.[83] Hayes was included in the Uxbridge Poor Law Union of 1836 and the poor transferred to the union workhouse in Hillingdon.[84] By 1864 the Hayes workhouse was occupied as a private cottage.[85]

The vestry minutes cease between 1842 and 1864, but the vestry presumably continued to administer the parish. After 1864 it met about 6 times a year and its business was mainly to elect officers and to propose rates.[86] A parish council was formed[87] in 1894 when a chairman and 9 councillors, consisting of 'five socialists and four gentlemen',[88] were elected. The council met monthly at Dr. Triplett's school in Church Walk, their officials being a paid clerk and an unpaid treasurer. Workmen employed by the council were to have a minimum wage of 20s. a week. Finance and Watch committees were formed in 1895.[89] The council dealt with much parish business, such as allotments, a fire service, and providing a village hall, drainage, and sewage. They produced a sewage scheme in 1898 but nothing had been done before 1903. In 1902 an attempt to adopt the Lighting and Watching Act was defeated by a large majority. Widespread demands in 1903 for local control over building expansion and objections to the Hayes contributions to the Uxbridge rural district being spent outside the parish led to the formation in 1904 of Hayes U.D.[90]

The urban district council consisted of 9 members and met fortnightly at 'Fairfield'. Four salaried officers were appointed, a clerk, surveyor, inspector of nuisances, and a medical officer. Two committees, for highways, sewage, and sanitation, and for general purposes and finance, were formed, and one of their first acts was to continue the sewage scheme that had been undertaken by the parish council.[91] In 1934

[65] M.R.O., Acc. 401/1, m. 11.
[66] Ibid. /2.   [67] S.C. 2/191/32.
[68] Environs of Lond. iii. 320, quoting deeds communicated by the steward.
[69] M.R.O., Acc. 401/8, m. 17. For Cotman's Town see p. 22.
[70] S.C. 6/1128/1.
[71] B.M. Add. MS. 38856, f. 40.
[72] M.R.O., Acc. 180/11.
[73] Ibid. /107.
[74] Sta. Cha 2/16/114.
[75] See p. 49.
[76] M.R.O., Acc. 659; Vestry Min. Bk. 1823–60.
[77] Rep. Cttee. on Rets. by Overseers, 1776, Ser. 1, ix, p. 396.
[78] Rets. on Expense and Maintenance of Poor, H.C. 175, pp. 294–5 (1803–4), xiii (demi-folio).
[79] Rep. Poor Law Com. App. B(2), H.C. 44, pp. 101 f-k (1834), xxxv–vi.

[80] M.R.O., Hayes Incl. Award and Map.
[81] O.S. Map 1/2,500, Mdx. xv. 9 (1865 and later edns.).
[82] Rep. Poor Law Com. App. B(2), H.C. 44, pp. 101 f-k (1834), xxxv–vi.
[83] M.R.O., Acc. 659.
[84] See p. 84.
[85] Hayes and Harlington U.D.C., Hayes Valuation (1864).
[86] Hayes and Harlington U.D.C., Par. Meeting Min. Bk. 1864–1904.
[87] The following paragraph, except where noted, is based on the Par. Coun. Min. Bks. 1894–1904, and the Par. Meeting Min. Bk. 1864–1904 penes Hayes and Harlington U.D.C.
[88] Char. Com. files.
[89] Ibid.
[90] Census, 1911.
[91] Hayes and Harlington U.D.C., Hayes U.D.C. Min. Bk. 1904–6.

Hayes U.D. became Hayes and Harlington U.D. and about an acre of Hayes civil parish was added to

Southall Borough.[92] In 1958 the council consisted of 24 members, Hayes parish forming 6 of the 8 wards into which the district was divided.[93] In 1965 the urban district was incorporated in the new London Borough of Hillingdon.[94]

URBAN DISTRICT OF HAYES AND HARLINGTON. *Vert, a silver pall, its lower limb cut short, between in chief two wings joined together argent, and on each side a cog-wheel argent in front of two rays of lightning or*
[Granted 1950]

Barra Hall, a residence at Wood End known in 1865 as Grove Lodge, was purchased by the council in 1923 and afterwards used as the town hall. In 1948 the department of the borough engineer and surveyor moved into the Chestnuts, formerly Grove Cottage, which is situated nearby at the junction of Botwell Lane and Woodend Green Road. From 1954 until its demolition in 1960 Wood End House accommodated the departments of parks and public health, which then moved to Springfield House in Hayes End Road.[95] In 1968 the former town hall of Hayes was used as the town hall of the London Borough of Hillingdon.

CHURCHES. In 1086 there was a priest on the Archbishop of Canterbury's manor of Hayes,[96] where the church was possibly already exempt from the Bishop of London. In 1272 Hayes was counted as part of the Archbishop of Canterbury's peculiar deanery of Croydon[97] and so remained until the abolition of the Middlesex peculiars in 1845.[98]

Throughout the Middle Ages the archbishop normally presented to the rectory,[99] except *sede vacante* when the Crown did so.[1] A papal provision to the church in 1351[2] seems to have been without effect, since the provisor was not yet in possession in 1366, when he petitioned the archbishop for it.[3] In the 15th century the advowson of the church, with the chapel of Norwood, was included in the farm of the manor.[4] In 1545 it passed with the manor to the king, who sold it to Sir Edward North.[5] In spite of this transaction it was granted by Cranmer to William Herbert, Earl of Pembroke, who claimed the right to exercise it in 1557.[6] William Jones, perhaps a servant of Lord Pembroke, presented in 1565[7] and

Thomas Higate held the advowson in 1589 and 1591 under a grant to his father Thomas from the earl.[8] In 1601 Lord Pembroke's grandson presented[9] but Higate again presented in 1608.[10] In 1656 the 'minister' had been appointed by Bulstrode Whitelocke, presumably as commissioner of the great seal.[11]

Miles Wolfe and John Knight were the patrons in 1661 and Ralph Hawtrey and Christopher Cratford presented in 1685 and again in 1689. Two lords of the manor, James Jenyns in 1727 and George Cooke in 1730 and 1739, owned the advowson, and a lawyer, Edward Jennings, presented in 1759.[12] In 1770, when the manors were offered for sale by the Cooke family,[13] the advowson was said to be annexed to the lordship of Hayes. This may have been the origin of the statement that the advowson had belonged to the lords of Hayes manor until 1777,[14] for it was not included in the sale of the Cooke property to the Ascoughs in that year. It must soon have changed hands, as James Clitherow of Boston House, New Brentford, presented in 1788, and James and Thomas Graham were the patrons in 1807. John Hambrough, a local landowner, held the patronage in 1858, but in 1860 William Randall was both patron and rector. Henry Bellinhurst, Samuel Wickens, and Frederick Owen presented in 1872,[15] as trustees of the rector, John Godding, who later became the patron.[16] In 1938 the advowson was bequeathed by Mr. J. W. S. Godding to Keble College, Oxford, which first exercised its right in 1957.[17]

The medieval rectors seldom, if ever, served the cure themselves but a vicarage was not ordained until 1520.[18] The rectory was then leased: by 1520 the lessee John Osborne had been replaced by a lawyer, Thomas Gold.[19] In 1656 the rectory was described as having cure of souls,[20] but in 1661 it was once again clearly a sinecure.[21] In the 18th century the patron normally appointed a rector who then leased the 'capital mansion house', glebe, and tithes to the patron. From this income the patron, who was thus also the effective impropriator, paid the salaries of the rector and vicar of Hayes and the curate of Norwood.[22] As early as 1656 part of the minister's salary was said to come from the farmers of the parsonage.[23] John Hambrough, the patron of the rectory, was said to be the lay impropriator in 1845;[24] James Townsend, described as the last sinecure rector, died in 1858,[25] from which time the benefice has been held by working rectors.

The tithes of the benefice are first mentioned in 1260 when the rector made an agreement with the Prior of Ruislip, whose house, like Ogbourne Priory (Wilts.), was a dependency of the Abbey of Bec. The rector was to have all the tithes but was to pay 8*s*.

92 *Census*, 1931.
93 *Hayes and Harlington Official Guide*, 25.
94 London Govt. Act, 1963, c. 33.
95 O.S. Maps 1/2,500, Mdx. xv. 9 (1865 and later edns.); ex inf. the Town Clerk, Hayes and Harlington U.D.C.
96 *V.C.H. Mdx.* i. 119.
97 Lambeth Palace, Estate MS. 1212, pp. 368–9.
98 *Lond. Gaz*, 1845, p. 2541.
99 e.g. C 145/263/22; Lambeth Palace, Estate MS. 1218.
1 *Cal. Pat.* 1396–9, 267.
2 *Cal. Papal Letters*, iii. 364.
3 *Reg. Langham* (Cant. & York Soc. liii), 101.
4 Lambeth Palace, Estate MS. 1218.
5 E 305/D/78; C 66/781/45.
6 Lambeth Palace, Reg. Pole, f. 74.
7 Lambeth Palace, MS. V/1.
8 C 142/222/48; /229/139.
9 Newcourt, *Repertorium*, i. 640.

10 Lambeth Palace, Reg. Bancroft, f. 288v.
11 *Home Cnties. Mag.* iii. 32.
12 Hennessy, *Novum Repertorium*, 209.
13 M.R.O., Acc. 264/123.
14 Brewer, *Beauties of Eng. and Wales*, x(5), 555–6.
15 Hennessy, *Novum Repertorium*, 209.
16 *Crockford* (1896, 1907).
17 Ex inf. the secretary to the Advowsons Cttee., Keble Coll.
18 For the vicarage see p. 34.
19 G. R. Elton, *Star Chamber Stories*, 181.
20 *Home Cnties. Mag.* iii. 32.
21 *Cal. S.P. Dom.* 1660–1, 520.
22 M.R.O., Acc. 264/123.
23 *Home Cnties. Mag.* iii. 32.
24 *Home Cnties. Dir.* (1845).
25 Hennessy, *Novum Repertorium*, 209.

a year to the prior.[26] In 1291 the gross income of the benefice was reckoned at £42 13s. and the net income at £21 17s.[27] The benefice was then taxed at £23 6s. 8d., and was charged with portions of £13 6s. 8d. to the monks of Rochester and of £2 6s. 8d. to Ogbourne.[28] It is possible that Osbert de Bilcheham of Yeading, who about 1200 gave some tithes to Rochester, may have been responsible for the first of these payments.[29] It is not known how Ogbourne Priory acquired rights in the benefice but it seems certain that the land subject to this payment lay in fact in Norwood.[30] In 1340 the church was taxed at £26 6s. 8d.[31] and it was valued and taxed at 35 marks in 1362 and 1428.[32] At the latter date the tax on the Ogbourne estate, at 46s. 8d., was larger than the 20s. levied on the Rochester property. Another annual payment in the late 15th century was 7s. 6d. free alms to the nuns of St. Sepulchre, Canterbury, which had been ordered by Archbishop Boniface of Savoy (d. 1270).[33] In 1535 the rectory was valued at £40.[34] Other income accrued from offerings customarily given on church-going, marriage, and burial, and some obits.[35] The advowson was reckoned to be worth 20s. a year in 1589[36] and the value of the parsonage, about £640 in 1656,[37] had risen to about £700 by 1866.[38]

A dispute over the tithes of corn and lambs reached its height in 1530, when the parishioners carted away their corn before the rector's share could be checked.[39] The incumbent was allowed one lamb in every 10, and those over were added to the lambs of the following year.[40] Alternatively if there were 6 odd lambs the tithe was 2d. a lamb.[41] Every tenth sheaf of corn was likewise to be laid aside when it was bound, or to be bound together in separate sheaves. This was said to be the local custom in Harlington, Heston, Ealing, and other neighbouring places.[42] In 1710 the tithes were owned by the patron, John Jenyns, who had sublet the small tithes of wool and lambs, called the town tithes, first to Henry Pigg, and then to William Fellowes. In that year he sold both the town tithes and the corn, grain, and hay tithes, together with other property, to Priscilla and Joseph Reynardson.[43] In 1770 the lay rector owned all the Hayes tithes, the great tithes amounting to over £344, divided into 12 lots, among them being the Botwell, Court, Home, and Yeading divisions. They were said to be considerably under-let and could be raised to about £125 a year, while the small tithes, if collected, were reckoned to produce at least £120 a year.[44] The tithes were ex-

tinguished at the inclosure award of 1814, when over 764 a. were allotted in lieu of tithe, 625 a. being granted to the rector, Elias Taylor. This amount, however, included property in Norwood.[45] A building called the Old Tithe Yard, owned by John Hambrough, was standing in 1827,[46] and corn rents of over £311 were owned by the rector in 1864.[47]

Little is known of the glebe land of Hayes rectory, which presumably originated from the hide held by the priest in 1086.[48] In 1413 the manor court granted a small piece of land in perpetuity to the churchwardens,[49] and in 1530 an inclosed field called Sherfield formed part of the glebe.[50] The rector held about 74 a. in 1598[51] and in 1656 the glebe was said to be 99 a.[52]

As early as 1367 the Archbishop of Canterbury had ordered an absentee rector to provide a chaplain, as the parish was neglected.[53] In 1426 there was a chaplain of the parish as well as a rector,[54] but it was not until 1520 that a vicarage was ordained by Archbishop Warham, uncle of William Warham, Archdeacon of Canterbury and Rector of Hayes. The vicarage was endowed with a £20 stipend, paid by the rector, which was considered sufficient to maintain the vicar and to supply a chaplain for Norwood chapel. The advowson was reserved to the archbishop, who was to pay the stipend during vacancies of the rectory. The rector was to build a vicarage and the vicar was not entitled to tithes or mortuaries.[55] Although the archbishop granted the advowson of the vicarage, with the manor, to the Crown in 1545, his successors acted as patron until 1608,[56] and thereafter the patronage seems to have been exercised by the rector[57] or, as in 1656, by his lessee.[58] The last patron was John Hambrough, who exercised his right in 1858, but no vicar was appointed thereafter.[59] In the early 16th century the value of the vicarage was reckoned at £20;[60] in 1770 an annual stipend of £60 was paid to the vicar by the patron.[61] This stipend was commuted at inclosure in 1814 for 16 a. of land. Four acres of glebe were augmented by a further 7 a., allotted in lieu of a salary augmentation from John Hambrough, the patron.[62] Hambrough had also attempted to augment the vicarage of Hayes and the Norwood curacy by a private Bill which failed from lack of support.[63] In 1855 the vicarage was valued at £120.[64]

There was probably a rectory house in the parish before the ordination of the vicarage in 1520, but it is first mentioned in about 1598 when it stood in Cotman's Town.[65] In 1656 Mrs. Patrick Young, the

[26] Hist. MSS. Com. 9th Rep. App. 41a; Newcourt, Repertorium, i. 638–9.
[27] Val. of Norw. ed. Lunt, 590, 599.
[28] Tax. Eccl. (Rec. Com.), 17–18.
[29] Red Bk. of Exch. (Rolls Ser.), 751.
[30] Public Works in Medieval Law, ii (Selden Soc. xl), 7.
[31] Inq. Non. (Rec. Com.), 195.
[32] Cal. Papal Petitions, i. 391; Feudal Aids, iii. 380.
[33] M.R.O., Acc. 76/2431.
[34] Valor Eccl. (Rec. Com.), i. 434.
[35] Sta. Cha. 2/8/90.   [36] C 142/222/48.
[37] Home Cnties. Mag. iii. 32.
[38] Kelly's Dir. Mdx. (1866).
[39] Elton, op. cit., 182–6.
[40] Sta. Cha. 2/25/69.
[41] Ibid. /145. Another account of tithe lambs is in L. & P. Hen. VIII, vii, pp. 208–9.
[42] Sta. Cha. 2/16/107; /17/89–90.
[43] M.L.R., 1710/1/60–1.
[44] M.R.O., Acc. 264/123.
[45] M.R.O., Hayes Incl. Award and Map.

[46] Hayes and Harlington U.D.C., Hayes Valuation (1827).
[47] Hayes Valuation (1864).
[48] V.C.H. Mdx. i. 119.
[49] M.R.O., Acc. 401/2, m. 22.
[50] Sta. Cha. 2/25/69.
[51] B.M. Add. MS. 24812.
[52] Home Cnties. Mag. iii. 32.
[53] Reg. Langham (Cant. & York Soc. liii), 163–4.
[54] Reg. Chichele (Cant. & York Soc. xlv), i. 214.
[55] Newcourt, Repertorium, i. 639; Canterbury Cathedral Libr., Reg. Tl, f. 172v.
[56] Hennessy, Novum Repertorium, 209–10.
[57] Ibid.; Newcourt, Repertorium, i. 639.
[58] Home Cnties. Mag. iii. 32.
[59] Hennessy, Novum Repertorium, 209–10.
[60] Valor Eccl. (Rec. Com.), i. 434.
[61] M.R.O., Acc. 264/123.
[62] M.R.O., Hayes Incl. Award.
[63] L.J. i. 332a, 384b.   [64] Home Cnties. Dir. (1855).
[65] B.M. Add. MS. 24812. For Cotman's Town see p. 22.

widow of a former rector,[66] had leased the parsonage to Thomas Jennings, the patron of the vicarage.[67] It is uncertain where this house stood. A building called the 'glebe dwelling house' which stood on Church Road in 1814 is probably identifiable with the Rectory of the 1860s.[68] In 1841 the curate of the parish lived in Manor House,[69] which was later claimed to have been a residence of Archbishop Cranmer and, being situated on the glebe, to have been the rectory house until its sale in 1860.[70] This was probably the building on the north side of Freeman's Lane, known in 1865 as Manor House but by 1914 as Manor Lodge; it was still standing in 1940[71] but its site is now covered by the gardens adjoining the Town Hall. A house on the north side of Hemmen Lane, near the junction with Church Road, had been reconstructed in 1862[72] and in 1864 was occupied by the rector.[73] This was called the Rectory in 1865 but 30 years later it was described as Rectory Manor House and, by 1914, simply as Manor House. The present rectory, further north but on the same side of Church Road, was in use by 1935.[74] Manor House, which in 1961 was the Education Office of the Hayes and Harlington U.D.C., is of 16th-century origin;[75] on the north side is some exposed timber framing, much restored. A vicarage house was ordered to be built when the vicarage was ordained in 1520,[76] and by 1531 it had been built and occupied.[77] It was in the secular ownership of Richard Millett in 1553,[78] and is mentioned as standing in Cotman's Town in 1598.[79] The vicarage house was situated on the vicarial glebe in Freeman's Lane in 1814,[80] and was occupied by the vicar in 1842.[81] Presumably the Manor House occupied by the curate in 1841 was a different dwelling.

In the mid 16th century the church had acquired $2\frac{1}{2}$ a. towards maintaining the fabric, while another 5 a. supported two lamps.[82] Throughout the Middle Ages the rectory was often held by pluralist or non-resident clergy. The earliest known, Rayner de Vitio in 1290, was a pluralist,[83] and his successor, Guy de Vitio, was a papal tax collector in Ireland.[84] Vitio was arraigned of 'divers trespasses' in 1307[85] but died still holding the living. He was succeeded by a pluralist who was provided to the benefice in 1312,[86] but in the same year Adam Murimuth, a distinguished historian, was collated to Hayes.[87] Many other pluralists held this rich archiepiscopal living during the late 14th and 15th centuries.[88] In 1537 William Warham was licensed to remain abroad to study and to be non-resident on his return.[89]

Other distinguished rectors in the late 15th and early 16th centuries included Thomas Jane, Bishop of Norwich 1499–1500, Thomas Ruthall, Bishop of Durham 1509–23, and Dr. John Young, Master of the Rolls.[90] Robert Wright, chaplain to Elizabeth I and James I, and later Bishop of Bristol (1623–32) and Lichfield (1632–43), held the rectory from 1601 to 1623 together with a residentiary canonry of Wells and, from 1613, the wardenship of Wadham College, Oxford.[91] He was succeeded by Patrick Young, chaplain of All Souls College, Oxford, librarian to James I and Charles I, and treasurer of St. Paul's.[92] Both Young, 'the most celebrated Grecian of his Age' and his vicar, Edmund Reeve, were sequestered in 1645,[93] and Timothy Hall, the succeeding vicar, was ejected in 1661.[94]

Nothing is known of the conduct of services in the parish. In 1530 there were riots against the farmer of the rectory, Thomas Gold, his brother Henry, the vicar, and the curate, Peter Lee. A band of parishioners, hoping to embarrass the Golds, vainly tried to secure Lee's dismissal.[95] Ornaments and vestments were removed from the church, and mass was not celebrated for a fortnight.[96] These disturbances were closely connected with an attack on the archbishop's authority in the parish and with the tithe disputes mentioned above. In the mid 18th century the vicar complained that his parishioners attended cock-fights, swore, and rioted in the churchyard during Shrove Tuesday services.[97] At about the same date he was having trouble both with his choir, which upset the congregation by singing the wrong psalms, and with the bellringers, who rang the bells during the services and spat from the belfry upon the seated congregation.[98] Large, serious, and well-behaved congregations, however, are said to have listened to the preaching of Charles and John Wesley between 1748 and 1751.[99] A curate, Frederick Sturmer, was blamed in 1839 for a fight among his pupils in which a boy was killed, but despite a petition from the parish for his removal, the archbishop refused to censure him.[1]

The church of *ST. MARY* stands behind a small green on the west side of Church Road; the churchyard was much enlarged in the 1860s[2] and in the 20th century. The building is of flint rubble with stone dressings and consists of chancel, nave, north and south aisles, south porch, and three-storied west tower. The chancel and the west end of the north arcade of the nave date from the later 13th century.[3] The chancel, which is built at a slight angle to the

[66] For Young see below.
[67] *Home Cnties. Mag.* iii. 32.
[68] M.R.O., Hayes Incl. Award.
[69] M.R.O., Acc. 659.
[70] *Mdx. and Herts. N. & Q.* (1897), iii. 156.
[71] O.S. Maps 1/2,500, Mdx. xv. 9 (1865, 1914, and 1940 edns.).
[72] S. G. Short, *Southall and its Environs*, 62.
[73] Hayes and Harlington U.D.C., Hayes Valuation (1864).
[74] O.S. Maps 1/2,500, Mdx. xv. 9 (1865 and later edns.).
[75] Hist. Mon. Com. *Mdx.* 70.
[76] See above.
[77] Sta. Cha. 2/8/85.
[78] M.R.O., Acc. 76/222a.
[79] B.M. Add. MS. 24812.
[80] M.R.O., Hayes Incl. Award.
[81] Hayes and Harlington U.D.C., Hayes Valuation (1842).
[82] E 301/34/165.
[83] *Cal. Papal Letters*, i. 514.

[84] *Reg. Winchelsey* (Cant. & York Soc. li), i. 141–2; *Cal. Close, 1302–7*, 271–2.
[85] *Cal. Close, 1302–7*, 483.
[86] *Cal. Papal Letters*, ii. 90.
[87] *Reg. Winchelsey* (Cant. & York Soc. lii), ii. 1226–7.
[88] *Reg. Sudbury* (Cant. & York Soc. xxviii), ii. 178; *Cal. Pat. 1396–9*, 28; *Reg. Bourgchier* (Cant. & York Soc. liv), 247–8; *Cal. Papal Letters*, xiii(1), 9–10.
[89] *L. & P. Hen. VIII*, xii(2), p. 168.
[90] Sta. Cha. 2/25/145.
[91] Newcourt, *Repertorium*, i. 640 n.   [92] *D.N.B.*
[93] *Walker Revised*, ed. Matthews, 261, 262.
[94] *Calamy Revised*, ed. Matthews, 243.
[95] Elton, op. cit., 209–10.
[96] Sta. Cha. 2/8/79–84.
[97] Par. Recs., Register 1707–84, *sub* 1752, 1754.
[98] Ibid. *sub* 1751.
[99] Ibid. *sub* burials, 1748–51. See below, p. 37.
[1] M.R.O., Acc. 659.   [2] Tablet on wall.
[3] *T.L.M.A.S.* xviii (2), no. 95; Hist. Mon. Com. *Mdx.* 68–70.

rest of the church and originally extended further west, has in its side walls lancet windows with rear-arches supported on carved corbels. The piscina and sedilia in the south wall are of the same date and nearby is an inserted 14th-century window. A new belfry is mentioned in 1422[4] and the west tower was probably built or altered at this time. In the late 15th century the north aisle was rebuilt and both aisle and nave were extended eastwards, adding two bays to the north arcade. The chancel roof and its east window are also of the 15th century. The south aisle and the nave roof, which has later dormer windows, date from the early 16th century; the timber south porch and the lychgate to the churchyard are probably of the same period.[5]

Views of the church in 1798 show the north aisle and the tower faced with brick-work while the other walls were apparently plastered.[6] The fabric was extensively restored in 1873 by Sir Gilbert Scott and further repairs were carried out by W. E. Troke in 1937.[7] In 1968 restoration of the nave roof was in progress.

Of the fittings in the church the oldest is the circular font bowl dating from c. 1200.[8] A former altar-table, dated 1605,[9] appears to have been removed to the vestry in 1909.[10] In 1726 a painting of the Adoration of the Shepherds was presented by James Jenyns, lord of the manor, and this constituted the altar-piece until 1873.[11] A three-decker pulpit of painted deal, said to have been made in 1726,[12] once formed the lofty centre-piece of a three-arched screen between nave and chancel; it was still in existence in 1853, although it had been removed to the tower arch.[13] An organ, financed by voluntary subscriptions, was first installed in 1812,[14] and in 1833 increasing congregations necessitated the erection of seats in the central aisle.[15] The charity board dates from the early 19th century. During Sir Gilbert Scott's restoration of 1873 the surviving box pews were removed and two wall paintings, a 13th- or 14th-century chequer-pattern on the north arcade and a 15th-century St. Christopher in the north aisle, were discovered.[16]

Memorial brasses in the church include one of c. 1370 to Robert Lenee, rector, said to be the earliest in Middlesex, and an inscription to Robert Buryges, rector (d. 1421–2). A stone tomb-chest with traceried sides and brasses on the lid commemorates Sir Walter Green (d. 1456) and a slab with brasses on a brick tomb is to Thomas Higate (d. 1576) and his wife. An elaborate monument of marble and alabaster with a reclining effigy in judge's robes commemorates Sir Edward Fenner (d. 1612) and a mural tablet with a half-figure laying one hand on

his helmet is ascribed to Edward Fenner (d. 1615). There are also mural tablets and floor slabs of the later 17th and 18th centuries.[17] There are six bells: one of 1793, three of 1798, and two which were re-cast in 1890.[18] The plate includes a chalice and paten of 1623 and an alms dish of 1693.[19] The registers, which are complete, date from 1557.[20]

A district chapelry at Botwell was established in 1910, when a chapel was built in Golden Crescent on a site given by the Shackle family.[21] In the following year a stipend was granted to the incumbent of Hayes in order to provide a curate at Botwell.[22] In 1914 a new mission church, provided out of the London Diocesan Fund,[23] was built on the corner of Nield Road and Station Road. This was replaced by the permanent church of ST. ANSELM, built on the same site and consecrated in 1929 when the parish of St. Anselm was created. Built in yellow brick to a design by H. C. Corlette, the church consists of a chancel, nave, north and south aisles, and a bell-turret with one bell.[24] The patron is the Bishop of London.[25]

A mission church in Yeading, described in 1890 as having formerly been a day school, was styled a mission room in 1908.[26] A small wooden hut in Yeading Lane was dedicated in 1932. This was removed in the following year and replaced by a larger timber hall built by the London Diocesan Mission.[27] It was demolished in 1961 when the permanent church of ST. EDMUND OF CANTERBURY, built on an adjoining site, was consecrated. The church, designed by Antony Lewis, is of yellow brick and is not orientated, its long axis lying north to south. The chancel is raised by 3 steps above the broad nave, and a Lady chapel is situated on the west side of the chancel. An octagonal hall at the south end is curtained off from the nave. There is one bell in the west bell tower, which is connected to the church only at the ground floor level.

The first church of ST. NICHOLAS was consecrated in 1937.[28] It consisted of a rectangular wooden hut set on the corner of Balmoral Drive and Raynton Drive. A new church on the corner of Raynton and Lansbury Drives was consecrated in 1961. This was built by the architect responsible for St. Edmund's and substantially to the same design.[29]

Although the church of ST. JEROME, Dawley, lies on Judge Heath Lane within the boundary of Hayes parish, its history has been included with that of the parish of Harlington.[30]

ROMAN CATHOLICISM. The wife of a Hayes parishioner in 1581 and a Hayes man in 1617 were

[4] Reg. Chichele (Cant. and York Soc. xlii), ii. 234.
[5] T.L.M.A.S. xviii (2), no. 95; Hist. Mon. Com. Mdx. 68–70.
[6] Illustrated copy of Lysons, Environs of Lond. ii(3), 592, in Guildhall Libr.
[7] T.L.M.A.S. xviii (2), no. 95.
[8] Hist. Mon. Com. Mdx. 70. See plate facing p. 36.
[9] T.L.M.A.S. xiii. 639.
[10] Par. Recs. faculty (1909).
[11] Brewer, Beauties of Eng. and Wales, x (5), 554–5; Thorne, Environs of Lond. 335–6.
[12] Mills, Hist. of Hayes, 21, and plate 10.
[13] J. H. Sperling, Church Walks in Mdx. (1853), 69.
[14] Brewer, Beauties of Eng. and Wales, x (5), 554–5.
[15] M.R.O., Acc. 659.
[16] Thorne, Environs of Lond. 335–6.
[17] Hist. Mon. Com. Mdx. 70; Pevsner, Mdx. 106; R. Gunnis, Dict. Brit. Sculptors, 1660–1851, 381, 426.

[18] T.L.M.A.S. xviii (2), no. 95.
[19] E. Freshfield, Communion Plate of Mdx. 30.
[20] The marriage registers from 1557 to 1812 have been printed in Mdx. Par. Reg., ed. Phillimore and Gurney, ii. 79–102.
[21] Except where otherwise stated the following section is based on information provided by the vicar. The chapel built in 1910 formed part of the public library, Golden Crescent, in 1966.
[22] Lond. Gaz. 4 Feb. 1911.
[23] Char. Com. files.
[24] T.L.M.A.S. xviii (2), no. 96.
[25] Lond. Dioc. Bk. (1965).
[26] Kelly's Dirs. Mdx. (1890–1908).
[27] Lond. Dioc. Bk. (1965); ex inf. the priest-in-charge.
[28] Ex inf. Mr. E. J. G. Beasley.
[29] Ex inf. the builder's foreman.
[30] V.C.H. Mdx. iii. 272.

1.   2.

3.   4.

1. Harmondsworth: south doorway of St. Mary's Church, 12th century
2. Hayes: font in St. Mary's Church, *c.* 1200
3. Ruislip: bread cupboard in St. Martin's Church, 1697
4. Ickenham: monument in St. Giles's Church, 1665

CHURCH DETAILS

SOUTHALL: THE INTERSECTION OF ROAD, CANAL, AND RAILWAY AT WINDMILL BRIDGE

WESTERN AVENUE AT PERIVALE

Ealing Golf Course and the River Brent are in the foreground, with St. Mary's Church among the trees on the left

presented for recusancy.[31] By 1640 no recusants were known in the parish, but one woman, Isabel Millett, never attended Communion, supposedly upon some 'Popish ground', although she regularly attended other church services.[32] There were two known Papists in 1706, when it was predicted that they would soon fall upon parish relief; another man, who owned an estate at Dorney (Bucks.), had recently apostatized.[33]

The parish of the Immaculate Heart of Mary, Botwell, was founded in 1912,[34] and a church was first registered in 1915.[35] It was rebuilt in 1954 and in 1960 was served by the Claretian Missionaries.[36] The church was replaced in 1961 by a much larger brick building fronting on Botwell Lane. It adjoins the early-19th-century Botwell House, whose grounds also contain a school. Further north along Botwell Lane, Bell House is occupied by the Poor Servants of the Mother of God,[37] whose chapel on the ground floor was registered in 1952.[38]

The parish of St. Raphael, Ayles Road, Yeading, was created in 1957, and the yellow brick church was consecrated in 1961. It consists of a nave, east and west aisles, and a small south gallery, lighted by hexagonal clerestory windows. A small north-western bell tower is connected to the aisle, and the raised porch is supported on six columns. The parish includes parts of Hayes, South Harrow, and Hillingdon. Services were formerly held in a school hall and in the priest's residence at Northolt.[39]

PROTESTANT NONCONFORMITY. In 1672 a house was licensed for Presbyterian worship.[40] Little further is known of dissenting activity in Hayes until 1831, when there was said to be a place of worship for Independents.[41] During the 1830s and early 1840s several houses were licensed for meetings of unidentified dissenters. These included Gothic House, Hayes, and two cottages at Wood End Green.[42]

John and Charles Wesley preached in Hayes church on at least ten occasions between 1748 and 1753,[43] and George Whitefield also visited the parish in 1750.[44] It has been assumed that John Wesley was married to Mrs. Vazeille at Hayes in 1751[45] but there appears to be no proof of this. By 1816 the Methodists had erected a small chapel in Hayes;[46] and in 1874 the Morgan's Lane Tabernacle was said to be in existence.[47] Nothing else is known of the

Methodist congregation until 1906, when the Hayes Tabernacle at Wood End Green was registered by Wesleyan Methodists.[48] The registration was cancelled in 1927 when the Methodist church in Morgan's Lane, Hayes End, was opened.[49] This in turn was closed when the church in Uxbridge Road was registered in 1935.[50] In 1961 the church was a large north-facing red-brick building with a slate roof. A Methodist church, about which nothing more is known, was opened in Clayton Road in 1909.[51] The registration (dated 1927) of another Methodist church, in Station Road,[52] was cancelled in 1930 on the registration of the Queen's Hall, Station Road.[53]

A Baptist chapel had been erected in Hayes by 1835[54] and one still existed in the mid 19th century.[55] The Salem Baptist chapel, which belonged to John Weekly, was registered in 1843,[56] and may be identifiable with the earlier chapel. By 1849 the trustees of the Salem chapel had acquired land fronting on Uxbridge Road to hold for the order of the Particular Baptists of Strict Communion. During the 19th century there was a chapel school next door to the Uxbridge Road chapel, and by 1943 the old chapel was itself used as the school.[57] The Salem chapel in Uxbridge Road was registered again in 1897 and in 1908[58] when the present small building was erected.[59] The Particular Baptists registered the Hayes Tabernacle at Wood End Green in 1872.[60] It was licensed for marriages in 1873,[61] but the registration was cancelled in 1906.[62] A Baptist Tabernacle hall was said to have been in existence in 1913[63] in Station Road. This was probably the forerunner of the Baptist chapel which was opened in Station Road, at Botwell, in 1922,[64] and was called the Baptist Tabernacle in 1923. This registration was cancelled in 1934,[65] after a new Tabernacle had been built in Coldharbour Lane.[66] In 1960 the chapel had 96 members.[67] The Baptists set up a mission church in Lansbury Drive, Grange Park, in 1934[68] and the church was officially founded in 1946. In 1960 it had 105 members.[69] In 1961 the brick building consisted of a single story with a hall at the rear.

The Hayes Town Congregational chapel, founded in 1788,[70] was first mentioned in 1841 when a piece of land in Church Road was in the hands of the chapel trustees. Before this date it was known as the Hayes Town chapel, but the name was then altered to the Hayes Congregational chapel.[71] The chapel was in existence in 1874[72] and was registered by the Congregationalists in 1884.[73] By 1939, however, it

[31] Mdx. Cnty. Recs. i. 123; ii. 127.
[32] B.M. Add. MS. 38856, f. 40.
[33] Guildhall MS. 9800.
[34] Catholic Dir. (1960)
[35] Gen. Reg. Off., Wship. Reg. 46469.
[36] Catholic Dir. (1960).
[37] Ibid.
[38] Gen. Reg. Off., Wship. Reg. 63600.
[39] Ex inf. the priest-in-charge.
[40] Cal. S.P. Dom. 1672, 473.
[41] Lewis, Topog. Dict. (1831), ii. 346.
[42] Lambeth Palace, MS. V/P/1/1/8/2/, ff. 18, 20, 37; M.R.O., C.P. Reg., Catholic Congregations, p. 8.
[43] Par. Recs. Reg. 1707-84.
[44] Ibid.
[45] Diary of John Wesley, ed. N. Curnock, iii. 515 n.
[46] Brewer, Beauties of Eng. and Wales, x (5), 557.
[47] Mills, Hist. of Hayes, 46.
[48] Gen. Reg. Off., Wship. Reg. 42040.
[49] Ibid. 50827.
[50] Ibid. 56330.
[51] Ibid. 43767.

[52] Ibid. 50758.
[53] Ibid. 52696.
[54] Lambeth Palace, MS. V/P/1/1/8/2, ff. 22-23.
[55] National Gazetteer, v. 225.
[56] Lambeth Palace, MS. V/P/1/1/8/2, f. 37.
[57] Char. Com. file; M.R.O., Acc. 180/11, pp. 451-2.
[58] Gen. Reg. Off., Wship. Reg. 35868, 43422.
[59] Foundation stones.
[60] Gen. Reg. Off., Wship. Reg. 20856.
[61] Lond. Gaz. 21 Feb. 1873, p. 737.
[62] Gen. Reg. Off., Wship. Reg. 20856.
[63] Ex inf. the Botwell Sisterhood.
[64] Gen. Reg. Off., Wship. Reg. 48358.
[65] Ibid. 48922.
[66] Ibid. 55118.
[67] Baptist Handbk. (1960).
[68] Gen. Reg. Off., Wship. Reg. 55675.
[69] Baptist Handbk. (1960).
[70] Board outside chapel.
[71] Char. Com. files.
[72] Mills, Hist. of Hayes, 46.
[73] Gen. Reg. Off., Wship. Reg. 27825.

was disused and services were held in premises 'not far away'. Although the old premises had been damaged by fire the chapel, gallery, and basement were still used for Sunday schools, youth meetings, and other activities.[74] In 1955 a new chapel, on the corner of Church Road and St. Mary's Road, was registered[75] and a hall was to be added with the proceeds of the sale of the old building.[76] In 1959 the old chapel was demolished during road widening.

The Botwell Brotherhood and Sisterhood meetings were first started in 1913, the Brotherhood meeting in a cinema, and the Sisterhood in the Baptist Tabernacle hall, both in Station Road. The sites were acquired by Woolworths, and the meetings moved to a hall built by the Brotherhood members, also in Station Road, next to the Post Office. In the early 1930s, this hall was sold for Post Office extensions and the Central Hall, Coldharbour Lane, was built in 1932.[77] In 1961 the Brotherhood had a membership of about 40, and the Sisterhood one of 100, both organizations being non-sectarian and non-political.[78]

The Salvation Army registered a barracks in Hayes between 1887 and 1896,[79] and their hall in Coldharbour Lane was registered in 1927.[80]

The Hayes Spiritualist Society registered the Albert Hall, Albert Road, in 1947.[81] The Elim Church, in Keith Road, was registered in 1951 by the Elim Foursquare Gospel Alliance;[82] the single-story building, which presumably also dates from 1951, is of red brick. The Apostolic Church registered their chapel in Willow Tree Lane, Yeading, in 1954.[83] The Kingdom Hall of the Jehovah's Witnesses stood in 1961 behind Church Walk, almost opposite the council offices; it consisted of a long, low, prefabricated building with a small entrance porch, and was probably erected in the 1950s.

EDUCATION. In 1819 there were five fee-paying day schools in Hayes, together containing about 130 children, and two Sunday schools with 80 children.[84] A large school house in Hayes, unoccupied in 1829,[85] was still standing in 1834, although no longer called a school house.[86] By this date there were 9 day schools in the parish, one of which was a Lancasterian school started in 1832, with 60 boys and 40 girls, and supported by subscriptions and weekly fees. The other 8 schools were together attended by only 38 boys and 60 girls, and were all fee-paying institutions. There was one boarding-school, which had 24 boys.[87] None of the private and dame schools

in the parish during the 19th century seems to have been long-lived.[88]

A National school is said to have been opened in 1836 at Wood End Green.[89] The National or Church of England school received a government grant in 1837 when it was attended by 125 children[90] and in 1842 a schoolroom, owned by trustees, stood at Wood End Green.[91] In 1859 Charles Mills, the lord of the manor, sold some land to the trustees of Dr. Triplett's charity in order to erect new schools in Hayes.[92] The girls' school was secured by a trust deed of 1857 and the boys' by a deed of 1860. The building was erected in 1861, and the schools, called Dr. Triplett's Charity School, received the income from the old National school which Dr. Triplett's replaced. The school also owned an endowment income of £100 a year which came from the charity. In return one-third of the school pence went to the charity funds. An infants' school was in existence at the same date,[93] and an infants' school building was added to the schools in 1866, opening in 1867.[94] The master and mistress of the old National school remained in their positions in Dr. Triplett's school, and a certificated assistant master was added to their staff. There was one female teacher.[95] The school did not qualify for a government grant in 1866,[96] but it had one by 1870.[97] The infants' school had a government grant by 1871.[98] In 1910 the organization of Dr. Triplett's schools was separated from the charity endowments of Petersham and Richmond (Surr.), with which it had been linked, and was formed into a separate organization to be run as a public elementary school.[99] The school was closed in 1963, but the Gothic-style buildings, yellow brick with red brick dressings, were still standing in Church Walk in 1968.

There was a school at Yeading before 1861 when the master and mistress transferred to the Biscoe school at Norwood.[1] This may have been the day school which by 1890 had been converted into a mission church.[2] The Yeading National school is mentioned in 1903.[3] The Church of England school, opened in 1904,[4] was closed in 1924.[5] A temporary elementary school was built in Clayton Road and opened in 1906 by the local authority. Its pupils were drawn from the Triplett school and the Harlington and Dawley National schools. This building was replaced in 1908 by the permanent school, also in Clayton Road, to which all the pupils were transferred. It consisted of junior, mixed, and infant schools,[6] and was attended by about 300 children.[7] A second block of buildings was opened in 1913;[8]

74 Char. Com. files.
75 Gen. Reg. Off., Wship. Reg. 31585.
76 Char. Com. files.
77 Ex inf. the Botwell Brotherhood and Sisterhood; Gen. Reg. Off., Wship. Reg. 54178.
78 Ex inf. the Botwell Brotherhood and Sisterhood.
79 Gen. Reg. Off., Wship Reg. 30172.
80 Ibid. 51016.   81 Ibid. 61666.
82 Ibid. 63214.   83 Ibid. 64279.
84 Digest of Rets. on Educ. of Poor, H.C. 224, p. 537 (1819), ix (1).
85 M.R.O., L.T.A. 696.
86 M.R.O., Acc. 180/201, 204.
87 Educ. Enquiry Abstract, H.C. 62, p. 564 (1835), xlii.
88 Pigot, Gen. Dir. (1824); Lond. and Prov. Dir. (1833-4); Home Cnties. Dirs. (1845, 1855); Kelly's Dirs. Mdx. (1866 and later edns.).
89 Mills, Hist. of Hayes, 33-34.
90 Mins. of Educ. Cttee. of Council, 1849 [1215], H.C. p. 456 (1850), xliii.

91 Hayes and Harlington U.D.C., Hayes Valuation (1842).
92 M.R.O., Acc. 180/365. For Triplett see p. 39.
93 Ed. 7/86.
94 Ed. 7/87.
95 Ed. 7/86.
96 Rep. Educ. Cttee. of Council, 1865-6 [3666], H.C. p. 737 (1866), xxvii.
97 Schs. in Receipt of Parl. Grants [C. 165], H.C. p. 618 (1870), xxii.
98 Ibid. [C. 406], H.C. p. 497 (1871), xxii.
99 Char. Com. files.
1 Norwood Par. Recs., School Trustees Min. Bk. 1828-1909.
2 Kelly's Dir. Mdx. (1890).
3 List of Schs. under Admin. of Bd. 1903 [Cd. 2011], H.C. p. 169 (1904), lxxv.
4 Ed. 7/87.   5 Ed. 7/86.   6 Ibid.
7 Bd. of Educ. List 21 (1908), p. 336.
8 Ed. 7/86.

the school was closed in 1931 on the opening of the Pinkwell School in Harlington.[9]

In September 1963 the old parish of Hayes contained seventeen maintained schools, which are set out below. The date at which the school was opened is given in brackets after the name of the school, followed by the dates of any extensions; the next figure is the number of children on the roll at September 1963, and the final figure denotes the age-group of the pupils:

Dr. Triplett's C. of E. (1861, rebuilt 1963). 344. 5–11; Minet Junior and Infants (c. 1925–30, rebuilt 1954). 671. 5–11; Wood End Park Junior Mixed and Infants (1930). 712. 5–11; Townfield Boys Secondary (1930). 493. 11–16; Townfield Girls Secondary (1930). 466. 11–16; Botwell R.C. (1931, 1961). 661. 5–11; Yeading Junior (1932). 366. 7–11; Grange Park Junior (1938). 388. 7–11; Mellow Lane Comprehensive (1938, 1949, 1963). 1,000. 11–18; Grange Park Infants (1939). 345. 3–7; Yeading Infants (1939). 322. 5–7; Charville Junior and Infants (1947). 579. 3–11; Barnhill Secondary (1949). 819. 11–16; Hayes Park Junior and Infants (1954). 502. 3–11; Barnhill Junior and Infants (1955). 447. 5–11; Hayes County Grammar (1955). 612. 11–18; Our Lady and St. Anselm R.C. Secondary (1956). 452. 11–16.[10]

The Hayes Jewish Industrial School was probably opened in the mid 19th century.[11] Authority for the school was transferred to the school board in 1877, and the site of the school, with 12½ a., was bought from William Minet in 1899 by trustees or governors who included Lord Rothschild. It then stood at the corner of Uxbridge Road and Coldharbour Lane. In 1908 the school was ranked as a charity but it was later transferred to the Ministry of Education.[12] In 1908 the school was housed in a two-story red-brick building with a clock tower, surrounded by sports fields and gardens.[13] Later it appears to have been called the Hayes School for Jewish Boys,[14] but this was shut during the middle 1930s and in 1937 the buildings were occupied by St. Christopher's Approved School, which accommodated 100 boys under the auspices of the Middlesex County Council.[15]

CHARITIES FOR THE POOR. The earliest known charity in which Hayes was concerned was the Emmanuel Hospital in Tothill Fields, Westminster, which was founded by the will of Anne, Lady Dacre, in 1594.[16] One man and one woman from Hayes were allotted places as almspeople in the hospital,[17] as well as a boy and a girl to attend the school which she also founded. The school was not established until 1736, but two Hayes children were selected thereafter.[18]

Thomas Triplett's charity was founded by a deed of 1668 securing property in Suffolk to pay, among other charitable donations, £15 a year for apprenticing the poor children of Hayes. During the early 18th century the charity appears to have been unpaid although the trustees were receiving the profits from the estate. The irregularities were settled in 1757 and thereafter the charity was regularly paid and unapplied income was generally invested in stock. The normal apprenticeship fees in the early 19th century were £15 for a boy and £10 for a girl.[19] The paying of these fees appears to have lapsed when the school was opened in 1861;[20] this may not in fact have been the case, however, since the charity supplied an endowment of £100 a year to the school but also received a third of the school pence.[21]

Roger Lea, by will dated 1661, left a rent of 10s. a year charged on land in Hayes. The distribution of Lea's gift was later linked with Blencowe's charity. Two cottages with ground attached were given to the poor in 1720 by Robert Cromwell to provide 6 blue cloth gowns for widows every Michaelmas.[22] In 1820 the cottages were in good repair, the gardens being small orchards, and some 11 gowns of blue serge were distributed annually.[23] By 1858, however, the cottages were dilapidated and were considered an example of discreditable management by the parish officers. After being condemned by the authorities, the buildings were finally sold and demolished in 1926.[24] The Revd. William Blencowe founded a coal charity in 1810, by will dated 1802, out of the income from £500 stock. The distribution of this was linked with the Lea charity, and the amount spent, which often exceeded the income, was made up by the Blencowe family.[25] Other charities were founded by the will of Elizabeth Parker, dated 1824, who left £1,000 stock, and by the will of the Hon. Juliana Curzon, dated 1834, who left £400 stock for coal and blankets at Christmas.[26] In 1857 these five charities were consolidated as the Hayes Amalgamated Charities by a Middlesex County Court Scheme.[27] In 1894–5 there was a bitter local dispute when an attempt made by the newly formed parish council to take control of the parish charities was strongly resisted by the trustees.[28] Other coal charities, each of £500 stock, were founded by the will of Emma Rousby Thompson, dated 1899, and by the will of Ann Fleet, dated 1912. The latter, however, was abated and only £110 stock was finally acquired in 1926. Louisa Davis gave £100 for stock to provide grey calico sheets for the poor in 1889. In 1958 the income from the five Hayes Amalgamated Charities amounted to £79, which was distributed in 50 gifts of coal, 26 of money, 6 blankets, and 4 blue gowns.[29]

[9] Bd. of Educ. *List 21*, (1932) p. 268. For the Pinkwell schools see *V.C.H. Mdx.* iii. 274.
[10] Ex inf. Hayes and Harlington Dist. Educ. Officer.
[11] Char. Com. file, where there are references to deeds of 1851 and 1862.
[12] Char. Com. files.
[13] *Kelly's Dir. Mdx.* (1908).
[14] Ibid. (1933).
[15] Ibid. (1937).
[16] *2nd Rep. Com. Char.* H.C. 547, pp. 69–71 (1819), x(B).
[17] *10th Rep. Com. Char.* H.C. 103, p. 309 (1824), xiii.
[18] *2nd Rep. Com. Char.* H.C. 547, pp. 69–71 (1819), x(B).

[19] *10th Rep. Com. Char.* H.C. 103, p. 309 (1824), xiii.
[20] For the schools see p. 38.
[21] Ed. 7/86.
[22] Charity board in Hayes church.
[23] *10th Rep. Com. Char.* H.C. 103, pp. 309–10 (1824), xiii.
[24] Char. Com. files.
[25] *10th Rep. Com. Char.* H.C. 103, pp. 309–10 (1824), xiii.
[26] Charity board in Hayes church.
[27] Char. Com. files.
[28] Hayes and Harlington U.D.C., Par. Council Min. Bk. 1894–9, p. 11.
[29] Char. Com. files.

NORWOOD
INCLUDING SOUTHALL

IN 1961 the area of the civil parish of Norwood was conterminous with that of the municipal borough of Southall,[1] which is now part of the London Borough of Ealing.[2] Before 1859, however, the whole area of Norwood formed part of the ancient parish of Hayes, being an ecclesiastically dependent chapelry called the precinct of Norwood.[3] Norwood formed that part of Hayes parish lying east of the Yeading Brook and the Paddington Canal, and was bounded by Heston on the south and Hanwell and Greenford to the east and north respectively. In 1859 the precinct was created a separate parish, thus formalizing the distinction between Hayes and Norwood that had been apparent from the Middle Ages. Because of this *de facto* division between Hayes and Norwood it has been found more convenient to present a separate account of each area. In this article references to the parish of Hayes concern that part of Hayes ancient parish lying to the west of the Yeading Brook and the Paddington (later the Grand Union) Canal.

In the 1860s Norwood covered an area of 2,461 a.[4] On the western side the boundary ran south down the Paddington Canal and the Yeading Brook. Turning eastward it followed the canal, Western Road, and Clifton Road and, crossing the north end of Osterley Park, ran through the lake to the Brent. After turning north up the river it ran west across former open fields, turning north again up the line of the modern Allenby Road and finally west again to the canal, just south of Ruislip Road.[5] In 1894 the southern boundary of Norwood was altered to include that area of Heston which lay north of the canal,[6] so that the southern boundary was formed by the canal as far as Norwood Mill. This increased the area of the civil parish to 2,545 a. Other minor boundary changes involved the transfer of 30 a. to Heston and Isleworth in 1934 and, in 1936, a gain of one acre from Heston and Isleworth, 60 a. from Ealing, and less than one acre from Hayes.[7] The area administered by the Borough of Southall in 1961 was 2,608 a.,[8] which covered approximately $2\frac{1}{2}$ miles from east to west and $3\frac{1}{4}$ miles from north to south.

The parish is predominantly flat and nowhere rises to more than 50 feet above sea level. The soil in the north is heavy London Clay, but south of Uxbridge Road light loam and gravel predominate.[9] The parish is watered by the Yeading Brook on the western boundary, and by the River Brent in the east. A small stream also flows along part of the southern boundary in Osterley Park, and drains through the lake into the Brent. The Brent was bridged before 1396, when the bridge was ruinous.[10] In the 18th century repair of the bridge was said to

be the joint responsibility of the lord of the manor and the Bishop of London as lord of the adjacent manor of Hanwell. In 1762 the Uxbridge turnpike trustees repaired it, and by 1815 the county had assumed responsibility. Batford Bridge, which crossed the Yeading Brook between Hayes and Southall, was widened in 1755 and rebuilt in 1800 by the turnpike trustees. In 1826, however, repair was charged to the lord of the manor.[11]

The early history of Norwood parish is inextricably connected with that of Hayes.[12] Although it was not mentioned in 1086, the church, and presumably the settlement, existed by the 12th century.[13] The church stood in the centre of the southernmost part of the parish, almost on the southern boundary. Southall is mentioned in 1274,[14] and in 1384 the names of 'Dormoteswell' (Dorman's Well) and Northcott both occur in a court roll.[15] It is reasonable to assume, therefore, that all three of the later hamlets of Norwood, i.e. Norwood, Southall, and Northcott, were settled by the 14th century, and probably much earlier. The exact position of the hamlets is uncertain before the late 16th century, when Northcott lay on the main Uxbridge road, round the junction of South Road and High Street.[16] Southall in the mid 17th century appears to have been the area later known as Southall Green, centring on King Street and the Green.[17] In 1573 Northcote Field and Northcote Oaten Field are mentioned,[18] and Southall Street is mentioned in 1580.[19] The survey of Hayes, carried out between 1596 and 1598 for Roger, Lord North, the lord of the manor, although incomplete, includes part of Norwood. At this date Northcott consisted of at least 14 houses and 7 cottages, all situated on the south side of the main road and surrounded by 45 a. of inclosures. Further inclosures lying on the south side of the main road amounted to 277 a. Another 242 a. of inclosed land at Northcott had been owned principally by Anne, Lady Dacre, the owner of Dorman's Well, which therefore may have lain on the north side of the road. Nothing, however, is known of settlement on the north side of the road at this date. Southall consisted of 19 houses, none of which is described as a cottage, surrounded by 35 a. of inclosed land. The chief property owners in Southall were the Child family, Robert Millett, and Francis Awsiter. There were four open fields around Southall: South Field (229 a.), North Field (201 a.), East Field (139 a.), and Middle Field (118 a.).[20] All these presumably occupied the positions they held in the 19th century, when all but East Field lay in the area between the Yeading Brook and Southall

---

[1] This article was written in 1961; any references to a later time are dated.

[2] See p. 50.

[3] O.S. Area Bk.

[4] Ibid.

[5] O.S. Maps 1/2,500, Mdx. xv. 6, 7, 10, 11, 14, 15; xx. 3 (1865 edn.).

[6] *Census*, 1901.

[7] Ibid. 1931.

[8] *Southall Official Handbk.* 81.

[9] Geol. Survey Map, sheet 259 (drift).

[10] *Public Works in Medieval Law*, ii (Selden Soc. xl), 7.

[11] *Rep. Cttee. of Magistrates on Public Bridges in Mdx.* (1826), 220–1, 225.

[12] See p. 22.

[13] *T.L.M.A.S.* xviii (2), no. 145.

[14] J.I. 1/540, m. 14.

[15] M.R.O., Acc. 401/1, m. 6.

[16] B.M. Add. MS. 24812.

[17] M.R.O., Acc. 180/76–77.

[18] S.C. 2/191/32.

[19] M.R.O., Acc. 401/7, m. 14.

[20] B.M. Add. MS. 24812.

Green, with Uxbridge Road on the north. East Field lay between Southall Green and Tentelow Lane.[21] Southall manor-house, in 1961 the property of the borough council and occupied by the public health department, was built in 1587 and is the only surviving ancient dwelling of importance in the parish.[22]

A Norwood field is mentioned c. 1600,[23] but Norwood is again omitted from the survey compiled c. 1657. Northcott then consisted of 4 houses and 27 cottages, four of which were inns,[24] while Southall comprised 12 houses and 10 cottages. A lane led north from Northcott to Northolt, and other lanes mentioned are Long Lane, leading to Southall, and Butts Lane, Southall Lane, and Southall Street, all in Southall. Northcote West Field (122 a.) and Middle Field (95 a.) are both mentioned. The Southall fields occupied almost the same acreage as in 1598. On the north side of the main road were over 116 a. of inclosures at Northcott, and further north still Dorman's Well was entirely inclosed with 177 a. Wexleys and the Common Down provided another 87 and 71 a. of inclosures.[25] At this date, therefore, much of the east side of the parish was inclosed, while the open fields lay to the west. Watermill Lane, passing through the parish from Greenford to Brentford, is mentioned in 1731,[26] but by 1754 it was called Windmill Lane[27] and by 1961 the part in Norwood had been enlarged into the Greenford Road. The upper portion of it, however, was still called Windmill Lane.

During the 18th century the names of the hamlets seem to have changed gradually. In 1754, when the first detailed map covering the parish was published, Northcott formed the settlement on the north side of Uxbridge Road around North Road and opposite South Road; Southall was then said to comprise the houses on the south side of the main road. There was a large settlement round Southall Green, which was not identified, and Norwood Road led only to Norwood, which was grouped on and round Norwood Green and on the south side of Tentelow Lane. This lane continued to Heston. North Road and Dormer's Wells Lane were both in existence and Allenby Road ran in its present position up the eastern boundary. A lane in the approximate position of Cornwall Avenue led to Wexley, a large farm. There were a few houses at Mount Pleasant, and on the main road and east of Windmill Lane, which was called Chivy Chase. The field pattern of the parish was much the same as it was a century earlier, except for East Field which ran from Havelock Road (a field lane) across to Tentelow Lane.[28] By the end of the 18th century well over half the parish was arable, and the names of the hamlets were becoming final. There were 56 houses in Northcott alias Southall, 40 in Norwood village, and 33 in Southall Green.[29] Norwood Lodge, a late-18th-century house in Tentelow Lane, survives from about this time.

The appearance of the parish was altered by the cutting in 1796 of the Grand Junction Canal. This ran through the southern part of Norwood, through part of Heston, and then north-east between Norwood and Southall Green approximately parallel with Tentelow Lane until it crossed Windmill Lane. It turned east to the Brent, whose line it followed south to the Thames. In 1801 the Paddington Canal was opened. This left the Grand Junction Canal at Bull's Bridge in Norwood, and ran northward through the parish parallel to the Yeading Brook, and formed, to the north, part of the western boundary. Norwood was inclosed under the Hayes Inclosure Act of 1809, but the award was not made until 1814, when under 1,000 a. were inclosed. Roads and settlements had altered very little at this date. Norwood Road, then called Wolf Lane, had been extended down to Norwood Green where it joined Tentelow Lane (then called Duncot Lane), leading to Heston. Western Road was a small unnamed field lane, leading off Southall Green Lane (now King Street, the Green, and South Road), and another small field lane, Templewood Lane, left Tentelow Lane and ran along the line of Glade Lane. There were 9 farm-houses in the parish, of which one at Frogmore Green, next door to the 'Wolf', was named Manor Farm.[30] Almost all of the eastern half of the parish was owned by the Earl of Jersey, part of whose park of Osterley extended into the southern portion of Norwood. Two other people, Thomas Parker and John Brett, each owned about 150 a. There were several large houses, one of which was Southall Park, owned by Lord Jersey.[31] By 1816 wharfs had appeared on the Grand Junction Canal at the junction with the Paddington Canal at Bull's Bridge. Grouped round the triangular Green at Norwood were many 'respectable villas' of an 'ornamental character'.[32] By the 1960s a number of these in Norwood Road and Tentelow Lane had been replaced by modern buildings; those which survived included Vine Cottage in Tentelow Lane and, in Norwood Green Road, an attached pair of tall three-storied houses known as the Grange and Friars Lawn. Norwood Hall, standing in extensive grounds to the east of Friars Lawn, had been much altered and enlarged in the late 19th century and in 1968 was in use by the Ealing Borough Council as a horticultural institute. It is probable that all three houses were built in 1813.[33] A few early-19th-century houses of more modest character have survived at Frogmore Green. In 1821 there were only four farms in Norwood, of which three, Southall Lane, Dormer's or Dorman's Well, and Warren farms, were owned by Lord Jersey. The fourth, Waxlow Farm,[34] has provided the name for a modern local telephone exchange. By 1834 the houses in the parish were described as mainly labourers' cottages, although labour itself was fairly scarce.[35]

In the 1830s coaches ran along the turnpike four times a day between Holborn and Uxbridge,[36] but in 1839 Southall Station on the main G.W.R. line to

[21] M.R.O., Hayes Incl. Award.
[22] Hist. Mon. Com. Mdx. 99–100; see below, p. 44.
[23] M.R.O., Acc. 435/ED. 16.
[24] For the inns see below.
[25] M.R.O., Acc. 180/76–77.
[26] M.R.O., Acc. 264/118.
[27] J. Rocque, Map of Mdx. (1754).
[28] Ibid.
[29] Lysons, Environs of Lond. iii. 320.
[30] Cf. the positions of the manor-houses: p. 44.

[31] M.R.O., Hayes Incl. Award and Map.
[32] Brewer, Beauties of Eng. and Wales, x (5), 607–8.
[33] Tablets on the garden wall between Friars Lawn and Norwood Hall record its erection in 1813 by the owners of the two properties.
[34] Southall Bor. Libr., Norwood Valuation (1821).
[35] Rep. Poor Law Com. App. B(2), H.C. 44, pp. 166 f–k (1834), xxxv–vi; Rep. Cttee. on Agric.: Mins. of Evidence, H.C. 464, pp. 165–71 (1837), v.
[36] Mdx. and Herts. N. & Q. iv. 105.

Slough and the west was opened.[37] The railway ran through the southern portion of the parish, south of Uxbridge Road. Its most prominent feature, the Wharncliffe Viaduct, although in Norwood parish, has been described in the account of Hanwell.[38] A branch line from Southall to Brentford was opened to goods in 1859 and to passengers in 1860; passenger services were suspended from 1915 to 1920 and were finally withdrawn in 1942.[39] The Brentford branch line was one of the last undertakings of I. K. Brunel, who caused three modes of transport to intersect by carrying the railway under the Grand Junction Canal at Windmill Bridge.[40] During the 1850s brick-making licences frequently included the right to erect labourers' cottages,[41] and brick-making as an industry spread in the parish, particularly round Southall, during the mid 19th century.[42] At this time the parish was still predominantly agricultural,[43] and four farms still existed in the 1860s.[44]

During the 19th century a feature of Norwood parish was the number of lunatic asylums. The Hanwell Lunatic Asylum (now St. Bernard's Hospital) in Uxbridge Road was opened in 1831 as a county asylum to take 500 people,[45] under the superintendence of Dr. William Ellis, whose wife was the matron.[46] Almost immediately the buildings were found to be adequate only for 300 people and by 1833 extensive repairs had had to be undertaken.[47] In fact repairs, extensions, and rebuilding were carried out continually during the 19th century.[48] Ellis resigned in 1838 after disagreement with the governors. His successor, Dr. John Conolly, was the first man in England to discontinue the use of all restraining implements on a large scale.[49] When the hospital was handed over to the London County Council in 1888 under the Local Government Act of that year[50] it contained 1,891 patients.[51] Under the 1947 Health Act administration passed to the local hospital board. In 1961 the buildings stood in 74 a. and held approximately 2,200 patients.[52] The exterior is mainly of yellow brick; there is a high brick wall along Uxbridge Road, where the main entrance consists of an impressive arched gateway flanked by single-story lodges. The earliest quadrangle, dating from 1831, was originally two-storied and has round-headed windows and a stone pediment. The third floor and basement were opened later. The whole range of buildings was, however, added to repeatedly between 1831 and 1923 and there are also post-1945 additions on the western end of the property adjoin-

ing Windmill Lane.[53] Southall Park, the large house lying just south of the main road and opposite North Road, was owned by Lord Jersey and between 1809 and 1824 was occupied by Dr. John Collins, who kept a school there for foreign Roman Catholic boys.[54] By 1855 Southall Park had become a private lunatic asylum,[55] which between 1861 and 1881 had an average of 18 patients.[56] The house, a 'fine specimen of Queen Anne architecture',[57] was destroyed by fire in 1883 killing Dr. Boyd, the superintendent, his son William, and 4 patients.[58] Between 1861 and 1911 there were four other lunatic asylums, Vine Cottage being one for over 30 years, and both the Shrubbery and Featherstone Hall for over 20 years.[59]

During the later 19th century train services were improved,[60] and in 1867 horse trams were run by the Southall, Ealing, and Shepherd's Bush Tramway Co.[61] Electric trams, linking Southall with Shepherd's Bush in 1901 and with Uxbridge in 1904,[62] were said to be directly responsible for an increase in population.[63] Trolleybuses, which were introduced in 1931, replaced trams on the main road to Uxbridge in 1936.[64]

Suburban development started in the last decade of the century. In 1890 there were 960 inhabited houses in the parish and 32 empty ones; by 1894 there was none vacant and a demand for cottages was anticipated owing to the building of a factory. Southall Green was then the most densely populated area.[65] Widespread development started in 1894,[66] although in 1904 Southall was still said to have 'a few picturesque houses on the London Road'.[67] In 1914 the area immediately surrounding the Broadway, bounded on the south by Beaconsfield Road, was built up, as was the area between North Road and Dormer's Wells Lane. The Green and King Street were both built up,[68] while a line of factories had appeared along the railway. There was extensive building south of Havelock Road, the extension of a lane formerly known as Feder Lane,[69] but little in Norwood apart from a terrace at Frogmore Green and another nearly opposite the church on Tentelow Lane.[70] By 1906 the parish was described as 'a manufacturing district'.[71]

After the First World War development proceeded more slowly, and during the 1920s and 1930s the north-western corner of the parish was built up. This covered Mount Pleasant, where over 700 houses were built between 1926 and 1928,[72] and the Allenby Road area. By 1940 the area around Lady Margaret Road and between Somerset and Hillside roads was

[37] T. B. Peacock, *G.W. Suburban Services*, 46.
[38] *V.C.H. Mdx.* iii. 223.
[39] Peacock, op. cit. 4–5.
[40] P. Kirwan, *Southall*, 35. See plate facing p. 37.
[41] e.g. M.R.O., Acc. 405/1; *Census*, 1871.
[42] For the brick-making industry see p. 47.
[43] H. Tremenheere, 'Agric. and Educ. Statistics of several pars. in Mdx.', *Jnl. Stat. Soc. of Lond.* vi. 142.
[44] O.S. Map 1/2,500, Mdx. xv. 6, 7, 10, 11, 14, 15 (1865 edn.).
[45] M.R.O., MJ/OC, 25, pp. 207–9.
[46] M.R.O., O.C. 24, pp. 488–9.
[47] Ibid. 25, pp. 504–7.
[48] e.g. M.R.O., M.B. 31, p. 285; 52, pp. 150–1, 158.
[49] Ibid. 31, pp. 341–58; Southall Bor. Libr., *News and Views* (St. Bernard's Hosp. Staff Mag.), Christmas 1953, pp. 2–6; G. Gibbon and R. W. Bell, *Hist. of the L.C.C. 1889–1939*, 344–5.
[50] File in M.R.O.
[51] M.R.O., M.B. 81, p. 55.
[52] Ex inf. the Group Secretary, St. Bernard's Hosp.
[53] Ex inf. the Group Secretary.
[54] M.R.O., Acc. 405/16/4; Pigot, *Gen. Dir.* (1824).
[55] *Kelly's Dir. Mdx.* (1855).
[56] *Census*, 1861–81.
[57] S. G. Short, *Southall and its Environs* (1910), 14.
[58] Ibid.; *Kelly's Dir. Mdx.* (1890); M.R.O., Acc. 402/2.
[59] *Census*, 1861–1911.
[60] Peacock, *G.W. Suburban Services*, 4–6, 12.
[61] M.R.O., Hist. Notes, 29/11/50.
[62] *Trans. Southall Local Hist. Soc.* i. 40.
[63] *Rep. Royal Com. on Lond. Traffic: Mins. of Evidence* [Cd. 2751], H.C. pp. 724, 907 (1906), xl.
[64] *Trans. Southall Local Hist. Soc.* i. 41.
[65] M.R.O., *Reps. of Local Inqs.* (1889–97), 355–6, 487.
[66] M.R.O., *Cnty. Development Plan* (1951), 74.
[67] *Home Cnties. Mag.* vi. 299.
[68] See plate facing p. 7.
[69] M.R.O., G.O.C., vol. 83/73.
[70] O.S. Maps 1/2,500, Mdx. xv. 6, 7, 10, 11, 14, 15; xx. 20 (1895–6 and 1914 edns.); M.R.O., Acc. 405/5.
[71] Char. Com. files.
[72] Ibid.

also built up. In Southall Green. Hillary Road and the east end of Havelock Road were developed, and there was also much building immediately north of Norwood Green.[73] By 1939 the local authority had erected 1,119 houses, and between 1945 and 1958 another 1,003 permanent dwellings were built.[74] In 1944 the overcrowding and congestion of Southall was described as 'acute' and no more industrial development was recommended.[75] Another industrial site was planned in 1951. Redevelopment was needed by 1951 for the area west of King Street and north of Western Road, principally for residential purposes and to provide open spaces.[76] Industry was almost wholly concentrated around Southall and Southall Green, while Norwood Green remained a comparatively open space, with Osterley Park extending on its eastern side. North of Uxbridge Road and east of Dormer's Wells Lane the course of the West Middlesex Golf Club was laid out in 1890.[77]

There are references to four inns at Northcott in the mid 17th century: the 'Harrow', the 'Walnut Tree', the 'Angel', and the 'Red Lion'.[78] The 'Angel' still stood in 1715,[79] while there has been a 'Red Lion' in Northcott or Southall ever since. The 'Plough' is probably the oldest inn in Norwood and incorporates a timber-framed building of the 17th century or earlier. There were eight inns in the parish in 1821.[80] In 1899 there is a reference to a house at Southall Green which was once called the 'Plough', afterwards the 'King's Head', and finally the 'King of Prussia', which was its name in 1814.[81]

Before the mid 16th century no population figures are available for Norwood and Southall, as these were included under the manor of Hayes.[82] In 1547 there were 140 communicants in the precinct of Norwood,[83] and 137 adult males took the protestation oath in 1642.[84] In 1653 the poor-rate was assessed on 59 people in Norwood.[85] Eleven years later 54 houses were charged to hearth tax and 38 were exempted.[86] In 1673 the poor-rate was levied on 32 people at Norwood and on 24 each at Northcott and Southall,[87] while hearth tax was rated on 40 houses at Norwood, 29 at Northcott, and 27 at Southall.[88] In 1801 the population numbered 697. During the remainder of the century the numbers rose steadily. The increase from 1,320 people in 1831 to 2,385 in 1841 is attributable in part to the opening of the Hanwell lunatic asylum, since by 1841 it contained 1,005 inmates. An increase in the population of nearly 2,000 between 1851 and 1861 was partly caused by the establishment of the St. Marylebone parochial school,[89] and

later increases followed the enlargement of the asylum and the spread of brick-making. The sudden rise from 7,896 in 1881 to 13,200 in 1901 was said to be a direct result of the opening of tramways along Uxbridge Road. During the earlier 20th century industrial development caused the population to leap upwards to 30,165 in 1921 and to 55,896 by 1951, although in 1961 it had fallen to 52,983.[90] Unlike many Middlesex councils, Southall Borough in 1948 reckoned that insured workers accounted for as much as 42·7 per cent. of its population.[91]

Many Commonwealth immigrants have been attracted to Southall by its light industries. Sikhs, who began to settle in 1953,[94] accounted for most of the 2,000 immigrants recorded in 1961. Their number rose shortly before the enforcement of the Commonwealth Immigrants Act of 1962 and was afterwards increased by arrivals from other parts of the United Kingdom.[93] In 1963, when racial tension was causing concern, it was thought that there were some 8,000 immigrants in Southall,[94] and by 1967 the Sikh community was estimated to number about 10,000.[95]

Norwood and Southall have had few well-known residents, apart from those mentioned elsewhere in this article. William Leybourn, the 17th-century mathematician and compiler of the earliest English ready-reckoner, settled at Northcott;[96] Josiah Wedgwood is said to have owned Norwood Court;[97] and the artist and book illustrator Henry Rountree, who died in 1950, lived for a time in Southall.[98]

MANORS. In 1212 William of Southall (*de Suhalle*) held a knight's fee in Southall of the Archbishop of Canterbury.[99] This was probably the origin of the manor of *SOUTHALL*. Alice of Southall conveyed some property in 1223[1] and in 1243 she paid scutage on a knight's fee in Hayes after a dispute over payment with the archbishop's bailiff at Harrow.[2] Harrow, Hayes, and other archiepiscopal manors were frequently organized as one unit.[3] In 1244 Alice conveyed her fee to William of Cranford, although she retained a life interest.[4] In 1245 and 1246 William acquired other land from Thomas of Newark and Matthew de la Wyke,[5] and in 1247 conveyed 70 a. in Southall to Thomas de Castre, who had bought other property in Southall in the same year.[6] Thomas sold a house, about 76 a., and 49s. rent in Southall to Robert Maynard in 1250.[7] This property probably passed by 1262 to Lawrence del Brok or Brook, who held at least 2 carucates in Southall which were to pass after his death to William del Brok.[8] The manor

[73] O.S. Maps 1/2,500, Mdx. xv. 6, 7, 10, 11, 14, 15; xx. 20 (1934–5 edn.).
[74] *Southall Official Handbk.* 22.
[75] Abercrombie, *Greater Lond. Plan* (1944), 148–9.
[76] M.R.O., *Cnty. Development Plan* (1951), 62.
[77] *V.C.H. Mdx.* ii. 281.
[78] M.R.O., Acc. 180/76.
[79] Southall Bor. Libr., Norwood Poor-rate Bk., 1687–1720.
[80] Southall Bor. Libr., Norwood Valuation (1821).
[81] M.R.O., Acc. 180/12, p. 170; Hayes Incl. Award and Map.
[82] For Hayes see p. 25.   [83] E 301/34/146.
[84] Hse. of Lords., Mdx. Protestation Rets.
[85] Southall Bor. Libr., Norwood Poor-rate Ass. and Disbursement Bk., 1653–86.
[86] M.R.O., H.T. 6.
[87] Southall Bor. Libr., Norwood Poor-rate Ass. and Disbursement Bk., 1653–86.
[88] M.R.O., H.T. 55.

[89] Kirwan, *Southall*, 46; see below, p. 54.
[90] *Census*, 1801–1961; *Rep. Royal Com. on Lond. Traffic: Mins. of Evidence* [Cd. 2751], H.C. p. 907 (1906), xl.
[91] M.R.O., County Development Plan (1951), 50.
[92] Ex inf. the President of the Sikh temple.
[93] Kirwan, *Southall*, 49.
[94] *The Times*, 10 Sept. 1963.
[95] Ex inf. the President of the Sikh temple.
[96] Kirwan, op.cit. 27.
[97] Short, *Southall*, 29.
[98] Kirwan, op.cit. 50.
[99] *Red Bk. of Exch.* (Rolls Ser.), ii. 471, 726.
[1] C.P. 25(1)/146/8/99.
[2] *Bk. of Fees*, ii. 897, 899.
[3] See p. 31.
[4] C.P. 25(1)/147/14/238.
[5] C.P. 25(1)/147/14/244; /147/15/271.
[6] C.P. 25(1)/147/15/273; /147/16/276.
[7] C.P. 25(1)/147/16/298.
[8] C.P. 25(1)/147/21/420; /147/24/498.

of Southall is first mentioned *eo nomine* in a lease of 1319 when it was the property of Roger, son of William del Brok.[9] In 1324 Roger del Brok conveyed the manor to John de Stonore, subject to a life interest granted by Roger de Bloxham[10] in 1319. Stonore evidently disposed of his interest to Bloxham, as in 1325 the succession to the manor was determined to fall to John and Robert, the sons of John de Bloxham.[11] In 1336 William, the son of Robert Hykeman of Bloxham (Oxon.), probably the Robert de Bloxham of 1325, granted all his rights in the manor of Southall to John Charlton, a London merchant.[12] In 1339 Thomas de Bloxham, a clerk, conveyed his interest in the manor to John Charlton, reserving a house and 26 a.[13] Robert de Bereford, son of John de Bloxham, finally granted the manor to Charlton in 1344.[14] Associated with Charlton in these and subsequent conveyances was Nicholas Shorediche, who had married Charlton's daughter Juette. Their heirs were to succeed, failing any issue to Charlton.[15] In 1361 Southall manor was in the hands of Sir Richard de Stanley and his wife Juette, who was almost certainly the widow of Nicholas Shorediche. At the same date members of a Bloxham family were still renouncing some rights in the manor.[16]

A grant of the manor of Southall, together with the manor of Poplar and lands in Cambridgeshire, in 1368 by Sir William Pulteneye to Nicholas de Louthe and 6 others[17] appears to have been a settlement of some kind, as in 1433 Robert and Margaret Shorediche were still in possession of the manor.[18] It was finally sold by Robert Shorediche in 1496 to Edward Cheeseman (d. 1510). The estate was then confirmed by Robert's son George Shorediche to Robert, son of Edward Cheeseman.[19] A quarter part of the manor appears to have been alienated, as in 1519 Elizabeth Godstone conveyed it without licence to John Makin,[20] but in 1547 Robert Cheeseman died holding both the manor of Southall and that of Norwood, which together passed to his daughter Anne and her husband Francis Chamberlain.[21]

Practically nothing is known of the earlier history of the manor of *NORWOOD*. It is first mentioned in 1481 when John Peke, Master of the London Ironmongers' Company, held a court for Norwood. In 1484 Thomas Grafton and others held a court for the manor and when Edward Cheeseman died in 1510 he was seised of the estate.[22] Robert Cheeseman held it at his death in 1547 when it passed with Southall to Anne and Francis Chamberlain, and thereafter, save on the death of Anne, Lady Dacre,[23] it descended with Southall.

In 1547 both manors were held from Sir Edward North and his manor of Hayes by Anne and Francis

Chamberlain.[24] Their son, Robert Chamberlain, sold the manors in 1578 to Gregory Fiennes, Lord Dacre, and his wife Anne.[25] Dacre died in 1594 and his widow in the following year, when 38 a. of Norwood were sold to Francis Awsiter of Southall by Anne's executors.[26] In 1602 they sold the manor of Norwood to Awsiter, and two months later he bought the manor of Southall from Gregory's sister and heir Margaret, Lady Dacre, and her husband Sampson Leonard.[27] Francis died in 1627 and was succeeded by his son Richard Awsiter. The manor was then said to be held of the manor of Dudley, Lord North, in Harrow.[28] The Awsiter family held the manors until 1754 when John Awsiter, who was in financial difficulties, sold both of them to Agatha Child of Osterley, the widow of Samuel Child.[29] In 1757 Agatha settled them on her son Francis Child,[30] on whose death they passed to Robert Child. Thereafter the descent of both manors follows that of Hayes manor, which passed in turn to the Earl of Jersey and the families of Blencowe and Mills.[31]

The manor-house on Southall Green was built or rebuilt by Richard Awsiter in 1587. The house of this date is a timber-framed structure consisting of a central hall range of two stories flanked by gabled cross-wings of unequal width. Projecting from the hall range on the entrance or west front are a two-storied porch and a two-storied bay window, both surmounted by gables. The front is of close-studded timbering, much restored. A north-east wing was added to the house in the early 17th century and part of its north front with twin gables and restored decorative framing can still be recognized. This wing was extended westward in the 18th century, the extension being later faced with imitation timbering. There are many 19th- and 20th-century alterations to the house, particularly at the rear, but two original chimneys have survived. The interior contains fireplaces and panelling of the late 16th and early 17th centuries.[32] The house was not included in the sale of the manors to Mrs. Child in 1754, but by 1816 it was unoccupied and decaying.[33] By 1821 the house, together with the remaining Awsiter estate, had been bought by William Welch,[34] and in 1847–8 it was extensively restored.[35] The house was again restored in the 1920s when it had been acquired by the Southall-Norwood U.D.C.,[36] and in 1961 it was occupied by the Public Health and Infant Welfare departments of Southall Borough Council.

The manor-house of Norwood on Frogmore Green is first mentioned in 1754.[37] It may have been so styled because John Awsiter had retained the Southall manor-house in his hands after the sale of the manors. A building called the Manor Farmhouse is marked on the inclosure map on the west

9 M.R.O., Acc. 435/ED. 16. This document is a 16th-cent. abstract of title to Southall manor. In the following descent reference has been given, where possible to conveyances of contemporary date.
10 C.P. 25(1)/149/51/318.
11 C.P. 25(1)/149/52/327.
12 W.A.M., 22798.
13 C.P. 25(1)/150/57/125.
14 C.P. 25(1)/150/60/178.
15 *Cal. Close*, 1346–9, 596–7.
16 C.P. 25(1)/150/68/391.
17 E 326/B 4908.   18 M.R.O., Acc. 436/11(2.)
19 M.R.O., Acc. 435/ED. 16, ff. 66v–68; see also Lambeth Palace, Estate MS. 478.
20 *L. & P. Hen.*, VIII, iii (1) p. 181.
21 M.R.O., Acc. 436/11(1).

22 Lysons, *Environs of Lond.* iii. 320–1.
23 See below.
24 M.R.O., Acc. 436/11(1).
25 M.R.O., Acc. 435/ED. 16, f. 12.
26 M.R.O., Acc. 436/11(1).
27 Ibid.
28 C 142/425/45.
29 M.R.O., Acc. 436/8(3).
30 Ibid./8(2).   31 See p. 26.
32 A detailed architectural description is given in Hist. Mon. Com. *Mdx.* 99–100: the date is on the building.
33 Brewer, *Beauties of Eng. and Wales*, x (5), 609.
34 Southall Bor. Libr., Norwood Valuation (1821).
35 Short, *Southall*, 27.
36 *Southall-Norwood and Hayes Official Guide* (1928), 22.
37 M.R.O., Acc. 436/8(3).

side of Norwood Road, approximately on the site of the present police station.[38] In 1821 the manor-house was owned by the Earl of Jersey and was occupied by Thomas Walton.[39] It is not mentioned again and had been demolished by the mid 19th century.[40]

The manor of *DORMAN'S WELL* seems to have developed in the late 16th and 17th centuries from the house and estate of Gregory Fiennes, Lord Dacre. It is said to have taken its name from the medicinal chalybeate springs in the neighbourhood.[41] A Ralph Dorman is mentioned in 1294[42] but nothing further is known of the family. In the early 16th century the Archbishop of Canterbury claimed some lands as part of Hayes manor from Thomas Burbage, probably a member of the Cowley and Hayes Park Hall family.[43] Among these was a house called Dormans, later called Burnt House, together with 21 a.; the archbishop claimed that the title deeds went back to 1401–2.[44] In 1554, however, the land belonging to this house was said to be in Botwell fields,[45] so it may have been unconnected with Dorman's Well. At all events the large house called Dorman's Well was in the possession of Robert Cheeseman on his death in 1547.[46] Cheeseman left the house or 'great hall' to Alice his relict as long as she remained a widow. The house descended as the manor of Southall, and became the seat of Lord and Lady Dacre, who had an inclosed park surrounding the house.[47] It was devised by Anne, Lady Dacre, together with Norwood, to Sir Edward Fenner and her other executors and when Fenner died in 1612 he was found to hold for his life the house called Burnt House.[48] Thereafter Dorman's Well followed the same descent as Norwood manor. In 1770 the land comprising Dorman's Well Farm, amounting to nearly 108 a., was principally arable.[49] By 1816 it was described merely as a farm.[50] There is no indication that the estate was styled a manor before the late 18th century.[51] In the early 16th century it probably formed the manor-house and demesne of Southall manor, and perhaps adopted the style of a manor after Southall manor-house, built by the Awsiters, had become divorced from its manor. There was a chapel, possibly a domestic one, at Dorman's Well in 1547.[52]

ECONOMIC AND SOCIAL HISTORY. Little is known of the value of the manors. In 1324 Southall manor was conveyed to John de Stonore with a rent of 14s. in Harrow,[53] and in 1433 the manor was said to consist of a house, a mill, 360 a., and 100s. rents in Hayes, Southall, Northcott, and Harrow.[54] The

same figures are given in 1510,[55] but in 1547, on the death of Robert Cheeseman, the manors of Southall and Norwood together contained 13 houses, 20 cottages, and 2,200 a.[56] It is possible that the Dorman's Well estate formed the demesne of Southall manor in the later 16th century;[57] 80 a. were expressly included in the sale to Agatha Child in 1754,[58] and 208 a. and a house in the settlement on Francis Child in 1757.[59]

Before the 16th century the economic identity of Norwood was indistinguishable from that of Hayes,[60] although there is a mention of Southall East Field in 1387.[61] In 1553 land in both Northcott and Southall hamlets and in their open fields was held customarily of Hayes manor,[62] and later in the century orders of the court were made expressly for Norwood. The cottagers were stinted at two cows or a cow and a horse on the common fields,[63] and cattle were not to be allowed on to the fields before July. Wheat was grown in Northcott,[64] and at least some sheep were kept.[65] In 1598 there were four open fields around Southall, North and South fields both being over 200 a., and East and Middle fields being over 100 a. Northcott West and Middle fields were both over 100 a., but the survey breaks off in the middle of the description of Norwood fields.[66] In the early 17th century peas and beans were grown in the precinct,[67] and sheep were stinted at the rate of 3 for every 2 a. of fallow.[68] A survey of c. 1657 shows that 899 a. lay in the open fields, of which all but 218 a. were in Southall open fields.[69] In the late 18th century the rotation of crops in the open fields was fallow, wheat, and barley or oats and clover, and in the inclosures it was wheat, barley and clover, and turnips.[70] Four years later the recommended rotation was wheat, beans, and peas; the wheat crop was said to be especially good as it was grown only once in 3 years.[71] At the end of the 18th century the precinct of Norwood was predominantly arable. The proportions then were: arable 1,354 a., meadow 981 a., waste 25 a.[72]

By c. 1657 there were 875 a. of inclosures in the precinct,[73] and inclosure continued to take place. Norwood was inclosed with Hayes under an Act of 1809 by an award of 1814, when 8 open fields amounting to well under 1,000 a. were inclosed. Nearly all the southern half of the precinct was in the hands of the Earl of Jersey, who owned over 966 a. Thomas Parker owned 158 a., John Brett owned 147 a. centred on Waxlow Farm, but the descendant of the lords of the manor, Robert Awsiter, owned only 58 a.[74] In 1821 there were 4 farms in the Southall Green area, cultivating between them 679 a.,

[38] M.R.O., Hayes Incl. Map.
[39] Southall Bor. Libr., Norwood Valuation (1821).
[40] O.S. Map 1/2,500, Mdx. xv. 14 (1865 edn.).
[41] Short, *Southall*, 17.
[42] J.I. 1/544, m. 52.
[43] See *V.C.H. Mdx.* iii. 173 and above, p. 27.
[44] Sta. Cha. 8/8/78.
[45] Ibid. 4/10/28.
[46] M.R.O., Acc. 436/11(1).
[47] J. Norden, *Speculum Britanniae*, pt. i (1593), 18.
[48] M.R.O., Acc. 401/8, m. 23.
[49] M.R.O., Acc. 264/123.
[50] M.R.O., Hayes Incl. Award and Map.
[51] M.R.O., Acc. 264/123; Lysons, *Environs of Lond.* iii. 322.
[52] M.R.O., Acc. 436/11(1).
[53] C.P. 25(1)/149/51/318.
[54] M.R.O., Acc. 436/11(2).
[55] M.R.O., Acc. 435/ED. 16, f. 14.
[56] M.R.O., Acc. 436/11(1).
[57] See below.
[58] M.R.O., Acc. 436/8(3).
[59] Ibid. /8(2).
[60] The medieval agric. of Hayes is discussed on p. 29.
[61] M.R.O., Acc. 401/1, m. 13.
[62] M.R.O., Acc. 76/222a, m. 20d.
[63] M.R.O., Acc. 401/7, m. 3d.
[64] Ibid. m. 17.
[65] Ibid. m. 7d.
[66] B.M. Add. MS. 24812.
[67] Sta. Cha. 8/41/18.
[68] M.R.O., Acc. 401/8, m. 20.
[69] M.R.O., Acc. 180/76–77.
[70] Foot, *Agric. of Mdx.* 11.
[71] Middleton, *View of Agric. of Mdx.* 151.
[72] Lysons, *Environs of Lond.* iii. 320 sqq.
[73] M.R.O., Acc. 180/76–77.
[74] M.R.O., Hayes Incl. Award and Map.

most of which was arable. There were no farms in the Norwood area.[75] Wheat for Uxbridge market was the main crop grown in the 1830s.[76] By 1842 the area around Norwood was said to be almost entirely pasture, with 180 cattle and 650 sheep; 545 a. produced hay; and of the remainder of the precinct 669 a. were arable, a third of which produced wheat. Other crops grown over a comparatively small acreage were beans, turnips, potatoes, oats, barley, mangel-wurzels, clover, tares, peas, and rye; these accounted for the remainder of the arable land. At this time there was one farm of over 250 a. which permanently employed 14 men, but there was a 'strong prejudice' against the use of modern farming implements due to a 'conscientious though mistaken solicitude' for the labourers' welfare.[77] In the 1860s there were 737 a. of arable to 1,085 a. of pasture out of a total parish acreage of over 2,460.[78] Throughout the 19th century there were market gardens in Norwood, and occasionally one in Southall. There were three market gardens at Top Lock in 1912, and one nurseryman was there in 1922.[79] Fruit was also grown to supply local jam factories.[80]

It is probable that the mill on the manor of Hayes in 1086, which was then valued at 4s., lay in Norwood,[81] but there is no further reference to a mill there until 1578 when a water-mill was leased out by Robert Chamberlain, the lord of the manor.[82] In 1596 the executors of Anne, Lady Dacre, reserved to themselves a water-mill and garden in Norwood and a windmill and one acre, both copyhold of Norwood manor.[83] There was still a mill in Norwood in 1611,[84] and in 1673 an overshot mill was said to be situated at Northcott. A Mr. Hamton owned or leased the mills in 1676,[85] and between 1680 and 1720 various millers were in possession. In 1716 the overshot mill came into the possession of Sir George Cooke, the future lord of the manor of Hayes;[86] this and the windmill, both corn mills, were offered for sale with the other Cooke property in 1770,[87] and in 1800 the overshot mill still comprised part of the manorial estate.[88] At that date it stood, together with a house and other property, at Dorman's Well.[89] The overshot mill, comprising a mill, house, mill-pond, and land, was owned by the Earl of Jersey in 1821,[90] and in the 1860s stood, as before, on Windmill Lane at Dorman's Well. Both mills were then flour mills.[91] A miller at Norwood is mentioned in 1866,[92] but by the end of the century the overshot mill had been converted into Mill Farm.[93] In 1912

the old water-mill on Windmill Lane was called Old Greenford mill, and although most of the machinery had disappeared, the wheelhouse and some of the old mill-stones still survived. The front premises then contained a baker's shop.[94] The site in 1961 was covered by the West Middlesex Golf Course.

There was a mill on the manor of Southall by 1433.[95] It was still there in 1496,[96] and may have been the windmill reserved to Lady Dacre's executors in the lease of 1596,[97] since in a conveyance of Southall manor in 1597 no mill is mentioned.[98] The corn windmill was included in the attempted sale in 1770,[99] and a windmill and Windmill Farm formed part of the Osterley estate in 1806.[1] Presumably the windmill was the one which Turner painted in 1806; it stood by the Grand Junction Canal[2] and was still there in 1821.[3] In the 1860s, however, a windmill seems to have stood in Windmill Lane at Dorman's Well, slightly to the north and on the opposite side of the road from the overshot mill. It had disappeared by the end of the century although its site is marked by an Ordnance Survey triangulation station.[4] Rocque's map of 1754 shows a mill standing on a small stream running through Osterley Park, on the southern boundary of Norwood parish, between Windmill Lane and the stream's confluence with the Brent.[5] There is no other record of a mill here, and as the overshot mill is not marked, he may possibly have confused its position. In the 1860s the Norwood Flour Mill stood on the north bank of the Grand Junction Canal immediately west of the bridge on Norwood Road.[6] It survived as a steam flour mill until about 1900,[7] and in 1906 was taken over by George Haigh as a plaster-moulding picture-frame factory. Haigh and Sons Ltd. still occupied the mill in 1961.[8]

In 1698 William III granted a Wednesday cattle market and two fairs a year to a local landowner, Francis Merrick of Southall. The fairs were for the exchange of horses, cattle, and grain.[9] The market was first rated in 1705,[10] and appears to have remained in the Merrick family until the early 19th century. In 1805 William Welch bought a lease of the market and built a market-place for showing the cattle.[11] The market-place occupied 3 a. at Southall in 1806[12] and in 1816 was said to be inferior only to Smithfield for the sale of fat cattle.[13] By 1843 the market had increased the value of the neighbouring land which was used for grazing. The coming of the Great Western Railway, however, caused much local

[75] Southall Bor. Libr. Norwood Valuation (1821).
[76] *Rep. Poor Law Com. App. B*(2), H.C. 44, pp. 166 *f–k* (1834), xxxv-vi; *Rep. Cttee. on Agric.: Mins. of Evidence*, H.C. 464, pp. 165–71 (1837), v.
[77] H. Tremenheere, 'Agric. and Educ. Statistics of several pars. in Mdx.', *Jnl. Stat. Soc. of Lond.* (1843), vi. 120–2.
[78] O.S. Area Bk.
[79] *Kelly's Dir. Mdx.* (1845–1922).
[80] M.R.O., County Development Plan (1951), 45.
[81] *V.C.H. Mdx.* i. 119.
[82] M.R.O., Acc. 435/ED. 16, f. 46.
[83] M.R.O., Acc. 436/11(2).
[84] M.R.O., Cal. Mdx. Recs. vi. 176.
[85] Southall Bor. Libr., Norwood Poor-rate Ass. and Disbursement Bk. 1653–86.
[86] Ibid. 1687–1720.
[87] M.R.O., Acc. 264/123.
[88] M.R.O., Acc. 436/16.
[89] M.R.O., Acc. 397/19.
[90] Southall Bor. Libr., Norwood Valuation (1821).
[91] O.S. Map 1/2,500, Mdx. xv. 11 (1865 edn.).
[92] *Kelly's Dir. Mdx.* (1866).

[93] O.S. Map 1/2,500, Mdx. xv. 11 (1896 edn.).
[94] Short, *Southall*, 12–13.
[95] M.R.O., Acc. 436/11(2).
[96] M.R.O., Acc. 435/ED. 16, f. 14; C.P. 25(1)/152/100/ 11 Hen. VII, East.
[97] M.R.O., Acc. 436/11(2).
[98] Ibid. 11(1).
[99] M.R.O., Acc. 264/123.
[1] M.R.O., Acc. 405/16/2.
[2] See frontispiece.
[3] Southall Bor. Libr., Norwood Valuation (1821).
[4] O.S. Map 1/2,500, Mdx. xv. 11 (1865 and 1896 edns.).
[5] Rocque, *Map of Mdx.* (1754).
[6] O.S. Map 1/2,500, Mdx. xv. 14 (1865 edn.).
[7] *Kelly's Dir. Mdx.* (1874–1906), *sub* Southall.
[8] *Southall Official Handbk.* 78–79.
[9] C 66/3398.
[10] Southall Bor. Libr., Norwood Poor-rate Ass. and Disbursement Bk., 1687–1720.
[11] Brewer, *Beauties of Eng. and Wales*, x(5), 608–9.
[12] M.R.O., Acc. 405/16/2.
[13] Brewer, op. cit. x(5), 608–9.

discontent, as it forced down the market prices by introducing West Country sheep and cattle.[14] The market further declined during the 1850s, and in 1860 a Bill, later abandoned, to establish a new cattle market at Southall was introduced in Parliament.[15] By 1869 the market had been transformed into a general, in place of a stock, market and was still losing ground to the London markets.[16] Cattle were still sold there in 1876,[17] but in 1910 Southall market was again said to be declining.[18] Leases of the market and market-house survive for the later 19th century.[19] In 1880 the premises covered just over 3 a. and were let together with another 69 a.[20] In 1929 a weekly livestock, poultry, corn, straw, and potato auction was held at Southall. This handled about 12,000 head a year, mainly of pigs. At that date it was the only livestock and poultry market in the county, and was held in both covered and uncovered premises by the owners, Steel Bros. of Southall. There was also a daily market for general retail produce, which was owned by S. Green of New Southall market.[21] In 1961 the Wednesday market was still held for horses, cattle, pigs, carts, and harness, and a general produce, shopping, and stall market was held every Saturday.

As in Hayes the first industry to make its appearance in Norwood was brick-making. As early as 1697 a London tiler and bricklayer, Robert Browne, had bought 3 a. in Bulls Bridge Field, Hayes, and in South Field, Norwood.[22] That the brick-making industry grew in the 19th century was due to the opening of the Grand Junction Canal in 1796 and of the Paddington Canal five years later.[23] The industry was slightly later in developing in Norwood than in Hayes and in 1821 there was only one small brick-field near Wolf Bridge.[24] In 1826 John Nash, the architect and builder, was licensed by Lord Jersey to dig brickearth in East Field,[25] and apparently he also made his bricks in Norwood. These are said to have been too rough and uneven for anything but thick walls. Nash supplied a great number of bricks for Buckingham Palace and may have sent some from Norwood.[26] In 1859 a Holborn builder developed a 14-acre brick-field in Norwood, paying Lord Jersey a royalty of 1s. 6d. on every thousand bricks over 2,666,666 a year. He also erected labourers' cottages on the site and built a dock on the canal.[27] In the 1860s the St. John's parochial school at Southall Green drew most of its pupils from the brick-makers. The school numbers fluctuated,[28] which may indicate a rapid turn-over of labour, and the speedy working-out of the brick-fields. The Southall Brick Co. was in existence by 1874 and three other brick-making firms were

centred on the Green in Southall.[29] At the end of the 19th century a 28-acre brick-field was opened in North Road, Southall, by Thomas Watson and between 1899 and 1901 this produced well over 2 million bricks a year.[30] A site for a brick-field in Havelock Road was advertised for sale in 1903,[31] and a brick-field behind Tudor Road was causing such smells in 1906 that there were complaints at a council meeting.[32] A new brick-field in North Road was let as late as 1910 at 2s. a thousand bricks,[33] and the East Acton Brick Co. held property at least until 1926.[34] In the late 19th century some gravel was also extracted.[35]

Norwood and Southall undoubtedly developed into a primarily industrial area because of their rail and canal communications. Both canals were open by 1802 and by 1816 there was already a large wharf with an extensive trade at Bull's Bridge,[36] where the Paddington and Grand Junction canals divide. The canal company owned 54 a. in 1821, together with warehouses and wharfs, and at least one factory, producing vitriol, was situated on the canal bank.[37] Industry did not immediately follow the opening of Southall railway station.[38] By the 1860s, however, as well as two brick-works and the vitriol factory, there was an oil-works by the canal.[39] The first gas-works was built near the canal by a private company in 1865. This was dismantled in 1869 by the Brentford Gas Co., which built on the site of the present gas-works immediately north of the railway. Most of the old installations were replaced in 1929–30.[40] In 1877 the pottery firm of R. W. Martin moved to a derelict soap factory on the canal bank at Southall. The four Martin brothers built a kiln and produced their salt-glaze pottery there until the First World War. The last brother died in 1923 and a later attempt to revive the business met with no success. The kiln was destroyed by fire in 1942.[41] In 1961 the Southall Library had a fine collection of Martin ware.

In the late 19th century the oil-works was turned over to chemicals and extended.[42] In 1893 a vast margarine factory on Margarine Road, afterwards Bridge Road, was opened by a Dane, Otto Mönsted. This factory was served by new railway sidings and a branch to the canal.[43] It later came under the Unilever group, and in 1961 the buildings were used by Thomas Wall's, a member of the Unilever combine, for storage.[44] In 1894 a factory to employ 300 people was about to be built[45] and a firm making picture-frame mouldings was opened in Norwood Mill in 1906.[46] By 1914 there were also factories producing jam, chemicals, wallpaper, paints, and telephones, as well as an engineering works. All these

[14] Jnl. Stat. Soc. of Lond. (1843), vi. 122.
[15] L.J. xcii. 45, 82.
[16] J. C. Clutterbuck, 'Farming of Mdx.', Jnl. R. Agric. Soc. (1869), Ser. 2, v. 26.
[17] Thorne, Environs of Lond. 559.
[18] Short, Southall, 19.
[19] M.R.O., Acc. 405/2.
[20] Ibid. /17/5.
[21] Markets and Fairs in Eng. and Wales (Min. of Agric. and Fisheries), iv. 69.
[22] M.R.O., E.M.C. 53/deeds 60–62.
[23] V.C.H. Mdx. ii. 123.
[24] Southall Bor. Libr., Norwood Valuation (1821).
[25] M.R.O., Acc. 180/174.
[26] J. Summerson, John Nash, 264.
[27] M.R.O., Acc. 405/1.
[28] Ed. 7/87.
[29] Kelly's Dir. Mdx. (1874).

[30] M.R.O., Acc. 405/1.
[31] Ibid. /5.
[32] Ibid. /2: cutting from The Gazette, 3 Mar. 1906.
[33] M.R.O., Acc. 405/1.
[34] Kelly's Dir. Mdx. (1926).
[35] M.R.O., Acc. 405/3–4.
[36] Brewer, Beauties of Eng. and Wales, x(5), 607–8.
[37] Southall Bor. Libr., Norwood Valuation (1821).
[38] See pp. 41–42.
[39] O.S. Map 1/2,500, Mdx. xv. 14 (1865 edn.).
[40] Trans. Southall Local Hist. Soc. i. 52–53.
[41] Country Life, 23 Mar. 1961, pp. 653–4; Kirwan Southall, 38–39.
[42] O.S. Map 1/2,500, Mdx. xv. 14 (1895 edn.).
[43] Kirwan, op. cit., 41.
[44] Ex inf. Unilever Ltd.
[45] M.R.O., Reps. of Local Inqs. (1889–97), 358.
[46] Southall Official Handbk. 77–78.

were situated on Rubastic Road, Scott's Road, and Johnson Street.[47] Kearley & Tonge opened their jam and marmalade factory on Brent Road in 1913, and later extended their business to include a great number of other foods. In 1961 the labour force numbered about 700, although it had occasionally reached 1,000.[48]

Other large firms which came to Southall after the First World War included the Crown Cork Co. Ltd., making bottle closures, which was established in Southall in 1922. In 1961 the firm had a labour force of about 600.[49] The heavy vehicle construction firm of A.E.C. Ltd. opened its main Southall factory, employing approximately 2,000 people, in 1927. Subsequently the company steadily enlarged its site, which lies off Windmill Lane and between the two railway lines, until in 1961 it employed about 5,000 people and was the largest single employer of labour in Southall. Its products include omnibuses for London Transport and other concerns, coaches, trucks, and lorries of all varieties.[50] The 1930s saw the establishment of two more large firms, that of Taylor Woodrow, the building contractors, in 1930 and of Quaker Oats in 1936. Taylor Woodrow first came to the area with the building of an estate of over 1,000 houses at Grange Park, Hayes, and set up its headquarters in Adrienne Avenue, Southall, on the banks of the Paddington Canal. New buildings were opened on the same site in 1954, 1958, and 1960, and a staff of 1,300 was employed there in 1961.[51] Quaker Oats, producing cereals, pig, and poultry foods, opened its works in 1936 in a building formerly belonging to the Maypole Dairy Co. Expansion after 1945 included a 20,000-ton grain silo, the grain being brought from the docks mainly by canal.[52] Other large firms in the borough include the building and engineering contractors, George Wimpey & Co. Ltd., who have a repair and maintenance depot on Lancaster Road, Southall, where over 400 people are employed,[53] and G. C. Cross & Co. Ltd., a sand, gravel, and building haulage firm which started in 1919 in a yard behind the 'White Hart' in Southall High Street. The firm prospered from work on the Wembley Exhibition of 1924 and moved to larger premises, first in Sussex Road and then to Uxbridge Road. In 1961 it employed over 100 people.[54] Ease of communication by water and rail, rather than by road, attracted many of these firms, most of which are situated along the railway or the canal.

In 1951 industrial premises covered over 228 a. in Southall and 56 per cent. of the employed population was occupied in vehicle and food production, or in the provision of gas, water, and electricity.[55] By 1961 firms owning premises in Southall covered a wide range of products, including paints and lacquers, steel radiators, engineering and electrical equipment (including radios and televisions), photocopying machinery, films for the Independent Television Authority, braille apparatus, packaging materials, and chemical engineering products of pure and commercial acids. There were also timber importers, joiners, sawmills, and building firms.[56]

Three newspapers were started in the late 19th century: the *Southall News*, which was published between 1885 and 1888;[57] the *Southall Guardian*, published between 1894 and 1895 and then incorporated in the *Middlesex and Surrey Express*; and the *Southall-Norwood Gazette*, published between 1894 and 1923, when it was continued as the *West Middlesex Gazette*. Another *Southall News* and the *Southall Post* were both published for the first time in 1954.[58] The Southall Local History Society, which publishes a newsletter, was founded in 1958.[59]

There was a friendly society with 48 members in 1803,[60] and in 1830 the Union Society had its registered meeting place at the 'Red Lion', Southall.[61] A friendly society met at the 'Wolf' at Norwood Green in 1846,[62] and in the 1870s and 1880s at least two masonic lodges were registered in Southall, the Gooch lodge meeting at the Prince Alfred Hotel and the Jersey lodge at the Coffee Tavern.[63] The working men's club in Featherstone Road was open by 1912 and a social club, the Conservative Association, and the Tariff Reform League were all established by 1922.[64] The Southall-Norwood Ratepayers' Association, which was non-political but 'definitely anti-Socialist', existed in 1932[65] and by 1939 had been joined by the Labour Club and Institute on the Broadway.[66] The oldest sports club in the parish is probably the Southall Football Club, which was founded in 1871 and joined the Athenian League in 1919–20.[67] The first football ground was in North Road but since 1906 the club has used its present ground in Western Road.[68] A Norwood cricket eleven played on the Green in 1876,[69] and the Southall Cricket Club was founded in 1887. After various moves from its original ground in Red Lion Fields, opposite the 'Red Lion', the club finally moved to Durdans Park in 1956.[70] There is a reference to the Workmen's Cricket Club, which also played on Norwood Green, in 1894.[71] A lawn tennis club was established by 1898,[72] and the West Middlesex Golf Club in 1890.[73] The Southall Electric Theatre opened in 1910; it was later known as the Gem cinema and, after being rebuilt in 1929, as the Century.[74] The Dominion cinema was opened in 1935[75] and the Odeon in 1936.[76] The greyhound racing stadium in Havelock Road was opened by 1939.[77]

47 O.S. Map 1/2,500, Mdx. xv. 14 (1914 edn.).
48 Ex inf. Kearley & Tonge Ltd.
49 Ex inf. Crown Cork Co. Ltd.
50 Ex inf. A.E.C. Ltd.
51 Ex inf. Taylor Woodrow Services Ltd.
52 Ex inf. Quaker Oats Ltd.
53 Ex inf. Geo. Wimpey & Co. Ltd.
54 Ex inf. G. C. Cross & Co. Ltd.
55 M.R.O., Cnty. Development Plan (1951), 58.
56 *Southall Official Handbk.* (n.d.), 65–79.
57 Kirwan, *Southall*, 40.
58 B.M. Newspaper Catalogue.
59 Southall Local Hist. Soc., *Newsletter* No. 11.
60 *Rets. on Expense and Maintenance of Poor*, H.C. 175, pp. 294–5 (1803–4), demifol. xiii.
61 M.R.O., C.P. Reg. of Socs. i. 3.

62 Ibid. ii. 24.
63 Ibid. v. 51, 321, 322, 329.
64 *Kelly's Dir. Mdx.* (1912–22).
65 *Southall-Norwood Official Guide* (1932), 24.
66 *Southall Official Guide* (1939), 28.
67 Ex inf. Southall F.C.
68 Southall F.C., *Official Handbk.* (1960–1), 5.
69 Thorne, *Environs of Lond.* 452.
70 Ex inf. Southall C.C.
71 M.R.O., Acc. 180/541.
72 *Kelly's Dir. Mdx.* (1898).
73 *V.C.H. Mdx.* ii. 281.
74 *Mdx. Cnty. Times*, 17 Aug. 1957.
75 Southall Bor. Libr., Programme of Opening.
76 Ibid. S.725 C.1.
77 *Southall Official Guide* (1939), 20.

LOCAL GOVERNMENT. A Norwood tithing was amerced by the justices in 1235.[78] According to Lysons courts for Norwood manor were held at the latest from 1481,[79] but even if this was the case the manor was clearly subordinate to that of Hayes.[80]

There seems to have been an independent vestry in Norwood by the mid 17th century, as at this date the poor-rate was levied not only on Norwood, Southall, and Northcott, but also on people residing in Heston, Hanwell, Greenford, and 'other out towns'.[81] The vestry, however, was not expressly mentioned until 1720.[82] In 1642 Norwood had two overseers, two constables, and a churchwarden,[83] but little is known of the local administration until the 19th century. In the late 18th century the poor-rates increased steadily from £252 in 1777 to £417 in 1785.[84] They reached a peak of £850 in 1821.[85] The parish had acquired a workhouse by 1803 when it had 12 inmates.[86] In 1814 the workhouse stood on the north side of what is now Featherstone Road.[87] There were 8 inmates in 1834,[88] but Norwood was included in the Uxbridge Union of 1836 and the workhouse poor were transferred to the union workhouse at Hillingdon. The Norwood vestry always remained an open one.[89] A vestry clerk was first appointed in 1857 because the population had then reached over 2,000.[90]

For the next thirty years little is known of the work of the vestry, which was probably not very active. A school board was formed in 1877,[91] and in 1877 and 1878 plans for water- and gas-works were being put into effect.[92] A Local Government Board order made in 1878 instructed the parish to find a permanent room for the vestry meetings.[93] In 1882 the first drainage proposals were introduced by the rural sanitary authority, but only for the area south of Norwood Green,[94] and in 1883 an Act for providing Norwood with mains water was passed.[95] By 1890 a complete drainage system for Norwood had been carried out and in the same year the parish applied to be created an urban district. At the ensuing inquiry it was found that since 1871 the rateable value of the parish had almost doubled from £22,000 to nearly £41,000, and that more than half of the latter figure was assessed on only 4 properties: the G.W.R. Co.'s line, the Grand Junction Canal, the Brentford Gas Works, and the Hanwell asylum. In addition to the rural sanitary authority and the lighting inspectors, there were 7 other parish bodies: the vestry, the guardians, the overseers, the assessment committee, and the highway, school, and burial boards. The vestry felt that all these bodies needed co-ordinating, and also that the inspector of

nuisances and medical officer of health ought to reside in the parish, as much of their work was within it. The burial board was certainly in existence by 1883. The highway board had 11 members and was responsible for the whole parish; there were about 13 miles of road, of which over 2 miles of Uxbridge Road were repaired by the county. The jurisdiction of the lighting committee did not extend over the whole parish, and to light the remainder would require a second committee.[96]

The Southall-Norwood U.D.C. was set up in 1894 with 14 members and 6 officers: a clerk, treasurer, surveyor, sanitary inspector, medical officer of health, and tax collector.[97] The council offices in the High Street were built in 1897–8.[98] The council proposed to build an isolation hospital in 1900,[99] and in 1904 the sanatorium on North Road, Mount Pleasant, was opened.[1] This later became the Mount Pleasant Hospital. In 1905 the electric lighting orders were confirmed,[2] and in the same year the public library in Osterley Park Road was opened.[3] By 1906 the council was meeting twice a month. It acquired some land in 1906 on which to erect a mortuary,[4] and in 1908 about 14 a. were acquired by the council from Lord Jersey as a recreation ground;[5] in 1924 there were three public open spaces: Southall Park (26 a.), the Recreation Ground (15 a.), and Norwood Green (8 a.).[6] The Recreation Ground, reached from Recreation Road or Tachbrook Road, lies in the ancient parish of Heston, but the area of the urban district and the Norwood civil parish had been extended in 1894 to cover the small part of Heston north of the canal.[7] An open-air swimming pool was built there in 1913 and reconstructed in 1930.[8] In 1924 the number of councillors was increased to eighteen. In 1925 the Southall–Norwood Hospital was first proposed and in 1930 a site on Uxbridge Road, behind Holy Trinity Church, was chosen. This site was later sold, and the hospital was opened in 1935 on its present site at the corner of the Green and Osterley Park Road.[9]

BOROUGH OF SOUTHALL. *Parted fesswise or and vert, two thorn-trees, the upper one proper and the lower or, between two palets wavy argent each charged with another such palet azure*

[Granted 1936]

In 1936 the municipal borough of Southall was formed, its area of jurisdiction being the same as the

[78] J.I. 1/539, m. 9.
[79] Lysons, *Environs of Lond.* iii. 320, quoting deeds communicated by the steward.
[80] See p. 32.
[81] Southall Bor. Libr., Norwood Poor-rate Ass. and Disbursement Bk. 1653–86.
[82] Southall Bor. Libr., Norwood Churchwardens' Acct. Bk. 1676–1744.
[83] Hse. of Lords' Mdx. Protestation Rets.
[84] *Rep. Cttee. on Rets. by Overseers, 1776*, Ser. 1, ix, p. 397; ibid., *1785*, p. 627.
[85] *Rep. Poor Law Com. App.* B(2), H.C. 44, pp. 166 f-k (1834), xxxv-vi.
[86] *Rets. on Expense and Maintenance of Poor*, H.C. 175, pp. 294-5 (1803-4), demi-fol. xiii.
[87] M.R.O., Hayes Incl. Map.
[88] *Rep. Poor Law Com. App.* B(2), H.C. 44, pp. 166 f-k (1834), xxxv-vi.   [89] Ibid.
[90] *Lond. Gaz.* 6 Jan. 1857, p. 77.

[91] Ibid. 17 July 1877, p. 4196.
[92] M.R.O., Deposited Plans, i. 1173; *L.J.* cx. 201-2, 235; cxii. 214, 283.
[93] *Lond. Gaz.* 26 Nov. 1878, pp. 6498-9.
[94] M.R.O., Acc. 405/4.   [95] *L.J.* cxv. 372.
[96] M.R.O., *Reps. of Local Inquiries* (1889-97), 487-95.
[97] *Kelly's Dir. Mdx.* (1898), *sub* Southall.
[98] Foundation stone on building.
[99] Char. Com. file.
[1] Southall Bor. Libr., *Programme of Opening*.
[2] *L.J.* cxxxvii. 163, 223.
[3] *Southall Official Handbk.* 24.
[4] M.R.O., Acc. 405/2.   [5] Ibid.
[6] *Southall-Norwood and Hayes Official Guide* (1924), 10 (copy in B.M.).
[7] *Census*, 1901. For boundary changes, see above, p. 40.
[8] *Southall Official Handbk.* 28.
[9] Southall Bor. Libr., *Programme of Opening*.

old urban district and the ancient parish of Norwood, the only civil parish being that of Norwood.[10] The borough council consisted of 18 members elected from 6 wards;[11] by 1960 membership had increased to 24, consisting of 6 aldermen and 18 councillors.[12] In 1965 Southall Borough was merged with the boroughs of Ealing and Acton to form the new London Borough of Ealing.[13]

CHURCHES. Until 1859 Norwood was ecclesiastically dependent on Hayes,[14] to which in the early 18th century it was said to form a chapel of ease.[15] Although there had been a chapel in Norwood since the 12th century,[16] the first mention of a priest in the precinct of Norwood is of Simon, the chaplain of Southall, in 1394.[17] In 1489 the advowson of the church of Hayes and the chapel of Norwood was vested in the farmer of the Archbishop of Canterbury's manor of Hayes.[18]

In 1520 the position of the Norwood chaplain was clarified in the ordination of Hayes vicarage by Archbishop Warham. The Vicar of Hayes was to be paid an annual stipend of £20 which was considered sufficient to maintain him and to supply the chaplain of Norwood, for which he was made responsible.[19] The appointment of chaplains may have remained in the hands of individual vicars of Hayes for some time, but it seems more likely that the patrons of the vicarage appointed them. Before 1656 Thomas Jennings, the farmer of Hayes rectory, had presented the resident 'preaching minister' of Norwood.[20] As early as 1656 there was a petition for Norwood to be made a parish in its own right, as it was distinct 'in all duties' from Hayes, and in 1775 Norwood curacy was endowed out of Queen Anne's Bounty, thus becoming a perpetual curacy.[21] In 1770 the advowson was declared, with that of Hayes, to be annexed to the lordship of Hayes.[22] In the early 19th century the incumbent, who was described as the curate, undertook all the duties himself.[23] The first new parish to be created in the precinct of Norwood was that of St. John, Southall Green, in 1850.[24] Nine years later Norwood precinct was created a parish separate from that of Hayes.[25] In 1860 Nathaniel Tertius Lawrence and John Hambrough of Hayes possessed the advowson of Norwood, and by 1866 the living was both held by and was in the gift of the Revd. Henry Worsley.[26] In the same year, 1866, the benefice of Norwood was elevated to a rectory.[27] Worsley ceded the advowson

in 1871, when it passed to John Robinson McClean,[28] who presented Donald Stuart McClean.[29] The advowson was held in 1880 by Maria Sophia McClean[30] and in 1890 by A. Henderson,[31] from whom it passed to the rector, James Leonard Macdonald.[32] In 1953 the patron was G. T. O'Neill, of Southend (Essex),[33] whose trustees owned the advowson in 1960.[34]

In 1656 there was only one minister, who received a stipend from Thomas Jennings, the patron, out of the tithes of the precinct. At this date the tithes were worth about £200 a year.[35] In 1770 the tithes, with barns, a rickyard, and a cart house, were worth only £210.[36] The tithes were extinguished by the inclosure award of 1814, when over 276 a. in Norwood were allotted in lieu of tithe to the Rector of Hayes.[37] The Curate of Norwood received just over 7 a. as glebe, nearly 17 a. in lieu of his former £40 stipend, and almost 9 a. as a gratuity to augment his living.[38] In 1815 an attempt to augment the curacy by a private Bill failed for lack of support[39] and in 1821 the glebe was still about 34 a.[40] The living had been augmented by £200 from Queen Anne's Bounty by 1831, and it had also had £210 from private benefactions.[41] In the later 19th century brickearth under the glebe was profitably extracted.[42] In 1961 the glebe consisted mainly of shops and houses in King Street, Southall, and some houses in Rectory and Westerham roads.[43]

It is not known when a house first became attached to the living; none was mentioned in the parliamentary survey of 1656.[44] Between 1657 and 1720 various people paid poor-rate on 'the parsonage' which at that time stood in Northcott.[45] A farmhouse which was bought in the mid 18th century[46] seems to have been the 'vicarage' which stood in 1814 on the site of the present rectory in Tentelow Lane.[47] In 1902 this was described as an 'interesting building in Tudor style, and nicely covered with ivy'.[48] The rectory, as it became, was destroyed by enemy action during the Second World War and, for lack of money, was not rebuilt until 1950-1. A 4-acre meadow at the rear of the house had been acquired earlier in order to prevent building behind the rectory.[49]

All that is known of the incumbents or religious life of the parish is that in the 1950s the patron was asked to appoint a 'Prayer Book Catholic' to the living in order to continue the traditions of the parish.[50]

[10] Census, 1951.
[11] Char. Com. files.
[12] Southall Official Handbk. 17.
[13] Lond. Govt. Act, 1963, c. 33.
[14] For the ecclesiastical hist. of Hayes see p. 33.
[15] Newcourt, Repertorium, i. 640.
[16] For the architectural hist. see below.
[17] M.R.O., Acc. 401/1, m. 29.
[18] Lambeth Palace, MS. E.D. 1218.
[19] Newcourt, Repertorium, i. 639.
[20] Home Cnties. Mag. iii. 32–33.
[21] C. Hodgson, Queen Anne's Bounty, 387.
[22] M.R.O., Acc. 264/123.
[23] Trans. Southall Local Hist. Soc. ii. 29.
[24] For St. John, Southall Green, see below.
[25] Index to Lond. Gaz. 1830–83, p. 1272; Census, 1861.
[26] Hennessy, Novum Repertorium, 354; Kelly's Dir. Mdx. (1866).
[27] Lond. Gaz. 20 Nov. 1866.
[28] Hennessy, Novum Repertorium, 354.
[29] Kelly's Dir. Mdx. (1874).
[30] Hennessy, Novum Repertorium, 354.
[31] Kelly's Dir. Mdx. (1890).

[32] Clergy List (1892).
[33] Par. Recs., P.C.C. Min. Bk. 1938–53.
[34] Crockford (1959–60).
[35] Home Cnties. Mag. iii. 32–33.
[36] M.R.O., Acc. 264/123.
[37] M.R.O., Hayes Incl. Award.
[38] Ibid.
[39] L.J. i. 332a, 384b; see above, p. 34.
[40] Southall Bor. Libr., Norwood Valuation (1821).
[41] Lewis, Topog. Dict. (1831), iii. 427.
[42] Char. Com. files.
[43] Ex inf. the rector.
[44] Home Cnties. Mag. iii. 32–33.
[45] Southall Bor. Libr., Norwood Poor-rate Assessment and Disbursement Bks. 1653–1720. For Northcott see p. 40.
[46] Trans. Southall Local Hist. Soc. ii. 14.
[47] M.R.O., Hayes Incl. Map.
[48] Home Cnties. Mag. iv. 312.
[49] Ex inf. the rector; Par. Recs., P.C.C. Min. Bk. 1938–53.
[50] P.C.C. Min. Bk. 1938–53.

The church of *ST. MARY THE VIRGIN* stands in Tentelow Lane at the corner of Norwood Green, and consists of a chancel, nave, north aisle, north transept, and south-west tower. The exterior owes its appearance almost entirely to 19th-century alterations and additions. The earliest parts of the building are the semicircular west arch and both responds of the north arcade; these date from the 12th century. In the south walls of both nave and chancel are single lancet windows of the 13th century, much restored, and the nave also contains two 14th-century windows. The church is said to have been reconstructed in 1439;[51] the chancel arch, the nave roof of crown-post construction, the south doorway, and several of the windows date from the 15th century, as do the font and a few original timbers in the restored south porch. There was formerly a wooden bell turret above the west end of the nave of which some of the supporting timbers survive.[52] A gallery installed by Francis Awsiter in 1612[53] still existed in 1863,[54] and a new pulpit was erected in 1638 by Christopher Merrick, the uncle of Francis Merrick.[55] The church was restored in 1824,[56] and in 1849 the north arcade is said to have been removed, the roof being propped on iron posts.[57] The arcade piers were probably rebuilt with their present 'Norman' capitals. It may have been at this time that a wider north aisle was built and the shallow north transept added. The church was again restored in 1864. At this or a subsequent restoration the south and east walls were faced externally with flint-work panels and red brick dressings. In 1896 the wooden belfry and spire were removed and the present south-west tower, also faced with flint and brick, was built.[58] The church and churchyard were closed for burials in 1883.[59] Another restoration was debated in 1950 when the tower required repointing and new floors were needed throughout.[60]

In the north-east corner of the chancel is a recessed and canopied tomb of the earlier 16th century, carved with intricate late medieval ornament; it is ascribed to Edward Cheeseman (temp. Henry VII) and his son Robert, with the date 1556, and perhaps served as an Easter sepulchre.[61] A brass (dated 1614) to Francis Awsiter on the south wall of the chancel and one to Matthew Hunsley (dated 1618) on the north wall both include figures. The handsome tomb of John Merrick (d. 1749) incorporates a full-size figure on a sarcophagus and supported by an urn. Four hatchments in the nave are said to come from the old gallery.[62] The registers, which are complete, date from 1654 and there are 6 bells. The pews have been removed and replaced by chairs. In 1961 the sacrament was being reserved in the Lady Chapel in

the north aisle and the stations of the cross had been hung on the walls of the nave.

A chapel of ease to Norwood church, dedicated to *ST. JOHN*, was built and endowed in 1838 at Southall Green by Henry Dobbs, owner of the vitriol factory,[63] and consecrated in 1841.[64] The parish of St. John, formed out of Norwood in 1850,[65] was extended in 1880.[66] The benefice, described in 1866 as a perpetual curacy,[67] received various charitable endowments during the late 19th century.[68] In 1874 the vicarage, as it was now called, was worth £120 a year.[69] In 1960 the patronage was held by the Church Patronage Society.[70] A vicarage-house which stood opposite the church in the 1860s[71] was still there in 1903.[72] The church, built of brown brick in the Gothic style in 1838, stood facing the west side of King Street and consisted of a chancel, nave, north and south aisles, and a small spire, later removed.[73] It was flanked on the north side by the St. John's parochial schools,[74] and in 1961 was being used as a hall for meetings and general parish purposes. The present church of St. John, on the south side of Church Avenue, was built by C. G. Miller in 1910 in the Perpendicular style. The exterior is of red brick with stone facings, and there is a single, small bell turret at the east end of the roof. It consists of a chancel, nave, north and south aisles, and an east chapel in the north aisle. A colonnade of 6 Gothic arches separates the nave from the aisles and there are 6 clerestory windows above. A tablet in the chancel commemorates the founder, John Henry Dobbs (d. 1843).[75] In 1939 a mission hall in Western Road was attached to the church.[76]

In 1874 the London Diocesan Home Mission were said to have 'recently' erected an iron church in Uxbridge Road.[77] This is probably the earliest mention of *HOLY TRINITY*, Uxbridge Road, which in 1881 stood on a site leased from the Earl of Jersey. One of the wardens was William Welch Deloitte,[78] who is commemorated by a tablet in the church as one of its founders. In 1960 the advowson was held by the Church Patronage Society.[79] The present church in Uxbridge Road was built by J. Lee in 1890 of brick, with white stone facings. It consists of a chancel, nave, north and south aisles, south transept, and apsidal baptistery.[80] The interior is of red and yellow brick, the aisles being divided from the nave by an arcade of five arches. There are five 3-light clerestory windows, and the chancel is separated from the nave by a carved wooden rood screen. The living was constituted a perpetual curacy in 1891, and the registers date from the same time.[81] A mission was founded by the church between 1928 and 1930 at Mount Pleasant.[82]

The church of *ST. GEORGE*, Lancaster Road,

[51] Hist. Mon. Com. *Mdx.* 98.
[52] *T.L.M.A.S.* xiv. 308; xviii(2), no. 145; Hist. Mon. Com. *Mdx.* 98–99. See plate facing p. 104.
[53] Plaque in church.
[54] Par. Recs., Sch. Trustees' Min. Bk. 1829–1909.
[55] Southall Bor. Libr., Churchwardens' Acct. Bk. 1676–1744.   [56] *T.L.M.A.S.* xviii(2), no. 145.
[57] J. Sperling, *Ch. Walks in Mdx.* (1849), 55–56.
[58] *T.L.M.A.S.* xviii(2), no. 145; plaque on tower.
[59] *Lond. Gaz.* 13 Nov. 1883.
[60] Par. Recs., P.C.C. Min. Bk. 1938–53.
[61] Sperling, *Ch. Walks.* 55–56.
[62] *T.L.M.A.S.* xviii(2), no. 145.
[63] Kirwan, *Southall,* 36.   [64] *Kelly's Dir. Mdx.* (1845).
[65] *Index to Lond. Gaz. 1830–83,* pp. 1272, 1579; *Census,* 1851.

[66] *Lond. Gaz.* 17 Sept. 1880.
[67] Ibid. 3 July 1866.   [68] Char. Com. files.
[69] *Kelly's Dir. Mdx.* (1874).
[70] *Crockford* (1959–60).
[71] O.S. Map 1/2,500, Mdx. xv. 14 (1865 edn.).
[72] M.R.O., Acc. 405/5.
[73] *Kelly's Dir. Mdx.* (1874).
[74] For the schools see p. 54.
[75] *T.L.M.A.S.* xviii(2), no. 148.
[76] *Southall Official Guide* (1939), 26.
[77] *Kelly's Dir. Mdx.* (1874).
[78] M.R.O., Acc. 405/2.   [79] *Crockford* (1959–60).
[80] *T.L.M.A.S.* xviii(2), no. 146.
[81] Hennessy, *Novum Repertorium,* 355.
[82] *Southall-Norwood and Hayes Official Guide* (1928), 15; (1930), 12.

was built by A. Blomfield in 1906.[83] It is said to have been financed by the sale of the site of the church of St. George, Botolph Lane (City of London).[84] The 17th-century oak pulpit and the organ case of 1753 by R. Bridge are both from this Billingsgate church.[85] In 1960 the patron was alternately the Crown and the Dean and Chapter of St. Paul's.[86] The exterior is of red brick with yellow brick and stone dressings. It consists of a chancel, nave, north and south aisles, a south-east chapel, and a small shingled turret at the west end. The church was altered in 1951. The interior is of red brick with arcades of five bays separating the aisles from the nave. A rood hangs in the chancel arch and the stations of the cross are hung in the aisles. There are six 2-light clerestory windows and six small aisle windows.[87]

Part of a wooden hut in Allenby Road erected out of the London Diocesan Fund in 1935 was set aside as a temporary church accommodating 250 people. The conventional district was known as that of Holy Redeemer, Greenford, and was staffed by a curate from Holy Cross church, Greenford. The parish of Christ the Redeemer, Southall, was formed in 1964 out of parts of the parishes of Greenford and Holy Trinity, Southall, and a detached part of Northolt parish. A permanent church of *CHRIST THE REDEEMER*, replacing the hut, then came into use.[88] In 1965 the Bishop of London was patron of the living.[89]

ROMAN CATHOLICISM. There is no record of Roman Catholicism in Norwood until the parish of St. Anselm, Southall Green, was founded in 1906.[90] The chapel, a temporary building, was opened in 1907.[91] In 1919–20 a new hall and church were opened.[92] The hall was used as a mixed junior and infants' school in and after 1921.[93] In 1930 a new church of St. Anselm was opened[94] but this too was considered temporary by 1961.[95] At that date it was a long, low, brick building with a separate small wooden bell turret; the roof was supported on iron girders and the east end was separated from the nave by 3 brick arches. The site for another church on the Green was being proposed in 1967.[96]

After the First World War the former St. Marylebone school in South Road[97] was bought as a Roman Catholic girls' school and renamed St. Joseph's.[98] The school, which was run by the Daughters of the Cross,[99] was offered for sale in 1931. The buildings were demolished soon afterwards and are now commemorated in St. Joseph's Drive.[1]

PROTESTANT NONCONFORMITY. In 1878 the Primitive Methodists registered a chapel in Western Road, Southall.[2] The present chapel building, standing on the corner of Western and Sussex Roads, was erected in 1876–7.[3] In 1961 it was a two-story building of yellow brick with a slate roof and a cement-rendered front. The Wesleyan Methodists opened a chapel in South Road in 1885[4] which was re-registered in 1907.[5] Before 1916 the chapel had been joined by the Wesley Hall.[6] At that date both chapel and hall were demolished, and the present King's Hall was erected and opened on their site, the architect being Sir Alfred Gelder of Hull.[7] The King's Hall formed the headquarters of Wesleyan Methodism in the area and provided a place for their social and religious meetings.[8] In 1961 the hall consisted of a large rectangular 3-story building with a red brick and stone front facing South Road.

The Baptists founded a church in Western Road in 1889,[9] which was registered in 1890.[10] Six years later the site and the chapel, a temporary one, were vested in trustees. A further piece of land, on the corner of Western and St. John's Roads, was added in 1898.[11] The chapel was rebuilt in 1901,[12] and the old corrugated iron chapel was then used as a Sunday school.[13] This building, an annexe to the church, was rebuilt in 1912–13.[14] The surviving trustees vested it in the London Baptist Property Board in 1930.[15] Branch Sunday schools were also held at the schools in Lady Margaret Road and Carlyle Avenue, and at the Norwood Green School.[16] In 1961 the church was a plain, yellow brick building, with red brick arches over the doors and windows and a small wooden central cupola. The annexe was a fairly large hall with offices attached. A Baptist mission station at the junction of Thorncliffe Road and Norwood Road, Norwood Green, was registered in 1946, but the registration was cancelled in 1954.[17]

The Congregationalists are said to have founded a congregation in a private house in 1909 although increased numbers eventually led to their renting a hall.[18] The church itself was formed in 1911[19] and a building in Villiers Road was registered in 1913.[20] This was an iron building given by the friends of Penge (Kent) Congregational Church.[21] The present building was erected adjoining it and registered in 1932.[22] In 1961 the church, which lay alongside Villiers Road, was a red brick building, with entrances at each end and a large free-standing centre façade of brick.

The Barn Mission took its name from evangelical

83 *T.L.M.A.S.* xviii(2), no. 147.
84 *Southall-Norwood and Hayes Official Guide* (1924), 12.
85 *T.L.M.A.S.* xviii(2), no. 147.
86 *Crockford* (1959–60).
87 *T.L.M.A.S.* xviii (2), no. 147.
88 Ex inf. the vicar.
89 *Lond. Dioc. Bk.* (1965).
90 *Catholic Dir.* (1960).
91 Gen. Reg. Off., Wship. Reg. 42375.
92 Ex inf. a sister.
93 Ed. 7/86.
94 Gen. Reg. Off., Wship. Reg. 52754.
95 Ex inf. the sister-in-charge.
96 Ex inf. Southall libr.
97 See p. 54.
98 Kirwan, *Southall*, 46.
99 *Catholic Dir.* (1925).
1 Kirwan, *Southall*, 46.
2 Gen. Reg. Off., Wship. Reg. 24206.
3 Foundation stone.
4 Gen. Reg. Off., Wship. Reg. 28758.

5 Ibid. 42193.
6 Ibid. 46853.
7 Ibid. 46912; *Southall Official Handbk.* (n.d.), 60.
8 *Southall-Norwood and Hayes Official Guide* (1924), 15.
9 *Baptist Handbk.* (1960).
10 Gen. Reg. Off., Wship. Reg. 31985.
11 Char. Com. files.
12 Foundation stone.
13 *Southall Official Guide* (n.d.), 59; Gen. Reg. Off., Wship. Reg. 38870.
14 Foundation stone.
15 Char. Com. files.
16 *Baptist Handbk.* (1960).
17 Ibid. (1950); Gen. Reg. Off., Wship. Reg. 61412.
18 *Southall Official Guide* (n.d.), 59.
19 *Congregational Yearbk.* (1960).
20 Gen. Reg. Off., Wship. Reg. 45816.
21 See below *sub* Southall Sisterhood Hall.
22 *Southall Official Guide* (n.d.), 59; Gen. Reg. Off., Wship. Reg. 53722.

services held in the 'old barn' of a Southall farm between 1862 and 1889, when the barn was burned down. A hall was used until 1898 when the founder and owner, H. Baxter, left Southall. Thereafter the mission used various premises including St. John's (church) hall and a carpenter's shop.[23] Between 1909 and 1921 their hall was situated behind 8–9 Alexandra Villas, Norwood Road. In 1921 a new hall was opened[24] on the present site in Norwood Road which apparently consisted of the re-erected St. George's school hall. The present building was erected in 1935–6. The Mission itself is affiliated to the Fellowship of Independent Evangelical Churches.[25]

A Salvation Army barracks in Waltham Road was first registered in 1885, and re-registered as a hall in 1897.[26] The Salvation Army Citadel in Adelaide Road is said to have been opened in 1883, but it was not registered until 1905;[27] it seems most likely in fact to have been the successor to the earlier Waltham Road barracks. In 1961 this remained the headquarters of the Army in Southall. Between 1913 and 1927 it also had a hall, the Athenaeum, on South Road.[28] In 1927 a second hall, which was still in use in 1961, was opened on the Broadway (Uxbridge Road).[29]

The Gospel Hall in Hammond Road, Southall, was erected in 1898,[30] although previously meetings had been held in various houses. The congregation termed itself 'brethren' and had no set order of service.[31] The hall was small and built of yellow brick, with a red brick front, and a round-arched porch in the centre. The Christian Brethren first met in 1904 and moved in 1935 to the Ebenezer Hall in Kingston Road.[32] The congregation had no paid minister and was registered for marriages and funerals.[33] The hall in 1961 was a small brick building with a tiled roof and central cupola. The Assemblies of God started a mission in Southall in 1920, and the Glad Tidings Hall at 15 Hortus Road, Southall, was opened in 1926.[34] At its registration the building was called the Ebenezer Hall, but it appears to have no connexion with the hall of the same name registered in 1935 by the Christian Brethren.[35] In 1961 the building was constructed of corrugated iron.

The Southall Spiritualist Church was founded as a meeting in a private house in Osterley Park Road in 1930,[36] and the church in Hortus Road was registered in 1932.[37] This building was rented by the congregation until 1954 when it bought the freehold.[38] In 1961 the church was a small corrugated iron building. Another Spiritualist centre, opened in 1938 in Featherstone Road, Southall, had evidently fallen into disuse by 1954.[39] The Pentecostal Assembly rented a room in 1934 in a building in Cambridge Road, Southall, describing themselves

simply as Christians. The registration was cancelled by 1954.[40] The Southall Sisterhood, an undenominational group which in 1961 met weekly, held their meetings in a corrugated iron hall which stood on the corner of Villiers Road and Park Avenue. This hall was the first Congregational church in Southall, and stands next to the present Congregational church.[41] The Southall Brotherhood met in the Norwood Road Sisterhood Hall opposite Endsleigh Road. The hall was built in 1929 of red and yellow brick with a small central porch. The Brotherhood and the Norwood Road Sisterhood, also an undenominational body, met weekly. The North Road Hall, apparently erected in the 1930s, was a meeting place of Christians every Sunday in 1961. The red brick building had a small south porch, a tiled roof, and a centre louvre.

SIKHS. The Sikhs, who previously had hired halls for their monthly meetings, acquired a temple on Southall Green in 1963.[42] This building was demolished in 1967 to make way for a new Roman Catholic church.[43] A larger temple was then opened in a converted dairy in Havelock Road.[44]

EDUCATION. In 1706 Francis Courtney devised two small cottages and a few acres of land in Heston to educate the poor children of the parish of Norwood.[45] No school appears to have been built with this endowment, although in 1784, when one of these cottages near Norwood Green was sold to Sarah Child, the money was to be paid by the churchwardens into the Courtney charity.[46] It seems probable that the charity was used mainly in cash payments to poor scholars, and possibly in grants of books and clothing. After 1909 exhibitions were awarded alternately to a boy and a girl either for tuition or entrance fees to a secondary school, or as a yearly maintenance allowance of £10. Other payments were made towards travelling expenses, books and other materials for children attending day or evening classes. In 1955 the income amounted to over £192, of which only £62 had been disbursed.[47]

The earliest school in Norwood was almost certainly that built in Tentelow Lane in 1767 by Elisha Biscoe,[48] who had been steward to the Awsiter family.[49] In 1772 he bequeathed £3,500 to pay a master and mistress to educate 34 boys and 6 girls from Heston, Hayes and Norwood.[50] The Biscoes owned property in Hayes and Heston,[51] and in 1801 Elisha Biscoe the younger was the largest landowner in and around Botwell.[52] By 1819 the school was said to be falling into decay; most of the trustees had

[23] Ex inf. the minister.
[24] Gen. Reg. Off., Wship. Reg. 43982, 48197.
[25] Ex inf. the minister.
[26] Gen. Reg. Off., Wship. Reg. 29074, 35858.
[27] Ibid. 40873; Southall Official Guide (n.d.), 60.
[28] Gen. Reg. Off., Wship. Reg. 45655.
[29] Ibid. 50862.   [30] Foundation stone.
[31] Ex inf. Mr. G. Retallick.
[32] Ex inf. the treasurer; Gen. Reg. Off., Wship. Reg. 55882.
[33] Ex inf. the treasurer.
[34] Ex inf. the minister; Gen. Reg. Off., Wship. Reg. 50370.
[35] See above.   [36] Ex inf. the secretary.
[37] Gen. Reg. Off., Wship. Reg. 54116.
[38] Ex inf. the secretary.
[39] Gen. Reg. Off., Wship. Reg. 58472.
[40] Ibid. 55228.   [41] See above.
[42] Ex inf. the President, Sikh temple.
[43] See p. 52.
[44] Ex inf. the President, Sikh temple; The Times, 23 Jan. 1967.
[45] Char. Com. file; Digest of Rets. to Cttee. on Educ. of Poor, H.C. 224, p. 539 (1819), ix(1).
[46] M.R.O., Acc. 289/433.
[47] Char. Com. files.
[48] Inscription on house.
[49] P. Kirwan, Southall, 28.
[50] Digest of Rets. to Cttee. on Educ. of Poor, H.C. 224, p. 539 (1819), ix(1).
[51] See p. 28; V.C.H. Mdx. iii, 90, 135.
[52] M.R.O., L.T.A. 671.

died, the capital had not been invested properly, and Elisha Biscoe, who now lived in Oxfordshire, was in sole charge.[53] In 1825 an action in Chancery established that most of the income had been devoted to the school but that no accounts had been kept. When new trustees were appointed under a Scheme of 1827, the school was attended by only 28 boys and 12 girls.[54] These figures were the same in 1833,[55] although children from Hayes soon ceased to attend, perhaps because of the foundation of the National School at Wood End Green.[56] Numbers were increased by 6 boys and 4 girls in 1858[57] and some 60 pupils were receiving free instruction in 1863;[58] the master eventually was allowed to take paying pupils but after 1870 numbers were gradually reduced to a maximum of 30 boys, 20 girls, and 10 children who paid fees. By this date the school buildings were apparently in urgent need of repair.[59] In 1909 the Southall-Norwood U.D.C. declared that the income from Biscoe's charity ought to be spent on higher education, but the school continued under its board of trustees, which pointed out that the charity also concerned Heston. More paying pupils were taken after the Second World War and the school was finally closed in 1950.[60] After the parish had refused to buy the building for use as a Sunday school,[61] it was sold to the last schoolmaster as a private residence.[62] In 1961 it consisted of a small, brown brick, two-story cottage with round-headed Gothic windows to the ground floor.

In 1819 there was an industrial school for 20 girls, supported by a £20 endowment and annual subscriptions.[63] In 1833 there were 7 day schools, excluding the Biscoe school, together educating 72 boys and 79 girls. Only one was endowed; the others were either fee-paying or subscription schools. There was also a Sunday school which had been started in 1827.[64]

The St. John's parochial school, Southall Green, was established in 1837–8 by Henry Dobbs. Boys, girls, and infants shared a single room, although it had dividing doors, and there was a room overhead for the master and mistress.[65] In 1845 an ex-mistress of the school, Ann Lawes, endowed it with £100 stock;[66] the endowment, however, was not settled in trust until 1855, when the five patrons of the living were selected as trustees. Numbers in the school were said to fluctuate, the children being drawn chiefly from brick-making families. In 1869, however, it was attended by 94 boys and 98 girls, who paid a weekly sum varying from 1d. to 3d.[67] The school was closed in 1891.[68] In 1961 the building, a single-story, yellow brick hall off King Street, was used for general parochial purposes.[69]

In 1858 a large school was opened on the west side of South Road[70] for poor children from the parish of St. Marylebone. The building, which sometimes held as many as 500 children, was used as a military hospital in the First World War and afterwards turned into a Roman Catholic girls' school.[71]

Norwood Bridge Church of England (National) School was opened in 1862. It was attended by 120 boys, girls, and infants, but had only one master. It was financed by a very small endowment and from other sources, including church collections.[72] The building remained the private property of the rector, who in 1873 set up a trust. The school was enlarged and reorganized in that year and a certificated master was appointed. He left in 1878, when the two rooms occupied by the school were very dilapidated, and was replaced by a master and mistress.[73] In the same year the school was leased to the Norwood School Board for 30 years.[74] In 1897 it had an average attendance of 217 children,[75] and it was finally closed in 1903 or 1904.[76]

The Dudley Road School was opened by 1897, when it was described as 'new'. There were at least three women teachers who were in charge of 8 classrooms.[77] By 1908 it had an average attendance of over 400 girls,[78] but this was halved after the First World War.[79] The school was reorganized as a junior mixed school in 1930; its separate existence ceased in 1958 when the building became an annexe to Southall Technical College.[80] The St. John's Temporary Council School was opened in 1905. It was closed in 1911 on the opening of the Western Road School. The freehold belonged to the trustees of St. John's church, who had leased it to the local authorities in 1877.[81] The school was probably held in the St. John's hall, the home of the former St. John's parochial school.[82] The temporary St. John's school was reopened in 1912 and finally closed in 1916.[83] The Hartington Road Temporary School was opened for infants in 1910, drawing children from the Featherstone Road Infants School. It was closed in 1911 on the opening of the Western Road School.[84]

A Roman Catholic school called St. Mary's was functioning in 1912,[85] but it is not mentioned again. The Roman Catholic school of St. Anselm was opened in 1921, drawing children from all over Southall and Norwood, and from Hanwell.[86] The county council opened a technical college in Beaconsfield Road in 1928 and greatly extended it in 1934, 1937, and after 1945.[87] The influx of Indians and Pakistanis in the early 1960s created an acute problem. In 1963 it was estimated that in the infants' department at Beaconsfield Road the number of

[53] *Digest of Rets. to Cttee. on Educ. of Poor*, H.C. 224. p. 539 (1819), ix(1).
[54] *Trans. Southall Local Hist. Soc.* i. 18–19.
[55] *Educ. Inquiry Abstract*, H.C. 62, p. 576 (1835), xlii.
[56] *Trans. Southall Local Hist. Soc.* i. 20; see p. 38.
[57] School Trustees' Min. Bk. 1828–1909.
[58] Ibid.; Char. Com. files.
[59] School Trustees' Min. Bk. 1828–1909; Char. Com. files.
[60] *Trans. Southall Local Hist. Soc.* i. 24–26.
[61] Par. Recs., P.C.C. Min. Bk. 1938–53.
[62] *Trans. Southall Local Hist. Soc.* i. 26.
[63] *Digest of Rets. to Cttee. on Educ. of Poor*, H.C. 224, p. 539 (1819), ix(1).
[64] *Educ. Inquiry Abstract*, H.C. 62, p. 576 (1835), xlii.
[65] Char. Com. files; Ed. 7/87.
[66] Char. Com. files.
[67] Ed. 7/87.
[68] Ex inf. London. Bor. of Ealing Educ. Officer.

[69] See below *sub* St. John's Temporary School.
[70] O.S. Map 6″; Mdx. xv. S.W.
[71] Kirwan, *Southall*, 46; see above, p. 52.
[72] Ed. 7/86.
[73] Ed. 7/87.
[74] Char. Com. files.
[75] Ed. 7/86.
[76] *List of Schs. under Admin. of Bd. 1903* [Cd. 2011], H.C. p. 169 (1904), lxxv.
[77] Ed. 7/86.
[78] Bd. of Educ., *List 21* (1908).
[79] Ibid. (1919).
[80] Ex inf. London Bor. of Ealing Educ. Officer.
[81] Ed. 7/87.
[82] See above.
[83] Ed. 7/86.
[84] Ibid.
[85] *Kelly's Dir. Mdx.* (1912).
[86] Ed. 7/86.
[87] *Southall Official Guide* (1939), 22–23; ex inf. Southall Divisional Educ. Officer.

immigrant children had risen in two years from about 55 to 130, while the number of English pupils had shrunk from 150 to 90. Plans were then made to disperse the immigrants among other primary schools, in order to avoid segregation.[88]

In September 1963 there were fifteen maintained schools in Norwood with Southall. These are listed below. The date of opening is given in brackets after the name of the school, followed by the dates of any extensions; the next figure is the number of children on the roll at September 1963, and the final figure denotes the age-group of the pupils:[89] North Road Junior Mixed and Infants (1851, 1879, 1914). 443. 5–11; Featherstone Road Infants (1890, 1901, 1953, 1962). 250. 5–7; Featherstone Road Junior Mixed (1901). 333. 7–11; Clifton Road Junior Mixed and Infants (1904). 347. 5–11; Tudor Road Junior Mixed and Infants (1907, 1925, 1930). 639. 5–11; Southall County Grammar (1907, 1927, 1938, 1963). 834. 11–18; Western Road Girls Secondary (1910, 1926). 463. 11–16; Beaconsfield Road Junior Mixed and Infants (1920). 540. 5–11;[90] Dormers Wells Boys Secondary (1934, 1963). 452. 11–16; Dormers Wells Girls Secondary (1934, 1947, 1959, 1963). 474. 11–16; Talbot Road Special (1936, 1957). 236. 8–16; Lady Margaret Road Junior Mixed and Infants (1938). 629. 5–11; George Tomlinson Junior Mixed and Infants (1953). 313. 5–11; Dormers Wells Junior Mixed and Infants (1954). 401. 5–11; Featherstone Boys Secondary (1958). 664. 11–16.

CHARITIES FOR THE POOR.[91] William Early, William Comyn, and Edward Hiller, in 1618 settled approximately 22 a. in Hayes in trust for the use of the poor. On this land or with this income was later erected a building called the Church House. In 1815 the Church House and the land on which it stood were exchanged by John Robins for a piece of ground at Norwood Green, fronting on Norwood Road, on which he erected four almshouses.[92] In 1901 the 4 occupants had one room each, with a communal outside convenience and cold water pump. By 1939 land at the corner of Ellison and Witley Gardens had been acquired by the trustees to erect five bungalows to replace the almshouses. Owing to the Second World War nothing was done and in the early 1950s the vacant Ellison Gardens site was bought by the borough council. The almshouses were repaired from time to time and in 1961 consisted of a row of 4 one-story cottages of yellow brick under one tiled roof.[93] They were finally demolished and rebuilt later in 1961 on the same Norwood Road site. They then consisted of 4 self-contained flats in a two-story, L-shaped block. In 1967 the trustees bought two more flats, in Wren Avenue.[94] Six other almshouses were given to the parish in 1897 by William Welch Deloitte in honour of Queen Victoria's diamond jubilee. The income with which Deloitte endowed them also provided gifts of money and coals. The almshouses stood in 1961 in North Road, Southall, opposite Masefield Avenue, and consisted of a terrace of one-story yellow- and red-brick cottages under a slate roof.[95]

Francis Awsiter, by will dated 1625, left a rent of 20s. for those poor widows of Norwood and Southall who attended an annual Good Friday Sermon which he also endowed. William Millett, by will dated 1631, left 8 a. to be divided equally between the poor of Heston and of Norwood and Southall. In 1863 the property also included a tramway toll on bricks, 3 cottages, and £2,600 stock.[96] An annual rent of 40s. was left by George Finch, by will proved 1641, and its payment, which had temporarily ceased, was enforced by a court order in 1677.[97] Robert Hampton, by will dated 1651, also left a rent of 40s. with which to provide 13 loaves every year, the surplus to be distributed in money. By will dated 1684 Robert Merrick left £100 to purchase bread for the needy who were 'not given to the novelties of the times'.[98] By will dated 1836 Anne Burrel left 20s. each to ten poor persons in Norwood and Southall. An annuity to provide bread and meat from stock worth nearly £112 was bequeathed by Henry Phelps, by will dated 1840.

By 1863 a number of the charities had already been combined, although not in an official Scheme, and the proceeds were used for gifts in money and kind, for contributions to penny banks and clothing clubs, and to support the Norwood and Southall schools. All the charities were consolidated in 1906 as the 'Almshouse and Eleemosynary Charities'. The principal charge was the upkeep of the almshouses and the payment of stipends to not more than four couples; other income was to be used for subscriptions and contributions to hospitals and provident clubs, and to provide nurses, annuities, clothes, bedding, fuel, and medicine. During the 20th century the charity land was gradually sold, and in 1964 the governing instrument was amended. The trustees could still appoint four couples, although in practice only two of the new flats were suitable for more than one occupant.[99] The gross income in 1966 was £567.

HILLINGDON
INCLUDING UXBRIDGE

HILLINGDON ancient parish lay on the north-west border of Middlesex approximately 16 miles from Charing Cross, 12 miles from Watford (Herts.), and 7 miles from Windsor.[1] In shape an irregular

[88] *The Times*, 15 & 16 Oct. 1963.
[89] Ex inf. Southall Divisional Educ. Officer.
[90] Ed. 7/86.
[91] Except where otherwise stated this section is based on Char. Com. files.
[92] Brewer, *Beauties of Eng. and Wales*, x(5), 610.
[93] There was also a low wall in front of the almshouses with an inscription briefly recording their history. See plate facing, p. 152.
[94] Ex inf. clerk of Norwood Charities.

[95] They are inscribed 'Deloitte Almshouses Jubilee 1897'.
[96] Southall Bor. Libr., Churchwardens' Acct. Bk. 1676–1744.
[97] C 93/36/17.
[98] Southall Bor. Libr., Churchwardens' Acct. Bk. 1676–1744.
[99] Ex inf. clerk of Norwood Charities.
[1] This article was completed in 1965. Any references to later years are dated.

rectangle, the old parish measured approximately 3 miles at its broadest point and, except where small rectangular areas projected from the north-west and south-east corners, roughly 5 miles from north to south.[2] The River Colne formed the county boundary with Buckinghamshire and the western parish boundary except in the extreme north-west where for about a mile both boundaries followed the Shire Ditch, a feeder of the Colne running between the parent stream and the Frays River or Cowley Stream, a branch of the Colne flowing parallel to and between ¼ and ½ mile east of the main stream. The other three sides were bounded by the parishes of Harefield and Ickenham[3] on the north, Hayes and Harlington to the east, and West Drayton and Harmondsworth to the south. Along the London–Oxford road (Uxbridge or London Road) south-east of the bridges carrying the highway over the Frays and Colne streams lay the hamlet and market-town of Uxbridge, whose inhabitants, relying on the town's tenuous claim to borough status, exercised an ill-defined franchise over an uncertain area of between 80 and 100 a. situated north of the modern Vine Street and mainly east of the Frays River. Until the 19th century the township was separated from Hillingdon by a 'borough ditch'.[4] South of Uxbridge, between the Frays stream on the west and the River Pinn to the east, lay Cowley parish, a fragmented 300-acre area entirely surrounded by and partly intermixed with Hillingdon.[5] Also insulated in Hillingdon, about 200 yards south of the junction of Swakeleys Drive and Long Lane, lay Chestlands, a 6-acre field belonging to Ickenham parish, while south-east of Ickenham village was a detached area of 12 a. belonging to Hillingdon. In 1841[6] Hillingdon parish, including the 99-acre 'chapelry' or township of Uxbridge, contained 4,944 a. and Cowley parish 306 a.

From medieval times Hillingdon, Uxbridge, and Cowley were for many purposes so closely related that it is almost impossible to consider them apart. Uxbridge and, later, the Domesday manor of Hillingdon were included in Colham manor;[7] from an early date Uxbridge hamlet extended into Hillingdon parish; parts of Cowley village lay until 1895 in Hillingdon.[8] Throughout the Middle Ages Uxbridge, jealously guarding its supposed privileges, maintained an uneasy administrative relationship with manor and parish authorities.[9] From the 17th century onwards, however, the economic growth of the hamlet gradually transcended the traditional framework of its parent parish. By 1830 the economic and administrative importance of Uxbridge had almost totally eclipsed that of Hillingdon parish and the town was virtually autonomous. This reversal in the administrative roles of hamlet and parish was recognized in the formation in 1836 of the Uxbridge Poor Law Union which comprised nine west Middlesex parishes including Hillingdon and Cowley.[10] The western portion of Hillingdon and the four northernmost detached parts of Cowley were included in the Uxbridge Local Board of Health District, constituted provisionally in 1849 and confirmed in 1853.[11] Under the Divided Parishes Act of 1882 the eight detached parts of Hillingdon and Ickenham were allotted to the parishes in which they were geographically situated.[12] In 1894 the Uxbridge Local Board of Health was replaced by an urban district council. Hillingdon old parish was then divided, the part within the new Uxbridge U.D. becoming the civil parish of Hillingdon West and the remainder Hillingdon East. In 1896 nearly 900 a. on the southern border of the old parish were separated from Hillingdon East to form the civil parish of Yiewsley.[13] At the same time the part of Hillingdon East west of the Pinn was transferred to Cowley parish and the part of Cowley east of the Pinn to Hillingdon.[14] Yiewsley became an urban district in 1911 and in 1929, after boundary changes involving the transfer of 193 a. from Hillingdon East and 33 a. of Cowley to Yiewsley and the addition of 29 a. of Yiewsley to Cowley, was joined with West Drayton and Harmondsworth civil parishes to form Yiewsley and West Drayton U.D.[15] By same order Uxbridge U.D. was extended to include the whole of the revised civil parishes of Hillingdon East (2,762 a.), Cowley (521 a.), and Harefield (4,622 a.).[16] In 1937 Uxbridge civil parish, co-extensive with the 10,240-acre urban district, was formed, and in 1955 the former urban district became the Borough of Uxbridge. 'Hillingdon' reappeared as the name of a major administrative unit in 1965 when the municipal borough of Uxbridge was merged with the urban districts of Hayes and Harlington, Ruislip–Northwood, and Yiewsley and West Drayton to form the new London Borough of Hillingdon.[17]

From at least as early as the 17th century the external boundary of Hillingdon parish was also, for most of its length, that of Colham manor. The only extant pre-19th-century survey, made in 1636,[18] traces the boundary from the Oxford road at Frays Bridge northward along the Shire Ditch, the Colne, and minor feeders of the Frays stream[19] to the southern edge of Cow Moor in Harefield, to Gospel Hill on the Harefield road, and along the edge of Swakeleys Park to Ickenham Bridge over the Pinn. Here the manor and parish boundaries separated. Nineteenth-century plans[20] show the parish boundary continuing eastward along the line of the modern Swakeleys Drive and just south of Ickenham

[2] Details of the parish boundaries appear below.
[3] In the 15th cent. there appears to have been some uncertainty over the boundaries between Ickenham and Hillingdon; see pp. 69–70.
[4] See below. The boundary of Uxbridge township was defined in 1727: M.R.O., Acc. 538/2, and is most clearly shown on the Hillingdon Inclosure Plan (1825) and the first edn. of the O.S. 1/2,500 Map of Hillingdon par. (1866).
[5] References to Cowley should be taken in conjunction with the history of that parish in *V.C.H. Mdx.* iii. 170–7. The boundaries of Cowley old par. are most clearly shown on O.S. Map 1/2,500, Mdx. xiv. 7, 8, 11 (1866 edn.).
[6] *Census*, 1841. Lysons, *Mdx. Pars.* 146, seems to be in error when giving the area of Hillingdon as *c.* 3,600 a.
[7] See p. 70.
[8] See p. 84.

[9] See p. 84.
[10] See p. 86.
[11] Act to confirm prov. orders of Gen. Bd. of Health, 16 & 17 Vic., c. 126; see below, p. 86.
[12] *Census*, 1891.
[13] For the creation in 1874 of the conterminous ecclesiastical par. of Yiewsley see p. 88.
[14] *Census*, 1901; *V.C.H. Mdx.* iii. 171.
[15] *Census*, 1931; *V.C.H. Mdx.* iii. 201.
[16] See p. 86; *V.C.H. Mdx.* iii. 237.
[17] London Govt. Act, 1963, c. 33.
[18] M.R.O., Acc. 448/1 (an 18th-cent. copy).
[19] These are shown on O.S. Map 1/2,500, Mdx. xiv. 11, 15 (1866 edn.).
[20] Ibid.; Hillingdon Incl. Plan (1825) in M.R.O.

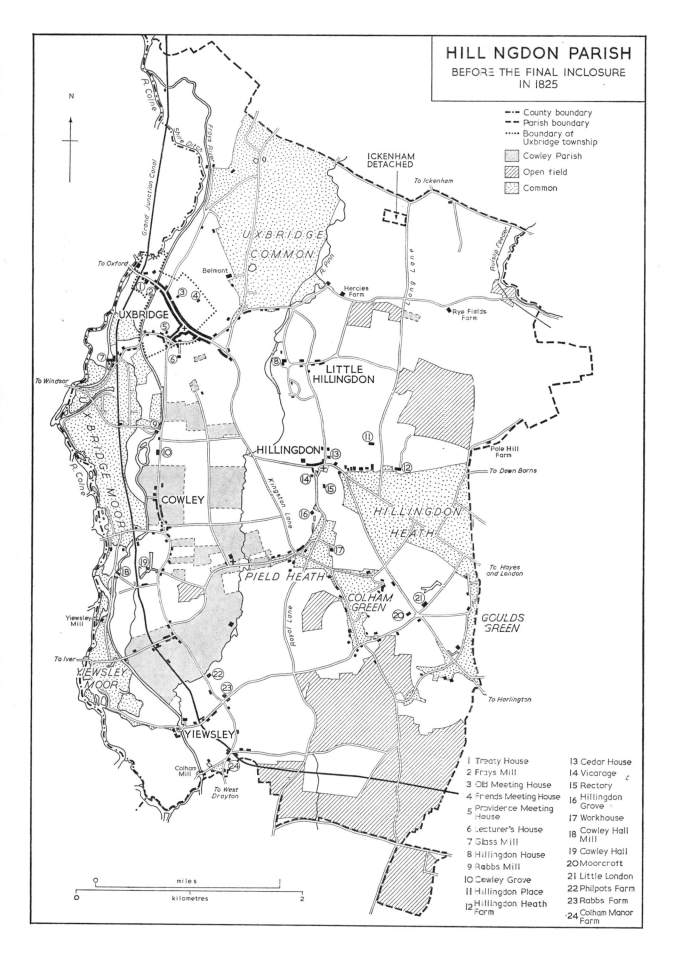

N

County boundary
Parish boundary
Boundary of
Uxbridge township
Cowley Parish
Open field
Common

ICKENHAM
DETACHED

To Ickenham

R. Colne

Shire Ditch

Frays River

Grand Junction Canal

UXBRIDGE
COMMON

Belmont

To Oxford

UXBRIDGE

Hercies
Farm

R. Pinn

Long Lane

Ruislip Feeder

Rye Fields
Farm

To Windsor

LITTLE
HILLINGDON

UXBRIDGE MOOR

R. Colne

HILLINGDON

Pole Hill
Farm

To Down Borns

COWLEY

Kingston Lane

HILLINGDON
HEATH

PIELD HEATH

COLHAM
GREEN

GOULDS
GREEN

Yiewsley
Mill

Royal Lane

To Hayes
and London

To Iver

YIEWSLEY
MOOR

To Harlington

YIEWSLEY

Colham
Mill

To West
Drayton

miles

0

kilometres 2

1 Treaty House
2 Frays Mill
3 Old Meeting House
4 Friends Meeting House
5 Providence Meeting House
6 Lecturer's House
7 Glass Mill
8 Hillingdon House
9 Rabbs Mill
10 Cowley Grove
11 Hillingdon Place
12 Hillingdon Heath Farm

13 Cedar House
14 Vicarage
15 Rectory
16 Hillingdon Grove
17 Workhouse
18 Cowley Hall Mill
19 Cowley Hall
20 Moorcroft
21 Little London
22 Philpots Farm
23 Rabbs Farm
24 Colham Manor Farm

57

Manor Farm to the Yeading Brook. After leaving this stream at its junction with a westward extension of Sweetcroft Lane the boundary passed across fields to Pole Hill Farm, where it rejoined the manor boundary, and then almost due south over Hillingdon Heath to the London road. South of the road the manor and parish boundary continued southward, passing east of the hamlet of Goulds Green, to Portway or Porter's Lane which ran east from Drayton towards Dawley. South of Portway Lane lay Hide Field, an almost detached 42-acre field protruding southward between Drayton and Harlington parishes. From the north-west corner of Hide Field the boundary ran along Portway Lane and northward up Falling Lane until it turned north-west to Colham manor-house. South of the house the boundary again ran south-westward to the Colne at its junction with the Colham mill stream. In 1636, as later, the Colne formed the western boundary of county, parish, and manor. Parts of the eastern boundary and, of course, the western boundary were perpetuated as the boundaries of Uxbridge Borough, but the remainder was completely obscured in the administrative reorganizations which began in 1896.[21]

Until natural divisions were blurred by modern housing this area was divisible into two distinct topographical zones, reflecting its underlying geological structure and lying north and south of the London–Oxford road, a medieval highway which crosses the parish in a north-westerly direction, passing through Hillingdon village and entering Buckinghamshire at Uxbridge. North of the road is an area of undulating clay country[22] at between 100 and 200 ft. Heavily wooded well into historic times,[23] this part of the parish remained largely uninhabited and partly uncultivated until the 20th century. Between Hillingdon village and Uxbridge a narrow tongue of clay extends southward as far as Cowley along the valley of the Pinn, a drainage stream flowing south-westward across the parish through Swakeleys lake in Ickenham to the Frays stream at Yiewsley. South of the London road the land falls uniformly to a south-draining plain at about 100 ft., the soil of which is almost entirely fertile brickearth overlying, to a depth of between 18 in. and 5 ft., valley gravels resting on a subsoil of London blue clay.[24] In this area lay most of the medieval open fields, the manor-houses, and many of the later principal residences.[25]

Archaeological evidence suggests that early settlement was largely confined to the well-drained lighter soils and concentrated at Hillingdon and around Colham and Yiewsley in the extreme south-west. Hillingdon, occupying a commanding position on a patch of glacial gravels at about 190 ft., has yielded evidence of Palaeolithic occupation. Similar remains have been recovered from the underlying gravels at Yiewsley,[26] and the discovery there, in Boyer's gravel-pit, of large quantities of Bronze or early Iron Age pottery suggests domestic occupation in the south of the parish by the early Iron Age.[27] Theories of Roman settlement in the area have been overstated, but at least one Roman road is thought to run through the parish from north to south.[28] Fragments of Roman ware have been found at Uxbridge, near Cowley church,[29] and, more recently, on the site of an unidentified earthwork at Coney Green, Hillingdon.[30] The incorporation of Saxon personal names in the place-names 'Hillingdon', 'Colham', 'Cowley', and 'Yiewsley',[31] and the probable association of Uxbridge with the 7th-century Wixan tribe[32] suggest areas of Saxon settlement. Attempts to interpret early forms of the place-name 'Uxbridge' as indicating the existence of a Saxon borough are inconclusive, and more reliable authorities suggest that the hamlet's name derives from its position at the eastern end of a ford and later bridge across the Colne.[33]

DEVELOPMENT BEFORE 1800. The first certain indications of the topography of the area appear in the Domesday Survey.[34] In 1086 the most prominent natural feature was an extensive tract of woodland, the bulk of which, probably confined to the heavy clays to the north, lay in Hillingdon manor.[35] Settlement seems to have been concentrated in hamlets at Hillingdon and Colham: the Survey mentions 33 persons in Colham manor and 10 in Hillingdon. Uxbridge is not included by name in the Survey although it was almost certainly in existence by 1086. When first mentioned in the 12th century it was already an important settlement.[36] A chapel of ease was built in the town in the early 13th century,[37] and in 1275 Uxbridge was one of the two Middlesex townships represented in Edward I's first parliament.[38] The vills of Colham and Uxbridge are mentioned in 1316.[39] In 1328, and probably earlier, separate courts were being held for the hamlet of Uxbridge,[40] and by the end of the 14th century Uxbridge, following the apparent decline of the hamlet at Colham,[41] had become the major settlement.

Early-14th-century surveys suggest that manorial demesne in the parish was divided almost equally between arable and pasture with smaller scattered areas of woodland.[42] The nature of the 'old park' which contained 200 a. of pasture in 1328[43] is unknown; it probably lay north of Hillingdon Heath in an area which was called Old Park as late as 1636.[44]

---

[21] See above.
[22] Geological description based on Geol. Survey Map, sheet 255 (drift); V.C.H. Mdx. i. 6.
[23] See below.
[24] Middleton, View, 18.
[25] See below.
[26] V.C.H. Mdx. i. 16–17.
[27] Ibid. 43–5, 58; C. E. Vulliamy, Arch. of Mdx. and Lond. 91.
[28] Sir M. Sharpe, Mdx. in British, Roman, and Saxon Times, 71, 87, reproduced by later writers, e.g. Borough Petition (1951), 8. For evidence of Roman roads in the par., see E. V. Parrott, 'Roman Roads in the Uxbridge Area', Uxbridge Record (Jnl. Uxb. Local Hist. Soc.), v. 7–8.
[29] V.C.H. Mdx. i. 74; Uxbridge finds in Uxb. Mus.
[30] Ex inf. Dr. F. Celoria.

[31] P.N. Mdx. (E.P.N.S.), 32, 41–42.
[32] Ibid. 49.
[33] Ibid.
[34] V.C.H. Mdx. i. 124.
[35] See p. 72.
[36] Grant of trading privileges penes Uxb. libr.; see p. 79.
[37] See p. 89.
[38] 'The First Parliament of Edward I', Eng. Hist. Rev (1910), 231–42.
[39] B.M. Harl. MS. 2195, f. 34.
[40] C 145/108/2; see p. 83.
[41] The vill of Colham is last mentioned in 1376; Lancs. Rec. Off., DDK/1746/2.
[42] e.g. C 131/3/3; C 145/108/2.
[43] C 145/108/2; see also C.P. 25(1)/152/90/64.
[44] M.R.O., Acc. 448/1.

Eight acres of woodland enclosed in 1328 by a ditch may be identifiable with the later Coney Green which was shown as a rabbit warren in 1675[45] and as completely surrounded by a low earthwork in 1733.[46] As early as 1311[47] the lord of Colham owned another warren on what later became known as Uxbridge Common.[48] During the 14th century, and presumably earlier, the lords of Colham also held more than 300 a. in Whatworth Field and Hanger Field and an unspecified acreage in Strode Field, Brodeappledore Field, Stone Field, and Rye Hill Field.[49] The exact location of the medieval open fields is uncertain, but most of them probably lay, as did the later common fields, south of the London road and east of the Frays stream. Only two medieval fieldnames, Rye Hill Field and Alton Field, survived into the 17th century. In 1777 Rye Hill Field apparently lay south of Rye Fields Farm in the triangle formed by Long Lane and Sweetcroft Lane.[50] Abutting Rye Hill Field to the south was High Field, said in the late 17th century to contain 67 a.[51] Hillingdon Field and Little Hillingdon Field possibly lay near the two settlements, but other fields mentioned in the 17th and 18th centuries all lay south of the London road.[52] South of the modern West Drayton Road were Hale Field, Beadle, Bedwell, or Bedewell Field, and Upper Field, a large field extending southward to the almost-detached Hide Field.[53] Between Upper Field and Falling Lane to the west was a small field known variously as Harlton, Horton, or Alton Field. Immediately to the north lay Hedging Field, separated by Falling Lane from Royal Field which covered the area between Colham Green and Royal Lane. The bulk of Colham, later Patcott or Padcot, Field probably lay north of Colham manor-house, although its exact limits are uncertain. Stretching northward from Cowley church almost to Uxbridge and bounded by Kingston Lane and Cowley Road to the east and west were more than 300 a. of open-field land known as Cowley Field. Approximately one-third of this, chiefly on the west bank of the Pinn, belonged, in the 18th century and presumably earlier, to the manor and parish of Cowley;[54] the rest belonged to the manors of Colham and Cowley Hall.

On the clay and gravels to the north and west of the open-field area were extensive tracts of common and waste. In 1636 these were said to comprise about 360 a.,[55] but more reliable 18th-century estimates give their area as almost 600 a.[56] Northolt or Ux-

bridge Common, which extended into Harefield parish in the north-west, and Hillingdon Heath, straddling the London road east of Hillingdon village, each contained about 200 a. West of the Frays stream were Uxbridge or Hog Moor (100 a.) south of the town and Yiewsley or Colham Moor (60 a.) stretching north of Yiewsley along the Middlesex bank of the Colne. Pield or Peel Heath north-west of Colham Green covered about 15 a., and Goulds Green, a southward extension of Hillingdon Heath, about 20 a.

By the time of the first parliamentary inclosure in 1795[57] approximately three-fifths of Hillingdon parish had already been inclosed.[58] Inclosure of small parcels of waste probably proceeded steadily from the late medieval period onwards: some open-field land had been inclosed before 1636, and the process accelerated during the 17th and 18th centuries.[59] Under the 1795 Act Cowley Field, comprising 331 a. in Hillingdon and Cowley parishes, was inclosed.[60] A second Act, passed in 1812 and executed in 1825, inclosed a further 1,400 a. and completed the inclosure of open-field and waste land, save for 15 a. of Uxbridge Common which were reserved as an open space.[61]

Until the construction at the end of the 18th century of the Grand Junction Canal the appearance of the parish remained substantially unchanged. Modifications were limited to the development, apparent from the 14th century onwards, of a simple pattern of internal communications. As a result of the natural barrier formed by the Colne and its tributary streams most of the major roads within the parish ran, until comparatively recent times, from north to south linking scattered settlement areas to the Oxford road, which crossed the river at High Bridge north-west of Uxbridge, or to the Bath Road in Harmondsworth parish to the south.[62] The London–Oxford road was an important national route by the 14th century. In 1358 Ellis Waleys of Uxbridge and two Acton men were granted rights of pavage in Uxbridge, Acton, and elsewhere between the two towns.[63] High Bridge was said to be ruinous in 1377,[64] and Stratford Bridge, carrying the Oxford road across the Pinn between Hillingdon and Uxbridge, was in existence by 1410.[65] A highway from Uxbridge to Rickmansworth is mentioned in 1384.[66] Contemporary navigation of the Colne as far as Uxbridge is suggested by the construction in 1419 of a wharf serving Mede mill.[67] By 1636[68] the river

[45] J. Ogilby, *Survey of Roads* (1675). It was called the Warren in 1647: Worcs. Rec. Off., Acc. 2636/44007.
[46] J. Seller, *Map of Mdx.* (1733). The earthwork, as it appeared in 1937, is described in Hist. Mon. Com. *Mdx.* 77; parts of it were still traceable in 1964.
[47] C 134/22/17.
[48] Its location is probably indicated by that of Warren House, shown on the Hillingdon Incl. Plan (1825). For the appointment of a warrener for Colham see p. 74. In *c.* 1690 there were in the warren 800 breeding rabbits worth £40: M.R.O., Acc. 591/29.
[49] C 131/3/3; C 145/108/2; Lancs. Rec. Off., DDK/1746/4.
[50] J. Andrews, *Map of Country 25 miles round Windsor* (1777).
[51] M.R.O., Acc. 180/649; the MS. is badly damaged. High Field had probably been partly inclosed by this date.
[52] In addition to the two sources cited above, field-names appear, usually without exact geographical location, in M.R.O., Acc. 448/1, /3; 180/625, 679; 276/1; *The Thame Cartulary*, ed. H. E. Salter (Oxford Rec. Soc. xxv), 161. The major open fields are shown on the Hillingdon Incl. Plan (1825).

[53] 42a. in 1913: O.S. Maps 1/2,500, Mdx. xiv. 16 (1914 edn.).
[54] M.R.O., Acc. 374/2; Hillingdon and Cowley Incl. Award (1796) *penes* Uxb. Bor.; and see *V.C.H. Mdx.* iii. 170–1.
[55] M.R.O., Acc. 448/1.
[56] Lysons, *Mdx. Pars.* 146.
[57] 35 Geo. III, c. 71 (Priv. Act).
[58] J. Rocque, *Map of Mdx.* (1754); M.R.O., Acc. 668/2a, 5; 538/2.
[59] e.g. M.R.O., Acc. 448/1; 180/676; 503/1; *Mdx. Cnty. Recs. Sess. Bks. 1689–1709*, 309; see also below, p. 59.
[60] See above; *V.C.H. Mdx.* iii. 171.
[61] Hillingdon Incl. Act, 52 Geo. III, c. 28; M.R.O., E.A./Hil./2.
[62] See p. 3.
[63] *Cal. Pat.* 1358–61, 25; 1361–4, 382.
[64] G. Redford and T. H. Riches, *Hist. of Uxbridge* (1885 edn.), 55–56.
[65] Lancs. Rec. Off., DDK/1746/7.
[66] *Cat. Anc. D.* v. 220.
[67] Lancs. Rec. Off., DDK/1746/8; see below, p. 77.
[68] M.R.O., Acc. 448/1.

had been bridged at a further three places between High Bridge and Yiewsley. The Uxbridge–Windsor road crossed the Colne at another High Bridge (later Long Bridge) south-west of the town. Further south were Rowley (later Cowley Moor) Bridge on the road from Cowley to Potters Cross, and Marsh or Huntsmoor Bridge on the road from Cowley to Iver. Responsibility for repairs to these three bridges was shared equally between the lords of Colham and Iver manor in Buckinghamshire. High Bridge on the London road was rebuilt as a seven-arch brick bridge about 1768 and Stratford Bridge as a brick bridge of three arches before 1726.[69] Although Long Bridge and Cowley Moor Bridge were both rebuilt before 1814 and all four Colne bridges improved or again rebuilt several times in the next one hundred and fifty years, there were still only four major bridges across the main river in 1964. Frays (later Mercer's) Bridge, carrying Uxbridge High Street across the Frays stream, was in existence by 1636.[70] It is shown on a plan of 1675[71] as a brick bridge with three arches. South-west of the town the road to Potters Cross crossed the Frays stream at Moorfield (later Rockingham) Bridge,[72] built before 1675[73] and rebuilt as a brick bridge of three arches in 1809.[74] By 1675 roads entering the parish by the Colne bridges were linked to Uxbridge and with West Drayton and Harmondsworth in the south by Cowley Road which ran south from Uxbridge roughly parallel to the Frays stream.[75] Other important 17th-century routes in the south of the parish were Royal Lane leading from Hillingdon through West Drayton to Harmondsworth, and Dawley Lane (later Harlington Road) running south-east from Hillingdon village towards Dawley and Cranford.[76] These three major north–south roads were joined by a network of lanes and access ways, chief of which were Falling or Fulling (later Kingston) Lane running from Stratford Bridge to Colham Green, Porter's or Portway Lane following the Drayton parish boundary towards Dawley, and lanes linking Goulds Green, Colham Green, and Hillingdon in the east, and Yiewsley with West Drayton in the south-west. North of the London road there were, until the 20th century, only two major roads: the road to Harefield (later Park Road) which joined the London road at the east end of Uxbridge, and Long Lane running south from Ruislip and Ickenham to the London road east of Hillingdon village. Between these Vine Lane, which ran north from Hillingdon church, may also have been of some importance. Pages or Peazes Lane left the Harefield road on Uxbridge Common and entered Uxbridge at the west end. East of the Pinn a number of minor lanes, including Sweetcroft Lane and Hercies Lane, linked the hamlets of Hil-

lingdon and Little Hillingdon and the scattered farms to the east. Except for the widening and improvement of former minor lanes, this pattern of road communications altered little until the urban developments of the 1930s.

Surveys made in the early 16th century stress the economic importance of Uxbridge. A market-house had apparently been built by 1513,[77] and an index to the relative prosperity of the town is provided by an assessment of 1522–3 to which 153 persons in Hillingdon parish were taxed, 77 of them from Uxbridge.[78] Describing Uxbridge in the 1530s, Leland stressed the town's dependence on its markets, fairs, and mills.[79] By this time Uxbridge seems to have assumed its later basic pattern of a ribbon settlement of timber-framed houses straggling for ½ mile along both sides of the Oxford road from the two wooden bridges carrying the highway over the Frays and Colne streams to its junction with Blind or Woolwind Lane (later Vine Street). Other houses probably lined both sides of the Lynch and Windsor Street for some 200 yards from the plot of waste known as the Lynch Green[80] to the junction with High Street. In 1555 three heretics from other parts of the country were burned on the Lynch Green, where a memorial was erected 400 years later.[81] At the intersection of Windsor Street with High Street, forming then, as later, the nucleus of the town, stood the old market-house and St. Margaret's chapel, a 13th-century foundation largely rebuilt in the 15th century.[82] The medieval chapel and a few surviving domestic buildings of the 15th and early 16th centuries to some extent qualify a description of the town in the 1580s as being 'of modern date'.[83] Nearly all the existing timber-framed buildings, many of which date from the 17th century, have altered or rebuilt frontages; they include several inns (see below) and one or two groups and individual houses in High Street. Windsor Street has suffered less alteration and retains for its size a larger proportion of such buildings. Two have also survived in Cross Street, overlooking what was formerly Lynch Green.[84]

The most notable 16th-century house in Uxbridge is the Treaty House, known in 1968 as the Crown and Treaty House Inn, which stands on the south-west side of High Street between the Frays and Colne streams. It is built of brick and the principal front, lying at right angles to the road, has two two-storied bay windows with moulded brick mullions and transoms. There are three chimney-stacks with clustered shafts at the rear and a curvilinear gable at the north-east end. The interior retains some original features. The present range is thought to represent little more than a single wing

[69] Rep. Cttee. of Magistrates on Public Bridges in Mdx. (1826), 239–46. [70] M.R.O., Acc. 448/1.
[71] Ogilby, Survey of Roads (1675).
[72] M.R.O., Acc. 538/2.
[73] Ogilby, Survey of Roads (1675).
[74] Rep. on Bridges in Mdx. 239–46.
[75] Many of the roads and minor ways are indicated in the survey of 1636: M.R.O., Acc 448/1. Ogilby's Survey of Roads (1675) shows the Lond.–Oxford road and the major roads joining it. 18th-cent. maps showing roads and bridges in the par. include J. Warburton, J. Bland, P. Smyth, Map of Mdx., Essex & Herts. (1746); Rocque, Map of Mdx. (1754); Andrews, Map of Country 25 miles round Windsor (1777).
[76] E. J. Dowdell, A Hundred Years of Quarter Sessions, 97 n. 2.

[77] M.R.O., Acc. 538/1. cf. Hist. of Uxbridge, 76, giving 1561 as the date of the erection of the market-house. This may have been a rebuilding of the earlier structure.
[78] E 179/141/115.
[79] J. Leland, Itinerary, ed. L. Toulmin Smith, i. 113–14. For the mills see below, p. 77.
[80] The name first appears in a grant dated 1509 penes Uxb. libr. as 'le lynche'.
[81] J. Foxe, Book of Martyrs, ed. S. G. Potter, 257, 272; Acts of P.C. 1554–6, 158.
[82] See p. 89.
[83] W. Camden, Britannia, ed. Gough, ii. 78.
[84] Hist. Mon. Com. Mdx. 129–31, plate 31. Several houses described in 1937 had been demolished by 1968; others were due for destruction during the redevelopment of the town centre.

The Treaty House in 1812

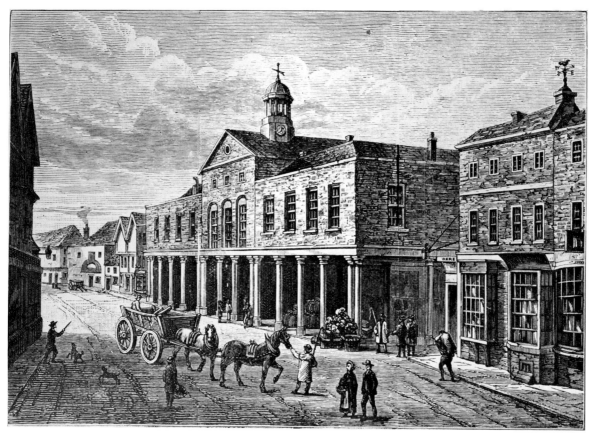

The Market House, built 1789

UXBRIDGE

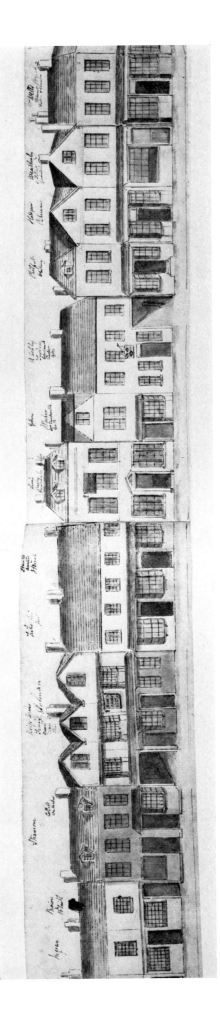

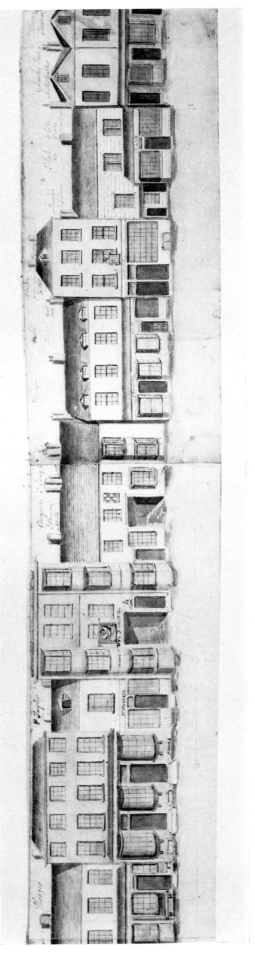

UXBRIDGE HIGH STREET, c. 1790

Part of the south-western side, showing (above) the 'King's Arms' and the 'Three Tuns', and (below) the 'Crown' and the 'Chequers'

of the 16th-century mansion,[85] originally the seat of the Bennet family.[86] In 1645 the house was used for meetings between Royalist and Parliamentary representatives negotiating the abortive 'treaty' of that year; it was then clearly of considerable extent.[87] A view published in 1789[88] shows the building reduced to its present size; it had two curvilinear gables above the bays on its principal front and a two-storied bay window at its north-east end. By the end of the century High Street had been diverted to run immediately past the house which at that time was let out in tenements.[89] In 1802 an Uxbridge sculptor, John Burgiss, was employed under Sir John Soane on masonry work at the Treaty House, perhaps in connexion with its conversion into an inn.[90] A watercolour of c. 1810 shows the walls partly faced with stucco; the front gables and the lower story of the end bay window had by then been removed. The view also includes a small octagonal building which may originally have formed part of a detached gatehouse.[91] By 1816 the house had become the Crown Inn, an earlier 'Crown' near the market having recently been demolished.[92]

Three surviving inns in High Street—the 'Three Tuns', the 'King's Arms', and the 'George'—incorporate 15th- and 16th-century work.[93] Two other inns, the 'Leg' and the 'Axe', mentioned in the 15th century,[94] probably changed their signs during the 17th century: the 'Axe' is last mentioned by name in 1647.[95] The 'Bull' and the 'Cross Keys' were in existence by 1548.[96] Other Uxbridge inns mentioned before 1648 include the 'Swan', standing in 1602,[97] the 'Black Bull' (1603),[98] the 'Spread Eagle' (1610),[99] the 'Chequer' (1620),[1] the 'Saracen's Head', built about 1619,[2] the 'Eagle and Child' (1632),[3] the 'Bell' near the market-house,[4] the 'Crown' and the 'White Horse', all three first mentioned in 1636,[5] the 'Rose', and the 'Queen's Head'.[6] A hundred years later there were twenty-nine licensed alehouses in the town.[7]

By 1664, despite severe visitations of the plague in the early years of the century,[8] 240 of the 431 houses in Hillingdon parish charged to hearth tax were situated in Uxbridge.[9] Further growth almost cer-

tainly followed the transfer to representatives of the townspeople in 1695 of the profits of Uxbridge manor.[10] Wooden pipes supplying the town with water from the Colne are said to have been laid in 1701,[11] and by 1727 twenty cottages, probably used as almshouses, had been erected in the Lynch.[12] In the 1730s, and probably earlier,[13] the main street extended south-eastward beyond Vine Street and the confines of the old borough ditch to form the contiguous district known as Hillingdon or Town End.[14] By 1782 there were said to be 366 houses within the borough ditch with a population of 1,712,[15] and the cramped and insanitary nature of High Street was causing inconvenience and concern.[16] Three years later the manorial trustees secured an Act[17] authorizing them to widen and improve High Street by demolishing the market-house and other buildings and by altering the course of the road between Mercer's Bridge over the Frays stream and High Bridge. A new market-house was completed in 1789[18] on a site slightly west of the old building. High Street was diverted at the west end of Mercer's Bridge to follow a new line about 52 yds. south-west of the old road, thus running immediately below the north-east gable-end of the Treaty House.[19] Provision was also made in the Act, which was reinforced by a second Act passed in 1806,[20] for the regulation of protruding signs, spouts, and steps, and for paving, lighting, and cleaning the streets.[21]

A panorama of Uxbridge High Street, probably drawn about 1790,[22] shows that it was then a neat road lined on both sides with Georgian frontages and a few shops.[23] The only significant non-domestic buildings shown are a chair factory at Hillingdon End, the recently completed market-house near the centre of the street, and a malthouse, a brewery, Mercer's (formerly Frays) mill, and Higgenson's bank, all at the north-west end of the town.[24] Apart from some of the inns, fifteen of which are shown, most of the old timber-framed domestic buildings appear to have been recently refronted or rebuilt.[25] The more imposing Georgian façades are shown at the north-west end of the street where several

[85] Ibid. 129, plates 31, 146.
[86] Lysons, *Mdx. Pars.* 179.
[87] Edw. Hyde, Earl of Clarendon, *Hist. of the Great Rebellion*, ed. Macray, iii. 472–3.
[88] *Gent. Mag.* 1789, lix, facing p. 685.
[89] See below; Lysons, *Mdx. Pars.* 179 and facing plate.
[90] R. Gunnis, *Dict. Brit. Sculptors, 1660–1851*, 70.
[91] See plate facing p. 60.
[92] Brewer, *Beauties of Eng. and Wales*, x(5), 532, 534.
[93] Hist. Mon. Com. *Mdx.* 130.
[94] C 1/41/265; /16/586. Camden, *Britannia*, ii. 78, commented on the many inns in Uxbridge in the 16th cent.
[95] M.R.O., Acc. 538/29–30.
[96] B.M. Harl. MS. 605, ff. 7v–9.
[97] C 142/304/12.
[98] C 142/366/187.
[99] M.R.O., S.R. 492/5.
[1] M.R.O., Acc. 88/56.
[2] M.R.O., Acc. 538/31–33.
[3] C.P.43/197/5.
[4] M.R.O., Acc. 448/1.
[5] *Mdx. & Herts. N. & Q.* iv. 78.
[6] M.R.O., Acc. 538/29–30.
[7] M.R.O., L.V. 6/84. A further 14 inns were said to be in Hillingdon par., but some at least of these were at Hillingdon End, included for most practical purposes in the town.
[8] See p. 63.
[9] M.R.O., H.T.6.
[10] See p. 72.

[11] TS. notes in Uxb. libr. section of original pipe in Uxb. Mus.
[12] M.R.O., Acc. 538/1; for the almshouses see below, p. 98.
[13] 17th-cent. houses on the east side of the highway are described in Hist. Mon. Com. *Mdx.* 78.
[14] J. Seller, *Map of Mdx.* (1733); T. Millward, *Map of Mdx.* (1742).
[15] Lysons, *Mdx. Pars.* 185.
[16] *Hist. of Uxbridge*, 76–77.
[17] Act for demolishing Uxbridge market-house, 25 Geo. III, c. 16; M.R.O., Acc. 473/6 (Bill). See also M.R.O., S.R. 3496/49.
[18] Lysons, *Mdx. Pars.* 177.
[19] The course of the old road is shown on Ogilby, *Survey of Roads* (1675).
[20] Act for more effectually paving streets of Uxbridge, 46 Geo. III, c. 60 (Local Act).
[21] For the execution of these provisions see M.R.O., Acc. 538/1, 2.
[22] The pen and ink drawing on two rolls, one for each side of the street, is in Uxbridge library. An endorsement recording the burning of Mercer's Mill in 1796 suggests that it was completed before that date; but cf. G. Hutson, 'Recollections of Uxbridge', MS. (c. 1884) penes Uxb. libr.
[23] See plate facing p. 61. Some trees were removed under the Act of 1806.
[24] For details of these see pp. 77, 81.
[25] cf. Brewer, *Beauties of Eng. and Wales*, x(5), 530.

substantial houses were evidently newly erected in the 18th and early 19th centuries. Examples which survived in 1968 were the Bank House (no. 64), no. 66, and no. 118, refronted. Some of the refronted buildings were structurally of the 15th and 16th centuries.[26] They included the Red House, demolished in 1967, and two houses adjacent to it; others further south on the same side of the street were still standing in 1968.

The present market-house, dating from 1789, is a two-storied building of brown brick with a long straight frontage to High Street of eleven bays.[27] The line of the rear wall is slightly concave in plan, with the result that St. Margaret's church, which lies immediately behind, is hemmed in and largely hidden from view. The market-house is supported on fifty-one Tuscan columns but the colonnades, originally open, are now glazed externally. The three central bays of the High Street front have round-headed first-floor windows, are raised by an extra story, and have a crowning pediment. The whole building is surmounted by a clock turret supporting a circular bell cupola.

Outside Uxbridge the pattern of settlement within the old parish changed little before the 19th century. In Hillingdon village, apart from the church,[28] few pre-19th century buildings have survived. Cedar House, north of the church, is a gabled brick building of the late 16th century with 18th-century alterations.[29] It stands in a walled garden at the junction of Uxbridge Road and Vine Lane and is entered from the south by an 18th-century wrought-iron gate flanked by rusticated brick piers. Samuel Reynardson, the eminent botanist, lived there from about 1678 until his death in 1721;[30] he is said to have planted the cedar tree after which the house is named.[31] To the west of Vine Lane a row of old houses on the north side of Uxbridge Road[32] was demolished when the road was widened and built up with shops in 1935-7. A surviving group opposite the west end of the church includes the Red Lion Inn, traditionally associated with Charles I,[33] and two houses to the south of it, both timber-framed and of 16th-century origin.[34]

Small hamlets at Little Hillingdon, Goulds Green, Colham Green, and Yiewsley were probably established by 1600.[35] A few surviving cottages and farm buildings incorporating 16th- and 17th-century features suggest scattered settlement around the hamlets in the east,[36] and mid-18th-century maps show a few houses south of Cowley and on the roads north of Uxbridge.[37] But as late as 1864 there were only four farm-houses—Hercies, Rye Fields, Pole

Hill, and Hillingdon Heath—in the area east of Little Hillingdon,[38] and, except for Philpots Farm, Rabbs Farm, and Colham Manor Farm on the east side of Cowley Road, the old open-field area south and west of Colham Green remained virtually uninhabited until after 1900.[39] On the commons, however, several plots were inclosed in the 17th and 18th centuries to provide sites for country residences. Blue House or Belmont on Uxbridge Common west of the Harefield road was probably built in the late 17th century. Between 1705 and 1712 the house was occasionally occupied by Richard, Lord Shannon.[40] William Wilberforce lived from 1824 to 1826 at the Chestnuts, an 18th-century house which still stands in Honeycroft Hill.[41] West of Little Hillingdon was a mansion known from the 18th century onwards as Hillingdon House. Said to have been built in 1617,[42] it was rebuilt in 1717 by the last Duke of Schomberg,[43] and again after being destroyed by fire in 1844.[44] Hillingdon House was described in 1907 as a brick and stone building, partly stuccoed, with extensive outbuildings and ornamental gardens covering in all 47 a.[45] An artificial lake of 5 a. bordering the gardens to the west was formed by damming the Pinn stream,[46] and the adjoining park, which then extended westward to Hillingdon End, comprised 158 a.[47] The Marchioness of Rockingham, widow of the prime minister, died at Hillingdon House in 1804;[48] members of the banking family of Cox later occupied the mansion,[49] which figures in Greville's diary and other memoirs.[50] In 1915 the house and park, after being on the market since 1908, were bought by the government, and an air force station was established there.[51] Seven gentlemen's residences had been built along the northern edge of Hillingdon Heath by 1825 when, under the inclosure award, their gardens were extended to the main road. The line was continued east of Long Lane by Hillingdon Heath Farm,[52] known by 1865 as Park Field.[53] All of these houses survived in 1968. A little to the north, on the west side of Long Lane, was Hillingdon Place, said to have been built in the 18th century by Admiral Drake,[54] and later occupied by members of the De Salis family.[55]

South of the London road was another large mansion, built shortly before 1878 by Peter de Salis, Count of the Holy Roman Empire,[56] and standing in an estate of more than 100 a. known variously as Coomes, Little London, and, in the 19th century, Hillingdon Park.[57] Nearby, at the junction of the modern Harlington Road and Drayton Road, Moorcroft perpetuates the name of an earlier house on the same site owned by Drew Saunders,[58] a 16th-century

[26] Hist. Mon. Com. *Mdx.* 130-1.
[27] See plate facing p. 60.
[28] See p. 89.
[29] Hist. Mon. Com. *Mdx.* 76-77; see plate facing p. 64.
[30] Lysons, *Mdx. Pars.* 156.
[31] Brewer, *Beauties of Eng. and Wales*, x(5), 545-6.
[32] See pl. facing p. 90.
[33] Lysons, *Mdx. Pars.* 152.
[34] Hist. Mon. Com. *Mdx.* 77.
[35] *Mdx. Sess. Recs.* ii. 200; iii. 29; M.R.O., Acc. 448/1; the evidence cited in *P.N. Mdx.* (E.P.N.S.), 41-42 should be used with care.
[36] Hist. Mon. Com. *Mdx..* 77.
[37] Warburton, *Map of Mdx., Essex & Herts.* (1746); Rocque, *Map of Mdx.* (1754).
[38] O.S. Map 1/2,500, Mdx. xiv. 4 (1866 edn.).
[39] Ibid. (1895 and 1914 edns.).
[40] Lysons, *Mdx. Pars.* 156.
[41] File in Uxb. libr.; ex. inf. Mr. K. R. Pearce.

[42] 18th-cent. copy of 1636 survey of Colham manor *penes* Uxb. libr.
[43] Lysons, *Mdx. Pars.* 155.
[44] Newspaper cutting *penes* Uxb. libr.
[45] M.R.O., Acc 503/107.
[46] Brewer, *Beauties of Eng. and Wales*, x(5), 538-9.
[47] M.R.O., Acc. 503/93a, 94, 107.
[48] *Complete Peerage*, xi. 62.
[49] M.R.O., Acc. 503/83, 107, 108.
[50] M. Robbins, *Middlesex*, 296.
[51] See below.
[52] M.R.O., Hillingdon Incl. Plan (1825).
[53] O.S. Map 6", Mdx. xiv. NE. (1865 edn.).
[54] Lysons, *Mdx. Pars.* 157; *D.N.B.*
[55] Lysons, *Mdx. Pars.* 157.
[56] M.R.O., Acc. 448/2.
[57] Lysons, *Mdx. Pars.* 157; Brewer, *Beauties of Eng. and Wales*, x(5), 547.
[58] See pp. 89, 91.

Merchant of the Staple. A mental home was established here about 1798 by Dr. Stilwell, whose descendants enlarged it and maintained it for 150 years. The property was bought in 1953 by the Middlesex County Council;[59] part is now used for old people and part as training centres for handicapped or disturbed adults and children. The core of the present house is an apparently 18th-century brick range of three stories and seven bays. Almost the only clue to its 16th-century origin is a Tudor-arched stone fireplace on the ground floor. This range was extended at both ends in the early and mid 19th century, and a detached doctor's house was built in the grounds. The large south-east wing of the main building dates from the late 19th century. Other 18th-century residences on Hillingdon Heath included Norringtons, with a freehold estate of about 80 a.,[60] and a house called Shammonds, apparently demolished between 1781 and 1785.[61] Another house called Newcrofts on Pield Heath was built in 1792 and demolished in the 1930s.[62]

Details of the population and economy of rural Hillingdon before the 14th century are confined to the Survey of 1086, which records 43 people in Hillingdon and Colham manors. The Domesday population of Colham comprised a priest on one hide, 6 villeins each on one virgate and 4 on two virgates, 10 bordars holding 5 a. each, 4 cottars, and 8 serfs. In Hillingdon there were 2 villeins on ½ hide, 2 bordars on 10 a., one cottar, and 2 Frenchmen who shared 1½ hide and had 3 men under them.[63] By the 14th century the population of Uxbridge had probably outstripped that of rural Hillingdon. For a muster of c. 1335 Colham was expected to contribute 57 footmen and Uxbridge 61 men under 3 officers, in all approximately one-eighth of the total county force.[64] Subsequent population increases reflect the disparity between the economic growth of town and rural parish. The relative prosperity of Uxbridge is indicated by an assessment of 1522–3 to which 153 persons in Hillingdon parish were taxed, 77 of them from Uxbridge.[65] In 1547 there were 320 communicants in Hillingdon,[66] but despite visitations of the plague in 1593,[67] and again in 1603, 1625,[68] and 1636,[69] the rate of expansion in Uxbridge continued to outpace that of the parish generally. In 1642 in Uxbridge 288 adult males took the protestation oath compared to 223 in the remainder of the parish.[70] By 1664 there were said to be 234 occupied houses in the town and only 179 in the rural parish.[71] In 1782 Hillingdon, excluding Uxbridge, contained 317 houses with a total population of 1,627 and the town 366 houses with a population of 1,712.[72]

DEVELOPMENT SINCE 1800. Significant changes in the topography of the parish began with the cutting at the end of the 18th century of the Grand Junction (later Grand Union) Canal. Numerous schemes for a navigable waterway linking London with the Colne near Uxbridge had been advanced from 1641 onwards.[73] The Act finally passed in 1793[74] provided for a canal passing Uxbridge to the west and running parallel with Cowley Road as far as Colham Manor Farm where it turned to flow eastward out of the parish. Excavations on Uxbridge Moor began in May 1793,[75] and the Middlesex section of the canal was completed by 1796.[76] The facilities offered by the canal for bulk transport to the metropolis and the industrial Midlands revitalized the commercial life of Uxbridge and facilitated the working, from about 1815, of the brickearth deposits in south Hillingdon.[77] By 1801 passenger barges were also running daily between Paddington and Uxbridge.[78] This development had little effect on the volume of traffic on the London road, described in 1798 as one of the busiest highways in the country.[79] An account of Uxbridge in the 1830s[80] describes the constant passage along High Street of pedestrians, cattle, waggons carrying farm produce from Buckinghamshire and flour from the Uxbridge mills to London, carriers' carts, and private carriages. More than 40 passenger and mail coaches running between London and the West also passed through the town between 4.30 a.m. and 10 p.m. The fastest coach, 'The Age', took 3 hours 20 minutes for the journey from Oxford to London. There were twelve daily coaches from Uxbridge to London:[81] two four-horse coaches left from the 'Kings Arm's' and two more from the 'Three Tuns'. Three carriers ran daily from Uxbridge to London and there were daily services to Drayton, Harefield, Pinner, and Windsor. In addition 33 long-distance carriers running between London and places as far distant as Bristol and Birmingham provided connexions to Uxbridge. Extensive stabling and refreshment accommodation was provided by the numerous inns along High Street: in 1853 there were 54 public houses and inns in the town.[82]

After the Inclosure Act of 1812 a number of small houses, many occupied by workers in the chair industry,[83] were built on allotments along both sides of the London road south of the 'Eight Bells'.[84] In 1828 strong criticism was levelled against the erection in Uxbridge by private speculators of large numbers of insanitary cottages.[85] At about the same time a line of middle-class residences was built along the London road south of Hillingdon End. The houses, terraced, detached, and in pairs, faced

[59] Mdx. Advertiser, 26 June 1953.
[60] M.R.O., Acc. 503/62–64, /90–91.
[61] Ibid. /201–3, /215, /216.
[62] Ex inf. Mr. N. W. Chenery, quoting the demolition contractors.
[63] V.C.H. Mdx. i. 124.
[64] M.R.O., F. 37/2–3.
[65] E 179/141/115.
[66] E 301/34/128.
[67] Acts of P.C. 1592–3, 348.
[68] Lysons, Mdx. Pars. 186.
[69] Cal. S.P. Dom. 1636–7, 86.
[70] Hse. of Lords, Mdx. Protestation Rets.
[71] M.R.O., H.T.6.
[72] Guildhall MS. 9558; Lysons, Mdx. Pars. 171.
[73] E. Forde, Design for bringing a Navigable River from Rickmansworth to St. Giles-in-the-Fields (1641); Plan for making Colne navigable from Watford and for cutting a canal

from Cowley Stream to Lond. (1694); Map of the Colne and the particular place whence the navigation is to be taken (? c. 1725): all in B.M. Map Room; Plan for the intended Canal from Uxbridge to Marylebone (1766): M.R.O., Acc. 668/1.
[74] Grand Junction Canal Act, 33 Geo. III, c. 80.
[75] Lysons, Mdx. Pars. 177.
[76] J. Carey, Inland Navigation (1795), 86, 119.
[77] Middleton, View, 403; see below, pp. 77–78.
[78] Prints penes Uxb. libr.; V.C.H. Mdx. ii. 123.
[79] Middleton, View, 396.
[80] Section based on Hutson, Recollections.
[81] Robson's Dir. (1839).
[82] Lake's Uxbridge Almanack (1853).
[83] See p. 80.
[84] Census, 1821; Hutson, Recollections.
[85] The Uxbridge Note Book (1828), 2, penes Uxb. libr. The reports of resulting poverty are probably exaggerated.

the park of Hillingdon House and bore such names as Pleasant Place (dated 1826), Park Villa and Rose Cottage.[86] Among larger residences built *c.* 1800 was Park Lodge, in Park Road, which was demolished in 1968.[87] Hillingdon Court, set in extensive grounds on the east side of Vine Lane,[88] was built in the 1850s by Charles Mills, founder of the banking house of Glyn, Mills and Co. Mills's wife was a daughter of Richard Cox, who lived on the opposite side of Vine Lane. In 1868 Charles Mills was created a baronet and in 1886 his son was created Lord Hillingdon.[89] The Hillingdon Court estate was sold on the death of the second baron in 1919: the house became a Roman Catholic school, while part of the grounds was used for building[90] and part acquired in 1928 by the council.[91]

By 1845 houses were said to be almost continuous along the road between Uxbridge and West Drayton.[92] Although this account is probably exaggerated, developments along Cowley Road and at Yiewsley certainly followed the completion in 1838 of the G.W.R. line to Bristol and the west and the opening of West Drayton station, which lay a few yards inside Hillingdon parish.[93] A regular connexion with Uxbridge was established when, between 1840 and 1842, William Tollit opened an omnibus service from the George Inn to West Drayton station, with six daily trips. By 1842 there were eight up and eight down trains daily, the fastest of which reached Paddington in 25 minutes.[94] Several abortive schemes for direct rail links between Buckinghamshire, Uxbridge, and London were advanced during the 1840s,[95] but not until 1853 did work begin on the G.W.R. line linking Uxbridge with the main line west of West Drayton station. The 2½-mile single track, with a terminus at Vine Street, was opened in 1856, regular trains reaching Paddington in 55 minutes.[96] Five years later a scheme to link Vine Street station with the proposed L. & N.W.R. line at Rickmansworth (Herts.) was formulated. Although work officially began in 1861 and further powers were obtained between 1862 and 1868 and again between 1881 and 1899, the scheme was eventually abandoned.[97]

Changes associated with the railways and canal were widespread. The volume of traffic along the London road fell away sharply during the period after 1840, and by 1880 road traffic through Uxbridge had almost ceased.[98] As a result several of the inns and adjoining stables in High Street were demolished or converted into private dwellings. Many of the buildings in High Street appear to have been refronted or more extensively altered between 1840 and 1880.[99] Further building and improvement

accompanied the commercial expansion which began about 1830. By 1839 Uxbridge supported a bank, library, and reading rooms, and was said to have the 'appearance of activity and great respectability'.[1] The public rooms in Vine Street (often called the Town Hall) were built in 1836 or 1837,[2] and a theatre was built in Windsor Street before 1839.[3] Six years later the town was described as 'large, well-built, and lighted with gas'.[4] Vine Street was widened about 1859 to accommodate traffic using the new station, which rivalled the market-house as the focus of activity in the town.[5]

Several industrial buildings, including a gas-works, oil mills, and mustard mills, were erected near the canal on Uxbridge Moor between 1830 and 1850,[6] and extensive wharves were built there and at the west end of Uxbridge.[7] Foundry Terrace, off York Road, was built about 1830 to house employees of an iron works in George Street.[8] By 1864 domestic building had also expanded westward to form the suburb of Uxbridge Moor, a straggling settlement along Rockingham Road, Waterloo Road, and in the triangle formed by St. John's Road and Cowley Mill Road.[9] Although the labourers' cottages erected at Hillingdon End after 1812 were demolished to make way for St. Andrew's church (completed in 1865) and a walled extension to Hillingdon House park to the east, further houses on the north side of the town were built between 1865 and 1870.[10] By 1871 there were more than 1,000 houses in the town and its environs, with a population of 5,329.[11]

Beyond the immediate vicinity of Uxbridge the establishment of new lines of communication significantly modified the traditional geography of the parish. The shape of the scattered settlements in the east, relatively remote from the canal and railways, altered little. But in the south-west and extreme west of the parish new buildings began to appear. By 1864[12] there were houses along Packet Boat Lane, at Little Britain on the Colne, and around the Trout Inn on Trout Lane west of Yiewsley. The erection of new houses, industrial premises, and St. Matthew's church (consecrated 1858) in Yiewsley itself began the process which in the 20th century was to transform the village into a peripheral district of the composite suburb of Yiewsley and West Drayton. In Yiewsley High Street many mid-19th-century middle-class houses were converted to commercial use by the building of shops on their front gardens. Further east the establishment, from about 1815 onwards, of brick-making industries associated with those in West Drayton[13] helped to transform the aspect of the south of the parish. The old open-field area from the Drayton boundary northward almost

[86] O.S. Map 6″, Mdx. xiv. NE. (1865 edn.).
[87] See plate facing p. 64.
[88] See plate facing p. 64.
[89] *P.O. Dir. Mdx.* (1862); *Complete Peerage.*
[90] R. de Salis, *Hillingdon through Eleven Centuries,* 99; see below.
[91] See below.
[92] *Home Cnties. Dir.* (1845).
[93] T. B. Peacock, *G.W. Suburban Services,* 47.
[94] *Lake's Uxbridge Appendix* (1842).
[95] M. Robbins, 'Railways and Railway Schemes at Uxbridge', *Rly. Mag.* cii. 295–8.
[96] Timetables *penes* Uxb. libr.
[97] H. L. Lewis, 'The Uxbridge and Rickmansworth Railway', *Rly. Mag.* xci.
[98] Hutson, *Recollections.*
[99] Ibid. Many inn yards, however, were not cleared until the 1930s: see below, p. 65.

[1] *Robson's Dir.* (1839); *Lake's Uxbridge Almanack* (1853).
[2] *Home Cnties. Dir.* (1845); see below, p. 81.
[3] Playbill *penes* Uxb. libr.
[4] *Home Cnties. Dir.* (1845). For the introduction of gas-lighting see below, p. 86.
[5] Notice of improvements to Vine St. *penes* Uxb. libr.
[6] See p. 80.
[7] *Home Cnties. Dir.* (1851).
[8] *Uxbridge Gaz.* 12 July 1935, recording the demolition of the terrace. See below, p. 80.
[9] O.S. Maps 1/2,500, Mdx. xiv. 3. (1866 edn.) (actual survey 1864).
[10] *Kelly's Dir. Mdx.* (1870).
[11] *Census,* 1871.
[12] O.S. Map 1/2,500, Mdx. xiv. 11 (1866 edn.).
[13] See p. 78.

1. Hillingdon: the Cedar House, *c.* 1580 and later 2. Uxbridge: Park Lodge, *c.* 1800, demolished 1968
3. Hillingdon Court, *c.* 1850 4. Harrow Weald: Grim's Dyke, 1872

COUNTRY RESIDENCES

to Colham Green and the whole of Hide Field were given over to the extraction of gravel and brickearth before 1894.[14] Elsewhere in the parish the railway encouraged horticultural specialization for the metropolitan market. By 1894 nurseries had been established on the London road south of Uxbridge, in Cowley Mill Road, Kingston Lane, and on Hillingdon Heath. The influx of labourers for the horticultural and brick-making industries was largely responsible for almost trebling the number of inhabited houses in the parish, excluding Uxbridge, between 1831 and 1891.[15]

Further growth in the population between 1891 and 1931 was accommodated by an expansion of council and speculative building which for the first time significantly affected the traditional pattern of settlement in the parish.[16] Most of the early building took place south and immediately east of Uxbridge and on the north side of Yiewsley. Between 1894 and 1913[17] private development spread southward from Uxbridge along Cowley Road to the Greenway and eastward with the opening of Montague Road and Honeycroft Hill. Further south at Yiewsley former agricultural land north and east of the village was laid out for building, and by 1913 the settlement extended northward almost as far as Falling Lane and to Horton Lane in the east. Council building under successive Housing Acts followed. Austin Waye, Frays Waye, and Westcott Waye on Uxbridge Moor were laid out between 1919 and 1939, and further housing complexes in Church Lane, Cowley Mill Road, Rockingham Road, and in the Lynch in Uxbridge itself were completed before the Second World War.[18] Developments completed during the same period at Cowley included houses in Station Road, Meadow View, and on the 21-acre Cowley Hall estate, formerly the manor-house site, which was acquired by the local authority in 1929.[19] Between Hillingdon End and Stratford Bridge a separate development took place on the west side of the main road (renamed Hillingdon Road) with the building of Nursery Waye, Manor Waye, and a complex between Orchard Waye and the Greenway. The effect of early-20th-century expansion in these areas together with private building north of Uxbridge was to transform the formerly distinct settlements of Uxbridge, Uxbridge Moor, and Cowley into an almost continuous suburb stretching from Uxbridge Common to Cowley Peachey. Further building after 1910 between Yiewsley and West Drayton achieved a similar result. In 1924 Yiewsley was said to have 'no community of interests' with Uxbridge, from which it was separated by a belt of open country.[20] Ten years later houses had completely filled the area between Falling Lane, Kingston Avenue, and the canal. Building south of the old village completed the transformation of the two autonomous settlements into a composite suburb,

centred on West Drayton station and the common main street formed by the High Street and Station Road. In the north and east of the parish building between 1920 and 1935 for the first time encroached significantly on the former open-field districts. By 1934 private housing estates and access ways covered much of the triangular area between Hillingdon village, Colham Green, and Goulds Green. Further private building was concentrated north of Hillingdon village along Long Lane and the east side of Vine Lane and further north on former agricultural land around Blossom Way and Sweetcroft Lane. Other private estates south and west of Swakeleys House in Ickenham extended southward into Hillingdon as far as Western Avenue.[21] More than 1,500 private dwellings were erected in Hillingdon and Cowley between 1931 and 1933, and the total had exceeded 5,000 by 1939.[22] Council building during the 1930s included 220 houses on the Oak Farm Estate (formerly Rye Fields Farm), which formed the nucleus of the new residential district of North Hillingdon south of Hillingdon Circus at the junction of Long Lane and Western Avenue. By 1939 the council had built about 1,200 dwellings in Hillingdon and Cowley.

The provision of social amenities to meet the rapid expansion of population after 1890 proceeded slowly. In Uxbridge the Court House in Harefield Road was completed in 1907.[23] The Savoy cinema, built on the site of the old public rooms at the junction of Vine Street and High Street, was opened in 1921,[24] and the Methodist Central Hall at the corner of Park Road was erected in 1930.[25] West of High Street County Buildings, which included accommodation for a library and museum, were completed about 1939.[26] A number of old and insanitary properties was demolished during the 1930s. Foundry Terrace was cleared in 1935,[27] and other dwellings were demolished to make way for the new London Transport station opened in 1938.[28] The construction of the station in axis with the market-house effectively emphasized the centre of the modern town. The station building, one of a notable series designed by Charles Holden for the London Passenger Transport Board in the 1930s,[29] has an impressive and spaciously planned interior. Between 1932 and 1939 the council demolished 435 slum dwellings in Hillingdon and Cowley, many of them houses in the old inn yards and crowded streets of Uxbridge.[30] Elsewhere in the parish hospital facilities established in the late 19th century were much expanded. Hillingdon Hospital in Royal Lane evolved from the infirmary of the Union workhouse which, in its turn, had replaced the parish workhouse established there in 1747.[31] Amenities were considerably extended during the 1930s and in 1945, after a number of temporary wards had been added, there were 806 beds. The building of a large new multi-story hospital

[14] O.S. Maps 1/2,500, Mdx. xiv. 12 (1866 and 1895 edns.).
[15] *Census*, 1831, 1891.
[16] Ibid. 1891, 1931.
[17] Cf. O.S. Maps 1/2,500, Mdx. xiv. 3, 4 (1895–6 and 1914 edns.).
[18] Information on housing developments after 1890 provided by Uxb. Bor. Council.
[19] Uxb. Bor., Reg. of Properties, M.D.28.
[20] Mdx. Cnty. Coun. Reps. 1924, G.P. Cttee. App. to meeting of 31 Jan. 1924.
[21] See p. 101.
[22] *Com. on Local Govt. in Greater Lond. Mins. of Evi-*

dence (1958).
[23] Ex inf. Sir Christopher Cowan, J.P.
[24] Programmes *penes* Uxb. libr. The cinema closed in 1960: file in Uxb. libr.
[25] See p. 94.
[26] Ex inf. the bor. librarian. The library moved into the building in 1940.
[27] *Uxbridge Gaz.* 12 July 1935.
[28] See below.
[29] I. Nairn, *Nairn's London*, 232.
[30] *Borough Petition* (1951), 63–65.
[31] See p. 83; ex inf. Uxb. Hosp. Group Sec.

was begun in 1962 on the opposite side of Pield Heath Road; by 1968 this catered for 799 patients.[32] The site was formerly the grounds of the Firs, an 18th- or early-19th-century country house which itself was adapted and extended for use as a school of nursing. A nurses' home was erected on part of the former workhouse site,[33] where the demolition of older buildings, including those of the mid-19th-century workhouse, was proceeding gradually in 1968. St. John's (formerly Uxbridge Joint) Hospital in Kingston Lane was opened in 1894[34] as a hospital for infectious diseases. Initially there was only a single ward in Kingston Lane with an attached small-pox hospital in Yeading Lane, Hayes.[35] Additional wards in Kingston Lane were built in the early 20th century and in 1968 the hospital accommodated 140 infectious and geriatric patients.[36] The large private mental home established by the Stilwell family at Moorcroft[37] had 40 inmates in 1845,[38] and this figure remained fairly constant until it was closed about 1947.[39]

At Hillingdon End topographical changes followed the purchase in 1915 by the government of the Hillingdon House estate.[40] In 1917 the Armament and Gunnery School of the Royal Flying Corps was established on the site. This unit was disbanded in 1919, and after 1920 the station was occupied by the Central Depot of the R.A.F. and, from time to time, other training, signals, and operational units. During the Second World War the station became an important Fighter Command Group headquarters controlling the air defence of London and south-east England. Buildings on the 180-acre site include a hospital, a sports stadium, and extensive living and recreational facilities. In 1963 there were 411 R.A.F. and W.R.A.F. personnel at Uxbridge, together with 274 civilians employed on the base.

The rapid expansion in population and building was paralleled, and is partly explained, by a significant improvement in communications after 1900. Despite the numerous plans advanced during the late 19th century, the only practical modifications to the rail system concerned the existing G.W.R. branch between Uxbridge and West Drayton.[41] This line was converted to standard gauge in 1871 and doubled nine years later. A station at Cowley was opened in 1904. Schemes to extend the Metropolitan line from the terminus at Harrow as far as Uxbridge and by the G.W.R. to link the Vine Street branch with the new main line from London to High Wycombe were approved in 1898. Work on the Metropolitan line, employing some 2,000 labourers, began in 1901. A terminus was built at Belmont Road, Uxbridge, and a station, Hillingdon (Swakeleys), to serve the northern part of the parish was

constructed in 1923 on Long Lane just inside the boundary with Ickenham. The line was opened for steam trains in 1904,[42] and these were replaced by electric trains in the following year. In 1910 District line trains were introduced as far as Uxbridge and in 1933 Piccadilly line trains also began to run along the same route. For a time all three services ran as far as Uxbridge, but District line services were later discontinued and in 1964 the town was served by the Metropolitan and Piccadilly lines only.[43] A new station opposite the market-house was opened in 1938 and the old Belmont Road station was then closed. The construction of the G.W.R. branch from the main line in Harefield began in 1900. Work on an iron bridge over High Street between the Frays and Colne streams and an approach embankment on the north side of the road was started. High Street station was opened for passenger traffic in 1907, but despite representations from the local council, the scheme to link the station with the Vine Street line was finally abandoned in 1914.[44] In the same year the High Street line was opened for goods traffic. The bridge over High Street was removed in 1922 and, following the closure in 1939 of the passenger service, which had been suspended between 1917 and 1919, High Street station was demolished. Goods traffic still used the line in 1964. On the branch line to West Drayton, Vine Street and Cowley stations were closed to passengers in 1962, and by 1966 the lines had been removed.

Although three separate rail termini had been built in Uxbridge by 1907, the railways served only the peripheral areas of the parish, and Hillingdon village and the settlements to the south-east relied on road and tramway communications. As early as 1871 the Hillingdon vestry approved a scheme advanced by the London and County Tramways Co. to run a line along the London road from Southall to Uxbridge.[45] Early schemes, however, were not pursued, and the London United Tramways Co.'s line to Southall was not extended to Uxbridge until 1904.[46] A terminus was built in High Street just north of the modern Odeon cinema and a depot housing 25 electric trams was constructed at Hillingdon Heath. The depot was closed about 1915 and has since been adapted for industrial purposes. The first bus service in the parish was instituted in 1921 when the Thames Valley Co. began to operate a route from High Wycombe to Uxbridge.[47] Other services, including one running alongside the tramway from Shepherds Bush, were instituted during the 1920s. A bus garage in Uxbridge was opened in 1922. In face of this competition more powerful trams were introduced, cutting the time for the journey from Shepherds Bush to Uxbridge

[32] *The Hospitals Year Book* (1969).
[33] See plate facing p. 105.
[34] Ex inf. the Hosp. Medical Officer.
[35] The later history of this establishment is unknown. It is said to have been opened as an emergency hospital during an epidemic in the Uxbridge area and may have been closed when the epidemic was over: ex inf. Mr. K. R. Pearce.
[36] *The Hospitals Year Book* (1969).
[37] See pp. 62–63.
[38] *Home Cnties. Dir.* (1845).
[39] *Census*, 1861–1911; ex inf. the bor. librarian.
[40] Paragraph based on information supplied by the Air Ministry.
[41] Section based on Peacock, *G.W. Suburban Services*, *passim*; R. K. Kirkland, 'The Railways of Uxbridge',

Rly. Mag. xcviii. 147 sqq.
[42] *Uxb. Gaz.* 30 June 1904; photograph of the opening *penes* Uxb. libr.
[43] Ex inf. Lond. Transport Exec.
[44] The line of the proposed track between the two lines is clearly shown in O.S. Map 1/2,500, Mdx. xiv. 3 (1914 edn.).
[45] Vestry Order Bk. 1867–94.
[46] *Uxb. Gaz.* 31 May 1904; following section, except where otherwise stated, based on 'Some Aspects of our Local Transport History', *Uxbridge Record* (Jnl. Uxb. Local Hist. Soc.), ii. 5–12.
[47] Ex inf. Mr. P. H. Grace. From 1917 to 1919, when the railway was closed as an economy measure, the G.W.R. ran a bus service from Uxbridge to Denham: ex inf. Mr. K. R. Pearce.

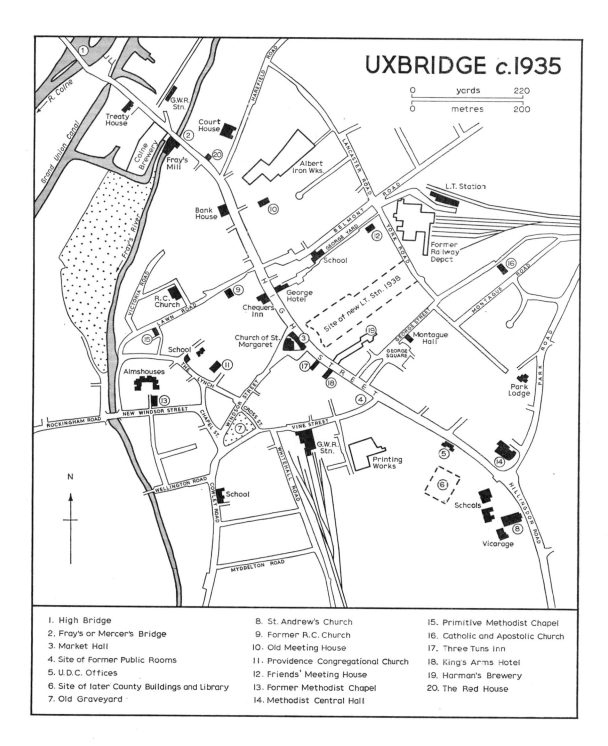

UXBRIDGE c.1935

0   yards   220

0   metres   200

R. Colne

Grand Union Canal

Treaty House

G.W.R. Stn.

Court House

Colne Brewery

Fray's Mill

Fray's River

Bank House

Albert Iron Wks.

HAREFIELD ROAD

LANCASTER ROAD

BELMONT ROAD

GEORGE YARD

YORK ROAD

L.T. Station

Former Railway Depot

School

Site of new L.T. Stn. 1938

VICTORIA ROAD

LAWN ROAD

R.C. Church

HIGH STREET

George Hotel

Chequers Inn

Church of St. Margaret

MONTAGUE ROAD

GEORGE STREET

GEORGE SQUARE

Montague Hall

PARK ROAD

Park Lodge

School

Almshouses

HELYNCH

CHAPEL ST.

WINDSOR CROSS ST.

ROCKINGHAM ROAD

NEW WINDSOR STREET

WELLINGTON ROAD

COWLEY ROAD

School

MYDDELTON ROAD

VINE STREET

WHITEHALL ROAD

G.W.R. Stn.

Printing Works

Schools

Vicarage

HILLINGDON ROAD

N

1. High Bridge
2. Fray's or Mercer's Bridge
3. Market Hall
4. Site of Former Public Rooms
5. U.D.C. Offices
6. Site of later County Buildings and Library
7. Old Graveyard

8. St. Andrew's Church
9. Former R.C. Church
10. Old Meeting House
11. Providence Congregational Church
12. Friends' Meeting House
13. Former Methodist Chapel
14. Methodist Central Hall

15. Primitive Methodist Chapel
16. Catholic and Apostolic Church
17. Three Tuns Inn
18. King's Arms Hotel
19. Harman's Brewery
20. The Red House

from 81 to 68 minutes. In 1931 improved trams were introduced on the Uxbridge line. These caused considerable congestion in High Street during the 1930s,[48] and in 1936 the trams were replaced by trolleybuses using a new terminus about a hundred yards beyond the old tram terminus. Trolleybuses continued to operate on this route until 1960. The most spectacular improvement in road communications, however, was the opening in 1934[49] of Western Avenue, the London–Oxford arterial road, which passed across the north of the parish. By 1933, when this road had been driven only as far as Hillingdon Circus, speculative building south of the roundabout had already begun.[50] Improvements to Long Lane, Uxbridge Road, Cowley Road, and, after the Second World War, the completion of Western Avenue and the reconstruction of Colham Green Road virtually completed the modern network of arterial roads.[51]

The process of urbanization, which almost ceased during the Second World War, accelerated again after 1946. Post-war housing development in Hillingdon was shared almost equally between local authority and speculative schemes. Council building was concentrated on the Violet Farm and Evelyns estates at Colham Green and on the Nine Elms and Cowley Manor estates at Cowley. Between 1945 and 1965 approximately 6,000 council and private dwellings were erected in Hillingdon and Cowley.[52] In Cowley Mill Road, between the canal and the Colne, the council developed a 26-acre industrial estate on the site of the former Uxbridge sewage works.[53] Since the opening of the estate in 1946 industrial building has been largely confined to this area and an adjoining 15-acre private trading estate.[54]

Despite industrial building and the proliferation of housing estates in the 20th century, approximately one-fifth of Hillingdon has been preserved as open space, parks, and recreation grounds, and as a result the areas north of the London road and along both banks of the Pinn to the south retain much of their rural character. Hillingdon village, although bisected by a dual-carriageway along which were built in the 1930s the 'Vine' roadhouse and a small complex of shops, retained in 1965 some of the character of an isolated rural village centred on the church and the 'Red Lion' and surrounded by largely undeveloped land. Coney Green, east of the churchyard, was acquired by the council in 1926[55] and has been preserved as an open space and cricket ground. North-west of the village the former Hillingdon House park was in 1965 shared between Hillingdon Golf Club, whose course was established here in 1892,[56] and the R.A.F. station. On the east side of Vine Lane the council laid out 56 a. of the former Hillingdon Court estate as a park.[57] Between Hercies Road and the Metropolitan line there was pasture in 1965, and almost the whole of the area between Long Lane and Uxbridge formed a distinctive residential district with large detached houses lining narrow lanes between parks and recreation grounds. North of the railway the area bounded by Park Road and Western Avenue has been preserved for agriculture and recreation. Fifteen acres of Uxbridge Common on the west side of Park Road were reserved as an open space under the inclosure award,[58] and in 1941 the council acquired 145 a. of the adjoining Hillingdon House Farm estate.[59] An open-air swimming pool off Park Road was opened in 1935,[60] and the council have since laid out the adjacent area as sports pitches.

In Uxbridge itself post-war clearance schemes resulted in the partial redevelopment of the town centre. On a 3-acre site immediately north of the London Transport station a bus station and car park were laid out and the approach roads to these facilities improved.[61] By the 1950s, however, it was clear that radical redevelopment was needed to relieve traffic congestion in the town, and with a view to an integrated scheme the local authority began to acquire possession of premises in High Street. Suggestions that the market-house should be demolished[62] were not adopted, but draft proposals for the town centre redevelopment published in 1961 provided for the eventual rebuilding of much of High Street as a pedestrian precinct with shops, restaurants, and markets, and the construction of a relief road to the south-west, leaving the old graveyard as a traffic island.[63] By 1968 wholesale clearance in the Lawn Road area west of High Street was in progress, while in High Street itself the presence of a number of empty buildings introduced a dilapidated note curiously at variance with its congested traffic and busy shops. Nursery land adjoining Kingston Lane, between Colham and Uxbridge, was acquired in 1963 for Brunel University, which received its charter in 1966. The first departments moved from Acton in 1967 and further buildings were under construction in 1968.[64]

Between 1801 and 1831 the number of houses in Uxbridge increased from 385 to 574, while the population rose from 2,111 to 3,043. In the same period the population of Hillingdon, excluding Uxbridge, rose from 1,783 to 3,842. Between 1831 and 1851 the number of dwellings in Uxbridge and its neighbourhood almost doubled and the population of that town rose by 2,055 to 5,098. In rural Hillingdon the growth during this period was even more spectacular: the number of occupied houses increased by 693 and the population by 3,760 to 7,602. The number of inhabited houses in the parish, excluding Uxbridge, had reached 2,117 by 1891, when there were 10,797 inhabitants. By 1921, after major boundary changes including the creation of Yiewsley parish, the population of Hillingdon was 12,843 and that of the 87-acre chapelry of Uxbridge 3,394. Extensive speculative and council building during the 1920s resulted in a sharp rise in the population of Hillingdon to 21,403 by 1931. In Uxbridge, however, commercial premises began to replace private dwellings, and the number of people living, as opposed to working, in the town, declined

[48] Photographs *penes* Uxb. libr.
[49] *The Times*, 15 Dec. 1934.
[50] O.S. Map 1/2,500, Mdx. ix. 16 (1934 edn.).
[51] Ex inf. Uxb. Bor Council.
[52] Ibid.
[53] See p. 80.
[54] *Greater Lond. Govt. Com. Evidence* (1958).
[55] Uxb. Bor., Reg. of Properties, M.D. 59.
[56] See p. 82.

[57] Uxb. Bor., Reg. of Properties, M.D. 50.
[58] M.R.O., E.A./Hil./2.
[59] Uxb. Bor., Reg. of Properties, M.D. 975.
[60] *Uxb. Gaz.* 30 Aug. 1935.
[61] *Borough Petition* (1951), 39.
[62] *Mdx. Advertiser*, 1 Feb. 1957.
[63] *Draft Proposals for Uxbridge Town Centre Redevelopment* (1961); ex inf. Uxb. Bor. Council.
[64] Ex inf. the academic registrar.

steadily after 1921. Thirty years later only 1,544 people lived in the 87-acre ward.[65]

Several well-known people have lived in or been associated with Hillingdon. Many of them inhabited mansions noticed above.[66] Others were incumbents, nonconformist preachers, Jesuit priests, or lords of Colham manor, and these are noticed briefly below.[67] Sir John Bennet (d. 1627), a member of the Council of the North and a judge of the Prerogative Court of Canterbury, lived at the house in Uxbridge later known as the Treaty House.[68] Impeached, he was imprisoned from 1621 to 1624, and died three years later.[69] John Lightfoot (1735–88), botanist and naturalist, was lecturer at Uxbridge from 1767 until his death and Curate of Cowley from 1768 to 1786.[70] Thomas Morten (1836–66), painter and book-illustrator, was born at Uxbridge. James Skinner (1818–81), author and hymn-writer, lived at Hillingdon for a time during 1859 when he was engaged in organizing the English Church Union. Sir John Barnard Byles (1801–84), a justice of the Common Pleas, who wrote several books and pamphlets on English law, lived in Uxbridge. John Dowson (1820–81), orientalist, was professor of Hindustani at University College, London, and between 1867 and 1877 published an eight-volume history of India.[71] Among members of the theatrical profession connected with Hillingdon were Barton Booth (1681–1733), actor, and John Rich (d. 1761), comedian and theatre manager, both of whom lived at Cowley Grove.[72] Rich's rococo sarcophagus is in Hillingdon churchyard,[73] where Thomas Harries (d. 1820), manager of Covent Garden theatre, is also buried.[74] The actress Ellen Terry (1847–1928) leased no. 84 High Street, Uxbridge, a 15th-century cottage, for use as a summer residence. It was also used for a time by her son Gordon Craig (1872–1966), whose first production, a translation of De Musset's 'On ne badine pas avec l'amour', took place at Uxbridge in 1893, in aid of the building fund of the Uxbridge National Schools.[75] The cottage was demolished in 1941.[76] Cecil J. Sharp (1859–1924), collector of English folk-music, lived at Dragonfield, Uxbridge High Street, in the early 20th century.[77] The actor Bernard Miles was born in 1907 at no. 2, Poplar Terrace, Hillingdon Heath; his family later moved to Charles Street and to Pole Hill Road.[78]

MANORS AND OTHER ESTATES. The tenurial pattern within the ancient parish and the relation-

ships of holdings in Hillingdon with estates in neighbouring parishes is at all periods complex and obscure. The 12 hides at which the manors of Hillingdon and Colham were together assessed in 1086[79] apparently bear little relation to the area of the later parish, given in 1801 as 4,944 a.[80] Whether this apparent discrepancy implies the omission from the Survey of one or more substantial estates, an inaccurate assessment, or the use of an uncommon unit of area measurement[81] is uncertain. A further possible explanation is that in 1086, as later, some areas of the parish formed appurtenances of manors lying elsewhere in west Middlesex or in Buckinghamshire. By the 15th century the manors of Colham Garden, Denham (Bucks.), Ickenham, Southcote, and Swakeleys all included land said to lie in Colham, Hillingdon, or Uxbridge,[82] and to these by the early 17th century, if not earlier, had been added holdings of the manors of Cowley Peachey, Harefield, Hayes Park Hall, and Stanwell.[83] In addition there were in the parish by 1400, and almost certainly earlier, a number of small freehold estates, particularly in and around Uxbridge town, of between 5 and 30 a., and at least one 200-acre holding.[84] Many of these small parcels of land had already been consolidated with one or more holdings outside the parish to form larger estates, described in subsequent conveyances only as a total acreage comprising property in a number of named parishes.[85] It is therefore impossible in most cases to assess what proportion of the land lay within Hillingdon parish.

The identity of the lands known throughout the Middle Ages as Tickenham is particularly obscure. The form 'Ticheham' first appears in the Survey of 1086,[86] and it has been generally assumed that the lands there described formed the medieval manors of Ickenham and Swakeleys,[87] and that the forms 'Ticheham' or 'Tickenham' and 'Ickenham' were subsequently used synonomously.[88] It seems almost certain, however, that part of one or more of the three Domesday fees of 'Ticheham' lay in Hillingdon ancient parish and that the name Tickenham was later used to describe an area, lying partly in Hillingdon and partly in Ickenham parish, in which the lords of Colham, Hillingdon, Cowley Hall, Ickenham, and Swakeleys all held land at various periods.[89] As early as 1235 John de Trumpinton granted a virgate in Tickenham to William Longe-spée, lord of Colham.[90] A number of 13th- and early 14th-century conveyances, involving particularly the Brok and Swalcliffe families,[91] include land described

[65] Census, 1801–1961. Until 1891 Uxbridge, for census purposes, included an uncertain area of Hillingdon par.
[66] See pp. 62–64.
[67] See pp. 70–72, 88–92.
[68] See pp. 60–61.
[69] D.N.B.
[70] Ibid.; memorial window in Cowley ch.; Lysons, Mdx. Pars. 184.
[71] D.N.B.
[72] Ibid.; Home Cnties. Mag. x. 133.
[73] Robbins, Middlesex, 296.
[74] D.N.B.
[75] E. G. Craig, Index to the Story of my Days, 138, 149.
[76] File in Uxb. libr.
[77] Ibid.; ex inf. Mr. K. R. Pearce.
[78] Ex inf. Sir Bernard Miles.
[79] V.C.H. Mdx. i. 124; for details and qualifications see below.
[80] Census, 1801.
[81] Such customary usages were not unknown in west

Mdx. during later periods: V.C.H. Mdx. iii. 197; below, p. 134.
[82] See, respectively, Cal. Pat. 1461–9, 197, 371; below (Colham Garden); Cal. Pat. 1385–9, 219; V.C.H. Bucks. iii. 256–9 (Denham); below, pp. 102–4 (Ickenham, Swakeleys); C.P. 25(1)/152/92/125; below, p. 136 (Southcote).
[83] C.P. 25(2)/10 Jas. I, Trin.; V.C.H. Mdx. iii. 172–4 (Cowley Peachey); C.P. 25(2)/21 Chas. II, Trin.; V.C.H. Mdx. iii. 240 sqq. (Harefield); C.P. 25(2)/1657, Mich.; see above, p. 27 (Hayes Park Hall); L. & P. Hen. VIII, xvii, p. 167; V.C.H. Mdx. iii. 36 sqq. (Stanwell).
[84] See p. 74.
[85] e.g. C.P. 25(1)/150/53/12; /150/62/240.
[86] V.C.H. Mdx. i. 124, 126, 128.
[87] Ibid. 82 n. 20; see also below, pp. 102–3.
[88] P.N. Mdx. (E.P.N.S.), 43.
[89] See pp. 70, 72–73, 102–3.
[90] C.P. 25(1)/146/10/136; for Jn. de Trumpinton see p. 103, for Colham see below.
[91] For the Swalcliffe holdings in Ickenham see p. 103.

as lying in Tickenham and Ickenham,[92] suggesting a distinction between the two places, and about 1260 land in Tickenham was clearly stated to lie in Hillingdon parish.[93] By 1332 the Brok or Brook family held land in Tickenham appurtenant to their manors of Cowley Hall and Hillingdon,[94] which later in the 14th century passed to the Charlton family, lords of Ickenham manor which also had appurtenances in Tickenham.[95] Further confusion surrounds a dispute in 1453 between the Rector of Ickenham and the Bishop of Worcester[96] as to tithes payable on approximately 50 a. in Tickenham.[97] Although the Rector of Ickenham had latterly received the tithes of this area, the disputed lands were adjudged to be in Hillingdon parish and the tithes due to Hillingdon church. Despite this decision, however, some at least of the fields mentioned were apparently always considered later to be part of Ickenham parish.[98] The identifiable fields lay east of the Yeading Brook, and the area known as Tickenham probably extended across the stream into the north-east corner of Hillingdon parish.[99] Lands in Tickenham are not mentioned after 1544,[1] although forms of the place-name survived until the 19th century.[2]

COLHAM manor was in 1086 assessed at 8 hides, 6 of which were in demesne. Associated with it (*jacet in* or *apposita est in*) at Domesday were four other estates held by Earl Roger in Harmondsworth (1 hide), Dawley (3 hides), Hatton (1½ hide), and 'Ticheham' (9½ hides).[3] The significance of this association is uncertain, although none of these estates had been linked with Colham in King Edward's time.[4] The value of Colham, including 46s. rents from 2½ mills, was given in 1086 as £8, a drop of £2 from its value in the Confessor's time. Part of the manor lands was probably granted away in the mid-13th century to form the basis of the sub-manor later known as Cowley Hall.[5] At some time before 1594, however, Hillingdon manor was incorporated in that of Colham.[6]

The location of the manor lands before the assimilation of Hillingdon manor is uncertain.[7] Fourteenth-century surveys of Colham include land in Great Whatworth Field, Hanger Field, and Strode Field, a warren on Uxbridge Common, and woodland at Highseat in the north-west.[8] This suggests that the bulk of the manor lands lay then, as later, south of the London road and west of the Pinn in the north-west of the old parish. By 1636, however, Colham and Hillingdon manors had been consolidated, so that the lands of Colham then covered approximately two-thirds of Hillingdon parish.[9] At this date the outer boundaries of Colham appear to have substantially respected those of the parish,[10] except in the north-east where the manor boundary followed the Pinn southward from Ickenham Bridge to Hercies Lane and then ran south-eastward to rejoin the parish boundary south of Pole Hill Farm.[11] Insulated within the lands of Colham lay the 'three little manors' of Cowley Hall, Colham Garden,[12] and Cowley Peachey,[13] and freehold estates belonging to a number of manors in other parishes,[14] including Swakeleys in Ickenham.[15]

In 1086[16] Colham manor, which before the Conquest had belonged to Wigot of Wallingford, was in the hands of the Conqueror's cousin, Roger de Montgomery, Earl of Shrewsbury.[17] On Roger's death in 1094 his fief, including Colham, passed to his son Robert de Bellême who retained the property until 1102 when, following his abortive rebellion, his lands were confiscated by Henry I. Colham was probably then granted to Miles Crispin (d. 1107).[18] After Crispin's death the manor probably descended to his widow Maud who shortly afterwards married Brian Fitz Count. In or about 1115[19] Colham was held *jure uxoris* by Brian as part of the honor of Wallingford. Brian and Maud had no heir and on their entering a religious community Henry, Duke of the Normans, later Henry II, seized the honor of Wallingford, retaining it after he became king in 1154.[20] The honor was farmed in 1178–9 by Thomas Basset and afterwards by Gilbert Basset,[21] who granted trading privileges to the men of Uxbridge.[22] By 1219 it had passed to William Longespée, a natural son of Henry II, who had married Ela (or Isabel), daughter of William, Earl of Salisbury, and become earl *jure uxoris* in 1198.[23] On William's death in 1226 his property passed to a second William Longespée,

[92] e.g. C.P. 25(1)/147/24/498; /148/38/341; /149/45/151; /149/52/351; /150/53/12; /150/56/96; *Cal. Close*, 1327–30, 373.
[93] *Cart. of Missenden Abbey*, pt. 3, ed. J. G. Jenkins (Bucks. Rec. Soc.), pp. 166, 170.
[94] C.P. 25(1)/150/55/64.
[95] C.P. 25(1)/150/56/96; see p. 102.
[96] For the appropriation of Hillingdon ch. to the bishop see p. 87.
[97] Worcs. Rec. Off., Acc. 2636/47884/2; Newcourt, *Repertorium*, i. 647–8; the original MS., part only of which is printed by Newcourt, is lost.
[98] Ickenham Incl. Award Map *penes* Uxb. Bor. Council; see p. 106.
[99] Lysons, *Mdx. Pars*. 154. No evidence has been found to support Lysons's assumption of a post-Domesday manor of Tickenham nor his statement (ibid. 166) that tithes of 300 a. were in dispute in 1453.
[1] C.P. 25(2)/27/185/36.
[2] M.R.O., E.M.C. 83/1.
[3] *V.C.H. Mdx*. i. 124. There is, however, a discrepancy of 1 hide 50 a. between the sum of the demesne hides and those occupied by the men and the total assessment of 8 hides.
[4] Ibid. 124.
[5] See p. 73.
[6] See below.
[7] For Hillingdon man. see p. 72. Lysons, *Mdx. Pars*. 151, apparently confuses the area of Colham with the manor's extensive honorial jurisdiction: see below, p. 83.

[8] C 145/108/2; Lancs. Rec. Off., DDK/1746/1, 4.
[9] M.R.O., Acc 448/1; 538/1.
[10] For the parish boundaries see p. 56.
[11] For estates in the north-east of the par. see above, p. 69 and below *sub* Hercies.
[12] See pp. 73–74.
[13] *V.C.H. Mdx*. iii. 170–4.
[14] See above.
[15] See p. 103.
[16] *V.C.H. Mdx*. i. 124.
[17] He is sometimes considered to have been Earl of Arundel as well: *Complete Peerage*, xi. 685 n.; D. C. Douglas, 'Companions of the Conqueror', *History*, xxviii. 135.
[18] *Chron. Abbatiae de Evesham* (Rolls Ser.), 97, states that Crispin's gift of land in Hillingdon to Evesham Abbey was made *temp*. Abbot Walter (d. 1086). This seems unlikely, since Earl Roger himself lived until 1094 and there is no reason to suppose that any part of his fief passed to the Crown until Robert de Bellême's forfeiture in 1102.
[19] *Chron. Evesham*, 75. Some authorities date Brian's grant of Hillingdon church to the 1140s, but a date between 1107 and 1115 seems more likely: the question is discussed in *V.C.H. Mdx*. i. 110 n. 51.
[20] *V.C.H. Berks*. iii. 524.
[21] *Pipe Roll* 1179 (P.R.S. xxviii), 100, 1180 (P.R.S. xxix), 47, 1184 (P.R.S. xxxiii), 57.
[22] Basset grant *penes* Uxb. libr.; B.M. Add. Ch. 9211. Both documents are undated, but see p. 79.
[23] *Bk. of Fees*, 272.

probably the eldest son of William and Ela (d. 1261).[24] William Longespée the younger was succeeded by his daughter Margaret (or Margery), wife of Henry de Lacy, Earl of Lincoln.[25] Henry died in 1311[26] and Colham descended to his daughter Alice, who had married Thomas, Earl of Lancaster, in 1294.[27] After the execution of Thomas in 1322, following the Battle of Boroughbridge, the king took the manor into his own hands and regranted it to Alice de Lacy, with remainder to Hugh le Despenser.[28] Before 10 November 1324 Alice married Ebulo Lestrange and in 1325 they entered into a new agreement, conveying Colham to Hugh le Despenser subject to Alice's life interest.[29] In 1328, however, Queen Isabel and Mortimer, who were attempting to win over the partisans of the late Earl of Lancaster, granted Colham, among other estates, to Ebulo for his life if he should survive Alice.[30] After the execution of Mortimer in 1330 Ebulo and Alice petitioned the king and council to consider their case, and eventually secured a grant of some of their lands on condition that they quit-claimed all the rest.[31] This agreement was embodied in a charter in 1331 whereby Colham manor, among other lands, was granted to Ebulo, Alice, and their heirs to hold as Henry de Lacy had held it of the king.[32] On the death of Ebulo Lestrange in 1335 Colham, with the hamlet of Uxbridge, was said to be held of the Earl of Cornwall as parcel of the honor of Wallingford.[33] Roger, Lord Strange, son of John Lestrange VI, Lord Strange (d. 1311), Ebulo's brother, was his heir.[34] Early in 1336, however, Alice, Ebulo's elderly widow, eloped with Sir Hugh de Frene, and Edward III, displeased, took her lands into his own hands. By 23 March 1336, however, they had married, been reconciled with the king, and received back their property. On 27 September 1336 they had licence to convey Colham, Uxbridge, and other lands to themselves for life with remainder to Roger Lestrange.[35] Hugh de Frene died in 1337 and Roger Lestrange than granted a life interest in Colham to Nicholas de Cantilupe, Alice's cousin, subject to Alice's life interest and with reversion to Roger's heirs.[36] Although Alice had surrendered all her property to Nicholas de Cantilupe by a deed dated 25 June 1337, the day before Roger's grant, she probably retained actual possession until her death in 1348.[37] Nicholas de Cantilupe died in 1355 and Colham then reverted to Roger, Lord Strange (d. 1382), son of Roger the heir of Ebulo who died in 1349. The

manors of Colham and Uxbridge were then said to be held of the Prince of Wales in chief, as part of the honor of Wallingford, by service of a knight's fee.[38] Roger Lestrange died in 1382, and his wife Aline two years later.[39] The manor then passed to their son John, Lord Strange (d. 1397)[40] and to his son Richard, Lord Strange (d. 1449).[41] After the death of Richard, his widow Elizabeth married Roger Kynaston.[42] On Elizabeth's death in 1453 Colham passed to John, Lord Strange, Elizabeth's son by her first marriage, although Kynaston petitioned in Chancery for rents which he claimed were due to him from the property.[43]

John Lestrange died in 1479 and Colham then descended to his only daughter and heir Joan (or Jane) who had married Sir George Stanley, the eldest son of Thomas Stanley, created Earl of Derby (d. 1504). George Stanley died in 1503 and Colham then passed to his eldest son Thomas (d. 1521), who succeeded his grandfather as Earl of Derby in 1504.[44] Members of the Stanley family continued to hold the manors of Colham and Uxbridge, as parcel of the honor of Wallingford (later Ewelme),[45] until 1636[46] when Alice, Dowager Countess of Derby, devised the property to her grandson George, Lord Chandos.[47] He died in 1654 or 1655, leaving his estates in the hands of Jane, his second wife, and trustees.[48] Jane then married George Pitt, a Hampshire landowner, and in 1669 they alienated Colham to Sir Robert Vyner, lord of Swakeleys manor,[49] and later Lord Mayor of London.[50] Colham remained in the Vyner family[51] until 1700 when Thomas Vyner sold it to Richard Webb and Samuel (later Sir Samuel) Dodd, afterwards Lord Chief Baron of the Exchequer.[52] Webb's interests in the manor were purchased between 1720 and 1740 by representatives of the Dodd family,[53] but after 1750 the property was frequently mortgaged.[54] In 1787 John Dodd of Swallowfield (Berks.) sold the whole manor to Fysh de Burgh, lord of the manor of West Drayton.[55] Fysh de Burgh died in 1800 leaving Colham, subject to the life interest of his widow Easter (d. 1823), in trust for his daughter Catherine (d. 1809), wife of James G. Lill who assumed the name of De Burgh, with remainder to their son Hubert.[56] The manor passed to Hubert de Burgh in 1832 and he immediately mortgaged the estate.[57] Hubert retained actual possession of the property, which was seldom if ever during this period unencumbered by mortgages,[58] until his death in 1872.

[24] Ibid. 473.
[25] *Plac. de Quo Warr.* (Rec. Com), 476.
[26] C 134/22/17.
[27] *Cal. Inq. p.m.* x, p. 195.
[28] *Cal. Pat.* 1321–4, 179, 182.
[29] Ibid. 1324–7, 103; C.P. 25(1)/286/32/249.
[30] *Cal. Pat.* 1327–30, 338.
[31] *Rot. Parl.* ii. 57b.
[32] *Cal. Chart. R.* 1327–41, 199, 213.
[33] C 135/43/10.
[34] *Cal. Close,* 1333–7, 444–5. For the Lestrange family see Hamon Lestrange, *Lestrange Records.*
[35] *Cal. Pat.* 1334–8, 319.
[36] Ibid. 463; C.P. 25(1)/287/39/223.
[37] *Cal. Close,* 1337–9, 19; *Cal. Inq. p.m.* ix, pp. 96–97.
[38] *Cal. Inq. p.m.* x, p. 195.
[39] Guildhall MS. 9171/1, ff. 70–71.
[40] C 136/40/47.
[41] C 139/134/29/16.
[42] C 139/153/18.
[43] C 1/40/143.
[44] E 150/472/4. For the Derby family see *Complete Peerage.*

[45] See pp. 82–83.
[46] C 142/40/64; /43/62; *L. & P. Hen. VIII,* iv(1), p. 929; B.M. Harl. MS. 760, f. 67; C.P. 25(2)/262/44–45 Eliz. Mich.; /527/6 Chas. I, Hil.
[47] Lysons, *Mdx. Pars.* 150.
[48] C.P. 43/235/98; /248/31; /286/186.
[49] See p. 103.
[50] C.P. 25(2)/21 Chas. II, Trin.
[51] C.P. 25(2)/32 Chas. II, Mich.
[52] Lysons, *Mdx. Pars.* 150.
[53] M.R.O., Acc. 742/69–72.
[54] Ibid. /79–93; C.P. 25(2)/6 Geo. III, Trin.; C.P. 43/735/133.
[55] M.R.O., Acc. 742/102, /103, /153; 538/22. Lysons, *Mdx. Pars.* 150, quoting Fysh de Burgh, gives 1782 as the date of sale, but this conflicts with the date given in both the schedule of deeds relating to the estate and Hubert de Burgh's abstract of title. For Fysh de Burgh see *V.C.H. Mdx.* iii. 192.
[56] M.R.O., Acc. 742/99.
[57] Ibid. /48, /49, /100–3, /153; 538/22.
[58] M.R.O., Acc. 538/22; 742/15, /64, /176.

Mention in 1245[59] of the 'court' of Colham surrounded by a hedge probably implies the existence by this date of a manor-house: such a dwelling was certainly standing in 1311.[60] Little is known of the medieval building. It was described in 1328 as having an adjoining garden,[61] but after the Lestrange family acquired the estate the house probably remained unoccupied. By 1386 the buildings on the site were valueless,[62] and in 1449 the manor-house was said to be beyond repair.[63] By 1521, however, when Thomas, Earl of Derby, died there,[64] the house had been rebuilt, probably on or near the site of the earlier building. The manor-house was described in 1547[65] as standing east of the Frays River about a mile north of the bridge carrying the Longford–Colnbrook road across the Colne. The Tudor dwelling, which probably stood in Patcott (Colham) Field on or near the site of the later Manor Farm, was still standing in 1636.[66] A large house at Colham is shown on a map of 1742,[67] but, since the manor-house was later said to have been demolished in the early 18th century,[68] it is not certainly identifiable with the Tudor building.

HILLINGDON manor, sometimes confused with the Bishop of Worcester's rectory estate or 'manor',[69] was assessed in 1086 at four hides, two of which were in demesne.[70] In King Edward's time the estate had belonged to the housecarl Ulf, but before 1086 it had been granted to Roger de Montgomery, Earl of Shrewsbury. For two hundred years after Domesday the history of Hillingdon manor is obscure and no further details of its extent or location have survived. The property may have descended, as parcel of the honor of Wallingford, to Earl Roger's son, and after his forfeiture to Miles Crispin.[71] By 1305[72] Hillingdon, with appurtenances in Colham, was in the hands of the Brook or Brok family which from at least as early as 1259 had been acquiring lands and rents in Uxbridge, Hillingdon, Cowley, and Ickenham.[73] Between 1332 and 1348[74] William, son of Roger del Brok, surrendered his interests in the manors of Hillingdon and Cowley Hall, together with lands in Tickenham, to John Charlton, a London merchant. Charlton obtained further interests in Hillingdon manor in 1345 from John Pain, Rector of Ickenham, who had secured an interest in the property in 1337,[75] and John de la (or atte) Pole.[76] The estate almost certainly remained in the possession of the Charlton family[77] until the attainder of Sir Richard Charlton following his death at Bosworth in 1485.[78] In 1486 Henry VII granted the

reversion on an estate including lands called Great and Little Hillingdon to Sir Thomas Bourchier, subject to the life interest of Elizabeth, Richard Charlton's widow.[79] In 1510 Bourchier granted his reversionary interest in Great and Little Hillingdon to Sir John Pecche and John Sharpe.[80] Sharpe died, and in 1521 Pecche transferred his interest to Henry Courtenay, Earl of Devon.[81] The subsequent history of the manor is uncertain. On his death in 1594 Ferdinando, Earl of Derby, was said to be seised of Hillingdon, Colham, and Uxbridge.[82] When the Stanley family acquired Hillingdon manor is unknown, but a date before 1522 seems unlikely.[83] The manor is not mentioned by name after 1594, and it was presumably merged by the Stanleys into their manor of Colham.[84]

Little is known of the early history of the so-called manor of *UXBRIDGE*. Neither manor nor hamlet was mentioned in 1086, but 13th-century sources suggest that at some time before 1242 Uxbridge manor may have formed part of the royal demesne.[85] By 1242 the Crown rights to tallage in the manor had been granted to William Longespée who at this date also held the manor of Colham as part of the honor of Wallingford.[86] Crown rights in Uxbridge are not mentioned after 1254, and the descent of the manor appears to have followed that of Colham[87] until 1669 when George Pitt sold Colham to Sir Robert Vyner but reserved the manor of Uxbridge.[88] In 1695 Pitt's son, also called George, sold the manor and its appurtenances to four trustees representing the inhabitants of the town.[89] In 1729 the surviving representatives conveyed the manor to seven trustees, known thereafter as the lords of the manor in trust, who were to use the manorial profits as a charitable fund for the benefit of the town. The trust was to be renewed whenever the number of trustees was reduced to three.[90] In 1963 the manor was still vested in trustees drawn from householders in the town.[91]

The only extant survey of the boundaries and customs of Uxbridge manor was presented at a court baron held in 1727.[92] By this date the boundaries of manor and township appear to have been conterminous, and whether they were anciently distinct is not known. Except for a small rectangular area lying across the Oxford road at the west end of the town, the area defined in 1727 lay east of the Frays stream and north of Blind or Woolwind Lane (later Vine Street). East of the Oxford road the boundary ran across open ground, and was, for some if not all of its length, marked by a ditch and bank, repaired,

[59] C.P. 25(1)/147/13/216.
[60] C 134/22/17.
[61] C 145/108/2.
[62] C 136/40/47.
[63] C 139/134/29/16.
[64] Lysons, *Mdx. Pars.* 150.
[65] J. Leland, *Itinerary*, ed. L. Toulmin Smith, . 114.
[66] M.R.O., Acc. 448/1.
[67] Thos. Millward, *Map. of Mdx.* (1742).
[68] Lysons, *Mdx. Pars.* 151.
[69] See p. 87.
[70] *V.C.H. Mdx.* i. 124.
[71] Ibid. 110.
[72] C.P. 25(1)/285/26/311; /148/38/345.
[73] See pp. 70, 73, 102; C.P. 25(1)/147/24/487; 147/2/498.
[74] C.P. 25(1)/150/55/64; *Cal. Close,* 1346–9, 547, 597, 603.
[75] *Cal. Close,* 1337–9, 109.
[76] C.P. 25(1)/287/42/370.
[77] *Cal. Close,* 1461–8, 132.
[78] *Rot. Parl.* vi. 276a.

[79] *Cal. Pat.* 1485–1509, 63.
[80] *L. & P. Hen. VIII,* i(1), pp. 289, 444. This grant seems to qualify the account given by Lysons, *Mdx. Pars.* 153.
[81] *L. & P. Hen. VIII,* iii(2), p. 750; iv(3), p. 2858.
[82] B.M. Harl. MS. 760, f. 67.
[83] Lysons, *Mdx. Pars.* 153, suggests that Thomas, Earl of Derby (d. 1521), was also seised of Hillingdon.
[84] The name of the manor had been lost by Lysons's day: *Mdx. Pars.* 148.
[85] *Cal. Close,* 1237–42, 406; 1242–7, 426; 1253–4, 14.
[86] Ibid. 1237–42, 406.
[87] *Cal. Chart. R.* 1257–1300, 436; *Cal. Pat.* 1334–8, 463; C.P. 25(1)/287/39/223.
[88] C.P. 25(2)/21 Chas. II, Trin.
[89] M.R.O., Acc. 538/1; see p. 98 for the conditions of sale.
[90] Ibid.
[91] *Kemp's Uxb. Dir.* (1962–3).
[92] M.R.O., Acc. 538/2.

until at least the end of the 18th century, by the lords in trust.[93]

The early history and extent of the estate later known as *COWLEY HALL* manor is uncertain. The manor is not mentioned by name until 1429,[94] but the fact that it was held, then as later, as a sub-manor of Colham at a rent of £5 a year[95] suggests that the estate is perhaps identifiable with property in Colham and Cowley granted by William Longespée in or shortly before 1245 to one Philip,[96] who was to hold the property of Colham manor at a yearly rent of £4 12s., rendering services of free tenancy and suit of court. Lawrence del Brok, the judge, who had obtained land in Ickenham in 1267,[97] received in 1271 a further six carucates in Hillingdon, Cowley, Tickenham, Ickenham, and Southall from William del Brok.[98] In 1327[99] Roger del Brok, perhaps Lawrence's grandson, mortgaged to Peter James, a London merchant, an estate described as 'the manor of Colham which is called Cowley'. The manor, almost certainly that later referred to as Cowley Hall,[1] comprised a capital messuage, rents, a fishery, three mills on the Colne, and 375 a. and was said to be held of the honor of Wallingford. In 1328 Roger del Brok was said to hold 1½ carucate of Colham manor by service of ⅙ knight's fee and an annual rent of 53s. 4d.[2] Later in the same year Peter James transferred his mortgage interest to John Charlton, another London merchant,[3] who four years later acquired further interests in what were called the manors of Cowley and Hillingdon from William, Roger del Brok's son.[4] Also included in the grant were two carucates and 66 a. in Tickenham. An interest in John Charlton's estate was acquired in 1337 by John Pain, Rector of Ickenham,[5] but he apparently reconveyed this interest to Charlton in 1345,[6] and Cowley Hall subsequently remained in the possession of the Charlton family.[7] In 1412 Alice, widow of Sir Thomas Charlton (d. 1410), held land worth £6 13s. 4d. in Colham and Uxbridge,[8] and in 1429 the estate of Thomas Charlton, possibly a nephew of the first Sir Thomas, included the manors of Cowley Hall and Cowley Peachey together with lands called Elys,[9] Barwell Field (12 a.), and a meadow (47 a.) called 'le Frays'.[10] Following the attainder of Sir Richard Charlton in 1486,[11] Cowley Hall was granted to Sir Thomas

Bourchier, subject to the life interest of Richard Charlton's widow.[12] In 1510 Bourchier granted the reversion on his estate in tail male to John Pecche and John Sharpe.[13] Sharpe died, and in 1521 Pecche transferred his reversionary interest in Cowley Hall to Henry Courtenay, Earl of Devon.[14] Courtenay, by now Marquess of Exeter, surrendered his interest at some time after 1530, and by 1546 the property had passed to George Stokes.[15] The manor changed hands at least once more before 1558 when Robert Hutton conveyed Cowley Hall, with appurtenances in Hillingdon, to Drew Saunders.[16] By 1582[17] the estate appears to have passed to Henry Chapman, Saunders's son-in-law,[18] who presumably held by right of his wife Sarah. In 1613 the Chapmans conveyed Cowley Hall to Walter Pritchet,[19] who in turn conveyed in 1639 at least part of his interest to Peter Gosfright.[20] The property then became the subject of several complicated mortgage settlements involving, among others, the Pritchet, Johnson, and Tower families.[21] Lancelot Johnson was said to be seised of Cowley Hall in 1669,[22] and Mary Johnson until about 1742[23] when her interest was assumed by Christopher Tower. Although the manor seems seldom to have been free from mortgage debts,[24] the Tower family retained Cowley Hall until at least as late as 1883,[25] after which the descent of the property is unknown.

Almost nothing is known of the medieval dwelling which probably occupied the site of the later Cowley Hall manor-house. A capital messuage is mentioned in a survey of 1327,[26] but whether there were buildings on the site at this date is uncertain. The Charlton family was living at a house called 'Couelehalle' in 1429,[27] although later in the 15th century their principal country residence seems to have been Swakeleys in Ickenham.[28] About 1465[29] the Charltons' smaller house, said to be situated at Uxbridge but possibly identifiable with the manor-house of Cowley Hall, comprised six principal rooms together with a kitchen, larder, and buttery. A map of 1742 shows a large house called Cowley Hall between Cowley Road and the Frays River about ¼ mile south of Cowley village.[30] Buildings on this site are shown on 19th-century maps: they were still standing as late as 1913, but the manor-house site was acquired by the local authority in 1929 and by 1934 had been

[93] *Hist. of Uxbridge*, 208.
[94] *Cal. Close*, 1429–35, 124.
[95] M.R.O., Acc. 448/3.
[96] C.P. 25(1)/147/13/216. The MS. is damaged. Possibly Philip de Cowley: *Cart. of Missenden Abbey*, pt. 3, ed. Jenkins (Bucks. Rec. Soc.), 166.
[97] C.P. 25(1)/147/22/450.
[98] C.P. 25(1)/147/24/498.
[99] C 131/3/3.
[1] It was not the manor of Cowley Peachey (*V.C.H. Mdx.* iii. 173) nor that of Colham (above, p. 70).
[2] C 145/108/2.
[3] *Cal. Close*, 1327–30, 373.
[4] C.P. 25(1)/150/55/64; see also *Cal. Close*, 1346–9, 547, 603.
[5] *Cal. Close*, 1337–9, 109.
[6] C.P. 25(1)/287/42/370.
[7] The will of Jn. Charlton, proved 1386, mentions tenements held of him at 'Couelebrok': Guildhall MS. 9171/1, f. 148.
[8] *Feudal Aids*, vi. 488.
[9] For the origin of this estate see E 210/9202.
[10] *Cal. Close*, 1429–35, 124; see also ibid. 1461–8, 132.
[11] See E 159/331/150.
[12] *Cal. Pat.* 1485–94, 63; *L. & P. Hen. VIII*, i(1), pp. 289, 444.

[13] Ibid.; C 66/612.
[14] *L. & P. Hen. VIII*, iii(2), p. 750; see also ibid. iv(3), p. 2858; C 66/656.
[15] C 54/335/57.
[16] C.P. 25(2)/74/630/P. & M. 4 & 5 Hil.
[17] *Cal. Inq. p.m. Lond.* iii, p. 65.
[18] Lysons, *Mdx. Pars.* 155.
[19] Ibid. A memorial in Harefield ch. to John Pritchett, Bp. of Gloucester 1672–81, describes him as the son of Walter Pritchett of Cowley Hall; see *V.C.H. Mdx.* iii. 254, 256, 271.
[20] C.P. 25(2)/15 Chas. I, Trin.
[21] C.P. 25(2)/1656, Trin.; Lysons, *Mdx. Pars.* 155; C.P. 43/600/346.
[22] Lysons, *Mdx. Pars.* 155.
[23] Ibid.; M.R.O., Acc 448/3.
[24] C.P. 25(2)/17 Geo. III, Hil.; C.P. 43/968/319.
[25] M.R.O., Acc 448/3; letters *re* Cowley Hall quit-rent *penes* Uxb. Bor. Council.
[26] C 131/3/3.
[27] *Cal. Close*, 1429–35, 124.
[28] See p. 104.
[29] W.A.M., 6646. The MS., which is undated, but said to be *temp.* Edward IV, is almost certainly an inventory of the goods of Sir Thos. Charlton (d. 1465).
[30] Millward, *Map of Mdx.* (1742).

obscured by a housing complex centring on Dagnall Crescent.[31]

The lands of *COLHAM GARDEN* manor lay, throughout its history, almost equally in West Drayton and Hillingdon, although the manor-house, Burroughs, stood in West Drayton parish.[32] In 1461, when Colham Garden is first so described, it comprised 89 a. in Colham, 20 a. and two messuages in Uxbridge, 90 a. in West Drayton, and 8 a. in Stanwell.[33] By 1872[34] there remained 55 a. in Hillingdon, 59 a. in West Drayton, and 4 a., first mentioned in 1512,[35] in Iver (Bucks.). From at least as early as the 16th century the lord of Colham Garden paid a yearly quit-rent of 20s. to Colham manor and one varying between 14s. and 20s. to West Drayton manor.[36] After 1506, when the manor came into the possession of Westminster Abbey,[37] the demesne was invariably leased. The Hillingdon portion was usually farmed separately at a yearly rent of £4.[38]

The origins of the estate later known as *HERCIES* manor are obscure. The property is first mentioned by name in 1386 when it formed part of the extensive estates of the Charlton family.[39] The Charltons still held Hercies in 1462,[40] and subsequently the descent of the manor appears to have followed that of Swakeleys manor in Ickenham.[41] After the death in 1643 of Sir Edmund Wright, however, Hercies passed to his daughter Elizabeth, wife of Sir John Trott.[42] The property thereafter passed in the female line to Sir Charles Shuckburgh, whose son John sold Hercies in 1709 to Edward Gibbon. Four years later Gibbon conveyed the manor to Sir Thomas Hardy (d. 1732), who was succeeded by his daughter Constance, wife of George Chamberlain who later adopted the name of Denton.[43] In 1778 or 1779[44] Constance Denton's representatives sold Hercies to the trustees of Thomas Bridges under whose will it descended to Thomas Clarke, Rector of Ickenham and lord of Swakeleys manor.[45] At the end of the 18th century Hercies or Herres Farm comprised 222 a. lying north of the farm buildings in the rectangular area bounded by Uxbridge Common, the Ickenham boundary, Long Lane, and Sweetcroft Lane.[46] In 1796 Thomas Clarke died and the property, then described as the site of the manor of Hercies, passed to his son Thomas Truesdale Clarke.[47] Under the inclosure award of 1825 Thomas Truesdale Clarke was allotted approximately 330 a. in lieu of Hercies and Rye Fields farms.[48] The property is not mentioned again until 1922 when Hercies Farm was acquired by the local authority.[49]

At all periods after the 14th century, and probably earlier, there was a number of freeholds in Hillingdon parish.[50] The location of most of the medieval estates is uncertain: some were certainly situated in and around Uxbridge itself,[51] others probably lay on the edges of the heaths to the north and east, and may have begun as assarts. By 1636 there were 35 freeholds in Colham manor,[52] together covering more than 300 a. Many were tenements in Uxbridge or small parcels of open-field land: only three estates exceeded 30 a. From the 17th century onwards a number of houses on Hillingdon Heath were owned by persons of importance: most of these estates deserve notice rather by virtue of their owners or the character of the houses and adjoining pleasure gardens, than for their size.[53] The largest estate was that attached to Hillingdon House, most of which was acquired by the Cox family after 1810.[54] When the estate was broken up in 1915 it comprised more than 500 a. in Hillingdon as well as land in Harefield and Ruislip.[55]

Among medieval estates which may be separately mentioned[56] was that which apparently attached in the 15th century to the office of warrener in Colham and Hillingdon manors. The estate in Colham, Cowley, and Hillingdon granted in 1434 by Richard Lestrange, lord of Colham, to John Pury, who paid £4 11s. 3d. for the office of warrener, comprised 8 messuages, a weir, pasture in Old Park, and more than 200 a. in Rye Hill Field, Bedewell Field, Boltons Mede, Jordans Mede, Colham Mede, and Broad Croft.[57] Three years later Pury's estate, which is not mentioned again, was said to comprise 20 marks in rent and land in Colham, Uxbridge, Hillingdon, and Cowley.[58]

Rabbs Farm, which until the dissolution of the chantries in 1547 probably formed part of the endowment of Rabb's chantry,[59] was acquired in 1553, together with other estates formerly belonging to the Savoy Hospital, by St. Thomas's Hospital.[60] From the late 16th century St. Thomas's Hospital leased the estate for 21-year terms at an annual rent which increased from £10 in 1594 to £105 in 1798. From 1594 until 1714 the estate was farmed by members of the Munsaugh family.[61] In 1636 Rabbs Farm was described as a freehold estate of 66 a.,[62] but in 1688[63] the Hospital estate, described as Rabbs

[31] O.S. Maps 1/2,500, Mdx. xiv. 7 (1866 and later edns.); Hillingdon Incl. Plan (1825).
[32] A full account and detailed descent of Colham Garden are given in *V.C.H. Mdx.* iii. 193–5.
[33] *Cal. Pat.* 1461–9, 371.
[34] Survey (1872) in Church Com. recs.
[35] W.A.M., Reg. Bk. ii, f. 36v.
[36] S.C. 6/Hen.VIII/2415; M.R.O., Acc 446/E.M. 37; E 178/1430; Lysons, *Mdx. Pars.* 35.
[37] *Cal. Pat.* 1494–1509, 517; W.A.M., 17028; *V.C.H. Mdx.* iii. 194.
[38] W.A.M., 4680, 4697.
[39] Guildhall MS. 9171/1, f. 148, which appears to throw doubt on the theory expressed in *P.N. Mdx.* (E.P.N.S.), 42.
[40] *Cal. Close,* 1461–8, 132.
[41] See p. 103.
[42] Lysons, *Mdx. Pars.* 153.
[43] Ibid., giving a detailed descent.
[44] Cf. ibid. and C.P. 43/783/147.
[45] See p. 104.
[46] Plan of Hercies (n.d.) *penes* Uxb. Bor. Council; M.R.O., F.54/1.
[47] C.P. 43/848/15.

[48] Hillingdon Incl. Award (1825) in M.R.O.
[49] Schedule of sale *penes* Uxb. Bor. Council.
[50] e.g. C.P. 25(1)/150/64/291; /150/53/8; /151/83/34; C 142/252/11; C.P. 25(2)/4 Jas. I, Easter.
[51] e.g. C 1/16/586; /29/470; /32/175; /47/117; C.P. 25(1)/285/28/19; /150/67/368; C.P. 25(2)/27/179/56.
[52] M.R.O., Acc. 448/1.
[53] For these houses see p. 62. See also M.R.O., Acc. 180/628, 645–7; 566/74.
[54] M.R.O., Acc. 503/83.
[55] Ibid. /107, /108.
[56] For the rectorial estate of the Bp. of Worcester see p. 87.
[57] C.P. 25(1)/152/90/64; /152/90/67; B.M. Harl. Roll D.22.
[58] C.P. 25(1)/152/91/76; /152/91/77.
[59] See p. 88.
[60] *Cal. Pat.* 1553, 283–4. For the Savoy Hosp. see *V.C.H. Lond.* i. 546–9.
[61] St. Thomas's Hosp., S2/55, 3/49, 8/27, 12/16, 20/4, 37/18, 40/29.
[62] M.R.O., Acc. 448/1.
[63] St. Thomas's Hosp., E2/12/1.

and Austen farms, comprised 94 a., of which 42 a. lay in Hedging Field, Hale Field, Upper Field, and Beadle Field. A quit-rent of 10s. was payable to Colham manor in respect of the house and close called Austen Farm which lay immediately south of Rabbs farm-house. The remaining land lay east of the farm buildings and to the west between Cowley Road and the Colne. The Hospital seems to have augmented its holding during the late 18th century,[64] and under the inclosure award of 1825 the Governors were allotted 110 a. at Yiewsley in lieu of their estate.[65] The Hospital acquired small areas of adjoining land during the 19th century, but the sale of plots for factory building and railway construction began in 1905. The remaining 157 a. of the Rabbs Farm estate were sold in 1928 and have since been used for houses and factories.[66]

About 1631, in answer to a writ of *quo warranto*, the inhabitants of Uxbridge claimed that the town was an ancient borough and corporation of 73 burgesses.[67] Judgment was given against them. In a second action, heard in Star Chamber in 1633, when the claims of the townspeople were again rejected, they based their case on a misinterpretation of the 12th-century document, which the town authorities were apparently unable to read, by which Gilbert Basset granted to the 'burgesses' of Uxbridge the right to hold a weekly market in the town.[68] This instrument also provided that holders of 1 a. in the town should be free from all tolls and customs on payment of 2s. a year, that ½-acre holders should have the same privileges in consideration of 1s. a year, and that both classes of tenant should have the right to alienate their holdings at will. Despite the judgments against them, the 'burgesses' of Uxbridge persevered with their claims and in 1657 petitioned Parliament for a charter of rights.[69] The matter was referred to a committee and nothing further is recorded. By the end of the 17th century, however, the tenuous claims of landholders in the town had again hardened into a form of customary holding. A rent roll of 1693 lists 86 'burgage' tenants;[70] in 1727 there were 88 such holdings in the town.[71] By 1809 there were 86 burgage holdings totalling 91 a.[72] By the 19th century the rights of pasture on wastes in Colham manor and on Cow Moor in Harefield, which the burgage holders had claimed as an incident of tenure as early as 1593, had also been established.[73] The King's Bench decision in a test case brought by the lords in trust before the execution of the 1812 Inclosure Act,[74] however, emphasized that the usage was only customary. The burgage holders were allotted 32 a. in Harefield in lieu of their pasture rights under the Harefield inclosure award of 1813.[75] In 1855 an Act was passed authorizing the sale by auction of this

land[76] and, despite a petition by the burgage holders, the sale was completed by the lords in trust in 1856.[77]

ECONOMIC AND SOCIAL HISTORY. Until the exploitation of brickearth deposits in south Hillingdon began in the early 19th century the economic history of Hillingdon outside Uxbridge is essentially agrarian. After Uxbridge emerged as a commercial centre in the early 12th century, economic expansion and most of the recorded social activity of the parish were concentrated there. Surviving population figures suggest that as early as the 14th century settlement also was concentrated in Uxbridge, and not until 1821 did the population of rural Hillingdon exceed that of the town.[78]

In 1086 the manors of Hillingdon and Colham together contained land for 9 ploughs. Earl Roger had 3 ploughs and room for one more on his 8 demesne hides, and the villagers and Frenchmen shared 4 ploughs. In addition there was sufficient meadow for 3 ploughs and 4 oxen, pasture for the cattle of the vill, woodland sufficient to support 1,400 pigs, and one arpent of vineyard.[79] In 1086, as at all later periods, mills were an important source of income. Two mills, presumably on the Colne, rendered 41s. and a further ½ mill, the other half of which probably lay in Buckinghamshire, was worth 5s.[80]

Commutation of services owed by tenants of Colham manor occurred during the 12th century.[81] By 1311 the customary obligations owed by many tenants had apparently been commuted for money payments.[82] In 1328, however, some tenants still rendered heavy services, including malting, brewing, threshing, shearing, mowing, harvesting, and the carriage of straw from the grange within the manor.[83] The continuation of such heavy labour services possibly resulted from difficulties in cultivating the extensive demesne.

In 1328 the demesne of Colham was said to comprise 325 a. of arable, 268 a. of pasture, 40 a. of meadow, and 18 a. of woodland.[84] Seven years later the demesne contained 670 a.,[85] but during the remainder of the 14th century its area appears to have declined. In Cowley Hall manor 234 a. of the 375-acre demesne were in cultivation by 1327.[86] By the 1370s the gross yearly value of Colham manor averaged £238 (£145 net), including rents from two mills at Colham and two at Uxbridge,[87] tolls of the twice-weekly market and the two statute fairs held at Uxbridge,[88] and perquisites of court worth approximately £12.[89] The manorial demesne was said to contain 449 a. in 1386,[90] but only 380 a. in 1449.[91] By the 1380s money payments had entirely replaced labour

[64] St. Thomas's Hosp., S37/18.
[65] Hillingdon Incl. Award (1825).
[66] Conveyances and schedules of sale *penes* St. Thomas's Hosp. Endowment Off.
[67] Album of documents (probably collected by Redford and Riches) *penes* Uxb. libr.; E. Walford, *Greater Lond.* (1882–4), 230.
[68] Original grant *penes* Uxb. libr.
[69] *Cal. S.P. Dom.* 1657–8, 229.
[70] M.R.O., Acc. 538/3.
[71] Ibid./1.
[72] Burgage roll *penes* Uxb. libr.
[73] *V.C.H. Mdx.* iii. 248; M.R.O., Acc. 538/1; /2/9.
[74] M.R.O., Hillingdon Incl. Award (1825).
[75] Harefield Incl. Award *penes* Uxb. Bor. Council.

[76] Uxbridge Burgage Lands Act, 18 & 19 Vic., c. 39 (Local Act).
[77] M.R.O., Acc. 538/4, /7.
[78] *Census*, 1801–21; see below.
[79] *V.C.H. Mdx.* i. 124.
[80] For the mills see p. 77.
[81] B.M. Add. Ch. 9211.
[82] C 134/22/17.
[83] C 145/108/2.   [84] Ibid.
[85] C 135/43/10.
[86] C 131/3/3.
[87] See p. 77.   [88] See p. 79.
[89] Lancs. Rec. Off., DDK/1746/1, /2, /3.
[90] C 136/40/47.
[91] C 139/134/29/16.

services.[92] At this period the demesne was divided into two parts, the northern estate administered from a grange called Northall. Each estate had a cowherd, swineherd, and ploughman, and a warrener was appointed for the whole manor.[93] In addition to the usual domestic and draught animals the stock included 60 cows, 100 pigs, and 400 sheep tended by a shepherd. Much of the demesne was in wheat, but small quantities of rye and oats were also grown. Of the total corn yield of 242 qr. in 1376, 105 qr. were sold, chiefly in London, 29 qr. sent to Uxbridge for malting and brewing, and 13 qr. milled for flour at Uxbridge and Colham. By *c.* 1690 the augmented demesne of Colham, all of which was apparently leased, totalled 536 a.[94] The manor was then said to be worth £931, including leasehold rents in Hillingdon worth £794, profits of court worth £20, and £68 from rents, tolls, and profits in Uxbridge.[95] By the 19th century the demesne had again been reduced to a little more than 300 a.[96]

Whether changes in land utilization following the inclosure of parcels of common and open-field land from the 16th century onwards[97] significantly retarded the growth of rural Hillingdon is uncertain. In 1670 large areas of the parish were in grass supplying hay for the London market,[98] and in the late 18th century the Colham leet still appointed a hayward for the manor.[99] But in 1801, when more than one-half of the total population was said to be employed in agriculture,[1] there were still 1,129 a. of arable in the parish.[2] Of this, 465 a. were in wheat, 292 a. in barley, 264 a. in peas and beans, and the remainder in oats, rye, turnips, and potatoes. Between 1801 and 1811 the population of rural Hillingdon increased by 469 to 2,252, and for the first time the number of families gaining a living by trade exceeded those employed in agriculture. In 1821, when the population of the remainder of the parish exceeded that of Uxbridge, 243 families were said to be employed in agriculture. Ten years later, following the opening of brick-fields in south Hillingdon[3] and the execution of the inclosure award in 1825,[4] the population of Hillingdon had risen to 3,842, but only 14 families were said to be employed in agriculture.[5] The sudden slump in agricultural employment reflected changes in land utilization and the beginning of industrial expansion in and near Uxbridge.[6] From the 1820s onwards an increasing amount of arable was leased for the extraction of gravel and brickearth,[7] and much of the remainder seems to have been turned over to grass.[8] In 1830 only 24 a. of the 103-acre Rye Fields Farm were arable,[9] and two years later the 129 a. of Colham Manor Farm were almost all meadow.[10] Further

north horticultural specialization for the metropolitan market followed the establishment in 1838 of a railway link with London.[11] By 1853 the Victoria and Hillingdon Nurseries had been established at Uxbridge by Thomas Appleby, and Robert Pain, who advertised as successor to James Griffin, owned the Uxbridge Nursery at Hillingdon End.[12] In 1876 there were said to be 'numerous' orchards in the parish,[13] and four years later there were nurseries in the Greenway, Kingston Lane, Harefield Road, Denham Road, and south of St. Andrew's church.[14] By 1894 the glass and orchards of the Uxbridge Nursery covered almost 40 a. between Hillingdon Road and the G.W.R. line.[15] There were then small areas of glass in Cowley Mill Road and Kingston Lane and a 5-acre nursery on Hillingdon Heath. The Kingston Lane premises of Joseph Lowe (later Lowe & Shawyer Ltd.), founded in 1864, were expanded during the 1890s and in the early 20th century the firm was said to be the largest cut flower nursery in the country, specializing in the growing of chrysanthemums for the London market.[16] A nursery at Pield Heath was established in 1895 by Milton Hutchings, a friend of Joseph Lowe.[17] By 1913 there were six nurseries, covering approximately 65 a., in the area bounded by Cowley Road, Hillingdon Road, and Royal Lane, and four smaller nurseries covering almost 20 a. on Hillingdon Heath.[18] All contained large areas of glass and chiefly produced flowers for the metropolitan market. Despite the rapid in-filling of the parish after 1900 and the encroachment of building estates on agricultural land, market-gardening and farming on a small scale continued.[19] Hercies Farm, north of Sweetcroft Lane, and Hillingdon House Farm to the west were not sold to the local authority until 1922[20] and 1941[21] respectively. In 1934 there were still large areas of glass along both sides of the railway between Uxbridge and Cowley and at Pield Heath.[22] Building after 1945 further reduced the land available for cultivation, but in 1963 there were still seven nurseries, five of them small, within the old parish.[23] In 1964 Milton Hutchings Ltd. employed between 80 and 100 people in their 25-acre nursery at Pield Heath.[24] At this date there were still patches of agricultural land north of Hercies Road and east of Hillingdon Circus.

Although there are references to mills in Hillingdon during all documented periods, the information is so fragmentary that many of the mills are unidentifiable, while others have more than one name. Hence it is seldom possible to say with certainty that a medieval mill remained in continuous use until the 19th century or later. In 1086 there were 2½ mills in

[92] Section based on Lancs. Rec. Off., DDK/1746/1, /2, /3.
[93] For the warrener's estate see p. 74.
[94] M.R.O., Acc. 591/29.
[95] Ibid. /28.
[96] M.R.O., Acc. 742/101.
[97] M.R.O., S.R. 106/2; Acc. 448/1; Cowley and Hillingdon Incl. Act, 35 Geo. III, c. 71.
[98] M.R.O., Acc. 180/696.
[99] M.R.O., Acc. 526/4.
[1] *Census,* 1801.
[2] H.O. 67/16.
[3] See below.
[4] See p. 59.
[5] *Census,* 1801–31.
[6] See p. 79.
[7] See below.
[8] Hutson, *Recollections.*
[9] M.R.O., Acc. 85/407.

[10] M.R.O., Acc. 742/101.
[11] See p. 64.
[12] *Lake's Uxb. Almanack* (1853); bill head in Uxb. libr.
[13] Thorne, *Environs of Lond.* 357.
[14] *Eele's Uxb. Dir.* (1881).
[15] O.S. Map 1/2,500, Mdx. xiv. 3, 4 (1895–6 edn.).
[16] Ex inf. Mr. N. W. Chenery; press cuttings in Uxb. libr. This flower was incorporated in the arms of Uxb. Bor.
[17] Ex inf. Mr. N. W. Chenery.
[18] O.S. Map 1/2,500, Mdx. xiv. 8 (1914 edn.).
[19] *Rep. on Decline in Agric. Population* [C. 3273], pp. 607 sqq. H.C. (1906), xcvi.
[20] Schedule of sale *penes* Uxb. Bor. Council.
[21] Uxb. Bor., Reg. of Properties, M.D. 975.
[22] O.S. Map 1/2,500, Mdx. xiv. 7, 8 (1934–5 edn.).
[23] *Kemp's Uxb. Dir.* (1962–3).
[24] Ex inf. Milton Hutchings Ltd.

Colham manor.[25] Presumably the third mill was driven by the main stream of the Colne, in which case the other half probably belonged to a manor on the Buckinghamshire bank.[26] The two other Domesday mills, however, were probably on the southern extension of the Frays river, known variously as the Cowley stream or Colham mill stream. During the medieval period the two mills belonging to Colham were called Port mill and Bury mill:[27] later they were known as Colham or Lower Colham mill and Yiewsley mill respectively. In the 19th century, and presumably earlier, Colham mill stood less than ½ mile west of Colham manor-house and about 1½ mile downstream from Yiewsley mill.[28] In 1265 Godfrey de Heddesore (probably Hedsor, Bucks.) was said to hold three mills in Uxbridge,[29] and in 1327 three water-mills called Crouch mill, Wode mill, and Town mill were included in an extent of Cowley Hall manor.[30] There was a windmill belonging to Colham manor in 1328[31] and at least from the late 14th century the lord of Colham owned, in addition to his two mills south of Uxbridge, two watermills under one roof in the town.[32] A mill called Mede mill, also belonging to the lord of Colham, is first mentioned by name in 1409 when it was apparently horse-powered.[33] A wharf for Mede mill was being constructed in 1419 and thereafter it is described as a water-mill.[34]

In the 1530s there were two mills, one driven by the Frays and the other by the Colne, near the Oxford road at the west end of Uxbridge.[35] In the 17th century a water-mill at Uxbridge belonged to Stanwell manor,[36] and two unidentified mills at Hillingdon were included in grants of Swakeleys manor in Ickenham.[37] In the 18th century, and possibly earlier, one or more of the Uxbridge mills were possibly used for paper-making.[38] Town (later Frays or Mercer's) mill on the Frays at the west end of Uxbridge and Crouch mill, presumably identifiable with the two 14th-century mills of the same name,[39] were again mentioned in 1636[40] and 1649[41] respectively. In 1649 Crouch mill and the adjoining mill-house were leased to Samuel Bonsey, a London mealman. Rabbs or Robbs mill (later Cowley mill), sited on the Frays stream at the junction of Cowley Road and the modern Cowley Mill Road, is first mentioned by name in 1636[42] although it had almost certainly been in existence since the Middle Ages. Cowley Hall mill on the Frays west of Cowley Hall, although not mentioned by name until 1733,[43] is

shown on a map of 1541.[44] By this date the Frays river powered at least five mills—Town or Frays mill, Rabbs mill, Cowley Hall mill, Yiewsley mill, and Colham mill—and before 1746 another mill on an arm of the Colne west of Uxbridge had apparently been built.[45] The demesne mill at Colham was separated from the manor in 1771 and sold to John Hubbard, a mealman, members of whose family had leased the mill and an adjoining close called Wharf Mead as early as 1690.[46] Hubbard's son John, Rector of Shepperton, owned Colham mill in 1800,[47] but by 1842 it had been acquired by the firm of Thomas Smith and Son.[48]

There were said to be 13 corn mills in the neighbourhood of Uxbridge during the 1840s,[49] but the location of some of these is uncertain. A map of 1842 shows eight corn mills on the Hillingdon stretch of the rivers.[50] Of these three were in Uxbridge, including Frays mill then in the possession of John Mercer, members of whose family had probably owned this mill and Drayton mill in West Drayton parish since about 1796.[51] In addition to the four ancient mills on the Frays stream a mill called Upper Colham mill, probably identifiable with the mill marked on a map of 1746,[52] is shown on the Colne west of Uxbridge.[53] Cowley Hall mill and an unidentified mill called Kelsey's were burned down in 1864 and 1873 respectively,[54] but Cowley Hall mill had been rebuilt before 1895 when it was one of four flour mills still standing on the Frays south of Uxbridge.[55] The mill on the Colne west of the town was purchased by the Bell Punch Co. in 1919 and incorporated in their industrial premises.[56] By 1934 only Rabbs or Cowley mill and Frays mill in Uxbridge were still certainly standing.[57] Rabbs mill was acquired by the local authority from Grimsdale and Sons, the Uxbridge brewers, in 1949.[58] Frays mill was modernized at the beginning of the 20th century and remained in use as a flour mill until the Second World War. In 1954 the buildings were bought from the millers E. and J. Fountain by Glaxo Ltd. and later converted into a training centre.[59]

Apart from milling there is no evidence of any industry in rural Hillingdon before the opening of the Middlesex section of the Grand Junction Canal at the end of the 18th century. The establishment of facilities for bulk transport stimulated the exploitation of brickearth deposits in the south of the parish. Brick-making on a commercial scale probably began shortly after 1815 with the opening of small fields

[25] V.C.H. Mdx. i. 124.
[26] Ibid. 96.
[27] Lancs. Rec. Off., DDK/1746/1.
[28] The position of these and other mills on the Frays stream is most accurately shown on the Hillingdon Incl. Award Plan (1825) in M.R.O.; see plate facing p. 90.
[29] C 145/28/37.
[30] C 131/3/3; see below.
[31] C 145/108/2. See also a grant of a mill in Colham dated 1314: C.P. 25(1)/149/45/150.
[32] Lancs. Rec. Off., DDK/1746/1-10.
[33] Ibid. 1746/6.
[34] Ibid. 1746/8-10.
[35] Leland, Itinerary, ed. L. Toulmin Smith, i. 113-14.
[36] C.P. 25(2)/1657-8, Hil.
[37] C.P. 25(2)/6 Jas. I, Mich.; /21 Jas. I, Easter.
[38] Cal. S.P. Dom. 1636-7, 409. See also A. H. Shorter, Paper Mills and Paper Makers in Eng. 1495-1800, 213, 215.
[39] See above.
[40] M.R.O., Acc. 448/1.
[41] C 3/459/64.
[42] M.R.O., Acc. 448/1.

[43] C.P. 43/600/346.
[44] Forde, Design for River from Rickmansworth to St. Giles in the Fields.
[45] It is first shown on Warburton, Map of Mdx. (1746).
[46] M.R.O., Acc. 591/29.
[47] Lysons, Mdx. Pars. 152.
[48] M.R.O., F.32.
[49] Robson's Dir. (1839); Home Cnties. Dir. (1845).
[50] M.R.O., F.32.
[51] Sketch penes Uxb. libr. recording the burning of Mercer's mill in 1796; V.C.H. Mdx. iii. 196.
[52] See above.
[53] Its location is confirmed by O.S. Map 1/2,500, Mdx. xiv. 3 (1866 edn.).
[54] S. Springall, Country Rambles Round Uxbridge (1907), 154.
[55] Cf. plan penes Uxb. Bor. Council; O.S. Map 1/2,500, Mdx. xiv. 7 (1896 edn.).
[56] Ex inf. Bell Punch Co.; see p. 80.
[57] O.S. Map 1/2,500, Mdx. xiv. 7 (1934 edn.).
[58] Uxb. Bor., Reg. of Properties, M.D. 1164.
[59] Ex inf. Mr. N. W. Chenery.

between Cowley Hall and Yiewsley.[60] In 1818 'several hundred' men were employed in the brick-fields south of Uxbridge.[61] In 1832 45 a. of Philpots Bridge Farm, 44 a. of Colham Manor Farm, and 22 a. in Pole Sturges meadow were leased for brick-working, and by 1836 a number of cottages for labourers in the brick-fields had been built south of the canal.[62] The extensive Hillingdon brick-field was said in 1853 to be a source of great wealth to Uxbridge.[63] By 1856 more than 240 a. in Hillingdon, including 100 a. of the rectorial glebe south of Colham Green leased to Samuel Pocock, were being worked for brickearth. All brick-field lessees paid a royalty on every thousand bricks and two tenants, as a condition of their lease of a total of 58 a., undertook to produce between them at least 5 million bricks a year.[64] By 1866 smaller brick-fields had been opened north-west of Colham Green and south of Uxbridge.[65] Eight years later, however, deposits near Uxbridge were said to have been exhausted.[66] In 1872 Samuel Pocock extended his Hillingdon brick-field southward into West Drayton parish, and between 1876 and 1879 he constructed a dock on a branch of the canal to serve the extended field.[67] Pocock had six stools in Hillingdon in 1877, when the bricks from the whole field were being fired in Hillingdon.[68] In 1884 Pocock conveyed his interests to C. B. Broad and G. Harris, of South Wharf, Paddington, and the field continued to be leased by Broad & Co. until 1935, when the company bought the freehold. The company's land included, as well as the West Drayton field, about 100 a. in Hillingdon parish.[69] At its peak, about 1890, Broad's brick-field was working 18 to 20 stools and gave seasonal employment to between 400 and 500 men.[70] At this period gravel associated with the brickearth deposits was also being extracted west of Starveall Lane and in the extreme south-east of the parish.[71] The Hillingdon brickearth was becoming worked out at the beginning of the 20th century and the Stockley brick-works began to decline. Brickearth was still being extracted from Hide Field in 1913, but processing was apparently carried out only at the Stockley works in the north-east corner of West Drayton parish.[72] By 1930 the Stockley works were producing only 2 million bricks a year, and the brick-field was closed in 1935.[73]

A number of other industries, about which little is known, were established during the 19th century along the canal in south and west Hillingdon. The Victoria oil mills on the canal at Yiewsley were in existence before 1855. By 1886 the works were occupied by Graham Walter & Co., a firm of oil cake manufacturers, who continued production there until about 1900.[74] The Hillingdon Varnish Works on the canal east of Yiewsley had been established by 1868,[75] and was still operating in 1895[76] when the chief industries of the Yiewsley area were described as brick-making, milling, tanning, rubber, varnish, and chemical works.[77] The Para rubber mill (established before 1898)[78] was sited on the canal north of Yiewsley, and a coconut fibre mill, which was converted to a leather works before 1913, stood north of Cowley Bridge.[79] The varnish and rubber factories were still operating in 1913.[80] An unidentified chemical works on the east side of Horton Lane which is shown on a map of 1864[81] was occupied in 1874 by Thomas Reynolds and Alfred White, manufacturing chemists. From 1890 the premises were described as the chemical works of Alfred White and Sons. The factory ceased production between 1910[82] and 1915 when the premises were opened by the Queen of Roumania as the Sonic engineering works. Here George Constantinescu (1881–1965), also a Roumanian, conducted experiments on his wave transmission system of interrupter gear for machine guns firing through the propellers of aircraft.[83] The premises were taken over in 1920 by the Admiralty for use as an engineering laboratory specializing in experimental work for the Navy. Stores, offices, and canteen buildings were added after 1920 and the number of persons employed on the site increased from 150 in 1920 to 350 in 1958.[84] Land formerly owned by St. Thomas's Hospital[85] was acquired in 1921 by two industrial concerns called Lactine Ltd. and Hobdellway & Co. Ltd., whose premises were purchased in 1928 by the Kenilworth Chemical Manufacturing Co. and the English Metal Powder Co. The English Metal Powder Co., producing flake and atomized aluminium powders and aluminium pastes, began operations on the site in 1932. In 1965 the firm employed approximately 80 persons. The premises in Trout Road originally occupied by the Metal Powder and Kenilworth companies were taken over after 1935 by the Middlesex Oil and Chemical Works Ltd., an associate company manufacturing oils, petroleum jellies, and resins. The Kenilworth and Metal Powder companies then moved to an adjoining site in Trout Road. In 1965 the Middlesex Oil and Chemical Works employed approximately 100 persons.[86] A large number of smaller industries, chiefly engaged in manufacturing chemicals, plastics, and engineering components, were established at Yiewsley, and particularly in Trout Road, after 1930. By 1960 there were more than forty such concerns in the area.[87] Among these was the factory of Bux Ltd. (formerly the Buckinghamshire Paper and Box Co. Ltd.) which was established in Bentinck Road in 1942 and later moved to a 6-acre site in Horton Road. In 1965

[60] *Hist. of Uxbridge*, 75; M.R.O., E.A./Hil./2; *Pigot's Nat. Com. Dir.* (1826–7).
[61] *Hist. of Uxbridge*, 75.
[62] M.R.O., Acc. 742/105, 107.
[63] *Lake's Uxb. Almanack* (1853).
[64] M.R.O., Acc. 742/32, 176.
[65] O.S. Map 1/2,500, Mdx. xiv. 3 (1866 edn.); note of land occupied for brick-making purposes (1866) *penes* Uxb. Bor. Council.
[66] *Kelly's Dir. Mdx.* (1874). [67] *V.C.H. Mdx.* iii. 199.
[68] Case *re* rating of brick-field *penes* Uxb. Bor. Council.
[69] Church Com. recs. [70] Ex inf. Broad & Co. Ltd.
[71] O.S. Map 1/2,500, Mdx. xiv. 12, 16 (1895 edn.).
[72] Ibid. (1914 edn.).
[73] Ex inf. Broad & Co. Ltd.
[74] *Kelly's Dir. Mdx.* (1855–1902).

[75] Terrier of land in Hillingdon of Hubert de Burgh *penes* Uxb. Bor. Council.
[76] Plan of civil par. of Hillingdon East *penes* Uxb. Bor. Council.
[77] M.R.O., *Reps. of Local Inquiries* (1889–97), 411–20.
[78] *Kelly's Dir. Mdx.* (1898).
[79] O.S. Map 1/2,500, Mdx. xiv. 7 (1896 edn.).
[80] Ibid.
[81] O.S. Map. 1/2,500, Mdx. xiv. 12 (1866 edn.).
[82] *Kelly's Dir. Mdx.* (1874–1910).
[83] Ex inf. Imperial War Mus.; *The Times*, 14 Dec. 1965.
[84] Ex inf. Admiralty Engineering Lab.
[85] See pp. 74–75.
[86] Ex inf. Eng. Metal Powder Co. and Mdx. Oil and Chemical Works Ltd.
[87] *Yiewsley and West Drayton Official Guide*.

the company, which manufactured fibreboard corrugated containers, employed approximately 150 people.[88] The coachbuilding firm of James Whitson & Co. moved into premises in High Street, Yiewsley, in 1952. The firm then manufactured chiefly coaches and fire engines and employed approximately 350 people. By 1965, however, the demand for luxury coaches had declined and the firm employed only about 50 people in manufacturing glass fibre components for commercial vehicles.[89] Further north, at Cowley, the Cowley Bridge works of Cape Building Products Ltd. was erected in 1935. Initially the factory produced flint bricks only, but in 1949 the company also began to manufacture asbestos insulation boards. In 1963 the factory had a labour force of approximately 550 persons, said to be drawn from an area within an 8-mile radius of Cowley.[90]

Uxbridge emerged as the economic focus of the ancient parish in the late 12th century when Gilbert Basset granted the right to hold a Thursday market in the town to the 'burgesses' of Uxbridge.[91] Basset's grant also provided that holders of one acre in the town should be free from all tolls and customs on payment of 2s. a year, that ½-acre holders should have the same privileges in consideration of 1s. a year, and that both classes of tenant should have the right to alienate their holdings at will. By 1281 the town also had an annual fair held on St. Margaret's day (20 July).[92] The right to hold a second annual fair at Michaelmas and a Monday market was granted to the lord of Colham in 1294.[93] Until the 19th century the importance of Uxbridge rested almost wholly on its markets, fairs, and mills. A market-house seems to have been built by 1513,[94] and the importance of the Uxbridge mills and markets was stressed by Leland, writing in the 1530s.[95] By the late 16th century the town was a market and milling centre for a wide area extending into Buckinghamshire and Hertfordshire.[96] Despite disputes over the right to dispose of the market tolls,[97] the Uxbridge corn market and flour mills seem to have retained their importance during the 17th and 18th centuries. The market-house was rebuilt in 1789,[98] and the corn trade was further stimulated by the opening of the Middlesex section of the Grand Junction Canal in 1796.[99] In 1799 almost 10,000 tons of grain and flour were carried on the canal between Uxbridge and the Thames.[1] The Thursday market was then said to be one of the largest pitched corn markets in the country, the market tolls realized more than £400 a year, and the town 'abounded' with mealmen and corn merchants.[2] About 1830

corn was brought to the Uxbridge market from places as far distant as Edgware and Hendon to the east, Staines, Hampton, and Kingston (Surr.) to the south, and Amersham, Missenden (Bucks.), and Chinnor (Oxon.) to the west.[3] On a good day more than 2,700 sacks of corn were sold, almost all of which was milled at Uxbridge. Street markets associated with the Thursday corn market and a market held on Saturdays sold fruit, vegetables, meat, and a variety of consumer goods. The corn market and mills began to decline about 1840 with the transfer to market-gardening, meadow, and brick-working of large areas of corn-growing land. The Uxbridge Corn Exchange Co. was instituted in 1859, and sale by sample superseded the old method of sale in bulk.[4] The Thursday street market also declined but in 1883 the corn and flour trade was still described as the staple business of Uxbridge.[5] In 1890, when there was still some street trading, the Thursday and Saturday markets were said to deal in corn, provisions, meat, vegetables, old clothes, and 'other petty commodities'.[6] By this date annual fairs, said in 1839[7] to be held on 25 March, 31 July, 29 September, and 11 October, had been discontinued.[8]

Although the commercial life of Uxbridge centred on the corn and flour trade, a number of minor industries existed in the town before 1800. Brewing seems to have been an important industry by the 14th century.[9] Uxbridge beer-brewers and breweries, presumably supplying the many inns and beerhouses in the town, are mentioned at all later periods.[10] In the 1580s Camden commented on the large number of inns in the town,[11] and with the increase in traffic on the London–Oxford road stabling and victualling became an important local industry. By 1648 there were approximately twenty inns in Uxbridge,[12] and a hundred years later nearly forty licensed alehouses in and around the town.[13] In 1853 there were 54 public houses, beerhouses, and inns in Uxbridge.[14] The first commercial brewery was apparently established in the early 18th century by George Harman (d. 1744).[15] Norton's brewery, which is said to have been established about 1750,[16] is shown on a late-18th-century plan at the north end of High Street,[17] and the brewing firm of G. B. Hetherington had premises in the town before 1847.[18] There were 4 breweries in Uxbridge in 1851,[19] 5 in 1869, but only 3 by 1909.[20] Of these the last, Harman's Uxbridge Brewery Ltd., was closed in 1964.

A tannery in Uxbridge is mentioned in 1672,[21] and one of the town mills may have been converted for paper-making by Joseph Grainger about 1793.[22]

[88] Ex inf. Bux Ltd.
[89] Ex inf. Jas. Whitson Ltd.
[90] Ex inf. Cape Building Products Ltd.
[91] Original grant in Uxb. libr.; see *Uxb. Record* (Jnl. Uxb. Local Hist. Soc.), i. 6–13. The witnesses included Henricus de Druvall and Fulk Basset, who may have been the Hugh de Druvall and Fulk Basset mentioned in 1188: *Eynsham Cartulary* (Oxf. Hist. Soc. xlix), 71–72.
[92] St. Paul's MSS. box 35/986.
[93] *Cal. Chart. R.* 1257–1300, 436; *Plac. de Quo Warr.* (Rec. Com.), 476.
[94] See p. 60.
[95] Leland, *Itinerary*, ed. L. Toulmin Smith, i. 113–14.
[96] *Acts of P.C.* 1586–7, 369.
[97] See below.
[98] See p. 61.   [99] See p. 63.
[1] Lysons, *Mdx. Pars.* 177.
[2] Ibid. 177–8.
[3] Section based on Hutson, 'Recollections'.
[4] Corn Exchange Min. Bk. 1859–86 *penes* Uxb. libr.

[5] E. Walford, *Greater Lond.* 233.
[6] *Rep. Com. on Market Rights & Tolls*, H.C. (1890–1) xl.
[7] *Robson's Dir.* (1839).
[8] *V.C.H. Mdx.* ii. 87.
[9] Lancs. Rec. Off., DDK/1746/1–3.
[10] e.g. M.R.O., Acc. 276/1; 526/61; C.P. 25(2)/8 Geo. I, Hil.
[11] *Britannia*, ii. 78.   [12] See p. 61.
[13] M.R.O., L.V. 6/84.
[14] Lake's Uxb. Almanack (1853).
[15] Ex inf. Mr. N. W. Chenery.
[16] *Hist. of Uxbridge*, 74.
[17] Sketch of High Street in Uxb. libr.
[18] Bill head in Uxb. libr.
[19] *Home Cnties. Dir.* (1851).
[20] Ex inf. Mr. N. W. Chenery.
[21] M.R.O., Acc. 499/1.
[22] A. H. Shorter, *Paper Mills and Paper Makers in Eng. 1495–1800*, 213, 215.

An establishment at Hillingdon End manufacturing Windsor chairs was in existence before 1800,[23] and a small firm manufacturing cutlery was established in High Street in 1798.[24] The opening of the Grand Junction Canal in 1796[25] not only revitalized the Uxbridge milling industry but also opened up the town and parish to industrial development. By 1814 a plate-glass mill had been established on the site of the old waterworks just north of Dolphin Bridge,[26] and between 1830 and 1850 a number of industrial premises, including a gas-works,[27] parchment works, oil mills, and mustard mills, were erected near the canal on Uxbridge Moor.[28] Extensive wharves were built along the canal on Uxbridge Moor and at the west end of Uxbridge. In 1851 the town was said to derive much of its importance from the redistribution of foreign timber, slate, and coal to west Middlesex and Buckinghamshire. Facilities for bulk transport also resulted in the establishment of several iron foundries in the town.[29] The firm of Grainge, Rogers, and Grainge occupied premises off High Street from 1800,[30] and the Uxbridge Iron Works of Stacey and Son were erected in George Street in the 1820s. Stacey's foundry employed about 50 men, whose families were housed in Foundry Terrace, York Road (demolished in 1935).[31] In 1853 both firms were described as agricultural implement makers.[32] A third foundry, the Albert Iron Works, had been built in Falcon Yard, east of Harefield Road, by 1894.[33] At this date the Uxbridge Iron Works, which has been sold in 1889, was still standing, but the factory is said to have been burned down before 1900.[34] Other 19th-century industries included the coach-making firm of Edward Hood, which was established in High Street about 1829 and moved to premises in Windsor Street shortly after 1840.[35] By 1853 a second coach-building firm had been established in High Street.[36] The firm of Brownie, rick-cloth and rope manufacturers, was established by 1830 and served both King William IV and Queen Victoria.[37] In 1868 the smell from Hetherington's tallow factory was causing discomfort in the town.[38] By 1880 two firms manufacturing clocks and watches and a branch of J. A. Harling & Co., a London firm of piano makers, had been set up in Uxbridge.[39] Boat-building yards in Waterloo Road are first mentioned in 1881,[40] and saw- and planing-mills two years later.[41] A factory in Waterloo Road manufacturing steel barrels opened about 1898. In c. 1905 the concern, then known as the Steel Barrel Co., employed between 40 and 50 men.[42]

After the First World War a number of industries moved to Uxbridge from the metropolitan area. The largest of these was the Bell Punch Co. (established 1878) which in 1919 moved from premises in the City of London to the site of an old mill on an arm of the Colne west of Uxbridge. In 1963 the firm, which manufactured ticket machines, taxi-meters, and other technical instruments, employed approximately 1,500 persons in workshops covering 8 a.[43] Other industrial building was concentrated on a 26-acre industrial estate between the canal and the Colne which was opened by the local authority in 1946.[44] An industrial trading estate association was formed in 1958, and by 1964 the estate comprised more than 50 companies, most of which were general or light engineering concerns specializing in the manufacture of component parts.[45] The average labour force in most of the factories was between 50 and 80 in 1963, but several larger concerns employed more than 200 persons. F. T. Products Ltd. was established in Rockingham Road in 1949 to manufacture components for the motor industry. Additional premises in Wallingford Road were opened in 1956, and in 1963 the company employed 315 persons.[46] A chemical engineering firm, Nordac Ltd., moved from a factory at Park Royal, Acton, to premises in Wallingford Road in 1950. By 1963 the factory area was approximately 41,000 sq. ft. and the firm had a labour force of 240.[47]

Social activity during the 16th and 17th centuries seems to have centred on the efforts of the inhabitants of Uxbridge to enforce and extend their customary privileges. A fatal quarrel between town and manorial officials occurred in the early 16th century,[48] and in 1561 the Vicar of Hillingdon and 17 others were indicted for breaking down fences on Cow Moor in Harefield on which Uxbridge burgage tenants claimed rights of common pasture.[49] About 1630 the townspeople engaged in a further dispute, this time with Alice, Dowager Countess of Derby, lady of Harefield and Colham manors, over her right to collect and dispose of the Uxbridge market tolls.[50] Although these profits belonged to the lords of Colham it had apparently been customary for the lord to allow the bailiffs of Uxbridge to collect the tolls for distribution for 'public and charitable purposes'. In 1631 the Countess accused the bailiffs of appropriating the tolls for their own benefit and declared her intention of distributing them herself. Her right to do so was disputed by the town authorities who, in answer to a writ of *quo warranto*, claimed that Uxbridge was an ancient borough and corporation of 73 burgesses holding the tolls by ancient privilege. Their claim was rejected, and the townspeople then created a series of disturbances and prevented the collection of the tolls. The Countess referred the matter to Star Chamber which in 1633 rejected the townspeople's interpretation of the 12th-century market grant[51] and fined them £200. They then

[23] Sketch of High Street in Uxb. libr.; *Hist. of Uxbridge*, 74.
[24] Ex inf. Mr. N. W. Chenery; *Hist. of Uxbridge*, 74.
[25] See p. 63.
[26] Survey of the canal (1814) *penes* Uxb. libr.
[27] See p. 66.
[28] *Home Cnties. Dir.* (1851).
[29] Ibid.
[30] Sign in Uxb. libr.
[31] *Uxb. Gaz.* 12 July 1935.
[32] *Lake's Uxb. Almanack* (1853).
[33] O.S. Map 1/2,500, Mdx. xiv. 3 (1896 edn.).
[34] *Uxb. Gaz.* 12 July 1935.
[35] *Lake's Uxb. Almanack* (1840).
[36] Ibid. (1853).
[37] Bills and ledger in Uxb. libr.
[38] Uxb. Local Bd. Min. Bk. 1859–72.
[39] Bill heads in Uxb. libr.
[40] *Eele's Uxb. Dir.* (1881).
[41] Walford, *Greater Lond.* 233.
[42] *To Uxbridge from the City* (n.d.), copy in Uxb. libr.
[43] Ex inf. Bell Punch Co. Ltd.
[44] See p. 68.
[45] Association booklet.
[46] Ex inf. F. T. Products Ltd.
[47] Ex inf. Nordac Ltd.
[48] See p. 84.
[49] M.R.O., S.R. 106/2; Acc. 538/2/9.
[50] Section based on album of contemporary documents in Uxb. libr.
[51] See above.

petitioned the Countess for the remission of the fine and relinquished their claim to the market tolls. In 1652, however, George, Lord Chandos, a Royalist sympathizer, who had succeeded his grandmother as lord of Colham, left the country,[52] and the towns-people again appropriated the tolls. An action for restitution was brought against the town authorities in 1665 and seven years later the case again came before the courts. Nothing further is recorded until a settlement was reached in 1695 with the sale of the manor and profits to representatives of the town.[53] Burgage tenants continued to exercise their custo-mary pasture rights on the Colham waste and on Cow Moor in Harefield until the 19th century.[54] Their pasture rights in Colham were extinguished on the inclosure of the commons in 1812, and under the Harefield Inclosure Act of 1813 they were allotted 32 a. in Harefield in lieu of their customary rights.[55] Despite protests from the burgage tenants this land was sold by the lords in trust in 1856 under powers conferred by an Act passed in 1855.[56]

Further details of the social life of Hillingdon during this period are confined to the activities of Parliamentary soldiers,[57] who garrisoned Uxbridge almost continuously between 1644 and 1651.[58] In 1688 disbanded soldiers from James II's army were said to be concentrated around Uxbridge and to be responsible for assaults, murders, and arson in the district.[59] Four years later additional watches were mounted in Cowley Street and at the 'Red Lion', Hillingdon, to combat the increasing number of larcenies.[60] The activities of highwaymen and smugglers in the Uxbridge area were frequently reported in the early 18th century,[61] and it was later said that in the 1750s notorious highwaymen lived openly in the town while travellers made a detour to avoid its thieves and pickpockets.[62]

The economic developments which followed the opening of the Grand Junction Canal in 1796 were accompanied by a significant expansion in the com-mercial and social facilities of Uxbridge. The Ux-bridge universal tontine was established in 1791,[63] and the first meeting of freemasons was held at the 'Crown' in 1796.[64] By 1836 two freemasons' lodges had been established in Uxbridge.[65] A bank, occupying premises on the west side of High Street, was founded in 1791 by members of the milling families of Norton and Mercer. A sub-branch at Southall was established as early as 1879, and by 1900, when it was taken over by Barclays & Co., the bank had branches at Pinner, Northwood, Brentford, Slough, Eton, and Windsor.[66] A printing press was set up in Uxbridge by Thomas Lake about 1770,[67] and by 1824 a second press was operating at Hillingdon End.[68] During the 1820s Lake's press

published literature attacking the local administra-tion,[69] but the town does not seem to have had a regular newspaper until the publication at Amer-sham (Bucks.) about 1840 of *Broadwater's Bucking-hamshire Advertiser and Uxbridge Journal* (after 1853 called the *Buckinghamshire Advertiser*). By 1870 the town had two further newspapers, the *Uxbridge Chronicle* and Hetherington's *Uxbridge Marvel*.[70] In 1880 the Uxbridge firm of John King began to print the *Uxbridge Gazette*. From 1860 the *Buckingham-shire Advertiser* was printed in offices in the King's Arms yard, Uxbridge. The paper was taken over in 1903 by W. J. Hutchings (d. 1917) who had also established a printing works in High Street in 1880, and the two newspapers continued in competition until 1916 when the King family bought the *Advertiser*. The two firms of King and Hutchings amalgamated in 1919, and the combined business subsequently acquired and published a number of local and county newspapers. The firm was acquired by the Westminster Press group in 1955. In 1965 the Uxbridge premises in Cricket Field Road com-prised a newspaper and general printing works employing more than 500 persons.[71]

Cultural activities in Uxbridge flourished in the early 19th century. The Uxbridge Book Society, which provided a lending library and reading room, was founded in 1811 with a limited membership of 60. On the creation in 1836 of the Literary and Scientific Institution, the Book Society was dissolved and its books transferred to the library of the new institution.[72] A savings bank was instituted in 1816 by a group of philanthropic townspeople,[73] and a friendly society in the following year.[74] Public rooms in Vine Street were opened in 1837, and the Theatre Royal in Windsor Street, said to have been opened by Edmund Keane, the actor, was in use by 1839.[75] The town was then said to have the 'appearance of activity and great respectability'.[76] A second theatre, the Prince of Wales, had opened by 1849[77] and other dramatic entertainments were staged in the public rooms and in the magistrates' room at the 'King's Arms'.[78] A building society had been formed by 1845 and a young men's improve-ment society by 1847. From about 1847 the im-provement society published a literary journal, the *Attempt*, which lasted until 1853. It overlapped with the *Uxbridge Pioneer*, which first appeared in 1849. The improvement society was still in existence in 1899 as the Uxbridge Young Men's Literary Insti-tute.[79] The Uxbridge branch of the Conservative Association was formed in 1870.[80]

Stags were hunted on Uxbridge Common as late as 1826 and Her Majesty's Staghounds met at Hillingdon until 1879. Cock fights were held at

[52] *Hist. of Uxbridge*, 28.
[53] See p. 72.
[54] Survey of the manor and bor. *penes* Uxb. libr.; M.R.O., Acc. 538/2/9; 448/1; burgage roll (1809) in Uxb. libr.
[55] M.R.O., Harefield Incl. Award.
[56] M.R.O., Acc. 538/4, 7; see p. 75.
[57] See p. 88.
[58] *Cal. S.P. Dom.* 1644, 91, 143, 533; 1645-7, 434, 463, 593; 1651, 413, 414; B.M. Add. MS. 5461; Harl. MSS. 22, 24; Lysons, *Mdx. Pars.* 179-80.
[59] Hist. MSS. Com. *15th Rep. App. I*, 135.
[60] M.R.O., M.S.P. 1692/Dec./11.
[61] File of early newspaper cuttings in Uxb. libr.
[62] Uxb. Note Bk. (1828), *penes* Uxb. libr, 26.
[63] M.R.O., Acc. 538/2.
[64] J. Lane, *Masonic Records, 1717-1886*, p. 65.

[65] M.R.O., TS. Reg. of Freemasons' Lodges.
[66] Ex inf. Barclays Bank Ltd.
[67] *V.C.H. Mdx.* ii. 200; *Lake's Uxb. Almanack* (1840).
[68] M.R.O., Printer's Declarations, box 2.
[69] Uxb. Note Bk. (1828) *penes* Uxb. libr.
[70] Bill heads in Uxb. libr.
[71] Ex inf. Mdx. County Press and Mr. K. R. Pearce.
[72] Uxb. Book Soc. Min Bk. *penes* Uxb. libr.
[73] Min Bk. *penes* Uxb. libr.
[74] Rules *penes* Uxb. libr.
[75] File in Uxb. libr.
[76] *Robson's Dir.* (1839).
[77] File in Uxb. libr.
[78] Cuttings in Uxb. libr.
[79] File in Uxb. libr.
[80] Min Bk. *penes* Uxb. libr.

Hillingdon until at least as late as 1839.[81] During the 19th century Uxbridge C.C., founded in 1789, played matches against important national teams on the club's ground in the modern Cricket Field Road.[82] Hillingdon C.C., playing on Coney Green, was in existence before 1865.[83] The Uxbridge amateur football club was formed in 1870, and has since played in many leagues and on various grounds in the town.[84] Hillingdon Golf Club was instituted in 1892 and a nine-hole course was laid out over 23 a. of Hillingdon House park.[85]

A military association for the Uxbridge division of Elthorne hundred was formed at Uxbridge in 1797.[86] The force, styled the Uxbridge Yeomanry Cavalry, consisted of two troops of horse which exercised and had their field days on Uxbridge Common. The troop founded in 1797 was disbanded four years later, but in 1830 a corps of 98 yeomanry cavalry was again raised at Uxbridge to meet the threat of agrarian discontent in the district. From about 1840 an annual race-meeting in connexion with the Uxbridge Yeomanry was held at Harefield Place, on Harefield Moor, and, later, at West Drayton. More than 10,000 people were said to have attended the 1846 meeting. In 1871 the strength of the volunteer corps was increased to four troops and the style changed to the Middlesex Yeomanry Cavalry. The 'Chequers' at Uxbridge, however, remained the headquarters of the corps until 1878 when the headquarters were moved to London. There were then said to be no more than five Uxbridge men in the regiment, and its subsequent history is that of a county rather than a local force.

The proliferation of cultural facilities in Uxbridge in the early 19th century contrasted strongly with social conditions in the town and parish during the same period. Complaints in 1828 drew attention to the declining reputation of Uxbridge. Increasing poverty in the town was attributed mainly to the erection by private speculators of large numbers of insanitary cottages. Prostitutes were said to be on the increase, and the opening of shops on Sunday mornings was also criticized.[87] Although criticism was probably exaggerated, the extinction of common grazing rights and changes in land utilization following inclosure in 1825, the introduction of industry into the parish, and the presence of labourers working in the brick-fields probably aggravated prevailing hardship. Unrest west of the Colne, where bands of 'swing rioters' were destroying machinery, farm implements, and ricks, resulted in the re-formation in December 1830 of the Uxbridge Yeomanry Cavalry to protect private property.[88] In Uxbridge town a vestry committee headed by the Vicar of Hillingdon was formed to suppress Sunday business and disturbances caused by drunken brick-field and railway workers.[89] In 1841 there were said to be 146 seasonal labourers living in barns in Hillingdon and population increases since 1831 were largely attri-

buted to the influx of brick-workers.[90] In the later 19th century urbanization, stimulated by the introduction of trams and railways, proceeded steadily. In 1904 the surveyors of the Hillingdon House estate considered that the development of 'smaller class property on the main road frontage' would inevitably follow the laying of the tramway.[91] Extensive speculative and council building during the 1920s accompanied the sharp rise in the population of Hillingdon, although the number of people living in Uxbridge had already started to decline.[92]

Despite the large-scale urbanization of rural Hillingdon after 1900 Uxbridge maintained its position as the economic and social focus of the parish. In 1964 the town, despite uncertainty over redevelopment plans, was a business and transport centre for north-west Middlesex and part of east Buckinghamshire.[93] Shops and industries in and around Uxbridge provided employment for a considerable part of the population of Hillingdon and adjoining parishes, and the location in the town of the branch offices of several government taxation and welfare departments further emphasized its wider importance. Local trade and industry also contributed significantly to the social life of the district by providing clubs and associations for sport and cultural activities. The Uxbridge chamber of trade and commerce (formed in 1908) had 265 members in 1963,[94] and a second chamber of commerce for the north Hillingdon district was formed in 1936.[95] In 1964 there were also several traders' organizations, a trades' council, two residents' associations, and ex-service, political, trade union, and youth organizations. A room in the county library was furnished as a museum, which was named after H. T. Hamson, for many years editor of the *Middlesex Advertiser* and a prominent benefactor of the museum.[96] A local history society was formed in 1949, and by 1964 the parish also supported opera, music, and drama societies. An Uxbridge festival of arts mounted in 1963 staged exhibitions of painting, books, and handicrafts, plays, and operatic and music recitals by international artists in the Regal cinema.[97] In 1962 the thirty-seventh annual Uxbridge Show, held on the show ground in Park Road, attracted approximately 10,000 people.[98]

LOCAL GOVERNMENT. From the early 12th century Colham manor, which probably included the hamlet of Uxbridge, formed part of the honor of Wallingford[99] and presumably owed suit to the view of frankpledge for the honor instead of to the hundred court. In 1293, and probably earlier, the frankpledge court for the Middlesex bailiwick of the honor met at Uxbridge.[1] At this date Hillingdon manor apparently owed suit to the hundred court,[2] but by the early 15th century Hillingdon also was attending the annual view for the honor at Uxbridge.[3]

[81] Newspaper cuttings in Uxb. libr.
[82] Press cuttings in Uxb. libr.
[83] Fixture card *penes* Uxb. libr.
[84] Ex inf. the club treasurer.
[85] *V.C.H. Mdx.* ii. 281; M.R.O., Acc. 503/107.
[86] C. Stonham and B. Freeman, *Historical Recs. of the Mdx. Yeomanry*, 4 sqq.
[87] Uxb. Note Bk. (1828) *penes* Uxb. libr.
[88] Stonham and Freeman, *Mdx. Yeomanry*, 12.
[89] Hutson, 'Recollections'.
[90] *Census*, 1841.
[91] M.R.O., Acc. 503/107.   [92] See pp. 68–69.

[93] *Borough Petition* (1951); *Kemp's Uxb. Dir.* (1962–3).
[94] Ex inf. the secretary
[95] Ex inf. the chairman.
[96] Ex inf. the bor. librarian.
[97] Programme in Uxb. libr.
[98] Ex inf. Uxb. Bor. Council.
[99] See p. 70. For the composition of the honor in 1235 see *Bk. of Fees.* 473–4.
[1] *Plac. de Quo Warr.* (Rec. Com.), 477.
[2] J.I.1/544, m. 51d.
[3] The broken series of Wallingford court rolls begins in 1422 and ends in 1673: S.C. 2/212/2–31.

Courts for the Middlesex division of the honor of Wallingford (later Ewelme)[4] were held at Uxbridge until the early 19th century.[5]

How far the jurisdiction of the honor court overlapped that of the local manorial courts is unknown since no manorial court records have survived. In 1245 the lord of Colham apparently claimed the right to hold a court to which his free tenants owed suit,[6] and from the 14th century onwards he was usually described, although holding of the honor of Wallingford, as having pleas and perquisites of courts leet and baron and, occasionally, the right to hold view of frankpledge.[7] Fourteenth-century manorial accounts appear to indicate that medieval lords of Colham held leet courts and views of frankpledge for Colham and Uxbridge in addition to those held annually by the steward of Wallingford.[8] Perquisites of 'portmoots' held for Uxbridge are also included in an early-14th-century extent of Colham.[9] Courts baron for Colham were held in the 17th century,[10] and in 1800 courts leet and baron were said to be held annually at the 'Red Lion', Hillingdon.[11] Courts baron for the manor continued to meet until at least as late as 1872.[12]

Which of the courts appointed local officers is also uncertain. In 1536 the honor court appointed 2 constables and 6 headboroughs for the Middlesex bailiwick,[13] and in the 19th century was said to have always appointed the officers for Uxbridge town.[14] A hayward for Colham was appointed at the manorial leet in the late 18th century,[15] but by this time control of local administration had almost certainly been assumed by the parish. The constables of Hillingdon are mentioned in 1609,[16] and again in 1642 when there were 2 constables and 2 overseers.[17]

The functions of the constables and churchwardens of Hillingdon seem to have overlapped during the 17th century. The churchwardens were administering the 'church-houses' in 1676 and perhaps as early as 1636.[18] Repairs to the parish property were paid out of the church-rate and most of the balance was spent on out-relief.[19] The parish property, later described as almshouses, seems to have been used as a poor-house or workhouse before 1747 when a new workhouse was built in Royal Lane.[20] The new premises comprised 9 rooms, together with a kitchen, dining-room, brewhouse, outbuildings, and hospital room. By 1768 a workroom equipped with tools and spinning wheels had been added. Six years later the house contained 58 paupers, and by 1796 there were 65 inmates. Further

extensions before 1810, when there were 47 persons in the house, included rooms for cobblers and weavers and a schoolroom.[21] During the 18th century both workhouse and out-poor were maintained out of the poor-rate. The Hillingdon poor-rate yielded £263 in 1739; six years later the amount realized was £404, the bulk of which was spent on occasional relief.[22] Thirty years later the poor-rate yielded £414, of which £320 was spent on the poor.[23] After 1790 the usual rate was 1s. in the £, but occasionally, as in 1800, 1819, and between 1830 and 1833, a 1s. 6d. rate was levied.[24] In 1802–3 the rate realized £1,553, of which £722 was spent on the workhouse. During the year 32 parishioners received regular relief out of the workhouse and a further 416 persons, including 60 non-parishioners, were given occasional relief.[25]

Efforts to reduce poor-relief expenditure began with the revival of the Hillingdon vestry as an effective administrative body in 1806. For administrative purposes the parish was divided into four divisions—Hillingdon East, Hillingdon Town, Goulds Green, and Yiewsley—to each of which the vestry usually appointed 3 overseers. In addition the vestry elected 4 constables and 11 headboroughs for the parish.[26] Early vestry activity was marked by the formation of procedural rules and attempts to encourage the attendance of parishioners at the monthly meetings. In 1809 the vestry was instrumental in the formation of an association, consisting of Hillingdon, Cowley, and West Drayton parishes, for rewarding the apprehension and prosecution of felons.[27] Apart from this early interest in law and order the staple business of the vestry, throughout its history, was the election of parish officers and the administration of the poor law and settlement Acts. In 1807 the vestry farmed out the maintenance of the parish poor, both in and out of the workhouse, for approximately £900 and employed a doctor to attend the poor at a salary of £26 a year. Annual contracting continued until 1810 when the vestry entered into a separate contract for the maintenance of the workhouse at £605 a year. Responsibility for out-relief was then transferred to the overseers. The overseers violently opposed the change, refusing to submit their accounts or to attend vestry meetings,[28] and during 1811 only 41 persons received occasional relief.[29] The vestry petitioned the local bench for assistance and, shortly afterwards, discontinued the allowance traditionally paid to the overseers for their refreshment at inns after the vestry meeting.[30]

[4] For the transfer of the rights of the honor of Wallingford to the new honor of Ewelme in 1540 see *V.C.H. Berks.* iii. 528.
[5] M.R.O., note of documents at Oxon. Rec. Off. concening the honor of Ewelme 1790–1813; see below.
[6] C.P. 25(1)/147/13/216.
[7] e.g. C 145/108/2; C 136/40/47; C 139/134/29, m. 16.
[8] Lancs. Rec. Off., DDK/1746/1–10: Colham manor bailiffs' accts. 1373–1419.
[9] C 145/108/2.
[10] M.R.O., Acc. 180/679.
[11] Lysons, *Mdx. Pars.* 152.
[12] M.R.O., Acc. 448/10.
[13] S.C. 2/212/18.
[14] See below.
[15] M.R.O., Acc. 526/4.
[16] *Mdx. Cnty. Recs.* ii. 52.
[17] Hse. of Lords, Mdx. Protestation Rets.
[18] The survey of Colham manor, made in 1636 (M.R.O., Acc. 448/1) includes a tenement owned by the churchwardens.

[19] Par. Recs., Churchwardens' Accts. 1676–1716.
[20] Note on 18th-cent. copy of 1636 survey in Uxb. libr. recording that £70 was allowed for the 'old house'. The location of the early building is unknown.
[21] Inventories of Hillingdon workhouse 1758–1810 *penes* Uxb. Bor. Council.
[22] Hillingdon Poor-rate Bks. 1738–49 *penes* Uxb. Bor. Council.
[23] *Rep. Cttee. on Rets. by Overseers, 1776*, Ser. i, ix. 396–7.
[24] Hillingdon Poor-rate Bks. 1738–1851 are *penes* Uxb. Bor. Council; Overseers' Acct. Bk. 1779–1803 is in Uxb. libr.
[25] *Rets. on Expense and Maintenance of Poor*, H.C. 175, pp. 294–5 (1803–4), xiii.
[26] Vestry Min. Bks. 1806–37 *penes* Uxb. Bor. Council. Occasionally the number of officers elected was increased by 2–3.
[27] Vestry Order Bk. 1806–17 *penes* Uxb. Bor. Council.
[28] Ibid.
[29] Overseers' Acct. Bks. 1811–30 *penes* Uxb. Bor. Council.
[30] Vestry Order Bk. 1806–17.

Following further increases in poor relief expenditure during the 1820s[31] the vestry introduced a scheme in 1829 for the temporary employment of the parish poor by individuals and for the purchase of land where they might be set to work. In the following year the workhouse was enlarged so that male and female paupers could be housed separately.[32] A 22-acre field adjoining the workhouse was rented in 1833, and the vestry appointed a special committee, the Parish Land Allotment Committee, to supervise the introduction of 'spade husbandry'.[33] The workhouse was again enlarged in 1834, but two years later Hillingdon became part of the Uxbridge Poor Law Union[34] and the workhouse was sold to the guardians.[35] The building then became the union workhouse and was further enlarged.[36] In 1841 it contained 169 paupers; thirty years later the number of inmates had risen to 232 and in 1911 reached a maximum of 282 persons.[37] At a later date the workhouse infirmary became the nucleus of Hillingdon Hospital.[38]

Other wider units of local government began to assume the responsibilities of the parish shortly after its inclusion in the Uxbridge Union. Despite a vestry resolution in 1839 that the inclusion of Hillingdon in the Metropolitan Police District was undesirable,[39] the parish was added to the District in 1840.[40] By 1864 there were police stations in Kingston Lane and at Goulds Green.[41] The western portion of Hillingdon was included in the Uxbridge Local Board of Health district constituted provisionally in 1849 and confirmed four years later,[42] and the remainder of the parish was covered by the Uxbridge Rural Sanitary Authority created in 1875.[43] The formation in 1878 of a board of management for highways under the Highways Act (1835)[44] relieved the vestry of another duty.[45] The vestry finally ceased to exist in 1894 when that part of Hillingdon old parish lying within the new Uxbridge U.D. (formerly the local board district) became the civil parish of Hillingdon West and the remainder, which was included within the new Uxbridge R.D. (replacing the rural sanitary authority's area), became the civil parish of Hillingdon East.[46] Two years later Yiewsley civil parish was created from the southern portion of Hillingdon East.[47] From 1895 until 1928 Hillingdon East had a parish council. The council met several times each month in various

schools in the parish and was largely concerned with the election of officers and routine business connected with highways and street lighting.[48] Larger projects were undertaken by the rural district council which began work on a joint sewerage disposal scheme for Hillingdon East, Cowley, and West Drayton in 1898. The council was also responsible for the beginnings of public housing in Hillingdon under the Government Assisted Housing Act.[49] In 1929 Uxbridge R.D. was dissolved and Hillingdon East parish was added to Uxbridge U.D. At the same time Yiewsley, which had been created an urban district in 1911, became part of Yiewsley and West Drayton U.D. Responsibility for local administration in these areas was then assumed by the two larger units of government.[50]

The importance of Uxbridge as an administrative centre is first indicated in the 13th century when meetings of the Wallingford honor court were being held in the town.[51] From the mid 16th century petty sessions of the Middlesex justices also met in Uxbridge,[52] and from 1750[53] alternate meetings of the county court were held at the 'George'.[54] In 1853 the former petty sessional division of Elthorne hundred was renamed the Uxbridge division.[55] During the 19th century the magistrates met in the 'King's Arms' and, later, in the public rooms. From 1907 both magistrates' and county courts were held in the Court House, Harefield Road.[56]

Whether Uxbridge enjoyed some form of autonomous government during the Middle Ages is not known.[57] Constables of Uxbridge appear to have been at variance with manorial officials as early as Henry VIII's reign when one of them was attacked and killed by the bailiff of Colham and his men.[58] It was later said[59] that as early as 1572 the constable was the chief officer of the town. A constable and headborough of Uxbridge are mentioned in 1613,[60] when there were both stocks and a pillory in the town,[61] and there were 2 constables, 2 churchwardens, and 4 collectors in 1642.[62] In the 1650s and again in the 19th century it was stated that, although Uxbridge remained technically part of Hillingdon parish, the townspeople had always elected their own officers and maintained their poor independently of the parent parish. In neither instance was the basis of this claim stated.[63] In the early 19th century the town was governed by 2 constables, 4 headboroughs,

31 Overseers' Acct. Bks. £2,693 was spent on the poor in 1830.
32 Vestry Mins. 1829–37 penes Uxb. Bor. Council.
33 Hillingdon Poor's Allotments Min. Bk. 1833–7 penes Uxb. Bor. Council.
34 See below.
35 Vestry Mins. 1828–37.
36 M.R.O., BG/U/1.
37 Census, 1841–1911.
38 See p. 65 and plate facing p. 105.
39 Vestry Mins. 1838–51.
40 Lond. Gaz. 1840, p. 2250.
41 O.S. Map 1/2,500, Mdx. xiv. 8, 12 (1866 edn.).
42 Act to confirm prov. orders of Gen. Bd. Health, 16 & 17 Vic., c. 126.
43 Bealby's Uxb. Almanack (1875).
44 5 & 6 Wm. IV, c. 50.
45 Vestry Order Bk. 1867–94. The Mdx. Cnty. Council assumed responsibility for main roads in 1891: Reps. of Local Inquiries (1889–97), pp. 393–408.
46 Copy of resolution of Mdx. Cnty. Council penes Uxb. Bor. Council; see above, p. 56.
47 See p. 56.
48 Hillingdon East Par. Council Order and Min. Bks. penes Uxb. Bor. Council.

49 Mdx. Cnty. Council Rep. of Local Inquiry relating to Uxb. R.D. (1923).
50 For Yiewsley and West Drayton U.D. see V.C.H. Mdx. iii. 202; for Uxb. U.D. and the later Borough of Uxbridge see below.
51 See above.
52 M.R.O., Acc 71/176 (S.R. 70); S.Reg.I, f. 55; Mdx. Cnty. Recs. Sess. Bks. 1689–1709, 73.
53 Act 23 Geo. II, c. 33.
54 Hist. of Uxbridge, 111–12. An early-19th-century building, said to have been the court-house, was still standing behind the 'George' in 1968.
55 M.R.O., O.C. 44/346–54.
56 Ex inf. Sir Christopher Cowan, J.P., and the county court registrar; see also Sir Christopher Cowan, 'The Magistrates of Uxbridge', Uxbridge Record (Jnl. Uxb. Hist. Soc.), v. 3–6.
57 For claims to borough status see p. 85.
58 Sta. Cha. 2/19/63.
59 Hist. of Uxbridge, 110.
60 Mdx. Sess. Recs. i. 235.
61 Ibid. 219; Mdx. Cnty. Recs. iii. 48.
62 Hse. of Lords, Mdx. Protestation Rets.
63 Lysons, Mdx. Pars. 176; M.R.O., Acc. 538/2.

and 2 ale-conners,[64] said to be appointed in the Wallingford court leet held at Uxbridge in Easter week each year.[65] After the honor court was discontinued about 1813[66] the town officers were presumably appointed by the Uxbridge vestry. The lords in trust, who were said in 1727 to have the right to hold a court baron and a 'burgage' court every three weeks,[67] appointed and paid a hogsherd and the keeper of the pound and shared with the vestry the right to appoint a beadle and town crier.[68]

In the late 17th century the poor-rate at Uxbridge, which, under an agreement made in 1624 between the townspeople and the authorities of Hillingdon parish, was levied on the occupiers of approximately 300 a. lying in and around the town,[69] was disbursed by the overseers as occasional relief to sick and needy paupers.[70] Almshouses and, possibly, a workhouse, had apparently been built in the Lynch before 1727.[71] After the reorganization of the manorial trust in 1729 the new trustees covenanted to rebuild the almshouses and to add a workhouse.[72] Of the management of the town workhouse in the 18th century almost nothing is known. It contained 60 paupers in 1775,[73] and 76 inmates in 1803.[74] The maintenance of workhouse and out-poor was farmed out by the vestry on a contract basis.[75] In 1795 the contractor agreed to maintain the poor both in and out of the workhouse for £450; by 1808 the contract was worth £1,050.[76] The poor-rate, which had yielded £410 in 1775–6,[77] raised £1,033 in 1803, all of which was spent on the poor.[78] During the year 59 parishioners received regular out-relief and a further 32 persons, of whom 5 were non-parishioners, were given occasional relief. Relief provided out of the poor-rate was augmented by the chapel wardens who administered the church-rate and the Uxbridge charities[79] and by the lords in trust who devoted an increasingly large part of the manorial profits to the provision of out-relief. In 1743 a total of £58 was spent by the trustees on occasional relief to 95 'townspeople', 12 'out town people', and 16 tenants of the almshouses.[80] Thirty years later almost two-thirds of the manorial profits of £378 were spent on the poor.[81] During the 1790s weekly payments were made to widows, paupers, and to 8 inmates of the workhouse: in 1801 widows received 2s. a week and workhouse poor 6d.[82]

During the early 19th century the Uxbridge vestry made several attempts to reduce the cost of poor relief. From 1814 the workhouse was farmed separately, administration of out-relief being undertaken by the overseers. Four years later the town entered into a contract with a married couple who agreed to live in the workhouse and to manage the establishment, under the supervision of the overseers, at a weekly salary of 12s.[83] The management of out-relief, however, was apparently left in the hands of unpaid officers and this probably led to some embezzlement. In 1819 weekly relief was being given to more than 100 persons. By the 1820s expenditure on the poor had risen to nearly £3,000 a year,[84] and the administration of poor relief was being greatly criticised. An overseer was defined as 'one who overlooks the advantage of the town' and a lord in trust as 'one who refuses to give account of his trust to any but the Lord'.[35] The vestry too was attacked for awarding the workhouse contract to John Keen, who had submitted a tender of 4s. 3d. a head. Another tender of 4s. was submitted but Keen, who was said to be a notorious drunkard, received the votes of eight Uxbridge publicans and was awarded the contract.[86] In 1833 protests were made in the vestry that part of the poor-rate was being used for road repairs.[87] Despite further public agitation for the appointment of a salaried overseer to live in the workhouse, the vestry apparently continued to farm out the maintenance of the workhouse until the transfer of the Uxbridge poor to Hillingdon workhouse.[88] The town workhouse was used by the Uxbridge volunteer police force[89] until the introduction of metropolitan police in 1840.[90] Two years later the trustees sold the workhouse premises.[91] The building seems to have been demolished before the 1880s when the site was said to be occupied by the fire station and almshouses.[92]

Apart from their interest in the poor the lords in trust were chiefly concerned with the provision of amenities for the town. Wooden pipes supplying the town with water from the Colne are said to have been laid by the manorial trustees in 1701.[93] A fire engine costing £48 was purchased in 1770 and a further £14 spent on erecting an engine-house. The scheme was financed by contributions from the Sun Fire Office, private subscribers, and the church-rate.[94]

[64] Lysons, *Mdx. Pars.* 179; *Hist. of Uxbridge,* 109–12. According to Redford and Riches the two bailiffs included in the list of town officers given by Lysons were not appointed after the late 17th cent.

[65] *Hist. of Uxbridge,* 111. This is the only evidence for the appointment of the town officials in the honor court and ought perhaps to be treated with caution.

[66] Ibid.; Hillingdon Vestry Order Bk. *penes* Uxb. Bor. Council.

[67] M.R.O., Acc. 538/1; Lysons, *Mdx. Pars.* 181. There is no evidence that courts baron were held after 1728.

[68] *Hist. of Uxbridge,* 111, 208. The office of town crier was discontinued in 1906: M.R.O., Acc. 538/4.

[69] M.R.O., Acc. 538/2.

[70] Overseers' Acct. Bk. 1694–1703 *penes* Uxb. libr.; Overseers' Accts. 1772–1817 in M.R.O.

[71] The survey of 1727 states that a workhouse had been built on the Lynch Green by this date; M.R.O., Acc 538/1.

[72] M.R.O., Acc. 538/7. It had apparently been built by 1732: Chapelwardens' Accts. in M.R.O.

[73] *Rep. Cttee. on Rets. by Overseers, 1776,* Ser. i, ix. 396–7.

[74] *Rets. on Expense and Maintenance of Poor,* H.C. 175, pp. 294–5 (1803–4), xiii.

[75] Chapelwardens' Accts. 1770 record a vestry meeting for letting the workhouse.

[76] *Hist. of Uxbridge,* 95–96.

[77] *Rep. Cttee. on Rets. by Overseers, 1776,* Ser. i, ix. 396–7.

[78] *Rets. on Expense and Maintenance of Poor,* H.C. 175, pp. 294–5, (1803–4), xiii.

[79] Chapelwardens' Accts. 1708–1807 in M.R.O. For the charities see below, p. 98.

[80] M.R.O., Acc. 538/1: Man. and Bor. Min. Bk. 1693–1787.

[81] Ibid. See also Guildhall MS. 9558.

[82] M.R.O., Acc. 538/4: Man. and Bor. Min. Bk. 1786–1803.

[83] *Hist. of Uxbridge,* 95–96; Vestry Mins. 1819–36 in M.R.O.

[84] Uxbridge Note Bk. *penes* Uxb. libr.; Hutson, 'Recollections'.

[85] Uxbridge Note Bk.   [86] Ibid.

[87] Vestry Mins. in M.R.O.

[88] Hutson, 'Recollections'; see above, p. 84.

[89] Hutson, 'Recollections'.   [90] See below.

[91] M.R.O., Acc. 538/4: Man. and Bor. Min. Bk. 1841–71.

[92] Hutson, 'Recollections'. A photograph in Uxb. libr. taken *c.* 1920 of a building reputed to be the old workhouse shows a small brick and weather-boarded house at no. 10 the Lynch, then in process of demolition.

[93] File in Uxb. libr. Section of original pipe in Uxb. Mus.   [94] File in Uxb. libr.

Little seems to have been done, however, to alleviate the congestion and the insanitary nature of High Street[95] until 1785 when an Act was passed[96] authorizing specially appointed trustees to widen the main street by demolishing the market-house and other buildings.[97] Provision was also made for removing protruding signs and spouts and for paving, lighting, and cleaning the streets. Until the institution of the Uxbridge Board of Health in 1849 all major improvements in the town were undertaken by trustees exercising powers conferred by the Acts of 1785 and 1806.[98] Land and houses involved in the widening of High Street were valued by a specially appointed jury and purchased by the trustees who also assessed compensation for land taken for the Grand Junction Canal. The trustees also appointed a highways surveyor with a salaried assistant and requested from the justices authority to levy an additional 3d. rate for road repair.[99] Improvements to the town water supply, which since 1701 had been drawn from the Colne,[1] began in 1800 with the sinking of two wells in the town. A third well was sunk in 1853, and these formed the basis of the municipal supply until the 20th century.[2] In 1801 the trustees resolved that the system of oil-fired street lighting was inadequate and appointed a committee to improve and extend the existing arrangements.[3] An application from the British Gas Light Co. to light the town was considered in 1824,[4] but nothing had been done by 1828 when the trustees were criticized for not introducing gas.[5] About 1832, however, a private speculator, James Stacey (d. 1879), built a gas-works near the canal on Uxbridge Moor,[6] and by 1833 some streets were apparently lighted by gas.[7]

During the 1830s Uxbridge began to assume a wider administrative importance.[8] An unofficial local board or sanitary authority for the town and its immediate neighbourhood may have been in existence as early as 1832.[9] Four years later the Uxbridge Poor Law Union was formed.[10] The union, which comprised the parishes of Hillingdon, Harefield, Ruislip, Ickenham, Cowley, West Drayton, Hayes, Norwood, and Northolt, was administered by three guardians meeting weekly in the 'White Horse', Uxbridge.[11] Hillingdon workhouse was adapted as the union workhouse for the reception of paupers from the constituent parishes.[12] Shortly after the formation of the Uxbridge Union a volunteer police force was created under the supervision of the town watch committee, and a police station was set up in the recently vacated workhouse.[13] This volunteer force was disbanded in 1840 when Uxbridge was added to the Metropolitan Police District.[14] Responsibility for the town's amenities, exercised since 1785 by trustees, was assumed by the Uxbridge Local Board of Health which was formed provisionally in 1849 and confirmed four years later.[15] The board was preoccupied with the provision of adequate sewerage and water-supply systems; other committees were appointed to deal with lighting and paving, rates, and the location and suppression of nuisances.[16] Until the 1850s gas lighting in the town was provided by the Uxbridge Old Gas Co., which had succeeded the private venture started in the 1830s.[17] In 1854, however, a second gas company, the Uxbridge and Hillingdon Consumers' Co., was incorporated,[18] and for a time both companies competed for the town lighting contract. Competition became acrimonious in 1860 when the Gas Consumers' Co. accused the local board of partiality towards the Old Gas Co. A police report on the state of street-lighting in the town was submitted to the government and an Act passed in 1861[19] provided for the purchase of the Old Gas Co. by the Gas Consumers' Co. and the incorporation of the amalgamated concern.[20] A burial board was formed when burials in St. Margaret's church ceased and the cemetery at the bottom of Windsor Street was closed in 1855.[21] The board opened a cemetery in Kingston Lane in 1853 and an adjoining cemetery for Hillingdon burials in 1866.[22] A volunteer fire brigade, with a station in Windsor Street, was formed in 1864.[23]

Under the Local Government Act (1894) the local board became an urban district council and the rural sanitary authority, created in 1875,[24] a rural district council.[25] Uxbridge R.D.C. was dissolved in 1929 and the urban district extended to include Harefield, Ickenham, and the whole of Hillingdon and Cowley civil parishes.[26] In 1951 the population of the new district was 55,944.[27] From 1949 the district was divided into seven wards, increased to nine in 1952, together returning 27 councillors.[28] In 1951 there were eight standing committees, for allotments, civil defence, finance and general purposes, housing, parks and open spaces, public health, rating and

[95] *Hist. of Uxbridge*, 76–77.
[96] 25 Geo. III, c. 16.
[97] See p. 61.
[98] M.R.O., Acc. 538/1, /2: Acct. and Min. Bks. of Trustees under Act 25 Geo. III (Town Improvement), 1785–1848.
[99] Ibid. For early-19th-cent. improvements see above, p. 61.
[1] See above.
[2] File and photographs *penes* Uxb. libr.
[3] M.R.O., Acc 538/4. The trustees paid a man to light the lamps each evening: ibid. /1.
[4] Ibid. /5.
[5] Uxb. Note Bk. (1828).
[6] Hutson, 'Recollections'; press cuttings in Uxb. libr.
[7] M.R.O., Acc. 538/5.
[8] For the town's importance as an administrative centre at earlier periods see above.
[9] Hillingdon Vestry Mins. 1828–37.
[10] *Lond. Gaz.* index.
[11] M.R.O., BG/U/1–28: Bd. of Guardians Min. Bks. 1836–1930. The number of guardians was increased to 5 in 1858 and again reduced to 3 in 1875: copies of local govt. bd. orders *penes* Uxb. Bor. Council.

[12] See p. 84.
[13] Hutson, 'Recollections'; *Lake's Uxb. Almanack* (1840).
[14] *Lond. Gaz.* 1840, p. 2250; *Lake's Uxb. Almanack* (1842).
[15] Act to confirm prov. orders of Gen. Bd. of Health, 16 & 17 Vic., c. 126.
[16] Uxb. Local Bd. Min. Bk. 1859–72 *penes* Uxb. Bor. Council.
[17] Hutson, 'Recollections'; see above.
[18] M.R.O., Acc. 638/18.
[19] Uxbridge Gas Act, 24 & 25 Vic., c. 53 (Local Act).
[20] M.R.O., Acc. 638/15; Hutson, 'Recollections'.
[21] Hutson, 'Recollections'; inscription on gateway of former cemetery.
[22] *Com. on Local Govt. in Greater Lond. Mins. of Evidence* (1958).
[23] Local Bd. Min. Bk. 1859–72; file and photographs in Uxb. libr.
[24] *Bealby's Uxb. Almanack* (1875).
[25] The Min. Bks. of the U.D.C. and R.D.C. are in the custody of Uxb. Bor. Council.
[26] *Borough Petition*, 6.
[27] Ibid. 16.
[28] Ibid. 21, 26.

valuation, and works and town planning.[29] The warding arrangements remained unchanged after the incorporation of Uxbridge Borough, co-extensive with the former urban district, in 1955.[30] The borough council administered five departments in 1958: those of the town clerk, treasurer, surveyor, public health, and parks, all of which were housed in converted dwellings in High Street. The council employed a permanent staff of 115, and 299 manual workers.[31] In 1929 the rate was 12s. in the £, and had risen to 21s. in the £ by 1962. The product of a penny rate rose from £845 in 1929–30 to £4,800 in 1961–2.[32]

URBAN DISTRICT (LATER BOROUGH) OF UXBRIDGE. *Or, on a pile gules between two roundels barry wavy argent and azure, an eagle displayed or* [Granted 1948]

The main task facing the rural district council and its successors was the provision of housing and amenities to meet the population expansion after 1890. Work on a joint sewerage disposal scheme for Hillingdon East, Cowley, and West Drayton began in 1898.[33] Council building also began in the 1890s with the completion of a small estate in Austin Waye.[34] By 1962 successive councils had erected 4,702 dwellings in the borough, of which approximately two-thirds were sited in Hillingdon old parish.[35] Amenities provided by the local authorities included municipal shops on some estates, a swimming-pool (opened in 1935) on the Hillingdon House Farm estate, and an industrial estate (opened in 1946) in Cowley Mill Road.[36] By 1962 there were also more than 2,000 a. of open spaces, parks, and recreation grounds, representing approximately 20 per cent. of the area of the borough, including nearly 80 a. of permanent and temporary allotments.[37]

In 1965 Uxbridge Borough was merged with the urban districts of Hayes and Harlington, Ruislip-Northwood, and Yiewsley and West Drayton to form the new London Borough of Hillingdon.[38]

CHURCHES. Shortly after 1100 Hillingdon church was granted by Brian Fitz Count, lord of Colham manor, to the Worcestershire abbey of Evesham. The gift also included a hide of land, a dwelling-house (*mansio*), and one-third of the tithes of Colham.[39] Evesham apparently appropriated the church property and exercised the right of presentation until the mid 13th century.[40] About 1247 the Abbot of Evesham was said to exercise the patronage and to have a pension of one mark from Hillingdon vicarage.[41] In 1248, as part of the settlement of a long-standing jurisdictional dispute between the abbey and the Bishop of Worcester, the abbey agreed to surrender the patronage of Hillingdon and an annual pension of one mark from the church property to the bishop, while retaining some of the tithes.[42] How far this compromise was put into effect is uncertain. The bishop's right to present to the living was confirmed by Henry III in 1266,[43] but the matter seems to have remained in dispute until 1281 when the Bishop of London confirmed the rights in Hillingdon of the bishops of Worcester.[44] The vicarage was then endowed by the Bishop of Worcester and the right of presentation vested in the Bishop of London and his successors. The Bishop of London still retained the advowson in 1964.[45]

The nucleus of the medieval rectorial estate was probably contained in Brian Fitz Count's grant of land, tithes, and a house to Evesham Abbey.[46] The rectory was valued at 30 marks about 1250[47] and at £21 in 1291.[48] The bishop paid several visits to the 'manor-house' between 1398 and 1401, and subsequently the estate was usually styled a manor.[49] The rectory was taxed at 31 marks in 1428,[50] and valued at £33 in 1547.[51] Tithes payable on about 50 a.[52] in Tickenham[53] were the subject of a dispute in 1453 between the Rector of Ickenham, who had for some years appropriated them, and the Bishop of Worcester. After litigation the disputed land was assigned to Hillingdon parish and the tithes to the bishop as proprietor of Hillingdon church.[54] From the 16th century the rectory house and estate were leased at an annual farm of between £33 and £34.[55] In 1647[56] the rectorial glebe comprised at least 60 a. in Horse Close, Nether Close, Little Hillingdon Field, and the warren of Coney Green, said to have been granted to Thomas, Bishop of Worcester, in 1427.[57] South of Coney Green, on a moated site almost certainly identifiable with that of the medieval 'manor-house', stood the rectory house, which had been rebuilt in brick about 1604.[58] Two-thirds of the great tithes were payable to Christ Church, Oxford,

[29] Ibid. 27.   [30] M.R.O., F. 62b.
[31] *Com. on Local Govt. Mins. of Evidence* (1958).
[32] *Uxb. Official Handbk.* (1963).
[33] *Mdx. Cnty. Council, Rep. of Local Inquiry relating to Uxb. R.D.* (1923).
[34] *Borough Petition*, 61.
[35] Ibid. 61–63; *Uxb. Official Handbk.* (1963); see above, p. 65.   [36] *Borough Petition, passim.*
[37] *Official Handbk.* (1963); *Com. on Local Govt. Mins. of Evidence* (1958).
[38] Lond. Govt. Act, 1963, c. 33.
[39] B.M. Cott. MSS. Vesp. B.24, ff. 12v, 17; *Chron. Abbatiae de Evesham* (Rolls Ser.), 75. The date of the charter is disputed, but it was probably issued between 1107 and *c.* 1115. One-half of the hide attaching to the church is stated (ibid. 97) to have been given to the abbey *temp.* Abbot Walter (1077–86), but this seems most unlikely. For a discussion of both questions see *V.C.H. Mdx.* i. 110 n 51. Fitz Count's charter (B.M. Cott. MSS. Vesp. B.24, f. 14) is printed in W. Kennett, *Parochial Antiquities.* i. 117.   [40] *Cal. Pat.* 1232–47, 159, 173.
[41] St. Paul's MS. W.D. 9, f. 84v.
[42] *V.C.H. Worcs.* ii. 19, 119.
[43] Worcs. Rec. Off., Acc. 3332/3/213.

[44] St. Paul's MSS. boxes 30/429, 35/986, 40/1441; M.R.O., Acc. 538/1 (translation of 35/986).
[45] *Crockford* (1963–4).   [46] See above.
[47] St. Paul's MS. W.D. 9, f. 84v.
[48] *Tax. Eccl.* (Rec. Com.), 17.
[49] *Cal. Pat.* 1396–9, 386; 1399–1401, 343. In the 19th cent. it was established that the bp. had no legal right to style the estate a manor: Worcs. Rec. Off., 47883/4.
[50] *Feudal Aids*, iii. 378.
[51] E 301/34/128.
[52] The figure of 300 a. given in Lysons, *Mdx. Pars.* 166, seems to be much exaggerated.
[53] See above.
[54] Worcs. Rec. Off., Acc. 2636/47884/2; Newcourt, *Repertorium*, i. 647; see below, p. 106.
[55] C.P. 25(2)/5 Jas. I. Trin.; C 3/324/24; Worcs. Rec. Off., Acc. 2636/44007, /47217, /47221–9, /43808, /47230–31; M.R.O., Acc. 566/60–70; Lysons, *Mdx. Pars.* 166.
[56] Worcs. Rec. Off., Acc. 2636/47884/1, /44007.
[57] M.R.O., Acc. 448/1.
[58] In 1647 it was described as 'recently rebuilt': Worcs. Rec. Off., Acc. 2636/44007. Lysons. *Mdx. Pars.* 166, cites the date 1604 over a window in the house. A view in Uxb. libr. shows the building in 1858.

and the remainder was payable to the bishop in 1772.[59] Under the inclosure award of 1825 the Bishop of Worcester's tithes were commuted for 470 a. of land and the tithes due to Christ Church for 21 a. in Hide Field.[60] The rectorial estate, consisting of the house and approximately 600 a., and the 21 a. belonging to Christ Church, were farmed by the Boston family until 1828[61] when the Bishop of Worcester's land was sold.[62] The rectory house was retained by the bishop and leased separately until 1855 when it too was sold. Later in the 19th century the house was rebuilt and named Bishopshalt; subsequently it passed through several hands until in 1925 it was purchased by the county authorities and converted into a school.[63]

The priest mentioned in 1086 held one hide in Colham manor.[64] About 1247 the vicarage, from which the Abbot of Evesham took an annual pension of one mark, was valued at 100s.[65] Under the appropriation grant of 1281[66] small tithes, including offerings made in the chapel of ease at Uxbridge on St. Margaret's day,[67] were assigned to the vicar, and the Bishop of Worcester endowed the vicarage with $\frac{1}{2}$ mark yearly and 2 a. of freehold to build a vicarage-house.[68] Ten years later the vicarage was worth £5[69] and in 1428 it was taxed at 8 marks.[70] In 1535 and 1547 the vicarage was valued at £16.[71] In 1650 the living comprised the vicarage-house, 2 a. of glebe, and small tithes, together worth £35.[72] The incumbent complained in 1678 that the vicarage was in need of repair.[73] It was rebuilt in the late 18th or early 19th century, when it was given a symmetrical front of brown brick with sash windows and a central pediment.[74] Under the inclosure award of 1825 the vicar was allotted 234 a. in lieu of tithes and glebe.[75] During the 19th century most of the glebe was leased and in 1835 the net income of the living was £489.[76] Three acres of glebe were purchased by the Grand Junction Canal Co. in 1880,[77] and a further 10 a. were sold in 1890 and 1923 to form extensions to Hillingdon cemetery.[78] The bulk of the remaining glebe land has since been sold.[79] The vicarage-house in Royal Lane was vacated about 1959 and demolished three years later. In 1965 the vicar lived in a modern detached dwelling south of the site of the old house.[80]

A lady chapel in Hillingdon church was constructed about 1380,[81] and a chantry in the chapel was endowed for the soul of Henry (or Walter) Rabb in 1397.[82] Sums for obits and lights in Hillingdon church were included in the wills, proved 1398, of John Ely of Hillingdon[83] and John atte More of Uxbridge.[84] William Knightcote, Vicar of Hillingdon in 1452,[85] gave land worth 23s. for an obit in the church,[86] and a light, said to have been dedicated to Thomas of Lancaster, is mentioned in 1523.[87] Rabb's chantry was worth £5 in 1547.[88] The church had a chaplain or chantry priest from the 14th century,[89] and a curate is mentioned in 1586.[90] There is no evidence that any of the medieval incumbents were pluralists. Henry Mason (vicar 1611–12) wrote a number of anti-Catholic works.[91] In 1642 Parliamentary forces burned the service book from Uxbridge chapel and took the surplice from Hillingdon church to make handkerchiefs.[92] Two years later a Commonwealth sympathizer was installed in the living. Richard Taverner, who held the living from 1650,[93] took part in a public dispute with Quakers at West Drayton in 1658.[94] A 'registrar' for the parish was appointed in 1653, but the registers, which begin in 1559, were mutilated and badly kept during the Commonwealth. They were frequently used by Thomas Boston (vicar 1660–77) to record comments on the morals of his parishioners.[95] A library of 16th- and 17th-century works on divinity, natural history, and medicine was bequeathed by the botanist Samuel Reynardson (d. 1721) to the parish.[96] The books, which were deposited in a specially built room in the tower, were, with one exception, destroyed by the incumbent about 1940.[97] Reynardson also left the interest on a mortgage debt to provide a sermon on Good Friday.[98] In 1790 morning service only was held at Hillingdon. The vicar officiated at evening service in Uxbridge chapel and parishioners attended at either Cowley or Uxbridge.[99] Hillingdon parish continued to be served in this way until 1827 when the Uxbridge chapelry district became a separate parish. Eleven years later the new parish of St. John was formed from the Uxbridge Moor area of Hillingdon. A chapel of ease at Yiewsley was consecrated in 1858, and in 1874[1] a separate parish of St. Matthew, Yiewsley, was formed from the southern

[59] Worcs. Rec. Off., Acc. 2636/47882/6. The date at which the college first appropriated $\frac{2}{3}$ of the tithes is uncertain. Lysons, *Mdx. Pars.* 167, quoting the lessee of the rectory, says that they were those formerly belonging to Thame Abbey (Oxon.) and granted to Christ Church at the Dissolution. The tithes payable to Thame in 1349 are listed in *The Thame Cartulary*, ed. H. E. Salter (Oxford Rec. Soc. xxv), 161.
[60] M.R.O., E.A./Hil./2.
[61] Worcs. Rec. Off., Acc. 2636/18558, /18560; M.R.O., Acc. 566/82, /83; 742/15; Lysons, *Mdx. Pars.* 167.
[62] Worcs. Rec. Off., Acc. 2636/47235.
[63] Deeds *penes* Mdx. Cnty. Council. For the subsequent history of the house see p. 97.
[64] *V.C.H. Mdx.* i. 124.
[65] St. Paul's MS. W.D. 9, f. 84v.
[66] See above.   [67] See below.
[68] St. Paul's MSS. boxes 35/986, 40/1441.
[69] *Tax. Eccl.* (Rec. Com.), 17.
[70] *Feudal Aids.* iii. 378.
[71] *Valor Eccl.* (Rec. Com.), i. 434; E 301/34/128.
[72] *Home Cnties. Mag.* ii. 280.
[73] Par. Recs.
[74] Photograph in Uxb. libr.
[75] M.R.O., E.A./Hil./2.
[76] *Rep. Com. Eccl. Rev.* [67], H.C. (1835), xxii.
[77] Par. Recs. terrier of glebe (1889).
[78] Letters *penes* Uxb. Bor. Council.

[79] Ex inf. the vicar.
[80] *The Times*, 24 Apr. 1962; ex inf. the vicar.
[81] Par. Recs., ref. to will (1386) of Jn. Charlton asking to be buried in '*capella beate Marie recenter constructa*'.
[82] Guildhall MS. 9531/3, f. 152.
[83] Guildhall MS. 9171/1, f. 412.
[84] Ibid. f. 414v.
[85] Newcourt, *Repertorium*, 648.
[86] E 301/34/128.
[87] Par. Recs., note of communication from Somerset Hse.
[88] E 301/34/128; B.M. Harl. MS. 601, f. 44. Rabbs Farm, which was probably included in the endowment of the medieval chantry, comprised 66 freehold a. in 1636: M.R.O., Acc 448/1. For the later history of Rabbs Farm see pp. 74–75.
[89] Guildhall MS. 9171/3, f. 27v; *Cal. Pat.* 1436–41, 277; B.M. Harl. Roll. D.22.
[90] Guildhall MS. 9537/6.   [91] *D.N.B.*
[92] *Cal. S.P. Dom.* 1641–3, 372.
[93] Newcourt, *Repertorium*, 647–8.
[94] See p. 91.   [95] Par. Recs.
[96] The rarer books are listed in Lysons, *Mdx. Pars.* 168–9.
[97] Ex inf. the vicar. The surviving volume was in 1965 among the Par. Recs.
[98] Lysons, *Mdx. Pars.* 168.
[99] Guildhall MS. 9558.
[1] Par. Recs.; *Crockford* (1963–4).

portion of Hillingdon parish. St. Andrew's parish, Uxbridge, was taken from the parent parish in 1865. In 1884, before a similar change was effected in the civil boundaries,[2] the area of Hillingdon west of the Pinn and south of St. Andrew's was transferred to Cowley ecclesiastical parish.[3] Part of Hillingdon parish north of the London road became the parish of All Saints in 1934.[4]

The parish church, dedicated to *ST. JOHN THE BAPTIST*, stands on high ground at the junction of Royal Lane and Uxbridge Road.[5] It is built mainly of flint rubble with stone dressings and consists of chancel, aisled nave, north and south transepts, west tower, and vestries. The oldest part of the building is the re-set chancel arch which has 'stiff-leaf' foliage capitals of the 13th century. The nave arcades, each of three bays, date from the mid 14th century but little medieval work survives in the aisles except for their 15th-century roofs. The impressive west tower, of four stages, was rebuilt in the Perpendicular style in 1629; it is surmounted by a wooden bell cupola. The church was thoroughly restored by G. G. (later Sir Gilbert) Scott in 1847–8 when the nave was lengthened, the transepts were added, and the present east end, including the chancel with flanking chapels, was built.[6] A vestry at the west end of the south aisle also dates from the 19th century; it replaced a porch given by William Munsaugh (d. 1655) which formerly provided the main entrance to the church. The building was restored in 1902 and again in 1953–5,[7] and a new north-east vestry was added in 1964.[8]

Monuments in the church include a notable brass which was formerly part of an altar tomb in the old chancel. It has figures of John, Lord Strange, and his wife beneath a double canopy; a smaller figure represents their daughter, Jane, who erected her parents' tomb in 1509. Other brasses commemorate Henry Stanley (d. 1528), John Marsh (d. 1561), Anne Wilson (d. 1569), Drew Saunders (d. 1579), William Gomersall (d. 1597), and John Atlee (d. 1599). Among many later monuments the most striking are those against the side walls of the chancel. On the south side a tomb of marble and alabaster has kneeling figures of Sir Edward Carr (d. 1636) and his wife, flanked by Ionic columns and surmounted by an elaborate and unusual canopy; in front of the central prayer desk a pedestal supports the figures of two daughters. Against the north wall of the chancel a large classical monument to Henry Paget, Earl of Uxbridge (d. 1743), includes a reclining figure in Roman costume. A mural tablet in

the nave to Thomas Lane (d. 1795) is the work of John Bacon the elder. In the 16th century the tower contained five bells.[9] The peal was increased to six after the reconstruction of the tower in 1629, to eight in 1731, and finally, in 1911, to ten.[10] The plate includes two silver cups with paten covers given by Rose Wood and date-marked 1636 and 1638, and a silver flagon made in 1686.[11] The registers, which are complete, record baptisms, marriages and burials from 1559.[12]

A chapel, presumably the one dedicated to St. Margaret by 1281,[13] was built in Uxbridge before 1248[14] and possibly as early as 1200.[15] During the late 14th century several Uxbridge inhabitants left sums for repairs to and lights in St. Margaret's.[16] The chapel appears to have been largely rebuilt in the early 15th century.[17] Later in the 15th century the south aisle was rebuilt as a guild chapel for the guild of St. Mary and St. Margaret, founded in 1448.[18] The guild provided a chaplain and two chapelwardens and acquired land and rents in the town. In 1548 the possessions of the guild, including land in Cowley Field, the George Inn, and shops and houses in Uxbridge, were worth £11.[19] A chantry for the soul of Walter Shiryngton, Chancellor of the Duchy of Lancaster, was endowed in 1459[20] with 27 a. of land and tenements in the town.[21] Shiryngton's chantry was worth £7 in 1535,[22] and in 1548 the chantry possessions, which included the 'Bull' and the 'Cross Keys' in Uxbridge, were valued at £11.[23]

Although the living of St. Margaret's was described in 1547 as a vicarage valued at £5,[24] it was apparently administered until 1827 as a chapel of ease to Hillingdon church.[25] Until 1575 Uxbridge dead were buried at Hillingdon, but under an agreement concluded in 1576 the Bishop of London and the Vicar of Hillingdon consented to the burial of Uxbridge inhabitants in St. Margaret's and in a burial ground to be built at the bottom of the Lynch (later Windsor Street). The townspeople agreed to contribute to the repair of Hillingdon church and churchyard and to pay 6s. 8d. to the vicar for each burial in Uxbridge chapel.[26] The ground was enlarged and enclosed by a brick wall in 1776. It was closed for burials in 1855[27] and later became a public garden. A brick gateway with inscribed tablets of 1776 and 1855 has survived. In 1650 the living comprised only small tithes and the inhabitants petitioned for the creation of a separate parish of Uxbridge.[28] Nothing was done, but the situation improved after the institution, under the will (dated

[2] See p. 56.
[3] *Lond. Gaz.* 1885, p. 7.
[4] Ex inf. the vicar.
[5] It is fully described in Hist. Mon. Com. *Mdx.* 75–76.
[6] Vestry Mins. 1838–51. For the early-19th-century church, see plate facing p. 90.
[7] Programme in Uxb. libr.
[8] F. C. Tyler, *Hillingdon Parish Church* (2nd edn.).
[9] *T.L.M.A.S.* ii. 77.
[10] Par. Recs.
[11] Inventory of plate among Par. Recs.; E. Freshfield, *Communion Plate of Mdx.* 33.
[12] Ex inf. the vicar.
[13] See above. The dedication is mentioned by name in 1393: Guildhall MS. 9171/1, f. 280.
[14] St. Paul's MSS. W.D. 9, f. 84v.; box 35/986.
[15] *Cart. of Missenden Abbey*, pt. 3, ed. Jenkins (Bucks. Rec. Soc.), p. 166.
[16] e.g. Guildhall MS. 9171/1, ff. 280, 321, 414v.
[17] See below.

[18] *Cal. Pat.* 1446–52, 186. Newcourt, *Repertorium*, i. 650, wrongly dates the building of St. Margaret's chapel to 1447.
[19] B.M. Harl. MSS. 601, f. 44; 605, ff. 7v–9. For the disposal of the guild's possessions after the Dissolution see *Cal. Pat.* 1553, 75, 251.
[20] *Cal. Pat.* 1452–61, 513. The date of Shiryngton's death is given as 1449: *Handbk. of Brit. Chron.* ed. F. M. Powicke and E. B. Fryde, 140.
[21] Lysons, *Mdx. Pars.* 185.
[22] *Valor Eccl.* (Rec. Com.), i. 434.
[23] B. M. Harl. MSS. 601, f. 44; 605, ff. 7v–9. For the sale of the chantry's lands see *Cal. Pat.* 1547–8, 411–13; 1548–9, 417, 422.
[24] E 301/34/128.
[25] St. Paul's MSS. W.D. 9 f. 84v; box 35/986.
[26] Guildhall MS. 9531/13, ff. 82v–84.
[27] Inscription on gateway.
[28] *Home Cnties. Mag.* ii. 280–81.

1682) of George Townsend, of a trust for the maintenance of ministers in the chapels at Uxbridge and Colnbrook (Bucks.). By 1685 the living, augmented under Townsend's will by rents from houses in the parish of St. Martin-in-the-Fields, Westminster, was worth approximately £50.[29] A further improvement in the administration of the cure was effected in or about 1706 when the parishioners of Uxbridge and Hillingdon instituted a lectureship in the chapel and provided a lecturer's house in Cowley Field south of Vine Street.[30] The lecturer, nominated by the Vicar of Hillingdon and the chapelwardens of Uxbridge, was to assist in the administration of the cure and to instruct 6 poor boys, or to pay £6 a year towards their teaching. In 1766 the minister appointed under Townsend's will officiated at morning service on Sundays only, while the lecturer, who at this date was also Vicar of Hillingdon, celebrated monthly communion and Sunday evensong and also administered the cure.[31] From 1768 to 1786 John Lightfoot, the naturalist, combined the ministry of Uxbridge with the curacy of Cowley.[32] In 1820 the lecturer was non-resident and his house was said to be let.[33] Seven years later the 99-acre chapelry district was created a separate parish of St. Margaret, Uxbridge. The patronage was vested in the trustees of the Townsend trust, and in 1835 the net income of the living was £111.[34] Numbers attending the church declined significantly after 1930 as business premises replaced private dwellings in the town. In 1965 the church was placed in the charge of the Vicar of St. Andrew's, Uxbridge. By this date the patronage had passed to the Bishop of London.[35]

The church of *ST. MARGARET* occupies part of a cramped island site at the junction of High Street and Windsor Street. It is hidden from High Street by the market-house and is hemmed in by streets on its south and west sides. The building is of flint rubble with stone dressings and consists of chancel, nave, north and south aisles, north vestry, and a north tower, the base of which forms a porch.[36] The tower is of 14th-century origin, but the upper part has been rebuilt. The nave, north aisle, and both the nave arcades date from the early 15th century. The building of a wider south aisle later in the same century nearly doubled the size of the church. The aisle is a lofty structure with a fine hammer-beam roof of nine bays. The chancel was probably rebuilt and extended at the same period. The chapel to the north of the chancel, now used as an organ chamber, is apparently of early-16th-century date and retains three original windows. Traditionally this was the site of Walter Shiryngton's chantry chapel.[37] On visitation in 1673 the west door of the church and windows in the south aisle were found to be blocked by shops built against the walls.[38] The tower was largely rebuilt *c.* 1820, when it was given its present buttresses, belfry windows and embattled parapet,[39] and when the domed cupola was probably renewed. At about the same time the north-west angle of the church was cut back to widen Windsor Street.[40] The building was thoroughly restored in 1872. Most of the windows were then replaced, including the east and west windows of the south aisle and three in its south wall, all with Perpendicular tracery. A north vestry was built on the site of the former chicken market in 1882.[41] Fittings in the church include a late-15th-century font and two carved chairs, one of which is dated 1679. The most important monument is an alabaster and marble altar tomb in the chancel commemorating Leonora Bennet (d. 1638). The tomb-chest supports a reclining female figure above which an inscribed tablet is flanked by columns and surmounted by a pediment. Behind bars at the front of the tomb-chest a circular aperture reveals realistically carved skulls and bones. The peal of six bells, recast in 1716, was increased to eight in 1902.[42] The plate includes a silver cup date-marked 1686 or 1696, a flagon dated 1720 and three silver patens date-marked 1716, 1717 and 1726.[43] The registers, which are complete, record baptisms, marriages, and burials from 1538.[44]

The church of *ST. JOHN THE EVANGELIST*, St. John's Road, Uxbridge Moor, was opened in 1838. The church was designed by Henry Atkinson; it is executed in yellow stock brick with cement facings and has a Gothic bell turret at its west end. A single bell, said to have been brought from Flanders Green (Herts.), is dated 1578.[45] Additions to the church include a late-19th-century chancel of variegated brick and a 20th-century vestry. The Bishop of London is patron of the living.[46]

The church of *ST. ANDREW*, High Street, Uxbridge, was opened in 1865. The living is vested in the Bishop of London.[47] The church, built of local Cowley brick with stone dressings and contrasting brick ornament, was designed by G. G. (later Sir Gilbert) Scott in an early Gothic style.[48] It consists of chancel, aisled nave and south porch; the vestry and the south-east tower with its lofty broach spire were slightly later additions. Internally decorative use has been made of exposed masonry and brickwork. The church was restored in 1952–7. The vicarage, which stands south-west of the church, was originally a private house, built about 1827 and known as Maryport Lodge. It was conveyed to the Ecclesiastical Commissioners when the church was built. A mission-room, dedicated to St. Peter, was built in the Greenway in 1906,[49] and a parish hall north of the church in 1923.[50]

A chapel of ease, dedicated to *ST. MATTHEW*,

[29] Guildhall MS. 9537/20; Lysons, *Mdx. Pars.* 184; *9th Rep. Com. Char.* H.C. 258 (1823), ix.
[30] The date given by Lysons, *Mdx Pars.* 184, conflicts with that given in *9th Rep. Com. Char.* H.C. 258 (1823), ix. Chapelwardens' Accts. 1718, in M.R.O., suggest that the earlier date is correct.
[31] Guildhall MS. 9558.   [32] *D.N.B.*
[33] *9th Rep. Com. Char.* H.C. 258 (1823), ix.
[34] *Rep. Com. Eccl. Rev.* [67], H.C. (1835), xxii.
[35] *Lond. Dioc. Bk.* (1965).
[36] The church is fully described in Hist. Mon. Com. *Mdx.* 127–9.
[37] Ex inf. the vicar; A. D. Perrott, *The Story of Uxbridge Parish Church*, 6–7.
[38] Guildhall MS. 1537/20.

[39] Perrott, op. cit. 13. Late-18th-century watercolours in Uxb. libr. show the earlier tower.
[40] Perrott, op. cit. 17–18.
[41] M.R.O., Acc 538/4.
[42] Redford and Riches, *Hist. Uxbridge* (1885 edn.), 124–5; Perrott, op. cit. 18.
[43] Freshfield, *Communion Plate of Mdx.* 53.
[44] Perrott, op. cit. 14–16. The registers, together with most of the Par. Recs., are now in the custody of M.R.O.
[45] *Ruislip-Northwood Gaz.* 4 Aug. 1960.
[46] *Crockford* (1963–4).
[47] Ibid.
[48] Pevsner, *Mdx.* 111.
[49] Ex inf. the vicar.
[50] Programme in Uxb. libr.

St. John the Baptist's Church, *c.* 1805, with the Red Lion Inn on the right. The houses shown along Uxbridge Road were demolished in the 1930s

Colham Mill, *c.* 1805

HILLINGDON

Providence Chapel in 1818; built 1795

Interior of the Friends' Meeting House, built 1818

UXBRIDGE

in High Street, Yiewsley, was consecrated in 1859. The early building formed the Lady Chapel and north aisle of the enlarged church, opened in 1898. The church, designed by Sir Charles Nicholson, is executed in yellow stock brick with a red tile roof. The Vicar of St. John the Baptist, Hillingdon, is patron of the living.[51]

The church of *ALL SAINTS*, Long Lane, North Hillingdon, was opened in 1934 to replace a temporary building which had been used for worship since 1930.[52] The Bishop of London is patron of the living.[53] The church, which stands at the junction of Long Lane and Ryefield Avenue, is built of red brick with stone facings.

ROMAN CATHOLICISM. Although there was almost certainly no large organized body of Roman Catholic opinion in Hillingdon until the late 19th century,[54] available evidence suggests that from about 1580 one or more secluded houses in the parish were being used as centres for Jesuit activity. Following the examination of Edmund Campion in 1581 a house near Uxbridge belonging to a woman referred to as Mrs. Griffin and said to have been visited by Campion was searched. The same investigation led to the arrest of John Eden, a former attorney at the Guildhall, who had been dismissed for recusancy and who lived near Uxbridge.[55] The centre of 16th-century activity was possibly the house near Colham Green known as Morecrofts or Moorcroft.[56] It was here that Henry Garnett (1555–1606), Jesuit Superior of the English province from 1587 until his execution as an accomplice of the Gunpowder plotters, was living in 1597.[57] Apart from local disturbances perpetrated in 1688 by Irish Catholic members of James II's disbanded army,[58] there is no further evidence of Roman Catholicism until 1706, when two papists, one living in Uxbridge and the other in Hillingdon parish, are mentioned in a parochial return.[59]

No further Roman Catholic activity is recorded until the late 19th century: there was apparently no provision for Roman Catholic worship in 1851.[60] The church of Our Lady of Lourdes and St. Michael is said to have been formed in 1891,[61] but premises in Lawn Road, Uxbridge, were not registered for Roman Catholic worship until 1893.[62] A new church, on a site south of Osborn Road, was consecrated in 1936 but had been built some years earlier.[63] St. Bernadette's church in Long Lane was

registered for worship in 1937,[64] and rebuilt on the same site in 1961.[65] Part of south-east Hillingdon was included in the parish of St. Raphael, Yeading, created in 1957.[66]

PROTESTANT NONCONFORMITY. In 1658 Richard Taverner, Vicar of Hillingdon, together with other local clergy, including Robert Hall, Perpetual Curate of Colnbrook (Bucks.), engaged in a public dispute with Quakers at West Drayton.[67] Although both Taverner and Thomas Godbolt of St. Margaret's, Uxbridge, probably remained in the district for a time after their ejection in 1660,[68] early nonconformist activity centred on three ministers ejected from livings outside the Uxbridge area. Of these the most influential was Hezekiah Woodward (1590–1675), ejected minister of Bray (Berks.), a noted schoolmaster and educational reformer.[69] Woodward was joined in Uxbridge by Hugh Butler, ejected from the living of Beaconsfield (Bucks.), 'a solid divine, and very grave person',[70] and Robert Hall, former soldier, schoolmaster, and Curate of Colnbrook.[71] The precise date of the earliest Uxbridge meetings is uncertain. Woodward was said in 1669 to have been preaching in the town for three or four years,[72] but his activities probably began between 1662 and 1664 when the Vicar of Hillingdon reported two 'very great sectaries' in the parish and mentioned burials and home baptisms conducted without his knowledge.[73] By 1669 seven regular nonconformist conventicles had been established in Hillingdon and Uxbridge. Three of these were probably Quaker meetings,[74] but the remaining four appear to have been related and are probably identifiable as early meetings of what subsequently emerged as the Presbyterian (later Congregational) body.[75] The most important conventicle was said to be held in the house of one Nicholls (probably William Nicholl). Robert Hall preached in another Uxbridge house, and also acted as a schoolmaster,[76] while Hugh Butler held meetings in a house in Hillingdon. Woodward was said to live in the house of a rich tanner named Buscold,[77] and to preach regularly on Sundays and some weekdays to 'the best of the town'.[78] Uxbridge meetings held by the three preachers continued to be persecuted until 1672,[79] when William Nicholl, who seems to have organized and co-ordinated their work, was granted licences permitting Woodward, Hall, and Butler to worship in private houses in the town.[80] In the following year

---

[51] *Crockford* (1963–4).
[52] Ex inf. the vicar.
[53] *Crockford* (1963–4).
[54] Two Uxbridge recusants were presented at quarter sessions in 1581 and 1584: *Mdx. Cnty. Recs.* i. 123, 150.
[55] *Acts of P.C.* 1581–2, 187–8, 1586–7, 21.
[56] See p. 62. See also R. de Salis, *Hillingdon Through Eleven Centuries*, 57–59.
[57] *D.N.B.*
[58] Hist. MSS. Com. *15th Rep. App. I*, 135.
[59] Guildhall MS. 9800.
[60] *Census*, 1851.
[61] *Cath. Dir.* (1965).
[62] Gen. Reg. Off., Wship. Reg. 33937.
[63] Ibid. 53336; *Cath. Dir.* (1965); ex inf. Mr. K. R. Pearce.
[64] Gen. Reg. Off., Wship. Reg. 57302.
[65] Ibid. 68191.
[66] See p. 37.
[67] *V.C.H. Mdx.* iii. 205; *Calamy Revised*, ed. Matthews, 476, mistakenly gives Taverner's Christian name as Philip.
[68] For Taverner's later nonconformist activity see *V.C.H.*

[69] *D.N.B.*; Irene Parker, *Dissenting Academies in Eng.* 37–39; *Trans. Congreg. Hist. Soc.* vi. 26; *Calamy Revised*, ed. Matthews, 545; R. T. Jones, *Congregationalism in Eng. 1662–1962*, 86–87.
[70] *Calamy Revised*, ed. Matthews, 93.
[71] Ibid. 242.
[72] Lambeth Palace, MS. 639, f. 222v.
[73] Guildhall MS. 9628.
[74] See p. 93. A churchwardens' return of 1669 (Guildhall MS. 9583/1A) lists 15 nonconformists, including Woodward, Hall, and members of the Nicholl and Biscoe families, in Uxbridge and 4 in Hillingdon.
[75] See below.
[76] Jones, *Congregationalism in Eng.* 86.
[77] Probably Richard Biscoe: *Cal. S.P. Dom.* 1672, 55; M.R.O., Acc. 499/1. Some of the Nicholl family, to which the Biscoes were related by marriage, were also tanners in Uxbridge: *V.C.H. Mdx.* iii. 194.
[78] Lambeth Palace, MS. 639, f. 222v.
[79] Guildhall MS. 9583/1A; *Mdx. Cnty. Recs.* iv. 13, 19.
[80] *Cal. S.P. Dom.* 1672, 55.

Mdx. iii. 131.

all three were said to be holding regular meetings at the 'Swan'.[81]

Little is known of nonconformist activity during the period of persecution which began in 1675.[82] There were said to be three nonconformists and 397 conformists in Hillingdon in 1676,[83] but the sect or sects to which the nonconformists belonged is not stated. Hezekiah Woodward died in 1675, and Robert Hall two years later. Hugh Butler probably continued to preach privately until his death in 1682, but after this date nothing is known of the leadership of the body. The congregation probably had no ministerial guidance until 1692, when James Waters (d. 1725), a Presbyterian minister from Reigate (Surr.), was invited to assume leadership of what had by then merged as the Uxbridge Presbyterian body. Meetings were held in private houses[84] until 1716 when the first chapel was built near the west end of the High Street.[85] The building was licensed for Presbyterian worship in 1717.[86] A view of the chapel published a hundred years later shows an unpretentious rectangular brick building with a double-gabled roof and a small doorway under a flat hood in the centre of one of its long sides.[87]

A period of decline seems to have followed the intense nonconformist activity of the 17th century, and by 1766 the number of Protestant dissenters in Uxbridge was said to be decreasing rapidly.[88] The Presbyterian congregation, however, had in 1753 purchased land adjoining the chapel, and by vesting the property in a trust for supporting a resident minister guaranteed future leadership of the body. This steady income was probably instrumental in attracting to the pastorate Dr. William Rutherford (minister 1769–89), the Scottish divine and writer. Rutherford purchased a large house in Park Road in which he established 'a very numerous and respectable' school known as Uxbridge School.[89] The foundation was continued by the succeeding minister, Thomas E. Beasley, and by 1792 a Sunday school had also been established. New school premises adjoining the chapel were built in the early 19th century,[90] and structural alterations to both school and chapel were made in 1828. These increased the capacity of the chapel to about 220 places.

The Presbyterian congregation seems to have adopted the style Old Meeting House during the early 19th century, and during the ministry of Thomas Barker (1833–8) Congregational church practices were adopted. Thomas H. Riches (co-author of *The History of Uxbridge*) was appointed deacon, and a system of monthly church meetings established. Three services were held every Sunday, and Communion once a month. By 1851 evening worship had been discontinued, but approximately 80 persons attended each of the other two services.

Of 19th-century ministers the most notable was Dr. Robert Vaughan (1795–1868) who held the Uxbridge pastorate from 1857 to 1861. An outstanding Congregationalist divine and writer, Vaughan was Professor of Modern History at University College, London, and the author of works on 17th-century England.[91] During his ministry membership seems to have declined, but after a period of intense activity, it had increased to 70 by 1871. Activities undertaken by the congregation then included tract distribution, cottage prayer meetings, and sick visiting, and in 1878 a Band of Hope was instituted. The Old Meeting Church joined the London Congregational Union in 1922, and about 1930 the first church constitution was drafted.[92]

In 1883 the Old Meeting House was enlarged at a cost of nearly £1,300. The west wall was rebuilt, the three remaining 18th-century walls were raised to support a new roof, and a small square tower and vestries were added; part of the school premises were pulled down at this time, but an extension was opened for the Sunday school in 1889.[93] Services were still held in the Old Meeting House in 1968, when there were plans to demolish it and build a new Congregational church in Belmont Road.[94]

A second Congregational body, later known as Providence Congregational Church,[95] was formed in Uxbridge about 1777. Many of the original members seem to have been drawn from the Anglican congregation of St. Margaret's chapel. Meetings were held in the 'George' until 1795 when the first meeting-house was built near the Lynch Green,[96] in the garden of J. A. Glover, a wealthy merchant who largely financed the project. The land around the building was consecrated as a burial ground.

The first resident minister was appointed in 1803, and during the ministry of George Redford (1812–27)[97] membership increased from 27 in 1813 to 54 in 1818. A number of members at this period manifested Baptist leanings, and these are thought to have seceded about 1840 to form a Baptist church.[98] The meeting-house was refronted in the middle of the 19th century in the neo-classical style and renovated about 1890 and again in 1902. By 1926 the congregation had increased to 319 members. After 1933, however, membership declined rapidly.[99]

A mission organized by Providence Church was established in a community room in Peachey Lane, Cowley, in 1955 to serve the new council estate at Cowley Peachey. The adult work, however, was not a success, and no evening services were held after 1960. A Sunday school continued to meet in the community room until 1963 when all work in the

[81] Guildhall MS. 9537/20.
[82] Subsequent account based on K. R. Pearce, *Old Meeting Congregational Church*.
[83] William Salt. Libr., Stafford, Salt MS. 33, p. 40. The figures given probably exclude Uxbridge.
[84] Gen. Reg. Off., Dissenters' Places of Wship. 1689–1852: Dioc. of Lond., cert. of 25 Nov. 1703; *Mdx. Cnty. Recs.* v. 240; Guildhall MS. 9579.
[85] M.R.O., Acc. 807.
[86] Guildhall MS. 9579.
[87] Print of 1818 in Uxbridge libr.
[88] Guildhall MS. 9558. This was probably a subjective view.
[89] *Hist. of Uxbridge*, 226; undated prospectus *penes* Uxb. libr.
[90] M.R.O., Acc. 807: plan of Uxbridge School (c. 1820).

The school was closed in 1880.
[91] *D.N.B.*
[92] Pearce, *Old Meeting Congreg. Ch.* 12–13, 16–17.
[93] Ibid. 14.
[94] Ex inf. the minister.
[95] Account based on L. D. Jarvis, *Free Church Hist. of Uxbridge*, 23–29; R. J. Reeves, 'Providence Congregational Church', *Uxbridge Record*, iii. 7–21; Hutson, 'Recollections'.
[96] Gen Reg. Off., Dissenters' Places of Wship. 1689–1852: Dioc. of Lond. cert. of 18 Nov. 1795; Guildhall MS. 9580/1. See plate facing p. 91.
[97] Co-author, with T. H. Riches of Old Meeting, of *The History of Uxbridge*.
[98] See below.
[99] *Congreg. Year Bk.* (1962); ex inf. Mr. K. R. Pearce.

building ceased. The children of Cowley nonconformists subsequently attended Sunday school in Uxbridge.[1]

From the late 1950s discussion centred on plans for the amalgamation of the two Congregational churches in Uxbridge. They were finally united in 1962 as Uxbridge Congregational Church, which thenceforth worshipped in the former Old Meeting premises. In 1963 services were still occasionally held in Providence Church[2] but soon afterwards the building became derelict and was demolished in 1969. It had a tall two-storied cement-rendered front with round-headed windows, pilasters, and a central pediment flanked by scrolls above the parapet.

Quaker activity in Uxbridge probably dates from about 1655 when Edward Burrough, a pioneer of the sect, was holding meetings at the house of William Winch.[3] Burrough established a monthly meeting in the town, but by 1658 he had left the district, and John Sands of Hillingdon wrote to George Fox requesting guidance for the Uxbridge meeting. Whether Fox visited the parish is unknown, but in 1659 he issued an encouraging broadside to the Uxbridge Friends. Meetings probably continued to be held in private houses in the parish. By 1669, despite sporadic persecution, meetings were being held in at least three houses in Uxbridge and in one in Hillingdon. The Quaker society at this time appears to have been organized by three Uxbridge tradesmen—Timothy Fry, a cooper named Edward Swift, and Richard Hale, a collar-maker, said to be a 'stiff sectary'.[4] By this date the Uxbridge meeting was organized as part of the Longford Monthly Meeting, and Uxbridge preachers attended the Longford meetings.[5]

From about 1677 meetings were held in a rented room in the 'George'. The congregation was frequently ejected and its ministers prosecuted during this period,[6] but both George Fox and William Penn visited the Uxbridge meeting. A meeting-house in the George Close (off the modern York Road) was built in 1692, and an adjoining plot was set aside as a burial ground. At this date the meeting also owned three cottages near the 'Catherine Wheel' and other property on the Lynch Green. By 1724, however, the Uxbridge meeting was in debt and poorly attended. The meeting-house was found to be in a dangerous state and had to be rebuilt, with the help of contributions from individuals and other meetings, in 1755. The meeting-house was again rebuilt in 1818.

Enthusiasm in the Uxbridge meeting did not revive until the late 18th century when the Hulls and other wealthy Quaker families settled in the town and assumed the care of the meeting.[7] The Hulls were related by marriage to Joseph Pease, the first

Quaker M.P., and were friends of Elizabeth Fry, the prison reformer, who visited the Uxbridge meeting in 1823.[8] During the early 19th century Uxbridge Friends played a prominent part in philanthropic activities in the town, serving on the committees of the school of industry, the savings bank, the board of health, and other institutions. By 1851 the average attendance at the morning meeting was 33.[9] Fourteen years later the Longford Monthly Meeting was joined with Westminster and the Uxbridge meeting became independent. Subsequently the meeting, now reduced to about 20 members, concerned itself with educational and temperance work. In 1880 a free library was opened at the meeting-house, and in 1883 a Sunday school for poor children was instituted. Five years later an adult school was established.

During the early 20th century the meeting again declined, and by 1929 only about 4 persons regularly attended the monthly meeting. With the influx of population after 1930, however, interest again revived and weekly meetings were instituted. In 1962 the meeting-house was extended by the addition of a schoolroom, kitchen, and cloakrooms.[10] The meeting-house, a plain rectangular building of brown stock brick with a hipped roof and round-headed windows, stands in its former burial ground, now made into a garden. Apart from the additions of 1962, the building has remained almost unaltered since 1818. Internally it is divided by a cross passage into a larger and a smaller meeting room, said to have been planned for the separate worship of men and women. The wooden partitions of the passage incorporated a number of double-hung panels which could be raised when a combined meeting was held. The larger room retains its original benches and other fittings.[11]

During the 18th century nonconformist activity in the parish seems to have been limited to meetings of the established Quaker and Presbyterian (later Congregational) bodies.[12] John Wesley preached in Hillingdon and Uxbridge in 1754 and 1758,[13] but there is no other evidence of 18th-century Methodist activity. By 1851, however, there were five Methodist meetings in Hillingdon parish with a total morning attendance of 290 persons.[14] In 1807 a house in Uxbridge was registered as a meeting-place for 'Calvinists'.[15] This was possibly a Calvinistic Methodist meeting,[16] identifiable with that described as 'Methodist' in 1810 when it was attended by a family of Cowley dissenters.[17]

A room in Uxbridge was licensed for the use of Wesleyan Methodists in 1821,[18] but meetings were probably discontinued shortly afterwards.[19] There is no evidence of further Methodist activity in the parish until 1845 when meetings in Uxbridge were re-established by members of a Wesleyan congregation

[1] Ex inf. Mr. K. R. Pearce.
[2] Ibid.
[3] Except where otherwise stated, this section is based on Mins. of Longford Monthly Meeting and Swarthmore MSS., both in Friends House, Euston Road, N.W.1. The author is indebted to Mrs. Celia Trott for allowing him to see the draft of her article on the Uxbridge meeting.
[4] Lambeth Palace, MS. 639, f. 222v; *Mdx. Cnty. Recs.* iv. 14. See also Guildhall MS. 9583/1A.
[5] *Mdx. Cnty. Recs.* iv. 219.
[6] Ibid. 202, 207–8, 219.
[7] Hutson, 'Recollections'.
[8] Susanna Corder, *Life of Elizabeth Fry* (1853), 336.
[9] *Census*, 1851.

[10] Ex inf. Mrs. Celia Trott.
[11] See plate facing p. 91.
[12] Guildhall MS. 9558.
[13] *Works of John Wesley* (Zondervan edn.), ii. 434, 812.
[14] *Census*, 1851.
[15] Guildhall MS. 9580/3; Gen. Reg. Off., Dissenters' Places of Wship. 1689–1852: Dioc. of Lond. cert. of 17 Nov. 1807.
[16] F. L. Cross, *Oxford Dict. of the Christian Ch.* 221.
[17] Guildhall MS. 9558.
[18] Gen. Reg. Off., Dissenters' Places of Wship. 1689–1852: Dioc. of Lond. cert. of 5 Mar. 1821.
[19] Subsequent account based on Jarvis, *Free Church Hist.* 30–36.

from Iver (Bucks.). Services were held in a room in Baker's Yard until the erection in 1847 of a permanent chapel in New Windsor Street, a building of brown stock brick with Gothic features.[20] The new Methodist Central Hall was erected in 1930 at the junction of High Street and Park Road,[21] and the chapel in New Windsor Street became a Masonic Hall. In 1957 Lawn Road Primitive Methodist congregation[22] was amalgamated with the former Wesleyan connexion in the Central Hall premises.[23]

A Primitive Methodist congregation was established in Uxbridge about 1864.[24] Services were held initially in the open air, and later in the Belmont Hall and the Union Hall, Windsor Street. A permanent chapel in Lawn Road was opened in 1876,[25] and meetings were held there until 1957 when the congregation was united with the Central Hall Methodist body.[26]

Two further Methodist bodies were established in the 20th century in areas of expanding population. Yiewsley Central Methodist Hall, Fairfield Road, was opened in 1927. It replaced a building (in 1964 the public library) which had been used since about 1873 by a small Primitive Methodist congregation.[27] Building costs were met by private subscription and a gift from Sir Joseph Rank, the flour miller. The Central Hall was renovated and extended in 1959.[28] Methodist meetings were held in a private house in Park Way, Hillingdon, from 1932. A hall in Long Lane was opened in 1933[29] when the congregation had 20 members.[30] In 1965 a permanent chapel with seating for 120 persons was opened on an adjoining site.[31]

Houses at Hillingdon and Colham Green were registered for Baptist worship in 1817 and 1828 respectively.[32] Little is known of the organization of the Baptist congregation during the 19th century.[33] Two cottages in Bonsey's yard were used for Baptist worship during the 1830s,[34] and the Uxbridge Baptist body appears to have been joined about 1840 by former members of Providence Congregational Church.[35] Meetings were held in the market-house until a chapel (Montague Hall), a plain yellow brick building in George Street, Uxbridge, was opened in 1856.[36] A Salem Baptist congregation at Hillingdon Heath is said to have been founded in 1847, although details of its history are obscure.[37] By 1851 there were five Baptist meetings in Hillingdon parish with a total morning attendance of 294 persons.[38] Meetings of the Uxbridge

Baptist body seem to have been discontinued about 1900. Hillingdon Park Baptist Chapel in Hercies Road was opened in 1931,[39] and extended in 1951.[40] In 1963 the Hillingdon Heath Salem Baptist congregation met in premises in Uxbridge Road.[41] Members of the West Drayton Baptist congregation began missionary work in Yiewsley in 1897. Early meetings were held in a cottage in Colham Avenue. A church, styled the Tabernacle, in Colham Avenue, was opened in 1900, and meetings were held there until 1954 when a new chapel, also in Colham Avenue, was erected.[42]

From about 1851[43] a gospel mission[44] was organized in conjunction with the Uxbridge Moor Ragged School[45] which had occupied premises in Waterloo Road since about 1846. Premises in Waterloo Road were licensed for worship in 1858.[46] The mission was then described as a Primitive Methodist connexion, although its work at all periods appears to have been of an undenominational character. A new building in Waterloo Road was opened in 1864 to house the mission services, reading room, and Sunday and day schools. The late 19th century was marked by a decline in membership, and the day school was closed in 1892. In 1903, however, a committee representing the Uxbridge free churches was formed to administer the mission. The premises were extended in 1913, and a new mission hall on the opposite side of Waterloo Road was opened in 1932.[47] The congregation operated as the Waterloo Road Mission until 1963, when the style Waterloo Road Free Church was adopted.[48]

Some other nonconformist sects have held meetings, about which few details are known, in Uxbridge, Hillingdon, and Yiewsley at various periods since the mid 19th century. In 1850 there were said to be meeting-houses in the parish for Independents, Presbyterians, Quakers, and Wesleyans. Baptists met in the market-house and the Mormons had a room in George Yard.[49] Evening service in a Catholic Apostolic church in Uxbridge, probably the successor of an Irvingite congregation founded in the 1830s,[50] was attended by an average of 30 persons in 1851.[51] Premises in Montague Road were licensed for Catholic Apostolic worship in 1858, and continued in use until the building was rendered unsafe by enemy action in 1940. It was demolished in the following year.[52]

Meetings of the Latter Day Saints in Uxbridge were attended by an average of 30 persons in 1851.[53]

[20] Gen. Reg. Off., Wship. Reg. 4831.
[21] Ibid. 52686.
[22] See below.
[23] Ex inf. the minister.
[24] Section based on Jarvis, *Free Church Hist.* 37–42.
[25] Gen. Reg. Off., Wship. Reg. 27328.
[26] See above. For the subsequent history of the Lawn Rd. Hall see below.
[27] Gen. Reg. Off., Wship. Reg. 21200.
[28] Ex inf. the minister.
[29] Gen. Reg. Off., Wship. Reg. 54254.
[30] Jarvis, *Free Church Hist.* 76–81.
[31] Ex inf. the minister, Hayes End Methodist Church.
[32] Gen. Reg. Off., Dissenters' Places of Wship. 1689–1852: Dioc. of Lond. certs. of 28 Aug. 1817, 28 Mar. 1828.
[33] Subsequent account based on Jarvis, *Free Church Hist.* 71–75; Hutson, 'Recollections'.
[34] Hutson, 'Recollections'.
[35] See above.
[36] Gen. Reg. Off., Rets. of Q.S. for Mdx. no. 36; *Bealby's Uxbridge Almanack* (1868); inscription on building; see below *sub* Uxbridge Salvation Army corps.
[37] Possibly the meeting described as 'Particular': Gen.
Reg. Off., Wship. Reg. 6619; *Baptist Handbk.* (1963).
[38] *Census*, 1851.
[39] Photographs of this and other Hillingdon chapels *penes* Uxb. libr.
[40] Ex inf. the minister.
[41] *Baptist Handbk.* (1963).
[42] Ex inf. the church treasurer; cf. *Baptist Handbk.* (1964–5).
[43] M.R.O., *Clerk of Peace's Reg.* x.
[44] Section based on *Waterloo Rd. Mission Centenary Handbk.* (1946).
[45] See p. 97.
[46] Gen. Reg. Off., Wship Reg. 8497.
[47] Ibid. 54193.
[48] Ex inf. the superintendent.
[49] *Home Cnties. Dir.* (1851); *Lake's Uxbridge Almanack* (1853).
[50] Hutson, 'Recollections'.
[51] *Census*, 1851.
[52] Gen. Reg. Off., Wship. Reg. 16541, 18898; ex inf. Mr. K. R. Pearce.
[53] *Census*, 1851.

Other 19th-century sects met in Emmanuel Church, Yiewsley, which was registered between 1879 and 1893 for the worship of members of the Free Church of England, and in the Mission Hall, Horton Lane, Yiewsley, registered for undenominational worship from 1885 to 1896.[54] The Blue Ribbon Gospel Temperance Mission met in the Public Rooms in Uxbridge High Street from 1884 to 1896.[55] Other premises registered for undenominational worship during the 20th century included 156a High Street, Uxbridge, for the Uxbridge Pentecostal Mission (1943), and Wimpole Hall, Wimpole Road, Yiewsley (1956).[56] The Brethren registered Rockingham Hall, the Lynch, in 1914, and the Gospel Hall, Cowley Road, in 1927.[57] The Cowley Road premises were still used by Exclusive Brethren in 1962.[58]

The Uxbridge Salvation Army corps was instituted in 1887.[59] Meetings were held in Jubilee Hall, Bell Yard (on the site of the London Transport station), until about 1899 when the corps appears to have exchanged places of worship with the declining Baptist congregation, meeting in Montague Hall. Salvationist activity has since been concentrated in the George Street premises.[60] The Yiewsley Salvation Army corps was founded in 1886 by Salvationists from Hounslow. Meetings were held in a disused engine-house in Horton Road and later in an adapted cattle shed in St. Stevens Road. The present hall in Horton Road was opened in 1914.[61] During the early 20th century about 100 persons attended Sunday evening services. The premises were extended in 1957, when the congregation had about 35 members. By 1963 attendance had dwindled to an average of 15 persons.[62] The Hillingdon Salvation Army corps was founded in 1932. Meetings were held in a house in Nelgrove Road until 1938 when a wooden hall in Uxbridge Road was registered.[63] This was demolished in 1965 and a permanent hall, built on the same site, was opened in 1966.[64]

Christian Science meetings were held in private houses in Uxbridge and Hillingdon from 1941 until 1959 when the former Lawn Road Methodist chapel was purchased and reopened for Christian Science worship.[65]

Spiritualist meetings were held in Villiers Hall, Villier Street, Uxbridge, during the 1940s.[66] The House of the Good Shepherd in Hinton Road, registered in 1950 as a Spiritualist church, was still in use in 1962.[67]

EDUCATION. The earliest evidence of organized education in Hillingdon parish dates from the 1660s

when Robert Hall, an ejected schoolmaster, was said to be giving tuition to the children of Uxbridge dissenters.[68] Two licensed schoolmasters, one of whom was Nathaniel Snell,[69] are mentioned in a parochial visitation of 1673.[70] Further denominational tuition for six poor boys of Uxbridge was provided under the trust of 1706 instituting the Uxbridge lectureship.[71] By this date the manorial trustees were also providing limited, and probably undenominational, teaching for poor girls in premises in the Lynch.[72] Subsequent 18th-century developments centred on the efforts of the Uxbridge manorial trustees to extend educational facilities in the town. They covenanted in 1728 to rebuild the school-house in the Lynch,[73] and from about 1730 applied part of the market tolls towards the education of 20 boys and 22 girls.[74] Teaching was undenominational;[75] the boys' classes were held in a room over the market-house; the girls probably continued to use the old building in the Lynch. Numbers attending each establishment during the 18th century fluctuated between 20 and 30.[76] During the 1780s part of the proceeds of Townsend's charity[77] seems to have been applied to the upkeep of the free schools.[73]

In 1809 the lords in trust resolved to reorganize their early foundations. The old schools for boys and girls were united in one institution housed in the market-house schoolroom, and styled the Uxbridge Lancasterian or British School. A special school committee was elected to supervise the new institution, and a master and mistress appointed at annual salaries of 80 guineas and £15 respectively. Children 'of all labouring people or mechanics' were eligible for entry, and the school contained 204 pupils during the first year.[79] A school of industry was also established, and a mistress appointed at an annual salary of £40. The school was supervised by female members of the school committee, and until new premises in Belmont Road were erected in 1816, classes were conducted in the market-house room.[80]

By 1819 the average attendance at the Uxbridge British School, renamed in 1816 the Uxbridge Free School, had declined to 140, and about 80 girls attended the school of industry. In addition there were said to be several small day-schools in the parish where parents paid 'about 4d. a week' for their children's tuition.[81] By 1816 a small school for Protestant girls seems to have been established at Hillingdon End under the patronage of Thomas Clarke of Swakeleys, Ickenham.[82]

No further schools were established until 1827 when the West Drayton British School was built at Hockey Hole in the extreme south of Hillingdon

54 Gen. Reg. Off., Wship. Reg. 24594, 29063.
55 Ibid. 27682.
56 Ibid. 60616, 65605.
57 Ibid. 45982, 51054.
58 Kemp's Uxbridge Dir. (1962–3).
59 Jarvis, Free Church Hist. 55–60.
60 Gen. Reg. Off., Wship. Reg. 30202, 37085, 49778.
61 Ibid. 46104.
62 Section based on inf. supplied by Yiewsley S.A.
63 Gen. Reg. Off., Wship. Reg. 54371, 58298.
64 Hillingdon Mirror, 2 Aug. 1966.
65 Ex inf. the deputy clerk, Uxb. Christian Science Soc.
66 Borough Petition, 40.
67 Gen. Reg. Off., Wship. Reg. 62722; Kemp's Uxbridge Dir. (1962–3).
68 See p. 91. For the history of Uxbridge (nonconformist) School see p. 92. For an abortive 16th-cent. attempt to provide a school in Uxbridge see p. 98.

69 See p. 99.
70 Guildhall MS. 9537/20.
71 See p. 90; Lysons, Mdx. Pars. 184.
72 M.R.O., Acc. 538/7.
73 Ibid.
74 M.R.O., Acc. 538/3.
75 Guildhall MS. 9558.
76 M.R.O., Acc. 538/3,/4.
77 See p. 90.
78 M.R.O., Acc. 538/4.
79 M.R.O., E. Mdx. 2/1; Brewer, Beauties of Eng. and Wales, x(5), 536–7; V.C.H. Mdx. i. 231–2.
80 M.R.O., Acc. 538/4; Ed. 7/86; Digest of Rets. to Cttee. on Educ. of Poor, H.C. 224, p. 538 (1819), ix(1).
81 Rets. of Educ. of Poor, H.C. 224, p. 538 (1819), ix(1). For fees at the British Sch. see V.C.H. Mdx. i. 231–2.
82 Brewer, Beauties of Eng. and Wales, x(5), 536–7.

parish.[83] In the following year the Hillingdon vestry conveyed a plot in Uxbridge Road to the vicar for the purpose of erecting a parish school for poor girls.[84] Building was completed in 1829, and the school, known initially as Hillingdon St. John's Girls School, and supported by church collections and parental contributions, opened with approximately 100 pupils.[85]

By 1835 there were said to be ten day-schools in Hillingdon parish, accommodating in all 261 boys and 185 girls, and serving a population of 3,842. There were also two private schools. Uxbridge, with a population of 3,043, had five day-schools, of which the largest was the British School with 187 pupils. One hundred and seven girls attended the school of industry; a third establishment had 51 boys; and two smaller institutions, established in 1827 and 1832 respectively, together accommodated 63 pupils. The three smaller schools were supported by parental contributions. In addition three girls' boarding schools together accommodated 137 children.[86]

Reorganization of existing facilities began in 1834 when the lords in trust declared the market-house schoolroom inadequate. New buildings were erected on a site in Cowley Road, and the British or Free School vacated the market-house in 1835. In 1836 the old premises were being used for meetings of the Mechanics' Institute.[87] The British School received its first Government grant in 1836;[88] and until the 1870s seems to have contained between 80 and 100 pupils.[89] By 1879, however, the institution was in financial difficulties, the master's salary was reduced, a pupil teacher absconded, and it was thought that the school would have to close at the end of the year.[90] Further Government grants, however, enabled it to continue, and attendance began to improve. By 1903 the establishment, then known as Cowley Road school, and controlled by the county council, had an average attendance of 193.[91] The school continued in the Cowley Road premises until 1928 when the pupils were transferred to Greenway County School.[92] Until about 1942 the school buildings were used as a county library (transferred in 1940) and domestic science centre for the Uxbridge district. Since 1942 the premises have been used as a school meals kitchen.[93]

Attendance at the girls' school of industry during the 19th century seems to have remained constant at between 100 and 120. The school was receiving Government grants by 1903 when it contained 127 girls.[94] The school premises were extended in 1910,

and attendance had increased to 168 by 1926. In 1928, as part of an extensive reorganization of educational facilities in Uxbridge, the pupils in the school of industry were transferred to the Whitehall and Greenway county schools.[95] The old building was then used as an infants' department, and subsequently known as Belmont Road Infants School.[96]

To meet the needs of a steadily increasing population the Hillingdon church school was considerably expanded during the late 19th century. An infant girls' department in Royal Lane opened in 1869,[97] and a boys' school was built on the Uxbridge Road site in 1895.[98] By 1906 the Hillingdon church schools accommodated 140 boys, 128 girls, and 124 infants.[99] The girls' department was transferred in 1924[1] to the newly built Uxbridge Road County School, which was itself reorganized in the early 1930s as Hillingdon Junior (mixed) School.[2] The former girls' department of the church school was used by the boys' department until 1928, when the whole school was reorganized as an infants' department. The infants' school in Royal Lane was then converted into a church hall (opened 1930), and the pupils transferred to the Uxbridge Road premises. By 1934 there were more than 300 pupils and the building was much overcrowded. Church control ceased in 1938 when the establishment became a county school. Three years later the premises were damaged by enemy action.[3] After the war the school was renovated and continued in use as Hillingdon Infants School.[4]

A number of new schools were also established after 1835 to relieve pressure on existing institutions. New Windsor Street Infants School was built in 1839,[5] and accommodated between 140 and 170 infants until its closure in 1911, when the pupils were transferred to the new Whitehall County School in Cowley Road.[6] Hillingdon and Cowley National Boys School in Hillingdon Road was built in 1841 to provide education for poor children from the two parishes.[7] Attendance increased from 65 in 1865 to 123 in 1927.[8] The school seems to have been closed shortly after the latter date. St. John's Church of England School, built on glebe land in St. John's Road, was erected in 1846 under the auspices of the National Society.[9] Initially the school accommodated 28 boys and 62 girls, drawn chiefly from the Uxbridge Moor district;[10] but the premises appear to have been extended about 1865, and in 1903 there were 157 pupils.[11] Senior departments were transferred to Whitehall County School in 1911,[12] and in 1963 the church school accommodated 70 children.[13]

[83] Ed. 7/87. The subsequent history of the school is unknown. It was still in existence in 1881.
[84] Vestry Mins. 1828–37 penes Uxb. Bor. Council.
[85] Nat. Soc. files; Ed. 7/86.
[86] Educ. Enquiry Abstract, H.C. 63, p. 565 (1835), xlii. Some inaccuracy may have resulted from uncertainty over the boundaries of Uxbridge chapelry.
[87] M.R.O., Acc. 538/5; E. Mdx. 2/2; see below.
[88] Mins. of Educ. Cttee. of Coun. 1849 [1215], H.C. (1850), xliii.
[89] Rep. Educ. Cttee. of Coun. 1865–6 [3666], p. 743, H.C. (1866), xxvii; 1870 [C. 406] p. 503, H.C. (1871), xxii.
[90] M.R.O., E. Mdx. 2/2.
[91] Schs. under Admin. of Bd. 1903 [Cd. 2011], p. 170, H.C. (1904), lxxv.
[92] See below.
[93] Ex inf. Div. Educ. Officer.
[94] Schs. under Admin. of Bd. 1903 [Cd. 2011], p. 170, H.C. (1904), lxxv.
[95] M.R.O., E/N.W. 5.
[96] See below.

[97] Par. Recs. terrier of benefice (1889).
[98] Ed. 7/86.
[99] Pub. Elem. Schs. 1906 [Cd. 3510], p. 448, H.C. (1907), lxiii.
[1] Bd. of Educ. List 21 (1927), p. 238.
[2] Ex inf. Div. Educ. Officer.
[3] M.R.O., E/N.W.4.
[4] Ex inf. Div. Educ. Officer.
[5] Ed. 7/87.
[6] Ed. 7/86; M.R.O., E/N.W.3/1, 2; Pub. Elem. Schs. 1906 [Cd. 3510], H.C. (1907), lxiii.
[7] Ed. 7/86.
[8] Rep. Educ. Cttee. of Coun. 1865–6 [3666], p. 555, H.C. (1866), xxvii; Bd. of Educ. List 21 (1927), p. 239.
[9] Ed. 7/86.
[10] Nat. Soc. files.
[11] Digest of Schs. under Admin. of Bd. 1903 [Cd. 2011], p. 170, H.C. (1904), lxxv.
[12] Ed. 7/86.
[13] See below.

Education for the children of Uxbridge Moor dissenters was provided from about 1846 in temporary premises near the canal. The school, known as the Moor Ragged School, was organized as part of the Waterloo Road mission,[14] whose members appointed a mistress at a salary of 8s. a week. Premises in Waterloo Road were occupied in 1864, and until the closure of the day-school in 1892 the institution accommodated about 60 pupils.[15] St. Margaret's, Uxbridge, National School was opened in 1864 as a mixed school for 300 children. The adjoining infants' department was added in 1869,[16] and by 1870 the school had 213 pupils. In 1906 the average attendance was 289.[17] The school seems to have closed about 1927.[18] St. Andrew's National School, erected on a site adjoining the church, was opened in 1869 to serve the new St. Andrew's ecclesiastical parish.[19] The school received an annual grant, and in 1870 had 55 pupils.[20] The premises were considerably extended in 1897,[21] and by 1927 accommodated 128 girls and 117 infants.[22] About two years later the school was reorganized as an infants' department, and in 1930 the girls' school building was converted into a parish hall.[23] St. Mary's Roman Catholic School, Rockingham Road, was built in 1895 to serve the Uxbridge district.[24] Since that date it has accommodated between 50 and 70 children.[25]

Until about 1870 educational facilities for the Yiewsley district of the parish were inadequate. West Drayton British School, which was just within Hillingdon parish, provided education for local dissenters' children, but many Hillingdon children attended the National school in Station Road, West Drayton.[26] In 1872, however, St. Matthew's C. of E. School was built in High Street, Yiewsley.[27] By 1887 a second church school, known as Starveall Infants School, had been opened.[28] This school seems to have been situated near Stockley Bridge, Yiewsley, but details of its history and closure are unknown.[29] St. Stephen's County Infants School, St. Stephen's Road, Yiewsley, was built in 1905, and in 1910 a second county school was opened in Providence Road. Some of the pupils from the St. Matthew's and St. Stephen's schools were then transferred to the new premises.[30] This virtually completed school building in Hillingdon parish until the 1930s when a number of new schools[31] were opened to meet the rapidly expanding population.

Bishopshalt Grammar School developed from the Uxbridge County School which occupied premises in the Greenway from 1907. This building was vacated in 1928 when the school was transferred to the house in Royal Lane which had been built on the site of the old rectory house owned by the bishops of Worcester.[32] The school then adopted the name Bishopshalt and was constituted a grammar school. The Greenway premises were subsequently occupied by the Greenway County Secondary School. A second grammar school, Vyners Grammar School, Warren Road, just inside the northern boundary of Hillingdon old parish, was opened in 1960.[33]

In September 1963 there were nineteen maintained schools in the old parish of Hillingdon. They are set out below. The date at which the school was opened is given in brackets after the name of the school, followed by the date of any extension; the next figure is the number of children on the roll at September 1963, and the final figure denotes the age-group of the pupils:[34]

St. John's C. of E. (1846, c. 1865). 70. 5–11; St. Andrew's C. of E. (1869, 1897). 171. 5–11; St. Matthew's C. of E. (1872). 311. 7–11; St. Mary's R.C. (1895). 140. 5–11; St. Stephen's County Infants (1905). 225. 5–7; Bishopshalt Grammar (1907). 784. 11–19;[35] Providence Road County Primary (1910). 238. 5–11; Whitehall County Primary (1911, 1927). 511. 5–11; Hillingdon Junior (1924). 279. 7–11; Belmont Road Infants (1928). 84. 5–7; Hillingdon Infants (1928). 226. 5–7; Greenway County Secondary (1928). 705. 11–16;[36] Oak Farm County Primary (1934). 734. 5–11; Evelyns County Secondary (1936). 840. 11–16; St. Bernadette's R.C. Primary (1939, 1961). 268. 5–11; Colham Manor County Primary (1951). 467. 5–11; Abbotsfield (Boys) County Secondary (1952). 768. 11–17;[37] Ryefield County Primary (1960). 384. 5–11; Vyners Grammar (1960). 604. 11–17.

Small select private schools and dame-schools have existed in the district since at least the beginning of the 19th century.[38] In 1840 Mrs. Moore's boarding-school for 'young ladies' gave instruction in English, history, geography, writing, arithmetic, and needlework for 20 guineas a year, and a M. Godard advertised French and dancing lessons.[39] There were said to be eight private schools in Hillingdon parish in 1870, together accommodating 124 children.[40] Some of these schools provided organized preparatory education for boys entering the large public schools. Possibly the most important was Evelyns School at Colham Green, which was founded in 1872, and maintained close connexions with Eton until it was closed in 1931.[41] Of the independent schools in Hillingdon in 1963 the largest were Rutland House School (125 boys), established in 1951 in The Cedars, the house in Vine Lane occupied during the early 18th century by Samuel Reynardson the botanist,[42] and Frays College in Harefield Road. This school was founded about 1926 as Uxbridge High School, and occupied

---

[14] See p. 94.
[15] Ex inf. the Superintendent, Waterloo Rd. Free Church.
[16] Ed. 7/86; Nat. Soc. files.
[17] Rep. Educ. Cttee. of Coun. 1870 [C. 406], H.C. (1871), xxii; Pub. Elem. Schs. 1906 [Cd. 3510], H.C. (1907), lxiii.
[18] Ex inf. Div. Educ. Officer.
[19] Ed. 7/86.
[20] Rep. Educ. Cttee. of Coun. 1870 [C. 406], H.C. (1871), xxii.
[21] Ex inf. Div. Educ. Officer.
[22] Bd. of Educ. List 21 (1927), p. 239.
[23] Nat. Soc. files.
[24] Ed. 7/86.
[25] Pub. Elem. Schs. 1906 [Cd. 3510], H.C. (1907), lxiii.
[26] V.C.H. Mdx. iii. 205.
[27] Ed. 7/86.
[28] Ed. 7/87.
[29] Ex inf. Div. Educ. Officer.
[30] Ed. 7/86.
[31] See below.
[32] See p. 88.
[33] Section based on information supplied by the Div. Educ. Officer.
[34] Ex inf. Div. Educ. Officer.
[35] See above.
[36] Ibid.
[37] See p. 109 sub Ickenham County School.
[38] Rets. on Educ. of Poor, H.C. 224, p. 538 (1819), ix(1).
[39] Lake's Uxb. Almanack (1840).
[40] Notes penes Uxb. Bor. Council.
[41] Mdx. & Bucks. Advertiser, 11 Sept. 1931.
[42] See p. 62.

several buildings in Uxbridge before moving to the present premises about 1929. Eric Blair (George Orwell) the novelist taught French at the school for a short time about 1934. In 1963 the school had 210 pupils, aged between 5 and 16 years, and a staff of 12.[43]

Two Roman Catholic girls' schools were established in Hillingdon in the early 20th century. The Sacred Heart of Mary Convent School, Hillingdon Court, accommodated 130 girls, some of whom were boarders, in 1963.[44] All Souls School in Pield Heath Road was opened in 1902 as a residential school for mentally defective girls. Subsequently the premises were considerably extended, and in 1963 basic education and domestic training were given to approximately 100 girls aged between 7 and 16 years.[45]

Technical education in the parish began about 1830 with the formation of a mechanics' institute in Uxbridge.[46] Lectures on astronomy and scientific and industrial topics were held at first in a room in the market-house and, after 1835, in the room formerly occupied by the British School.[47] Nothing further is known of the Uxbridge Mechanics' Institute: some of its functions were apparently assumed by the Literary and Scientific Institution which was formed in 1836.[48] In 1895 a committee, probably of nonconformist sympathies, was formed to organize 'technical' education in Uxbridge. A system of evening courses was established, and classes including book-keeping, art, shorthand, cookery, horticulture, and French were held in various Uxbridge schools. In 1904 a day centre for pupil teachers was instituted in the Old Meeting House, and two years later transferred to the Primitive Methodist chapel. The entire scheme seems to have been discontinued in 1907.[49] In 1963 evening institutes were held in the Greenway, Abbotsfield, and Evelyns secondary schools and in Vyners grammar school.[50]

In 1937 the county education committee approved the purchase of 5 a. of the Hillingdon Farm estate, with access to Park Road, for the building of a technical institute. Revised plans were drawn up in 1957 and work on the site began in 1961. A principal was appointed from 1965, when the first staff members moved into the new administrative block. Uxbridge Technical College opened in September 1965 with 40 full-time teaching staff and 1,323 full- and part-time students, divided between the Commerce and General Studies Department and the Engineering and Science Department.[51]

CHARITIES FOR THE POOR.[52] The earliest known Uxbridge charity is that of John Marsh, who, by will dated 1557, left the interest on £200 vested in the Mercers' Company to provide 2s. worth of bread every Sunday for 24 Uxbridge paupers. In 1908 Marsh's gift comprised an annuity of £5 and the interest on £113 stock.[53] Robert Woolman, a London mercer, by will dated 1570, left a rent-charge on land in Uxbridge, Hillingdon, and Cowley to build

a school in Uxbridge and to give £5 annually to the Uxbridge poor. The clause providing for a school in the town was subject to a two-year limitation period, and the school was never built. John Garrett, an Uxbridge brewer, by deed dated 1589, granted an annuity of 5 marks chargeable on his property in Uxbridge to the bailiffs and freemen of Kingston (Surr.) to the use of the Uxbridge poor. In 1908 the gift was represented by a rent-charge of £3 6s. 8d. on Dunstans Mead. William Skydmore, a London ironmonger, by will dated 1600, left premises in Uxbridge to his heirs on condition that they should give 1s. in bread to the poor each Sunday morning after divine service in Uxbridge chapel. In 1908 the gift comprised a rent-charge of £2 12s. on no. 66 High Street. Sir George Garrett, by will dated 1648, left 4 a. in Moor Field to the use of the Uxbridge poor. Part of the land was sold in the 19th century to the G.W.R. Co. and the proceeds were invested in £273 stock.[54]

In 1695 George Pitt sold the manor and borough of Uxbridge for £550 to four trustees who covenanted to pay £20 a year to 6 Uxbridge paupers and £10 a year to be distributed weekly in Uxbridge chapel as bread to 6 male and 6 female paupers. The trust was apparently varied in 1729 when the number of trustees was increased to seven and the manorial profits vested in a charitable fund for the general benefit of the town. In 1906 the manor and borough charity, worth £689 a year, consisted of the site of the 20th-century almshouses, the building in the Lynch used as almshouses until 1907, the fire-engine station, the market-house, cottages in Chapel Street, the Lynch, and New Windsor Street, and £43 stock.

John Bennet, Lord Ossulston (d. 1695), left £100 to put out apprentice poor children from Uxbridge. The money was used to buy 3 a. at Yiewsley which were exchanged in 1780 for 13 a. at Norwood. Part of the land was sold to the Grand Junction Canal Co. in 1795 and a further portion to the G.W.R. Co. in 1859.[55] In 1906 the gift was worth £126 a year and consisted of 10 houses in Ossulston Villas, a cottage and 5 a. at Norwood, a £100 share in the Grand Junction Canal Co., and £1,379 stock. Michael Pearce, by will dated 1695, left tenements in Uxbridge, subject to the life interest of his sister, in trust for the maintenance of the Uxbridge poor. In 1778 the gift was distributed as small cash payments to 124 paupers; in 1823 £23 was distributed among 172 paupers.[56] In 1906 Pearce's gift, worth £180 a year, consisted of an allotment, a house in High Street, and £160 stock. John Hill, by will dated 1744, left a rent-charge of £1 a year on the George Inn to provide 40 Uxbridge paupers with a 6d. loaf each Christmas Day. In 1821 the gifts of Marsh, Woolman, John Garrett, Skydmore, Sir George Garrett, and Hill were together worth £30. The whole amount, overlooking the specific directions of some of the donors, was distributed as bread, except for 3s. given away each Sunday in part satisfaction of Sir George Garrett's gift.

43 Section based on information supplied by the headmasters.
44 Ex inf. Div. Educ. Officer.
45 Ex inf. the sister-in-charge.
46 Hutson, 'Recollections'.
47 See above.
48 Hutson, 'Recollections'; see above, p. 81.
49 M.R.O., E/N.W.1.
50 Mdx. Educ. Cttee. Educ. List (1963).

51 Paragraph based on inf. supplied by the principal.
52 Except where otherwise stated, the authority for this section is either 9th Rep. Com. Char. H.C. 258 (1823), ix, or Char. Com. files. For Townsend's gift and the trust instituting the Uxbridge lectureship see above, p. 90.
53 M.R.O., Acc. 538/8.
54 Ibid.
55 M.R.O., Acc. 538/12.
56 Ibid. /9, /11.

Henry Fell Pease, by will dated 1820, left an uncertain amount to assist in the education of poor children. By 1915 Pease's gift consisted of two exhibitions tenable at the Greenway secondary school.[57] Under the 1825 inclosure award 4 a. on Uxbridge Moor were allotted to the Uxbridge poor. One acre was sold in 1903 and the proceeds invested in £313 stock.[58] William Wells, by will proved 1835, left the proceeds of £600 stock to the use of the Uxbridge poor. Emily James, by will proved 1920, left the income of £300 stock for the relief of the poor. Sarah Hunter of Fulham House, Hillingdon Heath, by will proved 1922, left the income on £300 to be devoted to the purchase of coal for the inmates of the Uxbridge almshouses. Charles Woodbridge, by will proved 1924, left £100, which was invested by his executors, to provide coal for the inmates of the almshouses.

By a Scheme of 1906, which introduced 5 representative trustees appointed by Uxbridge U.D.C. and 6 co-optative trustees drawn from persons living in or near Uxbridge, the gifts of Ossulston and Pearce and the manor and borough charity were consolidated as the Uxbridge United Charities.[59] The income of the charities was made available for the support of and payment of pensions to 20 poor in the almshouses and for the general benefit of the Uxbridge poor. The premiums for apprentices supported from Ossulston's gift were fixed at £20 to £25 for outdoor apprentices and £30 for indoor apprentices. In 1907 the terms of the gift were extended to include poor children from the whole of Uxbridge Urban District, and in 1920 another Scheme increased the amounts payable as apprenticeship premiums. By a further Scheme in 1939 the original intention of Ossulston's gift was modified to allow financial assistance to be given to poor persons under 21 years of age who needed fees for instruction, travelling expenses, or outfits when entering or engaged in trade or service.

By a Scheme of 1907 the charities of Clarke, Sir George Garrett, John Garrett, Hill, Marsh, Skydmore, Wells, and Woolman, and the Poor Allotment were consolidated as the Charities of Clarke and Others. The charities were to be administered by the trustees of the Uxbridge United Charities and their income, after the payment of insurance, repairs, and other necessary charges, was to be applied as if it were income from the United Charities.

In 1961 the income of the United Charities amounted to £8,265, used mainly to provide pensions to the almspeople and to maintain and insure the almshouses and market-house. The Charity of Clarke and Others realized £394 and Ossulston's gift £403. The income of the gifts of Hunter and Woodbridge together realized £11, all of which was spent on coal for the poor, and the income from the Pease charity was £95.

The early history of the Uxbridge almshouses is obscure. Almshouses in the Lynch were in existence before 1727.[60] Two years later the manorial trustees covenanted to rebuild the almshouses,[61] but whether they did so is uncertain. In 1743 there were 16 tenants in the Lynch almshouses.[62] Eight new almshouses, apparently built on the same site, were completed in 1846.[63] A Scheme for new almshouses was prepared in conjunction with the Charity Commissioners in 1905.[64] The new buildings were built next to the Methodist chapel in New Windsor Street at a cost of more than £3,000, which was met by temporarily appropriating the income from the Ossulston and Pearce charities. The new almshouses were occupied in 1907, and the 19th-century almshouses seem to have been demolished about 1920.[65]

The earliest known charity in Hillingdon parish outside Uxbridge is that of Nathaniel Snell who, by will dated 1692, left £5 a year for apprenticing a poor child from the parish. Thomas Tisdale, who was churchwarden of Hillingdon in 1692,[66] at an uncertain date left a 2-acre close called Honey Hill to the use of the Hillingdon poor. Under the inclosure award of 1825 this land was exchanged for 6 a. at the corner of Royal Lane and Cowley Church Road. Robert Brigginshaw, by will dated 1715, left a rent-charge of 30s. a year on his property in Hayes parish to be distributed on 30 January (the testator's birthday) in food among those Hillingdon poor who were not receiving parochial relief. Lady Sarah Winford, by will dated 1732, left £50 to purchase land, the rent from which was to be used in repairing her father's tombstone. Any surplus was to be distributed among the parish poor. Two acres in the common fields were purchased in 1743 and exchanged under the inclosure award of 1825 for 2 a. at the corner of Kingston Lane and Green Lane. Anthony Brown, by will dated 1800, left a sufficient sum to realize £5 a year to buy cheese for distribution each Christmas among the parish poor and a further £5 to be applied towards educating pauper children. In 1823 the gift was represented by £500 stock. Under the 1825 inclosure award 4 a. in front of the Hillingdon workhouse were allotted to the Hillingdon poor. The land was later sold to the Uxbridge guardians and in 1870 the allotment was represented by £643 stock. In 1823 the income from the gifts of Brown, Brigginshaw, Tisdale, and Winford was lumped together as one fund, which then realized £26 a year, and the total amount distributed at Christmas as bread and cheese among all the parish poor.

Under a Scheme of 1870 the Hillingdon charities were consolidated under the administration of the parish authorities. The income, after the payment of management expenses, was divided into 10 equal parts, 5 of which were apportioned to the ecclesiastical parish of St. John, Hillingdon, 3 to the parish of St. John, Uxbridge Moor, and 2 to St. Andrew's parish. The proceeds were to be used to provide the poor with clothes, bedding, fuel, and medical and other assistance. Representative trustees were introduced in 1898 and were defined in 1932 as 9 members appointed by Uxbridge U.D.C. and 3 by Yiewsley and West Drayton U.D.C., together with the vicars of the three parishes and that of St. Matthew, Yiewsley. In 1954 the vicars of All Saints, North Hillingdon, and St. Jerome, Dawley, were included, and the number of representatives appointed by Uxbridge Borough Council was reduced

[57] Ibid. /1.
[58] Ibid. /8.
[59] See also M.R.O., Acc. 538.
[60] Ibid. /1.
[61] Ibid. /7.
[62] Ibid. /1.
[63] Ibid. /4. The 19th-cent. buildings are shown on a photograph (c. 1905) in Uxb. libr.
[64] M.R.O., Acc. 538/4.
[65] In 1962 the almshouses were renamed 'Woodbridge House' in recognition of the service given to Uxbridge United Charities by the Woodbridge family.
[66] Par. Recs., Churchwardens' Accts. 1692.

to 8. In 1962 the income of the Charity of Brigginshaw and Others was £112, all of which was distributed as clothes, fuel, food, medical aid, and temporary financial assistance in cases of special hardship.

Charles Sims, by will proved 1918, left numbers 1 and 2 Rosslyn Villas in trust to provide coal and blankets for the poor of Hillingdon East civil parish. Under a Scheme of 1933 the property, which was then represented by £581 stock, was vested in 5 trustees, 4 of whom were appointed by Uxbridge U.D.C. and the other by Yiewsley and West Drayton U.D.C.

ICKENHAM

THE ANCIENT parish of Ickenham[1] lay approximately 14 miles west of Hyde Park Corner and two miles north-east of Uxbridge. The old parish[2] was situated between the River Pinn to the west and the Yeading Brook to the east.[3] Covering an area of 1,458 a. in 1801,[4] the parish measured roughly two miles from north to south at its longest, and a little over one mile at its broadest point. In Hillingdon parish, about 200 yards south of the junction of the modern Swakeleys Drive and Long Lane, was Chestlands, a 6-acre field included in Ickenham parish. South-east of the centre of Ickenham village was an area of 12 a. belonging to Hillingdon. Under the Divided Parishes Act of 1882 these fields were transferred to the parishes in which they were geographically situated.[5] In 1937, after further boundary changes, the civil parish of Ickenham was merged in that of Uxbridge.[6] Since 1965 it has formed part of the London Borough of Hillingdon.[7] The name Ickenham survives as the name of the London Transport station in Glebe Lane. This article deals with the area of the old parish before any of the later changes were made.

Ickenham appears as 'Ticheham' in the Survey of 1086,[8] and it has been generally assumed that the forms 'Ticheham', 'Tickenham', and 'Ickenham' were subsequently used synonymously to describe Ickenham parish.[9] It seems almost certain, however, that part of one or more of the three Domesday fees called 'Ticheham' lay in Hillingdon ancient parish and that the name Tickenham, forms of which survived until the 19th century, was used to describe an area lying partly in the north-east corner of Hillingdon and partly east of the Yeading Brook in Ickenham.[10]

The parish lies 136 ft. above sea level at its highest point in the north and 101 ft. at its lowest in the south.[11] Most of the soil is London Clay but a narrow strip of alluvium follows the course of the Pinn stream.[12] The Pinn, which formed the northern and western boundaries of the old parish, runs into an artificial lake in Swakeleys Park and thence through Hillingdon parish to join the Colne at Yiewsley. The Yeading Brook entering the parish a little to the north of Northolt airfield, runs west-

ward for about a mile and then gradually turns back to run in the opposite direction. About 400 yards south of Western Avenue the stream divides, one branch flowing towards Ruislip parish, the other towards Hillingdon. In the 18th century there were two woods on the banks of this brook: Great Ditch Wood, known later as Gutteridge Wood,[13] and Catthroat or Cutthroat Wood,[14] most of which was cleared during the 19th century.[15] On the south bank of the Pinn was Beeton Wood and to the south-west, around the lake, the wooded part of Swakeleys Park. Since 1816 a feeder from Ruislip reservoir to the Grand Junction Canal has also run from north to south through the parish.[16]

Until 1934 no major road passed through the parish. Long Lane, running roughly parallel with and about ½ mile east of the Pinn, connected Hillingdon, Ickenham, and Ruislip. From the centre of the village Back Lane led past the church in a westerly direction to the Pinn and eventually to a lane leading to Uxbridge. Other lanes led into the fields. The most important of these were Glebe Lane and Austin Lane which ran south-east from the centre of the village and joined after about ½ mile. At their junction lay the field which until 1882 belonged to Hillingdon parish. By 1935, when Ickenham was becoming a residential area, Long Lane had been widened[17] and Western Avenue, the London–Oxford arterial road opened in 1934, driven through the southern part of the old parish.[18] Rail communications were established in 1904 when the Metropolitan line, which had hitherto terminated at Harrow, was extended as far as Uxbridge. In the following year electric trains replaced steam engines on this line and a station was opened in Glebe Lane.[19] In 1910 District line trains were introduced and in 1933 Piccadilly line trains also began to run along the same route. For a time all three services ran through Ickenham, but District line services were later discontinued and in 1965 the parish was served by the Metropolitan and Piccadilly lines only.

At the inclosure of 1780 the open fields of Ickenham amounted to 683 a.[20] They began near the junction of Glebe and Austin lanes and covered the south of the parish.[21] To the north of the Yeading

[1] This article was written in 1961; any references to a later time are dated.
[2] M.R.O., Acc. 599: map of Ickenham *c.* 1760.
[3] M.R.O., EA/Hil./2.
[4] *Census,* 1801.
[5] Ibid. 1891.
[6] Ibid. 1951.
[7] See p. 106.
[8] *V.C.H. Mdx.* i. 124, 126, 128.
[9] *P. N. Mdx.* (E.P.N.S.), 43.
[10] For a detailed discussion see pp. 69–71.
[11] O.S. Maps. 1/2,500, Mdx. ix. 12, 16; x. 13; xv. 1

(1914 edn.).
[12] Geol. Survey Map, sheet 255 (drift).
[13] M.R.O., Acc. 599; Ickenham Incl. Award Map *penes* Uxb. Bor. Council.
[14] Ibid.
[15] O.S. Maps 1/2,500, Mdx. ix. 12, 16; x. 13 (1865 edn.).
[16] M.R.O., Acc. 85/4/281; see p. 128.
[17] O.S. Maps 1/2,500, Mdx. ix. 12, 16 (1934 edn.).
[18] *V.C.H. Mdx.* iii. 208.
[19] Ex inf. Lond. Transport Exec.
[20] M.R.O., Ickenham Incl. Award.
[21] Ickenham Incl. Award Map *penes* Uxb. Bor. Council.

Brook were Tipper Hill and Woe Acres. Two meadows in the parish were called Brook Mead. One was on the Ickenham bank of the Pinn near Beeton Wood, the other lay along the southern bank of the Yeading Brook where it entered the parish north of the modern airfield. Adjoining this Brook Mead was Ickenham Marsh. Middle Field and Bleak or Black Hill were inside the loop of the Yeading Brook on the banks of which were also Tottingworth Field, Swillingtons, Further Field, and Down Barnes Hill, which lay further to the south. Many of these fields are visible from the point where Western Avenue crosses the Yeading Brook. Bleak Hill, mentioned as early as 1367,[22] rises gradually to about 8 ft. above the level of the road and is topped by a clump of trees.

There were two common meadows in the old parish, Ickenham Green and Ickenham Marsh. Ickenham Green was a long narrow strip extending north-westward from the present Ickenham High Road to the Pinn. In 1836 some paupers inclosed part of it for gardens, and although given notice to quit in 1847, remained there until, by 1860, they had apparently established squatters' rights.[23] By 1865 a few houses and a chapel occupied the frontage of the Green bordering the High Road.[24] In 1906 the parish council was granted a lease of the Green by the lord of the manor, and succeeding local authorities have inherited this interest.[25] In 1950 the local authority leased part of the Green to Ickenham Cricket Club;[26] the remainder was preserved as an open space.

In 1860, and presumably earlier, every householder had the right to pasture one horse or two cows a day from May Day to Martinmas on Ickenham Marsh.[27] These rights were abused during the late 19th century and by 1892 the Marsh was severely overcropped. The parish council therefore attempted to gain control of the land by claiming that the inhabitants of Ickenham owed their rights on the Marsh to two women and appealing to the Charity Commissioners to have the Marsh declared a charity. The appeal failed through lack of supporting evidence,[28] but in 1906 the council took a lease of the Marsh and was able thereafter to regulate its use. Its successor, Uxbridge Borough Council, obtained full control in 1957 when it acquired the manorial rights.[29] In 1961 the Marsh was still used for grazing cattle.

About 1453 John Charlton inclosed part of Brook Mead as a park.[30] This was presumably the Brook Mead which lay on the banks of the Pinn, and Charlton's close possibly formed the nucleus of the later Swakeleys Park. It was probably in this area that John Pecche in 1517 inclosed arable land for his park.[31] The history of other early inclosure is uncertain. At inclosure in 1780 there were a number of 'old inclosures'. The most important of these were the land lying between the glebe and the lands of Ickenham manor, Middle Field, and the area be-

tween Cutthroat and Gutteridge woods. All the common fields were inclosed in 1780; Ickenham Green and the Marsh remained open.[32]

Ickenham village was situated at the junction of the modern Swakeleys Road and Long Lane. At this point Long Lane widened to form a roughly triangular village centre. Until the 1930s most of the houses were grouped around this space, with others on either side of Back Lane (now Swakeleys Road). There were also a few groups of cottages in the fields, connected with the main roads by private paths. Around the central space stood St. Giles's church, the Home Farm, a small post office and shop, and the 'Coach and Horses' with an attached smithy. In the middle of the space were the village pump and pond. The church school stood on the road to Ruislip and the almshouses were in Back Lane. Behind the latter was the rectory house, connected with the road by a private pathway.[33] Outside the village were the two manor-houses[34] and a few scattered farms.

The appearance of Ickenham began to change after the sale of most of the Swakeleys estate in 1922.[35] By 1934 the western part of the parish had acquired the character of a residential suburb. At the old village centre a row of shops had been built on the south side of Swakeleys Road (formerly Back Lane). Swakeleys Road was lined with houses on both sides as far as the parish boundary and beyond, and residential roads led from it. Larger dwellings and blocks of flats had been built near Swakeleys House and along Long Lane. More expensive detached dwellings were soon to be erected around a spacious green at Milton Court. Further north three more residential roads led off Ickenham High Road and there was a row of houses at the east end of Glebe Avenue (formerly Glebe Lane). There were also houses along the south side of Austin Lane.[36] Part of Northolt airfield[37] abutted on the south of the parish, but topographical change was less marked in this area, much of which was still used for agriculture. Thirty years later the old village centre had become a busy traffic junction and the shopping parade had been extended along Swakeleys Road. To the north of Swakeleys Road a large new estate of private houses had been laid out, resulting in the demolition of the former rectory and of Ivy House Farm.[38] There were houses along most of Glebe Avenue and to the south of it several new suburban streets encroached on the former open-field area.

In spite of the rapid development of Ickenham a number of its older buildings still survive (1968). The parish church was enlarged in 1958 but its ancient appearance has not been impaired. To the east of the church Home Farm has a jettied and gabled wing of c. 1500 and the 'Coach and Horses' incorporates 17th-century work.[39] There are some brick cottages near the pond, including the former post office. The Gothic canopy over the village pump was erected in 1866.[40] The Buntings, a substantial house in a large garden immediately west of the

[22] Cal. Inq. Misc. i, pp. 241–2.
[23] See p. 105.
[24] O.S. Map. 1/2,500, Mdx. ix. 12 (1865 edn.).
[25] Leases penes Uxb. Bor. Council.
[26] Lease penes Uxb. Bor. Council.
[27] Abstract of title of T.T. Clarke (1860) penes Uxb. Bor. Council.
[28] See p. 109.
[29] See p. 104.
[30] Newcourt, Repertorium, i. 647.

[31] C 147/7/2/14.
[32] M.R.O., Ickenham Incl. Award.
[33] O.S. Map 1/2,500, Mdx. ix. 12 (1914 edn.).
[34] See pp. 103–4.
[35] See p. 104.
[36] O.S. Maps 1/2,500, Mdx. ix. 12, 16; x. 13 (1934 edn.).
[37] For the history of the airfield see p. 132.
[38] Hist. Mon. Com. Mdx. 84; ex inf. Mr. G. W. Davies.
[39] Hist. Mon. Com. Mdx. 84.
[40] Inscription.

church, was rebuilt between the two world wars,[41] but its stable block, converted into two dwellings, has survived. Further west along Swakeleys Road are the mid-19th-century almshouses.[42] Swakeleys Cottage, standing at the junction of Swakeleys Road and the Avenue, was formerly a lodge at the main approach to Swakeleys manor-house. It is partly timber-framed and partly of brick and has a late-18th-century doorcase with an enriched frieze; the mullioned windows with round-headed lights are probably of the same date. A pair of cottages to the east of the Avenue has similar windows. Swakeleys itself is largely unaltered, although no longer in private occupation.[43] Ickenham manor-house,[44] of 16th-century origin, has survived together with part of its earlier moat, and Long Lane Farm nearby is an early-18th-century house, now roughcast. Ickenham Hall in Glebe Avenue is slightly later in date and has a symmetrical red brick front and a walled fore-court; in 1968 it was in use as a Youth Centre for North-West Middlesex.

In 1086 thirty-one people were listed on the three estates called 'Ticheham'.[45] Three of these were knights, and there were also 3 Englishmen, 13 villeins, 9 bordars, and 3 cottars. Until the 20th century the population of the parish increased only slowly. In 1547 there were said to be 80 communicants in Ickenham.[46] In 1642 54 adult male parishioners took the protestation oath,[47] and in 1664 37 persons were assessed to hearth tax.[48] About 1723 there were said to be 30 families in the parish.[49] The population in 1801 was 213; in 1841 it was 396, the highest figure for the 19th century. Ten years later the population was 364, but by 1861 it had again declined to 351. It increased to 386 by 1871 but then dropped steadily to 329 in 1901. The civil parish of Ickenham, which contained 443 inhabitants in 1921, was incorporated into Uxbridge U.D. in 1929, when its boundaries were considerably extended. In 1931 there were 1,741 people in the revised civil parish, which was absorbed into that of Uxbridge in 1937. The population of Ickenham ward was 7,107 in 1951 and 10,370 in 1961.[50]

Most of the prominent people associated with Ickenham have been lords of Swakeleys manor and are noticed briefly below. Roger Crab, a hermit and vegetarian, lived at Ickenham for a time during the Interregnum and acquired a small following through his reputation as a seer and physician.[51] After his retirement in 1886 Admiral the Hon. Arthur Cochrane, Commander-in-Chief, Pacific Station (1873–5), lived at the Buntings.[52]

MANORS. Three fees called 'Ticheham' are included in the Survey of 1086.[53] The largest of these, assessed at 9½ hides, was held by three knights and an Englishman from Roger de Montgomery, Earl of Shrewsbury, lord of the adjoining manors of Colham and Hillingdon.[54] In the Confessor's time this estate had been divided into three holdings: Tochi, a housecarl, then held 2 hides, Alwin, a man of Ulsi son of Manni, had one hide and 3 virgates, and two sokemen, men of Wulfweard, held 2 hides and one virgate. All were free to sell their land. After the Conquest, however, these three holdings were apparently consolidated and the estate associated, perhaps for administrative purposes only,[55] with Earl Roger's manor of Colham in which it was said to lie (iacet modo in) in 1086.

A second holding called 'Ticheham', assessed at 3½ hides, was held in 1086 by two Englishmen from Geoffrey de Mandeville. In King Edward's time this holding had also been divided into two estates, one of 2½ hides held by a man of Earl Leofwine and the remaining hide by a man of Ansgar the Staller. Ansgar's man could not sell without his lord's permission; the other man was free to do so.

The smallest of the 'Ticheham' fees, assessed in 1086 at 2 hides, was then held by Robert Fafiton. In the Confessor's time it had been held by Ælmer, a man of Wlward 'White', who was free to sell it.

The later history of the Domesday holdings is obscure, but Earl Roger's Domesday fee of 'Ticheham' almost certainly formed the nucleus of the later manor of ICKENHAM. To this was probably joined part of the 3½-hide Mandeville holding, since later in the Middle Ages lords of Ickenham owed suit to the honor courts of both Wallingford and Mandeville.[56] On Earl Roger's death in 1094 his fief, presumably including 'Ticheham', passed to his son Robert de Bellême. Robert retained the property until 1102 when, following his abortive rebellion against Henry I, his lands were confiscated. The descent of 'Ticheham' then probably followed that of Colham[57] until the seizure of the honor of Wallingford by Henry, Duke of the Normans. After becoming king as Henry II in 1154, Henry seems to have granted out the manors of the honor. By 1196 Ickenham had apparently passed to Ralph de Harpenden,[58] members of whose family still held the estate of the honor of Wallingford at the end of the 13th century.[59] In the early 14th century Ickenham was apparently acquired by the Brok or Brook family, since in 1334 William del Brok, lord of the manors of Hillingdon and Cowley Hall,[60] conveyed Ickenham to John Charlton, a London merchant and a considerable landowner in west Middlesex.[61] Between 1332 and 1348 Charlton also acquired Cowley Hall and Hillingdon.[62] On Charlton's death Ickenham descended to his daughter Juette who had married Nicholas Shorediche.[63] The estate then descended in the Shorediche family until the early 19th century.[64] Michael Shorediche, who was lord of the manor in 1800,[65] apparently mortgaged most of his property while at university,[66] and by 1812 Ickenham, prob-

[41] Ex inf. Mr. G. W. Davies.
[42] See p. 109.
[43] See p. 104.
[44] See p. 103.
[45] V.C.H. Mdx. i. 124–6, 128.
[46] E 301/34/183.
[47] Hse. of Lords, Mdx. Protestation Rets.
[48] M.R.O., H.T. 6.
[49] Guildhall MS. 9557.
[50] Census, 1801–1961.
[51] D.N.B.
[52] Who Was Who, 1897–1916; Kelly's Dir. Mdx. (1886), where his Christian name is given wrongly as Thomas.
[53] V.C.H. Mdx. i. 124–6, 128. For 'Ticheham' see above, pp. 69–70.

[54] See pp. 70, 72.
[55] See V.C.H. Mdx. i. 125.
[56] See pp. 82, 118.
[57] See p. 70.
[58] Chanc. R. 1196 (P.R.S. n.s. i), 160.
[59] Boarstall Cart. (Oxf. Hist. Soc. lxxxviii), 301.
[60] C.P. 25(1)/150/56/100.
[61] See pp. 72–73.
[62] Ibid.
[63] C.P. 25(1)/150/56/96.
[64] e.g. M.R.O., Acc. 640/2,/5,/8; C 142/149/72; /207/65.
[65] Lysons, Mdx. Pars. 190.
[66] Letters from Paul, son of Michael Shorediche, written in 1844 penes the rector.

ably as the result of foreclosure on a mortgage debt, has passed to George Robinson.[67] In an attempt to repair his fortunes Michael Shorediche married a West Indian heiress in 1813,[68] but by the time their grandson, Edward Ricaut Shorediche, came to Ickenham from Antigua in 1859 to see whether any of the family property could be recovered the manor had again changed hands and it was too late to take legal action.[69] In fact George Robinson's will had been disputed. In the end all his property was sold under a Chancery order of 1857. At the sale, held in 1859, Ickenham was bought by Thomas Truesdale Clarke and subsequently merged with his manor of Swakeley's.[70]

Little is known of the extent of the manorial property. In 1334 the Ickenham demesne amounted to over 80 a.,[71] to which 20 a. were added a few years later.[72] Subsequently much of this seems to have been granted away. In 1751 Robert Shorediche held land in Further Field, Bleak Hill, and Home Field.[73] In 1841 all that remained of the manorial demesne was a strip of land along the Hillingdon boundary near the manor-house.[74]

Ickenham manor-house stands about ¾ mile south-east of the church at the end of a lane leading off Long Lane. The building, begun in the early 16th century, was originally L-shaped and of close-studded timber framing. It has been partly refaced with brick and two gabled brick wings were added in the late 17th or early 18th century. There are some internal features of the original date and a 17th-century staircase. A moat formerly surrounded the house and there is a large outer moat, now incomplete, to the west of it. The house, previously known as Manor Farm, had been divided into two dwellings by 1968.[75]

The early history of the estate later known as *SWAKELEYS* manor is obscure. The nucleus of the medieval estate was probably Robert Fafiton's 2-hide Domesday fee of 'Ticheham',[76] but land in Speraskescroft and Layfield, held in the late 12th century by William de Tikeham, may have been distinct from this holding and, if so, was probably consolidated with it during the 12th century.[77] In the early 13th century the estate seems to have passed to John de Trumpinton whose son, also called John, still held it about 1260.[78] By 1329, however, part of this land had apparently been acquired by Robert Swalcliffe of Swalcliffe (Oxon.).[79] Four years later Robert and his wife conveyed their lands to William

le Gauger of London,[80] but the family name Swalcliffe, later contracted to Swakeleys, continued to attach to the estate.[81] Swakeleys changed hands at least once more before 1350 when Boniface Lapyn released the former Swalcliffe estate to John Charlton,[82] whose father, also called John, had held Ickenham manor since 1334.[83] Swakeleys then descended in the Charlton family until the forfeiture of Sir Richard Charlton following his death at Bosworth in 1485.[84] In 1486 Henry VII granted the reversion on an estate including Swakeleys manor to Sir Thomas Bourchier, subject to the life interest of Elizabeth, Richard Charlton's widow.[85] In 1510 Bourchier granted his reversionary interest in Swakeleys to Sir John Pecche and John Sharpe.[86] Sharpe died, and in 1521 Pecche transferred his interest to Henry Courtenay, Earl of Devon.[87] Ten years later Courtenay alienated the manor to Ralph Pexall and his wife Anne.[88] On Pexall's death in 1537[89] the manor passed to his son Sir Richard Pexall[90] who died in 1571 leaving four daughters among whom the property was apparently divided. Most of the estate eventually came into the possession of Pexall Brocas, son of Sir Richard's daughter Anne. Pexall married Margery, daughter of Sir Thomas Shirley of Westmeston (Suss.),[91] and some time before his death in 1583[92] he and his wife made over ten of the twelve parts of the manor to Sir Thomas Shirley.[93] By 1595 Shirley had sold Swakeleys to John Bromley,[94] who in 1606 sold it to John Bingley.[95] Two years later Bingley sold the manor to Edmund Brabazon.[96] This conveyance seems to have been invalid since Swakeleys was still in Bingley's possession in 1616.[97] In 1629 he sold Swakeleys to Edmund Wright, a London alderman and later lord mayor.[98] On Wright's death in 1643 the manor passed to his daughter Catherine, wife of Sir James Harrington.[99] Harrington was one of the judges of Charles I and after the Restoration was forced to leave the country.[1] In 1665 he or his representative attempted to sell Swakeleys to John Morris and Robert Clayton,[2] but the sale seems to have been invalid. By September 1665, when Pepys went to Swakeleys,[3] the house and manor were in the possession of Sir Robert Vyner, a London financier and later lord mayor. Sir Robert died in 1688 and the manor passed to his nephew Thomas Vyner,[4] whose son Robert inherited it in 1707.[5] In 1741 Robert sold Swakeleys to Sarah Lethieullier, a Huguenot widow, and Benjamin Lethieullier, her brother-in-law, who were to hold it

[67] M.R.O., EA/Hil. /2.
[68] Letter *penes* the rector.
[69] Photocopy of letter from Edw. Ricaut Shorediche *penes* Uxb. libr.; indenture *penes* Uxb. Bor. Council.
[70] Indenture *penes* Uxb. Bor. Council. For Swakeleys see below.
[71] C.P. 25(1)/150/56/96.
[72] C.P. 25(1)/150/58/130.
[73] M.R.O., Acc. 85/13/625a/5.
[74] M.R.O., T.A./ICK.
[75] Lysons, *Mdx. Pars.* 191; Hist. Mon. Com. *Mdx.* 84; Pevsner, *Mdx.* pl. 35a.
[76] See above.
[77] *Cart. of Missenden Abbey, pt. 3* (Bucks. Rec. Soc. xii), 164, 165.
[78] *Red. Bk. Exch.* (Rec. Com.), 543; *Cart. Missenden Abbey*, 163, 166.
[79] C.P. 25(1)/149/52/351; /150/53/12; the Oxfordshire place-name is pronounced 'Swaycliff'.
[80] C.P. 25(1)/150/56/91.
[81] *Cal. Inq. Misc.* iii, p. 241.
[82] *Cal. Close*, 1349–54, 235.
[83] See above.

[84] *Rot. Parl.* vi. 276a.
[85] *Cal. Pat.* 1485–1509, 63.
[86] *L. & P. Hen. VIII*, i(1), p. 289.
[87] Ibid. iii(2), p. 750.
[88] Ibid. v, p. 148.
[89] P.C.C. 14 Oyngley.
[90] P.C.C. 46 Holney.
[91] *Visitations of Sussex* (Harl. Soc. liii), x. 7; W. H. Godfrey, *Swakeleys* (Lond. Survey Cttee.).
[92] Par. Recs., Reg. 1.
[93] C.P. 25(1)/173/33 Eliz. I, Mich.
[94] C 2. W. w. 15/26 Eliz. I.
[95] E 112/99/1065.
[96] C.P. 25(2)/323/6 Jas. I, Mich.
[97] E 112/99/1065.
[98] C 66/2522/86.
[99] P.C.C. 21 Crane.
[1] *Cal. S.P. Dom.* 1660–1, 413.
[2] C.P. 25(2)/689/17 Chas. II, Mich.
[3] Pepys, *Diary*, 7 Sept. 1665.
[4] Godfrey, *Swakeleys.*
[5] M.R.O., Acc. 85/4/353.

in trust for Sarah's son Benjamin, then a minor.[6] Benjamin the younger came of age in 1750[7] and in the following year sold the estate to the Revd. Thomas Clarke, Rector of Ickenham.[8] Members of the Clarke family held Swakeleys for over a century. Thomas Clarke died in 1796 and was succeeded by his son Thomas Truesdale Clarke. Thomas Truesdale's son, another Thomas Truesdale, succeeded in 1840[9] and bought the manor of Ickenham in 1859.[10] He died in 1890 and was succeeded by his son William Capel Clarke, who had married Clara Thornhill and had added his wife's name to his own. William Capel Clarke-Thornhill died in 1898[11] and in 1922 his son Thomas Bryan Clarke-Thornhill sold most of the Swakeleys estate to agents for development as a residential suburb.[12] In 1927 the agents sold the remaining undeveloped land and the manorial rights to David Pool, who was then owner of the old Ickenham manor-house.[13] At this time the manorial rights still included rights over what had been the manorial waste at Ickenham Green and Marsh. David Pool died in 1956 and in 1957 his executors vested the manor or lordship of Ickenham in the borough of Uxbridge.[14]

The extent of Swakeleys in the Middle Ages is unknown: from the 14th century the manor included much land outside the parish. In 1531 it was said to comprise more than 1,000 a. and in 1608 over 2,000 a.[15] At inclosure in 1780 Thomas Clarke held 368 a. in Ickenham.[16] A park is mentioned in 1453[17] and again in 1517.[18] This presumably was that surrounding Swakeleys manor-house. An inventory[19] of the goods of Sir Thomas Charlton (d. 1465) includes details of what is almost certainly the medieval manor-house. At this date the dwelling contained nineteen rooms and a chapel, as well as stables and outbuildings. Nothing further is known of Swakeleys manor-house until 1616 when John Bingley had a dispute with William Cragg, who was then living in the house as a tenant. Bingley had reserved for his own use the great chamber known as the king's chamber with an adjoining inner chamber, the kitchen, buttery, hall, great parlour, and a room required for dressing meat, as well as stabling for his horses.[20] Most of these rooms are identifiable in the inventory of c. 1465.

The present mansion was built by Sir Edmund Wright between 1629 and 1638,[21] presumably on the same site as the medieval dwelling. It was altered by Sir James Harrington and again by the Clarkes at the end of the 18th century.[22] From 1894 the house was rented to tenants,[23] and in 1923 it was sold to estate agents. To prevent it from being demolished it was bought by H. J. Talbot in 1924 and then resold to the Foreign Office Sports Association.[24] During the Second World War it was occupied by the Army and after 1945 stood derelict. The London Postal Region Sports Club obtained the house in 1955 as a sports pavilion and social centre, while the grounds were used as playing fields.[25] The house as it stands today is substantially that erected by Sir Edmund Wright between 1629 and 1638. It has been little altered and remains one of the most notable mansions of its period in Middlesex. The building has an H-shaped plan and is of two stories and attics. The walls are of brick with dressings mostly of plaster to simulate stone; a few of the windows and door-surrounds, however, are of black marble. There are central entrances on both east and west fronts, the latter masked by a projecting porch of two stories. Both in its plan and in its unconventional use of classical detail, the house is typically Jacobean in character. External features include two-storied bay windows at both ends of the two cross-wings, a continuous entablature to each story with pediments above the windows, and curvilinear attic gables with crowning pediments. The roof line is further broken by tall clustered chimneys and, on the two principal fronts, by central niches with shell heads and flanking volutes. Internally two carved newels with shaped finials have been preserved from the original staircase and some of the panelling is of the same date. The hall screen, which has three round arches, columns painted to simulate marble, a central broken pediment, and carvings of lions and cherubs, is said to have been inserted by Sir James Harrington between 1643 and 1665. He may also have been responsible for the fine ornamental ceiling in the saloon on the first floor. Murals above the staircase representing scenes from the *Aeneid* are attributed to Robert Streater (1624–80). Other internal fittings are of the later 17th and 18th centuries. Alterations by the Clarkes in the late 18th century include two ground-floor windows on the south front. Immediately north of the house is a stable court enclosed by low buildings of the 17th century and later; the north range has been converted into three cottages and the east range includes an 18th-century orangery. A square brick dovecote with an ice-house below it, which formerly stood north of the courtyard,[26] was demolished in the early 1960s. The interior was partially restored in 1955 and the outside and roof were restored in 1961.[27]

ECONOMIC AND SOCIAL HISTORY. Until the second decade of the 20th century Ickenham was an exclusively agricultural community. Few details of the economy of the parish have, however, survived. In 1086 there were four ploughs on Earl Roger's demesne, with room for two more. In addition there was on his estate meadow for four ploughs, pasture for the cattle of the vill, and sufficient woodland to support 200 pigs. On the Mandeville fee there were two ploughs in demesne, meadow for two ploughs, pasture for the beasts, and woodland to support 40 pigs. On Robert Fafiton's land there had been one plough but it was no longer

[6] M.R.O., Acc. 85/4/349–51.   [7] Ibid. /352.
[8] Ibid. /13/623.
[9] Inscriptions in Ickenham church.
[10] See above.
[11] Inscriptions in Ickenham church.
[12] Abstracts of title *penes* Uxb. Bor. Council.
[13] Ibid.
[14] Letters *penes* Uxb. Bor. Council.
[15] C.P. 25(2)/181/22; /323/6 Jas. I, Mich.
[16] Ickenham Incl. Map *penes* Uxb. Bor. Council.
[17] Newcourt, *Repertorium*, i. 647.
[18] C 47/7/2/2/14.   [19] W.A.M., 6646.
[20] E 112/99/1065.
[21] The house is described in Hist. Mon. Com. *Mdx.* 82–84 and illustrated in plates 156–60. See also plate on facing page.
[22] Hist. Mon. Com. *Mdx.* 83.
[23] M.R.O., Acc. 85/13/632–3.
[24] Godfrey, *Swakeleys.*
[25] Ex inf. Lond. Postal Region Sports Club.
[26] Hist. Mon. Com. *Mdx.* pl. 49.
[27] Ex inf. Lond. Postal Region Sports Club.

NORWOOD: ST. MARY'S CHURCH, *c.* 1800

ICKENHAM: SWAKELEYS FROM THE SOUTH-EAST IN 1800

NORTHOLT GREEN

HILLINGDON HOSPITAL, *c.* 1966
Part of the 19th-century workhouse is seen on the left

there in 1086. There was meadow for one plough, pasture for the cattle of the vill, and sufficient woodland to support 30 pigs.[74] Three ploughs on the demesne are mentioned in 1220,[75] but nothing further is known of the medieval economy. Inclosure seems to have begun about 1453,[76] but until 1780 most of the arable was cultivated in open fields.[77] The use of these was regulated in the manor court and enactments of 1632, 1670, and 1685 were enforced by penalties.[78] In 1801 the main crops grown in Ickenham were beans (149 a.), wheat (126 a.), and oats (48 a.), while 313 a. were lying fallow. In all about 1,200 a. were under cultivation but about 250 a., including some of the best land in the parish, were said to be in common and used by some of the farmers instead of being put at the disposal of all.[79]

In 1855–6 Swakeleys Farm, owned by the Clarkes, made a profit of £595 on the sale of grain and £255 on the sale of stock. Crops sold in that year were mainly wheat and hay.[80] At the end of 1855 the stock included 16 horses, 54 cattle, 120 sheep, and 8 pigs. In addition to the profit made on sales there were enough animals to supply the Clarkes' table. Thus in 1865 69 sheep, 9 pigs, and 2 cows were slaughtered for the household.[81] Profits had declined by the end of the 19th century. In 1890 £254 was made on the sale of animals, £178 on wheat and hay, £31 on dairy produce, and £17 on root crops.[82]

At the beginning of the 20th century Ickenham still conveyed the impression of 'an old-fashioned country village . . . with farm houses that look the very picture of comfort and prosperity'.[83] Nine farms survived in 1922.[84] Between 1923 and 1927, however, much of the Swakeleys estate was laid out as a residential suburb[85] and arable in the northern part of the old parish was built over. After the Second World War more building took place in the neighbourhood of Glebe Lane and elsewhere. By 1961 Ickenham had become a residential suburb of Uxbridge Borough. But although much of the arable had been covered with houses, some farming continued. There were still two farms in 1961: Long Lane Farm, near the old Ickenham manor-house, and Home Farm, adjoining the pond in the centre of the old village.[86]

In the 1830s a cattle fair was held at Ickenham on 3 April and one for pleasure on 4 June.[87] They do not seem to have been of ancient origin and are not mentioned after 1839. Little else is known of social life in the old parish. From the returns of 1834[88] it appears that the overseers were chiefly concerned with relieving agricultural labourers in times of seasonal unemployment. In the same year a number of persons on poor relief came into conflict with the

lord of the manor. William Bunce and eighteen others inclosed without permission part of the waste on Ickenham Green for gardens. In 1837 they were allowed to remain as tenants on sufferance, paying 1s. a rood to the lord of the manor.[89] In the following year they were granted leases from year to year and in 1844 it was decided that they should bear the cost of preparing their leases at 6s. 8d. a rood. Payment was to be made by March 1845. The lessees, by pleading poverty, were able to obtain several postponements, but in March 1847 they were given final notice to quit.[90] A settlement seems to have been reached since in 1859, when Thomas Truesdale Clarke bought Ickenham manor,[91] he was informed that part of Ickenham Green had been turned into garden allotments and that the occupiers paid £1 a year.[92] It seems likely that these occupiers were the lessees of 1837 or their successors.

Little is known about relations between the parishioners and successive lords of the manor. Edmund Wright, Sir James Harrington, and Sir Robert Vyner were probably more often in London than at Ickenham.[93] But Thomas Clarke, who became rector in 1747 and obtained Swakeleys four years later, probably exercised considerable influence on the life of the parish. The only indication of his attitude to his flock, however, is the clause in his will directing that some money should be distributed among the poor of the parish, but none of it spent on drink.[94] Ickenham church school depended largely on the financial support of the Clarke family during the 19th century,[95] and William Capel Clarke-Thornhill, who succeeded as lord of the manor in 1890,[96] maintained some of the traditions of his predecessors although himself living in Kettering (Northants.). He continued to support the school, and donations to the Ickenham poor appear in his accounts.[97] An annual dinner for the tenants of the estate was provided at the rent audit until 1905.[98]

LOCAL GOVERNMENT. Courts baron were held for Ickenham manor from at least as early as 1415.[99] Lords of the sub-manor of Swakeleys owed suit at the Ickenham court. In 1434 Sir Thomas Charlton of Swakeleys was fined for non-attendance and in 1472 the bailiff of the manor was ordered to distrain upon Sir Richard Charlton for the same offence.[1] In 1595 Michael Shorediche took to court a tenant of Swakeleys who had refused to pay services owed to Ickenham manor.[2] Lords of Ickenham asserted their rights over the younger manor until 1860.[3]

Ickenham courts baron concerned themselves exclusively with manorial business and the regulation of the open fields.[4] After 1731 there is a hiatus

[74] V.C.H. Mdx. i. 124–6, 128.
[75] Bk. of Fees. i. 315.
[76] Newcourt, Repertorium, i. 647.
[77] M.R.O., Acc. 599.
[78] M.R.O., Acc. 640/5.
[79] H.O. 67/16.
[80] M.R.O., Acc. 85/14/637.
[81] Ibid. /14/636.
[82] Ibid. /13/632.
[83] Thorne, Environs of Lond. 374–5.
[84] Kelly's Dir. Mdx. (1922).
[85] See p. 101.
[86] Ex inf. Uxb. Bor. Council.
[87] Pigot's National Commercial Dir. (1834, 1839).
[88] Rep. Poor Law Com. App. B (2), H.C. 44, pp. 104 f–k (1834), xxxv–vi.

[89] M.R.O., Acc. 640/9, pp. 41–52.
[90] Ibid. pp. 68–78.
[91] See p. 103.
[92] Abstract of title (1860) penes Uxb. Bor. Council.
[93] See p. 103.
[94] M.R.O., Acc. 640/24.
[95] See p. 108.
[96] See p. 104.
[97] M.R.O., Acc. 85/13/632–3.
[98] Ibid.
[99] M.R.O., Acc. 640/1–6, /9.
[1] Ibid. /5.
[2] Ibid.
[3] Ibid. /9.
[4] Ibid.

in the court records until 1819 when George Robinson, the new lord, held a court baron at Ickenham manor-house. Courts continued to be held annually throughout the early 19th century.[5] In addition to the usual manorial business courts in the 19th century asserted the right of the lord to three pews in the parish church[6] and dealt with the encroachment of unauthorized persons on the manorial waste.[7] After Ickenham manor had been bought by Thomas Truesdale Clarke,[8] courts baron met in the 'Coach and Horses' but no longer every year. In 1865 the court recorded the grant of land on the manorial waste near the church for erecting a pump in the centre of the village.[9] The last court baron was held at the 'Coach and Horses' in 1878.[10]

Leet business was apparently transacted in the honorial court of Wallingford (later Ewelme) meeting at Uxbridge[11] and in the franchise court of Northolt manor.[12] In the 15th century Ickenham sent jurors to the view of frankpledge at Uxbridge[13] and attendance at the honor court was enforced until 1813.[14] From at least as early as 1461 lords of Ickenham owed suit to the leet at Northolt.[15] Here constables and headboroughs for Ickenham manor were appointed.[16] In 1660 it was stated that Richard Shorediche was bound, on inheriting Ickenham manor, to pay a relief of £1 6s. 8d. to the lord of Northolt and the same sum as an annual quit-rent.[17] This rent was paid as late as 1860.[18] The Northolt jurisdiction probably grew out of the 11th-century Mandeville holding in Ickenham.[19] In the later Middle Ages Northolt exercised a similar jurisdiction in other former Mandeville lands in the county.[20]

Little is known of the parochial government which succeeded manorial organization. A constable, two overseers, and two churchwardens are mentioned in 1642,[21] but their function and the method by which they were appointed are uncertain. The overseers presumably collected the poor-rate which was being levied by 1750,[22] and they may also have administered the poor-house which was probably built in the 18th century. All that is known of this building is that it stood in Back Lane in front of the churchyard and that it had been demolished by 1837 when the site was sold.[23] In 1834, the first year for which detailed evidence is available, poor relief was administered by the vestry. In 1833–4 eighteen able-bodied paupers were given work repairing and procuring gravel for the parish roads. This was the average number so assisted each year. The vestry appointed two overseers, drawn, like the paupers who applied to them, from the agricultural labourers

of the parish.[24] Ickenham became part of the Uxbridge Union in 1836[25] and the workhouse poor were transferred to the union workhouse at Hillingdon.

Apart from the administration of poor relief little is known of vestry business. In 1892 the vestry tried to limit grazing rights on Ickenham Marsh and later to have it declared a charity.[26] In 1894 Ickenham became part of Uxbridge R.D. and was thereafter administered by a parish council. The only record of the council's work are the regulations for Ickenham Marsh, which the council leased from the lord of the manor in 1906.[27] In 1929 the parish was incorporated into Uxbridge U.D. and ceased to exist as a unit of local government.[28] Under the London Government Act of 1963, Uxbridge was included in the London Borough of Hillingdon.[29]

CHURCH. There was a church in Ickenham by the mid 13th century.[30] Little is recorded of its early history or of the area it served until 1453 when the Rector of Ickenham came into conflict with the Bishop of Worcester, who had appropriated Hillingdon church,[31] about the tithes of 'Tickenham'. The dispute was apparently decided in favour of Hillingdon and the area assigned for ever to that parish. In fact those fields which can be identified remained in Ickenham parish,[32] and in one of them, Tottingworth Field, the Rector of Ickenham had glebe land in 1610.[33] At that date, as also in 1961, Ickenham church served the whole area of the ancient parish.

The benefice seems always to have been a rectory. Reynold Cabus held the advowson in the earlier 13th century,[34] but in 1257 John Cabus, perhaps his son, sold it to Lawrence del Brok.[35] His family presumably retained the advowson until 1334 when William del Brok conveyed it to John Charlton.[36] From this date until the 20th century the advowson was usually held by lords of Ickenham manor. From 1452 until 1464 the widow of John Shorediche exercised the right together with her two successive husbands.[37] In 1531 the Bishop of London presented for one turn only; in 1635 and 1660 the Crown presented; and two women had a turn in 1686.[38] After that the Shorediche family held the advowson until 1743 when it was purchased by Thomas Clarke, a London merchant, who in 1747 presented his son, Thomas.[39] The Clarkes held the advowson throughout the 19th century, although in 1859 the Revd. Henry St. John Beauchamp Pell was presented by Oliver Claude Pell and William Ford.[40] In 1923 Thomas Bryan Clarke-Thornhill transferred the

[5] M.R.O., Acc. 640/9.
[6] Ibid. p. 24.
[7] See p. 105.
[8] See p. 103.
[9] M.R.O., Acc. 640/9, p. 121.
[10] Ibid. p. 132.
[11] See p. 82.
[12] See pp. 117–18.
[13] S.C. 2/212/2,/8,/11.
[14] M.R.O., E.M.C. 83/1.
[15] W.A.M., N. 1–22; see p. 118.
[16] Ibid.; see p. 118.
[17] W.A.M., N. 22.
[18] Extract of title (1860) penes Uxb. Bor. Council.
[19] See p. 102.
[20] For a full discussion of this jurisdiction see p. 118.
[21] Hse. of Lords, Mdx. Protestation Rets.
[22] M.R.O., Acc. 85/13/624.
[23] Ibid. /11/548.
[24] Rep. Poor Law Com. App. B (2), H.C. 44, p. 104 f

(1834), xxxv–vi.
[25] 2nd Annual Rep. Poor Law Com. H.C. 595, p. 534 (1836), xxix(1).
[26] See p. 109.
[27] Lease penes Uxb. Bor. Council.
[28] Census, 1931.
[29] London Govt. Act, 1963, c. 33.
[30] St. Paul's MS. W.D.9, f. 83v.
[31] Newcourt, Repertorium, i. 647; see above, p. 87.
[32] See p. 100.
[33] Newcourt, Repertorium, i. 663.
[34] St. Paul's MS. W.D. 9, f. 83v.
[35] C.P. 25(1)/147/22/450.
[36] C.P. 25(1)/150/56/100.
[37] Newcourt, Repertorium, i. 663.
[38] Ibid.
[39] Lysons, Mdx. Pars. 193; Hennessy, Novum Repertorium, 227.
[40] Hennessy, Novum Repertorium, 227.

advowson to Eton College,[41] which was still the patron in 1961.[42]

In the Middle Ages Ickenham church had no endowments, obits, or lights, but the abbey of Chertsey maintained a chantry priest there. In 1547 this priest was described as a 'Frenchman'.[43] After the Dissolution he was paid out of the Augmentations until the chantries were suppressed.

Ickenham church was valued at £2 10s. in the mid 13th century.[44] In 1291 its value was assessed at £2.[45] In 1535 the annual value of the rectory was £13 and the tithes were worth 26s.[46] In 1610 the rectory included a house with a garden and orchard, barn, stable, three closes of meadow, and land in the common fields.[47] In 1650 there were 25 a. of glebe in five lands in the common fields and two leets of meadow, the whole valued at £31 a year.[48] In 1751 the Revd. Thomas Clarke in a survey of the glebe listed 14 allotments in the common fields, Chestlands,[49] a close near Beeton Wood, the parsonage house, and the land surrounding it.[50] In 1760 much of the glebe was concentrated in a block along the south-west side of Glebe Lane.[51] At inclosure twenty years later the rector was allotted land in the loop of the Yeading Brook in lieu of tithes.[52] In 1800 the rectorial glebe covered 240 a., most of which was farmed out.[53]

In 1760 the parsonage house stood among the fields on Glebe Lane.[54] It was described in 1800 as an 'ancient wooden building' consisting of four rooms.[55] From 1751 the rector, Thomas Clarke, lived at Swakeleys House and the parsonage house was leased to a tenant who farmed the glebe. By 1800 it had long been used as a farm-house, and it was clear that the attached dwelling was an inducement when a tenant was being sought to farm the glebe. The rector therefore petitioned the bishop for permission to build a rectory nearer to the parish church and the village centre. It was to stand near Back Lane on land obtained in exchange with Thomas Truesdale Clarke. A faculty for the change was granted in 1800[56] and the new rectory was built soon afterwards. In 1927 the house was sold to the Ickenham High School for Girls,[57] and the present rectory in Swakeleys Road was then built.[58] The old rectory was demolished in 1965.[59]

The rector in 1547 was resident in the parish.[60] On examination in 1586 the Rector of Ickenham was found to be 'simple'.[61] By 1642 the rector was assisted by a curate.[62] Three years later Andrew Clare was deprived of the benefice for deserting his cure and joining the Royalist army.[63] Nathaniel Nicholas, his Puritan successor, was in turn ejected in 1660.[64] Thomas Clarke, who was presented in 1747,[65] bought the manor of Swakeleys in 1751. He con-

tinued as rector and owner of the manor until his death in 1796.[66] One of the reasons advanced in 1800 for building a new rectory was that it would encourage the clergy to reside.[67]

In Thomas Clarke's time services were held twice on Sundays and there were four Communion services a year. Children were catechized during Lent, 'but with little success'.[68] At the end of the 18th century there were between 20 and 30 communicants.[69]

The church of *ST. GILES* stands near the pond in the centre of the old village. It consists of nave, chancel, north aisle, south porch, north-west chapel, and modern vestries.[70] The walls are of flint rubble, mostly roughcast, and of brickwork. The medieval church consisted of a chancel (16 ft. by 12 ft.) and a nave (32 ft. by 16½ ft.), both built in the later 14th century; they retain a south doorway and several restored windows of this date. A timber bell turret was added at the west end of the nave in the 15th century. In the late 16th century the church was found to be too small and a large north aisle was built by William Say, the old north wall being pierced to form an arcade. The aisle is of brick and consists of two bays, roofed under transverse gables. In the north wall each bay has a square-headed window with an oval window above it. The timber-framed south porch is of about the same date, representing, with the aisle, the only surviving work of this period in a Middlesex church.[71] The present chapel of St. John was built at the west end of the north aisle in the mid 17th century, probably by the Harringtons of Swakeleys.[72] The walls are of brick, plastered internally. It was designed as a mortuary chapel, the west, north, and south walls being lined with arcading to form arched recesses to house the coffins; there is an original oval window in the north gable. In 1914 thirty coffins, dating from 1647 to 1892, were removed from the chapel and interred in the churchyard; the building then became a vestry. In 1960, after new vestries had been provided, it was renovated and dedicated as the chapel of St. John.[73] The church was restored in the 1870s,[74] the chancel arch and the north arcade being refashioned in the 'Early English' style. After the Second World War the church was again found to be too small. An extension of two bays was therefore built at the west end of the nave; the new windows were copied from those of the 14th century already in the church, and old timbers were obtained for an internal roof truss. To the north of this extension a new vestry and a room for the choir were built, the work being completed in 1958.[75] In 1962, during external repairs, the cement was stripped

[41] Eton Coll. Recs.
[42] *Crockford* (1961).
[43] E 301/34/183.
[44] St. Paul's MS. W.D. 9, f. 83v.
[45] *Tax. Eccl.* (Rec. Com.), 20.
[46] *Valor Eccl.* (Rec. Com.), i. 433.
[47] Newcourt, *Repertorium*, i. 663.
[48] *Home Cnties. Mag.* ii. 282.
[49] See p. 100.
[50] M.R.O., Acc. 85/13/625a.
[51] M.R.O., Acc. 599.
[52] M.R.O., Ickenham Incl. Award.
[53] M.R.O., Acc. 85/11/547.
[54] M.R.O., Acc. 599.
[55] M.R.O., Acc. 85/11/547.
[56] Ibid.
[57] See p. 109.
[58] Ex inf. the rector.

[59] Ex inf. Mr. G. W. Davies.
[60] E 301/34/183.
[61] Guildhall MS. 9537/6, f. 173v.
[62] Hse. of Lords, Mdx. Protestation Rets.
[63] *Walker Revised*, ed. Matthews, 229.
[64] *Calamy Revised*, ed. Matthews, 365.
[65] Hennessy, *Novum Repertorium*, 227.
[66] See p. 104.
[67] M.R.O., Acc. 85/11/547.
[68] Guildhall MS. 9550.
[69] Ibid. 9558.
[70] It is fully described in Hist. Mon. Com. *Mdx.* 80–82.
[71] M. Robbins, *Middlesex*, 302.
[72] See p. 103.
[73] P. D. Kingston, *Parish and Church of St. Giles, Ickenham* (2nd edn.), 10–12.
[74] Thorne, *Environs of Lond.* 375; Hist. Mon. Com. *Mdx.* 80–82.   [75] Kingston, op. cit. 13.

from the east wall of the chancel to expose the flint rubble. In the same year the porch was restored and glazed, the ancient south door being rehung in the outer arch. In the course of the work a coped stone coffin lid bearing a raised cross, thought to date from the 14th century, was found beneath the floor.[76]

The church has a number of monuments, notably of lords of the manor and their families. There are several late-16th-century brasses commemorating Edmund Shorediche and members of the Say family.[77] A marble effigy of 1665 represents the infant son of Sir Robert Clayton, whose own monument is at Bletchingley (Surr.).[78] There are two mural tablets by Thomas Banks, one commemorating Thomas Clarke, rector (d. 1796), and the other J. G. Clarke (d. 1800). The carved wooden font dates from the late 17th century and is believed to have come from Swakeleys.[79] The oldest pieces of plate are a silver flagon and a paten, dated 1682 and given by Sir Robert Vyner. There is also a cup dated 1782 and a metal dish of the same period.[80] The registers, which are complete, record baptisms, marriages, and burials, and date from 1539.

The church hall, standing in Ickenham High Road to the north of the churchyard, was built in 1932; it was partly financed by the sale of the former church school.[81]

NONCONFORMITY. In 1584 Bernard Brocas, father of Pexall Brocas,[82] was fined for not attending the parish church.[83] Elizabeth Waters was fined several times for the same offence between 1593 and 1597,[84] but this is the last evidence of opposition to the established church until the 19th century. In 1801 the parish was said to have no papists and no dissenters.[85]

In 1831 Independent prayer meetings began to be held on Sunday afternoons in a private house. Five years later an Independent chapel was opened. In 1961 this stood on the Ickenham High Road in front of Ickenham Green. It is built of brick, plastered externally, and the windows are pointed in rough imitation of the Gothic style. Throughout the 19th century the congregation had no minister, and the Ickenham chapel was served from Providence Chapel at Uxbridge.[86] From the time the Ickenham chapel was built a Sunday school was held in an attached schoolroom, which was enlarged in 1921.[87] The first minister was appointed in 1927.[88] The old chapel was then becoming too small and in 1928 a site for a new building on Swakeleys Road was bought.[89] From 1930 until the new church was opened in 1936[90] services were held in the village hall.[91] The old

chapel in the High Road was sold in 1937,[92] and later became a scrap-merchant's store.

After 1947 Spiritualist meetings were held in a temporary building in Swakeleys Road.[93]

EDUCATION. In 1819 there was a Lancasterian school in Ickenham providing clothing and elementary education for 50 children.[94] This was almost certainly the only school in the parish until the foundation of Ickenham Church of England School in 1823 on land belonging to Thomas Truesdale Clarke, who also maintained it.[95] Ten years later this school was described as a fee-paying establishment for 10 boys and 20 girls.[96] By 1846 the children were instructed by a mistress and a schoolroom had been built.[97] A new building was erected by public subscription on part of the waste of Ickenham manor in 1866.[98] Standing on the south side of the modern Ickenham High Road close to the centre of the village,[99] it accommodated 108 children.[1] It was a church school, although not in union with the National Society.[2] In 1873 there were 37 pupils, taught by a salaried mistress who had been given a house adjoining the schoolroom. In addition to elementary subjects the girls were taught needlework. The school was maintained by subscriptions and school pence, any deficiency being met by Thomas Clarke, the owner.[3] The school was still classed as privately owned in 1907.[4]

Other 19th-century schools in the village were short-lived, since they had to compete with large schools in Ruislip and Uxbridge, attended by many Ickenham children.[5] A school for 12 girls founded in 1828, with a lending library attached, was still in existence in 1833 when it was supported by a private individual.[6] After this date, however, no more is heard of it. In 1846 there was a dame school in Ickenham attended by 14 children.[7]

By 1928 Ickenham Church School was overcrowded and the Board of Education hired the village hall to accommodate the older children. The school in the hall was styled the Ickenham Temporary Council School, and although not a church school was under the same headmaster as the old school across the road. In 1929 the site of the old church school was required for road widening and the institution was closed. The older children were transferred to a new building in Long Lane and the village hall was used for infants. Both schools ceased to be church schools and were taken over by the county council. That in Long Lane was styled the Ickenham County Council School; that in the village hall the Ickenham Temporary Council

[76] Kingston, op. cit. 8–9.
[77] Hist. Mon. Com. *Mdx.* 81.
[78] *V.C.H. Surr.* iv. 264. See plate facing p. 36.
[79] Kingston, op. cit. 12.
[80] E. Freshfield, *Communion Plate of Mdx.* 35.
[81] Kingston, op. cit. 7; see below.
[82] See p. 103.
[83] *Mdx. Cnty. Recs.* i. 150.
[84] Ibid. 216–17, 219, 221, 236.
[85] Guildhall MS. 9557.
[86] See p. 92.
[87] L. D. Jarvis, *Free Church Hist. of Uxbridge,* 65–70.
[88] Ibid.
[89] Char. Com. files.
[90] Gen. Reg. Off., Wship. Reg. 56948.
[91] Jarvis, *Free Church Hist.* 65–70.
[92] Char. Com. files.
[93] Ex inf. Ickenham Spiritualist Centre.

[94] *Digest of Rets. on Educ. of Poor,* H.C. 224, p. 538 (1819), ix(1).
[95] Bd. of Educ. *List 32* (1907). Clarke also maintained a school at Uxbridge: see above, p. 95.
[96] *Educ. Enquiry Abstract,* H.C. 62, p. 565 (1833), xlii.
[97] Nat. Soc. *Ret. of Schools* (1846, priv. print).
[98] Letters *penes* the rector.
[99] See p. 101.
[1] *Schs. in receipt of Parl. Grants, 1899* [Cd. 332], H.C. (1900), lxiv.
[2] Nat. Soc. files.
[3] Ed. 7/86.
[4] Bd. of Educ. *List 32* (1907).
[5] *Educ. Enquiry Abstract,* H.C. 62, p. 565 (1833), xlii; Nat. Soc. *Ret. of Schools* (1846, priv. print).
[6] *Educ. Enquiry Abstract,* H.C. 62, p. 565 (1833), xlii.
[7] Nat. Soc. *Ret. of Schools* (1846, priv. print).

School. Both were, for the first few months of their existence, under the same headmaster.[8] In 1937 the infants in the village hall and the juniors at Long Lane were transferred to the new Breakspear Primary Junior and Infant School in Bushey Road. In 1952 the boys from the Ickenham County Council School were transferred to Abbotsfield County Secondary School in Hillingdon[9] and their school building in Long Lane given to the new Swakeleys Secondary Modern Girls School. In 1961 this school had 682 girls on the roll; Breakspear School contained 654 boys and girls. In 1952 a new infant school, the Glebe Primary Junior and Infant School off Glebe Lane, was opened. It had 263 children in 1961.

Ickenham High School for Girls was founded in 1925. Two years later the school bought the old rectory house which it still occupied in 1961. The school then had 150 pupils, mainly girls aged between 4 and 17 years, but also including a few small boys who were given preparatory education.[10]

The Douay Martyrs Secondary Modern Roman Catholic School in Long Lane, designed to accommodate 450 children, was opened in 1962.[11]

CHARITIES FOR THE POOR.[12] In 1806 there were said to be no charities for the poor of Ickenham.[13] Charlotte Gell, by deed dated 1857, founded the Ickenham almshouses for five couples on land given by herself in Back Lane. By her will, proved 1864, she increased the endowment from £3,000 to £4,000 and stipulated that inmates must be members of the Church of England. Preference was to be given to persons who had lived in her own or her husband's family for five years, and then to inhabitants of the parish of Ickenham. In 1897 part of the site was sold. The proceeds were invested in £52 stock and added to the capital endowment, which in 1956 yielded £624. In 1959–60 the almshouses, a gabled range with flint walls and red brick dressings, were repaired and modernized to accommodate 8 almspeople and a warden.[14] Mrs. Gell also left £1,565 stock, the income of which was to be applied to gifts of coal to the poor at Christmas. In 1953 the income amounted to £485, and 10 cwt. of coal were distributed to 24 persons.

In 1892 the Ickenham parish council tried to show that Ickenham Marsh was a charity. The claim was based on a tradition, fifty or more years old, that two women had given the land for each householder in the parish to graze one horse and two cows. The claim was abandoned when no documentary evidence could be adduced in its support.[15]

NORTHOLT

THE ANCIENT parish of Northolt lay to the north-west of Ealing.[1] It had the shape of an irregular triangle lying along a north-east south-west axis approximately 3½ miles in length. In 1871 the parish contained 2,230 a.[2] The northern parish boundaries followed those of Ruislip and Ickenham and of Gore hundred. The Yeading Brook formed the western boundary and the other two sides were bounded by the parishes of Hayes and Southall to the south and Greenford in the east. From at least as early as the 18th century two detached areas of Northolt parish lay in Greenford. The larger area, comprising 47 a. was situated to the west of Greenford village immediately north of the Ruislip road and west of Oldfield Lane. A further 2½ a., called Mill Field in 1775, lay along the southern boundary of Greenford.[3] These detached parts were transferred to Greenford in 1882 and 1887 respectively, and in 1891 the area of Northolt parish was 2,180 a.[4] Northolt formed part of Uxbridge R.D. from 1894 until 1928. On the dissolution of the rural district an area of 100 a. in the extreme north-east of Northolt parish was transferred to Harrow-on-the-Hill U.D. The remainder of Northolt civil parish was absorbed into the municipal borough and civil parish of Ealing, which now forms part of the London Borough of Ealing.[5]

Except for a low ridge which runs in a north-easterly direction from Down Barns to Harrow and reaches more than 150 ft. north-west of Northolt village, most of the parish lies below 125 ft. The old village is sited in a shallow depression between this ridge and further rising ground which inclines gradually north-east to the slope of Harrow Hill. With the exception of two areas of brickearth in the extreme south, the soil is exclusively London Clay.[6]

There appears to have been a settlement at Northolt at least as early as the 8th century. Three burials and several dwellings of the early Saxon period have been found on and near the site later occupied by the medieval manor-house. The archaeological evidence suggests that the earliest settlement was sited on higher ground north-east of the church, and was replaced in the late 13th century, shortly before the first stone manor-house was built, by a settlement in the shallow valley to the west.[7] By 1500 settlement had assumed the pattern which it retained until the topography of the parish was

[8] Ex inf. Alderman A. H. Streets, Uxbridge.
[9] See p. 97.
[10] Ex inf. the principal.
[11] Ex inf. Uxbridge Educ. Office.
[12] Except where otherwise stated this section is based on Char. Com. files.
[13] Guildhall MS. 9557.
[14] Ex inf. Mr. I. Wild; see plate facing p. 152.
[15] See p. 101.
[1] This article was written in 1963. Any references to a later time are dated.
[2] Census, 1871.
[3] King's Coll. Cambridge, Map T. 46; W.A.M., N.

137C; O.S. Map 1/2,500, Mdx. xv. 11 (1865 edn.); V.C.H. Mdx. iii. 206–7.
[4] Census, 1891. See V.C.H. Mdx. iii. 206–7 and corrigenda to vol. iii.
[5] Ex inf. Mdx. Cnty. Council; Census, 1931; see below, p. 119.
[6] Geol. Survey Map, sheet 256 (drift).
[7] Ex inf. Mr. J. G. Hurst; J. G. Hurst, 'The Kitchen area of Northolt Manor', Medieval Archaeology, v. 211–99; C. H. Keene, 'Northolt Manor: an Archaeological & Historical Survey', Greater Ealing Local Hist. Soc., Members' papers no. 1; Anglo-Saxon Charters, ed. A. J. Robertson, 90.

blurred by 20th-century housing development.[8] There appear to have been five distinct areas of settlement in the medieval parish. Northolt village itself lay around a small green dominated by the church and manor-house complex sited on rising ground to the east. North of the village a small settlement called Eliots Green developed around the house known in the Middle Ages as Ruislips Place and later as Islips.[9] In the west of the parish the hamlet of West End was situated about ¼ mile south of the manor-house of Down. It seems possible that in the early Middle Ages a second settlement may have been sited immediately south of the Down manor site, but there is no evidence of its existence after the 15th century.[10] The smaller hamlet of Wood End in the extreme north-east seems to have grown up around the capital messuage of a freehold estate held from the 13th century by the Hospital of St. Thomas of Acon.[11] In the south-east corner of the parish the settlement of Goslings End (later Elm) centred on the junction of the roads from West End to Greenford (later Ruislip Road) and that running from Northolt to Greenford (now Kensington Road).

Apart from these roads and internal networks in the settlement areas, there seem to have been only four ancient roads of any importance. Sharvel or Charville Lane or Riggeway, running from Uxbridge to Harrow, crossed the Yeading Brook in the extreme north-west corner of the parish by Golding or Golden Bridge which was out of repair in 1504.[12] The road then ran parallel to the parish boundary, passing the north-west of Northolt village, until it left the parish in the extreme north-east corner. It was bisected east of Down manor by Ruislip Road running from West End to Ruislip. The road from Eastcote, known as Ruislip Way and later as Eastcote Lane, joined Sharvel Lane north of Northolt village, and the settlements of Wood End and Northolt were connected by Northolt or Wood End Lane, which continued to West End and Hayes as Janes Street.

Almost the whole of the parish west of Northolt village was covered by the open fields. Although a number of field names—Wood End Field, Sharpe's Field, Dowders Field, Priors Field—are mentioned in the 15th and 16th centuries in connection with smaller areas, or without any exact geographical location,[13] there appear to have been at all later periods six principal fields. About 1700 these covered approximately 900 a. Great or Church Field, comprising about 435 a., lay south and west of Northolt village. Mill Post Field (90 a.) lay in the south-east corner of the parish, and was adjoined to the west by Tunlow Field (115 a.). West End Field (112 a.) covered the area bounded by Janes Street, Ruislip Road, and Sharvel Lane. Hollow Field (68 a.) and Batsey or Batcher Field (63 a.) to the east lay north of Sharvel Lane.[14] Parts of Great and Tunlow fields, and the whole of West End lay within the manor of Down.[15]

Between the 15th and 16th centuries the topography of the parish remained substantially unchanged. Small areas of the waste and village greens were inclosed from the early 16th century onwards.[16] By 1700 there is evidence that the old pattern of open-field arable cultivation was being replaced by inclosure for pasture and hay farming. The large farm-houses of Court, Moat, and Down Barns farms all dated from the early 18th century.[17] By the early 19th century sections of Sharvel Lane, which in 1754 was shown as a continuous road,[18] were under cultivation, and much of the remainder served only as field access paths.[19] A further 700 a. were inclosed in 1835 under an Act of 1825,[20] and the transition to large-scale hay farming continued slowly. The opening in 1801 of the Paddington branch of the Grand Union Canal, which followed the 100-foot contour across the south-east corner of Northolt, did little to alter the rural character of the parish as a whole. The population was temporarily augmented after about 1830 by labourers working the brickearth deposits along the canal, and several new houses were built at West End. Many of the brickworkers left after the industry declined in the 1860s, and there were fewer inhabited houses in 1881 than there had been forty years earlier.[21] Between 1837 and 1937 only three houses were erected at West End, and the area to the north-east of the hamlet was in 1845 said to be one of the remotest areas in Middlesex.[22] As late as 1896, apart from the localized brick industry in the south, Northolt was still a lightly populated agricultural parish with five compact settlements and only isolated farm-houses elsewhere.[23]

An inadequate water supply and the poor state of the roads were the chief reasons advanced during the 19th century for the slow pace of development. The road from Harrow to Wood End was in the 1890s known alternatively as Love or Mud Lane, and during the early 20th century the parish council frequently complained to the rural district authorities about the condition of roads in Northolt.[24] Until 1791, when a well was sunk near the vicarage, Northolt village seems to have had no spring water.[25] Piped water was not brought to the village until 1898, and the supply remained inadequate until the 1920s.[26] By 1914 the village also had gas street-lighting, and electricity supplied by the Uxbridge and District Supply Co.[27] In 1903 the Great Western Railway Co. opened a loop line which

---

[8] This section is based on W.A.M., N. 1–16 (Northolt Ct. Rolls, 1461–1748) and N. 130 (terrier of lands of Edith Attewoode, 1489).
[9] See p. 115. Some 13th-cent. pottery was found when Eliots Green Farm (a 17th-cent. building) was demolished in 1954: ex inf. Mr. C. H. Keene.
[10] W.A.M., N. 2.
[11] See p. 115.
[12] W.A.M., N. 2.
[13] Ibid. 1–5.
[14] Ibid. 120, 134; Par. Recs., Matthew Hart Survey.
[15] M.R.O., Acc. 180/564.
[16] W.A.M., N. 3, 5, 8, 9.
[17] Ibid. 131; Par. Recs., Matthew Hart Survey, 1700, 1760; J. Rocque, Map of Mdx. (1754); Hist. Mon. Com. Mdx. 98.

[18] Rocque, Map of Mdx. Golden Bridge is mentioned as late as 1780: M.R.O., Acc. 180/567.
[19] M.R.O., Northolt Incl. Map (1835).
[20] W.A.M., N. 141, 143.
[21] Census, 1841–81.
[22] E. C. Willatts, Mdx. & the Lond. Region, 209; Robson, Home Cnties. Dir. (1845).
[23] Thorne, Environs of Lond. 452; O.S. Maps 1/2,500, Mdx. x. 15; xv. 1, 2, 3, 5, 6 (1895–6 edn.).
[24] H. J. Foley, Our Lanes & Meadowpaths, 89; Northolt Par. Council Mins. 1894–1928 penes Ealing Bor. Council.
[25] Lysons, Environs of Lond. iii. 307.
[26] Par. Council Mins.: a pump installed on the Green in 1873 was still in use during the 1920s.
[27] Ibid.; Electric Lighting Orders Confirmation (no. 7) Act, 1903, copy penes Ealing Bor. Council.

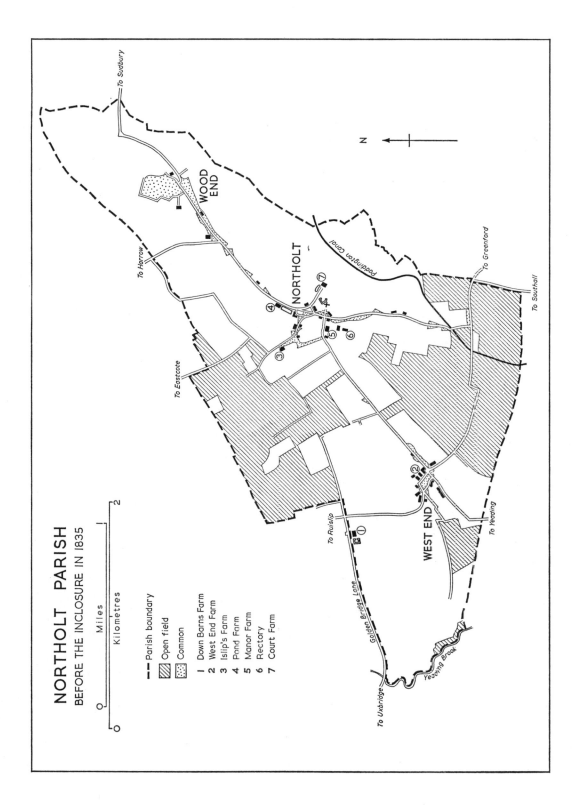

NORTHOLT PARISH
BEFORE THE INCLOSURE IN 1835

Miles
Kilometres

- - - Parish boundary
Open field
Common

1 Down Barns Farm
2 West End Farm
3 Islip's Farm
4 Pond Farm
5 Manor Farm
6 Rectory
7 Court Farm

To Sudbury
WOOD END
To Harrow
NORTHOLT
To Eastcote
To Ruislip
Golden Bridge Lane
To Uxbridge
Yeading Brook
WEST END
To Yeading
To Southall
To Greenford
Paddington Canal

N

connected the High Wycombe and Birmingham main lines and bisected the parish north of Northolt village. A halt at Northolt was opened in 1907,[28] and this was rebuilt as Northolt Station in 1948 when the Central line was extended from Greenford to West Ruislip along the G.W.R. route.[29] The Great Central Railway's passenger line to High Wycombe, passing across the north-east corner of the parish, was opened in 1906. A station at Northolt, initially called South Harrow and Roxeth Station, was opened in 1926, and renamed Northolt Park Station in 1929.[30]

Despite the provision of these amenities there was little residential development until the sale of the Manor Farm and Hillingdon Court estates in 1920 opened the way for the first speculative building.[31] In 1928 Northolt became part of the borough of Ealing and the pace of development accelerated.[32] A pony-racing track at Northolt Park was opened in 1929.[33] Western Avenue, running from east to west through the centre of the parish, was opened in 1934 and by 1936 two trunk roads—Whitton Avenue and Mandeville Road—had been driven across the north of the parish and Yeading Lane and Church Road widened to complete the network of arterial roads. Extensive ribbon development followed, and other areas developed by speculative builders before 1939 included former open-field land lying immediately west of Northolt village, and the area between Mandeville Road and Whitton Avenue to the north. The first Northolt planning scheme appeared in 1937,[34] and the first industrial premises in Rowdell and Belvue roads were established in the same year.[35] Further building was halted by the outbreak of the Second World War. After 1945 Northolt was extensively developed as a dormitory area for the borough of Ealing. Only 52 council dwellings were erected at Northolt between 1928 and 1939, but by 1946 building had begun on five council estates, the largest of which, together accommodating 442 housing units, were the South-East Northolt and Bridge Farm estates in the old brick-field area. In 1946 the borough council acquired the 124-acre Northolt Park estate, and building began there in 1951. By 1963 1,084 of the planned 1,150 housing units on this estate, including a number of multi-story flat blocks, had been completed.[36] Other council estates begun since 1949 include the Northolt Grange (1951), Medlar Farm (1949), and Lime Trees (1951) estates in the West End area, and the Fair View estate (1953) west of Eastcote Lane. By 1963 the council had built about 3,423 housing units in the area. This represented more than one-half of the total dwellings erected in Ealing Borough since 1945.

Twentieth-century expansion transformed the old pattern of distinct and autonomous settlements into a peripheral district of the borough of Ealing. In 1958 Moat Farm, the last of the 17th- and early-18th-century farm-houses, was demolished to make way for private housing developments, and no important domestic buildings of pre-19th-century date now survive. The 'Plough' and 'Crown' at Northolt and the 'White Hart' at West End were all licensed by 1746,[37] but all have been extensively modernized or rebuilt. By 1963 almost the entire area north of Western Avenue had been built over, with the exception of a wireless station in Wood End Lane (established c. 1926) and Belvue Park which includes the site of the medieval manor-house to the north-east of the parish church. To the west of the churchyard, where the ground falls away to a small stream, the remnants of Northolt Green have been preserved to give the old village centre an almost rural character.[38] Overlooking the green are the former church school, the Crown Inn, and, mixed with modern development, several houses and cottages of the earlier 19th century. Willow Cottages, a single-storied pair now used as sheds in a small public garden, were first mentioned in 1817.[39] The district of former open-field land to the south and west remains less heavily built over. A belt of predominantly agricultural land extends from Western Avenue to the Yeading Brook, and includes the West London Shooting Grounds west of the Down manor site. Lime Tree Park, lying west of Church Road, and Rectory Park, north of Ruislip Road, comprise the bulk of the 150 a. developed by the municipal authority as sports and recreation grounds. A further area lying between Kensington Road and Western Avenue was leased to Kensington Borough in 1938 for use as playing-fields. Areas of agricultural and undeveloped land, interspersed with small estates of prefabricated houses and pre-1939 residential building, give the south of the parish an unplanned appearance.[40] Nevertheless, Northolt in 1963 was a typical suburban, residential parish, with few local industries and a population chiefly employed in London or by industrial concerns in adjoining parishes.

The Domesday Survey mentions 32 people at Northolt. Twenty-two of these were described as villeins, but the size of their holdings varied considerably. There was one single-hide holding, another 5 villeins each had half a hide, 8 held a virgate each, and a further 8 half a virgate each. In addition there was a priest on half a hide, 3 cottars, and 6 serfs.[41] For a muster of c. 1335 Northolt was expected to contribute 30 footmen under 3 officers, or approximately $\frac{1}{30}$ of the total county force.[42] Twenty-seven persons were taxed for the subsidy of 1522-3,[43] and there were 100 communicants in 1547.[44] Ninety adult male parishioners took the protestation oath in 1642,[45] and in 1664 there were 54 occupied houses, as well as the church-house, which was inhabited by five widows.[46] Lists of 1659,

[28] W.A.M., N. 85; T. B. Peacock, *G.W. Suburban Services*, 45.
[29] Ex inf. London Transport Exec.
[30] Ex inf. Mr. H. V. Borley.
[31] W.A.M., N. 115; Partics. of Sale *penes* Ealing libr.
[32] Section based on information supplied by Ealing Bor. Council.
[33] See p. 117.
[34] Ealing (Northolt) Planning Scheme, copy *penes* Ealing Bor. Council.
[35] See p. 117.
[36] *Mdx. Cnty. Times*, 2 Feb. 1957.

[37] M.R.O., L.V. 6/84. The 'Plough' has been completely resited.
[38] See plate facing p. 105.
[39] C. H. Keene, 'Willow Cottages', *Northolt Vanguard* (par. mag.), Sept. 1964.
[40] In 1963 much of this land was scheduled for development as an extensive housing estate.
[41] *V.C.H. Mdx.* i. 126.
[42] M.R.O., F. 37/6.
[43] E 179/141/115.   [44] E 301/34/186.
[45] Hse. of Lords, Mdx. Protestation Rets.
[46] M.R.O., H.T.6.

1666, and 1669 enumerate about 60 free and copy-hold tenants, of whom approximately one half were said to be living out of the manor.[47]

The growth of Northolt's population from 336 in 1801 to 658 in 1861 was due largely to the influx of labourers which followed the establishment of the brick-making industry. Migration of workers after the closure of some of the brick-fields during the 1860s had reduced the population to 479 in 1871. Until the 1920s there was little significant increase. But between 1921 and 1931, although the area of the civil parish had been reduced after its incorporation into Ealing Municipal Borough, the population jumped from 904 to 3,047. Since 1945 development of the parish as a middle-class dormitory area has continued steadily; in 1951 the population of North-olt ward, covering an area considerably smaller than the ancient parish, was 19,201, and by 1961 it had reached 25,897.[48]

Most of the notable residents of Northolt have been either incumbents or lords of the manor, and are noticed briefly below.[49] Goronwy Owen (1723–69), the Welsh poet and first Secretary of the Cymmro-dorion Society of London, was Curate of Northolt from 1755 to 1758.[50] Stephen Demainbray (1710–82), who discovered the influence of electricity in stimu-lating the growth of plants and was astronomer at the Kew observatory from 1768 to 1782, is buried at Northolt.[51] Several writers have attempted to prove that John Hart (d. 1585), Chester Herald and author of two books on English phonetics, belonged to the Hart family which was living at Northolt as early as 1460. This identification has been doubted, and the available evidence is inconclusive.[52]

MANORS AND OTHER ESTATES. In 1086 *NORTHOLT* was held by Geoffrey de Mandeville and in the time of King Edward it had belonged to Ansgar the Staller.[53] The estate of fifteen hides, of which eight were in demesne, recorded in Domesday Book seems likely to have comprised most of the ancient parish. There is no mention in the Survey of subsidiary estates nor of the manor later known as Down or Down Barns.[54]

The Mandeville family retained Northolt until some time between 1227 and 1230, when Maud, daughter of Geoffrey Fitz Peter, Earl of Essex (d. 1213), alienated it to Thomas d'Eu or de Augo. In 1231 D'Eu released the manor to Peter Botiler (*Pincerna*) at a yearly rent of one pound of pepper.[55] Northolt then descended in the Botiler family[56] until 1339, when Stephen Botiler leased the manor at an annual rent of twenty marks to John Russell, the

first of a succession of London merchants to acquire the estate.[57] Stephen Botiler quitclaimed the mano to Russell in 1342;[58] the significance of the trans-action is uncertain, however, since in the same year William, Stephen's brother, quitclaimed an estate called the manor of Northolt to Geoffrey de Wychingham, later Sheriff and Mayor of London.[59] Wychingham acquired other interests in the manor from Stephen Botiler in 1346[60] and from John Waleys of Great Waltham (Essex) in 1343.[61]

John Russell released the manor to Simon Francis, another London merchant, in 1346,[62] and in 1352 Agnes, Russell's widow, surrendered her rights of dower to Francis.[63] In 1355 Simon Francis caused Northolt to be released to himself and one Thomas Loughtborough.[64] On Francis's death in 1357 Northolt, which was then worth, as it had been in 1086, £5 a year, passed to his son Thomas,[65] and on his death in 1368 to Alice, his widow, for life with reversion to Thomas's sister, also called Alice, who was married to Sir Thomas Travers.[66] The manor was mortgaged several times between 1368 and 1370;[67] and in 1370 the Sheriff of Middlesex instituted an enquiry into the sale and destruction of the manor-house and lands by Alice Francis.[68]

During the 1370s Nicholas Brembre, several times Mayor and Sheriff of London, gained control of the capital estate by acquiring the interests of Thomas Loughtborough and of the Travers family.[69] Brembre continued to hold the manor until he was convicted of treason in 1388. After his execution his wife Idony was permitted to retain his estate and to purchase the moveables forfeit to the Crown.[70] By this date the manorial demesnes of Northolt and Down comprised in all 595 a.,[71] together with land and rents in Stickleton and Greenford.[72] Idony Brembre probably continued to hold Northolt until after 1390, but the manor seems to have changed hands several times before 1396,[73] when it was rati-fied in the possession of Sir Richard Waldegrave, Speaker of the House of Commons, and others.[74] Three years later the Crown's claim to the forfeited estate was exercised, and Northolt was granted in free alms to Westminster Abbey.[75] The abbey retained possession of the estate until 1540.

No leases of the manor are recorded before 1489, and it seems probable that the abbey farmed the estate directly. From 1489 to 1540 Northolt was leased to one or more lessees at an annual farm of £15 8s. Fines and perquisites of court were always reserved to the abbot.[76] In 1535 woods in the manor were valued at £1 and perquisites of courts at 16s. 6d.[77] By 1540–1 the value of the manor had increased slightly.[78]

[47] W.A.M., N. 22–24.
[48] *Census*, 1801–1961.
[49] See pp. 113–14, 120.
[50] *D.N.B.; Dict. Welsh Biog.* 704.
[51] *D.N.B.*
[52] B. Danielsson, *John Hart, Chester Herald* (1958); cf. E. J. D. Obson, *English Pronunciation 1500–1700* (1957), ii. 1023.
[53] *V.C.H. Mdx.* i. 126.   [54] See below.
[55] C.P. 25(1)/146/8/78; *Bk. of Fees*, i. 474.
[56] *Feudal Aids*, iii. 373; *Cal. Close*, 1337–9, 238, 279, 386, 403; C.P. 25(1)/150/55/63.
[57] W.A.M., 386; B.M. Add. Ch. 7559.
[58] W.A.M., 405.   [59] Ibid. 384.
[60] C.P. 25(1)/150/61/216; W.A.M., 385, 390.
[61] C.P. 25(1)/150/59/175.
[62] W.A.M., 362.

[63] *Cal. Close*, 1349–54, 468; W.A.M., 392; N. 20.
[64] W.A.M., 392; C.P. 25(1)/150/66/343.
[65] C 135/140/6.
[66] W.A.M., 392; C.P. 25(1)/151/71/461.
[67] W.A.M., 366, 367, 399, 415.
[68] Ibid. 416; see below.
[69] W.A.M., 363, 365, 415; C.P. 25(1)/151/77/73; B.M. Add. Ch. 1658, 7558; *Cal. Close*, 1374–7, 358; *Cal. Chart. R.* 1341–1417, 231.
[70] *Cal. Pat.* 1385–9, 481; *Cal. Close*, 1385–9, 580.
[71] C 145/243/5.
[72] C.P. 25(1)/151/80/145.   [73] Ibid.
[74] *Cal. Pat.* 1391–6, 690.
[75] W.A.M., 7579; *Cal. Chart R.* 1341–1417, 376, 378.
[76] W.A.M., 394, 396; Reg. Bks. i, ii.
[77] *Valor Eccl.* (Rec. Com.), i. 417.
[78] S.C. 6/Hen. VIII/2415, m. 19d.

In January 1540 the abbey surrendered its estates to Henry VIII.[79] A year later Northolt was granted to Thomas Thirlby, Bishop of Westminster, as part of the endowment of the new bishopric.[80] In 1550 Thirlby, who had fallen into disfavour, surrendered his bishopric to Edward VI,[81] and the king granted Northolt, together with other manors included in the endowment, to Sir Thomas Wroth, a gentleman of the Bedchamber.[82] Members of the Wroth family continued to hold the manor until 1616 when the executors of Sir Robert Wroth conveyed Northolt to Sir John Bennet, a master of the Court of Chancery and Judge of the Prerogative Court of Canterbury.[83] In 1622 Bennet sold the manor to William Pennifather, Sheriff of London,[84] who in 1638 conveyed it to John Hulse.[85] Hulse died in 1653 leaving an only daughter, Lettice, who, under a marriage settlement made in 1647, became entitled to the property subject to the life interest of Elizabeth her mother.[86] Lettice, who had married Charles Goode of Malden (Surr.), died without issue in 1667. Her mother, remarried to Christopher Eyre, died in 1675, so that Charles Goode, despite the attempts of the Hulse family to deprive him,[87] succeeded to the reversion. Between 1675 and 1700 Goode frequently mortgaged the estate,[88] and in 1701 it passed to John Walker, Clerk Assistant of the House of Lords.[89] On Walker's death in 1715 Northolt was purchased by James Brydges, Earl of Carnarvon (later Duke of Chandos). He conveyed the manor to William Peere Williams, a Chancery lawyer, in 1722 and Williams's son, Sir Hutchins Williams, sold the property to Agatha Child, a member of the London banking family, in 1756.[90] The Childs continued to hold Northolt until 1804 when Sarah Sophia Fane married George Villiers, Earl of Jersey.[91] In 1827 Villiers sold Northolt manor, which then comprised only 269 a.,[92] to Sir Lancelot Shadwell, last Vice-Chancellor of England.[93] The manor remained in the hands of the Shadwell family[94] until the estate was split up and sold for building purposes during the early 20th century.[95]

Archaeological excavation on a moated site north-east of Northolt church, started in 1950, has revealed much of the structure of the medieval manor-house.[96] The neck of land which later formed the manor site appears to have been occupied at least as early as the 8th century. A moat was probably dug shortly after 1300, and enlarged later in the century when the first stone buildings were erected. In 1370

an inquiry was instituted into the partial demolition of the manor-house by Alice, widow of Thomas Francis. She was alleged to have dismantled and sold the timbers of a hall and inner court, four chambers, a grange, and a cattle shed, valued in all at more than £250, and to have destroyed oak, apple, and pear trees.[97] Buildings said to have been bought at Northolt were erected on the manor of Sutton (in Chiswick) about 1400.[98] Subsequently the manor-house appears to have been rebuilt on a smaller scale. Substantial repairs and rebuilding, probably to farm buildings adjacent to the manor-house, were effected in the 1530s.[99] The house seems to have been seldom occupied during the 16th century. It was possibly still standing in 1637,[1] but had been demolished by 1718.[2] Late-17th-century references to a manor-house[3] probably refer to a house called Northolt Court at which the manor lord was living in 1653.[4] The site and date of demolition of this building are unknown, but in 1700, when it was still occupied by the lord of the manor, the house was said to stand next to the church.[5] In 1935 the manor site was acquired by the local authority for preservation as an open space, and in 1963 it formed part of Belvue Park.

The origins of the manor of *DOWN* or Down Barns, which covered some 300 a. in the west of Northolt parish, are uncertain. Roger de la Downe (Dune), who is mentioned as early as 1203,[6] held freehold land in Northolt in 1212,[7] assessed at 32s. in 1220.[8] His land is mentioned several times during the 1230s,[9] but the descent of the holding during the later 13th century is obscure. In 1293 Down was in the possession of William de Scaccario.[10] By 1326 the bulk of his estate seems to have been acquired by Ralph Basset of Drayton,[11] who shortly afterwards sold what was henceforth called the manor of Down to John de Bohun, Earl of Hereford and Essex. On Bohun's death in 1336 the manorial demesne comprised 300 a. of arable, 5 a. of meadow, and 20 a. of woodland.[12] The Bassets seem to have retained some interest in the manor since Joan, widow of Ralph Basset, released her rights to one Edmund de Bereford in 1348.[13]

In 1354 Sir Thomas Holland and his wife Joan, later the wife of the Black Prince, sold Down to Simon Francis,[14] who had already purchased Northolt manor.[15] In the following year Francis acquired from Ralph, grandson of Ralph Basset of Drayton, the interest which he had retained in Down.[16] From

[79] *L. & P. Hen. VIII*, xv, p. 24.
[80] Ibid. xvi, p. 243.
[81] Rymer, *Foedera*, xv. 219–20.
[82] W.A.M., N. 58.
[83] C 66/14 Jas. I, no. 44.
[84] C 66/22 Jas. I, no. 48.
[85] C 66/13 Chas. I, no. 32.
[86] B.M. Add. Ch. 1628.
[87] B.M. Add. MS. 11318/7.
[88] B.M. Add. Ch. 1643, 1644, 1646, 1650.
[89] Ibid. 1655.
[90] B.M. Add. MS. 11318/20; W.A.M., N. 65–67.
[91] W.A.M., N. 70, 72; see above, p. 26.
[92] M.R.O., M.L.R. 1828/3/89.
[93] W.A.M., N. 73, 76–79.
[94] Ibid. 80–82, 84, 85.
[95] For partics. of sales in 1879, 1895, 1907, 1919, and 1920 see W.A.M., N. 115.
[96] *V.C.H. Mdx.* ii. 8; C. H. Keene, 'Northolt Manor: an Archaeological and Historical Survey', *Greater Ealing Local Hist. Soc.*, Members' papers no. 1 (1961); J. G. Hurst, 'The Kitchen Area of Northolt Manor', *Medieval Archaeology*, v. 211–99.

[97] W.A.M., 416.
[98] E 101/502/23. The roll is undated. L. F. Salzman, *Building in England down to 1540*, 199, dated it to 1401. He also identified the manor as that of Sutton in Surrey.
[99] W.A.M., 373, 31938.
[1] W.A.M., N. 10.
[2] Bodl. Libr., Rawlinson MSS. D. 896, ff. 2, 3.
[3] B.M. Add. Ch. 1629–1656.
[4] Bodl. Libr., Rawlinson MSS. D. 715.
[5] W.A.M., N. 131; for Islips as a residence of 17th-cent. lords of the manor see p. 115.
[6] C.P. 25(1)/146/3/35; *Cart. of Missenden Abbey, pt. 3* (Bucks. Rec. Soc. xii), 166.
[7] *Red Bk. Exch.* (Rolls Ser.), ii. 543.
[8] *Bk. of Fees*, 1242–93, 1440.
[9] Ibid. 1198–1242, 474; King's Coll., Q. 1, 3; J.I. 1/536, m. 1.
[10] J.I. 1/544, m. 51d.
[11] *Cal. Pat.* 1324–7, 292.
[12] C 135/48/2.
[13] W.A.M., 410.
[14] Ibid. 388.
[15] See above.
[16] B.M. Add. Ch. 19895.

this date until 1616 the descent of Down followed that of Northolt manor.[17] During the lordship of Westminster Abbey, although the two manors submitted a joint account,[18] Down was leased separately at an annual farm of £13 6s. 8d. In 1535 woods in the manor were valued at £3, and perquisites of court at 3s. 4d.[19]

After 1616 the descent of Down is obscure. By 1659 the manor was in the possession of one Samuel Carlton, in whose family it passed until 1717, when it was alienated to Andrew Hawes of Chatham (Kent) and John Harvey of Ickwell Bury in Bedfordshire.[20] Representatives of these two families continued to hold the manor jointly until it was broken up and sold in the early 20th century.[21]

There is little documentary evidence of the existence of a manor-house on the moated site at Down Barns, 1½ mile west of Northolt village.[22] A capital messuage was said to be of no value in 1336.[23] The early manor-house, which was probably in existence before 1388,[24] seems to have been abandoned during the 16th century, and a new house was built east of the moated site. Parts of the Tudor building were incorporated in a farm-house which replaced earlier buildings in the late 17th or early 18th century.[25] This house was demolished in 1954, and a smaller farm-house was built nearby.[26]

The freehold estate later known as *ISLIPS* manor was so named after the Ruislip family who held copy- and freehold land in Northolt as early as 1301.[27] In 1489 the property comprised a house called Ruislips Place, presumably standing north-west of the village on or near the site of the later Islips Manor, 71 a. in the common fields, 54 a. of pasture in six closes, and 9 a. of woodland in the north-east of the parish.[28] The estate passed in the Ruislip family until about 1493, when Christopher Morton, son by her first marriage of Edith Ruislip who had later married John Attewood (d. 1489), a London grocer, succeeded to the estate on the death of his mother.[29] Christopher Morton (d. 1517) was succeeded by his son John. John, son of John Morton, died in 1523 while still a minor, and the copyhold then passed to Margaret King of Hayes, cousin to John Morton the elder. The freehold estate, to which the copyhold lands were never reunited, descended to Catherine, John Morton's widow, who in 1517 married Thomas Roberts (d. c. 1543), a counsellor to the Abbot of Westminster. The estate, referred to as Ruislips and comprising a house and orchard, 20 a. of pasture, and 60 a. of common-field arable, passed on Thomas Roberts's death to his son Michael (d. 1544), and then to Michael's brother Edmund, subject to the life interest of Michael's widow Ursula (d. by 1565). Edmund

Roberts sold his reversionary interest in 1565 to Alan Horde of Ewell in Surrey, who shortly afterwards sold the estate to John Gifford of Northolt.[30] It then descended in the Gifford family until 1629 when William Pennifather, lord of Northolt manor, purchased the bulk of the Islips estate from William Gifford.[31] The descent of Islips subsequently followed that of Northolt manor[32] until about 1690 when Charles Goode sold the estate to Charles Hawtrey of Ruislip. During the late 17th century the house, referred to variously as Islips or Gifford's Farm, seems to have served as a manor-house to Northolt manor, and in consequence the estate was frequently styled a manor.[33]

The descent of Islips during the early 18th century is obscure. By 1740 it was in the possession of John Gibson, later Vicar of Heston. Successive members of the Gibson family held the estate until 1853[34] when it was sold to the antiquary George Harris.[35] The property then comprised the house and garden and 123 a.[36] The house, thereafter called Islips Manor, was rebuilt in 1865. Harris devised Islips to his wife who died in 1895, and the estate then passed to her cousin George Innes. Members of the Innes family leased out the estate until 1927. It was then sold to Robert Rowles, who in the following year sold the whole estate to Ealing Borough Council.[37] The house has since been used as a clinic and the bulk of the estate turned into recreation grounds.

The estate known in the Middle Ages as Le Freres or Frere Place[38] and later as Wood End Green Farm originated in an early-13th-century grant of freehold in Northolt to the Hospital of St. Thomas of Acon. The Hospital's Northolt property was valued at £4 11s. in 1291.[39] After 1521 the estate was leased to Thomas Turner who was also farming Northolt manor from Westminster Abbey.[40] At the Reformation the estate called Frere Place, which then comprised a farm-house, about 120 a. lying in the north-east of Northolt parish, and 25 a. in the common fields, together with land in Harrow and Greenford, was alienated by the Crown to Richard Andrews and Leonard Chamberlain of Woodstock (Oxon.).[41] In 1542 Andrews and Chamberlain sold Frere Place to John Thornton who had farmed Northolt manor from Westminster Abbey.[42] Subsequently the estate, which seems to have remained fairly constant at between 90 and 100 a., passed rapidly through a succession of owners including members of the Gerard and other Harrow families, and, in the early 20th century, to W. H. Perkin, the Greenford chemist.[43] From about 1800 the estate was known consistently as Wood End Green Farm.[44] When the Perkin estates were sold in 1907 the farm comprised a

[17] See above.
[18] W.A.M., 394, 400, 401, 33269–79.
[19] *Valor Eccl.* (Rec. Com.), i. 417.
[20] M.R.O., Acc. 180/561–5.
[21] Ibid. /566–70.
[22] *V.C.H. Mdx.* ii. 8.
[23] C 135/48/2.
[24] *Cal. Pat.* 1385–9, 481.
[25] Hist. Mon. Com. *Mdx.* 98; a brick from the house, dated 1754, was found by Mr. C. H. Keene and deposited in Wembley museum.
[26] Ex inf. Mr. C. H. Keene.
[27] W.A.M., N. 126; C.P. 25(1)/149/39/1; /149/42/97; /150/59/173.
[28] W.A.M., N. 130. For a description and analysis of this terrier, and details of the descent of Islips see C. H. Keene, 'A History of Islips Manor Estate', copy *penes* Ealing libr.

[29] W.A.M., N. 1, 2.
[30] Ibid. 2–5, 90b.
[31] Ibid. 5–9.
[32] See p. 114.
[33] W.A.M., N. 9–14.
[34] Ibid. 90b.
[35] Deeds to Islips estate *penes* Ealing Bor. Council.
[36] O.S. Bk of Reference to Northolt Plan (1865).
[37] Deeds to Islips estate *penes* Ealing Bor. Council.
[38] W.A.M., N. 130.
[39] *Tax. Eccl.* (Rec. Com.), 13.
[40] S.C. 6/Hen. VIII/2396, m. 8.
[41] *L. & P. Hen. VIII*, xvii, p. 259.
[42] Ibid. p. 320; see above, p. 114.
[43] *Cal. Pat.* 1563–6, 3; W.A.M., N. 131, 132, 115.
[44] W.A.M., 115, 132; M.R.O., Northolt Tithe Award.

substantial house and outbuildings, with approximately 90 a. of land lying between Wood End Lane and the parish boundary.[45] During the period 1920–39 the estate was broken up and sold for building, and by 1963 the farm-house had been demolished and the area completely covered by houses.

ECONOMIC AND SOCIAL HISTORY. Until the 19th century Northolt was almost exclusively an agricultural community. There seems to have been no other industry in the parish until after the opening of the Paddington Canal in 1801, and there was no corn-mill.

The manorial demesne in 1086 was assessed at 8 hides on which there were two ploughs. The villeins shared a further six ploughs, with room for two more. There was pasture for the cattle of the vill, and the woodland was sufficient to support 200 pigs.[46] After the Domesday Survey there is no information about the inhabitants or their land until the early 14th century. In 1336 the manorial demesne of Down consisted of 300 a. of arable, 5 a. of meadow, and 20 a. of woodland worth 10s. a year.[47] In 1388 the demesnes of Northolt and Down together comprised 595 a., including 320 a. of arable, of which 160 a. were sown with corn, and 240 a. of pasture. At this time the agrarian practice on the two manors was almost identical. The chief crops were wheat, oats, and beans, with the addition of peas at Northolt. Both manors supported substantial numbers of sheep—362 at Northolt, 393 at Down—as well as domestic and draught animals. The inventory of each manor included two ploughs. Northolt was valued at £57 and Down at £62.[48]

After the manors passed to Westminster Abbey in 1399, nothing is known of their economy until 1492 when the demesnes of Northolt and Down were leased separately at an annual farm of £15 8s. and £13 6s. 8d. respectively.[49] Oats from Northolt were delivered to Westminster in the early 16th century,[50] and in 1534 the abbey paid for the erection of new farm buildings on the manor.[51] A year later the two manors were together valued at £34.[52]

Regulations governing the use of the open fields and the conditions of copyhold tenure were repeated in the manor courts of Northolt and Down at intervals during the 16th and 17th centuries. Copyholders were entitled to fell timber on their land, and to lease their land for three years without leave. They were liable for the maintenance of gates, and to observe the regulations governing the pasturing of cattle, geese, and sheep on the common fields, the ringing of hogs, and the gathering of acorns.[53] The pattern of arable farming probably remained substantially unchanged throughout the 17th century, although small areas of the waste and village greens were inclosed from the early 16th century onwards.[54]

By 1700 there is evidence that the demands of the London market were resulting in changes in the agrarian economy. Inclosure for intensive hay farming seems to have replaced the old pattern of open-field cultivation in some areas during the early 18th century.[55] In 1801, however, there were still 257 a. of wheat, 206 a. of beans, and 128 a. of peas in the parish.[56] Changes in the pattern of land utilization continued slowly after the inclosure under the 1835 award of about 700 a. of the parish, including almost 600 a. in the open fields.[57] Much of the inclosed land was turned over to hay for the London market, and by 1876 most of the parish was said to be in grass.[58] In 1834[59] the average wage of an agricultural labourer in the parish was 10s.–12s. a week. Women and children were employed in summer in bird-scaring and haymaking. Labourers from Ireland and Oxford also helped with the haymaking.[60] This annual influx continued after 1900, and William Crees, who farmed Court Farm from 1900 to 1919, commented on the absence of mechanization and the general backwardness of farming methods in Northolt at this time. By introducing new methods, including manuring with London refuse brought by barge up the Paddington Canal, Crees built up a neglected stock farm into a prominent milk-producing establishment.[61] After 1920, however, building developments began to encroach on the agricultural land, and several 18th-century farm-houses were demolished to make way for speculative building.[62] Development was halted temporarily by the Second World War, but after 1945 a number of council estates further diminished the area available for agriculture. In 1963 farming on a limited scale was practised only in the west of the parish between Western Avenue and the Yeading Brook.

Exploitation of brickearth deposits in the south of the parish followed the opening of the Paddington Canal, and the first licence to dig brickearth was granted in 1834.[63] By 1851 there were 55 brick-workers living in the parish,[64] and four years later the Northolt field was described as 'extensive.'[65] During the 1860s, however, some of the brickearth deposits were becoming worked out, and the industry suffered a temporary decline. Two of the three brick-fields near the canal were described as 'old' in 1865,[66] and more than 150 labourers engaged in brick-making left the parish between 1861 and 1871.[67] By 1876 quantities of superior quality Northolt bricks were being despatched by barge from a specially constructed wharf for use in the construction of London sewers.[68] Improved brick-making methods were introduced in the late 19th century by the New Patent Brick Co., which until 1901 worked a field between Ruislip and the canal. The premises, sold in 1901, covered approximately 35 a., and included machine and engine rooms, a German kiln, and wharf on the canal. The field was then said

[45] W.A.M., 115.
[46] V.C.H. Mdx. i. 126.
[47] C 135/48/2.
[48] C 145/243/5; Cal. Pat. 1385–9, 481.
[49] W.A.M., 394, 396, 400, 401.
[50] Ibid. 32205.
[51] Ibid. 32017.
[52] Valor Eccl. (Rec. Com), i. 417.
[53] M.R.O., Acc. 180/562,/565; W.A.M., N. 5, 12, 14, 15.
[54] W.A.M., N. 3, 5, 8, 9.
[55] Ibid. 131; Par. Recs., Matthew Hart Survey, 1700, 1760.
[56] H.O. 67/16.

[57] W.A.M., N. 141, 143.
[58] Thorne, Environs of Lond. 452.
[59] Rep. Poor Law Com. App. B(2), H.C. 44, p. 165h (1834), xxxvi.
[60] Census, 1841.
[61] MS. Diary of F. W. Crees penes his daughters.
[62] See p. 112.
[63] W.A.M., Northolt Ct. Min Bk.
[64] H.O. 107/656.
[65] Kelly's Dir. Mdx. (1845).
[66] O.S. Map 1/2,500, Mdx. xv. 6 (1865 edn.).
[67] Census, 1861, 1871.
[68] Thorne, Environs of Lond. 452.

to be capable of producing ten million bricks yearly; but this estimate was probably exaggerated.[69] By the beginning of the 20th century the local brickearth was becoming worked out, although smaller concerns—the West End and Middlesex Brick companies, the Southern Brick and Tile Works, and the Northolt Brick Works—continued to operate until the final closure in 1939.[70]

Outside the brick-fields only a few firms in the parish appear to have employed a labour force of more than one hundred. The Greenford Dye Works at West End and a factory manufacturing patent leather are mentioned in 1918,[71] but both seem to have closed after a short time and no further trace of the premises can be found. In 1936 Gaumont British Pictures opened a temporary film studio off Eastcote Lane. No substantial industry was established in Northolt until 1937 when the Walter Kidde Co. and Tampax Ltd. occupied the first of a group of new premises in Belvue Road on the west side of the canal. The Walter Kidde Co., engaged in the manufacture of fire protection equipment, then employed a labour force of about fifty. The firm's premises were considerably extended during the 1950s, and the number of employees had increased to about 500 by 1963.[72] At this date the premises formerly occupied by Tampax Ltd. were being used as a Metropolitan Police store. Although other small industries, chiefly light mechanical and electrical engineering concerns, have been established since 1937, forming a small complex near the canal in Belvue Road and the adjoining Rowdell Road, they are not on a sufficient scale to affect the predominantly residential character of the parish.

Part of the former brick-field area on the border with Southall parish was purchased in 1940 by Taylor Woodrow Ltd., a large civil and mechanical engineering concern who had erected offices on the Southall bank of the Paddington Canal in 1934. Offices in Northolt were built in 1954 at the junction of Ruislip Road and Adrienne Avenue. A further office block was built on the west side of the canal in 1958, and the two blocks were connected over the canal by a two-story building erected in 1960.[73] Population growth has been accompanied by very little growth of industry, and only a limited provision of social amenities. In 1922 there was only one shop in the parish.[74] No theatre or cinema had been established by 1963, and for entertainment and shops, as well as for employment, Northolt remains partially dependent on neighbouring areas.

Details of social life before the 20th century are almost entirely lacking. Until communications with London were established by the cutting of the Paddington Canal in 1801 Northolt was remote and largely unaffected by outside influences. A bowling-alley near the churchyard is mentioned in 1661,[75] but during the 17th and 18th centuries information on recreational activities is limited to those enjoyed

by lords of the manor. In 1722 Northolt was advertised as an outstanding manor for game, and as including several large fish ponds stocked with perch, carp, and tench.[76]

The opening of the canal in 1801 and the coming of the brick-making industry introduced new elements into the social life of the parish. During the 19th century workers bathed in the canal, and a scheme to hold a fair on the village green was rejected in 1899 on the ground that it would attract undesirable people.[77] After 1900 the parish was developed increasingly as a recreation area for the metropolis. Between 1900 and 1920 the West London Shooting Grounds were established on land to the south-west of Down manor site, point-to-point races were held at Court Farm, and the Middlesex draghounds also met there.[78] In 1929 pony racing was started over a $1\frac{1}{2}$-mile course opened at Northolt Park, between the L.N.E.R. and G.W.R. lines. The venture was financed by the Northolt Racecourse Co., which had been formed in 1928 for the purpose of concentrating pony racing at one track. Extensive cantilever stands were built, and other facilities added during the 1930s included an electric totalizator, a totalizator stand, and an artificial watering system for softening the course. For a time the track was extremely popular;[79] the course was extended in 1935 by the addition of a bridge over Dabbs Hill Lane; and a meeting was televised in 1938. Racing ceased shortly after the outbreak of the Second World War, and the course was taken over as an ordnance depot. Plans to reopen the course after the war did not materialize, and in 1946 the 124-acre estate was purchased by Ealing Borough Council. The stands were demolished in 1950, and the area has since become a housing estate.[80]

LOCAL GOVERNMENT. At the end of the 13th century Peter Botiler claimed various liberties in his manor of Northolt, including view of frankpledge and the assize of bread and ale. Similar liberties were claimed by William de Scaccario in the manor of Down.[81] No Northolt court rolls appear to have survived from before 1461,[82] but after this date the series is substantially unbroken until manorial courts were discontinued in 1919.[83]

From 1461 until the 1520s it was customary for the lord of Northolt to hold courts leet and baron annually in October. During the 16th and 17th centuries this annual meeting normally took place in April or May. The activities of the leet declined during the 18th century, and the court met with increasing irregularity until the last leet was held in 1828. Courts baron and special courts baron continued to meet, with varying regularity, until 1919.[84]

In 1461 the lord of Northolt and Down was exercising a leet jurisdiction over what were called the manors of Greenford, Perivale, and Ickenham.[85]

[69] Plan and advertisements of sale *penes* Ealing libr.; *The Times*, 17 Nov. 1901.
[70] Ex inf. Ealing Bor. Council.
[71] Ibid.
[72] Ex inf. Ealing Bor. Council and Walter Kidde Co.
[73] Ex inf. Taylor Woodrow Ltd.
[74] Ex inf. Ealing Bor. Council.
[75] Par. Recs.
[76] W.A.M., N. 62.
[77] Northolt Par. Council Mins. *penes* Ealing Bor. Council.
[78] MS. Diary of F. W. Crees *penes* his daughters.

[79] *Illustrated Sporting & Dramatic News*, 15 May 1936.
[80] L. Jayne, *Pony Racing* (1949); C. H. Keene, 'Northolt Park Estate', *Northolt Vanguard*, Jan. 1959; Plan of the Northolt Park Race Course *penes* Ealing libr.
[81] J.I. 1/544, m. 51d.
[82] Two copies of extracts from rolls date from 1451 and 1460: B.M. Add. Ch. 1606, 1607.
[83] W.A.M., N. 1–22.
[84] Ibid. 38: Index of courts, 1461–1919.
[85] This section should be read in conjunction with the accounts given in *V.C.H. Mdx.* iii. 200–2; iv. 105–6, 125.

The basis and precise nature of this jurisdiction are uncertain, but the available evidence suggests that it may have originated in an administrative grouping of Mandeville holdings in this area during the 11th and 12th centuries.[86] Claims to jurisdiction over the estate consistently described as the manor of Greenford probably refer not to the capital manor of that name but to a smaller estate in the south of Greenford parish known variously as the manor of Stickleton or Greenford. Land which seems later to have formed the basis of Stickleton manor was held of the honor of Mandeville from at least as early as 1212.[87] During the 1530s Stickleton manor was farmed by one James Cole,[88] and he appears to be identifiable with a James Cole who made returns at the Northolt court from 1534 to 1543 as constable for the so-called manor of Greenford.[89]

During the 15th and early 16th centuries officers for five manors were appointed at Northolt court. In 1461 Greenford and Perivale each had a single head-borough; two each were appointed for Northolt and Ickenham; and three for Down. By 1505 the court was also appointing constables for Northolt and Greenford, and a constable and ale-taster for Ickenham. Apart from the election of manorial officers and occasional presentments, the Northolt court seems to have had little administrative connection with Perivale and Greenford. For several years there are no returns, and the constables, headboroughs, and tenants of both manors were frequently in default for non-appearance. After 1547 returns for Greenford and Perivale cease to appear in the Northolt rolls. The court continued to appoint officers for Ickenham and Down until 1616, when Down seems to have been granted separate courts leet and baron. The earliest surviving Down court roll dates from 1659, and courts leet were held there until the end of the 17th century.[90] After the separation of Down the Northolt court continued to appoint a constable and headboroughs for Ickenham until 1708. The lord of Ickenham manor was said in 1660 to owe fealty, suit of court, and a rent of £1 6s. 8d. to the lord of Northolt.[91] This rent was still being paid in 1878.[92] Although Northolt was described in 1722 as 'a manor paramount' to the manors of Ickenham, Greenford, and Perivale, the connection was by this time of little practical importance.[93]

Business in the Northolt and Down manor courts after 1700 was concerned almost entirely with admission to copyhold and the regulation of common-field usage. A manorial constable and headboroughs for Northolt were appointed as late as 1804, but by this date, and probably earlier, their functions appear to have overlapped those of the overseers of the poor and churchwardens. In 1642 there were two parish constables, a churchwarden, and two overseers of the poor.[94] A 'church-house' on the Green, said to have been built in 1572,[95] and presumably administered by the overseers, accommodated five widows in 1664,[96] and three widows and a poor man in 1715.[97] The church-house remained in use as a parish poor-house until 1806. General poor relief was financed by a rate on the parish. The poor-rates rose from £169 in 1775-6 to £423 in 1803-4, when 28 persons were on permanent relief and 20 received occasional payments.[98] Poor-relief expenditure rose to a maximum of £503 in 1806.[99] In that year, however, the vestry resolved to build a workhouse to replace the now inadequate church-house, and the cost of poor relief for the period 1809-22 fell to about £170 a year[1] The workhouse, built on a site taken from the waste in the modern Mandeville Road, was a substantial building of nine rooms, including a shop and brewhouse. The number of inmates fluctuated between 12 and 22.[2] Administration was entrusted to a governor to whom the parish farmed out the workhouse at an annual rent of between £200 and £290. The appointment of successive governors and the fixing of the annual farm provided the staple business of the vestry in the early 19th century. In 1834 regular out-relief was given each week during winter to an average of 17 agricultural workers. Able-bodied out-poor were employed on the roads.[3] After the 1834 Act the parish was included in the Uxbridge Union, and in 1838 the inmates of the Northolt workhouse were removed to the union workhouse at Hillingdon.[4] The building was then sold, and after conversion licensed as the 'Load of Hay'. The present public house replaced the earlier building in 1930.[5]

The surviving minutes suggest that the vestry was never more than a routine administrative body. Business in the early 19th century was limited to regulation of the workhouse farm, the appointment of officers, and the provision of poor relief. During this period there were seldom more than five meetings a year, attended by the vicar and parish officers. By 1850 there were only two meetings, held in the schoolroom, for the appointment of officers and the sale of the road-repair contract. With the occasional addition of repairs to the church and village pump, the nature of vestry business remained substantially unchanged until the end of the 19th century.[6]

In 1894 Northolt became part of Uxbridge R.D. and had a parish council, composed of a chairman and six councillors, and meeting in the schoolroom. Throughout its existence the council was concerned primarily with the organization of petitions against

[86] *V.C.H. Mdx.* i. 126; *Red Bk. Exch.* (Rolls Ser.), ii. 543; *Bk. of Fees*, i. 474; *Feudal Aids*, iii. 375; B.M. Harl. MS. 2195, f. 34.
[87] *Red Bk. Exch.* (Rolls Ser.), ii. 543; *Cal. Inq. p.m.* xiii, p. 142; *Feudal Aids*, vi. 584.
[88] For details of the 16th-cent. ownership see *V.C.H. Mdx.* iii. 211.
[89] W.A.M., N. 3.
[90] M.R.O., Acc. 180/561-70.
[91] W.A.M., N. 22.
[92] Ibid. 54.
[93] Ibid. 62.
[94] Hse. of Lords, Mdx. Protestation Rets.
[95] W. H. L. Shadwell, *Northolt* (1905), copy *penes* Ealing libr.
[96] M.R.O., H.T.6.
[97] Par. Recs., Dr. Cockburn's 'Register of the Par.'.
[98] *Rep. Cttee. on Rets. by Overseers, 1776*, Ser. 1, ix. 396; *Rets. on Expense and Maintenance of Poor*, H.C. 175 (1803-4), xiii (demi-folio).
[99] Poor Rate Bk. 1796-1807 *penes* Ealing Bor. Council.
[1] Overseers' Account Bks. 1809-24 *penes* Ealing Bor. Council.
[2] Par. Recs., Inventory of the Poor House, 1820; List of inmates of the workhouse; Vestry Mins. 1814.
[3] *Rep. Poor Law Com. App B(2)*, H.C. 44, p. 165h (1834), xxxvi.
[4] Par. Recs., Contractors' Agreements, 1806-28; Vestry Mins.
[5] C. H. Keene, 'The Old Northolt Workhouse' *Northolt Vanguard*, May 1958.
[6] Par. Recs., Vestry Mins. 1814-96.

the inclusion of the Mount Park estate in the then Harrow-on-the-Hill U.D., and the provision of amenities for Northolt village. Continued attempts to bring water to the village resulted in the first houses being connected to the main supply in 1898. The council also entered into an agreement in 1914 with the Harrow Gas Co. to provide gas street-lighting in the village, and made frequent representations to the rural district authorities about the condition of roads in the parish.[7]

LONDON BOROUGH OF EALING. *Argent, an oak-tree proper fructed or growing out of a grassy mount; on a chief gules three Saxon crowns or* [Granted 1965]

Uxbridge R.D. was dissolved in 1928. The Mount Park estate was then incorporated in the urban district and civil parish of Harrow, and the remainder of Northolt civil parish transferred to the municipal borough and civil parish of Ealing.[8] The more recent history of local administration in Northolt therefore belongs to the boroughs of Harrow and Ealing,[9] which since 1965 have been part of the London Boroughs of Harrow and Ealing.[10]

CHURCHES. There was a priest at Northolt in 1086.[11] A church is mentioned *c.* 1140, although the oldest parts of the present building have been assigned to the 13th century.[12] The church served the whole of the parish until 1954 when the new parish of St. Barnabas was formed from the north-east area of St. Mary's parish and part of the Greenford parish of Holy Cross.[13]

Northolt church formed part of the endowment of the priory of Walden in Essex, founded by Geoffrey de Mandeville about 1140.[14] Walden continued to exercise its rights to Northolt until some time between 1241 and 1251[15] when the prior's claims were disputed by the Dean and Chapter of St. Paul's. The matter was referred to Peter de Newport, Archdeacon of London, and it was agreed that a vicarage should be instituted and the patronage vested in the Bishop of London and his successors. Vicars of Northolt were to pay 12 marks annually towards the maintenance of St. Paul's Cathedral, and the Dean and Chapter of St. Paul's were to present to the living during vacancies of the London see.[16] About 1247 there was said to be no

vicarage,[17] and the exact date of its ordination is unknown. According to an early-15th-century source the vicarage was ordained in 1388,[18] but since the first recorded vicars date from the late 13th century,[19] the document referred to is almost certainly the confirmation of an earlier ordinance. The Bishop of London continued to exercise the patronage of Northolt until 1864, in which year it was transferred to Brasenose College, Oxford.[20] The college still held the advowson in 1963.

The benefice of Northolt was valued at 12 marks in the mid 13th century. The Abbot of Walden received two marks from the profits of the benefice, and the Prior of Hurley in Berkshire half a mark.[21] In 1291 the church was valued at £5; the Prior of Hurley still received his annual pension, and no payment to the Abbot of Walden is recorded.[22] Presumably the vicar then enjoyed the rectorial estate. An agreement made in 1518 between the Bishop of London and the Vicar of Northolt confirmed the vicar's right to great and small tithes in consideration of £4 paid annually to this bishop.[23] In 1535 the living was valued at £15.[24] Twelve years later the 'parsonage' was worth £26 and the vicar held 31 a. in the common fields. There were then no charities, obits, or lights, and the vicar furnished the cure himself.[25] By 1610 the vicarage estate comprised a vicarage-house, with two barns, stable, orchard, and garden, three closes of meadow containing 20 a., lands in the Northolt common fields, and houses and land in Greenford parish.[26] The living, which then included 48 a. of glebe, was worth £205 in 1650 when the great and small tithes were valued together at £170.[27] During the early 18th century the amount of glebe seems to have remained fairly constant at about 50 a., and the income from tithes and glebe at approximately £250.[28] Under the 1835 inclosure award two closes called Hedges Meadow and Catherine Mead to the south and east of the vicarage-house were allotted to the vicar in lieu of common-field land, and the glebe then comprised 44 a.[29] After the Greenford inclosure award of 1816 the Vicar of Northolt's right to tithes payable on old common-field land in Greenford parish was disputed by the Rector of Greenford. In 1841 the Greenford tithes were redeemed, the whole of the rent-charge apportioned to the Rector of Greenford, and the tithes payable to Northolt extinguished.[30] The Northolt tithes were redeemed for £682 in 1842.[31] The net value of the living in 1835 was £539.[32] Most of the glebe was sold for building after 1920.[33]

A vicarage-house at Northolt is first mentioned in 1610.[34] Its location is uncertain. In 1692 the old house was demolished by Charles Alston, the

[7] Northolt Par. Council Mins. 1894–1928 *penes* Ealing Bor. Council.
[8] Ex inf. Mdx. Cnty. Council.
[9] For Harrow see p. 245. The history of Ealing is reserved for treatment as part of Ossulstone hundred.
[10] London Govt. Act, 1963, c. 33.
[11] *V.C.H. Mdx.* i. 126.
[12] B.M. Harl. MS. 3697, f. 1; cf. Hist. Mon. Com. *Mdx.* 97.
[13] Ex inf. the vicar.
[14] B.M. Harl. MS. 3697, f. 1. The date of the foundation charter is discussed in *V.C.H. Essex*, ii. 111.
[15] Roger II, a party to the agreement, was Abbot of Walden 1241–51: Dugdale, *Mon.* iv. 134.
[16] Newcourt, *Repertorium*, i. 701; St. Paul's MSS. box 34/851; box 38/1297; Guildhall MS. 9531/11, f. 121.
[17] St. Paul's MS. W.D. 9, f. 83v.   [18] W.A.M., 425.

[19] *Cal. Inq. Misc.* 1219–1307, p. 246; Newcourt, *Repertorium*, i. 701.   [20] *Lond. Gaz.* 12 July 1864.
[21] St. Paul's MS. W.D. 9, f. 83v.
[22] *Tax. Eccl.* (Rec. Com.), 17. Two marks, however, were paid to Ralph de Bohun.
[23] Guildhall MS. 9531/9, f. 138v.
[24] *Valor Eccl.* (Rec. Com.), i. 433.
[25] E 301/34/186.   [26] Guildhall MS. 9628.
[27] *Home Cnties. Mag.* iii. 32.
[28] Par. Recs., Accounts of the Tithe and Glebe; Guildhall MS. 9556.
[29] Par. Recs.; M.R.O., Northolt Incl. Award.
[30] Par. Recs.; M.R.O., Greenford Tithe Award; W.A.M., N. 125.   [31] M.R.O., Northolt Tithe Award.
[32] *Rep. Com. Eccl. Rev.* [67], H.C. (1835), xxii.
[33] Par. Recs.; ex inf. the vicar.
[34] Guildhall MS. 9628.

incoming vicar, and a new vicarage built on a site off the modern Ealing Road.[35] This was described in 1715 as a brick-built house with seven principal rooms, kitchen, dairy, cellars, outbuildings, and walled garden.[36] Minor additions to the house were made during the 19th century, but after 1900 it was allowed to fall into disrepair. The house was demolished in 1928.[37] In 1963 the vicar was living in a semi-detached house in Church Road.

Little is known of the religious life of the parish before the 17th century. Some of the medieval and later incumbents seem to have been pluralists.[38] In 1302 the Vicar of Northolt was included in a list of Middlesex incumbents excommunicated for non-payment of the papal tenth.[39] Changes during the Interregnum occasioned some dissatisfaction in the parish. George Palmer (vicar 1638–43) was sequestered in 1643 on the grounds that he spoke against Parliament, enjoyed incestuous relations with his sister-in-law, and had deserted his cure to join the Royalist Army.[40] Palmer seems to have enjoyed considerable popularity among the parishioners, who described his successor, Robert Malthus (vicar 1643–61), as 'a factious preacher'. Although the parishioners petitioned Cromwell for his removal, alleging that he was an unsatisfactory speaker, preached against the army in Scotland, and failed to observe national thanksgiving, Malthus retained the living until the Restoration.[41] The years after 1661 are marked by laxity in the administration of the cure and in the maintenance of the church fabric. William Brabourne (vicar 1661–84) was frequently absent from the parish. During his absence the cure was served by a curate whose office is first mentioned in 1617.[42] By 1664 parts of the church were falling into disrepair. There was no chalice, and the plate consisted of one silver cup and a pewter plate. The churchyard was unfenced, so that pigs entered. Little was done to remedy these defects until 1685, when it was ordered that adequate plate be provided and the churchyard new-railed.[43] The churchyard was still open to incursions by pigs and sheep in 1715, but the church was said to be in reasonable repair. Pews had recently been installed and a new gallery erected at the west end for the use of singers and servants.[44] Several 18th-century vicars were absentees and the cure was served by the curate. Goronwy Owen, the Welsh poet, served as curate from 1755 to 1758.[45] During this period services were held twice on Sundays, and there were between 5 and 7 Communions a year. By 1790 the annual number of Communions had fallen to 4, and there were only 10 communicants.[46] In 1965 evensong and Communion were celebrated daily, and there were four Sunday services, the chief of which was Parish Communion at 9 o'clock.[47]

The church of *ST. MARY*, standing on high ground east of the village green, dates in part from the early 14th century with early-16th-century additions.[48] The chancel is built of brick and the nave of flint and ironstone rubble with stone dressings, all now roughcast externally. The building consists of chancel, nave, bell turret, a south porch partly rebuilt in 1909, and a south vestry added in 1945. The nave dates substantially from the 14th century, but incorporates late-13th-century fragments. The chancel and nave roof were rebuilt in the early 16th century, and the square bell turret, which is weather-boarded and finished with a broach spire, dates from the same period. Buttresses, including the massive ones of brick at the west end, were added in the 18th century, and the church was restored in the 19th century.[49] The octagonal stone font dates from the 14th century.[50] The bowl is decorated with simple relief carving, and the wooden cover is dated 1624. There are four early-17th-century bells, including a sanctus cast in 1626. A wooden gallery of three bays, supported on Doric columns and said to have been constructed in 1703, is built across the west end of the nave. Other fittings include an 18th-century painting of the Adoration of the Magi on the north wall of the chancel, and a 17th-century carving of the Stuart arms, executed in painted wood, on the east wall of the nave. There are brasses with figures to Henry Rowdell (d. 1452) and Isaiah Bures (vicar 1596–1610). A 16th-century palimpsest brass commemorates the Gifford family. Wall tablets in the chancel and nave commemorate a number of 18th- and 19th-century incumbents and successive members of the Shadwell family.

The plate consists of a silver paten and cup dated 1702, and an electroplate dish of 1839.[51] Permission to sell the plate was refused in 1919, and the plate was subsequently deposited in a Harrow bank.[52] The registers, which are complete, record baptisms from 1560, marriages from 1575, and burials from 1583.

Rapid increases in population during the 1930s and extensive council development after 1945 led to the formation of three daughter churches between 1940 and 1960. The church of *ST. JOSEPH*, serving the West End area, first met in 1942 in temporary premises off Watery Road. These were demolished in 1944 to make way for houses, and the congregation continued to meet in a variety of buildings. In 1957 services were being held in Arundell School and in the church-house in Hawtrey Avenue. The first permanent church, a brick-built dual-purpose hall behind the 'White Hart' in Ruislip Road, was dedicated in 1959. In 1963 land in Yeading Lane had been purchased for the erection of a new church.

From about 1948 occasional services were held in a builder's hut in south-east Northolt. A semi-permanent hut at the junction of Kensington Road and Ruislip Road was dedicated in 1954 as the church of *ST. HUGH*. In 1963, although the future

[35] Par. Recs., Register 1560–1700.
[36] Ibid. Dr. Cockburn's 'Register of the Par.'.
[37] Ex inf. Mr. C. H. Keene.
[38] Newcourt, *Repertorium*, i. 701; *Rep. Com. Eccl. Rev. 67*], p. 664, H.C. (1835), xxii.
[39] W.A.M., 5810.
[40] *Walker Revised*, ed. Matthews, 261.
[41] Par. Recs., Register 1560–1700; *Calamy Revised*, ed. Matthews, 335; Lysons, *Environs of Lond.* iii. 313.
[42] Par. Recs.
[43] Guildhall MSS. 9628, 9537/20.

[44] Par. Recs., Dr. Cockburn's 'Register of the Par.'.
[45] See p. 113.
[46] Guildhall MSS. 9550, 9557, 9558.
[47] *Lond. Dioc. Bk.* (1965).
[48] It is fully described in Hist. Mon. Com. *Mdx.* 96–97 and illustrated in ibid. pl. 1.
[49] See plate facing p. 105.
[50] Hist. Mon. Com. *Mdx.* pl. 12.
[51] E. Freshfield, *Communion Plate of Mdx.* 41.
[52] *Par Mag.* Sept. 1919.

of the church was said to be uncertain, plans were published for a new church on the site.

In 1958 services were being held in a youth club hut on the Northolt Park housing estate. The hut was burnt down in 1959, and the congregation then met in Vincent School. A dual-purpose hall-church in Haydock Avenue was consecrated in 1960 as the church of *ST. RICHARD*.[53]

Work began on the church of *ST. BARNABAS*, the Fairway, in 1940. Building was suspended during the Second World War, and the church was not completed until 1954. During this period services were held in temporary premises.[54] The church, built of yellow stock-brick, is of simple design and consists of a nave, transept, and south porch. An open tower at the west end contains a single bell. The interior of the church is simply furnished and the texture of much of the structural material has been retained. The patron of the living is the Bishop of London.[55]

NONCONFORMITY. In 1599 Andrra or Andrea Gifford, wife of William Gifford, was indicted at Quarter Sessions for not attending the parish church.[56] Apart from this isolated case there is little evidence of opposition to the Established Church in Northolt until the 19th century. There were said to be no papists or reputed papists in 1706, one dissenter in 1766, and no papists or dissenters in 1770.[57] Plans for a Roman Catholic church to be built in Mandeville Road were approved by the local authority in 1963,[58] and the building, dedicated to St. Bernard, was consecrated in 1965.[59]

A house in Northolt was registered as a Baptist meeting-place in 1817, and one at West End for the use of Wesleyans in 1834.[60] The exact locations and subsequent history of both these meeting-houses are unknown.

In and shortly after 1869 Charles H. Harcourt, a member of the West Ealing Baptist Church, established a chain of six undenominational village missions in the remoter parts of Northolt and Greenford. These were served and supported by Baptists and Methodists in Ealing.[61] In 1869 Harcourt founded two missions: in Oldfield Lane, Greenford, and in Ealing Road (now Kensington Road), Northolt.[62] The Northolt mission continued to meet in these premises until 1944 when the building was burnt down. Since that date the congregation has met in a private house in Eastmead Avenue, Greenford.[63]

Shortly after 1869 three further missions were established in Ruislip Road, West End, Yeading Lane, and Hayes Road. After Harcourt's death (*c.*

1901), a new hall, known as the Harcourt Memorial, was built on the Ruislip Road site, but after 1929 nothing further is known of these three missions.[64]

There is no further evidence of nonconformist activity in Northolt until 1933 when a Methodist chapel was erected on a site in Church Road.[65] A Congregational fellowship, under a student pastor, met in the Downe Manor school from 1955 to 1958, when a permanent church was built in Tithe Barn Way.[66] A Baptist chapel in Eastcote Lane was registered for worship in 1958.[67]

EDUCATION. In 1715 Dr. John Cockburn, Vicar of Northolt, commented on the absence of educational facilities in the parish, and instituted a scheme for the education of poor children. Three collections were made, and the money raised used to provide schooling for 6 children in part of the parish poor-house. Cockburn continued to finance the venture, increasing the number of children to 16, until his death in 1729.[68] Several other 18th-century incumbents seem to have attempted to revive Cockburn's scheme. Gilbert Bouchery (curate 1738–49) observed that the parish children were 'surprisingly perverse and inattentive to all manner of instruction, exhortation and example'.[69] After 1780 some Northolt children undoubtedly attended the school founded by Edward Betham in Greenford.[70] In 1818 the Vicar of Northolt was financing a day school at which 37 poor children were taught by a single mistress.[71]

The mixed school opened in 1835 was that generally known in the early 19th century as Northolt National School.[72] The school was housed in the converted poor-house, which stood immediately west of the churchyard[73] and was described later as 'three wooden cottages, gutted, and made into one'. Under the auspices of the National Society tuition was given to 18 boys and 27 girls. Efforts to educate Northolt children were said, however, to be largely frustrated by the parents' practice of putting children out to work before they had learned to read.[74] The poor-house was used as a school until 1868 when the premises were declared inadequate. A new building to accommodate 88 mixed pupils was erected in the same year on a site adjoining the playground of the old school.[75] Subsequently the school was known as Northolt Church School. It was receiving a government grant by 1870, when the average attendance was 39 children.[76] A new classroom was added in 1881,[77] and the average attendance increased to 72 in 1899, and to 105 by 1906.[78] In the following year the Church School was closed and the pupils

[53] Section based on inf. supplied by the Vicar of St. Mary's, Northolt, and *Northolt Vanguard* (par. mag.), *passim.*   [54] Ex inf. the vicar.
[55] *Crockford* (1961–2).
[56] *Mdx. Cnty. Recs.* i. 254.
[57] Guildhall MSS. 9800, 9558, 9557.
[58] Ex inf. Ealing Bor. Council.
[59] Souvenir booklet *penes* the parish priest.
[60] Gen. Reg. Off., Dissenters' Places of Wship. 1689–1852: Dioc. of Lond. certs. of 1 July 1817, 22 May 1834.
[61] Section based on inf. supplied by Messrs. C. H. Keene and A. Platt. It should be read in conjunction with *V.C.H. Mdx.* iii. 218–19.
[62] For the later history of the Greenford Mission see *V.C.H. Mdx.* iii. 218, *sub nom.* 'Gospel Assembly'.
[63] Northolt Village Mission Min. Bk. 1929–63, *penes* Mrs. Robinson.   [64] Ibid.

[65] Ex inf. the minister.
[66] Ex inf. the church secretary.
[67] Gen. Reg. Off., Wship. Reg. 66918.
[68] Par. Recs., Dr. Cockburn's 'Register of the Par.'.
[69] Par. Recs.
[70] *V.C.H. Mdx.* iii. 219.
[71] *Digest of Rets. to Cttee. on Educ. of Poor*, H.C. 224 (1819), ix(1).   [72] Ed. 7/87.
[73] O.S. Map 6", Mdx. xv. NW. (1868 edn.).
[74] Nat. Soc. files.
[75] M.R.O., Acc. 289/5; Nat. Soc. files.
[76] *Rep. Educ. Cttee. of Co. 1870* [C. 406], H.C. (1871), xxii.
[77] Nat. Soc. files; date on building.
[78] *Schs. in receipt of Parl. Grants, 1899* [Cd. 332], p. 169, H.C. (1900), lxiv; *Public Elem. Schs. 1906* [Cd. 3510], H.C. (1907), lxiii.

transferred to the new Northolt County Primary School, erected in 1907 at what is now the junction of Church Road and Western Avenue.[79] The former school, now called the Memorial Hall, is used as an old people's work centre and hired out for meetings.[80]

Northolt Primary School, built to accommodate 296 pupils, was, until 1931, the only school in the parish. The school's capacity was increased by the addition of prefabricated huts in the late 1930s, and by 1945 it accommodated 656 children. Since that date a number of new schools have been built in the parish, and in 1963 the Primary School, which was then scheduled for closure, accommodated only 341 pupils.[81]

The school now known as Wood End Secondary Girls' School was built in 1931 as an all-age department. In 1935 the infants were transferred to new premises erected on an adjoining site in Wood End Way. The infants' department was in turn re-organized in 1939, when it was taken over as a junior girls' school and the infants were transferred to the new Wood End Infants' School.[82]

Eliots Green Grammar School was erected in 1956 on a site in Eastcote Lane. In 1963 the school accommodated 590 pupils, of which approximately one-half were girls, and a full-time staff of 33. Pupils were prepared for the General Certificate and London University entrance examinations.[83]

In February 1963 there were fourteen maintained schools, excluding grammar schools, in the old parish of Northolt. They are set out below. The date at which the school was opened is given in brackets after the name of the school, followed by the date of any extension; the next figure is the number of children on the roll at February 1963, and the final figure denotes the age-group of the pupils:

Northolt Primary (1907, 1939). 341. 5–11; Wood End Secondary Girls (1931). 328. 11–16; Wood End Junior Boys (1935, 1939). 269. 8–11; Wood End Junior Girls (1935). 216. 8–11; Wood End Infants (1939). 378. 5–8; Downe Manor Junior and Infants (1948). 317. 5–11; Islip Manor Infants (1948). 240. 5–8; Islip Manor Junior (1951). 368. 8–11; Gifford Junior and Infants (1951). 607. 5–11; Arundell Primary (1952). 288. 5–11; Barantyne Junior (1952). 368. 8–11; Vincent Secondary (1953). 773. 11–16; Walford Secondary (1955). 771. 11–16; Northolt Park Infants (1960). 210. 5–8.[84]

CHARITIES FOR THE POOR.[85] Thomas Arundell (d. 1697) left 7 a. to the use of the poor. This gift yielded £5 yearly in 1697 and £9 10s. in 1810. The land forming Arundell's charity was sold to the lord of the manor in 1887, and in 1890 the gift was represented by £535 stock.[86] An unknown donor, by an instrument probably made before 1770,[87] conveyed a further 2 a. to the use of the poor. The land was sold to the Great Western Railway Co. in 1900, and in 1948 the gift was represented by £319 stock. Martha Jackson, by will proved 1836, left £44 stock to provide bread which was to be distributed among the poor every New Year's Day. Suggestions during the 1920s that the Northolt charities should be consolidated were not carried out, and the charities continued to be administered severally by the parish authorities. In 1958 the three charities together yielded £131.[88]

PERIVALE

THE ANCIENT parish of Perivale or Little Greenford[1] lay to the north of Ealing in the extreme east of Elthorne hundred.[2] It had the shape of an irregular rectangle measuring approximately one mile from north to south and ¾ mile from east to west, and contained 633 a.[3] The River Brent formed the southern parish boundary and the boundary of Ossulstone hundred. The other three sides were bounded by Gore hundred to the east and north and by Greenford parish to the west. Perivale formed part of Greenford U.D. from 1894 until 1926, when it was incorporated in the civil parish and municipal borough of Ealing and ceased to have any independent existence.[4] It now forms part of the London Borough of Ealing.[5]

Apart from a small area in the north-west on the lower slope of Horsenden Hill, all the parish lies below 100 ft. The land slopes uniformly from the Paddington Canal, following the 100-foot contour across the north of the parish, to approximately 50 ft. along the course of the Brent.[6] Except for a narrow deposit of flood plain gravel and an even narrower strip of alluvium along the river, the soil is London Clay.[7]

Little is known of the topography of the parish before the 19th century. An early-13th-century document mentions Eastfield, Westfield, Lukemere, and a field extending south to the Brent.[8] A 14th-century source further implies the existence of a system of open-field arable cultivation,[9] but the area and exact location of the fields are not known. The pattern of early settlement is also uncertain. At all recorded periods before 1890 there were fewer than 50 people living in the parish. Nine persons

[79] Ed. 7/86.
[80] Ex inf. the vicar.
[81] *Educ. in Ealing*, 1877–1945, copy *penes* Ealing libr.; ex inf. Borough Educ. Officer.
[82] Ex inf. Borough Educ. Officer.
[83] Ex inf. the headmaster.
[84] Ex inf. Borough Educ. Officer.
[85] Except where otherwise stated this section is based on Char. Com. files.
[86] Par. Recs., Register 1560–1700; Guildhall MS. 9558.
[87] Guildhall MS. 9557.
[88] Northolt Par. Council Mins. 1894–1928 *penes* Ealing Bor. Council.
[1] The name 'Perivale' ('pear tree valley') does not appear

in connexion with the parish before the early 16th cent.: *P.N. Mdx.* (E.P.N.S.), 46. It is used throughout this article, although in the Middle Ages the parish was referred to as Little or East Greenford.
[2] This article was written in 1963. Any references to a later time are dated.
[3] *Census*, 1871.
[4] Ibid. 1931.
[5] See p. 125.
[6] O.S. Map 1/25,000, 51/18 (1951 edn.).
[7] Geol. Survey Map, sheet 256 (drift).
[8] C.P. 25(1)/146/2/24.
[9] C 135/66/32.

were assessed for the subsidy in 1522–3[10] and four-teen adult male parishioners took the protestation oath in 1642.[11] In 1664 there were, as at all subse-quent periods until 1850, only five inhabited houses in the parish.[12] The population was 28 in 1801, 34 in 1881, and 60 in 1901.[13] A halt at Perivale on the Great Western Railway's suburban line from Paddington was opened in 1904,[14] but there were still only 114 people living in the parish in 1921.[15] In 1951 the population of Perivale ward, covering an area slightly larger than the ancient parish, was 9,979, but by 1961 it had decreased to 8,655.[16]

It seems probable that Perivale 'village' was never more than a small complex centred on the church, rectory, and manor-house in the south-west corner of the parish. By the time of the first detailed map in 1839[17] the manor-house had been demolished[18] and the only domestic buildings were five widely separ-ated farm-houses. Horsenden Farm lay in the extreme north-west corner of the parish, and Church and Grange farms in the south-west im-mediately north and west of the rectory. On the eastern boundary were Manor Farm and Apperton or Alperton Farm to the north.[19] At this time Peri-vale was said to be 'very secluded'.[20] The only roads in the parish were Horsenden Lane running parallel to the western boundary, and Apperton Lane, which passed just north of the rectory and continued east-ward to Hanger Hill and Alperton.[21]

During the 19th century the appearance of the parish altered little.[22] The opening in 1801 of the Paddington branch of the Grand Junction Canal had little effect on the isolation of the parish, and in 1876 Perivale was described as 'a curiously lonely-looking little place, lying in the valley of the Brent among broad meadows'.[23]

In 1903 the Great Western Railway's suburban line to High Wycombe was driven across the centre of the parish, and a halt at Perivale opened in the following year. This was enlarged and converted into a station in 1908, and continued to serve the parish until 1947,[24] when London Transport's Central line was extended from North Acton to Greenford alongside the G.W.R. line. Perivale station was then rebuilt and the local steam train service discontinued.[25] Despite the coming of the railway virtually no residential or industrial develop-ments occurred before 1930. In that year Sanderson's wallpaper factory in Horsenden Lane was com-pleted, and a section of Western Avenue driven across the parish along the line of Alperton Lane.[26] Between 1931 and 1939 the area bounded by Western Avenue, Horsenden Lane, and the Paddington Canal was almost entirely covered by factories and houses. Industrial building was concentrated in an

area immediately north of the railway line in and around Wadsworth Road and Bideford Avenue. Residential development was concentrated along the north side of Western Avenue and in the central area of the parish between the railway line and the canal. All the pre-1939 housing schemes were speculative. By 1939 the development of the parish was virtually completed.[27] Since 1945, although some factories have been extended and a number of private houses built, the pattern of settlement has remained substantially unchanged.

Open spaces have been preserved on three sides of the central developed area. The area between Western Avenue and the Brent forms part of the course of the Ealing Golf Club (established 1898),[28] and that between the Paddington Canal and the parish boundary part of Sudbury Golf Course. The area west of Horsenden Lane between Western Avenue and the railway is leased by the local authority to the Kensington Borough Council as a sports ground.

MANOR. In 1086 3½ hides in Greenford, which in the time of King Edward had belonged to Ansgar the Staller, were held of Geoffrey de Mandeville.[29] A further half hide in Greenford was held in free alms of the king by Elveve, the wife of Wateman of London. This estate had been held in King Edward's time by Levric, the man of Earl Leofwine.[30] Part at least of these estates seems to have been situated in Perivale parish, although the subsequent descent of the holdings is obscure. Several holdings seem to have been consolidated during the 12th and 13th centuries to form the estate known in the early 14th century as the manor of *LITTLE GREENFORD* or *CORNHILL*. Lands in Perivale which together may have formed the basis of the manor were acquired by the Hinton family during the early 13th century and held by it of the honor of Mandeville until at least 1245.[31] The Hinton estate appears to have passed to the Ruislip family of Northolt in the late 13th century. Early in 1307 the brothers Hugh and Simon Ruislip conveyed the property, then called the manor of Greenford, with appurtenances in Ealing and Harrow, to Walter de Langton, Bishop of Coventry and Lichfield.[32] Langton was imprisoned in July 1307 and his estates confiscated by Edward II.[33] Although he petitioned the king on his release in 1309, Langton was not restored to his estates.[34] The king retained the manor of Little Greenford until 1313, when he granted it to Henry Beaumont (d. 1341).[35] Henry Beaumont was suc-ceeded by his son John who died in 1342. The manor then comprised a ruinous messuage, 120 a. of

[10] E 179/141/115.
[11] Hse. of Lords, Mdx. Protestation Rets.
[12] M.R.O., H.T.6.
[13] Census, 1801–1901.
[14] T. B. Peacock, *G.W. Suburban Services*, 45.
[15] Census, 1921.
[16] Ibid. 1951, 1961.
[17] M.R.O., Perivale Tithe Award (1839).
[18] See p. 124.
[19] J. A. Brown, *The Chronicles of Greenford Parva*, 96–97; description of Grange Fm. (1851) *penes* the rector.
[20] Robson, *Home Cnties. Dir.* (1839).
[21] J. Rocque, *Map of 10 miles round Lond.* (1746); M.R.O., Perivale Tithe Award Map (1839).
[22] O.S. Maps 1/2,500, Mdx. xv. 4, 8 (1865 and 1896 edns.).
[23] Thorne, *Environs of Lond.* 467.

[24] Peacock, *G.W. Suburban Services*, 45.
[25] *The Times*, 25 June, 1 July 1947.
[26] Plan of Ealing Borough (1931) *penes* Ealing Bor. Council.
[27] O.S. Map 1/2,500, Mdx. xv. 4, 8 (1935 edn.).
[28] See plate facing p. 37.
[29] *V.C.H. Mdx.* i. 126.
[30] Ibid. 129.
[31] C.P. 25(1)/146/1/20; /146/5/18; *Red Bk. Exch.* (Rolls Ser.), ii. 543; *Bk. of Fees*, i. 474; *Feudal Aids*, iii. 375, 381; St. Paul's MS. W.D.9, f. 84v.
[32] C.P. 25(1)/148/38/360; *Cal. Chart. R.* iii. 77, 81.
[33] *Cal. Fine R.* 1307–19, 33.
[34] *Cal. Close*, 1307–13, 89; *Cal. Pat.* 1317–21, 145; *Rot. Parl.* (Rec. Com.), ii. 400.
[35] *Cal. Chart. R.* 1300–26, 224; *Cal. Close*, 1318–23, 7.

arable, 5 a. of underwood, and a windmill, held of the honor of Mandeville.[36] Members of the Beaumont family continued to hold the manor[37] until 1386 when Sir John Beaumont quitclaimed it to Thomas Charlton of Folkingham (Lincs.).[38] At some time after Charlton's death in 1410 Little Greenford passed to Thomas and Henry Frowyk, two London mercers, and others. In 1429 they conveyed the manor to another Thomas Charlton, who was possibly a nephew of the first Thomas.[39] By 1435 the manor was in the possession of one William Hall, who in that year conveyed it to William Eastfield (d. 1438), another mercer, and twice Mayor of London.[40] The descent of the manor during the remainder of the 15th century is obscure, but the right of presentation to the rectory, which seems always to have been included in grants of the manor, was exercised by John Middleton (1453), John Bohun (1472, 1473), and Henry Collet (1490).[41] On his death in 1516, Little Greenford was in the possession of Sir Robert Southwell.[42] He was succeeded by Sir Humphrey Browne (d. 1562), a judge of the Common Pleas, who owned the manor at least from 1521 to 1559.[43] In 1566 Roger Townsend, who was probably Browne's grandson, sold what was then called the manor of Perivale or Little Greenford to Henry Millett, who also held land in Greenford parish.[44] Subsequently the manor descended in the Millett family, and by the female line to the families of Lane and Harrison.[45] In 1767 John Harrison sold the manor, which then comprised the whole parish with the exception of Manor Farm, to Richard Lateward (d. 1777).[46] He devised the property to his great-nephew John Schrieber, who assumed the name of Lateward, and held the manor until his death in 1814. John Lateward (Schrieber) was succeeded by his son Richard who died in 1815. The manor of Little Greenford then descended to Richard Lateward's daughter, Sophia Jane (d. 1890), and then by the female line to the Croft-Murray family, descendants of Sophia Jane Lateward by her first husband, Sir Thomas Croft.[47] The manor remained in the hands of the Croft-Murray family until the 1920s when the estate was broken up and sold for building purposes.

There appear to have been two manor sites within the boundaries of the ancient parish. Nothing is known of the partially moated site on the lower slope of Horsenden Hill immediately north of the Paddington Canal.[48] The site may be identifiable with a capital messuage which was ruinous in 1342.[49] A further site west of the church on land which in 1963 formed part of Ealing Golf Course was still partially moated in the early 20th century.[50] A manor-house, possibly of Tudor date, was still

standing on this site in 1746.[51] In the late 18th century the house was said to be a three-story structure of red brick. It seems to have been demolished about 1780.[52]

ECONOMIC AND SOCIAL HISTORY. Until the 1930s Perivale was a sparsely populated agricultural parish.[53] Little is known about the inhabitants or their land at any period before the 19th century. Domesday Book mentions five people living on Geoffrey de Mandeville's three-hide estate.[54] Of these, two were described as villeins and shared half a hide; two were cottars; and there was one serf. This holding supported one plough, with room for a further half plough, and the woodland was sufficient to support 40 pigs. The half hide held of Geoffrey by Ansgot had room for two oxen, and that held of the king by Elveve had room for a single plough which was not there at the time of the Survey.[55]

A document of 1342 implies the existence of a system of open-field arable cultivation. Mention at this date of a windmill on the manor may suggest that Perivale enjoyed an early period of prosperity.[56] A mill is not mentioned again, and 19th-century references to a 17th-century windmill near the Brent seem to refer to a site outside the parish.[57]

During the 16th and 17th centuries the area south of Harrow, including Perivale parish and known collectively as the 'Perivale' or 'Purivale', acquired a reputation as a high quality wheat-growing district.[58] Wheat seems to have remained the major crop in the parish until the late 18th century. By 1839, however, there were only 46 a. of arable in the parish, and the bulk of the remainder was in grass supplying hay for the London market.[59] In 1843 it was said that at least half of the parish had been turned over to grass within the last fifty years. The reasons adduced for this change in land utilization were the demands of the London market, the easy communications afforded by the Paddington Canal, and the poor returns from wheat growing. The pasture was understocked and it was customary to let the fields after the hay harvest as summer pasture for sheep from the Midland counties. The parish was at this date divided into five farms, the largest of which comprised 179 a. There were no other houses and hence no resident farm labourers.[60] As late as 1876 there were still no labourers' cottages and the land was devoted exclusively to hay farming.[61]

The construction in 1924 of Greenford Road, an arterial road running north–south to the west of Perivale parish, and in 1929–30 of Western Avenue, passing from east to west across the south of the

[36] C 135/66/32.
[37] Cal. Close, 1343–6, 88; Reg. Sudbury (Cant. & York Soc. xxxiv), 237; Cal. Pat. 1374–7, 259.
[38] C.P. 25(1)/151/78/83; Cal. Close, 1385–9, 291; Feudal Aids, vi. 488.
[39] C.P. 25(1)/152/89/40; Cal. Close, 1429–35, 124.
[40] Lysons, Environs of Lond. ii. 446.
[41] Hennessy, Novum Repertorium, 175–7.
[42] B.M. Harl. MS. 756.
[43] Hennessy, Novum Repertorium, 175–7; Sta. Cha. 2/6/200; 2/23/64.
[44] C.P. 25(2)/171/8 & 9 Eliz. Mich.; V.C.H. Mdx. iii. 211.
[45] Cal. Inq. p.m. Hen. VII, v, p. 265.
[46] Brown, Chronicles, 53.
[47] Ibid.
[48] O.S. Map 1/25,000, 51/18 (1951 edn.).

[49] C 135/66/32.
[50] V.C.H. Mdx. ii. 9.
[51] Rocque, Map of 10 miles round Lond. (1746).
[52] Brown, Chronicles, 92–95; Lysons, Environs of Lond. ii. 449.
[53] Plan of Ealing Borough (1931) penes Ealing Bor. Council.
[54] But see p. 123.
[55] V.C.H. Mdx. i. 126, 129.
[56] C 135/66/32.
[57] Brown, Chronicles, 100–106.
[58] Ibid. 107, quoting Drayton, Polyolbion.
[59] M.R.O., Perivale Tithe Award (1839).
[60] H. Tremenheere, 'Agric. & Educ. Statistics of several pars. in Mdx.', Jnl. Stat. Soc. of Lond. vi. 123–4.
[61] Thorne, Environs of Lond, 467.

parish, first opened up the area to speculative building. As one of the nearest undeveloped areas to London, and lying in close proximity to a labour force in Ealing and Hanwell, Perivale was quickly adopted as a site for industrial expansion.[62] In contrast to the pattern of development in many of the neighbouring suburban areas, the earliest factories preceded housing developments. In 1929 work began on a new factory for Sanderson Wallpapers Ltd. The new premises, sited in the junction of Horsenden Lane and the G.W.R. line, were opened in 1930, when the labour force was approximately 900 persons. Since that date the factory has been further extended, and in 1963 the firm employed 1,650 persons in premises covering 10 a.[63] In 1932 a large factory fronting Western Avenue was opened by Hoover Ltd. for the manufacture of cleaners and other domestic appliances. The administrative, sales, and engineering headquarters of the Hoover organization in Britain are sited at Perivale, and the premises also include a training school and recreational buildings. In 1963 the factory, which was then being extended, employed more than 3,000 persons.[64]

After 1934 the pace of factory construction quickened. Industrial building was concentrated in an area roughly $\frac{1}{2}$ mile square in and around Wadsworth Road and Bideford Avenue. A number of factories, warehouses, and laboratories, employing from 50 to 400 persons, were erected during the 1930s, and many were extended after the Second World War. Manufactures include a variety of light engineering products, scientific and optical instruments, paints, sewing silks, and cosmetics.[65] Industrial building has been accompanied by a proportionate increase in private housing developments.

Not much is known of the social life of the parish before the 19th century. Part of a rifle range lay on the Perivale side of the Brent in 1865.[66] Church sports, attended by the youth of Ealing, were held annually during the 1890s.[67] There was no public house in Perivale until the opening of the 'Myllet Arms' on the site of the former Church Farm in the 1930s. A temporary building to house the Perivale Community Centre was built at the north end of Horsenden Lane about 1939.[68] It was still in use in 1963. In 1948 the Ministry of Labour opened a training centre in Walmgate Road, giving instruction in leather work, tailoring, watch repairing, and similar trades.[69] For most social activities Perivale is dependent on neighbouring areas. A few small shops have been built on both sides of Western Avenue, but the nearest large general shopping centre is at Ealing.

LOCAL GOVERNMENT. At all periods local government machinery in Perivale appears to have been wholly neglected or of no practical importance. By 1461, and presumably earlier, the tenants of the manor of Perivale attended view of frankpledge at the Northolt manor court. This obligation was probably of little significance since the headboroughs, appointed at the Northolt court, and the tenants were invariably in default for non-attendance. In 1501–2 there were said to be no Perivale residents; but whether these entries indicate that there were during this period no tenants living at Perivale or that they were again in default is not certain.[70] Nothing is known of the courts held by medieval lords of the manor. A dispute c. 1538 between Sir Humphrey Browne, lord of the manor, and John Lyon, one of his tenants, suggests that the lord's right to hold courts baron was normally not exercised. Lyon alleged that at the court baron convened by Browne he was the only person present.[71] After 1547 returns for Perivale cease to appear in the Northolt rolls, and there is no further evidence to suggest that courts of any description were held in Perivale.

There appears to have been no vestry at Perivale until 1812. Throughout its existence the vestry seldom met more than once a year, and in some years no meetings were held. Until the 1880s there were never more than five ratepayers resident in the parish, and the rector frequently conducted the vestry meeting alone. A salary was voted to the parish clerk in 1812, and a salaried constable first appointed in 1820. The offices of churchwarden and overseer of the poor were frequently united in one person, who occasionally also acted as constable. A surveyor of highways was first appointed in 1817. Parish offices, particularly that of highways surveyor, were frequently unfilled or elections made from persons resident in Ealing. The vestry was almost wholly concerned with the appointment of officers and the raising of church- and poor-rates.[72]

Until the practice was discontinued after a petty sessional order of 1675, the inhabitants of Perivale appear to have contributed towards the upkeep of the poor of Greenford parish.[73] By 1776 the Perivale poor-rate yielded £11, of which £9 was spent on the poor.[74] In 1803 the rate yielded £88. During the year four parishioners received permanent relief, and three other persons were given occasional relief.[75] The poor-rate fluctuated between 1s. and 3s. in the £ during the early 19th century, but there were seldom any paupers in the parish.[76] In 1836 Perivale became part of the Brentford Poor Law Union.[77]

In 1894 Perivale became part of the new Greenford U.D. Subsequently the vestry met only once each year, and was wholly concerned with the election of parish officers.[78] When the urban district was dissolved in 1926, the civil parish of Perivale was incorporated in the municipal borough and civil parish of Ealing. The more recent history of local administration in Perivale therefore forms part of the history of the municipal borough of Ealing[79] and, since 1965, of that of the London Borough of Ealing.[80]

[62] D. H. Smith, *Industrialization of Greater London*, 79.
[63] Ex inf. Sanderson Wallpapers Ltd.
[64] Ex inf. Hoover Ltd.
[65] *Kemp's Dir. of Ealing and Hanwell* (1961).
[66] O.S. Map 1/2,500, Mdx. xv. 8 (1865 edn.).
[67] Brown, *Chronicles*, 99.
[68] Local information.
[69] *Kemp's Dir. of Ealing and Hanwell* (1961).
[70] W.A.M., N. 1–4; see pp. 117–18.
[71] Sta. Cha. 2/23/64; 2/6/200.
[72] Vestry Mins. quoted in Brown, *Chronicles*, 74, 125–30.

There were no 19th-cent. vestry mins. in the parish in 1963.   [73] *Cal. Brentford Petty Sessions*, 77.
[74] *Rep. Sel. Cttee. on Rets. by Overseers, 1776*, Ser. 1, ix, p. 396.
[75] *Rets. on Expense and Maintenance of Poor*, H.C. 175, p. 294 (1803–4), xiii.
[76] *Digest Rets. on Educ. of Poor*, H.C. 224 (1819), ix(1).
[77] *2nd Rep. Poor Law Com.* H.C. 595 (1836), xxix(1).
[78] Par. Recs., Vestry Min. Bk. 1906–24.
[79] Reserved for treatment as part of Ossulstone hundred.
[80] London Govt. Act, 1963, c. 33.

CHURCHES. No church or priest at Perivale is mentioned in Domesday Book, but a document of 1203, which refers to Perivale as East Greenford, mentions a church near the Brent.[81] In the mid 13th century the patronage was vested in the priory of St. Helen, Bishopsgate.[82] The advowson descended with the manor of Perivale from the time of the first recorded presentations in the 14th century until 1911, when it was conveyed to the Society for the Maintenance of the Faith.[83] In 1963 the patronage was still exercised by the Society. Although the church was described as St. James's in the 19th century,[84] the original dedication was not known;[85] in 1951, after the discovery of a reference to 'the churchyard of St. Mary of Little Greenford' in a 15th-century will, the church was dedicated to St. Mary the Virgin.[86]

The benefice of Perivale is a rectory and seems never to have been appropriated. The benefice was valued at 6 marks in the mid 13th century.[87] It was worth £2 in 1291,[88] and £6 13s. 4d. in 1535.[89] In 1650 the income of the benefice, which included all the tithes, was valued at approximately £55.[90] There was said to be 2 a. of glebe in 1705,[91] and 3 a. in 1839.[92] During the late 18th century the value of the benefice increased slowly to £185 in 1831.[93]

The rectory-house, adjoining the churchyard to the north, dated in part from the 15th century, with 17th- and 18th-century additions.[94] The house is not mentioned before 1828 when it was said to be unfit for habitation.[95] During the 19th century the house was further extended and modernized for use as a lay residence.[96] After 1900, however, it was allowed to fall into disrepair, and despite local attempts to preserve it, was finally demolished in 1958.[97] Little is known about the religious life of the parish, but the available evidence suggests that at almost all periods before the mid 19th century the rector was non-resident and the cure neglected. In 1302 the Rector of Perivale was excommunicated for non-payment of papal tenths.[98] Complaints of the inefficiency of John Pearson (rector 1573–87) led to his being examined in the scriptures in 1586.[99] The Interregnum seems to have been marked by laxity in the administration of the cure. On visitation in 1685 the church registers were found to be deficient and the fabric out of repair.[1]

During the 18th century the rector, who normally lived in London, combined the cure with the enjoyment of the chapel at West Twyford. A single Sunday service was held, with a second service, provided for by an annual gift of £6 made in 1722, on the afternoon of the first Sunday in each month.[2] There were no children to be catechized,

and Communion was celebrated four times a year.[3] In 1790 the sacrament was said to have been long neglected, the registers had disappeared, and all the communicants accompanied the rector from London.[4] From about 1786 a curate, living at Ealing, assisted with the cure,[5] and probably served the parish during the incumbency of F. J. Lateward (rector 1812–61). Lateward was non-resident and combined the cure with a London living.[6] During his absence the church fittings seem to have fallen into disrepair. In 1836 the parish vestry resolved to purchase a second-hand bible and prayer book for use in the church. A motion to provide a new font and cover was negatived on the grounds that there were no christenings in the parish.[7]

During the incumbency of Charles Hughes (rector 1861–1907) the use of vestments was introduced and the Eucharist was sung on Sundays.[8] Attendance by non-resident communicants was encouraged, and grave-plots offered to strangers at exorbitant prices.[9] In 1904 attendance was said to be full.[10] High church practice was maintained after 1907, and in 1965 the main Sunday service was sung Mass.[11]

The church of *ST. MARY THE VIRGIN* stands among the trees on the south side of Church Lane in the extreme south-west of the parish.[12] It is approached through a timber lychgate, erected in 1904, and by a footpath which continues southward across the River Brent. The churchyard is surrounded on three sides by the course of the Ealing Golf Club. The church, one of the smallest in the county, consists of chancel, nave, west tower, and south porch. The nave and chancel, which may date from the later 13th century, have walls of flint and rubble, stuccoed externally; the roofs are tiled. A single 13th-century window survives in the chancel, but the earliest features visible in the nave are of 15th-century date; they include the crown-post roof, the west doorway, and two windows in the north wall. The weather-boarded west tower, which is of timber construction and has a pyramidal tiled roof, was probably added in the early 16th century, together with the narrow gallery at the west end of the nave. The chancel arch and most of the window and door openings in the church date from the 19th century. The south porch was probably added in the 17th century and rebuilt in 1875 when the interior of the church was much restored.[13] At that time an architectural authority advocated that 'all the rest of the Puritanical and Georgian anomalies, especially the Punch and Judy construction called the tower' be removed.[14]

A single brass in the floor of the nave shows

[81] C.P. 25(1)/146/2/24; and see *V.C.H. Mdx.* iii. 216.
[82] St. Paul's MS. W.D. 9, f. 84.
[83] Hennessy, *Novum Repertorium,* 175–7; ex inf. S.M.F.
[84] O.S. Map 1/2,500, Mdx. xv. 8 (1865 edn.).
[85] Hist. Mon. Com. *Mdx.* 100.
[86] E. Beavis, *Perivale, Its Manor, Church and Patronage,* 8. [87] St. Paul's MS. W.D. 9, f. 84
[88] *Tax. Eccl.* (Rec. Com.), 20.
[89] *Valor Eccl.* (Rec. Com.), i. 433.
[90] *Home Cnties. Mag.* ii. 284.
[91] Lysons, *Environs of Lond.* ii. 448.
[92] M.R.O., Perivale Tithe Award (1839).
[93] *Rep. Com. Eccl. Rev.* [67], p. 646, H.C. (1835), xxii.
[94] Hist. Mon. Com. *Mdx.* 101.
[95] Guildhall MS. 9560. [96] Brown, *Chronicles,* 91.
[97] Ex inf. the rector; letters and plans of the house *penes* J. L. Petingale, Greenford.

[98] W.A.M., 5817, 5820.
[99] Guildhall MS. 9537/6.
[1] Ibid. 9537/20. [2] Ibid. 9558; Par. Recs.
[3] Guildhall MSS. 9550, 9557. [4] Ibid. 9558.
[5] Ibid. 9557. [6] Ibid. 9560.
[7] Vestry Mins. quoted in Brown, *Chronicles,* 129.
[8] Par. Recs., Service Bks.; original vestments in vestry.
[9] Par. Recs., Graveyard Plan recording sales of grave-plots to non-residents.
[10] *Rep. Com. on. Eccl. Discipline, 1906* [Cd. 3069], p. 521, H.C. (1906), xxxiii.
[11] *Lond. Dioc. Bk.* (1965).
[12] It is fully described in Hist. Mon. Com. *Mdx.* 100–1, and see pl. 47. See also plate facing p. 126.
[13] Survey of the structure (1947) *penes* Ealing libr.; Brown, *Chronicles,* 57.
[14] *Builder,* xxvi (1868), p. 736.

EDGWARE: ST. MARGARET'S CHURCH IN 1792

PERIVALE: ST. MARY'S CHURCH, *c.* 1900
The Rectory, demolished 1958, is seen on the left

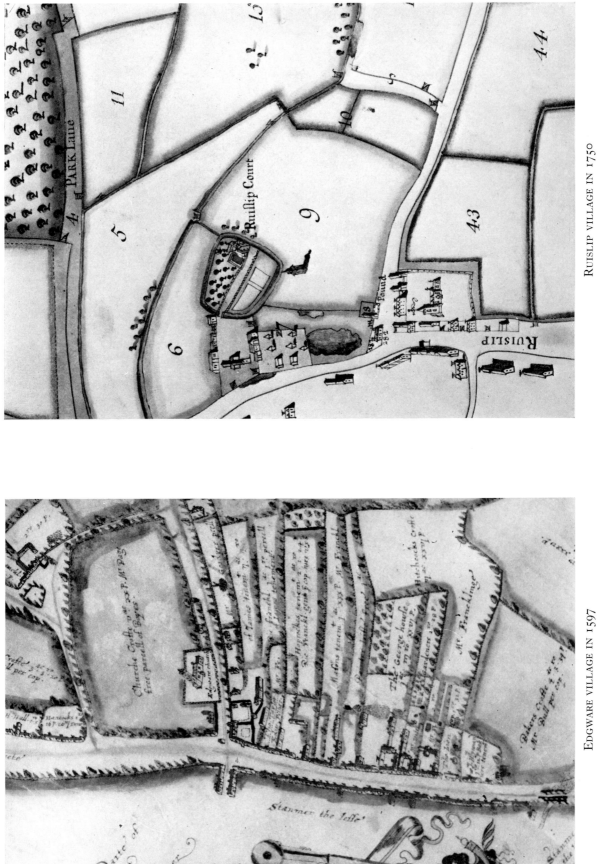

RUISLIP VILLAGE IN 1750

EDGWARE VILLAGE IN 1597

Henry Millett (d. 1505), with his two wives and their sixteen children. Wall monuments in the church commemorate members of the families of Millett, Lane, and Lateward. Monuments in the nave include one to Lane Harrison (d. 1740) by Thomas Ady,[15] and one incorporating figure sculpture to Ellen Nicholas (d. 1815), signed by Richard Westmacott. The small octagonal font is of late-15th-century date, with an elaborate carved wooden cover given by Simon Coston in 1665. One window in the church has re-set fragments of 15th-century glass. The church plate, part of which was dated 1625, consisted in 1685 of a silver chalice and cover, flagon, and plate.[16] These were exchanged by the incumbent in 1875 for a French silver-gilt cup and paten.[17] In 1937 there were two bells: (i) 1699, by William Eldrid; (ii) inscribed 1834. These were recast and, with the addition of a third bell, rehung in 1948.[18] The registers, some of which are said to have been sold in the early 19th century,[19] record baptisms from 1707, and marriages and burials from 1720.

The rapid increase in population during the 1930s and the remoteness of the parish church from the bulk of the parish necessitated the erection of an additional building to serve the new housing areas to the north and east. The daughter church of *ST. NICHOLAS*, a brick-built hall-church off Federal Road, was consecrated in 1934. In 1963 work began on a permanent church and vicarage sited immediately west of the old building. By this date St. Nicholas's church had largely replaced the old parish church as the centre of worship in Perivale. In 1963 three assistant priests helped the rector in the general administration of the parish and in religious and social work in the Perivale factories.[20]

NONCONFORMITY. From 1938 until 1960 a small Methodist community met in a scout hut, and later in the Perivale Community Centre in Horsenden Lane. A permanent church in May Gardens was opened in 1960 and in 1963 the congregation included members from Ealing, Acton, and Wembley.[21]

EDUCATION. The school founded at Greenford in 1780 by Edward Betham was intended to have at least thirty pupils,[22] of whom three were to come from Perivale.[23] In the first fifty years of its existence, when thirty-seven Perivale children are known to have attended, there was often a vacancy for the parish.[24] William Pearson, Rector of Perivale 1810-12, is said to have bequeathed £200 towards the education of ten poor girls,[25] but in 1871 all the children went to Greenford.[26] Founded in 1934 as an all-age department, the Perivale Junior and Senior Mixed and Infants' School in Sarsfield Road was reorganized in 1937 as a junior mixed and infants' department. In 1963 it accommodated 437 pupils. A senior girls' school, later known as Perivale Secondary Modern Girls' School, was opened in 1937, and in 1963 had approximately 270 pupils.[27]

CHARITIES FOR THE POOR. No charities are known to have been endowed in Perivale.

RUISLIP

THE ANCIENT parish of Ruislip[1] lay in the extreme north-west of Middlesex about 4 miles west of Harrow and 14 miles from London. The later urban district of Ruislip-Northwood was substantially coextensive with the ancient parish, and contained 6,583 a.[2] Both had the shape of an irregular quadrangle lying along a north-west south-east axis and measuring approximately 5 miles from north to south with a maximum breadth of 2½ miles. The northern and eastern parish boundaries followed the boundaries of Hertfordshire and Gore hundred respectively. The other two sides were bounded by Northolt parish in the south and Ickenham and Harefield to the west. Ruislip formed part of Uxbridge R.D. until 1904 when Ruislip-Northwood U.D. was constituted. An unsuccessful petition for incorporation as a municipal borough was lodged in 1953.[3] In 1965 Ruislip-Northwood U.D. was merged with the urban districts of Hayes and Harlington and Yiewsley and West Drayton and the municipal borough of Uxbridge to form the new London Borough of Hillingdon.[4]

The subsoil of the parish is predominantly London Clay with deposits of Reading Sand and Clay. Minor gravel deposits occur in the extreme north-east and north-west and to the west around Ducks Hill. A narrow alluvium deposit follows the course of the Pinn stream which roughly bisects the parish from west to east.[5] North of this stream the ground rises gradually. Haste Hill, north-east of the 'lido', and a ridge to the north called the Hogsback rise to over 300 ft. and form part of the north-facing escarpment overlooking the River Colne in Hertfordshire. The high ground is broken by a north–south valley in which lies an artificially constructed lake of some 50 a. This originally served as a compensating

[15] Pevsner, *Mdx.* 131.
[16] Guildhall MS. 9537/20.
[17] E. Freshfield, *Communion Plate of Mdx.* 42.
[18] Ex inf. the rector.
[19] Par. Recs., J. Farthing, 'An Illustrated History of Perivale Church' (MS. *c.* 1863).
[20] Ex inf. the Rector of Perivale.
[21] Gen. Reg. Off., Wship. Reg. 67989; ex. inf. the minister.
[22] *V.C.H. Mdx.* iii. 219.
[23] J. E. Wilson, 'Perivale' (TS. in Ealing Cent. Ref. Libr.), 29.

[24] Ibid. 30.
[25] *Gent. Mag.* 1847, 2nd ser. xxviii. 661.
[26] Wilson, op. cit. 35.
[27] Ex inf. Ealing Bor. Educ. Officer.
[1] The article was written in 1962. Any references to a later time are dated.
[2] *Census*, 1951. Two acres were transferred to Ickenham in 1934: ex inf. Ruislip-Northwood U.D.C.
[3] *Borough Status Petition* (1953) *penes* Ruislip-Northwood U.D.C.
[4] London Govt. Act, 1963, c. 33.
[5] Geol. Survey Map, sheet 255 (drift).

reservoir for the Grand Junction Canal, to which it was connected by a feeder, and came into operation in 1816.[6] The reservoir and the surrounding land, amounting in all to nearly 100 a., were purchased from the British Transport Commission in 1951 by the urban district council[7] which has since developed it as a lido. Eleven acres of low-lying ground at the north end of the lake were constituted a nature reserve in 1959.

East and west of the 'lido' are extensive areas of woodland. In 1086 there was sufficient woodland to support 1,500 pigs, and there was also a park for wild beasts (*parcus ferarum*).[8] At this time, and much later, what is now Park Wood probably extended southward at least as far as the Pinn. In 1565 Ruislip Common Wood, which seems to have included Copse Wood and much of what later became part of Ruislip Common to the east, contained 860 a. Of this area only 341 a. were still wooded in 1721, the rest having become open common.[9] During the 17th and 18th centuries the total area of Copse and Park woods was usually given as between 500 and 550 a.[10] In 1865 Park Wood covered an area stretching from just north of the Pinn to Haste Hill, and was bounded by the reservoir and Bury Street to the west and Frog Lane (Fore Street) in the east. Copse Wood then stretched from the reservoir to Northwood and was bounded by Ducks Hill Road to the west. Further woodland almost covered the area between Ducks Hill Road and the Harefield boundary.[11] Copse Wood covered 335 a. and Park Wood 408 a. in 1750;[12] in 1953 their total area was 396 a.[13] At this date Mad Bess Wood, between Ducks Hill Road and Harefield parish, covered 186 a.

North and south of Mad Bess Wood the narrow area between Ducks Hill Road and the parish boundary is almost wholly pasture land. South of the Pinn is a low ridge rising to 200 ft at Windmill Hill and Kingsend, and then sloping gradually to the Yeading Brook which runs parallel to the Pinn roughly mid-way between Eastcote Road and the Northolt boundary. South of this stream the land is uniformly flat and was, until the 20th century, devoted wholly to agriculture.[14]

From at least the 14th century until the topography of the parish was blurred by 20th-century development, there were three distinct areas of settlement. The villages of Ruislip and Eastcote developed on sites just south of the Pinn in the west and east of the parish respectively. The hamlet of Northwood grew up along the north side of the Rickmansworth–Pinner road which passes across the north-east of the parish. Apart from this road and internal networks in areas of scattered settlement to the east and west, there were only three ancient roads of any importance. Ducks Hill Road probably followed the course of the modern road from its junction with the Rickmansworth road in the north-west corner of the parish. It then ran south through Ruislip village as Bury Street and continued through the open fields as Down Barns Road (now West End Road) to West End in Northolt.[15] Eastcote Road, running south of the Pinn, connected Ruislip village with Eastcote, and Joel Street ran north from Eastcote to join the Pinner road near the eastern boundary. Field End Road, running south from Eastcote Road near the eastern boundary, probably originated as an access road to the Eastcote open fields. On Rocque's map of 1754 it appears to mark the western boundary of East Field.[16]

Long Bridge at Eastcote, which probably carried Eastcote Road across the Pinn, was out of repair as early as 1355. Liability for repairs was vested in the inhabitants of Ruislip village.[17] By 1611 the bridge, responsibility for which had been transferred to the lord of the manor, was again ruinous.[18] A brick and timber structure, maintained at the expense of King's College, Cambridge, as lords of the manor, was in existence by 1758. The college was also responsible for the upkeep of Cannons' Bridge and Parson's Bridge in Bury Street and a wooden bridge at White Butts on the road to Northolt. The responsibility for Clack Bridge across the Pinn at the west end of Clack Lane near the western boundary was divided equally between the college and the lord of Southcote manor.[19] All these were cart bridges, the parish being responsible for repairs to numerous foot bridges.[20]

This broad pattern of settlement and communications remained virtually intact until the coming of the railway at the end of the 19th century and the laying down of access roads to housing estates at the beginning of the 20th. The divisions within the parish are perpetuated in the modern districts of Ruislip, Eastcote, and Northwood. These, with the addition of the later developed areas of Northwood Hills and South Ruislip, comprised the modern urban district.

The origins and early history of settlement in the parish are uncertain. No reliably documented finds of pre-Roman date have been made within its boundaries,[21] and the theories of Roman settlement are largely unsubstantiated.[22] Further conjecture has centred upon the exact nature and extent of the park for wild beasts mentioned at Domesday.[23] This most probably covered much of the heavily-wooded area north of the Pinn. Its boundaries may possibly be inferred from otherwise inexplicable

[6] L. E. Morris, 'Notes on the History of Ruislip Reservoir', *Jnl. Ruislip and District Nat. Hist. Soc.* (1960).
[7] Ruislip-Northwood U.D.C., Terrier 278.
[8] *V.C.H. Mdx.* i. 126.
[9] King's College, Cambridge, Muniments, R. 36. Until *c.* 1750 all assessments are complicated by the use in the parish of a customary acre of 18 ft. to the pole. See letter from John Doharty in 1750: King's Coll., Q. 42/34.
[10] King's Coll., R. 36, R. 38a; B.M. Add. MS. 9368.
[11] O.S. Map 1/2,500, Mdx. ix. 4, 8 (1865 edn.).
[12] King's Coll., Survey 34.
[13] *Petition* (1953).   [14] See p. 139.
[15] And see n. 22.
[16] The earliest maps showing the parish's roads are J. Rocque, *Map of Mdx.* (1754); Map of the 1806 Inclosure: M.R.O., F. 4, F. 5; O.S. Maps 1/2,500, Mdx. ix, x (1865 edn.).

[17] *Public Works in Medieval Law*, ii (Selden Soc. xl), 28.
[18] M.R.O., Acc. 249/4335.   [19] See p. 137.
[20] King's Coll., Q. 42/37; cf. *Rep. of Cttee. of Magistrates on Public Bridges in Mdx.* (1826).
[21] C. E. Vulliamy, *Archaeology of Mdx. and Lond.*
[22] These are contained in Sir M. Sharpe, *Mdx. in British, Roman and Saxon Times, passim*, and have been reproduced in various forms by later writers. Excavations in 1963 on the conjectural line of a Roman road running from Rickmansworth through Ruislip parish along the course of Ducks Hill Road and Bury Street established the existence of a section in Rickmansworth parish: E. V. Parrott, 'A Possible Roman Road Through Ruislip', *Jnl. Ruislip and District Nat. Hist. Soc.* (1963).
[23] H. Braun, 'Earliest Ruislip', *T.L.M.A.S.* vii. 99–123; Hist. Mon. Com. *Mdx.* 108.

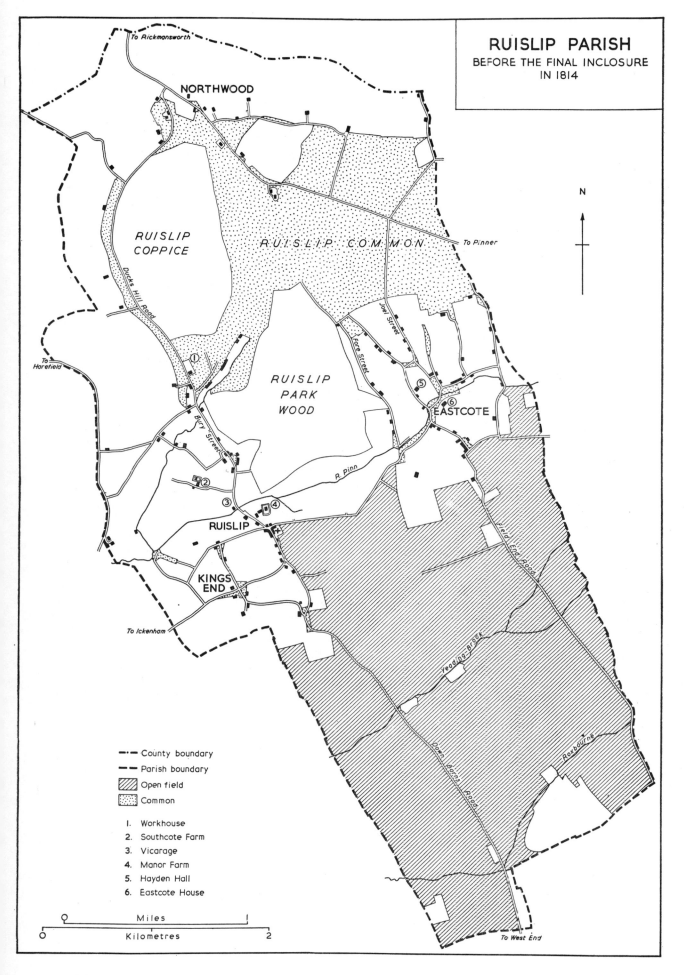

RUISLIP PARISH
BEFORE THE FINAL INCLOSURE IN 1814

To Rickmansworth

NORTHWOOD

RUISLIP COPPICE

RUISLIP COMMON

To Pinner

N

Ducks Hill Road

To Harefield

RUISLIP PARK WOOD

Fore Street

Joel Street

5

6

EASTCOTE

Bury Street

R. Pinn

2

3 4

RUISLIP

KINGS END

Field End Road

To Ickenham

Yeading Brook

Down Barns Road

Roxbourne

To West End

—··— County boundary

— — — Parish boundary

▨ Open field

⁙ Common

1. Workhouse
2. Southcote Farm
3. Vicarage
4. Manor Farm
5. Hayden Hall
6. Eastcote House

Miles 0 — 1

Kilometres 0 — 2

deviations in two of the oldest roads in the parish. Bury Street, running north from Ruislip village, curves west towards the Harefield border before regaining its general northerly direction; Eastcote Road, running parallel to and south of the Pinn, makes a wide sweep southward between Ruislip and Eastcote. Before 20th-century widening traces of a bank are said to have been visible along the north side of Eastcote Road.[24] The construction of the original closure cannot be reliably dated.[25] The park was stocked with deer in 1270,[26] and seems still to have been in existence in 1436 when the boundary palings were repaired.[27] A suggestion that further earthworks enclosed the village and some 90 a. around it[28] appears to be unfounded, although the remains of an unidentified earthwork are visible in the south of Park Wood. Ruislip village itself probably developed from an early settlement south of a crossing place on the Pinn.[29] There was a manorial grange at Northwood in 1248,[30] which may have occupied the site of the later Grange.[31] Northwood, however, separated from the rest of the parish by a belt of woodland, was slow to develop. Eastcote appears as a hamlet by 1323.[32]

By 1565 settlement had assumed the approximate pattern which it presented when the first detailed maps of the parish were made in the mid 19th century.[33] Ruislip village centred upon the church, which was in existence by the end of the 12th century,[34] and the Manor Farm occupying the site of an earlier manor-house[35] at the junction of Bury Street and Eastcote Road. South and north of the road junction scattered settlement lay along Bury Street, and was concentrated near Cannons' Bridge. Between Bury Street and Harefield parish lay South-cote Farm, near the site of Southcote manor-house.[36] A network of minor roads and trackways linked further farms and cottages along Clack Lane, near the western boundary, with Field End and Kings-end to the south-west of Ruislip village. The approximate geographical centre of Eastcote was the junction of Field End Road and Eastcote Road, but settlement followed no definable pattern. Houses and farms lay along both sides of the Pinn following a network of paths and minor roads, chief of which were Joel Street, Wiltshire Lane, Field End Road, and Cheney Street.

Almost the whole of the parish south of Eastcote Road was covered by the open fields. When these were inclosed under the 1804 Act they contained about 2,200 a.[37] The principal fields were Church Field, south of Ruislip church, Great Windmill Field, south-east of Ruislip village, Marlpit Field, which contained 175 a. in the mid 17th century,[38] to the east of the present West End Road, Bourne (Bone) Field to the south, and Roxbourne Field in

the extreme south-west corner of the parish. These lay in the Westcote division of the parish. In the Eastcote division were eastward extensions of Great Windmill Field and Marlpit Field known respectively as Little Windmill Field and Steen (Stone) Field. Well (Cognorth) Field and East Field lay south of Eastcote village. Field boundaries appear to have fluctuated and other field names—Prior's Field, Alderston Field, Tybber Field, Hill Field, Whitingrove Field—are mentioned in connexion with smaller areas or without any exact geographical location.[39] A dispute in 1519 about inclosure in Bourne and Windmill fields indicates that the names of the principal fields and the tenants' rights in them were established at least as early as the beginning of the 14th century.[40] The former open-field area remained unpopulated, except for two or three farmhouses, until the construction of Northolt aerodrome and the development of estates at South Ruislip after 1914.[41] In 1962 there was still grassland south of the Yeading Brook and along the Northolt boundary.

Northwood, separated from the main areas of development by Park and Copse woods and Ruislip Common, which in 1754 extended almost across the whole parish and covered most of the area now known as Northwood Hills, retains much of its autonomous character. A few cottages at Northwood are mentioned in the 1565 survey. Two hundred years later the shape of the hamlet, composed of a few farms and dwellings scattered along the Rickmansworth road, had altered little except for the addition of Holy Trinity church.[42]

An unusual number of timber-framed buildings, dating from the 15th, 16th, and 17th centuries, has survived in the parish. More than fifty were listed in a survey published in 1937[43] and many of these, adapted to modern use, are still in existence. Several are grouped near the church in the old village of Ruislip. Nos. 1–3 and 5–7 High Street are two irregular blocks flanking the west entrance to the churchyard; the former contains work of c. 1500, but both have been much altered on their street frontages. An adjacent range of similar date, nos. 9–15 High Street, has a long east front towards the churchyard with a jettied upper story of exposed close-studded timbering and a moulded bressummer. This building, together with no. 7, was acquired in 1931 by the newly formed Ruislip Village Trust.[44] In 1964 a thorough restoration was carried out by the Trust, the street front being reconstructed and the interior adapted for use as professional offices.[45] The group round the churchyard is completed by the range of former almshouses in Eastcote Road.[46] On the opposite side of High Street the Old Swan Inn and adjacent houses have been much altered but are of 16th- and 17th-century construction. A pair

24 Local information.
25 For a Roman dating see Sharpe, op. cit.
26 Cal. Close, 1268–72, 232.
27 S.C. 6/917/26.
28 Sir M. Sharpe, *Antiquities of Mdx.* 111.
29 *P.N. Mdx.* (E.P.N.S.), 47.
30 B.M. Add. MS. 24316.
31 See below.
32 *Cat. Anct. D.* iv. 555.
33 Except where otherwise stated,the following paragraph is based on a survey of the manor made in 1565: King's Coll., R. 36; Rocque, *Map. of Mdx.*; 1806 Incl. Map: M.R.O., F. 4, F. 5; O.S. Maps 1/2,500, Mdx. ix, x (1865 edn.).
34 See p. 142.
35 See p. 135.
36 See p. 137.
37 M.R.O., F. 4.
38 King's Coll., R. 36.
39 e.g. Rocque, *Map of Mdx.*; King's Coll., R. 36. For the area of some of these in 1565 see J. S. Cockburn, 'An Elizabethan Survey of Ruislip', *Jnl. Ruislip and District Nat. Hist. Soc.* (1963).
40 M.R.O., Acc. 249/39.
41 See p. 132.
42 See p. 144.
43 Hist. Mon. Com. *Mdx.* 108.
44 See p. 140.
45 Date given by occupier.
46 See p. 147.

of farm cottages at the junction of High Street and Bury Street are also timber-framed but were faced with red brick in the earlier 19th century and are now used as shops. The Manor Farm, a house of 16th-century origin,[47] was given to the people of Ruislip by King's College in 1937 together with the farm buildings. Two well-preserved weather-boarded barns stand to the west of the house; the smaller was extensively restored after 1937 and opened as a branch library.[48] Several old buildings survive among modern houses in the Bury Street area. They include a 16th-century farm-house to the north of Cannons' Bridge and Little Manor Farm, the latter incorporating the remains of a medieval hall.[49] The Old House near the south end of Bury Street was refronted c. 1700 and has a coved eaves cornice and a pedimented doorway. On the east side of the street are Woodman's Farm and the Plough Inn. The 'Plough', which has a medieval core, has been much extended; it was licensed in 1746, as was the 'Old Swan' in High Street.[50] There was a tavern at Ruislip in 1636,[51] demolished by 1865, and the 'Black Horse' and the 'Bells' are mentioned in 1732 and 1741 respectively.[52] Other inns licensed at least as early as this date were the 'Sun', the 'Red Lion', the 'White Hart', and the 'Leather Bottle'.[53] The 'Black Pots' stood just north of the present 'Six Bells' on the west side of Bury Street. It was still in existence at the 1804 inclosure,[54] but had been demolished by 1865.[55]

The only substantial old house in Northwood is Northwood Grange at the junction of Green Lane and Rickmansworth Road; it may occupy the site of a manorial grange mentioned in 1248.[56] The present building incorporates a 15th-century block with a crown-post roof, a cross-wing of the same date, and a long range of c. 1600. In 1934 the house was purchased and the lower portion dedicated for the use of parochial organizations.[57] After the war the building was acquired by the council which has converted the upper story into flats. The lower story is still used for cultural and similar meetings.[58]

At Eastcote there are many 16th- and 17th-century timber-framed buildings scattered among modern residential development. They occur mostly in the area north of the River Pinn and in Field End Road. The former include Cuckoo Hill Farm and Mistletoe Farm in Cuckoo Hill, St. Catherine's Farm in Catlins Lane, the Woodman Inn in Joel Street, and Fore Street Farm in Fore Street. Old Cheyney Cottage in Wiltshire Lane (dated 1663) was demolished c. 1960 but Ivy Farm opposite, which retained medieval roof timbers, was still standing in 1968. The Grange in Eastcote High Road is an extensive house of 16th-century origin with 18th-century and later additions; towards the road it has a walled forecourt, a 17th-century cottage, and a weather-boarded barn. Near it is a timber-framed

house called Ramin with an overhanging gable-end and a 16th-century barn. Eastcote House, standing at the junction of Eastcote High Road and Field End Road, was originally a building of the late 16th or early 17th century, refaced and extended in the 18th century. It was the seat of the Hawtrey family, who settled at Eastcote in the 16th century and were lessees of Ruislip manor from 1669 until the 19th century.[59] The house and grounds were purchased by the Middlesex County Council in 1937 and leased to the local authority.[60] For some years they were used for garden parties and other social gatherings, but public use ceased in 1962 and the house was demolished in 1964. In Field End Road are Park Farm, Field End Farm, and Eastcote Cottage; the two latter were partly faced with brick in the mid 19th century. Part of a large timber-framed barn in the garden of the Retreat has been converted into a cottage. A nearby house called the Barns, which may have been of medieval origin, was demolished in 1967. Eastcote, unlike Ruislip village, shows signs of residential occupation in the 18th and earlier 19th centuries. The most imposing house was Hayden Hall standing in its own grounds to the east of Joel Street. It was owned by the Franklin family during the 18th century;[61] by 1962 it had been leased to the Middlesex County Council for civil defence purposes. In 1968 it was unoccupied and rapidly becoming derelict. The oldest part of the house is the central block which is a rebuilding of c. 1700.[62] This rectangular red-brick structure, of two stories and seven bays, has closely set windows, a dentil cornice, and a steeply pitched hipped roof; the central doorway on the south front is surmounted by a scrolled pediment. Flanking the original building are two large Victorian wings. The Old Shooting Box in Eastcote High Road and Southill Farm in Southill Lane are both 18th-century houses with symmetrical red-brick fronts. The mid 19th century is represented by several pairs of smaller residential houses in Field End Road, formerly known as Eastcote Villas.[63]

Between the 16th and the 19th centuries the topography of the parish altered little. By 1754 Ruislip Common had encroached on Park and Copse woods in the north and covered the whole of the central area now known as Northwood Hills. A few dwellings had been built along Bury Street and at Kingsend and Field End to the south and west of Ruislip village.[64] Some 350 a. in the manor of St. Catherine's[65] were inclosed under the first Middlesex Inclosure Act in 1769. All the land affected lay west of Ducks Hill Road. It included West Wood (now Mad Bess Wood) which was common ground.[66] A further 3,000 a. of the parish were inclosed in 1804. Open-field land lying between Eastcote Road and the Northolt boundary made up the bulk of this, but further areas of common land to the north-east of

[47] See p. 135.
[48] Programme of the opening in Ruislip libr.
[49] See p. 136.
[50] M.R.O., L.V. 6/84.
[51] Mdx. and Herts. N. & Q. iv. 79.
[52] M.R.O., Acc. 249/1574.
[53] M.R.O., L.V. 6/84.
[54] M.R.O., Acc. 261/1.
[55] O.S. Map 1/2,500, Mdx. x. 5 (1865 edn.).
[56] B.M. Add. MS. 24316.
[57] Mdx. Advertiser, 12 Oct. 1934.
[58] Ex inf. Ruislip-Northwood U.D.C.
[59] See p. 135.

[60] Ex inf. Ruislip-Northwood U.D.C.
[61] For fuller descriptions of these and other old houses in the parish see Pevsner, Mdx. 44–45, 134–6; Hist. Mon. Com. Mdx. 108–10.
[62] There was a house on the site in the early 17th cent.: B.M. Add. MS. 9367; L. E. Morris, 'Eastcote', Bull. Mdx. Local Hist. Council, v. 8.
[63] O.S. Map 6", Mdx. x. NW. (1865 edn.).
[64] Rocque, Map of Mdx.
[65] See p. 135.
[66] St. Catherine's Inclosure Act: copy penes Ruislip-Northwood U.D.C.

Park and Copse woods were also included.[67] Thirty-nine acres of the Common were purchased from the inclosure commissioners in 1805 by the Grand Junction Canal Co. To this was added a similar area of Park Wood purchased from King's College in 1807. Damming works began a few years later, and the reservoir so formed came into operation in 1816. Some cottages standing between Park Wood and the present Reservoir Road were inundated.[68] Beyond this, inclosure had little effect on the topography of the parish. Eastcote was described as a 'deeply retired and rural' hamlet in 1816,[69] and Ruislip as 'most romantically situated' in 1826.[70] About 1825, however, the Rickmansworth road was turnpiked just north of its junction with Joel Street,[71] and in 1887 the Metropolitan Railway was extended from Pinner to Rickmansworth across the north-east corner of the parish. A station on this line was opened at Northwood, and remained the only station in the parish until that opened in 1904 at Ruislip on the Harrow and Uxbridge Railway Co.'s line between Harrow-on-the-Hill and Uxbridge. Electrification followed in 1905, and the Uxbridge line was incorporated in the Metropolitan Railway system in the same year. Halts on this line were opened at Eastcote in 1906 and Ruislip Manor in 1912. The District Railway opened a through passenger service to the West End and City along this line in 1910. From 1933 Piccadilly line trains ran along the same route, and the two lines operated together for a short time. After the Second World War this service was provided by the Piccadilly line only. Northwood Hills Station on the Metropolitan line, which had been electrified in 1925, was opened in 1933. By the following year three stations on the Great Western Railway's Birmingham line—West Ruislip (1906), South Ruislip (1932), and Ruislip Gardens (1934)—were serving the south of the parish. Following the extension of the Central line from Greenford to West Ruislip in 1948 these three stations were rebuilt and the local steam train service adjusted.[72] A short section of Western Avenue, the London–Oxford arterial road opened in 1934,[73] was driven across the extreme south-west corner of the parish.

Improved railway communications opened up the parish for residential building. In the last decade of the 19th century large houses in their own grounds began to appear near the new station in Green Lane and in newly formed roads to the north of it. Between Green Lane and Rickmansworth Road several streets had been laid out and partly built with smaller houses and continuous terraces.[74] By 1900 King's College had realized the potential value of the manorial estates. Purchases and the taking up of leases between 1901 and 1905 consolidated their estate with a view to future building development. A new road to the west of High Street, giving improved access to Kings End Fields adjoining Ruislip Station, was completed in 1907. The first houses

were built in the same year, and the college formed a company, the Ruislip Building Co., to manage further developments. An agreement with a private company, Garden Estates Ltd., replaced this arrangement in 1910,[75] and houses were advertised at freehold prices ranging from £700 to £800.[76] Most of these appear to have been small detached residences on narrow frontages. In 1911 a town planning competition was organized jointly by the college and the local authority. Plans by A. and J. Soutar[77] were adopted as the basis for the future development of some 6,000 a. of the parish, and finally approved by the local government board in 1914. A new company, Ruislip Manor Ltd., took over the organization of development from Garden Estates in 1911.[78] Further roads, including those across the corner of Copse Wood between Rickmansworth Road and Ducks Hill Road, and Manor Way and Park Way north of Ruislip Manor Station, were laid down in 1912–13. Building sites on an estate between Park Wood and the Pinn were available by 1928, and until the Second World War sales of land for building purposes brought the college a steady income.[79]

Further residential development followed the erection of R.A.F. establishments serving Northolt airfield, which had been established in 1915 on a site in Ruislip parish west of West End Road between the Yeading Brook and the Northolt boundary. During the First World War the airfield served as a training and defensive base. After improvement and extension westward into Ickenham parish, it became an important Fighter Command operational base in 1939. During the later stages of the war the base was further extended, and entered service as London's war-time airport in 1943. From 1945 the airport was devoted completely to civil aviation. After 1952, as operations were gradually transferred to the new London Airport at Heathrow, it ceased to be the country's major terminal. In 1954 Northolt officially ceased to be a civil airport and the base reverted to the R.A.F.[80]

Despite rapid developments in the south of the parish and the encroachment of housing estates into the south of Park Wood and the north of Copse Wood, the area north of the Pinn retained much of its rural character. Nearly 100 a. between Copse and Park woods and the Rickmansworth road were leased by King's College to the Northwood Golf Club in 1899.[81] The Gravel Pits, an area of 14 a. adjoining the golf course to the north-west in the angle of Ducks Hill and Rickmansworth roads, was scheduled by the urban district council in 1905 for preservation as an open space. Between 1905 and 1953 the council acquired a further 660 a. for open spaces, including the area laid down in 1929[82] as Haste Hill Golf Course (1927), King's College Fields between Park Avenue and the Pinn (1938), Poors Field between Copse Wood and Ruislip Lido (1939), and

[67] M.R.O., F. 4, F. 5.
[68] Morris, 'History of Ruislip Reservoir'.
[69] Brewer, *Beauties of Eng. and Wales*, x(5), 577.
[70] Pigot, *Lond. Dir.* (1826).
[71] O.S. Map 1/2,500, Mdx. x. 1 (1865 edn.); Par. Recs., Vestry Mins. 1825.
[72] This section is based on information supplied by the London Transport Executive.
[73] *The Times*, 15 Dec. 1934.
[74] O.S. Map 6", Mdx. v. SW. (1899 edn.); x. NW. (1897 edn.).

[75] King's Coll., *Memoranda Bk.* i.
[76] Brochure of Associated Garden Estates *penes* Ruislip libr.
[77] M.R.O., Acc. 364/40.
[78] King's Coll., *Memoranda Bk.* ii.
[79] Ibid. ii, iii.
[80] Section based on P. Brooks, 'The Northolt Story' *B.E.A. Mag.* nos. 71–73.
[81] King's Coll., *Memoranda Bk.* i.
[82] *Mdx. and Bucks. Advertiser* ,2 Aug. 1929.

Breakspear Road (1949).[83] Permanent preservation of the Manor Farm site and Park and Copse woods was assured by their transference to the Middlesex County Council and the urban district council in 1932 and 1936 respectively.[84] Open spaces in the parish totalled nearly 1,500 a. in 1953.[85] Much of this has been developed by the local authority as sports and recreation grounds. Ruislip Golf Course is laid out over the old Clack Lane to the north of West Ruislip Station. Facilities for most sports are provided at the Cavendish Recreation Ground and the adjoining Bessingby Fields south of Eastcote Station, and an athletics track was laid down in 1953 in King's College Fields. Similar facilities for Northwood and Northwood Hills are provided by the Northwood Recreation Ground in Chestnut Avenue. The Ministry of Health Sports Ground is situated south of Eastcote Station, and the Air Ministry owns another private sports ground, used by local R.A.F. units, in Shenley Avenue south of Ruislip Station.[86]

The open nature of the district attracted several hospitals to the parish. Mount Vernon Hospital, a branch of the North London Consumption Hospital founded in 1860, was built between 1902 and 1904 on a site south of the Rickmansworth road, in the extreme north-west corner of the parish. Initially the hospital had 130 beds and was confined to the treatment of tuberculosis patients. It was constituted a general hospital in 1929, and has since specialized in plastic surgery and cancer treatments. In 1962 the hospital had approximately 550 beds.[87] The first cobalt unit for the treatment of deep-seated cancer to be installed in this country was given to the hospital by a Canadian organization and has been operating since 1954.[88] St. Vincent's Orthopaedic Hospital, which had been established at Clapham in 1910 under the care of the Sisters of Charity of St. Vincent de Paul, took over a private house in Wiltshire Lane at the north end of Park Wood in 1912. At this date the hospital comprised 100 beds housed in wooden huts. These have been rebuilt in brick, and in 1962 there were 164 beds for orthopaedic cases of all types.[89] The Northwood, Pinner and District Hospital in Pinner Road, Northwood, was originally housed in a small hut-like building erected in 1919 as a war memorial. A more substantial building was erected in 1925, and extended in 1930. The hospital now provides beds for 36 patients, and houses physiotherapy and X-ray departments.[90]

After 1930 the pace of development accelerated. In that year a second town planning scheme covered those parts of the urban district not included in the 1914 plan.[91] Private building accounted for a majority of the new houses between the two wars, but since 1945 more than 2,000 dwellings have been erected by the council. Among the chief areas of

post-war building were Northwood Hills, Wiltshire Lane, Woodlands Avenue, and Pine Gardens in Eastcote, and the Dean estate at South Ruislip.[92] About one-half of the council's post-war houses are situated in South Ruislip. The only industries in the parish[93] are also sited in this district on small industrial areas provided for by the 1914 planning scheme. The original industrial estate has been reduced in size and now covers 65 a. south of Victoria Road. Of this, 30 a. are now occupied by the United States 3rd Air Division Headquarters.[94] These installations, established on their present site between 1949 and 1951, include a hospital and social and recreational facilities.[95] South Ruislip lacks the residential character preserved in the earlier-developed districts north of the Piccadilly line. It has no shopping centre to compare with High Street, Ruislip, Field End Road, Eastcote, and Northwood Hills, and almost no pre-20th-century buildings.[96] Many of the houses are compact, semi-detached dwellings of the standardized type built in the 1930s. Much of Ruislip and Eastcote, now joined by houses built along Eastcote Road, is devoted to spacious residential properties in quiet, tree-lined roads. Riverside walks have been preserved along both banks of the Pinn. The rural nature of Northwood, with extensive views over the rest of the parish, has attracted much high-class property, particularly in and around Copse Wood Way, along Green Lane and at the northern end of Ducks Hill Road.

The Domesday Survey mentions 53 people at Ruislip.[97] A mid-13th-century custumal lists more than 120 tenants.[98] For a muster of c. 1335 Ruislip was expected to contribute about 60 footmen, or approximately $\frac{1}{20}$ of the total county force.[99] A series of early-15th-century rentals lists between 105 and 130 tenants of the manor.[1] In 1547 there were 480 communicants in the parish;[2] 254 adult male parishioners took the protestation oath in 1642,[3] and there were 210 occupied houses in 1664.[4] There were said to be about 150 houses in Ruislip village in 1778,[5] and the number of inhabitants in the parish was little more than 1,000 in 1790.[6] The total population had reached only 1,413 by 1841, when there were 136 occupied houses in Ruislip village, 99 in Eastcote, and 41 in Northwood. Between 1891 and 1901 the number of houses in the parish, which had remained fairly constant throughout the 19th century, increased from 383 to 703, while the population rose from 1,836 to 3,566. Continued residential development almost doubled the number of inhabitants over the following decade, and further increases accompanied the establishment and extension of Northolt airfield. Between 1921 and 1931 the population rose from 9,112 to 16,042; by 1951 it had risen to 68,288 and by 1961 to 72,791.[7]

[83] Petition (1953).
[84] Ibid.; King's Coll., Memoranda Bk. iii; Programme of the opening of Park Wood penes Ruislip libr.
[85] Petition (1953).
[86] Ibid.; Ruislip-Northwood U.D. Official Guide (1959).
[87] Ex inf. the Hospital Secretary.
[88] Mdx. Advertiser, 12 Oct. 1955.
[89] Ex inf. the Hospital Secretary; the hospital's Annual Report (1960) classifies the patients treated.
[90] Ex inf. the Administrative Officer.
[91] Plan penes Ruislip-Northwood U.D.C.
[92] Ex inf. Ruislip-Northwood U.D.C., revising figures given in Petition (1953).
[93] See p. 139.

[94] Ex inf. Ruislip-Northwood U.D.C.
[95] Ex inf. the Command Historian.
[96] Hist. Mon. Com. Mdx. 109.
[97] V.C.H. Mdx. i. 126.
[98] B.M. Add. MS. 24316. Parts of the MS. are decayed.
[99] M.R.O., F. 37/1.
[1] King's Coll., R. 39, 40, 41, 44.
[2] E 301/34/180.
[3] Hse. of Lords, Mdx. Protestation Rets.
[4] M.R.O., H.T. 6.
[5] Guildhall MS. 9557.
[6] Ibid. 9558.
[7] Census, 1841–1961.

Among well-known residents mention may be made of Dr. Adam Clarke (1762–1832), an eminent Methodist theologian, who lived intermittently at Hayden Hall from 1805 until his death. He was three times president of the Wesleyan body, and published a number of theological works, the most important of which was an eight-volume scriptural commentary.[8] In 1961 Peter and Helen Kroger were each sentenced to twenty years imprisonment for operating a spy ring dealing in Britain's naval secrets from a house in South Ruislip.[9]

MANORS AND OTHER ESTATES. Before the Norman Conquest the manor of *RUISLIP* was held by Wlward Wit, a thegn of King Edward, who also held the manors of Kempton and Kingsbury in Middlesex and considerable estates elsewhere. By 1086 it had passed to Ernulf of Hesdin (*de Hesding*),[10] who *c.* 1087 granted it to the Abbot and Convent of the Benedictine Abbey of Bec in Normandy.[11] Bec enjoyed possession of it until 1211 when King John sequestrated the properties of the abbey.[12] From 1295,[13] and particularly after the outbreak of the wars with France in 1337, the English properties of alien priories were frequently sequestrated by the Crown.[14] The Prior of Ogbourne, as Bec's proctor in England, was permitted to retain the abbey properties only in return for a heavy annual farm.[15]

The Bec properties were finally confiscated in 1404, and Henry IV granted Ruislip manor, with reversion to the king and his heirs, jointly to his third son John, later Duke of Bedford, William de St. Vaast, Prior of Ogbourne, and Thomas Langley, Bishop of Durham 1406–37.[16] The prior shortly afterwards died, and no successor was appointed.[17] Langley exchanged his interest in Ruislip for other property,[18] leaving John in sole possession of the manor. On his death in 1435 the manor reverted to the Crown, and although Bec petitioned the king for the restoration of their property,[19] Henry VI in 1437 leased Ruislip manor, with a plot called Northwood, for seven years, later extended to a grant for life, to his chancellor John Somerset.[20] In 1438 the king granted the reversion on this estate to the University of Cambridge.[21] The University surrendered its interest in 1441, and the king granted the reversion to his new foundation, the College of St. Mary and St. Nicholas, later King's College, Cambridge.[22]

In 1451, shortly after a Commons petition requesting the dismissal of Somerset,[23] Ruislip manor was granted outright to King's College.[24] In 1461, however, Henry VI was defeated by Edward of York and the Lancastrian grants were declared void. King's College was not included in the list of exemptions;[25] but in the following year Edward IV granted Ruislip manor, with Northwood, in free alms to King's College,[26] in whose possession it remained until the break-up of the college estates in the early 20th century.[27]

In 1086 Ruislip manor was assessed at 30 hides, and valued at £20. There were 11 hides in demesne.[28] Although the bulk of this later consisted of Copse and Park woods and open-field land south of Ruislip village,[29] part of the demesne lay in the north of the parish and was farmed from a grange at Northwood.[30] By 1294, when the area of the demesne, excluding woodland, was estimated at about 1,000 a., the value of the manor had increased to £81.[31] In 1435 its value was £103.[32] The demesne contained 1,074 a. in 1642,[33] and 1,097 a. in 1745.[34] After the replacement of the customary acre by statute measurement in 1750,[35] the acreage in demesne was assessed at 1,455 a.[36]

Although Bec normally farmed the manor, leases of the demesne occur from an early date. Peter Fountain leased it in 1251 at an annual farm of one mark.[37] For a period during the 14th century the demesne lands at Northwood were leased separately.[38] After the manor came into the possession of King's College, however, it was continuously in the hands of lessees, and the demesne lands, including the woods, were normally leased in their entirety.[39] Roger More, Henry VIII's baker, leased the demesne in 1529 at an annual rent of £69.[40] More held some rights in the manor, and was to be presented each year with a new gown such as the gentlemen of the college wore. The college reserved the right to hold courts and the privileges and profits thereof until 1565 when they were granted, with a lease of the demesne and woodland, to Robert Christmas.[41] A lease to Robert Cecil, Earl of Salisbury, in 1602 included the mansion house and the right to dig marl. The terms of the farm then included a money-rent of £46 and a food-rent of 30 qr. of wheat and 52 qr. of malt,[42] and this remained substantially unchanged until 1810 when the money-rent was increased to £86.[43] The lease remained in the

[8] *D.N.B.*
[9] *The Times,* 23 Mar. 1961.
[10] *V.C.H. Mdx.* i. 101, 126.
[11] H. E. Salter, 'Two Deeds about the Abbey of Bec', *Eng. Hist. Rev.* xl. 74–75; *V.C.H. Mdx.* i. 114.
[12] *Pipe R.* 1211 (P.R.S. N.S. xxviii), 136. For a discussion of this, and later confiscations see M. Morgan, 'Suppression of the Alien Priories', *History,* xxvi. 204–12.
[13] E 106/2 (1–6).
[14] M. Morgan, *English Lands of the Abbey of Bec,* 47.
[15] For the relationship between the priors of Ruislip and Ogbourne see *V.C.H. Wilts.* iii. 395–6 and *V.C.H. Mdx.* i. 202–4.
[16] St. George's Chapel, Windsor, White Book, f. 91.
[17] *V.C.H. Wilts.* iii. 396.
[18] St. George's Chapel, x. 4. 2.
[19] A. A. Porée, *Histoire de l'Abbaye du Bec* (Evreux, 1901), ii. 217–18.
[20] King's Coll., Q. 9.
[21] Ibid. 11.
[22] *Cal. Pat.* 1436–41, 557.
[23] *D.N.B.* xviii. 653; J. C. Wedgwood and Anne D. Holt, *History of Parliament. Biographies of members of Commons 1439–1509,* p. 781.

[24] King's Coll., A. 35.
[25] *Rot. Parl.* v. 463–75. For the effect on King's Coll. see *V.C.H. Cambs.* iii. 379.
[26] *Cal. Pat.* 1461–7, 74.
[27] See p. 132.
[28] *V.C.H. Mdx.* i. 126.
[29] King's Coll., R. 36, R. 38, R. 38a; M.R.O., Acc. 668/75.
[30] B.M. Add. MS. 24316; S.C. 6/1126/5.
[31] E 106/2/1.
[32] S.C. 6/917/27. cf. S.C. 6/917/26.
[33] King's Coll., R. 38.
[34] Ibid. 38a.
[35] See p. 128.
[36] King's Coll., Surveys and Terriers, 1565–1753.
[37] Porée, op. cit. ii. 214.
[38] King's Coll., Q. 8; Morgan, *English Lands of Bec,* 115.
[39] King's Coll., Ledger Bk. i. Occasionally the woods were leased separately: King's Coll., Q. 13.
[40] King's Coll., Q. 13.
[41] King's Coll., Ledger Bk. ii.
[42] Ibid. iii.
[43] Ibid. xiv.

Cecil family until 1669 when it was acquired by Ralph Hawtrey of Eastcote.[44] The Hawtreys and their descendants, the Rogerses and Deanes, retained the farm until it was taken up by the college in the late 19th century.[45]

It has been suggested that a Norman motte-and-bailey castle occupied the site of the present Manor Farm.[46] The theory is, however, based entirely on topographical evidence, all of which is open to alternative interpretation. After the transfer of Ruislip to Bec a small monastic cell was established there in the 12th century.[47] The nature of the early building is uncertain, but during the 13th century Ruislip became an important administrative centre for Bec's English properties,[48] and a manor-house incorporating a chapel was in existence by 1294.[49] Silver plate valued at £17, linen, and furniture are mentioned in 1324.[50] An inventory of 1435 indicates that the building was extensive, containing a hall, counting-house, prior's chamber, lord's chamber, forester's chamber, and chapel, together with a scullery and bakehouse.[51] The site of this building was probably a few yards west of the present Manor Farm where early masonry has been dug up.[52] In 1613 King's College, with the consent of the lessee of Ruislip manor, licensed the demolition of the Friar's Hall, presumably the remains of the earlier building.[53] The present Manor Farm is a two-storied, timber-framed building of early-16th-century date with 18th-century and later alterations.[54] A moat completely encircled the site in 1750.[55] This was still intact in 1865, but by 1896 the northern portion had been filled in and the moat had acquired roughly its present dimensions.[56] The Manor Farm is now owned by the local authority,[57] and is used by cultural and health organizations.

The manor of *ST. CATHERINE'S*, also called St. Catherine End or Little Manor, seems to have originated in an estate in Ruislip parish held of the manor of Harmondsworth. A charter of c. 1087, confirming Ernulf of Hesdin's gift to the Abbey of Bec of the whole of Ruislip manor, excluded one hide held at this date by the Abbey of the Holy Trinity, or St. Catherine's, at Rouen.[58] This land probably passed to the abbey with the manor of Harmondsworth[59] which had been granted to Holy Trinity in 1069.[60]

Subsequently St. Catherine's manor seems to have passed as a sub-manor of Harmondsworth. In 1391 the Abbey of Holy Trinity had licence to sell all its English possessions.[61] St. Catherine's manor, as a parcel of Harmondsworth, was acquired by William

of Wykeham, Bishop of Winchester, and formed part of the endowment of Winchester College.[62] The college retained the Harmondsworth properties until 1543 when they were surrendered, in exchange for other lands, to Henry VIII.[63] Four years later, in 1547, the manor and lordship of Harmondsworth, including the woods called Westwood and Lowyshill in Ruislip parish, were granted to William, later Lord Paget,[64] and the Ruislip estate then descended with the other Paget properties.[65]

St. Catherine's manor was included in a list of Harmondsworth properties in 1588. It was then referred to as the manor of Ruislip, and was valued at 100 marks, exclusive of woodland.[66] In 1603 William, Lord Paget, sold the manor of Ruislip, with Westwood and Lowyshill, to Henry and Catherine Clarke.[67] The instrument describes the property as formerly held by Winchester College, and must refer to St. Catherine's manor since the Pagets never held the capital manor of Ruislip and the Southcote estate in Ruislip parish had passed to Clarke in 1597.[68]

During the early 17th century the descent of the manor is obscure. By 1680 it was in the hands of one John Reeves,[69] who may have held it as early as 1654.[70] The estate seems to have passed with that of Southcote, first to Reeves's widow and then c. 1700 to Robert Seymour.[71] In 1719 Henry Seymour of Hanford (Dors.) sold an estate called the manor of Ruislip, or Catherine-end, to John Child, the London banker. The property then passed to Child's son Christopher who devised it to his four nieces. One of these, Sarah Mico, married John Lewin who purchased the other three moieties in 1768 and was sole lord of the manor at the inclosure of the following year.[72] In 1800 the property was in moieties between Sarah Lewin and William Sheppard, husband of Susanna, the daughter and co-heir of John Lewin.[73] The manor remained in the hands of the Sheppards and the Cox family of Uxbridge until it was broken up later in the 19th century.

St. Catherine's manor lay in the west of the parish between Bury Street, Ducks Hill Road, and the parish boundary. Until the 1769 inclosure, however, precise details of its extent are lacking. The Abbey of Holy Trinity was involved in a dispute over land in Ruislip as early as 1238.[74] By 1587 the area of the manor seems to have been approximately 300 a., including 160 a. of commons. There were then nine free and fifteen copyhold tenants.[75] An undated document of c. 1740 lists twenty free and eighteen

[44] Ibid. vi.   [45] Ibid. vi–xv.
[46] H. Braun, 'Earliest Ruislip', *T.L.M.A.S.* vii. 99; quoted in Hist. Mon. Com. *Mdx.* 108, and Pevsner, *Mdx.* 136.
[47] *V.C.H. Mdx.* i. 202.
[48] Morgan, *English Lands of Bec, passim*; *V.C.H. Mdx.* i. 202.
[49] E 106/2/1.
[50] S.C. 6/1126/5.
[51] S.C. 6/917/26.
[52] Sir Cyril Flower, 'The Religious Houses of West Middlesex', *T.L.M.A.S.* ii. 203–4.
[53] King's Coll., Q. 41.
[54] Hist. Mon. Com. *Mdx.* 107.
[55] See plate facing p. 127.
[56] O.S. Map 1/2,500, Mdx. x. 9 (1865 and 1896 edns.).
[57] See p. 131.
[58] Salter, 'Two Deeds about the Abbey of Bec', *E.H.R.* xl. 74–75. A copy of the charter is in the Arundel White Book: St. George's Chapel, iv. B. 1, f. 153.

[59] For the position of the Prior of Harmondsworth as Proctor of St. Catherine's Abbey see *V.C.H. Mdx.* i. 201.
[60] J. A. Deville, *Cartulaire de l'Abbaye de la Sainte-Trinité du Mont de Rouen* (Paris, 1840), 455; *Regesta Regum Anglo-Normannorum*, i, ed. H. W. C. Davis, no. 29.
[61] *Cal. Pat.* 1388–92, 374, 434.
[62] Ibid. 471; Winchester Coll., Titley drawer, no. 20(17).
[63] *L. & P. Hen. VIII*, xviii(2), p. 124.
[64] *Cal. Pat.* 1547–8, 45.
[65] See above.
[66] M.R.O., Acc. 446/EM. 40.
[67] M.R.O., Acc. 446/ED. 103.
[68] M.R.O., Acc. 249/153; and see below.
[69] B.M. Add. MS. 9368.
[70] Ibid. 9367.   [71] See below.
[72] Copy of St. Catherine's Inclosure Act *penes* Ruislip-Northwood U.D.C.; M.R.O., Acc. 249/2707.
[73] Lysons, *Mdx. Pars.* 210.
[74] *Close R.* 1237–42, 148.
[75] E 178/1430.

copyhold tenants.[76] By 1769 St. Catherine's manor included more than 400 a., but by this date it had been merged with the Southcote estate[77] and their respective areas are uncertain. Included in the composite manor were 150 a. of woodland in and around the present Mad Bess Wood and some 200 a. of commons called West Wood.[78] The manor boundaries are shown on a map of the 1804 inclosures.[79] Ducks Hill Road and the parish boundary mark the eastern and western limits of the manor. The northern boundary runs just north of the present Mad Bess Wood, and the southern follows a line extended from Clack Bridge due east to Bury Street.

There is no documentary evidence for the existence of a manor-house in St. Catherine's manor. Little Manor Farm, standing to the west of Bury Street about half-a-mile north of Ruislip village, appears to incorporate part of the roof of a single-storied medieval hall between two gabled cross-wings.[80] It is not possible, however, to identify the building definitely as belonging to St. Catherine's manor.

The relationship of the manor or freehold estate of *SOUTHCOTE* to the parishes of Harmondsworth and Ruislip and to the manor of St. Catherine's is complex. Southcote manor appears to have evolved out of the holdings of the Southcote family who held land in Ruislip and Harmondsworth from at least the 13th century.[81] The land held initially by the Southcotes can be identified with the messuage attaching to their hereditary office of forester of Harmondsworth,[82] whose land is mentioned in 1230.[83] In 1248 Roger de Southcote and Avice his wife held three virgates in the capital manor of Ruislip.[84] A rental of Richard II's time refers to a tenement in Ruislip parish held of the lord of Harmondsworth, attaching to which were 80 a. at Eastcote held of the Prior of Ogbourne and 80 a. held of John Shorediche. The holder in serjeanty of this tenement was to be woodward of the lord of Harmondsworth.[85] In 1390 Richard Palmer, forester of Harmondsworth, did fealty for a tenement in Ruislip said formerly to have been held by Roger, son of Roger de Southcote, and in Edward III's time in farm by Alice Perrers and two clerks, Thomas Spigurnel and Adam de Hertingdon.[86]

In the late 13th century Roger de Southcote, son of Roger and Avice, had received 16 a. of land lying in Sipson in Harmondsworth from Roger de Cruce of Sipson,[87] and further property from William de la Logge,[88] William's widow,[89] and others.[90] Hence by 1300 there were Southcote holdings in both Harmondsworth and Ruislip parishes. Roger de Southcote's son, Robert, acquired in 1310 three houses and three carucates of land from Henry Spigurnel, lying not only in Southcote and Har-

mondsworth, but also in Stanwell, Harrow, Hillingdon, Uxbridge, Ickenham, and Ruislip.[91] Elizabeth, Robert de Southcote's widow, was holding land described as her manor of Ruislip in 1338,[92] but in 1341 their son, John de Southcote, sold the reversion on the whole property to William and Isabel Pycot. The property, held at this date by Elias de Saunford for the life of his wife Elizabeth, consisted of two houses and four carucates and 49 a. of land situated in Harmondsworth, Sipson, Southcote by Colnbrook, Ruislip, and elsewhere in Middlesex and Buckinghamshire.[93] This same property passed from Pycot some time before 1349, as in that year it was quitclaimed to Thomas de Colle and John de Padbury by Denise, widow of John Durant.[94]

In 1342 Elias and Elizabeth de Saunford also quitclaimed to William and Isabel their rights in property called the manors of Southcote and Ruislip which had been held by both John de Southcote and his mother.[95] The instrument implies a distinction between the Harmondsworth properties, called Southcote, and those lands lying in Ruislip. The manors called Southcote and Ruislip passed in 1348 from William Pycot's widow and her second husband, Edmund Blackwater, to Thomas de Colle and John de Padbury.[96] In 1349, therefore, Padbury and Colle held two different properties which together appear to have formed the manor of Southcote by Colnbrook which lies in Harmondsworth.

Padbury inherited Colle's interest, and in 1364 sold the manor of Southcote by Colnbrook to Odo Purchace, a London draper. The conveyance is dated from Ruislip, and the two grants of the Southcotes' lands, by Denise Durant and by the Blackwaters, are given as the source of the manor of Southcote by Colnbrook.[97] In the same year Purchace disposed of the manor to John atte Mulle, John Lessy, Vicar of Drayton, and William de Grendon, another clerk.[98] In 1375 Purchace's daughter, Christine, and her husband, Walter Aubrey, bought back the manor from two Londoners, John de Hilingford and Stephen de Kendale, to whom Lessy and Grendon had sold it.[99] At some time before 1375 what appear to be the Southcote lands in Ruislip had passed to Adam de Hertingdon and Thomas Spigurnel,[1] who were said in 1390 to have been holding jointly with Alice Perrers, Edward III's favourite.[2] By 1378 the Ruislip property had been divided between Alice Perrers and William Smith (or Southcote) of Ruislip. Alice's moiety was described as the manor of Southcote in Ruislip, and included the site of the manor, with a ruinous building on it, and 112 a. of land. This she held from several lords, including the priors of Harmondsworth and Ogbourne.[3]

After the confiscation of the Perrers properties in

[76] A list of tenants in the manor of St. Catherine End *penes* Ruislip-Northwood U.D.C.
[77] See below.
[78] Copy of St. Catherine's Inclosure Act *penes* Ruislip-Northwood U.D.C.
[79] Map of Ruislip, as inclosed by Act of Parliament *penes* Ruislip-Northwood U.D.C.
[80] Hist. Mon. Com. *Mdx.* 109.
[81] *Feet of F. Lond. and Mdx.* i. 221.
[82] M.R.O., Acc. 446/L1/14.
[83] Ibid. /L1/17.
[84] B.M. Add. MS. 24316.
[85] S.C. 12/11/20; M.R.O., Acc. 446/L1/16.
[86] Winchester Coll. Muns., 22988 a, b; M.R.O., Acc. 446/L1/14. See also M.R.O., Acc. 446/L1/16.

[87] E 210/D 3247, 3580, 4004. For Roger see p. 8.
[88] E 210/D 3236.   [89] Ibid. 6839.
[90] Ibid. 5608, 7904.
[91] C.P. 25(1)/285/28/27.
[92] S.C. 11/443.
[93] C.P. 25(1)/150/58/144; Winchester Coll., 11470.
[94] E 326/B 4526.
[95] E 210/D 1612.
[96] C.P. 25(1)/150/63/255.
[97] *Cal. Close*, 1360-4, 562-3.
[98] E 210/D 9599.
[99] Ibid. 8217.
[1] *Cal. Pat.* 1374-7, 89.
[2] Winchester Coll., 22988 a, b. See above.
[3] C 145/213/50.

1378, Southcote manor was leased to Peter Petrewogh,[4] who held it until 1379 when the forfeited properties were regranted to William of Windsor whom Alice had married.[5] The manor was then said to include lands in Ruislip, Harrow, Stanwell, and Colnbrook.[6] In 1400 part of the property was sold by John Kirkham of London to Thomas Arthington.[7] What appears to have been the remainder of the manor came into Arthington's hands in 1407 when William Smith quitclaimed to him all the lands and rents that had been the property of Robert and Richard Southcote, and of John, William's father.[8] Margery Southcote, however, had an interest in the manor of Southcote in 1446 when she transferred it to Nicholas Bolnehull.[9]

There still seems to have been a division within the manor. In 1454 William Chamber, a Yorkshire gentleman, granted to William Morton all the lands in Ruislip belonging to him as cousin and heir of Thomas Arthington.[10] Morton acquired further property, described as Southcote manor and the lands belonging thereto in Ruislip, from Robert Manfeld and Thomas Redehough in 1458.[11] A Southcote rental of Henry VI's time called it the manor of Ruislip,[12] and a Harmondsworth rental of 1549 includes the manor of Southcote in Ruislip, held of Harmondsworth manor.[13] It seems that Southcote manor is here confused with the Ruislip manor of St. Catherine's which had been granted to William Paget, together with Harmondsworth manor, in 1547.[14] In 1597 Richard Vincent, John Coggs, and Richard Melham conveyed Southcote manor to Henry Clarke,[15] who purchased the manor of St. Catherine's from Lord Paget in 1603.[16]

Subsequently the Southcote and St. Catherine's estates seem to have passed together, although details of the descent during the early 17th century are obscure. By 1680 John Reeves was holding 135 a. in Ruislip, including 90 a. of coppice at Southcote.[17] Some at least of this land he held as early as 1654.[18] On his death the property passed to his widow, and, about 1700, to Robert Seymour.[19] In 1719 Henry Seymour sold a capital messuage in an estate called Southcote to John Child who at the same time purchased the manor of St. Catherine End.[20] The descent of Southcote then followed that of St. Catherine's.[21]

There seems to have been a manor-house of Southcote in the 14th century. Whether or not the ruined building standing on the manor site in 1378 was the manor-house is uncertain.[22] Buildings on a moated site covering almost an acre are shown on a map of 1806 immediately north of Southcote Farm between Bury Street and the parish boundary.[23] Later 19th-century maps show no buildings.[24] The moat still existed in 1937,[25] but had been filled in by 1962.

In 1685 ten acres at Ducks Hill in Ruislip parish were said to belong to the manor of Bucknalls (More) in Hertfordshire.[26] This seems to represent the remainder of land at Northwood which in 1428 had been seized by the lord of the manor of More in exercise of a leet jurisdiction granting the right to confiscate felons' goods.[27] The estate then consisted of three messuages belonging to Guy atte Hill, and a messuage with 12 a. called Whiteslands which were Guy's and had formerly belonged to William White.[28] In 1520 the estate was referred to as a messuage, formerly two messuages, called Guy atte Hilles and Whytts in Ruislip parish;[29] and in 1601 as Gyett Hills in Ruislip.[30] In 1695 Ralph Hawtrey of Eastcote sold an estate called Gyetts Hills, consisting of approximately 90 a., to Sir Bartholomew Shower.[31] Nothing further is known of the property, although its name apparently survived in that of Gatehill Farm, Northwood, in the north-east corner of the parish. By 1937 the farm-house was said to be mainly of brick.[32]

ECONOMIC AND SOCIAL HISTORY. The population recorded in 1086 comprised a priest, 29 villeins, seven bordars each on four acres, eight cottars, four serfs, and four Frenchmen who shared three hides and one virgate.[33] By 1248 there were at least two free tenants of the manor. One of these, Roger de la Downe (Dune), lord of the manor of Down Barns in Northolt, held a hide and there was one other single-hide holding. Twelve tenants each held half a hide and two had three-virgate holdings. Thirty-six tenants each held a virgate each, six held half a virgate, and 59 had holdings of less than half a virgate. Manorial servants at this date included a cookboy at the manor and one at each of the granges at Bourne and Northwood.[34] In 1294 there were a mace-bearer, door-keeper, cook, baker, gardener, and carpenter in the manor-house.[35] At least one miller lived in the parish by 1250.[36] Among the customary tenants in 1324 were four men employed in carrying goods between Ruislip and London, a swineherd, cowherd, and hayward, as well as a woodward and a tile-counter.[37] By the 1430s there were two shopkeepers,[38] a joiner,[39] and a smith working a smithy near the manor-house gate.[40] Until the 19th century, however, the economic history of Ruislip is predominantly agrarian. Almost one-half of the total population in 1801 was

4 *Cal. Fine R.* 1378, 74.
5 B.M. Add. MS. 38810.
6 *Cal. Pat.* 1377–81, 503.
7 C.P. 25(1)/290/59/5.
8 *Cal. Close,* 1405–9, 251.
9 C.P. 25(1)/152/92/125.
10 *Cal. Close,* 1447–54, 500.
11 Ibid. 1454–61, 349.
12 S.C. 11/447.
13 M.R.O., Acc. 446/EM. 37.
14 See above.
15 M.R.O., Acc. 249/153.
16 M.R.O., Acc. 446/ED. 103; and see above.
17 B.M. Add. MS. 9368.
18 Ibid. 9367.
19 Ibid. 9368.
20 See above.
21 See above.
22 C 145/213/50. See above.

23 Ruislip Incl. Map (1806).
24 O.S. Maps 1/2,500, Mdx. x. 1, 5 (1865 and later edns.).
25 Hist. Mon. Com. *Mdx.* 107; cf. *V.C.H. Mdx.* ii. 9.
26 B.M. Add. MS. 9368.
27 King's Coll., Q. 51.
28 King's Coll., Q. 51, R. 39, R. 42.
29 S.C. 2/178/5.
30 M.R.O., Acc. 249/184.
31 MS. *penes* Soc. of Genealogists.
32 Hist. Mon. Com. *Mdx.* 109.
33 *V.C.H. Mdx.* i. 126.
34 B.M. Add. MS. 24316.
35 E 106/2/1; *V.C.H. Mdx.* i. 203.
36 B.M. Add. MS. 24316.
37 S.C. 6/1126/5.
38 King's Coll., R. 41.
39 Ibid. 44.
40 Ibid. 40.

employed in agriculture. By 1831 when 206 families were so employed, only 48 families were said to gain a living by trade.[41] During the late 19th and 20th centuries, however, the opening of communications stimulated residential development and a proportionate decrease in the amount of agricultural land. Minor industrial settlement has not balanced the rapid increase in population, and the parish has developed as a residential and dormitory suburb.[42]

In 1086 there was land for 20 ploughs on the manor. The lord had 3 ploughs on his 11 demesne hides, and the villeins and Frenchmen shared 12 ploughs with room for 5 more. There was pasture for the cattle of the vill, and the woodland was sufficient to support 1,500 pigs.[43] During the period of demesne farming in the 12th and 13th centuries the amount of arable in demesne seems to have remained constant at about 900 a.[44] For convenience of working this had been divided by 1250 into three parts, directed from the manor-house at Ruislip and from granges at Northwood and Bourne in the open fields to the south.[45] Difficulties in cultivating the extensive demesne probably account for the heavy services rendered by Ruislip tenants. Although some commutation of labour services had taken place in the early 13th century,[46] in 1250 most of the tenants owed customary services. There seems to have been no consistent relationship between the size of holdings and the services rendered, but tenants holding less than half a virgate generally owed only the standard obligation to provide labour on ploughing and harvest boondays and to pay pannage. At least 27 tenants, however, rendered in addition heavy weekly services of manuring, ploughing, harrowing, reaping, shearing, and other general farm maintenance work. They also had to provide carriage to the Thames for produce exported to Bec, and transport and maintenance for monks journeying from Ruislip. About 40 tenants held 'assized' land, for which they paid an increased rent when not rendering customary services.[47] While Bec farmed the demesne, the manorial economy was dependent rather on the sale of corn and wood than on raising livestock. Wheat (961 qr.), oats (912 qr.), and peas and beans (190 qr.) were the main crops in 1289. Out of a total revenue of about £121, £31 accrued from the sale of corn and beans, £30 from wood, and £4 from wool and fleeces. Pannage brought in an additional £4.[48] Five years later, of the 907 a. cultivated in demesne, 330 a. were sown with wheat and 330 a. with oats. Animals mentioned were used chiefly for farm operations, but the stock included 121 pigs, 25 cows, and 89 sheep. Pannage was then worth 100s.[49] In 1324 the stock included 100 sheep and 30 cows in addition to draught animals. By this date labour services were not being fully utilized, since the accounts include payments to men hired for harrowing, threshing, and winnowing.[50]

During the 14th century Bec gradually lost contact with its English estates.[51] Relaxation of control during Crown confiscations seems to have encouraged disorder and changes in the agrarian economy. The demesne lands were said to be lying wholly uncultivated after disturbances in 1343,[52] and there were further disorders, apparently over land holdings, in 1391.[53] By 1435 money payments seem to have entirely replaced labour services, and much of the demesne arable had been leased to the tenants.[54]

How far the economy of the demesne arable is reflected in that of the open fields is uncertain. By 1517 inclosure for pasture in Ruislip had resulted in the destruction of four holdings of ploughland. Twelve persons were said to have been dispossessed, and four messuages had become ruinous, 'the people turned out and the praise of God decayed'.[55] A dispute between the copyhold tenants and King's College over rights of common pasture in and passage through the common fields was taken to arbitration in 1521. It seems that from about 1500 the lessees of the demesne had denied the tenants' rights in Bourne and Windmill fields and in a meadow called Bourne Wyck. Six arable holdings were said to have been turned over to pasture, 30 persons had been deprived of work, and 15 cottages had been deserted. The arbitrators supported the tenants' rights against the college, but advised them to enter the fields only by the normal access roads and not to pull down hedges.[56] About 1545 the free and copyhold tenants filed a bill in Chancery alleging that Guy Wade, the farmer of the demesne, had again denied their customary rights of pasture and passage in the common fields.[57]

Disagreements over rights in the open fields were superseded about 1570 by a prolonged dispute between the lessee, Robert Christmas, and his tenants over the precise meaning of copyhold tenure. The excessive fines he levied on the admission of copyhold tenants and other abuses of manorial custom occasioned complaints to the college.[58] In 1579 and again in 1583 the copyhold tenants and the college agreed on a scale of payments in composition of customary duties,[59] but the matter dragged on until c. 1605 when the composition agreement was ratified by Act of Parliament. The college consented to stabilize fines on admission at one year's rent, and the tenants agreed to pay double rent on rents of £40 or over.[60] Other conditions of tenure were defined in 1640. Copyholders were said to have rights of common herbage and to the soil of the waste, and to be entitled to fell trees and pull down buildings on their lands.[61]

Regulations governing the use of the open fields were normally enforced in the manor court.[62] An agreement made between the tenants in 1651 suggests, however, that the activity of the leet may have been declining. The agreement provided for a scale of fines for overloading the stubble with cattle, allowing cattle to stray in the corn, and permitting

[41] Census, 1801, 1831.
[42] See above, p. 132; Census, 1891–1951.
[43] V.C.H. Mdx. i. 126.
[44] E 106/2/1.   [45] B.M. Add. MS. 24316
[46] King's Coll., Q. 2.
[47] B.M. Add. MS. 24316.
[48] Eton Coll. Muns., drawer D.5 (uncalendared).
[49] E 106/2/1.
[50] S.C. 6/1126/5; cf. C 47/18/1/12.
[51] Morgan, English Lands of Bec, 117–18. See also V.C.H. Mdx. i. 203.

[52] Cal. Pat. 1343–5, 174.
[53] Ibid. 1388–92, 519.
[54] S.C. 6/917/26,/27.
[55] V.C.H. Mdx. ii. 89.
[56] M.R.O., Acc. 249/39.   [57] Ibid. /21.
[58] King's Coll., Q. 42/4, /6.
[59] King's Coll., Ledger Bk. ii; Q. 25; M.R.O., Acc. 249/107.
[60] M.R.O., Acc. 249/200; and see Acc. 249/4004–4216.
[61] M.R.O., Acc. 249/875, Acc. 538/1.
[62] e.g. M.R.O., Acc. 446/M.100, Acc. 249/4335, /4183.

strangers to enter the common fields.[63] These regulations, with the addition of others governing the ringing of hogs, the marking of cattle and sheep, and the mending of hedges, were repeated in a leet presentment of 1742 setting out thirteen 'bye-laws' of the manor.[64]

The pattern of arable farming remained substantially unchanged during the 17th and 18th centuries. Ralph Hawtrey paid tithes on 600 a. of wheat and 600 a. of beans grown in 1722 on land leased from King's College.[65] Corn tithes paid by Elizabeth Rogers in 1756 on 1,623 a. of arable included £109 on wheat and £100 on beans.[66] In 1801 there were still 452 a. of wheat and 439 a. of beans in the parish, as well as small amounts of oats, barley, potatoes, and peas.[67] By this date, however, approximately 350 a. west of Bury Street had been inclosed under the 1769 award;[68] 557 a. of meadow and 245 a. of arable, some of which was in the open fields,[69] were said to have been inclosed by 1798.[70] In that year John Middleton advocated wholesale inclosure of the open fields, pointing out that although the open-field system had been modified in most areas by the abolition of fallow, there was still one field in Eastcote and one in Ruislip laid down to fallow every third year.[71] About 3,000 a. of the parish, including more than 2,000 a. in the open fields, were inclosed under the 1804 award, which was executed in 1814.[72] Changes in the pattern of land utilization followed and much of the inclosed land was turned over to hay. By 1880 some 4,232 a. were under mowing grass. There were also 868 cattle, 1,056 sheep, and 353 pigs.[73] In 1920, although Northolt airfield and building estates were encroaching on the arable,[74] there were still 3,328 a. of grass, 727 cattle, 555 sheep, and 247 pigs in the parish.[75] As late as 1931 there were 236 people in Ruislip still engaged in agriculture,[76] and in 1962 farming on a small scale was still practised in the north and extreme south of the parish.

There seems to have been a water-mill at Ruislip before 1248 when Roger de Southcote was paying rent for a millpond called Sitteclak.[77] In 1294 there were two mills in the manor, a windmill and a water-mill, valued together at 40s.[78] A mill of unspecified type is mentioned in a rental of 1442.[79] After this date there are no further references to mills in Ruislip, although a miller is mentioned in 1565.[80] The location of all these mills is uncertain, although Windmill Hill south of Ruislip village may indicate the site of the 13th-century windmill. The remains of what appears to be a mill leet were, and in part still are, traceable starting from a point on the Pinn near Fore

Street in Eastcote, and then running north of the Manor Farm to rejoin the Pinn west of Bury Street.[81] A water-mill may possibly have been sited on Bury Street where it crosses this ditch.[82]

There was little industry in Ruislip before 1930, and only limited industrial development has occurred since that date. During the 14th century oak from the demesne woods was used for making springolds (catapults) and other military engines, and in extensions to the Tower of London.[83] Further supplies of timber were ordered in 1344 for building at Windsor Castle, and at Westminster Palace in 1346 and 1347.[84] Sales of timber and firewood were said to realize £26 a year in 1442.[85] The woods seem to have been much depleted in 1538 as the result of personal animosity and indiscriminate felling by two of the royal purveyors engaged in requisitioning timber for fencing St. James's Park.[86] Further areas of woodland were grubbed up during the 17th century.[87] In 1796, however, the lessees' sales of wood for stakes and firing were worth £119,[88] and as late as 1870 many of the inhabitants of Northwood were engaged in supplying firewood to the metropolis.[89]

Tile- and brick-making industries existed in Ruislip from at least as early as the 14th century. A tile-counter is mentioned in 1324,[90] and in 1366 Simon Molder of Ruislip sold 3,000 flat tiles at 3s. a hundred.[91] Customary rents in 1565 and 1593 included payments of tiles and bricks.[92] Three tenants keeping tile-kilns in St. Catherine's manor in 1587 had to pay the lord 1,000 tiles annually in consideration of the right to dig brickearth on the common.[93] Seven Ruislip tile-makers were presented at sessions in 1572 for infringing a 15th-century statute governing the preparation of earth for tile-making.[94] On Rocque's map of 1754 a brick-kiln is marked adjoining the modern Tile Kiln Lane.[95] In 1865 there was a brick-field in West End Road, but it appears to have closed down shortly afterwards.[96] Another brick-field at Cheney Street, Eastcote, was worked from 1899 until its closure about ten years later.[97]

There were no other industries in the parish until the 1930s, and few of the firms whose premises have since been established at Ruislip have employed a labour force of more than a hundred. The organ-building firm of J. W. Walker & Sons, established in 1828, moved from premises in Soho to a new factory in Braintree Road in 1937. The firm has an international reputation, and buildings housing Walker organs include St. George's Chapel, Windsor, York Minster, and cathedrals all over the world. In 1962 the firm employed a labour force of

[63] M.R.O., Acc. 249/4113.
[64] Ibid. /1582.
[65] Ibid. /2281.
[66] Ibid. /2544.
[67] H.O. 67/16.
[68] See p. 131.
[69] M.R.O., Acc. 261/2.
[70] J. J. Roumieu, *A History of Ruislip* (1875), 7.
[71] Middleton, *View*, 151.
[72] M.R.O., Acc. 261/1.
[73] Ex inf. Min. of Agric.
[74] See p. 132.
[75] Ex inf. Min. of Agric.
[76] *Census*, 1931.
[77] B.M. Add. MS. 24316.
[78] E 106/2/1.
[79] King's Coll., R. 45.
[80] Ibid. 36.
[81] J. Doharty, Map of the Demesne Lands (1750): photostat copy in M.R.O.; O.S. Map 1/2,500 Mdx. x. 5, 9 (1865

edn.).
[82] No evidence has been found in support of the statement that the foundations of the mill were discovered in the early 20th cent.: Braun, 'Earliest Ruislip', *T.L.M.A.S.* vii. 120.
[83] *Cal. Close*, 1339–41, 59.
[84] *Cal. Pat.* 1345–8, 319.
[85] King's Coll., R. 45.
[86] *L. & P. Hen. VIII*, xiii(1), p. 526.
[87] King's Coll., R. 36.
[88] M.R.O., Acc. 249/2682.
[89] *Kelly's Dir. Mdx.* (1870).
[90] S.C. 6/1126/5.
[91] *V.C.H. Herts.* iv. 265; and see W.A.M., 32017.
[92] King's Coll., R. 36, 48.
[93] E 178/1430; cf. King's Coll., Q. 42/5.
[94] M.R.O., S.R. 170/1.
[95] Rocque, *Map of Mdx.*
[96] O.S. Map 1/2,500, Mdx. x. 9 (1865 edn.).
[97] Ex inf. Mr. L. E. Morris.

about 120.[98] Air Control Installations Ltd., whose premises for the manufacture of heating and ventilating equipment were established at South Ruislip in 1937, employed nearly 600 persons in 1962.[99] A new factory was built in 1954 in Victoria Road, South Ruislip, for Hivac Ltd., an electrical engineering firm. Approximately 450 people were employed there in 1962.[1] Although other light industries, chiefly printing and engineering undertakings, have been established at South Ruislip in the 20th century,[2] they are not on a sufficient scale to affect the predominantly residential character of the parish.

Few details survive of social life in the parish before the 19th century. Before 1300 the Abbot of Bec seems to have regularly given food to the poor of Ruislip. Complaints that the practice had been discontinued stimulated an inquiry in 1331, but the abbot apparently proved that he gave the food only at pleasure, and the custom does not seem to have been revived.[3] Successive abbots of Bec in the 13th century also had rights of free warren in the Ruislip demesne lands,[4] part of which had been enclosed for hunting purposes as early as 1086.[5] The park was stocked with deer in 1270.[6] Although deer in the park are not mentioned again, during the 19th century Park Wood, covering much of the old hunting enclosure, was a favourite resort for fox-hunting.[7] Disorders at Ruislip in 1576 involving more than 100 people were attributed to the playing of football, then an unlawful game.[8] Cricket was played at Moor Park, just over the Hertfordshire boundary with Northwood, as early as 1854 when an eleven led by Lord Ebury entertained visiting teams. Northwood C.C. took over their present ground in Rickmansworth Road about 1900.[9] Eastcote C.C., founded at least as early as 1865, still plays in the grounds of Hayden Hall.[10] The Northwood Golf Club, whose eighteen-hole course at Haste Hill was said in 1911 to be one of the best within easy reach of London, was founded in 1891.[11]

The presence of Northolt airfield and attendant air force installations has had some effect on the social life of the parish. Russian cadets trained at the airfield during the First World War, and during the Second World War units manning the R.A.F. station included Polish, Belgian, and Canadian contingents.[12] After 1945 the number of R.A.F. personnel living in the area was considerably reduced, but in 1949 the United States Air Force set up a command headquarters at South Ruislip and this was

further augmented in 1951. By 1962 there were 1,733 people employed at the base. Of these 487 were United Kingdom civilians, and the remainder United States air force and civilian personnel. In addition United States nationals working at South Ruislip had 2,339 dependants living in and around Ruislip parish.[13] After some initial opposition[14] the United States personnel have been integrated into the social life of the parish.

The Ruislip Residents' Association, instituted in 1919, has played an important part in the preservation of open spaces and historic buildings, and in opposing a scheme to drive a ring-road through the parish during the 1950s.[15] Other residents' associations now exist at Eastcote, Northwood Hills, and South Ruislip.[16] The Ruislip Village Trust was founded in 1931 in order to protect the cottages near the church;[17] capital was raised through ordinary shares and the directors were to receive no remuneration. The trust, probably the first limited company of its kind to be formed, remains active in the preservation of old buildings.[18]

LOCAL GOVERNMENT. In 1246 the Abbot of Bec was exercising various liberties in his manor of Ruislip, including view of frankpledge and the assize of bread and ale.[19] During the 13th century the single manorial court was attended by both free and unfree tenants. The court met twice yearly under the supervision of an itinerant steward who toured Bec's English manors after Easter and again about Martinmas.[20] Occasionally additional courts might be held, usually during the summer months.[21] Further informal meetings may have been held under the lord's bailiff who is first mentioned in 1280 and who discharged many of the functions of local government.[22] There were two bailiffs in the manor by 1296.[23]

A curious case argued in the royal courts in 1305 seems to call in question the abbot's right to demand suit of court from Ruislip freeholders.[24] The result of the case is not recorded, but freeholders appear to have continued to render suit until the end of the 14th century, when a separate court leet was established.[25]

By 1300 the court was appointing reeves for Ruislip and Northwood, a hayward, and a forester.[26] Four reeves were elected in 1394, but two of them paid a fine for release,[27] and by 1334 some of their duties appear to have been assumed by two

[98] Ex inf. J. W. Walker & Sons Ltd.
[99] Ex inf. Air Control Installations Ltd.
[1] Ex inf. Hivac Ltd.
[2] Cf. *Petition* (1953); Ruislip-Northwood U.D.C. *Official Guide* (1958).
[3] *Cal. Close*, 1330–34, 406, 419.
[4] *Cal. Chart. R.* 1226–57, 409.
[5] *V.C.H. Mdx.* i. 126.
[6] *Cal. Close*, 1268–72, 232; see below, p. 222.
[7] *Kelly's Dir. Mdx.* (1862).
[8] M.R.O., S.R. 196/18.
[9] Ex inf. the treasurer; W. A. G. Kemp, *The Story of Northwood and Northwood Hills.*
[10] *Petition* (1953), 15; W. A. G. Kemp, *History of Eastcote*, 109–22.
[11] *V.C.H. Mdx.* ii. 279.
[12] P. Brooks, 'The Northolt Story', *B.E.A. Mag.* nos. 71–73.
[13] Ex inf. the Command Historian.
[14] *Mdx. Advertiser*, 22 Apr. 1949.
[15] Ruislip Residents' Assoc. *Minute Bks.*
[16] Ruislip-Northwood U.D.C. *Official Guide.*

[17] See p. 130.
[18] Ex inf. the chairman, Ruislip Village Trust Ltd.
[19] King's Coll., C. 1. An almost unbroken series of court rolls from 1246 to 1925 is preserved in King's Coll.: C. 1–15, Q. 44–85, R. 1–35, Court Bks. i–xxviii (1671–1935). The earliest rolls are printed in *Select Pleas in Manorial Courts* (Selden Soc. xi). B.M. Add. MSS. 9367–9 contain details of leases and fines paid into court from c. 1589–1681.   [20] Morgan, *Eng. Lands of Bec*, 3–5.
[21] Three additional meetings were held in 1290: King's Coll., C. 9.
[22] Ibid. 8.   [23] Ibid. 11.
[24] The implications of the case are not clear. It is discussed in *Select Cases in the Court of King's Bench* (Seld. Soc. lviii), p. xcv, where it is cited as an illustration of the doctrine that 'if there ceased to be two freeholders owing suit, the manorial court perished'. It is doubtful whether the case supports this theory, but it may conceal a general attack on the abbot's privileges.
[25] King's Coll., Q. 46/10.
[26] King's Coll., C. 11; E 106/2/1.
[27] King's Coll., Q. 48.

foresters.[28] Both of these seem to have presented trespasses in the Ruislip court, but one of them also held land in Ruislip of the lord of Harmondsworth and presented trespasses on the Harmondsworth land in Ruislip at the Harmondsworth court.[29] This official was said to owe suit of court at Harmondsworth, but appears to have held a largely autonomous position in Ruislip. About 1390 Richard Palmer, the Harmondsworth forester, felled large amounts of timber in abuse of his rights of housebote and firebote, and subsequently became involved in a series of disturbances in the parish.[30] The Harmondsworth forester is not mentioned again, but a forester, presumably the Ruislip official, had a room in the manor-house in 1435,[31] and was said to be paid 5s. 2d. a year in 1442.[32]

Tenants on the Harmondsworth land in Ruislip were generally bound to make suit of court at Harmondsworth.[33] Occasionally, however, licences were granted in the Ruislip court for Ruislip tenants to live on Harmondsworth land on condition that they continued to pay services to the lord of Ruislip.[34]

After the manor came into the possession of King's College, Cambridge, in the mid 15th century, courts leet and baron were held in no clearly defined sequence, but rarely at less than quarterly intervals. A franchise coroner was appointed by the college for Ruislip and two other manors in 1455,[35] but there is no evidence of his activities. Until 1565 leases of the manor generally reserved the courts to the college, but after this date, although there were continued complaints of the exactions of lessees,[36] court perquisites normally accompanied grants of the manor. During the 16th and early 17th centuries at least two courts leet and baron seem to have been held each year.[37] In 1693, however, the constables of Ruislip had to petition quarter sessions for their discharge, since the lord of the manor had not held a leet during the preceding year.[38] A court leet was held annually during the 19th century,[39] and courts continued to meet, with varying regularity, until 1925.[40]

There were stocks and a pillory at Ruislip in 1296.[41] The stocks were still in use in 1617.[42] Little is known of the parish administration which superseded the manorial organization. By 1582 there were two constables for the parish,[43] and by 1634, and presumably earlier, two overseers of the poor and two churchwardens.[44] During the early 17th century, however, the lessee of Ruislip manor was responsible for repairs to the pound in Eastcote Road.[45] Extensive alterations to the 'parish house' took place in 1616.[46] Full responsibility for the parish house was assumed by the overseers from about 1670, and their

accounts for the late 17th century include payments for flax and other materials for the use of the poor. A scheme for schooling poor children seems to have been discontinued about 1705, perhaps in consequence of a rapid increase in the sums laid out on the poor. The poor-rates rose from about £50 a year in the 1660s to more than £100 in 1709, and to £130 in 1711.[47] By 1776 the poor-rate was £477, and in 1803 £605.[48]

From the late 18th century, and presumably earlier, the vestry was in effective control of the parish. Records of the vestry are preserved, with gaps in the earlier years, from 1787.[49] The vestry seldom met more than five times a year, and there were usually fewer than ten people present. Adjournments from the church to the 'Bell' or 'Black Horse' at Eastcote were better attended. Vestry business was concerned mainly with the provision of clothing for the poor and the apprenticing of pauper children. Cheap or free dwellings for poor families were provided in the almshouses in Eastcote Road on the north side of the churchyard. The history of these 'church-houses' is obscure, but extensive alteration of the old parish house in 1616 probably resulted in its conversion into the small, two-roomed dwellings which comprise the present almshouses.[50] During the 18th century the almshouses seem to have been used as a workhouse, and in 1776 they accommodated about 30 paupers.[51] By 1787 this limited accommodation was inadequate and in 1789 the vestry resolved to erect a workhouse on land taken from the Common just north of Reservoir Road and granted to the parish by King's College.[52] The parish farmed out the administration of the workhouse to a governor at an annual rent of £353. The appointment of successive governors and the fixing of the annual farm, which increased to 550 guineas in 1805 and to £780 by 1810, provided the staple business of the vestry during the first two decades of the 19th century. Numbers in the workhouse during these years fluctuated between 20 and 30.[53] After the 1834 Act the parish was included in the Uxbridge Union, and in 1838 the inmates of the Ruislip workhouse were removed to the union workhouse at Hillingdon.[54] The building was then sold, later converted into flats, and after renovation in the early 20th century became a private house.[55] It is approached from Ducks Hill Road and is a red-brick structure with a symmetrical front of two stories and five bays. A plaque above the door is dated 1789 and gives five names, presumably those of members of the vestry.

About 1820 a revival took place in the vestry, and, until the ending of parochial responsibility for poor relief, monthly meetings became the rule. No select

[28] Ibid. 49.
[29] S.C. 12/11/20.
[30] Winchester Coll., 22988 a, b; *Cal. Close*, 1389–92, 391.
[31] S.C. 6/917/27.
[32] King's Coll., R. 45.
[33] See p. 16.
[34] King's Coll., C. 2.
[35] King's Coll., Ledger Bk. i.
[36] See p. 138.
[37] B.M. Add. MSS. 9367–9.
[38] M.R.O., Sessions Bk. 506, p. 44.
[39] *Pigot's Dir. Mdx.* (1832).
[40] King's Coll., Court Bk. xxviii.
[41] King's Coll., C. 11.
[42] M.R.O., S.R. 561/123.
[43] M.R.O., S.R. 246/43.

[44] M.R.O., Acc. 249/797.
[45] Ibid. /549.
[46] Ibid. /234, /235.
[47] Ibid. /1574.
[48] *Rets. on Expense and Maintenance of Poor*, H.C. 175 (1803–4), xiii.
[49] The surviving vestry records are in St. Martin's church.
[50] See above, and L. E. Morris, 'Ruislip Almshouses', *Jnl. Ruislip and District Nat. Hist. Soc.* (1956).
[51] *Rep. Cttee. on Rets. by Overseers*, 1776, Ser. 1, ix, p. 397.
[52] King's Coll., C. 48.
[53] *Rets. on Expense and Maintenance of Poor*, H.C. 175, (1803–4), xiii; H.C. 82 (1818), xix.
[54] M.R.O., Min. Bk. Gb(v), no. 1, p. 24.
[55] *Uxbridge Weekly Post*, 23 Jan. 1952.

vestry was ever formed, and meetings were still normally attended only by the vicar and parish officers. The vestry dealt with removal and bastardy cases and with the provision of outdoor relief. They

also regulated rights of pasture on common and the poor's land. From 1820 poor labourers were permitted to cultivate potatoes and vegetables on land at Ducks Hill for the support of their families. With the ending of parochial responsibility for poor relief, vestry meetings again became less frequent, and the appointment of officers was their principal duty.

URBAN DISTRICT OF RUISLIP-NORTHWOOD. *Argent, a hurst of oak-trees proper growing out of a grassy mount, and above them a roundel azure charged with a star of five points or; on a chief gules a silver mitre between two fleurs-de-lis or* [Granted 1937]

After 1894 Ruislip became part of Uxbridge R.D., and had a parish council. In 1904 the parish was separated from the rural districts to form Ruislip-Northwood U.D. The council administered three departments in 1904, with a staff of five, some of whom were part-time, and 15 manual workers. There were four departments in 1962—those of the clerk and solicitor, engineer and surveyor, treasurer, and medical officer of health. These employed an indoor staff of 154, and an outside staff of 280, increased to 340 for seasonal work. With the exception of the housing section of the clerk's department and the health department at 76 High Street, Northwood, the council's offices were in Oaklands Gate.

The number of standing committees varied from 3 in 1904 to 16, including two advisory committees, in 1962. In 1904 the rate was 2s. 2d. in the £, and had risen to 10s. 4d. in the £ by 1929. The product of a penny rate rose from £649 in 1929–30 to £6,010 in 1960–61. Between 1919 and 1962 almost 2,500 council dwellings were completed, 2,000 of them in the period following the Second World War. There were approximately 1,500 a. of open spaces and recreation grounds in 1953, including 72 a. of permanent and temporary allotments.[56]

Nine councillors were elected in 1904, and by 1920, when the first warding of the District took place, there were 15 councillors. The allotment of councillors between wards was varied in 1929 and again in 1936 when the South Ruislip Ward was created. The number of councillors was increased to 24 in 1939 and to 27 in 1950. In 1954 the number of wards was increased from 4 to 9 with 3 councillors

for each ward.[57] Since 1965 Ruislip and Northwood have formed part of the new London Borough of Hillingdon.[58]

CHURCHES. There was a priest at Ruislip in 1086,[59] and a church is referred to about 1190.[60] The church continued to serve the whole parish until 1854 when the new parish of Holy Trinity was formed from the Northwood area of Ruislip parish and parts of the Hertfordshire parishes of Rickmansworth and Watford. Emmanuel parish, Northwood, was taken from that of Holy Trinity in 1909, and the parish of St. Lawrence, Eastcote, from Ruislip parish in 1931. Part of Ruislip parish formed the parish of St. Paul, Ruislip Manor, in 1936, and the area of St. Paul's lying south of the Yeading Brook became the parish of St. Mary in 1952.

Accounts of the early history of the church are confused,[61] but the church probably accompanied Ernulf of Hesdin's grant of Ruislip manor to the Abbey of Bec in the late 11th century.[62] The appropriation of Ruislip church to Bec was confirmed by Richard Fitz Neal, Bishop of London 1189–98,[63] and later bishops reconfirmed the grant during the 13th and early 14th centuries.[64] Except during periods of Crown confiscation[65] Bec continued to appropriate the church property until about 1400, and the advowson passed to the Crown on the final confiscation of Bec properties in 1404.[66] The date of the ordination of the vicarage is unknown, but the first recorded vicar was holding office during the early 14th century, and the Abbot of Bec was exercising the patronage at the time of the first dated presentation in 1327.[67] Ruislip church was included in Henry IV's grant of the confiscated manors of Ruislip and Ogbourne to John, Duke of Bedford.[68] In 1421 John granted the spiritualities of Ruislip and Ogbourne to the Dean and Canons of St. George's Chapel at Windsor.[69] St. George's still retained the advowson in 1962.

The rectory was valued[70] at £17 in 1291.[71] In 1547 the 'parsonage', said at this date to be in the possession of Winchester College, was worth £18.[72] That the college had any interest in the rectorial estate is most unlikely, since the Dean and Canons of St. George's consistently farmed out the rectory after 1476, first to the Waleston family, and from 1532 to the Hawtreys of Eastcote.[73] In 1650, when it was farmed by John Hawtrey, the 'parsonage' was worth about £300.[74] The great tithes were said to be worth £250 in 1718.[75] Under the inclosure award of 1814 the rectorial tithes were commuted for almost 300 a. of land in the old open-field area.[76] Immediately before its transfer to the Ecclesiastical Commis-

[56] *Petition* (1953).
[57] Section based on information supplied by Ruislip-Northwood U.D.C.
[58] London Govt. Act, 1963, c. 33.
[59] *V.C.H. Mdx.* i. 126.
[60] St. George's Chapel, xi. G. 6.
[61] Cf. Newcourt, *Repertorium*, i. 723, and A. A. Porée, *Histoire de l'Abbaye du Bec*, ii. 574.
[62] See p. 134; Morgan, *Eng. Lands of Bec*, 147. Newcourt, in assuming that the church was appropriated to Ogbourne Priory and passed with it to Bec in the mid 12th century, appears to be misled by the later relationship between the Bec properties of Ogbourne and Ruislip: *V.C.H. Mdx.* i. 202 (a more accurate dating of the grant of Ogbourne to Bec, St. George's Chapel, xi. G. 1, given by Newcourt as *temp.* Henry II, seems to be between 1122 and 1147: *V.C.H. Wilts.* iii. 394).

[63] St. George's Chapel, xi. G. 6.
[64] Ibid. G. 51, 52, 64.
[65] See p. 134.
[66] *Cal. Pat.* 1399–1401, 368; 1401–5, 446; see above, p. 134.
[67] Newcourt, *Repertorium*, i. 724.
[68] See p. 134.
[69] St. George's Chapel, x. 4. 1.
[70] The figure given in *Val. of Norw.*, ed. Lunt, 361, as the valuation in 1254 is based on a misreading of St. Paul's MS. W.D. 9.
[71] *Tax. Eccl.* (Rec. Com.), 17.
[72] E 301/34/180.
[73] St. George's Chapel, xv. 31. 65–73, xvi. 1. 58–80.
[74] *Home Cnties. Mag.* ii. 281.
[75] M.R.O., Acc. 249/2280.
[76] M.R.O., F. 4, 5; Acc. 261/1.

sioners in 1867 the rectorial estate consisted of 392 a. of arable and pasture on Bourne and Northwood farms, leased to Francis Deane, and valued at £684.[77]

The vicarage was valued at £5 in 1291,[78] and at £12 in 1535.[79] In 1547 the vicar furnished the cure himself; there were then no charities, obits, or lights, and the vicarage was worth £8 a year.[80] In 1650 the living comprised the vicarage house with a barn, stable, orchard, garden, and 29 a. of glebe, worth in all £37, and small tithes worth £23.[81] The value of the living in 1778 was only £90,[82] but by 1835 the net income had increased to £462.[83]

The priest mentioned at Domesday was said to hold half a hide.[84] In the mid 13th century the Vicar of Ruislip held land which had formerly belonged to Robert de Rading, and for which he paid an annual rent of twelve pence.[85] During the 15th century successive vicars were said to hold a house and 13 a. in Copwell Mede in Eastcote at the same rent.[86] There was said to be no land for the maintenance of the priest in 1547,[87] but the vicar was holding land in both Eastcote and Westcote common fields in 1565.[88] By 1650 there were 29 a. of glebe land.[89] Under the inclosure award of 1814 the Vicar of Ruislip was allotted approximately 160 a. in lieu of tithes, and a further 75 a., including 25 a. of Park Wood, in settlement of an old dispute with the lords of the manor over tithes of underwood.[90] In 1875 there were 230 a. of glebe,[91] and in 1887 259 a.[92] Sales for building purposes in the late 19th and 20th centuries[93] had reduced the glebe to about 100 a. by 1933.[94] The bulk of the remaining glebe land has since been sold.[95]

Early-15th-century rentals mention a house held by the vicar.[96] A vicarage house is first mentioned by name in 1565, when it was described as lying between Cannons' Bridge and Ruislip Wood.[97] A map of 1750 showed the vicarage on or near its present site on the west side of Bury Street.[98] The present vicarage, which was still in use in 1962, was rebuilt in 1881.[99]

Religious activity from the 12th to the 14th centuries was probably influenced by the foundation at Ruislip of a small cell of the Abbey of Bec.[1] No conventual priory was ever founded, and the designating of St. Martin's church as a 'priory' church[2] is inaccurate. Ruislip became an important administrative centre for Bec properties in England, and separate Priors of Ruislip were appointed during the 12th and early 13th centuries. About 1300 food

appears to have been regularly distributed among the poor of Ruislip by order of the Abbot of Bec.[3] A chapel in the manor-house is mentioned in 1294,[4] and again in 1336 and 1435.[5] Although Ruislip manor was, for some purposes, merged with the abbey's Ogbourne estate[6] after the mid 13th century, it remained an important administrative centre until the end of the 14th century. Audits for Bec's English manors seem to have been held at Ruislip,[7] and a counting house and counting board in the manor-house are mentioned in 1435.[8]

Little is known of the religious life of the parish during the 15th century. Whether early vicars resided in the parish is uncertain, but some later incumbents seem to have been pluralists, and several combined the cure with other livings nearby. George Gard (vicar 1482–92) was Rector of Ickenham for a time in 1486.[9] Complaints during the early 16th century that the praise of God was decayed seem to reflect agrarian discontent rather than lack of interest on the part of incumbents.[10] Dissatisfaction during the incumbency of Thomas Smith (1565–1615), however, resulted in his being examined in the scriptures in 1586. His performance was described as 'tolerable', and he retained the living for another 29 years.[11] Daniel Collins (vicar 1616–39), who was a canon of Windsor, held the living of Cowley during part of his incumbency, and seems to have resided there occasionally.[12] John Ellis, who replaced Collins as Vicar of Ruislip from 1633 to 1639, also held the church at Isleworth.[13] Nathaniel Giles, who was vicar for a time about 1647, was said to preach with a pistol hanging at his neck.[14] In 1706 profaneness and immorality were said to be increasing rapidly.[15] This may have occasioned the appointment of the curate who was serving in the parish by about 1723. The vicar was then said to be much indisposed, and received help with his parish from the Rector of Cowley.[16] Services were held twice on Sundays and there were four Communions a year.[17] In 1778 the curate's salary was £36: the arrangement of services was unchanged, and there were between 30 and 40 communicants. An additional Sunday sermon during the six summer months was being delivered by 1790.[18]

The parish church was dedicated to *ST. MARTIN* before 1250.[19] The present building, at the corner of Eastcote Road and Ruislip High Street, dates in part from the 13th century, with 15th- and 16th-century additions.[20] It is built of flint rubble with stone

77 St. George's Chapel, xvii. 21. 3.
78 *Tax. Eccl.* (Rec. Com.), 17.
79 *Valor Eccl.* (Rec. Com.), i. 434.
80 E 301/34/180.
81 *Home Cnties. Mag.* ii. 281.
82 Guildhall MS. 9557.
83 *Rep. Com. Eccl. Rev.* [67], H.C. (1835), xxii.
84 *V.C.H. Mdx.* i. 126.
85 B.M. Add. MS. 24316.
86 King's Coll., R. 40, 41, 43; S.C. 6/917/27.
87 E 301/34/18.
88 King's Coll., R. 36.
89 *Home Cnties. Mag.* ii. 281.
90 M.R.O., Acc. 261/1; King's Coll., Q. 24.
91 Roumieu, *Hist. of Ruislip*, 7.
92 *Rep. Com. Eccl. Rev.* H.C. 307, p. 92 (1887), lxiv.
93 St. George's Chapel, iii. K. 3.
94 *Kelly's Dir. Mdx.* (1953).
95 Ex inf. the vicar.
96 King's Coll., R. 40, 43.
97 Ibid. 36.
98 King's Coll., P. 38.

99 *Kelly's Dir. Mdx.* (1886).
1 For a detailed study see *V.C.H. Mdx.* i. 202.
2 Board outside church.
3 See p. 140.
4 E 106/2/1.
5 C 47/18/1/12; S.C. 6/917/27.
6 *V.C.H. Wilts.* iii. 394.
7 King's Coll., Q. 45.
8 S.C. 6/917/27.
9 Newcourt, *Repertorium*, i. 663.
10 See p. 138.
11 Guildhall MS. 9537/6.
12 *V.C.H. Mdx.* iii. 175.
13 Newcourt, *Repertorium*, i. 676.
14 *Calamy Revised*, ed. Matthews, 222.
15 Guildhall MS. 9800.
16 *V.C.H. Mdx.* iii. 175.
17 Guildhall MS. 9550.
18 Ibid. 9557.
19 B.M. Add. MS. 24316.
20 It is fully described in Hist. Mon. Com. *Mdx.* 104–5.

dressings, and consists of chancel, nave, north and south aisles, south chapel, west porch, and a south vestry added in 1954. The parapeted tower, built in the 15th century, stands at the south-west corner of the church. The chancel and south aisle, dating originally from the 13th century, were rebuilt in the 15th century. About 1500 the north aisle was also rebuilt and the south aisle re-roofed and perhaps extended to form the south chapel. The exterior of the church was much restored in 1869–70, and the west porch, built in 1875, was replaced in 1896. After slight bomb damage during the Second World War, further restoration work was carried out in 1954. The Purbeck marble font dates from the 12th century.[21] The tower contains six bells, which were recast by Thomas Mears of Whitechapel in 1801.[22] In the nave and north aisle are traces of 15th-century wall paintings depicting an unidentified saint, and the Virgin with St. Michael and St. Lawrence.[23] The plate includes a fine silver parcel-gilt cup and silver cover dated 1595, a silver flagon of before 1685,[24] and two other flagons date-marked 1725.[25] There are brasses with figures to Ralph Hawtrey (d. 1574) and John Hawtrey (d. 1593). Other monuments to the Hawtreys and their descendants include an alabaster wall monument to Ralph Hawtrey (d. 1638) and his wife (d. 1647) by John and Matthias Christmas. A baroque mural tablet commemorates Thomas Bright (d. 1673/4), vicar, and some of his descendants. There are several 14th- and 15th-century slabs including one of early-14th-century date inscribed to Roger de Southcote. The church contains two 16th-century iron-bound chests, and an inscribed bread cupboard in the north aisle records the gift of Jeremiah Bright in 1697.[26] The registers, which are complete, record baptisms from 1689, marriages from 1694, and burials from 1695.

The church of *HOLY TRINITY*, Northwood, was opened in 1854 on a site given by Lord Robert Grosvenor.[27] A chapel in the Grange is said to have been used as a place of worship by the inhabitants of Northwood before this date.[28] In 1961–2 the living was vested in trustees.[29] A vicarage house adjoining the church was built in 1856. The church, which is built of flint rubble with stone dressings, was designed by S. S. Teulon in a restrained Victorian Gothic style. It consists of a nave and well-proportioned north and south aisles, with a small tower at the east end. An extension to the north aisle was consecrated in 1895, and the south aisle and baptistry added in 1928. A memorial window to the Grosvenor family was executed by Burne-Jones and installed in 1886.[30]

The church of *EMMANUEL* in Church Road, Northwood, was opened in 1904 on the initiative of the Vicar of Holy Trinity. An iron church, tended by a curate-in-charge had been opened in 1896, and after the completion of the permanent building this remained in use as a church hall until 1958, when it was replaced by the present building.[31] The church was designed by Sir Frank Elgood and is executed in red brick with stone dressings. The chancel was added about 1906, and vestries for clergy and choir were built in 1961. In 1961–2 the living was vested in trustees,[32] and in 1965 the cure was administered by a vicar and a curate.[33]

The church of *ST. LAWRENCE*, Eastcote, was opened in 1933. A mission church on the site of the present parish hall (opened 1955) had been in use since 1920.[34] The Bishop of London is patron of the living.[35] The church, which stands near the junction of Field End Road and Bridle Road, was designed by Sir Charles Nicholson. It is built of red brick, and consists of a nave and north and south aisles. The white-washed interior is richly appointed. In 1965 the cure was served by the vicar and an assistant priest.[36]

The church of *ST. PAUL*, Thurlstone Road, Ruislip Manor, was opened in 1937. The Bishop of London is patron of the living.[37] The church, built of dark-red brick with small windows and a tiled roof, consists of a nave and north and south aisles. The roof is supported by brick pillars, and the walls and roof have been white-washed in an attempt to lighten the interior.

The church of *ST. EDMUND THE KING* was opened in 1935 as a mission church. The Bishop of London is patron of the living.[38] Services were held in a tent during the building of a semi-permanent structure in Pinner Road,[39] a few yards inside the parish boundary. A permanent church on an adjoining site had been completed by 1968. The parish of St. Edmund was created in 1952.[40]

The church of *ST. MARY*, South Ruislip, was opened in 1959. From 1931 services had been conducted in a wooden hall. The Bishop of London is patron of the living.[41] The church is of brick and concrete construction, and consists of a lofty nave and a small north chapel. The main external features are a shallow gabled clerestory, a small latticed polygonal spire and a figure of Christ crucified against the west window. Internally, the texture of much of the structural material is retained. The church is connected to the adjoining vicarage by a covered way.

ROMAN CATHOLICISM. Five suspected papists were indicted at Quarter Sessions in 1581 for non-attendance at the parish church,[42] and two Ruislip recusants were presented at sessions in 1625.[43] Apart from these isolated cases there is little evidence of Roman Catholicism before the 20th century. There were said to be no papists or reputed papists in the parish in 1706,[44] and only one family of papists by 1810.[45]

The Roman Catholic parish of Ruislip, co-exten-

21 Hist. Mon. Com. *Mdx.* 106 and pl. 10.
22 Par. Recs., Vestry Mins.
23 Hist. Mon. Com. *Mdx.* 107 and pl. 143.
24 Guildhall MS. 9537/20.
25 E. Freshfield, *Communion Plate of Mdx.* 43.
26 See p. 147 and plate facing p. 36.
27 This section is based on information supplied by the vicar.
28 *Northwood Advertiser and Gazette*, 16 Sept. 1932.
29 *Crockford* (1961–2).
30 Pevsner, *Mdx.* 126.
31 Section based on information supplied by the vicar, and *Golden Jubilee Booklet* (1953).

32 *Crockford* (1961–2).
33 *Lond. Dioc. Bk.* (1965).
34 Section based on information supplied by the vicar and *Silver Jubilee Programme* (1958).
35 *Crockford* (1961–2).
36 *Lond. Dioc. Bk.* (1965).
37 *Crockford* (1961–2).   38 Ibid.
39 Ex inf. the vicar.
40 *Lond. Dioc. Bk.* (1965).
41 *Crockford* (1961–2).   42 M.R.O., S.R. 231/10.
43 *Mdx. Cnty. Recs.* iii. 23.
44 Guildhall MS. 9800.
45 Ibid. 9558.

sive with the urban district and taken from the Roman Catholic parish of Uxbridge, was formed in 1921. A temporary brick building housing a church and priest's house was erected in Ruislip High Street and registered for worship in 1921.[46] In 1933 the Roman Catholic population of Ruislip was said to be about 200. A Roman Catholic primary school in Herlwyn Avenue was opened in 1937. The old church in the High Street was replaced by the present Church of the Most Sacred Heart in Pembroke Road, which was built and consecrated in 1939. The Roman Catholic parish of St. Matthew's, comprising the Northwood area of the urban district, was founded in 1923. Services were held initially in a small building later used as a church hall. The present St. Matthew's church in Hallowell Road was opened in 1924 and consecrated in 1954.[47] The Church of St. Thomas More in Field End Road, Eastcote, was opened in 1937. The parish of St. Thomas More, to which a priest was assigned, was formed in 1952. For several years services were held in a scout hut in South Ruislip,[48] and in 1958 the parish of St. Gregory the Great was created in the area south of the Yeading Brook.[49] In 1962 services were being held in the Swithun Wells and Bourne Primary Schools.[50] The church of St. Gregory the Great, in Victoria Road, was consecrated in 1967.[51]

Sisters of Charity of Ste Jeanne Antide established a convent in Green Lane, Northwood, in 1928. A convent school was opened in the same year.[52] In 1962 there were ten sisters.[53] St. Vincent's Orthopaedic Hospital, under the care of the Sisters of Charity of St. Vincent de Paul, was opened in 1912.[54] The hospital chapel, destroyed by enemy action in 1940, was rebuilt in 1962.[55]

PROTESTANT NONCONFORMITY. In the late 17th century at least two Ruislip tradesmen were attending Quaker meetings in Uxbridge.[56] There were said to be three Presbyterians and about as many Methodists in Ruislip in 1766.[57] Methodists were said to be decreasing in number in 1778, but there were still about ten Presbyterians in the parish.[58] A return of 1810 stating that there were no dissenters in the parish[59] was inaccurate to the extent that Dr. Adam Clarke (1762–1832), an eminent Methodist theologian, had taken up residence at Hayden Hall in 1805.[60] There was no meeting-house for dissenters in 1816,[61] but during the 1820s several houses were licensed for nonconformist worship. A house in Ruislip was certified for public worship on behalf of the Wesleyans in 1823.[62] Premises in Eastcote were licensed for Baptist worship in 1825, and a house in Ruislip on behalf of

the Independents in the following year. Another house in Ruislip was licensed on behalf of the Calvinistic Particular Baptists in 1832.[63]

The early 19th century was also marked by increased Methodist activity. A Methodist congregation at Eastcote, formed about 1825 by Dr. Clarke, met in the house now called 'Sunnyside' until his death in 1832. In 1848 the first Methodist chapel, seating about 100 people, was built opposite the present chapel in Pamela Gardens. This served the Eastcote congregation until the new chapel, the building of which had been delayed by the Second World War, was substantially completed. The chapel was occupied in 1950 and building work finished in 1962.[64] A building in Bury Street opposite the present Reservoir Road, said to have been licensed for nonconformist worship about 1854, and possibly originally licensed in 1850,[65] was taken over for Methodist use in 1882. It became known as Ruislip Common Chapel.[66] In Northwood Primitive Methodists met in a house called 'Elthorne' in the modern High Street from about 1896. In that year a school chapel to accommodate 250 people was built on the corner of High Street and Hallowell Road. The present church next to the school chapel was completed in 1903. It was further extended in 1910, and a new vestry added in 1927. Enemy action caused considerable damage to the building in 1944.[67] From 1905 a group of about 20 Wesleyan Methodists worshipped in a house in Chester Road. Two years later a temporary corrugated iron church was erected in Hallowell Road. After the construction of a permanent building in Oaklands Gate in 1924, the temporary structure was transferred there for use as a church hall. A new hall and classrooms costing £22,500 were completed in 1962. After the Methodist Union in 1932 these two churches became known as the High Street and Oaklands Gate Methodist churches.[68] Other Methodist churches were opened in Ickenham Road (1923), Torrington Road (1937), and Queen's Walk, South Ruislip (1951).[69]

The Ruislip Baptist church, a member of the Baptist Union, was formed in 1937, and a temporary wooden building in West Way, accommodating 150 people, was opened in the same year. This was replaced in 1954 by a permanent church seating 250.[70] The Northwood Hills Congregational church was formed in 1955. Until 1958, when the church in Joel Street was completed, services were held in schools and halls.[71] St. John's Presbyterian church, Northwood, was founded in 1905. The congregation met in a 'tin' church until 1914, when the present building in Hallowell Road was opened. From 1914 to 1918 the church was used as a hospital.[72]

[46] Gen. Reg. Off., Wship. Reg. 48305.
[47] Ex inf. the R.C. Rector of St. Matthew's.
[48] Cath. Dir. (1951).
[49] Westminster Year Bk. (1969).
[50] Cath. Dir. (1962).
[51] Westminster Year Bk. (1969).
[52] See p. 147.
[53] Ex inf. the sister-in-charge.
[54] See p. 133.
[55] Ex inf. the Hospital Secretary.
[56] Trust deed penes Uxbridge meeting.
[57] Guildhall MS. 9558.
[58] Ibid. 9557.
[59] Ibid. 9558.
[60] L. D. Jarvis, Free Church Hist. of Uxbridge, 62.
[61] Brewer, Beauties of Eng. and Wales, x(5), 583.
[62] Gen. Reg. Off., Dissenters' Places of Wship. 1689–

1852: Dioc. of Lond. cert. of 14 June 1823; cf. Guildhall MS. 9580/5.
[63] Gen. Reg. Off., Dissenters' Places of Wship. 1689–1852: Dioc. of Lond. certs. of 30 July 1825, 18 Dec. 1826, 8 June 1832.
[64] Ex inf. the minister.
[65] Gen. Reg. Off., Rets. of QS. for Mdx., ret. of 6 Dec. 1850; cf. M.R.O., A Register of the Places of Meeting of Protestants.
[66] Methodist Dir. Harrow Circuit (1962).
[67] Ex inf. the Trust Secretary; Jubilee Souvenir Bookle (1946).
[68] Ex inf. the minister.
[69] Methodist Dir. (1962).
[70] Ex inf. the minister; 21st Anniversary Booklet (1958).
[71] Ex inf. the minister.
[72] Ex inf. the minister.

A gospel assembly, founded in 1925, met in a tea-garden called 'the Poplars' and later in a dance-hall in Ruislip High Street. A hall called the West Way Hall was erected in 1935.[73] A similar assembly was formed at Northwood in 1948. Its members met in the Darby and Joan hut in Pinner Road, which they hired from the local authority. A temporary hall in Windsor Close was opened in 1951, and replaced by a permanent building in 1961.[74] From 1954 members of the Lutheran church met in the South Ruislip Community Centre, and in 1955 a group of 22 communicants founded the Lutheran church of St. Andrew under a resident minister. The congregation continued to meet in the South Ruislip Community centre until 1960 when a permanent church was erected at the junction of Whitby Road and Queen's Walk.[75] Jehovah's Witnesses registered the Kingdom Hall in Victoria Road in 1941.[76]

JEWS. The Ruislip Jewish community was founded in 1940. Its members worshipped in various premises until 1950, when a permanent synagogue was built in Shenley Avenue. In 1962 almost 1,000 people were said to use the synagogue.[77]

EDUCATION. Although there was said to be no school in the parish in 1778,[78] there had been a school at Ruislip as early as 1655.[79] In 1812 the parish vestry appointed a committee consisting of the vicar, churchwarden, overseers, and six parishioners to consider the free education of poor children. A master and two mistresses were appointed to provide education for some 50 children in a room in the churchyard.[80] By 1819 four schools providing for 110 children had been established. About 50 of these children were said to be clothed and educated from a voluntary subscription fund, and presumably this referred to the parish scheme.[81] Two of the schools seem to have closed before 1835, when there were only two charity schools in the parish. A small girls' school then had 32 pupils, and the other, a mixed school opened in 1833, contained 60 pupils under a master and mistress.[82] In 1846, although the number of children in both schools showed a slight increase, the National Society observed that there was insufficient financial support to meet the educational needs of the poor.[83]

The mixed school opened in 1833 was that generally known in the early 19th century as Ruislip National School,[84] and later replaced by Ruislip C. of E. School. From about 1848 further tuition under the auspices of the National Society was given in a schoolroom which was the private property of Lord Ebury. A permanent building to accommodate

66 mixed pupils was built in Rickmansworth Road in 1862, and this became known as Holy Trinity C. of E. School. Additional classrooms were erected in 1898 and the school served the whole of Northwood until 1910, when the primary school in Pinner Road was opened.[85] In 1906, when it became known as Ruislip-Northwood C. of E. School, the school contained 233 pupils.[86] Ruislip C. of E. School, attached to St. Martin's church, had been providing tuition in temporary premises since about 1850. A permanent building to accommodate 45 boys and 35 girls was erected in Eastcote Road in 1862.[87] The school received government grants from 1870, when it contained 71 pupils.[88] In 1899 the Vicar of Holy Trinity church, Northwood, was holding classes in the church mission room pending the completion of a new school.[89] The first half of the new Half Mile Lane Infants' School, built with a loan of £400 obtained from the vicar's personal friends, was opened later that year.[90] In 1899 the school received a government grant[91] and by 1903 it contained 43 pupils.[92]

Together these three church schools accommodated about 380 children in 1903.[93] Under the 1902 Act Ruislip came under the county council, and the Northwood County Primary School in Pinner Road was opened in 1910 to relieve pressure on Holy Trinity School. Some of the pupils from the Half Mile Lane Infants' School were also transferred here,[94] and the school took children from 5 to 15 years of age until the erection of Northwood Secondary School in 1934. About 1929 Ruislip C. of E. School was also declared inadequate to meet the demands of the rapidly increasing population, and the Bishop Winnington Ingram C. of E. School was built on the same site to replace the old school. The new premises, accommodating 280 pupils, were opened in 1931. Senior pupils from the old church school were transferred to the Manor Secondary School, opened in 1928 and further extended in 1936. Several other schools were built during the 1930s to meet the rapidly expanding population of the parish. These included Ruislip Gardens Primary (1939) and Whiteheath Primary (1938). The Roman Catholic primary school in Herlwyn Avenue was opened in 1937. On the outbreak of the Second World War the Ruislip Gardens school was closed because of its proximity to Northolt airfield, and the Bourne Secondary School at South Ruislip was closed after one week when the Air Ministry took over the building. Work also ceased on the new Deanesfield Primary School in Queen's Walk.

The Ruislip Gardens school was reopened in 1941. The Bourne school also reopened at the same time on the first floor of the Ruislip Gardens school, where it remained until 1946, when it removed to

[73] Ex inf. the secretary.
[74] Ex inf. the secretary.
[75] Ex inf. the minister; *British Lutheran*, Oct. 1960; *Ruislip-Northwood Gazette*, 1 Apr. 1955, 19 Nov. 1959.
[76] Gen. Reg. Off., Wship. Reg. 59953.
[77] Ex inf. the secretary.
[78] Guildhall MS. 9557.
[79] *Walker Revised*, ed. Matthews, 259.
[80] Par. Recs., Vestry Mins.
[81] *Digest of Rets. to Sel. Cttee. on Educ. of Poor*, H.C. 224, p. 540 (1819), ix(1); Brewer, *Beauties of Eng. and Wales*, x(5), 583.
[82] *Educ. Enquiry Abstract*, H.C. 62, p. 578 (1835), xlii.
[83] Nat. Soc. *Ret. of Schools* (1846, priv. printed).
[84] *Kelly's Dir. Mdx.* (1845).

[85] Nat. Soc. files; ex inf. the Divisional Educ. Officer.
[86] *Pub. Elem. Schs. 1906* [Cd. 3510], H.C. p. 449 (1907), lxiii.
[87] Ed. 7/86.
[88] *Rep. of Educ. Cttee. of Coun., 1870* [C. 406], H.C. (1871), xxii.
[89] Ed. 7/86.
[90] Nat. Soc. files.
[91] *Schs. in receipt of Parl. Grants, 1899* [Cd. 332], H.C. (1900), lxiv.
[92] *List of Schs. under Admin. of Bd. 1903* [Cd. 2011], H.C. (1904), lxxv.
[93] Ibid.
[94] Ed. 7/86.

new premises in Southbourne Gardens. Temporary huts on the Deanesfield school site were opened in 1943 and were still used by the junior school in 1962. Construction work began again in 1951 and the permanent school was opened and occupied by infants in the same year. St. Nicholas's Boys' Grammar School in Wiltshire Lane was opened in 1955, and a complementary girls' school, St. Mary's Grammar, on an adjoining site in 1957. In 1962 there were 700 pupils and a staff of 38 in the boys' establishment, while the girls' school, which had not yet fully developed, contained 583 pupils.[95]

In April 1962 there were nineteen maintained schools, excluding grammar schools, in the old parish of Ruislip. They are set out below. The date at which the school was opened is given in brackets after the name of the school, followed by the dates of any extensions; the next figure is the number of children on the roll at April 1962, and the final figure denotes the age-group of the pupils:

Holy Trinity C. of E. (1862). 119. 5–11; Emmanuel C. of E. (Half Mile Lane Infants) (1899). 63. 5–7; Northwood Primary (1910). 370. 5–11; Manor Secondary (1928, 1936, 1948). 637. 11–16; Coteford County Primary (1929, 1952). 429. 5–11; Bishop Winnington Ingram C. of E. (1930). 343. 5–11; Bourne Primary (1931, 1962). 337. 5–11; Northwood Secondary (1934). 653. 11–17; Lady Bankes County Primary (1936). 606. 5–11; Sacred Heart R.C. Primary (1937). 248. 5–11; Whiteheath County Primary (1938, 1947, 1958). 310. 5–11; Bourne County Secondary (1939, 1946). 796. 11–16; Ruislip Gardens County Primary (1939). 423. 5–11; Deanesfield County Primary (1943, 1951). 472. 5–11; Field End County Primary (1947, 1952). 551. 5–11; Newnham County Primary (1951). 429. 5–11; Queensmead County Secondary (1953). 774. 11–16; Harlyn Primary (1957). 240. 5–11; Blessed Swithun Wells R.C. Primary (1962). 125. 5–11.[96]

The residential character of the district has attracted a large number of private schools. In 1953 there were 18 kindergarten and independent schools in the parish, six of which contained more than 100 pupils.[97] Of these St. Philomena's Convent in Green Lane, Northwood, opened in 1928 by the Sisters of Charity of Ste Jeanne Antide, catered for about 125 children in 1962.[98] St. Helen's School, founded in 1899 in premises in Chester Road, Northwood, moved to its present site in Eastbury Road in 1902, and has since been much extended. The school began with 15 pupils in 1899, but by 1962 it contained 600 girls aged between 5 and 18 years. Another girls' school was moved from London to a site in Maxwell Road, Northwood, in 1892 or 1893, and became known as Northwood College. In 1962 the school contained 360 girls. The pupils in both of these schools are prepared for General Certificate and university entrance examinations.[99]

In 1962 there were three evening institutes at the Bourne, Manor, and Northwood Secondary Modern Schools.[1] Battle of Britain House on Ducks Hill was opened in 1948 by the Middlesex County Council as a short-course residential college. The building was occupied as a private house from its erection about 1909 until 1939 when it was requisitioned for war use. During the Second World War the house was used as a training centre for saboteurs and secret agents. A post-war scheme to furnish the entire house as an R.A.F. memorial failed through lack of financial support. The Middlesex County Council agreed to administer a modified scheme, and the dining-room was panelled with the badges of R.A.F. squadrons. After 1948, although the chief function of the college was to provide a wide variety of adult courses, some connexion with the R.A.F. was maintained in the form of youth leadership courses. The house and grounds are also used as the field centre of the Ruislip and District Natural History Society.[2]

CHARITIES FOR THE POOR.[3] The early history of the almshouses in Eastcote Road is uncertain. Extensive alteration to the 'parish house', probably to convert an earlier building into a series of two-roomed dwellings, took place in 1616.[4] A number of minor repairs are recorded later in the century.[5] Lady Mary Franklin, by will proved 1737, left £100 for the purchase of land, the income of which was to be applied to clothing the inhabitants of the church houses. No land was bought, and the money was invested in stock. In 1895 the gift yielded £3 interest, which was distributed by the vicar on St. Thomas's Day. The two-storied building, which may be of 16th-century origin, stands at the north-west corner of the churchyard. The partly exposed timbering of the upper floor incorporates large curved braces; the ground floor has been faced with brickwork. The former almshouses, each with an upper and a lower room, were arranged back to back, five facing the churchyard and five facing Eastcote Road. By 1968 four dwellings at the west end had been converted into a verger's house and two in the centre were occupied as a cottage by the curate.[6]

The earliest charity known in the parish is that of Richard Coggs, who in 1717 conveyed 3 a. in Frog Lane, Eastcote, to the use of the churchwardens for the relief of poor families. The land was converted into stock in 1889, at which date the gift yielded £4 yearly.

On consideration of £150 paid to them by Jeremiah Bright in 1721, the Leathersellers' Company covenanted to pay £6 annually to provide bread for the poor. The vicar was to receive 10s. from this sum for his care in administering the charity.[7]

Ralph Hawtrey, by will proved 1725, left £200, the interest on which was to be disposed of by the vicar in the relief of the poor. This gift yielded £8 annually, which was paid by Elizabeth Rogers, Hawtrey's granddaughter, until 1803 when she invested £267 stock, yielding an annual interest of £8. By 1897, however, the annual income had fallen to £7.

[95] Ex inf. the head teachers.
[96] Ex inf. the Divisional Educ. Officer.
[97] Petition, 55.
[98] Ex inf. the sister-in-charge.
[99] Ex inf. the headmistresses.
[1] Except where otherwise stated, this section is based on information supplied by the Divisional Educ. Officer.
[2] Ex inf. the Warden, Battle of Britain Hse., and Miss A. M. Pollard, Harrow libr.

[3] Except where otherwise stated, the authority for statements in this section is either 9th Rep. Com. Char. H.C. 258 (1823), ix, or Char. Com. files.
[4] M.R.O., Acc. 249/234, 235; L. E. Morris, 'Ruislip Almshouses', Jnl. Ruislip and District Nat. Hist. Soc. (1956).
[5] M.R.O., Acc. 249/1574.
[6] See plate facing p. 152.
[7] See p. 144.

Elizabeth Rogers, by will proved 1803, left £380 stock, from the interest on which the vicar was to receive two guineas a year on condition that he preached a sermon each Good Friday morning. The residue was to be divided among the poor, preference being given to regular church-goers. Rogers's charity yielded £16 in 1895.

Henrietta Howard, the date of whose will is unknown, left £100 stock to provide beef and bread for 25 poor families in Eastcote on Christmas Eve, and £60 stock to purchase blankets for six Eastcote families every New Year's Day. The gift was administered by the vicar and churchwardens, and yielded £4 yearly in 1897.

Lady Juliana Campbell, by will proved 1886, left sufficient money to yield, when invested, £10 yearly, to be devoted to the purchase of coal for the poor of Eastcote. In 1895 the gift consisted of £333 stock.

By a scheme of 1897, which introduced representative trustees, the gifts of Lady Juliana Campbell, Howard, Hawtrey, Bright, and Coggs, together worth £49 yearly, were consolidated as the Ruislip Non-Ecclesiastical Charities, and the income made available for the parish poor in general. In 1952 the income of the charities amounted to £358, used to provide coal and food vouchers, bread, and gifts of money.

Under the inclosure award of 1814 60 a. were allotted to the use of cottagers whose rents did not exceed £5 a year. Administration of the Ruislip Cottagers' Allotments Charity was vested in a representative committee. In 1880 95 cottagers were licensed to pasture cattle on this land. In 1960 the income of this charity was £319, applied to the general benefit of cottager families selected by the trustees.

THE HUNDRED OF GORE

THE hundred of Gore lies north of the River Brent on the Hertfordshire boundary of Middlesex. Bisected by Watling Street, it is bounded by Elthorne hundred on the west and by Ossulstone to the south and east.[1] In 1881 it covered 29,185 acres.[2]

In 1086 the hundred was assessed at 149 hides, equivalent to one hundred and a half.[3] It was then made up of five manors: Harrow, Hendon, Kingsbury, and the two manors of Stanmore. The Stanmore estate held at Domesday by Roger de Rames[4] was that later known as Little Stanmore, Whitchurch, or 'the other' Stanmore to distinguish it from the neighbouring manor and parish of Great Stanmore. The manor of Kingsbury, most of which the Survey assigns to Elthorne,[5] may be assigned in its entirety to the hundred of Gore in which it was included by the early 12th century.[6] Edgware, which was included in Gore by 1274,[7] was not mentioned in 1086. Its omission from the Survey is inexplicable, although it may have been included in the assessment for Little Stanmore or Kingsbury.[8]

The constituents of the hundred varied little after 1086. By 1316 Edgware was invariably included in surveys of the hundred.[9] Subsequently the only modification in the composition of the hundred was the occasional inclusion of the so-called manor of Pinner, a member of Harrow manor.[10] By the end of the 15th century the number of manors in Gore had increased to about 22.[11] In the early 19th century the hundred comprised the parishes of Edgware, Harrow, Hendon, Kingsbury, Great Stanmore and Little Stanmore.[12]

From an early date the jurisdiction exercised by the hundred was severely limited. Only Great Stanmore of its constituent manors did not, at some period before 1300, enjoy or claim exemption from the hundred court. Harrow, including Pinner, was included in the franchise owned by the Archbishop of Canterbury,[13] and until they were alienated about 1150 Hendon and Kingsbury formed part of the franchise of Westminster Abbey: Hendon was regranted to the abbey in 1312.[14] In 1274 Hendon, Edgware, Great Stanmore, and Little Stanmore were said to owe suit to the hundred court.[15] In 1293, however, Henry de Lacy, Earl of Lincoln, claimed view of frankpledge and other liberties in his manor of Edgware while the Prior of St. Bartholomew's, Smithfield, was apparently exercising similar liberties in his manor of Little Stanmore.[16]

A number of place-names suggest that the meeting-place of the hundred was near the border between Harrow and Kingsbury. Gore Field, Gore Mead, Gore Lane, and Gore Farm lay in Kingsbury[17] and there was also a Gore Field in Kenton.[18] The headborough of Preston was in mercy in 1421 for failing to prevent an obstruction of the watercourse at Gore hundred,[19] and land in Preston was described throughout the Middle Ages[20] by

---

[1] H. Braun, 'The Hundred of Gore and Its Moot-Hedge', *T.L.M.A.S.* xiii. 218–28.
[2] *Census*, 1881.
[3] *V.C.H. Mdx.* i. 83–84.   [4] Ibid. 128   [5] Ibid. 83.
[6] B.M. Add MS. 14252, f. 126; *V.C.H. Mdx.* i. 83.
[7] J.I. 1/540, m. 17.
[8] C. F. Baylis, 'The Omission of Edgware from Domesday', *T.L.M.A.S.* xvii. 62–66; see below, p. 155.
[9] *Feudal Aids*, iii. 373.
[10] *L. & P. Hen. VIII*, iv(1), p. 422.
[11] These figures are from the par. histories below, and from Lysons, *Environs of Lond.* iii. 2–7, 231–3, 392–4, 404–6.

[12] Greenwood, *Map of Mdx.* (1819).
[13] J.I. 1/544, m. 50; see pp. 237–8.
[14] *Flete's Hist. of Westminster Abbey*, ed. J. A. Robinson, 89; E. T. Evans, *Hist. of Hendon*, 23, 26; Lysons, *Environs of Lond.* iii. 231.
[15] J.I. 1/540, m. 17.
[16] *V.C.H. Lond.* i. 476; *Feudal Aids*, iii. 382.
[17] M.R.O., Kingsbury Tithe Map.
[18] M.R.O., Acc. 166(1)/1, /2.
[19] P. Davenport, 'Two Mdx. Hundred Moots', *T.L.M.A.S.* xvi. 145–9.
[20] Harrow court rolls, e.g. M.R.O., Acc. 76/2417, m. 87d; /2420, m. 1.

reference to 'le Moothegge' which abutted North Field, to 'Eldestretshote on Goredon', and to the 'Gaderbrok'. The 'Gaderbrok' must have been one of the eastern tributaries of the Lydding Brook and the hundred meeting-place may well have been at the northern end of Preston East Field, between 'Eldestrete' or Honeypot Lane (the north–south route from Stanmore to Kingsbury)[21] and a small stream which was perhaps the

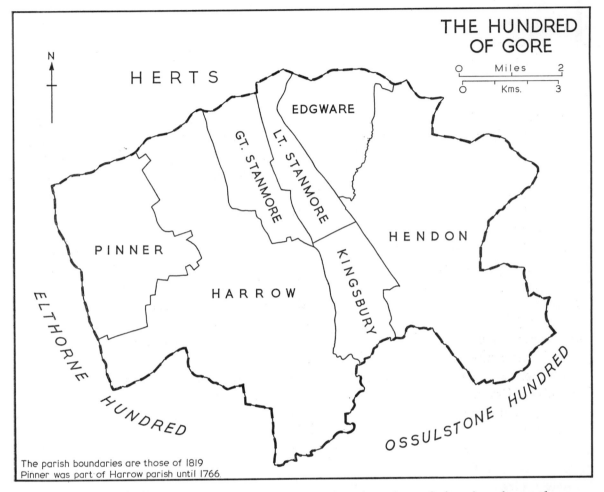

THE HUNDRED OF GORE

N

HERTS

EDGWARE

GT. STANMORE

LT. STANMORE

PINNER

HENDON

KINGSBURY

HARROW

ELTHORNE HUNDRED

OSSULSTONE HUNDRED

Miles 0 — 2
Kms. 0 — 3

The parish boundaries are those of 1819
Pinner was part of Harrow parish until 1766.

'Gaderbrok'.[22] The evidence, which includes the elevation of the site above the surrounding marshy ground, is reinforced by the Harrow map of 1759,[23] which marks a hedged area in the midst of common fields at this point. A survey of Kenton in 1547,[24] however, clearly describes Kenton Gore Field as abutting Stanmore and Kingsbury on the north and Preston North Field on the east. Gore Field also lay on the ancient north–south route, and the stream shown as separating Kenton and Preston common fields in the inclosure map[25] may have been the 'Gaderbrok'. The total disappearance of this area in housing development makes it impossible to trace the site on the ground.

[21] Marked clearly on Greenwood, *Map of Mdx.* (1819).
[22] H. Braun, 'The Hundred of Gore and its Moot-Hedge', *T.L.M.A.S.* xiii. 218–28.
[23] M.R.O., Acc. 643, 2nd deposit, Messeder map A.
[24] M.R.O., Acc. 166(1)/1, /2. See p. 186.
[25] M.R. 612.

EDGWARE

THE ANCIENT parish of Edgware[1] lay on the northern boundary of Middlesex. The extreme width of the parish was 1½ mile and the extreme length 2½ miles. In 1931, before Edgware became part of Hendon U.D., the area of the parish was 2,089 a.[2] The old parish was bordered on the north by Elstree (Herts.), on the west by Little Stanmore, and on the east by Hendon. The northern boundary followed roughly the line of Grim's Dyke,[3] and the western boundary ran from Elstree village southward along the modern Watling Street until it reached the Edgware Brook, which it followed until it joined Dean's Brook; it then turned towards the north and followed Dean's Brook until that stream petered out within a few hundred yards of Grim's Dyke and the eastern end of the northern boundary. This eastern edge of the parish followed the boundary of an estate in Hendon granted to Westminster Abbey severally by King Edwy (955–9) and King Edgar (959–75).[4] In the 12th and 13th centuries the vill of Edgware included the present parish and also that part of Little Stanmore north of the old road that branched off Watling Street in the direction of Watford along the line of the present Canons Drive.[5] The parish included part of the village of Elstree in its north-western corner, while that part of the village of Edgware which stands on the western side of Watling Street has always been in the parish of Little Stanmore.[6] Edgware was included in Hendon R.D. on its formation in 1895 and was transferred to Hendon U.D. in 1931. Hendon was incorporated in 1932 and has formed part of the London Borough of Barnet since 1965.[7]

The soil of Edgware consists mainly of London Clay. There is a narrow strip of alluvium along Dean's Brook, and the higher lands in the extreme north-west of the parish, together with Brockley Hill and Woodcock Hill, are composed of the sand and loam of the Claygate Beds, capped with pebble gravel.[8] The southern tip of the parish is only 150 ft above sea level; a gentle ascent is maintained northward for 2 miles, but beyond Edgwarebury the land rises sharply to reach over 475 ft near Elstree. Brockley Hill, probably the site of the Roman station of Sulloniacae,[9] and Woodcock Hill, in the north-east corner of the parish, are both over 450 ft high. Dean's Brook, the product of several small springs on the south-eastern slopes of Deacon's Hill, is joined by a small stream from Brockley Hill and Edgwarebury at a point some 500 yards north of the junction of Dean's Brook and Edgware Brook, which there combine to become Silk Stream. In modern times none of these streams has been great

enough to be more than an impediment to travellers, but the fact that the name of the village has been construed to mean 'Ecgi's weir or fishing pool' may well indicate that either Dean's Brook or Edgware Brook was at one time of far greater volume.[10] Moreover, the bridge known as Edgware Bridge, which carries Watling Street over Edgware Brook, has always been important by reason of the great amount of traffic moving along that highway. In 1370 it was claimed that the Prior of St. Bartholomew's, Smithfield, at that time holding land in Edgware, ought to repair a wooden bridge called 'Eggewerebrigge' and that his default had made the king's road there impassable for a year past. The prior claimed that he was not bound to repair the bridge, and after several postponements the jury declared in his favour, stating that the bridge was reparable by the alms of the men of the country and others crossing it.[11] A map of 1597 shows a bridge, of a considerably narrower track than the actual road, crossing the Edgware Brook; the stream, narrow on the left-hand or Stanmore side of the bridge, is wide and presumably shallow on the right-hand or downstream side. It seems probable, therefore, that the normal means of crossing the brook at that date was by fording, with the bridge used perhaps only by foot passengers and at times when the stream was in flood.[12] W. S. Tootell, writing in 1817, said that until recently the cost of repairing the bridge had been divided into four portions, two to be paid by the lord of Little Stanmore manor and one each by the lords of Hendon and Edgware manors. In 1814 these lords were indicted in King's Bench for not repairing the bridge. A witness for the prosecution said that a bar across the bridge was invariably kept shut except in time of floods. The judge declared that this showed that the public had the right to use the bridge only in time of flood, and as the indictment stated that the public might use it at their own free will and pleasure the defendants were acquitted.[13] Only one other bridge is shown on the map of 1597, that taking Edgwarebury Lane over the tributary of Dean's Brook. There was presumably a ford where Hale Lane crossed this stream, and until 1926, when the first bridge was built, there was a watersplash and regular winter flooding at the point where Hale Lane went through Dean's Brook.[14]

Watling Street, the Roman road from London to St. Albans (Herts.), has always been by far the most important of the roads touching Edgware. Sulloniacae lay exactly half-way between London and St. Albans, and Edgware, situated a mile or so to the south of the Roman station, has also had all the

---

[1] This article was written in 1963. Any references to a later time are dated.

[2] *Census*, 1931.

[3] H. Braun, 'Some Earthworks of North-West Middlesex', *T.L.M.A.S.* xiii. 379 sqq.

[4] *P.N. Mdx.* (E.P.N.S.), 220.

[5] C. F. Baylis, *Short Hist. of Edgware and the Stanmores in the Middle Ages*, 5.

[6] It is impossible to decide whether some early documents refer to the village of Edgware or only to the parish, and some figures given in this history are subject to that qualification. A few houses on the west side of Watling Street in Edgware village are mentioned in this article, but detailed treatment is reserved for the article on Little Stanmore.

[7] See p. 163.

[8] Geol. Survey Map, sheet 256 (drift).

[9] *V.C.H. Mdx.* i. 66.

[10] *P.N. Mdx.* (E.P.N.S.), 50.

[11] *Public Works in Medieval Law*, ii (Seld. Soc. xl), 49 sqq.

[12] All Souls Coll., Oxford, map of Edgware manor, 1597; see plate facing p. 127.

[13] Hendon Cent. Libr., 'A Brief Sketch of the Town of Edgware' by W. S. Tootell, 1817, pp. 42–43 (hereafter referred to as Tootell MS.).

[14] D. G. Denoon, 'Hendon Highways: Their Development and Administration', *Trans. Mill Hill Hist. Soc.* no. 2, p. 6.

obvious advantages of this medial position. Tootell mentions 'a few large stones which by tradition were dropped by the Romans on their passage through the island, to enable them to find their way back'.[15] Another tradition is that Edgware was used as a resting-place by pilgrims on their way from London to St. Albans.[16] The road was certainly important in the Middle Ages, and from time to time various grants of tolls and pavage were made to further its repair.[17] In 1597 the width of the road through the village varied from 60 to 105 feet, and between Edgware and Brockley Hill there were wide verges on either side for considerable stretches.[18] A petition to the Commons in 1711 stated that the part of the London–Watford road from Great Stanmore to Kilburn, which included the section of Watling Street in Edgware parish between Canons and Edgware Bridge, was so damaged by the multitude of carriages and passengers that it was almost impassable for six months of the year, and in the same year the Edgware–Kilburn turnpike trust was established.[19] The turnpike road apparently extended from Kilburn to Sparrow's Herne (Herts.),[20] but the 'Edgware' tollgate was actually situated in Hendon, 200 yards south of the Edgware parish boundary.[21] The turnpike seems to have made little difference to the state of the road, for in 1798 it was said to have four inches of mud after heavy rain in summer and nine inches all the winter.[22] The trust was absorbed into the Metropolitan Turnpike Roads Trust in 1827[23] and the road was disturnpiked in 1872.[24] Other roads in the parish, while not so ancient as Watling Street, have a certain documented antiquity.[25] The road now known as Station Road (Church Lane in 1845) and Hale Lane has remained unaltered in course since it appeared on the map of 1597, and is presumably the same highway for the making of which Richard Nicholl the elder left 20s. in 1498.[26] In 1597 Green Lane or Piper's Green Lane[27] ran north-west from Piper's Green along its present course, but joined Watling Street some 400 yards north of the present junction. Edgwarebury Lane held the same course in 1597 as it did in 1963, but from Edgwarebury it continued north-west to join the twisting track which is now Fortune Lane. This connexion with Fortune Lane was severed by the inclosure award of 1854, and a new way was adopted north from Edgwarebury across the common to meet the Elstree–Barnet road 750 yards east of Elstree crossroads, being for the greater part of its length a public footway only and not a public carriageway.[28] Clay Lane in 1597 followed its modern course. The modern development of Edgware has

caused roads to proliferate within the built-up area. The first new road of more than local importance was Edgware Way, part of the Watford by-pass, which runs athwart the parish and was completed in 1927.[29] There were proposals in 1928 and 1933 for a major road to run from the junction of Watling Street and Edgware Way across Edgware to the junction of the Barnet by-pass and the northern boundary of the parish, but the project lapsed.[30] A section of the M1 motorway, cutting north-west from Mill Hill and westward across the parish north of Bury Farm, was opened in 1967.[31]

During the coaching age Edgware enjoyed good communications with London. In 1791 one stage coach and two other coaches passed through Edgware each day to London and back, and another coach passed through on four days a week.[32] By 1839 there were nine coaches from London passing through each weekday, and three on Sundays; seven carters went daily, with one extra on Saturdays, together with one wagon each day and two more on three days a week.[33] By 1851 five omnibuses were running daily to London.[34] There was no station in Edgware on the Midland Railway's main line from London to Bedford, opened in 1868, which ran north-east across the parish and through a tunnel under Woodcock Hill.[35] An Act to authorize the construction of a branch of the Great Northern Railway from Finsbury Park to Edgware, however, was passed in 1862;[36] the original plan seems to have been to place the Edgware station in Hendon, just to the south of Dean's Brook and near the turnpike house, but eventually it was sited in its present position between Station Road and Dean's Brook. The line was opened in 1867.[37] By 1869 it was showing a weekly increase in traffic and paying its way.[38] Evidently Edgware was considered to be the end of the line for economic suburban traffic, however, as the proposal to extend the line to Watford was abandoned in 1870.[39] The parishioners, at least, seemed to want no further connexion with Hertfordshire, for in 1871 the vestry refused permission to the Common Road Conveyance Co. to lay a tramway along the highway from Watford to London.[40] During the next fifty years there were several abortive proposals to build railways connecting Edgware with Harrow, Stanmore, and Watford,[41] but the only important move came in 1902, when an Act 'for incorporating the Edgware and Hampstead Railway Co., and for empowering them to construct railways partly underground from Edgware to Hampstead' was passed.[42] When the extension of the underground reached Golders Green in 1907, however, there was no mention in the

---

[15] Tootell MS. p. 8.
[16] Edgware libr., 'Notes on the Church and Parish of Edgware' by H. S. Geikie, vol. ii (hereafter ref. to as Geikie MS.).
[17] *Cal. Pat.* 1313–17, 220; 1388–92, 38; *Cal. Chanc. Writs,* i. 410.
[18] All Souls Coll., map of Edgware, 1597.
[19] *Trans. Mill Hill Hist. Soc.* no. 2, p. 12; Mdx. and Hertford Highway Act, 10 Anne, c. 3.
[20] Kilburn Road Act, 19 Geo. III, c. 120.
[21] *Trans. Mill Hill Hist. Soc.* no. 2, p. 13.
[22] Middleton, *View,* 395.
[23] *Trans. Mill Hill Hist. Soc.* no. 2, p. 15; Mdx. Turnpike Trust Consolidation Act, 7 Geo. IV, c. 142.
[24] Hendon libr., TS. notes on hist. of Hendon.
[25] Baylis, *Edgware and the Stanmores,* claims that most of the roads there in 1597 existed *c.* 1200 as minor trackways.
[26] *Trans. Mill Hill Hist. Soc.* no. 2, p. 6.
[27] On 19th- and early 20th-cent. O.S. maps it is called

'Greene Lane' except at its extreme southern end.
[28] M.R.O., Edgware Incl. Award.
[29] Robbins, *Middlesex,* 83.
[30] *North Mdx. Regional Planning Scheme* (1928); *2nd Rep. Greater Lond. Regional Planning Cttee.* (1933).
[31] *The Times,* 25 May 1967.
[32] *Universal Brit. Dir.* iii. 36.
[33] *Kelly's Dir. Mdx.* (1839).
[34] *Post Office Dir. Mdx.* (1851).
[35] *Historical Notes of the Midland Railway* (1903), 55.
[36] *L.J.* xciii. 122.
[37] *The Times,* 26 Aug. 1867.
[38] Ibid. 22 Feb. 1869.
[39] Ibid. 12 Feb. 1870.
[40] Par. Recs., Vestry Min. Bk.
[41] *L.J.* cvi. 236; cxiv. 44; cxxix. 408; cxxv. 350; *The Times,* 12 May 1897; *Mdx. & Herts. N. & Q.* iii. 4, 167.
[42] *L.J.* cxxxiv. 38.

1.

2.

3.

4.

1. Ruislip, 16th century   2. Norwood Green, c. 1815, demolished 1961   3. Day's Almshouses, Edgware, 1828   4. Ickenham, 1857

ALMSHOUSES

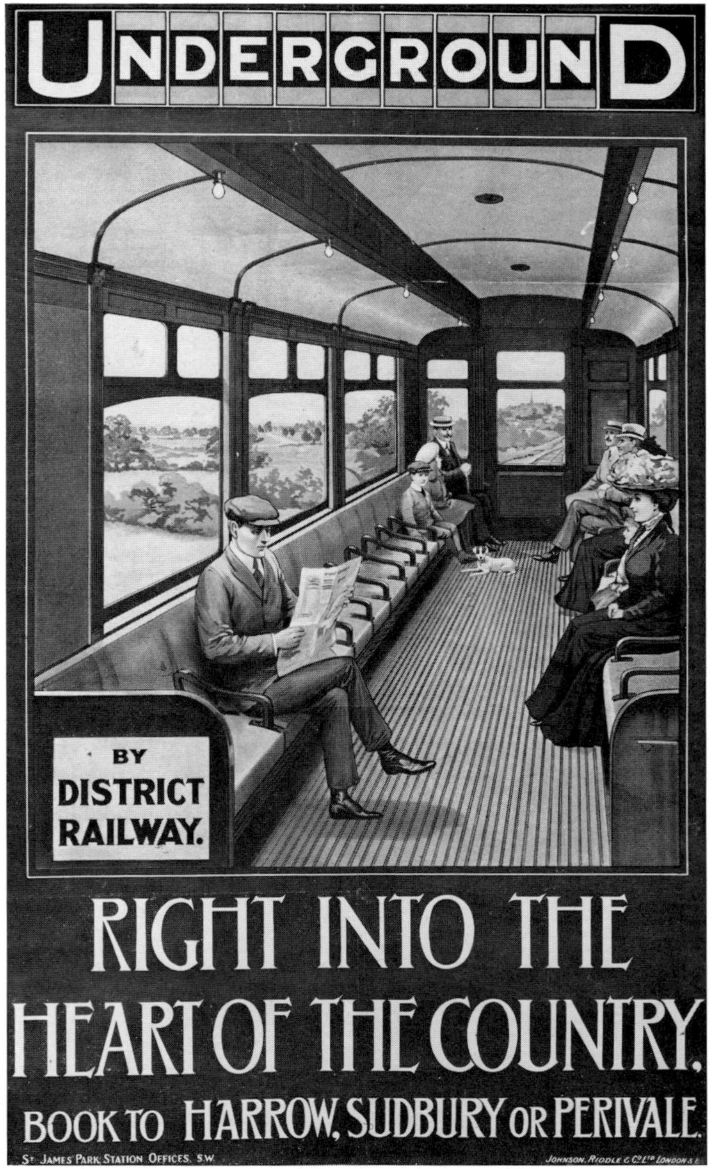

1904

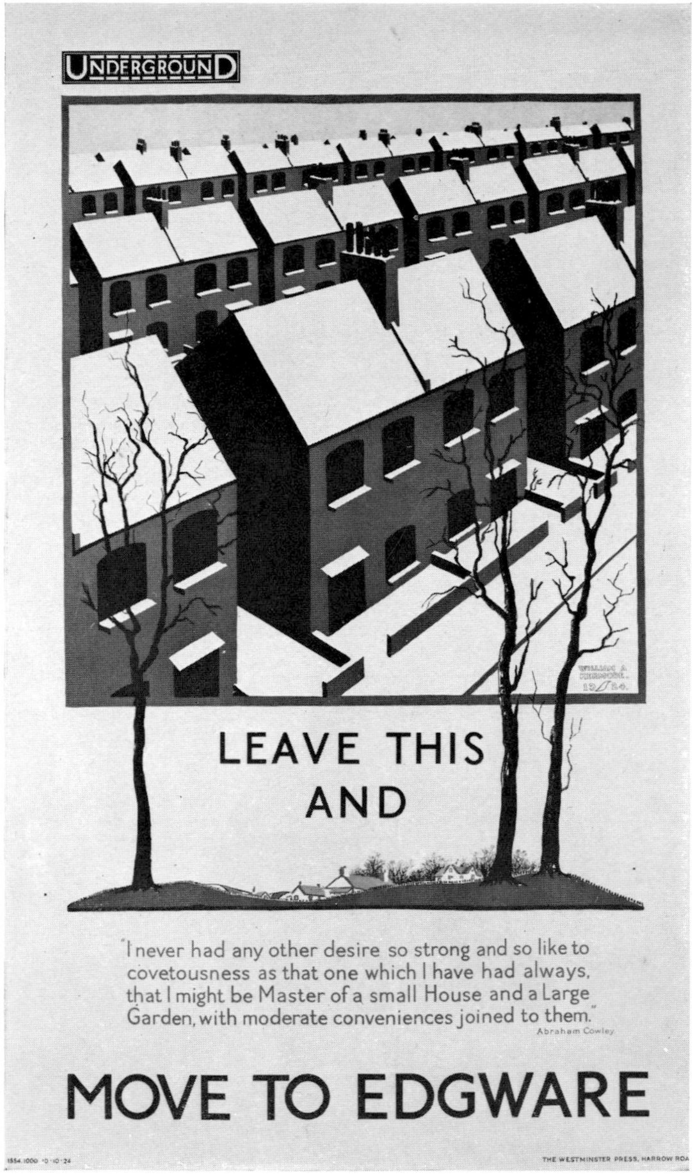

1924

UNDERGROUND POSTERS

official publicity of extensions to Edgware and Watford.[43] In fact, the surface extension of the tube from Edgware to Watford, authorized by an Act of 1903,[44] was never built, and in 1912 powers were obtained by the London Electric Railway to absorb the authorized Edgware and Hampstead Railway.[45] Work was begun on the extension of the tube from Golders Green in 1922, and in 1924 Edgware station was opened.[46] The intended New Works Programme of 1935–40, which proposed among other things the electrification of the L.N.E.R. line to Edgware and the extension of the tube to Aldenham (Herts.), was never carried out as regards works in Edgware, and the unfinished portions of the original scheme were finally abandoned in 1954.[47] In 1963 the line of the proposed extension could still be traced on the ground as far as Brockley Hill. In the meantime road transport had been developing. In 1904 the Metropolitan Electric Tramways Co. opened a service from Cricklewood to Edgware, which was extended to Canons Park in 1907.[48] By 1914 motor omnibuses were serving the village.[49] In 1936 the tramway beyond Edgware village was abandoned, and in the same year the tram service from Edgware to Acton was replaced by a trolleybus route. In 1938 the trolleybus service was extended to Canons Park. The last trolleybus was replaced by diesel omnibuses in 1962.[50]

Settlement in Edgware has been chiefly influenced by Watling Street. There is a possibility that the general unrest of the late 10th century had led to a certain amount of movement away from the highway, but there is no evidence that the village was ever sited away from Watling Street for any length of time.[51] The map of 1597[52] shows the village stretched on both sides of Watling Street between Edgware Bridge and the church, the houses cramped together and for the most part fronting the road, although on the Stanmore side there are seven with their gable-ends to the road, and on the Edgware side some detached houses and outbuildings stand in the gardens and crofts behind the houses lining the road. There are a few houses on Watling Street north of the church, and a square structure standing actually in the road is probably the pound, but otherwise the only settlements of significant size are the farm-houses and buildings at Piper's Green and Edgwarebury.

Over most of the parish there was little change in this pattern of settlement until the great expansion of the 20th century. At Elstree, in the extreme northwest corner, several houses were built along the east side of Watling Street in the 18th century. By 1866 sporadic residential development had taken place at Stone Grove on Watling Street and at Newlands in Green Lane. There was also at least one large house in its own grounds, Deacon's Hill, on the Elstree–Barnet road near the northern boundary of the parish.[53] In the late 19th century this area, occupying

high ground with fine views both to north and south, became a favourite site for such residences.[54] This trend has continued although the houses and their gardens have tended to become progressively smaller. Early in the 20th century the built-up area of Elstree was extended both eastward along the Barnet road and southward along Watling Street.

Edgware itself resisted wholesale development until after the First World War. In 1914 it could still be called a village although several streets of small terraced houses had been laid out on the site of Manor Farm to the north of St. Margaret's church, and also on the Stanmore side of Watling Street.[55] The want of quick railway communications was a reason given in 1924 to account for its backwardness,[56] but although the estate agents and developers began to invade Edgware after 1924,[57] the year in which the extension to the underground railway was completed, the railway itself was a symptom rather than a cause of the suburbanization of the parish. Once the first breach had been made, the southern end of the parish soon began to fill up with houses and shops,[58] more, perhaps, as a northern extension of Hendon than as a separate development of Edgware village. Until the outbreak of the Second World War building was confined mainly to the area south of Edgware Way[59] and after the war the northern part of the parish was included in London's Green Belt, thus ensuring the preservation of open spaces at Elstree, Deacon's Hill, and Scratchwood. The construction of the M1 motorway across this area made less visual impact than might have been expected owing to the deep cutting in which most of it lies. Some building estates have been planted north of Edgware Way in the post-war period, but they have been largely confined to the area between Edgwarebury Lane and the main railway line. The borough council's Spur Road estate was built only after bitter local opposition; it is dominated by five tall blocks of flats, the first of which, of eleven stories, was opened in 1957.[60]

The Edgware General Hospital is outside the old parish at Burnt Oak, Hendon.[61] The Anglican Convent of St. Mary at the Cross (Sisters of the Poor),[62] until 1931 known as the Convent of St. Mary of Nazareth, was founded in 1865 in Shoreditch by the Revd. H. D. Nihill. In 1873 land was bought at Edgware to the north of Hale Lane, and by degrees the work of the convent and its hospital at Shoreditch were given up. In 1937 a new hospital block, providing 50 extra beds, was opened at Edgware. It is now a home for sick and incurable children, who are taken in up to the age of 18 and then kept for life if they have no other home.

Apart from the tower of St. Margaret's church the only ancient buildings which survive in the old village lie on the Stanmore side of Watling Street.[63] About ten timber-framed houses, including the

[43] C. E. Lee, *Fifty Years of the Hampstead Tube*, 17.
[44] *L.J.* cxxxv. 350; *The Times*, 19 July 1906.
[45] Lee, *Hampstead Tube*, 23.
[46] Ibid. 24.
[47] Ibid. 27–28.
[48] Ex inf. London Transport Exec.
[49] *Kelly's Dir. Mdx.* (1914).
[50] Ex inf. London Transport Exec.
[51] Baylis, *Edgware and the Stanmores*, 1, 2.
[52] All Souls Coll., map of Edgware, 1597.
[53] O.S. Map 6″, Mdx. vi. NW. (1868 edn.).
[54] Ibid. (1898 edn.).
[55] O.S. Map 1/2,500, Mdx. vi. (1913–14 edn.).

[56] T. J. Relf, *Ye Booke of Olde Edgware*, introd.
[57] Sale cats. of Broadfields Manor Estate 1924, Hendon libr., R.L. 942.1911; other cats. R.L. 728.8, DD MHS 1/21.
[58] Map of proposed development 1927, B.M. Maps 4190(24).
[59] Hendon Planning Scheme no. 1, pp. 67–69.
[60] *Edgware Times and Guardian*, 7 June 1957.
[61] Reserved for treatment under Hendon.
[62] The following account is based on P. F. Anson, *Call of the Cloister*, 398–403; for the chapel see below, p. 166.
[63] This and the following paragraphs were revised in 1969.

former 'Chandos Arms' were recorded here in the 1930s.[64] A few of these, dating from the 16th and early 17th centuries, were still standing in 1969. The inn called the 'George', which stood on the Edgware side of Watling Street half-way between Edgware and the church, is first mentioned in 1454.[65] It probably continued to be used as an inn until its demolition in 1931, but this function is obscured by the fact that the small farm attached to the 'George' was obviously more important both to its lessees and the lords of the manor.[66] Henry Hayley, a lessee of the 'George' in the early 17th century, was in 1617 described as a brewer and indicted for uttering drink beyond the rate.[67] Tootell does not include the 'George' in his list of alehouses in 1753, but states that it was licensed in 1771 in lieu of the 'Red Lion'.[68] It was called an inn in 1791[69] and although in 1834 it was called only a tavern or public house[70] its fortunes seemed to revive in the later 19th century.[71] In 1597 the premises had consisted of four buildings, one of them fronting Watling Street, enclosing a courtyard; a long barn, also facing the road, stood to the north of the house, leaving a passageway through it to the enclosed land at the back, which contained a pond, outhouses, brewhouses, and an orchard.[72] A photograph of c. 1880–90[73] shows an agglomeration of two-story buildings, brick-built and of uncertain age, presenting to the road two gable-ends separated by two bays, the first consisting of a door and a shallow brick bow-front, the second of a room over a high, wide passage, the whole suggesting a plan not unlike that shown on the map of 1597. By 1900 most of the front had been covered with roughcast;[74] after the First World War the courtyard was covered over and made into a dance hall, and the whole house was demolished c. 1931 for road widening.[75] Two other inns in Edgware were founded in the 18th century. The 'Boot', standing at the corner of Station Road and Watling Street, is probably the same as the 'Boot and Spur' mentioned in 1753.[76] About 1880–90 the inn was a plain brick building of two stories with attics,[77] but this house has since been demolished and a modern public house occupies its site. The 'Leather Bottle' existed in 1753; apparently 'silenced' in 1759, it does not appear again until the early 20th century, and the present building replaced an earlier and smaller house in 1925.[78] Other 18th-century inns in Edgware were the 'Bell', the 'Red Lion', and the 'Green Man' alias the 'Greyhound'.[79]

Edgware Place, which stood in the village at the junction of Watling Street and the road now called Manor Park Crescent, was built c. 1803 by the Hon. John Lindsay, partly, at least, from materials obtained by the demolition of the buildings at Bermondsey Spa.[80] The house afterwards became the residence of Charles Day, who built for it a lodge

known as Blacking-Bottle Lodge, because its shape represented one of the bottles in which Day and Martin packed their liquid boot-blacking.[81] The house had been demolished by 1845 but the lodge remained for long after that date.[82] Nicoll's Farm, a brick house of c. 1700 which stood at the junction of Watling Street and Mill Ridge,[83] has disappeared but its partly timber-framed barn survives. Further north at Stone Grove are Day's Almshouses, dating from 1828.[84] Atkinson's Almshouses beyond them, originally built in 1680, were entirely reconstructed in 1957.[85] Two early-19th-century stucco residences in what is now Piper's Green Lane, Newlands Grange and Bromfield House, have been pulled down since the Second World War.

In the northern part of the parish two outlying farm-houses, Bury Farm at Edgwarebury[86] and Brockley Grange Farm, are partly timber-framed buildings probably dating from the early 17th century. The older houses on the east side of Watling Street at Elstree Hill South were built in the 18th century. They include a uniform range of five two-storied brick cottages with a central feature consisting of a doorway surmounted by a fanlight and a Venetian window above it; the range was unoccupied and partly derelict in 1969. Further south stands Hill House, a red brick building of two stories and attics. The front of its original block has a central doorway and a central Venetian window, flanked by projecting two-storied bays. A rainwater-head on one of the bays is dated 1779, but the core of the house and a long south wing may have been built earlier in the 18th century. Additional wings to the north were probably added after Hill House became a preparatory school in the late 19th century.[87] Several imposing 19th-century mansions were still standing in 1969 on the south side of the Elstree–Barnet road, although Deacon's Hill had been demolished and its site was being used for the erection of a close of neo-Georgian houses. Edgwarebury House, now a country club, and the Dower House date from the late 19th century and are both elaborately half-timbered externally. Other large houses of similar date in the area include the Chantry, Abbots Mead, and Penniwells. Much of the road frontage between them has been built up with 20th-century residences, mostly detached and standing in large gardens.

Until the 20th century there were no violent fluctuations in the population of Edgware. In the manor of Edgware in 1277 there were 8 free tenants (excluding the Grand Priory of Clerkenwell) and 52 customary tenants; the survey from which these figures are taken, however, includes lands appurtenant to the manor lying in Kingsbury.[88] In 1425–6 the manor of Edgware had three free and 29 customary tenants in the parish,[89] and in 1525–6 the num-

[64] Hist. Mon. Com. *Mdx.* 115.
[65] All Souls Coll., Edgware Old Lease no. 2.
[66] See p. 159.
[67] *Mdx. Sess. Recs.* iv. 160.
[68] Tootell MS. p. 49.
[69] *Universal Brit. Dir* (1791), iii. 36.
[70] *Pigot's Commercial Dir.* (1832–4), 898.
[71] O.S. Map 1/2,500, Mdx. vi. 13 (1896 edn.); Hendon libr., L. 506.
[72] All Souls Coll., map of Edgware, 1597.
[73] Hendon libr., L. 506.
[74] Ibid. 3704.
[75] Ibid. 5574; *Hendon Times*, 19 May 1933.
[76] Tootell MS. p. 49.
[77] Hendon libr., L. 510.
[78] Ibid. 1043; Geikie MS. vol v.
[79] Tootell MS. p. 49; M.R.O., Mdx. Sess. Papers, 1725 Dec./15.
[80] Tootell MS. p. 48; Lysons, *Environs of Lond.* i. 558.
[81] Geikie MS. vol. iv.
[82] M.R.O., Edgware Tithe Award.
[83] Hist. Mon. Com. *Mdx.* 17.
[84] See plate facing p. 152.
[85] See p. 168.
[86] See p. 157.
[87] *V.C.H. Herts.* ii. 349, where several houses on the Middlesex side of the boundary are noted.
[88] *T.L.M.A.S.* xiii. 158 sqq.
[89] All Souls Coll., Edgware Rental 2.

bers were two or three free and 26 customary tenants.[90] In 1547 there were 120 communicants in the parish.[91] In 1597 there were between 60 and 70 houses in the parish, and 44 more in the village of Edgware but on the west side of Watling Street and therefore within the parish of Little Stanmore.[92] In 1599 there were six free and 25 customary tenants of the manor within Edgware.[93] In 1642 the protestation oath was taken by 103 adult males.[94] In 1664 there were 73 houses in the parish, but the hearth tax of 1672 gives only 66.[95] During the 18th century the average numbers both of baptisms and burials declined gently but steadily; in the period 1717–26 the average number of baptisms was between 15 and 16 a year and the average number of burials 20, but by 1801–10 the figures were 11 and 9 respectively.[96] There were said to be 69 houses in the village in 1766 and 76 houses in 1792.[97] At the first census in 1801 the population was 412. Throughout the 19th century numbers rose slowly, except for the years between 1851 and 1871; the censuses of 1861 and 1871 show successive declines of 7 per cent., attributed in 1871 to migration and to the absence of direct railway communication with London. Ten years later the losses had been more than made good, and in 1901 the figure of 868 had been reached. By 1921 the population had grown to 1,516, but the great infilling of the southern part of Edgware after 1924 caused the most spectacular increase. In 1931 the population was 5,352; this had increased to 17,513 by 1951 and to 20,127 by 1961.[98]

Apart from a few incumbents,[99] there have been no well-known residents in the parish. The Anglo-Irish writer Richard Edgeworth (1744–1817) and his daughter Maria (1767–1849), the novelist, believed that their ancestors had lived in Edgware before settling in Ireland, where Edward Edgeworth (d. 1595), Bishop of Down and Connor, had founded the family's fortune.[1]

MANORS. The manor of *EDGWARE* is first mentioned in 1216.[2] Edgware does not occur in Domesday Book; either it was omitted by accident or included in Kingsbury or Stanmore. One possibility is that Edgware was reckoned part of Stanmore at the time of the Survey, although later in its history the manor certainly had close connexions with the manor of Kingsbury.[3] Stanmore was part of the barony of Roger de Rames at the time of Domesday. Roger's son William had two sons, Roger and Robert, between whom the Stanmore property was divided at some time before 1130. Adeliza de Rames, probably the daughter of the younger Roger, married

Edward of Salisbury as his second wife, possibly bringing with her part of the Domesday manor '*in Stanmera*' east of Watling Street, that is to say the greater part of Edgware. Edward's grandson Patrick, created Earl of Salisbury in 1149, was the first of the Salisbury family definitely known to have owned land at Edgware.[4] The Rames family continued to own the north-west corner of the parish together with the northern part of Little Stanmore.[5]

A royal writ of 1216 ordered that Eleanor, Countess of Salisbury, mother of Isabel, should be permitted to hold her manor of Edgware in peace.[6] Eleanor died in 1232 or 1233 and Ela (or Isabel), Countess of Salisbury, succeeded.[7] She had married William Longespée (d. 1226) and some time before 1240 she gave the manor to her fourth son Nicholas Longespée, later Bishop of Salisbury, at a quit-rent.[8] In 1261 Ela died and five years later Nicholas Longespée devised the manor to the money-lender Adam de Stratton, who in 1272 obtained their interests in the manor from Henry de Lacy and his wife Margaret, daughter and coheir of William, eldest son of the Countess Ela.[9] After the disgrace of Adam in 1290 the manor was forfeit to the king who regranted it to Henry de Lacy.[10] Henry de Lacy died in 1311 and the manor passed to his daughter Alice, who had married Thomas, Earl of Lancaster, in 1294.[11] After the death of Thomas in 1322, following the battle of Boroughbridge, the king took the manor into his own hands and regranted it to Alice de Lacy.[12] Before 10 November 1324 she married Ebulo Lestrange, and in 1325 a licence was granted to them to enfeoff Hugh le Despenser of the manor and for Hugh to regrant it to them for the life of Alice.[13] In 1328 Isabel and Mortimer, who, in order to consolidate their authority, were attempting to gain the allegiance of the partisans of the late Earl of Lancaster, granted the manor, among other estates, to Ebulo for his life if he survived Alice.[14] However, in 1330 Ebulo and Alice found it necessary to petition the king and council to consider their case, and eventually they secured a grant of some of their lands on condition that they quitclaimed all the rest.[15] The agreement was embodied in a charter in 1331 whereby Edgware manor, amongst others, was granted to Ebulo, Alice, and Ebulo's heirs to hold as Henry de Lacy had held it of the king.[16] This grant was perhaps a recognition of Ebulo's contribution to the overthrow of Isabel and Mortimer.[17]

On the death of Ebulo Lestrange in 1335 the manor of Edgware with the hamlet of Kingsbury was said to be held in chief, as parcel of the earldom of Salisbury, at half a knight's fee. Roger Lestrange, Lord Strange, son of John Lestrange VI,

[90] Ibid. 9.
[91] Hennessy, *Novum Repertorium*, 141.
[92] All Souls Coll., map of Edgware manor, 1597.
[93] All Souls Coll., Edgware MS. 52 (Martin, *Cat. All Souls*, 37).
[94] Hse. of Lords, Mdx. Protestation Rets.
[95] M.R.O., H.T.6
[96] Figures based on par. regs.
[97] Guildhall MS. 9558, p. 430; Edgware libr., Geikie MS. vol. i.
[98] *Census*, 1801–1961.
[99] See below.
[1] *D.N.B.*
[2] *Rot. Litt. Claus.* (Rec. Com.), i. 285.
[3] This paragraph is based on C. F. Baylis, 'The omission of Edgware from Domesday', *T.L.M.A.S.* xi. 62.
[4] E. A. Webb, *Recs. of St. Bartholomew's Priory*, i. 102.

[5] Cf. C. F. Baylis, *Short Hist. of Edgware and the Stanmores in the Middle Ages*, 9.
[6] *Rot. Litt. Claus* (Rec. Com.), i. 285.
[7] *Complete Peerage*.
[8] Baylis, *Edgware and the Stanmores*, 3; B.M. Harl. Chart. 53 B.12.
[9] *Cat. Anct. D.* i. A 1737; ii. A 2154; iv. A 7290.
[10] *Rot. Parl.* (Rec. Com.), i. 54a; *Cal. Close*, 1288–96, 63; *Cal. Fine R.* 1272–1307, 270.
[11] *Cal. Inq. p.m.* x, p. 195.
[12] *Cal. Close*, 1318–23, 575; *Cal. Pat.* 1321–4, 179, 180, 182; H. le Strange, *Le Strange Recs.* 273.
[13] *Cal. Pat.* 1324–7, 103; *Cal. Close*, 1323–7, 269.
[14] *Cal. Pat.* 1327–30, 338.
[15] *Rot. Parl.* (Rec. Com.), ii. 57b.
[16] *Cal. Chart. R.* 1327–41, 199; *Cal. Pat.* 1377–81, 83.
[17] Le Strange, *Le Strange Recs.* 276.

Lord Strange (d. 1311), the brother of Ebulo, was his heir.[18] In 1336, however, Sir Hugh de Frene eloped with Alice, now aged 55, and the king, displeased, took their lands into his hands; but by 23 March 1336 they had married and had made peace with the king, receiving back their property, and on 27 September 1336 they had licence to convey Edgware and other lands to themselves for life with remainder to Roger Lestrange.[19] In 1337 Hugh de Frene died, and Roger granted his interest in the manor to Nicholas de Cantilupe to remain with him for life after the death of Alice,[20] who by a deed of 25 June 1337, the day before Roger's grant, divested herself of all her castles and goods as a gift to her cousin, Nicholas de Cantilupe, although she probably retained actual possession until her death in 1348.[21] Nicholas died in 1355 and left Roger Lestrange, Lord Strange (d. 1382), son of the heir of Ebles who had died in 1349, in full possession of the manor. In 1377 he granted it for life to his son Roger,[22] who still held it in 1412.[23] In 1413 a grant of the reversion of rent in Edgware was made by Richard, Lord Strange (d. 1449),[24] and in 1422 he granted the reversion of the manor to Richard Ulverston, Richard Colfox, and John Wythyton,[25] presumably feoffees, for when Roger Lestrange died in 1426 the manor reverted to Lord Strange.[26] He held it only until 1430, however, for in that year he granted it to William and Elizabeth Davell.[27] This grant was supplemented by another in 1431, which gave a rent of 100 marks from Richard's manor of Dunham (Ches.) to Davell and his wife, not to be paid as long as they held the manor of Edgware.[28] In 1441 the manor was sold by the Davells to Thomas Chichele and other feoffees,[29] who surrendered it in 1442 to the king; in the same year the king granted it to All Souls College, Oxford, in whose hands it has remained ever since.[30] In 1475 a manor of Edgware was granted by the king to Queen Elizabeth, the Bishop of Salisbury, and the Dean of Windsor;[31] in 1483 the Dean and Chapter of Windsor enfeoffed the king of the manor of 'Eggeware',[32] but there is no indication in either transaction which of the Edgware manors was concerned nor how it came into the possession of the grantor. There is no evidence among the documents at All Souls that the college relinquished and regained the manor at any time during the reign of Edward IV. On the other hand, if the manor concerned was Edgware Boys, it must have returned to the Knights Hospitallers between 1483 and 1535, when it appears among the possessions of the Grand Priory of Clerkenwell.[33]

From the 13th to the 18th century the manor of Edgware included the greater part of the parish.

Throughout this period the manor had appurtenances in Kingsbury parish; the close connexion between the manors of Edgware and Kingsbury, which led to the intermingling of details of the manors in court rolls, rentals, and surveys, makes it impossible to determine the extent of these appurtenances. It would seem, however, that the acreage in Kingsbury belonging to the manor of Edgware was never greater than one-fifth of the total acreage of the manor,[34] and was for the greater part of the history of the manor under one-twentieth. In the early 17th century two small manors in other parishes were stated to be held as of the manor of Edgware at quit-rents: the manor of Coffers in Kingsbury,[35] 100 a. held by knight service, and the manor of Tokyngton in Harrow.[36]

It has been estimated that in 1277 the manor of Edgware contained 453 a. of demesne, 270 a. held by free tenants, and 814 a. held by customary tenants, but this can only be an approximation to the actual extent of the manor.[37] The rents for the Earlsbury farm in 1436[38] suggest that all the demesne was farmed out in one portion; in 1443, a year after the manor was acquired by All Souls College, the 'manor farm' was leased to Richard Kynge of Aldenham (Herts.), husbandman, for ten years at a rent of £8 a year.[39] An unstated amount of woodland was reserved to the lords, and in 1454 the demesne underwent a further division when the George Inn was leased to Henry Abell for ten years at a rent of £5 6s. 8d. a year, together with 200 oak faggots, on condition that the horse-mill and millstones at the inn were kept in repair.[40] This seems to have been the beginning of the George farm, which continued to be leased until the 19th century. A lease of 1532 states that the lessees had fire- and plough-bote; they were to keep in good repair the vessels of the brewhouse there and to provide food and drink for the manorial court.[41] A lease of 1541 included the same terms, but added that no fire-bote was to be expended in the common brewhouse.[42] In 1548 the rent was increased to £8[43] but in 1583 it was reduced to £5 6s. 8d. and the balance made up with 4 qr. of wheat and 5 qr. and 3 bu. of malt.[44] This rent continued unchanged until at least 1800. From 1554 leases ran for 20 years, although until at least 1625 they were always renewed well before they fell due. Earlsbury, a name which first occurs in 1436 and whose origin seems to have been as a complement to Kingsbury,[45] remained the chief demesne farm. The next surviving lease after that of 1443 is one dated 1540, when the rent was £6 15s. 4d.[46] Thereafter the rent rose slightly until in 1584 it stood at £8 a year plus 6 qr. of wheat and 8 qr. of malt,[47] at which

---

[18] Cal. Close, 1333–7, 444–5; Cal. Inq. p.m. vii, p. 464; Complete Peerage.
[19] Cal. Pat. 1334–8, 319; Complete Peerage.
[20] Cal. Pat. 1334–8, 463.
[21] Cal. Close, 1337–9, 19; Cal. Inq. p.m. ix, pp. 96–97.
[22] All Souls Coll., Edgware MS. 3 (No. 3 in C. T. Martin, Cat. Archives of All Souls Coll. p. 35).
[23] Feudal Aids, vi. 487.
[24] All Souls Coll., Edgware MS. 5 (Martin, Cat. All Souls, p. 35).
[25] Edgware MS. 6.
[26] Cal. Fine R. 1422–30, 130.
[27] All Souls Coll., Edgware MS. 8 (Martin, Cat. All Souls, p. 35).
[28] Edgware MS. 11.
[29] Edgware MSS. 12–16.
[30] Cal. Pat. 1441–6, 19–20, 99.
[31] Ibid. 1467–77, 543.
[32] Cat. Anct. D., v. A 10768; Cal. Close, 1476–85, 296.

[33] Valor Eccl. (Rec. Com.), i. 403.
[34] All Souls Coll., Edgware Rental 37 (1680).
[35] Reserved for treatment under Kingsbury.
[36] All Souls Coll., Edgware MS. 54 (Martin, Cat. All Souls, p. 37); Edgware Rentals 14, 34; see below, p. 208.
[37] D. G. Denoon and Trelawny Roberts, 'The Extent of Edgware, A.D. 1277', T.L.M.A.S. xiii. 160.
[38] See below.
[39] All Souls Coll., Edgware Old Leases 1.
[40] Ibid. 2.
[41] Ibid. 4.
[42] Ibid. 6.
[43] Ibid. 10.
[44] Ibid. 17.
[45] Edgware MS. 46; cf. Baylis, Edgware and the Stanmores, 2. No evidence has been found to support the assertion that the village was once called Earlsbury.
[46] All Souls Coll., Edgware Old Leases 5.
[47] Ibid. 18.

figure it remained until 1826, when it was increased to £25 with 8½ qr. of wheat and 11 qr. of malt.[48] The fine for entry in 1805 was £367, and by 1826 it had risen to £800.[49] Other parts of the demesne were leased in the 16th century, notably the so-called 'common wood' let to Robert Strensham of Wilton (Wilts.) in 1575.[50] The woods were leased to Christopher Hovenden, brother of the warden of the college, at £20 a year in 1580; the almost immediate surrender of the lease did not prevent the queen from citing it as a precedent when in 1587 she asked for a lease of the Middlesex woods of the college in favour of Jane, widow of Sir Robert Stafford. After a long and acrimonious dispute the college maintained its right not to lease the woods unless it wished to do so.[51]

There was no manor-house as such at Edgware. Edgwarebury always seems to have been the centre of the manor and of Earlsbury Farm, and a condition of the lease of Earlsbury in 1602 was that the lessee should lodge the lords or their representative when they came to the manor on college business,[52] although the manor court seems to have been held at the 'George'.[53] The house at Edgwarebury is mentioned in 1548,[54] and a house and farm buildings are shown on the map of 1597,[55] north and east of the pond. The existing house on the site, known as Bury Farm, has an older portion which probably dates from the early 17th century; this is partly timber-framed with external weather-boarding and a jettied upper story. A projecting brick wing was added on the west side in the 18th century.[56] Dick Turpin is said to have stolen the silver, raped the daughter of the householder, and poured boiling water over her father.[57] A second farm-house, which stood to the west of Bury Farm until after the Second World War, was an 18th-century brick building known as Edgwarebury Farm.

The origins of the manor of *EDGWARE BOYS* or *EDGWARE AND BOYS* are obscure,[58] but they may possibly be found in a grant by Henry Bocuinte to the Order of St. John of Jerusalem (Knights Hospitallers) between 1231 and 1238 of land in Edgware.[59] In 1277 the order held land as free tenants of the manor of Edgware, paying a rent of 7s. 7d.,[60] but the earliest mention of a separate manor of Boys occurs in a terrier of 1397.[61] In a rental of the manor of Edgware dated 1425–6 and in some later documents belonging to that manor the manor of Boys is said to have been formerly held by the Earl (or Countess) of Lincoln, but there is no other evidence that either Henry de Lacy or his daughter Alice ever had possession of the manor of

Boys.[62] Lysons states[63] that this was the manor granted by the Dean and Chapter of Windsor to the king in 1483, but there is no evidence for this identification, and the order still held the manor at the Dissolution.[64] In 1543 it was granted to Sir John Williams and Anthony Stringer at a rent of 20s. a year,[65] but it was immediately alienated by them to Henry Page of Harrow.[66] Henry's son John disposed of it to John Scudamore c. 1631, and it was sold to Thomas Coventry, Lord Coventry, in 1637.[67] It continued in the Coventry family until 1762, when it was sold to William Lee of Totteridge Park,[68] from whom it descended to his son William, who in pursuance of the terms of the will of Richard Antonie of Colworth (Beds.) took the surname of Antonie.[69] From Antonie it passed to his nephew John Fiott (son of Harriet, second daughter of William Lee of Totteridge Park), who assumed the name of Lee under the will of William Lee Antonie.[70] The descent of the estate after the death of John Lee in 1866 is obscure.

A terrier of the manor of Edgware Boys made in 1397 estimates the extent of that manor at 288 a.[71] About one-sixth of the manor appears to have been in Hendon. It contained one field of 60 a., three fields of 40 a. each, and thirteen smaller fields. No court records seem to be extant. The estate continued to be called a manor until after 1741,[72] but from the time of its acquisition by William Lee in 1762 it appears to have been known as the Edgware Estate.[73] In 1764 the estate yielded £180 in rent, which rose to £500 in 1780 and to £570 in 1797.[74] In 1845 the estate contained 216 a.[75] John Lee, the owner of the estate, was the impropriator of all tithes of corn, which were worth £25 a year. There does not appear to have been a manor-house at any time.

Part of the north-eastern corner of the parish, around the village of Elstree, belonged to the manor of Titburst and Kendalls in Aldenham (Herts.).[76] In 1845 the estate in Edgware amounted to 90 a.; the owner, William Phillimore, younger brother of the lawyer Joseph Phillimore,[77] lived in his mansion at Deacon's Hill, just on the Elstree side of the parish and county boundary.[78] The house was demolished after the Second World War. By 1175 the Priory of St. Bartholomew's, Smithfield, held a small amount of land in Edgware,[79] which soon after became part of their manor of Wimborough in Little Stanmore.[80]

ECONOMIC AND SOCIAL HISTORY. Traces of Celtic fields have been observed to the north of

[48] Ibid. 69.
[49] Ibid. 48, 69.
[50] Ibid. 15; see p. 160.
[51] The dispute is described at length in *Oxf. Hist. Soc. Collectanea* (1885), 236 sqq.
[52] All Souls Coll., Edgware Old Leases 21.
[53] Ibid. 4, 6, 7.
[54] Ibid. 9.
[55] All Souls Coll., map of Edgware, 1597.
[56] Hist. Mon. Com. *Mdx.* 17.
[57] Geikie MS. vol. v.
[58] Baylis, *Edgware and the Stanmores*, 11.
[59] *Cat. Anct. D.*, ii. A 2316.
[60] *T.L.M.A.S.* xiii. 163; Lysons, *Environs of Lond.* ii. 244.
[61] B.M. Cott. MS. Nero E.VI, ff. 82v–83.
[62] All Souls Coll., Edgware Rentals 2, 5–7, 9; Edgware MS. 53 (Martin, *Cat. All Souls*, p. 37).
[63] *Environs of Lond.* ii. 244.
[64] *Valor Eccl.* (Rec. Com.), i. 403.
[65] *L. & P. Hen. VIII*, xviii(1), pp. 130–1; *Cal. Pat.* 1553, 125.
[66] *L. & P. Hen. VIII*, xviii(1), p. 198.
[67] All Souls Coll., Edgware Rental 34; Edgware MS. 54 (Martin, *Cat. All Souls*, p. 37).
[68] Lysons, *Environs of Lond.* ii. 245.
[69] Burke, *Land. Gent.* (1849), iii. 199.
[70] Ibid.
[71] B.M. Cott. MS. Nero E.VI, ff. 82v–83.
[72] M.R.O., Acc. 768(2).
[73] Herts. Rec. Off., MSS. 68654–68771.
[74] Ibid. 68655, 68660, 68661.
[75] M.R.O., Edgware Tithe Award.
[76] See *V.C.H. Herts.* ii. 155–6 for the descent of this manor.
[77] Burke, *Peerage* (1959), 1784.
[78] M.R.O., Edgware Tithe Award.
[79] E. A. Webb, *Recs. of St. Bartholomew's*, i. 102, 479; Baylis, *Edgware and the Stanmores*.
[80] Reserved for treatment under Little Stanmore.

Edgwarebury,[81] and part of Brockley Hill appears to have been cultivated for a time in the 4th century A.D.,[82] but it seems likely that a great part of the parish was covered by forest until the 12th century.[83] Nothing is known about the agriculture of Edgware before 1277, but it is probable that by 1227, by which date Middlesex had obtained total exemption from the forest laws,[84] the greater part of the parish had been cleared of wood. A survey of the manor made in 1277 provides the earliest definite evidence.[85] It does not distinguish between land in Edgware and land in Kingsbury appurtenant to the manor, but the acreage of the latter was not large. The demesne consisted of 357 a. of arable, 90 a. of woodland, and 6½ a. of meadow. Nine free tenants held between them a carucate, 4½ virgates, and at least 115 a. of land. Fifty-two customary tenants held 21¾ virgates and 184 a. of land. The holdings were not big; one of the free tenants held a carucate, another held two virgates, while two free and nine customary tenants held one virgate each, six customary tenants three-quarters of a virgate, and eleven customary tenants half a virgate each. The main arable fields of the demesne were grouped around Edgwarebury: Milepondfeld (54 a.) to the south between Edgwarebury and Piper's Green Lane, Blanchepetfeld (100 a.) to the west, Mapeldereherst (30 a.) directly to the north, and Berihel (66 a.) to the north-east.[86] Melcheburnefeld (53 a.) cannot be identified, unless it is Great and Little Misburn (to the east of Edgwarebury and now bisected by the main railway line) which in 1597 were part of the manor of Edgware Boys. If any open fields existed, they must have been in the southern half of the parish.

All the customary tenants owed services to the lord, but these services did not run the whole gamut of agricultural practice. Every customary tenant owed reaping and binding services, and most of them owed carrying, hoeing, harrowing, and hedging services. A total of 598 days' work was due: 358 days of reaping, 79 days of binding, 68 days of hoeing, 33 days of hedging, 32 days of harrowing, and 28 days of carrying. In addition 29 tenants owed 80 averages between them. It is possible that such works as ploughing and sowing had already been commuted. These works were worth just under £3 a year, and with rents of £11 and the profits of the demesne the annual yield of the manor was almost £18.[87] An account of c. 1370 gives the gross income of the manor as £41, including £14 12s. from rents, £2 12s. from services, £10 13s. from the farm of the demesne, and £9 9s. from sale of stock and profits of the court.[88]

A rental of the manor of Edgware shows that in 1426 there were 3 free and 29 customary tenants.[89] It is certain that by this time much of the land must

have been parcelled out, for there were no fewer than 81 crofts, fields, and pightles. Many of the crofts and fields and even a few of the half-virgates are named, and by comparing them with the maps of 1597–9 it is possible to identify 46 out of the 111 pieces of land listed, a total of some 350 a. If there were any open fields they lay immediately to the north and south of Hale Lane. The common Broad Field is mentioned four times between 1484 and 1493 in the court rolls,[90] but it is impossible to discover its location. The common wood mentioned in 1483[91] seems to have been part of what was later called Brockhill Wood. Of the free and customary tenants in 1426, twelve (41 per cent.) held under 20 a., ten (35 per cent.) between 20 and 50 a., and seven (24 per cent.) over 50 a. Rents and services were worth together over £24, with a net income to the lord of £17 9s.[92] In 1525–6 there were 2 or 3 free and 27 customary tenants.[93] Nine half-virgates, 14 quarters, and 3 half-quarters were held by the customary tenants, together with 81 crofts, fields, pightles, and the like. Out of the 107 pieces of land listed, 60, including 7 of the half-virgates, can be identified. There is a blank space in the Hale Lane area where the remnants of the open fields, if there were any, were situated. The holdings of the tenants had become more differentiated in size. Fifteen (54 per cent.) held under 20 a., eleven (39 per cent.) between 20 and 50 a., and only two (7 per cent.) over 50 a.; one of these two tenants, William Blackwell, held about 118 a. and the other, William Goodyer, about 138 a. These figures do not include the demesne land and its farmers or the free land held by the Prior of Clerkenwell. Rents and services in 1483[94] and 1525–6[95] were valued at just over £11, and the net profit of the manor in one year between 1533 and 1536 was estimated to be just under £15.[96] Quit-rents for the manor in 1548 were reckoned to be worth nearly £22,[97] and in 1613 quit-rents for the manor of Edgware and Kingsbury 'by the ancient rule' were worth £21 and decayed rents 'by way of purchase and excheat' £4 or £5.[98] The annual value of the copyhold land in Edgware manor in 1599 was reckoned to be £276[99] and by 1680 this had increased to £1,161, although at the same date the total rents for the manor were worth under £16.[1] The manorial income must have depended more and more on fines for entry, for in 1751 the combined rents for the manors of Edgware and Kingsbury were worth under £24.[2] A good deal of enfranchisement occurred during the late 18th and early 19th centuries, and by 1845 only 604 a. were owned by the college.[3]

Surveys made during the reign of Elizabeth I show that the demesne land was divided into five portions.[4] Earlsbury Farm, with the house at Edgwarebury, was reckoned to contain 191 a. in 1574

[81] G. J. Copley, *Archaeology of South-East Eng.* 284.
[82] *T.L.M.A.S.* xvii. 261.
[83] Walsingham, *Gesta Abb. Mon. St. Albani* (Rolls Ser.), i. 39; Baylis, *Edgware and the Stanmores*, 1.
[84] M. L. Bazeley, 'Extent of the English Forest in the 13th century', *T.R.H.S.* 4th ser. iv. 152; cf. *V.C.H. Mdx.* ii. 224.
[85] *T.L.M.A.S.* xiii. 158 sqq.
[86] Identification based on field-names on maps of 1597–9 at All Souls Coll.
[87] *T.L.M.A.S.* xiii. 160.
[88] All Souls Coll., Edgware Rental 1.
[89] Ibid. 2.
[90] All Souls Coll., Edgware Court Roll 10, 2 Ric. III, 1 Hen. VII, 2 Hen. VII, 8 Hen. VII.
[91] Ibid. 1 Ric. III.
[92] All Souls Coll., Edgware MS. 46 (Martin, *Cat. All Souls*, p. 37).
[93] All Souls Coll., Edgware Rental 9.
[94] Ibid. 5.   [95] Ibid. 9.
[96] All Souls Coll., Valor and Extent (Martin, *Cat. All Souls*, p. 394).
[97] All Souls Coll., Edgware Old Leases 8.
[98] All Souls Coll., Edgware Rental 14.
[99] All Souls Coll., Edgware MS. 52 (Martin, *Cat. All Souls*, p. 37).
[1] All Souls Coll., Edgware Rental 37.
[2] Ibid. 40.
[3] M.R.O., Edgware Tithe Award.
[4] The subsequent two paragraphs are based on the

and 216 a. in 1597. The George farm, which included the inn of that name, contained 74 a. in 1574 and 56 a. in 1597. Both these farms had been leased since the mid 15th century at the latest. Another farm, called Strensham's Farm, contained 65 a. in 1597, and a fourth contained 27 a. There are no leases surviving for either of these farms. The remainder of the demesne, 251 a., was woodland in the hands of the lords, who made it their usual practice, at least in the 16th century, to sell the standing timber. By 1597 the manor was totally inclosed; most of the fields were small, and, apart from Brockhill Wood (137 a.), only three fields were reckoned at more than 20 a.—Bury Bush (28 a. of wood in the hands of the lords), Great Broadfield (24 a.), and Long Broadfield (21 a.), both belonging to Earlsbury Farm. Around most of the fields were hedgerows wide and thick enough to produce valuable timber; many were retained by the lords when the fields which they surrounded were leased. In addition to the leaseholders there were 28 tenants. Six held 91 a. of free land and 27 held 757 a. of copyhold, and with the tenants of 29 a. not specified the total extent of the manor was 1,493 a. Nineteen of the free and customary tenants (68 per cent.) held under 20 a., four (14 per cent.) held between 20 and 50 a., and five (18 per cent.) held over 50 a. Apart from Earlsbury Farm, there were two other large holdings: Richard Franklin's of 238 a., and William Blackwell's of 177 a. Earlsbury Farm was arranged compactly around Edgwarebury. Blackwell's holding consisted mainly of land in the middle of the parish between Piper's Green Lane, Edgwarebury, and Clay Lane, but Franklin's was more scattered, the main portions being situated in the extreme north of the parish around Deacon's Hill and Woodcock Hill, in the middle between Clay Lane and Edgwarebury Lane, and in the extreme southern tip of the parish.

In 1597 the agriculture of the parish was still very mixed. Only 21 per cent. of the land was used as arable; 32 per cent. was pasture, 13 per cent. was meadow, and 29 per cent. was woodland. Even if the large acreage of demesne wood is not included, 15 per cent. of the rest of the manor was woodland, a figure which contrasts strongly with the $1\frac{1}{2}$ per cent. (11 per cent. if the demesne wood is included) of Kingsbury manor, also in the hands of All Souls College, at the same date.[5] The woodland was for the most part situated on the northern heights of the parish. The arable land was spread fairly evenly over the manor, but pasture occupied most of the central area and the meadowland was concentrated in the flat and well-watered area in the south. Apart from Franklin's holding, which, perhaps on account of its disposition over the three areas of the manor, was divided evenly between meadow, pasture, arable, and wood, those holdings which were more than 50 a. concentrated on arable or pasture or both. Earlsbury Farm had 61 per cent. pasture and 33 per cent. arable;

the George farm was 80 per cent. pasture, while Strensham's Farm of 65 a. was 70 per cent. arable and had no pasture at all. The larger holdings of free and copyhold land were used in a similar way. Lynford's holding of 50 a. was 58 per cent. pasture and 31 per cent. arable, and Blackwell's holding of 183 a. contained 47 per cent. pasture, 18 per cent. arable, and 18 per cent. wood. A common feature of the larger holdings was the relatively small amount of meadow, only Franklin's containing more than the average acreage for the manor. In all the holdings of under 20 a. 36 per cent. of the land was meadow, while pasture and arable accounted for only 22 per cent. and 18 per cent. respectively. Seven of the smaller tenants held meadowland, six held pasture, five held arable, and only one held woodland. The use to which four of the smaller tenants put their land is not stated. Again, there is a contrast with the land use of the manor of Kingsbury. In that manor 50 per cent. of the land was pasture, 32 per cent. was arable, and only 7 per cent. was meadow. In Kingsbury there was little significant difference in the uses to which the land was put by large or small tenants; moreover, only one of the fourteen tenants holding under 20 a. had any meadow, while ten held some pasture and seven some arable. It is probable that by this date Edgware was beginning to assume an important role as a supplier of hay to the London market, and it is certain that cattle intended for Smithfield were grazed there.[6]

Some occupations of Edgware men other than those engaged directly in agriculture can be gathered from the Middlesex sessions records. Between 1608 and 1617 nine individuals were licensed as badgers, kidders, or drovers.[7] Ralph Haley, collier (i.e. a vendor of coal or charcoal), is recorded in 1612; he is mentioned again in 1616, along with two other colliers of Edgware, and in 1618.[8] In 1612 Thomas Wilson of Edgware, tailor, was sentenced to be hanged for stealing from a house in Edgware.[9] In 1615 Edward Wharton of Edgware, draper, was taken at Uxbridge for abusing the constable of Little Stanmore, telling him that he would not come to the musters and dissuading others, 'asking them if they would go see a football play'.[10] A brewer of Edgware was indicted in 1617, and butchers are mentioned in 1610 and 1613.[11] A surgeon resided in Edgware in 1608.[12] In 1621 John Pooley of Edgware, carrier, was indicted for driving more than five horses in his cart.[13] The parish was visited by the plague in 1630; the constable neglected to keep the sick persons isolated and finally abandoned his office altogether.[14]

A survey of the woods of Earlsbury Farm and the George farm in 1662 shows that 1,236 out of 1,256 trees counted by the surveyors were oaks.[15] Brockhill Wood seems to have continued to be woodland until the end of the 18th century. Rocque's map of 1754[16] appears to indicate that the woods had been cleared and inclosed, but the field boundaries bear so little

following documents at All Souls Coll.: Terriers 26–29 (Martin, *Cat. All Souls*, p. 287); Edgware MS. 52 (Martin, *Cat. All Souls*, p. 37); Maps of Edgware manor, 1597 and 1599.
  [5] All Souls Coll., Edgware MS. 52.
  [6] P. V. McGrath, 'Marketing of food, fodder and livestock in the London area in the seventeenth century' (London Univ. M.A. thesis, 1948), 238.
  [7] *Mdx. Sess. Recs.* i. 255; ii. 120; iii. 69, 120, 237; iv. 286; M.R.O., Cal. Mdx. Recs. i. 83; ii. 131; iii. 75; iv. 54; v. 131; viii. 125.

  [8] M.R.O., Cal. Mdx. Recs. ix. 70; *Mdx. Sess. Recs* iii. 120; iv. 314, 340.
  [9] M.R.O., Cal. Mdx. Recs. x. 34.
  [10] *Mdx. Sess. Recs.* ii. 344.
  [11] Ibid. i. 5, 234; M.R.O., Cal. Mdx. Recs. v. 35.
  [12] M.R.O., Cal. Mdx. Recs. i. 68.
  [13] *Mdx. Cnty. Recs.* ii. 159.
  [14] Ibid. iii. 33; *Cal. S.P. Dom.* 1629–31, 375.
  [15] All Souls Coll., Edgware MS. 56 (Martin, *Cat. All Souls*, p. 37).
  [16] Rocque, *Map of Mdx.* (1754).

resemblance to those of the 1845 tithe award, or, indeed, to those of the 1597–9 maps that Rocque's map must be regarded as extremely untrustworthy. Brockhill Wood was leased, along with two other and smaller pieces of woodland, in 1795[17] and again in 1802[18] but in the latter year, although the 140 a. was still called Brockhill Wood, Rush Wood, and Rush Mead Wood, it was noted that it was now 'for the most part stocked up, grubbed up, and converted into arable, meadow or pasture land'. The lessee of this demesne land also had all common of pasture for all commonable cattle on all fields and commonable pastures in Edgware, but there is no indication of the practical extent of these rights. It is obvious, however, that timber was no longer regarded as a very profitable crop for most of the land in Edgware. In 1791 it was remarked that the fields between Edgware and London were kept constantly in grass; there was scarcely any arable land, and it was chiefly from here that London was supplied with hay, 'so that it is no uncommon thing to see one hundred loads of hay go up to London on a market-day, and each of the teams bring back a load of dung for dressing the land, which preserves the ground in good heart'.[19] Middleton, writing in 1798, considered these upland meadows and pastures to be of the finest quality.[20] In 1808 Samuel Ridge of Edgwarebury Farm was one of many farmers and landowners in the neighbourhood who signed a protest against hunting over the area. The land was of great value, they said, and hunting over it by 100–150 horsemen was injurious. Fences were broken, cattle were allowed to stray, lasting damage was wrought on the heavy, retentive soil, and trespasses were committed by huntsmen who were not even residents or neighbours. The hunt pledged itself to make good any damage, but in 1809 Mr. Ridge suffered fresh trespasses upon lands 'which had been recently hollow-drained, and were thereby materially injured'. Several legal actions were brought against the hunt and damages were awarded to the plaintiffs.[21]

In 1811 there were 55 families chiefly employed in agriculture, 61 in trade, manufactures, or handicrafts, and 33 in neither category. In 1821 the figures were 58, 45, and 49 respectively, and by 1831 they had become 34, 45, and 56. Although the population figures showed a steady rise over this period (543, 551, 591), the number of families declined (149, 142, 135).[22] During the hay harvest the population was swollen by the influx of a large number of labourers; in July 1816 upwards of 300 poor Irish and other strangers were found to be 'almost in a starving condition, the weather having been so unfavourable as to prevent their being able to earn anything for many days'. A subscription was opened, and within six hours £39 was collected.[23] The Revd. Thomas Hitchin recalled that when he and his family arrived in Edgware for the first time (c. 1833) it was pouring with rain, and they had to witness 'a most savage encounter between the English and Irish labourers'.[24]

A commercial directory of 1832–4 gives the names of 56 individuals engaged in 31 different trades, and includes 5 grocers, 5 shoemakers, 6 shopkeepers, 2 innkeepers, 4 tavern keepers, and 4 retailers of beer. Besides other traders to be found in any village of this size there were a cabinet maker, a breeches maker, a straw-hat maker, a watchmaker, and a printer.[25]

The tithe award of 1845 shows how completely the agriculture of the parish had been given over to the production of grass. Taking the area within the bounds of the manor for the purpose of comparison with earlier figures, it can be estimated that only 105 a., or 7 per cent. of that area, were arable, while 1,376 a., or 86½ per cent., were meadow or pasture. There were only 18 a. of woodland left. In the whole of the parish, 1,683 a. (83 per cent.) were grassland, 172 a. (8½ per cent.) were arable, 63 a. (3 per cent.) were built over or used as gardens. Only three farms contained more than 30 a. of arable each. The largest farm was that of Henry Child, who held 391 a. from 11 different owners, and six other farms were between 100 and 200 a. These seven farms contained almost two-thirds of the agricultural land of the parish. Only 15 per cent. of the land was occupied by its owner. The common land mentioned in the tithe award was inclosed in 1854.[26] In 1597 this land had been leased by All Souls College as part of Strensham's Farm, and although two-thirds of it had borne the name 'common wood' only seven acres were in fact woodland, the remainder being cultivated by Strensham as arable.[27] Both in 1845 and 1854, however, it was clearly regarded as common land and not as part of the manor.

It was said of Edgware in 1862 that 'all its importance as a market town has long since vanished, and it may now be ranked among the suburban districts of the metropolis'.[28] The market had indeed vanished, but it was a little premature to call the village a suburb, for it was not until its expansion began in the 1920s that Edgware really became a part of the London sprawl, and in 1963 two-thirds of the parish was still outside the blanket of suburban housing, thanks largely to the preserving influence of the Green Belt. Edgware still had some local importance in the later 19th century. Lysons could find no charter for the weekly market,[29] but a market certainly existed in 1607.[30] The market-house, or at least the site of the market, was conveyed by Sir Lancelot Lake to trustees for a public school for Little Stanmore in the mid 17th century.[31] No market-house is readily distinguishable on the map of 1597, but if the school house on the tithe map (1838) of Little Stanmore is on the 17th-century site, it seems that the market-house in 1597 was one of the few houses on the Stanmore side of Watling Street showing its gable-end to the road, being almost exactly half-way between Edgware Bridge and Whitchurch Lane.[32] In spite of the loss of its site, however, the market was still being held in

[17] All Souls Coll., Edgware Old Leases 41 (Martin, *Cat. All Souls*, p. 38).
[18] Ibid. Lease 47.
[19] *Univ. Brit. Dir.* (1791), iii. 39.
[20] Middleton, *View*, 223–5.
[21] *Mdx. and Herts. N. & Q.* iii. 75–76, 159–62.
[22] *Census*, 1811–31.
[23] Tootell MS. p. 37.
[24] Hendon libr., MS. DD MHS 823, p. 2.
[25] Pigot, *Comm. Dir.* (1832–4), p. 897. These figures

probably include some shops and traders on the Stanmore side of the High St.
[26] M.R.O., Edgware Incl. Award.
[27] All Souls Coll., map of Edgware manor, 1597.
[28] *Kelly's Dir. Mdx.* (1862).
[29] Lysons, *Environs of Lond.* ii. 241.
[30] M.R.O., Acc. 2193/219b.
[31] Tootell MS. p. 41; *Kelly's Dir. Mdx.* (1878); Lysons, *Environs of Lond.* iii. 417.
[32] All Souls Coll., map of Edgware, 1597.

the earlier 18th century.[33] It seems to have been discontinued at some date between 1792 and 1795.[34] In 1867 the Privy Council licensed the holding of a cattle market on the last Thursday in every month,[35] but no market was noted by the Royal Commission in its report of 1888.[36]

There is no record of a fair in Edgware before 1760. On Ascension Day in that year a large fair for cattle was held in the yard and field belonging to the George Inn, but the dealers, finding their horses detained for the payment of toll and standing, 'naturally forsook it to return no more'.[37] The fair continued but degenerated into a pleasure fair with bull-baiting and throwing at cocks, until it eventually became extinct. In 1810, however, the lack of amusement for the inhabitants induced some of the principal tradesmen to organize a fair for the first three days of August, when a large quantity of cattle, shows, booths, and stalls was displayed in the field just above Edgware Bridge called Bakers Croft. Apart from the sale of animals, events such as 'wheeling barrows blindfolded for a new hat, jumping in sacks for a smock frock, grinning through horse collars for tobacco, and climbing a lofty pole for a shoulder of mutton' amused 'a very numerous attendance of the respectable families in the neighbourhood'.[38] The fair continued to be held, with an increasing emphasis on its lighter side, on the first Wednesday, Thursday, and Friday in August until about 1855; from at least 1834 to 1855 races were held on the Thursday and Friday,[39] but attempts to revive them in 1869 and 1873 did not succeed.[40]

In spite of its relatively small population in the 19th century the village of Edgware seems to have prospered commercially. In 1870, for instance, there were six insurance agents in the village.[41] The opening of the Great Northern Railway branch in 1867,[42] however, seems to have had little effect on the expansion of the village, and plans to extend the railway met with strong local opposition. A Bill to establish a line from Watford to Edgware, brought before Parliament in 1896 and 1897,[43] was opposed by residents, and it was said that the real harm of the railways was the opening up of building sites 'which are quickly covered with architectural atrocities'.[44] By this time the parish had begun to display a tendency to split into an opulent north and a workaday south, separated by a buffer of agricultural land. By 1896 several large houses had been built in the Elstree area or along the Elstree–Barnet road, while the old village gained the post office, the infants' school, the station, and the Railway Hotel.[45] The southern part of the parish was unable to repel the tide of suburban development, but the threatened dichotomy of the parish was to a large extent averted

by the nature of new buildings erected between the two world wars. Although the Elstree region of Edgware remained almost exclusively an area of large and expensive houses, the new estates which spread northward from the old village were widening ripples of working-class housing, and of the detached and semi-detached dwellings favoured by the middle classes. The shopping facilities of Edgware grew in proportion to the increasing size and diversity of the population. A branch of the Hendon Chamber of Commerce was formed in 1929 with an initial membership of 37, and in 1931 the Edgware Chamber of Commerce was founded. After the Second World War it was re-founded, and in 1963 it had 200 members,[46] including perhaps half the business and trading concerns in Edgware.

Industry has never played an important part in the economy of Edgware. Gravel pits were probably being worked by 1802[47] and certainly by 1834, partly at least by the labour of the able-bodied poor as a parish employment,[48] and in 1963 gravel was still being extracted on the eastern side of the parish. In 1831 there were no persons engaged in manufacturing in the parish,[49] and in fact there were no industries until in 1900 the firm of Chas. Wright Ltd., manufacturing engineers, moved from Clerkenwell to Edgware. During the First World War this firm was employed on government contracts and after the war it struck some two million Mons Stars and Victory medals. During the Second World War the most remarkable contract was for metal parts of respirator filters, $94\frac{1}{2}$ million being made between 1937 and 1943. In 1963 the company was chiefly engaged in the manufacture of motor car registration plates. There were 70 workmen employed, together with an office staff of 30. The firm of A.E.W. Ltd., founded in 1923 and established in Edgware in 1927, has a labour force of 50 and manufactures laboratory and industrial electric ovens and furnaces.[50]

LOCAL GOVERNMENT. During the Middle Ages and, indeed, up to the beginning of the 19th century the government of Edgware was in practice in the hands of the court of Edgware manor. By the late 13th century the lord of the manor was holding a view of frankpledge,[51] and a court leet continued to be held with a court baron until modern times. From at least the late 13th century Kingsbury was associated with Edgware manor.[52] In 1393–4 the court was called 'Eggeswere et Kyngesbury'.[53] In 1421–3 the jury consisted of 6 men from Edgware and 6 from Kingsbury.[54] Although this practice did not continue long, after All Souls College became the lord of both

[33] G. Miège, *Present State of Great Britain* (1716–48), gives a market at Edgware.
[34] Lysons, *Environs of Lond.* ii. 241; Tootell MS. p. 41; *Univ. Brit. Dir.* iii. 36; *Rep. Com. on Market Rights and Tolls* [C. 5550], p. 184, H.C. (1888), liii.
[35] Robbins, *Middlesex* 242.
[36] *Rep. Com. on Market Rights and Tolls* (1888), p. 184.
[37] Tootell MS. p. 39.
[38] Ibid. pp. 39–40.
[39] Pigot, *Comm. Dir.* (1832–4), 897; *Kelly's Dir. Essex* (1845), 424; ibid. (1855).
[40] E. Walford, *Greater Lond.* i. 286.
[41] *Kelly's Dir. Mdx.* (1870).
[42] See p. 152.
[43] See p. 152.
[44] *Mdx. and Herts. N. & Q.* iii. 4.

[45] O.S. Map 1/2,500, Mdx. vi. (1896 edn.).
[46] *Edgware and District Chamber of Commerce Year Book and Trades Dir.* (1959–60), and ex inf. the secretary.
[47] Herts. Rec. Off., 68673, 68676, 68678, 68718, 68752.
[48] *Rep. Poor Law Com. App. B*(2), H.C. 44, p. 93 (1834), xxxvi.
[49] *Census*, 1831.
[50] Ex inf. firms.
[51] S.C. 2/188/54; *Plac. de Quo Warr.* (Rec. Com.), 476. There are a few early court rolls in the P.R.O., but the great majority of the court documents, including rolls dating from the late 13th cent., are at All Souls Coll., Oxford.
[52] *T.L.M.A.S.* xiii. 158 sqq.
[53] All Souls Coll., Edgware Court Roll No. 5.
[54] Ibid. No. 6.

manors in 1443 it was natural that their administration should in practice be conducted at the same court. By the 17th century they were being dealt with as one manor, although they continued to have separate juries and officials.

In 1330–5 the court met on average 5 times a year;[55] in 1440–5 the average was thrice.[56] At the beginning of the 18th century the court was still meeting regularly twice a year.[57] By 1770 tenants could normally secure a meeting at any time by payment to the lord's steward.[58] The court continued to meet until the 20th century. The size of the jury varied considerably from year to year, particularly in the Middle Ages, when it ranged in number between 8 and 15.[59] For the view of frankpledge in 1421 the jury consisted of 12 capital pledges from Edgware and Kingsbury, while in 1433 it was made up of 6 inquisitors *ex officio*, and 6 inquisitors on oath, but there is no indication that either of these juries represented the normal composition.[60] By the beginning of the 18th century the jury for the two manors combined was of full size when the court leet and court baron were held on the same day, but considerably smaller when the court baron was held on its own.[61] The permanent officers of the manor were appointed by the lords and consisted of a steward and a bailiff. Other manorial officials were elected in the court, although such elections are recorded only fitfully in the rolls. The election of an ale-conner is mentioned in 1457, 1471, 1478, 1479, and 1543;[62] the election of capital pledges occurs in 1434, 1457, 1460, 1470, and 1479.[63] The election of a constable is first mentioned in 1470;[64] in only 5 of the years between 1483 and 1510 is this recorded, although one year was the theoretical term of office.[65] Constables continued to be elected at the leet until the 19th century, and were sworn both there and before the justices in sessions.[66]

In 1630, when the plague came to Edgware, the constable deserted the village leaving no deputy, and much disaster followed.[67] In 1667 the constable chosen at the manor court informed the justices that he was now ensign to the colonel of a regiment of foot and consequently unable to execute his office, and it was ordered that he should be discharged and some other person chosen.[68] In 1686 Joseph Cooper, pleading that a very great business occasioned his absence from Edgware where he was constable, petitioned the justices that a headborough might be chosen to assist him, and an order was made appointing a headborough.[69] The constables and headboroughs of Edgware were mentioned in 1617,[70]

and in 1642 there were two constables and two overseers.[71] In 1735 both a constable and a headborough were chosen in the court,[72] and again in 1737 a headborough was named.[73] From 1798 a constable was chosen and a headborough appointed,[74] and from 1831 to 1842 the practice was to appoint a constable and 2 headboroughs for Edgware.[75] It seems probable, therefore, that the headborough had taken over the functions of the medieval capital pledge as an assistant or complement to the constable, for the 'Memorandums touching the Court Baron and Court Leet' (1810–20) gives as the officials concerned with public justice only constables and tithingmen.[76] This document states that treason and felonies were enquirable in the court leet; things both enquirable and punishable included all matters of public concern within the manor, constables, tithingmen, breach of the pound, repair of the stocks, public peace, common barrators, scolds, eavesdroppers, public trade, breach of assize, false weights and measures, forestallers, nuisances, highways, watercourses, disorderly houses, and offensive trades. Constables were elected by the leet to serve the parish, and provision was made for swearing before a justice an elected constable who did not come to court to take up the office. Instruments of punishment were provided by the lord of the manor; in 1470 the cucking-stool and the stocks were in bad repair,[77] and in 1543 and 1544 there was neither a pillory nor a cucking-stool.[78] There was a pillory at Edgware in 1773 and 1739.[79]

It seems probable that the vestry, first mentioned in 1817,[80] was concerned mainly with the administration of poor relief. A sum of £170, representing 87 per cent. of the money raised by rates, was expended on the poor in 1776.[81] In 1783–5 the average expenditure on the poor was £175 (81 per cent.),[82] and it continued to rise to £283 in 1803 (79 per cent.),[83] an average of £367 in 1813–15 (77 per cent.),[84] and an average of £393 in 1822–4.[85] In 1835–6 the average amount was £272, 71 per cent. of the total.[86] There was no workhouse at any period. In 1803 there were 22 adults and 37 children (14 per cent. of the population in 1801) permanently receiving relief, and in addition 21 persons were relieved occasionally. There was one friendly society with 45 members.[87] It is probable that the able-bodied poor were employed in the gravel-pits at this time, for the owner of the Edgware Boys estate paid a 'gravel rate' on several occasions between 1802 and 1815.[88]

In 1813–15 the average number of persons per-

[55] All Souls Coll., Edgware Court Roll No. 1.
[56] Ibid. No. 8.
[57] All Souls Coll., Edgware Court Book No. 1.
[58] W. O. Ault, 'Village Assemblies in Medieval England', *Album Helen Maud Cam.* 32.
[59] e.g. All Souls Coll., Edgware Court Rolls Nos. 8, 9.
[60] Ibid. No. 6.
[61] All Souls Coll., Edgware Court Book No. 1.
[62] All Souls Coll., Edgware Court Rolls Nos. 8, 9, 13.
[63] Ibid. Nos. 7b, 8, 9.
[64] Ibid. No. 10.
[65] Ibid.
[66] *Mdx. Sess. Recs., passim.*
[67] *Cal. S.P. Dom.* 1629–31, 375; *Mdx. Cnty. Recs.* iii. 33.
[68] Cal. Mdx. Sessions Bks. iv. 38.
[69] Ibid. vii. 161.
[70] *Mdx. Sess. Recs.* iv. 207.
[71] Hse. of Lords, Mdx. Protestation Rets.
[72] All Souls Coll., Edgware Court Book No. 1, p. 101.
[73] Ibid. p. 108.

[74] Ibid. No. 5.
[75] Ibid. No. 6.
[76] M.R.O., Acc. 507/31.
[77] All Souls Coll., Edgware Court Roll No. 9.
[78] Ibid. No. 13.
[79] Cal. Mdx. Sessions Bks. xvi. 61; xviii. 50.
[80] Tootell MS. 34.
[81] *Rep. Sel. Cttee. on Rets. by Overseers, 1776*, Ser. 1, ix, p. 396.
[82] *Rets. on Expense and Maintenance of Poor*, H.C. 175 (1803–4), xiii (demi-folio).
[83] Ibid.
[84] *Ret. on Expenses and Maintenance of Poor*, H.C. 82 (1818), xix (demi-folio).
[85] *Rep. Cttee. on Poor Rates*, H.C. 334, p. 232 (1825), iv.
[86] *2nd Annual Rep. Poor Law Com.* H.C. 595, pp. 212–13 (1836), xxix (II).
[87] *Rets. on Expense and Maintenance of Poor* (1803–4), xiii.
[88] Herts. Rec. Off., MSS. 68673, 68676–8, 68718, 68752.

manently relieved was 27 (5 per cent. of the population), a figure which did not include children, and an average of 15 persons received occasional relief.[89] The friendly society had disappeared, but in 1818 the Revd. James Proctor was organizing a Poor Club.[90] In 1834 two overseers, generally farmers or tradesmen, were appointed annually; there had been previously for some years a paid assistant overseer, but the farmers were opposed to the practice on account of the expense. The numbers of the poor relieved varied; they were generally widows, orphans, decayed tradesmen, agricultural labourers, and illegitimate children. The parents of the infant poor were given a weekly allowance. The officers were disheartened by the ease with which the poor obtained orders for relief from the magistrates, and the worst characters obtained as much temporary relief as the deserving, for 'the extent of the applicant's family is the scale by which the relief is administered, without regard to character'. Able-bodied paupers were employed on the parish roads or in a gravel-pit, 'and, without any person properly to look after them, they idle away the day, and earn not one half of the sum they receive'. Relief was frequently given to the able-bodied on their promise not to come again for a certain time, sometimes from a plea that they were starving, but more commonly from not having any employment. The agricultural labourers were most subject to distress, for the local concentration on grassland gave them little employment during the winter months; their average wage was 12s. a week, and there was little work for their families. Considerable payments were made to casual paupers, but it was considered inadvisable to discontinue such allowances as there was not sufficient parish employment for so many persons.

There was a considerable number of small houses let to the poor at high rents by tradesmen. An average of 3 bastards received maintenance every year between 1827 and 1832, at an initial expense of 2s. 6d. a week for every child.[91] After the Act of 1834 Edgware was placed in the Hendon Poor Law Union.[92] By 1817 there were six houses held in trust for the benefit of the poor. They were situated to the east of the churchyard, and the choice of occupants rested with the vestry.[93]

The only surviving minute book of the vestry begins in 1849. In 1859 a scheme to light the 800 yards of Watling Street between Edgware Bridge and Hill House was carried out, and rates were collected for the maintenance of this service.[94] In 1885 it was resolved that the overseers should provide fire-fighting equipment at a cost of not more than £10 a year. In 1894 a poll was held to decide which of 7 candidates should be appointed paid assistant overseer.[95] After the Local Government Act of the same year a parish council was formed and the parish was placed in the rural district of Hendon. Edgware became part of Hendon U.D. in 1931 and became a ward of the borough of Hendon on its incorporation in 1932.[96] Under the London Government Act of 1963, Hendon was included in the London Borough of Barnet.[97]

CHURCHES. In the 12th and 13th centuries there was a small church or chapel belonging to the Hospital of St. Bartholomew in the north-west corner of the parish near the village of Elstree,[98] but the church of Edgware proper is first mentioned in the mid 13th century, when with Kingsbury it was stated to be appropriated to the use of the Knights Hospitallers.[99] The first substantial grant of land in the parish to the hospital had been made between 1231 and 1238.[1] There is no mention of the church in the taxation of 1291. The first known chaplain was Saer de Stevenage, whose will, proved in 1375, contained bequests of half a mark to the light of St. Margaret and of a cow towards the upkeep of the church.[2] In the clerical subsidy of 1428 the church of Kingsbury with the chapel of Edgware is mentioned as being not taxable.[3] The minister of the parish continued to be described as a chaplain or curate until the 19th century. The benefice was first described as a donative in 1685.[4] From the 14th century until the beginning of the 20th century, with the exception of a short period centred on 1800, the advowson remained with the holders of the manor of Edgware Boys, who appointed a chaplain or curate. In leases of the manor in 1397, 1506, 1511, and 1522 a condition was that the lessee should provide the chaplain.[5] After the Dissolution the manor passed through the hands of a number of lay owners, and it was not separated from the gift of the curacy until 1772, when the Earl of Coventry sold the manor to William Lee but apparently retained the presentation. By 1859, however, the gift was in the hands of the lord of the manor, John Lee.[6] From 1892 ministers were presented by members of the Phelps family, but by 1926 the patronage was in the hands of the Martyrs' Memorial Trustees, with whom it has remained.[7] In 1915 there was some debate on the status of the living; on the induction of John Consterdine the bishop in his address said that the

[89] *Ret. on Expenses and Maintenance of Poor* (1818), xix.
[90] Herts. Rec. Off., MSS. 68770, 68771.
[91] *Rep. Poor Law Com. App B(2),* H.C. 44, p. 93 f (1834), xxxv–vi.
[92] *Census,* 1851.
[93] Tootell MS. 34; Geikie MS. vol. i; M.R.O., Edgware Tithe Award.
[94] Hendon libr., MS. L. 5717.
[95] Vestry Min. Bk. *penes* the rector.
[96] Subsequent history is reserved for treatment under Hendon.
[97] London Govt. Act, 1963, c. 33.
[98] E. A. Webb, *Recs. of St. Bartholomew's Priory,* i. 479, 485; *V.C.H. Herts.* ii. 351. This section owes much to

Mr. H. S. Geikie's MS. history of the church and parish of Edgware, deposited in Edgware libr. and here cited as Geikie MS.
[99] St. Paul's MS. W.D. 9, f. 85v; *V.C.H. Mdx.* i. 199.
[1] *Cat. Anct. D.* ii. A 2316.
[2] B.M. Cott. MS. Nero E.VI, f. 81.
[3] *Feudal Aids,* iii. 380.
[4] Guildhall MS. 9537/70, f. 105.
[5] B.M. Cott. MS. Nero E.VI, f. 82; Cott. MS. Claudius E.VI, ff. 44, 85v, 216v.
[6] Bacon, *Liber Valorum* (1786); *Valor Ecclesiasticus* (1788); *Clerical Guide* (1822); *Clergy List* (1859).
[7] *Clergy List* (1892, 1905, 1915); *Crockford* (1896 and later edns.).

conclusion of the church's legal advisers was that it was a vicarage and not a rectory, and for the present he was advised to use the former term.[8] In spite of this opinion, however, the ministers since then have continued to call themselves rectors.[9]

In 1397 the tithes of the parish belonged to the manor of Edgware Boys and were worth 7 marks a year. The chaplain was provided with a suitable house and garden, with altarage, and 2½ marks a year.[10] In 1535 the appropriation was worth £12.[11] The chantry certificate of 1545 gives the value to the lay rector as £9.[12] In c. 1650 the parsonage tithes were said to be worth £50 a year at an improved rent and the small tithes, together with the house, to be worth £40 a year. There is only a faint suggestion that the minister received the small tithes.[13] The minister's stipend was evidently insufficient at this period, for in 1657 he was granted an augmentation of £20, besides the £10 already granted by the Trustees for the Maintenance of Ministers.[14] In 1788 Edgware was said to be a curacy, worth £80 a year.[15] During the 19th century the value of the living fluctuated. The tithe award of 1845 gave a rent-charge of £25 to the owner of Boys manor in lieu of corn tithes, a rent-charge of £450 to the vicar (that is, the resident minister, now beginning to promote himself) in lieu of all other tithes, and £2 to the vicar in lieu of vicarial tithes arising from the glebe lands.[16] This theoretical value continued to be quoted almost to the end of the century, but in 1896, although the tithe rent-charge was still £450 the average was £336, which with the glebe gave a gross income of £360. No great increase in the minister's income came until the 1930s brought building development to the glebe; in 1935 the gross income was £726, but by 1940, helped by new ground-rents of £525, it had risen to £1,317.[17]

In 1375 Saer de Stevenage left a house with garden, dovehouse, and meadow to the Hospitallers.[18] In 1397 John Wetynge, who was not the chaplain, held this house.[19] No rectory, vicarage, or curate's house is named on the map of 1597, although there is an L-shaped house on the site where the 18th-century house was to stand, between the west end of the church and the crossroads.[20] There was a 'vicarage house' in 1649, and in 1664 and 1672 the curate, Samuel Smith, occupied a house of five hearths.[21] An engraving of 1807 shows a substantial three-storied house to the west of the church, which was still standing in 1824.[22] In 1817 the curate hired by Thomas Martyn, the non-resident curate appointed to the donative, lived in the 'parsonage', which must have been this house.[23] In 1828, however, part of Katefield, a few hundred yards northeast of the church along what is now Station Road, was bought by John Lee, the owner of Boys manor, and in the following year it was sold to his brother

the Revd. Nicholas Fiott,[24] who built what later became known as the 'rectory house' on the site.[25] This house, built of white brick, had some twenty rooms, as well as stables and outbuildings.[26] The old house was demolished, and the new house continued to be used as a vicarage or rectory until, at some time shortly before 1919, it was sold. It has since been pulled down and houses, shops, and the Ritz Cinema have replaced it. The present house was built in 1920, and in 1953 a house was bought for one of the assistant curates.[27] Before 1829 the glebe consisted of about one acre at the back of the church, but by the purchase of Katefield it was increased to just over nine acres.

Thomas Disney, curate in the reign of Elizabeth I, was certified 'old and ignorant' in 1586.[28] John Whiston was turned out of the curacy in 1644, and at the Restoration complained that he was kept out of the parish by Richard Swift.[29] Swift, described by Whiston as a weaver, was appointed curate by the Triers in 1656 and ejected in 1660. Although he was without a degree he had the reputation of a learned man, and after his ejection he moved to Mill Hill, where he founded a school for Quakers.[30] In 1730 both the minister and the churchwardens showed some independence of mind. The curate complained that for some years the bishop's officials had taken undue, unreasonable, and unexplained fees, while the churchwardens showed irritation at the visitation articles. There was not at present, they said, a printed table of the prohibited degrees, but the minister 'will take care of it in a little time'. They had no chest for keeping the register, 'because we think it safer in the minister's custody. But if your Lordship insists upon it, we will get one'. They went on: 'If by the black hearse-cloth he meant a black pall, we have not one belonging to the parish: nor are we certain that the parish is obliged to have one. If it is, we will buy one. But there is always one in the town to be hired for a shilling'.[31] Francis Coventry, author of the satire *History of Pompey the Little* and a relative of the Earl of Coventry, was curate between c. 1750 and 1759. Thomas Martyn, the botanist and one of the earliest English disciples of Linnaeus, was the minister from 1787 to 1825. Martyn, who was non-resident, was described as the perpetual curate. In 1816 a false report of his death brought six candidates for his professorship at Cambridge, and sent his curate at Edgware, after a morning service in which he made several omissions and mistakes, in haste to London to sue for the incumbency during the minority of Nicholas Fiott, for whom the living was intended.[32]

H. A. H. Lea, rector 1925–48, made a determined effort to cope with the problems of a modern suburban parish. A strong evangelical, heartened by the success of the local clergy in preventing 'the threat-

[8] *Hendon Times*, 3 Sept. 1915.
[9] *Crockford* (1915 and later edns.).
[10] B.M. Cott. MS. Nero E.VI, ff. 82–83.
[11] *Valor Eccl.* (Rec. Com.), i. 203.
[12] Hennessy, *Novum Repertorium*, 141.
[13] *Home Cnties. Mag.* i. 320.
[14] *Cal. S.P. Dom.* 1657–8, 72.
[15] J. Lloyd, *Thesaurus Eccl.* 227.
[16] M.R.O., Edgware Tithe Award.
[17] *Crockford* (1896, 1935, 1940).
[18] B.M. Cott. MS. Nero. E.VI, f. 81.
[19] Ibid. ff. 82–83.
[20] All Souls Coll., map of Edgware, 1597.
[21] *Home Cnties. Mag.* i. 320; M.R.O., H.T.6.

[22] Guildhall Libr., interleaved copy of Lysons, *Environs of Lond.* ii.
[23] Hendon libr., Tootell MS. p. 23.
[24] See p. 157.
[25] Geikie MS. vol. iv; maps in Hendon libr.
[26] Geikie MS. vol. iv.
[27] Ibid.
[28] Guildhall MS. 9537/6.
[29] *Mdx. Cnty. Recs.* iii. 308.
[30] Geikie MS. vol. iv; E. Calamy, *Nonconformist's Memorial* (1802 edn.), ii. 446, which does not mention any connexion with Quakers.
[31] Guildhall MS. 9583/10.
[32] Tootell MS. p. 22; *Gent. Mag.* 1825, xcv (2), 87 sqq.

ened greyhound menace', he led the resistance to Sunday opening of the cinema in 1933. This time the united efforts of the churches failed, but the rector organized a counter-attack in the form of gatherings on Sunday evenings which included music, singing, lantern lectures, reading, and conversation. These meetings were held in the new church hall which had been built in 1931 on a site conveyed by the Martyrs' Memorial Trustees and the Church of England Trust out of newly acquired glebe. It replaced an old army hut in Hale Lane and augmented the Truth Hall, a small building of plain brick at the west end of the churchyard, which had been built in 1833 for use as a church school. The parochial church council expressed a particular wish that the new hall should not be used for the encouragement of dancing or card-playing.[33] In 1936 there were queues for getting into the church, although there were two services each Sunday evening.[34] In 1955 the Revd. J. M. Scutt organized a campaign among the 'no-mads of the Edgware milk-bars' and invited them to a meeting in the Truth Hall. On the appointed day a queue gathered outside the hall and the police, apparently misled by the appearance of some of the participants, warned the rector that his church was in danger.[35] The meetings were continued with some success.

The church of *ST. MARGARET* stands on the north-west side of Station Road near its junction with High Street. It consists of a west tower, chancel, aisled nave, north and south transepts, and vestries. The tower, which is the only ancient part of the building, is of ragstone rubble and flint with dressings of Reigate stone and has diagonal buttresses and a north-east turret; it probably dates from the 15th century, although 14th-century bricks were found when repairs were made to the newel turret in 1960.[36] A map of the manor made in 1597 shows the church to consist of the tower, much the same as it is today, with nave, chancel, and south porch.[37] In 1673 the tiles of the nave were fallen away[38] and in 1715 the foundations were reported to be defective. In 1727 the churchwardens presented that 'the church is old, and decayed; but is propped up' and in 1730 they said that 'the church (although much decayed) is in as good repair as we can keep it unless it were rebuilt'.[39] By 1760 the church was so ruinous that the inhabitants were afraid to gather in it. With funds collected partly on a brief, a new body of brick was built on to the old tower in 1763 and 1764.[40] The new building consisted of a nave, with three round-headed windows in the south wall and two in the north wall, short north and south transepts each with a square-headed door, an open pediment on the end wall and round-headed windows, and a shallow chancel with a round-headed east window and open pediment. The walls were of red brick and the roof of red tiles.[41] The nave, chancel,

and transepts were rebuilt in 'a debased Perpendicular style' in 1845.[42] The 18th-century plan appears to have been followed and the work was carried out in brick with stone dressings. In 1907 the church was closed when it was discovered that coffins were floating in up to three feet of water under the floor of the nave. During the subsequent excavations the foundations of a smaller and more ancient building were uncovered, but the vaults were filled in before they could be properly examined. The church was reopened in 1908.[43] By 1927 the church was obviously too small for a parish of some 5,000 inhabitants, and it was decided to enlarge the building to seat 450 people. The plan involved the addition of north and south aisles, each of two bays, and internal alterations to the chancel, at a total estimated cost of £13,500. The aisles are of brick with stone dressings and are built in a contemporary version of the Perpendicular style. The present vestries were built in 1939 and extended in 1960.[44]

A west gallery was erected in 1791 by the lord of the manor of Boys for the use of the Sunday school children.[45] A few years before 1817 a 'clumsy' gallery was built on the north side of the nave for the use of the parishioners, but subsequent rebuildings have removed all trace of it.[46] The small 18th-century marble font was removed from the aisle to a pew at the entrance of the church and its place supplied in the year 1809 by a stove.[47] In 1816 a barrel organ, with three barrels giving a choice of thirty tunes in all, was purchased and placed in the west gallery. It was removed to the north transept in 1850, where it was erected in a new case, with gilt front pipes, as a one-manual organ. There were no pedal pipes, and only half an octave of pedals. In 1915 a new organ was built by P. G. Phipps of Oxford, when the old pipes of the 1850 rebuilding were retained and augmented; an electric blower was installed in 1951.[48] The church was lit by candles until 1852, when twelve oil lamps were bought. In 1863 gas was introduced, although oil and candles continued to be used, and at the last remodelling in 1928 electric light was installed.[49]

In 1542 William Goodyer left 6s. 8d. in his will 'to the building of the steeple and to the reparations of the bells at Edgware'. There were three bells and a little broken bell in 1547.[50] The present peal of six bells, each with a motto and the name of the founder, was cast in 1769 by Thomas Janaway, an itinerant founder who set up his foundry in the churchyard near the tower.[51] There was a clock at the church in 1673, but in 1756 an eight-day ting-tang clock was fitted to the tower. By the beginning of the 20th century the inhabitants could stand its striking no longer and they successfully petitioned to have it silenced. The clock was repaired in 1961.[52]

There is a large mural tablet to Randall Nicholl

[33] Geikie MS. vol. iv.
[34] *Christian Herald and Signs of Our Times*, 6 Aug. 1936, quoted in Geikie MS. vol. iv.
[35] *The Christian*, 20 Jan. 1956, quoted in Geikie MS. vol. iv.
[36] Hist. Mon. Com. *Mdx.* 16; Geikie MS. vol. iii.
[37] All Souls Coll., map of Edgware, 1597.
[38] Guildhall MS. 9537/20.
[39] Ibid. 9583/5, /8, /10.
[40] Tootell MS. p. 11.
[41] Description based on engravings in Guildhall Libr., interleaved copy of Lysons, *Environs of Lond.* ii; see plate facing p. 126.

[42] *Kelly's Dir. Mdx.* (1890).
[43] Geikie MS. vol. iii.
[44] Ibid. vols. iii, iv.
[45] Plaque in church.
[46] Tootell MS. p. 17.
[47] Ibid.
[48] Ibid. p. 37; Geikie MS. vol ii.
[49] Ibid. vol. ii.
[50] Ibid. vol. iii; Browne Willis, *Hist. of Mitred Parliamentary Abbies*, app. p. 18.
[51] Geikie MS. vol. iii.
[52] Ibid.; Guildhall MS. 9537/20.

(1595–1658) who lived at Jervis, a house and farm on the Hendon side of Dean's Brook at Hale Lane. A man of considerable learning, he established by his will an annual commemoration sermon for the sum of 20s. to be given in Edgware church. The sermon is still preached.[53] There are several other mural tablets of the 18th and early 19th centuries. There are two small brasses: one carries an inscription to Sir Richard Chamberlain (d. 1532); the other commemorates Anthony Child (d. 1599/1600) and shows an infant in swaddling clothes. A silver Communion cup is date-marked 1562, and a silver paten may be a unique example of Marian plate, made about 1557. The remainder of the plate, except for a silver paten of 1715, is of the 19th century.[54] The registers are complete from 1717. The churchyard appears to have been enclosed by a stone or brick wall in 1597, but by 1792 it was fenced.[55] In 1817 it was considered to be too small, 'being every time the earth is broken for the internment of a corpse, in a state too painful to describe'.[56] There have, however, been many burials there since 1817.

The church of *ST. ANDREW*, Broadfields, in Lynford Gardens, is a red-brick building with round-headed windows and a pantile roof, built as a mission church to serve the area north of Edgware Way. The site and £4,000 were given by Miss Violet Wills, and the first curate-in-charge was appointed in 1937.[57]

The mission church of *ST. PETER*, on the east side of Watling Street, serves primarily the new council estate at Spur Road. It is a small building designed in a mid-20th-century style, having at its entrance a detached wooden framework supporting a bell and a large cross. The building was opened for worship in 1963 and is served by a curate-in-charge.

The Convent of St. Mary at the Cross[58] moved from Shoreditch to land north of Hale Lane, Edgware, between 1873 and 1877. The chapel, designed as the Lady Chapel to a conventual church which was never built, was not completed until 1890. The buildings, which are in a Victorian Gothic style and of red brick with stone dressings, are the work of James Brooks. From the beginning the rule was founded on that of St. Benedict. The Convent of St. Mary has claimed to be the first Anglican community to recite the Day Hours in Latin; since 1929 the whole of corporate worship has been in that tongue. In 1929 the community was affiliated to the Benedictines of Nashdom Abbey (Burnham, Bucks.), where it found a refuge during the Second World War.

ROMAN CATHOLICISM. In 1610 John Lodge of Edgware, butcher, was proclaimed a recusant.[59] There are no further references to Roman Catholicism in Edgware until 1913, when the church of St. Anthony of Padua was built in Garrett Road.[60] It is a red-brick building with stone dressings, designed in a Perpendicular style. Services were first held on the Broadfields estate in 1960 at the 'Sparrow Hawk', and in 1963 a temporary hut was in use while the church of St. Mathias was being built.[61]

PROTESTANT NONCONFORMITY. There are no references to Protestant nonconformists in Edgware before 1702, when a meeting of Quakers at the house of Thomas Prentice and a meeting of Baptists at the house of Roger Carter and Richard Rogers were certified and permitted to be held by the Middlesex Sessions.[62] There is no evidence that either of these congregations flourished, and by 1766 there were no dissenters in the parish.[63] On 20 October 1798 the house of Sarah Kent was registered as an Independent meeting-house. W. S. Tootell, writing in 1817, said that on 25 October the curate John De Veil (who 'when abroad fought with a tiger and mastered it') issued printed notices to the inhabitants 'to put them on their guard against the artful insinuations and designs of these itinerant preachers, reminding them that a like attempt had been made some years before, which nearly occasioned the house then occupied by a widow Hastings to be pulled down'.[64] Tootell declared that De Veil's action had been effective in preventing dissent from spreading to Edgware, but in 1799 Mrs. Hastings again risked having her house demolished when she registered it as an Independent meeting-house.[65] The congregation, however, did not prosper; in 1802 services were conducted by the Hoxton Itinerant Society in a room rented in a cottage on the Edgware side of the main road but this was given up after about three months, and in 1810 it was reported that there were not more than one or two dissenters in the parish.[66] In 1826 a brick building was registered as a meeting-house, but no denomination was given.[67] In 1829 the North Middlesex and South Hertfordshire Association fitted an upper room for worship in a cottage to the west of the main road near the turnpike; this was served by the students of Highbury College until the Association, at some time before 1833, invited the Revd. Thomas Hitchin to preach at Edgware. His first congregation in the upper room consisted of only three persons besides his family, and on his way about the village he was insulted by the populace, until the ringleader of the opposition died in agony only a few days after discharging a volley of abuse at the minister. After this the surviving persecutors no longer molested the minister and his family.[68] On 4 January 1833 a church was formed on the Congregational plan and land with a cottage was bought.[69] The first church was built on the Little Stanmore side of the village and was opened in 1834.[70] The increase in the congregation alarmed the Curate of Edgware, who called on Hitchin to enquire the reason why a certain woman had

[53] Geikie MS. vol. ii; P.C.C. 15 Wootton.
[54] E. Freshfield, *Communion Plate of Mdx.* 13–14.
[55] All Souls Coll., map of Edgware, 1597; Guildhall Libr., interleaved copy of Lysons, *Environs of Lond.* ii.
[56] Tootell MS. p. 16.   [57] Geikie MS. vol. iv.
[58] This paragraph is based on P. F. Anson, *Call of the Cloister*, 398–403; for an account of the hospital of the convent see above, p. 153.
[59] *Mdx. Cnty. Recs.* ii. 67, 215.
[60] Gen. Reg. Off., Wship. Reg. 45943.
[61] Ex inf. the priest.

[62] *Mdx. Cnty. Recs.* iv. 246.
[63] Guildhall MS. 9558, p. 430.
[64] Tootell MS. 20, 25–26; Gen. Reg. Off., Wship. Reg. 480.
[65] Gen. Reg. Off., Wship. Reg. 492.
[66] Geikie MS. vol. v; Hendon libr., DD MHS 823; Guildhall MS. 9558, p. 430; Tootell MS. 25.
[67] Gen. Reg. Off., Wship. Reg. 1482.
[68] Hendon libr., DD MHS 823; Geikie MS. vol. v.
[69] Geikie MS. vol. v.
[70] Ibid.

joined his congregation. Hitchin does not state whether this clergyman was Nicholas Fiott,[71] but writes that 'he loved darkness better than light'.[72] Hitchin left the parish some time after 1834, as the maintenance was insufficient.[73] The chapel continued to be used until, some time after 1881, it was closed; in 1893, however, it was reopened under the auspices of the London Congregational Union and the North Finchley Congregational Church, which helped and served it. A resident evangelist was appointed in 1900, and in 1914 the first full-time minister since 1881 was appointed.[74] In 1915 a hall with classrooms was built in Grove Road. From 1915 it was used for services, and in 1937 the interior was redesigned to form the present church.[75] In 1951 a new church hall was completed. From 1953 to 1961 the church was without a resident minister, but in the latter year it joined with the Watling Congregational Church to invite a minister to take up a joint pastorate.[76]

Other Protestant nonconformist denominations have had a much shorter history than the Congregationalists. A barn at Purcell's homestead was registered in 1884 as a place of worship for the Salvation Army, but there is no evidence that the congregation became established.[77] The first Wesleyan Methodist service was held in 1924 in the Old Court Hall in the High Street. A church hall was built in 1926 in Garrett Road and was used for worship until 1959, when a new church was built. Another church hall was built in 1950.[78] At the beginning of 1932 Presbyterian services began in Edgware in temporary premises, conducted by the ministers of neighbouring congregations, and in December of that year the North London Presbytery approved the steps taken by the Church Extension Committee to establish a congregation in the parish. Work on the building began at the end of 1932, and in 1933 a preaching station was established. At the first Communion service there were 70 communicants. Since the church was intended to be a Free Church for the immediate neighbourhood, its communicant members include many who are not strict Presbyterians. A manse was built in 1935 and extensions were made to the church in 1950 and 1952.[79]

JEWS. The Jewish congregations in Edgware were late in establishing themselves, but the parish has become something of a centre for the Jews of north Middlesex. In 1930 there were reckoned to be only 30 Jewish families in Edgware.[80] In 1929 the Edgware Synagogue, a constituent of the United Synagogue, was founded and in 1934 a temporary building, now used as a Jewish day school, was erected in Mowbray Road. The congregation expanded rapidly

towards the end of the Second World War and during the immediate post-war period, and in 1957 the present large building in Edgware Way, which contains seats for 1,000 worshippers and 14 classrooms, was built at a cost of £180,000.[81] The congregation of the Edgware and District Reform Synagogue was founded in 1935, when Friday evening services were held in a local schoolroom; later a room in the Congregational church was used. The community was disrupted during the war, but was revived after 1945. Sidbury Lodge, in Stone Grove, was purchased in 1951. The house was registered for worship in 1953 but a modern synagogue, with pews for 250, and a large adjoining hall have been built since that date. In 1961 most of the synagogue's 680 members lived in Edgware and Stanmore, but some came from Elstree, Boreham Wood, Harrow Weald, Pinner, Bushey, and Watford. In 1963 there were plans to replace Sidbury Lodge itself with a new communal hall and a classroom.[82] The Yeshurun Synagogue, a member of the Federation of Synagogues catering for the more traditionally inclined members of the Jewish faith, was built in Fernhurst Gardens in 1948, for a congregation founded in that year, and was licensed for worship in 1950.[83]

EDUCATION. In 1791 a Sunday school, supported by voluntary contributions, was instituted.[84] William Lee Antonie, owner of Edgware Boys and patron of the living, contributed 3 guineas a year[85] and also built the west gallery in the church for the use of the children who attended the school.[86] In 1818 the Revd. James Proctor—described by a contemporary resident as very assiduous and zealous in promoting Christianity and in enforcing the attendance of the poor at church[87]—reported that the Sunday school was the only school in the parish and there were no endowments for education, observing obscurely that 'the poor have the means of educating their children'.[88]

In 1833 a brick building was erected at the southwest corner of the churchyard for use as a school; from the single word in large capitals on its modest gable, it later became known as Truth Hall.[89] In 1834 there were 41 children attending the infant school and 3 attending the new day school, both apparently using Truth Hall. Fifty-one children attended the Sunday school. Parents paid 2d. a week for each child at the infant school, while the day and Sunday schools were supported by contributions.[90] In 1855 a National school was built in Little Stanmore[91] and from that date the educational history of Edgware was linked firmly with that of Stanmore. In 1869 the schools in Truth Hall catered for 60 children, and the annual income consisted of £46

[71] See p. 164.
[72] Hendon libr., DD MHS 823.   [73] Ibid.
[74] Geikie MS. vol. v.
[75] Ibid.
[76] Ex inf. the minister.
[77] Gen. Reg. Off., Wship. Reg. 28243.
[78] Ibid. 50420, 67424; Geikie MS. vol. v; ex inf. the minister.
[79] G. H. Williams, *St. James's Presbyterian Church of England, Edgware*.
[80] Geikie MS. vol. v.
[81] Ex inf. the minister; Geikie MS. vol. v.
[82] Ex inf. the minister.
[83] Ex inf. the minister. Gen. Reg. Off., Wship. Reg. 62868.

[84] Plaque in church. The school founded by Sir Lancelot Lake in 1656 was for children of parishioners of Little Stanmore and tenants of that manor, and its history before 1850 is therefore reserved for treatment under Little Stanmore.
[85] Herts. Rec. Off. MSS. 68714, 68755, 68760.
[86] Board in church.
[87] Tootell MS. 22.
[88] *Digest of Rets. to Sel. Cttee. on Educ. of Poor*, H.C. 224, p. 535 (1819), ix(1).
[89] Geikie MS. vol. iv. In 1969 the building was used for parish activities.
[90] *Educ. Enquiry Abs.* H.C. 62, p. 559 (1835), xlii.
[91] *Kelly's Dir. Mdx.* (1882).

from voluntary contributions, £10 from school pence, and £8 from collections in church. The school was managed by the vicar, and the solitary schoolmistress, a former apprentice pupil-teacher without training but with 5 years' teaching experience, received a salary of £50 a year with free lodgings.[92] In 1870 68 children attended the Truth Hall school, and 66 attended the public school in Little Stanmore.[93]

In 1875 a school board was compulsorily formed for the united district of Edgware, which consisted of Edgware and Little Stanmore,[94] and under its auspices an infant board school was built in 1877 with accommodation for 150 children, although the average attendance in 1882 was apparently only 70.[95] In 1893 three schools served the united district of Edgware:[96] the infant board school (accommodation for 150 children), situated at the end of Thorn Bank off the High Street,[97] the 'Parochial' girls' school in Truth Hall (80 children), and the National school in Stanmore (143 boys). New buildings were erected in 1895 on the site off the High Street[98] and in 1899 there was stated to be accommodation for a total of 415 children, although the average attendance was only 285. More than one-half of the annual income of £945 came from voluntary contributions.[99] Even by 1912 the school was becoming overcrowded, for although the accommodation was then stated to be sufficient for 340 children the average attendance was 350.[1] With the swift growth of population after 1924 the situation became still more serious, and in 1928 further building raised the accommodation to 700.[2]

In 1938 a new building on the High Street site was provided under the Hadow scheme for a separate junior and infant school with accommodation for 450 children. The Broadfields Primary School, built to serve the new housing estate, was opened in 1942 and originally accommodated junior and infant pupils in one department. In 1952 the junior school building was opened. In order to accommodate the extra secondary school pupils after the raising of the school leaving age, two additional buildings were erected on the High Street site in 1948. Between 1948 and 1957 the growing school population was catered for by temporary expedients, but in 1957 the new secondary school was opened at Green Lane with a roll of 920. At the same time the primary school was reorganized, the infant school, with a roll of 220, being located in the building of 1938 and the junior school, with a roll of 370, occupying the remainder of the buildings on the High Street site. In 1963 there were 890 pupils at the secondary school, 427 at the junior school, 267 at the infant school, 340 at the Broadfields Junior School, and 211 at the Broadfields Infant School.[3]

There are a few small independent schools in Edgware, the most important being the Rosh Pinah Jewish Day school in Mowbray Road; it came into

being in 1957 when the Edgware synagogue moved from the buildings in Mowbray Road to its present home on Edgware Way, and in 1963 had 200 children on the roll in kindergarten, infant, and junior sections.[4]

CHARITIES FOR THE POOR.[5] Samuel Atkinson, by will proved 1680, left £600 in trust to buy land in Edgware on which to build four almshouses. The almshouses were built on Watling Street at a cost of £240[6] and the remaining sum was used to purchase an endowment of 12 a. in the parish of Oakley (Bucks.). Thomas Napier of Brockley Hill, by will dated 1707, left £100 with which were purchased 3 a. in Harrow parish. The rent was to be applied as 4s. every month to each of the four almspeople, and the remainder in annual payments of 1s. 6d. each to the parish poor. By 1897 Napier's gift was represented by 3 a. in Harrow and £60 stock. A man named Watts, by an instrument of uncertain date, left copyhold called Harrods Green in Harrow to the use of the Edgware poor. Until c. 1820 the income was used in aid of the church- and poor-rates, but after that date the proceeds of the gift were added to the endowment of the Atkinson almshouses. By 1823 the almshouses' endowment was worth in all £33. Each of the four almspeople received 10s. a month and coals. The endowment was augmented under the will (dated 1875) of Harriet Hurst, who left the proceeds of her estate in trust for the upkeep of the church, the voluntary school, and the Atkinson and Day almshouses.[7] In 1897 her gift to the Atkinson almshouses was represented by £977 stock.

Under a Scheme of 1897 the gifts of Atkinson, Napier, Watts, and Hurst were consolidated as the Almshouse Charities of Atkinson and Others. The income of £50 a year, with the exception of 30s. payable under Napier's will to the parish poor, was to be applied to the upkeep of the Atkinson almshouses. Napier's gift was converted to £345 stock before 1915. Under a Scheme of 1932 the almspeople were defined as paupers who were unable to maintain themselves and had been resident in the parish for not less than two years. They were to receive an allowance of 5s. a week from the income of the Atkinson charities, which then amounted to £90 a year. The Atkinson almshouses were severely damaged by enemy action in 1940. They consisted of a single-storied brick range, having a central curvilinear gable on the front with an inscribed panel commemorating their foundation in 1680.[8] The ruins were demolished in 1955 and new almshouses, built on the same site, were opened in 1957. A Scheme of that year provided that almspeople were to contribute at least 10s. a week towards their own upkeep.

Miss Margaret Abel of Cricklewood, by will proved 1943, left £7,250 stock and £491 in cash in

[92] Ed. 7/86.
[93] *Rep. of Educ. Cttee. of Coun. 1870*, H.C. 201, p. 242 (1871), lv.
[94] *Lists of Sch. Boards and Sch. Att. Cttees.* [C. 2561], H.C. (1880), liv.
[95] *Kelly's Dir. Mdx.* (1882).
[96] *Rets. Rel. to Elem. Educ.* [C. 7529], H.C. (1894), lxv.
[97] O.S. Map 1/2,500, Mdx. vi. 13 (1896 edn.).
[98] Ex inf. Bor. Educ. Officer.
[99] *Rets. Rel. to Elem. Educ.* [Cd. 315], H.C. (1900), lxv (2).

[1] *Kelly's Dir. Mdx.* (1912).
[2] Ex inf. Bor. Educ. Officer; *Edgware Gaz.* (supplement), 1 May 1931.
[3] Ex inf. Bor. Educ. Officer.
[4] Ex inf. Bor. Educ. Officer and the headmaster.
[5] Except where otherwise stated this section is based on Char. Com. files and *9th Rep. Com. Char.* H.C. 258 (1823), ix.
[6] Geikie MS. vol. iv.
[7] See below.
[8] Hist. Mon. Com. *Mdx.* 17.

trust to build almshouses in the borough of Hendon. Under a Charity Commission Scheme of 1959 the gift was used to erect two almshouses, to be known as the Abel Homes, at the rear of the Atkinson almshouses. Occupation of the Abel Homes was limited to elderly poor who had been resident in Hendon Borough for at least 5 years, and the foundation was to be administered by the trustees of the Atkinson charities. In 1964 the income of the Atkinson charities amounted to £433, all of which was spent on the upkeep of the almshouses.

Charles Day (d. 1836) built, probably in 1828,[9] eight almshouses on a 1-acre plot fronting on Watling Street at Stone Grove which he bought in 1829 from All Souls College. During his lifetime Day selected the almspeople; by his will, which was proved in 1840, he conveyed the almshouses and land to trustees, leaving sufficient money to provide an endowment of £100 a year for the upkeep of the property and weekly payments to the almspeople. In selecting almspeople the trustees were to give preference to parishioners of Edgware and Little Stanmore, providing that they did not sell or drink intoxicants, swear, or break the Sabbath. Harriet Hurst[10] left £1,350 stock for the upkeep of the Day almshouses, and in 1958 the endowment comprised the site of the almshouses and £4,793 stock. One of the almshouses was burned down and rebuilt c. 1886, and the buildings were restored in 1959. They consist of a long single-storied range in an early-19th-century Gothic style with steep gables, pinnacled buttresses and a slate roof. The front is faced with stone ashlar and has Gothic arcading below the eaves and verges. In the central gable, which is flanked by two smaller ones, is a clock and the date 1828.[11] In 1964 the income of the endowment was £278. Expenditure was limited to the upkeep of the buildings and no payments were made to the occupants.

William Blasson, by will proved 1904, left the income on £200 to provide coal for the Edgware poor. In 1963 the income of £9 was used to buy 2 cwt. of coal for each of the eight almspeople.

HARROW
INCLUDING PINNER

THE archiepiscopal manor and ancient parish of Harrow, of which parish until 1766 Pinner was a chapelry, covered an area 6½ miles long and 4½ miles wide in the eastern half of Gore hundred. The parish, called Harrow in the account that follows to distinguish it from the hamlet of Harrow-on-the-Hill or Harrow Town, stretched south from the Hertfordshire border to the River Brent. It was bounded by Elthorne hundred on the west and by Great Stanmore and Kingsbury parishes on the east. Parts of the parish, notably Pinner and Harrow-on-the-Hill, attracted wealthy residents as early as the 17th century. Harrow School, founded in 1572, contributed to the growth of Harrow-on-the-Hill from the end of the 18th century. Railways were followed in the late 19th century by housing estates and factories. After the British Empire Exhibition of 1924–5, for which Wembley Stadium was built, the site was developed and building spread over the south-east of the parish.

In the 19th century the total area was 13,809 a., divided between Harrow (10,027 a.) and Pinner (3,782 a.). In 1931, when part of Northolt parish was added, the whole area, then administered by four district councils, consisted of 13,909 a. In 1961 this area, divided into wards totalling 13,983 a., formed part of the municipal boroughs of Harrow (12,555 a.) and Wembley (6,294 a.).[1] In 1965 Harrow became the London Borough of Harrow, and Wembley became part of the London Borough of Brent.[2] The account below relates to the area comprised in the parishes of Harrow and Pinner before the boundary changes of the 20th century.

Harrow forms part of the London Clay plain, overlain in patches by Claygate and Reading Beds and Bagshot Sands. Terrace gravels and alluvium are found along the water-courses. The London Clay produces gently undulating country with sluggish streams and bad drainage. The heavy soils once supported dense forest, and, when cleared, were especially suitable for grass. Hills, like Harrow Hill, Barn Hill, the Weald, and Pinner, rise where gravels and sands overlie the clay. Drainage is better in these areas, which were originally covered with light woodland and heath. The north, where there are hills of over 500 ft., contrasts with the clay plains of the south, less than 100 ft. above sea level. The main system of drainage is that of the tributaries of the Brent, which flow south-eastward from the Weald and Harrow Hill. A second system, that of the River Pinn, flows south-westward from the hills of Pinner and the Weald.[3]

Settlement probably began on the higher ground and later grew from homesteads in clearings by the streams. There was a Celtic earthwork on Barn Hill[4] and possibly another at Pinner. Roman coins, pottery, and brick- and stonework have been found at Waxwell, Bury Pond (Barrow Point) Hill, and Pinner Road in Pinner, in the grounds of Bentley Priory in Harrow Weald, and in the church of Harrow-on-the-Hill. Honeypot Lane on the eastern border of Kenton was probably an ancient trackway. There are sarsen

[9] Geikie MS. vol. iv.
[10] See above.
[11] See plate facing p. 152.
[1] Census, 1831–1961. Earlier censuses give the area of Harrow as 9,870 a. and Pinner as 3,720 a. For the 1961 boundaries of Harrow and Wembley boroughs, excluding wards formerly in Stanmore and Kingsbury parishes, see map on p. 201.
[2] See p. 246.

[3] Geol. Survey Map, sheet 256 (drift); G. B. G. Bull, 'Changing Landscape of Rural Mdx. 1500–1850' (Lond. Univ. Ph.D. thesis, 1958); A. J. Garrett, 'Historical Geography of Upper Brent Valley' (Lond. Univ. M.A. thesis, 1935); D. H. Smith, 'The Recent Industrialization of N. & W. sectors of Greater Lond.' (Lond. Univ. Ph.D. thesis, 1932).
[4] Ex inf. Mr. A. D. Lacaille.

stones in Harrow, of which the most famous, Sudbury stone and Weald stone, served as mile and boundary stones, although there is no evidence that they were so used in the Celtic or Roman periods.[5] The most puzzling of the early remains is Grim's Dyke or Ditch, a ditch and bank visible in north Pinner and Harrow Weald. Partly because of its name, an epithet for Woden, the earthwork has usually been dated to the 5th or 6th century and variously described as a defensive barrier or a political or hunting boundary.[6] Excavations in 1957, however, uncovered a large amount of Belgic pottery, dating Grim's Dyke to a much earlier period.[7]

The Domesday survey mentions 113 people at Harrow;[8] 223 people were listed for the 1522–3 subsidy,[9] and there were 1,545 communicants in the parish in 1547.[10] The earliest rental, dated 1553,[11] lists 122 free and customary head tenants; 623 adult male parishioners took the protestation oath in 1642.[12] There were 484 occupied houses in 1664[13] and allegedly 'about 400', of which one-third were in Pinner, in 1795.[14] The estimate was almost certainly too low, for there were 504 inhabited houses in 1801, and in 1805 478 houses were listed in claims under the Inclosure Act.[15] By 1821 there were 777 houses, by 1851 1,103, and by 1891 2,993. The population rose from 3,246 in 1801 to 4,093 in 1821, to 6,261 in 1851, and to 15,715 in 1891. From 25,321 in 1901, it rose still more sharply to 59,006 in 1921, to 135,970 in 1931, and to 277,615, its peak, in 1951. Thereafter it declined to 264,317 in 1961.[16]

In the Middle Ages there were 12 centres of settlement, excluding the lost hamlet of Norbury. Around Harrow-on-the-Hill were Pinner, in the north-west of the parish, Harrow Weald, in the north, Kenton, Preston, Uxendon, and Wembley, in the east, and Tokyngton and Alperton in the south-east; closer to the centre were Sudbury and Roxeth, respectively south-east and south-west of Harrow-on-the-Hill, and Greenhill, to the north.[17]

The hamlets of Harrow parish were linked together by rough tracks whose upkeep became a heavy burden upon the tithings and later upon the vestry. Bequests were made by Robert Hatch, by will proved in 1490,[18] for the road from Weald hamlet to Harrow church, Richard Parson, by will proved in 1539,[19] for Gore Lane in Preston, and John Lyon (d. 1592)[20] for the highway in Preston between Goreland Gate and Hyde

House. Bequests were also made by Richard Page, by will proved in 1551,[21] for East Lane in Sudbury, and Sir John Lyon, by will proved in 1564,[22] and John Lyon of Preston (d. 1592) for Deadman's Hill and its extension northward.[23] Some of the road-names are descriptive: Rough Street in Weald,[24] Watery Lane in Alperton, Dirty Lane in Greenhill,[25] and Mud Lane[26] in Pinner. The 'badness' of the route from Harrow-on-the-Hill to Pinner, Roxborough Lane, which had to cross a branch of the Yeading Brook at Hooking Green, was mentioned in 1650,[27] and in 1734 labourers were sent to mend it and dig ditches. In 1768 the inhabitants of Harrow parish were fined £500 for failing to repair Northolt Road but two years later both this and Uxbridge Road were in very bad repair.[28] Anthony Trollope remembered the 'miserably dirty lanes' of his boyhood in the Weald,[29] and in 1841 the road from Harrow Town to the Weald was especially poor. Part of the Preston–Kingsbury lane was flooded and impassable in winter in 1854.[30] Harrow-on-the-Hill was itself badly drained: Hog Lane, whose state had contributed to the cholera epidemic of 1848, was impassable for school-children in 1867 and Waldron Road, which joined it, was 'a ploughed field'. As late as 1898 Pinner could be described as a typical Middlesex village where 'roads are impassable for mud for 5 months out of 12'.[31] Among other hazards a well in the highway of Harrow-on-the-Hill was unfenced in 1724 and dangerous to travellers.[32]

The local roads were constantly shifting course. Inclosure, especially in the 16th and 17th centuries in the south-east, resulted in many changes, as in 1655 when Richard Page obstructed the old road and altered the route through Preston East Field.[33] The creation of Wembley Park in 1810 also changed the road pattern, and obstruction in Pinner Marsh and new paths in Pinner Park and Woodhall was frequent in the first decade of the 19th century.[34] In 1759 Oxhey Lane was a continuation northward of the road (later Headstone Lane) at Hatch End.[35] In 1767 because of the very bad condition of part of Weald Common,[36] the lower part of the lane was altered by two landowners to run eastward, along the higher ground.[37] Maps of 1759 and 1817 suggest that similar changes took place elsewhere, for example in Rayners Lane, Sheepcote Lane, and the entrance to Weald Copse Farm. Probably the most striking change was in the

[5] E. M. Ware, *Pinner in the Vale*, 52, 57, 189; W. W. Druett, *Pinner*, 3; *V.C.H. Mdx.* i. 71.
[6] *V.C.H. Mdx.* i. 76, 79; R. E. M. Wheeler, *London & the Saxons*, 67 sqq.; Pevsner, *Mdx.* 59.
[7] *Wembley Observer & Gaz.* 29 Aug. 1957; *Harrow Observer*, 22 & 29 Aug. 1957; Pinner South Residents' Assoc. *The Resident*, xxvii (Nov. 1957); ex. inf. Miss Jean MacDonald and Prof. W. R. Grimes. Mr. P. F. Suggett, the director of excavations, suggests that Grim's Dyke was built by the Catuvellauni after Julius Caesar's invasion, but the type of pottery found persisted over a long period.
[8] *V.C.H. Mdx.* i. 120.
[9] E 179/141/115.
[10] E 301/34 ff. 28v, 31. Includes Tokyngton, see p. 191.
[11] M.R.O., Acc. 76/222a.
[12] Hse. of Lords, Mdx. Protestation Rets.
[13] M.R.O., H.T. 5.
[14] Lysons, *Environs of Lond.* ii. 577.
[15] M.R.O., Acc. 76/1400. Of the total, 14 were described as mansions, 35 as farm-houses, 147 as cottages, 18 as inns, and the rest as houses, messuages, or tenements.
[16] *Census*, 1801–1961.
[17] See map on facing page.
[18] P.C.C. 36 Milles.
[19] Ibid. 3 Alenger (Person).

[20] Wemb. Hist. Soc., Acc. 713.
[21] P.C.C. 20 Welles.
[22] *Wembley News*, 1 Jan. 1953.
[23] i.e. 'the highway of Harrow from Hangers Wood to the highway thence to Uxbridge' (1564) and 'the highway between Preston and Deadman's Hill' (1592).
[24] M.R.O., Acc. 76/2417, m. 90.
[25] O.S. Map 1/2,500, Mdx. x. 8, xvi. 1 (1865 edn.).
[26] Alternate name for Love Lane: Robbins, *Middlesex*, 75.
[27] *Home Cnties. Mag.* i. 321–2; see below, p. 256.
[28] Except where otherwise stated, this and the next 3 paragraphs are based upon Barbara Jordan, 'The Roads round Harrow in the late 18th & 19th centuries' (TS. *penes* Harrow Cent. Ref. Libr.).
[29] A. Trollope, *Autobiography* (Oxford Crown edn. 1950), 11.
[30] M.R.O., Acc. 590/2, no. 484.
[31] Pinner Assoc. *The Villager*, vi.
[32] M.R.O., Acc. 76/873.
[33] Ibid. /1640.
[34] M.R.O., D.R.O. 8/CI/1.
[35] M.R.O., Acc. 643, 2nd deposit, Messeder map A.
[36] M.R.O., Acc. 76/1691.
[37] M.R. 612.

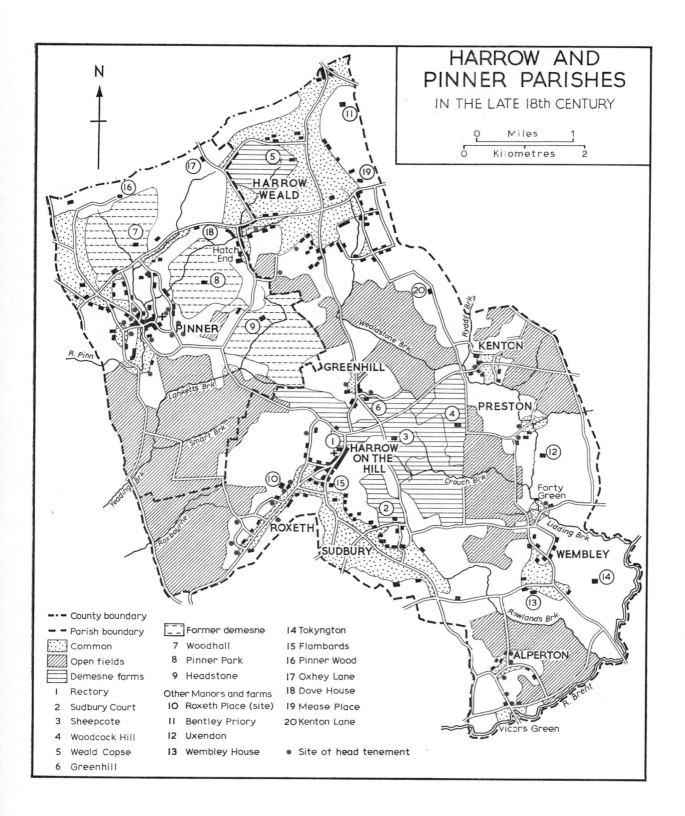

HARROW AND PINNER PARISHES
IN THE LATE 18th CENTURY

```
0        Miles        1
0     Kilometres      2
```

HARROW
WEALD

Hatch
End

PINNER

R. Pinn

Lanketts Brk.

Smart Brk.

Yeading Brk.

Roxbourne

ROXETH

SUDBURY

GREENHILL

Wealdstone Brk.

HARROW
ON THE
HILL

Crouch Brk.

KENTON

PRESTON

Ryddy Brk.

Forty
Green

Liding Brk.

WEMBLEY

Rowlands Brk.

ALPERTON

R. Brent

Vicars Green

—·— County boundary
— — Parish boundary
Common
Open fields
Demesne farms
1 Rectory
2 Sudbury Court
3 Sheepcote
4 Woodcock Hill
5 Weald Copse
6 Greenhill

7 Woodhall
8 Pinner Park
9 Headstone
Other Manors and farms
10 Roxeth Place (site)
11 Bentley Priory
12 Uxendon
13 Wembley House

Former demesne
14 Tokyngton
15 Flambards
16 Pinner Wood
17 Oxhey Lane
18 Dove House
19 Mease Place
20 Kenton Lane

• Site of head tenement

Harrow road, the main link with London. Sixteenth-century bequests clearly distinguish the 'London or Harrow way' from 'the highway in Hanger Wood', and Ogilby's map of 1675 shows two routes. The first ran from Harrow-on-the-Hill, across Sudbury Common, along the Harrow–Greenford boundary to Vicar's Bridge and thence to Harlesden, Paddington, and London.[38] A branch from Wembley Hill through Hangers Wood to Harlesden was presumably Deadman's Hill, which crossed the river at Stonebridge, originally by a ford or wooden bridge. The stone bridge was built between 1660 and 1700[39] and it seems to have diverted the main London road from the Vicar's Bridge route to Deadman's Hill, which took the name Harrow Road. By 1801 the route ran from Stonebridge, along the bottom of Wembley Green, and across Sudbury Common to Harrow Town.

The London or Harrow road attracted bequests from John Marshall, by will proved in 1507,[40] Thomas Page, by will proved in 1512,[41] Hugh Enystoo, by will proved in 1548,[42] and Henry Page, by will proved in 1558.[43] John Lyon (d. 1592) left 38 a. in Marylebone to Harrow School in trust for the repair of the road.[44] In 1754 it was said to be so bad that Harrow residents went to London via Acton[45] and in 1801, when it was 'narrow and incommodious', an Act was passed to set up a turnpike trust.[46] The trustees, whose survey stressed the inadequate drainage of the road in the south and its narrowness on Harrow Hill, erected a toll-gate and house near Harrow pound in 1801, and later erected turnpike gates at Roxborough and the northern entry to Sheepcote Lane.[47] After the misuse of funds by the highway surveyor in 1823,[48] the Harrow Road Trust was indicted by Quarter Sessions for the very bad state of the road from Harlesden to Harrow-on-the-Hill. James Macadam, son of the engineer, was elected surveyor and another survey described the road as 'circulous, dangerously narrow, confined by high banks with plantations and houses and with turnings almost at right angles', and as often impassable at the Brent crossing.[49] An Act was passed in 1826[50] to make a more direct road from the 'Swan' at the edge of Sudbury Common to the crossing at Stonebridge,[51] but in the same year the trust was absorbed into the Metropolitan Roads Commission.[52] The river was diverted, the road was resurfaced with stone and the gradient of Harrow Hill was reduced. In 1830 the road to Harrow led to nowhere else 'of note' and therefore was not much used and in good repair. Harrow turnpike house and gate were abolished in 1847, but the commission administered Harrow Road until 1872.[53]

There was a slight rise in traffic before the railways killed the coach trade. In 1681 a coach left Harrow-on-the-Hill daily for Holborn and in 1690 'Mr. Page's waggon' left every other day. It still took a whole day for a waggoner to drive a team to London from Harrow c. 1800.[54] By 1826 there were two daily coaches from Harrow-on-the-Hill, from the 'Crown and Anchor' and the 'King's Head' to and from London.[55] The 'Crown and Anchor' coach continued to the 'Queen's Head' at Pinner. By then Pinner Road (formerly Roxborough Lane) had been much improved, mainly because of its link with Rickmansworth. In 1809 an Act[56] was passed to widen and improve the turnpike road from Rickmansworth through Pinner to the Harrow road at Roxborough and a toll-bar was erected at Pinner Green.

Continuous settlement in the parish probably dates from the Saxon period. There were three phases: firstly, settlement in farms and hamlets around village greens and their gradual growth by encroachment on the waste; secondly, after Parliamentary inclosure in 1817, building on former waste and common, especially alongside roads, but still within the original hamlets; thirdly, the development of farm-land as housing estates and new districts. The first two phases are dealt with under individual hamlets; the last phase, which was closely connected with the railways, is treated in a further section.

The Growth of the Hamlets

HARROW-ON-THE-HILL. In 767 Offa made a grant of land between the Lydding and 'geminga hergae'. The latter, generally interpreted as 'the temple of the tribe or sons of Gumen', appears to have been a specific landmark.[57] The gravel-capped hill, rising abruptly above the wooded plain, was an obvious site for a heathen, probably Saxon, temple or sacred grove.[58] The name Harrow, therefore, seems to have been first applied to the hill, and then to the whole parish, 'on-the-Hill' being added from the end of the 14th century to distinguish the original area.[59]

In spite of its temple and well-water,[60] there is no evidence that Harrow-on-the-Hill was the first permanent settlement in the area. A major factor in the growth of Harrow Town was the presence of the parish church and priest. It would have been natural for the Church to have founded its first mission on the site of the pagan sanctuary. There was a priest by 1086[61] and the probable identification of his holding

[38] Ogilby, *Map of Mdx.* (1675).
[39] H. W. R. Elsley, *Tokyngton*, 26.
[40] P.C.C. 33 Adeane.
[41] Ibid. 8 Fetiplace.
[42] Ibid. 11 Populwell.
[43] Ibid. 35 Noodes.
[44] Wemb. Hist. Soc., Acc. 713.
[45] *Wembley News*, 1 Jan. 1953.
[46] 41 Geo. III c. 129 (Local and Personal Act).
[47] M.R.O., Acc 590/1–4, nos. 362, 449.
[48] See p. 239.
[49] Christ Church, Oxford, MS. Estates 47/278.
[50] 7 Geo. IV c. 91 (Local and Personal Act).
[51] See plan in B.M. Add. MS. 12543 A.
[52] Under the Metropolis Roads Act, 7 Geo. IV c. 142 (Local and Personal Act).
[53] Metropolis (Kilburn and Harrow) Roads Act, 35 & 36 Vic. c. 49 (Local and Personal Act). See p. 243.
[54] *Wembley News*, 1 Jan. 1953.
[55] Pigot, *Lond. Dir.* (1826), 448–9.

[56] 49 Geo. III c. 51 (Local and Personal Act).
[57] *Cart. Sax.* ed. Birch, i, p. 284; *P.N. Mdx.* (E.P.N.S.), 51–52; W. D. Bushell, 'The Harrow of the Gumenings', *Harrow Octocentenary Tracts*, iii.
[58] A few bricks embedded in St. Mary's church may have come from a Roman temple on the site: *Harrow Octocent. Tracts*, iii. 12.
[59] *P.N. Mdx.* (E.P.N.S.), 52. The distinction is used here wherever possible, although the parish, as well as the town, was often called Harrow-on-the-Hill.
[60] In 1554 100 carp were taken from Harrow Well: *Mdx. Cnty. Recs.* i. 20. The well, 'a great benefit to the inhabitants', was in 1724 'in the highway in this town': M.R.O., Acc. 76/893. At the end of the 16th cent. Harrow-on-the-Hill was said to have water on one side (presumably S.) of the hill, although those living near the church had to fetch water: B.M. Harl. MS. 570, f. 23. For later drainage and water-supply, see p. 248.
[61] *V.C.H. Mdx.* i. 20.

with the later rectory demesne[62] suggests that he lived on the hill. The account of the consecration of the first church of St. Mary, in 1094, does not mention a village, but it does indicate something resembling the later pattern of roads around the hill.[63]

The 'tenants of the church', mentioned in 1233–40,[64] were probably the 13 capital tenants[65] who held messuages in Harrow Town and virgate estates north of the hill.[66] By the 14th century the head tenements had been permanently split up among many under-tenants,[67] often smallholders of servile status who subsisted on the produce of a few selions and by animal husbandry. Eighteen people were charged pannage on Rectory manor in December 1368.[68] There were also some freehold estates, the most important of which was Flambards manor.[69] By 1553[70] there were 12 capital tenements, five lesser tenements, and four freehold estates. In 1724[71] there were 21 and by 1800[72] 25 tenants of Rectory manor.[73] Growth was helped by the grant of a weekly market and annual fair in 1261.[74] One of the appurtenances of Rectory manor in 1553 was the farm of three shops. Brewing and the leather trades were especially prominent: boots were sold without the lord's licence in 1394 and uncured shoes were sold in 1507.[75] A tailor was mentioned in 1557,[76] a brick-maker in 1589,[77] and a bricklayer in 1640.[78]

The original settlement of Harrow-on-the-Hill was probably along High Street south of the church and along Hog Lane, later Crown Street, and West Street. Six tenements, four of them capital messuages, were among the endowment granted by John Lyon to Harrow School in 1575.[79] They can probably be identified with the land held by the school at inclosure, mostly in the corner formed by West Street and High Street, and in two blocks on the east side of High Street. Other customary and capital tenements, enfranchised in the 19th century, were in High Street, at the corner of Middle Row and Byron Hill Road, and in West Street.[80] In West Street, too, was Pie-Powder House,[81] where cases arising from the market held at the corner of West Street and High Street were tried. There were 8 increments or parcels of waste in 1553 and 16 by the end of the century.[82] Some of these were for new houses or cottages. Twelve out of 14 wasteheld parcels in 1681[83] involved buildings, one of them a 'house newly erected'. Nine cottages, six messuages, and two inns, were among 18th-century wasteheld property.[84] Eighty-one

houses were listed for the 1664 hearth tax,[85] of which more than half were not charged. Three were large: Flambards, with 25 hearths, the Rectory, with 17 hearths,[86] and a house with 10 hearths owned by Daniel Waldo. Thirty-four houses had only one hearth. Fifty-three houses were charged in 1672.[87]

In 1759 settlement was concentrated along High Street between the churchyard and the junction with West Street, with buildings presenting a continuous front to the street. A more scattered string of buildings lay on either side of High Street, south of West Street, and between Hog Lane and West Street. A few houses lay north of West Street and south of Byron Hill Road, in which also were the brick-kilns leased to the Bodymeads.[88] Isolated, east of London Road, almost opposite the shooting butts, stood Flambards, marked as 'Mrs. Stapleton's'.[89]

Opposite the church the road divided and, as Church Hill and Grove Hill, formed a loop around some rectory land, on which were some houses and a hanging garden.[90] The road ran northward to Tyburn Hill, where it split into three: Roxborough Lane[91] or Lowlands Road, which ran alongside the Rectory estate to Pinner,[92] Greenhill[93] or Harrow Lane, which formed the eastern boundary of the Rectory lands and joined Harrow with Greenhill and the north, and Tyburn Lane, which ran eastward through demesne lands.[94] On either side of Tyburn Lane in its Harrow section lay Redings and Dodses, 50 a. of demesne land.[95] South of its junction with Church Hill, High Street divided into two, forming the north-eastern corner of a square of roads linking Harrow-on-the-Hill, Roxeth, and Sudbury. The southern continuation of High Street was London Road, which linked Harrow-on-the-Hill with Sudbury. Parallel with it on the west was Lower Road, a continuation of the road running northward from Northolt to join Lowlands Road and Pinner. Joining London Road and Lower Road were West Street, and, south and parallel with it, London or Roxeth Hill. Hog Lane or Crown Street was a diagonal road running south-westward from West Street, which at the centre of the square looped back, as West Hill or Byron Hill Road, to join London Road.

There were at least three inns in 1759. The 'Crown and Anchor' in High Street[96] was mentioned, as 'le Anker', in 1683[97] and may have been much older. The 'Castle' in West Street[98] existed by 1716[99] and the 'King's Head', on the west side of High Street, was

[62] See p. 250.
[63] *Eadmer's History of Recent Events in England*, ed. G. Bosanquet, 46 sqq. See below, p. 250.
[64] W. D. Bushell, 'The Vicarage', *Harrow Octocent. Tracts*, ix. 15. See p. 250.
[65] M.R.O., Acc. 974/I, m. 74.
[66] e.g. Blythes: M.R.O., Acc. 76/1909, /1912, /1939; Capers: Acc. 590/1, no. 353.
[67] For a discussion of head and under-tenants, see p. 224.
[68] M.R.O., Acc. 76/2427, m. 4.
[69] See p. 209.
[70] M.R.O., Acc. 76/222a. Under-set holdings are not recorded.
[71] M.R.O., Acc. 76 /1015.   [72] Ibid. /1126.
[73] Probably including some in Greenhill and Roxeth.
[74] See p. 225.
[75] M.R.O., Acc. 974/I, mm. 16, 77d.
[76] *Mdx. Cnty. Recs.* i. 31.
[77] M.R.O., Acc. 76/386.
[78] Ibid. /217.
[79] Ibid. /205, /222a.
[80] Ibid. /992, /1909, /1912, /1929, /1944.
[81] Robbins, *Middlesex*, 280, 284; *Harrow Observer & Gaz.* 18 July 1963; see below.

[82] M.R.O., Acc. 76/205, /222a.
[83] Ibid. /707.   [84] Ibid. /1109.
[85] M.R.O., H.T. 5.
[86] Cf. M.R.O., Acc. 76/848.
[87] M.R.O., H.T. 26.   [88] See p. 232.
[89] M.R.O., Acc. 643, 2nd deposit, Messeder maps A and B.
[90] *Harrow School*, ed. E. W. Howson and G. T. Warner, 51; 'le Hangyngardyn' was mentioned in 1451: M.R.O., Acc. 76/2417, m. 104.
[91] Rocque, *Map of Mdx.* (1754).
[92] The lane formed the northern line of a rectangle formed by Lowlands Road, High Street, West Street, and Bessborough Road.
[93] M.R.O., Acc. 76/217.
[94] The eastward extension of Tyburn Lane, in 1548 called the Churchway (*Cal. Pat.* 1547–8, 335) was, after 1896, called Kenton Road: Pinner Assoc. *The Villager*, lii.
[95] See p. 251.
[96] M.R.O., Acc. 590/1, no. 5.
[97] M.R.O., Acc. 210/46–47.
[98] M.R.O., Acc. 590/1, no. 156.
[99] M.R.O., Acc. 76/1109. Still there in 1967.

licensed from 1751.[1] The 'Bricklayers' Arms', licensed in 1751,[2] may be identified with an unnamed beershop in Crown Street, mentioned in 1852,[3] and with a beershop of the same name which was closed in 1907.[4] Other inns which may have been located in Harrow Town were the 'Queen's Head', licensed in 1759,[5] and a second 'King's Head', licensed 1751–1800[6] and perhaps identifiable with a messuage on the east side of High Street, which was described in 1872[7] as 'many years since called the Upper King's Head Inn'. The 'Plough' in Hog Lane, licensed in 1760,[8] may be identifiable with the Crown Inn,[9] first licensed under that name in 1785.[10]

The basic road pattern has remained unaltered. The main developments between 1759 and 1817[11] was the extension of Hog Lane, as Middle Row or Road, to the south-west corner of the square. The expansion of Harrow Town down the southern slope of Harrow Hill gathered impetus after inclosure.[12] Small, terraced houses were built fronting Crown Street, West Street, Byron Hill Road, and London Road. The population in 1831[13] was given as 1,345. In 1841[14] it was 1,359, when 167 houses were inhabited, but some of the items for Harrow Town were probably included in those for Roxeth. In 1851[15] Harrow Town had a population of 1,660 in 203 houses and four inns, giving a very high density of 8 people to a house. This is partly explained by the existence of large houses for the Harrow schoolboys and many servants. There was also much overcrowding in the centre, where insanitary conditions led to cholera outbreaks in 1847 and 1848 and a subsequent public health inquiry.[16]

Public buildings in 1852[17] included a Baptist chapel, post office, police station, and fire-engine house. There were also three forges, a slaughter-house, the 'King's Head', 'Crown and Anchor', 'Castle', and 'Crown', two beerhouses, the 'Wheatsheaf'[18] at the junction of Middle Row and Byron Hill Road, and the 'White Hart'[19] in High Street. A beer-shop in Crown Street, probably the 'Load of Hay', was later called the 'Wheatsheaf' and may be identifiable with the 'Bricklayers' Arms' or the 'North Star'.[20]

West Hill,[21] of which only the northern part existed in 1852, was completed by 1859,[22] as was Brickfields, as yet unnamed. By 1865 two other small roads, Waldron Road and Victoria Terrace, had been built within the main square, and Nelson Road led from West Street to Trafalgar Terrace. East of High Street, the south section of Peterborough Road had appeared, but Northwick Walk and Football Lane were still only paths through fields.[23] Houses were being built on any available space in the town,[24] but mainly in the north, on the former Rectory demesne on either side of Lowlands Road. Roxborough Villas were built between 1852 and 1860[25] on the eastern side of a path from St. Mary's church to the junction of Lowlands and Bessborough roads. Between Lowlands Road and Greenhill Lane (by 1871 called Station Road)[26] a series of roads, College, Roxborough, Kymberley, Headstone,[27] New (later Clarendon), Byron, and the still unnamed St. Anne's Road, had been laid out by 1865, although there were still only a few houses, mainly between St. Anne's and College roads and north of Lowlands Road.

The opening of Harrow-on-the-Hill station just north of Lowlands Road in 1880 accelerated development nearby.[28] Some houses in Roxborough Park existed by 1882[29] and by 1887 the land west of it was divided into building lots.[30] A Roman Catholic church was built there in 1894[31] and development was well advanced by 1897.[32] Peterborough Road had been continued up to its junction with Station Road by 1889 and the land between it and Grove Hill was also divided into lots.[33] By 1898[34] houses extended solidly northward to Greenhill and westward along the Metropolitan Railway line towards Pinner and Headstone.

In spite of the spread of building, Harrow-on-the-Hill itself has remained remarkably free from wholesale development. Much of the credit for this is due to Harrow School. It was during the 19th century, especially, that the school's influence was extended over the town. At inclosure the largest estates were still those of the Rectory held by James Edwards,[35] and Flambards, which Lord Northwick divided and leased out.[36] In comparison with most properties the school estate, then comprising the school-house, a master's house (probably Druries), 11 messuages, some of them divided into several tenements, a butcher's shop, and some pasture land,[37] was quite large. During the 19th century several mansions were leased or purchased as boarding houses, each usually containing a master and his family, a number of servants, and from 13 to 50 pupils. In 1851 there were seven of these houses,[38] including Harrow Park, the successor to Flambards.[39] In 1884 the lease of Harrow

[1] M.R.O., Acc. 590/1, no. 67; L.V. 7/1. See below.
[2] M.R.O., L.V. 7/1.
[3] M.R.O., Acc. 590/1, no. 165.
[4] M.R.O., P.S. G/H5/1.
[5] M.R.O., L.V. 7/37. See below.
[6] Ibid. 7/1; 9/2; 10/88.
[7] M.R.O., Acc. 76/1942; M.R. 612, no. 675.
[8] M.R.O., L.V. 7/44.
[9] M.R.O., Acc. 59 0/1, no. 168.
[10] M.R.O., L.V. 9/131.
[11] M.R. 612.
[12] Ibid.; M.R.O., Acc. 590/1.
[13] M.R.O., D.R.O. 3/F13/2.
[14] Census, 1841; see below, p. 196.
[15] H.O. 107/1700, ff. 1–20, 63–89, M.R.O., Acc. 590/1, /4.
[16] See p. 243.
[17] M.R.O., Acc. 590/1, nos. 181, 9, 137, 178, 102, 147, 153, 117 respectively.
[18] Ibid. no. 198; Acc. 76/992; P.S. G/H5/1.
[19] M.R.O., Acc. 76/1910; Acc. 590/1, no. 80.
[20] M.R.O., Acc. 590/1, no. 165; P.S. G/H5/1; Harrow Gaz. 1858. The 'North Star' in 1967 was used for storing borough archives.

[21] Joining Byron Hill Road and Roxeth Hill.
[22] Harrow Cent. Ref. Libr., Sales Particulars, ii (1859).
[23] O.S. Map 1/2,500, Mdx. x. 7, 8, 11 (1865 edn.).
[24] Harrow Cent. Ref. Libr., Sales Partics. ii (1859, 1866).
[25] Kelly's Dir. Mdx. (1860).
[26] Harrow Bor., High St., Local Bd. of Health, Min. Bk. (1870–5), 52–53.
[27] Only north as far as Kymberley Road.
[28] See p. 198.
[29] Kelly's Dir. Mdx. (1882).
[30] Harrow Cent. Ref. Libr., Sales Partics. i (1887).
[31] See p. 261.
[32] O.S. Map 6", Mdx. x. SE. (1897 edn.).
[33] Harrow Cent. Ref. Libr., Sales Partics. ii.
[34] O.S. Map 1", sheet 256 (1898 edn.).
[35] M.R. 612; M.R.O., Acc. 794/8. See p. 252.
[36] See p. 210.
[37] M.R.O., Acc. 76/1400. In the 17th cent. the school received rents, totalling £28, from 14 people: B.M. Harl. MS. 2211, f. 33.
[38] H.O. 107/1700, ff. 1–20, 32v–42. Probably the same number as in 1831: M.R.O., D.R.O. 3/F13/5.
[39] See p. 210.

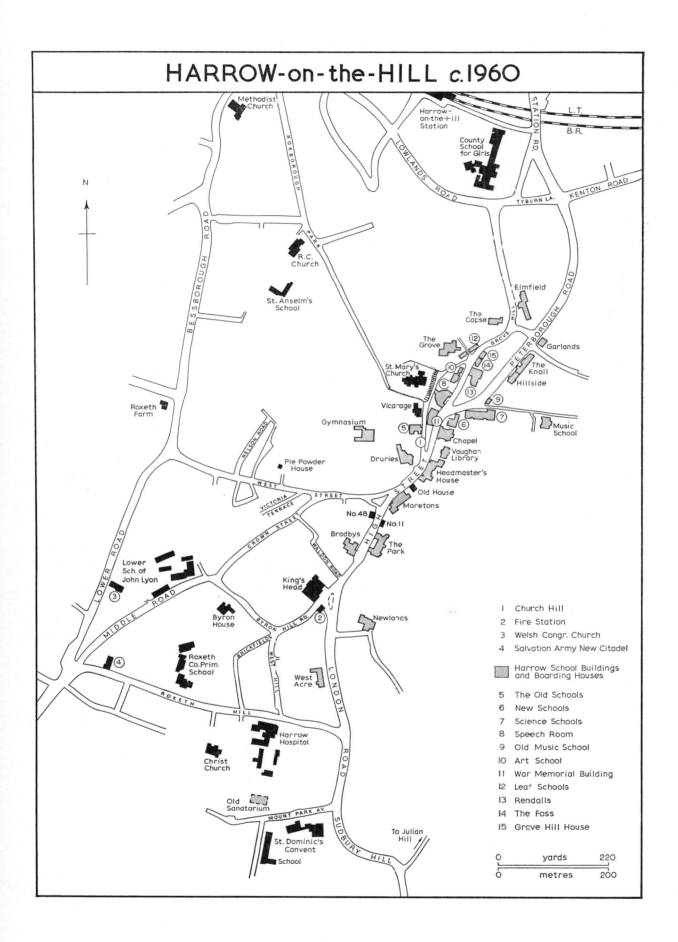

HARROW-on-the-HILL c.1960

N

Methodist Church

Harrow-on-the-Hill Station

County School for Girls

STATION RD.

L.T.
B.R.

TYBURN LA.

KENTON ROAD

ROXBOROUGH ROAD

PARK ROAD

LOWLANDS ROAD

R.C. Church

St. Anselm's School

BESSBOROUGH ROAD

Elmfield

The Copse

GROVE HILL

PETERBOROUGH ROAD

Garlands

The Grove

⑫

⑮

⑭

St. Mary's Church

⑩

⑧

⑬

The Knoll

Hillside

Roxeth Farm

Vicarage

⑨

⑤

⑪

⑥

⑦

Music School

NELSON ROAD

Gymnasium

Druries

①

Chapel

Vaughan Library

Pie Powder House

Headmaster's House

WEST STREET

VICTORIA TERRACE

Old House

Moretons

No. 48

No. 11

LOWER ROAD

CROWN STREET

WALDON ROAD

HIGH STREET

Bradbys

The Park

Lower Sch. of John Lyon

③

King's Head

MIDDLE ROAD

Byron House

BYRON HILL RD.

②

Newlands

BRICKFIELDS

WEST HILL

LONDON ROAD

Roxeth Co. Prim. School

④

West Acre

ROXETH HILL

Harrow Hospital

Christ Church

SUDBURY HILL

Old Sanatorium

MOUNT PARK AV.

To Julian Hill

St. Dominic's Convent

School

1   Church Hill
2   Fire Station
3   Welsh Congr. Church
4   Salvation Army New Citadel

    Harrow School Buildings and Boarding Houses

5   The Old Schools
6   New Schools
7   Science Schools
8   Speech Room
9   Old Music School
10   Art School
11   War Memorial Building
12   Leaf Schools
13   Rendalls
14   The Foss
15   Grove Hill House

0   yards   220
0   metres   200

Park expired,[40] and, lest building should spread southward from north Harrow, the Harrow Park Estate Trust was set up to buy property for the school.[41] Between 1884 and 1898 220 a. were acquired, including portions of the old demesne lands of the Rectory and Sudbury manors.[42] This has resulted in the preservation of large open spaces around the town, giving it a setting of parkland, playing fields, and gardens.

A few buildings have survived from the 17th century and earlier. The oldest is the former Pie-Powder House, probably dating from the 15th century, the remains of which stand in a yard at the rear of no. 75 West Street.[43] The rectangular timber-framed structure, originally single-storied, retains a fine arch-braced tie-beam roof truss, incorporating a crown-post with four-way struts. The King's Head Hotel, at the junction of High Street and Byron Hill Road, has a Georgian and Victorian frontage but parts are reputed to date from 1533. Further north in High Street no. 48, perhaps formerly the White Hart Inn,[44] is a timber-framed building behind a brick façade. In West Street no. 13 has a jettied gable-end and is part of a timber-framed house, probably of the 17th century. At the Old House (no. 5 High Street) a 19th-century tile-hung and gabled top story has been added above the original eaves cornice but the structure is otherwise of c. 1700 with traces of earlier work internally; it is thought to have been the Queen's Head Inn,[45] mentioned in 1759. With the adjoining buildings the Old House forms a group of dignified Georgian and Regency frontages on the east side of High Street. Further south is no. 11, a detached late-18th-century house of yellow brick with a symmetrical three-storied front and a pedimented doorway.[46] Many of the late-18th- and early-19th-century domestic buildings are small dwellings in High Street, West Street, and Crown Street, often altered and with inserted shop fronts. There are also several detached residences, both large and small, on the slope of the hill west of High Street. Many of the larger private dwellings in and around the town are or have been used as boarding houses for Harrow School; the more important of them are mentioned below. The growth of the school in the 19th century and the increased prosperity of the town led to considerable rebuilding and infilling along High Street. This is particularly noticeable round the small square at the junction of High Street, Byron Hill Road, and London Road; here Victorian frontages predominate. There are also many middle-class houses of this period, detached and in pairs, on both sides of London Road. The 20th century, on the other hand, has made little impact. In this respect Harrow-on-the-Hill forms a striking contrast to the suburban areas surrounding it.

As High Street leads northward to the parish church it becomes increasingly dominated by Harrow School until, at the foot of Church Hill, the main group of school buildings is reached. Older houses here were cleared away as the school expanded, so that no strict demarcation between town and school has ever been apparent. The principal buildings, erected singly over a considerable period, are mostly of red brick and show a variety of architectural styles, the favourite being a scholastic Tudor in all its 19th- and early-20th-century forms.[47]

The original school building, designed according to John Lyon's instructions but not completed until 1615, stood on the steep slope to the west of Church Hill. It was a rectangular brick structure of two stories, basement, and attics. A small wing, containing the entrance and staircase, projected from the east side.[48] The schoolroom occupied the first floor, with a governor's room and living rooms for the master and usher above it. In 1819–20 the building was more than doubled in size by the addition of a new east wing of approximately the same dimensions as the original school; the architect was C. R. Cockerell. Both old and new wings were embellished with oriel windows and crow-stepped gables. The entrance was moved to the centre of the south front where it is approached from the school yard by a long flight of steps and an arcaded porch. The roof is crowned by a combined clock turret and bell cupola. The building, known as the Old Schools, contains the original schoolroom with many of its fittings intact; they include the boys' benches, the masters' canopied chair and desk, the usher's table, and wainscotting on which generations of boys carved their names between 1701 and 1847.

Cockerell also designed the first school chapel, built on the east side of High Street in 1838–9. It was a red-brick building with a south-west bell turret and a curvilinear west gable above a large Perpendicular window.[49] The old chapel was replaced in stages between 1854 and 1857 by the present building, designed by G. G. (later Sir Gilbert) Scott in the Decorated style and built of flint with Bath stone dressings. When complete the chapel consisted of nave, north and south aisles of different widths, and an apsidal chancel; the spired bell turret was added in 1865 and the transepts and porches in 1902. Flanking the chapel to north and south respectively are the New Schools (1855) and the Vaughan Library (1861–3). The former, by F. Barnes, is of diaper-patterned red brick in a domestic Tudor style; it was extended in the 20th century. The Vaughan Library was designed by Scott as a symmetrical Gothic Revival building of variegated brick with elaborate stone dressings.[50] In 1874–7 the Speech Room was built on the opposite side of the road with funds raised to celebrate the tercentenary of John Lyon's charter. As the principal assembly hall of the school it was built on a semi-circular plan, the vaulted interior having tiers of seats following the curve of the back wall. The exterior design incorporates Venetian Gothic features, made popular by John Ruskin; the architect was William Burges. The straight front has a balcony on massive stone brackets with an arcaded row of Gothic win-

[40] i.e. the parkland as well as the house.
[41] *Harrow Sch.* ed. Howson and Warner, 43–52.
[42] i.e. Grove Fields, Northwick Walk Fields, and Football Field: ibid. 152–4; M.R.O., Acc. 794/17. For the school property in Harrow-on-the-Hill, see the map in Robbins, *Middlesex*, 283.
[43] In 1969 occupied by S.R.M. Engineering Ltd.
[44] Tablet on building. [45] Hist. Mon. Com. *Mdx.* 67–68.
[46] Although now called Flambards the house stands some distance from the site of the former manor-house and by 1806 was not even part of the Flambards estate: M.R.O.,

Acc. 643, 2nd deposit, survey of Northwick's estate (1806), no. 671; M.R. 612, no. 671.
[47] Unless otherwise stated the following account of the school buildings is based on E. D. Laborde, *Harrow Sch. Yesterday and Today*, chaps. iii–iv. The history of the school is given in *V.C.H. Mdx.* i. 299–302.
[48] Laborde, *Harrow Sch.* pl. on p. 68; R. Ackermann, *Free-Sch. of Harrow* (Hist. of the Colleges of Winchester etc. 1816), plates facing pp. 1, 17.
[49] Laborde, *Harrow Sch.* pl. on p. 93.
[50] See plate facing p. 180.

dows above it. Of the two angle towers, that to the south was not completed until 1924; the statue of Queen Elizabeth on its front wall was brought from Ashridge Park in the following year. Soil excavated from the foundations of the Speech Room was used to build up the terraces on the slope behind the chapel. At the north end of the terraces stand the Science Schools, built in 1874–6 to the design of C. F. Hayward and much enlarged later, and the tall gabled building housing the Museum Schools. The latter, completed in 1886, was designed by Basil Champneys in the 17th-century 'Dutch' style then fashionable; its lavish use of moulded brickwork and the arcaded angle staircase were much admired.[51] The Art School was built to the north of the Speech Room in 1896 to the design of W. C. Marshall and was extended in 1913. The most conspicuous 20th-century contribution to the school group is the War Memorial Building, erected in 1921–6. It stands behind a paved forecourt at the junction of Church Hill and High Street on a site previously occupied by older buildings used as boarding houses. The ground floor contains a memorial shrine and a ceremonial corridor leading from the forecourt to the south entrance of the Speech Room. The architect, Sir Herbert Baker, tried to harmonize his design with the adjacent buildings by using red brick, flint, stone dressings, and a mainly 17th-century style. The attempt to introduce some formal relationship between the school buildings was carried further in 1929 when houses and shops on the west side of High Street were demolished. This opened up a view of the Old Schools and gave them an axial approach from the south. The sloping site was laid out with flights of steps, lawns, and balustrades.

The Headmaster's House, on the opposite side of High Street, occupies the site of a dwelling already being rented by the schoolmaster in the 17th century. It was later enlarged to accommodate boarders, and early in the 19th century was remodelled at a cost of over £6,000. A print of 1816 shows a two-storied gabled front in the 'Tudor' style of the period with a central porch, embattled parapets, and two flanking bay windows;[52] a long wing to the north housed studies for the boys. The house was destroyed by fire in 1838, only an addition of 1836 being saved. Rebuilding took place in 1840 and a few years later a boys' wing was added and the street front was raised to three stories. Further additions were made in 1866 and 1897. The present red-brick front is largely of the mid 19th century. Tudor features include the projecting porch, the small gables to the parapet, and the hood-moulds and four-centred heads to several windows.

The main school group is continued north-eastward by a number of boarding houses built between 1850 and 1900. Nearly all are tall gabled buildings of red brick, some with Gothic features. Also in this area are the Old Music School (1873), the Copse (1901–4), and the Leaf Schools (1936). On the fringes of the group are the gymnasium and workshop (1874–6) and the New Music School (1890). The old sanatorium, opened in 1867 and now derelict, stands in Mount Park Avenue.

Several of the school boarding houses were first opened in existing houses in the town. The Grove, standing on the ancient rectory site at the summit of the hill,[53] was acquired c. 1820. It was burnt down in 1833 and rebuilt, the symmetrical Georgian front of seven bays being preserved. The building has been altered and extended at several periods. The former hanging garden belonging to the rectory occupied the steep slope between the house and what is now Grove Hill. Druries, set back from the west side of High Street at its north end, originated in a house called the Abbey. It became a boarding house at the end of the 18th century and was rebuilt in a Victorian Gothic style by C. F. Hayward in 1864. Moretons, which has a long stucco front facing the east side of High Street, was opened in 1811, rebuilt in 1828, and enlarged later. The Park stands further south and has extensive grounds falling away eastward to an ornamental lake. It was built in 1795 to replace the manor-house of Flambards and was enlarged for Lord Northwick in 1803.[54] The original approach was by a long drive from Sudbury Hill, leading to a main entrance on the east front. This front, stucco-faced like the rest of the building, retains two flanking bay windows with first-floor iron balconies. It was enlarged three times in the 19th century, after becoming a boarding house, and part was given an extra story in 1906. At this date an enriched tympanum and a Coade stone relief of a lion guardant (part of the Northwick arms) were moved from the centre of the east front to the street wall of the south wing. Bradbys, opposite the Park, is a building of grey brick with stone dressings and a classical porch, dating from 1849; it has two distinct wings which were combined as a single boarding house in 1864. Byron House in Byron Hill Road, formerly called Pond House, is no longer a boarding house but was used as such for most of the 19th century; it was the home of Matthew Arnold for a few years c. 1870. Its nucleus is a red-brick structure of three stories which may have been built by Thomas Brian, headmaster from 1691 to 1730.[55] On the west side of London Road is West Acre, converted to a boarding house from a pair of private dwellings in 1847; it was rebuilt after a fire in 1908. Other houses, including Newlands (1888), stand in Harrow Park, a cul-de-sac on the east side of London Road.

PINNER, in the north-eastern corner of Harrow parish, was on gravel-capped high land, with a river and wells.[56] Except for some Roman finds,[57] however, there is little evidence of early settlers and the etymology of the name is obscure. As a family name, 'de Pinnora', it first appears in 1232.[58] The first element may represent a personal name or the Old English *pinn*, 'pin' or 'peg', while the second element could be the Latin for 'bank or slope'. The river name, Pinn, is generally supposed to be a late back-formation.[59] Although evidence of Anglo-Saxon and early medieval occupation is completely lacking, Pinner appears in 1315–16 as one of the largest hamlets, with at least two tithings.[60] A new chapel was consecrated in 1321[61] and in 1336 Pinner was granted a weekly market and

[51] *Harrow Sch.* ed. Howson and Warner, 33–34.
[52] R. Ackermann, *Free-Sch. of Harrow*, pl. facing p. 18.
[53] See p. 252.   [54] See p. 210.
[55] *Harrow Sch.* ed. Howson and Warner, 51–52.
[56] e.g. Waxwell (*P.N. Mdx.* (E.P.N.S.), 64) and a large well in Chapel Lane (Pinner Assoc. *The Villager*, v).
[57] See above.

[58] *Cal. Chart. R.* 1226–57, 151. The family was apparently of Anglo-Saxon origin, e.g. Christian names Alfwin and Godmar. It was still associated with Pinner in 1399: *Cal. Close.* 1396–9, 492.
[59] *P.N. Mdx.* (E.P.N.S.), 5, 63–64.
[60] M.R.O., Acc. 76/2410, m. 3.
[61] See p. 255.

an annual fair.[62] In March 1383 24 people were presented for breaking the assize of ale, twice as many as in any other hamlet.[63] By 1547 there were said to be 300 communicants in Pinner, nearly 20 per cent. of the total for Harrow parish.[64] In addition to the copyhold tenements, there were 10 freehold houses and one wastehold house.[65]

The settlement pattern, small hamlets and farms linked by a maze of lanes across a large common, was apparent by the 14th century. Eleven of the 21 head tenements can be located: there were four in West End, Sweetman's Hall,[66] Clogges, Neoles,[67] and Aldridges;[68] one, Roughheads, in Love Lane[69] and another in Bridge Street;[70] two in East End, Marshes[71] and Cockparkers;[72] three around Nower Hill, of which one was called Nower Hill[73] and another Newhouse;[74] one at each end of Pinner Marsh,[75] and one, Gardiners, in the extreme north, between Potters Street and the shire ditch.[76] Others probably lay near Paines Lane,[77] East End,[78] and on the highway from Pinner to London.[79] Place-names further suggest the scattered character of the medieval settlement. Waxwell is recorded in 1274,[80] East End and Nower Hill in 1315–16,[81] Pinner Marsh in 1333,[82] Pinner Hill in 1334, and West End in 1448.[83] The surname 'de la Hacche' indicates the existence of Hatch End c. 1300.[84] Hatch End formed the boundary between Pinner and Harrow Weald, and for assessment, tithing, and open-field purposes seems always to have been divided between them. Headstone is first recorded c. 1300 as 'Hegton' or 'Heggeton',[85] home of the de la Hegge or de la Haye family mentioned as early as 1233–40.[86] There was probably a small settlement before the creation of the demesne farm here.[87]

Conversion of the forest to arable south and west of Pinner Town seems to have been well advanced by 1232.[88] It is probable that the three-field system was then already in existence. From the early 14th century, at least, the common fields were East or Long Field, Middle Field, and Down Field.[89] They were roughly rectangular and lay side by side south of Pinner Town and north of Roxeth common fields; Down Field, on the Ruislip border, was in the west, and Long Field

in the east.[90] Nower Field, which lay to the east of Pinner Road, south of Pinner Park, was by 1817 a small, isolated field.[91] Hyde and Roxborough Field, first mentioned in the early 16th century,[92] which joined Long Field on the east, and Hill and Home Field, mentioned in the 18th century,[93] were probably all associated with the small hamlet at Hyde End. Blakehall Field, which occurs from the 14th to the 16th century, can probably be identified with Roxeth Newden Field.[94] The 1547 survey[95] lists 541 a. of inclosed mainly freehold land, and 540 selions of openfield, mainly copyhold land, but not all holdings are described. At inclosure Pinner common fields covered 940a.[96] In the north and east two demesne manors had been created out of the forest by 1273–4.[97] Pinner Park probably remained woodland for most of the Middle Ages, since it was primarily a hunting enclosure,[98] but Woodhall, already in existence by 1236,[99] was an arable area of about 312 a. in the north of Pinner by c. 1285.[1] Headstone was converted into another predominately arable demesne farm after 1344.[2] There was also some assarting and inclosure and the creation of small estates which were held by socage or leased out, either separately or with one of the large demesne farms. In 1489–90 there were eight of these, mostly in the north,[3] the names of many of them retaining the element 'riding' or 'redding', which indicates their origin in clearings.[4] The most important of these was Woodridings, 158 a. to the east of Woodhall,[5] and Pinner Wood, 120 a. in the extreme north-west.[6] The northern part of Pinner at the end of the 16th century was still 'hilly and woody'[7] and even in the 1830s Albert Pell's boyhood memories of Pinner Hill stressed the loneliness of life in the house 'at the edge of a great wood'.[8]

Medieval Pinner was a settled area bounded on the north and east by demesne farms and assarts, on the west by closes, and on the south by open fields. It consisted of moderately sized estates: virgates and ½-hides. By 1547 some consolidation had taken place: the 21 head tenements were held by 15 tenants, many of whom also held freehold land, of which there were 320 a. and 54 selions.[9] Most of the land was held by the

[62] See p. 225.
[63] M.R.O., Acc. 76/2413, m. 6. There was no court at Rectory manor in 1383, but in July 1382 12 people at Harrow-on-the-Hill were presented: Acc. 974/I, m. 5.
[64] E 301/34, f. 28v.
[65] M.R.O., Acc. 1052, ff. 427–39.
[66] M.R.O., Acc. 76/2387; M.R. 612, no. 1497.
[67] M.R.O., Acc. 1052, ff. 433–9.
[68] M.R.O., Acc. 76/1941; M.R. 612, nos. 1250–2.
[69] M.R.O., Acc. 1052, f. 433. Possibly identifiable with Lyon's Mead, enfranchised in 1732: M.R.O., Acc. 76/437; M.R. 612, nos. 1508–10.
[70] M.R.O., Acc. 76/2382; M.R. 612, no. 1500.
[71] M.R.O., Acc. 76/1400, /1938; M.R. 612, no. 1450.
[72] M.R.O., Acc. 76/459–60; Acc. 794/8; M.R. 612, no. 1456.
[73] M.R.O., Acc. 76/646–7; M.R. 612, nos. 1374–6.
[74] M.R.O., Acc. 76/1904; M.R. 612, no. 1466. The third was recorded in M.R. 612, no. 1369; M.R.O., Acc. 76/1400.
[75] i.e. Pinner Marsh: M.R.O., Acc. 76/964; M.R. 612, no. 1472; Cannons: M.R.O., Acc. 76/434–5; M.R. 612, no. 1268.
[76] M.R.O., Acc. 1052, ff. 433–9.
[77] M.R.O., Acc. 76/432; Acc. 1052, ff. 433 sqq.
[78] M.R.O., Acc. 76/429.
[79] Ibid. /1902.
[80] P.N. Mdx. (E.P.N.S.), 64.
[81] M.R.O., Acc. 76/2410, m. 1.
[82] B.M. Add. Ch. 37365.
[83] P.N. Mdx. (E.P.N.S.), 65.

[84] Canterbury, Eastbridge Hosp. Archives, H(3); M.R.O., Acc. 76/2410, mm. 1, 6; P.N. Mdx. (E.P.N.S.), 64.
[85] Canterbury, Eastbridge Hosp. Archives, H(10–13).
[86] Harrow Octocent. Tracts, ix. 14.
[87] For its connexion with the lost hamlet of Norbury, see below.
[88] Cal. Chart. R. 1226–57, 151.
[89] B.M. Add. MSS. 37363, 37365; M.R.O., Acc. 76/222a, /2413, m. 77. [90] M.R. 612.
[91] Nower Field was first recorded in 1547 (M.R.O., Acc. 1052, ff. 433–9), but 'atte Nore' is mentioned in 1315–16 (Acc. 76/2410, m. 1d).
[92] Lambeth Palace, Estate MS. 477.
[93] M.R.O., Acc. 76/461–2, /646–7. See p. 196.
[94] See p. 195.
[95] M.R.O., Acc. 1052, ff. 427–39.
[96] M.R.O., Acc. 784/8.
[97] B.M. Add. MS. 29794. [98] See p. 205.
[99] Lambeth Palace, Estate MS. 1193.
[1] Ibid. 2068. [2] See p. 204.
[3] Lambeth Palace, Estate MS. 1219, mm. 9–9d. 'Tanrudine' already existed c. 1285: ibid. 2068. Tan Redding and Wat Redding were later part of Barrow Point (Bury Pond) estate: Pinner Assoc. The Villager, li.
[4] P.N. Mdx. (E.P.N.S.), 203.
[5] M.R.O., Acc. 76/222a, /397b.
[6] B.M. Add. Ch. 24494.
[7] B.M. Harl. MS. 570, f. 13.
[8] Pinner Assoc. The Villager, vii.
[9] M.R.O., Acc. 1052, ff. 427–39.

Edlins, Streets, Readings, and Birds, who dominated Pinner during the 16th and 17th centuries,[10] but by the end of the period important newcomers were building country houses. The interest of outsiders was already apparent in the 16th century when the Bacon family leased Pinner Park.[11] In the 17th century there were Sir Christopher Clitherow (d. 1641), Lord Mayor of London and Governor of the East India Company, and his son, also a London merchant, who owned Pinner Hill and Pinner Wood,[12] Sir Edward Waldo (d. 1707),[13] Simon Rewse of Headstone, the Royalist,[14] and Sir Bartholomew Shower (d. 1701) of Pinner Hill, a judge at the trial of the seven bishops.[15] In the 18th century there were Lord and Lady Hunsdon at Church House and at Cannons mansion-house,[16] which existed by c. 1630,[17] the poet laureate Henry John Pye (d. 1813), who gave occasion for the nursery rhyme 'Sing a song of sixpence', who lived at East End House,[18] and Sir Michael Foster (d. 1763), a justice of the King's Bench, at the Grove in Pinner Marsh.[19] John Zephaniah Holwell (d. 1798), Governor of Bengal and survivor of the Black Hole of Calcutta, lived at Pinner Place.[20] James Lightboun (d. 1738), Master of Chancery, and Lady Jane Brydges, lived in Pinner Hill, [21]Admiral John O. Spranger at Pinner Hall,[22] and Charles Palmer (d. 1777) at Paines Place[23] and the 18th-century Pinner House.[24] Farm-houses on the site of ancient head tenements, for example Nower Hill Cottage[25] and Sweetman's Hall,[26] illustrated the prosperity of local families. Cottages included one newly erected near Waxwell in 1655,[27] which was part of an underset holding, and no. 33 Love Lane, built in the late 17th century.[28] Several of the medieval farm-houses on the demesne manors were rebuilt.[29] Wastehold properties multiplied from 16 in 1553,[30] including 3 barns and a smith's house and forge, to 33 c. 1600.[31] There were 44 c. 1642,[32] when 186 adult males took the protestation oath.[33] Twenty-two years later 143 houses were listed for the hearth tax, 61 more than in Harrow Town,[34] although only 64 were charged. John Hawtrey was assessed for 15 hearths[35] and John Hutchinson for 14;[36] two others were assessed for 10 hearths and John Edlin for 8 hearths.

There were 85 parcels of wastehold by the end of the 17th century,[37] many of which had been granted recently for the first time. They included 13 cottages, among them one at Bury Pond Hill (1665), one at Pinner Green (1672), one each at Pinner Marsh and

Pinner Bridge (1682), one in Pinner Street near the church (1696), one in Waxwell Lane, and three on Pinner Common at an unknown date. Other wastehold properties included 17 barns and cart- or woodhouses, a shop and slaughter-house, a smith's shop, a bowling-alley, and a long walk planted with elms before Cannons mansion-house. Most of the other parcels were yards or orchards, usually adjoining a dwelling-house. Encroachment continued when 46 new parcels were granted, mostly in the first and third decades of the 18th century.[38] Twenty-seven supported cottages or larger houses, including a nonconformist meeting-house and the poor-house. Three cottages were at Bury Pond Hill, two at Hatch End, two at Pinner Green, and one each in the Marsh, West End, Pinner Town, and Pinner Wood Lane Green. Very few barns or cart-houses were erected, most of the other parcels being small inclosures and including two rows of trees which probably formed a drive to Pinner Hall. In addition to the wastehold property there were new cottages or messuages at West End in 1747[39] and Bury Pond Hill in 1755.[40]

By 1759 Pinner had a complicated system of roads.[41] There were two north–south routes: one on the west side, from Potters Street Lane across Pinner Common, through West End and the common fields, where it became Bourne or Rayners Lane,[42] to Roxeth; the other route, on the east, ran from Oxhey Lane, through Hatch End and Hooking or Hooken Green to Harrow-on-the-Hill,[43] and was connected to Pinner Town through Nower Hill. A road ran from west to east along the southern edge of Woodhall Farm to Hatch End and the Weald. The hamlets of Pinner, Pinner Hill, West End, Pinner Town, East End, Pinner Marsh, and Bury Pond Hill, were linked by a series of access roads.

Two branches of the Pinn joined just north of Pinner Town, to flow southward through the town and Pinner Marsh and then turn west at Cannons Farm. Further south, the Yeading Brook flowed from east to west across the common fields into Ruislip parish. One of the earliest bridging points must have been at the western end of Pinner Town. The 1759 map shows the Pinn running across a broad road from Pinner Town to Pinner Marsh. At each side of this ford there was a footbridge, which in 1686[44] was the responsibility of the lord of the manor. The ford was inadequate for the traffic from Harrow to Rickmansworth, and in 1809 a brick bridge of two arches was

---

[10] See pp. 214–15.
[11] C 3/152/6; /222/48; Cal. S.P. Dom. 1581–90, 2, 5; Hist. MSS. Com. 11th Rep. App. IV, 5.
[12] Ware, Pinner, 153–6, 169; M.R.O., Acc. 76/409; Home Cnties. Mag. v. 213–20.
[13] See p. 216.
[14] See p. 204.
[15] Ware, Pinner, 153–6.
[16] Ibid. 84; M.R.O., Acc. 310(4). Grace, Lady Hunsdon, was the daughter of Sir Edward Waldo: M.R.O., Acc. 76/2433, ff. 166, 322.
[17] M.R.O., Acc. 76/210.
[18] Ware, Pinner, 66, 95. The rhyme, supposedly by some M.P.s, alluded to the poet's extravagant expressions about birds.
[19] Ware, Pinner, 111.
[20] Ibid. 76, 165.
[21] Ibid. 154. Cf. M.R.O., Acc. 643, 2nd deposit, Messeder map A.
[22] At Pinner Hall 1795–1819: Ware, Pinner, 113; M.R.O., Acc. 76/493.
[23] There was a freehold tenement called Paynes to the east of Paynes Lane in 1547: M.R.O., Acc. 1052, ff. 427 sqq.

[24] Ware, Pinner, 156; M.R.O., Acc. 76/212. See p. 182.
[25] A 16th-cent. timber-framed cottage: Pinner Assoc. The Villager, ix.
[26] See p. 214.
[27] M.R.O., Acc. 854/12.
[28] Pinner Assoc. The Villager, lvii.
[29] See pp. 204–5.
[30] M.R.O., Acc. 76/222a.
[31] Ibid. /205.
[32] M.R.O., Acc. 794/2.
[33] Hse. of Lords, Mdx. Protestation Rets.
[34] M.R.O., H.T. 5.
[35] Pinner Hill, see p. 182.
[36] Pinner Park, see p. 181.
[37] M.R.O., Acc. 76/210, /707.
[38] Ibid. /210, /1109.
[39] M.R.O., Acc. 310(3).
[40] M.R.O., Acc. 76/696–7.
[41] M.R.O., Acc. 643, 2nd deposit, Messeder map A, the earliest accurate map.
[42] Ware, Pinner, 178–9.
[43] See p. 256.
[44] M.R.O., Acc. 76/1653–4.

built by the trustees of the Rickmansworth turnpike, who repaired it in 1820. It was unsatisfactory by 1894, and a few years later a new bridge was built by Pinner Parish Council.[45] Pinner Marsh, to the south-west of Pinner Town, was especially subject to flooding, and no road across it is marked in 1759. In 1728, however, Lady Hunsdon rebuilt a bridge near Cannons Farm, which may be identifiable with Pinner Marsh Bridge, a wooden footbridge mentioned in 1686–7. Before inclosure a road from Hunsdon Bridge led south-westward through the open fields to Eastcote. In 1806 it became a cul-de-sac, and Rayners Lane to the east became the main route to Roxeth, while a new road to Eastcote was built to the west. Where previously the road to West End had run beside the river to Cannons Farm, it was diverted northward to join the new road just north of its bridging point. The road across Pinner Marsh appears on post-inclosure maps, which show it bridging the Pinn again just north of Pinner Grove.[46] The eastern branch of the Pinn was crossed by Paines Lane at Paine's Bridge, which was repaired by the lord of the manor in the late 17th century,[47] although in 1814 Lord Northwick asserted that the vestry was responsible.[48] There were at least two other crossings over the branches of the Pinn along the Uxbridge road in 1686: Lewis Bridge, at Bury Pond Hill, was a wooden footbridge by a ford, and Woodhall Bridge was a stockbridge repaired by Mr. Wilkinson, the owner of Woodhall Farm.[49] In 1825 there were said to be three fords and footbridges on this road.[50] Except at Headstone manor, by whose entrance a new bridge was built c. 1466,[51] the Yeading Brook had only Hooking Green Bridge, a footbridge on the London–Pinner road. In 1685 it was a 'danger to life and goods', but the lord of the manor, who was urged to repair it, seems to have denied responsibility.[52] To the west of Hooking Green, Bourne (later Rayners) Lane crossed the Yeading Brook but was unbridged until the late 19th century.[53]

By 1759 the common had been reduced to little more than 260 a., made up of Pinner Common or Green (195 a.) and a number of small commons:[54] Bury Pond Hill (25 a.), Pinner Marsh (26 a.), Pinner Hill Green (11 a.), and Hooking Green[55] and Hatch End.[56] There were about 184 buildings in Pinner.[57] Houses and shops presented a continuous front on either side of Pinner High Street, thinning out slightly along Church Lane, the southern part of Paines Lane, Bridge Street, and Marsh Road. There were smaller groups in West and East End, at Pinner Wood Lane Green,[58] and at Hatch End. There were scattered settlements at Bury Pond Hill, along the northern

part of Waxwell Lane, in Pinner Marsh, Nower Hill, and Pinner Hill, and along the southern edge of Pinner Common where the Bell Inn already stood. Isolated farms were Headstone, Pinner Park, Woodhall, Cannons, Dove House, and Oxhey Lane.

There were several inns in 1759.[59] The 'Queen's Head' at the upper end of the High Street, was licensed from 1751.[60] The 'Red Lion' in Bridge Street existed by 1737;[61] it was rebuilt in 1875 and demolished in 1963.[62] The 'George' in Marsh Road, which was rebuilt in 1889, was also licensed from 1751,[63] as was the 'Bell' on Pinner Green in the north, which has been rebuilt several times, most recently in 1930.[64] The Crown Inn (closed in 1896)[65] and the White Hart beershop, both in the High Street, were first licensed in 1759. The 'Crown' may be identifiable with the 'Lower Queen's Head', which was licensed in 1751 but disappeared from the lists after 1759. Other Pinner inns, whose whereabouts are unknown, were the 'Chequers', licensed from 1751, a second 'Chequers', licensed in 1759, and the 'Crooked Billet', licensed 1759–60.[66]

In 1801 there were 140 inhabited houses and a population of 761.[67] These figures, compared with those of 1664, suggest that the 18th century was a period of rebuilding rather than of expansion. The distribution of houses in 1805 was essentially the same as in 1759.[68] There were about 52 houses in Pinner Town, including the inns and the poor-house. Eighteen houses, mostly cottages but including a windmill and the Bell Inn, were scattered across Pinner Common, mainly along the southern edge. West End, with two farms and 11 houses, was the next most densely populated area, followed by Pinner Wood Lane Green with about 13 cottages, and Hatch End, with a farm and about 8 other houses.[69] East End also had about 9 houses, and there were between 3 and 5 houses in each of the other hamlets, Pinner Marsh, Bury Pond Hill, Waxwell, Nower Hill, and Pinner Wood. Apart from a few farm cottages at Headstone, the isolated farms were as in 1759. More houses were built early in the 19th century,[70] especially on the waste, which was further reduced by 1817 to 196 a., 162 a. of which formed Pinner Common.[71] In 1811 there were 1,078 people in 167 houses but by 1821 there were still only 1,076 people in 181 houses. Ten years later there was a population of 1,270. In 1841 the 1,331 inhabitants included 56 haymakers living in barns, which explains the apparent drop to 1,310 in 1851, when there were 258 inhabited houses. The opening of Hatch End railway station in 1844 created new settlement areas, and made Pinner attractive to

[45] Rep. of Pub. Bridges in Mdx. (1825), 211–14 penes M.R.O.; Ware, Pinner, 41–42.
[46] Ware, Pinner, 45–46, 138–9; M.R.O., Acc. 76/1653–5; Acc. 643, 2nd deposit, Messeder map A; M.R. 612; O.S. Map 1/2,500, Mdx. x. 6 (1865 edn.).
[47] M.R.O., Acc. 76/1654.
[48] Ibid. /1296–9.
[49] Ibid. /1653, /1655.
[50] Rep. of Pub. Bridges in Mdx. (1825), 211–14.
[51] Lambeth Palace, Estate MS. 1214.
[52] M.R.O., Acc. 76/1649, /1653.
[53] Ware, Pinner, 178–81.
[54] M.R.O., Acc. 643, 2nd deposit, Messeder map A.
[55] Included in 109 a. of roads and small greens.
[56] Reckoned with Weald Common: see p. 185.
[57] The number is approximate because of dense concentration in Pinner Town.
[58] i.e. later Bridge Street and lower part of Waxwell Lane.
[59] See article in Pinner Assoc. The Villager, xliv.

[60] M.R.O., L.V. 7/1; O.S. Map 1/2,500, Mdx. x. 3 (1865 edn.).
[61] Ware, Pinner, 182.
[62] Panorama of Pinner Village, ed. E. J. S. Gadsden (1969).
[63] M.R.O., L.V. 7/1; J. W. Perry, Panorama of Pinner Village (pamphlet, 1947); O.S. Map 6", Mdx. x. NW. (1897 edn.).
[64] O.S. Map 1/2,500, Mdx. x. 2 (1865 edn.); Pinner Assoc. The Villager, xxvii.
[65] M.R.O., P.S. G/H5/1.
[66] M.R.O., L.V. 7/1, /37.
[67] Census, 1801.
[68] M.R.O., Acc. 76/1400.
[69] i.e. on the Pinner side.
[70] Unless otherwise stated, the rest of this paragraph is based upon Census, 1801–51.
[71] M.R.O., Acc. 794/8.

HARROW-ON-THE-HILL FROM THE SOUTH-EAST IN 1805
Showing Harrow Park on the extreme left and the Grove to the right of St. Mary's Church

HARROW SCHOOL
The Vaughan Library between the Chapel and the Headmaster's House

PINNER: HIGH STREET FROM THE WEST IN 1828

HARROW-ON-THE-HILL FROM THE SOUTH IN 1824

Showing High Street, St. Mary's Church, the Old Schools as remodelled in 1819–20, and, in the right
foreground, the wall of Harrow Park

wealthy Londoners. In 1851 there were six landed proprietors,[72] three 'proprietors of houses', five 'fundholders', three merchants, seven members of the legal and three of the medical profession, a publisher, a portrait-painter, a civil engineer, an army magistrate, a 'gentleman', and an 'independent lady'.[73] Nineteenth-century inhabitants included the Milman family of the Grove, of whom the first, Sir Francis Milman (1746–1821), was physician to Queen Charlotte,[74] Edward Bulwer-Lytton, who wrote *Eugene Aram* in 1831–3 at Pinnerwood House,[75] Mrs. Beeton (d. 1865) who lived at Woodridings,[76] and Mrs. Horatia Nelson Ward (d. 1881), the daughter of Nelson and Lady Hamilton, who lived in West Lodge and Woodridings.[77] The eye specialist Dr. Edwin Chesshire (b. 1819) at Dingles[78] and the historian James Gairdner (d. 1912) at Arden[79] were among those who built or rebuilt houses.[80] Other inhabitants include the novelists George Gissing (d. 1903),[81] and Ivy Compton-Burnett (d. 1969), who was born in Pinner in 1884,[82] Sir Ernest Jelf, King's Remembrancer, who from 1898 until his death in 1949 lived in turn at Acorn, Pinner Road, at Church Farm, and at St. Mary's Cottage in Waxwell Lane,[83] and Howard Spring the novelist, who in the late 1930s contributed to *The Villager*, the journal of the Pinner Association.

In 1861 there were 337 inhabited houses and a population of 1,849. This increase was explained by the opening of the Royal Commercial Travellers' Schools in 1856 and by the building of villas, probably on the first housing estate, at Woodridings.[84] By 1871 there were 2,382 people and 396 houses. When the Metropolitan line was driven through the centre of Pinner in the 1880s, the Baptist chapel and other buildings were destroyed, and the Rugby House estate was acquired by the Metropolitan Railway Co. as building land.[85] By 1893 the working class was said to be having difficulty in finding cottages in Pinner, partly because the cottages were being replaced by new housing estates. Cecil Park estate, south of the railway, was begun just before the First World War, and by 1916 building covered most of central Pinner.[86] The new settlements at Headstone, Woodridings, and Royston Park grew at the same time, and the population rose from 2,729 in 1891 to 3,366 in 1901, 7,103 in 1911 and 9,462 in 1921. By 1951, when Pinner was divided into three wards totalling 3,381 a.,[87] there was a population of 44,392. Ten years later the number had risen to 46,651. There were then 15,579 dwelling-houses, and a density of 13·7 per acre, compared with

2·5 in 1921, and 0·8 in 1901. Since most of Pinner Town was already settled by 1920, high-density housing and flats were substituted for cottages and large houses, especially when the latter had extensive grounds. Among property demolished were Bridge House (1932),[88] cottages in High Street (1933)[89] and Chapel Lane,[90] Dear's Farm,[91] Pinner Green Lodge (1935),[92] cottages in Marsh Road,[93] Paines Lane,[94] and Bridge Street (1939),[95] the Grove (1950),[96] Antoneys (1952),[97] West End Lodge and Howard Place (1953),[98] Pinner Place (1954),[99] Pinner Hall,[1] cottages in Pinner Hill Road, Love Lane (1956) and West End Lane, and East House (1957).[2]

Although by 1968 it had become part of suburban Middlesex, a residue of the older Pinner has remained, largely because of the work of the Pinner Association.[3] Parks and other recreational open spaces, of which the largest are Pinner Hill Golf Course and the sports ground at Headstone Manor, have helped to preserve a rural aspect. Three farms, Pinner Park,[4] Oxhey Lane, and Pinnerwood, survive, although the extensive pasture land at Pinner Park has been cut in two by George V Avenue and has been entirely surrounded by modern building. Headstone Manor House,[5] probably the oldest surviving domestic building in Pinner, also enjoys something approaching its original setting.

At the same time the town centre, still known locally as the 'village', retains much of its earlier character, with its ancient street pattern and many old buildings. In 1968 High Street was designated a Conservation Area under the Civic Amenities Act.[6] The street, widening at both ends, rises gradually towards the east where the vista is closed by the 15th-century tower of the parish church. In spite of the insertion of shop fronts and some incongruous rebuilding, the original scale of the street has in general been maintained.[7] Early houses on the south side include an L-shaped timber-framed building (nos. 4 and 6) which is dated 1580 but may well be older; it is jettied on two sides and has a moulded angle post supporting a heavy curved bracket. No. 26 is also timber-framed and no. 32 is an 18th-century brick house with a symmetrical two-storied front, a central pediment, and an arched recess enclosing the doorway and semi-circular fanlight. Nos. 34 and 36 are timber-framed, consisting of a jettied and gabled cross-wing and a main block which, with its chimney, was probably rebuilt in the 17th century; at the rear is a 17th-century timber barn. On the north side of the street no. 7 is a narrow gabled building, refronted in brick

[72] Excluding those who called themselves farmers.
[73] H.O. 107/1700, ff. 173–220.
[74] Ware, *Pinner*, 111; *D.N.B.*
[75] Ware, *Pinner*, 169; Robbins, *Middlesex*, 321.
[76] Ware, *Pinner*, 221; Pinner Assoc. *The Villager*, xix.
[77] Ware, *Pinner*, 141.
[78] Ibid. 92.
[79] Ibid. 104.
[80] For the more important of these houses, see below.
[81] Robbins, *Middlesex*, 321.
[82] *The Times*, 28 Aug. 1969.
[83] Ware, *Pinner*, 129–30; Pinner Assoc. *The Villager*, vii.
[84] See p. 199. Except where otherwise stated, this paragraph is based on *Census*, 1861–1961.
[85] M.R.O., *Reps. of Local Inqs.* (1889–97), p. 327; Pinner Assoc. *The Villager*, viii, xvi, xxv, xxx.
[86] O.S. Map 6″, Mdx. x. NW. (1916 edn.).
[87] See p. 245.
[88] Ware, *Pinner*, 41.
[89] Pinner Assoc. *The Villager*, xxv.
[90] Ware, *Pinner*, 51, 180.

[91] Pinner Assoc. *The Villager*, xxix.
[92] Dating from the 18th century: Ware, *Pinner*, 134–5.
[93] Ibid. 180.
[94] Ibid.; Pinner Assoc. *The Villager*, iv.
[95] Ibid. v.
[96] Ibid. xxx, xxxv; Ware, *Pinner*, 112.
[97] Pinner Assoc. *The Villager*, xxviii, xxxiii; Ware, *Pinner*, 10–11. A house called Antoneys existed in 1658; M.R.O., Acc. 276/3/49.
[98] Ware, *Pinner*, 213, 125.
[99] Ibid. 167; Pinner Assoc. *The Villager*, xli, xlvii.
[1] Ware, *Pinner*, 113; Pinner Assoc. *The Villager*, xix, lii.
[2] Pinner Assoc. *The Villager*, lviii, lvii, lix.
[3] See p. 237.
[4] See p. 205.
[5] See p. 205.
[6] *Panorama of Pinner Village*, ed. Gadsden, preface.
[7] See pl. on facing page. For further details of buildings in High Street and elsewhere dating from before 1714, see Hist. Mon. Com. *Mdx.* 103–4.

and dated 1721. No. 11, a much-restored timber-framed house, retains an early-16th-century mullion-ed window. Nos. 25 and 27 were brick-faced in the 18th century, but are structurally of timber. The 'Queen's Head' and the adjoining house probably date from the late 16th century, the former having a long jettied front with restored timbering and an inn sign spanning the pavement. Next to it another timber-framed house has two front gables. The street front-age ends with two brick houses of the 18th and early 19th centuries.

At the east end of High Street Paines Lane and Church Lane branch off to north and south of the church. On the north side of this junction a small green, bordered with chestnut trees, was given to the town as a permanent open space in 1924.[8] Set behind the green is Church Farm, a long low roughcast building roofed with old tiles. The east end, with its gabled cross-wing, is timber-framed and probably 17th century, while wings to the north and west are 18th-century additions. The group by the church is completed by a much-restored timber-framed build-ing, now Cornerways Restaurant, and a plain three-storied 18th-century house with a tile-hung addition designed by Sir Ernest George in 1878;[9] the latter was once the Cocoa Tree Tavern and later the Conserva-tive Club.

Church Lane is a winding road containing detached houses of various dates and sizes with some modern infilling in the formerly large gardens. Next to the churchyard is Chestnut Cottage, a gabled and plastered house probably of 18th-century origin with early-19th-century additions. Further east stands Pinner House, dated 1721. The three-storied red brick front is of five bays, the central bay being crowned by a pediment and flanked on the upper stories by tall pilasters.[10] The house became an old people's home in 1948.[11] Mount Cottage is of 18th-century red brick and Grange Cottage is an altered timber-framed structure perhaps of 16th-century origin. Several medium-sized houses were built during the first half of the 19th century. Two of the largest, which date from the middle of the century, are Elmdene (formerly New House) and the Grange (formerly Rugby House).[12]

The junction of Church Lane, Nower Hill, and Moss Lane is marked by a small triangular green on which stands a Gothic drinking fountain erected in memory of W. A. Tooke in 1886.[13] The house known as Nower Hill (formerly Nower Hill Cottage), which had been enlarged by Ambrose Heal in 1895,[14] was demolished c. 1960. Heal's architect was Cecil Brewer who also designed the Fives Court opposite, a good example of the domestic architecture of the first decade of the 20th century; it was built for Heal's son, later Sir Ambrose Heal.[15] A group of 16th-century buildings in Moss Lane probably represents the nucleus of the former hamlet of East End. At East End Farm are two weather-boarded barns of the 16th

and 17th centuries and a small timber-framed house, East End Farm Cottage, dating from the early 15th century with 16th-century additions. The additions include a rare porch of foiled barge-boards and tiled roof and an exceptionally fine wall-painting.[16] Further south East End House is an altered 18th-century building of red brick, and Tudor Cottage is an irregu-larly shaped timber-framed house with the date 1592 on its chimney. Moss Lane and Paines Lane are residential roads similar in character to Church Lane but with a higher proportion of modern buildings. At their junction stands Moss Cottage, a partly timber-framed and weather-boarded house of 17th-century origin, refronted and enlarged by Judge William Barber in 1887.[17] Further west Waxwell Lane con-tains several timber-framed cottages and some small terraced houses of the 19th century. Waxwell Farm-house is a large early-17th-century timber building with a brick extension of the 18th century. In West End Lane a few houses have survived from the former hamlet of West End. They include Sweetman's Hall,[18] the remains of West House,[19] which was presented to the urban district council in 1948 by the Pinner War Memorial Fund Committee,[20] and two brick houses (nos. 32 and 40) of the earlier 19th century.

At Hatch End the only old building still standing is Letchford House, a timber-framed farm-house of the mid 17th century, with later brick additions, inserted sash windows, and a Georgian porch. It may owe its name to Dr. Letchford (d. 1665) who, with his wife, is buried in the chancel of the parish church.[21] At the Woodridings estate, on the south side of Uxbridge Road, nearly all the original houses, which were built in pairs and completed by 1855,[22] have been replaced by modern villas and blocks of flats. The few which remain are plain but substantial three-storied dwell-ings with round-headed windows to their second floors. The Railway Hotel, facing the main road, is in the same style.

In the northern part of the parish, formerly a thinly populated area, only a few pre-20th-century buildings survive. They include the 18th-century farm-house at Oxhey Lane Farm and the former farm-house at Woodhall.[23] Clonard, which was built in Oxhey Lane by Sir Alexander Edward Miller in the 1890s[24] and later became the Convent of Our Lady of Lourdes, was pulled down in 1968. The house at Pinner Hill or Pinner Wood owned by the Clitherow family in the mid 17th century is likely to have been the building on which John Hawtrey was assessed for 15 hearths in 1664.[25] No house of this description has survived in the area, nor can its site now be identified. The isolated group of buildings at Pinner Wood is still surrounded by fields and woodland. Pinnerwood House is a timber-framed structure of c. 1600, con-sisting of a range of two bays with a single original chimney and a cross-wing which has evidently been reduced in length at some period. The entrance hall contains 17th-century panelling but carving on the

8 Tablet on tree-trunk.
9 Ware, *Pinner*, 87–88.
10 Photo. in Pinner Assoc. *The Villager*, xliv.
11 Ware, *Pinner*, 157.
12 O.S. Map 1/2,500, Mdx. x. 6 (1865 edn.); Pinner Assoc. *The Villager*, xvi, xxx.
13 Inscription on fountain.
14 O.S. Map 1/2,500, Mdx. x. 6 (1865 edn.); Ware, *Pinner*, 142.
15 Ware, *Pinner*, 142–3; *Country Life*, 7 Oct. 1909.
16 Ex inf. Dept. of Architecture, Greater London

Council.
17 Ware, *Pinner*, 139.
18 See p. 214.
19 See p. 211.
20 Bor. of Harrow, *Facts & Figures* (1963–4), 79.
21 Ware, *Pinner*, 134.
22 See p. 199.
23 See p. 204.
24 Ware, *Pinner*, 139. Miller was Commissioner of Railways and Master in Lunacy.
25 See p. 179.

staircase and elsewhere is thought to be Italian work recently introduced. Although the house was formerly of greater extent it is a comparatively modest two-storied structure and is unlikely to have formed part of the Clitherow mansion. Pinnerwood Farm, with a farm-house dating from the later 19th century, lies east of the house. Also in the group is Pinnerwood Cottage, a mid-19th-century brick residence said to have replaced an earlier building destroyed by fire.[26] The existing mansion at Pinner Hill, now the club house of Pinner Hill Golf Club, stands on much higher ground about half a mile further west. Its oldest part dates from the late 18th century and is a brown brick building of two stories and attics, having a symmetrical east front with a central pediment; bay windows and a verandah at the south end may be early-19th-century additions. In 1844 the estate, which included Pinner Hill Farm to the south and 185 a. of farmland, woods, and parkland, was bought by William Tooke for his son A. W. Tooke.[27] The latter was probably responsible for adding a new west front and an octagonal kitchen to the house, both elaborately designed in a mixture of Gothic and Tudor styles. Pinner Hill Golf Club acquired the property in 1927 and laid out their 18-hole course over part of the grounds.[28] The approach roads were built up with architect-designed houses in large gardens, forming one of the most select residential areas of Pinner. Woodhall Towers, built by A. W. Tooke in 1864 to the east of what is now Woodhall Drive, was demolished in 1965. Known locally as Tooke's Folly, it was an ornate, almost grotesque, structure of multi-coloured brick with Gothic features derived from French or German models.[29] A clock tower, built by Tooke in a similar style, was still standing at the former Pinner Hill Farm in 1968.

HARROW WEALD, known for most of its history as the Weald, was originally a large forested area unfavourable to settlement.[30] Although the lord's main profit long remained the wood and its products,[31] tenants were holding arable land from the early 13th century.[32] There were 12 medieval head tenements: one hide, eight ½-hides, and three virgates.[33] The messuages of some of them can probably be identified. One was on the site of Waldo's Farm, east of Hatch End,[34] where the miser Daniel Dancer (1716–94) lived, surrounded by farm-land which he left fallow in order to avoid the expense of cultivation.[35] There

were several head tenements between Hatch End and Wealdstone: Astmiss,[36] one at Causeway Gate,[37] and probably two others.[38] Weeles[39] and Deerings[40] were situated further east. The position of the head tenements and the description of their open fields suggests that there was never one nucleated hamlet. Clearing of woodland proceeded from the south, and a settlement grew up south-east of the forest, at Harrow Weald or, as it was called in the 18th century,[41] the Lower End of Weald. This was probably the earliest hamlet, to which were attached the main common fields on the south, separated from Greenhill common fields by the Lidding or Wealdstone Brook.[42] Great Field, an elongated field, and its western neighbour Middle Field are recorded in the 14th century.[43] The third field, Church Field, which joined Middle Field on the west, is not mentioned before 1507–8,[44] but it can probably be identifield with Bridge Field (Breggefeld 1383)[45] and North Field (1485–6), described as 'next to Churchbridge'.[46]

The second area of settlement straggled along the south-western edge of the forest, with slightly denser concentrations at Hatch End and north Wealdstone. Its common fields have all the appearance of assarting. At inclosure they were small, irregular blocks lying west and north of the main common fields.[47] Broad Field, the northernmost, lay south-east of Hatch End. As 'le Brodefelde in Hatch-end', it was in 1462[48] apparently a close, part of Wolsey's virgate;[49] it was a close in 1649[50] but had become an open field by the early 19th century.[51] The other open fields were Bugbeards or Bugbirds Field, which joined Broad Field on the south-east and took its name from an old local family,[52] Hatchets or Hatches Field, Smynells, Swinnells, or Spinnells Field, and Bingers or Byngers Field. All occur in the 18th century[53] and Byngers was part of Greenhill copy-hold in 1547.[54] Hampet Field, mentioned in 1383,[55] and partly inclosed by 1629,[56] still existed in 1719;[57] it may have been another name for one of the common fields marked on the inclosure map, or it may have been one of many assarted fields which were later inclosed. In 1817 the common fields of the Weald amounted to 538 a.[58]

The eastern side of the forest was granted, probably in the early 13th century, to the newly founded priory of Bentley,[59] whose estate stretched into Great Stanmore parish. By 1248 some at least of the

[26] Ex inf. Mrs. L. M. Craven, occupier of Pinnerwood House in 1969.
[27] Harrow Cent. Ref. Libr., Sales Partics. For Wm. Tooke F.R.S. (d. 1863) see *D.N.B.*
[28] Pinner Hill Golf Club, *Official Handbook* (1967), 5.
[29] Ware, *Pinner*, 155, 219; Druett, *Pinner*, 130–1; *Panorama of Pinner Village* (1969), illustration and caption.
[30] *P.N. Mdx.* (E.P.N.S.), 53.
[31] See pp. 221–2.
[32] Lambeth Palace, Estate MS. 1193.
[33] M.R.O., Acc. 76/222a. From 1573–4 three hides were described as ½-hides: ibid. /214.
[34] M.R.O., Acc. 76/1633; M.R. 612, no. 371.
[35] He always wore rags and once lost a lawsuit against a tradesman over 3d. After his death in 1794 his farm was ransacked and his grave opened in the search for his supposed wealth: M.R.O., D.R.O. 3/B2/3; *D.N.B.*
[36] M.R.O., Acc. 76/1920; Acc. 794/8; M.R. 612, no. 330.
[37] M.R.O., Acc. 76/1920; M.R. 612, no. 333.
[38] M.R.O., Acc. 76/634–5.
[39] Ibid. /625–6.
[40] Ibid. /641–2.
[41] M.R.O., Acc. 643, 2nd deposit, Messeder map A;

Acc. 76/641–2, /625–6.
[42] M.R. 612.
[43] M.R.O., Acc. 76/2413, mm. 61, 73, 77.
[44] Lambeth Palace, Estate MS. 477.
[45] M.R.O., Acc. 76/2413, m. 6.
[46] Ibid. /2420, m. 3.
[47] M.R. 612.
[48] M.R.O., Acc. 76/2418, m. 2.
[49] Wolsey, a head tenant, was probably responsible for the story that Cardinal Wolsey was connected with Pinner.
[50] M.R.O., Acc. 643, m. 2 and d.
[51] The evidence of the inclosure map is reinforced by an enfranchisement of 1820 which mentions an allotment in Broad Field: M.R.O., Acc. 76/1633.
[52] Mentioned in 1315–16: M.R.O., Acc. 76/2410, m. 6.
[53] M.R.O., Acc. 76/1513, /634–5.
[54] M.R.O., Acc. 1052, ff. 263 sqq. The survey does not describe Harrow Weald's common fields.
[55] M.R.O., Acc. 76/2413, m. 6.
[56] Ibid. /1010.
[57] Ibid. /1513.
[58] M.R.O., Acc. 794/2.
[59] See p. 206.

woodland had been cleared for arable farming[60] and by the 16th century the whole estate seems to have been converted into farm-land.[61] The priory's tenants and labourers probably built cottages along the eastern edge of the common. One of the lord's assarts survives in Old Redding, now a road.[62] The rentals suggest that the waste and wood still extended far south at the end of the Middle Ages. Apart from the Bentley Priory estate, described as a freehold carucate, the oldest holdings were the customary head tenements, which had their messuages in the settlements of the Lower End of Weald, north Wealdstone and Hatch End, and their lands in the common fields. Assarting, in some cases in the early 14th century,[63] produced freehold estates, mainly small and situated in the south-east.[64] By 1553 there were 16 free tenements, most of them closes.[65] From the Middle Ages, the Weald's population was second only to that of Pinner. By 1316 it had at least two tithings[66] and 9 people were presented for breaking the assize of ale in 1383.[67] Charcoal-burning also helped to support the population.[68]

Settlement seems to have expanded in the 1540s and 1550s. Three parcels inclosed out of the waste were granted as copyhold under Henry VIII, and thereafter inclosures were granted as wastehold. By 1553 there were already 17 wasteholds,[69] including Cornerhall, 'Brookes' cottage, and an unnamed house. There were 36 wastehold parcels c. 1600, including at least five more dwellings, some of them held by junior members of families who held the head tenements—the Warrens, Bugbeards, or Hatches.[70] The erection of unlicensed cottages and hovels explains an apparent drop in wastehold properties, to 35 in 1629,[71] and the small rise, to 42 by c. 1642.[72] An enquiry in 1618 revealed that 10 people had built houses and another 12 had encroached on the lord's waste.[73] They were all ordered to open their encroachments on pain of a 40s. fine, but in 1629 the order had to be repeated.[74] Sir Gilbert Gerard complained that his trees had been cut down in 1638 by men 'of mean condition, who live upon spoil and rapine', whom George Pitt had bribed by agreeing to grant by copy of court roll the illegal cottages which they had erected in Weald Wood.[75] Between 1633 and 1696 55 parcels of waste were granted, mostly in the 1680s;[76] 40 undated

parcels were also granted, probably before 1681.[77] In 1664, of the 106 houses in the Weald, 43 were not chargeable with hearth tax.[78] Of the 95 wastehold properties by the end of the 17th century, 50 were cottages, sometimes with barns and orchards, but often described as little. There were also two houses, six tenements, two inns, the 'Bell' (c. 1642)[79] and the 'Knight's House', two smith's shops, a millhouse, and many carthouses and barns. Their location is rarely known, but cottages were being built in the extreme north-east, on 'Bushey Heath', and at Brookshill, as well as in the area more vaguely described as 'Weald Wood'. There were few large houses, apart from Cornerhall.[80] Sir Edward Waldo's house had 9 hearths in 1664;[81] Henry Coghill also had a house, presumably Bentley Priory, with 9 hearths, while two others had 8 hearths. Weald Common was also diminished in the 17th century by the creation of the demesne farm of Weald Coppice or Copse.[82] Sixty-five grants of wastehold property were made during the 18th century,[83] nearly three-quarters of them by 1730. The properties included 30 cottages, of which at least three were at Brookshill, three at Bushey Heath, and four in Weald Wood. There were also new inns: the 'Green Head' (1703), the 'Hare' (1706),[84] the 'Red Lion' (1712),[85] and the 'Nag' (1728);[86] there were two smith's shops, and probably a new windmill.[87] Nine more cottages were erected by 1750. Further encroachments were made in the 40 years before inclosure but were not legalized.[88]

In 1759 a road from Watford, entering the parish in the north-east corner, crossed Weald Common and ran due south to Greenhill and Harrow-on-the-Hill,[89] crossing the Wealdstone Brook by the medieval 'church bridge'.[90] Another road, linked to it by a lateral road, went south-eastward, through the Lower End of Weald and, as Kenton Lane, on to Kenton, Wembley, and Willesden. The main east–west route led from Great Stanmore across the southern edge of the common to Hatch End, Pinner, and Uxbridge. Other roads linked the hamlets that made up the Weald. Apart from the Wealdstone Brook, which rose in Weald Common, branches of the Pinn rose in the high land of the Weald,[91] and there were many springs sufficient to form ponds[92] and, in the 19th century, ornamental lakes.[93]

[60] Matt. Paris, *Chron. Majora* (Rolls Ser.), v. 33.
[61] P.C.C. 19 Blamyr.
[62] For the meaning of 'redding', see p. 178.
[63] Lands belonging to Geof. Marlpits and Walter Pluckyngton. See p. 178.
[64] e.g. the New College estate near Colliers Lane and Rammes, probably identical with Reams: M.R.O., Acc. 794/8; M.R. 612, nos. 141–8b.
[65] M.R.O., Acc. 76/222a.
[66] Ibid. /2410, m. 3.
[67] Ibid. /2413, m. 6. Compared with 24 for Pinner and 2 each for Wembley, Sudbury, and Roxeth.
[68] M.R.O., Acc. 76/2413, m. 6; Acc. 643, 2nd deposit, Messeder map B. See p. 232.
[69] M.R.O., Acc. 76/222a.
[70] Ibid. /205.
[71] Ibid. /208.
[72] M.R.O., Acc. 794/2.
[73] M.R.O., Acc. 76/1008.
[74] Ibid. /1010.
[75] Ibid. /791.
[76] Ibid. /210, /707, /2019.
[77] They include the older wastehold properties, listed in rentals since 1553.
[78] M.R.O., H.T. 5. They were not all wastehold cottages.

[79] M.R.O., Acc. 794/2; Acc 590/1–3, no. 570.
[80] See above.
[81] M.R.O., H.T. 5.
[82] See p. 228.
[83] M.R.O., Acc. 76/210, /1109.
[84] Cottage at Brookshill leased to Thos. Clutterbuck: M.R.O., Acc. 76/1109. For the position of the 'Hare', see Acc. 590/1–3, no. 646; O.S. Map 1/2,500, Mdx. v. 15 (1865 edn.).
[85] M.R.O., Acc. 590/2, no. 914. Cottage leased to Wm. Smith: Acc. 76/1109. The Smiths of the 'Red Lion' were licensed throughout the 18th cent.: L.V. 3/94; 7/1; 9/2; 10/88.
[86] On the site of Harrow Weald Lodge, see below.
[87] In 1721 a windmill was to be built on a site where an earlier one had stood: M.R.O., Acc. 76/210.
[88] M.R.O., Acc. 310(1)
[89] M.R.O., Acc. 643, 2nd deposit, Messeder maps A and B.
[90] M.R.O., Acc. 76/2420, m. 3. Named presumably because the road led to St. Mary's church.
[91] Rocque, *Map of Mdx.* (1754).
[92] M.R.O., Acc. 643, 2nd deposit, Messeder map B.
[93] M.R.O., 590/2; O.S. Map 1/2,500, Mdx. v. 11, 15, 16 (1865 edn.).

Weald Common and Hatch End Green contained 749 a. in 1759, when 169 buildings are recorded. These were scattered mainly along the eastern and southern edges of the common, with clusters around the roads at north Wealdstone and Lower End of Weald and, in the extreme north, at Bushey Heath.[94] Bentley Priory stood by itself on the border with Great Stanmore, approached from the north and east by tree-lined avenues, and Weald Coppice farm-house stood at the eastern end of the farm. North-east of the farm were two groups of buildings, presumably Brookshill and the brick-works of the Bodymead family.[95] There were a few isolated houses along the road over the common from Hatch End to Stanmore. In contrast to Pinner, the Weald was not yet the home of many wealthy people, and apart from Bentley Priory, only Cornerhall[96] and 'Lady Egerton's'[97] are marked. There were five inns:[98] the 'Bell',[99] the 'Hare', the 'Red Lion', the 'Plough',[1] and the 'Seven Balls' or 'Bells'.[2] The 'Windmill' at Bushey Heath was first licensed in 1760.[3]

By 1817[4] Weald Common had been reduced to 685 a. and Hatch End to 5 a. Despite some inclosure since 1759[5] there is little indication of much building on the common. Dwellings recently erected at inclosure included two farm-houses[6] belonging to Drummond. Eight cottages 'at Harrow Weald Common', which were claimed by Mary Ann Blackwell in 1805, may have been the first to be built at 'the City', a group erected by the Blackwells for employees at their brick-works.[7] Some cottages on the east of the common may even have been pulled down during the landscaping of the Bentley Priory estate,[8] although Brookes House existed in 1780[9] and Woodlands was probably built shortly afterwards.[10]

Inclosure released a large amount of pleasant woodland, some of which was bought by Londoners for country houses. The most notable was Harrow Weald Park, later the Manor, rebuilt in 1870 in the Victorian Gothic style, on an ambitious plan and embellished with stone battlements and pinnacles.[11] Others, like Wealdstone House and Brookshill, were older houses which were altered. The Weald began to attract residents similar to those of Pinner. In 1851 they included an East India merchant at Woodlands, a merchant at Harrow Weald House, and a solicitor and landed proprietor at Kynaston Lodge,

as well as three 'fundholders', a 'proprietor of houses', two more solicitors, a 'gentleman', a portrait-painter, and a 'dramatic author'.[12] Other residents have included Sir Roger Kynaston at Kynaston Court, William Crockford of the gambling club at Harrow Weald Park, Sir William Gilbert,[13] and Earl Jellicoe at Hanworth House.[14]

The population rose gradually to 824 in 1831, when 30 families lived in 'the City',[15] and to 1,031 in 1841, when there were 184 inhabited houses.[16] In 1851 the population was 1,090.[17] In addition to the five inns of 1759, there were the 'Queen's Arms'[18] and two beershops, the 'Duck in the Pond'[19] and the 'Rose and Crown'.[20] Harrow Weald was within easy reach of both Harrow station, opened in 1837, and Pinner station, opened in 1844. 'Accommodation' land was advertised,[21] and many more large, detached residences had been built by the end of the 19th century.[22] By 1901 there were 331 houses and a population of 1,315. A rise in population to 2,220 by 1911 was partly due to an overflow of people working in Wealdstone. The residents of Harrow Weald, jealous of its superior character, refused any amalgamation with Wealdstone,[23] but numbers leaped from 2,814 in 1921 to 10,928 in 1931. The population density rose from 0·5 per acre in 1901 to 1·1 in 1921, and 4·6 in 1931. Harrow Weald ward (1,219 a.), from which the eastern part of the Weald was excluded, supported 16,951 people in 1951, a density of 13 per acre. In 1961 there were 14,913 people and 4,422 dwellings in the area.

Most of the development between the wars consisted of infilling on farm-land, especially to the south of Uxbridge Road. The northern area was more sporadically developed and even after the Second World War retained much of its former rural and wooded character.[24]

Architectural evidence of the earlier settlements of the Weald area is slighter than in neighbouring Pinner. Two 16th-century farms, Wealdstone House and Harrow Weald House in Elms Road, disappeared in the 1930s.[25] Priory House (formerly Priory Farm), on the southern edge of Bentley Park, has been almost entirely rebuilt but incorporates the base of a 16th-century chimney; its garden wall, as well as outbuildings at Lower Priory Farm to the south, appear to be of 17th-century brick.[26] The

[94] Marked on the map (M.R.O., Acc. 643, 2nd deposit, Messeder map B) as 'Upper end of Weald Common (erroneously called Bushey Heath)', but consistently called Bushey Heath in 18th-cent. documents.
[95] See p. 232.
[96] At the SE. corner of the common.
[97] A large house, the northernmost one along the E. edge of the common.
[98] M.R.O., L.V. 7/1, /37.
[99] A 17th-cent. building, pulled down in the 1930s: W. W. Druett, The Stanmores & Harrow Weald, 222.
[1] Licensed 1751–60: M.R.O., L.V. 7/1, /37, /44. Possibly identifiable with 'Plough and Harrow', licensed 1775 but gone from the lists by 1785: L.V. 9/2, 131. Its whereabouts is unknown.
[2] First licensed in 1759: M.R.O., L.V. 7/37; Acc. 590/2, no. 900; O.S. Map 1/2,500, Mdx. v. 16 (1865 edn.). See below.
[3] M.R.O., L.V. 7/44; Acc. 590/2, no. 750; O.S. Map 1/2,500, Mdx. v. 11 (1865 edn.).
[4] M.R.O., Acc. 794/8.
[5] M.R.O., Acc. 76/2205.
[6] i.e. c. 1817: ibid. /1145b.
[7] Ibid. /1400; see p. 233.
[8] M.R.O., Acc. 76/1597.
[9] M.R.O., Acc. 507/1.

[10] Druett, Weald, 245.
[11] Pevsner, Mdx. 104. In 1932 the British Israel World Federation bought the Manor for use as a college: Druett, Weald, 175–7. The house was subsequently demolished.
[12] H.O. 107/1700, ff. 106–46. Only servants occupied Bentley Priory and Harrow Weald Park when the census was taken.
[13] Druett, Weald, 172, 175 sqq., 242. For Gilbert's residence, see below.
[14] Pevsner, Mdx. 104.
[15] M.R.O., D.R.O. 3/F13/1, /3.
[16] Except where otherwise stated, this paragraph is based on Census, 1831–1961.
[17] H.O. 107/1700, ff. 106–46; M.R.O., Acc. 590/2, /4.
[18] Ibid. /2, /4, no. 484.
[19] Ibid. /2, /4, no. 874.
[20] Ibid. /2, /4, no. 843.
[21] e.g. Harrow Cent. Ref. Libr., Sales Partics. ii (1865); M.R.O., Acc. 507/37.
[22] O.S. Map 6", Mdx. v. SE., x. NE. (1897 edn.).
[23] Harrow Bor., North Star, Hendon R.D.C., Wealdstone extension inquiry, 1912.
[24] Land Util. Survey Map 1", sheet 106 (1931–2 edn.).
[25] Druett, Weald, 213–14, 220.
[26] Hist. Mon. Com. Mdx. 68.

buildings at Copse (formerly Weald Copse) Farm include a timber-framed and weather-boarded barn. The farm-house, which has been much altered and faced with red brick, may be of late-17th-century origin. About a mile to the south of Uxbridge Road the surviving farm-house at Kenton Lane Farm is of early-19th-century red brick. A timber-framed house in Boxtree Lane was ruinous by 1969, and the Seven Bells Inn in Kenton Lane, also structurally timber-framed,[27] had been modernized. The 'Hare', perhaps containing original brickwork, still stood at the junction of Brookshill and Old Redding. The 'Nag' or 'Nag's Head', also built in the early 18th century,[28] had changed its name by 1759 to 'Cold Harbour'.[29] It was probably rebuilt soon afterwards and in the earlier 19th century it was converted into a private residence known as Harrow Weald Lodge.[30] The building, which stands in Uxbridge Road to the east of Brookshill, was occupied in 1969 as council offices by the London Borough of Harrow. It has a two-storied red brick front of nine bays, surmounted by a dentil cornice and a central pediment; the original ground-floor windows were set in arched recesses, but two bay windows and the present door-way are additions of the early 19th century.

In the Brookshill area some evidence still remains of the 18th- and 19th-century brick-making activities of the Bodymead and Blackwell families.[31] The house called the Kiln is a two-storied bay-windowed building of red brick, dating from the mid 18th century; it has been considerably altered and one wing was pulled down in the late 1950s. In the garden are the ruins of a kiln, the foundations of another, and a range of drying sheds. By 1851 and in 1913 there was a second building on what later became the lawn.[32] The cottages known as 'the City' formed irregular groups on both sides of the lane later called Old Redding.[33] Only one or two have survived together with an inn named 'The Case is Altered'.

Of the many large private houses built or re-modelled in the later 19th century several to the north of Uxbridge Road are still standing. The most notable, Bentley Priory, is described elsewhere.[34] Woodlands, much altered in the late 19th century, is now occupied by the engineer's and surveyor's departments of the London Borough of Harrow. Mid-Victorian domestic architecture was once par-ticularly well represented in the area.[35] One of the best examples, Grim's Dyke, was built in the woodland to the north of Old Redding in 1872 for Frederick Goodall R.A., and was occupied by Sir William Gilbert from 1890 until his death in 1911. It was designed by Norman Shaw as a large country house in the domestic Tudor style which was to become so fashionable towards the end of the

century. It has a rambling plan, stone and tile-hung walls, tall chimneys, and many half-timbered gables.[36] The property was bought by the local authority in 1937 and used as a rehabilitation centre for tuberculosis patients,[37] but since 1962 the house has stood empty except when leased to film com-panies. Of another important house, the Manor (formerly Harrow Weald Park), only a stone lodge survives. To the north of it Hillside stands derelict, a gaunt building of diapered brick with curvilinear gables. Large houses which had completely disap-peared by 1969 included Brookshill (later the Hall), the Hermitage, the Cedars, Harrow Weald House, and Kynaston Lodge.

KENTON was a small hamlet on the eastern borders of Harrow south of Harrow Weald. It was typical of the settlements of the London Clay region, which grew out of isolated farms in clearings of the forest, especially along the Lidding or Wealdstone Brook.[38] Kenton, whose original meaning was probably 'farm of the sons of Coena',[39] was first mentioned, as 'Kenington', in 1231,[40] when it was already a town-ship and the home of Adam of Kenton. By 1316 the inhabitants formed a tithing,[41] but there were only two ancient head tenements, Wapses and Jacketts, whose messuages lay together on the west of Kenton Green.[42] By 1547 the two head tenements were held by the same man and the messuage of Jacketts had decayed, leaving only a close. At this time there were seven other tenements with gardens and orchards, one cottage, and a barn. They probably lay around the small green, which was also surrounded by 9 closes, containing 32 a.[43]

North of the hamlet lay Great Field, 7 furlongs made up of 112 selions and 26 a., bounded by Great Stanmore parish and the Weald common fields on the north and west, by Kenton Green on the south and east, and by Gore Field on the east. Little Field, 102 selions divided into 6 furlongs, lay east of Kenton Green, bounded by Preston North Field on the east, and by Gore Field on the north and east. Gore Field, 5 furlongs made up from 105 selions, was bounded on the north by Kingsbury and Great Stanmore parishes, on the east by Preston North Field, on the south by Little Field, and on the west by Great Field.[44] In the 17th and 18th centuries the three fields were Little Field, Great alias West Field, and Old Street Field alias Middle alias North Field.[45] The last, also described as abutting Preston Field on the east, was probably the 16th-century Gore Field, which may have been connected with the meeting-place of the hundred of Gore.[46] Inclosure during the 17th and early 18th centuries[47] had re-

[27] Hist. Mon. Com. *Mdx.* 68.   [28] See above, p. 184.
[29] M.R.O., Acc. 643, 2nd deposit, Messeder map A.
[30] M.R.O., Acc. 76/1850; Druett, *Weald*, 177–8; Pevsner, *Mdx.* 104–5.   [31] See pp. 232–3.
[32] M.R.O., Acc. 590 /2; O.S. Map 1/2,500, Mdx. v. 15 (1913 edn.).
[33] O.S. Map 1/2,500, Mdx. v. 15 (1865 edn.).
[34] See p. 206.
[35] Pevsner, *Mdx.* 104–5.   [36] See pl. facing p. 64.
[37] Pevsner, *Mdx.* 104; Druett, *Weald*, 172; ex inf. Mr. J. Churchill Day, chairman of the Gilbert and Sullivan Soc. (1968).
[38] At least two tributaries of the Lidding Brook flowed through Kenton's common fields, i.e. the Ryddy Brook in the north, near the Weald, and a stream separating Kenton and Preston fields.

[39] *P.N. Mdx.* (E.P.N.S.), 23, 53.
[40] *Cur. Reg. R.* xiv. 273.
[41] M.R.O., Acc. 76/2410, m. 3.
[42] Ibid. /222a; Acc. 166(1)/1. Wapses may possibly be identified with the house just W. of Kenton Green on the road leading to Kenton Lane: M.R. 612, no. 896; M.R.O., Acc. 76/1593; Acc. 794/8.
[43] M.R.O., Acc. 166(1)/1; Acc. 1052, ff. 221–61.
[44] M.R.O., Acc. 166(1)/1; Priestmead (cf. O.S. Map 1/2,500, Mdx. x. 8 (1865 edn.) was a 'shot' in Great Field. So was Brokesmere (Bloxman): M.R. 612, nos. 212–13, 221.
[45] M.R.O., Acc. 166/146/53; Acc. 276/3/49.
[46] See pp. 149–50.
[47] M.R.O., Acc. 166/146/31; Acc. 166/Box 3; Acc. 276/3/49.

duced Old Street Field to 14 a., Great Field to about 126 a., and Little Field to 50 a. by 1817.[48]

In 1547 the open fields and closes belonged to two ancient head tenements of a virgate each,[49] part of a head tenement of a hide,[50] and lands held freely and in free alms from Harrow, Uxendon, and Roxeth manors.[51] The land was held by 8 landholders, of whom John Parson (108 selions and 7 a.), Henry Spilman (108 selions and 6 a.), the chantry[52] (61 selions and 34 a.), and William Greenhill (26 selions) were the most important. During the 16th century most of the land passed to the Page family, one branch of which lived as yeoman farmers in Kenton.[53] From the Pages it went mostly to the Smiths and Walters[54] and thence, at the beginning of the 18th century, to the Grahams.[55] The main change during the two centuries from 1547 was in the inclosure of the common fields. There was a little encroachment on the common, mostly for barns but possibly also for cottages. By 1721 there were seven parcels of wastehold:[56] the Grahams had built a house and there were several cottages and a smith's shop.[57] In 1759 there were 29 buildings, all on the edge of the 18-acre green and closest together in the west, along the southern road leading to Kenton Lane.[58] Some were almost certainly outbuildings, but they included the Grahams' house, in 1801 a brick and tiled house on the south side of Kenton Green,[59] which can possibly be identified with the later Kenton Farm.[60] Another building can be identified with the Plough Inn, which was licensed by 1751 and possibly from 1722.[61] The inn, which was sold to Thomas Clutterbuck in 1801,[62] survived until 1926.[63]

No major road passed through Kenton village, although by 1759 local roads from Kenton Green led to Edgware, Kingsbury, and Preston on the east and south, and to Kenton Lane, part of a route from Wembley to Watford, on the west. The eastern boundary of the hamlet and parish was formed by Honeypot Lane or 'Old Street', a prehistoric track.[64] The road pattern survived until after the First World War.[65]

In the early 19th century the Grahams' estate was sold.[66] By 1817[67] there were 13 estates in Kenton, of which the two largest were held by outside landowners but most belonged to small, local farms. Inclosure, although it created rectorial and vicarial estates,[68] made little difference to methods of husbandry.[69] In 1831 there was a population of 83 and ten years later 99 people lived in 17 houses, which probably included Kenton Lane Farm and Woodcock Hill Farm.[70] In 1852 Kenton village consisted of Kenton Farm, four houses, eleven cottages, the Plough Inn, a National school, and a blacksmith's shop.[71] The population, 109 in 1851, consisted mainly of people who were born locally and lived by agriculture.[72] There was one solicitor, and an artist who lived in the large house south of the village street,[73] which was called Kenton Lodge in 1851–2.[74] Kenton was not one of the hamlets where Londoners built villas, mainly because of its distance from the railway. By 1897 Kenton Grove had appeared near Honeypot Lane and there were two new farms, Black Farm, belonging to Christ Church,[75] on the road leading west, and the vicarial Glebe Farm on the road to the east.[76] A second Kenton Farm was built to the north of the hamlet between 1897 and 1916,[77] the original one being renamed Kenton Grange Farm. A beershop, the 'Three Horseshoes', was licensed from 1873 but demolished in 1900. It was replaced by the 'Travellers' Rest', which, as the Rest Hotel, Kenton, the largest public house in Middlesex, was rebuilt in 1933.[78]

Between c. 1928 and 1938 Kenton was rapidly transformed from a small village to part of a large suburban area, and all trace of the old settlement vanished. The population of Kenton ward in Wembley U.D. rose from 268 in 1921 to 6,171 in 1931. After 1934 Kenton formed two wards, the northern one in Harrow and the southern in Wembley. By 1951 the combined population was 27,680, a density of 23·1 persons to an acre, compared with 0·2 in 1921 and 5·8 in 1931. In spite of further building after 1951, the population dropped to 27,572 in 1961.[79]

PRESTON, 'the farm belonging to a priest',[80] lay south of Kenton, on the eastern borders of the parish. It may have been part of the lands and

[48] M.R.O., Acc. 794/8. The inclosure map reverses the position of the Great and Little Fields of 1547 but if inclosure had left Great Field smaller than the others it would be logical to change the names: M.R. 612.
[49] i.e. Wapses and Jacketts.
[50] Mostly in Preston, see below.
[51] Roxeth and Uxendon manors had been held by the same lord in the 14th cent.: see pp. 205–6.
[52] See p. 253.
[53] M.R.O., Acc. 76/222a, /774; Acc. 794/2. The Pages acquired the chantry lands and those of Henry Spilman: Acc. 276/9/5. They had acquired one of the copyhold virgates by c. 1642: Acc. 794/2.
[54] M.R.O., Acc. 76/1646; Acc. 166(1)/7; Acc. 166/146/33, /35; Acc. 276/3/49, /5/11.   [55] See p. 207.
[56] M.R.O., Acc. 76/222a, /205, /210, /707.
[57] M.R.O., Acc. 166/146/37, /43; Acc. 166/Box 3, 1801 abstract.
[58] M.R.O., Acc. 643, 2nd deposit, Messeder map A.
[59] M.R.O., Acc. 166/Box 3, Sales Partics. 1801.
[60] Lysons, Environs of Lond. Suppl. 191.
[61] In 1751 an inn of that name was licensed to Wm. Higgs: M.R.O., L.V. 7/1. In 1722 an inn licensed to John Giggs: L.V. 3/94. Giggs appears in later licences (e.g. 1785: L.V. 9/131). Higgs was a local name in the 19th cent.
[62] M.R.O., Acc. 166/Box 3, abstract 1801.
[63] M.R.O., Acc. 794/21–23.
[64] M.R.O., Acc. 643, 2nd deposit, Messeder map A; ex inf. Mr. A. D. Lacaille.

[65] O.S. Map 6″, Mdx. x. NE., xi. NW. (1865 and later edns.).
[66] See p. 207.
[67] M.R.O., Acc. 794/8; M.R. 612.
[68] In 1852 Christ Church had 140 a. and the Vicar of Harrow 129 a. in Kenton: M.R.O., Acc. 590/4.
[69] M.R.O., D.R.O. 3/F13/1, /4.
[70] Census, 1841.
[71] M.R.O., Acc. 590/1–4.
[72] H.O. 107/1700, ff. 94v–97. Thirty-three people had been born in Kenton, 13 elsewhere in the parish, 29 in other parishes in Mdx. or London.
[73] M.R.O., Acc. 590/3, no. 1074.
[74] A large house east of the village and north of the main street is also identified as Kenton Lodge: Greenwood, Map of Mdx. (1819); O.S. Maps 6″, Mdx. x. NE., xi. NW. (1865 and later edns.). From 1865 the southern house is marked as Kenton Grange: O.S. Map 1/2,500, Mdx. x. 8 (1865 edn.).
[75] Built between 1878 and 1896: Christ Church, Harrow maps 5, 19.
[76] O.S. Map 6″, Mdx. x. NE., xi. NW. (1897 edn.).
[77] Ibid. (1865 and 1916 edns.).
[78] M.R.O., P.S. G/H5/1; Wembley Hist. Soc., Acc. 907/106.
[79] Census, 1921–61; O.S. Maps 1″, sheet 106 (1920, 1940, 1958 edns.); 6″, Mdx. x. NE., xi. NW. (1916, 1935, 1938 edns.); TQ 18 NE. (1951, 1967 edns.); Land Util. Survey Map 1″, sheet 106 (1931–2 edn.).
[80] P.N. Mdx. (E.P.N.S.), 53.

dwelling-house on the east bank of the Lidding, granted by Offa to Abbot Stidberht in 767,[81] but its connexion with the Church appears to have been lost before 1086.[82] First recorded by name in 1220,[83] Preston was a township in 1231.[84] It had its own tithing in 1316,[85] but had only three head tenements,[86] two of which later developed into farms, and a few cottages occupied by under-tenants at Preston Green.

North Field, East Field, South Field, and Crouch Field were mentioned in 1381.[87] The last two, which apparently served as common fields for both Preston and Uxendon,[88] lay south and west of the hamlet. North Field was a triangular-shaped field north-east of the hamlet, bounded on the east by Honeypot Lane and separated from Kenton common fields by a stream and from East Field[89] by the road from Kingsbury to Kenton.[90] The meeting-place of the hundred of Gore may have been at the northern end of East Field.[91] By 1547 North Field was the largest field, with 110 selions in five furlongs, compared with 79 selions in five furlongs in East Field.[92] By 1817, however, after inclosures during the 16th and 17th centuries,[93] there were 13 a. in North Field and 90 a. in East Field.[94]

By the mid 15th century the head tenements had been consolidated into two estates. There were probably also some freehold and other lands that were entered under Uxendon. One head tenement, called successively Preston's and Preston Dicket after two medieval families,[95] had become part of Uxendon manor by the late 15th century. A one-hide estate, of which a small part lay in Kenton, it was split up when Uxendon was sold by the Bellamys. The house and 80 a. of inclosed land passed to Richard Page; the Kenton portion was bought by Robert Walter.[96] Although part of the Uxendon estate, Preston Dicket, which retained its identity as a farm and was even called a manor-house,[97] was sold before 1799 to the Bocket family.[98] The house may be identified with Preston House, in the south-west corner of Preston village at the junction of Preston Road,

Preston Hill, and Woodcock Hill.[99] Preston House may have been used by members of the Page family, while the farm was leased out. Between c. 1642 and 1681 a new farm-house, Hillside Farm, was built on the waste at Preston Green, south of the road.[1] Before its demolition in 1960 it was a much altered two-storey building of brick and plaster with a tiled roof.[2] The other two head tenements were held by the Lyon family by 1435–6.[3] John Lyon's farm-house, probably on the site of one of the ancient head tenements, lay on the edge of Preston Green, north of the road.[4] Described in 1547 as a beautiful building,[5] it was re-built in red brick with a symmetrical two-storied front in the late 17th or early 18th century, and survived until 1960.[6] There were probably also a few cottages belonging to under-tenants and later to farm labourers.[7] From 1553 to 1628 there was only one wasehold property, where a barn was built.[8] By 1681 there were five encroachments on the waste and at least as many houses.[9]

In 1759 Preston Green (7½ a.) lay where the Lidding Brook was crossed by a road, later called Preston Hill, running from Honeypot Lane and Kingsbury in the north-east to the main north–south route from Watford to Willesden in the west.[10] Nine buildings, including the Horseshoe Inn, licensed from 1751, were spaced along the road and around the green.[11] By 1817 the green had been reduced to just over 5 a., but the number of houses was unchanged,[12] and in 1820 the brook had a ford and a footbridge.[13] There were 64 people in 1831[14] and 57 in 1851.[15] There is no evidence of any inn or beerhouse after 1759 in Preston, which remained unaltered throughout the 19th century. The Metropolitan line passed nearby but a proposal for a station in 1896 was rejected because there were not enough residents.[16] There was a halt at Preston from 1910 and a few houses were built in 1912. Most development dates from the 1930s, although more houses were built, especially north and east of Preston Road, after the Second World War.[17] In the course of the 20th century all old buildings have been demolished.[18] By 1951

[81] *Cart. Sax.* ed. Birch, i. p. 284. See below, p. 203.
[82] See p. 249.
[83] *Cur. Reg. R.* ix. 39. The entry cited in *P.N. Mdx.* 53 *sub* 1194 almost certainly refers to Preston in Suffolk.
[84] *Cur. Reg. R.* xiv. 273.
[85] Possibly with Uxendon: M.R.O., Acc. 76/2410, m. 3.
[86] Only two head tenements, both ½-hides, are entered in the rentals, but at least one of the 4 head tenements listed *sub* Uxendon was in Preston: M.R.O., Acc. 76/205, /208,/222a.
[87] E. J. L. Scott, *Recs. of Grammar Sch. at Harrow on Hill,* 4.   [88] See below.
[89] Scott, *Recs. of Grammar Sch.* 4.
[90] M.R.O., Acc. 76/2417, m. 87d; Acc. 166(1)/1; Acc. 166(2)/146/70–156; Acc. 643, m. 69d; M.R. 612.
[91] See p. 150.
[92] M.R.O., Acc. 1052, ff. 200–21. There were 164 a. of inclosed land.
[93] M.R.O., Acc. 76/1646; Acc. 166(2)/146/70–156; Acc. 853/11; H. W. R. Elsley, *Wembley Through the Ages,* 134–5.
[94] M.R.O., Acc. 794/8. For South Field and Crouch Field, see p. 189.
[95] The Prestons flourished in the 13th–15th cent.; M.R.O., Acc. 76/2420, m. 13; Acc. 76/388; *Cur. Reg. R.* xiv. 273; the Dickets in the 14th cent.: Canterbury, Eastbridge Hosp. Archives, H(13); *Cal. Close,* 1337–9, 535; 1349–54, 476.
[96] M.R.O., Acc. 76/208.
[97] M.R.O., Acc. 276/6. See p. 260.
[98] M.R.O., Acc. 76/209.
[99] M.R.O., Acc. 590/3, no. 1163; M.R. 612, no. 965; O.S. Map 1/2,500, Mdx. xi. 9 (1865 edn.).
[1] M.R.O., Acc. 76/707.

[2] Hist. Mon. Com. *Mdx.* 132. Sold in 1960, it was demolished and replaced by 80 flats: Wemb. Hist. Soc., Acc. 471; Acc. 907/172; ex. inf. Mr. A. H. Murgatroyd (1968).
[3] See p. 213.   [4] M.R. 612, n. 951.
[5] M.R.O., Acc. 1052, f. 201.
[6] Hist. Mon. Com. *Mdx.* 132. Some Tudor bricks found: Wemb. Hist. Soc. *Jnl.* i (5). On the death of the owner, F. J. Perrin, in 1958, the house passed by bequest to Wembley Bor. Council: Wemb. Hist. Soc., Acc. 907/67; Acc. 510.
[7] In 1547 there was only one tenement other than Preston Dicket and Lyon's house: M.R.O., Acc. 1052, f. 201.
[8] M.R.O., Acc. 76/205, /208, /222a.
[9] Ibid. /707.
[10] M.R.O., Acc. 643, 2nd deposit, Messeder map A.
[11] M.R.O., L.V. 7/1.
[12] M.R.O., Acc. 794/8; M.R. 612.
[13] *Rep. of Pub. Bridges in Mdx.* (1825).
[14] M.R.O., D.R.O. 3/F13/4. The figure may include Uxendon Farm or Woodcock Hill Farm.
[15] H.O. 107/1700, ff. 160–72. The figure of 105 in 1841 includes Uxendon: *Census,* 1841.
[16] Brent Town Hall, Wembley U.D.C., Min. Bk. i (1894–7), p. 314.
[17] Land Util. Survey Map 1″, sheet 106 (1931–2 edn.); Land Util. Survey Map 6″, sheet 223 (1961, unpubl., by courtesy of Miss Alice Coleman); O.S. Maps 6″, Mdx. xi. SW. (1938 edn.); TQ 18 N.E. (1967 edn.); O.S. Maps 1″, sheet 256 (1877, 1898 edns.); sheet 106 (1920, 1940, 1958 edns.); Wemb. Hist. Soc., *Jnl.* N.S. i (3).
[18] Ex inf. Mr. A. H. Murgatroyd. Some are described in Hist. Mon. Com. *Mdx.* 132.

Preston ward (790 a.) had a population of 12,408, giving a density of 15·7 persons to an acre. Ten years later the population had dropped to 11,810.[19]

UXENDON, south of Preston, is first recorded in a transaction by Hugh of 'Woxindon' in 1257.[20] The second element in the place-name is the Old English *dun*, 'hill', and probably refers to Barn Hill on the Kingsbury border. The first, as in Uxbridge, may come from an Anglo-Saxon tribe, the Wixan, or from the Celtic for 'water',[21] referring to the Lidding Brook or to nearby springs.[22] The possibility of a Celtic derivation is strengthened by the presence of a Celtic earthwork and an ancient trackway on the eastern border.

Uxendon seems always to have been sparsely settled. Hugh may have lived in an isolated farm-house, possibly on the site of the later Uxendon manor, on the eastern bank of the Lidding. The ancient head tenements were large units so that they can never have been numerous. It was not a tithing in 1316[23] but apparently it was one 20 years later.[24] During the 14th and 15th centuries a few families, the Aylwards, atte Okes, Pargraves, and Uxendons, formed a small settlement, probably at Forty Green.[25] Forty Green, called variously Uxendon Forty, Wembley Forty, or even Preston Forty,[26] lay at the southern end of Uxendon, where Forty or Chalkhill Lane, continuing a route from Sudbury in the west, crossed the Lidding at Forty Bridge and ran eastward to Kingsbury. The main north–south route ran parallel with the Lidding from Preston to Wembley, crossing Forty Lane south of Forty Bridge. A 'Flax Lane', mentioned in 1417,[27] may have been Forty Lane or one of the small lanes at Forty Green.

Five open fields are listed in 1547:[28] Crouch Field, South Field (both mentioned in 1381),[29] Barnet Field, Uxendon Field, and Bushy Down Field. Crouch Field,[30] the largest, 6 furlongs comprising about 120 selions, lay west and slightly north of Uxendon manor, in a block bounded on the north and east roads from Uxendon to Harrow-on-the-Hill and from Wembley to Watford, on the south by Crouch Brook, a western tributary of the Lidding,[31] and on the west by the Sudbury demesne land; one furlong jutted out in the north-west. South Field, which consisted of 52 selions in three furlongs, lay east of Crouch Field and extended as far as Uxendon manor-house. The other open fields lay to the east of the manor-house, stretching down the Kingsbury border as far as Forty Green in the south. Bushy

Down Field had three furlongs comprising 33 selions, and Uxendon Field, which bordered Wembley on the south, had 40 selions in four furlongs.

'Bushybarnet' was mentioned in 1469–70[32] and the whole of the region around Barn Hill was well wooded. Nevertheless inclosure seems to have proceeded from the east, perhaps influenced by the proximity of Kingsbury, which was inclosed much earlier than Harrow. In 1547[33] there were 86 a. of inclosed land around Uxendon manor-house with a further 58 a. (including Hill Field) belonging to the same estate in closes on the Kingsbury border. Bushey Down was inclosed in the 17th century, although its name survived in closes.[34] Barnet Field was still a single, arable field in 1693,[35] but by 1724 it had been divided into four and a barn had been built upon it.[36] In 1817 Barnetts was a large field of 56 a., east of Uxendon Forty between Forty Lane and Barn Hill.[37] In 1648 45 a. were inclosed out of South, later called Long, Middle, or Uxendon Field,[38] but although an Uxendon Field was mentioned in 1724,[39] both the South and Uxendon Fields of 1547 had entirely disappeared before 1817.[40] By this date the total area of open-field land was 127 a.,[41] confined to the western Crouch Field which had scarcely changed since 1547. The history of Uxendon until the 19th century shows not the expansion of a village, but the development of a few farms. By the mid 16th century the whole of Uxendon was held by two men, one of whom lived at Uxendon manor-house.[42] The other landowner was John Page, who held a one-virgate head tenement called Pargraves. The Uxendon estate, built up by inclosure, was described in 1599 as 'that whole manor, capital messuage, and farm of Uxendon'.[43] Pargraves developed as Forty Farm, whose farm-house in 1629 was 'newly erected'.[44] It was acquired by the Pages in 1649 but managed by them as a separate unit. A second Uxendon manor farm was built, probably between 1724[45] and 1759,[46] at Barn Hill.

In 1759 there was a complex of buildings at Uxendon manor-house, with a building on Barn Hill and five others, including Forty Farm, on the west of Forty Green, which covered 8 a.[47] Neither the number of buildings nor the area of the common had changed by 1817.[48] In 1851[49] there were 10 people at Forty Farm and one empty cottage at Forty Green, 13 people at Uxendon Farm, in the farm-house and one farm cottage, and three people at Barn Hill, then described as a cottage.

Uxendon remained a small, rural community until the destruction of Forty Green by the Metropolitan

---

[19] *Census*, 1951–61.
[20] *Ft. of F. Lond. and Mdx.* i. 37.
[21] *P.N. Mdx.* (E.P.N.S.), 49, 54; Elsley, *Wembley*, 41; *V.C.H. Mdx.* i. 78. See above, p. 58.
[22] M.R.O., Acc. 853/18.
[23] M.R.O., Acc. 76/2410, m. 3.
[24] Ibid. /2412, m. 6.
[25] Ibid. /216, /222a; Acc. 853/15.
[26] *P.N. Mdx.* 52; M.R.O., Acc. 853/23; H.O. 107/1700, f. 160.
[27] M.R.O., Acc. 853/15.
[28] M.R.O., Acc. 76/213; Acc. 1052, ff. 165–98.
[29] Elsley, *Wembley*, 38. They were also mentioned in 1445: M.R.O., Acc. 76/2417, m. 87d.
[30] Wm. atte Crouch was in 1316 a former reeve of Woodhall: M.R.O., Acc. 76/2410, m. 4.
[31] M.R.O., Acc. 76/2420, m. 13.
[32] M.R.O., Acc. 794/8; M.R. 612.
[33] M.R.O., Acc. 1052, ff. 165–72.
[34] M.R.O., Acc. 76/2434.

[35] M.R.O., Acc. 250/18.
[36] M.R.O., Acc. 76/871.
[37] M.R.O., Acc. 794/8; M.R. 612, no. 999.
[38] M.R.O., Acc. 853/18.
[39] M.R.O., Acc. 76/871.
[40] M.R.O., Acc. 794/8; M.R. 612.
[41] There were 313 a. of old inclosures.
[42] M.R.O., Acc. 76/213, /222a. There were three under-tenants but one of them, John Lyon of Preston, lived elsewhere: see above.
[43] M.R.O., Acc. 853/5.
[44] Ibid./15.
[45] M.R.O., Acc. 76/871, which mentions a barn but no farm at 'Barnetfield'.
[46] M.R.O., Acc. 643, 2nd deposit, Messeder map A; Acc. 76/1400.
[47] M.R.O., Acc. 643, 2nd deposit, Messeder map A.
[48] M.R.O., Acc. 794/8; M.R. 612.
[49] H.O. 107/1700, ff. 160–72; M.R.O., Acc. 590/3–4.

Railway in the 1880s and of Uxendon Farm with the building of the Wembley Park–Stanmore line in 1932. Forty Green was developed in the 1920s and Uxendon Farm, except Barn Hill, in the 1930s.[50]

WEMBLEY, 'Wemba lea' or Wemba's clearing in 825,[51] had well-wooded surroundings for much of the Middle Ages.[52] It gave its name to a 13th-century family[53] and in 1212 was a township.[54] In 1316 it contained two tithings,[55] but they included the Tokyngton people and it is unlikely that the medieval settlement was very large. There were only four head tenements, a half-hide and three virgates,[56] and freehold land amounting to one carucate, one virgate, and 6 a.[57] Upright's tenement was next to Wembley Green[58] but the position of the other head tenements is unknown. The village of Wembley seems to have grown up not around the Lidding but on the top of Wembley Hill, at the south-west corner of the large, triangular-shaped green. The green was enclosed by roads on two, and, by the early 19th century, on three sides;[59] it extended towards Tokyngton on the south-east, covering 60 a. in 1759 and 48 a. in 1817.[60]

North-west of the green lay the common fields. From the 15th century[61] they were Middle Field, Old Field, and Bitton or Church Field, so-called because it lay next to the path to Harrow church. Middle Field, the northernmost and largest, with 184 selions in 13 furlongs in 1547,[62] adjoined Uxendon Crouch Field[63] and on the east abutted Uxendon Forty Green. Old Field, which in 1547 comprised 88 selions in 5 furlongs, joined Middle Field on the south, abutting Staple Lane on the west;[64] Bitton Field, which in 1547 had 159 selions in 9 furlongs, in 1549[65] abutted Rowland's Brook on the south. Acre Croft, mentioned in 1449,[66] which abutted Forty Lane on the west, had 34 selions in 3 furlongs in 1547 but in 1807 was described as 'hitherto common field'.[67] Cynes Croft, consisting of only 9 selions, was included among the common fields in 1547. 'Brodenfeld', which appears in the 15th century,[68] may have been an alternative name for Old Field. Earlier stages can be glimpsed behind the fully developed field systems of the east Harrow hamlets of the late Middle Ages. As clearance of the forest proceeded, one open-field system was probably adopted for the whole area of scattered farms along the Lidding Brook. The original fields may have corresponded to Wembley Old Field, Uxendon *alias* South Field, Kenton's Great or West Field and Preston's North and possibly East Field. The inconvenience of distant fields, the growth of hamlets in place of isolated farmsteads, and the extension of arable, finally led to the creation of separate open-field systems for each hamlet. Traces of the earlier system remained: boundaries were particularly vague, some fields remained common to several hamlets, and landowners frequently had land, including selions making up one head tenement, in the open fields of more than one hamlet.[69] Consolidation of holdings was continuous, taking the form of inclosure from the Middle Ages. In 1547 there were 231 a. of inclosed and 596 selions of open-field land.[70] Forty Closes[71] were inclosed out of Middle Field between 1634 and 1650,[72] and encroachment on Wembley common fields, particularly by the Pages, proceeded throughout the 17th and early 18th centuries,[73] until in 1817 there were 288 a. of open fields left in Wembley.[74]

In 1547 there were 72 communicants attached to Tokyngton chapel, most of whom probably lived in Wembley,[75] although only six houses were listed in 1547.[76] Smaller than Pinner and the Weald, Wembley was nevertheless one of the richest hamlets in Harrow. Seven inhabitants were assessed for subsidy in 1550, two of them, Harry Page and John Lamb, on £100 worth of goods, the highest in the parish.[77] Both men, however, probably owned property elsewhere, and there were no very large houses. Eighteen people were assessed for hearth tax in 1672, Robert Page being assessed for 10 hearths and Henry Snowden for 7.[78] Page probably lived at Wembley House, mentioned as early as 1510[79] and the chief home of the Wembley Pages.[80] Probably this was the 'house of her master, John Page, in Wembley', where in 1580 Elizabeth Edlin gave birth to an illegitimate baby; the child was murdered by Francis Shoesmith, brewer, of Wembley, and buried in Rogers Croft, one of John Page's fields.[81] In 1865 a building called Wembley House lay south of Wembley Green.[82] Henry Snowden's house was probably the farmhouse, abutting south on Wembley Green, leased from the Claxton and later from the Arnold family.[83] Robert Cannon had a small farm-house at Wembley

[50] Land Util. Survey Map 1", sheet 106 (1931–2 edn.); 6", sheet 223 (1961, unpubl. edn.); O.S. Maps 1", sheet 106 (1920, 1940, 1958 edns.); 6", Mdx. xi. SW. (1935, 1938 edns.); TQ 18 NE. (1967 edn.).
[51] *Cart. Sax.* ed. Birch, i. 528–33; *P.N. Mdx.* (E.P.N.S.), 55.
[52] *Cal. Close,* 1399–1402, 293–7; M.R.O., Acc. 853/15.
[53] *Pipe R.* 1212 (P.R.S. N.S. xxx), 25–26; C.P. 25(1)/147/16.
[54] *Pipe R.* 1212, 25–26.
[55] M.R.O., Acc. 76/2410, m. 3.
[56] Including Pargraves, listed *sub* Uxendon.
[57] M.R.O., Acc. 76/222a. The survey of 1547 lists a carucate, 'certain lands' and part of a hide belonging to Uxendon: M.R.O., Acc. 1052, ff. 101–5.
[58] M.R.O., Acc. 1052, f. 104.
[59] M.R.O., Acc. 643, 2nd deposit, Messeder map A.
[60] M.R.O., Acc. 794/8.
[61] M.R.O., Acc. 76/871, /1835, /2416, m. 45d, /2420, m. 13; Acc. 276/6; Acc. 441/37; Acc. 853/15.
[62] M.R.O., Acc. 1052, ff. 105–161v.
[63] M.R.O., Acc. 853/15; M.R. 612.
[64] M.R.O., Acc. 441/26.
[65] M.R.O., Acc. 853/15.
[66] Ibid.
[67] M.R.O., Acc. 76/1097.
[68] M.R.O., Acc. 853/15; Acc. 76/2416, m. 45d, /2417, m. 100.
[69] e.g. an action in 1231 about 5 virgates in Preston and Kenton: *Cur. Reg. R.* xiv. 273.
[70] Including 32 selions and an unknown amount of inclosed land belonging to Wembley manor in Tokyngton: M.R.O., Acc. 1052, ff. 101–61v.
[71] i.e. from Uxendon Forty, not from 40 closes: M.R. 612, nos. 1017–18.
[72] M.R.O., Acc. 853/15, /19.
[73] M.R.O., Acc. 76/871; Acc. 276/3/49; Acc. 441/33.
[74] M.R.O., Acc. 794/8.
[75] Elsley, *Wembley,* 111, quoting 'a chantry roll', which cannot be located.
[76] M.R.O., Acc. 1052, ff. 101–5.
[77] E 179/142/169.
[78] M.R.O., H.T. 26. For the hearth tax of 1664, Wembley was assessed jointly with Alperton.
[79] Lambeth Palace, Estate MS. 478.
[80] *Cal. Pat.* 1547–8, 211; M.R.O., Acc. 76/1109.
[81] *Mdx. Cnty. Recs.* i. 119–20.
[82] O.S. Map 1/2,500, Mdx. xi. 13 (1865 edn.).
[83] M.R.O., Acc. 76/205, /208, /707, /1859; Acc. 794/2. John Read was another of Arnold's tenants: ibid. Acc. 76/1080.

Green, leased from the Pages. The Pages' property included Wembley manor or Dairy Farm, south of the green, which one of them usually farmed, Botnall Farm, and a farm-house leased to the Newmans.[84] Apart from one cottage and a smith's shop, which seem to have been taken in from the waste between 1672 and 1681, there was apparently no encroachment for building throughout the 17th and 18th centuries.[85]

In 1759 there were 42 buildings along the southern and eastern edges of Wembley Common and along a road leading north and west from Wembley Hill, roughly on the line of Manor Drive.[86] One of those on Wembley Green was an inn, which probably existed by 1722; in 1745 and 1751 it was called the 'Barley Mow'[87] and by 1785 the 'Green Man'.[88] The old weather-boarded inn was destroyed by fire and rebuilt in 1906.[89] Wembley Hill in 1759 was an area of common, marked out on two sides by converging roads. From the south-west corner a road led to Sudbury and Greenford. From the south-eastern corner a road, Deadman's Hill (later the Harrow road), led to Tokyngton and Willesden, bridging the Brent at Stonebridge in Tokyngton. In 1820 the two-arched bridge of brick and stone was described as an ancient one, built by the lords of Tokyngton and East Twyford manors. About 200 yards to the north was a brick bridge, Harrow Bridge, built c. 1800 by the parish of Harrow and the neighbouring landowners. It was in decay in 1818 and its arches were bricked up by the trustees of the turnpike road.[90] From the north corner of Wembley Hill a road ran northward to Watford, crossing the east–west road (Forty Lane and East Lane) from Kingsbury to Sudbury at Forty Green. Staple Lane ran northward from East Lane to the common fields[91] and another road ran north and then west to join Forty Lane south of Forty Green. Both Staple Lane and the road to Forty Lane had vanished and a new road, Blind Lane,[92] had appeared by c. 1820 as a result of the break-up of the Page estates and of inclosure. John Gray, who bought 327 a. of Richard Page's property[93] in 1810, made his chief residence the White House to the east of Wembley Green, and turned the surrounding estate into Wembley Park with the aid of the landscape gardener, Humphrey Repton.

In 1805 there were at least 22 houses, two of them described as mansions and three as farm-houses.[94] There was one blacksmith's shop, the Green Man Inn, and a tithe barn on the green. In 1831 there was a population of 208,[95] and in 1841 it was said to be 232, living in 40 houses,[96] although the figure almost certainly includes Forty Green and Tokyngton. In 1851 the population of Wembley and Tokyngton was

still only 203,[97] for the opening of a station in 1845[98] made little immediate difference. Excluding Tokyngton, there were five farms or houses in addition to Wembley Park mansion-house, Gray's bailiff's house, 25 cottages, a blacksmith's shop, the 'Green Man', and a beershop.[99] Wembley remained an area of farms and cottages until towards the end of the 19th century, when some large houses, like the Gables, Cumberland House, and Elm Lodge, were built in the corner near Wembley Hill Farm.[1] It was during the first decade of the 20th century that Wembley began to develop as a suburban and industrial area. In the 1920s the choice of Wembley Park for the British Empire Exhibition led to the building of what became Wembley Stadium, to be followed in the next decade by the Empire Pool and Arena.[2] The developments involved the wholesale destruction of the old houses and farms. Apart from the rebuilt 'Green Man', all that remained of old Wembley was the original street pattern, a skeleton beneath the maze of new streets covering the whole region.

TOKYNGTON. In the south-east corner of Harrow, separated from Willesden and Kingsbury by the Brent and its tributary, the Lidding, and from Alperton by another tributary, Rowland's Brook,[3] was Tokyngton or Oakington, first mentioned in 1171.[4] Tokyngton, 'the farm of the sons of Toca',[5] was divided among Wembley, Tokyngton, and Freren (Kingsbury) manors, and Tokyngton chapel. There is no evidence that Tokyngton was ever large enough to be considered a hamlet, although there was probably a community of naifs belonging to the manor farms.[6]

The lands of the three manors and chapel lay intermingled in common fields which probably stretched along the eastern border from Uxendon Forty to the River Brent. Yelne Field, South Field, and Hill Field[7] were mentioned in 1236[8] and Woodfurlong, Seven Acres, Stony Field, Brent Field, and Grove Field in 1400[9] and 1547.[10] Pekingborow Field, which abutted Uxendon Field on the north and east, belonged to the Freren estate in 1511–12.[11] The consolidation of estates led to the reduction and final disappearance of the open fields. In 1400 Wembley manor was divided between 50 a. of inclosed and 86 a. of open-field land; by 1547 it had 109 a. inclosed and only 35 a. in the open fields. The Dissolution may have hastened the process. Richard Bellamy, owner of Tokyngton manor, leased Freren manor in 1540[12] and by 1597[13] he had probably exchanged the Tokyngton portion of the Freren estate for the Kingsbury lands belonging to Tokyngton

[84] M.R.O., Acc. 276/3/49; Acc. 601/3; Acc. 853/19; Acc. 854/7.
[85] M.R.O., Acc. 76/210, /707, /1109.
[86] M.R.O., Acc. 643, 2nd deposit, Messeder map A.
[87] M.R.O., L.V. 7/1; Wembley News, 15 Jan. 1953.
[88] M.R.O., L.V. 9/131.
[89] Wemb. Hist. Soc., Acc. 907/101.
[90] Rep. Pub. Bridges in Mdx. (1825), 211–14 penes M.R.O.; Lond. & Mdx. Arch. Soc. Bulletin, v. 11.
[91] M.R.O., Acc. 441/26.
[92] Name altered to Park Lane in 1910: Brent Town Hall, Wembley U.D.C., Min. Bk. (1908–11), ix. 327.
[93] M.R.O., Acc. 794/8; M.R. 612, nos. 1120–44; Elsley, Wembley, 143.
[94] M.R.O., Acc. 76/1400.
[95] M.R.O., D.R.O. 3/F13/4.
[96] Census, 1841.
[97] H.O. 107/1700, ff. 152–8, 160–72.
[98] See p. 198.
[99] M.R.O., Acc. 590/3–4.
[1] Wemb. Hist. Soc., Acc. 380/2.
[2] See p. 235.
[3] M.R.O., Acc. 853/15.
[4] Kent Recs. xviii. 7.
[5] P.N. Mdx. (E.P.N.S.), 53.
[6] Cal. Close, 1399–1402, 293–7.
[7] Possibly Hall Field from Hall Lane, another name for Old Street or Honeypot Lane.
[8] C.P. 25(1)/146/10.
[9] Cal. Close, 1399–1402, 293–7.
[10] M.R.O., Acc. 1052, ff. 102–4.
[11] S.C. 2/191/45.
[12] S.C. 6/Hen. VIII /2402, m. 9d.
[13] All Souls Coll., Oxford, Hovenden Maps, Portfolio II, nos. 10–15.

manor. By 1609 both the former Wembley and Tokyngton manors and the chapel were in the hands of the Pages, who created the later pattern of farms.[14] Any small medieval settlement must have been destroyed in the process. There was one isolated farm, Tokyngton manor, in 1759[15] but the Great Central Railway cut across the farm-land in 1906 and the house was destroyed in 1939.

ALPERTON, first recorded in 1199 as 'Alprinton', possibly 'the farm of Eahlbeorht',[16] was in the south-west corner of Harrow parish, separated from Tokyngton on the north-east by Rowland's Brook. Since it was not a tithing in 1316, it may still have been little more than an isolated farmstead.[17] There was probably a small community by the mid 14th century, when there were six head tenements, five of which can be located. One was in Watery Lane, north of the main village,[18] another in the fork at the junction of Watery Lane with Honeypot Lane,[19] and another south of Alperton Green;[20] two, Alperton Lodge[21] and a cottage at Brentside,[22] lay to the south, at a second area of settlement at Vicar's Green, near the bridging point of the Brent. The pattern suggests that a comment in 1845 that Alperton was a 'straggling place'[23] would also have been true in the Middle Ages.

Alperton was always an area of small estates. Originally eight, there were six head tenements in 1553,[24] four ½-hides, one virgate, and one of three virgates. After some consolidation, probably at the end of the 15th and beginning of the 16th century, the six head tenements were held in 1553 by Thomas Page, John Hedger, and John Cannon.[25] By the end of the century one member of the Page family held the virgate, and another the 3-virgate and one ½-hide holding,[26] and the three together were from 1629 reckoned as a single head tenement of one hide. From 1629 there were only four head tenements,[27] one of the ½-hides having disappeared.[28] There were still four head tenements, held by four tenants, in 1698.[29] Freehold tenure in Alperton was not reckoned in hides and virgates, but there were several freehold estates that were probably medieval in origin. Most of the freehold land in 1553 was held by Sir Thomas Cheyney,[30] apart from 40 a. held by John Lyon of London.[31] Although the estates were small, there always seems to have been a good deal of sub-letting, sometimes to landowners there or

elsewhere but also to under-tenants who lived in cottages.[32]

In 1547[33] the four open fields of Alperton were Brent Field, Hill Field (both mentioned in 1470–1),[34] North Field, and Ham Field. Brent Field, then consisting of 137 selions in four furlongs, took its name from the river which formed its southern boundary. The even larger Hill Field, which had 181 selions in eight furlongs, joined it on the north. Of the smaller fields, Ham Field, with 51 selions in four furlongs, lay to the west of Brent Field, while North Field, consisting of 84 selions in six furlongs, lay to the north of the hamlet, joining Hill Field on its eastern border. Compared with 453 selions of open-field, there were 204 a. of mostly freehold inclosed land, including Snowden Hill Field[35] and Wood Field. Inclosure at Alperton before the 19th century was not nearly as extensive as in other hamlets, and at the time of parliamentary inclosure in 1817[36] only the south-west corner, about 296 a., was inclosed. Open fields, which formed an arc on three sides of the hamlet, still occupied 377 a. Alperton, unlike Uxendon and Wembley, had no dominating family. The Cheyney property, which in 1553 included a mansion and might have formed the nucleus for a large estate, was split up in the 17th century,[37] leaving Alperton a village of small, scattered farms and cottages. In 1672 the largest assessment was for Andrew Wright, with 7 hearths, and of the 14 people assessed seven had only one hearth.[38] There was some encroachment on the waste during the 16th and 17th centuries.[39] Three cottages, one 'new-built with brick', provided increments of rent in 1681.[40] A smith's shop was erected in 1680, two cottages were built in 1688, and single cottages in 1689, 1697, 1711, and 1714.[41] The last two were in Watery Lane[42] and Honeypot Lane.[43]

In 1759 the main north–south route from Harrow-on-the-Hill and Sudbury ran through Alperton to cross the Brent at Vicar's Bridge,[44] named in 1507–8[45] and apparently the bridge recorded in 1432–3.[46] The bridge, known as 'Vicarebrygge' in 1507–8, was also called Alperton or Brent Bridge during the 16th and 17th centuries,[47] when the lord made an allowance for repairs. It was wooden and was mended in 1796 by the lords of Harrow and Ealing, but in 1818, when it was impassable, they tried to avoid the expense of building a new one. In 1822 they reluctantly rebuilt the bridge, in timber,[48] and in 1874 it

[14] See p. 226. An 18th-century 'view of the village of Oackington' is unlikely to represent the Middlesex Tokyngton: Bodl. Maps Gough 18, f. 5v; Wemb. Hist. Soc., Acc. 411/14.
[15] M.R.O., Acc. 643, 2nd deposit, Messeder map A.
[16] Ft. of F. Lond. & Mdx. i. 1; P.N. Mdx. (E.P.N.S.), 52.
[17] M.R.O., Acc. 76/2410, m. 31.
[18] Ibid. /1400; M.R. 612, no. 1170.
[19] M.R.O., Acc. 76/1400; M.R. 612, no. 1172.
[20] M.R.O., Acc. 76/1844, /2388; M.R. 612, no. 1185.
[21] M.R.O., Acc. 76/1845; M.R. 612, no. 1195.
[22] M.R.O., Acc. 76/1400; M.R. 612, no. 1194.
[23] Home Cnties. Dir. (1845), 452.
[24] M.R.O., Acc. 76/222a. Originally 4 ½-hides and 4 virgates, see p. 224.
[25] Ibid. /2418, mm. 24, 47, /2420, m. 67d; Acc. 853/15.
[26] M.R.O., Acc. 76/205.
[27] Ibid. /208.
[28] i.e. that held in 1553 by John Hedger.
[29] M.R.O., Acc. 794/2.
[30] i.e. 'certain lands late Christiane Cheeseman', a mansion, 2 closes 'Rydyng', late John Best, and certain lands, and 1 tenement and lands late Ric. Goldington, said to be held of Roxeth manor.

[31] John Lyon atte Brugg was mentioned in 1432–3: M.R.O., Acc. 76/2416, m. 45d.
[32] M.R.O., Acc. 76/2418, mm. 24, 46, /2420, m. 67d; Acc. 441/38; Acc. 854/2.
[33] M.R.O., Acc. 76/2418, m. 24.
[34] Ibid. 222a. Snowden as a place-name in Alperton was recorded in 1384: Acc. 76/2413, m. 15.
[35] M.R.O., Acc. 854/2, /10.
[36] M.R.O., Acc. 794/8; M.R. 612.
[37] The Cheyney estate passed to the Draper family (M.R.O., Acc. 76/205, /208, /222a) who sold part in 1601 (Acc. 854/1) and part in 1632 (Acc. 854/2). And see Acc. 76/208; Acc. 899.
[38] M.R.O., H.T. 26.
[39] M.R.O., Acc. 76/205, /208, /222a; Acc. 899.
[40] M.R.O., Acc. 76/707.
[41] Ibid. /210, /1109.
[42] M.R. 612, no. 1163.   [43] Ibid., no. 1181.
[44] M.R.O., Acc. 643, 2nd deposit, Messeder map A.
[45] Lambeth Palace, Estate MS. 477.
[46] M.R.O., Acc. 76/2416, m. 45d.
[47] Ibid. /1985, /2007.
[48] Ibid. /917, /919, /921, /928–32, /940, /942; Lond. & Mdx. Arch. Soc. Bulletin, v. 11.

had to be rebuilt again, this time in concrete and brick.[49] Other roads in 1759 ran from Alperton Green westward[50] to join the main north–south road, and northward, as Watery Lane,[51] to join the east–west road from Wembley to Sudbury, and east and then south to the river near Twyford House. In the extreme south of the hamlet, a road ran parallel with the river from Perivale, across Vicar's Green and the road near Twyford House to join Deadman's Hill in Tokyngton. Thirty-five buildings, some of them almost certainly barns, formed a straggling pattern north, south, and east of Alperton Green, with a few on either side of the southern portion of Watery Lane, a few in Honeypot Lane, and six, as well as the three buildings of Alperton Lodge, at Vicar's Green. There were 20 a. of common land at Alperton and Vicar's greens.[52] Among the buildings were two inns, the 'Chequers', licensed from 1751, rebuilt in 1901,[53] and still in existence in 1967, and the 'Plough' on the Ealing road, licensed from 1722.[54] The road pattern changed with the cutting of the Paddington branch of the Grand Junction Canal across the southern corner of Alperton in 1801.[55] The southern road running eastward along the river stopped at the entry to the common fields[56] and, after inclosure, at Vicar's Bridge.[57] The road which had turned east and south to Twyford House changed course. At inclosure it extended far enough south to cross the canal by a 'wing' (sic) bridge but by 1852 this crossing had disappeared.[58] Instead the road, Honeypot Lane,[59] turned eastward, initially as an entry to the common fields, but by 1852 as the entry to Alperton Cottage.

On the eve of inclosure Thomas Bowler, who was hanged for manslaughter in 1812,[60] had the largest farm (175 a.), covering the south-west corner of Alperton and with cottages and farm buildings in Watery Lane and Honeypot Lane.[61] There were two other farms of just under 80 a., two estates of just under 40 a., and 9 less than 20 a., most of them under 10 a. After inclosure farms were similar in size but more compact. In 1851 there were four, the largest (100 a.) employing 4 labourers; no labourers were employed on two of the farms (of 60 a. and 15 a. respectively) and numbers on the fourth (88 a.) are not known.[62] After inclosure one new estate (176 a.) was allotted to Christ Church, Oxford, as tithe-owners, and a cottage was built in the middle of the land.[63]

In 1805 Alperton had at least 21 houses.[64] In 1831 the population was 199[65] and ten years later it was 242, in 41 houses.[66] In 1851 there were 234 people and 36 houses;[67] besides the two inns there was a beershop[68] at Vicar's Bridge and another, the 'Pleasure Boat', closed in 1901, which took most of its custom from trippers on the canal.[69] A tile-works, south of the canal, provided some industry. Alperton Cottage had been built by 1852,[70] and Exhibition Cottage on the western border with Perivale and new cottages at Vicar's Green and near the tile-works had been added by 1865.[71] More houses were built between 1880 and 1910, a number of which survive.[72] Rapid expansion of both industrial premises and housing estates took place after the First World War and again after the Second World War. The population rose from 2,468 in 1921 (a density of 4·3 persons to an acre) to 6,444 in 1931 and 14,432 (25·1 an acre) in 1951. Thereafter it declined to 12,804 in 1961.[73]

SUDBURY, a large, undefined hamlet, lay north-west of Alperton. The name, first recorded in 1273–4,[74] may derive from its position south of Harrow-on-the-Hill, or from its relationship to Rectory manor, the one being the north, the other the south manor.[75] The hamlet was intimately connected with the manor in its midst, with cotlanders, the only ones in Harrow,[76] providing regular labour on the demesne, which stretched from Sudbury village eastward across the centre of the parish. There were no open fields and the cotlanders depended upon their small crofts and upon their animals on the common. The medieval settlement apparently consisted of cottages in 5-acre closes along the edge of the large, wooded,[77] and, even in the 18th century, deserted Sudbury Common.[78] The centre of settlement was Sudbury Court itself and much 14th-century pottery was found at the top of Mutton Lane (Elm Lane) in 1963.[79] By the late 13th century there were 17 cotlanders[80] and in 1316 two tithings.[81] In 1547 there were 173 communicants in Sudbury.[82] By 1547 the 17 cotlands had been divided and combined and only seven still possessed messuages. The cotlands contained 88 a., compared with 463 a. of freehold land and 13 other houses.[83] The Hermitage, granted to Henry Bett, a London grocer, in 1540,[84] may have been the hermitage of St. Edmund and St. Katharine, said in 1529 to have been held by the lord

[49] M.R.O., Acc. 76/1979–80.
[50] i.e. the northern section of the modern Manor Farm Road.
[51] i.e. the northern section of the modern Ealing Road.
[52] There were only 12 a. by 1817: M.R.O., Acc. 794/8.
[53] M.R.O., L.V. 7/1; Wemb. Hist. Soc., Acc. 907/102.
[54] Still existing in 1913, on the E. of the road, midway between the canal and the Brent: M.R.O., Acc. 590/3, no. 1525; L.V. 3/94; L.V. 7/1; P.S. G/H5/1.
[55] See below, p. 198.
[56] M.R. 612.
[57] O.S. Map 1/2,500, Mdx. xvi. 5 (1865 edn.). The section left today is called Alperton Lane.
[58] M.R.O., Acc. 590/3.
[59] Not the Honeypot Lane in Kenton and Preston.
[60] M.R.O., Acc. 76/270, /713.
[61] Ibid. /1400; Acc. 794/8; M.R. 612.
[62] M.R.O., Acc. 590/3–4; H.O. 107/1700, ff. 152–8, 172.
[63] Christ Church, Oxford, Harrow Maps 5.
[64] M.R.O., Acc. 76/1400.
[65] M.R.O., D.R.O. 3/F13/4.
[66] Census, 1841.
[67] H.O. 107/1700, ff. 152–8, 172; M.R.O., Acc. 590/3–4.

[68] Ibid. /3, no. 1531.
[69] Ibid., no. 1544; P.S. G/H 5/1; Wemb. Hist. Soc., Acc. 907/110.
[70] M.R.O., Acc. 590/3.
[71] O.S. Map 1/2,500, Mdx. xv. 4, xvi. 1, 5 (1865 edn.).
[72] e.g. Stanley Villas (dated 1888): ex inf. Mr. A. H. Murgatroyd; Robbins, Middlesex, 357.
[73] i.e. of Alperton ward (566 a. in 1921 and 1931, 573 a. in 1951 and 1961): Census, 1951–61.
[74] B.M. Add. MS. 29794, m. 1d.
[75] P.N. Mdx. (E.P.N.S.), 54.
[76] See p. 224.
[77] Called Southwood in 1270: Close R. 1268–72, 221; Sudbury Wood in 1435: M.R.O., Acc. 76/1013, /1622; Acc. 854/3.
[78] Sudbury, ed. H. Egan, 11–12.
[79] Wemb. Hist. Soc., Jnl. N.S. (9).
[80] Lambeth Palace, Estate MS. 2068.
[81] M.R.O., Acc. 76/2410, m. 3.
[82] E 301/34 f. 28v, no. 141.
[83] M.R.O., Acc. 1052, ff. 15–25. The figures do not include Sudbury Court Farm.
[84] M.R.O., Acc. 76/1645.

for many years past.[85] In 1547 it was described as a mansion[86] and in the 17th century it was a large house belonging to the Flambards estate.[87]

During the 16th and 17th centuries, besides the three demesne farms, there were estates like those centred around Sudbury Place, possibly to be identified with Hundred Elms Farm, and Ilotts Farm.[88] In the 17th century Sudbury Common covered about 300 a.,[89] but encroachments were being made on the eastern edge. There were 9 wastehold properties in 1553[90] and 15 in 1681.[91] A new house east of the common was mentioned in 1622,[92] two new freehold houses had appeared by 1629,[93] and another by c. 1642.[94] By 1664 there were 40 houses of which 23 were assessed for hearth tax, including one with 23 hearths belonging to Edward Claxton, probably Sudbury Place, and one with 17 hearths belonging to Sir Gilbert Gerard, presumably the Hermitage.[95] In 1672 36 houses were assessed, including 8 which had not been chargeable in 1664. Claxton still had Sudbury Place, while the Hermitage was held by Sir Charles Pim.[96] Three more cottages were built between 1727 and 1742,[97] and the 'Mitre' was built near the bowling green[98] in 1756 by Thomas Clutterbuck. The manorial mill had existed on Sudbury Common, between the Hermitage and Flambards, since the Middle Ages,[99] and in 1693 the miller lived in a cottage nearby.[1] The Windmill House, said, probably erroneously, to belong to Richard Page and later to John Gray, was granted and possibly built in 1738.[2] In 1755 it was claimed by Francis Otway, in the right of his wife, Sarah, daughter of Charles Hayes, perhaps the Mr. Hayes who was presented in 1725 for inclosing a considerable part of the common without licence.[3] The map of 1759 marks Richard Page's house on the eastern edge of Sudbury Common midway between the Hermitage and Sudbury Court Farm.[4]

In 1759 a north–south route (Sudbury Hill and Harrow Road) ran across Sudbury Common from Harrow-on-the-Hill to Alperton, Ealing, and London, and a west–east route (Sudbury Court Road and East Lane) to Wembley. Sheepcote Lane was merely a lane from Sheepcote Farm to Sudbury Court. Mutton Lane ran southward to Hundred Elms Farm and joined Harrow Road as a tree-lined drive, possibly a private road to the farm. Wood End Road, Greenford Road, and a road through Horsenden Wood ran westward from Sudbury Hill and Harrow Road. Seventy buildings existed in 1759, 22 of them belonging to the farms: Sudbury Court, Sheepcote, Woodcock Hill, Ilotts, Hundred Elms, and Vale farms. To the north, near the point where Sudbury joins Roxeth and Harrow-on-the-Hill, the Hermitage was set in its own inclosure in the middle of the common, with Harrow pound on the west and a common well on the south. South of the well was the old bowling green, with two houses, belonging to Mr. Saunders and John Bliss, in a small inclosure on the east. On the eastern edge of the common were two large houses with avenues, one belonging to Richard Page, the other to Major Matthews. One may be identifiable with the later Sudbury Grove. Apart from the Mitre Inn,[5] the other buildings were mainly cottages along the eastern edge of Sudbury Common. The densest concentration was in the triangle formed by Harrow Road, Mutton Lane, and Sudbury Court Road, where the 'Black Horse' had been licensed from 1751.[6] Among the very few buildings on the southern and western edge was the 'Swan',[7] a coaching inn at the junction of Harrow Road and Sheepcote Lane. Only about 25 a. of the common had been lost in the century before 1759,[8] and on the eve of inclosure there were 235 a. of common land.[9] A second western road, Maybank Avenue, had appeared by 1817, turning northward at the edge of the common to join Greenford Road. The pattern of settlement, however, remained essentially the same. One new mansion was built between 1759 and 1805: Crabs House or Sudbury Lodge, the home of John Copland.[10]

Sudbury's closeness to Harrow-on-the-Hill, and, after 1845, its connexion by horse omnibus with the London trains at Wembley, contributed to its development. The population rose from 378 in 1831[11] to 566 in 1841, when there were 96 inhabited houses.[12] Ten years later the population was 588.[13] In spite of some new cottages, its character in the mid 19th century was determined by the large houses and villas in spacious surroundings which were erected for gentry and businessmen, people like Thomas Trollope, a lawyer, who had built Julian Hill by 1819.[14] Aspen Lodge and Sudbury Grove had also been built by 1819,[15] Sudbury Priory in 1828,[16] Sudbury Hill House and the Mount by 1830,[17] and Sudbury House by 1852.[18] In 1851 there were gentry, a barrister, stockjobbers, and capitalists.[19] Oak Place and Elms Wood had been added by 1865,[20] and

85 M.R.O., Acc. 76/2421, m. 58.   86 Ibid. /1645.
87 Ibid. /208; Acc. 794/2.
88 See p. 212.
89 M.R.O., Acc. 76/779.
90 Ibid. /222a.   91 Ibid. /707.
92 M.R.O., Acc. 854/3.
93 M.R.O., Acc. 76/208.   94 M.R.O., Acc. 794/2.
95 M.R.O., H.T. 5.
96 Presumably as lessee: H.T. 26.
97 M.R.O., Acc. 76/1109.
98 A 'little house built on the bowling green' was mentioned in 1672: M.R.O., Acc. 76/854; Bowling Green House was built c. 1766: ibid. /954.
99 Ibid. /1010, /1985; Lambeth Palace, Estate MS. 1193; B.M. Add. MS. 29794; S.C. 6/1128/12, m. 5; C.P. 25(1)/150/65/314; John Seller, Map of Mdx. (1710).
1 M.R.O., Acc. 76/87.
2 Ibid. /1109.
3 Ibid. /1385, /2090.
4 M.R.O., Acc. 643, 2nd deposit, Messeder maps A and B.
5 M.R.O., Acc. 76/1109; Acc. 590/1, /4, no. 1289; L.V. 9/186. Rebuilt c. 1930, it was still there in 1967: Wemb. Hist. Soc., Acc. 907/112.

6 M.R.O., Acc. 590/1, /4, no. 1673; L.V. 7/1. Still there in 1895: ibid. P.S. G/H5/1.
7 M.R.O., Acc. 590/1, /4, no. 1595. Possibly earlier the 'White Swan' (M.R.O., L.V. 9/93, /186; L.V. 10/88; L.V. 28), the 'Admiral Vernon' (L.V. 9/2), or the 'Crooked Billet' (L.V. 7/37). Rebuilt: Wemb. Hist. Soc., Acc. 907/104.
8 M.R.O., Acc. 643, 2nd deposit, Messeder maps A and B. A 'considerable' part, inclosed without permission, was ordered to be thrown open in 1725; M.R.O., Acc. 76/2090.
9 M.R.O., Acc. 76/2205; Acc. 794/8.
10 M.R.O., Acc. 76/1400; Acc. 794/8; M.R. 612.
11 M.R.O., D.R.O. 3/F13/1.
12 Census, 1841.
13 H.O. 107/1700, ff. 21–32, 99–105, 147–52, 158–9.
14 See p. 212.
15 Greenwood, Map of Mdx. (1819).
16 Wemb. Hist. Soc., Acc. 714. Demolished by the Home Guard during the Second World War: Wemb. Hist. Soc., Catalogue 411/10.
17 M.R.O., D.R.O. 3/F2/1.
18 M.R.O., Acc. 590/1, /4, no. 1746.
19 H.O. 107/1700, ff. 21–32, 99–105, 147–52, 158–9.
20 O.S. Map 1/2,500, Mdx. x. 11, 12, 15, 16 (1865 edn.).

Dr. (later Sir) William H. Perkin, the chemist, built the Chestnuts *c.* 1873 next to the older Seymour Villa, which he turned into a laboratory.[21] Sudbury Hall had been built by 1873[22] and Kennet House by 1900.[23] Terraced and semi-detached houses were also built. By 1865 there were some along Greenford Road,[24] with the 'Rising Sun' beerhouse,[25] and others were built south of Hundred Elms Farm and in the extreme east where the railway crossed the hamlet. As a focus for the growing community, the Coplands built a workmen's hall near Seymour Villa in 1864, which Sir William Perkin later replaced by the New Hall.[26] Development gathered pace from the end of the 19th century[27] and large villas were sold and their grounds broken up into building lots.[28] With the extension of the railway in the next century, housing spread over the area, replacing the farms as well as the big houses, although some open spaces like Vale Farm Sports Ground and Barham Park have been preserved. The population density increased from 2·3 persons to an acre in 1921 to 9·8 in 1931 and 18·7 in 1951, decreasing slightly to 18 in 1961.[29]

In 1968 little remained of older Sudbury. Sudbury Lodge, later called Barham House, an 18th-century building with 19th-century alterations, was demolished in 1956.[30] The grounds have become a public park and the stable block and other ancillary buildings, much extended in the late 19th century, are partly occupied as a library, a club, and an old people's home. Sudbury Court Farm was demolished in 1957.[31] The former farm-house at Hundred Elms Farm is of the mid 19th century; near it a two-storied brick outbuilding of the early 16th century with brick-mullioned windows is still standing.[32] Some 19th-century terraced cottages remain in Greenford Road and there are similar cottages and semi-detached houses in Harrow Road and Elms Lane.[33] On the high ground to the north-west, where Sudbury joins Harrow-on-the-Hill, several larger residences have survived; they include Julian Hill and Kennet House, together with Sudbury Hill House (later Bowden House), which became the sanatorium for Harrow School in 1929.[34]

ROXETH lay south of Pinner and south and west of Harrow-on-the-Hill. The boundary with Harrow-on-the-Hill ran from the corner of London Road and Roxeth Hill to a point just west of the junction of Hog Lane and Byron Road (later Byron Hill Road), across West Street and roughly through the centre of the lands enclosed by Bessborough Road and Lowlands Road. The place-name Roxeth is compounded of the personal name Hroc or Rook, which also appears in Roxborough and Roxbourne, and the suffix *seap*, a pit or well.[35] In 845 Roxeth was apparently the name of fields which belonged to Greenford township.[36] It occurs in the 13th century as the estate of the Roxeth family[37] and by 1316 it had as many as three tithings.[38] Eight of the 13 medieval head tenements can be identified, all but one on the western side of Northolt Road.[39] They were scattered along the whole length of Roxeth,[40] one of them being in the extreme north-east, possibly on the site of the later Honeybourne's Farm.[41] In the centre, almost opposite the junction of Northolt Road with London (later Roxeth) Hill, stood the moated site of Roxeth manor.[42] The location of the head tenements suggests that the medieval settlement was straggling, like the later village. By 1547[43] there were 10 houses belonging to the head tenements, 14 underset cottages, and seven free tenements or cottages. A 'mansion' was built on the waste by 1553.[44]

The principal common fields lay in a block north and west of Roxeth hamlet.[45] Newden or Newton Field, mentioned in 1507–8,[46] was in the north and consisted in 1547[47] of 225 selions in nine furlongs. South-west of Newden Field lay Mead or Middle Field, which was mentioned in 1456,[48] and which in 1547[49] contained 188 selions in seven furlongs and another furlong which belonged exclusively to Roxeth manor farm. The southernmost field was Dobbs or Dabbs, mentioned in 1383,[50] which was divided from Ruislip common fields by Bourne Lane. In 1547[51] it had 11 furlongs and 263 selions. Blackhall Field, which occurs from the 14th to the 16th century, may be the later Newden Field, since in 1456 land in Blackhall Field was described as at 'Newedenhacche' and in 1553 Newden Field was described as lying at Blackhall cross.[52] There was a second field system attached to the dependent hamlet of Hyde End, in north Roxeth. In 1547[53] Hill Field, which projected south-eastward from Newden

[21] *Sudbury*, ed. Egan, 17–20. For Perkins, see *V.C.H. Mdx.* iii. 209, 214.
[22] See p. 268. The building was demolished in 1959: Wemb. Hist. Soc., Catalogue, D 464/9.
[23] M.R.O., Acc. 76/1319.
[24] O.S. Map 1/2,500, Mdx. x. 11, 12, 15, 16 (1865 edn.).
[25] M.R.O., Acc. 590/1, /4, no. 1612; P.S. G/H5/1.
[26] *Sudbury*, ed. Egan, 19–20.
[27] Harrow Cent. Ref. Libr., Sales Partics. i. (1885); Wemb. Hist. Soc., Acc. 714.
[28] M.R.O., Acc. 208/3; Harrow Cent. Ref. Libr., Sales Partics. ii (the Mount estate, 1876, 1879, 1885, 1898).
[29] *Census*, 1921–61. In 1921–31 Sudbury ward was 1,253 a., and the population rose from 2,890 to 12,335. In 1951–61 Sudbury and Sudbury Court wards together comprised 1,044 a., and the population fell from 19,550 to 18,860.
[30] Photographic record (1965) at National Monuments Record; ex inf. Dept. of Planning, Lord Bor. of Brent.
[31] See p. 204.
[32] Hist. Mon. Com. *Mdx.* 131; illustrated in *Sudbury*, ed. Egan, 8.
[33] Some are dated 1862 and 1866: ex inf. Mr. A. H. Murgatroyd.
[34] Laborde, *Harrow Sch.* 207.
[35] *P.N. Mdx.* (E.P.N.S.), 53–54. The form Roxey, which co-existed into the 20th century, may be a distinct name, meaning Rook's island, and there may originally have been

two distinct localities: T. L. Bartlett, *Roxeth*, 6.
[36] *Cart. Sax.* ed. Birch, ii. 29.
[37] Lambeth Palace, Estate MS. 1193; B.M. Add. MS. 29794, m. 1d.
[38] M.R.O., Acc. 76/2410, m. 3.
[39] Ibid. /1953; M.R. 612, no. 530.
[40] From south to north, Grove Farm, i.e. M.R. 612, no. 507 (see p. 196); M.R. 612, no. 512 (M.R.O., Acc. 76/1951); Golden Croft, i.e. M.R. 612, no. 497 (M.R.O., Acc. 76/445; Acc. 794/8); M.R. 612, nos. 476–7 (M.R.O., Acc. 76/1894); M.R. 612, nos. 437, 469 (M.R.O., Acc. 76/1907); M.R. 612, no. 448 (M.R.O., Acc. 76/996).
[41] M.R.O., Acc. 76/690–1.
[42] See pp. 205–6.
[43] M.R.O., Acc. 1052, ff. 311v–18v.
[44] M.R.O., Acc. 76/222a.
[45] M.R. 612.
[46] Lambeth Palace, Estate MS. 477.
[47] M.R.O., Acc. 1052, ff. 340v–68.
[48] Scott, *Recs. of Grammar Sch.* 11.
[49] M.R.O., Acc. 1052, ff. 400v–23.
[50] M.R.O., Acc. 76/2413, m. 6d.
[51] M.R.O., Acc. 1052, ff. 368v–400.
[52] M.R.O., Acc. 76/222a; Scott, *Recs. of Grammar Sch.* 11.
[53] M.R.O., Acc. 1052, ff. 319–40.

Field, was the main field with 79 selions in five furlongs. Great Peeles Field[54] had 45 selions in two furlongs, Little Peeles Field had 27 selions in two furlongs, and Six Acres Field had 22 selions in three furlongs. There was some inclosure in the 17th and 18th centuries and in 1629 the manorial court ordered the re-opening of Great and Little Peeles.[55] All the Hyde End fields, except Hill Field, which was also associated with Pinner, had disappeared by 1817, but there can have been little inclosure of the main open fields, since they still comprised 539 a.[56]

Wastehold parcels, few of them described, increased from five in 1553 to 18 at the end of the century.[57] There were 21 parcels by c. 1642[58] and in 1681, including two cottages, three houses, six barns, and several orchards.[59] There were 45 houses in 1664, of which 16 were assessed for hearth tax, but none was very large: John Cannon, a freeholder, had 8 hearths, William Greenhill had 7, and five people had 6 hearths.[60] In 1672 thirty-nine houses were assessed, including some which had not been chargeable in 1664.[61] At least four more cottages, a messuage, and two barns seem to have been built between 1681 and 1721.[62]

By 1759 one main route (Bessborough Road, Lower Road, and Northolt Road) ran from north-east to south-west through the length of Roxeth, linking Pinner and Harrow-on-the-Hill with Northolt and Eastcote. Another ran from Pinner through the open fields to join the Northolt road in a series of branch roads, giving it the appearance on the map of a river delta.[63] This road, Pinner Lane, later called Rayners Lane, appears to have slightly changed course by 1817.[64] In 1759 there were seventy-eight buildings, some of them outbuildings, most densely concentrated on the west side of Northolt and Lower Road, between the northernmost branch road and a point just south of the junction with West Street. The 'Three Horse Shoes', licensed from 1751,[65] stood in the angle of Northolt Road and a branch road, on the line of Stanley Road. On the east side of Northolt Road there were a few buildings at the junction with Roxeth Hill and a few more to the south but none between Roxeth Hill and West Street. To the north there were a few isolated buildings, mainly farms, including Roxborough, Honeybourne's, and Roxeth, on each side of Bessborough Road. Buildings were also concentrated at the southern end of Northolt Road, less densely than at its northern end, and on the western edge of the common and around the southernmost branch road. Two isolated farms, Parker's and Baker's, and another, possibly Eve's, lay on the east side of

Northolt Road, but there was nothing along either of the two roads to Pinner. The unifying factor was the Northolt road and the long stretch of Roxeth Green and common, which in 1759 consisted of 77 a. The common had been reduced to 58 a. in 1817, but there is little sign of a corresponding increase in the number of buildings.[66]

The indistinct boundary with Harrow-on-the-Hill makes it difficult to estimate the population. The population apparently rose from 609 in 1831[67] to 703, living in 147 houses, in 1851, if Roxeth in 1851 is defined as Northolt Road with its extensions, Lower and Bessborough Road, London Hill, and Middle Row. The higher figure of 842 people in 1841 evidently included some of the inhabitants of Harrow Town as living in Roxeth.[68] Most of the new building had been close to Harrow Town, notably in Middle Row, where 41 houses had been erected since inclosure; a further 7 cottages and a school were built along the east side of Lower Road, backing on Middle Row.[69] There were 10 farm-houses in 1851–2; in the south-west corner, on either side of Northolt Road were Grove[70] and Parker's[71] farms, with Tithe Farm standing by itself in Eastcote Lane;[72] Roxborough,[73] Honeybourne's[74] and Roxeth Farm[75] were in the north, and a farm and brick-works belonging to Richard Chapman stood on the west of Northolt Road,[76] with two farms almost opposite.[77] There were two beershops besides the 'Three Horse Shoes': one, at the corner of Middle Row and London Hill, may have been the 'White Horse', licensed 1873–89,[78] the other[79] lay behind the cottages in the corner of Northolt Road and London Hill. There was also a beerhouse attached to Roxeth House, the only large residence.[80] A few bigger houses had been built by 1865: the Grange, Dudley Lodge, Roxeth Lodge, Pleasant Place, and Ivy Lodge and Dabbshill Lodge in the former open-field area.[81] New buildings in the 1850s and 1860s[82] included a gas-works in Northolt Road[83] and Christ Church in London Hill.[84]

Roxeth retained its rural character in the later 19th century with 7 farms and some farm cottages. There were 30 shops, many along Middle Row, and, besides the four older public houses, the 'Half Moon', the 'Timber Carriage', and one unnamed beershop[85] erected partly for migrant haymakers.[86] In the last third of the century roads and houses were built north-east of Eastcote Lane, and some public buildings and installations appeared: a hospital for infectious diseases and a sewage farm in the north, a cottage hospital in Lower Road, replaced in 1905 by one in Roxeth Hill, a drill hall, and mission

---

54 John and Ric. Pele had land in Roxeth in 1445: M.R.O., Acc. 76/2417, m. 89.
55 Ibid. /1010; Acc. 188/9, /20.
56 M.R.O., Acc. 794/8.
57 M.R.O., Acc. 76/205, /222a.
58 M.R.O., Acc. 794/2.
59 M.R.O., Acc. 76/707.
60 M.R.O., H.T. 5.
61 Ibid. 26.
62 M.R.O., Acc. 76/210, /707.
63 M.R.O., Acc. 643, 2nd deposit, Messeder map A.
64 M.R. 612.
65 M.R.O., L.V. 7/1; Acc. 590/1,/4, no. 265. Licensed to 1912: P.S. G/H5/1.
66 M.R.O., Acc. 794/8; M.R. 612.
67 M.R.O., D.R.O. 3/F13/2.
68 M.R.O., Acc. 590/1–4; H.O. 107/1700, ff. 43–62, 90–93.
69 This area may have been counted as Harrow-on-the-Hill in 1841.

70 M.R.O., Acc. 590/1, /4, no. 288.
71 Ibid. /4, no. 1812.
72 Ibid. /4, no. 1835. Created at inclosure and existing as New Farm by 1822; O.S. Map 1", sheet 7 (1822 edn.).
73 M.R.O., Acc. 590/1, /4, no. 360.
74 Ibid. /4, no. 346.
75 Ibid. /4, no. 232.
76 Ibid. /4, no. 256.
77 Ibid. /4, nos. 1800, 1803.
78 Ibid. /4, no. 215; P.S. G/H5/1.
79 M.R.O., Acc. 590/1, /4, no. 1795a.
80 Ibid. /4, nos. 133–4.
81 O.S. Map 1/2,500, Mdx. x. 7, 11, 14, 15 (1865 edn.).
82 M.R.O., Acc. 76/1838, /1892, /1894, /1900, /1905, /1907, /1922, /1927, /1946.
83 See p. 249.
84 See p. 258.
85 M.R.O., P.S. G/H5/1.
86 Bartlett, Roxeth, 85–89.

hall.[87] The development was still along the line of the ancient village and on land that had formed Roxeth Common.[88] With the coming of the railway in the 20th century, however, building began to follow railway lines, and farm-land gave way to housing estates. By the 1930s Roxeth had been swallowed into the new dormitory area of South and West Harrow. Roxeth Farm in Bessborough Road, a two-storied weather-boarded house with a symmetrical front of five bays and a hipped, tiled roof, is the oldest surviving building; with its two timber barns it was probably built *c.* 1700. Dating from the 19th century are cottages in Middle Row and some larger houses in Bessborough Road, including one now occupied by the Middlesex New Synagogue.

GREENHILL, one of the smallest hamlets, lay to the north of Harrow-on-the-Hill. Greenhill first appears as a surname in Harrow parish in 1273–4[89] and as a place-name in the 1330s,[90] although the hamlet may have existed earlier as Norbury.[91] Greenhill usually was not a separate tithing.[92] During the Middle Ages there were five head tenements or farms, two hides, one ½-hide, and two virgate holdings. Some consolidation had taken place by 1553, when Henry Greenhill held one hide, and John Greenhill and Henry Finch each held a hide and a virgate.[93] In 1698 the lands of Finch and Henry Greenhill were still held by their descendants, one of whom, William Greenhill, had been a counsellor at law and secretary to General Monck.[94] All the estates developed into farms of 90–150 a. The 19th-century house sometimes called Greenhill Lodge,[95] in the elbow of Bonnersfield Lane, was probably on the site of a head tenement held by Henry Greenhill,[96] while one of the Finches' head tenements is probably represented by Hill's house, on the west of Greenhill Lane.[97] There were also a few estates held from Rectory manor, whose lands, and probably also messuages, lay west and south of the village.[98]

Five common fields are described in 1547.[99] West Field, which lay west of the hamlet, joining the Rectory lands on the south, had 24 selions in two furlongs. The main block of open-field land lay east of the hamlet, divided from Weald common fields by the Wealdstone (Weald or Greenhill) Brook. The northernmost was North Field, mentioned in 1399,[1] which in 1547 had 48 selions in three furlongs. Joining it on the east was East Field, mentioned in 1336,[2] which had 28 selions in two furlongs. Green-

hill Field, which lay to the south-east, contained 105 selions in five furlongs. In the south, joining Kenton, was Bandon Field with 88 selions in seven furlongs. In addition, 22 selions of Church Field, Harrow Weald, were described as belonging to Greenhill. From the 17th century, however, Greenhill's fields were Great, Middle, and Bennet or Bonner Field,[3] which approximated to North, East and Greenhill, and Bandon Field.[4] At inclosure they covered 113 a.[5] There is little evidence of many under-tenants, even after the head tenements had been consolidated and some of the original messuages had presumably decayed.[6] There was no wasthold until 1629 and then only one parcel,[7] probably the little cottage held by John Show, which was the only wasthold property in 1681.[8] In 1664 only six houses were assessed for hearth tax, the two head tenements, Greenhill's and Finch's, having six hearths each.[9] There is no sign of new building in the 18th century, and some of the 19 buildings marked in 1759 were outhouses.[10] Greenhill was at that time a small hamlet of modest farms regularly spaced around the 6-acre village green, which had been reduced to 3 a. in 1817.[11] Through the centre of the hamlet ran Greenhill Lane, part of the north–south route through the Weald, Harrow-on-the-Hill, and Sudbury to London. A second road, Sheepcote or Longshot Lane,[12] joining Greenhill Lane at the southern edge of the village and running south-westward, probably dated from the formation of Sheepcote Farm. A linking road joined the junction with Sheepcote Lane in 1759 and 1817 but afterwards disappeared. One other road is marked in 1759, a short, crooked road leading eastward. By 1817 as Bonnersfield Lane, it ran along the northern boundary of the demesne lands to the common fields. North of it Dirty Lane ran eastward as another entry to the common fields, while a short road on the west formed another field lane. On the west of Greenhill Lane was Finch's, later Hill's Farm, with three other houses south of it, one of them the Six Bells Inn, first mentioned in 1746[13] and after 1775 called the 'Marquis of Granby'.[14] Opposite the inn lay a farm sometimes called Greenhill Farm. To the east lay the farm soon to become the demesne or Manor Farm, with Greenhill's manor-house and two buildings, possibly cottages. Five cottages east of Greenhill Lane had appeared by 1805[15] and by 1841[16] there were 28 houses, supporting a population of 151. Eight houses, at least three of them farms, 17 cottages, and one inn, formed a nucleated village of only 141 people

[87] O.S. Map 6″, Mdx. x. SW., SE. (1897 edn.). See pp. 247–8.
[88] Some farming land was offered in 1858 as 'suitable for building', but there is no evidence of building there until much later: Harrow Cent. Ref. Libr., Sales Partics. ii.
[89] B.M. Add. MS. 29794, m. 1d.
[90] M.R.O., Acc. 76/2412, m. 5.
[91] See below.
[92] It was one in 1385 (M.R.O., Acc. 76/2413, m. 19) but usually it was included with Harrow Weald.
[93] M.R.O., Acc. 76/222a.
[94] M.R.O., Acc. 794/2.
[95] e.g. O.S. Map 1/2,500, Mdx. x. 8 (1865 edn.). Greenhill Lodge is identified with Lowlands in Greenwood, *Map of Mdx.* (1819).
[96] M.R.O., Acc. 76/1846; M.R. 612, no. 248.
[97] M.R.O., Acc. 76/980; M.R. 612, nos. 279–80.
[98] M.R.O., Acc. 76/1479.
[99] M.R.O., Acc. 1052, ff. 265–301. For open fields held from Rectory manor, which is not described in the survey, see below.

[1] M.R.O., Acc. 76/2413, m. 77.
[2] Ibid. /2412, m. 5.
[3] Ibid. /1680, /1846; Acc. 643, m. 3.
[4] M.R. 612.
[5] M.R.O., Acc. 794/8.
[6] In 1547 there were 5 tenements and one head tenement had decayed: M.R.O., Acc. 1052, ff. 263–301.
[7] M.R.O., Acc. 76/208.
[8] Ibid. /707.
[9] M.R.O., H.T. 5.
[10] M.R.O., Acc. 643, 2nd deposit, Messeder map A.
[11] M.R.O., Acc. 794/8.
[12] M.R.O., Acc. 76/404.
[13] Ibid. /1383; L.V. 7/1.
[14] M.R.O., L.V. 9/2; Acc. 590/2, /4, no. 391; Acc. 76/1479. One of the other houses was possibly the messuage described in 1812 as divided into three, abutting the 'Six Bells': M.R.O., Acc. 76/1479.
[15] M.R.O., Acc. 76/1400.
[16] *Census,* 1841.

in 1851–2,[17] with four more houses in the corner of Greenhill Lane and Roxborough Lane. Change in the late 19th century was rapid, because of Greenhill's position between two railway stations. St. John's church replaced one farm in 1866,[18] and development in Roxborough, North Harrow, and Wealdstone engulfed Greenhill between 1870 and 1900. In the next two decades it spread into the surrounding farm-land so that, apart from the road pattern, there was nothing left of the original village.

NORBURY. The hamlet of Norbury has not been identified with certainty. Lands there were recorded in deeds of *c.* 1300.[19] Abutments included 'the road which goes to Harrow on the west', the meadow of the Rector of Harrow on the south, and a messuage on the north. Most of the land consisted of crofts, but some lay in fields: East Field, West Field, La Breche, and Twelveacres. The transactions chiefly concerned William Aylward, or son of Aylward, his brother Simon, and William Carpenter, all 'of Norbury'. Other people involved were Roger Elys[20] and John Searle 'of Harrow', William le Knel of Headstone, and Roger Frowyk, goldsmith, of London.

Norbury probably stood in some relation to Sudbury, either as the 'north (i.e. Rectory) manor' or as 'north of the town', presumably Harrow-on-the-Hill.[21] All the land was held of the capital fee of the lord, but there is no indication which lord, while mention of a road to Harrow excludes any identification with Harrow-on-the-Hill itself. The land probably lay north of Harrow-on-the-Hill, between Roxborough Lane (later Pinner Road) on the west, the rectory estate on the south, Headstone on the north, and Greenhill on the east. The field names are common throughout the parish, but West Field and Twelveacres can be found together just north of the rectory estate.[22] Next to them was Broad Field,[23] which in 1645 was described as 'Northberry *alias* Broadfield'.[24] This land was held from the Rectory manor, whose court rolls mention selions on Norbury Hill.[25] The only croft of Norbury which can be located is Fisher's Croft, which lay east of West Field. The evidence suggests that the lost hamlet can be identified with Greenhill, and certainly land in West Field and Norbury *alias* Broad Field later belonged to copyholds of Rectory manor in west Greenhill.[26] Other possible sites for Norbury are Hooking Green in south Pinner, the only common in Harrow without a settlement, or Headstone, which lay north of the land in question but is mentioned by name in the same documents. Norbury was probably a very small hamlet at or near the site of the hamlet of Greenhill, probably on the west side of Greenhill Lane, with its fields lying north of the ancient glebeland and stretching towards Headstone. Possibly it lost some fields when Headstone became a demesne manor,[27] and the name Norbury[28] was superseded by Greenhill, the name of the leading local family.[29]

Suburban Development

The Paddington branch of the Grand Junction Canal, opened in 1801, crossed the south-west corner of Harrow parish.[30] It particularly affected Alperton where brick- and tile-making flourished, especially after the Brent Reservoir, which supplied the canal, was enlarged in 1851. The canal was also used to transport hay to London and bring back horse dung. It carried passenger traffic, mostly Londoners on pleasure trips: Greenford Green, where it was accessible from Pinner,[31] was one of the main stages, but passengers also stopped at Alperton, for refreshment at the 'Pleasure Boat'.[32]

The Grand Junction Canal Co. joined with local landowners in opposing the Birmingham and Manchester Railway Bill in 1831.[33] The London & Birmingham (later the London & North Western)[34] Railway was opened in 1837 from Euston Square to Boxmoor (Herts.), passing northward through the middle of the parish. Harrow (later Harrow & Wealdstone) station was opened in 1837, Pinner (later Hatch End) station in 1844, and Sudbury (later Wembley Central) station in 1845. Stations at Kenton and North Wembley were opened in 1912 and at Headstone a year later. South Kenton station was opened *c.* 1933. In 1890 a branch line from Harrow station to Stanmore was opened by a local company which in 1899 was absorbed by the L. & N.W.R. In 1917 the London Electric Railway[35] operated services (the Bakerloo line) on the L. & N.W.R. line as far as Watford.

The second line to be opened was the Metropolitan[36] which crossed the parish from east to west. A line opened from Willesden Green to Harrow in 1880, with a station at Harrow-on-the-Hill,[37] was extended to Pinner in 1885 and to Rickmansworth in 1887. A station was opened in the centre of Pinner Town in 1886[38] and one at Wembley Park in 1894. A branch line from a point near Roxborough Lane to Uxbridge was opened in 1904 by the Harrow and Uxbridge Railway Co.,[39] which was absorbed by

[17] M.R.O., Acc. 590/2, /4; H.O. 107/1700, ff. 17–19.
[18] Replaced in 1904. See p. 258.
[19] Canterbury, Eastbridge Hosp. Archives, H (1–14).
[20] Who possibly gave his name to the copyhold of Rectory manor called Alleys, a virgate holding which lay partly at least at 'Norbury Hill': M.R.O., Acc. 974/I, mm. 23, 74.
[21] *P.N. Mdx.* (E.P.N.S.), 54.
[22] M.R.O., Acc. 590/2, /4, nos. 385, 380, 374. There was an East Field in Greenhill in the 1330s: see above.
[23] M.R.O., Acc. 590/4, no. 384; Acc. 76/1945. In 1547 Greenhill's West Field abutted south on 'the parsonage lands called Broad Field': M.R.O., Acc. 1052, f. 265.
[24] M.R.O., Acc. 76/217, f. 46v.
[25] Ibid /2417, m. 102d; Acc. 974/I, mm. 23, 44, 72.
[26] M.R.O., Acc. 590/2, /4, no. 419.
[27] Abutments at Norbury Hill included 'the land of the lord archbishop of Canterbury', i.e. Headstone manor: M.R.O., Acc. 974/I, mm. 44 (1428).
[28] Last recorded in 1316: C.P. 25(1)/149/47.

[29] Since there is no hill in the area, the place may have taken its name from a family which originated elsewhere: *P.N. Mdx.* (E.P.N.S.).
[30] Robbins, *Middlesex*, 65; Wemb. Hist. Soc. *Jnl.* N.S. i (8).
[31] Pinner Assoc. *The Villager*, ix.
[32] See p. 193.
[33] M.R.O., Acc. 76/2289, /2303, /2307. See p. 231.
[34] Except where otherwise stated, this and the next 2 paragraphs are based upon Robbins, *Middlesex*, 77–81; *Kelly's Dirs. Mdx.* (1906–37); *Kelly's Dirs. Harrow* (1909–50); *Kelly's Dirs. Wembley* (1929–33); *Kelly's Dirs. Pinner* (1929–33); *London Transport System* (map publ. by London Transport).
[35] V. Sommerfield, *London Transport, A Record & Survey*, 15, 50–52.
[36] Ibid. 44–46.
[37] Robbins, *Middlesex*, 281.   [38] Ibid. 320.
[39] *Opening of Harrow & Uxbridge Rly.* (Harrow Cent. Ref. Libr.).

the Metropolitan in 1906. The whole system was electrified in 1905. Other stations opened on the main line were North Harrow in 1927, Northwick Park by 1929, and Preston, which had been a halt since 1910, by 1933. On the Uxbridge branch line West Harrow station was opened c. 1929. A branch of the Metropolitan Railway was opened in 1932 between Wembley Park and Stanmore. It became part of the Bakerloo line in 1939.[40]

The Metropolitan District line,[41] which skirted the west of the parish, opened an electric service between Park Royal and Roxeth, where a station, called South Harrow, was opened in 1903. The line was extended to Uxbridge in 1904 and a halt at Rayners Lane, later shared with the Metropolitan Uxbridge branch line, was in use by c. 1906–8. Other stations were opened in 1906 at Alperton (originally called Alperton & Perivale) and at Sudbury Town, and in 1910 at Sudbury Hill. The London Electric Co. inaugurated a service (the Piccadilly line) over the line as far as South Harrow in 1932 and beyond it in 1933. The Metropolitan District Railway ceased operation after the Second World War and the line became confined to the Piccadilly line. The Great Central Railway (later part of the L.N.E.R.)[42] opened a line from Greenford to Neasden in 1906. It crossed the southern part of the parish with stations at Sudbury and Harrow Road and at Wembley Hill. Another station, South Harrow (later Sudbury Hill) was opened in 1910. The line never became part of the underground system.

As the Harrow farmers had predicted, the London & Birmingham railway was chiefly a link with the Midlands and the north, not a commuters' line. Typical of its passengers was Thomas Port, a hat-manufacturer of Burton-upon-Trent (Staffs.) who in 1838 died after his legs had been severed by the train. In Harrow churchyard his epitaph reads:

Bright rose the morn, and vigorous rose poor Port,
Gay on the train he used his wonted sport;
Ere noon arrived his mangled form they bore
With pain distorted and o'erwhelmed with gore.
When evening came to close the fatal day
A mutilated corpse the sufferer lay.[43]

In 1845, when there were three stations in the parish, there were only three down and five up local trains each week-day, and three each way on Sundays. Only one train a day took third-class passengers. Since that was ideal for those who did not need to spend every day in the City or who wanted a country home for week-ends, the railway first produced large residences in existing villages. Nevertheless it inaugurated and helped to shape the third phase of settlement—the development of former farm-land. The London Clay offered a formidable challenge, which could be met properly only by local authorities or large companies who could pay for roads, drains,

and sewers, as well as build houses on whole estates at a time. That partly explains why development increased after 1884, when the Colne Valley Water Co. undertook to supply piped water, and after 1894 when the new local authorities tackled the problems of sewerage.

The three L. & N.W.R. stations formed nuclei for new settlements. Pinner station was situated north of Hatch End, where the railway crossed the Uxbridge road. Woodridings estate grew up west of it, south of the Uxbridge road, opposite Woodridings Farm. The first houses, mainly substantial villas, were ready in 1855, when the prospectus stressed that the station was three minutes' walk away.[44] By 1865 Woodridings was served by a temporary church and railway tavern.[45] The station that was opened on the Metropolitan line in 1886 was linked with the older one by a two-horse bus service.[46] Settlement spread westward from Woodridings, where several large houses were built,[47] and northward across the Uxbridge road, where there were new estates at Westfield Park and Royston Park by 1908.[48]

Harrow station was situated where the railway crossed the road from Harrow Weald to Harrow Town, north of Greenhill. By 1852[49] there were also a house and several cottages owned by the L. & N.W.R., some other cottages, and an inn. They formed the nucleus of Wealdstone, where brickearth deposits east of Headstone Farm[50] gave rise to a small brick-making industry.[51] By 1865 settlement at Wealdstone was well advanced, with new roads on both sides of the road from Harrow Weald to Harrow Town, which became Wealdstone High Street and Station Road. In 1881 Wealdstone was a compact hamlet of 211 houses around the station, with further development stretching towards Headstone on the west.[52] The factory of Kodak Ltd. expanded during the 20 years after its establishment at Wealdstone in 1890,[53] and a number of other firms opened factories, especially on the western side of the railway line. By 1912 six factories employed 1,418 people, most of whom lived in the locality.[54] There were 481 houses in 1891,[55] 991 in 1899, and 2,563 by 1911, while the rateable value rose from £18,808 in 1895[56] to £83,000 in 1912. There were 1,240 people in 1881,[57] 2,504 in 1891, 5,901 in 1901[58] and 11,923 in 1911, but the ratio of persons per house over the same period dropped from 5·8 to 4·6.[59] The decline in density resulted partly from the movement of people towards Harrow Weald as Wealdstone itself became overcrowded. Growth slackened and in 1921 the population had reached only 13,433. By 1916 building was continuous from Harrow Weald to Harrow Town, where it coalesced with development in the northern part of Harrow-on-the-Hill and Greenhill.[60] The Roxborough and Northwick estates in north Harrow-on-the-Hill were started in

[40] Wemb. Hist. Soc., Acc. 907/91.
[41] Sommerfield, Lond. Transport, 46–48.
[42] Ibid. 38.   [43] Robbins, Middlesex, 78.
[44] Harrow Cent. Ref. Libr., 94 Pinner; Pinner Assoc. The Villager, xviii, xix.
[45] O.S. Map 1/2,500, Mdx. x. 2 (1865 edn.). See p. 258.
[46] Replaced by a motorbus in 1914: Pinner Assoc. The Villager, xviii.
[47] O.S. Map 6″, Mdx. x. NW. (1916 edn.).
[48] Kelly's Dir. Mdx. (1908).
[49] M.R.O., Acc. 590/2.
[50] Harrow Cent. Ref. Libr., Sales Partics. i (1860).
[51] Ibid. ii (1892); O.S. Map 1/2,500, Mdx. x. 3 (1865 edn.).

[52] O.S. Map 1″, sheet 256 (1877 edn.); M.R.O., Reps. of Local Inqs. (1889–97), 327.
[53] Harrow Cent. Ref. Libr., Sales Partics. ii (1892). See p. 233.
[54] Harrow Bor., North Star, Hendon R.D.C., Wealdstone extension inquiry, 1912.
[55] M.R.O., Reps. of Local Inqs. (1889–97), 327.
[56] Ibid. 271.
[57] Ibid. 327.
[58] From 1895 the figures refer to Wealdstone U.D.C. which included north Kenton, but Kenton was still a small hamlet.
[59] Census, 1901–11.
[60] O.S. Map 6″, Mdx. x. NE. (1916 edn.).

the 1880s.[61] Houses stretched westward along Pinner Road, especially after the electrification of the Metropolitan line and the building of the Uxbridge extension line; they followed both lines and by 1920 reached as far as West Harrow station.[62]

The last area developed before the First World War was around Sudbury station, where the railway crossed the Harrow road just west of Wembley. The Copland sisters contributed by building a church, vicarage, and school on their estate, just west of the station. By 1852 there were nine buildings on the Harrow road between the 'Swan' and Sudbury station.[63] Although as early as 1866 land in Alperton was offered to builders as being near Sudbury station,[64] it was not until the end of the century that the area around the station was sold for building. After the death of General Copland Crawford in 1895, the Copland estate, then called Harrowdene estate, was open to development, mainly by the Conservative Land Co.,[65] and by 1897 many roads had been laid out on both sides of the Harrow road.[66]

Between 1899 and 1901 Wembley Hill estate, the triangle enclosed by High Road, Wembley Hill Road, and Park Lane, was developed for houses and shops.[67] The G.C.R. was built across it and a station opened at Wembley Hill in 1906, which encouraged building south of Wembley High Road. In 1909 the Wembley House estate was developed opposite Wembley Hill estate and in 1910 the Wembley Dairy Farm estate was divided into 505 lots and offered for sale.[68] A network of roads between the Harrow road and the L. & N.W.R. line had been already laid out.[69] At the same time building spread southward along Ealing Road until it joined up with Alperton hamlet.[70] By 1920[71] there was a continuous built-up area[72] from the canal, across Alperton station, up Ealing road and Wembley High Road from Wembley Central station to Wembley Hill station. Besides the railways there was an electric tram service along the Harrow road to Wembley by 1908 and to Sudbury by 1910.[73]

Wembley Park estate, north-east of the original hamlet, was sold in 1881. Part was acquired by the Metropolitan Railway Co. and in 1889 Sir Edward Watkin, chairman of the board, acquired 280 a. in association with the company. The Metropolitan Tower Construction Co. was formed to give effect to Watkin's vision of London's greatest pleasure ground, dominated by a tower which was to surpass the Eiffel Tower. The Metropolitan Railway opened a station at Wembley Park on the line from Baker Street in 1894 and the pleasure grounds were opened in 1896, but drainage proved difficult and the tower

had reached only 200 feet when funds ran out. Within two years the Tower company went into liquidation and the property was taken over by the Wembley Park Estate Co. Ltd. The first stage of the tower survived as 'Watkin's Folly' until it was dismantled in 1907.[74]

The pleasure grounds of Wembley Park continued to be used for various exhibitions, but it was not until 1924-5 that the British Empire Exhibition was held there. The site was chosen in spite of opposition from Wembley U.D.C., and most of the important buildings were designed in 1923 by J. M. Simpson and M. Ayrton.[75] Visitors poured into Wembley and permanent changes were effected. Roads were widened to accommodate the traffic, Forty Lane was transformed from a country lane to a main highway, and drainage of the site opened up the whole of eastern Wembley for development. Some of the exhibition buildings, including Wembley Stadium, were retained for sport while others were leased for light industry. The Empire Pool and Arena, designed by Sir Owen Williams, was built in 1934. Most of the wealthier inhabitants left the district, which developed as a mixed residential and industrial area.[76]

The large-scale development of farm-land elsewhere started when most of the big estates were sold in the 1920s and early 1930s. The electrification of the L. & N.W.R. line in 1917 and the running of Piccadilly trains over the Metropolitan District line from 1932 made commuting possible from most areas. By 1933 there were 21 stations in Harrow.[77] By 1926 roads had been laid out on the Northwick estates, although a substantial area, roughly co-extensive with Sheepcote Farm, was retained as Northwick Park open space.[78] Christ Church sold its estates in Preston, Kenton, the Weald, and Roxeth between 1921 and 1933,[79] and the vicarage and Harrow School estates in Preston were sold about the same time.[80] New College had begun to sell its land by 1926[81] and St. Thomas's Hospital sold its Pinner Park estate in 1931.[82] The Hemings estate had been sold by 1926[83] and Brookshill, Wealdstone Farm, Harrow Weald House, and land in Kenton Lane by 1926.[84]

Building was continuous from 1925 until 1939. Industry was attracted not only to the Wembley Park area but to the Wembley part of East Lane, where the British Oxygen Co. opened a factory as early as 1918 and other firms followed in the 1920s.[85] Most development, however, was residential, with local authorities for the first time building their own housing estates and drawing up overall schemes.

[61] Harrow Cent. Ref. Libr., Sales Partics. i (1887); ii (1889).
[62] O.S. Map 6″, Mdx. x. SE. (1916 edn.).
[63] M.R.O., Acc. 590/1, /3.
[64] Harrow Cent. Ref. Libr., Sales Partics. ii.
[65] Christ Church, Oxford, Harrow Maps 27.
[66] Wemb. Hist. Soc. Jnl. i (4).
[67] Wemb. Hist. Soc., Acc. 148-52; Acc. 380/2.
[68] Brent Town Hall, Wembley U.D.C., Min. Bk. ix (1908-11), 69, 90.
[69] Wemb. Hist. Soc., Acc. 156; Acc. 719/3.
[70] Brent Town Hall, Wembley U.D.C., Min. Bk. ix (1908-11), 156.
[71] O.S. Map 1″, sheet 106 (1920 edn.).
[72] In 1914 it was estimated that 764 a. out of a total of 4,564 a. in Wembley U.D. had been developed: Wemb. Hist. Soc., Acc. 727/1.
[73] Robbins, Middlesex, 356; Wembley News, 23 Oct. 1952, 8 Jan. 1953.

[74] T.C. Barker and M. Robbins, Hist. of London Transport i. 160, 205-6; Elsley, Wembley, 143 sqq.
[75] See pl. facing p. 203.
[76] Elsley, Wembley, 147-9, 203-7; Robbins, Middlesex, 356-7.
[77] Those at Sudbury Town, Sudbury Hill, and Alperton were designed by Charles Holden in 1932-3 in an advanced architectural style and were among the first of a series of London Transport stations said to have done much to establish the modern idiom in Britain: Pevsner, Mdx. 26.
[78] M.R.O., Acc. 794/19-27.
[79] Christ Church, Oxford, Harrow Maps 17-25.
[80] Wembley News, 15 Jan. 1953.
[81] New College, Oxford, MS. 307.
[82] St. Thomas's Hosp. Endowment Office, Pinner Park docs.
[83] Harrow Bor., North Star, Hendon R.D.C., Wealdstone boundaries, 1926.
[84] Ibid. docs. 1928.   [85] See p. 233.

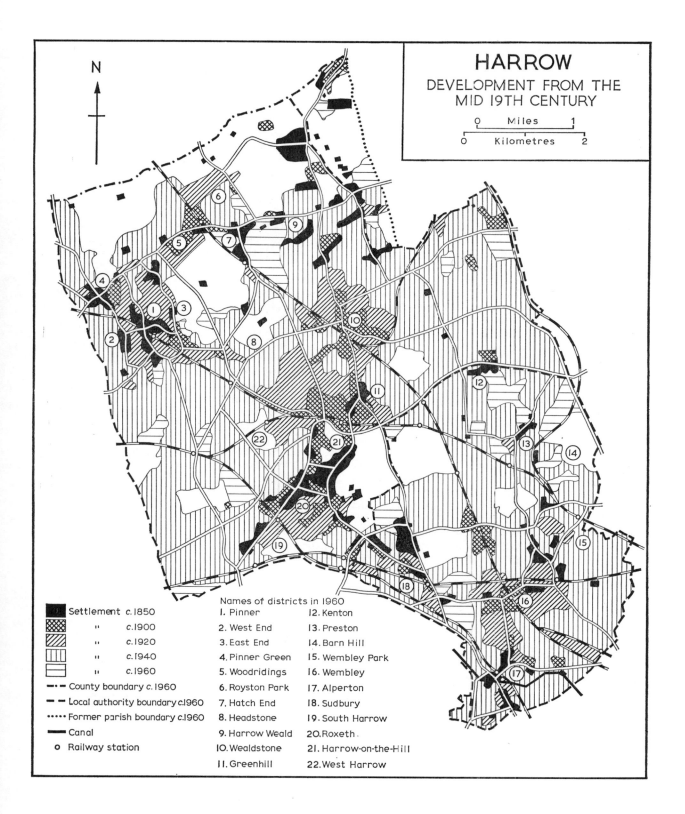

N

HARROW
DEVELOPMENT FROM THE MID 19TH CENTURY

0   Miles   1
0   Kilometres   2

	Settlement c.1850
	" c.1900
	" c.1920
	" c.1940
	" c.1960

–·– County boundary c.1960

– – Local authority boundary c.1960

····· Former parish boundary c.1960

—— Canal

o Railway station

Names of districts in 1960

1. Pinner
2. West End
3. East End
4. Pinner Green
5. Woodridings
6. Royston Park
7. Hatch End
8. Headstone
9. Harrow Weald
10. Wealdstone
11. Greenhill

12. Kenton
13. Preston
14. Barn Hill
15. Wembley Park
16. Wembley
17. Alperton
18. Sudbury
19. South Harrow
20. Roxeth
21. Harrow-on-the-Hill
22. West Harrow

Wembley's early plans for a high-class garden suburb[86] had been disrupted by the British Empire Exhibition. Hendon R.D. in 1925 and Harrow-on-the-Hill in 1933 produced residential schemes with densities of 12 houses an acre and less.[87] Both schemes included main roads, some of which, like Alexandra Avenue, Imperial Drive, and George V Avenue, were built. The necessity for large-scale planning was one reason why the four local authorities were reduced to two in 1934. Two new schemes were published by the enlarged Harrow U.D.C. in 1939, and in 1945 the local authorities of Harrow, Wembley, Hendon, and Willesden formed a joint planning committee.[88]

To remedy the shortage of working-class houses,[89] councils, under the Acts of 1919–25 built estates[90] at Pinner Hill (285 houses), in Eastcote Lane (272 houses)[91] in Roxeth, at North Harrow (53 houses) and Honeybun (202 houses and bungalows) between Roxeth and Harrow Town, at Elmgrove (169 houses) in Greenhill, in Canning Road (7 bungalows) and Weald Village (351 houses) in Wealdstone, and in Kenton Lane (22 houses) in Harrow Weald. Wembley built about 500 houses on the Christ Church estate and 200 houses on the Manor Farm estate in south-west Alperton in the late 1920s and early 1930s.[92]

Private building also flourished, with infilling in Harrow Weald,[93] Kenton, west Preston, Greenhill,[94] Headstone, and Wembley during the late 1920s. By 1931–2 building was continuous along the two main railway lines, the London & North Western (later the London, Midland & Scottish) Railway and the Metropolitan, except in the north and at Northwick Park, and along the main road from Pinner through North Harrow to Kenton and the Edgware road.[95] There was some development in Sudbury, especially on the Sudbury Court estate where 1,700 houses were built in 1928–34,[96] while building along Rayners Lane linked up with development westward from Roxeth. Most of the former open-field land between Pinner and Roxeth was built up during the 1930s, giving rise to entirely new districts, West, South, and North Harrow, by 1938.[97] Development also started along the eastern borders of Harrow,

especially the former open-field area of Kenton and Preston,[98] but some of it was incomplete when the Second World War brought work to a halt.[99] At Wembley infilling produced 1,130 houses in 1933 alone.[1] After the amalgamation of Wembley with Kingsbury in 1934 Forty Lane was chosen for a new town hall, which was opened in 1939.[2]

Of 35,000 houses in Wembley Borough, half were damaged in the Second World War.[3] Temporary houses were erected by both Harrow and Wembley boroughs, and in 1951 the population reached a peak.[4] The density for the whole area[5] was 19·8 persons an acre, varying from 8·0 an acre in Pinner North ward to 39·3 in Queensbury ward. Since only small areas were available for building, many old farm-houses and large Victorian residences were destroyed. Housing estates built by Wembley council since the war included Sudbury Farm (140 houses and old people's accommodation) in 1947,[6] Gauntlett Court (about 100 flats) in the 1950s,[7] and Sudbury Heights (65 flats) in 1964 in Sudbury,[8] and King's Drive (114 flats) in 1952–3 near Wembley Town Hall.[9] Estates built by Harrow council included Rayners Lane (252 houses and flats), Whittington Way (81 houses and flats), Chigwell Hurst[10] (36 flats), Latimer Close[11] (31 houses), Headstone Lane (24 flats), Towers[12] (40 flats), and Oxhey Lane (48 houses), all in Pinner, Alexandra Avenue (132 flats), Brookside (77 flats and houses), Northolt Road (46 flats and maisonettes), all in South Harrow, Wealdstone House (56 flats and houses), Kenton Road (24 flats), Kenton Lane (96 flats and houses), Woodlands (271 flats and houses) in Harrow Weald,[13] and Cullington Close (80 houses) in Greenhill.[14] The largest estate in Harrow since the war was built by the L.C.C. at Headstone, where 153 a. south of the Uxbridge road housed 5,000 people from London.[15] There was another large site (181 a.) in the area of Barn Hill and Chalkhill, where Brent council proposed to replace the few large houses with high-density dwellings, primarily to rehouse people from Willesden. Planning permission was refused by the Greater London Council, but the old authorites had already built some flats by 1964.[16]

Although houses and flats continued to be built

[86] Wemb. Hist. Soc., Acc. 351. A town planning cttee. was appointed in 1910: Brent Town Hall, Wembley U.D.C. Min. Bk. ix (1908–11), 262.
[87] Hendon R.D.C. *Rep. of Principal Activities, 1929–31*, and map *penes* Harrow Cent. Ref. Libr.
[88] Harrow U.D.C. *Year Bk.* (1946–7).
[89] Hendon R.D.C. *Rep. of Principal Activities, 1929–31.*
[90] Borough of Harrow, *Facts & Figures* (1963–4). The City, Harrow Weald, was taken for council housing and in 1964 the future of the site was uncertain; see above, p. 185.
[91] Built in 1928: M.R.O., LA. HW., Harrow U.D.C., Ledger (1928), ff. 7–8, 11.
[92] Ex inf. Housing Dept. of London Bor. of Brent (1968).
[93] In 1926 Whitefriars Bldg. Estate was rapidly developing: Harrow Bor., North Star, Hendon R.D.C., 1926. In 1928 there was considerable activity along Kenton Lane, at Whitefriars and Wealdstone Farm, Harrow Weald House and Brookshill estates: ibid. 1928.
[94] Bonnersfield Lane, Elmsgrove Rd. etc.: Harrow Bor. North Star, Hendon R.D.C., 1926.
[95] Land Util. Survey Map 1″, sheet 106 (1931–2 edn.).
[96] O.S. Maps 6″, Mdx. x. SE., NE., NW. (1935, 1938 edns.); Wemb. Hist. Soc., Acc. 446/15; ex. inf. church-warden of St. Cuthbert's church. See pl. on facing page.
[97] O.S. Maps 6″, Mdx. x. NW., NE., SE. (1935, 1938 edns.).
[98] Wemb. Hist. Soc. *Jnl.* i (3).
[99] e.g. *T.L.M.A.S.* N.S. vii. 288; x. 148.

[1] Wemb. Hist. Soc., Acc. 212.
[2] See p. 246.
[3] Including Kingsbury: Wemb. Hist. Soc., Acc. 176.
[4] See below.
[5] Area (13,958 a.) approximating to the original Harrow parish, i.e. Harrow Bor., excluding the 2 Stanmore wards, and Wembley Bor., excluding Roe Green, Fryent, and Chalkhill wards: *Census*, 1951.
[6] Between the Harrow road and the Piccadilly line.
[7] Between the Harrow road and the former G.C.R., west of Sudbury and Harrow station.
[8] Wemb. Hist. Soc., Acc. 907/167.
[9] Ex inf. Housing Dept. of London Bor. of Brent.
[10] Milman Close, near Little Common, built c. 1949: Pinner Assoc. *The Villager*, xxxiv.
[11] South of Pinner Hill Golf Course; 26 houses were sold in 1955.
[12] Lloyd Court off Eastcote Rd.
[13] Site being prepared in 1945: Pinner Assoc. *The Villager*, xxv.
[14] *Facts & Figures* (1963–4).
[15] *The Times*, 2 Oct. 1948, 3c; London Bor. of Harrow, *Official Guide* [1968]; ex inf. the Vicar of All Saints, Harrow Weald, 1965.
[16] Wemb. Hist. Soc., Acc. 524; Acc. 701/1; Acc. 907/79, 142, 145, 152, 179, 182, 184; *The Times*, 23 Feb. 1963, 4e; ex inf. Dept. of Planning & Research, London Bor. of Brent.

Ruislip: Frithwood Avenue, Northwood, early 20th century

Harrow: Sudbury Court estate, 1934

SUBURBAN DEVELOPMENT

WEMBLEY STADIUM AND THE BRITISH EMPIRE EXHIBITION IN 1924

after 1951, the population has steadily declined.[17] In 1961 the overall density was 18·9 an acre, after attempts to spread the burden more evenly[18] and after some migration, including the rehousing of families in new towns. Office, industrial, and civic buildings also helped to reduce congestion, as overhead costs forced many businesses to move out from London. In 1956–60 more than 250 applications for offices, covering 57 a., were granted within the present London Borough of Brent; about 38 a. lay in Wembley,[19] where some 53,000 people were employed by 1964.[20] There was similar office development in Harrow, whose population was also affected by plans for a civic centre to replace the houses and shops around Station Road and Marlborough Hill.[21] In central Wembley, south of the High Road, buildings of about the same date as those around Marlborough Hill were in 1968 being demolished to make way for a shopping precinct.[22]

One of the first actions of Harrow Local Board of Health, established in 1850, was to investigate possible recreation grounds.[23] By 1910 a special committee of the Harrow-on-the-Hill U.D.C. was administering Harrow and Roxeth recreation grounds.[24] Wembley U.D.C. opened the King Edward VII Park in Wembley in 1914 and One Tree Hill in Alperton soon afterwards.[25] Wealdstone preserved Byron Recreation Ground from the encroaching building.[26] E. B. Montesole, a member of the Hendon R.D.C., who lived in East House, Pinner, campaigned for a green belt in Middlesex and was responsible for some major acquisitions in Pinner and Harrow Weald, including Headstone in 1925 and Pinner Park in 1930.[27] By 1934, on the eve of the creation of Harrow U.D.,[28] the three local authorities administered 563 a. of open space within Harrow's boundaries.[29] More land was bought, especially in the north, and in 1938 Harrow decided to reserve 962 a. for the green belt.[30] By 1938 Wembley had acquired most of its open spaces.[31] After the opening of Mogden Sewage Works in 1936, the Harrow sewage farms were turned into Kenton recreation ground and Newton, Roxbourne, and Queensbury parks.[32] Apart from Harrow School's playing fields, land was also sold in the 1920s and 1930s to a number of schools, London stores, and other organizations for use as sports grounds.[33]

During the Second World War much of the land was given over to allotments, but in 1968 there were over 2,000 a. of open space out of a total of nearly 14,000 a.[34]

MANORS.[35] In 767 Offa, King of Mercia 757–96, granted 30 hides (*manentes*) between Harrow and the Lidding to Abbot Stidberht in exchange for land in Wycombe (Bucks.). An extra 6 hides and a dwelling-house east of the brook were added as a gift.[36] Although the charter was confirmed in 801 by Pilheard, an under-king of Cenwulf, King of Mercia 796–821, and although Cenwulf exempted the land from royal taxes and services,[37] the property had returned to the royal house by 824. At the Council of Clovesho, Cwenthryth, Abbess of Southminster (Kent) and daughter of Cenwulf, agreed to surrender 100 hides in Harrow, *Herefrething Land*,[38] Wembley, and Yeading in reparation for her father's spoliation of archiepiscopal property. Beornwulf, King of Mercia 823–5, agreed to free (*liberabat*) all of the property which had not been freed in 801, and Cwenthryth was instructed to deliver her landbooks to the archbishop, although she failed to hand over three hides and the books for 47 hides. In 825 the second Council of Clovesho ratified her reconciliation with Archbishop Wulfred, which was bought with the landbooks, 4 more hides at Harrow and 30 hides in Kent.[39] Wulfred gave the Harrow lands to his kinsman, Werhard, a priest, for life. Werhard in 845 exchanged one hide at Roxeth, formerly belonging to Greenford township, with Werenberht the thegn,[40] and devised the land to the monks of Christ Church, Canterbury. Harrow was held by King Harold's brother, Earl Leofwine, in 1066, but Canterbury regained it after the Conquest. When the Canterbury lands were divided by Lanfranc between the archbishop and Christ Church, Harrow and Hayes were allotted to the former.[41]

Except *sede vacante*, when it was administered by the Crown,[42] *HARROW* manor was held by the archbishops until Cranmer was forced to exchange it with Henry VIII on 30 December 1545. Six days later, the king sold it to Sir Edward (later Lord) North (d. 1564), Chancellor of the Court of Augmentations.[43] Dudley (d. 1666), the 3rd baron, who,

---

[17] Wembley Bor., pop. in 1951, 125,000, in 1964, 123,800; *Background to Brent* (Rep. by Dept. of Planning & Research, Lond. Bor. of Brent, 1967), 8. Harrow Bor., pop. in 1951, 219,463, in 1966, 208,730: *Facts & Figures* (1963–4); London Bor. of Harrow, *Official Guide* [1968].
[18] In Pinner North, Headstone, Wembley Park and Central, and Sudbury Ct. the pop. rose between 1951 and 1961, while in all other wards it fell: *Census, 1951–61*.
[19] *Background to Brent*, 41–45.
[20] Wemb. Hist. Soc., Acc. 907/155.
[21] In 1968 the old buildings had been demolished but the centre had not been built: ex inf. Harrow Bor. Town Planning Dept.
[22] Wemb. Hist. Soc., Acc. 907/125/129; Acc. 887/2; *The Times*, 2 Sept. 1962, 6c.
[23] Harrow Bor., High St., Local Bd. of Health, Min Bk. (1850–3).
[24] Ibid. Harrow U.D.C. Min. Bk. xxxiii (1900–1), 7, 104; M.R.O., LA. HW., Harrow U.D.C., Ledger (1910–11), ff. 25, 112. [25] Wemb. Hist. Soc., Acc. 727/1.
[26] O.S. Map 6″, Mdx. x. NE. (1916 edn.).
[27] Pinner Assoc. *The Villager*, x; Hendon R.D.C. *Rep. of Principal Activities, 1929–31*, penes Harrow Cent. Ref. Libr.; Ware, *Pinner*, 159. [28] See p. 245.
[29] *Rep. of Joint Advisory Cttee.* (1934) penes Harrow Cent. Ref. Libr.

[30] Including Stanmore: *Facts & Figures* (1963–4), 99.
[31] O.S. Maps 6″, Mdx. x. NE., SE., xi. NW., SW. (1938 edn.).
[32] Ibid. x. NE., SE., SW., xi. NW. (1938 edn.); TQ 18 NE., NW. (1966–7 edn.).
[33] M.R.O., Acc. 794/19–20; Christ Church, Oxford, Harrow Maps 17–25; *Background to Brent*, 85–96.
[34] *Background to Brent*, 85–96; *Facts & Figures* (1963–4); London Bor. of Harrow, *Year Bk.* (1967–8).
[35] Rectory manor is treated below, under Church.
[36] *Eng. Hist. Docs.* i. 461; *Cart. Sax.* ed. Birch i, p. 284; W. D. Bushell, 'The Harrow of the Gumenings', *Harrow Octocent. Tracts*, iii.
[37] Except for *trimoda necessitas*.
[38] For possible meanings, see Bushell, 'Early Charters', *Harrow Octocent. Tracts*, i. 14 n. 2; Elsley, *Wembley*, 17.
[39] *Harrow Octocent. Tracts*, i, ii; *Cart. Sax.* ed. Birch, i. 528–33.
[40] Both pieces of land were probably in Roxeth.
[41] *Harrow Octocent. Tracts*, i. 20–24; *V.C.H. Mdx.* i. 104–5. [42] See p. 219 n. 33.
[43] M.R.O., Acc. 76/897–8, /1005; Bushell, 'Alienation of the Harrow Manors', *Harrow Octocent. Tracts*, xiii. 5–33; *Narratives of the Days of the Reformation*, ed. J. G. Nichols (Camd. Soc. lxxvii), 264–5; *L. & P. Hen. VIII*, xxi, pt. 1, p. 72.

according to Camden, 'consumed the greatest part of his estate in the gallantries of King James's court',[44] sold Harrow manor in 1630 to Edmund Phillips and George and Rowland Pitt.[45] In 1636, after Phillips's death, Rowland Pitt quitclaimed his interest to George Pitt (d. *c.* 1653)[46] and his heirs.[47] George Pitt's son, Edmund, was dead by 1666 and the manor descended to Edmund's daughter, Alice, and her successive husbands, Edward Palmer[48] and Sir James Rushout, Bt. (d. 1698).[49] In spite of an attempted sale in 1764[50] it remained with the Rushouts, who acquired the barony of Northwick in 1797, until the 3rd baron, Sir George Rushout-Bowles, died in 1887.[51] His relict, Lady Elizabeth Augusta, sold some of the estate[52] but on her death in 1912 the bulk passed to her grandson, Capt. E. G. Spencer-Churchill. He sold the remaining land in the 1920s[53] but retained the manorial rights until his death in 1964,[54] when they passed to his executors.[55]

Until the creation of Rectory manor, which is discussed below,[56] 'Harrow manor' described both manorial rights over the whole area and the chief demesne farm in the centre of the parish. To distinguish it from the Rectory estate at Harrow-on-the-Hill, the demesne was, from the 14th century, called *SUDBURY* manor or *SUDBURY COURT*.[57] Its descent followed that of Harrow manor. Sudbury manor in the Middle Ages comprised about 620 a. and a grange, which may have been the archbishop's original residence since it included a chapel.[58] It was leased out from the late 14th century and afterwards divided into several farms, of which Sudbury Court Farm remained the most important.[59] Although there were traces of an earlier building,[60] the farm-house which stood on the north side of Sudbury Court Road until its demolition in 1957 dated from the late 16th or early 17th century, with additions made in the 18th century, 1842, and 1888.[61]

A second demesne farm, *WOODHALL* manor, consisting of a grange and 312 a. in north Pinner,[62] existed by 1236.[63] It descended with Harrow manor until 1630 when the manorial rights[64] were combined with those of Harrow and Sudbury and sold to Edmund Phillips and the Pitt brothers, while the demesne farm was sold to William Pennifather (d. 1658), Sheriff of London and lord of Northolt

manor.[65] In 1637 Pennifather conveyed Woodhall to William Wilkinson. It passed to Wilkinson's grandson, Henry Neville, but in 1754 Margaret Conyers and her nephew Cosmo Neville were ejected by the heir of Anthony Collins, sole surviving trustee of a settlement made by Wilkinson in 1655. Under this settlement Woodhall was sold in 1760 to John Lawes, who six years later alienated it to John Drummond. In 1795 the estate was held in trust for Drummond's grandson, George,[66] who was in possession in 1817.[67] In 1864 it was held by A. W. Tooke, of Pinner Hill.[68] Although the land was sold for modern housing, the farm-house, built in the early 19th century on the site of a 16th- or 17th-century predecessor and containing a Tudor fireplace, still stood to the west of Woodhall Drive in 1968.[69]

Although there was a small settlement at Headstone by the early 14th century, most of the land was probably still held by the de la Hegge or de la Haye family who had an estate there in the 13th century.[70] During the 1330s it passed to Robert Wodehouse, Treasurer of the Exchequer and Archdeacon of Richmond,[71] who in 1338 owed suit of court as tenant of the archbishop of Canterbury.[72] In 1344 Wodehouse (d. 1346),[73] granted a messuage, three carucates of land, 20 a. of meadow, 5 a. of wood, and 24s. rent in Harrow to the archbishop in mortmain.[74] By 1348 this was described as the manor of *HEADSTONE*, 'de novo perquisitum'.[75] Headstone manor, a grange and 235 a., descended with Harrow manor until 1630[76] when its manorial rights were detached and sold with Harrow and Sudbury manors. Headstone Farm was bought by Simon Rewse, the lessee. In 1647 it was sequestered by the Middlesex Committee for Compounding but in 1649 the order was discharged and the estate was sold to William Williams. He sold it in 1671 to Sir William Bucknall, in whose family it remained at least until 1823.[77] At inclosure the estate comprised a block of 388 a. between the Weald and Pinner.[78] By 1854 it was divided equally between Frederick Harrison and William Bush Cooper. Portions were alienated during the 19th century and in 1874 the rest of Harrison's portion, then consisting of the manor-house and 189 a., was conveyed to Edward Christopher York (d. 1885). York's executors sold some land in 1899

[44] Burke, *Peerage* (1907).
[45] M.R.O., Acc. 76/421, /423.
[46] Ibid. /1020; C.P. 25(2)/575.
[47] M.R.O., Acc. 76/705.
[48] Ibid. /1021–2, /1025.
[49] Foster, *Peerage* (1882).
[50] B.M. Add. MS. 29254, f. 6v. See p. 250.
[51] Foster, *Peerage* (1882); Burke, *Peerage* (1907).
[52] M.R.O., Acc. 794/17.
[53] See p. 200.
[54] *The Times*, 25 June 1964, 12e.
[55] Hist. MSS. Com. Manorial Reg.
[56] See p. 250.
[57] Thirteenth-cent. 'Harrow' has been identified with 14th-cent. 'Sudbury' by comparisons between Lambeth Palace, Estate MS. 2068 and *Cal. Inq. Misc.* vi, p. 123. For the court of Sudbury, see M.R.O., Acc. 76/2412, m. 5d (1337).
[58] Lambeth Palace, Estate MS. 1213. Probably identifiable with Harrow chapel, used for ordinations in the 13th and 14th centuries: *Reg. Winchelsey* (Cant. & York Soc. lii), 953; I. Churchill, *Canterbury Admin.* i. 100 n. 3. Sudbury manor chapel was said in 1397 to be of no net yearly value: *Cal. Inq. Misc.* vi, p. 123.
[59] See p. 228.
[60] In 1547 there was 'a mansion house meet for a farmer': M.R.O., Acc. 1052, p. 25.
[61] Wemb. Hist. Soc., Plans of Excavations, 1957; Wemb.

Hist. Soc. *Jnl.* N.S. i(9).
[62] Lambeth Palace, Estate MS. 2068.
[63] Ibid. 1193.
[64] i.e. 'all seignory rights, quit-rents, rents of assize, works, suits, services'.
[65] M.R.O., Acc. 76/421. See p. 114.
[66] Lysons, *Environs of Lond.* ii. 565.
[67] M.R.O., Acc. 794/8; C.P. 43/939A, ff. 78 sqq.; M.R. 612.
[68] Ware, *Pinner*, 219.
[69] Ex inf. the occupier (1968); Pinner Assoc. *The Villager*, xli.
[70] *Harrow Octocent. Tracts*, ix. 14; Canterbury, Eastbridge Hosp. Archives, H(1–14); see above, p. 178. The estate was similar in kind to that owned by the Roxeth family: see below.
[71] C.P. 25(1)/150/55/55, 62, 75.
[72] M.R.O., Acc. 76/2412, m. 4.
[73] *D.N.B.*; J. Le Neve, *Fasti, 1300–1541* (revised edn.), vi. 25.
[74] B.M. Add. MS. 15664, ff. 18–19; *Cal. Pat. 1343–5*, 328–9.
[75] S.C. 6/1128/12.
[76] M.R.O., Acc. 76/421.
[77] C.P. 43/961/123; Lysons, *Environs of Lond.*, Suppl. 190; Ware, *Pinner*, 115–18.
[78] M.R. 612; M.R.O., Acc. 794/8; C.P. 43/939A, ff. 78 sqq.

but the house and 148 a. were conveyed to his son, Edward, in 1922. Edward York sold the house and 63 a. in 1925 to Hendon R.D.C. for recreational uses.[79] The house, known until after the Second World War as Moat Farm, was occupied by the head groundsman in 1968.[80]

Headstone manor-house, a 'well-built site' in 1397,[81] replaced Sudbury as the archbishop's main Middlesex residence. By 1367 there was a chapel,[82] which was removed during rebuilding in 1488–9.[83] The house, which still stood within its moat in 1968, is largely timber-framed. At the centre a two-storied medieval wing survives, its steeply pitched gable-end facing north-east. It contains an original roof of three bays with collar purlin, crown-posts, and heavy arch-braced tie-beams. The date 1501 is marked out in bricks at the rear of the house but most of the structure was rebuilt late in the 16th century. The single-storied south-east block, the so-called chapel, is of this date, but it may occupy the site of one bay of the original open hall. Much of the house was faced with red brick in the 18th century and it is possible that the south-east block was truncated at this period. The north wing and the tall clustered shafts of the chimney date from the 17th century. South-west of the house is a timber-framed and weather-boarded barn of ten bays, dating from c. 1600.[84]

The last of the demesne estates,[85] *PINNER PARK*, was never a manor in the same sense as Sudbury, Woodhall, and Headstone.[86] First mentioned in 1273–4, it was a wooded area of approximately 250 a., enclosed by a bank and double ditch.[87] A house was built there by 1560 and the park transformed into a farm soon afterwards.[88] It descended with Harrow manor until 1630 when it was sold to Thomas Hutchinson (d. 1656) of London and his son, John.[89] John Hutchinson was in possession in 1674,[90] but Pinner Park had left the family before its purchase in 1731 by St. Thomas's Hospital.[91] The hospital leased out the estate as a farm until 1931, when 250 a. were sold to the local authority.[92] A small portion was conveyed to the R.S.P.C.A. in 1936 but the rest was from 1937 leased to the Hall family,[93] formerly tenant-farmers of Headstone.[94] The brick farm-house and extensive out-buildings of brick and timber date mainly from the 18th and 19th centuries.

ROXETH manor originated in freehold land held by the Roxeth family.[95] Hamo and Hugh Roxeth (de Rokeseie) were mentioned in 1233–40[96] but the estate was united in the hands of John Roxeth by 1319.[97] After William Roxeth was outlawed, the estate (166 a. and 45s. rent), escheated to the archbishop, who in 1371 granted it in tail to Sir Nicholas Brembre, Mayor of London and lord of Northolt manor.[98] After Brembre's attainder in 1388 an apparently unsuccessful action for novel disseisin was brought against his widow, Idony, by John Dereham and his wife Joan, who was William Roxeth's sister.[99] The property had reverted to the archbishop before 1430 when he leased it out on the same terms as his demesne estates.[1] Roxeth, by 1514 called a manor,[2] probably passed in 1546, when it consisted of 67 a. of inclosed and 130 selions of open-field land,[3] to Sir Edward North, who still leased it out in 1553.[4] In 1630 it was sold with Pinner Park to the Hutchinsons[5] and in 1678 John Hutchinson sold the manor of Roxeth Place (151 a.) to Thomas Smith and Robert Nichols.[6] After Chancery litigation it was conveyed in 1727 by devisees under the will of Thomas Nichols (d. 1705) to Thomas Brian, headmaster of Harrow School. The descent thereafter is obscure. In 1764 Brian Taylor alienated the estate to Percival Hart (d. 1773), distiller of Brentford,[7] whose widow held one-third in dower in 1795, when the remainder was held jointly by Emma, wife of David Garrick,[8] and Mary, relict of Charles Vaughan Blunt, presumably Hart's daughters.[9] In 1817 Mary Blunt had 150 a. in Roxeth, mostly in the open fields, together with a large building at the southern end of Northolt Road.[10] It was marked more prominently than were the buildings and rickyard held by her trustees in 1852.[11] The manor-house itself, with most of the estate, apparently lay elsewhere. In 1805 George Watlington claimed for the manor of Roxeth, including 110 a. of inclosed and 136 a. of open-field freehold.[12] The greater part was probably 113 a. of inclosed and 53 a. of open-field land in Roxeth, owned in 1817 by Henry Greenhill and in 1852 by Richard Chapman. The property included a square-moated site, well back from the road, west of the junction of Northolt Road and Roxeth Hill. Described in 1852 as 'homestall and ponds', it was almost certainly the site of the medieval Roxeth Place,[13] which had disappeared by

---

[79] Deeds, *penes* Town Clerk's Dept., Lond. Bor. of Harrow. The house passed in 1934 to Harrow U.D.C.: Harrow, *Official Guide* (n.d.); ex. inf. Harrow Bor.
[80] Ex inf. Mr. E. O'Brien, head groundsman (1968).
[81] *Cal. Inq. Misc.* vi, pp. 123–4.
[82] *Reg. Langham* (Cant. & York Soc. liii), 293.
[83] Lambeth Palace, Estate MS. 1218, m. 10d.
[84] Pevsner, *Mdx.* 133; Hist. Mon. Com. *Mdx.* 103; *Home Cnties. Mag.* ix. 296; ex inf. Harrow Bor. Illustrated in Robbins, *Middlesex*, pl. 31.
[85] For Weald Copse Farm, see p. 228.
[86] i.e. had rights to customary rents and services.
[87] B.M. Add. MS. 29794, m. 1d. See p. 222.
[88] C 3/222/48; Ware, *Pinner*, 158.
[89] M.R.O., Acc. 76/421.
[90] M.R.O., H.T. 53.
[91] Deeds in the Endowment Office of St. Thomas's Hosp. Ware (*Pinner*, 164) says that Obadiah and John Ewer, who owned land in Pinner, had Pinner Park after Hutchinson, but they may have been lessees.
[92] Harrow, *Official Guide* (n.d.).
[93] Ex inf. Town Clerk's Dept., Lond. Bor. of Harrow.
[94] Ex inf. Mr. A. W. Hall.
[95] Mentioned in ministers' accts. in 1236 (Lambeth Palace, Estate MS. 1193) and 1273–4 (B.M. Add. MS.

29794, m. 1d.).
[96] *Harrow Octocent. Tracts*, ix. 11, 14.
[97] *Year Bk.* 1319 (Selden Soc.), 19.
[98] *Cal. Pat.* 1370–4, 160; Canterbury Cathedral Libr., Register H, ff. 75v–76.
[99] *Year Bk.* 1387–8 (Ames Foundation), 268 sqq.; *Cal. Pat.* 1385–9, 481; *Cal. Inq. Misc.* v, pp. 130–1; *Cal. Close*, 1385–9, 580–1, 1389–92, 12.
[1] Cant. Cath. Libr., Reg. S, f. 105.
[2] Ibid. Reg. T1, f. 21.
[3] M.R.O., Acc. 1052, ff. 423 sqq.
[4] Ibid., Acc. 76/222a.
[5] Ibid. /421.
[6] Ibid. /658, /1658; C.P. 25(2)/691/30 Chas. II East.
[7] M.R.O., Acc. 507/1, unpag., 13, 16 Geo. III.
[8] Nephew of the actor.
[9] Lysons, *Environs of Lond.* ii. 567. Emma, the elder, was admitted to Hart's copyhold lands in 1776: M.R.O., Acc 507/1, unpag., 16 Geo. III.
[10] M.R.O., Acc. 794/8; M.R. 612, no. 506.
[11] M.R.O., Acc. 590/1, /4, no. 286.
[12] M.R.O., Acc. 76/1400.
[13] Ibid. /2420, m. 22; Acc. 590/1, /4, no. 258; Acc. 794/8; M.R. 612, no. 454; *V.C.H. Mdx.* ii. 6.

1547.[14] In 1873, when Chapman still owned 159 a., the site was in the grounds of his house, the Grange.[15]

Harrow was in many ways a classic manor, with a central demesne surrounded by customary land and fringed, at least on the east, by freehold estates. In the north-east, on the boundary with Stanmore, was *BENTLEY PRIORY*, an Augustinian house dependent upon the priory of St. Gregory, Canterbury, a foundation of Lanfranc. Bentley was probably founded in the early 13th century,[16] almost certainly by an archbishop of Canterbury.[17] The estate, described as one plough-land[18] and leased out by 1502,[19] was in 1535 valued at £4 10s. a year.[20] From c. 1510 there was apparently no prior or chaplain[21] and Bentley was probably little more than a source of income for St. Gregory's.[22] When St. Gregory's was dissolved in 1536, its property was granted to Archbishop Cranmer in exchange for land at Wimbledon and elsewhere,[23] but in 1542 he was forced to give these lands back to the king.[24] In 1546 the buildings and lands of the former Bentley priory were granted to Henry Needham and William Sacheverell,[25] who in the same year conveyed them to Elizabeth Colte.[26] The estate remained with the Colte family until between 1629 and c. 1642, when it passed to Henry Coghill.[27] It was left in 1734 by Thomas Coghill to his nephew Thomas Whittewrong, from whom it passed in 1761 to John Bennet.[28] In the following year Bennet sold an interest in Bentley to William Waller and in 1764 a subsidiary interest in land in Harrow, Little Stanmore, Pinner, and Edgware to John and Samuel Rudge.[29] Waller bought further interests in that part lying in Great Stanmore and Harrow in 1775,[30] and soon alienated his whole estate to James Duberly, who in turn sold it to John James Hamilton, Marquess of Abercorn (d. 1818), in 1788.[31] The estate, heavily mortgaged, was sold in 1857 to John Kelk (later Sir John Kelk, Bt.), a builder and railway engineer.[32] In 1882 Bentley Priory was acquired by Frederick Gordon, who unprofitably turned it into a residential hotel. After Gordon's death it became a private boarding school for girls, which was closed in 1924. In 1926 a syndicate bought about 240 a., part of which was used for building. The county council bought about 90 a., including the park, for inclusion in the green belt. A leasehold interest in this part was acquired by Harrow U.D.C. in 1936. The house with 40 a., was sold to the Air Ministry, which used it from 1936 as the administrative headquarters for Fighter Command, later Strike Command.[33] In 1943 Air Chief Marshal Sir Hugh Dowding (Air Officer Commanding-in-Chief, Fighter Command, 1936–40) was created Baron Dowding of Bentley Priory.[34]

The medieval priory probably stood near the site of Priory House, a 16th-century timbered farmhouse near Clamp Hill.[35] Further north, on higher ground, James Duberly built a house, which was altered and enlarged c. 1788–99 by Sir John Soane.[36] Lysons in 1795 thought it 'a noble mansion, in which convenience is united with magnificence' but in 1816 Brewer considered it 'an irregular range of brick building, destitute of architectural beauty, and of rather a gloomy character'. Its present appearance owes more to the 19th century, when a high clock-tower was added and the exterior was remodelled in the 'Italian' style; internally, however, a staircase and several rooms by Soane have survived.[37]

The manor of *UXENDON*, first so named in 1373,[38] consisted of a collection of interests and property on the eastern borders of Harrow parish. In 1357 Simon Francis, mercer of London, died seised of considerable property in Middlesex, including tenements in Harrow held of the Archbishop of Canterbury.[39] The estate passed to his son, Thomas (d. 1368) and to Alice, Thomas's widow, for life, with reversion to his sister, another Alice, wife of Sir Thomas Travers. In 1376 Sir Thomas's brother, Richard Travers, clerk, quitclaimed the reversionary interest to Sir Nicholas Brembre,[40] but the property was held in dower by Maud, Simon Francis's widow, from 1357 until her death in 1384. In 1385 Brembre acquired 2 hides in Preston from John Legge, a head tenant who had granted them to the Francis family, possibly on lease.[41] Another Preston family, the Dickets, granted their land in 1352 to Thomas Barnebieu, chaplain, who enfeoffed John Maselyn with it. The title passed to Maselyn's cousin, a clerk of the same name, who quitclaimed his interest to Brembre in 1384.[42] In that year Brembre settled much Middlesex property, including Uxendon manor, upon himself for life, with reversion to the grantors and to the heirs of Thomas Bere, parson of St. Michael Paternoster.

[14] M.R.O., Acc. 1052, f. 423.
[15] *Ret. of Owners of Land, 1873* [C. 1097], H.C. (1875), lxxii.
[16] First mentioned in 1229–30: *Cur. Reg. R.* xiii. 336. Not in the charter of Hubert, Abp. of Cant. 1193–1205, to St. Gregory's: Dugdale, *Mon.* (1846 edn.), vi. pt. 2, 615.
[17] *V.C.H. Mdx.* i. 169, quoting J. Tavernor-Perry, *Memorials of Old Mdx.* 11, which cites no source, gives Ranulf de Glanville as the founder. A Harrow court roll of 1512 states that the property had been granted by the archbishop in pure and perpetual alms: M.R.O., Acc. 76/2421, m. 3.
[18] e.g. M.R.O., Acc. 76/222a.
[19] P.C.C. 19 Blamyr (Thos. Downer).
[20] Listed *sub* St. Gregory's as 'farm of land called Bentley': *Valor Eccl.* (Rec. Com.), i. 25.
[21] The Prior of St. Gregory's was supposed to appoint a canon as celebrant and Prior of Bentley, but in 1512 he had not made an appointment for 2 years: M.R.O., Acc. 76/2421, m. 3.
[22] An 80-year lease of the 'whole priory of Bentley' for £4 10s. a year was granted to Arthur Darcy in 1532: S.C. 6/Hen. VIII/2105.
[23] Dugdale, *Mon.* (1846 edn.). vi, pt. 2, 614; Knowles and Hadcock, *Med. Religious Houses*, 132. On Cranmer's enforced exchanges, see F. R. H. Du Boulay, *Lordship of Cant.* 322 sqq.
[24] *L. & P. Hen. VIII*, xvii, p. 256; B.M. Add. Ch. 7490.
[25] Ibid. xxi(2), p. 92.
[26] Lysons, *Environs of Lond.* ii. 568.
[27] M.R.O., Acc. 76/205, /208, /222a; Acc. 794/2.
[28] Lysons, *Environs of Lond.* ii. 568–9.
[29] C.P. 25(2)/1361/4 Geo. III Hil.
[30] Ibid. /1363/15 Geo. III Hil.
[31] Lysons, *Environs of Lond.* ii. 569.
[32] M.R.O., Acc. 502/22–23, /27, /32, /34.
[33] 'Story of Bentley Priory, Stanmore' (TS. 1946, *penes* Bentley H.Q. Fighter Command); ex inf. Town Clerk's Dept., Lond. Bor. of Harrow.
[34] *Who's Who* (1968).
[35] Hist. Mon. Com. *Mdx.* 68; O.S. Map 1/25,000, Mdx. TQ 19 (1950 edn.).
[36] Lysons, *Environs of Lond.* ii. 569; Brewer, *Beauties of Eng. & Wales*, x(5), 678–9 (illustrated).
[37] H. M. Colvin, *Biograph. Dict. Eng. Architects (1660–1840)*, 561; Pevsner, *Mdx.* 104; M.R.O., Acc. 311/20; 'Story of Bentley Priory'.
[38] *Cal. Close, 1369–74*, 536.
[39] *Cal. Inq. p.m.* x, pp. 348–9.
[40] *Cal. Close, 1374–7*, 357.
[41] M.R.O., Acc. 2413, mm. 12, 22.
[42] *Cal. Close, 1349–54*, 467, 476; *1381–5*, 597.

After Brembre's attainder the manor, then worth £6 13s. 4d., was occupied by Thomas Goodlake in Bere's name,[43] but it escheated to the Crown and in 1394 was sold to Goodlake,[44] a London citizen who had other property in the district.[45] Although John Hadley died seised of an interest in 1410,[46] the capital interest descended to Goodlake's daughter, Thomasine (d. 1429), who married Sir John Boys (Boyce or Bosco) (d. 1447).[47] John Legge surrendered a hide in 1416 and John Weald surrendered ½ hide in Preston (called Bugbeards) in 1422 to the use of Sir John and Thomasine,[48] and the Boyses' copyhold land was described as 1½ hide in Preston and 1 hide in Uxendon until 1459.[49] John Boys's estate in Harrow and Kingsbury was worth £5 in 1412,[50] but although the family held the freehold of Uxendon manor,[51] there is no description of it before 1516. The freehold then comprised a carucate formerly belonging to Richard Uxendon, three hides and three virgates formerly belonging to Richard atte Oke,[52] and a virgate formerly belonging to Adam Aylward. The copyhold was ½ hide formerly Michael Uxendon's, ½ hide formerly Alice Uxendon's, a hide 'late John Lyon',[53] and two hides formerly John Preston's. The total property was estimated at about 1,000 a.[54] All these people, save Lyon, had held land in Preston and Uxendon in the 13th and 14th centuries.[55]

On Thomas Boys's death in 1516, all the property passed to his daughter, Mabel, the wife of Richard Bellamy.[56] The estate, although heavily mortgaged, remained with the Bellamys, until another Richard Bellamy conveyed his remaining interests to Joan Mudge and William Mascall in 1603.[57] Mascall quit-claimed to Joan Mudge in the same year and by 1608 Uxendon manor was in the hands of her son-in-law, Richard Page.[58] The Preston property, 80 a. around Preston or Preston Dicket manor-house,[59] was in 1603 delivered to Stanwardine Passey, one of Bellamy's creditors, but in 1609 it was acquired by Richard Page.[60] Part was held by Edward Halsey in 1770[61] and the rest was sold to the Bocket family before 1799.[62] At inclosure Martha Bocket and Mary Halsey had a farm-house and 72 a. of freehold at Preston.[63] By 1629 the Kenton portion of Uxendon manor had been alienated to Robert and Thomas Walter and merged in their other Kenton estate.[64] This passed to the Grahams at the beginning of the 18th century[65] but in 1797,[66] 1802, and 1803 their estate, 70 a. of inclosed meadow and 90 a. of common-field land, was broken up and sold.[67]

The Uxendon part of the estate, however, remained intact in the hands of the Page family and in 1817 consisted of 413 a. of inclosed land and 202 a. allotted in lieu of open-field land, north of Forty Lane and west of Blind Lane and Preston Road.[68] On the death of Richard Page in 1803 Uxendon manor passed to his brother Francis, who died unmarried in 1810, leaving his brothers William and Henry as his heirs. Henry Page married in 1813, when he and William entered into a conveyance for uses with Francis Fladgate, a solicitor. Fladgate died in 1821, followed three years later by William Page, who had never married, leaving Henry Page in possession. There is no evidence that Henry Page left any heir, but Henry Young of Essex Street, a junior partner of Fladgate, apparently obtained a deed of bargain and sale by fraud from Henry Page, who was of weak intellect and frequently drunk, in 1825. Page confirmed the deed in his will and when he died in 1829 Young entered into Uxendon, which he enjoyed until his death in 1869. He left instructions that the estates were to be sold for the benefit of his wife and children.[69] By 1914 the house was being used by the Lancaster Shooting Club.[70] It fell into decay and in 1933 the railway line from Wembley Park to Stanmore was built across the site.[71]

WEMBLEY manor originated in the estate in Wembley, Tokyngton, and Alperton which was acquired by the priory of Kilburn from the Huscarl and Tokyngton families.[72] William Huscarl, who paid £2 15s. annual rent for his lands to the archbishop in 1236,[73] granted 94 a. to the priory of St. Helen, Bishopsgate, in 1236[74] and 133 a. and £2 0s. 10d. rents to Kilburn in 1243.[75] A dispute between Kilburn and St. Helen's in 1249 suggests that the latter's Harrow property passed to Kilburn.[76] The most important grant to Kilburn, however, was probably that made by Ralph Tokyngton in 1246–7.[77]

[43] C.P. 25(1)/289/54/129; *Cal. Inq. Misc.* v, pp. 130–1; *Cal. Pat.* 1385–9, 481.
[44] *Cal. Pat.* 1391–6, 403.
[45] *Cal. Close*, 1389–92, 293, 1396–9, 492; Scott, *Recs. of Grammar Sch.* 5.
[46] Lysons, *Environs of Lond.* ii. 566n. Hadley may have inherited from one of the grantors of 1384, although they included no one of that name.
[47] *Mdx. Pedigrees* (Harl. Soc. lxv), 9. For the Boys family, see B.M. Add. MS. 45500, ff. 283–4.
[48] M.R.O., Acc. 76/2415, mm. 3d, 26.
[49] Ibid. /2417, m. 121d.
[50] *Feudal Aids*, vi. 490.
[51] C 1/39/49.
[52] Ric. de Oke (or attenoke) was the abp.'s bailiff in 1273–4: B.M. Add. MS. 29794.
[53] Probably identifiable with ½-hide called Bugbeards surrendered to John Boys by John Weald in 1422: M.R.O., Acc. 76/2415, m. 26. Weald's title is unknown, but by 1435–6 John Lyon was admitted as brother and heir of Agnes Bugbeard: ibid. /2416, m. 57.
[54] Including some land in Harrow Weald. The 1553 rental also lists 1½ hide of freehold *sub* Uxendon, formerly Ric. Uxendon's.
[55] *Ft. of F. Lond. and Mdx.* i. 37; M.R.O., Acc. 76/2412, mm. 3, 6. Transactions involving the Uxendon and atte Oke families are given *sub* Ed. III of the index to the court rolls (Acc. 76/216), but the relevant rolls are damaged or missing.
[56] M.R.O., Acc. 76/388; *Mdx. Pedigrees*, 9. Boys's step-daughter, Anna Wenne, became a nun of St. Helen's, Bishopsgate.
[57] W. D. Bushell, 'The Bellamies of Uxendon'. *Harrow Octocent. Tracts*, xiv. See below, p.260.
[58] M.R.O., Acc. 276/3/49; Acc. 853/1–12.
[59] M.R.O., Acc. 76/208.
[60] M.R.O., Acc. 853/13–14.
[61] M.R.O., Acc. 76/212.
[62] Ibid. /209.
[63] Ibid. /1400; Acc. 794/8; M.R. 612.
[64] M.R.O., Acc. 76/208.
[65] M.R.O., Acc. 166(1)/28; Acc. 166/146/33, /35, /48, /50, /53, /70–153.
[66] See p. 213.
[67] M.R.O., Acc. 166/Box 3.
[68] M.R.O., Acc. 76/1400; Acc. 794/8; M.R. 612.
[69] Wemb. Hist. Soc., Acc. 5. Estates leased out by Young, who lived at Sudbury Grove: M.R.O., Acc. 590/3, nos. 1213, 1232; *Wembley News*, 25 Dec. 1952. C. A. Loud, listed for Uxendon in 1866 and 1886, was probably only the lessee: *Kelly's Dirs. Mdx.* (1866, 1886).
[70] *Harrow Octocent. Tracts*, xiv. 1; Wemb. Hist. Soc., Acc. 351.
[71] Elsley, *Wembley*, 169.
[72] *Cur. Reg. R.* xiii. 526; C.P. 25(1)/146/10/131.
[73] Lambeth Palace, Estate MS. 1193.
[74] C.P. 25(1)/146/10/139.
[75] Ibid. /147/13/201.
[76] Ibid. /16/281.
[77] Ibid. /15/266; *Ft. of F. Lond. & Mdx.* i. 31.

A Ralph Tokyngton (de Tockint'), who held $1\frac{1}{6}$ knight's fee in Hayes, Southall, and Tokyngton c. 1171,[78] may have descended from one of the three knights who held 6 hides in Harrow in 1086.[79] Godfrey Tokyngton in 1210–12 held $\frac{1}{4}$ knight's fee,[80] which appears to have passed to Ralph by 1230.[81] In 1334 the Prioress of Kilburn did homage for 1 hide and 1 carucate of arable and 4 a. of meadow[82] which were held by fealty, suit of court, service, and £3 8s. rent.[83] After the Dissolution, however, Wembley was said to have been held by the priory in chief by service of $\frac{1}{20}$ knight's fee and rent.[84] The total value of Kilburn's property in Wembley and Tokyngton in 1535 was £8 10s. 6d., made up of the farm of the manor, rents, profits from woods, and perquisites of court.[85] In 1542 the annual value of the manor of Wembley was given as £7 7s.[86]

Kilburn Priory was dissolved in 1536[87] and in 1542 all its former lands in Wembley and Tokyngton were granted to Richard Andrews of Hailes (Glos.) and Leonard Chamberlain of Woodstock (Oxon.). They regranted the property in the same year to Richard Page, whose family had leased it from before the Dissolution.[88] Richard Page, the lessee of Sudbury Court, was licensed in 1547 to lease Wembley manor to Thomas Page, his son.[89] The manor was usually held in the Page family by the eldest son of the lessee of Sudbury Court.[90] Dairy Farm and 134 a. stretching southwards to the Brent, bounded on the east by the Harrow road and on the west by Alperton common fields, were sold by Richard Page in 1803 to Samuel Hoare.[91] In 1852 they were owned by Henry Hoare.[92] In 1910, when it was offered for sale as building land, Dairy Farm was called the Curtis estate.[93] The rest of Wembley manor was sold to John Gray.[94] The estate, which at inclosure consisted of 327 a. between Wembley and Forty greens,[95] passed to his son, the Revd. Edward Gray, who sold part of it to the Metropolitan Railway Co. in 1881. The remaining 280 a. were sold by his executors to Sir Edward Watkin in 1889.[96] In 1905 James Page, who stated that he was the heir of Henry Page, claimed the Wembley Park estate from the Metropolitan Railway and the Tower Co. Ltd., but the companies based their title on the sale to John Gray and the case was dismissed.[97]

The head of the Page family of Wembley seems to have lived in Wembley House, south of Wembley Green, first mentioned in 1510[98] and occupied in 1781 by Richard Page and later by John Gray.[99] The farm-house or Dairy in 1547 stood north of Wembley Green and south of the brook,[1] but it was later built to the east of Wembley House.[2] In 1810 John Gray built the White House, a mansion with two wings, a stucco front and Doric portico,[3] at Wembley Park. The house was used as a nunnery from 1905 until its demolition in 1908.[4]

TOKYNGTON or *OAKINGTON* manor[5] originated in a freehold estate built up by the Barnville family from the end of the 13th century.[6] In 1317 John Barnville received rents, nearly 100 a. and the advowson of Tokyngton chapel from Richard the Fair (le Blound).[7] Most of the estate was in Tokyngton, where it seems to have been interspersed with the Kilburn lands and Freren.[8] Part of it may originally have lain in Kingsbury and it was the only estate within Harrow parish of which the Archbishop of Canterbury was not overlord. In 1272 the overlordship of Edgware and Kingsbury manor was said to extend to Tokyngton[9] and from 1426 the estate appears in Kingsbury rentals as 100 a. of free land held from Edgware manor for 1d. rent a year.[10] When the Barnvilles leased Kilburn's Tokyngton property in the late 14th century, they apparently tried to create a single estate and it was only after prolonged litigation that Kilburn retained its lands in 1401.[11] In 1456 the Barnvilles tried to extend their estate by leasing the demesne of Kingsbury manor.[12] John Barnville was dead by 1482, when the Tokyngton estate was held by his daughter, Elizabeth, and her first husband Sir Thomas Frowyk, Chief Justice of the Common Pleas.[13]

Frowyk died in 1506[14] and Elizabeth had remarried by 1508[15] when she and her second husband, Thomas Jakes, conveyed an interest, possibly a reversion or mortgage, in over 2,300 a. in Middlesex, including Tokyngton manor and the advowson of Tokyngton chapel, to Richard Bellamy and others. After Elizabeth's death in 1515[16] the property was held by Frideswide (d. 1528), her daughter by her first husband, and by her husband, Sir Thomas Cheyney.[17] Cheyney was still holding one freehold[18]

[78] *Kent Recs.* xviii. 7.   [79] *V.C.H. Mdx.* i. 120.
[80] *Red Bk. Exch.* (Rolls Ser.), 471.
[81] *Cur. Reg. R.* xiii. 526.
[82] M.R.O., Acc. 76/2412, m. 1d.
[83] Specified as 5 marks and 16d.; 5 marks (£3 6s. 8d.) remained the rent for the carucate throughout the 16th and 17th cent.
[84] M.R.O., Acc. 276/9/8.
[85] *Valor Eccl.* (Rec. Com.), i. 432.
[86] M.R.O., Acc. 276/9/8.
[87] Knowles and Hadcock, *Med. Religious Houses*, 213. For Kilburn, see *V.C.H. Mdx.* i. 178–82.
[88] *L. & P. Hen. VIII*, xvii, pp. 259, 320.
[89] *Cal. Pat.* 1547–8, p. 211; M.R.O., Acc. 1052, ff. 101–4.
[90] P.C.C. 20 Welles, 18 Martyn, 35 Noodes; *Cal. Pat.* 1560–3, p. 605; M.R.O., Acc. 76/205, /208, /212, /1985; Acc. 794/2.
[91] M.R.O., Acc. 76/587, /739; Acc. 794/8; M.R. 612, no. 1069.
[92] M.R.O., Acc. 76/2374; Acc. 590/3, /4, no. 1419.
[93] Wemb. Hist. Soc., Acc. 156.
[94] Brewer, *Beauties of Eng. & Wales*, x(5), 680–1, says that it was sold in 1802 by Richard Page. Lysons, *Environs of Lond.* Suppl. 190, says that it was sold in 1804 by Page's executors.
[95] M.R.O., Acc. 794/8; M.R. 612; C.P. 43/939A, ff. 78 sqq.
[96] *Wembley News*, 15 Dec. 1952; T. C. Barker and M.

Robbins, *Hist. of London Transport*, i. 205–6. For the subsequent development of Wembley Park, see above, p. 200.
[97] Elsley, *Wembley*, 144–5.
[98] Lambeth Palace, Estate MS. 478.
[99] M.R.O., Acc. 76/1109.
[1] M.R.O., Acc. 1052, ff. 101–4.
[2] O.S. Maps 1/2,500 Mdx. xi. 13 (1865 edn.).
[3] M.R.O., D.R.O. 3/F2/5; Wemb. Hist. Soc., Acc. 351; Harrow Cent. Ref. Libr., Sales Partics. i (1834).
[4] Wemb. Hist. Soc., Acc. 351; Elsley, *Wembley*, 148.
[5] First called a manor in 1505: *Cal. Inq. p.m. Hen. VII*, iii, p. 282.
[6] C.P. 25(1)/26/148/36; *Cal. Close*, 1333–7, 735.
[7] C.P. 25(1)/149/48/231. Possibly an epithet for Richard Tokyngton.
[8] The Freren estate in Kingsbury is reserved for treatment in a later volume.
[9] C.P. 25(1)/147/24; /282/7.
[10] Bodl. MS., All Souls D.D. c56/2.
[11] *Cal. Close*, 1399–1402, 293–7, 299.
[12] Bodl. MS., All Souls D.D. c79/3.
[13] Ibid. c56/5.
[14] *Cal. Inq. p.m. Hen. VII*, iii, pp. 111–15.
[15] C.P. 25(1)/294/81.
[16] P.C.C. 13 Holder. Jakes was already dead.
[17] Bodl. MS., All Souls D.D. c38/13.
[18] Described in 1547 as Margaret Tokyngton's: M.R.O., Acc. 1052, ff. 101 sqq.

and one copyhold virgate in Wembley in 1553[19] but the bulk of the Tokyngton estate, consisting of a messuage, 210 a. and £3 rent, was the subject of a fine between the Cheyneys and Richard Stanerton and William Hale in 1522.[20] By 1528, however, Richard Bellamy was in possession.[21] Tokyngton was among the Bellamy property searched in the 1580s[22] and in 1588 it was mortgaged to William Gerard.[23] Philip Gerard, to whom it was again mortgaged in 1592,[24] effected a recovery in 1602[25] but by 1609 the manor was in the hands of the Pages.[26] In 1800 it was conveyed by Richard Page to Robert Tubbs,[27] who at inclosure in 1817 owned a compact 300 a. in the south-east corner of the parish.[28] By 1835 it had passed to Joseph Neeld,[29] who devised it by will proved 1856 to his brother John (later Sir John). The Neeld family retained Tokyngton manor, under the name of Oakington Park or Sherren's Farm, until the break-up of the estate in the 20th century. The Great Central Railway line was built through it in 1906 and in 1913 Sir Audley D. Neeld agreed with Wembley U.D.C. to develop the estate on garden city lines. In 1938 he conveyed 21 a., including the manor-house, to Wembley Borough Council for use as open space.[30]

The house of William Barnville was mentioned in 1400,[31] but the later manor-house dated from c. 1500, when it was leased to the wealthy John Lamb,[32] and was extended c. 1600. From the 16th century it was usually leased as a farm[33] and although a single building is marked in 1759,[34] farm buildings had been added by 1817.[35] The farm later became a park, when Col. Sir Patrick Wellesley Talbot was tenant,[36] and lodges were built near Wembley Hill Road and Harrow Road.[37] The estate reverted to farm-land at the end of the 19th century[38] and the buildings grew very dilapidated.[39] A proposal that the manor-house should become a public library was rejected, and in 1939 it was demolished.[40]

There was one sub-manor held from Rectory manor. This was *FLAMBARDS* or *FLAMBERTS* manor, so-called in 1486,[41] which originated in an estate of about 320 a. in Harrow, Northolt, and Greenford in the hands of the Flambard family by 1353.[42] After the death of Elizabeth Flambard in 1394, it passed to her daughter, Eleanor, the wife of Walter Tyrell.[43] The estate, which as 'the manor of Harrow' was disputed among the Tyrell family c. 1429,[44] was conveyed by Sir Thomas Tyrell and his wife, Anne, to Henry Frowyk, Thomas Charlton, and John Sturgeon in 1447–8.[45] Charlton and Sturgeon were both related by marriage to the Frowyks, to whom they seem to have quitclaimed their interest.[46] From the early 14th century various branches of the Frowyks had held property in Harrow,[47] where the family may have had more than one estate. Part descended from Sir Thomas Frowyk (d. 1506) to his daughter, Frideswide (d. 1519) and her husband, Sir Thomas Cheyney,[48] but most was inherited by the elder brother of Sir Thomas Frowyk, Henry Frowyk of Gunnersbury,[49] who died, seised of Flambards, in 1505.[50] Henry's son Thomas was dead by 1522 and the property descended to his sisters, Margaret, wife of Michael Fisher, and Elizabeth, wife of Sir John Spilman of Narborough (Norf.), Justice of the King's Bench.[51] John Spilman, grandson of the judge, conveyed Flambards in fee farm in 1573[52] to William Gerard, who seems to have been living there, probably as a lessee, by 1566.[53] Gerard paid an annual rent of £30 to John Spilman and his descendants. In 1656 John Spilman (d. 1663) sold the fee-farm rent to John Bernard and Daniel Waldo.[54] Elizabeth (d. 1766), only child of Charles Gerard (d. 1701), married Warwick Lake in 1709 and Miles Stapledon seven years later. In 1767 representatives of the Lake and Stapledon families sold Flambards to Francis Herne, whose heirs were his sisters, Mary, who seems to have lived at Flambards,[55] and Ann, the first wife of Richard Page. The property passed to Page's son, another Richard, by the will of Mary Herne c. 1787.[56] Richard Page sold some of his land in Roxeth and Northolt in 1803[57] to Samuel Hoare, who at inclosure in 1817[58] held 204 a. in Roxeth, including two farms. In 1852 the property was divided between Samuel and Hannah Hoare and the farms took the names of the lessees, Joseph

[19] M.R.O., Acc. 76/222a. This property was listed under Margery Draper c. 1600 (ibid. /205), Philip Gerard in 1629 (ibid. /208), and the heirs of Wm. Dwight c. 1642 (Acc. 794/2).

[20] *Ft. of F. Lond. & Mdx.* ii. 27.

[21] Bodl. MS., All Souls D.D. c56/11.

[22] Elsley, *Wembley*, 81.

[23] M.R.O., Acc. 853/17.   [24] Ibid. /16, /17.

[25] M.R.O., Acc. 276/6.

[26] Bodl. MS., All Souls D.D. c78/187.

[27] Elsley, *Tokyngton*, 15.

[28] M.R.O., Acc. 76/1400; Acc. 794/8; M.R. 612.

[29] M.R.O., LA. HW. Harrow Poor-rate Bk., ix.

[30] Abstract of title (1938) and information *penes* Town Clerk's Dept., London Bor. of Brent.

[31] *Cal. Close*, 1399–1402, 293–7.

[32] P.C.C. 1 Bucke. Assessed for the 1550–1 subsidy on £100 goods, the highest in the parish: E 179/142/169.

[33] M.R.O., Acc. 276/3/49; D.R.O. 3/B2/1, /F2/1; LA. HW. Harrow Poor-rate Bk. ix; Acc. 590/3, /4, no. 1345.

[34] M.R.O., Acc. 643, 2nd deposit, Messeder map. Several buildings are marked, though unreliably, on Rocque, *Map of Mdx.* (1754).   [35] M.R. 612.

[36] Elsley, *Wembley*, 172, says that Talbot was there from 1850 until 1887, but Jas. Gurney is recorded in 1852 and E. H. Sherren in 1886: M.R.O., Acc. 590/4, no. 1345; *Kelly's Dir. Mdx.* (1886).

[37] M.R.O., Acc. 590/3; O.S. Map 1/2,500, Mdx. xi. 13 (1865 edn.).

[38] Wemb. Hist. Soc., *Jnl.* i(4); *Kelly's Dirs. Mdx.* (1886, 1906).

[39] Pictures of house in *Wembley News*, 12 Feb. 1953; Wemb. Hist. Soc., Catalogue Acc. 99, 333/4, /8; 441/10–11.

[40] Elsley, *Wembley*, 172–3.

[41] *Cal. Inq. p.m. Hen. VII*, i, p. 74.

[42] C.P. 25(1)/150/65/314.

[43] M.R.O., Acc. 76/2413, mm. 52, 54; Acc. 974/1, mm. 16, 16d; and see mm. 1, 6d.

[44] C 1/32/178. The Rectory court rolls of 1446 refer to tenants of 'land formerly Edw. Tyrell's called Flambards': M.R.O., Acc. 76/2417, m. 102d.

[45] *Ft. of F. Lond. & Mdx.* i. 196.

[46] cf. e.g. *Cal. Close, 1461–8*, 132; *Mdx. Pedigrees*, 88–89.

[47] Roger and Idony Frowyk (c. 1300–16): C.P. 25(1)/148/38/355–6, /149/41/55–56, /47/199; Canterbury, Eastbridge Hosp. Archives, H(12–14).

[48] *Cal. Inq. p.m. Hen. VII*, iii, p. 111; M.R.O., Acc. 76/2421, mm. 8d. 58d.

[49] *Cal. Inq. p.m. Hen. VII*, i, p. 74.

[50] Ibid. ii, p. 282; M.R.O., Acc. 76/2420, m. 67; C. 142/21/114.

[51] M.R.O., Acc. 76/2421, mm. 26, 58d; Lysons, *Environs of Lond.* ii. 225; *Mdx. Pedigrees*, 88–89.

[52] M.R.O., Acc. 853/25.

[53] M.R.O., Acc. 76/811.

[54] M.R.O., Acc. 853/25.

[55] M.R.O., D.R.O. 3/B2/2.

[56] M.R.O., Acc. 76/570, /1884; Lysons, *Environs of Lond.* ii. 568.

[57] M.R.O., Acc. 76/587, /739.

[58] M.R.O., Acc. 794/8.

Baker[59] and George Atkins.[60] The devisees of Richard Page (d. 1803), in accordance with his will, sold the house and 90 a. around it in 1804 to George Heming. In 1807 Heming conveyed his Flambards estate, as part of an exchange involving Greenhill Farm, to Lord Northwick, who merged it with his neighbouring lands.[61] Northwick sold the house and 50 a. in 1825 to Gen. Alexander Murray Macgregor,[62] who mortgaged the property which in 1831 was bought by the Revd. W. W. Phelps, then a master at Harrow School. The property remained with the Phelps family until 1885 when it was purchased by Harrow Park Trust.[63]

The core of the Flambards estate consisted of free and copyhold land held from both Harrow and Rectory manor, on either side of the border between Harrow-on-the-Hill and Sudbury.[64] The estate reached its greatest extent under the Frowyks. When Henry Frowyk died in 1505 seised of the manor of Flambards, it consisted of a messuage, a windmill, 1,240 a. and £5 rent in Harrow, Sudbury, Pinner, Roxeth, Wembley, Greenhill, Great Greenford, and Northolt.[65] Except for the Wembley lands, which were held of Tokyngton manor,[66] the property, worth £10, was held of the Archbishop of Canterbury. Frowyk was also seised of a messuage, 113 a., and 10s. rent in Kenton, worth £3 and held of the archbishop, which may have been the other family estate. All his property seems to have passed to the Spilmans,[67] but the Gerards reorganized it[68] and in 1609, after the death of William Gerard, Flambards manor was described as three messuages, 610 a. and £3 rent in Harrow, Northolt, and Greenford, worth £4 a year.[69] Other property, Frere Place and Freemantels, comprised 233 a. in the three parishes, and Woodridings consisted of 158 a. in Pinner. From the 17th century Flambards manor was usually described as 16 messuages, a windmill, 800 a., and £2 rent in Harrow, Pinner, Greenford, and Northolt.[70] By 1807 it had shrunk to 90 a. on the borders of Sudbury and Harrow-on-the-Hill.[71]

Fourteenth-century brasses in St. Mary's church[72] suggest that the Flambards lived in Harrow. The Tyrells, an Essex family,[73] and the Frowyks, of London and South Mimms, seem to have leased out the property,[74] but at least one member of the Spilman family wanted to be buried in St. Mary's church[75] and Sir Gilbert Gerard stated in 1639 that the ancient manor-house of Flambards had been 'formerly the seat of persons of great worth and quality'.[76] The house, which was in Harrow-on-the-Hill, east of London Road,[77] was supplied with piped water in 1580.[78] Sir Gilbert spent £3,000 in 1619–39 in 're-edifying and beautifying' it and planting elms as shelter.[79] In 1664 Flambards, with 25 hearths, was the largest house in Harrow parish.[80] A new mansion, further north, was begun by Richard Page and finished on a larger scale by Lord Northwick. This was named Harrow Park[81] from its setting in landscaped grounds,[82] and became the Northwicks' principal Harrow residence.[83] In 1826 its purchaser, Gen. Macgregor, was said to be the greatest personage in Harrow and to have the finest house.[84] Although documents as early as 1736 record the original Flambards as occupying the site of 'the late manor-house',[85] it is clearly marked in 1806 as 'the Mansion House', with the new house to the north marked as 'The Park'.[86] Gerard's mansion, which may well have degenerated into farm buildings,[87] seems to have been pulled down and replaced by other houses between 1867 and 1896.[88]

The manor of *PINNER*, mentioned in 1486 and 1500, was probably *FEMALES* or *FEARNALS* manor, mentioned in 1573, an estate which the rentals describe as a freehold hide in Pinner. In 1486 it was held by Richard Barnet,[89] who was holding land in Pinner in 1477–8.[90] Barnet was the great-grandson of Richard Frowyk[91] and the estate may have originated in Frowyk lands, as did Brackenbury manor in Harefield.[92] In 1486 Thomas Rigby was among those seised of the property to the use of Richard Barnet. In 1500 Rigby's son, George, quitclaimed his interest to John Morton and others.[93] In the same year John Morton entered into a fine with William Draycote, clerk, and William Hyde whereby Pinner and Brackenbury manors and considerable property elsewhere in Middlesex were conveyed to Morton and his wife for life with remainder to Hyde's heirs.[94] The death of a Morton,[95]

59 M.R.O., Acc. 590/1, /4, no. 1803; M.R. 612, no. 534.
60 M.R.O., Acc. 590/1, /4, no. 346; M.R. 612, no. 427.
61 M.R.O., Acc. 76/565, /570–3, /586; Acc. 643, unsorted box of 19th-cent. documents.
62 M.R.O., Acc. 76/586.
63 *Harrow School*, ed. Howson and Warner, 48; C. Hole, *Life of W. W. Phelps*, ii. 86 sqq.
64 e.g. M.R.O., Acc. 76/2413, mm. 52, 54, /2417, m. 102d; Acc. 974/I mm. 1, 16, 17.
65 *Cal. Inq. p.m. Hen. VII*, iii, p. 282.
66 There was a Flambards Nook in Uxendon in 1648: Wemb. Hist. Soc., Acc. 900/1.
67 Hen. Spilman held 109 selions of freehold in Kenton in 1546–7, about half being parcel of Uxendon manor and half parcel of Harrow manor: M.R.O., Acc. 166/1.
68 e.g. exchange of land in Northolt c. 1579: M.R.O., Acc. 276/7/13.
69 M.R.O., Acc. 276/9/7.
70 M.R.O., Acc. 76/1884.
71 Ibid. /571–2, /576–9.
72 Hist. Mon. Com. *Mdx.* 66.
73 *Visitation of Essex* (Harl. Soc. xii), 110–1, 300–2.
74 M.R.O., Acc. 76/2417, m. 102d; Lambeth Palace, Estate MS. 477. This may explain the phrase 'formerly Edw. Chalkhill's': *Cal. Inq. p.m. Hen. VII*, i, p. 74. While the Chalkhills held land which probably passed to the Frowyks, they can only have been connected with Flambards as tenants. 75 P.C.C. 8 Home.
76 M.R.O., Acc. 76/791.

77 M.R.O., Acc. 643, 2nd deposit, Messeder map B; Rocque, *Map of Mdx.* (1754).
78 W. W. Druett, *Harrow*, 220.
79 M.R.O., Acc. 76/791.
80 M.R.O., H.T. 5.
81 Greenwood, *Map of Mdx.* (1819), marks it 'Harrow Villa'. 'Flamberts House', on the same map, is erroneous.
82 Anne Rushout made sketches of the house and grounds in 1805, 1807, and 1815: M.R.O., Acc. 643, 4th and 5th deposits. See plate facing p. 180.
83 M.R.O., Acc. 643, unsorted box of 19th-cent. documents; *Harrow School*, ed. Howson and Warner, 48; Hole, *Life of W. W. Phelps*, ii. 89.
84 Hole, op. cit. ii. 9. See above.
85 M.R.O., Acc. 76/1884a.
86 M.R.O., Acc. 643, 2nd deposit, Survey of Northwick's estate (1806).
87 Described in 1852 as house, building, stables and coach-house, owned but not occupied by Wm. Phelps: M.R.O., Acc. 590/1, /4, nos. 46–47.
88 O.S. Maps 1/2,500, Mdx. x. 11 (1867 and 1896 edns.).
89 *Cal. Inq. p.m. Hen. VII*, i, p. 35.
90 M.R.O., Acc. 76/2418, m. 47.
91 W.A.M. 439.   92 *V.C.H. Mdx.* iii. 243.
93 W.A.M. 440.   94 C.P. 25(1)/294/80/82.
95 No Christian name is given. There was a Wm. Morton of Chester who held property in Pinner whose will is dated 1525 (P.C.C. F38 Bodfelde) but the son named in his will was called Peter.

who held 'divers lands and tenements freely for rent', is recorded in 1530–1.[96] His son William of Morton (Ches.) disputed the title to a messuage, lands and tenements called Females worth £5 a year, with Robert Boreman of Chipping Wycombe (Bucks.), who alleged that Morton had sold the property to Thomas Boreman, his father.[97] Boreman presumably won, for in 1553 he held one freehold hide, 'formerly John Morton's', for £1 8s. 3½d.[98] In 1547 the property was described as a freehold house in West End and 56 a. on the borders of Ruislip.[99] In 1569 Boreman conveyed the manor or farm called Females in Pinner to John Page of Wembley.[1] It was held by Richard Page c. 1600[2] and in 1629[3] but by c. 1642 it had been broken up and sold to nine people, including two members of the Street family.[4] In 1707 John Street of West End held a close of meadow called Females and 57 selions in the open fields.[5]

A copyhold virgate called Aldridges, also in West End, held by Robert Boreman in 1535–6[6] and 1553,[7] apparently followed the same descent, being held in 1573–4 by John Page[8] and in 1629 by a branch of the Streets.[9] About 1642 they were called the Streets of West End[10] and the estate formed out of part of Females manor and Aldridges was probably the mainly freehold estate held by them at inclosure.[11] It then consisted of a farm-house and dwelling-house in West End, 21 a. of old inclosures, and 2 a. of open-field land. The messuage, 'new-built' in 1747 and 'the farm called Aldridges' in 1795,[12] was enfranchised in 1872 as the 'tenement called Alfridges . . . now called West End Cottage'.[13] The map accompanying the enfranchisement marks West End House and a smaller building nearby. It had passed to William Dickson by 1872. As West House it passed to Harrow U.D.C. in 1948 and the estate became part of Pinner Memorial Park.[14] The central part of the house was demolished in the early 1950s, when one wall was found to be timber-framed.[15] Two mid-19th-century wings survived in 1969.

The most obscure of the so-called manors was *MARLPITS*, named after a family which owned land in Harrow in the 14th century.[16] The estate, in Hatch End, the Weald, Pinner, and Uxendon, was acquired by the Boyses of Uxendon and so descended to the Bellamys.[17] The Uxendon portion had apparently become detached by 1547, when it was held by John Page.[18] The Pinner part, a close called

Marlpits, was held in 1547 by Hugh Wright[19] and in 1553 by William Winter,[20] who sold it to John Edlin of the Weald.[21] By c. 1600 it was in the hands of Richard Edlin of the Marsh and thereafter it descended with Pinner Place.[22] In 1805 'a meadow called Marlpit Wood' was part of this estate.[23] The bulk of the estate lay in the Weald, around Hatch End, and this was conveyed by the Bellamys before c. 1600 to John Edlin,[24] who had been William Bellamy's tenant in 1566.[25] When William Edlin, John's heir, died seised of the manor of Marlpits in 1606, it comprised 56 a., 32 selions and 5 furlongs in Broad Field and Hampet Field, the Lea, Galportes garden, and several closes, including Cannons and Marlpits.[26] Most of this property, which was held from Harrow manor for £1 9s. 6d. rent, remained with the Edlins of Northchurch (Herts.) at least until c. 1642.[27] This branch, described as of Weald and later of Northchurch, had also held a ½-hide head tenement called Blackwell's at Headstone or Wolff's Green, and 19 a. of freehold called East Field since 1553.[28] Most of their lands, and probably some of those still held c. 1642 by the Edlins of Parkgate, passed to the Waldo family.[29] Marlpits manor was the object of a recovery involving Israel Wollaston and Samuel Waldo in 1752,[30] and a Waldo paid £1 9s. 6d. quit-rent in 1770,[31] the same amount as John Edlin paid c. 1600.[32] Although Marlpits manor was freehold it was intermingled with copyhold lands, all of which were remodelled to form Waldo's Farm. When this was sold in 1817 it included fields called Marlpits, Lye Field, and Broad Field.[33] As part of the farm, Marlpits was sold by Charles Waldo in 1790 to Daniel Dancer. It passed in 1794 to Henry and Mary Sayer and in 1817 to Daniel Wilshin.[34]

OTHER ESTATES.[35] One of the few estates that was entirely freehold was the New College property, which can be traced back through the transactions of London citizens to 1410–11 when Richard Walworth and his wife Agnes conveyed land in Harrow and Great Stanmore to Henry Harburgh, clerk.[36] In 1420 Harburgh conveyed it to John Franks and others, who five years later granted it to Thomas Charlton and John Rich.[37] In 1436 Charlton granted it to Richard Cotes and others,[38] who in 1451 enfeoffed Helen Hall, a widow. Eight years later she granted it to several people, including Joan Langton, who conveyed it to her son, John, a saddler, and his wife,

---

[96] M.R.O., Acc. 76/2421, m. 63d. The court rolls do not normally record freehold property.
[97] C1/1029/54–55.
[98] M.R.O., Acc. 76/222a.
[99] M.R.O., Acc. 1052, f. 427.
[1] Ware, *Pinner*, 101–2.
[2] M.R.O., Acc. 76/205.
[3] Ibid./208
[4] M.R.O., Acc. 794/2.
[5] M.R.O., Acc. 310(3).
[6] M.R.O., Acc. 76/2421, m. 74d.
[7] Ibid. /222a.
[8] Ibid. /214.
[9] Ibid. /208.
[10] M.R.O., Acc. 794/2.
[11] Ibid. /8; M.R. 612. Cf. M.R.O., Acc. 310(3), (4).
[12] M.R.O., Acc. 310(3).
[13] M.R.O., Acc. 76/1941; Ware, *Pinner*, 214–15, seems to have confused West End Lodge and West End Hse.
[14] Bor. of Harrow, *Facts & Figures* (1963–4), 79.
[15] Local information.
[16] Canterbury, Eastbridge Hosp. Archives, H(4); *Cal. Close,* 1346–9, 373; B.M. Add. Ch. 37366.

[17] M.R.O., Acc. 76/388, /222a; Acc. 1052, f. 456; Lambeth Palace, Estate MS. 477.
[18] M.R.O., Acc. 76/213; Acc. 1052, ff. 165–98.
[19] M.R.O., Acc. 1052, f. 427.
[20] M.R.O., Acc. 76/222a.
[21] P.C.C. 36 Pyckeryng.
[22] M.R.O., Acc. 76/205. See below.
[23] Ibid. /1400.   [24] Ibid. /205.
[25] P.C.C. 13 Crymes.
[26] Wards 7/39/64. Cf. M.R.O., Acc. 76/2418, mm. 1, 1d.
[27] M.R.O., Acc. 76/205, /208; Acc. 794/2.
[28] M.R.O., Acc. 76/205, /208, /214, /222a.
[29] See p. 216.
[30] C.P. 43/678/456.
[31] M.R.O., Acc. 76/212.
[32] The rents of freehold usually remained constant, while those of copyhold increased.
[33] M.R.O., Acc. 507/3, pp. 261–4.
[34] See p. 216.
[35] For the Christ Church estate see p. 251.
[36] *Ft. of F. Lond. and Mdx.* i. 177.
[37] New College MSS., Lower Room, Harrow 21.
[38] *Cat. Anct. D* .i, C 539.

Agnes, in 1466.[39] Langton's title was challenged in 1478 by Thomas Cornyssh,[40] who apparently removed the title deeds from Saddlers' Hall and altered them,[41] and it was not until 1503 that Raphael Cornyssh, Thomas's son, acknowledged the title of Elizabeth Langton, widow,[42] and Robert Sherborne, Dean of St. Paul's (later Bishop of Chichester), who had been associated in 1501 in an instrument for uses.[43] In 1504 Sherborne and Elizabeth Langton granted the estate to New College, Oxford,[44] which leased it, as Mease Place, to Elizabeth for an annual rent of 1 lb. of pepper for 51 years.[45] Elizabeth was probably dead by 1520–1 and thereafter the estate was usually held on leases of 10–20 years.[46] It comprised 62 a. north of Colliers Lane,[47] with the farm-house in the west on the edge of Weald Common, and 53 a., called Levels or Lovells, along the Hertfordshire border.[48] During the late 18th century Mease Place Farm was leased to George Drummond, to whose executors the college surrendered it in 1807 in exchange for Anderson's Farm, an estate of equal size (116 a.),[49] lying further south, to the west of Kenton Lane. The farm-house of Mease Place was in 1782 a large lath and plaster house with several barns. It was rebuilt in brick by George Drummond and in 1807 was considered vastly superior to Anderson's house.[50] The old farm-house, at the Lower End of Weald, was leased to labourers and by 1837 a more commodious one had been built where Kenton Lane turns sharply to the east.[51] The estate continued to be leased out as a farm until the college began to sell land for building in 1926.[52]

A freehold virgate in Sudbury was granted in 1400–1 by John Sadler, a dyer, and his wife Matilda to Robert Twyere, a skinner of London.[53] It descended to Robert's son, Elias, and afterwards to his daughters, Alice and Joan. Alice, wife of Richard Chandler, a London draper, seems to have inherited the Sudbury estate, which was held by Cornyssh and sold in 1470 to Gilbert Clerk, a husbandman who had already inherited property there.[54] Gilbert's wife, Margaret, apparently remarried and the property descended before 1509 to her son, William Finch, a yeoman of Harrow.[55] In 1547 William Finch held two freehold virgates, Chandler's (20 a.) and Clerk's (20 a. and Acreman Field), two crofts known as Hyde crofts (10 a.), next to Flambards, and Acreman croft (1 a.).[56] A note beside this entry on a later rental reads 'Ilotts'.[57] Finch's estate was

therefore presumably the one described in 1599 as a messuage or tenement, Ilotts, with about 27 a. in closes, including Great Acreman Field.[58] The Finches, who lived in Watford, leased out Ilotts for most of the next 200 years. In 1640 they owned 39 a.,[59] which by 1663 had developed into two estates, one a messuage, a cottage with only one hearth, the other the messuage Ilotts, probably a small farm-house with three hearths and nearly 50 a.[60] In 1789 Ilotts Farm consisted of 56 a. in an arc around the north of Hempstall, the part of Sudbury Court Farm adjoining the farm-house. Ilotts farm-house stood on high ground at the western end of the estate, abutting Sudbury Common.[61] In 1800 Ilotts was sold to Richard Page,[62] whose devisees sold it in 1805 to George Heming.[63] He in turn conveyed it two years later to Lord Northwick.[64] In the next decade the boundaries were rearranged, although the old names survived. Thus Thomas Trollope, father of the novelist, leased 157 a. from Lord Northwick as Ilotts Farm, which also included land from the Sudbury Court and Flambards estates.[65] Trollope, who came to Sudbury between 1813 and 1815,[66] leased the property for 21 years from 1819.[67] On a commanding site to the north-west, but not on the original Ilotts land,[68] he built a house which he called Julian Hill, supposedly after an estate in Royston (Herts.) which he hoped to inherit.[69] When his expectations were disappointed, he let Julian Hill to John W. Cunningham,[70] and moved to a farm-house on the land, presumably the original Ilotts Farm, which Anthony used as the model for Orley Farm. After a few years at a farm in Harrow Weald, Thomas returned to Ilotts and apparently rebuilt the farm-house, spending more than £3,000.[71] The expense, combined with the agricultural depression, left him unable to pay his rent, and in 1834 the Trollopes fled to Belgium, taking with them as much as possible before the bailiffs arrived.[72] Ilotts Farm, its bounds still roughly following those of Trollope's estate but excluding Julian Hill, was leased to John Hinxman and then to Henry Green, each of whom combined it with Sudbury Court Farm.[73] The old farm-house had been a school for some time by 1900 and it disappeared soon afterwards.[74] In 1969 Julian Hill, although surrounded by modern houses, retained its secluded garden and was approached by a long tree-planted drive from the west. As originally built with a two-storied low window, verandah, and

[39] New Coll. MSS. L.R. Harrow 21.
[40] *Cat. Anct. D.* iii, B 4193.
[41] C1/226/3; /297/90.
[42] Probably John Langton's second wife.
[43] New Coll. MSS. L.R. Harrow 3, 6–8, 10, 12, 14–15, 20, Abstract of title (unnumbered).
[44] Ibid. Harrow 1–2, 4.
[45] Ibid. 5.
[46] New Coll. MSS. 306, 308–9; L.R. Harrow 18, 21, Abstract of title, leases (1507/8–1729, 1737–42).
[47] About 12a. stretched into Stanmore.
[48] New Coll. MSS. 312, 383, 2420; L.R. 24–26.
[49] Ibid. 306, 311, 1379–80.
[50] Ibid. 1379–80.
[51] Ibid. 311, 1382; M.R.O., Acc. 590/2, /4, no. 959.
[52] New Coll. MSS. 177, 307–8.
[53] *Ft. of F. Lond. and Mdx.* i. 169.
[54] M.R.O., Acc. 276/9/6.
[55] Ibid. /7/16–17.
[56] M.R.O., Acc. 1052, f. 15.
[57] M.R.O., Acc. 794/2.
[58] M.R.O., Acc. 276/7/14, /18.
[59] M.R.O., Acc. 76/1647.
[60] Ibid. /590; Acc. 276/3/49; H.T. 5.

[61] M.R.O., Acc. 76/607.
[62] Ibid. /609.
[63] Ibid. /567–9.
[64] Ibid. /571–2.
[65] Ibid. /565, /1361; M.R. 612, nos. 660–2, 810–19, 821–3, 825, 852.
[66] M.R.O., D.R.O. 3/B2/4.
[67] M.R.O., Acc. 76/59, where Holts is written for Ilotts.
[68] i.e. 'on other land and ground of Northwick near to the said farm': M.R.O., Acc. 76/61.
[69] By coincidence one of the Flambards fields which he leased was already called Julians: M.R.O., Acc. 76/565 (1805); Acc. 974/I, m. 16 (1394). Both the new house and the farm-house were called Julian Hill; Acc. 590/1, /4, nos. 1723, 1728.
[70] See p. 255.
[71] M.R.O., Acc. 76/2346.
[72] A. Trollope, *Autobiography* (Oxford Crown edn. 1950), 2–4, 7, 16, 26–27; M. Sadleir, *Trollope, A Commentary*, 42, 44–45, 54; M.R.O., Acc. 76/620, /1573–9, /2346. See below, p. 230.
[73] M.R.O., Acc. 76/42, /65, /376, /1318; H.O. 107/1700, 9ff. 9–105.
[74] M.R.O., Acc. 76/1319.

canopied balcony, the house may have inspired the drawing of Orley Farm by Sir John Millais in the first edition of Trollope's novel (1862).[75] The staircase hall, dining room, and bow-ended drawing room are all part of the original house. A northern extension, now a separate dwelling, was built in the mid 19th century and later an entrance hall and billiard room were added on the west. The former stable block, converted to a house, stands to the north of Julian Hill.

A small freehold estate of 62 a., Woodfield and Roses in Alperton,[76] was held in 1547[77] by John Lyon, grocer of London.[78] It remained with the Lyons of Twyford until 1637–8 when George Lyon sold it to Robert Moyle. After the death of Walter Moyle in 1687, it passed to his sister Margaret Bennet,[79] who conveyed it to the Newman family, which already held property in Alperton[80] and Wembley. Henry Newman's daughter and heir, Susannah, married Richard Page c. 1745 and their son, Richard, sold Woodfield c. 1800 to Thomas Bowler, who was related by marriage to another branch of the Pages.[81] At inclosure Bowler owned about 100 a., mostly in the south-west corner of Alperton.[82]

The nucleus of Dove House Farm or Tyndales was a messuage and 9 a. called Wapses, in Hatch End, held by Henry Sharp in 1547.[83] It had passed to Francis Tyndale by 1629[84] and possibly by 1613.[85] Other freehold closes were in Dean Tyndale's hands by c. 1642.[86] The property passed to John Norwood c. 1649[87] and may be represented by the 12 hearths which were chargeable to Norwood in 1664.[88] It was owned by the Boys family in 1770[89] and at inclosure the farm, 79 a. of inclosed land in north-east Pinner, was leased from John Boys.[90] Dove House farm-house stood by 1759[91] on a moated site, presumably that of a much earlier house.[92] In the early 19th century it was the home of Mr. Tilbury, the horse dealer, who gave his name to the two-wheeled carriage. Napoleon III visited Dove House and copied Tilbury's magnificent stables for his palace at Chantilly.[93] Tilbury apparently let his farm: in 1845 and 1851 it was in the hands of Richard Roadnight, farmer and head jockey.[94] New Dove House or the Mansion, Hatch End, was built for Tilbury's

brother.[95] Dove House was still standing at the end of the century,[96] although the building of the railway and the Royal Commercial Travellers' Schools split up the estate.[97] The house was demolished c. 1965, when a block of flats was built on the site.[98]

The Harrow School estate developed from a head tenement in Preston, described alternatively as $\frac{1}{2}$ hide and 1 hide, held by the Lyons at the end of the 14th century.[99] When Agnes Bugbeard, a sister of William Lyon, died in 1435–6, another copyhold $\frac{1}{2}$-hide passed to her nephew John Lyon.[1] In 1553 another John Lyon held the two head tenements in Preston and much underset land.[2] He bought a freehold messuage and some land in Alperton from Richard Nicholl and his wife Catherine in 1572[3] and acquired eight tenements, out of 25 listed in contemporary rentals, in Harrow-on-the-Hill.[4] In 1575 he settled his Preston and Harrow Town property on himself and his wife Joan for life, with remainder to the governors of Harrow School.[5] John Lyon was dead by 1592 and his widow died in 1608.[6] The governors leased out the property, which yielded £45 6s. 8d. a year in the mid 17th century.[7] In 1797 they acquired by exchange 66 a. in Kenton which John Hunter of Gubbins (Herts.) had just purchased from the Grahams.[8] In the 16th century John Lyon had begun to inclose common-field land in Preston[9] and on the eve of parliamentary inclosure Preston Farm consisted of 144 a. stretching north from the farm-house as far as Kenton. There were 7 a. scattered in Alperton village and 22 a. in Harrow Town. Allotments in lieu of open-field land totalled 115 a., mostly in Preston.[10] By 1852 Preston Farm consisted of 243 a., and there were 18 houses in the centre of Harrow Town.[11] Most of the land bought by the school around Harrow-on-the-Hill in the late 19th century was used for playing fields, but a small farm was created in the corner between Watford Road and Pebworth Road to replace Preston Farm, which was sold for development in the 1920s.[12]

The hamlets in the east of the parish, Kenton, Preston, Uxendon, Wembley, and Tokyngton, were dominated by sub-manors which became concentrated in the Page family from the 16th century onwards. In Pinner there were the Marshes, Edlins,

[75] Robbins, *Middlesex*, 284 and pl. 10. Alternatively Ilotts Farm, as altered by Thomas Trollope, may have served as a model for the drawing.
[76] Except where otherwise stated, the account of this estate is based upon M.R.O., Acc. 76/270.
[77] M.R.O., Acc. 1052, ff. 13 sqq.
[78] There were Lyons in Alperton in 1432–3: M.R.O., Acc. 76/2416, m. 45d.
[79] M.R.O., Acc. 974/VI, m. 52d (618d).
[80] Part of the freehold once held by Sir Thos. Cheyney was sold in 1632 by Jasper Draper to Arthur Newman: M.R.O., Acc. 76/208; Acc. 854/2; Acc. 899.
[81] M.R.O., Acc. 507/2, f. 145.
[82] Ibid. Acc. 76/1400; Acc. 794/8; M.R. 612. See p. 193.
[83] M.R.O., Acc. 1052, ff. 427 sqq.
[84] M.R.O., Acc. 76/208.
[85] Ibid. /210.
[86] M.R.O., Acc. 794/2.
[87] M.R.O., Acc. 76/210.
[88] M.R.O., H.T. 5.
[89] M.R.O., Acc. 76/212. No known connexion with the much earlier family of Uxendon.
[90] M.R.O., Acc. 794/8; M.R. 612. Boys's claim for 'a farm called Tindals *alias* the Dovehouse Farm' (Acc. 76/1400) refutes the identification of Tyndales with Pinner Hall (Ware, *Pinner*, 113).
[91] M.R.O., Acc. 643, 2nd deposit, Messeder map A.
[92] Druett, *Pinner*, 188.
[93] Ibid.; Ware, *Pinner*, 145.

[94] *Home Cnties. Dir.* (1845); H.O. 107/1700, ff. 173–84.
[95] Ware, *Pinner*, 145.
[96] O.S. Map 6″, Mdx. x. NE. (1897 edn.).
[97] Ware, *Pinner*, 145.
[98] Local information.
[99] Elsley, *Wembley*, 95 sqq. Worksilver and hen payments confirm the $\frac{1}{2}$-hide assessment.
[1] M.R.O., Acc. 76/2416, m. 57.
[2] e.g. the Uxendon survey lists 67$\frac{1}{2}$ selions and 4 a. in Uxendon as held by John Lyon from Wm. Bellamy: M.R.O., Acc. 76/213.
[3] P. M. Thornton, *Harrow School*, App. C, p. 405. Catherine was the daughter of Wm. Page, under whose name the property appears in 1553: M.R.O., Acc. 76/222a. It is not listed in subsequent rentals.
[4] M.R.O., Acc. 76/205.
[5] Thornton, *Harrow Sch.* App. C, pp. 406–7.
[6] *V.C.H. Mdx.* i. 299.
[7] B.M. Harl. MS. 2211, f. 33. Thornton (*Harrow Sch.*) dates the rental 1590, but Joan Lyon still held property at that time and surviving leases suggest that it must be dated 1646–51: Scott, *Recs. of Grammar Sch.* 67, 69.
[8] The school surrendered a farm in North and South Mimms: M.R.O., Acc. 398/22.
[9] Thornton, *Harrow Sch.* App. C, p. 408.
[10] M.R.O., Acc. 76/1400; Acc. 794/8; M.R. 612.
[11] M.R.O., Acc. 590/3, /4, no. 1139.
[12] See pp. 188, 200.

Readings, Streets, and Birds, although none became as powerful or persisted for so long as the Pages.[13] The Marshes, who took their name from Pinner Marsh, held small amounts of land in Pinner in the 14th century.[14] In 1463 Richard Marsh conveyed 3 messuages, 3 carucates, 300 a. of pasture, 20 a. of wood, and 40s. rent in Harrow and Pinner to Richard Danvers and others.[15] By 1553[16] most of his property was in the hands of the Edlins, including one freehold hide, which c. 1600 was described as 'late Richard Danvers'.[17] The Edlins had lived in Pinner and Harrow Weald at least since c. 1300.[18] Some had built up estates during the next two centuries,[19] and in 1522–3 they ranged from John, a labourer worth 20s. in wages, to Richard, the lessee of Woodhall manor, worth £20 in goods.[20] At least six Edlins held land[21] in 1553.[22] The two main branches were the Edlins of Woodhall manor, and later of Pinner Marsh, and those of Parkgate. Their principal home throughout the 16th century and possibly until 1623[23] was Woodhall manor, which was leased in 1553 and c. 1609–10[24] to Richard Edlin. In 1553 he also held one hide, ½ virgate, and 29 a. of freehold land, most of which had belonged to Richard Marsh, and a ½-hide head tenement, called Rowheads. By 1573–4[25] Richard Edlin of Woodhall had acquired another head tenement, Cockparkers,[26] from John Street. At the same date a Richard Edlin of the Marsh was holding a virgate head tenement, Clobbes in West End, which in 1553 had been held by Richard Fearne. With the exception of Rowheads and Cockparkers, which passed to Andrew Smith by 1629 and to Sir Charles Palmer by 1770, all this land had passed by 1629 to the Edlins of the Marsh.[27] They owned and later lived in the manor or farm known as Marshes Place in 1547[28] and 1685,[29] which can probably be identified with Pinner Place. They had lost some property by c. 1642[30] and by 1692 the house itself was in the hands of Mountjoye Kirton, whose son conveyed it in 1757 to Thomas Lord and Thomas Corne.[31] Corne relinquished his share to Lord, a paviour of London, in 1765.[32] There was a resident called Aldwin in 1767 and another called Budworth in 1792 at Marshes or Pinner Place, where John Zephaniah Holwell (d. 1798) also lived.[33] In 1805 the house and 50 a., mostly in old inclosures, were held by Edward Aubrey or Abrey.[34] By 1851 the property had passed

to James Garrard, described as a landed proprietor,[35] who was still there in 1886.[36] Another estate belonged to the Edlins of Parkgate. It seems to have been entirely freehold, including Richard Danvers's hide, and some of it lay on the borders of Pinner and Harrow Weald.[37] It was still in their hands c. 1642[38] but its descent thereafter is obscure, although it may have passed to the Waldos. In 1770 a Mrs. Edlin paid the highest rent in Pinner[39] and in 1795 William Edlin died seised of 24 a. at Bury Pond Hill, property which was granted to William Legge, Earl of Dartmouth (d. 1801) who surrendered it to John Spranger.[40]

Part of the Marsh lands passed to the Readings, who were mentioned in 1315–16.[41] One ½-hide head tenement, which had belonged to Thomas Eastend, descended in 1516–17 to his daughter, Elizabeth, wife of Nicholas Marsh. Their daughter Elizabeth married Thomas, son of Richard Reading of Headstone, to whom the property was surrendered in 1549–50.[42] On the death of Simon Reading in 1703 the holding passed to his daughter Mary, wife of John Davy.[43] The descent is thereafter obscure, but the property may be identifiable with the head tenement called Marshes in East End. Sarah Street died seised of it in 1793 and her heir, William Street, surrendered it in 1795 to William Burrows of Alperton,[44] who was still in possession in 1817.[45] When it was enfranchised in 1871, it was held by Henry John Pye.[46]

In 1527–8 Richard Marsh, who had married the widow of William Reading, conveyed a ½-hide head tenement called Downers to his stepson, Richard Reading.[47] In 1553, besides Headstone manor, which he had leased since 1535, Richard Reading held four head tenements and some freehold.[48] The property was held by his son Thomas in 1573[49] and most of it was still held by Readings c. 1600,[50] although they had lost almost all by the middle of the next century. The estate was split up into several farms, roughly corresponding to the ancient head tenements. One was Sweetmans or Swetmans, in West End, a ½-hide named from the Pinner family which held it in the 14th century.[51] It was in the hands of John Reading by 1393 and in 1593–4 was sold by Thomas Reading to Henry Nicholas (d. 1611) of Hayden in Ruislip. A descendant, also called Henry Nicholas, sold Sweetmans in 1720 to

---

13 See p. 226.
14 M.R.O., Acc. 76/216, /2412–3, *passim*; C.P. 25(1)/152/90/71.
15 C.P. 25(1)/152/96/4; *Cal. Close, 1461–8*, 256, 299–300, 368.
16 M.R.O., Acc. 76/222a.
17 Ibid. /205.
18 Canterbury, Eastbridge Hosp. Archives, H(4).
19 M.R.O., Acc. 76/216, /2410, /2413, m. 59 *et passim*, /2415, m. 28, /2418, mm. 9, 10d, 41d, 44, 45, 55d, /2420, mm. 9d, 44d, 57d.
20 E 179/141/115, ff. 6–7v. In 1558 Thomas Edlin was the servant of John Edlin: P.C.C. 48 Welles.
21 i.e. excluding under-set and leased holdings.
22 M.R.O., Acc. 76/222a.
23 When leased to Ric. Nicholas: M.R.O., Acc. 76/421.
24 Ibid. /222a and b.
25 Ibid. /214.
26 At enfranchisement in 1738, it consisted of a 3-acre close held by Gavin Stokes: M.R.O., Acc. 76/459–60.
27 Ibid. /208.
28 M.R.O., Acc. 1052, ff. 427 sqq.
29 M.R.O., Acc. 310(4)/2.
30 M.R.O., Acc. 794/2.
31 Ware, *Pinner*, 164.

32 M.R.O., Acc. 310(3)/3, (4)/3, /4.
33 Ware, *Pinner*, 164–7. For Holwell, see above, p. 179.
34 M.R.O., Acc. 76/1400; Acc. 794/8; M.R. 612.
35 H.O. 107/1700, ff. 185 sqq.
36 *Kelly's Dir. Mdx.* (1886).
37 Including 'Spynnels', 31 a. between the shire ditch and Woodhall: M.R.O., Acc. 1052, ff. 433–9.
38 M.R.O., Acc. 76/205, /208, /222a; Acc. 794/2.
39 i.e. £3 7s. 3d. Elizabeth Edlin paid £1 5s. 10d.: M.R.O., Acc. 76/212.
40 M.R.O., Acc. 507/2, ff. 294 sqq.
41 M.R.O., Acc. 76/2410.
42 Ibid. /2421, m. 11, /2422, m. 11.
43 Ibid. /2433, f. 120.
44 M.R.O., Acc. 507/2, pp. 247, 280–1, 410–11.
45 M.R.O., Acc. 76/1400; Acc. 794/8; M.R. 612.
46 M.R.O., Acc. 76/1938.
47 Ibid. /2421, m. 87.
48 M.R.O., Acc. 76/222a.
49 Ibid. /214.
50 Ibid. /205.
51 Except where otherwise stated, this account is taken from 'Sweetmans Hall', TS. *penes* M.R.O., which is based upon the court rolls.

Gideon Lot (d. 1731). Although it was sold in 1812 by John Lot to Daniel Wilshin, the house and 37 a., of which half was open-field land and half old inclosures, mostly in West End, was listed under Elizabeth Lot at inclosure.[52] When Wilshin died in 1822, most of his property, including Sweetmans, was left in trust for his family. In 1884 Emily Soames enfranchised the estate,[53] then comprising 18 a. inclosed out of Down Field in addition to the old inclosures. In 1887 it was sold to Henry Davison, from whom it passed after 1925 to Guy Berridge and Westbury Trust Ltd. In 1966 Sweetmans Hall was a 16th-century timber-framed building with a tiled roof.

Cannons Farm originated in a ½-hide head tenement named after the family which held it throughout the Middle Ages[54] until 1542–3, when George Cannon conveyed it to Richard Reading.[55] It was held by the Readings during the later 16th century[56] but passed before 1629 to Thomas Hutchinson,[57] whose descendant John sold it in 1682 to Sir Edward Waldo, whose grandchildren sold it to John Carter.[58] Joshua Glover bought it from Carter's son in 1763[59] and most, if not all, of the property was in the hands of Elizabeth Glover at inclosure. In 1760 it had consisted of Cannons mansion-house, a farm-house abutting the mansion,[60] a cottage called Dells, 45 a. of inclosure, and 70 selions and a virgate of common-field land.[61] In 1817 Elizabeth Glover owned 43 a. of open-field and 36 a. of inclosed land around Cannons Farm, at the point where the River Pinn turns westward.[62] In 1821 Cannons Farm, consisting of 80 a., was owned by Joshua Glover Etherington, possibly the son of Elizabeth Glover. A Miss Etherington was the owner in 1869, but the Etheringtons did not live in Pinner and the farm was leased out throughout the 19th century.[63] Most of the other Reading lands, including two head tenements, had passed to the Stanboroughs by c. 1642.[64] In 1732 Joseph Stanborough enfranchised one, a capital messuage abutting east on East End Green, with 6 a. of inclosures and 54 a. of open-field land.[65] The Stanboroughs had disappeared by 1770 and some at least of their property passed to Sir Charles Palmer,[66] who paid £1 18s. 7d. rent in 1770, the third highest in Pinner.[67] His property included Paines Place, East End, and Cockparkers. Cockparkers was a virgate which in 1553 was held by John

Street, whose family was mentioned in 1315–16[68] and which accumulated land between the 15th and the 17th century. The estate in West End was still held by Streets in the 19th century.[69] The branch represented in 1553 by John Street of Love Lane[70] had lost its property to the Edlins by c. 1600.[71] Other property passed to Elizabeth Aldwin on the death of her father, Henry Street, in 1743.[72]

The Birds, another local family, were mentioned in 1287.[73] In 1553 John Bird was the lessee of Pinner Park and Francis and Thomas held three head tenements and miscellaneous holdings.[74] One of Thomas's head tenements, a ½-hide called Crouches, was held by his descendants in 1698[75] but not in 1770.[76] A John Bird of the Marsh, however, was one of the principal inhabitants in 1720,[77] and Richard Bird owned a wastehold cottage and orchard in Pinner in 1736.[78] Some of Francis Bird's scattered property was in the north, including Galpers Grove and parcels of waste at Pinner Wood, upon one of which Edmund Bird built a house.[79] Of Francis Bird's head tenements, one had passed to John Fearne between c. 1600[80] and 1629,[81] and the other to Henry Sedgewick between 1629 and c. 1642.[82] The second, a ½-hide called Blakes or News, may be identifiable with a head tenement called News and 20 a. of old inclosures which were enfranchised by Philip Aldwin in 1733[83] and still in his possession in 1770.[84] The other head tenement was a virgate called Ponders or Eastends, near Nower Field.[85] It was probably one of three held by a Mr. Fearne at the end of the 17th century[86] and later it seems to have been confused with Howells and Hungerlands, freehold closes of 20 a. east of Hooking Green, which were disputed among the Bird family at the end of the 16th century.[87] Howells and Hungerlands were enfranchised by Matthew Fearne in 1733.[88] In 1770 Matthew Fearne paid the highest rent in Pinner after Mrs. Edlin.[89] Howells and Hungerlands were sold in 1772 to the Commissioners of Queen Anne's Bounty,[90] and the rest of Matthew's copyhold estate,[91] 13 a. of inclosed and 33 selions of open-field land, passed in 1788 to his daughter Mary, wife of Henry Sayer.[92] In 1817 Henry Sayer owned 36 a. of inclosed land in Headstone and 46 a. in Harrow Weald.[93]

Few families flourished for so long as those from Pinner. The Warrens, however, held a ½-hide head

[52] M.R.O., Acc. 76/1400; Acc. 794/8; M.R. 612.
[53] M.R.O., Acc. 76/2387.
[54] Family mentioned in the earliest court roll (1315–16): M.R.O., Acc. 76/2410.
[55] Ibid. /2421, m. 92.
[56] Ibid. /205, /208, /222a.
[57] Ibid. /208.
[58] Ibid. /433–4; Acc. 310(4).
[59] M.R.O., Acc. 310(4).
[60] Mentioned in 1682: M.R.O., Acc. 974/VI, m. 25d (591d).
[61] M.R.O., Acc. 310(4).
[62] M.R.O., Acc. 794/8; M.R. 612.
[63] M.R.O., Acc. 310(4).
[64] M.R.O., Acc. 794/2.
[65] M.R.O., Acc. 76/429.
[66] Ibid. /243, ff. 97v–100.
[67] Ibid. /212. Presumably all Palmer's property was freehold as his name is not in the index to the court rolls. His East End tenement was therefore probably the one enfranchised by Jos. Stanborough, possibly East House, held in 1817 by Chas. Lawrence: Acc. 794/8; M.R. 612, no. 1456.
[68] M.R.O., Acc. 76/2410.
[69] See p. 211.
[70] M.R.O., Acc. 76/222a.
[71] Ibid. /205.
[72] Ibid. /2434, f. 199.
[73] C.P. 25(1)/15 Ed. I/158.
[74] M.R.O., Acc. 76/222a.
[75] M.R.O., Acc. 794/2.
[76] M.R.O., Acc. 76/212.
[77] Ware, Pinner, 26.
[78] M.R.O., Acc. 76/1109.
[79] Ibid. /205, /222a.
[80] Ibid. /205.   [81] Ibid. /208.
[82] M.R.O., Acc. 794/2.
[83] M.R.O., Acc. 76/432.
[84] Ibid. /212.
[85] M.R.O., Acc. 1052, ff. 433 sqq.
[86] M.R.O., Acc. 794/2.
[87] Cal. Procs. in Chancery, Eliz. I (Rec. Com.), i. 78; M.R.O., Acc. 1052, ff. 427 sqq.
[88] M.R.O., Acc. 76/435, /1682.
[89] Ibid. /212.
[90] Ware, Pinner, 29. See below, p. 256.
[91] Except for a £10 annuity and part of his house in Pinner, which were bequeathed to his wife, Elizabeth, for life.
[92] M.R.O., Acc. 276/4/1.
[93] M.R.O., Acc. 76/1400; Acc. 794/8; M.R. 612.

tenement in Harrow Weald from 1395[94] until 1691–2, when it passed to William Warren's sister, Mary, wife of James Marsh.[95] In 1740 their son, James, secured the enfranchisement of the property, described as a head tenement called Weeles in the Lower End of Weald and 67 a.[96] Its later descent is obscure but by inclosure it was probably part of the large estate of George H. Drummond.[97] In 1553 another branch of the Warrens held a 1-hide head tenement, called Trums after a medieval family,[98] which by c. 1600 had passed to William Deering and by 1629 to Henry Finch, who was still the holder c. 1642. The property may have been a head tenement called Deerings which was enfranchised in 1742.[99] It was then held by John Street of West End and consisted of 28 a., mostly in old inclosures at the Lower End of Weald.

The Waldos were also of some importance. Daniel Waldo, a clothworker of London, acquired about 73 a. around Hooking Green, between Pinner and Roxeth, from Thomas Page in 1640–1.[1] Sir Edward Waldo of London bought Cannons in Pinner in 1682[2] and acquired property in Harrow Weald by 1688.[3] By 1695 all the property was united in his hands but some land in the Weald was apparently sold after his death in 1707.[4] A head tenement, 70 a. in Hatch End, was retained[5] until 1790 when Charles Waldo sold it, then totalling 97 a. and known as Waldo's Farm, to the miser Daniel Dancer.[6] After the death of Dancer in 1794,[7] a dispute between his brother Henry and Sir Henry Tempest, Bt.,[8] was finally settled in 1799.[9] Waldo's Farm was surrendered to Henry Sayer and his wife Mary, as trustees for both parties, and in 1817[10] they sold it to Daniel Wilshin, who obtained its enfranchisement in 1821.[11] On the eve of inclosure the estate consisted of 80 a. of inclosures at Hatch End and 30 a. in the open fields of the Weald.[12] After the death of Charles Waldo, before 1804,[13] his property in Pinner and Roxeth passed to his widow, Elizabeth Catherine, who, as Mrs. Charles Walsh, claimed in 1805 for a mansion-house, a farm-house, and 157 a.[14] She was dead by 1813[15] and in 1814 Richard Burnett, her

nephew and heir, and James Sharp, a trustee, sold the estate to William Smith of Hammersmith.[16] The property, which included Roxeth Farm, was owned by Smith's trustees in 1852.[17]

The Waldo property in Roxeth originated in underset holdings which became detached from their head tenements. In Roxeth, where land was held from both Harrow and Rectory manors and also from Roxeth manor,[18] considerable undersetting, fragmentation, and combination made it hard even for contemporaries to identify holdings.[19] One estate, less obscure than most, was built up by the Osmonds. In 1553 Richard Osmond held a ½-hide head tenement, Goodwyns, through his marriage with Joan Hurlock, whose family had been prominent in medieval Roxeth.[20] Between c. 1600[21] and 1629[22] Hurlocks passed to Henry Martin,[23] but meanwhile William Osmond acquired Webbs and Walters, and John Osmond acquired Margarets, all 1-virgate head tenements. By c. 1642[24] they were united by William Osmond, who had also acquired a ½-hide head tenement since 1629 from Thomas Burton. In the late 17th century a William Osmond exchanged land and built up a more compact estate out of selions scattered in the common fields.[25] He sold Margarets in 1664[26] but still had three head tenements in 1698.[27] In 1717[28] William Osmond sold everything but one head tenement to Samuel Sandford, who also acquired Margarets.[29] Isaac Hollis succeeded Sandford in 1746,[30] and in 1817[31] Isaac's son or grandson John (d. 1824)[32] possessed 35 a., mostly in old inclosures in the southern corner of the hamlet, between the common fields and Northolt Road. Field-names suggest that Hollis's farm-house, Grove Farm, might be Webbs head tenement.[33] 'The Grove' was the name given to the head tenement as early as 1721.[34] In 1852 Grove Farm was owned but not occupied by J. H. Antony,[35] who was still the owner in 1875.[36]

Hugh Millett, who had died by 1462–3, had 42 a. of freehold and one cotland in Sudbury.[37] His heirs, especially Richard Millett (d. 1525–6), acquired more land,[38] and by 1553 Henry Millett held 6½

[94] *Ft. of F. Lond. & Mdx.* i. 167. The head tenement was 'formerly Gilbert Warren's': M.R.O., Acc. 76/222a.
[95] M.R.O., Acc.. 76/205, /208, /222a, /2424, mm.'2, 2d, 9d; Acc. 794/2; Acc. 974/IV, m. 43d (450d).
[96] M.R.O., Acc. 76/625–6, /2424, m. 34d, /2434, ff. 172d, 173, 182–3. After enfranchisement the property no longer appeared in the court rolls.
[97] M.R.O., Acc. 76/1400; Acc. 794/8; M.R. 612.
[98] M.R.O., Acc. 76/222a.   [99] Ibid. /641–2.
[1] M.R.O., Acc. 974/IV, mm. 100–100d (507–507d). In the rentals 33 a. are listed as crofts in Pinner; the other 40 were an under-set holding of Thomas Maynard's ½-hide in Roxeth: Acc. 76/208; Acc. 794/2.
[2] M.R.O., Acc. 974/VI, m. 25d(591d). See above.
[3] Ibid. m. 55d(621d).
[4] M.R.O., Acc. 76/2425, m. 27d, /2433, f. 166. He had 4 tenements, an unspecified amount of land, and Hillhouse in Harrow Weald.
[5] M.R.O., Acc. 507/1, unpag. 25 Geo. II.
[6] Ibid. /2, p. 213.
[7] Ibid. pp. 264, 290, 334. See above, p. 183.
[8] By Dancer's will his property was to go to Lady Mary Tempest (d. by 1795), Sir Henry's mother.
[9] M.R.O., Acc. 507/2, pp. 374–7.
[10] Ibid. /3, pp. 361–4.
[11] M.R.O., Acc. 76/1633.
[12] Ibid. /1400. The farm-house can probably be identified with M.R. 612, no. 371.
[13] M.R.O., Acc. 507/3, pp. 71, 122.
[14] M.R.O., Acc. 76/1400.
[15] M.R.O. ,Acc. 507/3, p. 271.

[16] Ibid. pp. 273, 306–9, 448–50. The inclosure award lists the estate under Charles Walsh: M.R.O., Acc. 794/8.
[17] M.R.O., Acc. 590/1,/4, no. 232.
[18] In 1553, 20 parcels of free land were held from Roxeth manor: M.R.O., Acc. 76/222a. The land is not entered in subsequent rentals.
[19] e.g. M.R.O., Acc. 166/146/49; Acc. 188/44; Acc. 276/5/11.
[20] M.R.O., Acc. 76/222a.
[21] Ibid. /205.   [22] Ibid. /208.
[23] Martin had 3 head tenements but Osmond retained 20 selions from this holding: M.R.O., Acc. 188/5.
[24] Ibid.; Acc. 794/2.
[25] M.R.O., Acc. 188/1, /5, /7–10, /35.
[26] Then only 6 a.: Acc. 188/1. Osmond sold it to Eliz. Andrew, from whom it passed to Jos. Wilcocks, John Page, and Wm. Andrew: ibid. /35.
[27] M.R.O., Acc. 794/2.
[28] M.R.O., Acc. 188/33.
[29] From Wm. Andrew in 1721: M.R.O., Acc. 188/35.
[30] Ibid. /35–36.
[31] M.R.O., Acc. 794/8; M.R. 612.
[32] M.R.O., Acc. 188/46.
[33] Ibid. /30, /36, /38; M.R. 612, no. 507.
[34] M.R.O., Acc. 188/30.
[35] M.R.O., Acc. 590/1, /4, no. 288.
[36] M.R.O., Acc. 507/34.
[37] M.R.O., Acc. 76/2417, m. 113d, /2418, m. 3.
[38] Ibid. /2418, m. 53d, /2420, mm. 3d, 4, 17d, 57d, 59d, 65, /2421, mm. 5, 7, 32, 45d, 61d, 73, /2422, m. 19d.

cotlands, 42 a. of freehold and other small pieces of land.[39] Another cotland was acquired by *c.* 1600.[40] The property was held by the heirs of William Millett in 1629[41] but had passed by *c.* 1642 to Edward Claxton, a London mercer,[42] who already had a small estate in Sudbury. In 1513–14 William Wilkinson had conveyed a cotland once of Baldwin Harris to Roger Wright,[43] whose son Hugh by 1547 held a messuage north-east of Sudbury Common, 49 a. of freehold and 9 a. of copyhold.[44] His land passed to Sir Gilbert Gerard, Master of the Rolls and elder brother of William Gerard of Flambards, and by *c.* 1600 to Sir Thomas Gerard.[45] The estate, misleadingly called 'the manor or farm of Sudbury', was sold *c.* 1622 by Sir Charles Gerard to Edward Bryers, who in turn conveyed it to Edward Claxton.[46] In 1640, after acquiring the Millett estate, Claxton owned 90 a. held in demesne and 139 a. divided among 8 under-tenants,[47] but when the estate was sold after his death to Tanner Arnold in 1689 it comprised 320 a. in Sudbury, of which 157 a. were in hand, the rest being leased to 9 tenants.[48] The home farm of Sudbury Place, 'very large, built with timbers',[49] was probably the house with 23 hearths for which Claxton was assessed in 1664.[50] Claxton's total estate was nearly 400 a., including small estates in Wembley, Roxeth, and Alperton, some of them once part of the Millett property. The Wembley estate, two head tenements (1 virgate and ½ hide) totalling 71 a., had been held by the Wembley Pages in the 16th century but passed before 1629 to Thomas Nicholas and by *c.* 1642 to Edward Claxton.[51] At the end of the 17th century it was divided among 5 under-tenants. In 1707 besides the Sudbury Place farm (140 a.), which was then leased out, there were three smaller Sudbury farms:[52] one of 55 a. leased to Richard Watson,[53] one of 30 a. and one of 20 a.; there was one very small farm at Wembley which apparently followed the descent of the Sudbury property.[54] Another small farm abutting south on Wembley Green was sold in 1713 to Thomas Graham,[55] who acquired other property in 1728.[56] The three small Sudbury farms, all freehold, were sold to Rebecca Houblon in 1757, by which time Watson's farm-house had disappeared.[57] The farm, apparently leased by the Watsons throughout the century, passed to William Wright before 1784 and was sold by Edward and Mary Wright to Lord North-wick in 1805.[58] Some of Rebecca Houblon's property, however, formed the Houblon charity and in 1817

comprised 56 a. in the corner of Sheepcote Lane and East Lane.[59] Henry Arnold in 1806 said that his father had disposed of his considerable property to pay his father's debts,[60] but Sudbury Place apparently remained and may possibly be identified with Hundred Elms Farm.[61] In 1817 the farm-house and 32 a. around were held by Henry Arnold, but another 40 a. south-west of Sudbury Common was described as belonging to Henry Arnold and Walsh.[62] In 1852 the farm-house and 115 a. were owned by them and farmed by William Greenhill.[63]

In Greenhill the five medieval head tenements remained intact longer than in most hamlets. In 1553 two head tenements, a ½-hide called Finches or Coles and a virgate called Dyaches or Dyetts, and a tenement held from Rectory manor, were held by Henry Finch.[64] They descended in his family[65] until 1798 when Hannah, daughter of Henry Finch, surrendered all the Finch property in Greenhill and Pinner to the use of herself and her husband, Daniel Hill, for life.[66] In 1817 the Greenhill property included a mansion-house, 112 a. of inclosures and 62 a. in Greenhill and Harrow Weald common fields.[67] The house stood west of Greenhill Lane with most of the farm-land stretching westward to Headstone manor; another block lay to the east, south of Dirty Lane. In 1852 the farm-house, 179 a. and several cottages, were held by Henry Finch Hill,[68] who was still in possession in 1880.[69]

The other three Greenhill head tenements were in 1553 held by John and Henry Greenhill. Of the two head tenements held by John in 1553, one, a virgate called Lampitts, passed to John Uxton or Ortin by *c.* 1600[70] and was held by Greenhill Ortin in 1629 and *c.* 1642.[71] It then disappears from the rentals. The other head tenement, a hide called Hawkins, had passed *c.* 1600 to Simon Wilkins, who still held it in 1629.[72] It had passed to Simon's grand-daughter, Sarah, wife of John Anderson, by *c.* 1642.[73] Their son, John Anderson, still had an interest in the property in 1712[74] but Tanner Arnold held it in 1698[75] and Richard Hoare was admitted in 1738, after the death of his mother Sarah, who was said to hold during the life of John Arnold.[76] In 1763 John Arnold's widow, Elizabeth, and other relations conveyed the property to Sir John Rushout, Bt.,[77] to become a demesne farm.[78] The head tenement held in 1553 by Henry Greenhill was a hide which had once belonged to Thomas Hutton,[79] described *c.* 1692 as a house, farm-house, and 83 a., including 44

[39] Ibid. /222a.   [40] Ibid. /205.
[41] Ibid. /208.
[42] M.R.O., Acc. 794/2.
[43] M.R.O., Acc. 76/2421, m. 6. Wright also had land in Pinner and Roxeth: M.R.O., Acc. 76/2421, mm. 9d, 56, 84d.
[44] M.R.O., Acc. 1052, ff. 15–29v; Acc. 76/2423, m. 7d, /2422, m. 7d.
[45] M.R.O., Acc. 76/205; *Mdx. Pedigrees* (Harl. Soc. lxv), 19.
[46] C 3/378/8.
[47] M.R.O., Acc. 76/1647.
[48] Ibid. /2433, ff. 21v–23v.
[49] Ibid. /1080.   [50] M.R.O., H.T. 5.
[51] M.R.O., Acc. 76/205, /208, /222a; Acc. 794/2.
[52] M.R.O., Acc. 76/1859.
[53] Probably in existence at end of 17th cent.: M.R.O., Acc. 76/1080.
[54] Ibid. /1861.
[55] M.R.O., Acc. 166/146/52.
[56] M.R.O., Acc. 76/1083.   [57] Ibid. /1877.
[58] Ibid. /1, /14, /229, /1872, /1882.
M.R.O., Acc. 794/8; M.R. 612. In 1885 there was a

new farm-house: Wemb. Hist. Soc., Acc. 463.
[60] M.R.O., Acc. 76/1277.
[61] See p. 194.
[62] M.R. 612; C.P. 43/939A, ff. 78 sqq.
[63] M.R.O., Acc. 590/1, /4, nos. 1583–91, 1648–51.
[64] M.R.O., Acc. 76/222a.
[65] Ibid. /205, /208, /212; Acc. 794/2.
[66] M.R.O., Acc. 507/2, pp. 33–35, 180, 242, /3, pp. 355 sqq., 361.
[67] M.R.O., Acc. 794/8; M.R. 612, nos. 279–80.
[68] M.R.O., Acc. 590/2, /4, no. 419.
[69] M.R.O., Acc. 76/980.
[70] Ibid. /205.
[71] Ibid. /208; Acc. 794/2.
[72] M.R.O., Acc. 76/205, /208.
[73] M.R.O., Acc. 794/2; Acc. 974/IV, m. 135 (542).
[74] M.R.O., Acc. 76/2425, m. 45d.
[75] M.R.O., Acc. 794/2.
[76] M.R.O., Acc. 76/2434, f. 156.
[77] M.R.O., Acc. 507/1, unpag. 3 Geo. III.
[78] See p. 228.
[79] Described in the 18th-cent. court rolls as 53 a. and 53 selions.

selions in the open fields.[80] In 1803 it was conveyed by Elizabeth Greenhill and her son, Thomas, neither of whom lived there, to George Heming.[81] When Mary Ann Heming secured its enfranchisement in 1868, it consisted of a head tenement, three tenements, and 95 a. in Greenhill.[82] The tenements all lay in Greenhill village, west of Greenhill Lane. The land was in two blocks on the south-east and north-west of Greenhill Lane.

The Greenhill estate was only one among many acquired by the Heming family. In 1783 18 a. in Kenton common fields were surrendered to George Heming of New Bond Street, a silversmith.[83] He acquired 16 a. in Greenhill in 1787[84] and a small amount in Kenton in 1805,[85] when he was living in Stanmore. The next year he acquired all the property of Mrs. Jane Edlin,[86] probably Oxhey Lane Farm (116 a.) on the northern borders of Pinner and Harrow Weald.[87] In 1807 George Heming was succeeded by his cousin, Richard Heming,[88] who in 1817 owned four messuages, four cottages, and 400 a., divided into farms in north Pinner, Greenhill, and Kenton.[89]

The Drummonds of Charing Cross, who had a home in Stanmore, were also large landowners in Harrow. In 1766 John Drummond (d. 1774) bought Woodhall, and in 1774 a wasteheld cottage in Harrow Weald was surrendered to his use by Samuel Higgs.[90] Cornerhall Farm, about 60 a. in the south-east of Harrow Weald, which had been held by William Page in 1696 and passed in 1728 to his sister Sarah Daniel, and after her death in 1730 to her son, William Cranwell, was sold in 1782 by his son, Thomas Cranwell, to George Drummond (d. 1789).[91] A messuage called Roodes, near the farm, was conveyed to Drummond in the same year[92] and in 1787 he acquired another cottage and 13 a. and 43 selions in the common fields from Richard Smith.[93] In 1795 George Harley Drummond (d. 1855) received two head tenements from John Gibson.[94] One of them, Underhills, had been reduced to 7 a. and in 1694–5 had passed from Anna to Isaac Bennet, who in 1728 conveyed it to John Gibson.[95] The other, to which 89 a. were still attached, was called 'Richard Adownes' and may have been the ½-hide described as Richard Downers or atte Downes.[96] It was held in 1553 by Richard Downer but by 1573 had passed to Randall Nicholls, in whose family it remained until c. 1642.[97] Before 1688 John Hutchinson of Lichfield sold it to Sir Edward Waldo. The messuage, by this date known as Hillhouse,[98] was

sold by Waldo's trustees to John Gibson, whose grandson sold it to Drummond.[99]

A 50-acre farm, Mays Farm, which originated in a head tenement in Harrow Weald, was conveyed in 1796 by John Page of Finsbury Terrace to George H. Drummond.[1] Its history is unknown but by 1796 the premises formed one farm. Two more head tenements, Astmiss and Causeway Gate, were acquired by Drummond in 1800.[2] The origin of Astmiss, which comprised 14 a. and 10 selions, is obscure, but Causeway Gate, only a messuage and two pightles, may have been a virgate held in 1553 by Henry Hatch. It had passed by 1573 to Henry Finch and in 1785 a Henry Finch conveyed it to Daniel Dancer.[3] Under the settlement following the death of Dancer, Astmiss and Causeway Gate passed to Sir Henry Tempest, who in 1798 surrendered them to the Marquess of Abercorn,[4] who in turn conveyed them to Drummond in 1800. Drummond also acquired considerable freehold property and leased an estate from New College, becoming the largest landowner in Harrow after Lord Northwick.[5] Apart from Woodhall Farm in Pinner and a small amount in Greenhill, his estates lay in a block on the south-eastern borders of Harrow Weald, stretching into Stanmore.[6] In 1840, however, George H. Drummond, who was a spendthrift, sold his estates, mostly to the Marquess of Abercorn.[7]

After the Marquess of Abercorn had bought Bentley Priory[8] he began to extend the estate southwards by acquiring wasteheld property at Brookshill in the 1790s, by inclosing part of the waste himself, and by considerable purchases at the time of parliamentary inclosure.[9] In 1817 he had 297 a. on the north-east borders of Harrow.[10] The Drummond acquisitions included Kenton Lane Farm (280 a.), the Levels Farm (100 a.), and Dancer's Farm (30 a.), and by 1852[11] the Abercorn estates amounted to 1,344 a. in Harrow and Stanmore, of which over 800 a. lay in Harrow.[12] Most of the property was sold during the 1850s and early 1860s,[13] although the family still owned the two head tenements comprised in Dancer's Farm in 1863.[14]

ECONOMIC HISTORY.

AGRARIAN HISTORY TO 1545. In 1086 Harrow was assessed at 100 hides, which included land for 70 ploughs, pasture for the cattle of the vill, and woodland for 2,000 pigs. It was worth £60 T.R.E., £20 when Archbishop Lanfranc received it, and £56 in

80 M.R.O., Acc. 76/1678–80.
81 M.R.O., Acc. 507/3, pp. 28–30.
82 M.R.O., Acc. 76/1846.
83 M.R.O., Acc. 507/2, p. 85.
84 Ibid. p. 139.   85 Ibid. /3, pp. 114–15.
86 Ibid. pp. 134–5. A head tenement, held by Edw. Edlin (d. 1772) and then in turn by his daughters, Mary (d. 1801) and Jane: ibid. /1, unpag. 12 Geo. III, /2, p. 493.
87 M.R.O., Acc. 507/3, pp. 210–13; Acc. 794/8; M.R. 612.
88 M.R.O., Acc. 76/576–7; Acc. 507/3, pp. 210–13.
89 M.R.O., Acc. 76/1400; Acc. 794/8; M.R. 612.
90 M.R.O., Acc. 507/1, unpag. 15 Geo. III.
91 M.R.O., Acc. 76/2433, f. 74, /2434, ff. 36–37, 58; Acc. 507/1, unpag. 24 Geo. I, /2, p. 50.
92 M.R.O., Acc. 507/2, p. 215.
93 Ibid. pp. 137–8, 215.
94 Ibid. pp. 271–3.
95 M.R.O., Acc. 76/216, /2434, f. 45d; Acc. 794/2. It may have been a ½-hide called Weald, which was held by the Tanner family for most of the 16th century.
96 M.R.O., Acc. 76/214, /222a.

97 M.R.O., Acc. 794/2.
98 M.R.O., Acc. 974/VI, m. 55d (621d).
99 M.R.O., Acc. 76/2425, m. 27d, /2433, f. 166; Acc. 507/2, pp. 271–3.
1 M.R.O., Acc. 507/2, pp. 306–8.
2 Ibid. pp. 418–22.   3 Ibid. p. 108.
4 Ibid. pp. 264, 290, 418–22.
5 See p. 229.
6 M.R.O., Acc. 76/1400; Acc. 794/8; M.R. 612.
7 M.R.O., Acc. 502/22–23. Drummond once lost £20,000 to Beau Brummel at White's; H. Bolitho and D. Peal, The Drummonds of Charing Cross, 117.
8 See p. 206.
9 M.R.O., Acc. 502/1–10; Acc. 507/2, pp. 206–7, 334, 353, 421–2, 525–6.
10 M.R.O., Acc. 794/8; M.R. 612.
11 M.R.O., Acc. 590/2; LA. HW. Harrow Assess. Bk. 1852.
12 M.R.O., Acc. 502/22–23.
13 Ibid. /31, /34.
14 M.R.O., Acc. 507/6, pp. 348–50.

1086. There were 4 ploughs, and could be 5 more on the 30-hide demesne, and there were 45 ploughs, and could be 16 more, on the land held by the archbishop's tenants, both French (*franc*') and villeins. The tenants consisted of a priest, who held one hide, three knights, who held 6 hides and had 7 men under them, and villeins on various holdings: 13 each on ½ hide, 25 each on a virgate, 48 each on ½ virgate, and 13 on 4 hides. There were 2 cottars on 13 a. and 2 serfs. Apart from common and woodland, Harrow therefore was divided almost equally between the lord's demesne (30 hides) and the land of all the other holders (29¾ hides and 13 a.), although most of the arable (45 out of 49 ploughs) was held by tenants.[15]

In 1093–6 Harrow was farmed out, for £54 a year,[16] and it probably continued to be farmed out, like other archiepiscopal manors, for most of the 12th century.[17] Direct exploitation of the demesne, however, had started by 1231,[18] when a reeve is first recorded. The 'grange of Harrow' and the submanor of Woodhall existed by 1236.[19] In 1273–4 Harrow and Woodhall were grouped with Hayes, Lambeth, Wimbledon, and Croydon under one bailiff.[20] This grouping was somewhat haphazard until Archbishop Pecham (1279–92) organized his manors into six large bailiwicks, which remained unchanged for the rest of the Middle Ages. Harrow and its later sub-manors formed one of the richest estates in the valuable Middlesex and Surrey bailiwick.[21]

The 'Harrow' demesne *c.* 1285 was divided into three arable fields, called Bendenefeld (178 a.), Russalespirifeld (158 a.), and Wytingesbergh (186½ a.), five meadows, called Hempstall and Rylwyneslovehagh (34 a.), Rodlandesdene (12½ a.), Harerashdene (2½ a.) and Wolnothesdene (1½ a.), 'thirteen pastures' in Sevenacre and pasture in Lovenford (33 a.). Harrow or, more properly, Sudbury, manor seems to have been the original demesne manor,[22] and its arable, 482½ a., probably corresponds to the 4 ploughs in demesne of the Domesday Survey. The sub-manor of Woodhall was in *c.* 1285 divided into three arable fields, called Oldefeld and Chalvecroft (115½ a.), Middelfeld (73½ a.), and Fernover (90 a.), and five meadows, Langemed (5 a.), Westmed (3 a.), Tan Redding (Tanrudinge) (2¼ a.), Oxenlese (20 a.), and 'in the old pond and behind it' (3¼ a.). Woods were noted at Pinner Park, Weald, and Sudbury. The cultivable demesne had been extended since 1086 by creating Woodhall manor, but the total of the two manors (just over 920 a.) left much land that was still afforested.[23]

In the two demesne manors a mixed, but predominantly arable, economy was necessitated by the archbishops' continuous travelling. The one concession to the heavy clay soil seems to have been a larger proportion of oats to wheat than on the archbishops' more fertile Kentish manors.[24] In 1233 £43 8*s.* 4*d.* was spent on oats for seed and horse provender, and on wheat for wages at Harrow and Hayes.[25] Oats were sold and wheat was purchased in 1236–7, when ditches enclosed the wheat at Woodhall.[26] In 1273–4 the largest crop was oats: 123 qr. were produced by the two manors, 29 qr. were bought, and a small amount was confiscated from a felon, to give a total of 159 qr. 5 bu., of which 122 qr. 1 bu. was used in seeding 244 a. at Sudbury and Woodhall. Of a total of 55½ qr. of wheat, 44 qr. 6 bu. had to be bought and 43 qr. of this was used in seeding 172 a. Most of the maslin, 53 qr. 6½ bu. out of 70 qr. ½ bu., was also bought, but all the peas and beans, 7½ qr., were produced on the home manors.[27] The year 1273–4, however, seems to have been particularly bad for arable produce.[28]

In 1236 an ox-house at Harrow grange was mentioned, and 124 cheeses and the hides of a horse and 5 calves which had died from disease were sold.[29] In 1273–4 there were 15 cows, 17 steers, and 26 heifers; during the year 20 calves were born, 13 steers and 17 heifers were sent to Hayes, one heifer died, one cow and 6 calves were sold, and two calves were paid in tithe. There were 62 goats, of which 49 were she-goats; 21 died during the year and two were sent by the steward to the Earl of Winchester; the dead she-goats and 12 of their kids were sold for hides and four goats and 16 kids were also sold. In 4½ months 21 cows and 24 goats produced 18 gallons of butter, all of which was sold, and 160 cheeses, of which 151 were sold. Draught animals in 1273–4 comprised 3 carthorses, a mare and her foal, 7 stots, and 28 oxen; during the year one carthorse and 4 stots were bought, a stot was acquired as a heriot, and 4 oxen were sent from Canterbury, but the mare and foal and one dead stot were sold.[30] By 1278 there were 3 carthorses, 16 stots, and 38 oxen.[31]

In the 14th century wheat and oats continued as the chief crops of a three-field system. An account[32] made after the death of Archbishop Stratford (d. 23 Aug. 1348)[33] shows that wheat was sown on 101 a. of

15 *V.C.H. Mdx*, i. 120.

16 *Domesday Monachorum of Christ Church, Cant.* ed. D. C. Douglas (R.H.S. 1944), 99. For the Canterbury estates in the 11th cent., see R. V. Lennard, *Rural England, 1086–1135*, 118–20, 131.

17 F. R. H. Du Boulay, *Lordship of Cant.* 197.

18 Ibid. 213.

19 Lambeth Palace, Estate MS. 1193.

20 The early connexion with Hayes was particularly close and they were probably administered as one unit: *Cal. Lib. R.* 1226–40, 237.

21 Du Boulay, *Lordship of Cant.* 268 and map; Du Boulay, 'Abp. as Territorial Magnate', *Medieval Recs. of Abps. of Cant.* ed. E. G. W. Bill, 63; Du Boulay, 'Pipe Roll account of the See of Cant. after the death of Abp. Pecham, 1292–5', *Kent Recs.* xviii. 41 sqq.; D. Sutcliffe, 'Financial Condition of the See of Cant. 1279–92', *Speculum*, x. 53–68.

22 See p. 204 n. 57.

23 Lambeth Palace, Estate MS. 2068. Rentals and surveys, all now lost, were made of Canterbury estates in 1197–8, 1202–3, and *c.* 1213–20 (by steward Elias of Dereham). A large rental and custumal, based on Dereham's survey, was made in 1283–5, and survives, although not for Harrow, in a 15th-cent. copy (Cant. Cath. Libr., Lit. MS. E 24). An abbreviated version (Lambeth 2068) was made *c.* 1285–1325: Du Boulay, *Lordship of Cant.* 10 sqq., 206; Friends of the National Libraries, *Ann. Rep.*(1963), 14; Jane E. Sayers, 'A Rec. of the Abp. of Cant.'s Feudal Rights', *Jnl. of Soc. of Archivists*, iii(5), 215 sqq.

24 Du Boulay, *Lordship of Cant.* 209.

25 *Cal. Lib. R.* 1226–40, 237.

26 Lambeth Palace, Estate MS. 1193.

27 B.M. Add. MS. 29794, m. 2.

28 The dearth (*caristiam*) this year is specifically mentioned: B.M. Add. MS. 29794, m. 1d.

29 Lambeth Palace, Estate MS. 1193.

30 B.M. Add. MS. 29794, m. 2.

31 B.M. Cotton Galba MS. E. iv, f. 3 which lists draught animals only. The figures for Woodhall and Harrow are, respectively: 1, 2; 4, 12; 19, 19.

32 S.C. 6/1128/12, mm. 5 sqq.

33 The 14th-cent. extant accounts (for 1327, 1329, 1348) were made *sede vacante*, at different times of the year, and therefore are not comparable.

fallow land at Sudbury, 84½ a. at Woodhall, and 90 a. at Headstone. Probably never more than one third of the grain, and often considerably less, was sold.[34] A small amount of maslin at Woodhall was mentioned in 1348, and about 3 qr. of peas and beans on each manor were mixed with grain as payment for the manorial labourers.[35] All the manors produced a little hay,[36] and in 1348 the main Sudbury meadows, Hempstall and Ede Wyneloneshagh, were given over to pasture for the draught animals.[37] The animal stock probably remained much the same as in the 13th century, although the 1327 account lists animals only for Woodhall[38] and the 1329 account is concerned solely with crops.[39] The 1348 account mentions draught beasts only: 7 plough-horses (2 each at Sudbury and Woodhall, 3 at Headstone), 12 stots (4 each at the three manors), and 52 oxen (16 each at Sudbury and Woodhall, 20 at Headstone).[40] By 1397 there were sheep on the demesne, including 200 wethers at Sudbury and Headstone. The transformation of arable and meadowland into pasture is reflected in stocks of 10 qr. of wheat and 30 qr. of oats at Sudbury and 10 qr. each of wheat, oats, and beans at Headstone, and in the reduction of draught animals to two horses and 8 oxen at each manor. There were 31 cows and a bull at Sudbury, but no cattle at Headstone.[41] Very little is known about the subsequent agrarian history of Woodhall and Headstone, although a new sheep-house was erected at Sudbury c. 1500.[42]

In 1273–4 a reeve and a beadle were paid 8s. and 6s. a year respectively; the reeve also received 5½ qr. of wheat, and the reeve of Woodhall, perhaps a separate official, 1 qr. of wheat in autumn; the beadle received 1 qr. of wheat in autumn and 6 bu. of maslin in Lent. The bailiff of all the Middlesex and Surrey estates was paid £5 a year from the Harrow receipts.[43] Expenses had also to be paid when the archbishop's steward visited Harrow with his clerks.[44] A carpenter and smith, mentioned in 1273–4, were each paid wages and may have been hired as the occasion demanded. Permanent servants on the demesne included a cowherd, who was paid 3s. a year and 2 qr. 5½ bu. of maslin, a goatherd, paid 2s. 6d. a year and 4 qr. 3 bu. of maslin, an oxherd, paid 1s. 2d. and 3 bu. of maslin in autumn, and two dairy-men or -girls, who were paid 6s. 8d., one of them also receiving a cheese and 2 qr. 6 bu. of maslin. Seasonal workers included a carter and 8 ploughmen, a carter at Woodhall, men who hoed the corn, two men who made cheeses and a boy to scare birds away from the corn. Famuli, who were fed on porridge made from oats and salt,[45] may have been household servants descended from the Domesday serfs and settled on the demesne, although there is

no evidence of any base serjeanties.[46] Most famuli, however, especially the ploughmen and others whose work was mainly seasonal were probably small-holders, possibly under-tenants, cotmen, or the younger sons of head tenants.

The survey of c. 1285 describes the customary services in full. At Sudbury, 17 cotmen or cotlanders owed one work each a week for 48 weeks and 12 carting services each. Other customary tenants were divided into head and under-tenants.[47] The head tenants, called hidemen c. 1285, held 29 hides 1 virgate directly from the lord for rent, services, and heriot. The under-tenants held small parcels of land from the head tenant, to whom they paid rent, relief, and heriot. Customary works, calculated according to the one-hide unit, were demanded only from the head tenant, although, increasingly, the actual work was performed by hired under-tenants. Some services were also due from free tenants. Customary services from the head tenants included 655 threshing, 525 harrowing, 202 hoeing, 413 carrying, and 29¼ reaping works. Hempstall meadow was to be mown with 66 scythes. There were certain specialized ploughing and reaping services, including 'caulerth', 'niedbedrip', and 'rithrip'. Each free and customary plough had to plough one acre in winter (niederth) and one in Lent (righterth), for which bread, porridge, ale, and three dishes, were given. Three men were apparently assigned to each plough. Other services included sowing and winnowing.[48]

There were five boon-works for reaping and mowing. All the reapers within the manor had to attend the great boon-work, for which they were given wheaten bread, ale, and meat.[49] In 1381 a presentment was made at the Rectory court of a tenant who had not attended 'le heghbedrys'. A note accompanying a later translation of this passage explains that by ancient custom tenants owed 199 days' work at the 'general reap day (sometimes called magna precaria)' and that the bailiff summoned all who had a chimney to send a man.[50] Drink was also provided at the autumn reaping boon-work called alelove, to which 108 men were summoned. Another boon-work, performed by 70 men, was called meteleselove. The other two boon-works, performed by 149 and 137 men respectively, were 'dry' works, giving a total of over 3,116 works. There are details of the services due on one estate of 3 carucates and 25 a., and 24s. rent, in 1344: righterth, or ploughing one acre at the sowing season and 1½ a. at Lent, the free tenant's boon-work of ploughing with his own plough for one day, nedrip, or reaping one acre of wheat and 1½ a. of whatever other grain there was at Lent, and finding four men to hoe on one day and to reap at the autumn alelove boon-work, ten men to

[34] S.C. 6/1128/8, mm. 1–1d; /9; /12, mm. 5 sqq. In 1327 (probably Dec.) 5 qr. 1 bu. out of 80½ qr. of wheat were sold at Harrow and 63 qr. out of 183 qr. 3½ bu. at Woodhall. For oats the figures were 41 qr. (total 131 qr.) at Harrow and none (total 75 qr. 2 bu.) at Woodhall.

[35] S.C. 6/1128/12, mm. 5 sqq.; /8, mm. 1–1d.; /9 (where 4 qr. of pulse, haras', were sold at Woodhall).

[36] Ibid. /8, /9, /12.

[37] Ibid. /12, m. 5. Usually about 4 a. of hay on each manor was considered enough to keep animals during autumn.

[38] Ibid. /8, m. 1.

[39] Ibid. /9.

[40] Ibid. /12, m. 5.

[41] Cal. Inq. Misc. vi, pp. 123–4.

[42] M.R.O., Acc. 76/2131, m. 37d.

[43] B.M. Add. MS. 29794. 'Claviger' is mentioned with 'bedellus', but one man probably held both offices.

[44] For the steward, see Du Boulay, Lordship of Cant. 267.

[45] B.M. Add. MS. 29794. It is not clear whether the dairymaid's maslin was payment in kind or whether it was to be used for the servant's porridge.

[46] For the famulus see M. M. Postan, The Famulus (Ec. H.R., Supplement, ii).

[47] Lambeth Palace, Estate MS. 2068. As at Hayes, cotmen probably did not have to work for a week at each of the principal festivals: Cant. Cath. Libr., Lit. MS. E 24, f. 148.

[48] Lambeth Palace, Estate MS 2068.

[49] B.M. Add. MSS. 15664, ff. 18–19; 29794.

[50] M.R.O., Acc. 974/I, m. 4.

reap at the two autumn dry boon-works, and eight men to reap at the great autumn boon-work. The total value of these works was 4s.[51]

Alfwin, son of Godmar of Pinner, paid 19s. 7½d. 'de gabulo pro omni consuetudine' for 1½ hide in 1232.[52] In 1270 £2 16s. 8d. was received from the commutation of works and services,[53] but in 1273-4 only £1 14s. 1d. was received in lieu of 420 works, about 13 per cent. of the total due.[54] On the eve of the Black Death out of 828¾ reaping works due from both head tenants and cotmen, 680 had been commuted.[55] All the 437 threshing works due from head tenants[56] and 144½ from cotmen[57] had been sold. Thus about 40·5 per cent. of the original customary services had been commuted. Only niederth was still performed, 6 ploughs ploughing one acre each. There was also no allotment of grain for feeding boon-workers. Customary services, however, were never entirely commuted during the Middle Ages and strenuous efforts were made, especially on Rectory manor, to enforce them on the eve of the Peasants' Revolt.[58] In 1397 mowing, tedding, weeding, gathering, and stocking services were among the appurtenances of Sudbury manor, although other works had been released for £15. At Woodhall, all the tenants' works had been commuted for £15, but the cotmen's works, worth 10s. a year, had apparently been transferred to the new demesne manor of Headstone.[59] During most of the 15th and early 16th centuries, however, uncommuted works, especially those of cotmen, again formed part of the appurtenances of Sudbury manor.[60] In 1432 these were specified as making hay, and the boon-works of reaping and mowing.[61] In the 16th century autumn works of tenants were leased with Woodhall manor.[62] By the mid 15th century works were commuted at a rate of £1 a hide, yielding £15 at Harrow and £13 10s. at Woodhall.[63] This payment, worksilver, was still made in the mid 17th century at the rate of 5s. a virgate.[64] In 1553 six customary, but not cotland, tenements each paid 1s. 6d. to the farmer of Sudbury Court.[65] Even after the commutation of most services there were several distraints in the 15th century at both Sudbury Court and Rectory manor for not performing autumn and, occasionally, mowing works.[66] Autumn works were appurtenances of the Kilburn estate at Wembley as late as 1540-1.[67]

In 1327-8 the threshing and winnowing was done by hired labourers at piece rates, while the man who supervised the threshing was paid wages.[68] In the 14th century the permanent officials and manorial servants were paid in money and kind. In 1315 the former reeve of Woodhall was in mercy for not paying the wages of the lord's *famuli*.[69] On the three demesne manors in 1348 *famuli* received wheat, maslin, and beans, and a boy who made their porridge and a ploughman and four plough servants received payment in money and kind. There was also a hayward, paid in money and kind, at Headstone, and a harrower, paid in kind only, at Harrow. The animal-keepers of the 13th century may be comprised in the general category of *famuli*. Wheat was given to the reeves in charge of Sudbury and Woodhall, and to the serjeant at Headstone. The serjeant and the Sudbury reeve also received money, as did the beadle and the forester.[70] By 1466-7 the reeve and beadle were paid entirely in money, only the words 'wages and stipend' (*vadium et stipendium*) recalling the earlier payment in kind.[71] In the late 15th century skilled craftsmen, carpenters, smiths, tilers, and thatchers, were hired for specific jobs and paid money wages.[72]

A windmill and a water-mill existed by 1236.[73] The windmill probably stood close to the site of the later manorial mill, near Flambards,[74] and in 1353 a mill was mentioned in a fine between Edward Flambard and the Vicar of Harrow.[75] The water-mill was on the Brent at Alperton and gave its name to a field called Mill Acre.[76] The water-mill was repaired in 1273-4 and the windmill in 1348,[77] but the water-mill had disappeared by 1470-1[78] and perhaps by 1348.[79] Milling on the Brent was probably hazardous because of floods.[80] In 1273-4 apparently both mills were administered directly[81] but generally they were farmed out.[82]

In 1270 the northern part of the parish was mainly woodland and a large area called 'southwood' may have covered most of the later Sudbury Common.[83] There was a forester at least from 1236,[84] receiving 12s. a year wages and paying 13s. for the farm of the office.[85] Pinner Park, in existence by 1273-4,[86] was still part of the bailiwick of the forestership of Harrow in 1358.[87] In the 13th century the sale of honey from the woods fetched between 10d. and

---

[51] B.M. Add. MS. 15664, ff. 18-19.
[52] *Cal. Chart. R.* 1226-57, 151.
[53] S.C. 6/1128/1.
[54] B.M. Add. MS. 29794, m. 1d.
[55] S.C. 6/1128/12, m. 5. Calculated as one work due each day from each hide (29¾ hides) for 5 days a week for the 5 weeks before Mich., and one work due each week from each cotman (17 cotlands) during the same period.
[56] i.e. for 8½ weeks after Mich.
[57] i.e. one a week for 8½ weeks from each cotman.
[58] M.R.O., Acc. 974/I, m. 3 *et passim*.
[59] *Cal. Inq. Misc.* vi, pp. 123-4. See above, p. 204.
[60] M.R.O., Acc. 76/2431.
[61] Cant. Cath. Libr., Reg. S, f. 109v.
[62] Ibid. Reg. T1, ff. 131, 174. Cf. Reg. S, ff. 138, 193; T2, ff. 61v-62.
[63] Lambeth Palace, Estate MS. 1213, mm. 9, 10; M.R.O., Acc. 76/2431, *passim*. The £13 10s. was paid by head tenements in Weald and Pinner. Originally other hamlets paid £15 15s.: see table below. There is no evidence of customary works at Headstone: cf. leases, Cant. Cath. Libr., Reg. G, f. 223v; S, ff. 137v, 198v; T1, ff. 121v-2, 294v-5; T2, ff. 69-70.
[64] M.R.O., Acc. 899.   [65] M.R.O., Acc. 76/222.
[66] Ibid. /2417, mm. 91, 108, /2418, mm. 1-2, /2428, m. 2.
[67] S.C. 6/Hen. VIII/2344.

[68] S.C. 6/1128/8, m. 1.
[69] M.R.O., Acc. 74/2410, m. 4.
[70] S.C. 6/1128/12, mm. 5 sqq.
[71] Lambeth Palace, Estate MS. 1214, m. 9.
[72] M.R.O., Acc. 76/2431, mm. 41, 41d, 50, 51, 54.
[73] Lambeth Palace, Estate MSS. 1193, 2068; B.M. Add. MS. 29794.
[74] John Seller, *Map of Mdx.* (1710); J. Norden, *Speculum Britanniae*, pt. i (1593), map facing p. 10; M.R.O., Acc. 76/1010.
[75] C.P. 25(1)/150/65/314. The property lay in Harrow, Northolt, and Greenford.
[76] M.R.O., Acc. 76/2418, mm. 26, 47; B.M. Add. MS. 29794, m. 1d.
[77] B.M. Add. MS. 29794, m. 1d. S.C. 6/1128/12, m. 5.
[78] M.R.O., Acc. 76/2418, m. 26.
[79] The account mentions only the windmill: S.C. 6/1128/12, m. 5.
[80] Repairs in 1273-4 included raising timber 'submerged by the water'; B.M. Add. MS. 29794, m. 1d.
[81] Ibid. m. 2.
[82] e.g. Lambeth Palace, Estate MS. 1193.
[83] *Close R.* 1268-72, 221.
[84] Lambeth Palace, Estate MS. 1193.
[85] B.M. Add. MS. 29794, mm. 1d, 2.   [86] Ibid.
[87] *Cal. Close*, 1354-60, 532. See above, p. 205.

1s. 8d., and of nuts between 1s. 6d. and 9s. 6d.[88] In 1086 there was woodland for 2,000 pigs,[89] and an annual render to the archbishop of 30 pigs from Harrow was mentioned c. 1093–6.[90] Pigs are recorded only once on the demesne, at Woodhall in 1292–5.[91] Tenants with more than 10 pigs had to give one to the lord, while those with fewer than 10 had to pay 1d. for each pig.[92] The sale of pannage realized £2 10s. in 1270[93] and over twice as much in 1273–4.[94] About 1316 it was £3 13s. 4d.[95] No pannage was listed in 1348 for Harrow (Sudbury), probably because Sudbury Wood had shrunk;[96] 13s. 4d. was obtained for pannage in Pinner Park and 3s. from Headstone, the latter from allowing pigs to feed on the stubble in autumn.[97] In 1446 there was no pannage since the woods had been cut down to provide timber for Archbishop Chichele's foundation, All Souls College.[98] From 1485 'pannage, nothing' recurs in the accounts.[99]

William I forbade anyone to hunt on the archbishop's manor at Harrow.[1] Five roe-deer were sent to stock the Prior of Ruislip's park in 1270.[2] At Pinner Park one of the chief tasks of the keeper, first mentioned in 1348, or of the parker, first mentioned in 1443, was to maintain the deer.[3] In the late 15th century stock fluctuated between 97 and 120 beasts of which only about 6 or 7 were disposed of in a year.[4] Timber for fuel and charcoal,[5] and even for the chancel of Harrow church,[6] was granted by the king during vacancies in the archbishopric in the 13th century. The sale of wood and logs fetched £11 12s. 6d. in 1270[7] and £14 3s. 8d. in 1273–4.[8] The felling of trees by tenants without permission was an offence.[9]

There were fishponds at Harrow and Pinner,[10] and a dovecote at Headstone.[11] Gardens are recorded at Harrow and Woodhall in 1236,[12] and in 1270 profit from them was 2s.[13] The garden at Woodhall was mentioned in 1348,[14] that at Sudbury in 1397,[15] and at Headstone fruit was grown on the slopes of the moat in the 15th century.[16] Herbage was sold for £3 6s. 8d. in 1270[17] and £3 14s. 0½d. in 1273–4,[18] when it was almost equally divided between Sudbury, Pinner Park, and assarts. Only winter pasture was recorded in 1348.[19] At Sudbury a large common replaced the wood and in the north, in Pinner and Harrow Weald, 'ridings' were cleared, sometimes for crops[20] but usually for pasture.[21] Throughout the 15th and early 16th centuries herbage was one of the appurtenances leased with Pinner Park and Headstone.[22]

The total of fixed or assessed rents (rentata assisa),[23] payable at five terms[24] and rising only slightly as increments were added, ranged from £53 in 1270[25] to £64 throughout the 15th century.[26] By 1525–6 fixed rents were £64 5s., new rents 5d., and increments 10s.[27] Rents in kind were usually entered as customary or movable rents (consuetudines or redditus mobiles). Cotlanders owed hens at Christmas at a rate of 4 hens from a married man or 2 hens from a single man or widow.[28] In 1270 £1 1s. 4d. was received in lieu of 121 hens[29] but only 107 were rendered in 1273–4,[30] when a statement that the lord's poulterers were 24 free men probably meant that he had no more need for a render in kind. At the end of the 14th century the render, still 4 or 2 hens (commuted at 2d. each) from each cotlander, was divided between Sudbury and Headstone in the proportion of 120 and 33 respectively.[31] From 1485 and probably earlier, the number crystallized at 122, commuted at 3d. a hen,[32] and although a rent of hens from cotlanders was listed as an appurtenance of Sudbury manor in 1432,[33] there is no evidence that it was paid. By 1553 payment was exacted from all customary head tenants, usually at a rate of 4½d. for a virgate, 6d. for ½-hide, and 9d. for a hide, each hen being commuted for 3d.[34] Another rent in kind was 11 ploughshares, payable at Michaelmas, which had been commuted at 6d. each in 1270,[35] 8d. each in 1348,[36] and 1s. each by 1485.[37] By 1553 payment was

---

[88] Lambeth Palace, Estate MS. 1193; B.M. Add. MS. 29794, m. 1d; S.C. 6/1128/1.
[89] V.C.H. Mdx. i. 120.
[90] Domesday Monachorum, ed. Douglas, 99.
[91] E 372/141, m. 28d.
[92] M.R.O., Acc. 76/2431, m. 13.
[93] S.C. 6/1128/1.
[94] B.M. Add. MS. 29794, m. 1.
[95] M.R.O., Acc. 76/2410, m. 6.
[96] S.C. 6/1128/12, mm. 5 sqq. Sudbury Wood still existed in 1435: M.R.O., Acc. 76/1643.
[97] S.C. 6/1128/12, mm. 5 sqq.
[98] M.R.O., Acc. 76/2417, m. 90.
[99] Ibid. /2431, passim.
[1] Regesta Regum Anglo-Normannorum, i, ed. Davis, no. 265.
[2] Close R. 1268–72, 232.
[3] Cal. Pat. 1348–50, 141, 376, 1441–6, 168; Cal. Inq. Misc.. vi, pp. 123–4.
[4] M.R.O., Acc. 76/2431, mm. 7d, 10d, 16d.
[5] Close R. 1232–4, 95, 120; 1237–42, 415; 1268–72, 221.
[6] Ibid. 1237–42, 420.
[7] S.C. 6/1128/1.
[8] B.M. Add. MS. 29794, m. 1d.
[9] Cal. Pat. 1313–17, 245; M.R.O., Acc. 76/2410, mm. 1v, 2; /1643.
[10] Cal. Pat. 1321–4, 373; Cant. Cath. Libr., Reg. S, f. 137v.
[11] Cal. Inq. Misc. vi, pp. 123–4; S.C. 6/1128/12.
[12] Lambeth Palace, Estate MS. 1193.
[13] S.C. 6/1128/1.
[14] Ibid. /12, m. 5.
[15] Cal. Inq. Misc. vi, pp. 123–4.
[16] Lambeth Palace, Estate MS. 1213, m. 9d; 1214, m. 6; 1219, m. 10d.
[17] S.C. 6/1128/1.
[18] B.M. Add. MS. 29794.
[19] S.C. 6/1128/12, m. 5.
[20] e.g. 'Oteredyng'.
[21] e.g. 'Oxenlese'.
[22] S.C. 6/Hen. VIII/7153; M.R.O., Acc. 76/2431, mm. 2, 27, 28; Cant. Cath. Libr., Reg. S, f. 198v; Lambeth Palace, Estate MSS. 1213, m. 9d, 1214, mm. 6, 6d.
[23] Cf. Du Boulay, Lordship of Cant. 176, where the gabulum is suggested as equalling the fixed rent. Compare the £56 of 1086 and £54 of 1093–6 (see above) with the £57 of 1236.
[24] i.e. Martinmas, Christmas, Easter, Nativity of John the Baptist, and Michaelmas.
[25] S.C. 6/1128/1. Figures are given to the nearest £.
[26] Lambeth Palace, Estate MS. 1213, m. 9; M.R.O., Acc. 76/2431, mm. 1, 26. Between 1458–9 and 1497–8 they rose by 1s. ¼d. Entries at Martinmas and Michaelmas 1348 show an increase of 6s. 7¾d. on c. 1285: S.C. 6/1128/12, m. 5. The figure for 1397 (£72 5s.) is inaccurate: Cal. Inq. Misc. vi, pp. 123–4.
[27] S.C. 6/Hen. VIII/7153.
[28] Lambeth Palace, Estate MS. 2068.
[29] S.C. 6/1128/1.
[30] B.M. Add. MS. 29794, m. 1d.
[31] Cal. Inq. Misc. vi, pp. 123–4.
[32] M.R.O., Acc. 76/2431, passim.
[33] Cant. Cath. Libr., Reg. S, f. 109v. The render to Headstone, mentioned in 1397 (see above), was among the feudal dues reserved to the seneschal of the liberty from 1453: ibid. Reg. S, f. 198v.
[34] M.R.O., Acc. 76/222a.
[35] S.C. 6/1128/1.
[36] Ibid. /12, m. 5.
[37] M.R.O., Acc. 76/2431, passim.

being made for nine ploughshares, assessed mostly on free tenants in Sudbury and Roxeth.[38]

Other feudal dues included *gersenese*, perhaps merchet, which in 1273–4 produced seven pigs and a piglet, sold for 15s. 6d.,[39] and in 1348 £3 8s. 6d.[40] Merchet was being paid in cash in 1385.[41] As heriot, free tenants owed a horse, customary head tenants their best cloven-hoofed beast, and cotlanders one black sheep. If a tenant had no beast, 3s. 6d. was accepted for a cloven-hoofed animal and 10d. or 11d. for a sheep.[42] Although heriot was still sometimes paid in kind as late as 1553,[43] there were money payments by 1315–16[44] and, on the excuse that there was no beast, money payments became usual even for estates which almost certainly had suitable animals.[45] Perquisites of court usually yielded between £10 and £12 a year from the 13th to the 16th centuries.[46] They comprised fines and amercements, and heriots and reliefs, which were paid by the heir before entering a head tenement and which were calculated as one year's rent.[47] Entry fines were paid when a tenement passed to someone who was not the heir.

By the end of the 14th century the archbishops no longer needed directly to exploit their demesne manors and feudal services.[48] Throughout the 15th and 16th centuries the only mansion-house in the area which was maintained to receive the archbishop was Headstone manor,[49] where the lessee had also to provide for the archbishop's officials. Pinner Park, usually combined with timber rights, was reserved in the archbishop's hands until 1539, under a keeper or parker who was appointed for life. He was paid 3d. a day and allowed to appoint a deputy, so that the office was often a reward for service elsewhere.[50] The archbishop also reserved fixed rents and feudal dues, especially in the 16th century. Payments in commutation of customary services continued to be made to the manorial officials, even though the services were formally leased with the demesne manors.[51] With these exceptions, all the demesne lands and manorial rights within Harrow were leased out. A receiver was appointed to collect the

lessees' rents and the rents which tenants paid to the reeves and collectors.[52] The earliest extant lease is for Headstone, leased in 1383 for 20 years at £12 a year. Woodhall and Sudbury had both been leased out, at £23 13s. 4d. and £25 a year respectively, by 1397.[53] Roxeth, which had escheated to the archbishop, was leased in 1430 for 50 years at £1 13s. 4d. a year.[54] A slight rise in the annual rent issuing from the demesne manors during the late 15th and 16th centuries reflects the growing attraction of areas near London, and of the practice of leasing.[55] The estates of Kilburn Priory in Wembley,[56] of Uxendon manor,[57] and of Bentley Priory in the Weald[58] were also leased out. In 1539 Pinner Park was leased for 50 years at £20 a year and a payment of £66 13s. 4d. for all wood within the park. In 1541 Weald Wood was leased for 80 years at £3 6s. 8d. a year, and shortly after the acquisition of the Harrow estate by Sir Edward North, Pinner Wood was leased for 99 years at £10 a year.[59] By 1545 the archbishop was receiving £92 7s. 8d. annually in rent from his Harrow demesne.[60] His expenses were few: fixed items, like wages, totalling £3 11s. 8d., and other items varying from nothing to an exceptional £44 12s. but usually costing less than £10 a year. Feudal receipts gradually rose from £89 in 1485 to £114 1s. in 1553. In 1535 the annual value of the archbishop's Harrow property was £166 10s.[61] and by 1545 he could expect a clear annual profit of about £180.[62]

Cranmer used various devices, including refusal of ratification by the Canterbury Chapter, and long leases, to try to retain control of Harrow before its surrender in 1545.[63] He and his predecessors consistently granted leases to local men: fallow land was to be manured, enclosures, hedgerows, and wood were to be preserved, and the lessee was to repair any damages committed by him or his animals, although all the other repairs were the responsibility of the archbishop. Sub-letting was restricted to sons or brothers, and leases, since they were often made jointly to a father and son, tended to become hereditary.[64] Headstone was leased to the Readings in

---

[38] Ibid. /222a.   [39] B.M. Add. MS. 29794, m. 1d.
[40] S.C. 6/1128/12, m. 5.
[41] M.R.O., Acc. 76/2413, m. 20d.
[42] Ibid. /216; Bodl. MS. Gough Mdx. 4, ff. 21 sqq. Under-setters paid heriot to the head tenant. One subtenant, however, paid a heriot of a cow to the lord in 1337: M.R.O., Acc. 76/2412, m. 5d.
[43] M.R.O., Acc. 76/222a.
[44] Ibid. /1210, mm. 1, 2d, 8.
[45] In 1327 bulls and cows were sold at 8s. each: S.C. 6/1128/8, m. 1. An ox in 1512–13 was worth 10s.: M.R.O., Acc. 76/2421, m. 3.
[46] B.M. Add. MS. 29794, m. 1d; Lambeth Palace, Estate MSS. 1213, m. 9, 1214, m. 9; S.C. 6/1128/1, /12, m. 5; /Hen. VIII/7153; M.R.O., Acc. 76/2431, mm. 1, 26. The amount varied from £4 13s. 11d. in 1466–7 to £12 11s. 8d. in 1497.
[47] Bodl. MS. Gough Mdx. 4, ff. 31 sqq.; M.R.O., Acc. 76/2413, m. 7d.
[48] For the transition to leasing, see Du Boulay, *Lordship of Cant.* 218 sqq.; Du Boulay, 'Abp. as Territorial Magnate', *Med. Recs. of Abps. of Cant.* ed. E. G. W. Bill, 50–70. Unless otherwise stated, the following section is based upon copies of leases ratified by the Chapter of Canterbury Cathedral. Those relevant to the Harrow demesne are: Cant. Cath. Libr., Reg. G, f. 223v; S, ff. 105, 109v, 137v, 138, 143, 164, 192, 193, 198v, 206, 228v, 250, 355v; T1, ff. 106, 121–2, 131, 156v, 174, 216v, 294v–5, 297, 317v, 337; T2, ff. 2–2v, 61v–62, 69–70, 136v–7v, 149v–50v, 162v–3v; U1, ff. 2, 29v–30v, 81v, 124v–5v.
[49] M.R.O., Acc. 76/222a.

[50] Ibid. /2431, *passim*; *Reg. Bourgchier* (Cant. & York Soc. liv), 45–46; *Cal. Pat.* 1441–6, 168.
[51] The reeve and, for Woodhall, the collector of rents: Lambeth Palace, Estate MS. 1213, mm. 9, 10; M.R.O., Acc. 76/2431, *passim*.
[52] Du Boulay, *Lordship of Cant.* 261; *Med. Recs. of Abps. of Cant.* 50–70. There was one receiver for all the archbishop's Mdx. and Surrey manors.
[53] *Cal. Inq. Misc.* vi, pp. 123–4.
[54] M.R.O., Acc. 76/2431, mm. 2d. sqq.
[55] Du Boulay, 'A Rentier Economy in the late Middle Ages: the Archbishopric of Cant.', *Ec. H.R.* xvi. 427–38.
[56] S.C. 6/Hen. VIII/2344.   [57] S.C. 2/191/45.
[58] P.C.C. 19 Blamyr.
[59] M.R.O., Acc. 76/410, /1639. This lease probably superseded Cranmer's lease of all the woods within Woodhall manor, made to his servant in 1545: Cant. Cath. Libr. Reg. U1, ff. 124v–5v.   [60] M.R.O., Acc. 76/222a.
[61] i.e. farm of Sudbury, Woodhall, Headstone, and herbage of Pinner Park, and perquisites of court: *Valor Eccl.* (Rec. Com.), i. 3.
[62] S.C. 6/Hen. VIII/7153; M.R.O., Acc. 76/222a, /2431. Includes farm of Roxeth, Pinner Pk. and Weald Wood.
[63] For the speculation surrounding the Canterbury estates, see Du Boulay, *Lordship of Cant.* 319 sqq.; Du Boulay, 'Abp. Cranmer and the Cant. Temporalities', *E.H.R.* lxvii. 19–36; *Narratives of the Days of the Reformation*, ed. J. G. Nicholas (Camd. Soc. lxxvii), 264–5.
[64] Du Boulay, *Lordship of Cant.* 221 sqq.; Du Boulay, 'Who were farming the English demesnes at the end of Middle Ages?', *Ec. H.R.* xvii. 443–55.

1397[65] and from 1458 to 1569 and probably later.[66] Sudbury manor came into the hands of William Page between 1432[67] and 1458[68] and remained with his family until 1698.[69] From *c.* 1485 until 1503 Woodhall was leased by the Streets, and from 1520 by the Edlins.[70] Roxeth was held by the Webbs in 1523 and remained with them until the end of the 16th century.[71] The Bird family provided deputies for the parkers and keepers of Pinner Park from 1482–3;[72] one of the first lessees of the park was John Bird, whose descendants relinquished it between 1555 and 1559.[73] The Pages, Streets, Edlins, Readings, and Birds all sprang from the head tenants, the most important of the three classes of customary tenant recognized by the manor court, namely cotmen or cotlanders, head tenants, and under-

allowed widows to keep the whole of their husbands' inheritance for life was changed under Elias of Dereham (*c.* 1197–1240) to allow them one third, the rest passing to the heir at 22, and was later modified to allow them merely 'a reasonable value in money'.[79] By the 16th century, however, under-setting often had permanently alienated part of a head tenement, while the combination of free and cutomary holdings made it difficult to distinguish head tenements. Thus the rentals, dating from 1553, do not always correspond to the data in the table. They show 69 head tenements, made up of 9 hides, 30 $\frac{1}{2}$-hides, 24 virgates, and 6 irregular units.[80] Despite the changing amounts of open-field land belonging to head tenements, there seems to have been an attempt to preserve the site of the original

HEAD TENEMENTS: SIZE AND DISTRIBUTION

Hamlet	Hide	$\frac{1}{2}$-hide	Virgate	Total (in hides)
Pinner	..	10	11*	$7\frac{3}{4}$
Weald	1	8	3	$5\frac{3}{4}$
Kenton	..	..	2	$\frac{1}{2}$
Preston	..	2	..	1
Uxendon	1	3	..	$2\frac{1}{2}$
Wembley	..	1	3	$1\frac{1}{4}$
Alperton	..	4	4	3
Roxeth	..	5	8	$4\frac{1}{2}$
Greenhill	2	1	2	3
	4	34	33	$29\frac{1}{4}$

* One tenement, apparently a virgate, was split, probably after 1383–4, and thereafter only 3*s.* 4*d.* was paid for it as worksilver: M.R.O., Acc. 76/214, /2413, m. 15d.

tenants or under-setters. Whereas there were two cottars in 1086,[74] by the 13th century there were 17 cotlanders, each holding a cottage and 5 a.[75] All the cotlanders were at Sudbury, where they appear to have had an especially close relationship with the original demesne manor. Elsewhere the size and distribution of the head tenements can be reconstructed, as in the table below, from payments of worksilver, calculated at £1 a hide, and of hens, of which $1\frac{1}{2}$ were due from each virgate, 2 from each $\frac{1}{2}$-hide, and 3 from each hide.

Each of the 71 ancient head tenements consisted of a messuage within a close, usually on the edge of a village green, and several selions in the surrounding open fields. An 18th-century custumal[76] stated that each hide contained 100 a., selions, or lands, each selion being about 3 roods. Head tenements may once have approximated to a hide or a simple fraction of it, since 16th-century rentals sometimes refer to 50-acre head tenements instead of $\frac{1}{2}$-hides,[77] but the custumal recognized that the hide and similar terms were variable. If there was no male heir the eldest female inherited the whole.[78] The custom that

messuage, to which the rights and duties of the tenement were attached. Frequently the name of the holding, which was often derived from a 14th-century tenant, became attached to the messuage and, if that decayed, to the surrounding close.[81]

Under-tenants, who do not appear in rentals, were naturally more numerous than head tenants. The only evidence, dating from 1724, gives 103 under-setters, compared with 34 head tenants.[82] There is little sign of a permanent class of poor peasants, distinct from the other customary tenants. There were bond-tenants in the 14th century on all the Harrow manors, including Wembley, where there was a bond-tenant of Kilburn Priory as late as 1400,[83] and on the Canterbury estate they are perhaps to be identified with the *famuli*. In 1337 three bond-tenants were summoned to Sudbury court for giving their daughters in marriage to freemen without the lord's consent,[84] and in 1384 the goods of a bond-tenant of the Rectory estate were seized because he sent his son 'into remote parts to learn the liberal arts'.[85] Although the peasants withdrew their rents and services in 1381, when there were

[65] *Cal. Inq. Misc.* vi, pp. 123–4.
[66] Lambeth Palace, Estate MSS. 1213–21; M.R.O., Acc. 76/222a, /1985, /2431.
[67] When leased to Wm. Bray for 20 years: Cant. Cath. Libr., Reg. S, f. 109v.
[68] Lambeth Palace, Estate MS. 1213, m. 11.
[69] Lambeth Palace, Estate MSS. 1213–21; M.R.O., Acc. 76/222, /1647, /1985, /2003–4, /2006, /2431; Bodl. MS. All Souls D.D. c57/25. From *c.* 1640 the Pages held one of the farms into which Sudbury was divided.
[70] They still had it *c.* 1573–4: M.R.O., Acc. 76/214.
[71] Ibid. /205, /222b, /1985.
[72] Lambeth Palace, Estate MS. 1216.
[73] M.R.O., Acc. 76/2000; C 3/222/48.

[74] *V.C.H. Mdx.* i. 120.
[75] Lambeth Palace, Estate MS. 2068.
[76] Bodl. MS. Gough Mdx. 4, f. 31.
[77] e.g. M.R.O., Acc. 76/205.
[78] Bodl. MS. Gough Mdx. 4, ff. 31–40.
[79] Lambeth Palace, Estate MS. 2068.
[80] M.R.O., Acc. 76/205, /208, /214, /222a.
[81] e.g. Jacketts in Kenton: M.R.O., Acc. 166/1.
[82] M.R.O., Acc. 76/1015.
[83] i.e. Adam Hoppere, serf of the prioress: *Cal. Close, 1399–1400,* 293–7.
[84] M.R.O., Acc. 76/2421, m. 5.
[85] M.R.O., Acc. 974/I, m. 9d.

trespasses in Harrow and Pinner Park,[86] discontent cannot be assigned to any one class. One of the bond-tenants of 1337, John Swetman, gave his name to a head tenement in Pinner.[87] Many head tenants were themselves under-setters, and younger sons frequently held under-set lands from a father or brother. Although the head tenement could not be subdivided, a younger son often had his own house and lived on a small estate leased or under-set from the head tenement.[88] With the growth of population, however, there arose a class of landless labourers. Of the 224 people assessed for the subsidy of 1522–3, 26 were described as labourers, assessed on 20s. a year wages; 68 others, similarly assessed, probably were also labourers. Many names, Edlin, Rede, Bird, Hatch, and Street, are found among those landless men and in a rising class of prosperous yeomen. Most of the sixteen people who were assessed in 1522–3 on goods worth over £100 were descendants of Harrow peasantry. They included the lessees of the demesne manors, but also people like John Greenhill, John Lyon, and the Page family, whose wealth came from an accumulation of tenements, especially head tenements.[89] By 1553 the 71 head tenements were in the hands of 52 tenants, who also held free and under-set land.[90]

Harrow from early times had attracted London merchants and courtiers.[91] Some, like Sir Nicholas Brembre (d. 1388),[92] owned considerable estates. Most held leases and rents in freehold, and, occasionally, copyhold property. Landholders included Edward III's mistress, Alice Perrers,[93] and many tradesmen in the 14th, 15th, and early 16th centuries.[94]

As on the demesne, agriculture elsewhere was mixed but mainly arable. Each hamlet, except Harrow-on-the-Hill and Sudbury, was surrounded by open fields, mostly of wheat and oats. By the early 16th century wheat seems to have been grown more widely than oats in all parts of the parish. Animals tended to be kept nearer the home, on the common or in closes around the house. Pannage paid c. 1316 on Sudbury manor shows that 980 pigs were kept by 204 tenants.[95] In 1368 18 tenants of Rectory manor paid pannage for 68 pigs.[96] A few cattle were kept in all areas and draught animals included horses and oxen, even in the 16th century.[97] The mixed agriculture of Roxeth is shown in 1388: Sir Nicholas Brembre had a plough, 40 a. sown with wheat, 10 qr. each of wheat, oats, and peas, 20 qr. of beans and peas, 3 cartloads of

hay, 3 horses, 11 oxen, a bull, 24 cows, a boar, sow, and 9 piglets, a gander and two geese.[98]

Brembre himself had no sheep, although there were some in Roxeth, Pinner, Wembley, and Kenton,[99] and more in Harrow-on-the-Hill and Sudbury. Sheep were the animals most often presented for straying and trespass, especially in the lord's meadows and pasture at Sudbury.[1] In 1336 four men were presented, including Simon Francis (Fraunceys), a landowner in four counties,[2] who was presented for offences involving 100, 200, and 100 sheep.[3] In 1362 flocks of 50 and 80 sheep were recorded,[4] and Thomas Page had 80 sheep at Sudbury in 1512.[5] In 1380 four out of eight trespasses at Rectory manor were by sheep.[6] The fact that a black sheep was the customary heriot exacted from cotlanders at Sudbury suggests that sheep were numerous even before the clearing of Sudbury Wood increased the amount of common pasture available.[7]

A weekly market, on Mondays, and an annual fair on the vigil, feast, and morrow of the Nativity of the Virgin Mary (7–9 Sept.) were granted to the archbishop's tenants at Harrow in 1261.[8] From 1314 the market was held on Wednesdays and the fair was restricted to 7–8 Sept.[9] In 1336 Pinner was granted a weekly market and an annual fair on the vigil, feast, and morrow of the Nativity of St. John the Baptist (23–25 June).[10] In 1441 Archbishop Chichele remitted all market tolls, making his tenants free in other markets from toll, stallage, murage, pedage, and pontage.[11] The Harrow market still existed in Henry VIII's reign but it had apparently lapsed by the end of the 16th century.[12]

AGRARIAN HISTORY FROM 1545. The inhabitants were little affected by the transfer of the lordship and ownership of most of Harrow from ecclesiastical to lay hands. The demesne manors continued to be leased to the same men as before,[13] and in the south-east former lessees became the owners of the Wembley and Tokyngton estates. Lord North was apparently satisfied with profits from leasing, without speculating in reversions. In 1569 the year's profits were £205;[14] in 1604 £204.[15] In the late 16th century, however, Pinner Park, with its hunting and timber rights, was a rich prize, attracting influential people like the Bacon family.[16] Outsiders,[17] however, by no means displaced the local families, many of whom achieved their greatest prosperity during this period. Sixty-five people were assessed on goods worth £10 and upwards in 1550–1.[18] Of these,

[86] Cal. Pat. 1381–5, 77.
[87] See pp. 178–9.
[88] e.g. Cant. Cath. Libr., Reg. F, f. 35; P.C.C. 19 Blamyr, 8 Fetiplace, 33 Adeane, 3 Alenger.
[89] E 179/141/115, f. 6.
[90] M.R.O., Acc. 76/222a.
[91] e.g. John, son of Nicholas of London, claimed one virgate in Preston in 1220: Cur. Reg. R. ix. 39.
[92] Cal. Close, 1381–5, 218–19; see above, pp. 205–6.
[93] Cal. Pat. 1377–8, 503.
[94] Cal. Close, 1354–60, 517, 1429–35, 357, 362, 1500–1509, 8; E. J. L. Scott, Recs. of Grammar School at Harrow on Hill, 13.
[95] M.R.O., Acc. 76/2410, m. 6.
[96] Ibid. /2427, m. 18.
[97] P.C.C. 8 Fetiplace, 19 Blamyr, 3 Alenger, 33 Adeane.
[98] Cal. Pat. 1385–9, 481.
[99] P.C.C. 33 Adeane, 3 Alenger, 8 Fetiplace; Cant. Cath. Libr., Reg. F, f. 35.
[1] M.R.O., Acc. 76/222a, /1985, /2412, m. 4.
[2] Cal. Inq. p. m. x, pp. 348–9. See above, pp. 113, 206.

[3] M.R.O., Acc. 76/2427, m. 18.
[4] Ibid., m. 8.   [5] P.C.C. 8 Fetiplace.
[6] M.R.O., Acc. 974/I, m. 3.
[7] Bodl. MS. Gough Mdx. 4, ff. 31 sqq. Although often unreliable on ancient custom, the custumal here seems to be right: cf. M.R.O., Acc. 76/2412, m. 5.
[8] Cal. Chart. R. 1257–1300, 38.
[9] Ibid. 1300–26, 274.
[10] Ibid. 1327–41, 360.
[11] B.M. Lansdowne Ch. 180; Harrow Octocent. Tracts, xi. 8–9.
[12] J. Norden, Speculum Britanniae, pt. i (1593), 13; Camden, Britannia, ed. Gough, ii. 89.
[13] M.R.O., Acc. 76/222a and b, /1985, /2000.
[14] Ibid. /1985.
[15] Including Hayes: S.C. 12/1/20.
[16] C 3/152/6, /5/57, /222/48; Cal. S.P. Dom. 1581–90, 2, 5; Hist. MSS. Com. 11th Rep. pt. 4, p. 5.
[17] e.g. the Clitherows: see p. 179; Edw. Claxton: see p. 217; Sir Edw. Waldo: see p. 216.
[18] E 179/142/169.

twelve were assessed on goods worth from £20 to £30 and nine on goods worth more than £30. Only two out of 21 of the wealthiest people in Harrow were born outside the parish: Hugh Wright, gentleman, assessed on £60 in Sudbury, was a Londoner;[19] William Layton, assessed on £60 in Harrow, was the brother of the rector.[20] Only one other man, William Bellamy, assessed on £70 in Harrow and Uxendon, described himself as a gentleman. All the others, including the most highly assessed (on goods worth £100),[21] were local yeomen.[22]

Long-established families which accumulated land during the 16th and 17th centuries included the Greenhills of Greenhill and Roxeth, the Finches of Greenhill and Weald, the Edlins of Pinner and Weald, the Osmonds of Roxeth, the Bugbeards and Warrens of Weald, the Lyons of Preston, the Streets, Readings, and Birds of Pinner, and the Pages.[23] The most remarkable was the Page family, members of which held land in the neighbouring parishes of Edgware, Little Stanmore, Hendon, and Kingsbury in the 14th century.[24] The earliest recorded connexion with Harrow is of 1383,[25] and during the 15th century they began to accumulate property, mostly in Uxendon and Wembley but also in Sudbury and Roxeth.[26] From the mid 15th century Pages leased Sudbury manor,[27] before another branch acquired the Kilburn estate at Wembley.[28] Thomas Page, the lessee of Sudbury in 1537, had interests in Buckinghamshire almost equal in value to those which he had in Middlesex.[29] By 1553 at least seven Pages had land in Harrow parish: Richard leased Sudbury manor and held one ½-hide and one virgate in Roxeth; John held a ½-hide and one virgate in Wembley and one virgate and other lands in Uxendon; Thomas, who lived on Roxeth Common, held one carucate (Wembley manor) in Wembley and 1½ hide and several parcels of waste and tenements in Alperton; another Thomas, of Northall, had three selions in Roxeth; William, who lived at Sudbury where he held two cotlands and 20 a., also held land in Alperton and Wembley; Henry had property at Kenton; and Agnes had one cotland in Sudbury.[30] In 1544 Richard Page had acquired an interest in Uxendon and Tokyngton manor through the marriage of his daughter to William Bellamy. When another Richard bought Uxendon manor and the 80-acre estate at Preston,[31] the family interests became concentrated in the south-east corner of the parish, particularly after the expiry of the Sudbury lease and the purchase of Harrow manor by George Pitt. John Page of Wembley, who died in 1623, was said to have lived to see 75 children and grandchildren.[32] There were 18 Page households in the 1660s: two in Harrow, one in Sudbury, one in Roxeth, three in

Pinner, two in Weald, four in Kenton, Preston, and Uxendon, three in Wembley, and two in Alperton.[33] Some members were little more than cottagers; others, especially the main Wembley and Uxendon branches, ranked as gentry. William Page (d. 1642), Baron of the Exchequer, and Richard Page of Uxendon, knighted in 1645, were Royalists. Other Pages included two Roman Catholic martyrs[34] and Dr. William Page (1590–1663), who wrote a treatise justifying bowing at the name of Jesus. Two Pages were among the original six governors of Harrow School, and the connexion was maintained until the early 19th century.[35] Thomas Page in 1672 described himself as lord of many manors,[36] and the Pages of Wembley and Uxendon were among the first three or four landowners in Harrow throughout the 17th and 18th centuries.[37] Their importance declined after the death of Richard Page of Wembley in 1803. There were still Pages in the parish during the 19th century, but they were craftsmen.[38]

Most open-field land in Uxendon and Tokyngton and some in Wembley was inclosed during the 16th and 17th centuries by the Pages, and to a lesser extent, by their predecessors, the Bellamys.[39] Inclosure does not seem to have been an issue, for only 20 a. of converted arable and four persons were included in the returns of 1517.[40] Even in south-east Harrow inclosures seems to have been intended primarily to consolidate estates. Conversion from arable into meadow and pasture, a process taking centuries to complete, began on the demesne farms and large, inclosed, usually freehold estates. In 1547, of a total demesne of 1,448 a., only 531 a. and 130 selions were arable, mostly concentrated on the smaller farms of Headstone (71 per cent. arable), Pinner Park (64 per cent.), and Roxeth. On the larger and older farms of Woodhall and Sudbury, the proportion, 37 and 19 per cent., was much lower.[41] There is some evidence of dairy farming and the fattening of livestock[42] and during the 16th century presentments for overstocking sheep on Sudbury Common became more frequent. In 1585 servants were forbidden to keep sheep there unless they were branded with their masters' signs.[43] In the rest of the parish, however, and especially in the extensive open fields of Pinner, Roxeth, and Alperton, arable was predominant. Peas, beans, tares, and hay were grown, but cereals, especially wheat, were noted by 16th-century writers. Camden wrote of the rich land south of Harrow-on-the-Hill,[44] and, according to Norden, a man standing on Harrow hill before harvest-time might see 'such comfortable abundance of all kinds of grain, that it maketh the inhabitants to clap their hands for joy . . .'. He also noted that in wet weather the mud impeded travel-

[19] P.C.C. 35 Porch.
[20] P.C.C. 9 Powell. See p. 254.
[21] i.e. Harry Page, lessee of Wembley, and John Lamb of Tokyngton: P.C.C. 1 Bucke, 35 Noodes.
[22] P.C.C. 20, 48 Welles, 30 Wrastley, 35 Noodes; Scott, Recs. of Grammar Sch. 28.
[23] Most families were tenants of the manor from the 14th to 18th centuries: index to court rolls, M.R.O., Acc. 76/216.
[24] Elsley, Wembley, 126.
[25] M.R.O., Acc. 76/2413, m. 3.
[26] Ibid. /2415, mm. 7v, 17, /2417, m. 120v, /2418, mm. 13, 43v, /2420, mm. 34v, 38.
[27] See above.
[28] See p. 208.
[29] E 179/141/124.
[30] M.R.O., Acc. 76/222a.

[31] See p. 207.
[32] Lysons, Environs of Lond. ii. 574.
[33] M.R.O., H.T. 5, 26, 53, 75.
[34] See p. 251.
[35] Elsley, Wembley, 126–33; Wembley News, 11 Dec. 1952.
[36] M.R.O., Acc. 76/853.
[37] Ibid. /212, /891, /2005.
[38] M.R.O., D.R.O. 3/F13/3; H.O. 107/1700, ff. 21–32.
[39] See pp. 189–90.
[40] C 47/7/2/2, m. 14; V.C.H. Mdx. ii. 89.
[41] M.R.O., Acc. 1052, ff. 25–29v, 423–6, 439v–52v.
[42] P.C.C. 11, 16, 19 Populwell, 1 Bucke, 20, 48 Welles 13, 35 Noodes, 11 Stevenson, 36 Pyckering.
[43] M.R.O., Acc. 974/II, mm. 93(227), 135(270).
[44] Camden, Britannia, ed. Gough, ii. 78.

ling, and that the soil was very hard in spring, making it difficult for the oxen.[45] There may even have been a reversion to arable on the demesne farms in the 17th century, for accounts show that at Sudbury Court in 1637 wheat was sold for £99 7s. and oats for £61 6s., compared with only £25 9s. for cattle and sheep.[46] After the Harrow market had lapsed the capital came to dominate the local economy, and the need to feed London's expanding population brought prosperity to many farmers.[47]

It was during the 17th century that the greatest strain was placed upon the relationship between lord and tenant. In 1603 the manorial court rolls, the only source of traditional practice, were indexed and a custumal was extracted from them, probably by the steward, since it is slanted in favour of the lord.[48] In 1618 the homagers presented considerable encroachment and some digging of earth on the waste without the lord's permission. They upheld the right of copyholders to fell timber and erect cart-houses on the waste, declaring that they did not know whether the lord had free warren, and that the erection of cottages 'belongeth not to us to enquire of'.[49] There is a break in the court rolls from 1618 to 1629, after which the traditional copyhold formula, 'secundum consuetudines manerii', gave way to one favouring the lord, 'ad voluntatem domini secundum consuetudines manerii'.[50] In the same year orders were made against 22 encroachments on the waste, including the erection of 10 cart-houses.[51]

Disputes over the waste led to two cases between lord and tenants in the 1630s. The first concerned Weald Wood, about 700 a. of land common to lord and tenants alike, which had become so overgrown that it was useless as pasture. It was agreed that Lord North would inclose about 150 a. and that the tenants were to have the rest. In 1666 the lord of the manor was to claim that the agreement had taken place about 60 years previously[52] but in 1631 an order of the justices had been necessary, after Lord North claimed the right, under a recent statute, to bound off a quarter of Weald Wood. North seems to have won and c. 1637 his successor, George Pitt, was trying to inclose another third of the wood. He was advised against it but told that he could fell timber on the other three quarters, 'which will raise you a pretty sum of money and give your tenants good content'.[53] This Pitt did, but in 1666 six tenants threw down the lord's inclosure and claimed all the land as common. The lord won the subsequent lawsuit on the grounds of prescriptive right,[54] and Weald Wood, originally valued for its timber,[55] developed into the demesne farm of Weald Copse.[56]

The other case concerned Sudbury Common, which, in the absence of open fields, was especially precious to the near-by inhabitants. The common in the 1630s was a wooded area of about 300 a. About 1608 Lord North, with the consent of the homagers, had established a rabbit warren there and in 1633

George Pitt obtained their consent to enlarge it and erect a timber hunting lodge. Sir Gilbert Gerard objected that the rabbits ate up all the grass leaving none for the tenants' cattle and, claiming to champion the tenants, sent his servants to pull down the lodge. At the same time Pitt claimed that the Hermitage was wastehold and therefore subject to entry fine, while Gerard claimed that it was copyhold and exempt when inherited. In 1634 Pitt sent armed men, allegedly to turn out Gerard's leasehold tenant from the Hermitage and install one of his own. Gerard protested that they had broken the windows and left the gates open so that cattle from the common had destroyed his fruit trees. In 1637 the parliamentarian Gerard, who was a J.P., revived the feud by committing Pitt's warrener for supplying bowls at Sudbury on Whit Sunday. The warrener died in prison, whereupon his wife was sent by Gerard to the house of correction where ill treatment caused her to miscarry. Pitt and Gerard also quarrelled over rectorial rights, the lopping of trees, and the making of bricks. In 1638 Pitt cut down a row of elms in front of Flambards and Gerard brought an action in Star Chamber, the outcome of which is unknown. Gerard had exploited his position in the county to challenge Pitt, but the rights of common were genuinely in danger. In 1639 Pitt's tenants refused to allow him to inclose a quarter of Sudbury Common in order to fell trees, although he had obtained a similar right in Weald Wood. In 1640, however, the landowners and tenants of Sudbury agreed that his warren was beneficial and consented to the erection of another lodge on the common.[57]

In 1650 the under-set tenants denied that they owed suit or service to the court baron on the grounds that the head tenant alone was responsible.[58] There was more trouble over removing earth and wood from the waste in 1675; the homage upheld the tenant's right to plant and cut any ash or elm on the waste before his house.[59] In 1722 Sir John Rushout brought an action against John Street for lopping trees. Street replied that Rushout was violating the customs of the manor.[60] Street also brought an action, which was dismissed with costs, alleging that Rushout exacted unjust heriots; he relied on a recently made custumal challenged by Rushout which said that a tenant with more than one holding owed only a single heriot and that a horse could not be taken as heriot.[61] Until the relatively late written custumals, manorial usage remained 'in the heads of the tenants'[62] and interpretations therefore differed. In 1724 Rushout demanded any best beast or 40s. for heriot while Street took his stand on the later custumal, but the court rolls prove neither side wholly right. Horses and geldings were sometimes surrendered by freeholders[63] but usually 3s. 6d. was accepted instead and there may have been a new attempt by the lord to secure animals, and especially

[45] B.M. Harl. MS. 570, ff. 11–12v. Cf. Mdx. Cnty. Recs. ii. 169.
[46] M.R.O., Acc. 76/205.
[47] B.M. Harl. MS. 570, f. 15; E. J. Fisher, 'The Development of the London Food Market, 1540–1640', Ec. H.R. v. 51 sqq.
[48] M.R.O., Acc. 76/216.
[49] Ibid. /1008.
[50] M.R.O., Acc. 974/III, m. 103 (401), m. 6 (413d).
[51] M.R.O., Acc. 76/1010.
[52] Ibid. /1022.
[53] Ibid. /2195.
[54] Ibid. /1022–3, /2195.
[55] Ibid. /1020, /1025.
[56] See p. 228.
[57] M.R.O., Acc. 76/779–80, /783–5, /791, /800, /816, /826–7, /830, /836, /839, /1648. See p. 234.
[58] M.R.O., Acc. 76/1011–12.
[59] Ibid. /1013.
[60] Ibid. /903–4.
[61] Bodl. MS. Gough Mdx. 4, ff. 31–40; M.R.O., Acc. 76/216.
[62] Cal. Procs. in Chancery, Eliz. I (Rec. Com.), i. 78.
[63] e.g. M.R.O., Acc. 974/I, m. 3.

horses, as heriots in the mid 17th century.[64] Although payments of 3s. 6d. generally continued, the case against Rushout was dismissed with costs.

Where both custumals agreed that no entry fine was owed by the legal heir or by a purchaser who was already a tenant, the earlier custumal stressed that any other purchaser had to pay a fine at the will of the lord, where the later one mentioned a fine agreed between lord and tenant. The common law was increasingly insisting upon 'a reasonable fine', which was generally fixed at two years' improved value of the property concerned.[65] In 1728 Sir John Rushout, against the wishes of several copyholders, unsuccessfully petitioned the House of Lords for a bill to fix a fine not exceeding two years' value, to be settled between the lord and tenant.[66] In the early 19th century one tenant quoted the general law on copyhold, restricting the entry fine to two years' rent, while Lord Northwick claimed that he could charge any amount, or that both lord and tenants should be controlled and that all should pay an entry fine.[67] In 1809 Northwick demanded a fine on the admission of trustees, each of whom was already a tenant, but judgement was given against him.[68] In 1819 a dispute between Lord Northwick and George H. Drummond over timber rights on copyhold was referred to arbitration.[69] In 1723 Sir John Rushout enfranchised 52 copyhold estates[70] and 40 more enfranchisements were granted between 1730 and 1770.[71] By 1817 there were 7,455 a. of freehold, compared with 2,242 a. of copyhold.[72] Enfranchisements were still being made in the 1880s.

Agricultural prosperity was reflected in the number of 16th- and 17th-century farm-houses, some of which still exist.[73] The pattern of landholding did not become settled until the late 17th and early 18th centuries, when several farms of moderate size emerged. This was especially true of Sudbury, which had never had an open-field system, and Wembley, where a large area was in the hands of one family. Most striking was the splitting-up of the demesne lands of Sudbury manor into three farms: Sudbury Court, Sheepcote, and Woodcock Hill, and the development of new demesne farms at Greenhill and Weald Copse. Between 1620[74] and 1640 the Sudbury Court or manor estate was split up, for in 1640 the demesne was said to consist of 517 a., divided among six lessees. The largest estates, of 180 a., 130 a., and 100a., were held respectively by John Brittridge, William Page, and Thomas Walter.[75] These under-estates remained fluid throughout the

17th century. Sheepcote or Shipcot Farm is first recorded in 1661,[76] while the lands of Woodcock Hill or Ruff Leas Farm, as yet unnamed, were divided between two lessees in the early 1670s.[77] Sudbury Court Farm had emerged, in approximately its later form, by 1682,[78] and Sheepcote by 1704.[79] Woodcock Hill is first named in 1754.[80] Weald Copse Farm, which emerged in the late 17th or early 18th century, is marked on the map of 1754.[81] All the demesne farms, except Greenhill, which was a head tenement conveyed to Sir John Rushout in 1763, were recorded in 1759[82] and described in 1764.[83]

In 1700 grain, and especially wheat, was still predominant but the 18th century saw a shift from arable to meadow. By 1764, of 7,702 a. of farming land for which figures are available,[84] 46 per cent. was meadow, although in the open-field areas of Roxeth and Pinner it formed only 34 per cent. and 37 per cent. The highest proportion of meadow (55 per cent.) was in Wembley and Alperton, partly because of inclosure by the Pages and partly because of the water-meadows along the Brent. Meadow formed 49 per cent. of the demesne farms but only on Sudbury Court Farm did it exceed arable. At that time tithes were calculated at a rate of 2s. for meadow, 1s. 3d. for arable, and 1s. for leys.[85] By 1800 the position was reversed, for wheat was calculated at 8s. an acre and Lent corn at 6s., compared with 3s. 6d. an acre for inclosed and 3s. for open-field meadow. Since the arable land was fallow every third year, however, its annual value was reduced. In 1797, of 7,020 a. for which figures are available, 4,578 a. (65 per cent.) was meadow, and arable was restricted to the open fields and some inclosures in Pinner and Roxeth. Apart from the commons, pasture was found on the eastern borders of the parish, at Bentley and Uxendon.[86] The dating of the change varied from farm to farm. It took place in the 17th or early 18th century on the New College estate in Harrow Weald. In 1627 meadow formed 39 per cent. of the home farm and none of the northern block known as Levels,[87] and about half of the entire estate was exclusively arable. By 1735 arable formed only 35 per cent. and was confined to Levels, although by 1779 it had risen to 43 per cent., $\frac{9}{10}$ of it in Levels.[88] Except at Sudbury Court, an old centre of animal farming, the shift occurred on the demesne farms in the late 18th century. Meadow and pasture comprised 49 per cent. in 1764 and 73 per cent. in 1806.[89] By this date Lord Northwick owned 302 a. of arable, 746 a. of meadow, and 104 a. of

[64] e.g. M.R.O., Acc. 76/1646. A custumal included in the survey of 1547 reasserted the lord's right to the best beast, since tenants originally had been excused because of ploughing services which they no longer performed: M.R.O., Acc. 1052, f. 7.

[65] W. S. Holdsworth, Hist. of Eng. Law, vii. 307.

[66] L.J. xxiii. 327b, 356a, 362a, 389b; photostat copy of the bill penes M.R.O.

[67] M.R.O., Acc. 76/863.

[68] Ibid. /862.

[69] Ibid. /1131.

[70] M.R.O., Acc. 166(2)/146/70–156. The advantage to the lord was the immediate cash.

[71] M.R.O., Acc. 76/951. Many deeds of enfranchisement c. 1733–1886 are in the M.R.O., mainly in Acc. 76. Enfranchisements are also recorded in the later court books.

[72] M.R.O., Acc. 794/8, abstracted from incl. award. Estates which do not distinguish between freehold or copyhold (e.g. Drummond's) and wastehold have been excluded.

[73] See pp. 182, 185–6, 204–5.

[74] M.R.O., Acc. 76/205.

[75] Ibid. /1647.

[76] Ibid. /848, /2006. A field called 'Longshoyte alias Shipe Cotefelde' was mentioned in 1548: Cal. Pat. 1547–8, 335.

[77] M.R.O., Acc. 76/2003–4.

[78] Ibid. /79, /200.

[79] Ibid. /88.

[80] Rocque, Map of Mdx.

[81] Ibid. See p. 185.

[82] M.R.O., Acc. 643, 2nd deposit, Messeder maps A and B.

[83] M.R.O., Acc. 76/404–5.

[84] Estimates for tithe (Christ Church MS. Estates 47/7) and description of demesne farms (M.R.O., Acc. 76/404–5).

[85] Meadow includes 119 a. of leys and 60 a. of pasture. The division of arable and meadow is confirmed by Rocque, Map of Mdx. (1754).

[86] Christ Church MS. Estates 47/19; Milne, Plan of City of Lond. & Westminster, circumjacent towns & valleys (1800) (B.M. King's Topog. Col. VI. 95).

[87] See p. 212.

[88] New Coll. MSS. 312, 383, 1380, 2420; ibid., L.R. 25.

[89] M.R.O., Acc. 643, 2nd deposit, survey with maps of Northwick's estate (1806).

pasture. Meadow predominated on all farms, the amount of arable varying from 36 per cent. at Green-hill to 9 per cent. on Northwick's newly acquired estate at Harrow. Type of soil, the proportion of open-field to inclosed land, and individual preferences could also affect the change. In mid-18th-century Sudbury, which had a soil favourable to grass and no open fields, Sudbury Court, Jackson's, and Weston's farms were mainly meadow, but Sudbury Place and Watson's Farm still had more arable.[90] In the 1760s and 1770s Weald Copse Farm was already concentrating on stock raising and hay.[91]

The main reason for the change was London's need for hay and meat. Hay was grown as a crop, stored in large barns[92] and sold by the load (36 trusses, each of 56–60 lbs.) in London and Westminster.[93] At the end of the 18th century produce was also sold in markets and fairs at Pinner, Uxbridge, Barnet and Redbourn (Herts.), and Kingston (Surr.).[94] Cows were kept throughout the year but other cattle and sheep were bought in the spring and fattened on the commons and fallow open fields for sale in November. By this time the sheep provided the additional profit of a 7- or 8-months' growth of wool.[95] Horses and cattle from London were also agisted, and there was sometimes a danger of the land being over-stocked. The stint in 1654 for landholders of Sudbury manor was three sheep for each fallow, and 5 for each ley land.[96] In 1720 it was reduced to 2 sheep for each arable plough land[97] and 3 for each ley land.[98] Presentments for surcharging the common were made in the leet court,[99] and some leases forbade the pasturing of any great cattle other than the tenant's own.[1]

Crops in 1797 included wheat (1091 a.), beans (953 a.), peas (197 a.), oats (37 a.), and tares (85 a.); barley was not sown but clover, extensively grown on the demesne as early as 1753,[2] covered 81 a. and hay 4,578 a.[3] Extreme conservatism, which made arable farming less profitable, probably assisted the change-over to meadow.[4] There was a team of five oxen at Bentley Priory, although horses were the usual draught and plough animals. Leases repeated medieval clauses against conversion to arable, on pain of fines of up to £10 an acre, and traditional methods, notably the three-field system, with its rotation of wheat, broadcast beans, and fallow, were upheld.[5] Some of the regulations were aimed at conserving fertility, like those forbidding land to be sown with grain more than two years consecutively and directing that fallow must be manured, but the open-field

system meant that inadequate water-furrows were cut to drain the heavy soil.

An attempt to inclose the waste and common-field land in 1796 failed through disagreement on terms.[6] In 1802 the chief proprietors, led by Richard Page, agreed to support a Bill for inclosure. They were opposed by the lesser proprietors, led by J. Baker Sellon, serjeant-at-law, who formed an association and presented a petition signed by 101 landholders.[7] Despite the opposition, which was attributed to sinister motives,[8] an Act was passed in 1803[9] and, after many disputes and claims,[10] the award was made and plan published in 1817.[11] Allotments in lieu of tithe were made at a rate of $\frac{1}{9}$ of waste, $\frac{1}{5}$ of arable, and $\frac{1}{9}$ of meadow or pasture. Corn-rents, paid by proprietors who did not want to make an allotment, totalled £1,328. Lord Northwick received 10 allotments, totalling 71 a., as compensation for his rights in the commons as lord of the manor.[12] Seventy-four roads, footways, and watering-places and gravel-pits were allotted to the surveyors of the highways, a proportion was sold to defray the commissioners' expenses, and the rest of the 4,750 a. which were inclosed under the award was divided among the proprietors and commoners. There were 230 proprietors of old inclosures and 41 who held common-field land or had rights of common only. After the award Northwick (1,258 a.), Drummond (1,172 a.), Christ Church, Oxford (912 a.), and the devisees of Richard Page (642 a.) were the largest landholders in the parish. Nine proprietors held between 250 and 400 a., 18 between 100 and 250 a., 18 between 50 and 100 a., 63 between 10 and 50 a., and 118 had less than 10 a., of whom 49 had less than an acre. A few new farms appeared in the former open fields, for example, Tithe Farm in Roxeth and Down's Farm in Pinner.

From 1825 the price of grain fell steadily.[13] It was not only grain which suffered, for in 1827 almost all the farmers brought back their sheep unsold from Kingston fair.[14] Heavy rain in the autumn of 1828, the worst year they ever experienced,[15] left the fine crop of wheat mildewed and spoilt $\frac{7}{8}$ of the hay;[16] most of the sheep, too, were 'quite rotten'. All agricultural prices appear to have dropped and Thomas Trollope claimed that he could make no profit on his sheep.[17] At the same time popular distress caused an outbreak of terrorism: farmers tried to meet the demands of the labourers, to preserve their stacks from the flames,[18] and a warning came from 'Captain Swing' that Lord Northwick had

[90] M.R.O., Acc. 76/1080, /1859, /1861.
[91] Documents *penes* the Blackwell family, on loan to M.R.O.
[92] G. B. G. Bull, 'Changing landscape of Rural Mdx. 1500–1850' (Lond. Univ. Ph.D. thesis, 1958), 104.
[93] Foot, *Agric. of Mdx.* 57–58; Middleton, *View*, 102; M.R.O., Acc. 76/205.
[94] Blackwell docs., 18th-cent. acct. bks.
[95] Middleton, *View*, 102, 346; M.R.O., Acc. 76/1095 e–g; M.R.O., LA.HW., Harrow Poor-rate Bk. iii. (1722–67).
[96] M.R.O., Acc. 643, m. 30d.
[97] i.e. land, meaning selion, about 3 roods.
[98] M.R.O., Acc. 76/1508.
[99] Ibid. /882, /1508, /1644.
[1] M.R.O., Acc. 188/38.
[2] Thirty loads of clover were grown, compared with 20 loads of wheat, probably on Sudbury Court Farm only: M.R.O., Acc. 76/1683.
[3] Christ Church MS. Estates 47/19.
[4] Foot, *Agric. of Mdx.* 67; Middleton, *View*, 166.

[5] M.R.O., Acc. 76/93, /195, /199–202, /2003–4; Acc. 188/17.
[6] Middleton, *View*, 60; M.R.O., Acc. 76/2221, /2223–5.
[7] Ibid. /2216, /2218, /2221.
[8] M.R.O., Acc. 77/5, /6b.
[9] M.R.O., Acc. 310(1); Harrow Incl. Act, 43 Geo. III, c. 43 (Priv. Act).
[10] M.R.O., Acc. 76/1400; cf. Acc. 76/2170–4.
[11] Award: C.P. 43/939A, ff. 76–206. Abstract: M.R.O., Acc. 794/8. Plan: M.R. 612. Copy: M.R.O., Harrow Incl. Map, EA/HAR. In 1814 it was said that all the essential points of inclosure were over: Christ Church MS. Estates 47/215.
[12] M.R.O., Acc. 76/1489.
[13] Bull, 'Changing Landscape', 150.
[14] M.R.O., Acc. 76/1763.
[15] Ibid. /1792.
[16] Ibid. /1799–1800.
[17] Ibid. /1818.
[18] Ibid. /2273.

'ground the labouring man too long'.[19] The farmers could not even pay the rent.

The correspondence between Lord Northwick at Northwick Park (Worcs.) and his bailiff, Quilton, at Harrow, is almost entirely concerned with payments by the lessee farmers. Northwick complained of Quilton's supineness and threatened to withhold his salary,[20] while the bailiff, although generally obsequious, tried to persuade his master to reduce the traditional rents.[21] One grievance was that Northwick would not repair the farms; in particular James Hill at Sheepcote[22] and George Hicks at Wembley,[23] where windows were stopped up with paper, complained about the shocking state of their premises. In 1830 the lessees of Sudbury Court, Ilotts, Greenhill, and Woodcock Hill jointly drew Lord Northwick's attention to the general depression and asked for a reduction in rent.[24] Thomas Trollope wrote, separately, that in the 17 years during which he had had his farm the produce had never sufficed to pay the rent.[25] Northwick accused him of being the ringleader of a conspiracy,[26] and distraint was made on his crops.[27] The other lessees were also in difficulties. Perry of Greenhill said in 1831 that he had lost £100 each year he had been at the farm,[28] which he relinquished in 1832.[29] In the same year Northwick wanted to distrain on Thomas Hodson, the tenant of Woodcock Hill, but he was apparently dissuaded by Quilton.[30] At the end of 1833 Hicks of Wembley was caught while trying to do a moonlight flit, his goods were distrained, and he himself was ejected.[31] When Trollope finally left the parish in 1834 he too had his crops distrained.[32] Northwick, finding it difficult to attract new tenants,[33] was forced to lower his rents[34] and repair the premises. Repairs were carried out at Sheepcote in 1832, just after the lessee had surrendered against Northwick's will,[35] but in 1833 the new tenant complained that vermin had destroyed his beans, which had to be kept in the bed-room for lack of any other place.[36] Considerable improvements were effected at Greenhill in 1834, a year after it had been leased,[37] and in 1842 Sudbury Court was said to have been repaired at great expense.[38] As late as 1846 Lord Northwick claimed a loss of £3,270 on Greenhill Farm and about the same on Sheepcote Farm.[39]

On other estates the depression proved equally crippling. In 1829 Samuel Greenhill of Roxeth hanged himself and Thomas Foster, a small landowner in Pinner, Roxeth, and Harrow Weald, was 'all to pieces' because his estate had to be sold.[40] Anthony Trollope described his father's farm in Harrow Weald at about the same time: 'a wretched, tumble-down farm-house . . . one of those farmhouses which seem always to be in danger of falling into the neighbouring horse-pond. As it crept downwards from house to stables, from stables to barns, from barns to cowsheds, and from cowsheds to dung-heaps, one could hardly tell where one began and the other ended!'[41]

The depression was even worse for the farm labourers, and the warnings of those who had opposed inclosure seemed to have come true.[42] Lord Northwick mentioned a scheme in Worcestershire, whereby allotments were granted to labourers,[43] but Quilton replied in 1834 that it had already been tried in Pinner, Roxeth, and neighbouring places, without success.[44] In 1831 a small committee rented two fields (13 a.), one of them Roxborough Field, and sub-let them as allotments, but the soil was water-logged and the potato crop failed. In 1851 the Harrow Young Men's Society revived the scheme and by 1853 there were 49 allotments. The project was apparently successful until 1861, when the land was sold for building.[45]

Sometimes, particularly at the beginning of the depression, the poor were relieved in kind with soup or coal.[46] In the winter of 1819–20 Lord Northwick was thanked for a large distribution of wood and about 23 people benefited from a scheme whereby the poor were given material to make into clothing, which was sold at half-price.[47] Fifty guineas were also distributed to 30 needy families with more than three children, when a guinea was expected to buy a pair of blankets, a shawl, and a man's shirt.[48] In 1829 there was an experiment in baking bread at a low price for the poor,[49] but the increasing difficulties of the farmers curtailed poor-relief.[50] In 1832 the parish raised enough money to send six adults and three children to Canada,[51] but most of the poor remained in the parish, usually as paupers.[52]

Between 52 and 60 per cent. of all the families in Harrow parish depended upon agriculture in the early 19th century.[53] Even in 1851, after farming had recovered from the depression,[54] 75 farmers employed few more than 243 out of 530 agricultural labourers.[55] Since hay-making was seasonal, itinerant labourers were widely employed while many local

[19] The writer was almost illiterate: M.R.O., Acc. 76/2275.
[20] M.R.O., Acc. 76/2307, /2319, /2349. In 1844 Northwick contrasted the state of Harrow with that of 25 years previously, when he claimed to have got £2,100 to £2,300 every 6 months by his own management: Acc. 76/1366.
[21] M.R.O., Acc. 76/1763, /1792, /1800.
[22] Ibid. /1736, /1800.
[23] Ibid. /2299, /2300–1, /2337, /2344.
[24] Ibid. /2273.
[25] Ibid. /2274. See p. 212.
[26] M.R.O., Acc. 76/2276.
[27] Ibid. /2277, /2279.
[28] Ibid. /2290.
[29] Ibid. /2319, /2324.
[30] Ibid. /2316, /2318.
[31] Ibid. /2354–5, /2358.
[32] Ibid. /2375. See p. 212.
[33] M.R.O., Acc. 76/2292, /2296.
[34] Ibid. /43, /2346.
[35] Ibid. /2291, /2297, /2300, /2319, /2324, /2329.
[36] Ibid. /2351.
[37] Ibid. /63, /2268–9.
[38] Ibid. /1102.

[39] Ibid. /1356–7.
[40] Ibid. /1813.
[41] A. Trollope, Autobiography (Oxford Crown edn. 1950), 11.
[42] M.R.O., Acc. 77/5.
[43] M.R.O., Acc. 76/2349.
[44] Ibid. /2374; cf. /2331.
[45] M.R.O., D.R.O. 3/H2/1.
[46] Ibid. 8/C1/1; Acc. 76/1347–51. Mrs. Beeton made soup for poor children during the hard winter of 1858: Pinner Assoc. The Villager, xi.
[47] M.R.O., Acc. 76/1349, /1354.
[48] M.R.O., Acc. 1347–8.
[49] M.R.O., D.R.O. 3/C1/4.
[50] See p. 241.
[51] M.R.O., D.R.O. 3/C1/4.
[52] See p. 241.
[53] Census, 1801–51. The proportion was much higher in Pinner, Kenton, and Wembley, but was offset by varied occupations in Harrow-on-the-Hill.
[54] By 1859 the 'habitual intoxication' of some lessees of allotments was attributed to general prosperity and an increased demand for labour: M.R.O., D.R.O. 3/H2/1.
[55] H.O. 107/1700, ff. 1–220.

men remained paupers. In 1841 359 hay-makers, chiefly Irish, were living in barns and sheds at Harrow and 56 at Pinner, and Irishmen were still employed in the 1870s and 1880s.[56] After inclosure farming remained mixed. Fallowing continued into the 1830s, and into the 1860s leases enjoined leaving ⅓ of the arable fallow.[57] The Loudons, who leased Woodhall and Kenton Lane farms in the earlier 19th century, complained that Middlesex farms were badly run and the arable wretchedly managed.[58] The Loudons introduced Scottish farming methods, however, and a reference in Trollope's *Orley Farm* to new farming practice may indicate the use of guano, introduced into Middlesex in the 1840s by some Harrow farmers.[59] At Greenhill Farm in 1819[60] rye and tares were grown with the more traditional crops, and the equipment included a hay machine, a corn-dressing machine, two swing ploughs, and a drill plough.[61] There were nurseries in Roxeth and Sudbury during the 19th century, and mushrooms were grown at Alperton in the early 20th century, but market-gardening never became important.[62] Although there were pig dealers at Alperton from c. 1895,[63] the main trend of agriculture was the continued conversion to grass-land. Hay fields formed 70 per cent. of Sudbury Court Farm[64] and 67 per cent. of Weald Copse Farm in 1861[65] and 62 per cent. of Sheepcote Farm in 1863.[66] Outside the demesne the proportion was even higher, ranging from 70 per cent. at Pinner Hill in 1844[67] to 85 per cent. on the Rectory estates by 1845,[68] and 100 per cent. at Uxendon, Forty, and New College farms in 1852 and on small farms in Wembley (1856),[69] Roxeth (1860),[70] and Greenhill (1863).[71] Grass covered 83 per cent. of the agricultural land in Harrow in 1852,[72] 98 per cent. from 1887 to 1917, and 96 per cent. in 1937.[73] In 1867 the return of 117 farmers gave a total of 11,378 a. of farming land, of which 10,783 a. were meadow and permanent pasture. A further 152 a. were under clover or artificial grass and 75 a. under mangold-wurzels or turnips and swedes. Cereals accounted for 234 a., mostly oats and wheat, and beans for 37 a. Other vegetables, mostly cabbages and potatoes, occupied 35 a., and 60 a. lay fallow. There were 11,615 sheep, 808 cattle, 596 dairy cows, and 575 pigs. One farm dealt in livestock only, all the others being mixed. In 1887

183 farmers worked 11,448 a., of which 11,272 a. were under grass, 28 a. under clover or artificial grass, and 31 a. under fodder crops. Vegetables covered 40 a. and orchards and fruit 22 a., but there was no fallow and cereals occupied only 64 a. The number of sheep had dropped to 6,113, cows and pigs had remained about the same, and cattle had risen to 1,297. There were 416 horses.

Hay-farming was at its height in the 1880s. The main market was London, although some hay was retained to fatten stock.[74] Improved communications brought great prosperity to the farmers,[75] although, led by Lord Northwick, the landowners had opposed the railway in the 1830s,[76] in the belief that it would benefit farmers from further afield.[77] The demand for hay began to decline even before the arrival of motor traffic. In 1891 grass-keeping was said to have fallen[78] and by 1907 only 66 per cent. of grass-land was devoted to meadow as opposed to permanent pasture; from 61 per cent. in 1917 it dropped sharply to 33 per cent. in 1937. The place of hay was taken by livestock, for meat and especially for dairy produce.[79] Forty Farm in Wembley and Dove House Farm in Hatch End, where Tilbury, who invented the vehicle named after him, was a lessee, were noted for horses.[80] In the 1870s Parker's Farm in Roxeth was let to Daniel Hawkins, the 'well-known horse dealer'.[81] There were also trades dependent upon leather, especially saddlers and shoe-makers, of whom there were 55 in 1851.[82] Wheat was still important in Pinner and, for example, was predominant on Sweetman's Hall Farm in the 1880s. The wheat-straw was used for making straw hats, another local industry.[83] Dairying flourished with the growth of a suburban population. The Desiccated Milk Co. had been established by Thomas Grimwade, lessee of Sheepcote Farm, as early as 1862 and a model dairy farm was run at Sudbury by George T. Barham, chairman of the Express Dairy Co. from 1913 to 1937.[84] Pinner Park Farm changed c. 1920 from hay and livestock to dairy farming.[85]

The dominance of animal farming can be seen in the crop returns for 1907. In spite of a reduction in the meadow and pasture (10,090 a.) and of the total farming area (10,225 a.), the numbers of cows (736), other cattle (1,633), pigs (1,475), and horses (535) had risen over 20 years, although the number of

[56] By Col. Talbot of Oakington Farm: Wemb. Hist. Soc., Acc. 900/1.
[57] M.R.O., Acc. 76/364.
[58] Pinner Assoc. *The Villager*, xli.
[59] *Ec. Jnl.* lvii, 321.
[60] M.R.O., Acc. 76/55.
[61] For rye, tares, barley, and clover in the 1830s, see M.R.O., Acc. 76/2307, /2375; A. J. Garrett, 'Hist. Geog. of Upper Brent Valley' (Lond. Univ. M.A. thesis, 1935), 84.
[62] M.R.O., Acc. 76/1856; G. Bennet, *Horticultural Industry of Mdx.* 38. Market-gardens covered only 38¼ a. in 1947.
[63] *Kelly's Dir. Mdx.* (1906); Brent Town Hall, Wembley U.D.C., Min. Bk. i. (1894–7), 84.
[64] M.R.O., Acc. 76/364. Hay had covered 76 per cent. c. 1830 but by 1861 the farm had expanded from 230 a. to 341 a.: Acc. 76/1359; Acc. 643, 2nd deposit, survey of Northwick's estate (1806).
[65] M.R.O., Acc. 76/372.   [66] Ibid. /379.
[67] Harrow Cent. Ref. Libr., Sales Partics. i. This excludes acreage under wood (almost as much as arable).
[68] Christ Church MS. Estates 47/449.
[69] M.R.O., Acc. 76/24.
[70] M.R.O., Acc. 507/33.
[71] M.R.O., Acc. 76/1921.

[72] M.R.O., Acc. 590/4. The figures exclude Pinner, the area with most arable.
[73] Except where otherwise indicated, figures are from agricultural rets.: M.A.F. 68/136 (1867), /1105 (1887), /2245 (1907), /2815 (1917), /3827 (1937), /4021 (1942), /4465 (1954). Until 1892 returns were from occupiers of more than 5 a., thereafter from those of more than one acre: J. T. Coppock, 'Agricultural Rets. as a source of Local History', *Amateur Historian*, iv (2), 49–55.
[74] In 1828 Quilton referred to Tuesday as 'hay market day' (M.R.O., Acc. 76/1768), but there is no indication that the market was in Harrow.
[75] Bull, 'Changing Landscape', 110.
[76] M.R.O., Acc. 76/2307, /2289.
[77] Christ Church MS. Estates 47/328.
[78] Ibid. /696v, /698v.
[79] Pigot, *Lond. Dir.* (1826), 448–9; Robson, *Dir. of Home Cnties.* (1839); *P.O. Dir. of Six Cnties.* (1845); *Home Cnties. Dir.* (1851); *Kelly's Dirs. Mdx.* (1866, 1886, 1906, 1917).
[80] See p. 213.   [81] M.R.O., Acc. 507/34.
[82] H.O., 107/1700.
[83] Pinner Assoc. *The Villager*, xliv.
[84] Elsley, *Wembley*, 166; *Harrow Gaz.* June 1862, Mar. 1866.
[85] Pinner Assoc. *The Villager*, xlviii.

sheep (2,589) had again dropped. Apart from one acre of rye, there were no cereals, and only 30 a. were under vegetables, although fruit and orchards had increased to 48 a. and fodder crops to 81 a. By 1917 the spread of building had left only 8,596 a. of farming land, of which 8,426 a. were meadow and pasture, 20 a. heath, and 23 a. clover or artificial grass. Other fodder crops covered 31 a. The density of animals was still high: 625 cows, 1,019 other cattle, 927 pigs, 475 horses, and 3,604 sheep. There was a slight diversification with 9 a. of autumn wheat and 3 a. of oats, 85 a. of vegetables and 74 a. of fruit. The spread of fruit and vegetables was probably due to the allotments encouraged during the First World War.[86]

Many farms disappeared with the enormous expansion of suburban building. In 1907 there were 206 farms, of which 66 were in Wembley and 61 in Pinner. Five consisted of more than 300 a., 56 of from 50 to 300 a., 89 of between 5 and 50 a., and 50 less than 5 a.; only 12 per cent. of the farming land was owned by the farmer. By 1937 there were returns for 56 farms, of which only 9 were in Wembley, where 56 farmers had made returns in 1917. Where in 1917 there had been 10 farms of more than 100 a., in 1937 there was only one. Of 2,143 a. of farming land in 1937,[87] 2,073 a. were under grass; in addition 334 a. of heath-land were used for rough grazing. Fodder crops were reduced to $7\frac{1}{4}$ a.; there were no cereals but 44 a. of vegetables and 15 a. of fruit.

In 1942, during the Second World War and the 'dig for victory' campaign, there were returns for 53 farms involving 2,505 a. Grass covered 1,863 a. (74 per cent.), while another 320 a. were heath-land. The density of animals was greater than ever (251 cows, 483 cattle, 1,361 sheep, 681 pigs, 158 horses, and 3,961 poultry), and 117 a. of arable land were under fodder crops. For the first time since the early 19th century a considerable area supported cereals: 164 a. of wheat, 83 a. of oats, and 91 a. of mixed cereals. There were 164 a. of vegetables and 5 a. of flax, but only 12 a. under fruit. Many of the vegetables were grown on allotments, of which there were 5,905 plots in Harrow U.D. in 1942.[88] In 1954 there were still 149 a. of barley, 142 a. of wheat, and 88 a. of oats. Only 1,626 a., 69 per cent. of the total 2,342 a.[89] of farming land, was under grass, although there were 215 a. of clover and 7 a. of other fodder crops. Pigs (1,948) and poultry (9,955) reached a record number, but the numbers of all the other animals had fallen. There were 57 a. of vegetables and 40 a. of fruit. Heath-land covered 137 a.

By 1967 most of the land under cereals had reverted to grass, since the soil had proved too wet. At Pinner Park Farm, farmed by Hall & Sons, the entire 230 a. produced grass to support 240 Friesian cows.[90] The surrounding residential district formed a market for milk produced there and at Kenton Lane Farm. Pigs and cattle (40 Friesian cows and 40 heifers and calves) were kept at Harrow School's farm, horses, cows, sheep, and fowl at Oxhey Lane Farm in north Pinner, and horses and 120 Jersey cows at Pinner Wood Farm.[91] Of the old demesne farms, only Copse (formerly Weald Copse) Farm (210 a.), which had been sold to the former lessees, the Blackwell family, in 1895, survived. It passed to new management in 1947, and in 1967 it specialized in pigs and sheep for meat, and summer cattle for beef and milk.[92] No farms remained in Wembley, and the farm-house of Hundred Elms Farm had been absorbed by the United Dairies bottling station.[93] By 1937 only 123 people were employed in agriculture, a number which rose to 158 in 1942 but had dropped to 136 in 1954.

INDUSTRY. Charcoal burning[94] gave rise to two 'Colliers Lanes'.[95] There was a weaver in Harrow in 1436,[96] and there were several shoemakers, cordwainers, and weavers by the end of the 17th century, when Harrow boys were often apprenticed in London.[97] The only other industry recorded before the modern period was brick-making. Although there were no brickearth deposits, Claygate Beds and pebble gravel on the higher areas of Harrow Weald and Harrow-on-the-Hill provided the necessary clay and sand.[98] Chalk was being dug at Waxwell in the 17th century[99] and by the 18th century the Pinner lime-kilns were under the same management as the brick-kilns of Harrow Weald and Harrow-on-the-Hill.[1] Chalk was still being worked at Pinner in the mid 19th century.[2] A brick-maker of Harrow-on-the-Hill is recorded in 1589,[3] and the 'surreptitious getting of a great quantity of sand' to make bricks was an issue between Pitt and Gerard in the 1630s.[4] Gerard, having clay but no sand at Flambards, took over 100 loads of sand from Pitt's ground to make bricks, underselling Pitt by 6d. in the 1000. The castigation of this action as 'against the custom of the country' suggests that brick-making was already well established.

A brick-clamp in Weald Wood occurs in 1609–10,[5] when, as ten years later, it was leased to Thomas Tibbald.[6] By 1685 Matthew Bodymead owned a brick-, tile-, and lime-kiln on land leased to him on Weald Common near Bentley Corner.[7] Other members of this old Weald family maintained brickworks throughout the 18th century at Harrow Weald, Harrow-on-the-Hill, and Pinner, until at the end of the century their property passed by marriage to the Blackwells.[8] In 1767 and 1776 building bricks were the main product, but paving bricks and tiles

[86] Pinner Assoc. *The Villager*, xiii.
[87] Out of a total acreage including land formerly in Stanmore and Kingsbury parishes, see p. 245.
[88] Pinner Assoc. *The Villager*, xvi.
[89] Total acreage, 18,849 a.: *Census*, 1951.
[90] Ex inf. Hall & Sons; Pinner Assoc. *The Villager*, iv.
[91] Ex inf. Miss A. M. Pollard; *Harrow & Wealdstone Weekly Post*, 29 Nov. 1967.
[92] Ex inf. Mr. J. Rogers, Copse Farm.
[93] Ex inf. Brent Bor. Engineer and Surveyor.
[94] *Close R.* 1322–4, 95; *Cal. Lib. R.* 1226–40, 200; M.R.O., Acc. 76/2410, m. 4d.
[95] In Harrow Weald and Alperton: M.R.O., Acc. 76/2413, m. 6.
[96] Scott, *Recs. of Grammar Sch.* 9.

[97] Ibid. 61, 72 sqq.
[98] Geol. Survey Map, sheet 256 (drift).
[99] M.R.O., Acc. 76/1640–2.
[1] Ibid. /2200; Blackwell docs.
[2] Harrow Cent. Ref. Libr., Sales Partics. i (Pinner Hill, 1844).
[3] M.R.O., Acc. 76/386.
[4] Ibid. /836–7.
[5] Ibid. /222b.
[6] Ibid. /205.
[7] Ibid. /80. Possibly before 1677: Acc. 76/2006.
[8] The following section is based upon family documents on loan to the M.R.O. by the Blackwell family. For surviving buildings connected with the brick-works, see p. 185.

were also made. The Blackwells flourished throughout the 19th century, their prosperity growing with the demand for suburban villas and workmen's cottages. Several fine residences—Hillside, Brookside, and the Cedars—housed members of the family. Charles Blackwell built cottages for his own employees at the City of the Weald. In 1831 these housed 120 people, including the families of 26 brick-making labourers.[9] Twenty years later there were 52 workers at the Weald works.[10] In the 19th century the firm specialized in pots, pipes, and tiles. The Blackwells relinquished their interest in Harrow Weald in the 1890s, but brick-making continued at Clamp Hill into the next century.

By 1851 there was a tile-making works at Alperton and bricks were also made at Roxeth and Pinner. Brick-laying employed about 40 people, mostly in Harrow-on-the-Hill and Roxeth.[11] A brick-field was established by the canal in Alperton about 1848. The tile-works was owned by the Ainslie Tile-making Co., and chimney and flower-pots were still being made in 1886. It was owned by Woolleys at the end of the 19th century, when the occupier was Henry Haynes, a builder and contractor[12] who was still there in 1920.[13] The Harrow Brick & Tile Co., founded in 1884, opened a factory near the station at Wealdstone, although brick-making at Pinner ceased soon after 1886.[14]

Small factories have been opened within the old parish: a bacon, later a mattress, factory in Bessborough Road, a bicycle works (1887) in Northolt Road, Roxeth, an organ-makers at Courtfield Avenue in Greenhill, and factories for making machine-tools and engineering and household equipment in North and South Harrow.[15] Modern industry, however, is concentrated in Wealdstone, Wembley, and Alperton. The first large industrial premises at Wealdstone were erected in 1890 for the Kodak organization on a site north of Headstone Drive. The premises have been much enlarged since production began in 1891, and by 1965 they comprised over 100 buildings on a 55-acre site. About 5,500 people were then employed in research and producing film, chemicals, and other photographic accessories, but subsequent expansion has been limited by lack of space and has been diverted to new towns like Hemel Hempstead.[16]

When Wealdstone was growing in the 1890s and 1900s factories were opened by Gogswell & Harrison Ltd., gunsmiths of Ferndale Terrace, who employed 70 men in 1893,[17] Winsor & Newton Ltd. (1897), manufacturers of artists' materials, and two printing firms, David Allen Ltd., which operated there from 1896 until 1918, and G. Pulman & Sons Ltd., which opened in 1901.[18] David Allen's works were acquired by Her Majesty's Stationery Office, which in 1969 employed 1,000 people.[19] A

coffin factory, Messrs. Ingall, Parsons, Clive & Co., was opened in 1900 on a site in Mason's Avenue, directly backing upon the railway; it employed 70 men in 1900 and continued to make coffins until the beginning of the Second World War.[20] The brush-making firm of Hamilton & Co. Ltd. (established in 1811) occupied manufacturing premises in the modern Rosslyn Crescent in 1898. The company's offices and warehouses were moved to Harrow in 1951 and a further factory for the manufacture of household brooms was opened there in 1960; by 1965 the firm employed approximately 350 persons.[21] The glassworks of James Powell & Sons (Whitefriars) Ltd. was moved in 1923 from premises in the City of London, which it had occupied since 1680, to a new factory in Tudor Road. Production, which is entirely by hand, is largely of domestic glassware, thermometer tubing, and stained glass; the labour force, which has fluctuated little since 1923, was approximately 250 in 1965.[22] Bastian & Allen Ltd., electrical and mechanical engineers, began to manufacture electrode boilers in a former wooden toy factory in Ferndale Terrace in 1949; the premises were later extended and in 1965 the company employed 180 persons.[23]

Large-scale industrial development in Wembley began in the early 20th century and accelerated after the closure of the British Empire Exhibition released the buildings and site. Factories established after 1924 were chiefly for the manufacture of light engineering components and luxury goods. In 1965, 70 firms employed 6,300 people on the former exhibition site and 5 employed 6,600 people in East Lane.[24] The British Oxygen Co. opened a factory in East Lane in 1918 for the manufacture of gases and welding equipment; the premises were later much enlarged and the labour force, which was 55 in 1918, had increased to 700 by 1965.[25] The Wrigley Co. Ltd. (established in 1911) began to make chewing gum in East Lane in 1926; the company's Wembley factory employed approximately 300 persons in 1965.[26] Johnson, Matthey & Co. Ltd., refiners and fabricators of precious metals, opened research laboratories employing 24 people on a 5-acre site at the exhibition grounds in 1938. Manufacturing premises were later added and by 1965 more than 1,100 persons were employed in research and the manufacture of fine wires, electrodes, and electrical contacts in base and precious metals.[27]

The brick-works and agricultural industries[28] of Ealing Road, Alperton, had expanded by 1910[29] to include rubber and fire-proofing factories. Many factories, mainly concerned with engineering or motor cars, were opened in Ealing Road during the 1920s and 1930s.[30] By 1965 there were 31 firms employing 3,700 people.[31] The largest was the Glacier Metal Co. Ltd., which purchased the works

[9] M.R.O., D.R.O. 3/F13/3.
[10] H.O. 107/1700, *passim.*   [11] Ibid.
[12] Wemb. Hist. Soc. *Jnl.* N.S. i(8).
[13] *Kelly's Dir. Harrow* (1919–21).
[14] *Harrow Gaz.* 27 Mar. 1884; W. W. Druett, *The Stanmores and Harrow Weald,* 237; *Kelly's Dirs. Mdx.* (1886, 1906); J. Silvester, *Visible & Invisible* (pamphlet hist. of St. John's, Wembley), 17.
[15] Ex inf. Local Hist. Librarian, Harrow Cent. Ref. Libr.; *Harrow Official Guide* (n.d.).
[16] Ex inf. Kodak Ltd.
[17] *Harrow Gaz.* 18 Feb. 1893.
[18] *Harrow Official Guide* (n.d.).
[19] Ex inf. H.M.S.O.

[20] Ex inf. Local Hist. Librarian.
[21] Ex inf. Hamilton & Co. Ltd.
[22] Ex inf. Whitefriars Glass Ltd.
[23] Ex inf. Bastian & Allen Ltd.
[24] *Background to Brent,* 34.
[25] Ex inf. British Oxygen Co.
[26] Ex inf. Wrigley Co. Ltd.
[27] Ex inf. Johnson, Matthey & Co. Ltd.
[28] e.g. mushroom growers (see p. 231) and agricultural chemical works.
[29] *Kelly's Dir. Harrow* (1909–11).
[30] Ibid. (1919–21); *Kelly's Dirs. Wembley* (1930; 1937); ex inf. Rima Electric Ltd.
[31] *Background to Brent,* 34.

of the Wooler Engineering Co. Ltd. in 1923, the former Key Glass Works in 1960, and those of Crosby Valve & Engineering Co. Ltd. in 1968. By 1969 it employed 2,100 people in Alperton.[32] During the 1930s industry spread eastward from Ealing Road along Mount Pleasant and Beresford Avenue.[33] By 1965 there were 67 firms employing 5,200 people in the Beresford Avenue area.[34] Several firms which had long been established there, like Celotex Ltd. (opened 1936) and Rizla Cigarette Papers Ltd. (opened 1937),[35] moved from the area in 1969, when a new industrial estate, Northfield, was being built.[36]

SOCIAL HISTORY. Harrow was never a society composed solely of peasants and dominated by one lord, for even in the Middle Ages there were some influential residents, like the Flambards, Boyses, Bellamys, and Cheyneys. Apart from drawing rents from land, Elizabethan Londoners built houses in Middlesex 'for their recreation in the summer time and for withdrawing places in the times of common sickness'.[37] From the 17th century merchants and minor gentry increasingly lived in Harrow in addition to owning property there. By 1614 people like Master Bartholomew Cokes 'a tall young squire of Harrow o' the Hill' and Mistress Grace Wellborn 'of the same place' must have been common enough to have been recognized by Ben Jonson's audience.[38] Later in the century the Gerards and the merchant families of Claxton and Waldo dominated Harrow-on-the-Hill, Sudbury, Pinner, and Harrow Weald. The native-born Pages won a similar pre-eminence in Wembley, to be replaced in the early 19th century by the Grays, who were treated deferentially as the local squires.[39] The Copland sisters, of Sudbury Lodge, were great local benefactresses,[40] as was George T. Barham, who lived in a house on the site of Sudbury Lodge in the early 20th century.[41] Another Sudbury resident, Sir William Perkin, was active in nonconformist and social work.[42] Late-19th-century Alperton was dominated by Henry Haynes, whose brick-works provided work for almost everyone there.[43] Other villages, like Pinner and Harrow Weald, contained many 'gentlemen of wealth . . . mostly engaged in the City of London', who fought to protect Harrow Weald from the encroaching factories and terraced housing of Wealdstone.[44]

By 1826 the trade of Harrow-on-the-Hill was in a great measure dependent upon the school.[45] Harrow School also attracted new residents, especially old boys who needed to live near London. Sheridan, for example, entertained Fox and Burke at the Grove

when he was an M.P. in the 1780s.[46] There were also parents who could not always afford boarding fees. They included Anthony Trollope's mother,[47] and Mary Shelley, who in 1834 found Harrow a dull, inhospitable place.[48] In 1861 a large proportion of 'educated members of the upper classes' were in the parish because of the school.[49] Matthew Arnold and Charles Kingsley[50] were exceptional, but the Harrow schoolmasters, clergy, and booksellers, and the relatively numerous gentry and professional people, formed a cultivated, if conservative, society.

In 1826 it was claimed that 'families of the first distinction and opulence' lived in and around Harrow, but this was an exaggeration based on the presence of the marquesses of Abercorn.[51] The Norths in the 16th and the Rushouts from the end of the 18th century, who belonged to the nobility, were seldom resident. Lord Northwick once entertained Lord Nelson at Harrow,[52] but the most brilliant society was to be found at Bentley Priory under John James Hamilton, Marquess of Abercorn (d. 1818), an exotic figure who provided the model for Sheridan's Don Whiskerandos.[53] Between 1788, when he bought Bentley Priory, and his death, Abercorn entertained politicians such as Pitt, Canning, Liverpool, Sidmouth, and Wellington, writers like Wordsworth, Moore, Rogers, Scott, and Campbell, and distinguished members of the theatrical profession like Mrs. Siddons and John Kemble. Abercorn was succeeded by his grandson, a minor, whose step-father, Lord Aberdeen, lived at Bentley Priory. Under Aberdeen, Colonial Secretary 1834–5 and leader of the Conservative Free Trade Society, Bentley became a Conservative Party headquarters. Its last distinguished occupant was Queen Adelaide, who leased the house in 1846[54] and died there three years later.[55]

In spite of royal protection for Lanfranc's deer,[56] John in 1206 ordered ten greyhounds and three attendants to be kept at Harrow for his own use.[57] After the disappearance of the forest cover, the deer were maintained at Pinner Park partly to provide hunting for the archbishop, but after Pinner Park's conversion to farm-land only smaller game were hunted. Richard Layton, when Rector of Harrow, sent partridges killed by his hawk to Thomas Cromwell in 1537.[58] Sir Gilbert Gerard was accused in 1638 of hawking for partridges and pheasants.[59] In 1533 tenants were forbidden to ensnare those birds.[60] Snaring hares before St. George's Day with nets or 'harpipes' had been similarly forbidden in 1512.[61] A rabbit-warren was kept at Sudbury at the beginning of the 17th century.[62]

The Queen's hounds hunted over Pinner in the

[32] Ex inf. Glacier Metal Co. Ltd.
[33] *Kelly's Dir. Wembley* (1937).
[34] *Background to Brent*, 34.
[35] Ex inf. Rizla Cigarette Papers Ltd.
[36] Ex inf. Northfield Industrial Estate.
[37] B.M. Harl. MS. 570, f. 13v. The printed edn. is incomplete: J. Norden, *Speculum Britanniae*, pt. i (1593).
[38] Ben Jonson, *Bartholomew Fair*.
[39] Elsley, *Wembley*, 171.
[40] Wemb. Hist. Soc., Acc. 900/10; *Wembley News*, 22 Jan. 1953. See below, pp. 247, 257, 266.
[41] Elsley, *Wembley*, 166.
[42] See pp. 195, 262.
[43] Wemb. Hist. Soc., Acc. 907/13. See p. 233.
[44] Harrow Bor., North Star, Hendon R.D.C., Wealdstone extension inquiry, 1912.
[45] Pigot, *Lond. Dir.* (1826), 448–9.
[46] Druett, *Harrow*, 143; W. Sichel, *Sheridan*, i. 260.

[47] A. Trollope, *Autobiography*.
[48] Druett, *Harrow*, 164.
[49] M.R.O., Acc. 76/101.
[50] Druett, *Harrow*, 171.
[51] Pigot, *Lond. Dir.* (1826), 448–9.
[52] Druett, *Weald*, 158.
[53] In *The Critic*.
[54] Druett, *Weald*, 130 sqq., 160.
[55] *D.N.B.*
[56] See p. 222.
[57] *Rot. Litt. Claus.* (Rec. Com.), i. 65.
[58] W. D. Bushell, 'The Harrow Rectors', *Harrow Octocent. Tracts*, xi. 27.
[59] M.R.O., Acc. 76/829.
[60] Ware, *Pinner*, 151.
[61] W. O. Hewlett, 'Hist. of the manors of Harrow', *Harrow Sch.* ed. E. W. Howson and G. T. Warner, 1–10.
[62] M.R.O., Acc. 76/205; Acc. 794/2. See p. 227.

19th century[63] and between the two world wars the Household Brigade met twice a year with drag hounds at Pinner Park. The Pinner, later the Middlesex, Drag Hunt was formed in 1932.[64] In the 19th century coursing took place on Daniel Hill's land in north Pinner and prize-fighting and illegal cock-fighting also flourished,[65] while cock-shying had been carried on at Pinner in the 17th and 18th centuries.[66] Horse-breeding by farmers in the 19th century led to the establishment of racecourses. After the failure of one behind Sir William Perkin's house, the site was used by Perkin for religious meetings.[67] Race meetings held by the lessee of New College farm under the auspices of the licensed victuallers of London provoked an outcry in 1867 from the Vicar of Harrow, who alleged that they attracted 'the very off-scourings of the lowest London stables', and begged that racing should be forbidden when the lease fell in.[68] A proposal to open a racecourse at Wembley Park, after the collapse of the pleasure grounds scheme, was defeated by local opposition.[69] The best known racecourse, at Headstone, had to be suppressed in 1899 after a riot started by Londoners.[70] In 1925 a donkey derby was started in the grounds of Pinner Grove on the initiative of the jockey, Steve Donaghue.[71]

There were shooting butts in the corner of Roxeth Hill and London Road[72] by 1392.[73] During the 18th century the shooting by the Harrow schoolboys for the silver arrow attracted large crowds, but these included unruly elements from London and at the end of the century the contests were replaced by cricket.[74] A 'tenys court' is recorded in 1574,[75] but the most popular gentlemen's sport in the 17th century seems to have been bowling. In the 1630s bowls were probably played at Sudbury, just south of Flambards,[76] and there were also bowling greens in the late 17th century at Pinner Hill and in the north of Harrow Weald.[77] The cricket played by Harrow School drew crowds from miles around. Pinner Green and Rickmansworth Cricket Club existed by 1790[78] and Wembley Cricket Club was founded in 1860.[79] Barrow Point Cricket Club, which played on Judge William Barber's land, had been founded by 1888[80] and Pinner United Club was founded in 1895.[81] By 1928 there were 17 cricket clubs in Wembley.[82] A football club was formed in Pinner in 1892[83] and by 1928 there were 13 football clubs in Wembley.[84] Wembley Stadium, built as part of the British Empire Exhibition with under-cover accommodation for 100,000, was first used for the Football Association cup final of 1923. From this date Wembley became a household name until it achieved international fame as the site of the Olympic Games in 1948 and of the World Cup Final in 1966. In 1934 the Empire Pool and Sports Arena was built for indoor sports. Wembley has thus become one of the national centres for spectator sports.[85] There was a golf club in Wembley in 1896[86] and in 1968 there were golf courses at Grim's Dyke in Harrow Weald (opened in 1910) and at Pinner Hill.[87] Sudbury Golf Course, in spite of its name, lies outside the boundary of ancient Harrow and modern Brent alike. By 1968 there were clubs for almost every kind of sporting activity and over 2,000 a. of park and recreation ground.[88]

Mummers performed at Pinner at Christmas until the beginning of the 20th century,[89] and a pleasure fair developed out of Pinner's medieval fair. By the early 19th century wrestling, racing, 'gingling', climbing a greasy pole, and 'other manly and old English sports' accompanied the sale of cattle and hay.[90] The fair, as a pleasure fair only, flourished in 1968,[91] despite attempts to close it in 1829[92] and 1893[93] as a source of immorality. Presentments for breaking the assize of ale indicate many medieval inns and alehouses.[94] In 1517 presentments were made for permitting dicing within houses, and three 'common dice-players' were fined in 1521.[95] In 1577 alehouses were forbidden to open on Sundays or feast days during divine service, in 1610 anyone found drunk in an alehouse had to pay a fine of 5s., and a year later it was forbidden to serve drinks after 9.0 p.m., except to travellers.[96] In 1671 the licence of Richard King of Harrow-on-the-Hill was suppressed, supposedly because he could earn a living by other means but in reality because he entertained local servants 'to the great damage and disturbance of the neighbourhood'.[97]

In 1722 there were 22 victuallers in Harrow parish[98] and in 1751 there were 19 inns in Harrow and 6 in Pinner.[99] In 1787 Pinner vestry resolved to enforce a royal proclamation against frequenting alehouses during divine service and against unseemly behaviour and opening shops on Sundays,[1] and by 1800 the number of alehouses had dropped to 18 in Harrow and 5 in Pinner.[2] In 1827, when 'gross misconduct' was alleged against the landlord of the

[63] Pinner Assoc. *The Villager*, ix.
[64] Ibid. xlviii.
[65] Ibid. xli.
[66] Ware, *Pinner*, 87; Druett, *Harrow*, 79.
[67] *Wembley News*, 12 Feb. 1953.
[68] New College MS. 1381.
[69] Elsley, *Wembley*, 146 sqq. See above, p. 200.
[70] Druett, *Pinner*, 188; Ware, *Pinner*, 118.
[71] Pinner Assoc. *The Villager*, v.
[72] M.R.O., Acc. 643, 2nd deposit, Messeder map A.
[73] M.R.O., Acc. 76/2413, m. 38d.
[74] *V.C.H. Mdx.* i, illustration facing p. 300.
[75] *Harrow Sch.* ed. Howson and Warner, 6.
[76] M.R.O., Acc. 76/826, /854; Acc. 643, 2nd deposit, Messeder map A. See p. 227.
[77] M.R.O., Acc. 76/707.
[78] Pinner Assoc. *The Villager*, xxvii.
[79] Wemb. Hist. Soc., Acc. 637/16.
[80] Pinner Assoc. *The Villager*, lii.
[81] Ibid. xxvii.
[82] *Wembley Year Bk.* (1928).
[83] Pinner Assoc. *The Villager*, xxxi.
[84] *Wembley Year Bk.* (1928).
[85] Elsley, *Wembley*, 146 sqq.; Bor. of Wembley, *Handbk.*

(n.d.).
[86] Brent Town Hall, Wembley U.D.C., Min. Bk. i. (1894–7), 296.
[87] Ware, *Pinner*, 146; Pinner Assoc. *The Villager*, xxviii.
[88] London Bor. of Brent, *Official Guide* [1968]; *Background to Brent* (Rep. by Dept. of Planning & Research, Lond. Bor. of Brent, 1967); Lond. Bor. of Harrow, *Official Guide* [1968].
[89] Ware, *Pinner*, 141.
[90] Ibid. 97–99.
[91] Ex inf. Miss A. M. Pollard.
[92] M.R.O., Acc. 76/1804.
[93] Pinner Assoc. *The Villager*, xiv.
[94] M.R.O., Acc. 76/2413, m. 6; Acc. 974/1, mm. 1 sqq.
[95] *Harrow Sch.* ed. Howson and Warner, 1–10.
[96] Ibid. 6–7.
[97] N.R.A. and Harrow U.D.C., *Festival Exhib. of Docs.* (1951), 52.
[98] M.R.O., L.V. 3/94.
[99] Ibid. 7/1.
[1] M.R.O., D.R.O. 8/C1/1.
[2] M.R.O., L.V. 10/88.

'Bell', Major William Abbs of Pinner Hall pressed for the inn-keeper's removal.[3] The magistrates were asked to reduce the number of public houses in Pinner and it was proposed that no relief should be given to people who refused to attend divine service twice on Sundays. At the time there were five public houses in Pinner and a population of between 1,076 and 1,270, giving a ratio of *c.* 235 people to each public house.[4] Harrow, with 17 public houses and between 3,017 and 3,861 inhabitants, had a ratio of *c.* 200. In Pinner an exceptionally large vestry agreed, by 47 votes to 19, to rescind the call made four months earlier for the dismissal of the 'Bell's' landlord, but the temperance party was firmly in control in the 1830s, when the depression probably helped it. In 1830 constables were required to lay complaints against drunkards and against landlords or retailers who permitted drunkenness or who opened outside legal hours. A special committee was to visit ale-houses, and strict regard was to be paid to the habits of applicants for relief. A year later all shops were to shut on Sundays except during the summer, when, because of the influx of hay-makers, they could stay open until 9.0 p.m.[5]

By 1851, when the population of Pinner had risen to 1,331, there were still only five public houses, giving a ratio of 266 people to each public house. In Harrow, whose population had risen to 4,951, there were 36 inns and beershops, a ratio of 137 people to each public house or beershop.[6] In 1860 a petition claimed that Harrow fair was obsolete and 'productive of . . . serious injury to the morals of the lower classes',[7] and in 1872 the fair was abolished.[8] By 1873 there were 27 inns and 27 beershops in Harrow and 8 inns and 7 beershops in Pinner.[9] The population in 1871 was 8,537 for Harrow and 2,383 for Pinner, giving a ratio of 158 people to each inn and beershop in Harrow and the same proportion in Pinner. In 1873 the Vicar of St. John's, Wembley, complained that 'beer is the curse of the place',[10] and a census taken by the Harrow Temperance Association, founded in 1876, estimated that there was one drinking house to every 228 persons.[11] At first the association rented a room in the workmen's hall which had been erected *c.* 1861 in Crown Street, and offered coffee and literature. In 1879 it converted the room into the Royal Oak coffee tavern, and in 1883, when there were 245 adult and 250 junior members, established a coffee cart at the end of College Road to serve employees of the railway works. By 1885, however, trade was so bad that the committee felt free to close

the tavern, which from 1890 became St. Mary's temperance house.[12] A similar coffee tavern, the 'Cocoa Tree', was opened in Pinner in 1878 by Judge William Barber.[13]

Clubs founded by the workmen themselves often replaced the small benefit and friendly societies of the 1830s and 1840s.[14] Sometimes the initiative came from the upper and middle classes, who hoped to mix entertainment with instruction. One of the earliest public halls was founded in 1864 by the Copland sisters at Sudbury, where working men and mechanics over 16 were provided with a library and non-alcoholic drinks. The members subscribed 1*s.* a quarter and the hall was to be managed by a committee.[15] In 1930 the hall was replaced by the Wembley institute.[16] A parish hall in Pinner was used for concerts and penny readings from 1866 to 1897.[17] In addition to the workmen's hall in Harrow-on-the-Hill, opened *c.* 1861, there was a lecture hall in Roxeth, opened in 1869,[18] and a public hall and assembly rooms for 400 people at Harrow-on-the-Hill, opened in 1874.[19] In Greenhill there was a workmen's club from the 1860s and a Victoria Hall from 1888. The hall was enlarged in 1895 to include a reading room, library, and football and cricket facilities, and by *c.* 1898 it had a membership of about 200.[20] St. Mary's church leased a mission house from 1885 to be used for religious and social meetings.[21] Under the patronage of the middle and upper classes the Harrow Young Men's Society was founded in 1851 to provide evening classes and lectures and a library of 'instructive' books for the benefit of young workmen. It had a building by 1855 and 201 members by 1859, though few of them were labourers. Numbers then declined, although they rose again with a shift of emphasis from instruction to entertainment. The Society lasted until at least 1903.[22] Other clubs included a young men's institute in Pinner from 1866 to 1895,[23] a young men's literary institute at Wembley in 1886,[24] St. Mary's Social Club from 1903 to 1905 for men attending the Sunday afternoon services,[25] and a men's institute at Roxeth from 1909.[26]

Harrow Literary Institute, founded by 1851,[27] acquired a site in the High Street in 1864.[28] Its successor, Harrow Fifty Club, which survived from 1899 until 1914, was a conversational club restricted to elected members.[29] A poetical society existed in Harrow Weald in 1878[30] and St. John's Debating and Literary Society in Wembley from 1906.[31] There were horticultural societies in Harrow from 1853,[32] in Pinner from 1890,[33] in Wembley from 1893,[34] and

[3] M.R.O., D.R.O. 8/C1/1.
[4] M.R.O., L.V. 28–30; *Census,* 1821–31.
[5] M.R.O., D.R.O. 8/C1/1.
[6] H.O. 107/1700.
[7] M.R.O., Acc. 643, 2nd deposit.
[8] *Lond. Gaz.* 1872, p. 3207.
[9] M.R.O., P.S. G/H5/1.
[10] Christ Church MS. Estates 47/638.
[11] The following section is based upon reports and accounts of the society: M.R.O., D.R.O. 3/H3/2–4.
[12] M.R.O., D.R.O. 3/H3/5.
[13] J. W. Perry, *Panorama of Pinner Village* (pamphlet, 1947); Pinner Assoc. *The Villager,* xvi
[14] M.R.O., M.C./R1–2.
[15] *Sudbury,* ed. H. Egan, 19; Wemb. Hist. Soc., Acc. 900/10.
[16] Wemb. Hist. Soc., Acc. 907/134.
[17] M.R.O., E.M.C. 50/1/1; Ware, *Pinner,* 150; Pinner Assoc. *The Villager,* ii.
[18] *Kelly's Dir. Mdx.* (1886).
[19] Ibid. (1906).

[20] *Handbk. for use of Visitors to Harrow-on-Hill* (1898); G. Rowles, *Onward* (pamphlet hist. of St. John's, Greenhill); *Opening of New Victoria Hall, 9 Nov. 1963* (pamphlet).
[21] M.R.O., D.R.O. 3/H5/1–2.
[22] Ibid. /H2/1, /H4/1.
[23] Ware, *Pinner,* 223.
[24] *Kelly's Dir. Mdx.* (1886).
[25] M.R.O., D.R.O. 3/H4/1.
[26] *Kelly's Dir. Mdx.* (1917).
[27] *Home Cnties. Dir.* (1851).
[28] M.R.O., E.M.C. 50/5.
[29] Sir H. H. Lunn, *Chapters from my Life,* 229.
[30] *Contributions to the Harrow Weald Poetical Soc. for 1878–9.*
[31] J. Silvester, *Visible & Invisible.*
[32] Harrow Horticultural & Rose Soc. *Centenary Shows, 1853–1953.*
[33] Ware, *Pinner,* 102.
[34] Silvester, *Visible & Invisible,* 26.

at Wembley Hill from 1921.[35] A Liberal club was founded in Harrow in 1906[36] and a Conservative club at the 'Cocoa Tree' in Pinner after 1931.[37] Wembley Choral Society was founded in the 1880s but most musical and dramatic clubs started between the world wars.[38] Examples include the Vagabonds (1920), Pinner and Hatch End Operatic Society (1922), the Pinner Players (1936), and the Pinner Orchestra (1939).[39] After demands for a theatre the Coliseum was opened in 1940 in Station Road, Harrow, where it remained until its closure in 1955.[40] The Coliseum had itself replaced a cinema which had been opened on the site in 1922.[41] A cinematograph hall in Harrow High Street was rebuilt in 1911 to hold 480 people.[42] Nine cinemas had been closed down by 1964[43] but 7 remained in 1968.[44] Rapid development between the wars stimulated interest in the past. The Pinner Association was founded in 1932 to protect rural scenery and to secure good local government. In Wembley the local history society, which was founded in 1952, has collected archive material and surveyed buildings due for demolition, although attempts to preserve buildings have usually been unsuccessful. A similar society for Harrow was founded in 1932. Both Harrow and Brent have arts councils assisted by the local authority.[45]

The first local newspaper, the *Harrow Gazette*, was founded in 1855. A second weekly, the *Wealdstone, Wembley, and Harrow Observer*, more usually known as the *Harrow Observer*, was founded in 1895, and in 1912 the two amalgamated as the *Harrow Observer and Gazette*. The *Harrow Press* existed from 1892 to 1896. The *Harrow Post* had been founded by 1956. The *Wembley Observer and Gazette* was founded in 1912 and the *Wembley News* in 1923. All these newspapers were published in 1968.[46]

LOCAL GOVERNMENT AND PUBLIC SERVICES.

MANORIAL GOVERNMENT. The archbishop's jurisdiction over his tenants probably remained undefined[47] until Cnut in 1020 granted 'sake and soke, grithbreach, hamsocn, forestall, infangenetheof, and flymenafyrmth' over his own men and over as many thegns as the king allowed him.[48] These liberties were confirmed by William I, who added toll and team,[49] and by subsequent kings.[50] Henry II added geld and danegeld, hidage, *murdrum* fines, works of bridges, castles, parks, and closes, aid for the army, wardpenny, bloodwite, childwite, and exemption for

the archbishop's demesnes and villeinage from the hundred courts.[51] In 1202 John granted amercements of men from the archbishop's fees.[52] Return of writs, granted in 1235,[53] was duly noted in the hundred rolls, together with the observation that the township (*villata*) of Harrow and the other tenants of the archbishop had been subtracted from the county and hundred.[54]

In 1300 Archbishop Winchelsey threatened the sheriff with excommunication for freeing distresses made by his Harrow bailiffs and withdrawing pleas from the Harrow court to the county court.[55] A grant in 1314 made it clear that the archbishop was to have the fines and forfeitures of all his men and tenants, wherever they might reside.[56] Subsequent royal grants and confirmations, made in 1335,[57] 1382,[58] 1399,[59] and 1463,[60] set out the franchises and fiscal privileges in full to obviate the plea of non-user and to remove ambiguity. Despite a reiterated injunction against royal officials usurping the duties of the bailiff of the liberty and permission in 1463 for the archbishop to appoint constables for his own hundreds, the emphasis throughout was upon fiscal privileges. The archbishop's men could be tried in the royal courts but any fines or confiscated chattels had to be handed over. The 1399 grant even included the profits of attainder or Praemunire, eleven years after the property of one of the archbishop's foremost Harrow vassals, Sir Nicholas Brembre, had been forfeited to the Crown.[61] In 1378 the archbishop's Harrow and Hayes tenants were exempted from contributing to the expenses of the parliamentary knights of the shire.[62]

The surrender of Harrow by Cranmer in 1545 and the grant to Sir Edward North in 1547 included all the manorial privileges.[63] The liberty was by now equivalent to a grant of green wax, the right to fines and amercements exacted from tenants in the royal courts and paid to the Exchequer. A series of quietus rolls from 1617 to 1676[64] shows that repayments were claimed from the King's Bench, Common Pleas, Sessions of the Peace, and Clerk of the Market, usually amounting to £3–£12 a year. From 1665 the 'issues before the Barons', presumably in the Exchequer Court, were added, which in 1666 were as much as £115. Although the rolls show no lapse in the payments, the proprietors of Harrow manor in 1667 claimed all the archiepiscopal liberties in Harrow, quoting the medieval charters.[65] The claim was allowed on the basis of the grant to Sir Edward North, but the last quietus roll dates from 1676 and in 1680–1 the lords of several Middlesex liberties,

[35] Wemb. Hist. Soc., Acc. 299.
[36] *Kelly's Dir. Mdx.* (1906).
[37] Perry, *Panorama of Pinner Village.*
[38] Silvester, *Visible & Invisible*, 23.
[39] Pinner Assoc. *The Villager*, xxv, xxviii, xxx.
[40] Ibid. ii.
[41] Ibid. ix, lv.
[42] *Kelly's Dir. Harrow* (1911–12).
[43] Mdx. Local Hist. Council, *Bulletin*, xviii.
[44] i.e. in the ancient parish of Harrow: London Bor. of Harrow, *Official Guide* [1968]; London Bor. of Brent, *Official Guide* [1968].
[45] Pinner Assoc. *The Villager*, iv.
[46] *Willing's Press Guide* (1966); Wemb. Hist. Soc., *Guide to Wembley in Hist. Exhib.* (1953); London Bor. of Harrow, *Official Guide* [1968]; London Bor. of Brent, *Official Guide* [1968]; ex. inf. Harrow Post.
[47] *Anglo-Saxon Writs*, ed. F. E. Harmer, 181–2, referring simply to 'mund'.
[48] Ibid. 183–4; Du Boulay, *Lordship of Cant.* 280.

[49] *Cartae Antiquae* (P.R.S. N.S. xvii), 97.
[50] Ibid. 91, 99–100; *Cal. Chart. R. 1257–1300*, 178; 1327–41, 345–8.
[51] Ibid. 1327–41, 345–6.
[52] *Cartae Antiquae* (P.R.S. N.S. xvii), 85.
[53] *Cal. Close, 1234–7*, 117, 149.
[54] *Rot. Hund.* (Rec. Com.), i. 417, 432.
[55] *Cal. City of Lond. Letter Bk. C*, 80; *Reg. Winchelsey* (Cant. & York Soc. li), 396–7.
[56] *Cal. Chart. R. 1300–26*, 236.
[57] Ibid. 1327–41, 345–8.
[58] Ibid. 1341–1417, 278.
[59] Ibid. 384–6.
[60] Ibid. 1427–1516, 192 sqq.
[61] *Year Bk. 1387–8* (Ames Foundation), 268 sqq.
[62] *Cal. Close, 1377–81*, 150.
[63] W. D. Bushell, 'The Alienation of the Harrow manors *Harrow Octocent. Tracts*, xiii. 17.
[64] M.R.O., Acc. 76/219, /665,/1986–99, /2193.
[65] Ibid. /1883.

A HISTORY OF MIDDLESEX

including Harrow, had 'for many years past' been deprived of 'divers fines' in the King's Bench.[66] These had been paid to the court's coroner and thence to the Exchequer, and the Clerk of the Pipe had refused the claims of the bailiffs of the liberties. This time the Attorney General must have disallowed the claims, since no more green wax payments are recorded. Of the archiepiscopal liberties all that was left, apart from the ordinary manorial jurisdiction, was the right to take chattels, waifs, and estrays, which had always been accounted for by the bailiff of the liberty and not with other perquisites of court by the beadle.[67] As late as 1812 Lord Northwick claimed the chattels of a tenant who had been executed as a felon.[68]

The bailiwick or liberty covered a wider area than Harrow itself. Tenants by knight service in Hayes[69] and Berrick (Oxon.)[70] held from the bailiwick of Harrow and owed suit of court there. Perquisites are recorded in 1236–7[71] and courts at Harrow and Hayes, held by bailiffs or by a serjeant, in 1242;[72] a view of frankpledge is listed in 1273–4.[73] The earliest extant court rolls for the archiepiscopal manor of Harrow or Sudbury date from 1315. The rolls are complete from 1378 to 1721 and the court books from 1687 to 1913.[74]

A court was held at Weald Wood in 1316[75] and another at Roxeth in 1529[76] but most courts were probably held at the principal demesne manor of Sudbury, which from the 14th century was also called Sudbury Court.[77] The most important court, the leet and view of frankpledge, was usually held in the spring, and a second general court was held in the autumn. Other courts baron were held during the year, originally every three weeks.[78] The annual number of courts, sometimes 9 (1384, 1395) or 10 (1394) in the 14th century, was gradually reduced to one or two by the 17th century. Thus an early-18th-century custumal listed suit at two general courts, at Easter and Michaelmas, as an obligation of head tenants.[79] From the 14th century suitors could pay 2d. for each non-appearance or 1s. for relaxation of suit for a year. Whether the customary under-setters owed suit of court was one of the points at issue in the 17th and 18th centuries.[80]

Most customary offences were presented at the view of frankpledge, when the ale-tasters also made presentments. Criminal jurisdiction was exercised in the early views. From 1514 constables were appointed but invariably they reported that all was well.[81] The courts exercised the franchisal rights of the archbishop[82] until 1631. Thereafter, perhaps

because a new lord coincided with a new steward,[83] the only presentments were for default of suit of court. Business became entirely concerned with property transactions, while all other jurisdiction passed to the county and national courts. In 1660 two men who carried off some of Sir Gilbert Gerard's wood were convicted at the sessions of the peace, although they were to be punished at the whipping-post in Harrow.[84]

The chief early officials were the reeves and beadles, head tenants chosen at the Michaelmas general court by the homage. Reeves received 50s. and beadles 10s. a year. The reeve collected all the rents and presented them for audit; the beadle collected fines, amercements, and other perquisites of the court.[85] Presentments were made according to tithings, organized by hamlets and represented by the chief pledges or headboroughs. In 1316 Pinner, the largest hamlet, had at least three headboroughs, Harrow Weald and Roxeth at least two, Sudbury and Wembley two each, and Preston and Kenton one each.[86] Alperton, Uxendon,[87] Greenhill,[88] and Hatch End[89] were sometimes separate tithings. By the 16th century tithings had crystallized into six, for Pinner, Harrow Weald, Roxeth, Sudbury, Kenton and Preston, and Wembley and Alperton. Each had headboroughs, one or two ale-tasters or ale-conners, and a constable, all generally elected at the Easter view of frankpledge. Ale-tasters rarely made presentments in the mid 17th century and appear to have been dropped soon afterwards. Constables and headboroughs, one of each for each of the six tithings, continued to be appointed until 1896.[90]

The charter of 1233–40 did not specify perquisites of court although it mentioned 'homages, pannages, and other services of the church' among the appurtenances of the rectory.[91] The court rolls of Rectory or Harrow-on-the-Hill manor, with a few gaps, are complete from 1349 until 1678; court books are complete from 1629 to 1896.[92] Courts at Harrow-on-the-Hill were probably held at the rectory itself. The homage could then dine at the lord's expense,[93] and a lease of part of the 'rectory house' in 1682 provided for entertainment for the lord and tenants at two rent dinners and one audit dinner.[94] In the 14th century there was often only one court a year, a view of frankpledge and court baron, held in the winter or spring. In the 15th century there were more courts (as many as seven in 1483), when the view could be at any time, but after c. 1493 there were only one or two, the view in the spring and a general court or court baron at any other time. After Sudbury and Rectory

[66] E 372/525.
[67] e.g. M.R.O., Acc. 76/222a.
[68] Ibid. /270, /713.
[69] Bk. of Fees, 899.
[70] Cal. Inq. p.m. i, p. 250.
[71] Lambeth Palace, Estate MS. 1193.
[72] Cal. Lib. R. 1240–5, 131.
[73] B.M. Add. MS. 29794, m. 1d.
[74] All except two are in the M.R.O., Acc. 76/2410–426; 2433–4; Acc. 410/6, m. 11; Acc. 507/1–11; Acc. 643(1); Acc. 974, vols. II–VI. Those for 1507–10 are at Lambeth Palace, Estate MSS. 477–8.
[75] M.R.O., Acc. 76/2410, m. 4.
[76] Ibid. /2421, m. 59. The context makes it unlikely that this court belonged to Roxeth manor.
[77] e.g. 'the court of Sudbury': M.R.O., Acc. 76/2412, m. 5d (1337).
[78] M.R.O., Acc. 1052, ff. 2–6.
[79] Bodl. MS. Gough Mdx. 4, ff. 31–40.
[80] See p. 227.
[81] M.R.O., Acc. 76/2421, m. 6.
[82] Ibid. /216.
[83] M.R.O., Acc. 974/IV, m. 50 (457). Transition from Lord North and his steward, Simon Rewse, to George Pitt and a new steward, Percival Staple.
[84] Mdx. Cnty. Recs. iii. 282.
[85] Bodl. MS. Gough Mdx. 4, ff. 31–40.
[86] M.R.O., Acc. 76/2410, m. 3.
[87] Ibid. /2412, m. 6 (1334–7).
[88] Ibid. /2413, m. 19 (1385).
[89] Ibid. /2421, m. 58 (1531).
[90] M.R.O., Acc. 507/9.
[91] Harrow Octocent. Tracts, ix. 15.
[92] M.R.O., Acc. 76/217, /2416, m. 63, /2417, mm. 94, 102, 104, 110, 114, 118,/2427–30; Acc. 507/14–20; Acc. 643(2); Acc. 974,/vols. I–III.
[93] Bodl. MS. Gough Mdx. 4, ff. 31–40.
[94] M.R.O., Acc. 76/202. The lease makes it clear that this refers to the rectory- and not to the vicarage-house.

manors passed into the same hands, they were to some extent worked as a unit. Usually only one court a year, the view of frankpledge, was held for the Rectory manor after the mid 16th century, nearly always on the day after the Sudbury view. Occasionally a court baron, but never a general court, was also held, again usually one day after a Sudbury court. Thus the 18th-century custumal mentioned one general court of the Rectory manor, held at Easter.[95]

As with Sudbury court, the fine for non-attendance was 2d. The Rectory court rolls mention several offences not recorded at Sudbury: two butchers were presented in 1507 for selling expensive and unhealthy meat and a tawer was presented for selling shoes which were insufficiently tanned.[96] In the 14th century there were many presentments for violence and failure to perform feudal services. Development after the mid 16th century followed that of the main manor. One head tenant was elected by the homage to act as reeve and beadle, for 6s. 8d. a year.[97] A woman was elected in 1507.[98] There were usually two headboroughs, two ale-tasters, and a constable. Two constables are mentioned as early as 1368[99] and constables presented regularly at the view after 1419.[1]

The Prioress of Kilburn had a court on her Wembley manor[2] and courts baron were held by Wembley manor at the end of the 18th century.[3] There is one roll of a court baron of the manor of Uxendon, held in 1608.[4]

PARISH GOVERNMENT: HARROW. For Harrow, churchwardens' accounts and rate-books[5] date from 1729, with gaps for the years 1768–72. The overseers' accounts are complete from 1739 until 1831, except for 1798–9, and there are poor-rate books from 1684 until 1933.[6] Accounts of the surveyors of the highway date from 1768 to 1831 and highway-rate books from 1745 to 1868.[7] Vestry minutes begin in 1704 with a gap between 1757 and 1793.[8] Parish officers, were, however, active long before these dates. Two keepers and guardians of the goods of the parish church of St. Mary are mentioned in 1467.[9] There was a parish clerk by 1521–2,[10] and two churchwardens signed the parish registers as early as 1559.[11] By 1622 Pinner had its own parish officers.

A vestry was mentioned in 1701.[12] The annual number of vestry meetings[13] gradually rose from five or six in the first decade of the 18th century to twenty in 1829. By the early 20th century the vestry met every three or five years. The last meeting was held in 1924,[14] by which date the vestry had been superseded by the parish church council, formed in 1911.[15] Meetings were held at first in inns and later usually in the chancel and, after 1849,[16] in the vestry of the church. The vicar usually presided and attendance varied from six or seven in 1704 to 22 in May 1724. Most of the business concerned outrelief or the workhouse. The vestry authorized rates for the church, the poor, and the highways. It kept a firm control over the parish officers. In 1822, for example, they were forbidden to incur any expenses in eating and drinking upon parish business without previous permission.

The vicar and the vestry each elected a churchwarden. One churchwarden[17] dealt with Harrow Town, Roxeth, Sudbury, Wembley, and Alperton, and the other with Harrow Weald, Greenhill, Kenton, and Preston. Each collected the church-rate, usually 2d. to 6d. in the £, in the 18th century, and spent it in a variety of ways, on the church, on travelling, on killing vermin—pole-cats, for example, were still being caught in the 1820s—and on the salary of the parish clerk. The churchwardens continued to pay the salaries of parish officials into the 20th century.

The surveyors of the highway, first mentioned in 1718, were elected annually by the vestry. The office tended to run in respectable families, notably the Greenhills, Hills, and Blackwells.[18] In 1745 there were three surveyors and three parochial wards: Harrow Town and Roxeth; Sudbury, Wembley, and Alperton; and Harrow Weald, Greenhill, Kenton, and Preston. By 1750 a fourth surveyor had been appointed, the third ward being divided into Weald and Greenhill, and Kenton and Preston.[19] A highway-rate, levied by the vestry, is first mentioned in 1722 when it was 1d. in the £.[20] By 1780 it had been raised to 6d. which thereafter remained the usual rate.[21] From 1745 the rate was fixed retrospectively at the Quarter Sessions. After finding the highway surveyors' accounts unsatisfactory in 1823, the vestry appointed a salaried man to superintend the highways and act as an assistant overseer.[22]

From 1684[23] to 1896[24] three overseers of the poor were appointed by the vestry, one for Harrow Town, Roxeth, and Sudbury, one for Harrow Weald and Greenhill, and one for Wembley, Alperton, Kenton, and Preston.[25] A salaried assistant overseer appointed in 1832 had to live within ¼ mile of Harrow Town, to take his instructions from the vestry and the overseers, to interview applicants for relief, to employ

95 Bodl. MS. Gough Mdx. 4, ff. 31–40.
96 M.R.O., Acc. 974/I, m. 77.
97 M.R.O., Acc. 76/222a; Bodl. MS. Gough Mdx. 4, ff. 31–40.   98 M.R.O., Acc. 974/I, m. 78.
99 M.R.O., Acc. 76/2427, m. 4.
1 M.R.O., Acc. 974/I, m. 43.
2 C.P. 25(1)/147/16; Valor Eccl. (Rec. Com.), i. 432.
3 M.R.O., Acc. 812/Box 1, documents dated 15 May 1781 and 19 June 1795.
4 M.R.O., Acc. 276/9/5.
5 M.R.O., D.R.O. 3/B2/1–15.
6 M.R.O., LA.HW., Harrow Overseers' Accts. (8 vols.) and Poor-rate Bks.
7 M.R.O., LA.HW., Harrow Surveyors' Accts. (8 vols.) and Rate Bks. (11 vols.).
8 M.R.O., D.R.O. 3/C1/1–10.
9 W. O. Hewlett, The Church House, Harrow-on-the-Hill (pamphlet).
10 M.R.O., Acc. 974/I, m. 95(92).
11 Registers of St. Mary's Ch., Harrow-on-the-Hill, i. 75.
12 M.R.O., LA.HW., Harrow Poor-rate Bk. 1684–1707.

13 Unless otherwise stated, this paragraph is based upon the Vestry Min. Bks.: M.R.O., D.R.O. 3/C1/1–10.
14 M.R.O., D.R.O. 3/C1/9.
15 Harrow Par. Ch., D1/1–5.
16 W. D. Bushell, 'Intro. to the Arch. & Hist. of par. ch.', Harrow Octocent. Tracts, 13.
17 This section is based upon the Churchwardens' Acct. and Rate Bks.: M.R.O., D.R.O. 3/B2/1–15.
18 Barbara Jordan, 'The Roads round Harrow in the late 18th and 19th centuries' (TS. penes Harrow Cent. Ref. Libr.), 4.
19 M.R.O., LA.HW., Harrow Highway-rate Bk. i (1745–68).
20 Jordan, 'Roads round Harrow', 27; M.R.O., D.R.O. 3/C1/1, f. 83.
21 M.R.O., LA.HW., Harrow Highway-rate Bks. i, ii.
22 M.R.O., D.R.O. 3/C1/4.
23 See below. The rate may have been levied earlier.
24 M.R.O., D.R.O. 3/C1/8.
25 M.R.O., LA.HW., Harrow Overseers' Accts. and Poor-rate Bks. 1684–1834.

and pay labourers, and to collect rates.[26] For a short period from 1744[27] two stewards were appointed each month by the vestry, mainly to deal with the poor, and they alone signed most of the vestry minutes. The unpaid stewards, bearing an increasingly heavy burden, were apparently replaced, probably after 1754, by a master of the workhouse, who farmed the inmates and, by the 1820s, all the poor in the parish. His annual payment, £590 in 1795 and £1,400 in 1821, varied with the number of inmates and the general level of prices; in 1829 the rate was 4s. 6d. a head a week. The farmer had to provide for the poor at the workhouse at his own expense, to provide for the poor of the parish and, sometimes, to teach the workhouse children. In return he could benefit from the labour of the workhouse inmates.[28] A salaried medical officer was appointed as 'surgeon, apothecary, and midwife to the poor' in 1810.[29]

The five Harrow constables,[30] though appointed by the manor court, received their instructions and, in 1761, their 'new painted staves' from the high constable,[31] but were primarily parish officers who received expenses from the overseers.[32] Some of their equipment, including in 1824 a 'new pair of handcuffs',[33] belonged to the parish. The beadle, a salaried official until 1876,[34] became more completely a parish official than the constable, being elected by the vestry and occasionally combining his office with that of sexton.[35] He too received expenses, mainly for serving summonses and attending magistrates' courts.[36] He also received his uniform, in 1852 a blue cloth waistcoat and a 'Paris hat'.[37] Most police action was executed by the constable but the beadle provided straw for the cage in 1825[38] and was instructed to apprehend beggars in 1820.[39]

By the 1850s and 1860s salaried parish officials included the parish clerk, beadle, collector, lamplighter, organ blower, organist, bell-ringers, vestry clerk, and sexton.[40] Salaries were still being paid to the last four in 1921.[41] A woman who was elected sexton in 1866 had to find an assistant, her duties being mainly confined to pew opening.[42]

Vagrancy in the 16th and 17th centuries was dealt with by the county and manorial courts. In 1559 it was proclaimed in the Harrow court that no unmarried or masterless man or woman was to remain in the parish for more than 14 days on pain of a fine

of £1.[43] In 1574 six vagrants taken at Harrow-on-the-Hill were sentenced at the sessions to be flogged and burnt on the right ear.[44] By the 18th century much of the responsibility had passed to the parish vestry and its officers. A girl who had 'eloped' from her mistress in 1744 was brought back by force[45] and servants who entered clandestinely from other parishes were sent back.[46] Many settlement certificates survive,[47] but the number of removals decreased until by 1834 there was only one.[48]

During the late 17th and early 18th centuries poor relief took the form of monthly allowances, usually in money but occasionally in clothes or fuel.[49] Poverty was alleviated by remitting or reducing rents[50] and by providing rent-free parish houses for poor widows.[51] These 'poor houses' survived until the vestry's decision to sell them in 1845.[52] The church-house also served as a poor-house.[53] After an unusually large meeting in 1724 a workhouse was built in West Street, opposite the Crown Inn, with material from the old church-house.[54] Even under the farming-out system the parish officers exercised considerable control. In 1822 the churchwardens and overseers laid down in detail the food to be given to each workhouse inmate: a breakfast of milk porridge, broth, or water gruel, dinner and supper of 2 oz. of butter or 4 oz. of cheese with bread, made of 'good second flour', and 'wholesome butcher's meat' for three days' and pea soup for one day's dinner. Each person was allowed 3 pints of beer a day.[55] In 1776 [the workhouse] was said to accommodate 60 persons.[56] The average number rose gradually from 32 in 1758 to 43 in 1770 and 1780, and 49 in 1821, but the figures conceal seasonal variations, for in March 1819 there were 105 inmates. In summer and late autumn, when winter wheat was sown, numbers were low, while in winter and spring unemployment caused a large intake.[57]

Outdoor relief continued alongside the indoor relief provided by the workhouse. Money allowances increased from 19 cases in 1724[58] to 69 in 1821.[59] In 1795 the average allowance was 1s. 6d. a week but with rising prices this increased and in 1800 an allowance was made of 1s. 6d. a week for every child under 14.[60] In October 1821, compared with 35 people in the workhouse, there were 69 receiving outdoor relief of from 1s. to 8s. a week.[61] In 1834, out of £2,689 spent on the poor,[62] £1,607 went on

[26] M.R.O., D.R.O. 3/C1/4.
[27] Until 1754 at least: M.R.O., D.R.O. 3/C1/1. The minute bk. for 1757–93 does not survive.
[28] Cf. agreement made in 1822 between the vestry and the master: M.R.O., D.R.O. 3/F7/1.
[29] K. G. Charles, 'Hist. of Poor Law Admin. in Harrow-on-the-Hill, 1743–1900' (TS. penes Harrow Cent. Ref. Libr.), 1; M.R.O., D.R.O. 3/F7/1.
[30] i.e. one each for Weald and Greenhill, Kenton and Preston, Wembley and Alperton, Sudbury and Roxeth (M.R.O., D.R.O. 3/E1/1; Acc. /507/3 p. 63), appointed by Sudbury manor and one for Harrow-on-the-Hill, appointed by Rectory manor: M.R.O., Acc. 76/1480.
[31] M.R.O., LA.HW., Harrow Poor-rate Bk. 1722–67.
[32] e.g. M.R.O., LA.HW., Harrow Overseers' Accts. v (1800–13), ff. 1 sqq.
[33] M.R.O., D.R.O. 3/C1/4.
[34] Ibid. 3/B2/6.
[35] e.g. in 1744: ibid. 3/C1/1.
[36] Ibid. 3/C3/1; M.R.O., LA.HW., Harrow Overseers' Accts. v., ff. 1 sqq.
[37] M.R.O., D.R.O. 3/C3/1.   [38] Ibid.
[39] Ibid. 3/C1/3.
[40] Ibid. 3/B2/6, /15.
[41] Ibid. 3/B2/6.

[42] Ibid. 3/C1/7.
[43] M.R.O., Acc. 974/II, m. 1 (126).
[44] Mdx. Cnty. Recs. i. 87.
[45] M.R.O., D.R.O. 3/C1/1, pp. 225–30.
[46] Ibid. pp. 220–4.
[47] M.R.O., D.R.O. 3/F3/1–2.
[48] Charles, 'Poor Law Admin.', 7.
[49] M.R.O., LA.HW., Harrow Poor-rate Bks. and Overseers' Accts. 1684–1767; M.R.O., D.R.O. 3/C1/1.
[50] e.g. in 1553: M.R.O., Acc. 76/222a; in 1681: ibid. /707.
[51] Ibid. /2019.
[52] Charles, 'Poor Law Admin.', 3.
[53] Hewlett, Church House.
[54] M.R.O., D.R.O., 3/C1/1, f. 88.
[55] Ibid. 3/F1/1.
[56] Rep. Sel. Cttee. on Rets. by Overseers of Poor, 1776, pp. 396–7.
[57] M.R.O., LA.HW., Harrow Overseers' Accts. 1739–84; M.R.O., D.R.O. 3/C1/4.
[58] M.R.O., D.R.O. 3/C1/1.
[59] Ibid. 3/C1/4.
[60] Charles, 'Poor Law Admin.', 4.
[61] M.R.O., D.R.O. 3/C1/4.
[62] Ibid. 3/F1/3.

outdoor relief, consisting of £680 paid to widows and bastards, £424 on casual relief, usually of the sick, and £503 on labour on the roads.[63]

To deal with the increased number of unemployed during the agricultural depression, the vestry reduced outdoor relief and increased parish work, on the roads and at the mill or picking oakum.[64] Able-bodied paupers had repaired the highway in the mid 18th century but their wages are not recorded.[65] In 1817 15 male paupers were paid 1s. 6d. to 2s. a day for such work.[66] In 1831 there was a scheme to send single men from the workhouse to parishioners who agreed to employ and presumably pay them at a rate fixed by the vestry. From December 1831 out-relief was steadily reduced from 7s. a week (already reduced) for a man and his wife, 8s. for a family with one child, 9s. for two children, 10s. for three children, and 11s. for five or more children, until by 1835 a man and wife received 5s. a week, a family with one child 6s., with two to four children 7s., and with five or more children 8s.[67] Paupers with dogs were refused all relief.[68]

Apart from charities and exceptional measures[69] the burden of poor relief was normally borne by the poor-rate.[70] From 1684[71] to 1722 twice yearly rates, usually at 5d. in the £, raised £200–£300 each year. From 1723 a 6d. rate was usual, the number of rates varying from one in 1760, which raised £172, to three in 1740, which raised £521. From 1800 to 1826 there were usually five or six rates, which raised about £1,660–£2,040 a year, and the number increased from seven in 1827 to ten in 1831 and 1832, finally bringing the total raised to £3,331. This was during the depression which affected the rate-paying farmers, as well as the labourers.[72] Protests reduced the number of rates to nine in 1833 and 1834, making the amount raised in the year before the Poor Law Union £2,954. The 1834 Act confined outdoor relief to the sick and old. The able-bodied poor were offered work in the workhouse or in the parish, at wages fixed by the guardians. Harrow therefore spent less in casual relief and labour on the roads in 1835 than in 1834; only widows' pensions cost more.[73] Under the union there was a decline from nine 6d. rates in 1835 to five in 1837 and 1839.[74] In 1834–5 Harrow raised £2,888, of which £2,272 was spent on the poor; a year later £2,002 was raised and £1,655 was spent. A sharp increase in 1841 was due to the opening of the workhouse at Redhill and to the large numbers applying for outdoor relief. The

poor-rate in Harrow was raised from 2s. 3d. to 3s. in 1841, when the corresponding expenditure mounted from £1,960 to £2,820.[75] Expenditure, £2,309 in 1844, continued to rise until a new assessment of Harrow was made in 1851.[76]

PARISH GOVERNMENT: PINNER. Surviving parish records for Pinner include churchwardens' accounts from 1622, with gaps from 1757 to 1810,[77] a poor-rate book from 1773 to 1781,[78] and complete vestry minutes from 1787 to 1925.[79] Pinner, however, conducted its own administration long before it became a separate ecclesiastical parish in 1766.[80] From 1622 it had chapelwardens, overseers, and a parish clerk.[81] In 1699 Pinner asserted its 'immemorable immunity from [Harrow's] church rate',[82] and c. 1702–7 it was said to keep its own poor.[83] The vestry existed by 1773.[84] In the 18th and early 19th centuries there were usually one to four meetings a year but by the 1830s there were six to eight. In April 1827 resolutions were signed by one man only, Major William Abbs; in August there was an attendance of 66 to rescind them.[85] In the early 20th century the vestry met once a year, the last meeting being in 1925.[86] Meetings seem to have been held, at least at first, in the church[87] and generally were presided over by the vicar. In 1810 a chimney, new ceiling, and window were built for the vestry room, 'it being before a wretched hole'.[88]

There were two chapel- or churchwardens, who in 1696 were entitled 'the churchwardens of the poor'.[89] Poor relief was entered in their accounts[90] until 1773[91] and they continued to pay small sums until 1815,[92] after which they were more strictly confined to church affairs. Surveyors of the highway were mentioned in 1821.[93] In 1788 the two overseers of the poor were to serve for two years.[94] An assistant overseer was appointed at £12 a year in 1825 and £21 in 1829.[95]

From 1773 and probably earlier the vestry instructed the constable, although he was appointed at Sudbury manor court.[96] The constable had to execute special instructions, such as those against fireworks (1818), drunkenness (1787 and 1830), or the violation of the Sabbath (1831),[97] but his main function was as a police official. Prisoners were kept in the cage, which from c. 1775 to 1825 stood near the site of Pinner Metropolitan Police Station. It was moved and repaired in 1825, and in 1831 was ordered to be taken to the workhouse premises.[98] There were

[63] Ibid. /2.
[64] Ibid. 3/C1/4; /F7/1. In 1829 £236 was paid by the farmer of the workhouse to labourers at the mill: M.R.O., LA.HW., Harrow Labour Bk. 1829–30.
[65] e.g. 1744: M.R.O., D.R.O. 3/C1/1, pp. 220–4; 5 Mar. 1770: M.R.O., LA. HW., Harrow Overseers' Accts. 1769–84.
[66] Charles, 'Poor Law Admin.', 4.
[67] M.R.O., D.R.O. 3/C1/4–5; 3/C1/1. Charles, 'Poor Law Admin.', App. A–C.
[68] In 1834: M.R.O., D.R.O. 3/C1/5.
[69] In 1794 the churchwardens paid out £1 11s. to several poor people during severe weather; M.R.O., D.R.O. 8/B2/3.
[70] This paragraph is based upon M.R.O., LA.HW., Harrow Poor-rate Bks. 1684–1834. Annual figures are for the accounting year, Apr.–Apr.
[71] See below. The rate may have been levied earlier.
[72] See p. 230.
[73] M.R.O., D.R.O. 3/F1/2.
[74] Ibid. /3. A new survey was being prepared in 1838.
[75] M.R.O., D.R.O. 3/F1/3.
[76] Ibid. 3/F2/5.

[77] Pinner Church B1/1; M.R.O., D.R.O. 8/B1/2–3.
[78] M.R.O., D.R.O. 8/D1/1.
[79] Ibid. 8/C1/1–3.
[80] See p. 256.
[81] M.R.O., E.M.C. 120/B1/1; Ware, Pinner, 148–9, 172.
[82] See p. 256.
[83] Bodl. MS. Rawl. B 389B, f. 31.
[84] M.R.O., D.R.O. 8/D1/1, and see Ware, Pinner, 63.
[85] M.R.O., D.R.O. 8/C1/1.
[86] Ibid. 8/C1/3.
[87] e.g. in 1788: ibid.
[88] M.R.O., D.R.O. 8/C1/1.
[89] Ware, Pinner, 81.
[90] Ibid. 172–3.
[91] M.R.O., D.R.O. 8/D1/1.
[92] Ibid. 8/B1/2.
[93] Ibid. 8/C1/1.
[94] Ibid.
[95] Ibid.
[96] See above.
[97] M.R.O., D.R.O. 8/C1/1.
[98] Ibid.; Ware, Pinner, 171–2, 218.

also stocks, at the corner of High Street and Bridge Street.[99]

Other parish officials included a salaried sexton, who in the late 17th century was nominated by the churchwardens and later elected by the vestry,[1] and a salaried parish clerk, who was nominated by the vicar.[2] In 1801 'because of the great increase in the number of rates and other business', a vestry clerk was appointed at £10 a year,[3] and in 1810 a pound-keeper was appointed and allowed to take fees for each beast impounded.[4] A medical officer for the poor was paid 11 guineas a year in 1799 and 35 guineas in 1831.[5] In 1860 the churchwardens paid an organist, parish clerk, collector, and vestry clerk. By 1880 a pew-opener had replaced the last two;[6] there was a verger by 1892.[7]

A 'workhouse' in Pinner, with accommodation for 30 people, mentioned in 1776,[8] was probably a poor-house. The decision to erect a workhouse was taken in 1789 and the proposal 'that the first story shall re-main the same height as it now is' may mean that it was built on to the old poor-house.[9] The workhouse stood beside the River Pinn, near the George Inn. It was converted into tenements in 1858, sold to the Metropolitan Railway Co. in 1886, and demolished soon afterwards.[10] The practice of contracting out the poor for a fixed sum, in 1791 £240 a year and in 1818 £600, alternated with that of appointing masters of the workhouse, whose annual salary was £30 in 1794, £40 in 1825, and £13 in 1832.[11]

Since the 17th century Pinner had provided varied outdoor relief to its own poor and to those passing through.[12] In 1789, for example, it paid for a burial and for beer at the funeral, for a tin kettle, and 6d. to Mrs. Begg 'for altering Shuffle's girl's stays'.[13] Even general poverty was usually relieved in kind:[14] in 1799 a quartern loaf each week was allowed for each child to parishioners earning less than 10s. a week; pea soup was distributed to 95 families during the winter of 1799–1800; cheap coal was sold to the poor in 1806; bread was distributed or sold at a low price in 1822 and 1825; drink, a butt of old port in 1821 and two dozen pint bottles of wine in 1826, was bought for the sick; vaccination was another benefit. Money allowances were also made, especially in the 19th century; in 1821 one man was given as much as £1 1s. because he had a large family. In September 1817, 25 people were receiving outdoor relief. In 1800 all the able-bodied poor were to work at the order of the parish officers or the master of the workhouse and, of every 1s. earned, 1d. was to be returned to adults and ½d. to children. In 1812 those

in the workhouse were to pick oakum, while a list of able-bodied paupers receiving relief was to be pinned to the church door and the overseers were to con-tract with local farmers to employ them. Bad weather and economic depression caused unusually large numbers of unemployed in 1817, 1823, and the 1830s. Temporary work was given in road-making and after 1827 it was usual in winter to send paupers to work for parishioners at a fixed wage. In October 1832[15] all rate-payers were to employ and pay labourers or to make up the balance in rates. In December wages were raised from 8s. to 10s. a week, and one labourer was assigned to every £50 rental of house, 50 a. of meadow, or 30 a. of arable. Relief was refused to those with dogs as early as 1826 and a year later to boys who did not attend divine service twice each Sunday.

Poor relief was probably financed in the 17th century out of the church-rate, but from 1773 at the latest a poor-rate, normally 6d. and occasionally 3d. in the £, was levied between one and four times a year. One 6d. rate raised £92 in 1773 and £97 in 1780.[16] In 1776 £272 was raised, probably by three 6d. rates, of which £245 was spent on relief.[17] Pinner's reaction to the depression was not, like Harrow's, to increase the number of rates, but to raise the amount: in June 1831 it was 9d. and in September it was raised to 1s.[18] In 1835 £820 was raised and £773 spent on relief. Although only £487 was spent in 1836,[19] expenditure was £900 in 1844[20] and in 1845 Pinner joined with Harrow vestry in requesting the Poor Law Commissioners to investi-gate the heavy cost of the Hendon Union.[21]

LOCAL GOVERNMENT AFTER 1834. In 1835[22] Harrow and Pinner became constituent parishes of Hendon Union, created by the Poor Law Amend-ment Act of 1834. Parish overseers were subor-dinated to the union officials, who included not only the guardians, of whom four were elected by Harrow[23] and two by Pinner[24] every spring, but a salaried officer, responsible for outdoor relief. There was tension between the parish and union and a separate relieving officer for Harrow was appointed in 1838 following complaints by the vicar that visits to Harrow were infrequent. The Harrow workhouse was too small to be used as a union workhouse or as an infirmary, as proposed by the guardians, and after 1840 it was occupied by children only. Although Pinner workhouse was used to house paupers until 1858,[25] the main union workhouse was in Hendon.

Harrow Local Board of Health was created in

[99] N.R.A. and Harrow U.D.C. *Festival Exhib. of Docs.* (1951), item 81; Pinner Assoc. *The Villager*, xxxix, xl.
[1] Ware, *Pinner*, 81.
[2] Ibid. 148.
[3] M.R.O., D.R.O. 8/C1/1.
[4] Ibid. 4d. for each hoofed animal, 2d. for each pig, and 5d. for every score of sheep or geese.
[5] M.R.O., D.R.O. 8/C1/1.
[6] Ibid. 8/B1/2.
[7] Ibid. 8/B1/3.
[8] *Rep. Sel. Cttee. on Rets. by Overseers of Poor*, 1776, pp. 396–7.
[9] Grant in 1790 of 3 roods of waste 'where the poor-house now is' to the chwdns.: M.R.O., Acc. 76/1109.
[10] Ware, *Pinner*, 223; M.R.O., Acc. 310(3); Harrow Bor., North Star, Plan of workhouse, 1836; Pinner Assoc. *The Villager*, xlv.
[11] M.R.O., D.R.O. 8/C1/1.
[12] e.g. in 1730, 90 travellers recently released from

Algerian slavery: Ware, *Pinner*, 172.
[13] Ware, *Pinner*, 173.
[14] Except where otherwise stated, the remainder of this section is based upon the vestry minutes, 1787–1845: M.R.O., D.R.O. 8/C1/1.
[15] Adopting Act 2 & 3 Wm. IV, c. 96.
[16] M.R.O., D.R.O. 8/D1/1 for figures 1773–81.
[17] *Rep. Sel. Cttee. on Rets. by Overseers of Poor*, 1776, pp. 396–7.
[18] *Rep. Poor Law Com.* H.C. 595, pp. 212–13 (1836 Sess. II), xxv.
[19] Ibid.
[20] M.R.O., D.R.O. 3/F1/3.
[21] Ibid. 8/C1/1.
[22] M.R.O., D.R.O. 3/F1/3. Except where otherwise stated, this and the subsequent paragraphs are based upon Charles, 'Poor Law Admin.', 9 sqq.
[23] M.R.O., D.R.O. 3/C1/5.
[24] Ibid. 8/C1/1.
[25] See above.

1850. Outbreaks of cholera in Hog Lane in 1847 and 1848 resulted, at the instigation of Harrow School and its surgeon, Dr. Thomas Hewlett, in an inquiry[26] which revealed the insanitary conditions of the most populous part of the parish and the need for such a board.[27] It first met under the chairmanship of the vicar at Dr. Hewlett's house and later at other private houses or at the Savings Bank. The board administered about 1,000 a., comprising the whole of Harrow-on-the-Hill, most of Greenhill and Roxeth, and north Sudbury.[28] A clerk was appointed at £20 a year and a surveyor and inspector of nuisances at £40 a year. By 1870 there were committees for sanitation, sewage irrigation, slaughter-houses, gas, street-watering, street-naming, and the fire engine. A medical officer of health was being paid in 1877, and during the 1880s and 1890s committees were appointed to deal with roads and foot-paths, plans and works, finance and rate defaulters, legal questions and by-laws, boundaries, and allot-ments. A mortuary, public baths, and a steam roller were also provided. The board was financed by general and special district rates, and money was raised by the sale of crops from the sewage farms.

The River Pinn, which flowed through the centre of Pinner village, repeatedly flooded and harboured rubbish. A nuisance removal committee was set up in 1855, with a salaried inspector,[29] but in 1861 the vestry decided not to reappoint it, probably for financial reasons.[30] The duties of the committee passed to Hendon Union Board of Guardians. A nuisance removal committee for the part of Harrow parish outside Harrow Local Board District flourished from 1855 to 1865, when it relinquished its duties to Hendon Union Board.[31] The board's sanitary functions passed to Hendon Rural Sanitary Authority, which was set up under the Public Health Act of 1872.[32]

Until 1863 the responsibility for roads was divided among several authorities: the Metropolitan Roads Commission,[33] Harrow Local Board of Health, Harrow highway parish, which had four surveyors, and Pinner parish, which had one surveyor. In 1863 the last two were absorbed into Edgware Highway Board, created by the Highway Act of that year.[34] The board's district consisted of parishes in Hendon Union, each of which appointed waywardens in place of the surveyors: Harrow highway parish had two

and Pinner one.[35] Pinner vestry claimed that its roads were excellently maintained at moderate expense and in 1866 it asked for the separation of Pinner from Edgware Highway District,[36] but the application failed and costs steadily increased, especially after turnpike trusts were transferred from the Metro-politan Roads Commission to Edgware Highway Board and to Harrow Local Board[37] in 1872.[38] Complaints to the waywardens of the board were often still referred to the vestry.[39] After 1879 charges were apportioned among the parishes according to their rateable value[40] and rates were collected in Harrow by the assistant overseer instead of by the waywardens.[41] Harrow and Pinner contributed over 70 per cent. of the district's rates.[42]

Edgware Highway Board was superseded by Hendon Rural Sanitary Authority in 1879.[43] Harrow vestry accordingly reorganized its rates into cate-gories: the poor-rate, which embraced police and school board rates; general expenses (highway and establishment charges); and special expenses of the rural sanitary authority. Two assistant overseers were appointed, one for Harrow Local Board of Health and the other for Harrow Highway District. The first collected the poor-rate and executed all the orders of the Local Government Board and the Board of Guardians of Hendon Union. The second collected the poor-rate and all separate rates for Hendon Rural Sanitary Authority, and executed their orders and those of the Hendon guardians. Each assistant overseer received £2 10s. for every £100 collected.[44]

Under the Burials Act of 1852,[45] burial boards were set up in the parishes of Pinner in 1856,[46] St. John's, Wembley, in 1883,[47] St. Mary's, Harrow-on-the-Hill, in 1884,[48] Holy Trinity, Wealdstone, in 1888,[49] and Christ Church, Roxeth, in 1899.[50] Harrow vestry appointed a boundary committee,[51] which recommended in 1869 that perambulations should take place every 7 years or, where there was much building, every two to three years. Under the Lighting and Watching Act of 1833[52] lighting com-mittees were set up in Wealdstone in 1889,[53] and in St. John's, Wembley in 1890.[54]

Under the Local Government Act of 1894[55] Harrow Local Board of Health District became Harrow-on-the-Hill U.D. The parish of Holy Trinity, Wealdstone, became Wealdstone U.D.,[56]

[26] Jordan, 'Roads round Harrow', 8, 69; Elsley, *Wembley*, 184–5.
[27] This paragraph is based upon Local Bd. of Health minute books and letter books *penes* Harrow Bor., High St., and ledger books in M.R.O., LA.HW., Harrow. For the work of the board, see p. 248.
[28] Copy of 1850 map in Harrow Bor., North Star, Box H/HUDC, boundaries 1927–30. List of streets named in 1871 in Harrow Bor., High St., Local Bd. of Health, Min. Bk. (1870–5), 52–53.
[29] M.R.O., D.R.O. 8/C1/2.
[30] Ibid. 8/C1/3.
[31] Ibid. 3/C1/6–7.
[32] 35 & 36 Vic. c. 79.
[33] See p. 172.
[34] 25 & 26 Vic. c. 61.
[35] M.R.O., D.R.O. 3/C1/7; 8/C1/2; Jordan, 'Roads round Harrow', 10, 72.
[36] M.R.O., D.R.O. 8/C1/2, /3.
[37] Metropolis Rds. Act, 35 & 36 Vic. c. 49.
[38] M.R.O., LA.HW., Edgware Highways Bd., Parish Ledger (1863–79), 72; Act 33 & 34 Vic. c. 73; Elsley, article in *Wembley News*, 1 Jan. 1953.
[39] e.g. in 1878 and 1879 at Harrow: M.R.O., D.R.O. 3/C1/8, ff. 158, 177.

[40] M.R.O., LA.HW., Edgware Highway Dist., Ledger (1879–80).
[41] M.R.O., D.R.O. 3/C1/8.
[42] M.R.O., LA.HW., Edgware Highway Dist., Ledger (1879–80), 2, 5, 29.
[43] Wemb. Hist. Soc., Acc. 713.
[44] M.R.O., D.R.O. 3/C1/8.
[45] 16 & 17 Vic. c. 134.
[46] M.R.O., D.R.O. 8/C1/2.
[47] M.R.O., LA.HW., Wembley Burial Bd., Rate Bks. (1885–94); Brent Town Hall, Wembley Burial Bd., Min Bks. ii (1889–95); Wembley Hist. Soc. *Jnl.* i(4).
[48] M.R.O., LA.HW., Harrow Burial Bd., Min. Bks. (1884–1934); Ledgers and Rate Bks. (1887–1926).
[49] M.R.O., D.R.O. 8/C1/3.
[50] M.R.O., LA.HW., Roxeth Burial Bd., Min Bks. (1899–1934); Ledger (1900–23); Rate Bks. (1911–26).
[51] M.R.O., D.R.O. 3/C1/8.
[52] 3 & 4 Wm. IV. c. 90.
[53] M.R.O., LA.HW., Wealdstone Lighting Cttee., Rate Bk. (1889).
[54] Brent Town Hall, Wembley Lighting Cttee., Min. Bk. (1890–4).
[55] 56 & 57 Vic. c. 73.
[56] Local Govt. Bd. Order 31845.

an area of 2,072 a. To the south, Wembley, Sudbury, Alperton, Preston, south Kenton, and Kingsbury parish became Wembley U.D.[57] Hendon R.D. was formed out of those parishes in Hendon Rural Sanitary Authority which had not been converted into urban districts, the two largest being Pinner (3,791 a.) and Harrow Weald (2,384 a.). By an Act of 1899 Harrow Weald Common was to be administered by the Harrow Weald conservators, appointed by the four new district councils and by the parish councils of Pinner and Harrow Weald.[58] Lack of space induced authorities to press for more land.[59] Harrow-on-the-Hill U.D., which was developed earliest, successfully applied in 1895 for an additional 1,100 a., which gave it the whole of Roxeth and most of Greenhill, bringing its total acreage to 2,197.[60] A small part of northern Greenhill was surrendered to Wealdstone U.D. Between 1895 and 1914 Wealdstone developed most rapidly of all and therefore often sought a realignment of boundaries. Initially it had hoped to include Harrow Weald, but the opposition of prominent residents proved too powerful. A minor adjustment at Hindes Road in 1902[61] left Harrow-on-the-Hill with 2,028 a., Wealdstone with 1,061 a., Pinner with 2,782 a., and Harrow Weald with 2,373 a. In 1912 a petition by Wealdstone for an extra 2,795 a., mostly in Harrow Weald, was accepted by the county council but disallowed by the Local Government Board,[62] and various schemes for more land were unsuccessfully presented in 1926.[63] Separation from Kingsbury[64] left Wembley with 4,564 a., and in 1928 Harrow-on-the-Hill U.D. gained an extra 101 a., part of Mount Park estate in Northolt parish.[65]

Harrow-on-the-Hill U.D.C. at first comprised nine members.[66] At the beginning of the 20th century its nine committees were reduced to three, arranged according to the permanent officers, the clerk, surveyor, and inspector, and in 1903 the number of councillors was increased to 12.[67] By 1910 there were still three standing committees, as well as a by-law committee and special committees for Lowlands and Harrow recreation grounds. In the last years of its existence, 1933–4, the council still worked through committees attached to the clerk and surveyor, but separate committees for housing, public health, and maternity and infant welfare had replaced the inspector's committee; there were also

six other committees. Income rose from £6,023 in 1895–6 to £17,900 in 1910 and £37,615 in 1928, while expenditure mounted from £6,981 to £16,184, and then to £50,814.[68]

Wealdstone U.D.C., which consisted of 12 councillors, first met in the boys' school at Wealdstone.[69] In 1895 a sanitary inspector and building inspector were appointed and four committees were formed. By 1896 there were five more committees, a medical officer of health, and a collector. The committees had been reduced to three by 1901 and a new one, appointed in that year, had been absorbed by 1910. In 1933 there were eight standing committees. Income for the first year was £1,400 and total expenditure £2,805. By 1910 the figures were £9,505 and £11,958, and by 1928 £28,547 and £38,018.[70]

The 12 members of Wembley U.D.C. first met in the workmen's hall in Wembley.[71] Three standing committees had been increased to six by 1896. Officers included a clerk, a medical officer of health, a treasurer, and one man to act as engineer, highway surveyor, inspector of nuisances, and building surveyor. Parish overseers of the poor, 4 for Wembley and 3 for Kingsbury, were appointed early in 1895, and an assistant overseer was appointed soon afterwards. The early meetings were often turbulent,[72] mainly because Kingsbury, with only three councillors, alleged that all the revenue was spent on Wembley. Premises on the corner of Harrow Road and St. John's Road were leased as offices in 1896, but the heavy expense of the Wembley Park sewerage scheme caused further dissension and in 1897 Kingsbury became a separate assessment area, leaving Wembley to pay a special sewerage rate. In 1900 Kingsbury became a separate district and Wembley U.D.C. was reduced to nine councillors, with authority over Wembley civil parish.[73] The council formed only three committees in 1910 but a town planning committee was soon added and in 1911 a building inspector and an assistant surveyor were appointed. This was the beginning of Wembley's Town Planning Scheme, which was largely put into effect during the 1920s.[74] In 1927 Wembley U.D. was divided into six wards, Alperton, Sudbury, Kenton, Wembley Central, Wembley Hill, and Wembley Park, and the number of councillors was increased to 21.[75] At the same time four more committees were appointed.[76] The income for the

[57] Local Govt. Bd. Order 31385.
[58] Metropolitan Commons (Harrow Weald) Supplemental Act, 62 & 63 Vic. c. xxxvii (Local and Personal Act).
[59] For the boundaries in 1895, see O.S. map 6″, Mdx. v. S.W., S.E., x. N.W., N.E., S.W., S.E., xi. S.W., N.W. (1897 edn.) and Harrow Bor., North Star, Hendon R.D.C. Amalgam. map (1934).
[60] Local Govt. Bd. Order 33999; M.R.O., *Reps. of Local Inqs.* (1889–97), 291; (1895–1907), application by Harrow-on-the-Hill U.D.C., 1903; *Census*, 1901.
[61] Local Govt. Bd. Order 44414; M.R.O., *Reps. of Local Inqs.* (1895–1907), inquiry, 1901.
[62] Harrow Bor., North Star, Hendon R.D.C. Boundaries, 1910, 1912.
[63] Ibid. Applications by Wealdstone U.D.C. and Hendon R.D.C. 1926.
[64] See below.
[65] Harrow Bor., North Star, Harrow-on-the-Hill U.D.C. Boundaries 1927–30; Mdx. (Harrow-on-the-Hill U.D.) Confirmation Order, 72899; *Census*, 1931. See above, p. 119.
[66] This paragraph is based upon Harrow Bor., High St., Harrow-on-the-Hill U.D.C., Min. Bks. (1895–6), p. 2.; xxxiii (1910–11), pp. 102 sqq.; liii (1933–4), pp.

3 sqq.
[67] M.R.O., *Reps. of Local Inqs.* (1895–1907), inquiry, 1903.
[68] M.R.O., LA.HW., Harrow-on-the-Hill U.D.C., Ledgers (1895), p. 136; (1910), p. 112; (1928), p. 210.
[69] This paragraph is based upon Harrow Bor., High St., Wealdstone U.D.C., Min. Bks. i (1894–6), *passim*; vi (1900–1), pp. 160–1; xiv (1910–11), p. 100; xxxviii (1933), p. 106.
[70] M.R.O., LA.HW., Wealdstone U.D.C., Ledgers (1895), pp. 47, 51; xi. (1910–13), pp. 18, 59; xv (1926–9), pp. 192, 230. There was only one district rate in 1895, compared with two in other years.
[71] Except where otherwise stated, this paragraph is based upon Brent Town Hall, Wembley U.D.C., Min Bks. i (1894–7), *passim*; ix (1908–11), pp. 239, 262, 368, 446.
[72] Described as 'an object lesson in misgovernment' by the investigator into Kingsbury's application for separation: M.R.O., *Reps. of Local Inqs.* (1895–1907).
[73] Ibid. p. 392; Wemb. Hist. Soc., *Jnl.* i(4).
[74] Wemb. Hist. Soc., Acc. 351.
[75] Ibid. Acc. 719/4; Wembley U.D.C. Engineer & Surveyor's map (1932) *penes* Wemb. Hist. Soc.
[76] Wemb. Hist. Soc., Acc. 212, 351.

combined parishes of Wembley and Kingsbury in the year 1895–6 was £3,465.[77] In 1910 it was £9,806 from Wembley alone.[78]

Pinner and Harrow formed two-thirds of Hendon R.D. and by 1926 Pinner's rateable value was greater than that of all the other parishes together.[79] The rural district had eleven councillors, five of them elected by Pinner and two by Harrow Weald. The parishes enjoyed some autonomy through their own councils, each of 9 or 10 councillors. By 1930 the rural district council employed a clerk, an engineer and surveyor, a valuation officer, a sanitary inspector, and a medical officer of health.[80] Separate parish accounts recorded income collected by overseers, and general and special expenses. In 1910–11 the annual income of Hendon R.D.C. for general expenses was £6,584 and for special expenses £5,991. Of the latter £2,800 went to Pinner, mainly to repay loans made for the sewage works, and £890 was paid to Harrow Weald.[81] Ten years later Hendon R.D.C. had a total income from the parochial general rate of £8,187. Of this Pinner took £3,811 and Harrow Weald £1,681.[82] The special rate was abolished in 1930 and replaced by one general rate.

A district rate of 2s. 10d. in the £ was levied in the first year of Harrow-on-the-Hill U.D., as in the last year of Harrow Board of Health. For the same year, 1895–6, the rate for Wealdstone and Wembley urban districts was 3s. The peculiar circumstances of Wembley forced a rate of 7s. in 1898, but there was a general rise: in Wealdstone to 5s. in 1902 and in Harrow-on-the-Hill to 4s. in 1903. Thereafter there was a decline until in 1910 the rate was 2s. 8d. in Harrow-on-the-Hill, 2s. 9d. in Wealdstone, and 3s. in Wembley. Rates had risen to a new peak by 1922, when they were 4s. 10d. in Harrow-on-the-Hill, 4s. 6d. in Wealdstone, 5s. 4d. in Wembley, and 3s. 7d. in Harrow Weald. By 1928 they had dropped to 3s. 8d. in Harrow-on-the-Hill, 3s. 10d. in Wealdstone, and 2s. 6d. in Wembley. At this date the district rate represented rather less than half the total rate. After 1930 different accounting gives only the total rate, which in 1933 was 8s. 4d. in Harrow-on-the-Hill, 8s. 9d. in Wealdstone, 9s. 4d. in Wembley, 8s. 11d. in Harrow Weald, and 8s. 8d. in Pinner.[83]

In 1929 Hendon R.D.C., frustrated in its town-planning schemes by its boundary with Harrow-on-the-Hill and Wealdstone, proposed a Greater Harrow Urban District.[84] Five years later the Middlesex Review Order replaced the existing authorities by two new urban districts. Harrow U.D. was formed by amalgamating the urban districts of Harrow-on-the-Hill and Wealdstone with the parishes of Pinner, Harrow Weald, and Great and Little Stanmore from Hendon R.D. Wembley U.D. was formed from the old urban districts of Wembley and Kingsbury.[85] The western boundary was straightened, giving a small part of Ealing to Harrow and part to Wembley. The Brent ceased to be the southern boundary and part of Willesden was incorporated into Wembley. A rationalization of the boundary between Harrow and Wembley gave all the playing fields up to Watford Road to Harrow.[36] As a result Harrow U.D. consisted of 12,555 a.;[87] Wembley was 6,284 a., until a further adjustment in 1938 brought its total to 6,294 a.

Harrow U.D. was divided into 12 wards: Harrow-on-the-Hill and Greenhill, Harrow Weald, Headstone, Kenton, Pinner North, Pinner South, Roxeth, West Harrow, Wealdstone North, Wealdstone South, Stanmore North, and Stanmore South, each with three councillors.[88] The Harrow (Wards and Councillors) Order, made in 1948 by the Middlesex County Council, increased the number of wards to 15 and of councillors to 45. One new ward, Roxbourne, was formed out of Pinner South and Roxeth. The other two, Belmont and Queensbury, were created from Kenton, Stanmore North, and Stanmore South.[89] Although incorporation was mentioned in 1935,[90] it was not until 1954 that Harrow U.D. became a municipal borough.[91] In 1935 there were offices at Harrow Weald for the surveyor's, treasurer's, and clerk's departments, in Wealdstone for the valuation and housing departments, and in London Road, Harrow-on-the-Hill, for the public health department.[92] By 1946 there were council offices at Harrow Weald Lodge and in High Street, Harrow-on-the-Hill, but Stanmore had replaced Wealdstone for the third office. There were at that date five departments,

URBAN DISTRICT (LATER BOROUGH AND LATER LONDON BOROUGH) OF HARROW. *Or, a fess arched vert; in chief a pile gules charged with a clarion or, on the dexter side of the pile a torch sable with flames proper, and on the sinister side a quill pen sable; and in the base of the shield a hurst of trees growing out of a grassy mount*

[Granted 1938]

[77] Brent Town Hall, Wembley U.D.C., Min. Bk. i (1894–7), p. 132; Wemb. Hist. Soc., *Jnl.* i(3).
[78] Brent Town Hall, Wembley U.D.C., Min. Bk. ix (1908–11), pp. 228, 246, 306.
[79] Harrow Bor., North Star, Hendon R.D.C. Boundaries, 1926.
[80] Hendon R.D.C., *Rep. of Principal Activities, 1929–31, penes* Harrow Cent. Ref. Libr.; Ware, *Pinner*, 149–50.
[81] M.R.O., LA.HW., Hendon R.D.C., financial statement, ii (1905–11).   [82] Ibid. iv (1917–21).
[83] The rates for Harrow-on-the-Hill are taken from M.R.O., LA.HW., Harrow-on-the-Hill U.D.C., Ledgers (1895), f. 136; (1910), p. 112; (1928), f. 210; *Rep. of Local Inqs.* (1895–1907), inquiry, 1903. Those for Wealdstone are from ibid., Wealdstone U.D.C., Ledgers (1895), pp. 47, 51; (1910–13), pp. 18, 59; (1926–9), pp. 192, 230. Those for Wembley are from Brent Town Hall, Wembley U.D.C., Min. Bk. i (1894–7), p. 132; Wemb. Hist. Soc., *Jnl.* i(3); Wemb. Hist. Soc., Acc. 719/4; Acc. 907/174; Rates for Pinner and Harrow Weald and information about other authorities is from Harrow Bor., North Star, Harrow-on-

the-Hill U.D.C. Boundaries, 1927–30; Hendon R.D.C. Amalgam. 1934.
[84] Hendon R.D.C. *Rep. of Principal Activities, 1929–31.*
[85] *Kelly's Dir. Mdx.* (1937).
[86] Map in Harrow Bor., North Star, Hendon R.D.C. Amalgam. 1934.
[87] i.e. in addition to the combined acreage of Harrow-on-the-Hill and Wealdstone U.Ds. and the parishes of Hendon R.D.: *Census*, 1951.
[88] Harrow U.D.C. *Year Bk.* (1946–7). All except the last two are within the ancient parish of Harrow. For ward boundaries, see Harrow Bor., North Star, Map of Harrow U.D. 1935.
[89] Bor. of Harrow, *Mun. Year Bk.* (1959–60). For the new ward boundaries, see map in London Bor. of Harrow, *Year Bk.* (1967–8).
[90] Harrow Bor., North Star, Box Harrow U.D.C., TS. statement by chairman, 1935.
[91] Bor. of Harrow, *Mun. Year Bk.* (1959–60).
[92] Harrow Bor., North Star, Map of Harrow U.D. 1935; ibid. Box Amalgam. 1933/4, plan c. 1934.

those of the solicitor and clerk of the council, the engineer and surveyor, public health, the treasurer, and valuation. In 1946 there were eight standing committees, 17 sub-committees, and five other committees.[93] By 1959 there were 17 committees and 31 sub-committees, which dealt mainly with housing and education. There were still only five departments, education having replaced valuation, but these employed 31 senior staff.[94]

Wembley U.D., which was incorporated as Wembley Municipal Borough in 1937, was divided into 12 wards, Wembley Central, Wembley Park, Tokyngton, Alperton, Kenton, Preston, Sudbury, Sudbury Court, Roe Green, Fryent, Chalkhill, and the Hyde, the last four being formed out of Kingsbury parish.[95] At the first meeting in 1934,[96] attended by 12 new councillors elected from the wards, 11 standing committees and 3 sub-committees were appointed. At incorporation the governing body was designated a mayor, 12 aldermen, and 36 councillors. The foundation stone of Wembley (later Brent) Town Hall, in Forty Lane, was laid in 1937 and the building, consisting of offices, public hall, and library, was opened in 1939.[97] By 1959–60 there were 13 standing committees, 10 special committees, 4 sub-committees for education, and five departments.[98]

BOROUGH OF WEMBLEY. *Vert, two seaxes crossed saltirewise passing through a Saxon crown or* [Granted 1938]

In 1937 the rate in Harrow U.D. was 10s. in the £ and in Wembley Borough 10s. 2d.[99] During the Second World War it was fixed at 11s. 8d. in Harrow and 13s. in Wembley,[1] but it rose to 16s. 10d. in Harrow by 1948 and in Wembley by 1949. Harrow's rate dropped slightly in 1952 but reached a maximum of 20s. 4d. in 1954 and 1955, while Wembley's rose gradually to 20s. 10d. in 1954. A new assessment reduced it in 1956 to 12s. 10d. in Harrow and 13s. in Wembley but by 1961 it was 18s. in Harrow and 18s. 2d. in Wembley. In 1963 Harrow's rates reached a new maximum of 19s. 10d. Under a new assessment for 1964 Harrow had a rate of 7s. 4d. and Wembley one of 6s. 9d., making it the lowest rated borough in England and Wales.[2]

Under the London Government Act of 1963, which took effect from 1965, Harrow Municipal Borough became the London Borough of Harrow, while Wembley and Willesden were combined as the London Borough of Brent. In Harrow the wards were slightly changed but the total acreage remained the same. The new council had 11 committees and 20 sub-committees, mostly connected with the education and general purposes committees. Harrow Weald Lodge remained the office of the town clerk; the departments of the borough engineer and surveyor and of the architect and planner were in Stanmore, while that of the borough treasurer and those for children and for education were housed in Lyon Road, Harrow.[3] In its first year the London Borough of Harrow received £4,251,245 income out of a total raised from the rates of £5,758,404.[4] In 1966–7 the rate was 11s. 4d.[5] There were 26 wards in Brent,[6] of which Sudbury, Kenton, Preston, Barham, Tokyngton, Alperton, Queensbury, Kingsbury, and Chalkhill lay within the old borough of Wembley. In 1966 a plan was approved, with effect from 1968, to create 31 wards in all. Sudbury, Barham, Kenton, Kingsbury, Queensbury, Tokyngton, and Alperton were to be altered; Chalkhill would disappear, and new wards were to be created: Roe Green, Fryent, Town Hall, Wembley Park, Wembley Central, and two unnamed wards in the Sudbury and Preston area.[7] In 1965 there were 60 councillors and 11 committees. Wembley Town Hall, renamed Brent Town Hall, remained the mayor's parlour and the centre of local government, although there were other offices in Willesden and at Brent House and Chesterfield House on the Harrow Road in Wembley. The fusion of Conservative, low-rated Wembley with Labour-controlled and high-rated Willesden caused difficulties, notably in a bitter dispute over the development of Chalkhill.[8] In 1965, when the rate was 10s. 2d., an estimated £9,699,000 was raised.[9] In 1966–7 the rate was 10s. 7d.[10]

LONDON BOROUGH OF BRENT. *Per chevron gules and vert, a chevron wavy argent between in dexter chief an orb and in sinister chief two swords crossed saltirewise or points upwards and in base two seaxes crossed saltirewise passing through a Saxon crown or* [Granted 1965]

PUBLIC SERVICES. Buckets and rakes for fire-fighting were owned by Pinner parish in 1702.[11] Harrow had an engine, which was used with six men at Uxendon in 1828[12] and at the Grove in 1833, when other engines had to be summoned from Wembley, Stanmore, and Westminster.[13] An out-

[93] Harrow U.D.C. *Year Bk.* (1946–7).
[94] Bor. of Harrow, *Mun. Year Bk.* (1959–60).
[95] *Census*, 1951; Wemb. Hist. Soc., Acc. 274. For ward boundaries, see map in Bor. of Wembley, *Official Guide* (n.d.).
[96] Brent Town Hall, Wembley U.D.C., Min Bk. xxxiii (1934), pp. 20 sqq., 133.
[97] Wemb. Hist. Soc., Acc. 237; Bor. of Wembley, *Official Guide.*
[98] Bor. of Wembley, *Year Bk.* (1959–60).
[99] Wemb. Hist. Soc., Acc. 274. Except where otherwise stated, the figures in this paragraph are taken from *Whitaker's Almanack* (1951–67); Harrow U.D.C. *Year Bk.* (1946–7); Bor. of Harrow, *Facts & Figures* (1963–4).
[1] Pinner Assoc. *The Villager*, xv.
[2] *Wembley News*, 6 Mar. 1964.

[3] London Bor. of Harrow, *Year Bk.* (1967–8).
[4] Ibid. The steep rise was due to the transfer of education from the county to the borough.
[5] *Whitaker's Almanack* (1967).
[6] Except where otherwise stated, the rest of the paragraph comes from Wemb. Hist. Soc., Acc. 708/1, which includes a map.
[7] Wemb. Hist. Soc., Acc. 820/2, which includes a map.
[8] Wemb. Hist. Soc., Acc. 708/1; Acc. 907/140,/142,/145, /179, /182, /184.
[9] Ibid. Acc. 907/145.
[10] *Whitaker's Almanack* (1967).
[11] Ware, *Pinner*, 102.
[12] M.R.O., D.R.O. 3/B2/5.
[13] M.R.O., Acc. 76/2336.

break of fire in 1838 at the headmaster's house at Harrow School again revealed inadequacies: the parish's manual engine was aided by another small engine kept in the yard of Dr. Wordsworth's house, by the Marquess of Abercorn's engine, and finally by others from London and Brentford, but water ran short and the house was burnt down. Expenses amounted to £93 and after an investigation the vestry acquired a new engine, repaired the old one, and cleaned Harrow pond. The two engines, which were kept in an engine-house in Hog Lane,[14] were owned by the vestry until 1864 and afterwards by Harrow Local Board of Health.[15] A fire station was built at the southern end of High Street in 1877[16] and extended in 1889. The strength of the fire brigade was raised to 21 in 1895 and the station was rebuilt in 1914.[17] Pinner for some time depended upon fire hydrants but there was a fire brigade by 1881 and in the 1890s a manual engine was kept at Pinner Hall and later at the George Inn. A fire station was opened in 1903 at the Red Lion Inn to house a steam fire engine. New fire brigade head-quarters were opened in 1938 in Pinner Road.[18] One aim of Wembley Lighting Committee, formed in 1890, was to provide fire appliances at Wembley station, in East Lane, and at Alperton,[19] but it was not until 1895 that Wembley U.D.C. acquired an old manual engine from Harrow-on-the-Hill U.D.C. The equipment was housed in a corrugated iron shed in St. John's Road and manned by 12 volunteers. The brigade was given uniforms in 1909, when a permanent fire station was sanctioned.[20] The fire station is in Harrow Road, north of Wembley Hospital. Wealdstone U.D.C. set up a fire brigade committee in 1896 and made regular payments to the fire brigade.[21] Control of the fire service passed to the county council in 1948[22] and to the Greater London Council in 1965.[23] In 1968 Kodak had its own fire service which was sometimes used elsewhere.[24]

An association for the protection of property flourished in Harrow from 1801 to 1826.[25] The vestry opposed the Metropolitan Police Act in 1839, fearing heavy expense,[26] and in 1843 Pinner followed suit,[27] but both parishes became part of the Metropolitan Police District. A police station was built in West Street, Harrow, but despite protests from Pinner it was not until 1900 that a police station was opened in Bridge Street, Pinner.[28] Police stations were opened soon afterwards in High Road, Wemb-

ley,[29] and in High Street, Wealdstone, and, more recently, in Northolt Road, South Harrow.[30]

There was a pesthouse in Harrow by the 18th century;[31] it was sold in 1851.[32] A small infirmary was built in 1773 on Sudbury Common by John Hodsdon and Samuel Greenhill for 'such poor persons as should be afflicted with infectious diseases or labour under dangerous accidents'. Later the building was used as a casual ward, but by 1850 it was so dilapidated that it was pulled down.[33] In 1866 a cottage hospital was founded by Dr. W. Hewlett, mainly to serve Harrow, Roxeth, and Greenhill. It was managed by a board which included the Vicar of Harrow and the Headmaster of Harrow School. The hospital originally comprised two cottages on Roxeth Hill, which provided nine beds, but in 1868 the landlady gave notice to quit. A hospital with 11 beds, an operating room, and dispensary, was opened in Lower Road in 1872. A new site on Roxeth Hill was purchased in 1905 and a new hospital, with 18 beds, was opened in 1907.[34] In 1910 it was staffed by a matron and four nurses, and had an annual expenditure of £799. In 1935, after extensions in 1925, 1931, and 1934, there were 80 beds, a matron and 30 nurses.[35] By 1966 it had 121 beds.[36] In 1871 Miss Anne Copland founded Copland Village Hospital in the Harrow Road, opposite Blind (later Park) Lane. She endowed it with £3,500, and appointed a medical officer at £50 a year and a matron at £25 a year. The endowment proved inadequate; after 1875 the hospital was frequently closed and from 1883 no in-patients were admitted. The hospital became a dispensary, its property vested in 1913 in the Charity Commissioners.[37] A hospital for infectious diseases, later called Roxbourne Hospital, was opened at Rayners Lane, Roxeth, in 1896. It was financed by the councils of the surrounding urban districts.[38] In 1946 when it had 25 beds it was run as a unit with a hospital in Stanmore.[39] After the National Health Act of that year it became a hospital for the chronic sick. In 1956 it had 51 beds.[40]

Patients from Wembley went to London, Harrow, and Willesden until 1924 when the council's public health committee started a hospital fund. In 1925 the Copland Charity was incorporated into the proposed hospital by a Charity Commission Scheme. A site nearly opposite St. John's Church was conveyed by George T. Barham in 1926 and Wembley Hospital opened in 1928. It was a voluntary

[14] T. F. May, 'The Destruction by Fire of the Headmaster's House', *Lond. & Mdx. Historian*, i (July 1965), 5–11; M.R.O., D.R.O. 3/C1/5; /C4/1/1, /3, /27, /28. The outbreak was probably accidental, although Henry Drury, a master at the school, displayed an unhealthy delight in fires.

[15] M.R.O., D.R.O. 3/C4/1/51, /59.

[16] M.R.O., LA.HW., Harrow Local Bd. of Health, Ledger (1868–79), f. 113; *Kelly's Dir. Mdx.* (1886).

[17] Harrow Bor., High Street, Harrow-on-the-Hill U.D.C., Min. Bk. (1895–6), 14; *Kelly's Dirs. Mdx.* (1906, 1917).

[18] Ware, *Pinner*, 102.

[19] Brent Town Hall, Wembley Lighting Cttee., Min. Bk. (1890–4), 4.

[20] Ibid. Wembley U.D.C., Min. Bk. i (1894–7), pp. 134, 356; ix (1908–11), p. 125; Wemb. Hist. Soc., *Jnl.* i (4).

[21] Harrow Bor., High St., Wealdstone U.D.C., Min. Bk. i (1894–6), pp. 346, 387; M.R.O., LA.HW., Wealdstone U.D.C., Ledgers xi (1910–13), p. 59; (1920), p. 113; (1928), p. 230.

[22] Bor. of Harrow, *Facts & Figures of Harrow* (1963–4).

[23] London Bor. of Harrow, *Official Guide* [1968].

[24] Local inf.

[25] M.R.O., D.R.O. 3/H1/1.

[26] Ibid. 3/C1/5.   [27] Ibid. 8/C1/1.

[28] Ibid. 8/C1/2; Ware, *Pinner*, 172.

[29] Brent Town Hall, Wembley U.D.C., Min. Bk. ix (1908–11), p. 52.

[30] London Bor. of Harrow, *Official Guide* [1968].

[31] M.R.O., D.R.O. 3/F1/1.

[32] Ibid. /F8/2/9–10.

[33] Wemb. Hist. Soc., Acc. 719/3; Elsley, *Wembley*, 184.

[34] Ex inf. E. W. Tompson (Dep. Hosp. Sec. of Harrow Hosp. and author of history of hosp.); *Handbk. for use of visitors to Harrow-on-the-Hill* [1898] penes M.R.O.; O.S. Map 6", Mdx. x. SE (1897 and 1920 edns.); *Kelly's Dir. Mdx.* (1906).

[35] *Harrow Observer & Gaz. Jubilee Supplement*, 3 May 1935 penes M.R.O.

[36] *Hospitals Year Bk.* (1967). Figures are for 31 Dec. 1965.

[37] Wemb. Hist. Soc., Acc. 239; Acc 687/24; Christ Church MS. Estates 47/638.

[38] Brent Town Hall, Wembley U.D.C., Min. Bk. i (1894–7), p. 370; O.S. Map 6", Mdx. x. SE. (1897 edn.).

[39] Harrow U.D.C. *Yr. Bk.* (1964–7).

[40] *Hosp. Yr. Bk.* (1967).

hospital, built with the help of King Edward VII's Hospital Fund for London but entirely maintained by local organizations, chiefly by an area contribution scheme: by 1933 there were 10,409 subscribers, who paid 6d. a month and were entitled to free treatment. The hospital opened with 22 beds and was extended in 1932, 1934, 1937, 1938, 1940, and 1959,[41] until by 1966 there were 134 beds.[42] In 1948, when hospitals were grouped under management committees, there was a plan to rebuild Charing Cross Hospital at Northwick Park. Harrow and Wembley general hospitals, therefore, were placed in the Charing Cross Hospital Group. When a different site was found for Charing Cross Hospital in 1959, the other two hospitals, together with Grim's Dyke Rehabilitation Unit for about 40–50 patients, housed in Sir William Gilbert's house in Harrow Weald[43] and formerly maintained by the county council, were transferred to Harefield and Northwood Group. Roxbourne Hospital, together with Oxhey Grove in Oxhey Lane, Hatch End, a hospital with 30 beds for the chronic sick, and Harrow Chest Clinic in Station Road, belonged to the Hendon Group.[44] The Northwick Park site was reserved in 1961 for a large district hospital for 800 patients under the North-West Middlesex Regional Board and a clinical research centre for the Medical Research Council.[45] Building was in progress in 1967.

The new Harrow Local Board of Health[46] planned to bring water to 2,000 people, but its survey in 1850 revealed that Harrow-on-the-Hill could not be adequately supplied without heavy expense. The board's sub-committees[47] registered lodging-houses and slaughter-houses, and major sewerage works were completed early in 1853. A surveyor and inspector of nuisances supervised the main sewers and inspected all private drainage, and in 1852 it was proposed to borrow £2,000 'for the perfect drainage' of the district. Since many cottages had to buy water at ½d. a bucket[48] or collect rainwater from their gutters in underground tanks,[49] the newly formed Harrow Waterworks Co. was permitted to lay pipes, and a waterworks was built in Bessborough Road after an Act had been passed in 1854.[50] The company was taken over in 1884 by the Colne Valley Water Co.,[51] which retained the works but brought most of the water by pipe from Bushey.[52]

In 1854[53] Pinner vestry and the guardians of Hendon Union, under the Nuisances Removal Act of 1846,[54] resolved to clear the Pinn, to lay pipes and to unblock footpaths. In 1858 114 orders were made to clean and build cesspools and privies, many of which drained into the river. Before the Colne Valley Water Co. brought piped water, a lake and a pump house south of All Saints' church supplied the new Woodridings estate,[55] whose owners were constantly pressed to provide adequate drainage. In heavy rain the Pinn was often discoloured by streams from slaughter-houses on the hill, and in 1857 it was reported that 'the blood receptacle of the slaughter-house is insufficient'.[56] The Hendon guardians, who superseded the nuisances removal committee in 1861, appear to have been less assiduous. In 1864 the vestry complained about the brook at the bottom of the village and two years later pollution was held responsible for epidemic sickness. The guardians promised disinfectant, free medicine for diarrhoea, and £10 to whitewash the houses of the poor.[57]

Insanitary conditions were blamed for the 'amount of epidemic disease there always is in Harrow' by a surgeon in 1870.[58] There were frequent complaints about sewage and drainage under Harrow Local Board during the 1870s and 1880s, when even smallpox was attributed to bad smells. The sanitary committee and surveyor appear to have been conscientious, although faced with overcrowding and old buildings as well as farm-yards which were too close to the town. Gradually the board extended its powers, controlling building and ordering houses where smallpox had occurred to be disinfected.[59] The Infectious Diseases (Notification) Act had been adopted by 1889.[60] Among the authorities which were responsible for public health in the part of Harrow parish outside Harrow Local Board District,[61] Hendon Rural Sanitary Authority (1879–94) had to provide the sewerage required by the rapid spread of building, notably at Hatch End and Roxborough.[62]

From 1894 to 1934 sewerage and drainage were divided among four authorities, each with its own farms and outfall works. Harrow-on-the-Hill U.D. had inherited sewage farms at Greenhill[63] and in Newton (Newden) Field, Roxeth,[64] and also sewage tanks on Sudbury Hill.[65] Wealdstone U.D. built a large sewage farm just over its eastern border.[66] Wembley U.D. inherited a farm at Alperton and established a new one at Wembley Park.[67] Hendon R.D. had a sewage farm and outfall works in Pinner[68] and sewage disposal works at Harrow Weald.[69] The

41 Wemb. Hist. Soc., Acc. 239; Acc. 687/24.
42 *Hosp. Yr. Bk.* (1967).
43 See p. 186.
44 *Hosp. Yr. Bk.* (1951, 1961); Wemb. Hist. Soc., Acc. 687/24.
45 Wemb. Hist. Soc., Acc. 907/127.
46 Except where otherwise stated, this paragraph is based upon Harrow Bor., High St., Local Bd. of Health, Letter Bk. (1850–8); Min. Bk. (1850–3).
47 See p. 243.
48 N.R.A. Exhib. of Docs. (1953), item 93.
49 Twelve such tanks were excavated near Hundred Elms Farm: Wemb. Hist. Soc. *Jnl.* N.S. i(3).
50 Harrow Water Act, 17 Vic. c. 30 *penes* Harrow Cent. Ref. Libr.
51 Druett, *Harrow*, 220.
52 *Kelly's Dir. Mdx.* (1886).
53 Unless otherwise stated, this paragraph is based upon M.R.O., D.R.O. 8/C1/2.
54 9 & 10 Vic. c. 96.
55 Pinner Assoc. *The Villager*, xviii.
56 Ibid. xl.   57 M.R.O., D.R.O. 8/C1/3.
58 Harrow Bor., High St., Local Bd. of Health, Min. Bk.

(1870–5), p. 8.
59 Ibid. p. 72; Plans Cttee., Min. Bk. (1880–5).
60 Ibid. Min. Bk. xv (1889–91), p. 5.
61 See p. 243.
62 M.R.O., LA.HW., Hendon Rural Sanitary Authority, Gen. Ledger (1882–9), f. 8.
63 i.e. built 1852–3: Harrow Bor., High St., Local Bd. of Health, Letter Bk. (1850–8).
64 In existence by 1893: M.R.O., LA.HW., Harrow Local Bd. of Health, Ledger (1893–4), f. 40; O.S. Map 6″, Mdx. x. SE. (1897 edn.).
65 O.S. Map 6″, x. SE. (1897 edn.).
66 In existence by 1895: Harrow Bor., High St., Wealdstone U.D.C., Min. Bk. i (1894–6); O.S. Map 6″, Mdx. x. NE. (1897 edn.).
67 Brent Town Hall, Wembley U.D.C., Min. Bk. i (1894–7), p. 15; M.R.O., *Reps. of Local Inqs.* (1889–97), 327 sqq.
68 In existence by 1882: M.R.O., LA.HW., Hendon Rural Sanitary Authority, Gen. Ledger (1882–9), f. 17; O.S. Map 6″, Mdx. SW. (1897 edn.).
69 In existence by 1901: M.R.O., LA.HW., Hendon R.D.C., Ledger (1901), f. 10.

number of authorities, and especially their conjunction in the built-up area around Wealdstone, necessitated joint action. Harrow-on-the-Hill's Greenhill farm originally lay within Wealdstone;[70] Wealdstone's works were in Harrow Weald.[71] In 1897 Willesden tried to build a sewage farm in Wembley.[72] Drainage cut across the boundaries and sometimes, as in the Wembley Park scheme, there was a clash of interest within a district. The management of the sewage farm at Alperton was described by a local inquiry investigator in 1899 as terrible.[73] Sewage polluted the Brent and led to successful actions by Greenford and Ealing urban districts against Wembley in 1897 and 1898. Wembley also had to pay for a sewerage scheme started by Hendon Rural Sanitary Authority in Wembley Park,[74] on which nearly £25,000 was spent by the two authorities from 1894 to 1901. This scheme, which involved tunnelling under Harrow Road, the railway, and the Grand Junction Canal, was not finished until 1924.[75]

Under the West Middlesex Sewerage and Sewage Disposal Scheme of 1933, 27 sewage works were replaced by trunk sewers and one central works at Mogden, which since 1936 have served the whole area.[76] The former sewage farms were generally turned into recreation grounds or allotments, although at Alperton a refuse disposal works was opened in 1936 on the old site. From 1924 Wembley's refuse had been sent by barge at considerable expense to Yiewsley and West Drayton. In 1935 a public cleansing committee of Wembley council was set up and a cleansing officer appointed. This was Frank Fitton, who drew up the scheme for a refuse works and who invented 'Wembley Pudding', which was made there and sold as animal fodder.[77]

A public meeting discussed lighting in 1855 and a local ironmonger, John Chapman, undertook to build a small gas-works at Roxeth. Harrow Local Board of Health, which had already noted the problem of lighting in 1850,[78] encouraged him and in 1856 gas lamps replaced the oil street lamps. The gas-works were reconstructed in 1872 on the formation of the Harrow Gas, Light, and Coke Co. Ltd., which was incorporated in 1873 as Harrow District Gas Co. and, by an Act of 1894,[79] joined with Stanmore Gas Co. to become Harrow and Stanmore Gas Co. In 1924 it was absorbed by Brentford Gas Co., which in turn was taken over by the Gas, Light, and Coke Co. in 1926.[80] Pinner Gas Co., set up by 1881,[81] built gas-

works in Eastcote Road[82] and was absorbed by the Gas, Light, and Coke Co. in 1929.[83]

At first the streets of Harrow-on-the-Hill were lighted only during the winter. In 1870 the local board agreed, on conditions, that private roads should be lighted.[84] Pinner High Street had six gas lamps by 1880. In 1894 Pinner's traditional aversion to high rates prevented it from adopting the Lighting and Watching Act of 1833,[85] but by 1901 money was being paid by the parish to the Pinner and Harrow gas companies.[86] The ratepayers of Holy Trinity, Wealdstone, adopted the Act in 1889 and raised over £100 by a rate of 3¾d. in the £ on houses and 1¼d. on land.[87] Those of St. John's, Wembley, appointed a lighting and fire-fighting committee in 1890 but its estimate of £230 was too ambitious and in 1893 a more modest target was adopted. Gas mains and street lamps were beginning to be laid in 1894 although Wembley still had only six gas lamps in 1895.[88] All the new urban districts and Hendon R.D. adopted the Lighting and Watching Act and supplied public gas lighting. Harrow Local Board had an electric lighting loan account by 1893.[89] Private Acts provided for electricity in Harrow in 1894,[90] and in Wealdstone, Pinner, and Harrow Weald in 1906.[91] Harrow Electric Light and Power Co., which had a generating station at Harrow-on-the-Hill, was authorized to supply Wealdstone U.D. in 1911.[92] Pinner was supplied by the Colne Valley Electric Supply Co. in 1913[93] and Wembley by the North Metropolitan Electric Power Supply Co. in 1920.[94]

Cemeteries were provided by burial boards at Paines Lane, Pinner, in 1860,[95] next to St. John's churchyard, Wembley, in 1885,[96] at Pinner Road, North Harrow, in 1887, and at Roxeth Hill and Eastcote Lane, Roxeth, in 1900.[97] Local authorities provided those at Byron Road, Wealdstone, in 1899, Perivale Lane, Alperton, in 1928,[98] Pinner Road, Pinner, in 1931, and Clamp Hill, Harrow Weald, in 1937.

HARROW CHURCH. It is not known whether Werhard, the priest who owned land in Roxeth in the 9th century, had a church in Harrow.[99] A priest is recorded in Domesday Book.[1] In 1094 the consecration of a church built by Lanfranc provoked one of the first disputes over archiepiscopal peculiars. The archbishops assumed that Harrow was wholly under their jurisdiction, diocesan as well as manorial, but

[70] M.R.O., *Reps. of Local Inqs.* (1889–97), 291 sqq.
[71] Harrow Bor., North Star, Hendon R.D.C., Wealdstone extension inquiry, 1912; applic. for alteration of Wealdstone boundaries, 1926.
[72] Wemb. Hist. Soc. *Jnl.* i(4).
[73] M.R.O., *Reps. of Local Inqs.* (1895–1907).
[74] Wemb. Hist. Soc. *Jnl.* i(4); Brent Town Hall, Wembley U.D.C., Min. Bk. i (1894–7), p. 392.
[75] Wemb. Hist. Soc. *Jnl.* i(5).
[76] Ibid.; Wemb. Hist. Soc., Acc. 212; Hendon R.D.C. *Rep. of Principal Activities, 1929–31, penes* Harrow Cent. Ref. Libr.
[77] Wemb. Hist. Soc., Acc. 236; Acc. 907/76.
[78] Harrow Bor., High St., Local Bd. of Health, Min. Bk. (1850–3).
[79] 57 & 58 Vic. c. 208.
[80] Harrow Cent. Ref. Libr., Sales Partics. i (1896 shares of gas co.); *Harrow Observer*, 24 Oct. 1957.
[81] Act relating to Brentford, Pinner etc. gas, 44 & 45 Vic. c. 103.
[82] O.S. Map 6″, Mdx. x. NW. (1897 edn.).
[83] Transfer of Pinner Gas Co. Ltd., to Gas, Light & Coke Co., 19 & 20 Geo. V, c. 43.

[84] Harrow Bor., High St., Local Bd. of Health, Min. Bk. (1870–5), 14, 31.
[85] Pinner Assoc. *The Villager*, xvi, xlii.
[86] M.R.O., LA.HW., Hendon R.D.C. Ledger (1901), f. 11.
[87] Ibid. Wealdstone Lighting Cttee, Rate Bks. (1889–93).
[88] Brent Town Hall, Wembley Lighting Cttee., Min. Bk. (1890–4); Wemb. Hist. Soc. *Jnl.* i(3).
[89] Harrow Bor., High St., Local Bd. of Health, Min. Bk. xv (1889–91), p. 13; M.R.O., LA.HW., Local Bd. of Health, Ledger (1893–4), f. 64.
[90] 57 & 58 Vic. c. 50.
[91] 6 Edw. VII, cc. 110, 129.
[92] 1 & 2 Geo. V, c. 163.
[93] 3 & 4 Geo. V, c. 153.
[94] Wemb. Hist. Soc., Acc. 351.
[95] Bor. of Harrow, *Facts & Figures* (1963–4); Ware, *Pinner*, 48.
[96] Wemb. Hist. Soc., *Jnl.* i(4).
[97] Bor. of Harrow, *Facts & Figures* (1963–4).
[98] Wemb. Hist. Soc., Acc. 719/4.
[99] See p. 203.
[1] See p. 219.

Maurice, Bishop of London, claimed the right to consecrate the church since it lay within his diocese. Anselm carried out the ceremony in 1094 in spite of an abortive attempt by one of the Bishop of London's clerks to steal the consecration oil, and afterwards he won support from the last surviving English bishop, Wulfstan of Worcester.[2] Thereafter Harrow remained a peculiar of the archbishopric of Canterbury within the deanery of Croydon until 1845 when, on the abolition of the Middlesex peculiars, it became part of the London diocese.[3] There were medieval chapels of ease to Harrow church at Pinner and Tokyngton. Tokyngton chapel was suppressed with the chantries but Pinner survived to become an independent parish in 1766.[4] Nineteen parishes were founded in the 19th and 20th centuries within the original parish of Harrow.

Harrow had a landed estate, manorial rights, and tithes drawn from a large area; closely connected with the archbishop's residences, it was also accessible to London and on the route from Canterbury to the king's palace at Woodstock. Thus it always attracted ambitious and important men. Werhard was probably the first of many non-resident priests,[5] some of whom provided deputies. A vicar is mentioned in 1170,[6] although it was not until 1233–40 that a charter endowed the vicarage and regulated the endowments of the rectory.[7] The rectory continued, usually as a sinecure, until it was impropriated in 1546 to Christ Church, Oxford, and soon afterwards to the secular lords of Sudbury manor.

The advowson of the rectory was exercised by the archbishops of Canterbury, except *sede vacante* in 1278, 1294, 1366, and 1396, when the Crown made the appointment.[8] Once, *c.* 1170, the king usurped the advowson, whereupon his nominee was excommunicated by Becket.[9] In 1312–17 there were three claimants, presented respectively by the archbishop, by the king *sede vacante*, and by the pope. The archbishop's candidate, William de Bosco (Boys), won but had to pay £40 a year to the papal nominee, William de Testa.[10] In 1537 Cranmer granted the 'gift, collation, and free disposition of the parish churches of Harrow and Hayes' to Sir Roger Townsend and others,[11] but the rectory was impropriated before another vacancy occurred. The medieval rectors held the advowson of the vicarage[12] and after impropriation the lay rector normally presented.[13] In 1601, however, William Gerard of Flambards and in 1625 Simon Rewse of Headstone did so, Gerard probably because of the confusion

which followed the division of the rectory,[14] Rewse perhaps as a trustee.[15] In 1776 the advowson was exercised by Sir John Rushout and John Kennion, in accordance with an agreement made by Rushout in 1764 to sell all his Harrow property; Kennion paid part of the price, mortgaging the estate to Rushout, but Rushout foreclosed in 1782 on failing to receive the rest.[16] In 1806, expecting the decease of the vicar, Walter L. Williams, Lord Northwick conveyed the advowson for £3,500 to Robert Markland of Ardwick (Lancs.). When Williams died in 1810 Markland, for £5,000, released it back to Northwick, who made the next presentation.[17] Thereafter the advowson remained with the lords of the manor.

The hide of land which had been granted to the priest before 1086[18] was held from the archbishop for suit of court, payment of heriot, and 8s. a year.[19] This presumably became the rectory estate, which was described variously as one hide[20] or 1½ hide,[21] probably because the status of the land east of the parsonage was always ambiguous. From 1233–40 the rector was to have all the demesne of the church except the vicarage site, comprising land, houses, homage, pannage, and other services of tenants of the church, all the tithes of grain, herbage, and hay, except those from Roxeth and Headstone manors, and all mortuaries of beasts worth more than 2s.; he was also to receive 50 geese from the vicar on St. James's Day (25 July).[22] The reference to homage and services implies that Rectory manor already existed. The rector had sole manorial jurisdiction over Harrow-on-the-Hill and Roxborough, and part of Roxeth and Greenhill. His rectory was valued in 1291 at £40 and in 1535 at £88 4s. 4d. a year.[23]

Although most of the rectors were pluralists and absentees, it is unlikely that they were content with a modest residence. John Byrkhede, for example, entertained Archbishop Chichele at Harrow in 1440.[24] William Bolton, Prior of St. Bartholomew's, Smithfield, and Rector of Harrow, is said to have erected a fortress on Harrow hill in anticipation of a great flood in 1524. This may refer to a rebuilding of the parsonage-house, for in 1537 Richard Layton could offer Thomas Cromwell 12 beds there.[25]

In 1539 Layton leased the rectory to Thomas Wriothesley (later Earl of Southampton, d. 1550) for 60 years at £78 a year, reserving only the tithes of Pinner, the advowson of the vicarage, and repairs to the chancel.[26] In September 1544 Richard Coxe, a

[2] *Eadmer's History of Recent Events in England*, ed. G. Bosanquet, 46; W. D. Bushell, 'Consecration of church', *Harrow Octocent. Tracts,* iv.
[3] *Lond. Gaz.* 1845, p. 2541.
[4] See p. 256.
[5] Werhard probably resided at Hayes: *Harrow Octocent. Tracts,* i. 22 n.
[6] W. D. Bushell, 'St. Thos. of Cant.', *Harrow Octocent. Tracts,* vi. 23.
[7] *Harrow Octocent. Tracts,* ix. 10–16.
[8] W. D. Bushell, 'Harrow Rectors', *Harrow Octocent. Tracts,* x, xi.
[9] See below.
[10] *Harrow Octocent. Tracts,* x. 15–19. Wm. de Testa was apparently the earliest candidate, holding in 1309 and 1312 (Reg. Clem. V, nos. 4667, 8075; *Cal. Pap. Reg.* ii. 59, 96) but the final decision, by Abp. Reynolds (Camb. Univ. Libr., MS. Ee. v. 31, f. 184) in 1317 favoured De Bosco on the grounds that Harrow was with cure and required the presence of its rector.
[11] Cant. Cath. Libr., Reg. T2, ff. 93v–94v. The grant

was dated Nov., i.e. after the collation of Richard Layton.
[12] W. D. Bushell, 'The Vicarage', *Harrow Octocent. Tracts,* ix. 17–19.
[13] Ibid. 19–22.
[14] See below.
[15] *Harrow Octocent. Tracts,* ix. 20.
[16] M.R.O., Acc. 76/403, /406, /1089, /1697; Acc. 166(2)/146/20–156; B.M. Add. MS. 29254, f. 6v.
[17] M.R.O., Acc. 76/528, /534.
[18] *V.C.H. Mdx.* i. 120.
[19] M.R.O., Acc. 76/216, mm. 25, 67, 72; /222a; /2413, m. 72. Described *c.* 1645 as held in socage: ibid. /777.
[20] e.g. M.R.O., Acc., 76/216, mm. 67, 72; /2413, m. 72.
[21] e.g. ibid. /216, m. 25, /222a.
[22] *Harrow Octocent. Tracts,* ix. 10–16.
[23] *Tax. Eccl.* (Rec. Com.), 176; *Valor Eccl.* (Rec. Com.), i. 434; Newcourt, *Repertorium,* 636.
[24] *Reg. Chichele* (Cant. & York Soc. xlv), i. 301.
[25] *Harrow Octocent. Tracts,* xi. 18–19, 27.
[26] Cant. Cath. Libr., Reg. T2, ff. 162v–3v.

canon of Cardinal College (Christ Church), Oxford, was collated to Harrow rectory.[27] In November Cranmer surrendered its advowson to the king,[28] who in 1546 granted it to Christ Church,[29] of which Coxe had become dean. Coxe presumably surrendered his title and in 1547 the college alienated the rectory and the advowson of the vicarage to Sir Edward North, reserving the great tithes. The grant was made in fee farm in perpetuity for £13 6s. 8d. annually,[30] a payment which was still made, although charged exclusively on the rectory-house, in 1881.[31] In 1550 the 'parsonage and great tithes' were leased to North for 50 years at £74 17s. 8d. a year. The inclusion of the word parsonage, whether through doubt about the title in fee farm or through carelessness in drafting the lease, led to trouble. In 1566 a similar lease in reversion was made to Nicholas Todd for 99 years. After Todd surrendered his interest in 1569 it was granted to William Wightman, who was to pay a peppercorn rent until North's 50-year lease should expire.[32] Wightman possessed both the rectory and the tithes before 1553.[33] Sir Edward North paid a total of £88 4s. 8d.[34] annually to Christ Church, comprising the fee farm for the rectory and the rent for the tithes. He leased the rectory, with all appurtenances except manorial rights, to Wightman for £31 a year, and sub-leased the tithes to him for £74 18s. 10d. a year. Wightman in turn sub-leased some of the tithes, those of Sudbury being leased by Sir Gilbert Gerard for £8 6s. 8d. a year. After Gerard's executors sued Wightman's widow and daughters in 1593 the Wightman lease from Christ Church of the tithes passed to the Gerards,[35] while another action established that the parsonage was part of the fee farm grant to Sir Edward North.[36]

The parsonage nevertheless was claimed both by North and his successors and by Christ Church and their lessees. North enjoyed the rights and profits of the rectory; he had a seat in the chancel and received payments for burials there.[37] The rectory was conveyed to George Pitt in 1630 and thereafter descended with Sudbury Court until 1807, when it was sold by Lord Northwick to James Edwards. Pitt was challenged by Sir Gilbert Gerard, who leased the tithes and, as he thought, the parsonage from Christ Church. In 1550 the college had covenanted to do all the repairs to the chancel and tithe barns except 'the great walling and thatching',[38] while since 1569 the college's lessee had been held responsible for the chancel.[39] Gerard repaired it until c. 1632, when his tithes were sequestrated

before he could be induced to carry out the work,[40] but c. 1638, desiring the privileges as well as the duties of rector, he demanded the chancel, the parsonage-house, and the tithe geese. He went to Oxford to incite the college to question Pitt's title, removed the keys from the chancel, and nailed up the doors within the church to prevent Pitt from occupying his chancel pew.[41] The rectory was thus involved in the general dispute between the two men, until in 1657 Gerard admitted that the grant of 1569 was void because of the previous grant in fee farm to North. He surrendered his lease and took up a lease of tithes only,[42] for three lives and for the old rent of £74 17s. 8d., agreeing to repair 'the tithe barns and all demised premises with appurtenances and everything in Harrow' for which Christ Church was liable.[43] Gerard interpreted these as the tithe barns only and in 1661 asserted that the chancel should be repaired by Mrs. Pitt, who claimed that it was the tithe-holder's obligation.[44] In 1663 a decree ordered £66 13s. 4d. to be paid by the tithe-holder and £33 6s. 8d. by the rector,[45] but ten years later the issue was raised again. From 1678, after arbitration, the chancel was to be repaired jointly by the tithe-holder and rector,[46] but there were similar disputes in the 1780s, in 1829, and in 1847, chiefly because the lay rector was reluctant to pay.[47]

The rectory and the tithes were held separately after 1593.[48] In c. 1645 the annual value of the rectory, comprising the house, about 150–180 a., the advowson of the vicarage, and perquisites of court, was estimated at £303; in addition, wood on the manor was said to be worth £1,000.[49] At this time part of the glebe was leased out. Most of the original glebe—the one hide lying north of Roxborough Lane—was leased in 1654 for 21 years at £50 a year.[50] In 1671 all the glebe land, including the section east of the house, called Redings and Dodses, and part of the rectory-house called the Dairy, was leased for 21 years at £140 a year.[51] The lease was repeated in 1682 for a further 21 years at an annual rent of £165,[52] although for most of the 18th century the Rushouts leased out only Redings and Dodses.[53] There was an annual rent of £117 c. 1796, when the house and land in hand were valued at £150 a year.[54] In 1805 Northwick claimed that Redings and Dodses, 50 a. on either side of Kenton Road,[55] were glebe land and therefore exempt from tithe, saying that he had a map showing the glebe in 1611.[56] By 1805, however, the distinction between rectorial glebe and other manorial lands was vague, and the

[27] *Harrow Octocent. Tracts*, xi. 29.
[28] *L. & P. Hen. VIII*, xix(2), 383.
[29] Ibid. xxi(2), 335.
[30] *Cal. Pat.* 1547–8, 187; M.R.O., Acc. 76/1007, /1698.
[31] Christ Church MS. Estates 47/560, /562, /683.
[32] M.R.O., Acc. 76/1149.
[33] Ibid. /222a, /1985.
[34] *Recte* £88 4s. 4d.
[35] *Cal. Procs. in Chancery Eliz. I* (Rec. Com.), i. 345.
[36] The court upheld North's lessee, John Button, against Audrey Wightman, who claimed to hold as lessee of Christ Church: M.R.O., Acc. 76/400, /1175; *Acts of P.C.* 1592, p. 308. Wightman himself had assigned to his widow and daughter the lease of the parsonage, which he had 'by grant of Roger, Lord North', and the lease in reversion of the tithes, which he had 'by grant of Christ Church': P.C.C. 9 Arundell.
[37] M.R.O., Acc. 76/1701.
[38] Ibid. /1175.
[39] Ibid. /1149.
[40] Ibid. /1171.

[41] Ibid. /826–7, /829.
[42] The confusing phrase 'parsonage of Harrow with appurtenances and all tithes' was repeated, but from this date lessees recognized that they were only entitled to tithes.
[43] M.R.O., Acc. 76/1150, /1160, /1167.
[44] Ibid. /1152, /1155, /1160–6, /1174–5, /1701.
[45] Ibid. /1699.
[46] Ibid. /1177–81.
[47] Christ Church MS. Estates 47/11, /285, /496.
[48] M.R.O., Acc. 76/400.
[49] Ibid. /777.
[50] Ibid. /195.
[51] Ibid. /201.
[52] Ibid. /202.
[53] Ibid. /404–5.
[54] Ibid. /1124.
[55] Ibid. /234, /238, /242, /404; Acc. 643, 2nd deposit, Messeder map B.
[56] M.R.O., Acc. 76/1702–3; Christ Church MS. Estates 47/178, /180, /209.

inclosure commissioners rejected his claim. In 1807 Northwick sold the rectory-house and 121 a. north of it to James Edwards, retaining the disputed lands which became part of Harrow Park.[57]

The rectory- or parsonage-house was described c. 1645 as spacious.[58] Some £441 was spent on repairs between 1654 and 1663,[59] and in 1664 it was one of the largest houses in the parish, with 17 hearths.[60] The Pitts and Rushouts reserved most of it for their own visits, and also retained the advowson of the vicarage, the timber, and manorial perquisites. In the 1780s the mansion was occupied by Richard Sheridan[61] and c. 1796, amid large walled gardens and a pleasure ground, it commanded 'rich and delightful views'.[62] This house, known as the Grove after its once wooded close, became a boarding house for Harrow School c. 1820.[63]

The great tithes and tithe barns at Wembley, Alperton, Harrow Weald, and Pinner continued to be leased for £74 17s. 8d. throughout the 17th and 18th centuries on 21-year leases, renewable every seven years for a substantial fine, in 1793 as much as £1,790.[64] The lease was held by the Conyers family, the first of whom was an executor of Sir Francis Gerard, from 1709 to 1772, then by the Hernes until 1793 and by Richard Page from 1793 to 1803. All tithes were extinguished by the Inclosure Act of 1803. The inclosure commissioners' award to Christ Church of £1,005 annually in corn-rents and 897 a. of land seems to have been excessive,[65] for in 1657 the tithes had been valued at £800 a year[66] and in 1764 at only £711, although an 'improvable account' of £941 was also given.[67] Opponents of inclosure protested that the value of all tithes was only about £1,800 whereas the proposed rate of commutation would give the holders about £3,000–£4,000 a year.[68] They were probably correct, since a valuation kept by Richard Page gave them as worth £1,625 a year.[69] The estimate at the time of the award in 1817 was £1,400 for the land and £856 for the corn-rents.[70] The land allotted in lieu of rectorial tithe consisted of four blocks, mainly taken out of the open fields: 390 a. around Tithe Farm in Roxeth, 229 a. in Kenton and Harrow Weald later forming Black Farm, 176 a. in Alperton, and 104 a. in Preston.[71] The estate and corn-rents seem to have been leased to Page's executors after his death. From 1830 to 1872 or later they were leased to Henry Young of Essex Street and subsequently to his widow on 21-year leases, renewable every seven years for a fine of £5,700, although in 1831 the college, considering the fallen price of land and corn, assessed the fine at £2,690.[72] Young sub-leased the land which, in 1831, was divided among seven tenants who paid £1,169 in rent.[73] In 1845 there were still 7 under-tenants, and the net annual value of land and corn-rents was £2,555.[74] By 1866 there were only 5 tenants, most of the land being held by Thomas Goodchild, and the net annual value was £1,479 for the land and £674 for the fixed rent-charge.[75] Corn-rents, supposedly determined by the price of corn from year to year, were reviewed only in 1832, 1846 (at £846), 1902, and 1916,[76] but most were redeemed between 1893 and 1911.[77] Small amounts of the land were conveyed to the railways or local authorities in the 1860s, in 1881, and 1893,[78] but most of it was sold during the 1920s and 1930s for building.[79]

In 1233–40 Archbishop Edmund Rich, at the request of the rector, Elias of Dereham, endowed the vicarage with a house and a curtilage, with all the oblations of Harrow church and Pinner and Tokyngton chapels, and with all small tithes and mortuaries under the value of 2s. The vicarage was also granted the tithe of hay from Hamo and Hugh Roxeth (Roxeth manor) and of Ailwin and William de la Hegge (Headstone manor).[80] In 1291 it was valued at £6 13s. 4d.,[81] and in 1535 at £33 4s. 4d. a year.[82] In 1650 the profits were £50 a year, and a further £50 a year was granted by the committee for plundered ministers.[83] By c. 1796 the vicarage was said to be worth £200 a year.[84] The tithes due from Headstone manor were commuted at an early date for a modus of £3 6s. 8d. and a court decision of 1656 upheld this customary payment. Another case in 1731 established the modus for small tithes: 4d. for each cow, for each sow with piglets, and for each orchard, and 2d. for each garden.[85] In 1804 resources subject to vicarial tithe were about 1,600 a. of grazing waste, 300–400 a. of herbage from annually de-pastured land, 100 a. each of turnips and potatoes, 5 or 6 pigeon-houses, orchards, gardens, hot-houses and wall fruits, seeds, honey, wax, some 14,000 sheep, 400 cows, 20–30 colts, pigs, and various poultry; there was also the modus from Headstone Farm and another, of £1 10s., from Roxeth Farm.[86] At inclosure this was commuted for £323 a year in corn-rents and 188 a. of land.[87] The value of the vicarage c. 1811 was £1,080 a year, made up of £323 in corn-rents, 295 a. leased at £496 a year, a vicarage-house worth £80 a year and mortuaries worth £180 a year. The vicar also received £25 from Harrow School and £20 for preaching 10 sermons.[88] In 1835 his average

[57] M.R.O., Acc. 794/8; Acc. 643, 2nd deposit, survey of Northwick's estate (1806); Christ Church MS. Estates 47/187, /242, /245.
[58] M.R.O., Acc. 76/777.
[59] Ibid. /848.
[60] M.R.O., H.T. 5.
[61] See p. 234. For Sheridan's stables at Grove Hill in 1795, see Druett, Harrow, illustration facing p. 208.
[62] M.R.O., Acc. 76/1124.
[63] See p. 177.
[64] M.R.O., Acc. 76/1149–50, /1166; Christ Church Deeds, Harrow leases 1709–1810; Lysons, Environs of Lond. ii. 575.
[65] C.P. 43/939A.
[66] M.R.O., Acc. 76/1166.
[67] Christ Church MS. Estates 47/7.
[68] M.R.O., Acc. 77/5.
[69] Christ Church MS. Estates 47/19.
[70] Ibid. /225.
[71] Ibid. /306v, /449, /599; Christ Church Deeds, Harrow leases 1830–60, surrender 1872; Christ Church Harrow Maps 5.
[72] Christ Church MS. Estates 47/314.
[73] Ibid. /306v.
[74] Ibid. /449.
[75] Ibid. /599.
[76] Ibid. /565, /804.
[77] Christ Church Redemption Deeds.
[78] Christ Church Deeds, Harrow conveyances 1864, 1868; Christ Church Harrow Maps 5.
[79] Christ Church Harrow Maps 17–25.
[80] Harrow Octocent. Tracts, ix. 10–16. Confirmed in 1396 and 1512: M.R.O., Acc. 76/808.
[81] Tax. Eccl. (Rec. Com.), 176.
[82] Valor Eccl. (Rec. Com.), i. 434.
[83] Lambeth Palace MS. 913, Parl. Survey XII, p. 146.
[84] M.R.O., Acc. 76/1124.
[85] Ibid. /861, /2077.
[86] Ibid. /1095.
[87] C.P. 43/939A.
[88] M.R.O., Acc. 76/562.

net income was £627, and £160 was paid in stipends for two curates.[89] By 1851 the net income was £595.[90] Over 70 a. of vicarial glebe land in Harrow Weald were sold in 1861[91] and most of the corn-rents had been redeemed by 1967, although they still contributed about £50 to the endowment of £1,620. At least £1,000 has been surrendered by the vicars to help new parishes.[92]

The house granted in 1233–40[93] stood south of the burial ground, where the vicarage has remained ever since.[94] It was assessed for 6 hearths in 1664 and subsequently for 5 hearths.[95] Walter L. Williams (vicar 1776–1811) let the vicarage for use by boarders at Harrow School and lived at Pinner House.[96] In 1812, after £205 had been paid for repairs, the new vicar, John W. Cunningham, complained that the state of the wall between the playground and parson-age enabled schoolboys to climb in, and warned that it might deter a vicar from living there.[97] Cunning-ham moved first to a house at the corner of Roxeth Hill and later to Julian Hill.[98] Having been let as a boarding house for Harrow School for much of the 19th century, the former vicarage was largely re-built in 1870 and reverted to its original use.[99] The present house is of red brick with stone dressings; a south-east wing may date from c. 1812, the rest being a Victorian Gothic building of 1870.

Tokyngton, one of two chapels mentioned in 1234–40,[1] was a free chapel, dedicated to St. Michael and served by its own priest. About 1273–80 Joseph de Chauncey, Prior of Clerkenwell, granted to Bene-dict 'rector of the chapel of Tokyngton', a messuage with a house and one acre of arable land in 'Kukukes', between the land of Clerkenwell on the east and the road from the chapel to the Brent on the west for 3s. 4d. annual rent.[2] This was probably the 'priest-house' which abutted upon lands belonging to Kilburn Priory in 1400.[3] The chapel's endowments came from the Knights Hospitallers and possibly from Tokyngton manor, to which the advowson belonged.[4] After acquiring the advowson in 1317[5] the Barnville family presented a priest to the 'chantry' or 'perpetual chantry' of Tokyngton chapel in 1367 and 1419.[6] The chapel was worth £4 13s. 4d. a year in 1535.[7] The last priest, William Layton, brother of Richard, surrendered Tokyngton to the Crown in 1545,[8] but three years later John Finch claimed to hold the property, then worth £6 a year, by a grant from Layton made about two years earlier.[9] A decision not to interfere with Finch's occupation seems to have been followed until 1567,[10]

when the queen leased the property to Richard Read for £3 9s. 8d. The drop in value is explained by the complete ruin of the chapel, for Read undertook to repair and maintain the premises. In 1795 the build-ing was said to have been long since destroyed.[11] The lease was renewed, for fines of £10 9s. in 1585 and 1597, to Richard Read and his descendants.[12]

In 1607 the king granted the chapel of Tokyngton, a messuage, barn, three closes of meadow (10 a.), and 2 a. of wood in Tokyngton and Wembley, with a moiety of tithes of corn, grain, hay, and wood, issuing from these premises, in fee farm for £3 9s. 8d. a year to Sir William Herrick and Arthur Ingram, who conveyed them in the same year to John Page.[13] Thereafter this property descended with Tokyngton manor until in 1650 John Page sold the chapel, tithes, messuage, and lands to Humphrey Wigan, a London merchant tailor,[14] who in 1672 conveyed them to another tailor, Lawrence Wood of Holborn, for £360.[15] Wood surrendered his interest in 1724 to John Wyne, who surrendered it in the same year to William Stanlake.[16] In addition the fee farm rent of £3 9s. 8d. was granted out, being held in 1677 and 1703 by Francis and Richard Wilshaw.[17] The property apparently reverted to the Pages and was probably included in the conveyance of Tokyngton in 1800, for at inclosure Richard Page and Robert Tubbs claimed exemption from payment of half-tithe for lands in Wembley and Tokyngton formerly belonging to Kilburn Priory. While Kilburn may have had privileges which would account for Page's claim as lord of Wembley manor, Tubbs's interest derived from Tokyngton manor. This, too, may have been privileged, as its medieval lords were patrons of the chapel, but the claim is more likely to have derived from the post-Dissolution grant to the owners of the manor. Land allotted in lieu of this tithe was assessed at $\frac{1}{18}$ of waste, meadow, and pasture, and $\frac{1}{10}$ of arable land.[18]

In 1324 William de Bosco, rector from c. 1312 to 1324 and probably a member of the Uxendon family, founded a chantry chapel, dedicated to the Virgin, probably on the north side of Harrow church.[19] He endowed it with a messuage, 101 a. of arable, 5 a. of meadow, and 4s. 4d. rent to support a chaplain to celebrate mass daily.[20] The messuage was a chantry house at Hatch End. Most of the land, in 1547 a messuage and 39 a. of closes and 61 selions in the open fields, lay in Kenton, where it was said to be held in free and perpetual alms from the manor of Uxendon for a quit-rent of $\frac{1}{2}$ lb. of cumin.[21] The

[89] Rep. Com. Eccl. Rev. [67], pp. 196–7, H.C. (1835), xxii. [90] H.O. 129/135/1/1/1.
[91] M.R.O., Acc. 76/1906.
[92] Ex inf. the vicar (1967).
[93] Harrow Octocent. Tracts, ix. 15.
[94] Cf. M.R.O., Acc. 643, 2nd deposit, Messeder maps A and B.
[95] M.R.O., H.T. 5, 26, 53, 75.
[96] Druett, Harrow, 163.
[97] M.R.O., Acc. 76/1321, /1601, /1625.
[98] Druett, Harrow, 163. See p. 212.
[99] Harrow Sch. ed. Howson and Warner, 37.
[1] Harrow Octocent. Tracts, ix. 14.
[2] B.M. Harl. MS. 601, f. 48; presumably part of the Freren estate: see above, p. 191.
[3] Cal. Close, 1399–1402, 297.
[4] Elsley, Wembley, 54–56. See above, p. 208.
[5] C.P. 25(1)/149/48/231. See p. 208.
[6] Reg. Langham (Cant. & York Soc. liii), 281; Reg. Chichele (Cant. & York. Soc. xlv), i. 174.
[7] Valor Eccl. (Rec. Com.), i. 434.

[8] W. D. Bushell, 'The alienation of the Harrow manors and the surrender of the chantries', Harrow Octocent. Tracts, xiii. 36–37.
[9] E 301/34, f. 31.
[10] Harrow Octocent. Tracts, xiii. 40–41; E 310/19/91, f. 19.
[11] Lysons, Environs of Lond. ii. 575.
[12] Harrow Octocent. Tracts, xiii. 41–42.
[13] M.R.O., Acc. 276/6; Newcourt, Repertorium, 638; Lysons, Environs of Lond. ii. 576.
[14] Wemb. Hist. Soc., Acc. 465/2.
[15] C.P. 25(2)/691/1672 Mich.
[16] M.R.O., Acc. 210/48; Acc. 276/6. In 1722 Wood had agreed to sell the premises to John Halsey: Acc. 276/5/8.
[17] M.R.O., Acc. 521/Box IV/O.B. IX.
[18] M.R.O., Acc. 310(1).
[19] P.C.C. 7 Blamyr (Hugh Ives). Probably identifiable with the Wm. de Bosco (d. 1329) who was a prebendary of Chichester and Chancellor of Lichfield: J. Le Neve, Fasti, 1300–1541 (revised edn.), vii. 56, x. 9. See above, p. 207.
[20] Cal. Pat. 1321–4, 390; E 310/34, f. 31.
[21] M.R.O., Acc. 166/1, Acc. 1052, ff. 221–6.

chantry was valued in 1535 at £6 a year[22] but in 1548 the property was leased for £9 16s. 5d. a year.[23] The advowson was usually exercised by the parishioners and occasionally by the archbishop.[24] In 1548 the property was sold for £747 8s. 6d. to William Gyes of the Strand.[25] It was then a messuage with 104 a. in Kenton, all in the tenure of William Tanner, the chantry house and other lands in Hatch End, the wood called Thomas Hatches,[26] held by various members of the Edlin family, and a messuage in 'Harrow Street', held by William Finch. By the end of the 16th century the lands had been sub-divided[27] and only the name Priestmead or Priest's Meadow in Kenton[28] and the mistaken local tradition of a chantry in Hatch End recalled the medieval chapel.[29]

William de Bosco also left 10 a. of wheat, 2 oxen, 2 kine, and a horse, to augment the divine service in Harrow church. The church had one light and two obits: Henry Parson granted a close called Danyelles to maintain a lamp and for the relief of the poor, and a croft called Hamonds for an obit; Agnes Greenhill gave a piece of land, Highfield, to support an obit.[30] In 1548 Danyelles, probably in Pinner, was held by Robert Edlin for £1 2s. 8d. a year,[31] and Hamonds, 3 a. in Kenton, was leased to John Seles for 8s.;[32] Highfield, probably in the south of Harrow Weald, was held by Thomas Bugbeard for 8s. a year.[33] In 1548 all three closes, worth £1 15s. 1d. a year clear, were among property granted to Sir Michael Stanhope and John Bellowe.[34]

Other medieval chapels were wholly independent of Harrow church.[35] One belonged to Bentley Priory and, according to Camden, stood on Weald Common, detached from the monastery. A complaint in 1512 that the Prior of St. Gregory's, Canterbury, had not presented for 20 years, 'to the damage of the tenants of the manor', suggests that the chapel was used for public worship. The chapel was demolished, probably in the 16th century, and all trace of it disappeared.[36] There was also a hermitage, dedicated to St. Edmund and St. Katharine, on Sudbury Common, which in 1529 was said to have been in the hands of the lord for many years.[37]

Practically all the rectors were pluralists and absentees, although some stayed at Harrow[38] a few were buried in the church,[39] and some contributed

to its fabric[40] or to the welfare of the poor.[41] Some, like Elias of Dereham (c. 1205 to 1242)[42] or William Baunton (1390 to 1396)[43] became rector for their services as the archbishop's steward. Others, like Simon Offeham (c. 1242 to 1278),[44] Geoffrey of Everley (1278 to 1283),[45] and John de Bukingham (1366 to 1387),[46] were presented sede vacante by the king for their work as royal clerks, seal-bearers, ambassadors, or officials in the Exchequer or Chancery. Among these was Nigel de Sackville,[47] the king's seal-bearer, whom Henry II appointed when Becket was archbishop. Apart from William de Testa,[48] there was one foreign rector, Raymund Pelegrini de Rapistagno (1353–65), a cardinal and papal nuncio as well as a royal chaplain.[49] At least two rectors were builders, Elias of Dereham being concerned with Salisbury Cathedral,[50] and others included a Prior of St. Bartholomew's, Smithfield,[51] two chancellors of Oxford University,[52] and two bishops, one of them Cuthbert Tunstall, translator of the Bible.[53] In 1483 a papal bull permitted the rectors of Harrow to wear the furred almuce, as though they were canons.[54] The last rectors were among the most notorious: Richard Layton (1537–44) was one of Cromwell's visitors, the demolisher of Becket's shrine,[55] and Richard Coxe (1544–6) destroyed books and manuscripts in Oxford.[56]

Much less is known about the medieval vicars, most of whom seem to have been resident.[57] In 1401 there were three other celebrants,[58] and the will of John Byrkhede, rector, in 1468 mentions three chaplains, although one may have been a relation and unconnected with Harrow.[59] In 1521 a chaplain was fined as a common dice player.[60] Apart from the priests who served Pinner, Tokyngton, and the chantry chapel, there were clerks in minor orders, like Robert Baldock, 'holy water clerk', mentioned in 1434.[61] Arthur Layton (vicar 1528–c. 1551), who was probably related to Richard, in 1548 had found two priests to serve the cure.[62] His successor, Richard Dean (1551–9), seems to have been a pluralist.[63] William Launce, Headmaster of Harrow School 1615–21, was appointed vicar in 1625[64] but was apparently displaced in 1645 by Thomas Pakeman, a favourite of the Puritan Sir Gilbert Gerard who considered him a 'constant preaching mini-

[22] Valor Eccl. (Rec. Com.), i. 434.
[23] E 301/34, f. 31.
[24] Reg. Chichele (Cant. & York Soc. xlv), i. 281; Harrow Octocent. Tracts, x. 32.
[25] Cal. Pat. 1547–8, 299. The grant was made to Wm. Gyes and Michael Purefoy, but Purefoy quitclaimed his interest: Harrow Octocent. Tracts, xiii. 44–46.
[26] Probably identifiable with Hatchets, the common field in Harrow Weald (M.R. 612) (pace Cal. Pat. 1547–8, 299).
[27] M.R.O., Acc. 76/205; Acc. 276/9/5.
[28] M.R.O., Acc. 166/1; Acc 794/8; M.R. 612, no. 221; Lambeth Palace, Estate MS. 478.
[29] O.S. Map 1/2,500, Mdx. x. 3 (1865 edn.).
[30] E 301/34, f. 31.
[31] M.R.O., Acc. 76/205, /222a.
[32] M.R.O., Acc. 166/1. Said in the survey of 1546–7 to be held by the churchwardens.
[33] M.R.O., Acc. 76/205, /222a.
[34] Cal. Pat. 1547–8, 391–4.
[35] See also pp. 204–5.
[36] Druett, Weald, 103.
[37] M.R.O., Acc. 76/2421, m. 58.
[38] e.g. John Byrkhede: Reg. Chichele (Cant. & York Soc. xlv), i. 301; Wm. Bolton and Ric. Layton: Harrow Octocent. Tracts, xi. 18–27.
[39] e.g. Simon Marchford (1397–1437): Harrow Octocent. Tracts, xi. 1–4; John Byrkhede: ibid. 5–12.
[40] Simon Marchford: Cal. Papal L. vii. 472–3; Elias of

Dereham: Harrow Octocent. Tracts, x. 10–11, xii, passim; Wm. de Bosco: ibid. x. 15–19.
[41] e.g. John Byrkhede: Harrow Octocent. Tracts, xi. 11; P.C.C. 24 Godyn.
[42] See p. 224.
[43] Harrow Octocent. Tracts, xi. 27.
[44] Cal. Pat. 1232–47, 316.
[45] Harrow Octocent. Tracts, x. 12.
[46] Ibid. 23–25.
[47] Ibid. 9; vi. 20–21.
[48] See above.
[49] Harrow Octocent. Tracts, x. 23.
[50] Ibid. xii.
[51] Wm. Bolton: ibid. xi. 18–21.
[52] John Letch and Ric. Coxe: ibid. x. 21; xi. 30.
[53] Ibid. xi. 16–18.
[54] Reg. Bourgchier (Cant. & York Soc. liv), 61–62.
[55] Harrow Octocent. Tracts. x(2), 22–28.
[56] Ibid. 28–32.
[57] Ibid. ix. 15–22.
[58] Druett, Harrow, 61.
[59] P.C.C. 24 Godyn.
[60] Elsley, Wembley, 73.
[61] Cat. Pat. 1429–36, 313.
[62] E 301/34, f. 31.
[63] Harrow Octocent. Tracts, ix. 19.
[64] Ibid. 20.

ster'.[65] George Pitt, a royalist and possibly a Laudian, who erected communion rails at his own expense,[66] was less enthusiastic about Pakeman and in 1649 asked Gerard for his opinion of Mr. Lauglie as a prospective vicar.[67] Pakeman, ejected in 1662,[68] still resided in the vicarage in 1664,[69] when the new vicar, Joseph Wilcocks, was presented for the second time.[70] The parishioners expressed approval of Wilcocks[71] to Mrs. Pitt, but their relations with Francis Saunders, vicar 1727–76, were not so happy. Six years after establishing the *modus* for small tithe[72] they stopped the vicar from burying non-parishioners in the churchyard without their consent, Saunders having buried 91 in 10 years, compared with 21 in the previous 20 years.[73]

The parish was deeply divided over John William Cunningham, vicar 1811–61.[74] Cunningham was a well-known evangelical, member of the Clapham sect, and author of *The Velvet Cushion*, published in 1814, from which he was nicknamed 'Velvet' Cunningham. The first clash with the aristocratic, and, from 1836 to 1844, high-church Anglicans of Harrow School came in 1822, when Byron wished his illegitimate daughter Allegra to be buried in Harrow church. Although both the evangelicals and the School party agreed that there should be no commemorative stone, to safeguard the morals of the boys, Cunningham at the same time made himself ridiculous by obsequiously seeking Byron's friendship. He asked Byron's friend, Henry Drury, a tutor at the school, to compliment the poet on his recently published *Cain*. Drury repeated the story and his friend Frances Trollope, Anthony's mother, wrote a satirical poem.[75] In 1839, three years after Christopher Wordsworth became headmaster, Cunningham opposed the building of a school chapel, lest the boys should become papists.[76] In 1851 the vicar's popularity was attested by congregations of 1,500, 750, and 750 respectively at the three Sunday services.[77] The parish followed his funeral procession 'like one great family mourning for a father' in 1861, and a lychgate was erected to his memory.[78] Some parishioners, however, asked for a successor who was a gentleman and scholar, in view of the clergymen at the school,[79] and Lord Northwick rejected the candidate suggested by the late vicar and his curates, appointing Francis Hayward Joyce out of some 25 applicants.[80]

The parish church, dedicated to *ST. MARY THE VIRGIN*,[81] stands in a commanding position on the top of Harrow hill, possibly on the site of a pagan temple.[82] It is built of flint with stone dressings and consists of chancel, nave, north and south aisles, north and south transepts, a west tower and spire, a 19th-century north-east chapel and vestry. Nothing survives of Lanfranc's church, and the

earliest portion, the lower part of the tower and the west door, dates from c. 1140. Elias of Dereham was responsible for the chancel, roofed in oak from Harrow forest in 1242,[83] which retains its lancet windows, and probably also for the nave, with its five-bay arcades on low circular piers. The transepts were added at the end of the century. The next major period of building was probably during the rectory of John Byrkhede (1437–67), who, like Dereham, was known as a master builder.[84] The present clerestory and carved tie-beam roof were added, Perpendicular windows were inserted in the aisles, and an upper story and a tall, octagonal spire were built on the old tower. Frequent references were made during the 17th and 18th centuries to the ruinous state of the fabric. Large-scale restoration and alteration took place in the 19th century,[85] notably in 1846–9 when George Gilbert (later Sir Gilbert) Scott refaced the exterior with flint, added battlemented parapets, and reconstructed the chancel. Minor additions and alterations were made in the 20th century.[86]

The church contains 13 brasses, the most notable being those of Sir Edmund Flambard (d. c. 1370) and his wife, Sir John Flambard (d. c. 1390), John Byrkhede (d. 1468), George Aynesworth (d. 1488–9), and his three wives and 14 children, and John Lyon (d. 1592) and his wife. Of the monuments, the largest commemorate two William Gerards (d. 1584 and d. 1609). There is also a memorial of 1815 to John Lyon, carved in relief by John Flaxman, and one to Joseph Drury (d. 1835) by the younger Westmacott. The late-12th-century font is of Purbeck marble and there is a carved late-17th-century pulpit. The plate includes a cup and paten-cover of 1568, a flagon of 1633, and a large paten, paten-cover, and cup of 1638, the latter inscribed 1678. Except for the cup of 1568, which is silver-gilt, all the plate is silver.[87] The registers, which are complete, record marriages and burials from 1558 and baptisms from 1562.[88] There are eight bells: (i, ii, and iv) 1779; (iii) 1665; (v) 1805; (vi) 1683; (vii) 1869; (viii) 1759.[89]

PINNER CHURCH. Although Pinner chapel already existed by 1234–40,[90] it was almost entirely rebuilt before its dedication in 1321 by Peter, Bishop of Corbavia.[91] The consecration, which included the graveyard if not previously consecrated, stressed the authority of the mother church. The chapel had no separate endowment and was served by the Vicar of Harrow or his curate. In 1538, however, the tithes and profits of the rector annexed to the parsonage of Harrow 'as in the right of the chapel

[65] *Harrow Octocent. Tracts*, ix. 20; *Home Cnties. Mag.* i. 321.
[66] M.R.O., Acc. 76/1162.
[67] Ibid. /844.
[68] Matthews, *Calamy Revised*, 379; *D.N.B.*
[69] M.R.O., H.T. 5.
[70] *Harrow Octocent. Tracts*, ix. 21.
[71] M.R.O., Acc. 76/30.
[72] Ibid. /861, /2077.
[73] Bodl. MS. Eng. Misc. C. 31, ff. 76 sqq.
[74] *Harrow Octocent. Tracts*, ix. 21–22.
[75] M. Sadleir, *Trollope, A Commentary*, 47–48.
[76] H.O. 129/135/1/1/2; *V.C.H. Mdx.* i. 300.
[77] H.O. 129/135/1/1/1.
[78] *Harrow Octocent. Tracts*, ix. 22; Druett, *Harrow*, 162.
[79] M.R.O., Acc. 76/101.
[80] Ibid. /101–20.
[81] *T.L.M.A.S.* xviii(2), no. 77; Hist. Mon. Com. *Mdx.* 64–67; Pevsner, *Mdx.* 97; Robbins, *Middlesex*, 281–2.
[82] See p. 172.
[83] *Close R.* 1237–42, 420.
[84] *Harrow Octocent. Tracts*, xi. 5–12.
[85] M.R.O., D.R.O. 3/B4/1; Acc. 76/1152, /1155, /1179, /1699; Acc. 643, 2nd deposit; Robbins, *Middlesex*, 281.
[86] M.R.O., D.R.O. 3/F2/4.
[87] E. Freshfield, *Communion Plate of Mdx.* 29.
[88] See list in M.R.O. The registers from 1558 to 1653 have been edited and printed by W. O. Hewlett (1899).
[89] *T.L.M.A.S.* xviii(2), no. 77.
[90] *Harrow Octocent. Tracts*, ix. 14.
[91] Lambeth Palace, Reynolds's Reg., f. 126v. Printed in Ware, *Pinner*, 62.

of Pinner' were leased separately,[92] and in 1548 the communicants of Pinner were separately enumerated.[93] During the 17th century the inhabitants often had their own minister[94] and in 1650 they detained the small tithes for him, while the commissioners recommended that Pinner should be made a separate parish, 'considering the distance of the place and the illness of the way'.[95] In 1699 Pinner asserted its immunity from the Harrow church-rate,[96] but it was not until 1766 that it achieved full parochial independence as a perpetual curacy as the result of a benefaction from Queen Anne's Bounty.[97] From 1868 it was called a vicarage.[98]

The advowson of the perpetual curacy and later of the vicarage of Pinner was exercised by the Vicar of Harrow.[99] The first perpetual curate, Walter L. Williams (appointed 1764) retained Pinner on becoming Vicar of Harrow in 1776. When Williams presented a curate for Pinner, Lord Northwick was apparently annoyed that he had not been consulted.[1] In 1961–2 the benefice was served by a vicar and one curate.[2]

In 1548, under 'Pinner', the parsonage and vicarage were given as worth £18 and £13 6s. 8d. a year respectively.[3] The figures presumably represent the tithes and offerings drawn from the Pinner area, for the chapel was not yet endowed. By will dated 1622 John Dey, Curate of Pinner chapel, left property for the maintenance of a preaching minister, 'a man well qualified and a Master of Arts at the least',[4] but there is no evidence that his provision was carried out. The earliest known endowment was Francis Tyndale's gift in 1630 of Willat Street *alias* Howlis Close, 3 a. north of Hooking Green.[5] In 1642, when the inhabitants petitioned for a lecturer whom they would maintain at their own charge, their curate received £10 a year from the Vicar of Harrow,[6] representing the small tithes of Pinner, which, including those of Headstone, were worth £19 6s. 8d. a year in 1650. The parliamentary commissioners settled £60 on the Pinner minister.[7] In 1705 William Norrington gave £100 with which to buy a dwelling-house. A rent-charge of £4 on property at Ruislip was given by the will of Sir Thomas Franklin of Pinner Hill, dated 1728, and in 1731 two common-field lands were bought with money from the sale of wood in Willat Close,[8] which was later sold to redeem the land tax on other glebe lands.[9] From 1766 these endowments were supplemented by an annual payment of £8 made by the Vicar of Harrow.[10] In 1766 £200 from Queen Anne's Bounty was granted to

the minister, and in 1772 Howells and Hungerlands, 20 a. at Hooking Green which had been sold to the commissioners by Matthew Fearne, were added to the glebe.[11] Thus at inclosure Walter L. Williams, as Curate of Pinner, had 25 a. of old inclosure and 3 a. allotted in lieu of common-field land.[12] By will proved 1797, Mary Roberts bequeathed £600 stock to augment the curacy of Pinner, provided that the curate was resident. The benefaction came into effect after the death of a life annuitant in 1811 and a suit in Chancery.[13] At about this time the curacy was estimated to be worth £180 a year, consisting of a small house, 26 a. of old inclosures worth £100, and £80 in benefactions and perquisites.[14] In 1835 the average net income was said to be only £100[15] and in 1851 it was only £81, of which £71 came from endowments.[16] The parishioners tried hard to induce Christ Church to help their curate, who had 'the duties of a vicar and the stipend of a curate'. The college refused, since the chapelry had had no share in the vicarial tithes. Christ Church also declined to repair the chancel, and the Pinner inhabitants, who had to pay great tithes to the college as well as levy their own church-rate for repairs, became very bitter.[17] The glebe was sold in the 1930s.[18]

The first perpetual curate lived in Pinner House.[19] By 1875 the old vicarage, bought with the gift of 1705, was so dilapidated that a maid's leg came through the ceiling,[20] but repairs were effected with £750 from the Ecclesiastical Commissioners.[21] The old vicarage, which had 18 rooms, stood near the road in Church Lane, and in 1877 was also used as a school. It was demolished in 1937 and replaced by a building set further back on the same site.[22]

One obit in Pinner chapel was maintained from a messuage called Beale of Pinner, given by John Street. This was leased for 12s. in 1548 when two tenements in Pinner churchyard, whose origin had been forgotten, were leased for 8s. a year. In 1548 all this property was granted to Thomas Bouchior and Henry Tanner.[23] A church house was mentioned in 1628, 1634, and 1690.[24]

Little is known about the curates of Pinner. In 1642 the inhabitants complained that the curate, John Willis, seldom preached or provided anyone in his place. They appointed Philip Goodwin, but Willis, making up for his neglect, 'expanded' in Pinner chapel for the whole of the afternoon when Goodwin was to take up his appointment. Finally Willis was ordered by Parliament to give way.[25] The 'preaching minister' in 1650 was William Rolls or

[92] Cant. Cath. Libr., Reg. T2, ff. 114v–5.
[93] E 301/34, f. 28v; *Harrow Octocent. Tracts*, ix. 24.
[94] e.g. in 1622: M.R.O., Acc. 76/1095c; in 1642: Hist. MSS. Com. *5th Rep*. 66.
[95] Lambeth Palace MS. 913, Parl. Survey XII, pp. 147–50. Printed in *Home Cnties. Mag.* i. 321–2.
[96] Robbins, *Middlesex*, 319.
[97] M.R.O., Acc. 76/1095a.
[98] Druett, *Pinner*, 122.
[99] Hennessy, *Novum Repertorium*, 206.
[1] M.R.O., Acc. 76/538.
[2] *Crockford* (1961–2).
[3] E 301/34, f. 28v.
[4] M.R.O., Acc. 76/1095c.
[5] Ibid.; M.R. 612, no. 1360; Pinner church, B1/1; Lysons, *Environs of Lond.* ii. 586.
[6] Hist. MSS. Com. *5th Rep*. 66.
[7] *Home Cnties. Mag.* i. 321–2.
[8] Lysons, *Environs of Lond.* ii. 586.
[9] Druett, *Pinner*, 127.
[10] M.R.O., Acc. 76/1095a; *Ret. of Parishes divided . . .*

since 1866, H.C. 433, p. 43 (1870), liv.
[11] M.R.O., Acc. 76/1095a; M.R. 612, nos. 1292, 1294; Druett, *Pinner*, 127. See above, p. 215.
[12] M.R.O., Acc. 794/8.
[13] M.R.O., Acc. 76/464, /1616; *9th Rep. Com. Char.* H.C. 258, pp. 265–6 (1823), ix.
[14] M.R.O., Acc. 76/562.
[15] *Rep. Com. Eccl. Rev.* [67], pp. 196–7, H.C. (1835), xxii.
[16] H.O. 129/135/1/1/5.
[17] Christ Church MS. Estates 47/443, /520, /535, /537, /541.
[18] Druett, *Pinner*, 127.
[19] Ibid. 94, 111.
[20] Ware, *Pinner*, 41.
[21] *Lond. Gaz.* 1876, p. 2927; Druett, *Pinner*, 122.
[22] Ware, *Pinner*, 209. The frontage to Church Lane is illustrated in *Panorama of Pinner Village*, ed. Gadsden (1969).
[23] E 301/34, f. 28v; *Cal. Pat.* 1547–8, 410.
[24] Druett, *Pinner*, 94, 111.
[25] Hist. MSS. Com. *5th Rep*. 66; Druett, *Pinner*, 82.

Rowles,[26] who was ejected in 1662, and was later an Independent minister of Pinner.[27] James Cox became curate after his expulsion as Headmaster of Harrow School in 1746 for 'a disorderly, drunken, idle life'.[28] Later incumbents included Cunningham's protégée, John Venn (1830–3), son of the Rector of Clapham after whom the Clapham sect was named,[29] William St. Hill Bourne (1875–80), the hymn-writer, and William H. Pinnock (1880–5), the writer on church history.[30]

The church of *ST. JOHN THE BAPTIST*,[31] Pinner, built of flint with freestone and ironstone dressings, stands on a hill in the centre of old Pinner. It consists of chancel, nave, north and south aisles, north and south transepts, south-east chapel, and western tower, and dates largely from the early 14th century, although the plan and the lower part of the north-east wall may date from the 13th century. The tower and south porch were added in the 15th century and a large wooden cross, encased in lead, was erected on top of the tower in 1637. Considerable alterations were made in the 19th century, especially in 1811, 1859 when the south chapel was added, and 1880 when the whole building was 'renovated' by J. L. Pearson. A few repairs were effected in 1936 and 1949–53. The church contains a chrisom brass (1581) and a number of 17th-century wall monuments and floor slabs, notably those of John Dey (d. 1622), Thomas Hutchinson and his wife (both d. 1656), and Christopher Clitherow (d. 1685). There is a 15th-century font and a 17th-century chest. In the churchyard is the monument to William Loudon (d. *c.* 1810) which, from its strange shape, gave rise to a local legend.[32]

All the old silver plate was stolen in 1846 and replaced by a plated set in 1883.[33] The registers date from 1654 and are complete.[34] There are five bells dating from 1622, which have been recast, and three more which were added in 1771.[35]

MODERN CHURCHES. In 1815 a chapel of ease was dedicated to St. Andrew in the south-west corner of what later became the churchyard of All Saints. It was served by the curates of Harrow, of whom there were two in 1835.[36] One of them, Edward Monro, became in 1841 the first perpetual curate of the new church of *ALL SAINTS*, Harrow Weald,[37] built near the chapel of ease in 1842 and 1843 and consecrated in 1850.[38] A separate parish

was assigned to it in 1844, taken from St. Mary's, Harrow, and a small part of Bushey (Herts.).[39] The church is of stone and comprises chancel, built by J. T. Harrison in 1842, nave and south aisle, built by W. Butterfield in 1845, and north aisle and gabled tower, also by Butterfield, added in 1890 at the expense of T. F. Blackwell. Two vestries were added in 1958. Six bells date from 1890 and two from 1935. Registers of burial date from 1838 and of marriages and baptisms from 1845.[40] The living was a perpetual curacy until 1861 when it became a vicarage. The patronage is exercised by trustees.[41] The original building costs were met by subscription, mainly raised by the Vicar of Harrow, one of whose friends endowed the church with £1,500.[42] In 1963–4 the parish was served by a vicar and two curates.[43] St. Barnabas, Long Elmes, is a mission church within All Saints' parish. It originated in 1950 on a housing estate in north Headstone. A dual-purpose hall was built by the diocese and consecrated in 1955. It is a flat-roofed brick building, with a priest-in-charge.[44]

Anne and Frances Copland, who in 1843 inherited Sudbury Lodge and its estate, offered land nearby for a church to serve the southern part of Harrow parish. In spite of opposition from local farmers, who preferred a site on Lord Northwick's property on Wembley Hill, the sisters' offer was accepted since they would bear all the cost of building.[45] The church of *ST. JOHN THE EVANGELIST*, Wembley, designed by George Gilbert (later Sir Gilbert) Scott and W. B. Moffatt, was consecrated in 1846. It was built of flint with stone dressings, in the Gothic style, and comprised chancel, nave, north-east chapel, and wooden bell turret. A north aisle was added in 1859 and a south aisle in 1900; extensions were made to the west by G. P. Pratt in 1935. There is one bell and the registers date from 1846.[46] It became a separate parish in 1846; the living was a perpetual curacy until 1872, when it came to be called a vicarage.[47] The patronage is exercised by trustees, originally appointed by the Coplands and thereafter co-opted by the survivors.[48] The sisters endowed the church with £1,300, which with £200 from Queen Anne's Bounty and £30 a year charged on Harrow vicarage, gave an income in 1851 of £74. Even with pew rents and offerings, the annual income in 1851 was not more than £119,[49] and in 1859 the curate asked Christ Church to contribute, pleading that he had only £150 a year with which to keep a wife and 7 children, that the population had greatly

[26] *Home Cnties. Mag.* i. 321–2.
[27] Matthews, *Calamy Revised*, 416. See below, p. 261.
[28] Druett, *Pinner*, 108.
[29] Ware, *Pinner*, 207–8. See above, p. 255.
[30] Druett, *Pinner*, 122, 125.
[31] Hist. Mon. Com. *Mdx.* 101–3; Ware, *Pinner*, 57–84; Robbins, *Middlesex*, 320; *T.L.M.A.S.* xviii(2), no. 86; Pevsner, *Mdx.* 131–2.
[32] i.e. that the coffin was contained in the monument, above ground: *Panorama of Pinner Village*, ed. Gadsden.
[33] E. Freshfield, *Communion Plate of Mdx.* 42.
[34] See list in M.R.O., where most are deposited, D.R.O. 8/A1.
[35] *Parish church of Pinner* (pamphlet).
[36] *Rep. Com. Eccl. Rev.* [67], pp. 196–7, H.C. (1835), xxii.
[37] *Ret. of Parishes divided . . . since 1866*, H.C. 433, p. 43 (1870), liv; ex inf. the Vicar of All Saints.
[38] H.O. 129/135/1/1/4.
[39] *Lond. Gaz.* 1845, p. 2030; *Ret. of Parishes divided . . . 1818–56*, H.C. 557, p. 23 (1861), xlviii. The dates of the foundations of all the parishes in the following section are

in *London Diocesan Bk.* (1969).
[40] *T.L.M.A.S.* xviii(2), no. 781; Pevsner, *Mdx.* 103; Robbins, *Middlesex*, 285; ex inf. the vicar. See illustration in Druett, *Weald*.
[41] *Lond. Gaz.* 1882, p. 538; Hennessy, *Novum Repertorium*, 206.
[42] Christ Church MS. Estates 47/457, /464.
[43] *Crockford* (1963–4).
[44] Ex inf. the priest-in-charge (1965); ex inf. the Vicar of All Saints (1966).
[45] M.R.O., Acc. 76/154.
[46] Originally called Sudbury church: Elsley, *Wembley*, 191; J. Silvester, *Visible & Invisible* (pamphlet hist. of St. John's, Wembley); *T.L.M.A.S.* xviii(2), no. 203; Pevsner, *Mdx.* 170.
[47] *Ret. of Parishes divided . . . since 1866*, H.C. 433, p. 43 (1870), liv; Elsley, *Wembley*, 191–2; Christ Church MS. Estates 47/567.
[48] Hennessy, *Novum Repertorium*, 207.
[49] H.O. 129/135/1/1/3; Christ Church MS. Estates 47/515.

increased, and that the inhabitants either joined the dissenters 'or neglect the means of grace.'[50] In 1869, when the income was £175, the college was approached again[51] and in 1872 Christ Church endowed the Wembley vicarage with £50 from corn-rents.[52] C. Layard, who enlarged the church in 1859, attracted a large congregation as perpetual curate.[53] There were weekly meetings during the 1880s at Wembley Hill and in Honeypot Lane, Alperton, while services for men were held at the workmen's hall and for women in a house in Alperton and a room in East Lane. After such evangelism the high church innovations of J. W. P. Silvester (vicar 1896–1944) aroused controversy.[54]

Activity by the Vicar of Harrow and his curates led to the foundation in 1862 of *CHRIST CHURCH*, Roxeth. The church, accommodating 350,[55] was built of flint with stone dressings by George Gilbert (later Sir Gilbert) Scott. It consisted of chancel, nave, transepts, north aisle, and a tower with a small spire. A south aisle was added in 1866 and the whole building was restored by G. H. Jenkins in 1953–4.[56] In 1863 Christ Church became a district chapelry, created from the mother parish of Harrow and bordering the new chapelry of St. John the Evangelist, Wembley.[57] There was a perpetual curate until 1873, when a vicar was appointed.[58] In 1963–4 Christ Church was served by a vicar and curate.[59] The patronage was originally exercised by trustees[60] and in 1963–4 by the Church Patronage Society. The registers date from 1863.

Although Christ Church, Oxford, conveyed land for the purpose to the Church Commissioners in 1869,[61] it was not until 1882 that the church of *HOLY TRINITY*, Wealdstone, was built to serve the newly developed neighbourhood. The building, erected with the help of 'gentlemen of Harrow Weald', is of stone with brick dressings in the Gothic style by Roumieu & Aitchison. It comprises chancel, nave, and aisles,[62] accommodating 286.[63] The parish of Holy Trinity, a district chapelry, was created in 1881 out of the parishes of Harrow, Harrow Weald, and Pinner.[64] The incumbent is a vicar, appointed by trustees for the Diocesan Board.[65]

The Vicar of Harrow unsuccessfully tried to raise money for a church at Greenhill, south of Wealdstone, in 1864.[66] He held services, however, at the workmen's club room before the consecration in 1866 of *ST. JOHN THE BAPTIST*, Greenhill,[67] a small church 'of particoloured brick, with a prodigious roof',[68] built by Bassett Keeling. It was administered as a chapel of ease under the Vicar of Harrow until the curate was given sole charge in

1885. The church became a separate parish, created out of Harrow, in 1896 when the stipend of its vicar was £200. The church was rebuilt on a larger scale in 1904, to serve the population which had spread southward from Wealdstone. The nave, west porch, and turret of the old building were demolished and a new nave and aisles, built in the Decorated style by J. S. Alder, were consecrated in 1905; transepts were added in 1925 and a new chancel, by M. Travers, replaced that of the old church in 1938.[69] The registers date from 1869. The living is in the patronage of the Bishop of London, the Archdeacon of Middlesex, and the Vicar of Harrow. From 1897 the vicar was assisted by a curate and in 1963–4 there were two curates.[70]

All Saints, Woodridings, was erected in 1865 on the initiative of the Vicar of Pinner.[71] It functioned as a chapel of ease, with a curate appointed by the vicar and paid a stipend of £150. The building, of corrugated iron, was entered from Wellington Road and Devonshire Road. Although it was enlarged after a request by the Royal Commercial Travellers' Schools for additional accommodation for 100 children, subscriptions were raised for a new church, to accommodate 450, which was founded in 1894 on T. F. Blackwell's building estate. The church of *ST. ANSELM*, Hatch End, consecrated in 1895, was built by F. E. Jones of brick and flint in the Gothic style, and consisted of chancel, nave, and chapel; a north aisle was added in 1906.[72] A rood screen was dedicated in 1902 after an appeal to the Court of Arches against the chancellor, who had feared that it would encourage superstition.[73] St. Anselm's was a stipendiary curacy under the Vicar of Pinner until 1906, when it became a vicarage in the patronage of the Bishop of London. The new parish was formed in 1895 mostly from Pinner parish, with a small area from All Saints, Harrow Weald.[74] In 1963–4 it was served by a vicar and two curates.[75]

During the 1880s Alperton was served by missions from St. John's, Wembley. In 1890 the vicar, who had long deplored the 'careless state' of many in the village, persuaded W. R. Lane, a wandering missionary, to set up his tent in Alperton. It was replaced in 1893 by a mission room, and in 1896 by a corrugated iron church, which was administered by the Vicar of Wembley and a curate[76] until a separate parish, *ST. JAMES*, Alperton, was created in 1904.[77] The living is a perpetual curacy in the patronage of trustees.[78] A church, built by W. A. Pite in the Gothic style, was consecrated in Stanley Avenue in 1912. It is of yellow stock brick with red brick and stone dressings, and consists of chancel, nave, aisles,

[50] Christ Church MS. Estates 47/563, /567.
[51] Ibid. /612–13, /624, /626–32.
[52] Christ Church Deeds, Harrow 1872; *Lond. Gaz.* 1872, p. 5878.
[53] Christ Church MS. Estates 47/567.
[54] J. Silvester, *Visible & Invisible.*
[55] *Ret. of Districts . . . 1861–3*, H.C. 163, p. 507 (1865), xli. [56] *T.L.M.A.S.* xviii(2), no. 79.
[57] *Lond. Gaz.* 1863, p. 4497.
[58] Hennessy, *Novum Repertorium*, 206.
[59] *Crockford* (1963–4).
[60] *Ret. of Districts . . . 1861–3*, H.C. 163, p. 507 (1865), xli.
[61] Christ Church Deeds, Harrow conveyance 1869; ibid. MS. Estates 47/675.
[62] *T.L.M.A.S.* xviii(2), no. 8; Pevsner, *Mdx.* 169; ex inf. the vicar (1965).
[63] *Ret. of Parishes divided . . . 1880–90*, H.C. 386, p. 11 (1890–1), lxi.

[64] Ibid.; *Lond. Gaz.* 1882, pp. 537–8.
[65] Hennessy, *Novum Repertorium*, 207; *London Diocesan Bk.* (1969).
[66] Christ Church MS. Estates 47/589.
[67] G. Rowles, *Onward* (pamphlet history of St. John's, Greenhill, 1954).
[68] Robbins, *Middlesex*, 284.
[69] Ibid.; *T.L.M.A.S.* xviii(2), no. 83.
[70] *Crockford* (1963–4).
[71] Ware, *Pinner*, 7–9.
[72] Ibid. 195–200; *T.L.M.A.S.* xviii(2), no. 90; Christ Church MS. Estates 47/700, /788, /790.
[73] Ware, *Pinner*, 197–8.
[74] *London Diocesan Bk.* (1969).
[75] *Crockford* (1963–4).
[76] J. Silvester, *Visible & Invisible.*
[77] *Census*, 1931, *Eccl. Areas*, 77.
[78] *Crockford* (1963–4).

south transept, north-east chapel, north-west baptistery, narthex, and bell turret. It has one bell and contains an organ which came from St. Peter's, Clerkenwell. The registers date from 1904.[79]

In 1907, on the initiative of the Vicar of St. Anselm's, Hatch End, a corrugated iron church was erected to serve Headstone. Most of the new parish was formed in 1911 out of St. Anselm's, but small portions were taken from Pinner and Greenhill. Money was raised locally and the church of *ST. GEORGE*, Headstone, was consecrated in 1911. The building, by Alder, Turrill & Danvers, is of red brick with stone dressings in the Gothic style. It consists of chancel, nave, and aisles; a stained glass east window by M. Travers was added in 1935 and a reredos by J. Crawford in 1949.[80] The living is a perpetual curacy, in the patronage of the Bishop of London.[81]

A church extension scheme was inaugurated in 1904 to serve the expanding suburbs of London. Among the first mission churches was *ST. PETER*, North Harrow. In 1907 a temporary church was dedicated on a site fronting Sumner Road and Colbeck Road. It was run as a mission church of St. Mary's, Harrow, by London Diocesan Home Missionaries until a permanent building was erected in 1913, when a separate parish was created.[82] The church, built by G. H. Fellowes Prynne of stone with red brick dressings, consists of chancel, nave, aisles, transepts, north-east chapel, baptistery, and bell turret.[83] The living is a vicarage in the patronage of the Bishop of London.[84]

Another foundation under this scheme was the church of *ST. ANDREW*, Sudbury, consecrated in 1904. The building was designed by Arnold Mitchell for secular and religious purposes. A separate hall was built in 1911 but plans for a permanent church by J. S. Alder were interrupted by the war. A new church, designed by W. Charles Waymouth, architect of the London Diocesan Home Mission, was consecrated in 1926. It is of brick with stone dressings, with an open-timber interior, and consists of chancel, nave, aisles, north-east chapel, and bell turret.[85] Sudbury was a London Diocesan Home Mission, with a resident missioner from 1910 until 1925 when it became a separate parish, served by a vicar with the Bishop of London as patron.[86] The vicar was assisted by a curate from 1932.[87] Although founded on the initiative of one of the Harrow curates, St. Andrew's took its parish from St. John's, Wembley.

Another daughter of St. John's, Wembley, was the church of *ST. AUGUSTINE*, Wembley Park, opened as a mission church in 1912. A permanent church, built in the Byzantine style by G. P. Pratt, was opened in 1926 but the foundations were insecure and it was demolished in 1953.[88] A new church was built in 1954 by W. W. Todd and G. Briscoe in

Wembley Hill Road, a low brick and concrete building, consisting of chancel, narrowed at the sanctuary, nave, south-west chapel, and roof turret.[89] St. Augustine's was a mission church until 1926, when it became a separate parish and a vicarage in the patronage of the Bishop of London.[90] The church of The Annunciation, South Kenton, which was opened in 1938, has a conventional district within St. Augustine's.[91]

In 1927 a new parish in Kenton was formed from the parishes of St. Mary, Harrow, All Saints, Harrow Weald, St. John the Baptist, Greenhill, and St. Augustine, Wembley Park. A wooden church, dedicated to St. Leonard, was replaced by a permanent church in 1936,[92] with money from the sale of the site of St. Mary the Virgin, Charing Cross. The church of *ST. MARY THE VIRGIN*, Kenton, was built of yellow brick with stone dressings in the Gothic style by J. H. Gibbons. It consists of chancel, nave, north aisle, south passage aisle, a double north transept, north-east and east chapels, west gallery, and south tower. Fittings include a Calvary by A. Toft, a rood screen, the font from St. Giles, Cripplegate, fragments of glass from All Saints, North Street, York, and Italian glass in the baptistery.[93] The living is a vicarage in the patronage of the Bishop of London. In 1963–4 it was served by a vicar and two curates.[94]

In 1928 a mission church was founded by the clergy of Christ Church, Roxeth, to serve the new housing estate at South Harrow. In 1930 a conventional district was created from Christ Church parish for the church of *ST. PAUL*, South Harrow. It became a parish in 1937 when the temporary wood and asbestos structure was replaced with the aid of proceeds from the sale of Holy Trinity, Gray's Inn Road, and £4,000 raised locally.[95] The church, built by N. F. Cachemaille-Day in grey brick, consists of chancel, nave, north aisle, south chapel, west gallery, and east tower; it contains stained glass by C. Webb and an organ from St. Luke's, Berwick Street.[96] In 1967–8 it was served by a vicar and two curates, and the patron was the Rector of St. Bride's, Fleet Street.[97]

Another parish which began as a London Diocesan Home Mission is that of *ST. MICHAEL*, Tokyngton, which originated in a wooden church opened in 1926. The parish, with a curate-in-charge, was formed in 1925 from the parish of St. John the Evangelist, Wembley. It is a vicarage in the patronage of the Bishop of London.[98] A permanent church was built in 1933 with money raised locally and with £8,000 donated after the closing of Christ Church, Endell Street (W.C.1). The church, built of yellow brick with stone dressings by C. A. Farey, consists of an apsidal chancel and nave. It was damaged in the Second World War. The furniture and fittings come from Christ Church, Endell Street, and the bells,

[79] *T.L.M.A.S.* xviii(2), no. 206.
[80] Ware, *Pinner*, 202; *T.L.M.A.S.* xviii(2), no. 91; *Census*, 1911.
[81] *Crockford* (1963–4).
[82] *St. Peter's Church Golden Jubilee, 1913–63* (pamphlet).
[83] *T.L.M.A.S.* xviii(2), no. 87.
[84] *Crockford* (1963–4).
[85] *Parish church of St. Andrew, Sudbury* (pamphlet); *Sudbury*, ed. Egan, 21–27; J. Silvester, *Visible & Invisible*; *T.L.M.A.S.* xviii(2), no. 204.
[86] *Census*, 1931, *Eccl. Areas*; Wemb. Hist. Soc., Acc. 759.
[87] *Crockford* (1963–4).

[88] Elsley, *Wembley*, 193.
[89] *T.L.M.A.S.* xviii(2), no. 205.
[90] *Census*, 1931, *Eccl. Areas*, 85.
[91] *Crockford* (1963–4); Elsley, *Wembley*, 194; ex inf. the Rural Dean of Harrow (1967).
[92] Ex inf. the vicar (1967).
[93] *T.L.M.A.S.* xviii(2), no. 84; Robbins, *Middlesex*, 285; *Wembley News*, 29 Jan. 1953.
[94] *Crockford* (1963–4).
[95] Ex inf. the assistant curate (1965).
[96] *T.L.M.A.S.* xviii(2), no. 86.
[97] *Crockford* (1967–8).
[98] Ibid. (1963–4).

dating from 1828, from St. Thomas's, Portman Square.[99]

In 1930 a new parish was formed when mission services were organized by Pinner church in a hall in the new residential area of North Harrow. In 1937 a permanent church was consecrated at the Ridgeway and a district chapelry was assigned to it. The church of *ST. ALBAN*, North Harrow, designed by A. W. Kenyon, is considered one of the finest Middlesex churches of its time. Built with a re-inforced concrete frame, yellow brick walls, and barrel roofing, it comprises chancel, nave, passage aisles, north-east chapel, and a tall north-east tower; it contains a statue of St. Alban by J. C. Blair. The church was damaged in 1940.[1] From 1937 the living has been a vicarage in the patronage of the Bishop of London. In 1963–4 it was served by a vicar and a curate.[2] In 1960 a small mission church, combined with a hall, was built in Cannon Lane and dedicated to St. Martin. It was run from St. Alban's until the appointment in 1967 of a curate-in-charge.[3]

A wooden mission church, opened in 1938 to serve Sudbury Court estate, was destroyed by a bomb in 1940. Services were held in Byron Court until 1950 when a dual-purpose hall was erected by the London Diocesan Home Mission and a new parish was assigned to it from the parish of St. Andrew, Sudbury. In 1953 it became a vicarage in the patronage of the Bishop of London.[4] The present church of *ST. CUTHBERT*, North Wembley,[5] was consecrated in 1959, paid for by war-damage claims, the London Diocesan Fund, and money raised locally.[6]

A parish was formed in 1952 from the parishes of St. Alban's, North Harrow, and St. Paul's, South Harrow. The church of *ST. ANDREW*, Roxbourne, was built in 1957 in a traditional Gothic style, of pale stock brick with a tower and spire.[7] In 1963–4 the parish, of which the living was a vicarage in the patronage of the Bishop of London, was served by a vicar and two curates.[8]

Services held in a marquee by a priest sent by the Bishop of London in 1937 led to the foundation of the church of *THE ASCENSION*, Preston. The dual-purpose hall erected in the Avenue, Wembley, in 1937 became the church hall twenty years later, when a church was built alongside it. The church, paid for by local subscriptions and war-damage payments, is built of yellow stock brick with traditional stained glass.[9] In 1951 a parish was formed from the parishes of St. Augustine, Wembley Park, and St. Mary, Kenton; the living is a vicarage in the patronage of the Bishop of London.[10]

In 1934 a mission district was created to serve the houses on the former farm-land of New College, Oxford. The college gave a combined hall and church, Wykeham Hall, which was erected in 1935.[11] A permanent red brick church, dedicated to *ST.*

MICHAEL AND ALL ANGELS, Harrow Weald, was built in 1958 with money from the War Damage Commission.[12] The parish was formed in 1935 from the parishes of All Saints, Harrow Weald, and Holy Trinity, Wealdstone, and the vicarage is in the patronage of the Bishop of London.[13]

ROMAN CATHOLICISM. Early Roman Catholic activity centred on Uxendon manor-house, where, from the beginning of the Jesuit mission, priests sought refuge with the Bellamys.[14] William Bellamy (d. 1581) entertained Edmund Campion shortly before his capture in 1581, and Richard Bristow, author of *Motives Inducing to the Catholic Faith*, who was buried in Harrow churchyard under the pseudonym of Richard Springe, apparently lived in the house for some time. In 1583 William's widow, Catherine, and two of her sons, Richard and Jerome, were indicted as recusants[15] and another son, Robert, was imprisoned. Jesuits continued to visit Uxendon and in 1586 Anthony Babington was captured there. Catherine Bellamy died in the Tower, Jerome, 'a very clownish, blunt, wilful, and obstinate papist', was hanged for bringing food to the conspirators, and two other sons, Robert and Bartholomew, also died in prison. Richard, a married son, moved from Tokyngton manor-house to Uxendon after his mother's imprisonment and continued the family tradition.[16] His wife, Catherine and two of his sons, Faith and Thomas, were indicted for recusancy in 1587[17] and in 1592 his daughter Anne was committed to the Gatehouse of Westminster. There the notorious pursuivant Richard Topcliffe seduced her and forced her to betray the Jesuit Robert Southwell, who was arrested at Uxendon in 1592 and executed in 1595.[18] Possibly Topcliffe promised protection for Anne's relatives, for they were arrested but not executed and Richard was released for a time. Anne was married to an under-keeper of the Gatehouse prison and in 1594, after she had borne Topcliffe's child, Topcliffe asked her father for a marriage portion and for Preston manor-house as a residence for Anne and Nicholas Jones. The Bellamys seem to have been angered more by the marriage than by Topcliffe, but Richard's refusal brought further persecution. Richard and Catherine Bellamy, charged with receiving 15 or 16 priests, were committed to the Gatehouse, their two daughters, Audrey and Mary, were sent to the Clink, and Faith and Thomas to St. Catherine's prison. After 10 years' 'persecutions of extreme barbarity', Richard Bellamy conformed and was released, selling his Uxendon estates and dying in poverty in Belgium. Although there is a tradition that his wife died in prison, 'Catherine Bellamy of London, widow, late wife of Richard Bellamy', figured in a mortgage of Preston manor-house in 1609.[19] The two sons seem to have

[99] J. Silvester, *Visible & Invisible*; Elsley, *Wembley*, 194; *T.L.M.A.S.* xviii(2), no. 207; ex inf. the vicar (1965).
[1] Ware, *Pinner*, 193–5; *T.L.M.A.S.* xviii(2), no. 81; Robbins, *Middlesex*, 285, where the church is wrongly called St. Paul's; Pevsner, *Mdx.* 103; Bor. of Harrow, *Official Guide* (n.d.).
[2] *Crockford* (1963–4).
[3] Ex inf. the vicar (1967).
[4] *Crockford* (1963–4).
[5] Elsley, *Wembley*, 193; ex inf. churchwarden (1965).
[6] Ex inf. churchwarden.
[7] Ware, *Pinner*, 195.
[8] *Crockford* (1963–4).

[9] Elsley, *Wembley*, 194; *Church of The Ascension* (pamphlet). [10] *Crockford* (1963–4).
[11] *Parish Mag.* Oct. 1965, and MS. notes by the vicar.
[12] *T.L.M.A.S.* xviii(2), no. 85.
[13] *Crockford* (1963–4).
[14] The following section is based on W. D. Bushell, 'The Bellamies of Uxendon', *Harrow Octocent. Tracts*, xiv; Elsley, *Wembley*, 77–94.
[15] *Mdx. Cnty Recs.* i. 140.
[16] Ibid. 207; *Cal. S.P. Dom. 1591–4*, 403, 528.
[17] *Mdx. Cnty. Recs.* i. 171.
[18] *Cath. Rec. Soc.* v. 334.
[19] M.R.O., Acc. 853/13.

conformed but their fate and that of their sisters, who were apparently in prison for some time, is unknown. Three more recusants were indicted in 1587[20] and another was indicted in 1591;[21] at least one of those charged in 1587 served in the Bellamy household.[22] The Page family also provided some recusants. William Page, brother of the first Catherine Bellamy, lived in Uxendon manor-house and was imprisoned with the rest. Anthony Page (d. 1593) and Francis Page (d. 1692), both priests, became Roman Catholic martyrs.[23]

Apart from the Revd. Chetwood Eustace, an Irishman who assisted Dr. Collins in his school,[24] no more Roman Catholics appear until the late 19th century. In 1873 the church of Our Lady and St. Thomas of Canterbury was opened as an iron hut in Roxborough Park. In 1894 this was replaced by a church for 250 people, built in the Perpendicular style by Arthur Young, with stained glass by the Harrow artist, J. E. Nuttgens.[25] Monthly mass was offered by the Harrow priest in the public hall in Wealdstone from 1899 until 1901, when the Salvatorian mission, which took the name of St. Joseph, registered Avondale, a private house in the High Road, as a mass-centre. In 1902 the Salvatorians moved to the Elms, a neighbouring house, and in 1905 they bought a site in the same road, where a temporary church was opened a year later. A corrugated iron and wooden hall was built as a school and social centre in 1907 and a community house in 1911. A new church, designed by Adrian G. Scott in the Gothic style, was opened in 1931, from which date the temporary church became a school until its demolition in 1954. A Salvatorian college, started in 1926 in the community house, had by 1967 expanded over much of the site near St. Joseph's church, which is used by the college for its communal masses.[26] Roman Catholics from Wembley worshipped in Harlesden until a convent chapel from Harley Place (near Baker Street), was re-erected in 1901 at Wembley Green. The small brick chapel, also dedicated to St. Joseph, was replaced in 1957 by a new building.[27] Services in Pinner were held at Dudley House, Woodridings, before a church in Love Lane was dedicated to St. Luke in 1915. This church, which contained the shrine of St. Philomena, was replaced by a basilica church in 1957.[28] A mission was established in Sudbury in 1924 and a temporary church was opened two years later. St. George's church in Harrow Road, built of yellow brick in a Gothic style, was consecrated in 1928.[29]

St. Erconwald's in Carlton Avenue East, Wembley,[30] and All Hallows, later All Saints, in Clermont Avenue, Kenton,[31] were founded in 1932. All Saints was a small brick and asbestos structure until a yellow brick church with a free-standing tower was built in 1963.[32] St. Gabriel's in Northolt Road, Roxeth or South Harrow, was founded in 1933[33] and St. John Fisher in Imperial Drive, North Harrow, in 1939.[34] St. Gabriel's, a plain brick church with seating for 180, produced a daughter church, St. Bernard's, at Northolt in 1965.[35] St. John Fisher, whose congregation had previously attended St. Luke's, Pinner, was built in a Romanesque style.[36] Roman Catholics in north Pinner and Harrow Weald formerly attended mass at the convent of Our Lady of Lourdes but the chapel could not accommodate worshippers from the new Headstone Lane estate. A new parish was created in 1953 and a basilica church, dedicated to St. Teresa of the Child Jesus, was built by John E. Sterrett and opened in 1955.[37]

For three years from 1905 the White House in Wembley was occupied by nuns who had been expelled from France.[38] In 1947 Waxwell farm-house in Pinner was acquired by the Grail, a secular organization concerned with ecumenical and welfare work. A chapel, meeting-hall, and dormitory block were added to the original farm-house, which in 1967 was used for conferences and as the administrative centre of the society.[39] There was a Roman Catholic Radio and Television Centre at Hatch End in 1970.[40]

PROTESTANT NONCONFORMITY. William Rolls, the ejected minister of Pinner, was licensed as an Independent minister there in 1672,[41] the congregation meeting in the houses of Richard Stanborough, John Finch, John Winchester, and William Edlin. By 1684 there was an assistant, John Heywood, who described Rolls as 'a very faithful, laborious, ancient minister, whose strength is decayed'.[42] About 1691 the minister was Thomas Goodwin, author of several theological and devotional works, who also kept an academy for dissenting preachers.[43] A meeting-house was licensed in 1700[44] and a wastehold property was acquired in 1711.[45] The small meeting-house of the Pinner Independent congregation seems to have closed soon after 1795.[46] Quakers obtained a certificate for worship in Pinner in 1700,[47] and there were probably a few Baptists and Methodists there a hundred years later.[48]

[20] Mdx. Cnty. Recs. i. 171.   [21] Ibid. 198.
[22] i.e. Ric. Smith: Harrow Octocent. Tracts, xiv. 39.
[23] Harrow Octocent. Tracts, xiv. 4–5n; Elsley, Wembley, 129–30; Miscellanea, xii (Cath. Rec. Soc. xx), 123.
[24] Miscellanea, xii (Cath. Rec. Soc. xx), 280; see below, p. 268.
[25] Gen. Reg. Off., Wship. Reg. 21788, 34647; Ret. of churches, chapels ... H.C. 401, p. 172 (1882), i; Kelly's Dir. Mdx. (1886, 1906).
[26] Gen. Reg. Off., Wship. Reg. 45248, 45252, 53035; Kelly's Dir. Mdx. (1906); Westminster Dioc. Year Bk. (1966); Pevsner, Mdx. 169; ex inf. Father Paschal Green, S.D.S.
[27] Gen. Reg. Off., Wship. Reg. 38392, 66485; Wemb. Hist. Soc., Acc. 907/54, /56.
[28] Gen. Reg. Off., Wship. Reg. 47819, 66508; Ware, Pinner, 198, 202–3; Westminster Dioc. Year Bk. (1966).
[29] Gen. Reg. Off., Wship. Reg. 50315; Westminster Dioc. Year Bk. (1966).
[30] Gen. Reg. Off., Wship. Reg. 53883.
[31] Ibid. 53642, 61927.
[32] Ibid. 69066; Westminster Dioc. Year Bk. (1966).
[33] Gen. Reg. Off., Wship. Reg. 54852.   [34] Ibid. 58876.
[35] Opening of St. Bernard's church, Northolt (pamphlet, 1965); ex inf. Hon. Sec. of St. Gabriel's (1965).
[36] Ware, Pinner, 202–3.
[37] Gen. Reg. Off., Wship. Reg. 64989; Westminster Dioc. Year Bk. (1966).
[38] Wembley News, 25 Dec. 1952.
[39] Ex inf. Miss Philippa Craig of the Grail.
[40] The Times, 9 Jan. 1970.
[41] Cal. S.P. Dom. 1672, pp. 677, 680.
[42] Calamy Revised, ed. Matthews, 416.
[43] B.M. Add. MS. 24484, f. 372; A. Gordon, Freedom after Ejection, 72; D.N.B.
[44] Guildhall MS. 9579.   [45] M.R.O., Acc. 76/1109.
[46] Stephen Crisp (d. 1729) was a minister: Dr. Williams's Libr., MS. 34.4. Cf. ibid. MS. 34.5; Lysons, Environs of Lond. ii. 586.
[47] Gen. Reg. Off., Dissenters' Places of Wship. 1689–1852: Dioc. of Lond. cert. of 1700.
[48] Ware, Pinner, 103–4, 139.

Meeting-houses were registered at Roxeth in 1809 and 1812 and at Harrow in 1810.[49] The first two belonged to Baptists; the denomination of the last is uncertain.[50]

A Wesleyan chapel was erected in 1810 on the eastern side of Lower Road, Roxeth, near the cricket ground, and accommodated 218 people. In March 1851 an attendance of 190 at the afternoon and 116 at the evening service was said to be low because of bad weather.[51] The chapel, which was registered in 1856,[52] was replaced in 1905 by a red brick Gothic building, with accommodation for 650, in Bessborough Road.[53] The Wesleyans of Pinner, who worshipped in a cottage in Chapel Lane from the beginning of the 19th century,[54] built a brick chapel for 154 people in 1844. In 1851 there were 76 at the afternoon and 89 at the evening service.[55] A new building intended to serve as a school and chapel was erected in Love Lane in 1918, enlarged in 1926, and replaced by the present church at the junction of Love Lane and Avenue Road in 1937.[56]

A chapel to seat 160 people was erected in Byron Hill Road, Harrow-on-the-Hill, by the Particular Baptists in 1811 or 1812. In 1851 the average attendance at the three Sunday services was 80, 41, and 50.[57] In 1906 a chapel seating 750 was built in College Road and its predecessor was closed down.[58] Baptist activity in Alperton dates from 1824, and in 1828 a small chapel to seat 100 was erected in Ealing Road near the site later occupied by Alperton station. In 1851 the chapel was used by both Baptists and Independents, the congregation varying from 20 to 50 adults and from 10 to 25 Sunday school children.[59] New buildings, erected north of this chapel and on the other side of Ealing Road, were registered for worship in 1891. The church, a plain brick building, was rebuilt in 1937.[60] At Harrow Weald a room seating 50 people was opened by Particular Baptists in 1846. In 1851, 19 people attended the morning and 25 the evening service.[61] The congregation, which still existed in 1882,[62] later probably merged with the Baptists of Wealdstone.

From the mid 19th century Methodists have been the largest denomination. The congregations in Pinner and Roxeth were followed by others in Wembley, Harrow, Harrow Weald, Wealdstone, and Sudbury. A Wesleyan preaching-house was opened in Wembley in 1883[63] and replaced by a chapel in Water Lane in 1895; the chapel was closed in 1912.[64] There was a mission room in Harrow Weald from 1889 to 1935[65] and a chapel in Station Road, Wealdstone, from 1892[66] to 1904, when it was replaced by the present chapel in Locket Road.[67] Primitive Methodist chapels were opened in Welldon Crescent, Greenhill, in 1904[68] and in High Street, Wealdstone, in 1918.[69] In the 1860s Sir William Perkin had started an inter-denominational church for his German workers in a disused barn. In 1875 this was replaced at his own expense by a hall in Harrow Road,[70] which in 1913 his widow sold to the Methodists, with whom Perkin had had a particularly close connexion. The building was registered by them in 1924 and replaced by a church on the same site in 1933. The congregation grew with the development of Sudbury and the church was extended in 1939 and 1964.[71] Several Methodist churches were founded in the 1920s. In Park Lane, Wembley, a Wesleyan church was in use from 1925 to 1961,[72] and the Mabel Comben Memorial Hall from 1929 to 1961.[73] A Primitive Methodist church, opened in Ealing Road, Wembley, in 1927, survived in 1967.[74] A Wesleyan church was opened to serve the new Kenton estate in 1929 and replaced by another church and a hall on the same site in 1937.[75] Wesleyans in North Harrow and Headstone met in a private house in Southfield Park until a hall was built in Pinner Road in 1927. It was extended in the 1930s and a church was built next to it in 1957.[76] Relatively few churches have been founded since 1930. One was opened at the corner of Walton and Carlyon Avenues in South Harrow in 1937 and was rebuilt in 1957.[77] In Wembley, Methodist churches were opened in East Lane in 1938,[78] in Park Lane, Monks Park, in 1950,[79] and in Park Lane in 1962, although the last replaced the church which had closed in 1961.[80] The Calvinistic Methodists opened a hall in London Road in 1950 and replaced it by the Wembley Welsh Church on the same site five years later.[81]

[49] Guildhall MSS. 9580/3, /4. The meeting-houses were probably not built as chapels.
[50] Gen. Reg. Off., Dissenters' Places of Wship. 1689–1852: Dioc. of Lond. certs. of 7 Jan. 1809, 2 May 1812, and 20 Nov. 1810.
[51] *Ret. of churches, chapels* . . . H.C. 401, p. 172 (1882), i; H.O. 129/135/1/1/6; M.R.O., Acc. 76/1784; O.S. Map 1/2,500, Mdx. x. 11 (1865 edn.).
[52] Gen. Reg. Off., Wship. Reg. 7265.
[53] Ibid. 40890; *Kelly's Dir. Mdx.* (1906).
[54] Ware, *Pinner*, 139.
[55] *Ret. of churches, chapels* . . . H.C. 401, p. 172 (1882), i; Gen. Reg. Off., Wship. Reg. 13512; H.O. 129/135/1/1/7.
[56] Gen. Reg. Off., Wship. Reg. 47063, 57388; Ware, *Pinner*, 139.
[57] *Ret. of churches, chapels* . . . H.C. 401, p. 172 (1882), i; *Rep. of Royal Com. on non-parochial regs.* . . . *1838* [148], p. 436, H.C. (1837–8), xxviii; Gen. Reg. Off., Wship. Reg. 16534; H.O. 129/135/1/1/8.
[58] Gen. Reg. Off., Wship. Reg. 43296; *Kelly's Dir. Mdx.* (1917).
[59] H.O. 129/135/1/1/9; ex inf. secretary of church (1965).
[60] Gen. Reg. Off., Wship. Reg. 32716, 57685.
[61] H.O. 129/135/1/1/10.
[62] *Ret. of churches, chapels* . . . H.C. 401, p. 172 (1882), i; Gen. Reg. Off., Wship. Reg. 9583. The registration was cancelled in 1954 but it had probably lapsed long before.
[63] Gen. Reg. Off., Wship. Reg. 27237.
[64] Ibid. 34927.
[65] Ibid. 31618.
[66] Ibid. 33258.
[67] Ibid. 40750.
[68] Ibid. 40600. The small brick chapel was still there in 1966.
[69] Gen. Reg. Off., Wship. Reg. 47316. Registration cancelled after the Methodist church union in 1935.
[70] Probably the New Hall, Sudbury, registered for worship in 1887, whose registration was cancelled in 1924; Gen. Reg. Off., Wship. Reg. 29956.
[71] Gen. Reg. Off., Wship. Reg. 49318, 54843, 55564.
[72] Ibid. 49737.
[73] Ibid. 51701.
[74] Ibid. 51056.
[75] Ibid. 51837, 57601–2. The chapel in Kenton Road was still there in 1966.
[76] Gen. Reg. Off., Wship. Reg. 50990, 66038; Ware, *Pinner*, 139; ex inf. secretary of North Harrow Methodist Church (1965).
[77] Gen. Reg. Off., Wship. Reg. 57358, 66087.
[78] Ibid. 58169. Replacing two Nissen huts used since 1920: ex inf. senior steward, North Wembley Methodist Church (1967).
[79] Gen. Reg. Off., Wship. Reg. 62816. The church has been extended since 1964: ex inf. the minister of Park Lane Methodist Church (1967).
[80] Gen. Reg. Off., Wship. Reg. 68821; ex inf. the minister.
[81] Gen. Reg. Off., Wship. Reg. 62709, 64832.

In the extreme south Methodists met in the community hall in Alperton before opening the misleadingly named Perivale Church in May Gardens in 1960; the premises were extended in 1965.[82] In the north Methodists opened a church in Cannon Lane, Pinner, in 1956[83] and met in the Anglican church of All Saints, Harrow Weald, in 1967.[84]

It was not until 1859 that the Baptists in Pinner leased land in Chapel Lane, then called West End, where an iron chapel to hold 70 people was erected east of the Methodist chapel. The property was sold in 1875, and in 1885–6 a new chapel was erected in Marsh Road on a site leased from the Metropolitan Railway Co. The congregation moved to a 'handsome building' in the Gothic style in Paines Lane in 1910, when it broadened its membership and was re-registered as the United Free Church, Pinner.[85] Baptists met in various rooms in Wealdstone from 1875 and built a corrugated iron hall on land purchased in the High Street c. 1900. A permanent church to seat 500 was erected in 1905 and new halls were added in 1930.[86] The Baptists, unlike most denominations, had no chapel in Wembley, but in 1911 a chapel in Harrow Road, Sudbury, was called the Sudbury and Wembley Baptist Church. This was replaced in 1924.[87] Many Baptist congregations have been founded since the 1920s. A church in Northolt Road, Roxeth, was opened in 1927 and rebuilt in 1935.[88] Baptists established in Kenton in 1932 hired the Co-operative Society Hall, Kenton Road, and met in private houses until a hall was erected in Streatfield Road in 1933; the congregation, then called Belmont Free Church, was accepted by the national Baptist Union, which appointed a minister and registered the hall for worship in 1934. A year later a 'tin hut', which seated 300, was re-erected next to the existing church hall. The hut was replaced in 1939 by a brick building, registered as Kenton Free Church, and a new hall was added in 1965.[89] On the eastern borders Lindsay Park Baptist Church grew out of a Sunday school, held in 1943 in a builder's hut in Chantry Close by the minister of Kingsbury Free Church. A private house was used from 1945 until the dedication of the church in the Mall, Kenton, in 1949. A deaconess was in charge until a minister was appointed in 1958. An extension was planned in 1965.[90] Baptists from the newly developed Rayners Lane area met in a dance studio before a building was erected for worship in 1934 at the junction of Vicarage Way and Imperial Drive. Halls were added in 1953 and 1965.[91] In 1948 the Rayners Lane Baptist Church started a Sunday school in Roxeth, adding a Sunday evening service in 1957. In 1959 this became the Roxeth Green Free Church and in 1962 the present building was erected on the corner of Coles Crescent and Welbeck Road, on a site previously owned by the church. Although originally sponsored by the Baptists, Roxeth Green Free Church is an independent, non-denominational community.[92] A small Baptist chapel in Rowlands Avenue was erected in 1936 to serve Hatch End.[93]

Other nonconformist bodies were less prominent. The Harrow or Silver Street Congregational Church originated by migrants from Hampstead who worshipped in a private room in Harrow View in 1900. In 1903 services were held at the Gayton Rooms in Station Road. In 1911 a temporary steel building was erected in Hindes Road, Greenhill, with proceeds from the sale of the Falcon Square (City) Congregational Church. A permanent church was opened in 1929.[94] Wembley Park Congregational Church in East Lane, first registered in 1930, was rebuilt in 1934.[95] Harrow Welsh Congregational Church, a grey brick building, was built in Lower Road, Harrow, in 1949.[96]

English Presbyterians were established in Wembley in 1899 and a hall in Ealing Road was registered for worship in 1902. St. Andrew's Church was built in 1904, to seat 450 people, and enlarged in 1907.[97] Harrow Presbyterian Church was founded in Station Road, Greenhill, in 1902; services were held in a hall until Trinity Presbyterian Church, built by W. Gilbert Scott in the Gothic style, was opened in 1906. There were two mission rooms at Marlborough Hill from 1938 until 1941.[98] Kenton Presbyterian Church was registered for worship in 1931 and St. John's in Woodcock Hill was built in 1934.[99] All of these belonged to the Presbyterian Church of England. A Welsh Presbyterian congregation, established in Wembley in 1925, opened a hall in 1927.[1]

Quakers met in various places in Harrow from 1905 until they erected their own meeting-house in Rayners Lane, Pinner, in 1935.[2] A few Quakers also began meeting in Wembley in 1942.[3] Salvation Army barracks were opened in 1886 in Alperton,[4] in 1887 on Roxeth Hill, Harrow,[5] in Wealdstone,[6] and in High Street, Pinner.[7] Both the Alperton and Pinner groups had collapsed by 1896.[8] The Harrow corps met in a tent and then in a barn until a building on Roxeth or London Hill was obtained in 1906; a new hall was built next to it in 1959.[9] The Wealdstone

[82] Ibid. 67989; ex inf. the minister of Park Lane Methodist Church (1967).
[83] Gen. Reg. Off., Wship. Reg. 65781, 70280.
[84] Ex inf. minister of Wealdstone circuit (1967).
[85] Gen. Reg. Off., Wship. Reg. 31600, 44232; Ware, *Pinner*, 103–4.
[86] Gen. Reg. Off., Wship. Reg. 28722, 39374, 41446, 53094; *Kelly's Dir. Mdx.* (1906).
[87] Gen. Reg. Off., Wship. Reg. 44687, 49464.
[88] Ibid. 50624, 51498, 56425.
[89] Ibid. 55431, 57129; Kenton Free Church, *Opening & Dedication of the New Hall* (pamphlet, 1965).
[90] *Baptist Times*, 11 Apr. 1957; ex inf. the treasurer (1965).
[91] Gen. Reg. Off., Wship. Reg. 56418; Ware, *Pinner*, 181; ex inf. the minister (1965).
[92] Ex inf. editor of Roxeth Green Free Church Magazine (1967); Gen. Reg. Off., Wship. Reg. 68656, 69069.
[93] Gen. Reg. Off., Wship. Reg. 56684, 57009; ex inf. the secretary (1965).
[94] Gen. Reg. Off., Wship. Reg. 41395, 45053, 52537; *Story of Silver Street Congregational Church* (pamphlet).
[95] Gen. Reg. Off., Wship. Reg. 52720, 53765, 56105, 61479. The registration was cancelled and renewed several times.
[96] Gen. Reg. Off., Wship. Reg. 62455.
[97] Ibid. 38810, 40790; *Kelly's Dirs. Mdx.* (1906, 1917); Wemb. Hist. Soc., Acc. 555.
[98] Gen. Reg. Off., Wship. Reg. 39788, 42177, 58190.
[99] Ibid. 52894, 55542.
[1] Ex inf. Dr. R. Tudor Edwards (1966).
[2] Gen. Reg. Off., Wship. Reg. 55931; ex inf. the clerk (1965).
[3] Ex inf. Jane Hobbs (1965).
[4] Gen. Reg. Off., Wship. Reg. 29788.
[5] Ibid. 29828.
[6] Ibid. 30036.
[7] Ibid. 30487.
[8] Ibid. 29788, 30487.
[9] Ibid. 38546, 42424, 67615, 67658; ex inf. corps secretary (1965).

group, an offshoot from Harrow, met in several places before buying a former Baptist chapel in Palmerston Road, which was registered for worship by the Salvation Army in 1921. A hall was acquired nearby for young people in 1927 but in 1965 it was too small.[10] A Salvation Army hall was registered in 1938 in London Road, Wembley, where a new hall was opened in 1957.[11] Halls were registered by the Brethren in Love Lane, Pinner, from 1887 to 1917 and in High Street, Alperton, from 1897 to 1954.[12] Belmont Hall in Pinner Road, Harrow, was registered by them in 1911[13] and a hall in north Pinner, later called Pinner Hill or Pinner Green Chapel, in 1929.[14] Another hall was opened in Parkside Way, south Pinner, in 1932.[15] In Wembley, Plymouth or Christian Brethren met in an iron building in Alperton before a hall was opened in Ealing Road in 1924. This was registered for worship in 1930[16] and another, Uxendon Hall, was opened in Elmstead Avenue in 1938.[17] An evangelistic mission in 1934 led to the foundations of Elmfield Hall, Imperial Drive, North Harrow in 1934[18] and Glebe Hall, Loretto Gardens, Kenton, in 1935.[19] Headstone Hall in Headstone Road, registered in 1932 but active mainly after 1948,[20] and Oak Hall on the Cedars L.C.C. estate, Headstone, registered in 1951[21] by the Headstone Christian Fellowship, are also meeting-houses which have no formal ties with any denomination but follow the practice of the Christian Brethren.[22]

After the First World War spiritualist meetings were held in various halls in Harrow and in 1936 the Harrow Spiritualist Church, accommodating 180 people, was opened in Vaughan Road.[23] Home circles in the Wembley area developed in 1929 into the Wembley Spiritualists' Society. Rooms were hired until the Wembley Spiritualists' National Church was constructed in 1957 in St. John's Road.[24] In 1940 a Spiritualist church, meeting in a private house in Rayners Lane, was registered in Pinner[25] and a Christian Spiritualist church, St. Michael's, was registered in Northolt Road, Roxeth, and, later in that year, in Kenton Road, Kenton.[26] Another Christian Spiritualist church, founded in 1948, met initially in Cecil Park, Pinner, and, from 1949, in Bridge Street.[27] The Evangelicals met in a wooden building in Wealdstone from 1921 until a brick building was opened in Mason's Avenue in 1928.[28] A second church was opened in Charlton Road, Kenton, in 1959.[29] Jehovah's Witnesses were established in 1936 in Harrow, using hired rooms until a Kingdom Hall was erected in Peel Road, Wealdstone, in 1939.[30] A Kingdom Hall was opened in Oakington Manor Drive, Wembley,[31] in 1956 and a separate community was founded at Pinner in 1958.[32] The Assemblies of God opened the South Harrow Pentecostal Assembly in Northolt Road, Roxeth, in 1938 and re-registered it as the Full Gospel Church in South Hill Avenue in 1959.[33] They also registered rooms in 1941 in Wembley, first in Neeld Parade and then in Wembley Hill Road, but this registration was cancelled in 1954.[34] The one Seventh Day Adventist church grew out of services held in the Majestic Ballroom and other halls in Wembley in 1940; a house in Barham Close was bought and registered in 1941.[35] Christian Scientists first met in Oddfellows Hall, Maxwell Lane, Pinner in 1920. A Sunday school and reading room were erected in Elm Park Road in 1926 and the community was recognized as a branch of the First Church of Christ, Scientist, in 1929. The church was built and registered in 1937.[36] A Harrow branch was formed in 1953 and met in the Labour Hall, Railway Approach.[37]

The church of St. John the Divine in Watford Road, Wembley, was registered for worship by the Catholic Apostolic Church in 1963,[38] Cedar Hall in Station Grove, Wembley, was registered by the Church of God in 1962,[39] and Barnhill Lodge in Barnhill Road, Wembley, by the Church of Christ in 1964 and 1967.[40] A hall in Mason's Avenue, Wealdstone, was registered from 1932 until 1934 by the Brotherhood Movement.[41] The New Chapel in Pinner was registered in 1859 for Protestant dissenters using the new burial ground in Paines Lane.[42] In 1887 the Iron Room, Alperton[43] and a mission room in Peel Road, East Lane, Wembley[44] were registered for undenominational worship; both registrations were cancelled in 1954, as was that of a mission hall in High Street, Wealdstone, dating from 1899.[45] Meeting-places of unknown denomination are the Marlborough Mission on Marlborough Hill, Wealdstone, registered from 1942 until 1959,[46] a room at 128–30 Hindes Road, Harrow, registered in 1952,[47] another in Elm Park Road, Pinner, registered in 1962,[48] and another at the junction of Carlton Avenue East and Forty Avenue, Wembley, registered in 1965.[49]

[10] Gen. Reg. Off., Wship. Reg. 32046, 38547, 40308, 48088, 50834; ex inf. Brig. W. Wilson (1965).
[11] Gen. Reg. Off., Wship. Reg. 58042, 66257.
[12] Ibid. 30244, 55889.
[13] Ibid. 44849.
[14] Ibid. 52117.
[15] Ibid. 53771.
[16] Ibid. 52868; ex inf. Mr. F. W. Little.
[17] Gen. Reg. Off., Wship. Reg. 58091.
[18] Ibid. 55449.
[19] Ibid. 59915.
[20] Ibid. 53772; ex inf. Mr. E. W. Crabb of Glebe Hall (1967).
[21] Gen. Reg. Off., Wship. Reg. 63160.
[22] Ex inf. Mr. E. W. Crabb (1967).
[23] Gen. Reg. Off., Wship. Reg. 56459; ex inf. the secretary (1965).
[24] Gen. Reg. Off., Wship. Reg. 63373, 66728; ex inf. the president (1966).
[25] Gen. Reg. Off., Wship. Reg. 59263, 59680; ex inf. the president (1965).
[26] Gen. Reg. Off., Wship. Reg. 59419, 59476, 59594. Cancelled in 1954.
[27] Ex inf. the president (1965).
[28] Gen. Reg. Off., Wship. Reg. 48732, 51411; ex inf. the secretary (1965).
[29] Gen. Reg. Off., Wship. Reg. 67154.
[30] Ibid. 59074; ex inf. Mr. D. L. Bates (1965).
[31] Gen. Reg. Off., Wship. Reg. 65906.
[32] Ex inf. Mr. D. L. Bates (1965).
[33] Gen. Reg. Off., Wship. Reg. 58224, 67081.
[34] Ibid. 59709, 59910.
[35] Ibid. 59750, 66302; ex inf. the minister (1965).
[36] Gen. Reg. Off., Wship. Reg. 51521, 57291; ex inf. the clerk (1965).
[37] Char. Com. Reg. 236189.
[38] Gen. Reg. Off., Wship. Reg. 68946.
[39] Ibid. 68624.   [40] Ibid. 69869, 70840.
[41] Ibid. 54182.
[42] Ibid. 9037: Ret. of churches, chapels . . . H.C. 401, p. 172 (1882), 1; Ware, Pinner, 47–48.
[43] Gen. Reg. Off., Wship. Reg. 29955.
[44] Ibid. 29957.
[45] Ibid. 37354.
[46] Ibid. 60023.
[47] Ibid. 63439.
[48] Ibid. 68741.
[49] Ibid. 69999.

JEWS. The first synagogue was established in the area in 1918 and became a district member of the United Synagogue in 1933. Premises in Sheepcote Road were registered as the Harrow and Kenton Synagogue in 1935. In 1946, as the Harrow Hebrew Congregation, it acquired 3, Vaughan Road, Harrow.[50] During the 1930s numbers of Jews, mostly belonging to the United Synagogue, moved into Harrow, especially into the Kenton and Wembley districts. When the Vaughan Road premises were acquired, a group of Kenton Jews formed a second congregation which established a synagogue in Kenton Park Avenue in 1948, affiliated to the United Synagogue in 1949 and registered for worship a year later. A building was erected in Shaftesbury Avenue, Kenton, in 1958 and extended in 1962.[51] Other United synagogues were established in Forty Avenue, Wembley (1934)[52] and in Cecil Park, Pinner (1941).[53]

A Liberal synagogue was established in 1947 at 326 Preston Road, Preston, where it was originally called the Wembley Progressive Jewish Congregation.[54] In 1959 a Reform synagogue, under the title of the Middlesex New Synagogue, was established at 39 Bessborough Road, Harrow, a square, 19th-century building with a porch of Ionic columns.[55] From 1966 a Sephardi congregation held services in the Congregational church hall, the Broadway, Wembley.[56] It was estimated in 1965 that there were approximately 21,000 Jewish people in the London Borough of Harrow and the Wembley part of Brent. Of these, about 16,000 were connected with the synagogues in the area.[57]

EDUCATION. Richard Gerard, who entered Caius (Gonville and Caius) College, Cambridge, in 1567, attended a school at Harrow, and a letter of 1626 mentioned one there as early as Mary's reign. Before Harrow School, whose history is described elsewhere,[58] moved to a new building in 1615, it had been held in the 'school or church-house of the parish of Harrow',[59] which was probably in or near the churchyard and may have housed Harrow's earlier school.[60] In 1660 the governors of Harrow School appointed six 'school dames' at salaries of £4 a year, to teach the children of Harrow-on-the-Hill, Preston, Roxeth, Sudbury, Kenton, Wembley, and Harrow Weald to read.[61] Thomas Robinson, schoolmaster, of Roxeth, mentioned in 1754 and 1755,[62] may have been such a 'dame'. In 1711 Edward Robinson bequeathed £10 a year for clothing and for teaching reading and the catechism to 12 of the poorest children, ten boys and two girls, aged four to ten, in Harrow Weald under a dame who was to be a member of the Church of

England. The charity soon fell into disuse but was revived in 1770, when £70 of arrears was invested, and from 1772 a dame was paid £2 10s. a year.[63] Further stock was added in 1777 by the inhabitants of Harrow Weald, who had sold a parcel of waste. In the early 19th century the charity yielded £13 10s., which was distributed to the children by the overseers of Harrow Weald.[64]

At Pinner, in addition to the Independent academy run by Thomas Goodwin from c. 1696 to 1704,[65] there was apparently a school throughout the 17th and 18th centuries. A school building was repaired in 1635, 1675, and 1681, and £100 was left to Pinner 'where I once went to school' by William Norrington (d. 1705).[66] Schoolmasters are mentioned in 1749[67] and 1777,[68] and in 1764 Mrs. Goditha Martin left the interest on £100 to pay a schoolmistress to teach 6 poor children of Pinner to read.[69]

In 1818, however, it was Pinner rather than Harrow that was inadequately served. Apart from the endowed school for 6 children, there was only a Sunday school, supported by annual contributions and attended by 100 pupils. The poor of Pinner were much in want of a day school but at Harrow they were 'not without the means of education'. In addition to Harrow School and the small dame schools maintained by its governors, there was a Sunday school in Harrow Weald attended by 104 children and probably connected with the Robinson charity, a Sunday evening school for adults at Harrow, maintained by the vicar, and a day and Sunday school there supported by subscriptions.[70] The latter, the first National school in the parish, was especially important, at a time when Harrow School was becoming the preserve of fee-paying 'foreigners'.[71] Harrow or Roxeth National school, named from its position on Roxeth or London Hill,[72] was founded in 1812 through the efforts of the vicar, J. W. Cunningham. By 1816, when it had 160 pupils, it had joined the National Society as a day school. It is usually referred to in the plural, presumably because boys', girls', and infants' departments for most of the time were housed in separate buildings. By 1833 there were 133 pupils and a master and mistress.[73] In the 1830s the infants' classroom was used as a scullery and mothers were refusing to send their children there. The vicar tried to raise money for a new infant school at the back of the girls' school[74] and in 1837 one was erected with the aid of a £50 grant from the Treasury. The school was maintained by voluntary contributions, school pence, and £4 from the governors of Harrow School,[75] who presumably treated it as a continuation of the 1660 dame school. In 1853 the infant school was attended by an average of 70 children.[76] It is not clear when the

[50] Gen. Reg. Off., Wship. Reg. 56071, 61260; *Jewish Chron.* 7 Sept. 1934; *Jewish Year Bk.* (1964); ex inf. sec., Harrow District synagogue (1965).
[51] Gen. Reg. Off., Wship. Reg. 62715, 66813; *Jewish Year Bk.* (1964); ex inf. the minister (1965).
[52] Gen. Reg. Off., Wship. Reg. 55923, 66796; *Jewish Year Bk.* (1964).
[53] *Jewish Year Bk.* (1964).
[54] Ibid.; Gen. Reg. Off., Wship. Reg. 65977.
[55] Gen. Reg. Off., Wship. Reg. 69041.
[56] *Jewish Year Bk.* (1966–69).
[57] These figures include Kingsbury and Stanmore.
[58] *V.C.H. Mdx.* i. 299–302.
[59] Druett, *Harrow*, 105.
[60] Ibid. The house was demolished in 1724. There is no evidence for a medieval school.

[61] Edith M. Sturdy, 'Charity and State-aided Education in Harrow, 1384–1959' (TS. Harrow Local Collection), 3.
[62] M.R.O., Acc. 76/1384.
[63] Sturdy, 'Educ. in Harrow', 4–5; Druett, *Weald*, 228.
[64] *9th Rep. Com. Char.* H.C. 258, pp. 261–6 (1823), ix.
[65] Robbins, *Middlesex*, 133. See above, p. 261.
[66] Ware, *Pinner*, 190.
[67] M.R.O., Acc. 76/2434.   [68] M.R.O., Acc. 310(3).
[69] *Digest of Rets. on Educ. of Poor*, H.C. 224, p. 537 (1819), ix(1).
[70] Ibid.   [71] Sturdy, 'Educ. in Harrow', 6.
[72] O.S. Map 1/2,500, Mdx. x. 11 (1865 edn.).
[73] Sturdy, 'Educ. in Harrow', 7, 9–12.
[74] Christ Church MS. Estates 47/343, /413.
[75] Ed. 7/87.
[76] Ibid.; *Kelly's Dir. Mdx.* (1886).

Roxeth Hill site was acquired, but Cunningham was probably referring to it in 1850, when it was decided to buy the 'site of the present building', then rented yearly, and to put up new buildings.[77] In 1851 a boys' schoolroom was built in memory of A. F. A. Cooper (d. 1825), son of the Earl of Shaftesbury (d. 1851).[78] The infants' section was added in 1854 and a girls' section was built in 1870.[79] The average attendance in 1870 was 254.[80]

The National Society was making grants to Pinner, possibly to the Sunday school, in 1816.[81] A National school was discussed by the vestry in 1824,[82] but it was not until 1841 that one was erected. Perhaps the deficiencies of 1818 had been remedied by the opening of several small schools, especially in the 1830s. In 1833, in addition to the old Sunday school where 87 children were taught, there was a church infant school (revived in 1831) containing 25 boys and 33 girls, six day schools, one of them opened in 1832 and together containing 41 boys and 65 girls, and two private boarding schools containing 32 boys and 8 girls. In the whole of Harrow parish outside Pinner, there were three infant schools (opened in 1826) where 93 children were taught, 4 day schools with a total of 197 children, and two boarding schools with 76 children. There were also four Sunday schools: a Wesleyan school opened in 1825, two which 'recommenced' in 1830, and one opened in 1832. These taught a total of 409 children[83] of whom 199 attended the Wesleyan school in Lower Road.[84] Thus Pinner, with a population of 1,270, provided for 291 children, while Harrow, with a population of 3,861, provided only for 775.[85]

Pinner National School, with one room for girls and infants and another for boys, was built in 1841 at the bottom of the High Street. It was maintained by voluntary contributions, school pence, and an annual sermon. In 1866, when there were 107 pupils,[86] the vicar appealed for funds since he anticipated an increase in population, presumably at Woodridings.[87] In the same year the old school was sold[88] and another site acquired near Marsh Road. A new school, accommodating 300 children, was built[89] and was attended in 1870 by an average of 157 children.[90] The building was used by the Harrow College of Further Education from 1962 until 1967.[91]

In 1839 aid was sought from the National Society for a new Sunday and day school for 70 girls at Harrow Weald.[92] It was not, however, until 1845 that Harrow Weald National School was established next to All Saints' church. The school was controlled by the perpetual curate and maintained by voluntary contributions and school pence. Boys and girls, housed in separate rooms, were taught the Bible, 'ciphering', writing, needlework, and knitting. There were 185 pupils in 1846–7, 160 in 1856,[93] and an average of 157 in 1870.[94]

In 1846–7 a day school was run by a mistress in a house at Sudbury, attended by 16 boys and 19 girls, and another in a room at Greenhill, attended by 12 boys and 8 girls. These were infant schools, descendants of the dame schools.[95] At Sudbury John Brown, by will dated 1846, left money for the support of an infant school.[96] A National school, erected in Greenford Road in 1850, was variously known as Sudbury, Greenford Road, or Christ Church, Roxeth, District Church of England School.[97] It consisted of a schoolroom, classroom, and teacher's house, and was supported by endowment, possibly from Brown's charity, by voluntary contributions, and school pence. In 1863 there were 15 boys, 32 girls, and 5 infants,[98] and the average attendance in 1870 was 51.[99] The infant school at Greenhill was run by a Mrs. Witney, almost certainly in a cottage opposite Dirty Lane (Elmgrove Road). In 1859 the *Harrow Gazette* reported that 'hitherto the school has been carried on in a room better fitted for six children than for thirty-six, which is about the number on its books'.[1] A site on Roxborough Road was given to the Vicar of Harrow for a school for the poorer classes, and a mistress's house with three rooms was erected in 1860.[2] Greenhill Parochial or National School, supported by voluntary contributions and school pence, had 20 boys and 27 girls in 1861, although the average attendance was only 26.[3] Additions were built in 1866[4] and by 1870 the average attendance had risen to 62.[5]

A school was established next to the church of St. John the Evangelist, Wembley, by Frances and Anne Copland in 1849. It comprised a teacher's house, a schoolroom, and a classroom, and was maintained by endowment, voluntary contributions, and school pence. The premises were held in trust for the education of poor children in the principles of the Church of England, but the school was never connected with the National Society. In 1863 there were 94 pupils, drawn from within a radius of $2\frac{1}{2}$ miles.[6] There was an infant school in Kenton, supported by voluntary contributions and run by a mistress, by 1845.[7] A small National school was built on the south side of Kenton Road in 1852 with the help of a grant. It was maintained by voluntary contribu-

[77] Christ Church MS. Estates 47/542, /546, /548, /551; N.R.A. & Harrow U.D.C., *Festival Exhib. of Documents* (1951), 69.
[78] Christ Church MS. Estates 47/542; Sturdy, 'Educ. in Harrow', 12; *Kelly's Dir. Mdx.* (1886).
[79] *Kelly's Dir. Mdx.* (1886).
[80] *Rep. of Educ. Cttee. of Coun. 1870* [C. 406], H.C. p. 497 (1871), xxii.
[81] Sturdy, 'Educ. in Harrow', 7.
[82] M.R.O., D.R.O. 8/C1/1.
[83] *Educ. Enquiry Abstract, 1833*. H.C. 62, pp. 96, 110 (1835), xlii.
[84] O.S. Map 1/2,500, Mdx. x. 11 (1865 edn.).
[85] *Census*, 1831.
[86] M.R.O., D.R.O. 8/C1/1, vestry 1840; Acc. 76/1586; Ed. 7/86/52.
[87] Christ Church MS. Estates 47/586, /591.
[88] Thereafter used as a parish hall.
[89] Druett, *Pinner*, 94.
[90] *Rep. of Educ. Cttee. of Coun. 1870*, p. 497.
[91] Ex inf. the Registrar of Harrow Coll. of Further Educ.
[92] Sturdy, 'Educ. in Harrow', 10.

[93] Ibid. 11; Ed. 7/86/43; Druett, *Weald*, 227.
[94] *Rep. of Educ. Cttee. of Coun., 1870*, p. 497.
[95] National Society enquiry: Sturdy, 'Educ. in Harrow' 11.
[96] The 1850 handbook of Harrow lists Sudbury Infant School, supported by Mr. Brown's gift, with Miss Eleanor Page as mistress: Sturdy, 'Educ. in Harrow', 11. In 1851 Eleanor Page was listed as National school governess: H.O. 107/1700, ff. 43–62.
[97] O.S. Map 1/2,500, Mdx. x. 16 (1865 edn.); Christ Church MS. Estates 47/688v; Ed. 7/86/42.
[98] Ed 7/86/42.
[99] *Rep. of Educ. Cttee. of Coun. 1870*, p. 497.
[1] Sturdy, 'Educ. in Harrow', 12.
[2] *Festival Exhib. of Docs.* 69, no. 122.
[3] Ed. 7/86/41.
[4] Sturdy, 'Educ. in Harrow', 13.
[5] *Rep. of Educ. Cttee. of Coun. 1870*, p. 497.
[6] Ed. 7/87; Silvester, *Visible & Invisible*, 15; O.S. Map 1/2,500, Mdx. x. 16 (1865 edn.).
[7] *P.O. Dir. of Six Cnties.* (1845); Sturdy, 'Educ. in Harrow', 11.

tions, school pence, and a church-rate, and was attended by an average of 8 boys and 16 girls in 1859,[8] and of 21 children in 1865–6.[9] A National school was built in Grant Road, Wealdstone, in 1869 with the aid of a grant.[10]

In 1870 there were 9 schools connected with the Church of England or the National Society, but none linked with the British Society or any non-conformist or Roman Catholic body. Three schools had no religious ties. In Harrow there were six public schools with 781 children, one private voluntary school with 97 children, and four private 'adventure' schools with 100 children. There was one public school with 173 children in Pinner and one 'adventure' school with 14 children.[11] Under the 1870 Act, a school board was set up in Harrow in 1877. All the National and Church schools, except Pinner and Wembley, were transferred to the board in 1878, and Pinner became a contributory member in 1882.[12] The school at Roxeth Hill was enlarged in 1899,[13] to accommodate up to 899, after average attendance figures had risen to 611 in 1898.[14] It was still in existence in 1967.[15] At Pinner new infant schoolrooms were erected in 1876[16] and further enlargements in 1887[17] increased the accommodation to 398. The average attendance rose to 226 in 1898.[18] A new boys' schoolroom was erected in Harrow Weald in 1887,[19] so that by 1898 there was accommodation for 460 and an average attendance of 217.[20] The school was closed after the Second World War and the buildings were leased to the local education authority until 1968, when they were purchased by the parish church council.[21] At Greenhill, where all three departments had been mixed, a separate infants' department was erected in 1883 and a boys' department in 1896.[22] By 1898 there was accommodation for 544 and an average attendance of 330.[23] The school was still in use in 1967.[24] The school at Kenton was rebuilt in 1895,[25] but it still comprised a single schoolroom and the average attendance in 1898 was 28.[26] It was closed between 1938 and 1957.[27] The greatest expansion was at Wealdstone, where the school in the High Street (Grant Road) was enlarged in 1883, 1885, and 1895.[28] By 1898 the average attendance was 523.[29] It was closed between 1938 and 1957.[30]

The only school entirely unconnected with the Harrow School Board was the parochial school of St. John the Evangelist, Wembley. It was enlarged in 1876 and appeals were made to pay for the additions, to support three mistresses and a pupil-teacher, and to pay for a school in Pinner Road (later Watford Road), Sudbury.[31] The new school, intended as an infants' department to the parish school, was opened in 1877 in a single room. It was purchased by the board in 1880 and a room for girls was built.[32] A room for boys was added in 1894 when the old Greenford Road school, which was run by the board as a boys' school, was closed.[33] In 1898 the Pinner Road school, called Sudbury Board School, accommodated 542 and had an average attendance of 317.[34]

Harrow School Board erected two new schools, the first at Alperton, an area previously neglected. It was probably Alperton children who were meant by a note in 1870 that children from Harrow attended Twyford Abbey School.[35] A short-lived infants' schoolroom, attached to Wembley parish school, was opened in Alperton in 1876,[36] and a building with one room for boys and girls and another for infants was erected on a rented site in 1878. A permanent school was built on land bought in 1879, with a schoolroom and classroom for each of the three departments and with two teachers' houses.[37] By 1898 there was accommodation for 413 and an average attendance of 345.[38] It was replaced by Park Lane, Wembley, council school in 1911.[39] Bridge School was opened in Wealdstone in 1902; it was closed in 1966 and replaced by Elmgrove Junior School. An infant school was opened on the site.[40]

Under the 1902 Education Act, which replaced the board with the Middlesex County Council, provision also had to be made for secondary education.[41] The following primary schools were founded between the Acts of 1902 and 1944, the time of greatest suburban development in Harrow:[42] White-friars (1910) in Wealdstone, Vaughan (1910)[43] in West Harrow and Welldon Park (opened in 1911 as a temporary school in Northolt Road with infants from Roxeth Hill School and replaced by a new school at Welldon Park in 1912)[44] in South Harrow, Park Lane (1911) and St. Joseph's Roman Catholic (1929) in Wembley, Pinner Park (1931), Preston Park (1932), St. Anselm's Roman Catholic (1932) in Roxborough Park, Byron Court (1932) in Sudbury, Roxeth Manor Primary (1933), Oakington Manor

[8] Ed. 7/86/98.
[9] *Schs. aided by Parl. Grants, 1865–6* [3666], H.C. p. 737 (1866), xxvii.
[10] Sturdy, 'Educ. in Harrow', 14; *Rep. of Educ. Cttee. of Counc., 1870*, p. 497. No attendance figures are available.
[11] *Rets. relating to Elem. Educ.* H.C. 201, pp. 242–3 (1871), lv.
[12] *Kelly's Dir. Mdx.* (1886).
[13] Sturdy, 'Educ. in Harrow', 15.
[14] *Schs. in receipt of Parl. Grants, 1898* [C.9454], H.C. p. 168 (1899), lxxiv.
[15] List supplied by Educ. Officer of London Bor. of Harrow (1967).
[16] Christ Church MS. Estates 47/658, /660.
[17] Sturdy, 'Educ. in Harrow', 14.
[18] *Schs. in receipt of Parl. Grants, 1898*, p. 169.
[19] Ed. 7/86/43.
[20] *Schs. in receipt of Parl. Grants, 1898*, p. 168.
[21] Ex inf. Vicar of All Saints, Harrow Weald (1970).
[22] Ed. 7/86/41.
[23] *Schs. in receipt of Parl. Grants, 1898*, p. 168.
[24] List supplied by Educ. Officer of London Bor. of Harrow (1967).
[25] Ed. 7/86/98.
[26] *Schs. in receipt of Parl. Grants, 1898*, p. 168.

[27] Bd. of Educ. *List 21* (1938); Mdx. Cnty. Council, *List of Schs.* (1957).
[28] *Kelly's Dir. Mdx.* (1886, 1906).
[29] *Schs. in receipt of Parl. grants, 1898*, p. 168.
[30] Bd. of Educ. *List 21* (1938); Mdx. Cnty. Council, *List of Schs.* (1957).
[31] Christ Church MS. Estates 47/661.
[32] Ed. 7/86/100.
[33] Ibid.; *Ret. of Schs. 1893* [C.7259], H.C. pp. 426–7 (1894), lxv.
[34] *Schs. in receipt of Parl. Grants, 1898*, p. 168.
[35] *Rets. relating to Elem. Educ.* H.C. 201, pp. 242–3 (1871), lv.
[36] Ed. 7/87.
[37] Ed. 7/86/98.
[38] *Schs. in receipt of Parl. Grants, 1898*, p. 168.
[39] Ed. 7/86/99A.
[40] Ex inf. the Headmaster of Elmgrove Sch. (1967).
[41] Sturdy, 'Educ. in Harrow', 15.
[42] The following two paragraphs are based upon lists supplied by the Education Officers of the London Boroughs of Harrow and Brent (1967).
[43] Ed. 7/86/42A.
[44] Ibid. /42C; Ed. 7/87/42B.

(1933) in Wembley, Cannon Lane (1934) in Pinner, Glebe (1934) and Priestmead (1935) in Kenton, Longfield (1935) in North Harrow, Barham (1936) in Sudbury, Lyon Park (1936) in Alperton, St. Joseph's Roman Catholic (1937) in Wealdstone, Uxendon Manor (1937) in Preston, Roxbourne (1937), Belmont Primary (1938) in Harrow Weald, Kenmore Park (1938) in Kenton, Vicar's Green (1938) in Alperton, Grimsdyke (1939) in Hatch End, and Pinner Wood (1939). Secondary schools founded in the same period were: Harrow County for Boys (1910), Harrow County for Girls (1914), Wembley County (1922), East Lane (1928) in Sudbury, Headstone Secondary (1929), Claremont (1930) in Preston, the Roman Catholic Salvatorian College for boys (1931) in Wealdstone, Roxeth Manor Secondary (1932), Harrow Weald Grammar (1933), and Belmont Secondary (1935) in Harrow Weald, Pinner Grammar (1937), and Preston Manor County (1938).

Under the 1944 Education Act the area was divided between two divisional executives of the boroughs of Harrow and Wembley, and after the London Government Act of 1963, between those of the London Boroughs of Harrow and Brent. Primary schools built after 1945 were: Cedars (1948) and Chantry (1949) in Headstone, Grange (1949) in South Harrow, Weald (1950) in Robin Hood Drive, Mount Stewart (1951) in Preston, Wembley Manor (1952) and West Lodge (1954) in Pinner, St. George's Roman Catholic (1965) in Sudbury Hill, and Elmgrove (1966) in Wealdstone. Secondary schools founded during the same period are Lascelles Secondary Modern (1949) in Roxeth, Blackwell County (1950) in Hatch End, Copland (1952) in Wembley, St. Gregory's Roman Catholic (1956) in Preston, and Alperton Boys (1958) and Girls (1962).

Brent adopted a comprehensive scheme of education, with effect from September 1967. All schools in Wembley became co-educational, taking pupils from 11–18, except for one junior high school, East Lane, Wembley, with pupils from 11–16 and, after 1969, from 11–13, and two senior high schools, Copland and Preston Manor, which from 1968 were to take pupils of 13–18. Three schools, Wembley County, Alperton Boys, and Alperton Girls, were amalgamated as Alperton High School. In 1966 Harrow refused to adopt a comprehensive scheme, preferring to develop a collegiate system and to set up a junior college.[45]

From the 18th century there were probably always some small private schools. Dr. Collins had a school at Harrow before it was moved to Southall Park in 1806.[46] Between 1818 and 1826 two boarding schools for gentlemen were established at Pinner, one of them in Pinner House.[47] They were still flourishing in 1833,[48] when there were also six fee-paying day schools in Pinner and two fee-paying boarding schools in Harrow.[49] In 1851 there were seminaries in Harrow-on-the-Hill and Alperton, a

'ladies'' school at Pinner,[50] and 16 governesses, mostly in Harrow-on-the-Hill.[51] Edward Monro, Perpetual Curate (1842–60) of All Saints, opened a small college, St. Andrew's, at Harrow Weald, to train poor boys free of charge as schoolmasters or clergy. The institution ran into debt and closed after Monro left the parish.[52] In 1851 there were 29 boys at St. Andrew's College and 15 boys at the Nursery, an agricultural college in Harrow Weald.[53]

The Royal Commercial Travellers' Schools at Pinner derived from a small school for the orphans of commercial travellers founded on the initiative of John Robert Cuffley in 1845 at Wanstead (Essex). In 1855 the foundation stone of a larger school with accommodation for 140 was laid by the Prince Consort on a site in Hatch End.[54] The building, in red brick with stone dressings in the Gothic style, was enlarged in 1868, 1876–7, 1878, 1905, and 1907. There were 365 boys and girls, all of them boarders, in 1937.[55] The school, which provided a grammar school education, was renamed the Royal Pinner School, Hatch End, in 1965. By this date it was in financial difficulties[56] and it was closed in 1967, although a Royal Pinner School Foundation was set up to help pupils who had been receiving a free education. The buildings were divided between Harrow College of Further Education and a Roman Catholic primary school.[57]

Sudbury Home for Girls, which originated as a school established in Bloomsbury in 1852 by the National Refugees Society, moved in 1873 to Sudbury Hall, where it trained destitute girls for domestic service.[58] The number of girls varied between 73 and 87.[59] The school remained there until 1930 when it moved to Esher Place (Surr.).[60]

In 1876 after legislation had finally severed the links between Harrow School and the locality, the Lower School of John Lyon was established by the governors to provide secondary education for the inhabitants of Harrow.[61] After the changes in state secondary education made by the Act of 1902, the Lower School of John Lyon was too small. In 1909 after protracted discussions about expansion, the governors of Harrow School withdrew their contributions, and the Lower School raised its fees. In 1910 Middlesex County Council therefore opened a new secondary school, Harrow County. In 1966 John Lyon School, still an independent day school, was attended by about 400 boys.[62]

Dominican sisters opened a girls' boarding school in 1878 in the Mount, Harrow-on-the-Hill. Later it moved to a new building in the convent grounds and day pupils were admitted. There was an extension in 1937 but the boarding school closed in 1948 and the junior department shortly afterwards. By 1967 St. Dominic's was an independent grammar school for 200–240 girls.[63] Other 19th-century schools included a church school in Harrow in the 1850s and 1860s, which gave boys industrial training,[64]

[45] The Times, 22 Oct. 1966, 12e.
[46] Miscellanea, xii (Cath. Rec. Soc. xx), 280.
[47] Pigot, Lond. Dir. (1826), 448–9.
[48] See above.
[49] Educ. Enquiry Abstract, 1833, H.C. 62, pp. 96, 110 (1835), xlii.   [50] Home Cnties. Dir. (1851).
[51] H.O. 107/1700.
[52] D.N.B. sub Edw. Monro; Druett, Weald, 224.
[53] H.O. 107/1700, ff. 106–31.
[54] Ware, Pinner, 187–8.
[55] Kelly's Dir. Mdx. (1937).
[56] The Times, 19 July 1966, 10d.

[57] Ibid. 10 Mar. 1967, 3e; Evening Standard, 30 June 1967.
[58] Silvester, Visible & Invisible, 18–19; Ed. 7/87.
[59] Schs. in receipt of Parl. Grants, 1898, p. 168; Pub. Elem. Schs. 1906 [Cd.3510], H.C. p. 450 (1907), lxiii.
[60] Wembley News, 22 Jan. 1953.
[61] B. Pearce, 'The John Lyon School and the Origins of Harrow County School' (TS.).
[62] Schools Dir. (1966).
[63] Ex inf. the Prioress, St. Dominic's Convent (1967).
[64] Christ Church MS. Estates 47/546; Schs. aided by Parl. Grants, 1865–6 [3666], H.C. p. 737 (1866), xxvii.

and Sudbury College in Station Road, founded c. 1892.[65] Orley Farm School was founded in Ilotts Farm before 1900,[66] Southlands, a girls' boarding and day school, opened in 1900,[67] St. Margaret's School opened in Hindes Road in 1902 and moved in 1934 to Sheepcote Road,[68] and the Imperial Yeomanry School for Girls opened in Alperton Hall to educate the daughters of yeomanry soldiers killed during the Boer War.[69] By 1969 there were 27 private schools in the area, including Orley Farm and St. Margaret's.[70]

Apart from the evening classes held for adults in 1818,[71] there were those offered by the Harrow Young Men's Society.[72] A school of art was founded in 1887 in Harrow-on-the-Hill High Street by a member of the Hewlett family and in 1894 it was taken over by a local committee established by the county council. By 1897 there were 260 students and in 1901 the school moved to a new building in Station Road, which was extended in 1907 and 1932. Evening technical classes were held from 1901, a technical school was added in 1930, and in 1947 the institution was named Harrow Technical College and School of Art. A new eight-story building in Northwick Park was opened in 1959 for the technical college, the school of art occupying the whole of the Station Road premises and, in 1967, using Greenhill school in St. Anne's Road as an annexe while new accommodation was being built next to the technical college.[73] An annexe of Harrow Technical College was opened in the old Pinner National School in School Lane in 1962 as Pinner Day College. In 1964 it became a separate college, to which an engineering annexe was opened in High Road, Harrow Weald. It was renamed Harrow College of Further Education in 1965 and a year later a second annexe was opened in Wealdstone Bridge School. By 1966 there were 926 students. From September 1967 the main part of the college was housed in former premises of the Royal Pinner School and, of the old buildings, only the annexe in Harrow Weald was retained.[74]

CHARITIES FOR THE POOR.[75] The will of Werhard, dated 832, mentions a bequest by Archbishop Wulfred (d. 832) of food to be given daily and 2s. 2d. to be given annually for clothing to 5 poor people at Harrow.[76] One will of the 15th century[77] and several of the 16th century[78] contain small bequests to the poor. In 1580 John Lyon provided that the governors of Harrow School should give 60 of the poorest 'housekeepers' in Harrow 6s. 8d. apiece every Good Friday or otherwise at their discretion. Pinner was to be excluded unless there were insuf-

ficient paupers in Harrow. In the 19th century and later the governors paid £20 annually to the Vicar of St. Mary's, for distribution at Christmas and on Good Friday. Any surplus was to be devoted to the 'help and relief of poor marriages, and other such good and charitable purposes'. In the 18th and early 19th centuries the charity occasionally provided small sums for apprenticing poor children, as marriage portions, and to support a Sunday school at Pinner and the National school at Harrow.

In 1611 Catherine Clarke settled £240 in trust on the Mercers' Company to pay each year to the Vicar and churchwardens of Harrow £12, for distribution half-yearly among 6 paupers from Harrow and 6 from Roxeth. From 1696 until 1802 payments were in arrear but after the money had been re-invested in stock worth £324 the income of £22 was distributed annually in sums of 10s. In 1630 Barbara Burnell bequeathed £300 to the Clothworkers' Company[79] and in 1655 Thomas Burnell augmented the gift by £5 a year, the income to be paid to the poor of Stanmore. Later the gift, in the form of 2d. loaves, 3½d. cheeses, and clothes, was distributed among two poor women in Harrow Weald, two in Bushey, two in Edgware, and one in Stanmore. By will dated 1637 William Dwight left a rent-charge of £2 a year from property in Sudbury. This was augmented when Margaret, widow of Samuel Parr (d. 1825), left the interest on £200 stock in trust to be distributed annually in bread among the poor of Harrow, Roxeth, Sudbury, and Greenhill. Her bequest yielded £6 a year in the 19th century. Under a Charity Commission Scheme of 1888 the gifts of Clarke, Burnell, Dwight, and Parr were consolidated as the Harrow Pension Charities, vested in seven trustees who were to pay pensions to 3 paupers who had lived in the parish for more than 5 years. By 1965 the income was between £25 and £60 a year.

In 1791 Henry Burch, a London citizen, gave the interest on £200 stock for the use of the Wembley poor. In the early 19th century this gift was distributed by the vicar in sums not exceeding 10s. Martha Bowen, by will dated 1888, left £150 in trust to be distributed annually by the vicar in bread or money to paupers attending the parish church. In 1965 the income of about £4 was spent on bread. Ann Sahler, by will dated 1893, left £300 in trust to provide an annual gift for not more than 3 widows in Harrow Weald. In 1965 the income of between £10 and £25 was distributed as coal.

In Pinner Mary Franklin, by will dated 1735, left the interest on £50 to buy bread for paupers of the Established Church. In the early 19th century the income was distributed in bread at Christmas. Elizabeth Deering, by will dated 1781, left the

---

[65] Silvester, *Visible & Invisible*, 25.
[66] M.R.O., Acc. 76/1319. See p. 212.
[67] *Schools Dir.* (1966).
[68] Druett, *Weald*, 230.
[69] *Kelly's Dir. Mdx.* (1906).
[70] *Schools Dir.* (1969), i.e. excluding schools controlled or aided by the state.
[71] See above.
[72] See p. 236.
[73] Sturdy, 'Educ. in Harrow', 15; prospectuses of Harrow School of Art and Harrow Technical Coll. (1967-8). During the Second World War the Northwick Park site accommodated temporary huts housing government departments, including the Admiralty Record Office which was removed in 1959: ex inf. the Principal of Harrow Coll. of Technology and Art (1969).

[74] Prospectus of Harrow Coll. of Further Educ. (1967-8).
[75] Except where otherwise stated, the following section is based on Char. Com. files and *9th Rep. Com. Char.* H.C. 258, pp. 261-6 (1823), ix. Some charities have been treated under Church, Local Government, and Schools. Houblon's charity, which had land in Sudbury, does not appear to have been a Harrow charity; it may have been connected with the charity of that name, whose origin is obscure, in Great Hallingbury (Essex): *29th Rep. Com. Char.* H.C. 216, p. 191 (1835), xxi.
[76] *Harrow Octocent. Tracts*, i. 20-21.
[77] P.C.C. 24 Godyn (John Byrkhede, 1468).
[78] Ibid. 7 Blamyr (Hugh Ives, 1501); 13 Noodes (Ric. Lamb, 1557); 35 Noodes (Hen. Page, 1558); 28 Morrison (Robt. Crowley, 1565); 38 Pyckering (John Edlin, 1575).
[79] Wemb. Hist. Soc., Acc. 907/68.

interest on £100 to be distributed at Christmas to 10 widows 'who frequently receive the sacrament'. The charity was still in existence in 1810[80] but its history after that date is obscure. Mary Roberts, by will proved 1797, left the interest on £500 stock to be distributed at Christmas in portions of 30s. to 10 old people who received no parish alms. The gift was contingent on the death of Abraham Clarke, and Chancery proceedings after his death in 1811 reduced the amount to £364 stock. In the 1830s the interest of £17 a year was generally distributed in sums of 30s. Mary Elige, by will dated 1824, gave £50 to be distributed among out-poor in Pinner. In 1836 the legacy was invested and the interest was thereafter consolidated with Franklin's gift, the combined charity being called Elige's. In 1849 Thomas Hill, a Pinner farmer, gave £200 stock, the interest on which was to be distributed annually in blankets to Pinner paupers. Henrietta Howard in 1841 gave £100 stock, the interest on which was to be spent annually on bread and meat for 25 poor families in Pinner. By her will, proved 1855, she gave a further £60 stock, the interest on which was to be used to buy blankets for six poor families. Charlotte Howard, by will proved 1855, left the interest on £500 stock for distribution in fuel and blankets to the poor of Pinner at Christmas. The gift was to be styled the Edward Alexander Howard Charity in memory of her father. Christian Snow, by a codicil to his will, proved 1868, left the interest on £50 stock to be distributed each Christmas in bread to the resident poor. Benjamin Weall, by will proved 1868, left to the churchwardens the interest on £100, with which to buy blankets for such poor as they thought proper. John Weall, by will dated 1864, created a similar trust for the purchase of blankets for 6 poor parishioners. In 1962 the income of the Pinner non-ecclesiastical charities, comprising Roberts's gift and the 19th-century benefactions, amounted to £43, which was distributed in small sums and blankets.

[80] M.R.O., D.R.O. 8/C1/1.

INDEX

NOTE: A page-number in italic denotes an illustration; a number prefixed by a dagger † indicates a plate facing that page.

The following abbreviations have been used: adv., advowson; agric., agriculture; Alex., Alexander; And., Andrew; Ant., Anthony; abp., archbishop; Bart., Bartholomew; Benj., Benjamin; bp., bishop; bor., borough; Cath., Catherine; chant., chantry; chap., chapel; char., charity; Chas., Charles; Chris., Christopher; Chron., Chronicle; ch., church; coll., college; ctss., countess; ct., court; Dan., Daniel; dchss., duchess; econ., economy; Edm., Edmund; educ., education; Edw., Edward; Eliz., Elizabeth; f., father; fam., family; Fr., France; Fred., Frederick; Gaz., Gazette; Geof., Geoffrey; Geo., George; Gilb., Gilbert; Godf., Godfrey; Hen., Henry; Herb., Herbert; ho., house; hosp., hospital; Humph., Humphrey; inc., inclosure; ind., industry; Jas., James; Jos., Joseph; Lawr., Lawrence; ld., lord; man., manor; mchnss., marchioness; Marg., Margaret; mkt., market; m., married; Mat., Matthew; Mic., Michael; Min., Ministry; Nat., Nathaniel; Nic., Nicholas; nonconf., nonconformity; n, note; par., parish; pk., park; Phil., Philip; pop., population; Prot., Protestant; R.D., Rural District; rly., railway; Ric., Richard; riv., river; Rob., Robert; Rog., Roger; Rom., Roman; Sam., Samuel; sch., school; Sim., Simon; s., son; sta., station; Steph., Stephen; Thos., Thomas; U.D., Urban District; univ., university; vct., viscount; Wal., Walter; wid., widow; w., wife; Wm., William.

CORRIGENDA TO VOLUMES I AND III

Earlier lists of corrigenda will be found in Volumes I and III

Vol. I, frontispiece, *for* 1883 *read* 1833

page xxiii, line 3, *after* 'Cannings' *insert* 'Cross'

xxiii, line 8, *for* 'Oxoniensis' *read* 'Oxonienses'

xxiii, line 9, *for* 'C. J. Aungier' *read* 'G. J. Aungier'

xxiv, line 3, *for* 'préhistoire' *read* 'préhistorique'

xxiv, line 4 from end, *after* 'Society' *add* '. Consecutive numbers are used for the whole series, although Volumes vii–xvii (1905–54) appeared as N.S. i–xi'

17, lines 6, 23, and 4 from end, *for* 'Galloway' *read* 'Garraway'

23, note 60, *for* 'Record' *read* 'Records'

60, note 45, *for* 'Jahrbucher' *read* 'Jahrbücher'

65, note 7, *for* 'iii' *read* 'ix'

84, line 15, *for* 'Loefwine' *read* 'Leofwine'

91, line 5, *for* 'th c ii' *read* 'the *cotarii*'

126*b*, line 17 from end, *for* '; a beech-grove (*silva*' *read* 'and beasts of the chase (*silva-*'

160*a*, line 19, *for* 'Liège' *read* 'Liége'

168, note 19, *for* 'Seeley' *read* 'Seely'

182*b*, line 14 from end, *for* 'nun's' *read* 'nuns' '

219, line 6 from end, *for* 'words' *read* 'wands'

230, lines 24–25, *delete* ', the Royal Engineers' at Brompton,'

249, line 2 from end, *for* 'Aberbeen' *read* 'Aberdeen'

250, line 23, *for* 'Dodderidge's' *read* 'Doddridge's'

262, line 2 from end, *for* 'Enfield.' *read* 'Enfield,'

277, line 18, *for* 'Jew's' *read* 'Jews' '

281, line 3 from end, *for* 'Fortress' *read* 'Fortess'

289, line 32, *for* 'Surburban' *read* 'Suburban'

300*b*, line 34, *for* '1823–6' *read* '1823–4'

311, note 14, *for* 'Rosalie C. Grylls' *read* 'Rosalie G. Grylls'

363 *c*, *s.v.* Angers, *for* 'Maire-et-Loire' *read* 'Maine-et-Loire'

363*c*, *s.v.* 'Arnold's' wood, *delete whole entry and substitute* 'Arnos Grove ('Arnold's' wood), in Southgate, 169'

364*a*, *s.v.* 'Atherley's lands', *for* '169' *read* 'see London, City of'

368*a*, *between* 'Dodd' *and* 'Doding', *insert* 'Doddridge, Dr. Phil., 250'

369*c*, *s.v.* Fortress Road High Sch., *for* 'Fortress' *read* 'Fortess'

373*a*, *s.v.* Jews' College, *after* '263' *add* ', 277'

374*b*, *s.v.* London, City of, *before* 'Bank of England' *add* ' 'Atherley's lands', 169;'

379*b*, *s.v.* Royal Engineers, *delete whole entry*

380*c*, *s.v.* Seeley & Paget, *for* 'Seeley' *read* 'Seely'

381*a*, *s.v.* Southgate, *after* 'and see' *insert* 'Arnos Grove;'

385, line 13 from end, *for* '227*b*' *read* '277*b*'

Vol. III, page xx, line 2 from end, *after* 'date)' *add* '. Consecutive numbers are used for the whole series, although Volumes vii–xvii (1905–54) appeared as N.S. i–xi'